PLUTARCH'S LIVES

✦ THE BARNES & NOBLE LIBRARY OF ESSENTIAL READING ✦

PLUTARCH'S LIVES
Volume 1

—◆|◆—

PLUTARCH

TRANSLATED BY JOHN DRYDEN

EDITED BY ARTHUR HUGH CLOUGH

INTRODUCTION BY
CLAYTON MILES LEHMANN

BARNES & NOBLE

NEW YORK

THE BARNES & NOBLE
LIBRARY OF ESSENTIAL READING

Introduction and Suggested Reading
© 2006 by Barnes & Noble, Inc.

Originally published circa AD 110

This 2006 edition published by Barnes & Noble, Inc.

Barnes & Noble, Inc.
122 Fifth Avenue
New York, NY 10011

ISBN: 978-0-7607-8092-3

Printed and bound in the United States of America

3 5 7 9 10 8 6 4

Contents

INTRODUCTION

If a man were called to fix the period in the history of the world, during which the condition of the human race was most happy and prosperous, he would, without hesitation, name that which elapsed from the death of Domitian to the accession of Commodus. The vast extent of the Roman Empire was governed by absolute power, under the guidance of virtue and wisdom. The armies were restrained by the firm but gentle hand of four successive emperors, whose characters and authority commanded involuntary respect.

—Edward Gibbon, *Decline and Fall of the Roman Empire*

PLUTARCH OF CHAERONEA WROTE COMPARATIVE LIVES OF NOBLE GREEKS and Romans such as Pericles and Fabius, Demosthenes and Cicero, and Alexander and Caesar. He chose his subjects not for the greatness and interest of their careers so much as for the sake of the moral qualities revealed by the collision of formidable characters and powerful events. Fortunate himself to live at the dawn of the era Gibbon considered the happiest in human history, Plutarch took full advantage of the learning of his and past ages as well as his experience in public life to discover that which constitutes the best in a human being, and which, in turn, determines a person's role in the world. The subjects he chose as his examples live on memorably in his vivid narratives and strongly stated judgments. More than any other author from antiquity, Plutarch defined for all subsequent ages the character of Greek and Roman moral identity.

Ironically, we can recover the life of this most famous of biographers almost only from incidental references in his voluminous writings. For example, because he mentions that he was a young man when Nero visited Greece in 67 CE, Plutarch must have been born in the 40s CE. He came from a wealthy leading family in the small city of Chaeronea in Central Greece, famous not only for its biographer but also as the battlefield where Alexander's father, Philip, defeated the Greeks in 338 BCE and where the Roman general Sulla defeated the eastern monarch Mithridates VI in 86 BCE. Plutarch reports that relics of Sulla's battle continued to surface in the fields for two hundred years afterward, which means he was still alive in the 110s CE. Inscriptional evidence from Delphi, where he served as one of the two priests for life at the beginning of the sanctuary's second-century revival, suggests that he died before 125 CE. We meet several members of his family in his writings. His brother, father, grandfather (the witty, cultured Lamprias), and sons participate in some of the dialogs in the sprawling collection of essays called the *Moralia,* and he addressed the most touching of his essays, *Consolation,* to his wife, Timoxena, on the death of their daughter. Sympathetic to marriage, children, and women, Plutarch expected women to be literate and interested in philosophy. Proud of his origins even while he recognized their provinciality (see the opening of *Demosthenes*), he remained a lifelong resident of Chaeronea and held several municipal and regional offices. The people of Delphi and Chaeronea joined to honor Plutarch by setting up a statue of him in Delphi.

Plutarch also studied in Athens and traveled widely through Greece and the empire, from Alexandria to Rome. He had many friends in high positions within the imperial government, including Quintus Sosius Senecio, twice consul and dedicatee of several of the *Lives,* and Lucius Mestrius Florus, who evidently arranged for Plutarch to receive Roman citizenship; in gratitude Plutarch assumed the Romanized name Lucius Mestrius Plutarchus. Plutarch's interest in education has led many to believe he ran a school in Chaeronea, but there is little evidence for anything but widely ranging discussion at informal gatherings.

Plutarch lived at the beginning of the period Gibbon considered the most felicitous in human history. But, ironically, he grew up during the reign of Nero and lived through the calamitous eighteen months of civil war following it—the two surviving of Plutarch's *Lives* of the emperors from Augustus to Vitellius belong to this period. He also experienced the catastrophic year 79–80 when Vesuvius erupted, plague decimated the empire, fire swept Rome, and when he saw his friends suffer under the harsh rule of Domitian (81–96). While the Romans enjoyed unprecedented peace and stability in the following half century, they knew how easily bad days could return: as Gibbon observed, so much depended on the quality of the man who ruled the empire—and so the writers of the period weighed carefully the character of their rulers. Arnoldo Momigliano noted with appreciation the independence of the biographers of Plutarch's age: neither Tacitus, Suetonius, nor Plutarch became servants of imperial propaganda; rather they kept the emperors human.

Although he focused on individual lives and individuals' characters in his writings, Plutarch offered some comments on the larger world; several of the essays, notably *Precepts on Statecraft*, treat the Roman context explicitly. The Roman Empire functioned not by coercing its subjects but by co-opting local elites, giving them responsibility for ensuring good order at the local level in return for keeping them in their positions of privilege. Plutarch believed that he lived in a world not only of security but also of considerable liberty—which meant that those naturally suited to rule by virtue of wealth and birth had the freedom to control their cities without external interference. Liberty emphatically did not mean democracy, a system Plutarch attacked repeatedly in his writings: in his view, a democracy represents a city where the wise speak but fools decide. Notably, Flamininus' proclamation of Greek liberty at the end of the Second Macedonian War in 196 BCE constitutes the climax of his life, Sulla's liberation of Athens from Mithridates offsets his sack of the city in 86 BCE, and Nero's gesture in freeing the Greeks in 67 CE redeems the otherwise monstrous emperor. But Emperor Vespasian (69–79 CE) revoked Nero's grant, and Plutarch spent all his adult life as a subject and then citizen of Rome.

Plutarch had no illusions about any possibility of the Greeks recovering their ancient liberty. Instead, Plutarch insisted, the role of Greek leaders was to lead free men within the empire, ensure local order and cooperation among local elites and with the imperial authorities, and to strike a balance between the independence that might occasion intervention by the imperial authorities and excessive dependency that might annoy them. The glories of ancient Greece that fill the Greek *Lives* serve as background to the analysis of the characters of her heroes, not inspiration for revolutionary activity.

If the *Lives* furnishes any advice for the contemporary statesman, it comes perhaps in *Phocion*, where Plutarch compares the duty of the statesman to the sun's gentle declination, dispensing "his light and influence, in his annual revolution, at several seasons in just proportions to the whole creation." The ruler, by turns, must favor the people, but also hold them in check. "But if such a blessed mixture and temperament may be obtained, it seems to be of all concords and harmonies the most concordant and most harmonious. For thus we are taught even God governs the world, not by irresistible force, but persuasive argument and reason, controlling it into compliance with his eternal purposes."

Plutarch goes on to insist that the Greek statesman should not look beyond Greek politics by pursing positions within the imperial administration. Romans had long developed friendships with Greeks, but only in the second century do we find the Greeks on the verge of the period when they, like other non-Italians, could attain positions of power in the Roman order and not limit themselves to the role of learned Greeks advising Romans. Plutarch himself became the acquaintance of many powerful Romans who attended his lectures and discussions, but except for the grant of citizenship and, possibly, consular honors, he did not appear to have taken advantage of those connections in any way beyond the pleasure of cultivated company. Plutarch's own rather modest political career therefore constitutes a model for how the Greek statesman should work within the empire.

One wonders why Plutarch paired Greeks and Romans in his *Parallel Lives*. D. A. Russell argued it was to demonstrate the "parity and partnership of Greece and Rome, each with its contribution to make towards the development of political virtue," and to show how the humanity (*philanthropia*) that Greek moral education inculcated could modify Roman destructiveness. Others have seen in his project a reflection of the insecurity of the Greeks who wanted to equal the Romans on their terms—military and political greatness—rather than in the Greek sphere where the Romans acknowledged their inferiority: art and literature; thus Plutarch strove to prove the Greeks real men and the Romans civilized and not barbarian. C. P. Jones showed in *Plutarch and Rome* that this supposed diplomatic purpose never appears in the *Lives*. The very arrangement of the lives belies such a plan: it is haphazard, accidental, and dependent on chance just as much as life itself—the sort of arrangement that can serve a study of morality in human life, not an argument about culture. Plutarch did not need to build a bridge between Greeks and Romans; the bridge already existed, well integrating Greece into the Roman order. Plutarch, Jones said, was both "Greek, in that he saw himself as a Greek by birth and language, Roman, in that his interests and sympathies are bound up with the empire." Robert Lamberton argued that Plutarch actually helped create the Athenocentric interpretation of Greek culture that influenced Hadrian's program to elevate Athens to a position analogous to Rome's: "Plutarch's *Parallel Lives* constitute the principal document in the high empire's reinvention of Classical Greece." Plutarch's way of interpreting Greece and Rome proved so powerful that his became the standard way of understanding antiquity—as opposed to, say, the Virgilian model in which Rome prevails in law and government, Greece in arts and literature. The lives of the mythical heroes Theseus and Romulus, Lycurgus and Numa, for whom limited information enabled considerable flexibility on Plutarch's part, above all show the biographer's interest in elevating Greece into Rome's sphere of action: these lives really compare Athens and Rome and Greek and Roman institutions, not individuals.

Still, Plutarch's own stated purpose did not involve the elucidation of themes of cultural difference or liberty; morality constituted his primary interest, and he used great lives to reveal great character. Perhaps we should see Plutarch's biographical choices as the product not so much of a great Greco-Roman cultural project but rather as an exploration of character in those who most strongly demonstrated powerful moral qualities: the insatiable ambition of Marius, the pitiless inhumanity of Sulla, the sublime excessiveness of Alexander, the sheer power-hunger of Caesar, the futile idealism of the younger Cato, the charismatic immorality of Alcibiades, the uxorious helplessness of Antony, the impressive fairness of Aristides, the inhumane self-righteousness of Cato the Elder, the embarrassing self-importance of Cicero, the baffling bad luck of Sertorius. These biographical choices will be explored in the introduction to volume 2. Here we shall consider the lasting influence of Plutarch.

The last generation of scholars has credited Plutarch with great originality and creativity as he pursued his intellectual and moral projects. Earlier scholars, however, considered his work important not in itself, but for the way it transmitted antiquity to later generations. And indeed, no one can deny the fact that already in his own lifetime Plutarch's readers derived their understanding of their Greco-Roman past largely through his eyes. The *Parallel Lives* became an instant classic, widely quoted and excerpted in antiquity. The Byzantine scholar Planudes collected and edited all the Plutarchan manuscripts he could find about 1300. The *Lives* saw their first translations in the fourteenth (into Aragonese and Tuscan) and fifteenth (into Latin) centuries, often for political motives. Thus Bruni, interested in the Republican origins of Florence, translated the life of the last Republican, Cato the Younger; the Venetians, in contrast, interested in the maritime East, preferred the Athenian general Phocion. The sixteenth century saw many vernacular translations—even Queen Elizabeth translated one of the essays into English—but pride of place goes to Amyot's French translation (*Lives* in 1559, *Moralia* in 1572), which itself served as the source for Thomas

North's translation of the *Lives* (1579, with new editions in 1595 and 1603) into the English version Shakespeare knew, as did most English-speaking readers until the version edited by Dryden appeared a century later.

Thus the Plutarchan view of antiquity persisted through the end of the Roman Empire and was revived in the Renaissance and Early Modern Period when Shakespeare drew on his writings as his source for the Roman tragedies and Montesquieu proclaimed Plutarch "my man." After the heroic age of Rousseau and Franklin, Plutarch went into decline on account of what seemed excessive moralizing and unthinking borrowing of earlier authors; nevertheless, he has continued to impart political wisdom to statesmen such as Harry Truman and Eugene McCarthy as well as memorable vignettes of Greek and Roman history to undergraduate students.

John Dryden (1631–1700) himself contributed only an essay on the life of Plutarch to the great translation of the *Parallel Lives* that bears his name. Nevertheless, Dryden deserves credit for soliciting translations of the individual lives, editing them, and arranging for their publication by Jacob Tonson in five volumes from 1683 to 1686 (second edition in 1688, third in 1693). Arthur Sherbo has shown that in the last two decades of his life Dryden assembled a team of gentlemen, many of whom he knew from his days at Westminster School and Trinity College, Cambridge, where he first read Plutarch in the mid-1600s. They contributed original poetry as well as translations from the classics for a series of books (most of them proceeding from Tonson's press) from 1680 to 1711. Dryden's innovative thinking about the craft of translation appeared in the preface to the first of the series, *Ovid's Epistles* (1680), where he distinguished among close translation (metaphrase), free translation strictly preserving the sense of the original (paraphrase), and a substantially new composition in the style of the original but using its sense only as a starting point for new ideas (imitation). In the preface to another of these collaborative works, *Sylvae* (1685), Dryden characterized his translations of the sentiments of an ancient author: "if he were living, and an Englishman, they are such, as he wou'd probably have written." Dryden preferred Plutarch's sentiment to his "roughness of expression. . . . Yet, for manliness of eloquence, if it abounded not in our author, it was not wanting in him. He neither studied the sublime style, nor affected the flowery."

A. H. Clough revised the Dryden translation in the nineteenth century, rendering the version most accessible today. In the twentieth century the Loeb edition, with its facing Greek text and modern English translation, also enjoys wide use, and exclusively so for the *Moralia*. Otherwise we have

English translations only of individual lives removed from their parallel setting into collections meant for history classes treating various periods of Greece and Rome. Although useful in such courses, treating the lives individually destroys the effect Plutarch aimed at in his comparative, ethical approach. We shall turn to this aspect of Plutarch's *Parallel Lives* in the introduction to volume 2.

Clayton Miles Lehmann teaches history at the University of South Dakota. He has published widely on various topics in Greek and Roman history and archaeology.

THESEUS

As geographers, Sosius, crowd into the edges of their maps parts of the world which they do not know about, adding notes in the margin to the effect, that beyond this lies nothing but the sandy deserts full of wild beasts, unapproachable bogs, Scythian ice, or a frozen sea, so in this work of mine, in which I have compared the lives of the greatest men with one another, after passing through those periods which probable reasoning can reach to and real history find a footing in, I might very well say of those that are farther off: "Beyond this there is nothing but prodigies and fictions, the only inhabitants are the poets and inventors of fables; there is no credit, or certainty any farther." Yet, after publishing an account of Lycurgus the lawgiver and Numa the king, I thought I might, not without reason, ascend as high as to Romulus, being brought by my history so near to his time. Considering therefore with myself—

> Whom shall I set so great a man to face?
> Or whom oppose? Who's equal to the place?

(as Æschylus expresses it), I found none so fit as him that peopled the beautiful and far-famed city of Athens, to be set in opposition with the father of the invincible and renowned city of Rome. Let us hope that Fable may, in what shall follow, so submit to the purifying processes of Reason as to take the character of exact history. In any case, however, where it shall be found contumaciously slighting credibility and refusing to be reduced to anything like probable fact, we shall beg that we may meet with candid readers, and such as will receive with indulgence the stories of antiquity.

1

Theseus seemed to me to resemble Romulus in many particulars. Both of them, born out of wedlock and of uncertain parentage, had the repute of being sprung from the gods.

> Both warriors; that by all the world's allowed.

Both of them united with strength of body an equal vigour of mind; and of the two most famous cities of the world, the one built Rome, and the other made Athens be inhabited. Both stand charged with the rape of women; neither of them could avoid domestic misfortunes nor jealousy at home; but towards the close of their lives are both of them said to have incurred great odium with their countrymen, if, that is, we may take the stories least like poetry as our guide to the truth.

The lineage of Theseus, by his father's side, ascends as high as to Erechtheus and the first inhabitants of Attica. By his mother's side he was descended of Pelops. For Pelops was the most powerful of all the kings of Peloponnesus, not so much by the greatness of his riches as the multitude of his children, having married many daughters to chief men, and put many sons in places of command in the towns round about him. One of whom named Pittheus, grandfather to Theseus, was governor of the small city of the Trœzenians and had the repute of a man of the greatest knowledge and wisdom of his time; which then, it seems, consisted chiefly in grave maxims, such as the poet Hesiod got his great fame by, in his book of Works and Days. And, indeed, among these is one that they ascribe to Pittheus,

> Unto a friend suffice
> A stipulated price;

which, also, Aristotle mentions. And Euripides, by calling Hippolytus "scholar of the holy Pittheus," shows the opinion that the world had of him.

Ægeus, being desirous of children, and consulting the oracle of Delphi, received the celebrated answer which forbade him the company of any woman before his return to Athens. But the oracle being so obscure as not to satisfy him that he was clearly forbid this, he went to Trœzen, and communicated to Pittheus the voice of the god, which was in this manner,

> Loose not the wineskin foot, thou chief of men,
> Until to Athens thou art come again.

Pittheus, therefore, taking advantage from the obscurity of the oracle, prevailed upon him, it is uncertain whether by persuasion or deceit, to lie with his daughter Æthra. Ægeus afterwards, knowing her whom he had lain with to be Pittheus' daughter, and suspecting her to be with child by him, left a sword and a pair of shoes, hiding them under a great stone that had a hollow in it exactly fitting them; and went away making her only privy to it, and commanding her, if she brought forth a son who, when he came to man's estate, should be able to lift up the stone and take away what he had left there, she should send him way to him with those things with all secrecy, and with injunctions to him as much as possible to conceal his journey from everyone; for he greatly feared the Pallentidæ, who were continually mutinying against him, and despised him for his want of children, they themselves being fifty brothers, all sons of Pallas.

When Æthra was delivered of a son, some say that he was immediately named Theseus, from the tokens which his father had *put* under the stone; others that he had received his name afterwards at Athens, when Ægeus *acknowledged* him for his son. He was brought up under his grandfather Pittheus, and had a tutor and attendant set over him named Connidas, to whom the Athenians even to this time, the day before the feast that is dedicated to Theseus, sacrifice a ram, giving this honour to his memory upon much juster grounds than to Silanio and Parrhasius for making pictures and statues of Theseus. There being then a custom for the Grecian youth, upon their first coming to man's estate, to go to Delphi and offer first-fruits of their hair to the god, Theseus also went thither, and a place there to this day is yet named Thesea, as it is said, from him. He clipped only the fore part of his head, as Homer says the Abantes did. And this sort of tonsure was from him named Theseus. The Abantes first used it, not in imitation of the Arabians, as some imagine, nor of the Mysians, but because they were a warlike people, and used to close fighting, and above all other nations accustomed to engage hand to hand; as Archilochus testifies in these verses:

> Slings shall not whirl, nor many arrows fly,
>> When on the plain the battle joins; but swords,
> Man against man, the deadly conflict try
>> As is the practice of Eubœa's lords
> Skilled with the spear.

Therefore that they might not give their enemies a hold by their hair, they cut it in this manner. They write also that this was the reason why Alexander gave command to his captains that all the beards of the Macedonians should be shaved, as being the readiest hold for an enemy.

Æthra for sometime concealed the true parentage of Theseus, and a report was given out by Pittheus that he was begotten by Neptune; for the Trœzenians pay Neptune the highest veneration. He is their tutelar god; to him they offer all their first-fruits, and in his honour stamp their money with a trident.

Theseus displaying not only great strength of body, but equal bravery, and a quickness alike and force of understanding, his mother Æthra, conducting him to the stone, and informing him who was his true father, commanded him to take from thence the tokens that Ægeus had left, and sail to Athens. He without any difficulty set himself to the stone and lifted it up; but refused to take his journey by sea, though it was much the safer way, and though his mother and grandfather begged him to do so. For it was at that time very dangerous to go by land on the road to Athens, no part of it being free from robbers and murderers. That age produced a sort of men, in force of hand, and swiftness of foot, and strength of body, excelling the ordinary rate and wholly incapable of fatigue; making use, however, of these gifts of nature to no good or profitable purpose for mankind, but rejoicing and priding themselves in insolence, and taking the benefit of their superior strength in the exercise of inhumanity and cruelty, and in seizing, forcing, and committing all manner of outrages upon everything that fell into their hands; all respect for others, all justice, they thought, all equity and humanity, though naturally lauded by common people, either out of want of courage to commit injuries or fear to receive them, yet no way concerned those who were strong enough to win for themselves. Some of these, Hercules destroyed and cut off in his passage through these countries; but some escaping his notice while he was passing by, fled and hid themselves, or else were spared by him in contempt of their abject submission: and after that Hercules fell into misfortune, and, having slain Iphitus, retired to Lydia, and for a long time was there slave to Omphale, a punishment which he had imposed upon himself for the murder: then, indeed, Lydia enjoyed high peace and security, but in Greece and the countries about it the like villainies again revived and broke out, there being none to repress or chastise them. It was therefore a very hazardous journey to travel by land from Athens to Peloponnesus; and Pittheus, giving him an exact account of each of the robbers and villains, their strength, and the cruelty they used to all strangers, tried to persuade Theseus to go by sea. But he, it seems, had long since been secretly fired by the glory of Hercules, held him in the highest estimation, and was never more satisfied than in listening to any that gave an account of him; especially those that had seen him, or had been present at any action or saying of his. So that he was altogether in the same state of feeling as, in after ages, Themistocles was, when he said that he could not sleep for the trophy of Miltiades; entertaining such admiration for the virtue of Hercules, that in the night his dreams were all of that hero's actions, and in the day a continual emulation stirred him up to perform the like. Besides, they were related, being born of cousins-german. For Æthra was daughter of Pittheus, and Alcmena of Lysidice; and Lysidice and Pittheus were brother and sister, children of Hippodamia and Pelops. He thought it therefore a dishonourable thing, and not to be endured, that Hercules should go out everywhere, and purge both land and sea from wicked men, and he himself should fly from the like adventures that actually came in his way; disgracing his reputed father by a mean flight by sea, and not showing his true one as good evidence of the greatness of his birth by noble and worthy actions, as by the token that he brought with him the shoes and the sword.

With this mind and these thoughts, he set forward with a design to do injury to nobody, but to repel and revenge himself of all those that should offer any. And first of all, in a set combat, he slew Periphetes, in the neighbourhood of Epidaurus, who used a club for his arms, and from thence had the name of Corynetes, or the club-bearer; who seized upon him, and forbade him to go forward in his journey. Being pleased with the club, he took it, and made it his weapon, continuing to use it as Hercules did the lion's skin, on whose shoulders that served to prove how huge a beast he had killed; and to the same end Theseus carried about him this club; overcome indeed by him, but now in his hands, invincible.

Passing on further towards the Isthmus of Peloponnesus, he slew Sinnis, often surnamed the Bender of Pines, after the same manner in which he himself had destroyed many others before. And this he did without having either practised or ever learnt the art of bending these trees, to show that natural strength is above all art. This Sinnis had a daughter of remarkable beauty and stature, called Perigune, who, when her father was killed, fled, and was sought after everywhere by Theseus; and coming into a place overgrown with brushwood, shrubs, and asparagus-thorn, there, in a childlike innocent manner, prayed and begged them, as if they understood her, to give her shelter, with vows that if she escaped she would never cut them down nor burn them. But Theseus calling upon her, and giving her his promise that he would use her with respect, and offer her no injury, she came forth, and in due time bore him a son, named

Melanippus; but afterwards was married to Deioneus, the son of Eurytus, the Œchalian, Theseus himself giving her to him. Ioxus, the son of this Melanippus, who was born to Theseus, accompanied Ornytus in the colony that he carried with him into Caria, whence it is a family usage amongst the people called Ioxids, both male and female, never to burn either shrubs or asparagus-thorn, but to respect and honour them.

The Crommyonian sow, which they called Phæa, was a savage and formidable wild beast, by no means an enemy to be despised. Theseus killed her, going out of his way on purpose to meet and engage her, so that he might not seem to perform all his great exploits out of mere necessity; being also of opinion that it was the part of a brave man to chastise villainous and wicked men when attacked by them, but to seek out and overcome the more noble wild beasts. Others relate that Phæa was a woman, a robber full of cruelty and lust, that lived in Crommyon, and had the name of Sow given her from the foulness of her life and manners, and afterwards was killed by Theseus. He slew also Sciron, upon the borders of Megara, casting him down from the rocks, being, as most report, a notorious robber of all passengers, and, as others add, accustomed, out of insolence and wantonness, to stretch forth his feet to strangers commanding them to wash them, and then while they did it, with a kick to send them down the rock into the sea. The writers of Megara, however, in contradiction to the received report, and, as Simonides expresses it, "fighting with all antiquity," contend that Sciron was neither a robber nor doer of violence, but a punisher of all such, and the relative and friend of good and just men; for Æacus, they say, was ever esteemed a man of the greatest sanctity of all the Greeks; and Cychreus, the Salaminian, was honoured at Athens with divine worship; and the virtues of Peleus and Telamon were not unknown to anyone. Now Sciron was son-in-law to Cychreus, father-in-law to Æacus, and grandfather to Peleus and Telamon, who were both of them sons of Endeis, the daughter of Sciron and Chariclo; it was not probable, therefore, that the best of men should make these alliances with one who was worst, giving and receiving mutually what was of greatest value and most dear to them. Theseus, by their account, did not slay Sciron in his first journey to Athens, but afterwards, when he took Eleusis, a city of the Megarians, having circumvented Diocles, the governor. Such are the contradictions in this story. In Eleusis he killed Cercyon, the Arcadian, in a wrestling match. And going on a little farther, in Erineus, he slew Damastes, otherwise called Procrustes, forcing his body to the size of his own bed, as he himself was used to do with all strangers; this he did in imitation of Hercules, who always returned upon his assailants the same sort of violence that they offered to him; sacrificed Busiris, killed Antæus in wrestling, and Cycnus in single combat, and Termerus by breaking his skull in pieces (whence, they say, comes the proverb of "a Termerian mischief"), for it seems Termerus killed passengers that he met by running with his head against them. And so also Theseus proceeded in the punishment of evil men, who underwent the same violence from him which they had inflicted upon others, justly suffering after the manner of their own injustice.

As he went forward on his journey, and was come as far as the river Cephisus, some of the race of the Phytalidæ met him and saluted him, and upon his desire to use the purifications, then in custom, they performed them with all the usual ceremonies, and, having offered propitiatory sacrifices to the gods, invited him and entertained him at their house, a kindness which, in all his journey hitherto, he had not met.

On the eighth day of Cronius, now called Hecatombæon, he arrived at Athens, where he found the public affairs full of all confusion, and divided into parties and factions, Ægeus also, and his whole private family, labouring under the same distemper; for Medea, having fled from Corinth, and promised Ægeus to make him, by her art, capable of having children, was living with him. She first was aware of Theseus, whom as yet Ægeus did not know, and he being in years, full of jealousies and suspicions, and fearing everything by reason of the faction that was then in the city, she easily persuaded him to kill him by poison at a banquet, to which he was to be invited as a stranger. He, coming to the entertainment, thought it not fit to discover himself at once, but willing to give his father the occasion of first finding him out, the meat being on the table, he drew his sword as if he designed to cut with it; Ægeus, at once recognising the token, threw down the cup of poison, and, questioning his son, embraced him, and having gathered together all his citizens, owned him publicly before them, who, on their part, received him gladly for the fame of his greatness and bravery; and it is said, that when the cup fell, the poison was spilt there where now is the enclosed space in the Delphinium; for in that place stood Ægeus' house, and the figure of Mercury on the east side of the temple is called the Mercury of Ægeus' gate.

The sons of Pallas, who before were quiet upon expectation of recovering the kingdom after Ægeus' death, who was without issue, as soon as Theseus appeared and was acknowledged the successor, highly resenting that Ægeus first, an adopted son only of Pandion, and not at all related to the family of Erechtheus, should be holding the kingdom, and that after him, Theseus, a visitor and stranger, should be destined to succeed to it, broke out into open war. And dividing themselves into two companies, one part of them marched openly from Sphettus, with their father, against the city, the other, hiding themselves in the village of Gargettus, lay in ambush, with a design to set upon the enemy on both sides. They had with them a crier of the township of Agnus, named Leos, who discovered to Theseus all the designs of the Pallantidæ. He immediately fell upon those that lay in ambuscade, and cut them all off; upon tidings of which Pallas and his company fled and were dispersed.

From hence they say is derived the custom among the people of the township of Pallene to have no marriages or any alliance with the people of Agnus, nor to suffer the criers to pronounce in their proclamations the words used in all other parts of the country, Acouĕtĕ Leoi (Hear ye people), hating the very sound of Leo, because of the treason of Leos.

Theseus, longing to be in action, and desirous also to make himself popular, left Athens to fight with the bull of Marathon, which did no small mischief to the inhabitants of Tetrapolis. And having overcome it, he brought it alive in triumph through the city, and afterwards sacrificed it to the Delphinian Apollo. The story of Hecale, also, of her receiving and entertaining Theseus in this expedition, seems to be not altogether void of truth; for the townships round about, meeting upon a certain day, used to offer a sacrifice which they called Hecalesia, to Jupiter Hecaleius, and to pay honour to Hecale, whom, by a diminutive name, they called Hecalene, because she, while entertaining Theseus, who was quite a youth, addressed him, as old people do, with similar endearing diminutives; and having made a vow to Jupiter for him as he was going to the fight, that, if he returned in safety, she would offer sacrifices in thanks of it, and dying before he came back, she had these honours given her by way of return for her hospitality, by the command of Theseus, as Philochorus tells us.

Not long after arrived the third time from Crete the collectors of the tribute which the Athenians paid them upon the following occasion. Androgeus having been treacherously murdered in the confines of Attica, not only Minos, his father, put the Athenians to extreme distress by a perpetual war, but the gods also laid waste their country; both famine and pestilence lay heavy upon them, and even their rivers were dried up. Being told by the oracle that, if they appeased and reconciled Minos, the anger of the gods would cease and they should enjoy rest from the miseries they laboured under, they sent heralds, and with much supplication were at last reconciled, entering into an agreement to send to Crete every nine years a tribute of seven young men and as many virgins, as most writers agree in stating; and the most poetical story adds, that the Minotaur destroyed them, or that, wandering in the labyrinth, and finding no possible means of getting out, they miserably ended their lives there; and that this Minotaur was (as Euripides hath it)—

> A mingled form where two strange shapes combined,
> And different natures, bull and man, were joined.

But Philochorus says that the Cretans will by no means allow the truth of this, but say that the labyrinth was only an ordinary prison, having no other bad quality but that it secured the prisoners from escaping, and that Minos, having instituted games in honour of Androgeus, gave, as a reward to the victors, these youths, who in the meantime were kept in the labyrinth; and that the first that overcame in those games was one of the greatest power and command among them, named Taurus, a man of no merciful or gentle disposition, who treated the Athenians that were made his prize in a proud and cruel manner. Also Aristotle himself, in the account that he gives of the form of government of the Bottiæans, is manifestly of opinion that the youths were not slain by Minos, but spent the remainder of their days in slavery in Crete; that the Cretans, in former times, to acquit themselves of an ancient vow which they had made, were used to send an offering of the first-fruits of their men to Delphi, and that some descendants of these Athenian slaves were mingled with them and sent amongst them, and, unable to get their living there, removed from thence, first into Italy, and settled about Japygia; from thence again, that they removed to Thrace, and were named Bottiæans; and that this is the reason why, in a certain sacrifice, the Bottiæan girls sing a hymn beginning *Let us go to Athens.* This may show us how dangerous it is to incur the hostility of a city that is mistress of eloquence and song. For Minos was always ill spoken of, and represented ever as a very wicked man, in the Athenian theatres; neither did Hesiod avail him by calling him "the most royal Minos," nor Homer, who styles him *"Jupiter's familiar friend";* the tragedians got the better, and from the vantage ground of the stage showered down obloquy upon him, as a man of cruelty and violence; whereas, in fact, he appears to have been a king and a lawgiver, and Rhadamanthus, a judge under him, administering the statutes that he ordained.

Now, when the time of the third tribute was come, and the fathers who had any young men for their sons were to proceed by lot to the choice of those that were to be sent, there arose fresh discontents and accusations against Ægeus among the people, who were full of grief and indignation that he who was the cause of all their miseries was the only person exempt from the punishment; adopting and settling his kingdom upon a bastard and foreign son, he took no thought, they said, of their destitution and loss, not of bastards, but lawful children. These things sensibly affected Theseus, who, thinking it but just not to disregard, but rather partake of, the sufferings of his fellow-citizens, offered himself for one without any lot. All else were struck with admiration for the nobleness and with love for the goodness of the act; and Ægeus, after prayers and entreaties, finding him inflexible and not to be persuaded, proceeded to the choosing of the rest by lot. Hellanicus, however, tells us that the Athenians did not send the young men and virgins by lot, but that Minos himself used to come and make his own choice, and pitched upon Theseus before all others; according to the conditions agreed upon between them, namely, that the Athenians should furnish them with a ship and that the young men that were to sail with him should carry no weapons of war; but that if the Minotaur was destroyed, the tribute should cease.

On the two former occasions of the payment of the tribute, entertaining no hopes of safety or return, they sent out the ship with a black sail, as to unavoidable destruction; but now, Theseus encouraging his father, and speaking greatly of himself, as confident that he should kill the Minotaur, he gave the pilot another sail, which was white, commanding him, as he returned, if Theseus were safe, to make use of that; but if not, to sail with the black one, and to hang out that sign of his misfortune. Simonides says that the sail which Ægeus delivered to the pilot was not white, but—

> Scarlet, in the juicy bloom
> Of the living oak tree steeped,

and that this was to be the sign of their escape. Phereclus, son of Amarsyas, according to Simonides, was pilot of the ship. But Philochorus says Theseus had sent him by Scirus, from Salamis, Nausithoüs to be his steersman, and Phæax his look-out-man in the prow, the Athenians having as yet not applied themselves to navigation; and that Scirus did this because one of the young men, Menesthes, was his daughter's son; and this the chapels of Nausithoüs and Phæax, built by Theseus near the temple of Scirus, confirm. He adds, also, that the feast named Cybernesia was in honour of them. The lot being cast, and Theseus having received out of the Prytaneüm those upon whom it fell, he went to the Delphinium, and made an offering for them to Apollo of his suppliant's badge, which was a bough of a consecrated olive tree, with white wool tied about it.

Having thus performed his devotion, he went to sea, the sixth day of Munychion, on which day even to this time the Athenians send their virgins to the same temple to make supplication to the gods. It is farther reported that he was commanded by the oracle of Delphi to make Venus his guide, and to invoke her as the companion and conductress of his voyage and that, as he was sacrificing a she goat to her by the seaside, it was suddenly changed into a he, and for this cause that goddess had the name of Epitragia.

When he arrived at Crete, as most of the ancient historians as well as poets tell us, having a clue of thread given him by Ariadne, who had fallen in love with him, and being instructed by her how to use it so as to conduct him through the windings of the labyrinth, he escaped out of it and slew the Minotaur, and sailed back, taking along with him Ariadne and the young Athenian captives. Phercydes adds that he bored holes in the bottom of the Cretan ships to hinder their pursuit. Demon writes that Taurus, the chief captain of Minos, was slain by Theseus at the mouth of the port, in a naval combat as he was sailing out for Athens. But Philochorus gives us the story thus: That at the setting forth of the yearly games by King Minos, Taurus was expected to carry away the prize, as he had done before; and was much grudged the honour. His character and manners made his power hateful, and he was accused moreover of too near familiarity with Pasiphae, for which reason, when Theseus desired the combat, Minos readily complied. And as it was a custom in Crete that the women also should be admitted to the sight of these games, Ariadne, being present, was struck with admiration of the manly beauty of Theseus, and the vigour and address which he showed in the combat, overcoming all that encountered with him. Minos, too, being extremely pleased with him, especially because he had overthrown and disgraced Taurus, voluntarily gave up the young captives to Theseus, and remitted the tribute to the Athenians. Clidemus gives an account peculiar to himself, very ambitiously, and beginning a great way back: That it was a decree consented to by all Greece, that no vessel from any place, containing above five persons, should be permitted to sail, Jason only excepted, who was made captain of the great ship Argo, to sail about and scour the sea of pirates. But Dædalus having escaped from Crete, and flying by sea to Athens, Minos, contrary to this decree, pursued him with his ships of war, was forced by a storm upon Sicily, and there ended his life. After his decease, Deucalion, his son, desiring a quarrel with

the Athenians, sent to them, demanding that they should deliver up
Dædalus to him, threatening upon their refusal, to put to death all the
young Athenians whom his father had received as hostages from the city.
To this angry message Theseus returned a very gentle answer excusing himself that he could not deliver up Dædalus, who was nearly related to him,
being his cousin-german, his mother being Merope, the daughter of
Erechtheus. In the meanwhile he secretly prepared a navy, part of it at
home near the village of the Thymœtadæ, a place of no resort, and far
from any common roads, the other part by his grandfather Pittheus' means
at Trœzen, that so his design might be carried on with the greatest secrecy.
As soon as ever his fleet was in readiness, he set sail, having with him
Dædalus and other exiles from Crete for his guides; and none of the
Cretans having any knowledge of his coming, but imagining when they saw
his fleet that they were friends and vessels of their own, he soon made himself master of the port, and immediately making a descent, reached
Gnossus before any notice of his coming, and, in a battle before the gates
of the labyrinth, put Deucalion and all his guards to the sword. The government by this means falling to Ariadne, he made a league with her, and
received the captives of her, and ratified a perpetual friendship between
the Athenians and the Cretans, whom he engaged under an oath never
again to commence any war with Athens.

There are yet many other traditions about these things, and as many
concerning Ariadne, all inconsistent with each other. Some relate that she
hung herself, being deserted by Theseus. Others that she was carried away
by his sailors to the isle of Naxos, and married to Œnarus, priest of
Bacchus; and that Theseus left her because he fell in love with another—

> For Ægle's love was burning in his breast;

a verse which Hereas, the Megarian, says was formerly in the poet Hesiod's
works, but put out by Pisistratus, in like manner as he added in Homer's
Raising of the Dead, to gratify the Athenians, the line—

> Theseus, Pirithous, mighty son of gods.

Others say Ariadne had sons also by Theseus, Œnopion and Staphylus; and
among these is the poet Ion of Chios, who writes of his own native city—

> Which once Œnopion, son of Theseus built.

But the more famous of the legendary stories everybody (as I may say) has
in his mouth. In Pæon, however, the Amathusian, there is a story given,

differing from the rest. For he writes that Theseus, being driven by a storm upon the isle of Cyprus, and having aboard with him Ariadne, big with child, and extremely discomposed with the rolling of the sea, set her on shore, and left her there alone, to return himself and help the ship, when, on a sudden, a violent wind carried him again out to sea. That the women of the island received Ariadne very kindly, and did all they could to console and alleviate her distress at being left behind. That they counterfeited kind letters, and delivered them to her, as sent from Theseus, and, when she fell in labour, were diligent in performing to her every needful service; but that she died before she could be delivered, and was honourably interred. That soon after Theseus returned, and was greatly afflicted for her loss, and at his departure left a sum of money among the people of the island, ordering them to do sacrifice to Ariadne; and caused two little images to be made and dedicated to her, one of silver and the other of brass. Moreover, that on the second day of Gorpiæus, which is sacred to Ariadne, they have this ceremony among their sacrifices, to have a youth lie down and with his voice and gesture represent the pains of a woman in travail; and that the Amathusians call the grove in which they show her tomb, the grove of Venus Ariadne.

Differing yet from this account, some of the Naxians write that there were two Minoses and two Ariadnes, one of whom, they say, was married to Bacchus, in the isle of Naxos, and bore the children Staphylus and his brother; but that the other, of a later age, was carried off by Theseus, and; being afterwards deserted by him, retired to Naxos, with her nurse Corcyna, whose grave they yet show. That this Ariadne also died there, and was worshipped by the island, but in a different manner from the former; for her day is celebrated with general joy and revelling, but all the sacrifices performed to the latter are attended with mourning and gloom.

Now Theseus, in his return from Crete, put in at Delos, and having sacrificed to the god of the island, dedicated to the temple the image of Venus which Ariadne had given him, and danced with the young Athenians a dance that, in memory of him, they say is still preserved among the inhabitants of Delos, consisting in certain measured turnings and returnings, imitative of the windings and twistings of the labyrinth. And this dance, as Dicæarchus writes, is called among the Delians the Crane. This he danced around the Ceratonian Altar, so called from its consisting of horns taken from the left side of the head. They say also that he instituted games in Delos, where he was the first that began the custom of giving a palm to the victors.

When they were come near the coast of Attica, so great was the joy for the happy success of their voyage, that neither Theseus himself nor the pilot remembered to hang out the sail which should have been the token of their safety to Ægeus, who, in despair at the sight, threw himself headlong from a rock, and perished in the sea. But Theseus being arrived at the port of Phalerum, paid there the sacrifices which he had vowed to the gods at his setting out to sea, and sent a herald to the city to carry the news of his safe return. At his entrance, the herald found the people for the most part full of grief for the loss of their king; others, as may well be believed, as full of joy for the tidings that he brought, and eager to welcome him and crown him with garlands for his good news, which he indeed accepted of, but hung them upon his herald's staff; and thus returning to the seaside before Theseus had finished his libation to the gods, he stayed apart for fear of disturbing the holy rites; but, as soon as the libation was ended, went up and related the king's death, upon the hearing of which, with great lamentations and a confused tumult of grief, they ran with all haste to the city. And from hence, they say, it comes that at this day, in the feast of Oschophoria, the herald is not crowned, but his staff, and all who are present at the libation cry out *eleleu, iou, iou,* the first of which confused sounds is commonly used by men in haste, or at a triumph, the other is proper to people in consternation or disorder of mind.

Theseus, after the funeral of his father, paid his vows to Apollo the seventh day of Pyanepsion; for on that day the youth that returned with him safe from Crete made their entry into the city. They say, also, that the custom of boiling pulse at this feast is derived from hence; because the young men that escaped put all that was left of their provision together, and, boiling it in one common pot, feasted themselves with it, and ate it all up together. Hence, also, they carry in procession an olive branch bound about with wool (such as they then made use of in their supplications), which they call Eiresione, crowned with all sorts of fruits, to signify that scarcity and barrenness was ceased, singing in their procession this song:

> Eiresione bring figs, and Eiresione bring loaves;
> Bring us honey in pints, and oil to rub on our bodies,
> And a strong flagon of wine, for all to go mellow to bed on.

Although some hold opinion that this ceremony is retained in memory of the Heraclidæ, who were thus entertained and brought up by the Athenians. But most are of the opinion which we have given above.

The ship wherein Theseus and the youth of Athens returned had thirty oars, and was preserved by the Athenians down even to the time of Demetrius Phalereus, for they took away the old planks as they decayed, putting in new and stronger timber in their place, insomuch that this ship became a standing example among the philosophers, for the logical question of things that grow; one side holding that the ship remained the same, and the other contending that it was not the same.

The feast called Oschophoria, or the feast of boughs, which to this day the Athenians celebrate, was then first instituted by Theseus. For he took not with him the full number of virgins which by lot were to be carried away, but selected two youths of his acquaintance, of fair and womanish faces, but of a manly and forward spirit, and having, by frequent baths, and avoiding the heat and scorching of the sun, with a constant use of all the ointments and washes and dresses that serve to the adorning of the head or smoothing the skin or improving the complexion, in a manner changed them from what they were before, and having taught them farther to counterfeit the very voice and carriage and gait of virgins so that there could not be the least difference perceived, he, undiscovered by any, put them into the number of the Athenian maids designed for Crete. At his return, he and these two youths led up a solemn procession, in the same habit that is now worn by those who carry the vine-branches. Those branches they carry in honour of Bacchus and Ariadne, for the sake of their story before related; or rather because they happened to return in autumn, the time of gathering the grapes. The women, whom they call Deipnopheræ, or supper-carriers, are taken into these ceremonies, and assist at the sacrifice, in remembrance and imitation of the mothers of the young men and virgins upon whom the lot fell, for thus they ran about bringing bread and meat to their children; and because the women then told their sons and daughters many tales and stories, to comfort and encourage them under the danger they were going upon, it has still continued a custom that at this feast old fables and tales should be told. For these particularities we are indebted to the history of Demon. There was then a place chosen out, and a temple erected in it to Theseus, and those families out of whom the tribute of the youth was gathered were appointed to pay tax to the temple for sacrifices to him. And the house of the Phytalidæ had the overseeing of these sacrifices, Theseus doing them that honour in recompense of their former hospitality.

Now, after the death of his father Ægeus, forming in his mind a great and wonderful design, he gathered together all the inhabitants of Attica into one town, and made them one people of one city, whereas before they lived dispersed, and were not easy to assemble upon any affair for the common interest. Nay, differences and even wars often occurred between them, which he by his persuasions appeased, going from township to township, and from tribe to tribe. And those of a more private and mean condition readily embracing such good advice, to those of greater power he promised a commonwealth without monarchy, a democracy, or people's government, in which he should only be continued as their commander in war and the protector of their laws, all things else being equally distributed among them—and by this means brought a part of them over to his proposal. The rest, fearing his power, which was already grown very formidable, and knowing his courage and resolution, chose rather to be persuaded than forced into a compliance. He then dissolved all the distinct state-houses, council halls, and magistracies, and built one common state-house and council hall on the site of the present upper town, and gave the name of Athens to the whole state, ordaining a common feast and sacrifice, which he called Panathenæa, or the sacrifice of all the united Athenians. He instituted also another sacrifice called Metœcia, or Feast of Migration, which is yet celebrated on the sixteenth day of Hecatombæon. Then, as he had promised, he laid down his regal power and proceeded to order a commonwealth, entering upon this great work not without advice from the gods. For having sent to consult the oracle of Delphi concerning the fortune of his new government and city, he received this answer:

> Son of the Pitthean maid,
> To your town the terms and fates,
> My father gives of many states.
> Be not anxious nor afraid;
> The bladder will not fail to swim
> On the waves that compass him.

Which oracle, they say, one of the sibyls long after did in a manner repeat to the Athenians, in this verse:

> The bladder may be dipt, but not be drowned.

Farther yet designing to enlarge his city, he invited all strangers to come and enjoy equal privileges with the natives, and it is said that the common form, *Come hither, all ye people*, was the words that Theseus proclaimed when he thus set up a commonwealth, in a manner, for all nations. Yet he did not suffer his state, by the promiscuous multitude that flowed in, to be turned into confusion and be left without any order or degree, but was the first that divided the Commonwealth into three distinct ranks, the noblemen, the husbandmen, and artificers. To the nobility he committed the care of religion, the choice of magistrates, the teaching and dispensing of the laws, and interpretation and direction in all sacred matters; the whole city being, as it were, reduced to an exact equality, the nobles excelling the rest in honour, the husbandmen in profit, and the artificers in number. And that Theseus was the first, who, as Aristotle says, out of an inclination to popular government, parted with the regal power, Homer also seems to testify, in his catalogue of the ships, where he gives the name of *People* to the Athenians only.

He also coined money, and stamped it with the image of an ox, either in memory of the Marathonian bull, or of Taurus, whom he vanquished, or else to put his people in mind to follow husbandry; and from this coin came the expression so frequent among the Greeks, of a thing being worth ten or a hundred oxen. After this he joined Megara to Attica, and erected that famous pillar on the Isthmus, which bears an inscription of two lines, showing the bounds of the two countries that meet there. On the east side the inscription is,

Peloponnesus there, Ionia here

and on the west side,

Peloponnesus here, Ionia there.

He also instituted the games, in emulation of Hercules, being ambitious that as the Greeks, by that hero's appointment, celebrated the Olympian games to the honour of Jupiter, so by his institution, they should celebrate the Isthmian to the honour of Neptune. For those that were there before observed, dedicated to Melicerta, were performed privately in the night, and had the form rather of a religious rite than of an open spectacle or public feast. There are some who say that the Isthmian games were first instituted in memory of Sciron, Theseus thus making expiation for his death, upon account of the nearness of kindred between them, Sciron being the son of Canethus and Heniocha, the daughter of Pittheus; though others write that Sinnis, not Sciron, was their son, and that to his honour, and not to the other's, these games were ordained by Theseus. At the same time he made an agreement with the Corinthians, that they should allow those that came from Athens to the celebration of the Isthmian games as much space of honour before the rest to behold the spectacle in, as the sail of the ship that brought them thither, stretched to its full extent, could cover; so Hellanicus and Andro of Halicarnassus have established.

Concerning his voyage into the Euxine Sea, Philochorus and some others write that he made it with Hercules, offering him his service in the war against the Amazons, and had Antiope given him for the reward of his valour; but the greater number, of whom are Pherecydes, Hellanicus, and Herodorus, write that he made this voyage many years after Hercules, with a navy under his own command, and took the Amazon prisoner—the more probable story, for we do not read that any other, of all those that accompanied him in this action, took any Amazon prisoner. Bion adds, that, to take her, he had to use deceit and fly away; for the Amazons, he says, being naturally lovers of men, were so far from avoiding Theseus when he touched upon their coasts, that they sent him presents to his ship; but he, having invited Antiope, who brought them, to come aboard, immediately set sail and carried her away. An author named Menecrates that wrote the History of Nicæ in Bithynia, adds, that Theseus, having Antiope aboard his vessel, cruised for sometime about those coasts, and that there were in the same ship three young men of Athens, that accompanied him in this voyage, all brothers, whose names were Euneos, Thoas, and Soloon. The last of these fell desperately in love with Antiope, and, escaping the notice of the rest, revealed the secret only to one of his most intimate acquaintances, and employed him to disclose his passion to Antiope; she rejected his pretences with a very positive denial, yet treated the matter with much gentleness and discretion, and made no complaint to Theseus of anything that had happened; but Soloon, the thing being desperate, leaped into a river near the seaside and drowned himself. As soon as Theseus was acquainted with his death, and his unhappy love that was the cause of it, he was extremely distressed, and, in the height of his grief, an oracle which he had formerly received at Delphi came into his mind; for he had been commanded by the priestess of Apollo Pythius, that wherever in a strange land he was most sorrowful and under the greatest affliction, he should build a city there, and leave some of his followers to be governors of the place. For this cause he there founded a city, which he called, from the name of Apollo, Pythopolis, and, in honour of the unfortunate youth, he named the river that runs by it Soloon, and left the two surviving brothers intrusted with the care of the government and laws, joining with them Hermus, one of the nobility of Athens, from whom a place in the city is called the House of Hermus; though by an error in the

Dad —

I hope this is the right book.

Happy Father's Day!

Love,
Chris

accent it has been taken for the House of Hermes, or Mercury, and the honour that was designed to the hero, transferred to the god.

This was the origin and cause of the Amazonian invasion of Attica, which would seem to have been no slight or womanish enterprise. For it is impossible that they should have placed their camp in the very city, and joined battle close by the Pnyx and the hill called Museum, unless, having first conquered the country around about, they had thus with impunity advanced to the city. That they made so long a journey by land, and passed the Cimmerian Bosphorus, when frozen, as Hellanicus writes, is difficult to be believed. That they encamped all but in the city is certain, and may be sufficiently confirmed by the names that the places hereabout yet retain, and the graves and monuments of those that fell in the battle. Both armies being in sight, there was a long pause and doubt on each side which should give the first onset; at last Theseus, having sacrificed to Fear, in obedience to the command of an oracle he had received, gave them battle; and this happened in the month of Boedromion, in which to this very day the Athenians celebrate the Feast Boedromia. Clidemus, desirous to be very circumstantial, writes that the left wing of the Amazons moved towards the place which is yet called Amazonium and the right towards the Pnyx, near Chrysa, that with this wing the Athenians, issuing from behind the Museum, engaged, and that the graves of those that were slain are to be seen in the street that leads to the gate called the Piraic, by the chapel of the hero Chalcodon; and that here the Athenians were routed, and gave way before the women, as far as to the temple of the Furies, but, fresh supplies coming in from the Palladium, Ardettus, and the Lyceum, they charged their right wing, and beat them back into their tents, in which action a great number of the Amazons were slain. At length, after four months, a peace was concluded between them by the mediation of Hippolyta (for so this historian calls the Amazon whom Theseus married, and not Antiope), though others write that she was slain with a dart by Molpadia, while fighting by Theseus' side, and that the pillar which stands by the temple of Olympian Earth was erected to her honour. Nor is it to be wondered at, that in events of such antiquity, history should be in disorder. For indeed we are also told that those of the Amazons that were wounded were privately sent away by Antiope to Chalcis, where many by her care recovered, but some that died were buried there in the place that is to this time called Amazonium. That this war, however, was ended by a treaty is evident, both from the name of the place adjoining to the temple of Theseus, called, from the solemn oath there taken, Horcomosium; and also from the ancient sacrifice which used to be celebrated to the Amazons the day before the Feast of Theseus. The Megarians also show a spot in their city where some Amazons were buried, on the way from the market to a place called Rhus, where the building in the shape of a lozenge stands. It is said, likewise, that others of them were slain near Chæronea, and buried near the little rivulet formerly called Thermodon, but now Hæmon, of which an account is given in the life of Demosthenes. It appears further that the passage of the Amazons through Thessaly was not without opposition, for there are yet shown many tombs of them near Scotussa and Cynoscephalæ.

This is as much as is worth telling concerning the Amazons. For the account which the author of the poem called the Theseid gives of this rising of the Amazons, how Antiope, to revenge herself upon Theseus for refusing her and marrying Phædra, came down upon the city with her train of Amazons, whom Hercules slew, is manifestly nothing else but fable and invention. It is true, indeed, that Theseus married Phædra, but that was after the death of Antiope, by whom he had a son called Hippolytus, or, as Pindar writes, Demophon. The calamities which befell Phædra and this son, since none of the historians have contradicted the tragic poets that have written of them, we must suppose happened as represented uniformly by them.

There are also other traditions of the marriages of Theseus, neither honourable in their occasions nor fortunate in their events, which yet were never represented in the Greek plays. For he is said to have carried off Anaxo, a Trœzenian, and having slain Sinnis and Cercyon, to have ravished their daughters; to have married Peribœa, the mother of Ajax, and then Pherebœa, and then Iope, the daughter of Iphicles. And further, he is accused of deserting Ariadne (as is before related), being in love with Ægle, the daughter of Panopeus, neither justly nor honourably; and lastly, of the rape of Helen, which filled all Attica with war and blood, and was in the end the occasion of his banishment and death, as will presently be related.

Herodorus is of opinion, that though there were many famous expeditions undertaken by the bravest men of his time, yet Theseus never joined in any of them, once only excepted, with the Lapithæ, in their war against the Centaurs; but others say that he accompanied Jason to Colchis and Meleager to the slaying of the Calydonian boar, and that hence it came to be a proverb, *Not without Theseus;* that he himself, however, without aid of anyone, performed many glorious exploits, and that from him began the saying, *He is a second Hercules.* He also joined Adrastus in recovering the bodies of those that were slain before Thebes, but not as Euripides in his tragedy says, by force of arms, but by persuasion and mutual agreement and composition, for so the greater part of the historians write; Philochorus adds further that this was the first treaty that ever was made for the recovering of the bodies of the dead, but in the history of Hercules, it is shown that it was he who first gave leave to his enemies to carry off their slain. The burying-places of the most part are yet to be seen in the village called Eleutheræ; those of the commanders, at Eleusis, where Theseus allotted them a place, to oblige Adrastus. The story of Euripides in his suppliants is disproved by Æschylus in his Eleusinians, where Theseus himself relates the facts as here told.

The celebrated friendship between Theseus and Pirithoüs is said to have been thus begun; the fame of the strength and valour of Theseus being spread through Greece, Pirithoüs was desirous to make a trial and proof of it himself, and to this end seized a herd of oxen which belonged to Theseus, and was driving them away from Marathon, and, when the news was brought that Theseus pursued him in arms, he did not fly, but turned back and went to meet him. But as soon as they had viewed one another, each so admired the gracefulness and beauty, and was seized with such respect for the courage of the other, that they forgot all thoughts of fighting; and Pirithoüs, first stretching out his hand to Theseus, bade him be judge in this case himself, and promised to submit willingly to any penalty he should impose. But Theseus not only forgave him all, but entreated him to be his friend and brother in arms; and they ratified their friendship by oaths. After this Pirithoüs married Deidamia, and invited Theseus to the wedding, entreating him to come and see his country, and make acquaintance with the Lapithæ; he had at the same time invited the Centaurs to the feast, who growing hot with wine and beginning to be insolent and wild, and offering violence to the women, the Lapithæ took immediate revenge upon them, slaying many of them upon the place, and afterwards, having overcome them in battle, drove the whole race of them out of their country, Theseus all along taking their part and fighting on their side. But Herodorus gives a different relation of these things; that Theseus came not to the assistance of the Lapithæ till the war was already begun; and that it was in this journey that he had his first sight of Hercules, having made it his business to find him out at Trachis, where he had chosen to rest himself after all his wanderings and his labours; and that this interview was honourably performed on each part, with extreme respect, and goodwill, and admiration of each other. Yet it is more credible, as others write, that there were, before, frequent interviews between them, and that it was by the means of Theseus that Hercules was initiated at Eleusis, and purified before initiation, upon account of several rash actions of his former life.

Theseus was now fifty years old, as Hellanicus states, when he carried off Helen, who was yet too young to be married. Some writers, to take away this accusation of one of the greatest crimes laid to his charge, say, that he did not steal away Helen himself, but that Idas and Lynceus were the ravishers, who brought her to him, and committed her to his charge, and that, therefore, he refused to restore her at the demand of Castor and Pollux; or, indeed, they say her own father, Tyndarus, had sent her to be kept by him, for fear of Enarophorus, the son of Hippocoön, who would have carried her away by force when she was yet a child. But the most probable account, and that which has most witnesses on its side, is this: Theseus and Pirithoüs went both together to Sparta, and, having seized the young lady as she was dancing in the temple Diana Orthia, fled away with her. There were presently men sent in arms to pursue, but they followed no further than to Tegea; and Theseus and Pirithoüs, being now out of danger, having passed through Peloponnesus, made an agreement between themselves, that he to whom the lot should fall should have Helen to his wife, but should be obliged to assist in procuring another for his friend. The lot fell upon Theseus, who conveyed her to Aphidnæ, not being yet marriageable, and delivered her to one of his allies, called Aphidnus, and, having sent his mother, Æthra, after to take care of her, desired him to keep them so secretly, that none might know where they were; which done, to return the same service to his friend Pirithoüs, he accompanied him in his journey to Epirus, in order to steal away the king of the Molossians' daughter. The king, his own name being Aidoneus, or Pluto, called his wife Proserpina, and his daughter Cora, and a great dog, which he kept, Cerberus, with whom he ordered all that came as suitors to his daughter to fight, and promised her to him that should overcome the beast. But having been informed that the design of Pirithoüs and his companion was not to court his daughter, but to force her away, he caused them both to be seized, and threw Pirithoüs to be torn in pieces by his dog, and put Theseus into prison, and kept him.

About this time, Menestheus, the son of Peteus, grandson of Orneus, and great-grandson of Erechtheus, the first man that is recorded to have affected popularity and ingratiated himself with the multitude, stirred up and exasperated the most eminent men of the city, who had long borne a secret grudge to Theseus, conceiving that he had robbed them of their several little kingdoms and lordships, and having pent them all up in one city, was using them as his subjects and slaves. He put also the meaner people into commotion, telling them, that, deluded with a mere dream of liberty, though indeed they were deprived of both that and of their proper homes and religious usages, instead of many good and gracious kings of their own, they had given themselves up to be lorded over by a newcomer and a stranger. Whilst he was thus busied in infecting the minds of the citizens, the war that Castor and Pollux brought against Athens came very opportunely to further the sedition he had been promoting, and some say that by his persuasions was wholly the cause of their invading the city. At their first approach, they committed no acts of hostility, but peaceably demanded their sister Helen; but the Athenians returning answer that they neither had her there nor knew where she was disposed of, they prepared to assault the city, when Academus, having, by whatever means, found it out, disclosed to them that she was secretly kept at Aphidnæ. For which reason he was both highly honoured during his life by Castor and Pollux, and the Lacedæmonians, when often in aftertimes they made incursions into Attica, and destroyed all the country round about, spared the Academy for the sake of Academus. But Dicæarchus writes that there were two Arcadians in the army of Castor and Pollux, the one called Echedemus, and the other Marathus; from the first that which is now called Academia was then named Echedemia, and the village Marathon had its name from the other, who, to fulfil some oracle, voluntarily offered himself to be made a sacrifice before battle. As soon as they were arrived at Aphidnæ, they overcame their enemies in a set battle, and then assaulted and took the town. And here, they say, Alycus, the son of Sciron, was slain, of the party of the Dioscuri (Castor and Pollux), from whom a place in Megara, where he was buried, is called Alycus to this day. And Hereas writes that it was Theseus himself that killed him, in witness of which he cites these verses concerning Alycus—

> And Alycus upon Aphidnæ's plain,
> By Theseus in the cause of Helen slain.

Though it is not at all probable that Theseus himself was there when both the city and his mother were taken.

Aphidnæ being won by Castor and Pollux, and the city of Athens being in consternation, Menestheus persuaded the people to open their gates, and receive them with all manner of friendship, for they were, he told them, at enmity with none but Theseus, who had first injured them, and were benefactors and saviours to all mankind beside. And their behaviour gave credit to those promises; for, having made themselves absolute masters of the place, they demanded no more than to be initiated, since they were as nearly related to the city as Hercules was, who had received the same honour. This their desire they easily obtained, and were adopted by Aphidnus, as Hercules had been by Pylius. They were honoured also like gods, and were called by a new name, Anaces, either from the *cessation* of the war, or from the *care* they took that none should suffer any injury, though there was so great an army within the walls; for the phrase *anakos ekhein* is used of those who look to or care for anything; kings for this reason, perhaps, are called *anactes*. Others say, that from the appearance of their star in the heavens, they were thus called, for in the Attic dialect this name comes very near the words that signify *above*.

Some say that Æthra, Theseus' mother, was here taken prisoner, and carried to Lacedæmon, and from thence went away with Helen to Troy, alleging this verse of Homer to prove that she waited upon Helen—

Æthra of Pittheus born, and large eyed Clymene.

Others reject this verse as none of Homer's, as they do likewise the whole fable of Munychus, who, the story says, was the son of Demophon and Laodice, born secretly, and brought up by Æthra at Troy. But Ister, in the thirteenth book of his Attic History, gives us an account of Æthra, different yet from all the rest: that Achilles and Patroclus overcame Paris in Thessaly, near the river Sperchius, but that Hector took and plundered the city of the Trœzenians, and made Æthra prisoner there. But this seems a groundless tale.

Now Hercules, passing by the Molossians, was entertained in his way to Aidoneus the king, who, in conversation, accidentally spoke of the journey of Theseus and Pirithoüs into his country, of what they had designed to do, and what they were forced to suffer. Hercules was much grieved for the inglorious death of the one and the miserable condition of the other. As for Pirithoüs, he thought it useless to complain; but begged to have Theseus released for his sake, and obtained that favour from the king. Theseus, being thus set at liberty, returned to Athens, where his friends were not yet wholly suppressed, and dedicated to Hercules all the sacred places which the city had set apart for himself, changing their names from Thesea to Heraclea, four only excepted, as Philochorus writes. And wishing immediately to resume the first place in the commonwealth, and manage the state as before, he soon found himself involved in factions and troubles; those who long had hated him had now added to their hatred contempt; and the minds of the people were so generally corrupted, that, instead of obeying commands with silence, they expected to be flattered into their duty. He had some thoughts to have reduced them by force, but was overpowered by demagogues and factions. And at last, despairing of any good success of his affairs in Athens, he sent away his children privately to Euboea, commending them to the care of Elephenor, the son of Chalcodon; and he himself having solemnly cursed the people of Athens in the village of Gargettus, in which there yet remains the place called Araterion, or the place of cursing, sailed to Scyros, where he had lands left him by his father, and friendship, as he thought, with those of the island. Lycomedes was then king of Scyros. Theseus, therefore, addressed himself to him and desired to have his lands put into his possession, as designing to settle and to dwell there, though others say that he came to beg his assistance against the Athenians. But Lycomedes, either jealous of the glory of so great a man, or to gratify Menestheus, having led him up to the highest cliff of the island, on pretence of showing him from thence the lands that he desired, threw him headlong down from the rock, and killed him. Others say he fell down of himself by a slip of his foot, as he was walking there, according to his custom, after supper. At that time there was no notice taken, nor were any concerned for his death, but Menestheus quietly possessed the kingdom of Athens. His sons were brought up in a private condition, and accompanied Elephenor to the Trojan war, but, after the decease of Menestheus in that expedition, returned to Athens, and recovered the government. But in succeeding ages, besides several other circumstances that moved the Athenians to honour Theseus as a demigod, in the battle which was fought at Marathon against the Medes, many of the soldiers believed they saw an apparition of Theseus in arms, rushing on at the head of them against the barbarians. And after the Median war, Phædo being archon of Athens, the Athenians, consulting the oracle at Delphi, were commanded to gather together the bones of Theseus, and, laying them in some honourable place, keep them as sacred in the city. But it was very difficult to recover those relics, or so much as to find out the place where they lay, on account of the inhospitable and savage temper of the barbarous people that inhabited the island. Nevertheless, afterwards, when Cimon took the island (as is related in his life), and had a great ambition to find out the place where Theseus was buried, he, by chance, spied an eagle upon a rising ground pecking with her beak and tearing up the earth with her talons, when on the sudden it came into his mind, as it were by some divine inspiration, to dig there, and search for the bones of Theseus. There were found in that place a coffin of a man of more than ordinary size, and a brazen spearhead, and a sword lying by it, all which he took aboard his galley and brought with him to Athens. Upon which the Athenians, greatly delighted, went out to meet and receive the relics with splendid processions and sacrifices, as if it were Theseus himself returning alive to the city. He lies interred in the middle of the city, near the present gymnasium. His tomb is a sanctuary and refuge for slaves, and all those of mean condition that fly from the persecution of men in power, in memory that Theseus while he lived was an assister and protector of the distressed, and never refused the petitions of the afflicted that fled to him. The chief and most solemn sacrifice which they celebrate to him is kept on the eighth day of Pyanepsion, on which he returned with the Athenian young men from Crete. Besides which they sacrifice to him on the eighth day of every month, either because he returned from Trœzen the eighth day of Hecatombæon, as Diodorus the geographer writes, or else thinking that number to be proper to him, because he was reputed to be born of Neptune, because they sacrifice to Neptune on the eighth day of every month. The number eight being the first cube of an even number, and the double of the first square, seemed to be an emblem of the steadfast and immovable power of this god, who from thence has the names of Asphalius and Gæiochus, that is, the establisher and stayer of the earth.

ROMULUS

FROM WHOM, AND FOR WHAT REASON, THE CITY OF ROME, A NAME SO GREAT in glory, and famous in the mouths of all men, was so first called, authors do not agree. Some are of opinion that the Pelasgians, wandering over the greater part of the habitable world, and subduing numerous nations, fixed themselves here, and, from their own great *strength* in war, called the city Rome. Others, that at the taking of Troy, some few that escaped and met with shipping, put to sea, and driven by winds, were carried upon the coasts of Tuscany, and came to anchor off the mouth of the river Tiber, where their women, out of heart and weary with the sea, on its being proposed by one of the highest birth and best understanding amongst them, whose name was Roma, burnt the ships. With which act the men at first were angry, but afterwards, of necessity, seating themselves near Palatium, where things in a short while succeeded far better than they could hope, in that they found the country very good, and the people courteous, they not only did the lady Roma other honours, but added also this, of calling after her name the city which she had been the occasion of their founding. From this, they say, has come down that custom at Rome for women to salute their kinsmen and husbands with kisses; because these women, after they had burnt the ships, made use of such endearments when entreating and pacifying their husbands.

Some again say that Roma, from whom this city was so called, was daughter of Italus and Leucaria; or, by another account, of Telaphus, Hercules' son, and that she was married to Æneas, or, according to others again, to Ascanius, Æneas' son. Some tell us that Romanus, the son of Ulysses and Circe, built it; some, Romus, the son of Emathion, Diomede having sent him from Troy; and others, Romus, king of the Latins, after driving out the Tyrrhenians, who had come from Thessaly into Lydia, and from thence into Italy. Those very authors, too, who, in accordance with the safest account, make Romulus give the name of the city, yet differ concerning his birth and family. For some say, he was son to Æneas and Dexithea, daughter of Phorbas, and was, with his brother Remus, in their infancy, carried into Italy, and being on the river when the waters came down in a flood, all the vessels were cast away except only that where the young children were, which being gently landed on a level bank of the river, they were both unexpectedly saved, and from them the place was called Rome. Some say, Roma, daughter of the Trojan lady above mentioned, was married to Latinus, Telemachus' son, and became mother to Romulus; others that Æmilia, daughter of Æneas and Lavinia, had him by the god Mars; and others give you mere fables of his origin. For to Tarchetius, they say, king of Alba, who was a most wicked and cruel man, there appeared in his own house a strange vision, a male figure that rose out of a hearth, and stayed there for many days. There was an oracle of Tethys in Tuscany which Tarchetius consulted, and received an answer that a virgin should give herself to the apparition, and that a son should be born of her, highly renowned, eminent for valour, good fortune, and strength of body. Tarchetius told the prophecy to one of his own daughters, and commanded her to do this thing; which she avoiding as an indignity, sent her handmaid. Tarchetius, hearing this, in great anger imprisoned them both, purposing to put them to death, but being deterred from murder by the goddess Vesta in a dream, enjoined them for their punishment the working a web of cloth, in their chains as they were, which when they finished, they should be suffered to marry; but whatever they worked by day, Tarchetius commanded others to unravel in the night.

In the meantime, the waiting-woman was delivered of two boys, whom Tarchetius gave into the hands of one Teratius, with command to destroy them; he, however, carried and laid them by the river side, where a wolf came and continued to suckle them, while birds of various sorts brought little morsels of food, which they put into their mouths; till a cowherd, spying them, was first strangely surprised, but, venturing to draw nearer, took the children up in his arms. Thus they were saved, and when they grew up, set upon Tarchetius and overcame him. This one Promathion says, who compiled a history of Italy.

But the story which is most believed and has the greatest number of vouchers was first published, in its chief particulars, amongst the Greeks by Diocles of Peparethus, whom Fabius Pictor also follows in most points.

Here again there are variations, but in general outline it runs thus: the kings of Alba reigned in lineal descent from Æneas, and the succession devolved at length upon two brothers, Numitor and Amulius. Amulius proposed to divide things into two equal shares, and set as equivalent to the kingdom the treasure and gold that were brought from Troy. Numitor chose the kingdom; but Amulius, having the money, and being able to do more with that than Numitor, took his kingdom from him with great ease and, fearing lest his daughter might have children, made her a Vestal, bound in that condition forever to live a single and maiden life. This lady some call Ilia, others Rhea, and others Silvia; however, not long after, she was, contrary to the established laws of the Vestals, discovered to be with child, and should have suffered the most cruel punishment, had not Antho, the king's daughter, mediated with her father for her; nevertheless, she was confined, and debarred all company, that she might not be delivered without the king's knowledge. In time she brought forth two boys, of more than human size and beauty, whom Amulius, becoming yet more alarmed, commanded a servant to take and cast away; this man some call Faustulus, others say Faustulus was the man who brought them up. He put the children, however, in a small trough, and went towards the river with a design to cast them in; but, seeing the waters much swollen and coming violently down, was afraid to go nearer, and dropping the children near the bank, went away. The river overflowing, the flood at last bore up the trough, and, gently wafting it, landed them on a smooth piece of ground, which they now called Cermanus, formerly Germanus, perhaps from *Germani,* which signifies brothers.

Near this place grew a wild fig tree, which they called Ruminalis, either from Romulus (as it is vulgarly thought), or from *ruminating,* because cattle did usually in the heat of the day seek cover under it, and there chew the cud; or, better, from the suckling of these children there, for the ancients called the dug or teat of any creature *ruma;* and there is a tutelar goddess of the rearing of children whom they still call Rumilia, in sacrificing to whom they use no wine, but make libations of milk. While the infants lay here, history tells us, a she-wolf nursed them, and a woodpecker constantly fed and watched them; these creatures are esteemed holy to the god Mars; the woodpecker the Latins still especially worship and honour. Which things, as much as any, gave credit to what the mother of the children said, that their father was the god Mars; though some say that it was a mistake put upon her by Amulius, who himself had come to her dressed up in armour.

Others think that the first rise of this fable came from the children's nurse, through the ambiguity of her name; for the Latins not only called wolves *lupæ*, but also women of loose life; and such an one was the wife of Faustulus, who nurtured these children, Acca Larentia by name. To her the Romans offer sacrifices, and in the month of April the priest of Mars makes libations there; it is called the Larentian Feast. They honour also another Larentia, for the following reason: the keeper of Hercules' temple having, it seems, little else to do, proposed to his deity a game at dice, laying down that, if he himself won, he would have something valuable of the god; but if he were beaten, he would spread him a noble table, and procure him a fair lady's company. Upon these terms, throwing first for the god and then for himself, he found himself beaten. Wishing to pay his stakes honourably, and holding himself bound by what he had said, he both provided the diety a good supper, and giving money to Larentia, then in her beauty, though not publicly known, gave her a feast in the temple, where he had also laid a bed, and after supper locked her in, as if the god were really to come to her. And indeed, it is said, the deity did truly visit her, and commanded her in the morning to walk to the marketplace, and, whatever man she met first, to salute him, and make him her friend. She met one named Tarrutius, who was a man advanced in years, fairly rich, without children, and had always lived a single life. He received Larentia, and loved her well, and at his death left her sole heir of all his large and fair possessions, most of which she, in her last will and testament, bequeathed to the people. It was reported of her, being now celebrated and esteemed the mistress of a god, that she suddenly disappeared near the place where the first Larentia lay buried; the spot is at this day called Velabrum, because, the river frequently overflowing, they went over in ferry boats somewhere hereabouts to the forum, the Latin word for ferrying being *velatura*. Others derive the name from *velum*, a sail; because the exhibitors of public shows used to hang the road that leads from the forum to the Circus Maximus with sails, beginning at this spot. Upon these accounts the second Larentia is honoured at Rome.

Meantime Faustulus, Amulius' swineherd, brought up the children without any man's knowledge; or, as those say who wish to keep closer to probabilities, with the knowledge and secret assistance of Numitor; for it is said, they went to school at Gabii, and were well instructed in letters, and other accomplishments befitting their birth. And they were called Romulus and Remus (from *ruma*, the dug), as we had before, because they were found sucking the wolf. In their very infancy, the size and beauty of their bodies intimated their natural superiority; and when they grew up, they both proved brave and manly, attempting all enterprises that seemed hazardous, and showing in them a courage altogether undaunted. But Romulus seemed rather to act by counsel, and to show the sagacity of a statesman, and in all his dealings with their neighbours, whether relating to feeding or flocks or to hunting, gave the idea of being born rather to rule than to obey. To their comrades and inferiors they were therefore dear; but the king's servants, his bailiffs and overseers, as being in nothing better than themselves, they despised and slighted, nor were the least concerned at their commands and menaces. They used honest pastimes and liberal studies, not esteeming sloth and idleness honest and liberal, but rather such exercises as hunting and running, repelling robbers, taking of thieves, and delivering the wronged and oppressed from injury. For doing such things they became famous.

A quarrel occurring betwixt Numitor's and Amulius' cowherds, the latter, not enduring the driving away of their cattle by the others, fell upon them and put them to flight, and rescued the greatest part of the prey. At which Numitor being highly incensed, they little regarded it, but collected and took into their company a number of needy men and runaway slaves—acts which looked like the first stages of rebellion. It so happened, that when Romulus was attending a sacrifice, being fond of sacred rites and divination, Numitor's herdsmen, meeting with Remus on a journey with few companions, fell upon him, and after some fighting, took him prisoner, carried him before Numitor, and there accused him. Numitor would not punish him himself, fearing his brother's anger, but went to Amulius, and desired justice, as he was Amulius' brother and was affronted by Amulius' servants. The men of Alba likewise resenting the thing, and thinking he had been dishonourably used, Amulius was induced to deliver Remus up into Numitor's hands, to use him as he thought fit. He therefore took and carried him home, and, being struck with admiration of the youth's person, in stature and strength of body exceeding all men, and perceiving in his very countenance the courage and force of his mind, which stood unsubdued and unmoved by his present circumstances, and hearing further that all the enterprises and actions of his life were answerable to what he saw of him, but chiefly, as it seemed, a divine influence aiding and directing the first steps that were to lead to great results, out of the mere thought of his mind, and casually, as it were, he put his hand upon the fact, and, in gentle terms and with a kind aspect, to inspire him with confidence and hope, asked him who he was, and whence he was derived. He, taking heart, spoke thus: "I will hide nothing from you, for you seem to be of a more princely temper than Amulius, in that you give a hearing and examine before you punish, while he condemns before the case is heard. Formerly, then, we (for we are twins) thought ourselves the sons of Faustulus and Larentia, the king's servants; but since we have been accused and aspersed with calumnies, and brought in peril of our lives here before you, we hear great things of ourselves, the truth of which my present danger is likely to bring to the test. Our birth is said to have been secret, our fostering and nurture in our infancy still more strange; by birds and beasts, to whom we were cast out, we were fed, by the milk of a wolf and the morsels of a woodpecker, as we lay in a little trough by the side of the river. The trough is still in being, and is preserved, with brass plates round it, and an inscription in letters almost effaced, which may prove hereafter unavailing tokens to our parents when we are dead and gone." Numitor, upon these words, and computing the dates by the young man's looks, slighted not the hope that flattered him, but considered how to come at his daughter privately (for she was still kept under restraint), to talk with her concerning these matters.

Faustulus, hearing Remus was taken and delivered up, called on Romulus to assist in his rescue, informing him then plainly of the particulars of his birth, not but he had before given hints of it, and told as much as an attentive man might make no small conclusions from; he himself, full of concern and fear of not coming in time, took the trough, and ran instantly to Numitor; but giving a suspicion to some of the king's sentries at his gate, and being gazed upon by them and perplexed with their questions, he let it be seen that he was hiding the trough under his cloak. By chance there was one among them who was at the exposing of the children, and was employed in the office; he, seeing the trough and knowing it by its make and inscription, guessed at the business, and, without further delay, telling the king of it, brought in the man to be examined. Faustulus, hard beset, did not show himself altogether proof against terror; nor yet was he wholly forced out of all; confessed indeed the children were alive, but lived, he said, as shepherds, a great way from Alba; he himself was going to carry the trough to Ilia, who had often greatly desired to see and handle it, for a confirmation of her hopes of her children. As men generally do who are troubled in mind and act either in fear or passion, it so fell out Amulius now did; for he sent in haste as a messenger, a man, otherwise honest, and friendly to Numitor, with commands to learn from Numitor whether any tidings were come to him of the children being alive. He, coming and seeing how little Remus wanted of being received into the arms and embraces of Numitor, both gave him surer confidence in his hope, and advised them, with all expedition, to proceed to action; himself too joining and assisting them, and indeed, had they wished it, the time would not have let them demur. For Romulus was now come very near, and many of the citizens, out of fear and hatred of Amulius, were running out to join him; besides, he brought great forces with him, divided into companies each of an hundred men, every captain carrying a small bundle of grass and shrubs tied to a pole. The Latins call such bundles *manipuli,* and from hence it is that in their armies they still call their captains *manipulares.* Remus rousing the citizens within to revolt, and Romulus making attacks from without, the tyrant, not knowing either what to do, or what expedient to think of for his security, in this perplexity and confusion was taken and put to death. This narrative for the most part given by Fabius and Diocles of Peparethus, who seem to be the earliest historians of the foundation of Rome, is suspected by some, because of its dramatic and fictitious appearance; but it would not wholly be disbelieved, if men would remember what a poet fortune sometimes shows herself, and consider that the Roman power would hardly have reached so high a pitch without a divinely ordered origin, attended with great and extraordinary circumstances.

Amulius now being dead and matters quietly disposed, the two brothers would neither dwell in Alba without governing there, nor take the government into their own hands during the life of their grandfather. Having therefore delivered the dominion up into his hands, and paid their mother befitting honour, they resolved to live by themselves, and build a city in the same place where they were in their infancy brought up. This seems the most honourable reason for their departure; though perhaps it was necessary, having such a body of slaves and fugitives collected about them, either to come to nothing by dispersing them, or if not so, then to live with them elsewhere. For that the inhabitants of Alba did not think fugitives worthy of being received and incorporated as citizens among them plainly appears from the matter of the women, an attempt made not wantonly but of necessity, because they could not get wives by goodwill. For they certainly paid unusual respect and honour to those whom they thus forcibly seized.

Not long after the first foundation of the city, they opened a sanctuary of refuge for all fugitives, which they called the temple of the god Asylæus, where they received and protected all, delivering none back, neither the servant to his master, the debtor to his creditor, nor the murderer into the hands of the magistrate, saying it was a privileged place, and they could so maintain it by an order of the holy oracle; insomuch that the city grew presently very populous, for they say, it consisted at first of no more than a thousand houses. But of that hereafter.

Their minds being full bent upon building, there arose presently a difference about the place. Romulus chose what was called Roma Quadrata, or the Square Rome, and would have the city there. Remus laid out a piece of ground on the Aventine Mount, well fortified by nature, which was from him called Remonium, but now Rignarium. Concluding at last to decide the contest by a divination from a flight of birds, and placing themselves apart at some distance, Remus, they say, saw six vultures, and Romulus double that number; others say, Remus did truly see his number, and that Romulus feigned his, but when Remus came to him, that then he did indeed see twelve. Hence it is that the Romans, in their divinations from birds, chiefly regard the vulture, though Herodorus Ponticus relates that Hercules was always very joyful when a vulture appeared to him upon any action. For it is a creature the least hurtful of any, pernicious neither to corn, fruit-tree, nor cattle; it preys only upon carrion, and never kills or hurts any living thing; and as for birds it touches not them, though they are dead, as being of its own species, whereas eagles, owls, and hawks mangle and kill their own fellow-creatures; yet, as Æschylus says,

What bird is clean that preys on fellow bird?

Besides, all other birds are, so to say, never out of our eyes; they let themselves be seen of us continually; but a vulture is a very rare sight, and you can seldom meet with a man that has seen their young; their rarity and infrequency has raised a strange opinion in some, that they come to us from some other world; as soothsayers ascribe a divine origination to all things not produced either of nature or of themselves.

When Remus knew the cheat, he was much displeased; and as Romulus was casting up a ditch, where he designed the foundation of the city-wall, he turned some pieces of the work to ridicule, and obstructed others; at last, as he was in contempt leaping over it, some say Romulus himself struck him, others Celer, one of his companions; he fell, however, and in the scuffle Faustulus also was slain, and Plistinus, who, being Faustulus' brother, story tells us, helped to bring up Romulus. Celer upon this fled instantly into Tuscany, and from him the Romans call all men that are swift of feet Celeres; and because Quintus Metellus, at his father's funeral, in a few days' time gave the people a show of gladiators, admiring his expedition in getting it ready, they gave him the name of Celer.

Romulus, having buried his brother Remus, together with his two foster-fathers, on the mount Remonia, set to building his city; and sent for men out of Tuscany, who directed him by sacred usages and written rules in all the ceremonies to be observed, as in a religious rite. First, they dug a round trench about that which is now the Comitium, or Court of Assembly, and into it solemnly threw the first-fruits of all things either good by custom or necessary by nature; lastly, every man taking a small piece of earth of the country from whence he came, they all threw in promiscuously together. This trench they call, as they do the heavens, Mundus; making which their centre, they described the city in a circle round it. Then the founder fitted to a plough a brazen ploughshare, and, yoking together a bull and a cow, drove himself a deep line or furrow round the bounds; while the business of those that followed after was to see that whatever earth was thrown up should be turned all inwards towards the city; and not to let any clod lie outside. With this line they described the wall, and called it, by a contraction, Pomœrium, that is, *post-murum*, after or beside the wall; and where they designed to make a gate, there they took out the share, carried the plough over, and left a space; for which reason they consider the whole wall as holy, except where the gates are; for had they adjudged them also sacred, they could not, without offence to religion, have given free ingress and egress for the necessaries of human life, some of which are in themselves unclean.

As for the day they began to build the city, it is universally agreed to have been the twenty-first of April, and that day the Romans annually keep holy, calling it their country's birthday. At first, they say, they sacrificed no living creature on this day, thinking it fit to preserve the feast of their country's birthday pure and without stain of blood. Yet before ever the city was built, there was a feast of herdsmen and shepherds kept on this day, which went by the name of Palilia. The Roman and Greek months have now little or no agreement; they say, however, the day on which Romulus began to build was quite certainly the thirtieth of the month, at which time there was an eclipse of the sun which they conceived to be that seen by Antimachus, the Teian poet, in the third year of the sixth Olympiad. In the times of Varro the philosopher, a man deeply read in Roman history, lived one Tarrutius, his familiar acquaintance, a good philosopher and mathematician, and one, too, that out of curiosity had studied the way of drawing schemes and tables, and was thought to be a proficient in the art;

to him Varro propounded to cast Romulus' nativity, even to the first day and hour, making his deductions from the several events of the man's life which he should be informed of, exactly as in working back a geometrical problem; for it belonged, he said, to the same science both to foretell a man's life by knowing the time of his birth, and also to find out his birth by the knowledge of his life. This task Tarrutius undertook, and first looking into the actions and casualties of the man, together with the time of his life and manner of his death, and then comparing all these remarks together, he very confidently and positively pronounced that Romulus was conceived in his mother's womb the first year of the second Olympiad, the twenty-third day of the month the Ægyptians call Chœac, and the third hour after sunset, at which time there was a total eclipse of the sun; that he was born the twenty-first day of the month Thoth, about sunrising; and that the first stone of Rome was laid by him the ninth day of the month Pharmuthi, between the second and third hour. For the fortunes of cities as well as of men, they think, have their certain periods of time prefixed, which may be collected and foreknown from the position of the stars at their first foundation. But these and the like relations may perhaps not so much take and delight the reader with their novelty and curiosity as offend him by their extravagance.

The city now being built, Romulus enlisted all that were of age to bear arms into military companies, each company consisting of three thousand footmen and three hundred horse. These companies were called legions, because they were the choicest and most select of the people for fighting men. The rest of the multitude he called the people; an hundred of the most eminent he chose for counsellors; these he styled patricians, and their assembly the senate, which signifies a council of elders. The patricians, some say, were so called because they were the fathers of lawful children: others, because they could give a good account who their own fathers were, which not everyone of the rabble that poured into the city at first could do; others, from patronage, their word for protection of inferiors, the origin of which they attribute to Patron, one of those that came over with Evander, who was a great protector and defender of the weak and needy. But perhaps the most probable judgment might be, that Romulus, esteeming it the duty of the chiefest and wealthiest men, with a fatherly care and concern to look after the meaner, and also encouraging the commonalty not to dread or be aggrieved at the honours of their superiors, but to love and respect them, and to think and call them their fathers, might from hence give them the name of patricians. For at this very time all foreigners give senators the style of lords; but the Romans, making use of a more honourable and less invidious name, call them Patres Conscripti; at first, indeed, simply Patres, but afterwards, more being added, Patres Conscripti. By this more imposing title he distinguished the senate from the populace; and in other ways separated the nobles and the commons—calling them patrons, and these their clients—by which means he created wonderful love and amity betwixt them, productive of great justice in their dealings. For they were always their clients' counsellors in law cases, their advocates in courts of justice; in fine, their advisers and supporters in all affairs whatever. These again faithfully served their patrons, not only paying them all respect and deference, but also, in case of poverty, helping them to portion their daughters and pay off their debts; and for a patron to witness against his client, or a client against his patron, was what no law nor magistrate could enforce. In aftertimes, all other duties subsisting still between them, it was thought mean and dishonourable for the better sort to take money from their inferiors. And so much of these matters.

In the fourth month, after the city was built, as Fabius writes, the adventure of stealing the women was attempted; and some say Romulus himself, being naturally a martial man, and predisposed too, perhaps by certain oracles, to believe the fates had ordained the future growth and greatness of Rome should depend upon the benefit of war, upon these accounts first offered violence to the Sabines, since he took away only thirty virgins, more to give an occasion of war than out of any want of women. But this is not very probable; it would seem rather that, observing his city to be filled by a confluence of foreigners, a few of whom had wives, and that the multitude in general, consisting of a mixture of mean and obscure men, fell under contempt, and seemed to be of no long continuance together, and hoping farther, after the women were appeased, to make this injury in some measure an occasion of confederacy and mutual commerce with the Sabines, he took in hand this exploit after this manner. First, he gave it out as if he had found an altar of a certain god hid under ground; the god they called Consus, either the god of counsel (for they still call a consultation *consilium,* and their chief magistrates *consules,* namely, counsellors), or else the equestrian Neptune, for the altar is kept covered in the Circus Maximus at all other times, and only at horse-races is exposed to public view; others merely say that this god had his altar hid under ground because counsel ought to be secret and concealed. Upon discovery of this altar, Romulus, by proclamation, appointed a day for a splendid sacrifice, and for public games and shows, to entertain all sorts of people: many flocked thither, and he himself sat in front, amidst his nobles clad in purple. Now the signal for their falling on was to be whenever he rose and gathered up his robe and threw it over his body; his men stood all ready armed, with their eyes intent upon him, and when the sign was given, drawing their swords and falling on with a great shout, they ravished away the daughters of the Sabines, they themselves flying without any let or hindrance. They say there were but thirty taken, and from them the Curiæ or Fraternities were named; but Valerius Antias says five hundred and twenty-seven, Juba, six hundred and eighty-three virgins: which was indeed the greatest excuse Romulus could allege, namely, that they had taken no married woman, save one only, Hersilia by name, and her too unknowingly; which showed that they did not commit this rape wantonly, but with a design purely of forming alliance with their neighbours by the greatest and surest bonds. This Hersilia some say Hostilius married, a most eminent man among the Romans; others, Romulus himself, and that she bore two children to him—a daughter, by reason of primogeniture called Prima, and one only son, whom, from the great concourse of citizens to him at that time, he called Aollius, but after ages Abillius. But Zenodotus the Trœzenian, in giving this account, is contradicted by many.

Among those who committed this rape upon the virgins, there were, they say, as it so then happened, some of the meaner sort of men, who were carrying off a damsel, excelling all in beauty and comeliness and stature, whom when some of superior rank that met them, attempted to take away, they cried out they were carrying her to Talasius, a young man, indeed, but brave and worthy; hearing that, they commended and applauded them loudly, and also some, turning back, accompanied them with goodwill and pleasure, shouting out the name of Talasius. Hence the Romans to this very time, at their weddings, sing Talasius for their nuptial word, as the Greeks do Hymenæus, because they say Talasius was very happy in his marriage. But Sextius Sylla the Carthaginian, a man wanting neither learning nor ingenuity, told me Romulus gave this word as a sign when to begin the onset; everybody, therefore, who made prize of a maiden, cried out, Talasius; and for that reason the custom continues so now at marriages. But most are of opinion (of whom Juba particularly is one) that this word was used to new-married women by way of incitement to good housewifery and *talasia* (spinning), as we say in Greek, Greek words at that time not being as yet overpowered by Italian. But if this be the case, and if the Romans did at the time use the word *talasia* as we do, a man might fancy a more probable reason of the custom. For when the Sabines, after the war against the Romans were reconciled, conditions were made concerning their women, that they should be obliged to do no other servile offices to their husbands but what concerned spinning; it was customary, therefore, ever after, at weddings, for those that gave the bride or escorted her or otherwise were present, sportingly to say Talasius, intimating that she was henceforth to serve in spinning and no more. It continues also a custom at this very day for the bride not of herself to pass her husband's threshold, but to be lifted over, in memory that the Sabine virgins were carried in by violence, and did not go in of their own will. Some say, too, the custom of parting the bride's hair with the head of a spear was in token their marriages began at first by war and acts of hostility, of which I have spoken more fully in my book of Questions.

This rape was committed on the eighteenth day of the month Sextilis, now called August, on which the solemnities of the Consualia are kept.

The Sabines were a numerous and martial people, but lived in small, unfortified villages, as it befitted, they thought, a colony of the Lacedæmonians to be bold and fearless; nevertheless, seeing themselves bound by such hostages to their good behaviour, and being solicitous for their daughters, they sent ambassadors to Romulus with fair and equitable requests, that he would return their young women and recall that act of violence, and afterwards, by persuasion and lawful means, seek friendly correspondence between both nations. Romulus would not part with the young women, yet proposed to the Sabines to enter into an alliance with them; upon which point some consulted and demurred long, but Acron, king of the Ceninenses, a man of high spirit and a good warrior, who had all along a jealousy of Romulus' bold attempts, and considering particularly, from this exploit upon the women, that he was growing formidable to all people, and indeed insufferable, were he not chastised, first rose up in arms, and with a powerful army advanced against him. Romulus likewise prepared to receive him; but when they came within sight and viewed each other, they made a challenge to fight a single duel, the armies standing by under arms, without participation. And Romulus, making a vow to Jupiter, if he should conquer, to carry, himself, and dedicate his adversary's armour to his honour, overcame him in combat, and a battle ensuing, routed his army also, and then took his city; but did those he found in it no injury, only commanded them to demolish the place and attend him to Rome, there to be admitted to all the privileges of citizens. And indeed there was nothing did more advance the greatness of Rome, than that she did always unite and incorporate those whom she conquered into herself. Romulus, that he might perform his vow in the most acceptable manner to Jupiter, and withal make the pomp of it delightful to the eye of the city, cut down a tall oak which he saw growing in the camp, which he trimmed to the shape of a trophy, and fastened on it Acron's whole suit of armour disposed in proper form; then he himself, girding his clothes about him, and crowning his head with a laurel garland, his hair gracefully flowing, carried the trophy resting erect upon his right shoulder, and so marched on, singing songs of triumph, and his whole army following after, the citizens all receiving him with acclamations of joy and wonder. The procession of this day was the origin and model of all after triumphs. This trophy was styled an offering to Jupiter Feretrius, from *ferire*, which in Latin is to smite; for Romulus prayed he might smite and overthrow his enemy; and the spoils were called *opima*, or royal spoils, says Varro, from their richness, which the word *opes* signifies; though one would more probably conjecture from *opus*, an act; for it is only to the general of an army who with his own hand kills his enemies' general that this honour is granted of offering the *opima spolia*. And three only of the Roman captains have had it conferred on them: first, Romulus, upon killing Acron the Ceninensian; next, Cornelius Cossus, for slaying Tolumnius the Tuscan; and lastly, Claudius Marcellus, upon his conquering Viridomarus, king of the Gauls. The two latter, Cossus and Marcellus, made their entries in triumphant chariots, bearing their trophies themselves; but that Romulus made use of a chariot, Dionysius is wrong in asserting. History says, Tarquinius, Damaratus' son, was the first that brought triumphs to this great pomp and grandeur; others, that Publicola was the first that rode in triumph. The statues of Romulus in triumph are, as may be seen in Rome, all on foot.

After the overthrow of the Ceninensians, the other Sabines still protracting the time in preparations, the people of Fidenæ, Crustumerium, and Antemna joined their forces against the Romans; they in like manner were defeated in battle, and surrendered up to Romulus their cities to be seized, their lands and territories to be divided, and themselves to be transplanted to Rome. All the lands which Romulus acquired, he distributed among the citizens, except only what the parents of the stolen virgins had; these he suffered to possess their own. The rest of the Sabines, enraged hereat, choosing Tatius their captain, marched straight against Rome. The city was almost inaccessible, having for its fortress that which is now the Capitol, where a strong guard was placed, and Tarpeius their captain; not Tarpeia the virgin, as some say who would make Romulus a fool. But Tarpeia, daughter to the captain, coveting the golden bracelets she saw them wear, betrayed the fort into the Sabines' hands, and asked, in reward of her treachery, the things they wore on their left arms. Tatius conditioning thus with her, in the night she opened one of the gates, and received the Sabines. And truly Antigonus, it would seem, was not solitary in saying he loved betrayers, but hated those who had betrayed; nor Cæsar, who told Rhymitalces the Thracian, that he loved the treason, but hated the traitor; but it is the general feeling of all who have occasion for wicked men's service, as people have for the poison of venomous beasts; they are glad of them while they are of use, and abhor their baseness when it is over. And so then did Tatius behave towards Tarpeia, for he commanded the Sabines, in regard to their contract, not to refuse her the least part of what they wore on their left arms; and he himself first took his bracelet off his arm, and threw that, together with his buckler, at her; and all the rest following, she, being borne down and quite buried with the multitude of gold and their shields, died under the weight and pressure of them; Tarpeius also himself, being prosecuted by Romulus, was found guilty of treason, as Juba says Sulpicius Galba relates. Those who write otherwise concerning Tarpeia, as that she was the daughter of Tatius, the Sabine captain, and being forcibly detained by Romulus, acted and suffered thus by her father's contrivance, speak very absurdly, of whom Antigonus is one. And Simylus, the poet, who thinks Tarpeia betrayed the Capitol, not to the Sabines, but the Gauls, having fallen in love with their king, talks mere folly, saying thus:

> Tarpeia 'twas, who, dwelling close thereby,
> Laid open Rome unto the enemy,
> She, for the love of the besieging Gaul,
> Betrayed the city's strength, the Capitol.

And a little after, speaking of her death:

> The numerous nations of the Celtic foe
> Bore her not living to the banks of Po;
> Their heavy shields upon the maid they threw,
> And with their splendid gifts entombed at once and slew.

Tarpeia afterwards was buried there, and the hill from her was called Tarpeius, until the reign of King Tarquin, who dedicated the place to Jupiter, at which time her bones were removed, and so it lost her name, except only that part of the Capitol which they still called the Tarpeian Rock, from which they used to cast down malefactors.

The Sabines being possessed of the hill, Romulus, in great fury, bade them battle, and Tatius was confident to accept it, perceiving, if they were overpowered, that they had behind them a secure retreat. The level in the middle, where they were to join battle, being surrounded with many little hills seemed to enforce both parties to a sharp and desperate conflict, by reason of the difficulties of the place, which had but a few outlets, inconvenient either for refuge or pursuit. It happened, too, the river having overflowed not many days before, there was left behind in the plain, where now the forum stands, a deep blind mud and slime, which, though it did not appear much to the eye, and was not easily avoided, at bottom was deceitful and dangerous; upon which the Sabines being unwarily about to enter, met with a piece of good fortune; for Curtius, a gallant man, eager of honour, and of aspiring thoughts, being mounted on horseback, was galloping on before the rest, and mired his horse here, and, endeavouring for a while, by whip and spur and voice to disentangle him, but finding it impossible, quitted him and saved himself; the place from him to this very time is called the Curtian Lake. The Sabines, having avoided this danger, began the fight very smartly, the fortune of the day being very dubious, though many were slain; amongst whom was Hostilius, who, they say, was husband to Hersilia, and grandfather to that Hostilius who reigned after Numa. There were many other brief conflicts, we may suppose, but the most memorable was the last, in which Romulus having received a wound on his head by a stone, and being almost felled to the ground by it, and disabled, the Romans gave way, and, being driven out of the level ground, fled towards the Palatium. Romulus, by this time recovering from his wound a little, turned about to renew the battle, and, facing the fliers, with a loud voice encouraged them to stand and fight. But being overborne with numbers, and nobody daring to face about, stretching out his hands to heaven, he prayed to Jupiter to stop the army, and not to neglect, but maintain the Roman cause, now in extreme danger. The prayer was no sooner made, than shame and respect for their king checked many; the fears of the fugitives changed suddenly into confidence. The place they first stood at was where now is the temple of Jupiter Stator (which may be translated the Stayer); there they rallied again into ranks and repulsed the Sabines to the place called now Regia, and to the temple of Vesta; where both parties, preparing to begin a second battle, were prevented by a spectacle, strange to behold, and defying description.

For the daughters of the Sabines, who had been carried off, came running, in great confusion, some on this side, some on that, with miserable cries and lamentations, like creatures possessed, in the midst of the army and among the dead bodies, to come at their husbands and their fathers, some with their young babes in their arms, others their hair loose about their ears, but all calling, now upon the Sabines, now upon the Romans, in the most tender and endearing words. Hereupon both melted into compassion, and fell back, to make room for them betwixt the armies. The sight of the women carried sorrow and commiseration upon both sides into the hearts of all, but still more their words, which began with expostulation and upbraiding, and ended with entreaty and supplication.

"Wherein," say they, "have we injured or offended you, as to deserve such sufferings past and present? We were ravished away unjustly and violently by those whose now we are; that being done, we were so long neglected by our fathers, our brothers and countrymen, that time, having now by the strictest bonds united us to those we once mortally hated, has made it impossible for us not to tremble at the danger and weep at the death of the very men who once used violence to us. You did not come to vindicate our honour, while we were virgins, against our assailants; but do come now to force away wives from their husbands and mothers from their children, a succour more grievous to its wretched objects than the former betrayal and neglect of them. Which shall we call the worst, their lovemaking or your compassion? If you were making war upon any other occasion, for our sakes you ought to withhold your hands from those to whom we have made you fathers-in-law and grandsires. If it be for our own cause, then take us, and with us your sons-in-law and grandchildren. Restore to us our parents and kindred, but do not rob us of our children and husbands. Make us not, we entreat you, twice captives." Hersilia having spoken many such words as these, and the others earnestly praying, a truce was made, and the chief officers came to a parley; the women, in the meantime, brought and presented their husbands and children to their fathers and brothers; gave those that wanted meat and drink, and carried the wounded home to be cured, and showed also how much they governed within doors, and how indulgent their husbands were to them, in demeaning themselves towards them with all kindness and respect imaginable. Upon this, conditions were agreed upon, that what women pleased might stay where they were, exempt, as aforesaid, from all drudgery and labour but spinning; that the Romans and Sabines should inhabit the city together; that the city should be called Rome from Romulus; but the

Romans, Quirites, from the country of Tatius; and that they both should govern and command in common. The place of the ratification is still called Comitium, from *coire,* to meet.

The city being thus doubled in number, an hundred of the Sabines were elected senators, and the legions were increased to six thousand foot and six hundred horse; then they divided the people into three tribes: the first, from Romulus, named Ramnenses; the second from Tatius, Tatienses; the third Luceres, from the *lucus,* or grove, where the Asylum stood, whither many fled for sanctuary, and were received into the city. And that they were just three, the very name of *tribe* and *tribune* seems to show; each tribe contained ten curiæ, or brotherhoods, which, some say, took their names from the Sabine women; but that seems to be false, because many had their names from various places. Though it is true, they then constituted many things in honour to the women; as to give them the way wherever they met them; to speak no ill word in their presence; not to appear naked before them, or else be liable to prosecution before the judge, of homicide; that their children should wear an ornament about their necks called the *bulla* (because it was like a bubble), and the *prœtexta,* a gown edged with purple.

The princes did not immediately join in council together, but at first each met with his own hundred; afterwards all assembled together. Tatius dwelt where now the temple of Moneta stands, and Romulus, close by the steps, as they call them, of the Fair Shore, near the descent from the Mount Palatine to the Circus Maximus. There, they say, grew the holy cornel tree, of which they report, that Romulus once, to try his strength, threw a dart from the Aventine Mount, the staff of which was made of cornel, which struck so deep into the ground, that no one of many that tried could pluck it up, and the soil being fertile, gave nourishment to the wood, which sent forth branches, and produced a cornel stock of considerable bigness. This did posterity preserve and worship as one of the most sacred things; and therefore walled it about; and if to anyone it appeared not green nor flourishing, but inclining to pine and wither, he immediately made outcry to all he met, and they, like people hearing of a house on fire, with one accord would cry for water, and run from all parts with buckets full to the place. But when Caius Cæsar, they say, was repairing the steps about it, some of the labourers digging too close, the roots were destroyed, and the tree withered.

The Sabines adopted the Roman months, of which whatever is remarkable is mentioned in the Life of Numa. Romulus, on the other hand, adopted their long shields, and changed his own armour and that of all the Romans, who before wore round targets of the Argive pattern. Feasts and sacrifices they partook of in common, not abolishing any which either nation observed before, and instituting several new ones; of which one was the Matronalia, instituted in honour of the women, for their extinction of the war; likewise the Carmentalia. This Carmenta some think a deity presiding over human birth; for which reason she is much honoured by mothers. Others say she was the wife of Evander, the Arcadian, being a prophetess, and wont to deliver her oracles in verse, and from *carmen*, a verse, was called Carmenta; her proper name being Nicostrata. Others more probably derive Carmenta from *carens mente*, or insane, in allusion to her prophetic frenzies. Of the feast of Palilia we have spoken before. The Lupercalia, by the time of its celebration, may seem to be a feast of purification, for it is solemnised on the *dies nefasti*, or non-court days, of the month February, which name signifies purification, and the very day of the feast was anciently called Februata; but its name is equivalent to the Greek Lycæa; and it seems thus to be of great antiquity, and brought in by the Arcadians who came with Evander. Yet this is but dubious, for it may come as well from the wolf that nursed Romulus; and we see the Luperci, the priests, begin their course from the place where they say Romulus was exposed, But the ceremonies performed in it render the origin of the thing more difficult to be guessed at; for there are goats killed, then, two young noblemen's sons being brought, some are to stain their foreheads with the bloody knife, others presently to wipe it off with wool dipped in milk; then the young boys must laugh after their foreheads are wiped; that done, having cut the goats' skins into thongs, they run about naked, only with something about their middle, lashing all they meet; and the young wives do not avoid their strokes, fancying they will help conception and childbirth. Another thing peculiar to this feast is for the Luperci to sacrifice a dog. But, as a certain poet who wrote fabulous explanations of Roman customs in elegiac verses, says, that Romulus and Remus, after the conquest of Amulius, ran joyfully to the place where the wolf gave them suck; and that, in imitation of that, this feast was held, and two young noblemen ran—

> Striking at all, as when from Alba town,
> With sword in hand, the twins came hurrying down;

and that the bloody knife applied to their foreheads was a sign of the danger and bloodshed of that day; the cleansing of them in milk, a remembrance of their food and nourishment. Caius Acilius writes, that, before the city was built, the cattle of Romulus and Remus one day going astray, they, praying to the god Faunus, ran out to seek them naked, wishing not to be troubled with sweat, and that this is why the Luperci run naked. If the sacrifice be by way of purification, a dog might very well be sacrificed, for the Greeks, in their illustrations, carry out young dogs, and frequently use this ceremony of *periscylacismus,* as they call it. Or if again it is a sacrifice of gratitude to the wolf that nourished and preserved Romulus, there is good reason in killing a dog, as being an enemy to wolves. Unless, indeed, after all, the creature is punished for hindering the Luperci in their running.

They say, too, Romulus was the first that consecrated holy fire, and instituted holy virgins to keep it, called vestals; others ascribe it to Numa Pompilius; agreeing, however, that Romulus was otherwise eminently religious, and skilled in divination, and for that reason carried the *lituus,* a crooked rod with which soothsayers describe the quarters of the heavens, when they sit to observe the flights of birds. This of his, being kept in the Palatium, was lost when the city was taken by the Gauls; and afterwards, that barbarous people being driven out, was found in the ruins, under a great heap of ashes, untouched by the fire, all things about it being consumed and burnt. He instituted also certain laws, one of which is somewhat severe, which suffers not a wife to leave her husband, but grants a husband power to turn off his wife, either upon poisoning her children, or counterfeiting his keys, or for adultery; but if the husband upon any other occasion put her away, he ordered one moiety of his estate to be given to the wife, the other to fall to the goddess Ceres; and whoever cast off his wife, to make an atonement by sacrifice to the gods of the dead. This, too, is observable as a singular thing in Romulus, that he appointed no punishment for real parricide, but called all murder so, thinking the one an accursed thing, but the other a thing impossible; and, for a long time, his judgment seemed to have been right; for in almost six hundred years together, nobody committed the like in Rome; and Lucius Hostius, after the wars of Hannibal, is recorded to have been the first parricide. Let this much suffice concerning these matters.

In the fifth year of the reign of Tatius, some of his friends and kinsmen, meeting ambassadors coming from Laurentum to Rome, attempted on the road to take away their money by force, and, upon their resistance, killed them. So great a villainy having been committed Romulus thought the malefactors ought at once to be punished, but Tatius shuffled off and deferred the execution of it; and this one thing was the beginning of open quarrel betwixt them; in all other respects they were very careful of their conduct, and administered affairs together with great unanimity. The relations of the slain, being debarred of lawful satisfaction by reason of Tatius, fell upon him as he was sacrificing with Romulus at Lavinium and slew him; but escorted Romulus home, commending and extolling him for a just prince. Romulus took the body of Tatius, and buried it very splendidly in the Aventine Mount, near the place called Armilustrium, but altogether neglected revenging his murder. Some authors write, that the city of Laurentum, fearing the consequences, delivered up the murderers of Tatius; but Romulus dismissed them, saying one murder was requited with another. This gave occasion of talk and jealousy, as if he were well pleased at the removal of his co-partner in the government. Nothing of these things, however, raised any sort of feud or disturbance among the Sabines; but some out of love to him, others out of fear of his power, some again reverencing him as a god, they all continued living peacefully in admiration and awe of him; many foreign nations, too, showed respect to Romulus; the Ancient Latins sent and entered into league and confederacy with him. Fidenæ he took, a neighbouring city to Rome, by a party of horse, as some say, whom he sent before with commands to cut down the hinges of the gates, himself afterwards unexpectedly coming up. Others say, they having first made the invasion, plundering and ravaging the country and suburbs, Romulus lay in ambush for them, and having killed many of their men, took the city; but, neverthless, did not raze or demolish it, but made it a Roman colony, and sent thither, on the Ides of April, two thousand five hundred inhabitants.

Soon after a plague broke out, causing sudden death without any previous sickness; it infected also the corn with unfruitfulness, and cattle with barrenness; there rained blood, too, in the city; so that, to their actual sufferings, fear of the wrath of the gods was added. But when the same mischiefs fell upon Laurentum, then everybody judged it was divine vengeance that fell upon both cities, for the neglect of executing justice upon the murder of Tatius and the ambassadors. But the murderers on both sides being delivered up and punished, the pestilence visibly abated; and Romulus purified the cities with lustrations, which, they say, even now, are performed at the wood called Ferentina. But before the plague ceased, the Camertines invaded the Romans and overran the country, thinking them, by reason of the distemper, unable to resist; but Romulus at once made head against them, and gained the victory, with the slaughter of six thousand men, then took their city, and brought half of those he found there to Rome, sending from Rome to Camerium double the number he left there. This was done on the first of August. So many citizens had he to spare, in sixteen years' time from his first founding Rome. Among other spoils he took a brazen four-horse chariot from Camerium, which he placed in the temple of Vulcan, setting on it his own statue, with a figure of victory crowning him.

The Roman cause thus daily gathering strength, their weaker neighbours shrunk away, and were thankful to be left untouched; but the stronger, out of fear or envy, thought they ought not to give way to Romulus, but to curb and put a stop to his growing greatness. The first were the Veientes, a people of Tuscany, who had large possessions, and dwelt in a spacious city; they took occasion to commence a war, by claiming Fidenæ as belonging to them; a thing not only very unreasonable, but very ridiculous, that they, who did not assist them in the greatest extremities, but permitted them to be slain, should challenge their lands and houses when in the hands of others. But being scornfully retorted upon by Romulus in his answers, they divided themselves into two bodies; with one they attacked the garrison of Fidenæ, the other marched against Romulus; that which went against Fidenæ got the victory, and slew two thousand Romans; the other was worsted by Romulus, with the loss of eight thousand men. A fresh battle was fought near Fidenæ, and here all men acknowledge the day's success to have been chiefly the work of Romulus himself, who showed the highest skill as well as courage, and seemed to manifest a strength and swiftness more than human. But what some write, that of fourteen thousand that fell that day, above half were slain by Romulus' own hand, verges too near to fable, and is, indeed, simply incredible; since even the Messenians are thought to go too far in saying that Aristomenes three times offered sacrifice for the death of a hundred enemies, Lacedæmonians, slain by himself. The army being thus routed, Romulus, suffering those that were left to make their escape, led his forces against the city; they, having suffered such great losses, did not venture to oppose, but, humbly suing to him, made a league and friendship for an hundred years; surrendering also a large district of land called Septempagium, that is, the seven parts, as also their salt-works upon the river, and fifty noblemen for hostages. He made his triumph for this on the Ides of October, leading, among the rest of his many captives, the general of the Veientes, an elderly man, but who had not, it seemed, acted with the prudence of age; whence even now, in sacrifices for victories they lead an old man through the marketplace to the Capitol, apparelled in purple, with a *bulla,* or child's toy, tied to it, and the crier cries, *Sardians to be sold;* for the Tuscans are said to be a colony of the Sardians, and the Veientes are a city of Tuscany.

This was the last battle Romulus ever fought; afterwards he, as most, nay all men, very few excepted, do, who are raised by great and miraculous good-haps of fortune to power and greatness, so, I say, did he; relying upon his own great actions, and growing of an haughtier mind, he forsook his popular behaviour for kingly arrogance, odious to the people; to whom in particular the state which he assumed was hateful. For he dressed in scarlet, with the purple-bordered robe over it; he gave audience on a couch of state, having always about him some young men called *Celeres,* from their swiftness in doing commissions; there went before him others with staves, to make room, with leather thongs tied on their bodies, to bind on the moment whoever he commanded. The Latins formerly used *ligare* in the same sense as now *alligare,* to bind, whence the name *lictors,* for these officers, and *bacula,* or staves, for their rods, because staves were then used. It is probable, however, they were first called *litores,* afterwards, by putting in a *c, lictores,* or, in Greek, *liturgi,* or people's officers, for *leïtos* is still Greek for the commons, and *laös* for the people in general.

But when, after the death of his grandfather Numitor in Alba, the throne devolving upon Romulus, he, to court the people, put the government into their own hands, and appointed an annual magistrate over the Albans, this taught the great men of Rome to seek after a free and anti-monarchical state, wherein all might in turn be subjects and rulers. For neither were the patricians any longer admitted to state affairs, only had the name and title left them, convening in council rather for fashion's sake than advice, where they heard in silence the king's commands, and so departed, exceeding the commonalty only in hearing first what was done. These and the like were matters of small moment; but when he of his own accord parted among his soldiers what lands were acquired by war, and restored the Veientes their hostages, the senate neither consenting nor approving of it, then, indeed, he seemed to put a great affront upon them; so that, on his sudden and strange disappearance a short while after, the senate fell under suspicion and calumny. He disappeared on the Nones of July, as they now call the month which was then Quintilis, leaving nothing of certainty to be related of his death; only the time, as just mentioned, for on that day many ceremonies are still performed in representation of what happened. Neither is this uncertainty to be thought strange, seeing the manner of the death of Scipio Africanus, who died at his own home after supper, has been found capable neither of proof or disproof; for some say he died a natural death, being of a sickly habit; others that he poisoned himself; others again, that his enemies, breaking in upon him in the night stifled him. Yet Scipio's dead body lay open to be seen of all, and anyone, from his own observation, might form his suspicions and conjectures, whereas Romulus, when he vanished, left neither the least part of his body, nor any remnant of his clothes to be seen. So that some fancied the senators, having fallen upon him in the temple of Vulcan, cut his body into pieces, and took each a part away in his bosom; others think his disappearance was neither in the temple of Vulcan, nor with the senators only by, but that it came to pass that, as he was haranguing the people without the city, near a place called the Goat's Marsh, on a sudden strange and unaccountable disorders and alterations took place in the air; the face of the sun was darkened, and the day turned into night, and that, too, no quiet, peaceable night, but with terrible thunderings, and boisterous winds from all quarters; during which the common people dispersed and fled, but the senators kept close together. The tempest being over and the light breaking out, when the people gathered again, they missed and inquired for their king; the senators suffered them not to search, or busy themselves about the matter, but commanded them to honour and worship Romulus as one taken up to the gods, and about to be to them, in the place of a good prince, now a propitious god. The multitude, hearing this, went away believing and rejoicing in hopes of good things from him; but there were some, who, canvassing the matter in a hostile temper, accused and aspersed the patricians, as men that persuaded the people to believe ridiculous tales, when they themselves were the murderers of the king.

Things being in this disorder, one, they say, of the patricians, of noble family and approved good character, and a faithful and familiar friend of Romulus himself, having come with him from Alba, Julius Proculus by name, presented himself in the forum; and, taking a most sacred oath, protested before them all, that, as he was travelling on the road, he had seen Romulus coming to meet him, looking taller and comelier than ever, dressed in shining and flaming armour; and he, being affrighted at the apparition, said, "Why, O king, or for what purpose have you abandoned us to unjust and wicked surmises, and the whole city to bereavement and endless sorrow?" and that he made answer, "It pleased the gods, O Proculus, that we, who came from them, should remain so long a time amongst men as we did; and, having built a city to be the greatest in the world for empire and glory, should again return to heaven. But farewell; and tell the Romans, that, by the exercise of temperance and fortitude, they shall attain the height of human power; we will be to you the propitious god Quirinus." This seemed credible to the Romans, upon the honesty and oath of the relater, and indeed, too, there mingled with it a certain divine passion, some preternatural influence similar to possession by a divinity; nobody contradicted it, but, laying aside all jealousies and detractions, they prayed to Quirinus and saluted him as a god.

This is like some of the Greek fables of Aristeas the Proconnesian, and Cleomedes the Astypalasan; for they say Aristeas died in a fuller's workshop, and his friends coming to look for him, found his body vanished; and that some presently after, coming from abroad, said they met him travelling towards Croton. And that Cleomedes, being an extraordinarily strong and gigantic man, but also wild and mad, committed many desperate freaks; and at last, in a school-house, striking a pillar that sustained the roof with his fist, broke it in the middle, so that the house fell and destroyed the children in it; and being pursued, he fled into a great chest, and, shutting to the lid, held it so fast, that many men, with their united strength, could not force it open; afterwards, breaking the chest to pieces, they found no man in it alive or dead; in astonishment at which, they sent to consult the oracle at Delphi; to whom the prophetess made this answer,

> Of all the heroes, Cleomede is last.

They say, too, the body of Alcmena, as they were carrying her to her grave, vanished, and a stone was found lying on the bier. And many such improbabilities do your fabulous writers relate, deifying creatures naturally mortal; for though altogether to disown a divine nature in human virtue were impious and base, so again, to mix heaven with earth is ridiculous. Let us believe with Pindar, that—

> All human bodies yield to Death's decree,
> The soul survives to all eternity.

For that alone is derived from the gods, thence comes, and thither returns; not with the body, but when most disengaged and separated from it, and when most entirely pure and clean and free from the flesh: for the most perfect soul, says Heraclitus, is a dry light, which flies out of the body as lightning breaks from a cloud; but that which is clogged and surfeited with body is like gross and humid incense, slow to kindle and ascend. We must not, therefore, contrary to nature, send the bodies, too, of good men to heaven; but we must really believe that, according to their divine nature and law, their virtue and their souls are translated out of men into heroes, out of heroes into demi-gods, out of demi-gods, after passing, as in the rite of initiation, through a final cleansing and sanctification, and so freeing themselves from all that pertains to mortality and sense, are thus, not by human decree, but really and according to right reason, elevated into gods admitted thus to the greatest and most blessed perfection.

Romulus' surname Quirinus, some say, is equivalent to Mars; others, that he was so called because the citizens were called Quirites; others, because the ancients called a dart or spear Quiris; thus, the statue of Juno resting on a spear is called Quiritis, and the dart in the Regia is addressed as Mars, and those that were distinguished in war were usually presented with a dart; that, therefore, Romulus being a martial god, or a god of darts, was called Quirinus. A temple is certainly built to his honour on the mount called from him Quirinalis.

The day he vanished on is called the Flight of the People and the Nones of the Goats, because they go then out of the city and sacrifice at the Goat's Marsh, and, as they go, they shout out some of the Roman names, as Marcus, Lucius, Caius, imitating the way in which they then fled and called upon one another in that fright and hurry. Some, however, say this was not in imitation of a flight, but of a quick and hasty onset, referring it to the following occasion: After the Gauls who had taken Rome were driven out by Camillus, and the city was scarcely as yet recovering her strength, many of the Latins, under the command of Livius Postumius, took this time to march against her. Postumius, halting not far from Rome, sent a herald, signifying that the Latins were desirous to renew their former alliance and affinity (that was now almost decayed) by contracting new marriages between both nations; if, therefore, they would send forth a good number of their virgins and widows, they should have peace and friendship, such as the Sabines had formerly had on the like conditions. The Romans, hearing this, dreaded a war, yet thought a surrender of their women little better than mere captivity. Being in this doubt, a servant-maid called Philotis (or, as some say, Tutula), advised them to do neither, but, by a stratagem, avoid both fighting and the giving up of such pledges. The stratagem was this, that they should send herself, with other well-looking servant-maids, to the enemy, in the dress of free-born virgins, and she should in the night light up a fire signal, at which the Romans should come armed and surprise them asleep. The Latins were thus deceived, and accordingly Philotis set up a torch in a wild fig tree, screening it behind with curtains and coverlets from the sight of the enemy, while visible to the Romans. They, when they saw it, eagerly ran out of the gates, calling in their haste to each other as they went out, and so, falling in unexpectedly upon the enemy, they defeated them, and upon that made a feast of triumph, called the Nones of the Goats, because of the wild fig tree, called by the Romans Caprificus, or the goat-fig. They feast the women without the city in arbours made of fig tree boughs, and the maid-servants gather together and run about playing; afterwards they fight in sport, and throw stones one at another, in memory that they then aided and assisted the Roman men in fight. This only a few authors admit for true; for the calling upon one another's names by day and the going out to the Goat's Marsh to do sacrifice seem to agree more with the former story, unless, indeed, we shall say that both the actions might have happened on the same day in different years. It was in the fifty-fourth year of his age and the thirty-eighth of his reign that Romulus, they tell us, left the world.

THE COMPARISON OF ROMULUS
WITH THESEUS

THIS IS WHAT I HAVE LEARNT OF ROMULUS AND THESEUS, WORTHY OF memory. It seems, first of all, that Theseus, out of his own free-will, without any compulsion, when he might have reigned in security at Trœzen in the enjoyment of no inglorious empire, of his own motion affected great actions, whereas the other, to escape present servitude and a punishment that threatened him (according to Plato's phrase), grew valiant purely out of fear, and dreading the extremest inflictions, attempted great enterprises out of mere necessity. Again, his greatest action was only the killing of one King of Alba; while, as mere by-adventures and preludes, the other can name Sciron, Sinnis, Procrustes, and Corynetes; by reducing and killing of whom, he rid Greece of terrible oppressors, before any of them that were relieved knew who did it; moreover, he might without any trouble as well have gone to Athens by sea, considering he himself never was in the least injured by those robbers; whereas Romulus could not but be in trouble whilst Amulius lived. Add to this, the fact that Theseus, for no wrong done to himself, but for the sake of others, fell upon these villains; but Romulus and Remus, as long as they themselves suffered no ill by the tyrant, permitted him to oppress all others. And if it be a great thing to have been wounded in battle by the Sabines, to have killed King Acron, and to have conquered many enemies, we may oppose to these actions the battle with the Centaurs and the feats done against the Amazons. But what Theseus adventured, in offering himself voluntarily with young boys and virgins, as part of the tribute unto Crete, either to be a prey to a monster or a victim upon the tomb of Androgeus, or, according to the mildest form of the story, to live vilely and dishonourably in slavery to insulting and cruel men; it is not to be expressed what an act of courage, magnanimity, or justice to the public, or of love for honour and bravery, that was. So what methinks the philosophers did not ill define love to be the provision of the gods for the care and preservation of the young; for the love of Ariadne, above all, seems to have been the proper work and design of some god in order to preserve Theseus; and, indeed, we ought not to blame her for loving him, but rather wonder all men and women were not alike affected towards him; and if she alone were so, truly I dare pronounce her worthy of the love of a god, who was herself so great a lover of virtue and goodness, and the bravest man.

Both Theseus and Romulus were by nature meant for governors; yet neither lived up to the true character of a king, but fell off, and ran, the one into popularity, the other into tyranny, falling both into the same fault out of different passions. For a ruler's first aim is to maintain his office, which is done no less by avoiding what is unfit than by observing what is suitable. Whoever is either too remiss or too strict is no more a king or a governor, but either a demagogue or a despot, and so becomes either odious or contemptible to his subjects. Though certainly the one seems to be the fault of easiness and good-nature, the other of pride and severity.

If men's calamities, again, are not to be wholly imputed to fortune, but refer themselves to differences of character, who will acquit either Theseus of rash and unreasonable anger against his son, or Romulus against his brother? Looking at motives, we more easily excuse the anger which a stronger cause, like a severer blow, provoked. Romulus, having disagreed with his brother advisedly and deliberately on public matters, one would think could not on a sudden have been put into so great a passion; but love and jealousy and the complaints of his wife, which few men can avoid being moved by, seduced Theseus to commit that outrage upon his son. And what is more, Romulus, in his anger, committed an action of unfortunate consequence; but that of Theseus ended only in words, some evil speaking, and an old man's curse; the rest of the youth's disasters seem to have proceeded from fortune; so that, so far, a man would give his vote on Theseus' part.

But Romulus has, first of all, one great plea, that his performances proceeded from very small beginnings; for both the brothers being thought servants and the sons of swine-herds, before becoming freemen themselves, gave liberty to almost all the Latins, obtaining at once all the most honourable titles, as destroyers of their country's enemies, preservers of their friends and kindred, princes of the people, founders of cities, not removers, like Theseus, who raised and compiled only one house out of many, demolishing many cities bearing the names of ancient kings and heroes. Romulus, indeed, did the same afterwards, forcing his enemies to deface and ruin their own dwellings, and to sojourn with their conquerors; but at first, not by removal, or increase of an existing city, but by foundation of a new one, he obtained himself lands, a country, a kingdom, wives, children, and relations. And, in so doing, he killed or destroyed nobody, but benefited those that wanted houses and homes and were willing to be of a society and become citizens. Robbers and malefactors he slew not; but he subdued nations, he overthrew cities, he triumphed over kings and commanders. As to Remus, it is doubtful by whose hand he fell; it is generally imputed to others. His mother he clearly retrieved from death, and placed his grandfather, who was brought under base and dishonourable vassalage on the ancient throne of Æneas, to whom he did voluntarily many good offices, but never did him harm even inadvertently. But Theseus, in his forgetfulness and neglect of the command concerning the flag, can scarcely, methinks, by any excuses, or before the most indulgent judges, avoid the imputation of parricide. And, indeed, one of the Attic writers, perceiving it to be very hard to make an excuse for this, feigns that Ægeus, at the approach of the ship, running hastily to the Acropolis to see what news, slipped and fell down, as if he had no servants, or none would attend him on his way to the shore.

And, indeed, the faults committed in the rapes of women admit of no plausible excuse in Theseus. First, because of the often repetition of the crime; for he stole Ariadne, Antiope, Anaxo the Trœzenian, at last Helen, when he was an old man, and she not marriageable; she a child, and he at an age past even lawful wedlock. Then, on account of the cause; for the Trœzenian, Lacedæmonian, and Amazonian virgins, beside that they were not betrothed to him, were not worthier to raise children by then the Athenian women, derived from Erechtheus and Cecrops; but it is to be suspected these things were done out of wantonness and lust. Romulus, when he had taken near eight hundred women, chose not all, but only Hersilia, as they say, for himself; the rest he divided among the chief of the city; and afterwards, by the respect and tenderness and justice shown towards them, he made it clear that this violence and injury was a commendable and politic exploit to establish a society; by which he intermixed and united both nations, and made it the foundation of after friendship and public stability. And to the reverence and love and constancy he established in matrimony, time can witness, for in two hundred and thirty years, neither any husband deserted his wife, nor any wife her husband; but, as the curious among the Greeks can name the first case of parricide or matricide, so the Romans all well know that Spurius Carvilius was the first who put away his wife, accusing her of barrenness. The immediate results were similar; for upon those marriages the two princes shared in the dominion, and both nations fell under the same government. But from the marriages of Theseus proceeded nothing of friendship or correspondence for the advantage of commerce, but enmities and wars and the slaughter of citizens, and, at last, the loss of the city Aphidnæ, when only out of the compassion of the enemy, whom they entreated and caressed like gods, they escaped suffering what Troy did by Paris. Theseus' mother, however, was not only in danger, but suffered actually what Hecuba did, deserted and neglected by her son, unless her captivity be not a fiction, as I could wish both that and other things were. The circumstances of the divine intervention, said to have preceded of accompanied their births, are also in contrast; for Romulus was preserved by the special favour of the gods; but the oracle given to Ægeus commanding him to abstain, seems to demonstrate that the birth of Theseus was not agreeable to the will of the gods.

LYCURGUS

THERE IS SO MUCH UNCERTAINTY IN THE ACCOUNTS WHICH HISTORIANS
have left us of Lycurgus, the lawgiver of Sparta, that scarcely anything
is asserted by one of them which is not called into question or contradicted by the rest. Their sentiments are quite different as to the family he
came of, the voyages he undertook, the place and manner of his death,
but most of all when they speak of the laws he made and the commonwealth which he founded. They cannot, by any means, be brought to an
agreement as to the very age in which he lived; for some of them say that
he flourished in the time of Iphitus, and that they two jointly contrived the
ordinance for the cessation of arms during the solemnity of the Olympic
games. Of this opinion was Aristotle; and for confirmation of it, he
alleges an inscription upon one of the copper quoits used in those sports,
upon which the name of Lycurgus continued uneffaced to his time. But
Eratosthenes and Apollodorus and other chronologers, computing the
time by the successions of the Spartan kings, pretend to demonstrate that
he was much more ancient than the institution of the Olympic games.
Timæus conjectures that there were two of this name, and in diverse times,
but that the one of them being much more famous than the other, men
gave to him the glory of the exploits of both; the elder of the two, according to him, was not long after Homer; and some are so particular as to say
that he had seen him. But that he was of great antiquity may be gathered
from a passage in Xenophon, where he makes him contemporary with
the Heraclidæ. By descent, indeed, the very last kings of Sparta were
Heraclidæ too; but he seems in that place to speak of the first and more
immediate successors of Hercules. But notwithstanding this confusion and
obscurity, we shall endeavour to compose the history of his life, adhering

to those statements which are least contradicted, and depending upon those authors who are most worthy of credit.

The poet Simonides will have it that Lycurgus was the son of Prytanis, and not of Eunomus; but in this opinion he is singular, for all the rest deduce the genealogy of them both as follows:

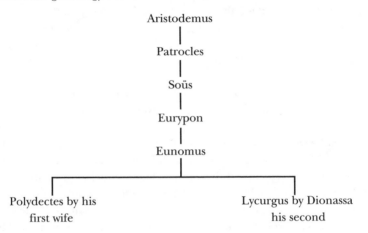

Aristodemus

Patrocles

Soüs

Eurypon

Eunomus

Polydectes by his first wife

Lycurgus by Dionassa his second

Dieuchidas says he was the sixth from Patrocles and the eleventh from Hercules. Be this as it will, Sous certainly was the most renowned of all his ancestors, under whose conduct the Spartans made slaves of the Helots, and added to their dominions, by conquest, a good part of Arcadia. There goes a story of this king Soüs, that, being besieged by the Clitorians in a dry and stony place so that he could come at no water, he was at last constrained to agree with them upon these terms, that he would restore to them all his conquests, provided that himself and all his men should drink of the nearest spring. After the usual oaths and ratifications, he called his soldiers together, and offered to him that would forbear drinking his kingdom for a reward; and when not a man of them was able to forbear, in short, when they had all drunk their fill, at last comes King Soüs himself to the spring, and, having sprinkled his face only, without swallowing one drop, marches off in the face of his enemies, refusing to yield up his conquests, because himself and all his men had not, according to the articles, drunk of their water.

Although he was justly had in admiration on this account, yet his family was not surnamed from him, but from his son Eurypon (of whom they were called Eurypontids); the reason of which was that Eurypon relaxed the rigour of the monarchy, seeking favour and popularity with the many.

They, after this first step, grew bolder; and the succeeding kings partly incurred hatred with their people by trying to use force, or, for popularity's sake and through weakness, gave way; and anarchy and confusion long prevailed in Sparta, causing, moreover, the death of the father of Lycurgus. For as he was endeavouring to quell a riot, he was stabbed with a butcher's knife, and left the title of king to his eldest son, Polydectes.

He, too, dying soon after, the right of succession (as everyone thought) rested in Lycurgus; and reign he did, until it was found that the queen, his sister-in-law, was with child; upon which he immediately declared that the kingdom belonged to her issue, provided it were male, and that he himself exercised the regal jurisdiction only as his guardian; the Spartan name for which office is *prodicus*. Soon after, an overture was made to him by the queen, that she would herself in some way destroy the infant, upon condition that he would marry her when he came to the crown. Abhorring the woman's wickedness, he nevertheless did not reject her proposal, but, making show of closing with her, despatched the messenger with thanks and expressions of joy, but dissuaded her earnestly from procuring herself to miscarry, which would impair her health, if not endanger her life; he himself, he said, would see to it, that the child, as soon as born, should be taken out of the way. By such artifices having drawn on the woman to the time of her lying-in, as soon as he heard that she was in labour, he sent persons to be by and observe all that passed, with orders that if it were a girl they should deliver it to the women, but if a boy, should bring it to him wheresoever he were, and whatsoever doing. It fell out that when he was at supper with the principal magistrates the queen was brought to bed of a boy, who was soon after presented to him as he was at the table; he, taking him into his arms, said to those about him, "Men of Sparta, here is a king born unto us"; this said, he laid him down in the king's place, and named him Charilaus, that is, the joy of the people; because that all were transported with joy and with wonder at his noble and just spirit. His reign had lasted only eight months, but he was honoured on other accounts by the citizens, and there were more who obeyed him because of his eminent virtues, than because he was regent to the king and had the royal power in his hands. Some, however, envied and sought to impede his growing influence while he was still young; chiefly the kindred and friends of the queen-mother, who pretended to have been dealt with injuriously. Her brother Leonidas, in a warm debate which fell out betwixt him and Lycurgus, went so far as to tell him to his face that he was well assured that ere long he should see him king; suggesting suspicions and preparing the way for an accusation of him, as though he had made away with his nephew, if the child should chance to fail, though by a natural death. Words of the like import were designedly cast abroad by the queen-mother and her adherents.

Troubled at this, and not knowing what it might come to, he thought it his wisest course to avoid their envy by a voluntary exile, and to travel from place to place until his nephew came to marriageable years, and, by having a son, had secured the succession; setting sail, therefore, with this resolution, he first arrived at Crete, where, having considered their several forms of government, and got an acquaintance with the principal men among them, some of their laws he very much approved of, and resolved to make use of them in his own country; a good part he rejected as useless. Among the persons there the most renowned for their learning and their wisdom in state matters was one Thales, whom Lycurgus, by importunities and assurances of friendship, persuaded to go over to Lacedæmon; where, though by his outward appearance and his own profession he seemed to be no other than a lyric poet, in reality he performed the part of one of the ablest lawgivers in the world. The very songs which he composed were exhortations to obedience and concord, and the very measure and cadence of the verse, conveying impressions of order and tranquillity, had so great an influence on the minds of the listeners, that they were insensibly softened and civilised, insomuch that they renounced their private feuds and animosities, and were reunited in a common admiration of virtue. So that it may truly be said that Thales prepared the way for the discipline introduced by Lycurgus.

From Crete he sailed to Asia, with design, as is said, to examine the difference betwixt the manners and rules of life of the Cretans, which were very sober and temperate, and those of the Ionians, a people of sumptuous and delicate habits, and so to form a judgment; just as physicians do by comparing healthy and diseased bodies. Here he had the first sight of Homer's works, in the hands, we may suppose, of the posterity of Creophylus; and, having observed that the few loose expressions and actions of ill example which are to be found in his poems were much outweighed by serious lessons of state and rules of morality, he set himself eagerly to transcribe and digest them into order, as thinking they would be of good use in his own country. They had, indeed, already obtained some slight repute among the Greeks, and scattered portions, as chance conveyed them, were in the hands of individuals; but Lycurgus first made them really known.

The Egyptians say that he took a voyage into Egypt, and that, being much taken with their way of separating the soldiery from the rest of the nation, he transferred it from them to Sparta, a removal from contact with those employed in low and mechanical occupations giving high refinement and beauty to the state. Some Greek writers also record this. But as for his voyages into Spain, Africa and the Indies, and his conferences there with the Gymnosophists, the whole relation, as far as I can find, rests on the single credit of the Spartan Aristocrates, the son of Hipparchus.

Lycurgus was much missed at Sparta, and often sent for, "for kings indeed we have," they said, "who wear the marks and assume the titles of royalty, but as for the qualities of their minds, they have nothing by which they are to be distinguished from their subjects"; adding, that in him alone was the true foundation of sovereignty to be seen, a nature made to rule, and a genius to gain obedience. Nor were the kings themselves averse to see him back, for they looked upon his presence as a bulwark against the insolence of the people.

Things being in this posture at his return, he applied himself, without loss of time, to a thorough reformation, and resolved to change the whole face of the commonwealth; for what could a few particular laws and a partial alteration avail? He must act as wise physicians do, in the case of one who labours under a complication of diseases, by force of medicines reduce and exhaust him, change his whole temperament, and then set him upon a totally new regimen of diet. Having thus projected things, away he goes to Delphi to consult Apollo there; which having done, and offered his sacrifice, he returned with that renowned oracle, in which he is called beloved of God, and rather God than man; that his prayers were heard, that his laws should be the best, and the commonwealth which observed them the most famous in the world. Encouraged by these things he set himself to bring over to his side the leading men of Sparta, exhorting them to give him a helping hand in his great undertaking; he broke it first to his particular friends, and then by degrees, gained others, and animated them all to put his design in execution. When things were ripe for action, he gave orders to thirty of the principal men of Sparta to be ready armed at the market place by break of day, to the end that he might strike a terror into the opposite party. Hermippus hath set down the names of twenty of the most eminent of them; but the name of him whom Lycurgus most confided in, and who was of most use to him, both in making his laws and putting them in execution was Arthmiadas. Things growing to a tumult, King Charilaus, apprehending that it was a conspiracy against his person, took sanctuary in the temple of Minerva of the Brazen House; but, being soon after undeceived, and having taken an oath of them that they had no designs against him, he quitted his refuge, and himself also entered into the confederacy with them; of so gentle and flexible a disposition he was, to which Archelaus, his brother-king, alluded, when, hearing him extolled for his goodness, he said, "Who can say he is anything but good? He is so even to the bad."

Amongst the many changes and alterations which Lycurgus made, the first and of greatest importance was the establishment of the senate, which having a power equal to the king's in matters of great consequence, and, as Plato expresses it, allaying and qualifying the fiery genius of the royal office, gave steadiness and safety to the commonwealth. For the state, which before had no firm basis to stand upon, but leaned one while towards an absolute monarchy, when the kings had the upper hand, and another while towards a pure democracy, when the people had the better, found in this establishment of the senate a central weight, like ballast in a ship, which always kept things in a just equilibrium; the twenty-eight always adhering to the kings so far as to resist democracy, and on the other hand, supporting the people against the establishment of absolute monarchy. As for the determinate number of twenty-eight, Aristotle states, that it so fell out because two of the original associates, for want of courage, fell off from the enterprise; but Sphærus assures us that there were but twenty-eight of the confederates at first; perhaps there is some mystery in the number, which consists of seven multiplied by four, and is the first of perfect numbers after six, being, as that is, equal to all its parts. For my part, I believe Lycurgus fixed upon the number of twenty-eight, that, the two kings being reckoned amongst them, they might be thirty in all. So eagerly set was he upon this establishment, that he took the trouble to obtain an oracle about it from Delphi, the Rhetra, which runs thus: "After that you have built a temple to Jupiter Helianius, and to Minerva Hellania, and after that you have *phyle'd* the people into *phyles,* and *obe'd* them into *obes,* you shall establish a council of thirty elders, the leaders included, and shall, from time to time, *apellazein* the people betwixt Babyca and Cnacion, there propound and put to the vote. The commons have the final voice and decision." By *phyles* and *obes* are meant the divisions of the people; by the *leaders,* the two kings; *apellazein,* referring to the Pythian Apollo, signifies to assemble; Babyca and Cnacion they now call Œnus; Aristotle says Cnacion is a river, and Babyca a bridge. Betwixt this Babyca and Cnacion, their assemblies were held, for they had no council-house or building to meet in. Lycurgus was of opinion that ornaments were so far from advantaging them in their counsels, that they were rather an hindrance, by diverting their attention from the business before them to statues and pictures, and roofs curiously fretted, the usual embellishments of such places amongst the other Greeks. The people then being thus assembled in the open air, it was not allowed to anyone of their order to give his advice, but only either to ratify or reject what should be propounded to them by the king or senate. But because it fell out afterwards that the people, by adding or omitting words, distorted and perverted the sense of propositions, Kings Polydorus and Theopompus inserted into the Rhetra, or grand covenant, the following clause: "That if the people decide crookedly it should be lawful for the elders and leaders to dissolve"; that is to say, refuse ratification, and dismiss the people as depravers and perverters of their counsel. It passed among the people, by their management, as being equally authentic with the rest of the Rhetra, as appears by these verses of Tyrtæus,

> These oracles they from Apollo heard,
> And brought from Pytho home the perfect word:
> The heaven-appointed kings, who love the land,
> Shall foremost in the nation's council stand;
> The elders next to them; the commons last;
> Let a straight *Rhetra* among all be passed.

Although Lycurgus had, in this manner, used all the qualifications possible in the constitution of his commonwealth, yet those who succeeded him found the oligarchical element still too strong and dominant, and to check its high temper and its violence, put, as Plato says, a bit in its mouth, which was the power of the ephori, established an hundred and thirty years after the death of Lycurgus. Elatus and his colleagues were the first who had this dignity conferred upon them in the reign of King Theopompus, who, when his queen upbraided him one day that he would leave the regal power to his children less than he had received it from his ancestors, said in answer, "No, greater; for it will last longer." For, indeed, their prerogative being thus reduced within reasonable bounds, the Spartan kings were at once freed from all further jealousies and consequent danger, and never experienced the calamities of their neighbours at Messene and Argos, who, by maintaining their prerogative too strictly, for want of yielding a little to the populace, lost it all.

Indeed, whosoever shall look at the sedition and misgovernment which befell these bordering nations to whom they were as near related in blood as situation, will find in them the best reason to admire the wisdom and foresight of Lycurgus. For these three states, in their first rise, were equal, or, if there were any odds, they lay on the side of the Messenians and Argives, who, in the first allotment, were thought to have been luckier than the Spartans; yet was their happiness of but small continuance, partly the tyrannical temper of their kings and partly the ungovernableness of the people quickly bringing upon them such disorders, and so complete an overthrow of all existing institutions, as clearly to show how truly divine a blessing the Spartans had had in that wise lawgiver who gave their government its happy balance and temper. But of this I shall say more in its due place.

After the creation of the thirty senators, his next task, and, indeed, the most hazardous he ever undertook, was the making a new division of their lands. For there was an extreme inequality amongst them, and their state was overloaded with a multitude of indigent and necessitous persons while its whole wealth had centred upon a very few. To the end, therefore, that he might expel from the state arrogance and envy, luxury and crime, and those yet more inveterate diseases of want and superfluity, he obtained of them to renounce their properties, and to consent to a new division of the land, and that they should live all together on an equal footing; merit to be their only road to eminence, and the disgrace of evil, and credit of worthy acts, their one measure of difference between man and man.

Upon their consent to these proposals, proceeding at once to put them into execution, he divided the country of Laconia in general into thirty thousand equal shares, and the part attached to the city of Sparta into nine thousand; these he distributed among the Spartans, as he did the others to the country citizens. Some authors say that he made but six thousand lots for the citizens of Sparta, and that King Polydorus added three thousand more. Others say that Polydorus doubled the number Lycurgus had made, which, according to them, was but four thousand five hundred. A lot was so much as to yield, one year with another, about seventy bushels of grain for the master of the family, and twelve for his wife, with a suitable proportion of oil and wine. And this he thought sufficient to keep their bodies in good health and strength; superfluities they were better without. It is reported, that, as he returned from a journey shortly after the division of the lands, in harvest time, the ground being newly reaped, seeing the stacks all standing equal and alike, he smiled, and said to those about him, "Methinks all Laconia looks like one family estate just divided among a number of brothers."

Not contented with this, he resolved to make a division of their movables too, that there might be no odious distinction or inequality left amongst them; but finding that it would be very dangerous to go about it openly, he took another course, and defeated their avarice by the following stratagem: he commanded that all gold and silver coin should be called in, and that only a sort of money made of iron should be current, a great weight and quantity of which was very little worth; so that to lay up twenty or thirty pounds there was required a pretty large closet, and, to remove it, nothing less than a yoke of oxen. With the diffusion of this money, at once a number of vices were banished from Lacedæmon; for who would rob another of such a coin? Who would unjustly detain or take by force, or accept as a bribe, a thing which it was not easy to hide, nor a credit to have, nor indeed of any use to cut in pieces? For when it was just red hot, they quenched it in vinegar, and by that means spoilt it, and made it almost incapable of being worked.

In the next place, he declared an outlawry of all needless and superfluous arts; but here he might almost have spared his proclamation; for they of themselves would have gone after the gold and silver, the money which remained being not so proper payment for curious work; for, being of iron, it was scarcely portable, neither, if they should take the means to export it, would it pass amongst the other Greeks, who ridiculed it. So there was now no more means of purchasing foreign goods and small wares; merchants sent no shiploads into Laconian ports; no rhetoric-master, no itinerate fortuneteller, no harlot-monger, or gold or silver-smith, engraver, or jeweller, set foot in a country which had no money; so that luxury, deprived little by little of that which fed and fomented it, wasted to nothing and died away of itself. For the rich had no advantage here over the poor, as their wealth and abundance had no road to come abroad by but were shut up at home doing nothing. And in this way they became excellent artists in common, necessary things; bedsteads, chairs, and tables, and such like staple utensils in a family, were admirably well made there; their cup, particularly, was very much in fashion, and eagerly bought up by soldiers, as Critias reports; for its colour was such as to prevent water, drunk upon necessity and disagreeable to look at, from being noticed; and the shape of it was such that the mud stuck to the sides, so that only the purer part came to the drinker's mouth. For this also, they had to thank their lawgiver, who, by relieving the artisans of the trouble of making useless things, set them to show their skill in giving beauty to those of daily and indispensable use.

The third and most masterly stroke of this great lawgiver, by which he struck a yet more effectual blow against luxury and the desire of riches, was the ordinance he made, that they should all eat in common, of the same bread and same meat, and of kinds that were specified, and should not spend their lives at home, laid on costly couches at splendid tables, delivering themselves up into the hands of their tradesmen and cooks to fatten them in corners, like greedy brutes, and to ruin not their minds only but their very bodies which, enfeebled by indulgence and excess, would stand in need of long sleep, warm bathing, freedom from work, and, in a word, of as much care and attendance as if they were continually sick. It was certainly an extraordinary thing to have brought about such a result as this, but a greater yet to have taken away from wealth, as Theophrastus observes, not merely the property of being coveted, but its very nature of being wealth. For the rich, being obliged to go to the same table with the poor, could not make use of or enjoy their abundance, nor so much as please their vanity by looking at or displaying it. So that the common proverb, that Plutus, the god of riches, is blind, was nowhere in all the world literally verified but in Sparta. There, indeed, he was not only blind, but like a picture, without either life or motion. Nor were they allowed to take food at home first, and then attend the public tables, for everyone had an eye upon those who did not eat and drink like the rest, and reproached them with being dainty and effeminate.

This last ordinance in particular exasperated the wealthier men. They collected in a body against Lycurgus, and from ill words came to throwing stones, so that at length he was forced to run out of the market place, and make to sanctuary to save his life; by good-hap he outran all, excepting one Alcander, a young man otherwise not ill accomplished, but hasty and violent, who came up so close to him, that when he turned to see who was so near him, he struck him upon the face with his stick, and put out one of his eyes. Lycurgus, so far from being daunted and discouraged by this accident, stopped short and showed his disfigured face and eye beat out to his countrymen; they, dismayed and ashamed at the sight, delivered Alcander into his hands to be punished, and escorted him home, with expressions of great concern for his ill-usage. Lycurgus, having thanked them for their care of his person, dismissed them all, excepting only Alcander; and, taking him with him into his house, neither did nor said anything severely to him, but, dismissing those whose place it was, bade

Alcander to wait upon him at table. The young man, who was of an ingenuous temper, without murmuring did as he was commanded; and being thus admitted to live with Lycurgus, he had an opportunity to observe in him, besides his gentleness and calmness of temper, an extraordinary sobriety and an indefatigable industry, and so, from an enemy, became one of his most zealous admirers, and told his friends and relations that Lycurgus was not that morose and ill-natured man they had formerly taken him for, but the one mild and gentle character of the world. And thus did Lycurgus, for chastisement of his fault, make of a wild and passionate young man one of the discreetest citizens of Sparta.

In memory of this accident, Lycurgus built a temple to Minerva, surnamed Optilĕtis; *optilus* being the Doric of these parts for *ophthalmus,* the eye. Some authors, however, of whom Dioscorides is one (who wrote a treatise on the commonwealth of Sparta), say that he was wounded, indeed, but did not lose his eye with the blow; but that he built the temple in gratitude for the cure. Be this as it will, certain it is, that, after this misadventure, the Lacedæmonians made it a rule never to carry so much as a staff into their public assemblies.

But to return to their public repast—these had several names in Greek; the Cretans called them *andria,* because the men only came to them. The Lacedæmonians called them *phiditia,* that is, by changing *l* into *d,* the same as *philitia,* love feasts, because that, by eating and drinking together, they had opportunity of making friends. Or perhaps from *phido,* parsimony, because they were so many schools of sobriety; or perhaps the first letter is an addition, and the word at first was *editia,* from *edode,* eating. They met by companies of fifteen, more or less, and each of them stood bound to bring in monthly a bushel of meal, eight gallons of wine, five pounds of cheese, two pounds and a half of figs, and some very small sum of money to buy flesh or fish with. Besides this, when any of them made sacrifice to the gods, they always sent a dole to the common hall; and, likewise, when any of them had been a hunting, he sent thither a part of the venison he had killed; for these two occasions were the only excuses allowed for supping at home. The custom of eating together was observed strictly for a great while afterwards; insomuch that King Agis himself, after having vanquished the Athenians, sending for his commons at his return home, because he desired to eat privately with his queen, was refused them by the polemarchs; which refusal when he resented so much as to omit next day the sacrifice due for a war happily ended, they made him pay a fine.

They used to send their children to these tables as to schools of temperance; here they were instructed in state affairs by listening to experienced statesmen; here they learned to converse with pleasantry, to make jests without scurrility and take them without ill humour. In this point of good breeding, the Lacedæmonians excelled particularly, but if any man were uneasy under it, upon the least hint given, there was no more to be said to him. It was customary also for the eldest man in the company to say to each of them, as they came in, "Through this" (pointing to the door), "no words go out." When anyone had a desire to be admitted into any of these little societies, he was to go through the following probation: each man in the company took a little ball of soft bread, which they were to throw into a deep basin, which a waiter carried round upon his head; those that liked the person to be chosen dropped their ball into the basin without altering its figure, and those who disliked him pressed it betwixt their fingers, and made it flat; and this signified as much as a negative voice. And if there were but one of these flattened pieces in the basin, the suitor was rejected, so desirous were they that all the members of the company should be agreeable to each other. The basin was called *caddichus,* and the rejected candidate had a name thence derived. Their most famous dish was the black broth, which was so much valued that the elderly men fed only upon that, leaving what flesh there was to the younger.

They say that a certain king of Pontus, having heard much of this black broth of theirs, sent for a Lacedæmonian cook on purpose to make him some, but had no sooner tasted it than he found it extremely bad, which the cook observing, told him, "Sir, to make this broth relish, you should have bathed yourself first in the river Eurotas."

After drinking moderately, every man went to his home without lights, for the use of them was, on all occasions, forbid to the end that they might accustom themselves to march boldly in the dark. Such was the common fashion of their meals.

Lycurgus would never reduce his laws into writing; nay there is a Rhetra expressly to forbid it. For he thought that the most material points, and such as most directly tended to the public welfare, being imprinted on the hearts of their youth by a good discipline, would be sure to remain, and would find a stronger security, than any compulsion would be, in the principles of action formed in them by their best lawgiver, education. And as for things of lesser importance, as pecuniary contracts, and such like, the forms of which have to be changed as occasion requires, he thought it the best way to prescribe no positive rule or inviolable usage in such cases, willing that their manner and form should be altered according to the circumstances of time, and determinations of men of sound judgment. Every end and object of law and enactment it was his design education should effect.

One, then, of the Rhetras was, that their laws should not be written; another is particularly levelled against luxury and expensiveness, for by it was ordained that the ceilings of their houses should only be wrought by the axe, and their gates and doors smoothed only by the saw. Epaminondas' famous dictum about his own table, that "Treason and a dinner like this do not keep company together," may be said to have been anticipated by Lycurgus. Luxury and a house of this kind could not well be companions. For a man might have a less than ordinary share of sense that would furnish such plain and common rooms with silver-footed couches and purple coverlets and gold and silver plate. Doubtless he had good reason to think that they would proportion their beds to their houses, and their coverlets to their beds, and the rest of their goods and furniture to these. It is reported that king Leotychides, the first of that name, was so little used to the sight of any other kind of work, that, being entertained at Corinth in a stately room, he was much surprised to see the timber and ceiling so finely carved and panelled, and asked his host whether the trees grew so in his country.

A third ordinance of Rhetra was, that they should not make war often, or long, with the same enemy, lest that they should train and instruct them in war, by habituating them to defend themselves. And this is what Agesilaus was much blamed for, a long time after; it being thought, that, by his continual incursions into Bœotia, he made the Thebans a match for the Lacedæmonians; and therefore Antalcidas, seeing him wounded one day, said to him, that he was very well paid for taking such pains to make the Thebans good soldiers, whether they would or no. These laws were called the Rhetras, to intimate that they were divine sanctions and revelations.

In order to the good education of their youth (which, as I said before, he thought the most important and noblest work of a lawgiver), he went so far back as to take into consideration their very conception and birth, by regulating their marriages. For Aristotle is wrong in saying, that, after he had tried all ways to reduce the women to more modesty and sobriety, he was at last forced to leave them as they were, because that in the absence of their husbands, who spent the best part of their lives in the wars, their wives, whom they were obliged to leave absolute mistresses at home, took great liberties and assumed the superiority; and were treated with over-much respect and called by the title of lady or queen. The truth is, he took in their case, also, all the care that was possible; he ordered the maidens to exercise themselves with wrestling, running, throwing the quoit and casting the dart, to the end that the fruit they conceived might, in strong and healthy bodies, take firmer root and find better growth, and withal that they, with this greater vigour, might be the more able to undergo the pains of child-bearing. And to the end he might take away their overgreat tenderness and fear of exposure to the air, and all acquired womanishness, he ordered that the young women should go naked in the processions, as well as the young men, and dance, too, in that condition, at certain solemn feasts, singing certain songs, whilst the young men stood around, seeing and hearing them. On these occasions they now and then made, by jests, a befitting reflection upon those who had misbehaved themselves in the wars; and again sang encomiums upon those who had done any gallant action, and by these means inspired the younger sort with an emulation of their glory. Those that were thus commended went away proud, elated, and gratified with their honour among the maidens; and those who were rallied were as sensibly touched with it as if they had been formally reprimanded; and so much the more, because the kings and the elders, as well as the rest of the city, saw and heard all that passed. Nor was there anything shameful in this nakedness of the young women; modesty attended them, and all wantonness was excluded. It taught them simplicity and a care for good health, and gave them some taste of higher feelings, admitted as they thus were to the field of noble action and glory. Hence it was natural for them to think and speak as Gorgo, for example, the wife of Leonidas, is said to have done, when some foreign lady, as it would seem, told her that the women of Lacedæmon were the only women in the world who could rule men; "With good reason," she said, "for we are the only women who bring forth men."

These public processions of the maidens, and their appearing naked in their exercises and dancings, were incitements to marriage, operating upon the young with the rigour and certainty, as Plato says, of love, if not of mathematics. But besides all this, to promote it yet more effectually, those who continued bachelors were in a degree disfranchised by law; for they were excluded from the sight of those public processions in which the young men and maidens danced naked, and, in wintertime, the officers compelled them to march naked themselves round the marketplace, singing as they went a certain song to their own disgrace, that they justly suffered this punishment for disobeying the laws. Moreover, they were denied that respect and observance which the younger men paid their elders; and no man, for example, found fault with what was said to Dercyllidas, though so eminent a commander; upon whose approach one day, a young man, instead of rising, retained his seat, remarking, "No child of yours will make room for me."

In their marriages, the husband carried off his bride by a sort of force; nor were their brides ever small and of tender years, but in their full bloom and ripeness. After this, she who superintended the wedding comes and clips the hair of the bride close round her head, dresses her up in man's clothes, and leaves her upon a mattress in the dark; afterwards comes the bridegroom, in his everyday clothes, sober and composed, as having supped at the common table, and, entering privately into the room where the bride lies, unties her virgin zone, and takes her to himself; and, after staying sometime together, he returns composedly to his own apartment, to sleep as usual with the other young men. And so he continues to do, spending his days, and, indeed, his nights, with them, visiting his bride in fear and shame, and with circumspection, when he thought he should not be observed; she, also, on her part, using her wit to help and find favourable opportunities for their meeting, when company was out of the way. In this manner they lived a long time, insomuch that they sometimes had children by their wives before ever they saw their faces by daylight. Their interviews, being thus difficult and rare, served not only for continual exercise of their self-control, but brought them together with their bodies healthy and vigorous, and their affections fresh and lively, unsated and undulled by easy access and long continuance with each other; while their partings were always early enough to leave behind unextinguished in each of them some remaining fire of longing and mutual delight. After guarding marriage with this modesty and reserve, he was equally careful to banish empty and womanish jealousy. For this object, excluding all licentious disorders, he made it, nevertheless, honourable for men to give the use of their wives to those whom they should think fit, that so they might have children by them; ridiculing those in whose opinion such favours are so unfit for participation as to fight and shed blood and go to war about it. Lycurgus allowed a man who was advanced in years and had a young wife to recommend some virtuous and approved young man, that she might have a child by him, who might inherit the good qualities of the father, and be a son to himself. On the other side, an honest man who had love for a married woman upon account of her modesty and the well-favouredness of her children, might, without formality, beg her company of her husband, that he might raise, as it were, from this plot of good ground, worthy and well-allied children for himself. And indeed, Lycurgus was of a persuasion that children were not so much the property of their parents as of the whole commonwealth, and, therefore, would not have his citizens begot by the first-comers, but by the best men that could be found; the laws of other nations seemed to him very absurd and inconsistent, where people would be so solicitous for their dogs and horses as to exert interest and to pay money to procure fine breeding, and yet kept their wives shut up, to be made mothers only by themselves, who might be foolish, infirm, or diseased; as if it were not apparent that children of a bad breed would prove their bad qualities first upon those who kept and were rearing them, and well-born children, in like manner, their good qualities. These regulations, founded on natural and social grounds, were certainly so far from that scandalous liberty which was afterwards charged upon their women, that they knew not what adultery meant. It is told, for instance, of Geradas, a very ancient Spartan, that, being asked by a stranger what punishment their law had appointed for adulterers, he answered, "There are no adulterers in our country." "But," replied the stranger, "suppose there were?" "Then," answered he, "the offender would have to give the plaintiff a bull with a neck so long as that he might drink from the top of Taygetus of the Eurotas river below it." The man, surprised at this, said, "Why, 'tis impossible to find such a bull." Geradas smilingly replied, "'Tis as possible as to find an adulterer in Sparta." So much I had to say of their marriages.

Nor was it in the power of the father to dispose of the child as he thought fit; he was obliged to carry it before certain triers at a place called Lesche; these were some of the elders of the tribe to which the child belonged; their business it was carefully to view the infant, and, if they found it stout and well made, they gave order for its rearing, and allotted to it one of the nine thousand shares of land above mentioned for its maintenance, but, if they found it puny and ill-shaped, ordered it to be taken to what was called the Apothetæ, a sort of chasm under Taygetus; as thinking it neither for the good of the child itself, nor for the public interest, that it should be brought up, if it did not, from the very outset, appear made to be healthy and vigorous. Upon the same account, the women did not bathe the new-born children with water, as is the custom in all other countries, but with wine, to prove the temper and complexion of their bodies; from a notion they had that epileptic and weakly children faint and waste away upon their being thus bathed, while, on the contrary, those of a strong and vigorous habit acquire firmness and get a temper by it, like steel. There was much care and art, too, used by the nurses; they had no swaddling bands; the children grew up free and unconstrained in limb and form, and not dainty and fanciful about their food; not afraid in the dark, or of being left alone; and without peevishness, or ill-humour, or crying. Upon this account Spartan nurses were often bought up, or hired by people of other countries; and it is recorded that she who suckled Alcibiades was a Spartan; who, however, if fortunate in his nurse, was not so in his preceptor; his guardian, Pericles, as Plato tells us, chose a servant for that office called Zopyrus, no better than any common slave.

Lycurgus was of another mind; he would not have masters bought out of the market for his young Spartans, nor such as should sell their pains; nor was it lawful, indeed, for the father himself to breed up the children after his own fancy; but as soon as they were seven years old they were to be enrolled in certain companies and classes, where they all lived under the same order and discipline, doing their exercises and taking their play together. Of these, he who showed the most conduct and courage was made captain; they had their eyes always upon him, obeyed his orders, and underwent patiently whatsoever punishment he inflicted; so that the whole course of their education was one continued exercise of a ready and perfect obedience. The old men, too, were spectators of their performances, and often raised quarrels and disputes among them, to have a good opportunity of finding out their different characters, and of seeing which would be valiant, which a coward, when they should come to more dangerous encounters. Reading and writing they gave them, just enough to serve their turn; their chief care was to make them good subjects, and to teach them to endure pain and conquer in battle. To this end, as they grew in years, their discipline was proportionately increased; their heads were close-clipped, they were accustomed to go barefoot, and for the most part to play naked.

After they were twelve years old, they were no longer allowed to wear any undergarments, they had one coat to serve them a year; their bodies were hard and dry, with but little acquaintance of baths and unguents; these human indulgences they were allowed only on some few particular days in the year. They lodged together in little bands upon beds made of the rushes which grew by the banks of the river Eurotas, which they were to break off with their hands without a knife; if it were winter, they mingled some thistle-down with their rushes, which it was thought had the property of giving warmth. By the time they were come to this age there was not any of the more hopeful boys who had not a lover to bear him company. The old men, too, had an eye upon them, coming often to the grounds to hear and see them contend either in wit or strength with one another, and this as seriously and with as much concern as if they were their fathers, their tutors, or their magistrates; so that there scarcely was anytime or place without someone present to put them in mind of their duty, and punish them if they had neglected it.

Besides all this, there was always one of the best and honestest men in the city appointed to undertake the charge and governance of them; he again arranged them into their several bands, and set over each of them for their captain the most temperate and boldest of those they called Irens, who were usually twenty years old, two years out of the boys; and the oldest of the boys, again, were Mell-Irens, as much as to say, who would shortly be men. This young man, therefore, was their captain when they fought and their master at home, using them for the offices of his house; sending the eldest of them to fetch wood, and the weaker and less able to gather salads and herbs, and these they must either go without or steal; which they did by creeping into the gardens, or conveying themselves cunningly and closely into the eating-houses; if they were taken in the fact, they were whipped without mercy, for thieving so ill and awkwardly. They stole, too, all other meat they could lay their hands on, looking out and watching all opportunities, when people were asleep or more careless than usual. If they were caught, they were not only punished with whipping, but hunger, too, being reduced to their ordinary allowance, which was but very slender, and so contrived on purpose, that they might set about to help themselves, and be forced to exercise their energy and address. This was the principal design of their hard fare; there was another not inconsiderable, that they might grow taller; for the vital spirits, not being overburdened and oppressed by too great a quantity of nourishment, which necessarily discharges itself into thickness and breadth, do, by their natural lightness, rise; and the body, giving and yielding because it is pliant, grows in height. The same thing seems, also, to conduce to beauty of shape; a dry and lean habit is a better subject for nature's configuration, which the gross and overfed are too heavy to submit to properly. Just as we find that women who take physic whilst they are with child, bear leaner and smaller but better-shaped and prettier children; the material they come of having been more pliable and easily moulded. The reason, however, I leave others to determine.

To return from whence we have digressed. So seriously did the Lacedæmonian children go about their stealing, that a youth, having stolen a young fox and hid it under his coat, suffered it to tear out his very bowels with its teeth and claws and died upon the place, rather than let it be seen. What is practised to this very day in Lacedæmon is enough to gain credit to this story, for I myself have seen several of the youths endure whipping to death at the foot of the altar of Diana surnamed Orthia.

The Iren, or under-master, used to stay a little with them after supper, and one of them he bade to sing a song, to another he put a question which required an advised and deliberate answer; for example, Who was the best man in the city? What he thought of such an action of such a man? They used them thus early to pass a right judgment upon persons and things, and to inform themselves of the abilities or defects of their country-men. If they had not an answer ready to the question, Who was a good or who an ill-reputed citizen, they were looked upon as of a dull and careless disposition, and to have little or no sense of virtue and honour; besides this, they were to give a good reason for what they said, and in as few words and as comprehensive as might be; he that failed of this, or answered not to the purpose, had his thumb bit by the master. Sometimes the Iren did this in the presence of the old men and magistrates, that they might see whether he punished them justly and in due measure or not, and when he did amiss, they would not reprove him before the boys, but, when they were gone, he was called to an account and underwent correction, if he had run far into either of the extremes of indulgence or severity.

Their lovers and favourers, too, had a share in the young boy's honour or disgrace; and there goes a story that one of them was fined by the magis-trate, because the lad whom he loved cried out effeminately as he was fight-ing. And though this sort of love was so approved among them, that the most virtuous matrons would make professions of it to young girls, yet rivalry did not exist, and if several men's fancies met in one person, it was rather the beginning of an intimate friendship, whilst they all jointly conspired to render the object of their affection as accomplished as possible.

They taught them, also, to speak with a natural and graceful raillery, and to comprehend much matter of thought in few words. For Lycurgus, who ordered, as we saw, that a great piece of money should be but of an inconsiderable value, on the contrary would allow no discourse to be cur-rent which did not contain in few words a great deal of useful and curious sense; children in Sparta, by a habit of long silence, came to give just and sententious answers; for, indeed, as loose and incontinent livers are sel-dom fathers of many children, so loose and incontinent talkers seldom originate many sensible words. King Agis, when some Athenian laughed at their short swords, and said that the jugglers on the stage swallowed them

with ease, answered him, "We find them long enough to reach our enemies with"; and as their swords were short and sharp, so, it seems to me,
were their sayings. They reach the point and arrest the attention of the
hearers better than any. Lycurgus himself seems to have been short and
sententious, if we may trust the anecdotes of him; as appears by his answer
to one who by all means would set up a democracy in Lacedæmon. "Begin,
friend," said he, "and set it up in your family." Another asked him why he
allowed of such mean and trivial sacrifices to the gods. He replied, "That
we may always have something to offer to them." Being asked what sort of
martial exercises or combats he approved of, he answered, "All sorts,
except that in which you stretch out your hands." Similar answers,
addressed to his countrymen by letter, are ascribed to him; as, being consulted how they might best oppose an invasion of their enemies, he
returned this answer, "By continuing poor, and not coveting each man to
be greater than his fellow." Being consulted again whether it were requisite to enclose the city with a wall, he sent them word, "The city is well fortified which hath a wall of men instead of brick." But whether these letters
are counterfeit or not is not easy to determine.

Of their dislike to talkativeness, the following apophthegms are evidence. King Leonidas said to one who held him in discourse upon some
useful matter, but not in due time and place, "Much to the purpose, Sir,
elsewhere." King Charilaus, the nephew of Lycurgus, being asked why
his uncle had made so few laws, answered, "Men of few words require but
few laws." When one, named Hecatæus the sophist, because that, being
invited to the public table, he had not spoken one word all supper-time,
Archidamidas answered in his vindication, "He who knows how to speak,
knows also when."

The sharp and yet not ungraceful retorts which I mentioned may be
instanced as follows. Demaratus, being asked in a troublesome manner
by an importunate fellow, Who was the best man in Lacedæmon?
Answered at last, "He, Sir, that is the least like you." Some, in company
where Agis was, much extolled the Eleans for their just and honourable
management of the Olympic games; "Indeed," said Agis, "they are
highly to be commended if they can do justice one day in five years."
Theopompus answered a stranger who talked much of his affection to
the Lacedæmonians, and said that his countrymen called him Philolacon
(a lover of the Lacedæmonians), that it had been more for his honour
if they had called him Philopolites (a lover of his own countrymen). And
Plistoanax, the son of Pausanias, when an orator of Athens said the

Lacedæmonians had no learning, told him, "You say true, Sir; we alone of all the Greeks have learned none of your bad qualities." One asked Archidamidas what number there might be of the Spartans, he answered: "Enough, Sir, to keep out wicked men."

We may see their character, too, in their very jests. For they did not throw them out at random, but the very wit of them was grounded upon something or other worth thinking about. For instance, one, being asked to go hear a man who exactly counterfeited the voice of a nightingale, answered, "Sir, I have heard the nightingale itself." Another, having read the following inscription upon a tomb—

> Seeking to quench a cruel tyranny,
> They, at Selinus, did in battle die,

said, it served them right; for instead of trying to quench the tyranny, they should have let it burn out. A lad, being offered some game-cocks that would die upon the spot, said that he cared not for cocks that would die, but for such that would live and kill others. Another, seeing people easing themselves on seats, said, "God forbid I should sit where I could not get up to salute my elders." In short, their answers were so sententious and pertinent, that one said well that intellectual much more truly than athletic exercise was the Spartan characteristic.

Nor was their instruction in music and verse less carefully attended to than their habits of grace and good-breeding in conversation. And their very songs had a life and spirit in them that inflamed and possessed men's minds with an enthusiasm and ardour for action; the style of them was plain and without affectation; the subject always serious and moral; most usually, it was in praise of such men as had died in defence of their country, or in derision of those that had been cowards; the former they declared happy and glorified; the life of the latter they described as most miserable and abject. There were also vaunts of what they would do, and boasts of what they had done, varying with the various ages, as, for example, they had three choirs in their solemn festivals, the first of the old men, the second of the young men, and the last of the children; the old men began thus:

> We once were young, and brave, and strong;

the young men answered them, singing:

> And we're so now, come on and try;

the children came last and said:

But we'll be strongest by and by.

Indeed, if we will take the pains to consider their compositions, some of which were still extant in our days, and the airs on the flute to which they marched when going to battle; we shall find that Terpander and Pindar had reason to say that musing and valour were allied. The first says of Lacedæmon—

> The spear and song in her do meet,
> And Justice walks about her street;

And Pindar—

> Councils of wise elders here,
> And the young men's conquering spear,
> And dance, and song, and joy appear;

both describing the Spartans as no less musical than warlike; in the words of one of their own poets—

> With the iron stern and sharp,
> Comes the playing on the harp.

For, indeed, before they engaged in battle, the king first did sacrifice to the Muses, in all likelihood to put them in mind of the manner of their education, and of the judgment that would be passed upon their actions, and thereby to animate them to the performance of exploits that should deserve a record. At such times, too, the Lacedæmonians abated a little the severity of their manners in favour of their young men, suffering them to curl and adorn their hair, and to have costly arms and fine clothes; and were well pleased to see them, like proud horses, neighing and pressing to the course. And, therefore, as soon as they came to be well-grown, they took a great deal of care of their hair, to have it parted and trimmed, especially against a day of battle, pursuant to a saying recorded of their lawgiver, that a large head of hair added beauty to a good face, and terror to an ugly one.

When they were in the field, their exercises were generally more moderate, their fare not so hard, nor so strict a hand held over them by their officers, so that they were the only people in the world to whom war gave repose. When their army was drawn up in battle array, and the enemy near, the king sacrificed a goat, commanded the soldiers to set their garlands upon their heads, and the pipers to play the tune of the hymn to

Castor, and himself began the pæan of advance. It was at once a magnificent and a terrible sight to see them march on to the tune of their flutes, without any disorder in their ranks, any discomposure in their minds, or change in their countenances, calmly and cheerfully moving with the music to the deadly fight. Men, in this temper, were not likely to be possessed with fear or any transport of fury, but with the deliberate valour of hope and assurance, as if some divinity were attending and conducting them. The king had always about his person someone who had been crowned in the Olympic games; and upon this account a Lacedæmonian is said to have refused a considerable present, which was offered to him upon condition that he would not come into the lists; and when he had with much to-do thrown his antagonist, some of the spectators saying to him, "And now, Sir Lacedæmonian, what are you the better for your victory?" he answered, smiling, "I shall fight next the king." After they had routed an enemy, they pursued him till they were well assured of the victory, and then they sounded a retreat, thinking it base and unworthy of a Grecian people to cut men in pieces, who had given up and abandoned all resistance. This manner of dealing with their enemies did not only show magnanimity, but was politic too; for, knowing that they killed only those who made resistance, and gave quarter to the rest, men generally thought it their best way to consult their safety by flight.

Hippius the sophist says that Lycurgus himself was a great soldier and an experienced commander. Philostephanus attributes to him the first division of the cavalry into troops of fifties in a square body; but Demetrius the Phalerian says quite the contrary, and that he made all his laws in a continued peace. And, indeed, the Olympic holy truce, or cessation of arms, that was procured by his means and management, inclines me to think him a kind-natured man, and one that loved quietness and peace. Notwithstanding all this Hermippus tells us that he had no hand in the ordinance, that Iphitus made it, and Lycurgus came only as a spectator, and that by mere accident too. Being there, he heard as it were a man's voice behind him, blaming and wondering at him that he did not encourage his countrymen to resort to the assembly, and, turning about and seeing no man, concluded that it was a voice from heaven, and upon this immediately went to Iphitus and assisted him in ordering the ceremonies of that feast, which, by his means, were better established, and with more repute than before.

To return to the Lacedæmonians. Their discipline continued still after they were full-grown men. No one was allowed to live after his own fancy;

but the city was a sort of camp, in which every man had his share of provisions and business set out, and looked upon himself not so much born to serve his own ends as the interest of his country. Therefore if they were commanded nothing else, they went to see the boys perform their exercises, to teach them something useful or to learn it themselves of those who knew better. And indeed one of the greatest and highest blessings Lycurgus procured his people was the abundance of leisure which proceeded from his forbidding to them the exercise of any mean and mechanical trade. Of the money-making that depends on troublesome going about and seeing people and doing business, they had no need at all in a state where wealth obtained no honour or respect. The Helots tilled their ground for them, and paid them yearly in kind the appointed quantity, without any trouble of theirs. To this purpose there goes a story of a Lacedæmonian who, happening to be at Athens when the courts were sitting, was told of a citizen that had been fined for living an idle life, and was being escorted home in much distress of mind by his condoling friends; the Lacedæmonian was much surprised at it and desired his friend to show him the man who was condemned for living like a freeman. So much beneath them did they esteem the frivolous devotion of time and attention to the mechanical arts and to money-making.

It need not be said that upon the prohibition of gold and silver, all lawsuits immediately ceased, for there was now neither avarice nor poverty amongst them, but equality, where everyone's wants were supplied, and independence, because those wants were so small. All their time, except when they were in the field, was taken up by the choral dances and the festivals, in hunting, and in attendance on the exercise-grounds and the places of public conversation. Those who were under thirty years of age were not allowed to go into the market place, but had the necessaries of their family supplied by the care of their relations and lovers; nor was it for the credit of elderly men to be seen too often in the market place; it was esteemed more suitable for them to frequent the exercise-grounds and places of conversation, where they spent their leisure rationally in conversation, not on money-making and market prices, but for the most part in passing judgment on some action worth considering; extolling the good, and censuring those who were otherwise, and that in a light and sportive manner, conveying, without too much gravity, lessons of advice and improvement. Nor was Lycurgus himself unduly austere; it was he who dedicated, says Sosibius, the little statue of Laughter. Mirth, introduced seasonably at their suppers and places of common entertainment, was to serve as a sort of sweetmeat to accompany their strict and hard life. To conclude, he bred up his citizens in such a way that they neither would nor could live by themselves; they were to make themselves one with the public good, and, clustering like bees around their commander, be by their zeal and public spirit carried all but out of themselves, and devoted wholly to their country. What their sentiments were will better appear by a few of their sayings. Pædaretus, not being admitted into the list of the three hundred, returned home with a joyful face, well pleased to find that there were in Sparta three hundred better men than himself. And Polycratidas, being sent with some others ambassador to the lieutenants of the king of Persia, being asked by them whether they came in a private or in a public character, answered, "In a public, if we succeed; if not, in a private character." Argileonis, asking some who came from Amphipolis if her son Brasidas died courageously and as became a Spartan, on their beginning to praise him to a high degree, and saying there was not such another left in Sparta, answered, "Do not say so; Brasidas was a good and brave man, but there are in Sparta many better than he."

The senate, as I said before, consisted of those who were Lycurgus' chief aiders and assistants in his plans. The vacancies he ordered to be supplied out of the best and most deserving men past sixty years old, and we need not wonder if there was much striving for it; for what more glorious competition could there be amongst men, than one in which it was not contested who was swiftest among the swift or strongest of the strong, but who of many wise and good was wisest and best, and fittest to be intrusted forever after, as the reward of his merits, with the supreme authority of the commonwealth, and with power over the lives, franchises, and highest interests of all his countrymen? The manner of their election was as follows: The people being called together, some selected persons were locked up in a room near the place of election, so contrived that they could neither see nor be seen, but could only hear the noise of the assembly without; for they decided this, as most other affairs of moment, by the shouts of the people. This done, the competitors were not brought in and presented all together, but one after another by lot, and passed in order through the assembly without speaking a word. Those who were locked up had writing-tables with them, in which they recorded and marked each shout by its loudness, without knowing in favour of which candidate each of them was made, but merely that they came first, second, third, and so forth. He who was found to have the most and loudest acclamations was declared senator duly elected. Upon this he had a garland set upon his head, and went in procession to all the temples to give thanks to the gods; a great number of young men followed him with applauses, and women, also, singing verses in his honour, and extolling the virtue and happiness of his life. As he went round the city in this manner, each of his relations and friends set a table before him, saying "The city honours you with this banquet"; but he, instead of accepting, passed round to the common table where he formerly used to eat, and was served as before, excepting that now he had a second allowance, which he took and put by. By the time supper was ended, the women who were of kin to him had come about the door; and he, beckoning to her whom he most esteemed, presented to her the portion he had saved, saying, that it had been a mark of esteem to him, and was so now to her; upon which she was triumphantly waited upon home by the women.

Touching burials, Lycurgus made very wise regulations; for, first of all, to cut off all superstition, he allowed them to bury their dead within the city, and even round about their temples, to the end that their youth might be accustomed to such spectacles, and not be afraid to see a dead body, or imagine that to touch a corpse or to tread upon a grave would defile a man. In the next place, he commanded them to put nothing into the ground with them, except, if they pleased, a few olive leaves, and the scarlet cloth that they were wrapped in. He would not suffer the names to be inscribed, except only of men who fell in the wars, or women who died in a sacred office. The time, too, appointed for mourning, was very short, eleven days; on the twelfth, they were to do sacrifice to Ceres, and leave it off; so that we may see, that as he cut off all superfluity, so in things necessary there was nothing so small and trivial which did not express some homage of virtue or scorn of vice. He filled Lacedæmon all through with proofs and examples of good conduct; with the constant sight of which from their youth up the people would hardly fail to be gradually formed and advanced in virtue.

And this was the reason why he forbade them to travel abroad, and go about acquainting themselves with foreign rules of morality, the habits of ill-educated people, and different views of government. Withal he banished from Lacedæmon all strangers who would not give a very good reason for their coming thither; not because he was afraid lest they should inform themselves of and imitate his manner of government (as Thucydides says), or learn anything to their good; but rather lest they should introduce something contrary to good manners. With strange people, strange words must be admitted; these novelties produce novelties in thought and on these follow views and feelings whose discordant character destroys the harmony of the state. He was as careful to save his city from the infection of foreign bad habits, as men usually are to prevent the introduction of a pestilence.

Hitherto I, for my part, see no sign of injustice or want of equity in the laws of Lycurgus, though some who admit them to be well contrived to make good soldiers, pronounce them defective in point of justice. The Cryptia, perhaps (if it were one of Lycurgus' ordinances, as Aristotle says it was), gave both him and Plato, too, this opinion alike of the lawgiver and his government. By this ordinance, the magistrates despatched privately some of the ablest of the young men into the country, from time to time, armed only with their daggers, and taking a little necessary provision with them; in the daytime, they hid themselves in out-of-the-way places, and there lay close, but in the night issued out into the highways, and killed all the Helots they could light upon; sometimes they set upon them by day, as they were at work in the fields, and murdered them. As, also, Thucydides, in his history of the Peloponnesian war, tells us, that a good number of them, after being singled out for their bravery by the Spartans, garlanded, as enfranchised persons, and led about to all the temples in token of honours, shortly after disappeared all of a sudden, being about the number of two thousand; and no man either then or since could give an account how they came by their deaths. And Aristotle, in particular, adds, that the ephori, so soon as they were entered into their office, used to declare war against them, that they might be massacred without a breach of religion. It is confessed, on all hands, that the Spartans dealt with them very hardly; for it was a common thing to force them to drink to excess, and to lead them in that condition into their public halls, that the children might see what a sight a drunken man is; they made them to dance low dances, and sing ridiculous songs, forbidding them expressly to meddle with any of a better kind. And accordingly, when the Thebans made their invasion into Laconia, and took a great number of the Helots, they could by no means persuade them to sing the verses of Terpander, Alcman, or Spendon, "For," said they, "the masters do not like it." So that it was truly observed by one, that in Sparta he who was free was most so, and he that was a slave there, the greatest slave in the world. For my part, I am of opinion that these outrages and cruelties began to be exercised in Sparta at a later time, especially after the great earthquake, when the Helots made a general insurrection, and, joining with the Messenians, laid the country waste, and brought the greatest danger upon the city. For I cannot persuade myself to ascribe to Lycurgus so wicked and barbarous a course, judging of him from the gentleness of his disposition and justice upon all other occasions; to which the oracle also testified.

When he perceived that his more important institutions had taken root in the minds of his countrymen, that custom had rendered them familiar and easy, that his commonwealth was now grown up and able to go alone, then, as Plato somewhere tells us, the Maker of the world, when first he saw it existing and beginning its motion, felt joy, even so Lycurgus, viewing with joy and satisfaction the greatness and beauty of his political structure, now fairly at work and in motion, conceived the thought to make it immortal too, and, as far as human forecast could reach, to deliver it down unchangeable to posterity. He called an extraordinary assembly of all the people, and told them that he now thought everything reasonably well established, both for the happiness and the virtue of the state; but that there was one thing still behind, of the greatest importance, which he thought not fit to impart until he had consulted the oracle; in the meantime, his desire was that they would observe the laws without any the least alteration until his return, and then he would do as the god should direct him. They all consented readily, and bade him hasten his journey; but, before he departed, he administered an oath to the two kings, the senate, and the whole commons, to abide by and maintain the established form of polity until Lycurgus should be come back. This done, he set out for Delphi, and, having sacrificed to Apollo, asked him whether the laws he had established were good, and sufficient for a people's happiness and virtue. The oracle answered that the laws were excellent, and that the people, while it observed them, should live in the height of renown. Lycurgus took the oracle in writing, and sent it over to Sparta; and, having sacrificed the second time to Apollo, and taken leave of his friends and his son, he resolved that the Spartans should not be released from the oath they had taken, and that he would, of his own act, close his life where he was. He was now about that age in which life was still tolerable, and yet might be quitted without regret. Everything, moreover, about him was in a sufficiently prosperous condition. He therefore made an end of himself by a total abstinence from food, thinking it a statesman's duty to make his very death, if possible, an act of service to the state, and even in the end of his life to give some example of virtue and effect some useful purpose. He would, on the one hand, crown and consummate his own happiness by a death suitable to so honourable a life, and on the other hand, would secure to his countrymen the enjoyment of the advantages he had spent his life in obtaining for them, since they had solemnly sworn the maintenance of his institutions until his return. Nor was he deceived in his expectations, for the city of Lacedæmon continued the chief city of all Greece for the space of five hundred years, in strict observance of Lycurgus' laws; in all which time there was no manner of alteration made, during the reign of fourteen kings down to the time of Agis, the son of Archidamus. For the new creation of the ephori, though thought to be in favour of the people, was so far from diminishing, that it very much heightened, the aristocratical character of the government.

In the time of Agis, gold and silver first flowed into Sparta, and with them all those mischiefs which attend the immoderate desire of riches. Lysander promoted this disorder; for by bringing in rich spoils from the wars, although himself incorrupt, he yet by this means filled his country with avarice and luxury, and subverted the laws and ordinances of Lycurgus; so long as which were in force, the aspect presented by Sparta was rather that of a rule of life followed by one wise and temperate man, than of the political government of a nation. And as the poets feign of Hercules, that, with his lion's skin and his club, he went over the world, punishing lawless and cruel tyrants, so may it be said of the Lacedæmonians, that, with a common staff and a coarse coat, they gained the willing and joyful obedience of Greece, through whose whole extent they suppressed unjust usurpations and despotisms, arbitrated in war, and composed civil dissensions; and this often without so much as taking down one buckler, but barely by sending someone single deputy to whose direction all at once submitted, like bees swarming and taking their places around their prince. Such a fund of order and equity, enough and to spare for others, existed in their state.

And therefore I cannot but wonder at those who say that the Spartans were good subjects, but bad governors, and for proof of it allege a saying of King Theopompus, who when one said that Sparta held up so long because their kings could command so well, replied, "Nay, rather because the people know so well how to obey." For people do not obey, unless rulers know how to command; obedience is a lesson taught by commanders. A true leader himself creates the obedience of his own followers; as it is the last attainment in the art of riding to make a horse gentle and tractable, so is it of the science of government, to inspire men with a willingness to obey. The Lacedæmonians inspired men not with a mere willingness, but with an absolute desire to be their subjects. For they did not send petitions to them for ships or money, or a supply of armed men, but only for a Spartan commander; and, having obtained one, used him with honour and reverence; so the Sicilians behaved to Gylippus, the Chalcidians to Brasidas, and all the Greeks in Asia to Lysander, Callicratidas, and Agesilaus; they styled them the composers and chasteners of each people or prince they were sent to, and had their eyes always fixed upon the city of Sparta itself, as the perfect model of good manners and wise government. The rest seemed as scholars, they the masters of Greece; and to this Stratonicus pleasantly alluded, when in jest he pretended to make a law that the Athenians should conduct religious processions and the mysteries, the Eleans should preside at the Olympic games, and, if either did amiss, the Lacedæmonians be beaten. Antisthenes, too, one of the scholars of Socrates, said, in earnest, of the Thebans, when they were elated by their victory at Leuctra, that they looked like schoolboys who had beaten their master.

However, it was not the design of Lycurgus that his city should govern a great many others; he thought rather that the happiness of a state, as of a private man, consisted chiefly in the exercise of virtue, and in the concord of the inhabitants; his aim, therefore, in all his arrangements, was to make and keep them free-minded, self-dependent, and temperate. And therefore all those who have written well on politics, as Plato, Diogenes, and Zeno, have taken Lycurgus for their model, leaving behind them, however, mere projects and words; whereas Lycurgus was the author, not in writing but in reality, of a government which none else could so much as copy; and while men in general have treated the individual philosophic character as unattainable, he, by the example of a complete philosophic state, raised himself high above all other lawgivers of Greece. And so Aristotle says they did him less honour at Lacedæmon after his death than he deserved, although he has a temple there, and they offer sacrifices yearly to him as to a god.

It is reported that when his bones were brought home to Sparta his tomb was struck with lightning, an accident which befell no eminent person but himself and Euripides, who was buried at Arethusa in Macedonia; and it may serve that poet's admirers as a testimony in his favour, that he had in this the same fate with that holy man and favourite of the gods. Some say Lycurgus died in Cirrha. Apollothemis says, after he had come to Elis; Timæus and Aristoxenus, that he ended his life in Crete; Aristoxenus adds that his tomb is shown by the Cretans in the district of Pergamus, near the strangers' road. He left an only son, Antiorus, on whose death without issue his family became extinct. But his relations and friends kept up an annual commemoration of him down to a long time after; and the days of the meeting were called Lycurgides. Aristocrates, the son of Hipparchus, says that he died in Crete, and that his Cretan friends, in accordance with his own request, when they had burned his body, scattered the ashes into the sea; for fear lest, if his relics should be transported to Lacedæmon, the people might pretend to be released from their oaths, and make innovations in the government. Thus much may suffice for the life and actions of Lycurgus.

NUMA POMPILIUS

THOUGH THE PEDIGREES OF NOBLE FAMILIES OF ROME GO BACK IN EXACT form as far as Numa Pompilius, yet there is great diversity amongst historians concerning the time in which he reigned; a certain writer called Clodius, in a book of his entitled Strictures on Chronology, avers that the ancient registers of Rome were lost when the city was sacked by the Gauls, and that those which are now extant were counterfeited, to flatter and serve the humour of some men who wished to have themselves derived from some ancient and noble lineage, though in reality with no claim to it. And though it be commonly reported that Numa was a scholar and a familiar acquaintance of Pythagoras, yet it is again contradicted by others, who affirm that he was acquainted with neither the Greek language nor learning, and that he was a person of that natural talent and ability as of himself to attain to virtue, or else that he found some barbarian instructor superior to Pythagoras. Some affirm, also, that Pythagoras was not contemporary with Numa, but lived at least five generations after him; and that some other Pythagoras, a native of Sparta, who, in the sixteenth Olympiad, in the third year of which Numa became king, won a prize at the Olympic race, might, in his travel through Italy, have gained acquaintance with Numa, and assisted him in the constitution of his kingdom; whence it comes that many Laconian laws and customs appear amongst the Roman institutions. Yet, in any case, Numa was descended of the Sabines, who declare themselves to be a colony of the Lacedæmonians. And chronology, in general, is uncertain; especially when fixed by the lists of victors in the Olympic games, which were published at a late period by Hippias the Elean, and rest on no positive authority. Commencing, however, at a convenient point, we will proceed to give the most noticeable events that are recorded of the life of Numa.

It was the thirty-seventh year, counted from the foundation of Rome, when Romulus, then reigning, did, on the fifth day of the month of July, called the Caprotine Nones, offer a public sacrifice at the Goat's Marsh, in presence of the senate and people of Rome. Suddenly the sky was darkened, a thick cloud of storm and rain settled on the earth; the common people fled in affright, and were dispersed; and in this whirlwind Romulus disappeared, his body being never found either living or dead. A foul suspicion presently attached to the patricians, and rumours were current among the people as if that they, weary of kingly government, and exasperated of late by the imperious deportment of Romulus towards them, had plotted against his life and made him away, that so they might assume the authority and government into their own hands. This suspicion they sought to turn aside by decreeing divine honours to Romulus, as to one not dead but translated to a higher condition. And Proculus, a man of note, took oath that he saw Romulus caught up into heaven in his arms and vestments, and heard him, as he ascended, cry out that they should hereafter style him by the name of Quirinus.

This trouble, being appeased, was followed by another, about the election of a new king; for the minds of the original Romans and the new inhabitants were not as yet grown into that perfect unity of temper, but that there were diversities of factions amongst the commonalty and jealousies and emulations amongst the senators; for though all agreed that it was necessary to have a king, yet what person or of which nation was matter of dispute. For those who had been builders of the city with Romulus, and had already yielded a share of their lands and dwellings to the Sabines, were indignant at any pretension on their part to rule over their benefactors. On the other side, the Sabines could plausibly allege, that, at their king Tatius' decease, they had peaceably submitted to the sole command of Romulus; so now their turn was come to have a king chosen out of their own nation; nor did they esteem themselves to have combined with the Romans as inferiors, nor to have contributed less than they to the increase of Rome, which, without their numbers and association, could scarcely have merited the name of a city.

Thus did both parties argue and dispute their cause; but lest meanwhile discord, in the absence of all command, should occasion general confusion, it was agreed that the hundred and fifty senators should interchangeably execute the office of supreme magistrate, and each in succession, with the ensigns of royalty, should offer the solemn sacrifices and despatch public business for the space of six hours by day and six by night; which vicissitude and equal distribution of power would preclude all rivalry amongst the senators and envy from the people when they should behold one, elevated to the degree of a king, levelled within the space of a day to the condition of a private citizen. This form of government is termed, by the Romans, interregnum. Nor yet could they, by this plausible and modest way of rule, escape suspicion and clamour of the vulgar, as though they were changing the form of government to an oligarchy, and designing to keep the supreme power in a sort of wardship under themselves, without ever proceeding to choose a king. Both parties came at length to the conclusion that the one should choose a king out of the body of the other; the Romans make a choice of a Sabine, or the Sabines name a Roman; this was esteemed the best expedient to put an end to all party spirit, and the prince who should be chosen would have an equal affection to the one party as his electors and to the other as his kinsmen. The Sabines remitted the choice to the original Romans, and they, too, on their part, were more inclinable to receive a Sabine king elected by themselves than to see a Roman exalted by the Sabines. Consultations being accordingly held, they named Numa Pompilius, of the Sabine race, a person of that high reputation for excellence, that, though he were not actually residing at Rome, yet he was no sooner nominated than accepted by the Sabines, with acclamation almost greater than that of the electors themselves.

The choice being declared and made known to the people, principal men of both parties were appointed to visit and entreat him, that he would accept the administration of the government. Numa resided at a famous city of the Sabines called Cures, whence the Romans and Sabines gave themselves the joint name of Quirites. Pomponius, an illustrious person, was his father, and he the youngest of his four sons, being (as it had been divinely ordered) born on the twenty-first day of April, the day of the foundation of Rome. He was endued with a soul rarely tempered by nature, and disposed to virtue, which he had yet more subdued by discipline, a severe life, and the study of philosophy; means which had not only succeeded in expelling the baser passions, but also the violent and rapacious temper which barbarians are apt to think highly of; true bravery, in his judgment, was regarded as consisting in the subjugation of our passions by reason.

He banished all luxury and softness from his own home, and while citizens alike and strangers found in him an incorruptible judge and counsellor, in private he devoted himself not to amusement or lucre, but to the worship of the immortal gods, and rational contemplation of their divine power and nature. So famous was he, that Tatius, the colleague of Romulus, chose him for his son-in-law, and gave him his only daughter, which, however, did not stimulate his vanity to desire to dwell with his father-in-law at Rome; he rather chose to inhabit with his Sabines, and cherish his own father in his old age; and Tatia, also, preferred the private conditions of her husband before the honours and splendour she might have enjoyed with her father. She is said to have died after she had been married thirteen years, and then Numa, leaving the conversation of the town, betook himself to a country life, and in a solitary manner frequented the groves and fields consecrated to the gods, passing his life in desert places. And this in particular gave occasion to the story about the goddess, namely, that Numa did not retire from human society out of any melancholy or disorder of mind, but because he had tasted the joys of more elevated intercourse, and, admitted to celestial wedlock in the love and converse of the goddess Egeria, had attained to blessedness, and to a divine wisdom.

The story evidently resembles those very ancient fables which the Phrygians have received and still recount of Attis, the Bithynians of Herodotus, the Arcadians of Endymion, not to mention several others who were thought blessed and beloved of the gods; nor does it seem strange if God, a lover, not of horses or birds, but men, should not disdain to dwell with the virtuous and converse with the wise and temperate soul, though it be altogether hard, indeed, to believe, that any god or dæmon is capable of a sensual or bodily love and passion for any human form or beauty. Though, indeed, the wise Egyptians do not plausibly make the distinction, that it may be possible for a divine spirit so to apply itself to the nature of a woman, as to imbreed in her the first beginnings of generation, while on the other side they conclude it impossible for the male kind to have any intercourse or mixture by the body with any divinity, not considering, however, that what takes place on the one side must also take place on the other; intermixture, by force of terms, is reciprocal. Not that it is otherwise than befitting to suppose that the gods feel towards men affection, and love, in the sense of affection, and in the form of care and solicitude for their virtue and their good dispositions. And, therefore, it was no error of those who feigned, that Phorbas, Hyacinthus, and Admetus were beloved by Apollo; or that Hippolytus the Sicyonian was so much in his favour, that, as often as he sailed from Sicyon to Cirrha, the Pythian prophetess uttered this heroic verse expressive of the god's attention and joy:

Now doth Hippolytus return again,
And venture his dear life upon the main.

It is reported, also, that Pan became enamoured of Pindar for his verses, and the divine power rendered honour to Hesiod and Archilochus after their death for the sake of the Muses; there is a statement, also, that Æsculapius sojourned with Sophocles in his lifetime, of which many proofs still exist, and that, when he was dead, another deity took care for his funeral rites. And so if any credit may be given to these instances, why should we judge it incongruous, that a like spirit of the gods should visit Zaleucus, Minos, Zoroaster, Lycurgus, and Numa, the controllers of kingdoms, and the legislators for commonwealths? Nay, it may be reasonable to believe, that the gods, with a serious purpose, assist at the councils and serious debates of such men, to inspire and direct them; and visit poets and musicians, if at all, in their more sportive moods; but for difference of opinion here, as Bacchylides said, "the road is broad." For there is no absurdity in the account also given, that Lycurgus and Numa, and other famous lawgivers, having the task of subduing perverse and refractory multitudes, and of introducing great innovations, themselves made this pretension to divine authority, which, if not true, assuredly was expedient for the interests of those it imposed upon.

Numa was about forty years of age when the ambassadors came to make him offers of the kingdom; the speakers were Proculus and Velesus, one or other of whom it had been thought the people would elect as their new king; the original Romans being for Proculus, and the Sabines for Velesus. Their speech was very short, supposing that, when they came to tender a kingdom, there needed little to persuade to an acceptance; but, contrary to their expectations, they found that they had to use many reasons and entreaties to induce one, that lived in peace and quietness, to accept the government of a city whose foundation and increase had been made, in a manner, in war. In presence of his father and his kinsman Marcius, he returned answer that "Every alteration of a man's life is dangerous to him; but madness only could induce one who needs nothing, and is satisfied with everything, to quit a life he is accustomed to; which whatever else it is deficient in, at any rate has the advantage of certainty over one wholly doubtful and unknown. Though, indeed, the difficulties of this government cannot even be called unknown; Romulus, who first held it, did not escape the suspicion of having plotted against the life of his colleague Tatius; nor the senate the like accusation, of having treasonably murdered

Romulus. Yet Romulus had the advantage to be thought divinely born and miraculously preserved and nurtured. My birth was mortal; I was reared and instructed by men that are known to you. The very points of my character that are most commended mark me as unfit to reign—love of retirement and of studies inconsistent with business, a passion that has become inveterate in me for peace, for unwarlike occupations, and for the society of men whose meetings are but those of worship and of kindly intercourse, whose lives in general are spent upon their farms and their pastures. I should but be, methinks, a laughing-stock, while I should go about to inculcate the worship of the gods and give lessons in the love of justice and the abhorrence of violence and war, to a city whose needs are rather for a captain than for a king."

The Romans, perceiving by these words that he was declining to accept the kingdom, were the more instant and urgent with him that he would not forsake and desert them in this condition, and suffer them to relapse, as they must, into their former sedition and civil discord, there being no person on whom both parties could accord but on himself. And, at length, his father and Marcius, taking him aside, persuaded him to accept a gift so noble in itself, and tendered to him rather from heaven than from men. "Though," said they, "you neither desire riches, being content with what you have, nor court the fame of authority, as having already the more valuable fame of virtue, yet you will consider that government itself is a service of God, who now calls out into action your qualities of justice and wisdom, which were not meant to be left useless and unemployed. Cease, therefore, to avoid and turn your back upon an office which, to a wise man, is a field for great and honourable actions, for the magnificent worship of the gods, and for the introduction of habits of piety, which authority alone can effect amongst a people. Tatius, though a foreigner, was beloved, and the memory of Romulus has received divine honours and who knows but that this people, being victorious, may be satiated with war, and, content with the trophies and spoils they have acquired, may be, above all things, desirous to have a pacific and justice-loving prince to lead them to good order and quiet? But if, indeed, their desires are uncontrollably and madly set on war, were it not better, then, to have the reins held by such a moderating hand as is able to divert the fury another way, and that your native city and the whole Sabine nation should possess in you a bond of goodwill and friendship with this young and growing power?"

With these reasons and persuasions several auspicious omens are said to have concurred, and the zeal, also, of his fellow-citizens, who, on understanding what message the Roman ambassadors had brought him, entreated him to accompany them, and to accept the kingdom as a means to unanimity and concord between the nations.

Numa, yielding to these inducements, having first performed divine sacrifice, proceeded to Rome, being met in his way by the senate and people, who, with an impatient desire, came forth to receive him; the women, also, welcomed him with joyful acclamations, and sacrifices were offered for him in all the temples, and so universal was the joy, that they seemed to be receiving, not a new king, but a new kingdom. In this manner he descended into the forum, where Spurius Vettius, whose turn it was to be interrex at that hour, put it to the vote; and all declared him king. Then the regalities and robes of authority were brought to him; but he refused to be invested with them until he had first consulted and been confirmed by the gods; so being accompanied by the priests and augurs, he ascended the Capitol, which at that time the Romans called the Tarpeian Hill. Then the chief of the augurs covered Numa's head, and turned his face towards the south, and, standing behind him, laid his right hand on his head, and prayed, turning his eyes every way, in expectation of some auspicious signal from the gods. It was wonderful, meantime, with what silence and devotion the multitude stood assembled in the forum, in similar expectation and suspense, till auspicious birds appeared and passed on the right. Then Numa, apparelling himself in his royal robes, descended from the hill to the people, by whom he was received and congratulated with shouts and acclamations of welcome, as a holy king, and beloved of all the gods.

The first thing he did at his entrance into government was to dismiss the band of three hundred men which had been Romulus' lifeguard, called by him Celeres, saying that he would not distrust those who put confidence in him; nor rule over a people that distrusted him. The next thing he did was to add to the two priests of Jupiter and Mars a third, in honour of Romulus, whom he called the Flamen Quirinalis. The Romans anciently called their priests Flamines, by corruption of the word Pilamines, from a certain cap which they wore, called Pileus. In those times Greek words were more mixed with the Latin than at present; thus also the royal robe, which is called Læna, Juba says, is the same as the Greek Chlæna; and that the name of Camillus, given to the boy with both his parents living, who serves in the temple of Jupiter, was taken from the name given by some Greeks to Mercury, denoting his office of attendance on the gods.

When Numa had, by such measures, won the favour and affection of
the people, he set himself without delay to the task of bringing the hard
and iron Roman temper to somewhat more of gentleness and equity.
Plato's expression of a city in high fever was never more applicable than
to Rome at that time; in its origin formed by daring and warlike spirits,
whom bold and desperate adventure brought thither from every quarter,
it had found in perpetual wars and incursions on its neighbours its after
sustenance and means of growth, and in conflict with danger the source
of new strength; like piles, which the blows of the hammer serve to fix into
the ground. Wherefore Numa, judging it no slight undertaking to mollify
and bend to peace the presumptuous and stubborn spirits of this people,
began to operate upon them with the sanctions of religion. He sacrificed
often and used processions and religious dances, in which most commonly he officiated in person; by such combinations of solemnity with
refined and humanising pleasures, seeking to win over and mitigate their
fiery and warlike tempers. At times, also, he filled their imaginations with
religious terrors, professing that strange apparitions had been seen, and
dreadful voices heard; thus subduing and humbling their minds by a sense
of supernatural fears.

This method which Numa used made it believed that he had been
much conversant with Pythagoras; for in the philosophy of the one, as in
the policy of the other, man's relations to the deity occupy a great place.
It is said, also, that the solemnity of his exterior garb and gestures was
adopted by him from the same feeling with Pythagoras. For it is said of
Pythagoras, that he had taught an eagle to come at his call, and stoop
down to him in his flight; and that, as he passed among the people assembled at the Olympic games, he showed them his golden thigh; besides
many other strange and miraculous seeming practices, on which Timon
the Philasian wrote the distich—

> Who, of the glory of a juggler proud,
> With solemn talk imposed upon the crowd.

In like manner Numa spoke of a certain goddess or mountain nymph
that was in love with him, and met him in secret, as before related; and professed that he entertained familiar conversation with the Muses, to whose
teaching he ascribed the greatest part of his revelations; and amongst
them, above all, he recommended to the veneration of the Romans one in
particular, whom he named Tacita, the silent; which he did perhaps in imitation and honour of the Pythagorean silence. His opinion, also, of images

is very agreeable to the doctrine of Pythagoras; who conceived of the first principle of being as transcending sense and passion, invisible and incorrupt, and only to be apprehended by abstract intelligence. So Numa forbade the Romans to represent God in the form of man or beast, nor was there any painted or graven image of a deity admitted amongst them for the space of the first hundred and seventy years, all of which time their temples and chapels were kept free and pure from images; to such baser objects they deemed it impious to liken the highest, and all access to God impossible, except by the pure act of the intellect. His sacrifices, also, had great similitude to the ceremonial of Pythagoras, for they were not celebrated with effusion of blood, but consisted of flour, wine, and the least costly offerings. Other external proofs, too, are urged to show the connection Numa had with Pythagoras. The comic writer Epicharmus, an ancient author, and of the school of Pythagoras, in a book of his dedicated to Antenor, records that Pythagoras was made a freeman of Rome. Again, Numa gave to one of his four sons the name of Mamercus, which was the name of one of the sons of Pythagoras; from whence, as they say, sprang that ancient patrician family of the Æmilli, for that the king gave him in sport the surname of Æmilius, for his engaging and graceful manner in speaking. I remember, too, that when I was at Rome, I heard many say, that, when the oracle directed two statues to be raised, one to the wisest and another to the most valiant man in Greece, they erected two of brass, one representing Alcibiades, and the other Pythagoras.

But to pass by these matters, which are full of uncertainty and not so important as to be worth our time to insist on them, the original constitution of the priests, called Pontifices, is ascribed unto Numa, and he himself was, it is said, the first of them; and that they have the name of Pontifices from *potens,* powerful, because they attend the service of the gods, who have power to command over all. Others make the word refer to exceptions of impossible cases; the priests were to perform all the duties possible to them; if anything lay beyond their power, the exception was not to be cavilled at. The most common opinion is the most absurd, which derives this word from *pons,* and assigns the priests the title of bridge-makers. The sacrifices performed on the bridge were amongst the most sacred and ancient, and the keeping and repairing of the bridge attached, like any other public sacred office, to the priesthood. It was accounted not simply unlawful, but a positive sacrilege, to pull down the wooden bridge; which moreover is said, in obedience to an oracle, to have been built entirely of timber and fastened with wooden pins, without nails or cramps of iron. The stone bridge was built a very long time after when Æmilius was quæstor, and they do, indeed, say also that the wooden bridge was not so old as Numa's time, but was finished by Ancus Marcius, when he was king, who was the grandson of Numa by his daughter.

The office of Pontifex Maximus, or chief priest, was to declare and interpret the divine law, or, rather, to preside over sacred rites; he not only prescribed rules for public ceremony, but regulated the sacrifices of private persons, not suffering them to vary from established custom, and giving information to everyone of what was requisite for purposes of worship or supplication. He was also guardian of the vestal virgins, the institution of whom, and of their perpetual fire, was attributed to Numa, who, perhaps, fancied the charge of pure and uncorrupted flames would be fitly intrusted to chaste and unpolluted persons, or that fire, which consumes, but produces nothing, bears an analogy to the virgin estate. In Greece, wherever a perpetual holy fire is kept, as at Delphi and Athens, the charge of it is committed, not to virgins, but widows past the time of marriage. And in case by any accident it should happen that this fire became extinct, as the holy lamp was at Athens under the tyranny of Aristion, and at Delphi, when that temple was burnt by the Medes, as also in the time of the Mithridatic and Roman civil war, when not only the fire was extinguished, but the altar demolished, then, afterwards, in kindling this fire again, it was esteemed an impiety to light it from common sparks or flame, or from anything but the pure and unpolluted rays of the sun, which they usually effect by concave mirrors, of a figure formed by the revolution of an isosceles rectangular triangle, all the lines from the circumference of which meeting in a centre, by holding it in the light of the sun they can collect and concentrate all its rays at this one point of convergence; where the air will now become rarefied, and any light, dry, combustible matter will kindle as soon as applied, under the effect of the rays, which here acquired the substance and active force of fire. Some are of opinion that these vestals had no other business than the preservation of this fire; but others conceive that they were keepers of other divine secrets concealed from all but themselves, of which we have told all that may lawfully be asked or told, in the life of Camillus. Gegania and Verenia, it is recorded, were the names of the first two virgins consecrated and ordained by Numa; Canuleia and Tarpeia succeeded; Servius afterwards added two, and the number of four has continued to the present time.

The statutes prescribed by Numa for the vestals were these: that they should take a vow of virginity for the space of thirty years, the first ten of which they were to spend in learning their duties, the second ten in performing them, and the remaining ten in teaching and instructing others. Thus the whole term being completed, it was lawful for them to marry, and, leaving the sacred order, to choose any condition of life that pleased them; but this permission few, as they say, made use of; and in cases where they did so, it was observed that their change was not a happy one, but accompanied ever after with regret and melancholy; so that the greater number, from religious fears and scruples, forbore, and continued to old age and death in the strict observance of a single life.

For this condition he compensated by great privileges and prerogatives; as that they had power to make a will in the lifetime of their father; that they had a free administration of their own affairs without guardian or tutor, which was the privilege of women who were the mothers of three children; when they go abroad, they have the fasces carried before them; and if in their walks they chance to meet a criminal on his way to execution, it saves his life, upon oath made that the meeting was an accidental one, and not concerted or of set purpose. Anyone who presses upon the chair on which they are carried, is put to death. If these vestals commit any minor fault, they are punishable by the high priest only, who scourges the offender, sometimes with her clothes off, in a dark place, with a curtain drawn between; but she that has broken her vow is buried alive near the gate called Collina, where a little mound of earth stands, inside the city, reaching some little distance, called in Latin *agger;* under it a narrow room is constructed, to which a descent is made by stairs; here they prepare a bed, and light a lamp, and leave a small quantity of victuals, such as bread, water, a pail of milk, and some oil; that so that body which had been consecrated and devoted to the most sacred service of religion might not be said to perish by such a death as famine. The culprit herself is put in a litter, which they cover over, and tie her down with cords on it, so that nothing she utters may be heard. They then take her to the forum; all people silently go out of the way as she passes, and such as follow accompany the bier with solemn and speechless sorrow; and indeed, there is not any spectacle more appalling, nor any day observed by the city with greater appearance of gloom and sadness. When they come to the place of execution, the officers loose the cords, and then the high priest, lifting his hands to heaven, pronounces certain prayers to himself before the act; then he brings out the prisoner, being still covered, and placing her upon the steps that lead down to the cell, turns away his face with the rest of the priests; the stairs are drawn up after she has gone down, and a quantity of earth is heaped up over the entrance to the cell, so as to prevent it from being distinguished from the rest of the mound. This is the punishment of those who break their vow of virginity.

It is said, also, that Numa built the temple of Vesta, which was intended for a repository of the holy fire, of a circular form, not to represent the figure of the earth, as if that were the same as Vesta, but that of the general universe, in the centre of which the Pythagoreans place the element of fire, and give it the name of Vesta and the unit; and do not hold that the earth is immovable, or that it is situated in the centre of the globe, but that it keeps a circular motion about the seat of fire, and is not in the number of the primary elements; in this agreeing with the opinion of Plato, who, they say, in his later life, conceived that the earth held a lateral position, and that the central and sovereign space was reserved for some nobler body.

There was yet a farther use of the priests, and that was to give people directions in the national usages at funeral rites. Numa taught them to regard these offices, not as a pollution, but as a duty paid to the gods below, into whose hands the better part of us is transmitted; especially they were to worship the goddess Libitina, who presided over all the ceremonies performed at burials; whether they meant hereby Proserpina, or, as the most learned of the Romans conceive, Venus, not inaptly attributing the beginning and end of man's life to the agency of one and the same deity. Numa also prescribed rules for regulating the days of mourning, according to certain times and ages. As, for example, a child of three years was not to be mourned for at all; one older, up to ten years, for as many months as it was years old; and the longest time of mourning for any person whatsoever was not to exceed the term of ten months; which was the time appointed for women that lost their husbands to continue in widowhood. If any married again before that time, by the laws of Numa, she was to sacrifice a cow big with calf.

Numa, also, was founder of several other orders of priests, two of which I shall mention, the Salii and the Fecials, which are among the clearest proofs of the devoutness and sanctity of his character. These Fecials, or guardians of peace, seem to have had their name from their office, which was to put a stop to disputes by conference and speech; for it was not allowable to take up arms until they had declared all hopes of accommodation to be at an end, for in Greek, too, we call it peace when disputes are settled by words, and not by force. The Romans commonly despatched the Fecials, or heralds, to those who had offered them injury, requesting satisfaction; and, in case they refused, they then called the gods to witness, and, with imprecations upon themselves and their country should they be acting unjustly, so declared war; against their will, or without their consent, it was lawful neither for soldier nor king to take up arms; the war was begun with them, and when they had first handed it over to the commander as a just quarrel, then his business was to deliberate of the manner and ways to carry it on. It is believed that the slaughter and destruction which the Gauls made of the Romans was a judgment on the city for neglect of this religious proceeding; for that when these barbarians besieged the Clusinians, Fabius Ambustus was despatched to their camp to negotiate peace for the besieged; and, on their returning a rude refusal, Fabius imagined that his office of ambassador was at an end, and, rashly engaging on the side of the Clusinians, challenged the bravest of the enemy to a single combat. It was the fortune of Fabius to kill his adversary, and to take his spoils; but when the Gauls discovered it, they sent a herald to Rome to complain against him; since, before war was declared, he had, against the law of nations, made a breach of the peace. The matter being debated in the senate, the Fecials were of opinion that Fabius ought to be consigned into the hands of the Gauls; but he, being forewarned of their judgment, fled to the people, by whose protection and favour he escaped the sentence. On this, the Gauls marched with their army to Rome, where having taken the capitol, they sacked the city. The particulars of all which are fully given in the history of Camillus.

The origin of the Salii is this. In the eighth year of the reign of Numa, a terrible pestilence, which traversed all Italy, ravaged likewise the city of Rome; and the citizens being in distress and despondent, a brazen target, they say, fell from heaven into the hands of Numa, who gave them this marvellous account of it: that Egeria and the Muses had assured him it was sent from heaven for the cure and safety of the city, and that, to keep it secure, he was ordered by them to make eleven others, so like in dimensions and form to the original that no thief should be able to distinguish the true from the counterfeit. He farther declared, that he was commanded to consecrate to the Muses the place, and the fields about it, where they had been chiefly wont to meet with him, and that the spring which watered the fields should be hallowed for the use of the vestal virgins, who were to wash and cleanse the penetralia of their sanctuary with those holy waters. The truth of all which was speedily verified by the cessation of the pestilence. Numa displayed the target to the artificers and bade them show their skill in making others like it; all despaired, until at length one Mamurius Veturius, an excellent workman, happily hit upon it, and made all so exactly the same that Numa himself was at a loss and could not distinguish. The keeping of these targets was committed to the charge of certain priests, called Salii, who did not receive their name, as some tell the story, from Salius, a dancing-master, born in Samothrace, or at Mantinea, who taught the way of dancing in arms; but more truly from that jumping dance which the Salii themselves use, when in the month of March they carry the sacred targets through the city; at which procession they are habited in short frocks of purple, girt with a broad belt studded with brass; on their heads they wear a brass helmet, and carry in their hands short daggers, which they clash every now and then against the targets. But the chief thing is the dance itself. They move with much grace, performing, in quick time and close order, various intricate figures, with a great display of strength and agility. The targets were called Ancilia from their form; for they are not made round, nor like proper targets, of a complete circumference, but are cut out into a wavy line, the ends of which are rounded off and turned in at the thickest part towards each other; so that their shape is curvilinear, or, in Greek, *ancylon;* or the name may come from *ancon,* the elbow, on which they are carried. Thus Juba writes, who is eager to make it Greek. But it might be, for that matter, from its having come down *anecathen,* from above; or from its *akesis,* or cure of diseases; or *auchmon lysis,* because it put an end to a drought; or from its *anaschesis,* or relief from calamities, which is the origin of the Athenian name Anaces, given to Castor and Pollux; if we must, that is, reduce it to Greek. The reward which Mamurius received for his art was to be mentioned and commemorated in the verses which the Salii sang, as they danced in their arms through the city; though some will have it that they do not say Veturium Mamuium, but Veterem Memoriam, ancient remembrance.

After Numa had in this manner instituted these several orders of priests, he erected, near the temple of Vesta, what is called to this day Regia, or king's house, where he spent the most part of his time performing divine service, instructing the priests, or conversing with them on sacred subjects. He had another house upon the Mount Quirinalis, the site of which they show to this day. In all public processions and solemn prayers, criers were sent before to give notice to the people that they should forbear their work, and rest. They say that the Pythagoreans did not allow people to worship and pray to their gods by the way, but would have them go out from their houses direct, with their minds set upon the duty, and Numa, in like manner, wished that his citizens should neither see nor hear any religious service in a perfunctory and inattentive manner, but, laying aside all other occupations, should apply their minds to religion as to a most serious business; and that the streets should be free from all noises and cries that accompany manual labour, and clear for the sacred solemnity. Some traces of this custom remain at Rome to this day, for, when the consul begins to take auspices or do sacrifice, they call out to the people, *Hoc age*, Attend to this, whereby the auditors then present are admonished to compose and recollect themselves. Many other of his precepts resemble those of the Pythagoreans. The Pythagoreans said, for example, "Thou shalt not make a peck-measure thy seat to sit on. Thou shalt not stir the fire with a sword. When thou goest out upon a journey, look not behind thee. When thou sacrificest to the celestial gods; let it be with an odd number, and when to the terrestrial, with even." The significance of each of which precepts they would not commonly disclose. So some of Numa's traditions have no obvious meaning. "Thou shalt not make libation to the gods of wine from an unpruned vine. No sacrifices shall be performed without meal. Turn round to pay adoration to the gods; sit after you have worshipped." The first two directions seem to denote the cultivation and subduing of the earth as a part of religion; and as to the turning which the worshippers are to use in divine adoration, it is said to represent the rotatory motion of the world. But, in my opinion, the meaning rather is, that the worshipper, since the temples front the east, enters with his back to the rising sun; there, faces round to the east, and so turns back to the god of the temple, by this circular movement referring the fulfilment of his prayers to both divinities. Unless, indeed, this change of posture may have a mystical meaning, like the Egyptian wheels, and signify to us the instability of human fortune, and that, in whatever way God changes and turns our lot and condition, we should rest contented, and accept it as right and fitting. They say, also, that the sitting after worship was to be by way of omen of their petitions being granted, and the blessing they asked assured to them. Again, as different courses of actions are divided by intervals of rest, they might seat themselves after the completion of what they had done, to seek favour of the gods for beginning something else. And this would very well suit with what we had before; the lawgiver wants to habituate us to make our petitions to the deity not by the way, and, as it were, in a hurry, when we have other things to do, but with time and leisure to attend to it. By such discipline and schooling in religion, the city passed insensibly into such a submissiveness of temper, and stood in such awe and reverence of the virtue of Numa, that they received, with an undoubted assurance, whatever he delivered though never so fabulous, and thought nothing incredible or impossible from him.

There goes a story that he once invited a great number of citizens to an entertainment, at which the dishes in which the meat was served were very homely and plain, and the repast itself poor and ordinary fare; the guests seated, he began to tell them that the goddess that consulted with him was then at that time come to him; when on a sudden the room was furnished with all sorts of costly drinking-vessels, and the tables loaded with rich meats, and a most sumptuous entertainment. But the dialogue which is reported to have passed between him and Jupiter surpasses all the fabulous legends that were ever invented. They say that before Mount Aventine was inhabited or enclosed within the walls of the city, two demigods, Picus and Faunus, frequented the springs and thick shades of that place; which might be two satyrs, or Pans, except that they went about Italy playing the same sorts of tricks, by skill in drugs and magic, as are ascribed by the Greeks to the Dactyli of Mount Ida. Numa contrived one day to surprise these demigods, by mixing wine and honey in the waters of the spring of which they usually drank. On finding themselves ensnared, they changed themselves into various shapes, dropping their own form and assuming every kind of unusual and hideous appearance; but when they saw they were safely entrapped, and in no possibility of getting free, they revealed to him many secrets and future events; and particularly a charm for thunder and lightning, still in use, performed with onions and hair and pilchards. Some say they did not tell him the charm, but by their magic brought down Jupiter out of heaven; and that he then, in an angry manner answering the inquiries, told Numa, that, if he would charm the thunder and lightning, he must do it with heads. "How," said Numa, "with the heads of onions?" "No," replied Jupiter, "of men." But Numa, willing to elude the cruelty of this receipt, turned it another way, saying, "Your meaning is, the hairs of men's heads." "No," replied Jupiter, "with living"— "pilchards," said Numa, interrupting him. These answers he had learnt from Egeria. Jupiter returned again to heaven, pacified and *ileos*, or propitious. The place was, in remembrance of him, called Ilicium, from this Greek word; and the spell in this manner effected.

These stories, laughable as they are, show us the feelings which people then, by force of habit, entertained towards the deity. And Numa's own thoughts are said to have been fixed to that degree on divine objects, that he once, when a message was brought to him that "Enemies are approaching," answered with a smile, "And I am sacrificing." It was he, also, that built the temples of Faith and Terminus, and taught the Romans that the name of Faith was the most solemn oath that they could swear. They still use it; and to the god Terminus, or Boundary, they offer to this day both public and private sacrifices, upon the borders and stone-marks of their land; living victims now, though anciently those sacrifices were solemnised without blood; for Numa reasoned that the god of boundaries, who watched over peace, and testified to fair dealing, should have no concern with blood. It is very clear that it was this king who first prescribed bounds to the territory of Rome; for Romulus would but have openly betrayed how much he had encroached on his neighbours' lands, had he ever set limits to his own; for boundaries are, indeed, a defence to those who choose to observe them, but are only a testimony against the dishonesty of those who break through them. The truth is, the portion of lands which the Romans possessed at the beginning was very narrow, until Romulus enlarged them by war; all those acquisitions Numa now divided amongst the indigent commonalty, wishing to do away with that extreme want which is a compulsion to dishonesty, and, by turning the people to husbandry, to bring them, as well as their lands, into better order. For there is no employment that gives so keen and quick a relish for peace as husbandry and a country life, which leave in men all that kind of courage that makes them ready to fight in defence of their own, while it destroys the licence that breaks out into acts of injustice and rapacity. Numa, therefore, hoping agriculture would be a sort of charm to captivate the affections of his people to peace, and viewing it rather as a means to moral than to economical profit, divided all the lands into several parcels, to which he gave the name of *pagus,* or parish, and over everyone of them he ordained chief overseers; and, taking a delight sometimes to inspect his colonies in person, he formed his judgment of every man's habits by the results; of which being witness himself, he preferred those to honours and employments who had done well, and by rebukes and reproaches incited the indolent and careless to improvement. But of all his measures the most commended was his distribution of the people by their trades into companies or guilds; for as the city consisted, or rather did not consist of, but was divided into, two different tribes, the diversity between which could not be effaced and in the meantime prevented all unity and caused perpetual tumult and ill-blood, reflecting how hard substances that do not readily mix when in the lump may, by being beaten into powder, in that minute form be combined, he resolved to divide the whole population into a number of small divisions, and thus hoped, by introducing other distinctions, to obliterate the original and great distinction, which would be lost among the smaller. So, distinguishing the whole people by the several arts and trades, he formed the companies of musicians, goldsmiths, carpenters, dyers, shoemakers, skinners, braziers, and potters; and all other handicraftsmen he composed and reduced into a single company, appointing everyone their proper courts, councils, and religious observances. In this manner all factious distinctions began, for the first time, to pass out of use, no person any longer being either thought of or spoken of under the notion of a Sabine or a Roman, a Romulian or a Tatian; and the new division became a source of general harmony and intermixture.

He is also much to be commended for the repeal, or rather amendment, of that law which gives power to fathers to sell their children; he exempted such as were married, conditionally that it had been with the liking and consent of their parents; for it seemed a hard thing that a woman who had given herself in marriage to a man whom she judged free should afterwards find herself living with a slave.

He attempted, also, the formation of a calendar, not with absolute exactness, yet not without some scientific knowledge. During the reign of Romulus, they had let their months run on without any certain or equal term; some of them contained twenty days, others thirty-five, others more; they had no sort of knowledge of the inequality in the motions of the sun and moon; they only kept to the one rule that the whole course of the year contained three hundred and sixty days. Numa, calculating the difference between the lunar and the solar year at eleven days, for that the moon completed her anniversary course in three hundred and fifty-four days, and the sun in three hundred and sixty-five, to remedy this incongruity doubled the eleven days, and every other year added an intercalary month, to follow February, consisting of twenty-two days, and called by the Romans the month Mercedinus. This amendment, however, itself, in course of time, came to need other amendments. He also altered the order of the months; for March, which was reckoned the first, he put into the third place; and January, which was the eleventh, he made the first; and February, which was the twelfth and last, the second. Many will have it, that it was Numa, also, who added the two months of January and February; for in the beginning they had had a year of ten months; as there are barbarians who count only three; the Arcadians, in Greece, had but four; the Acarnanians, six. The Egyptian year at first, they say, was of one month; afterwards, of four; and so, though they live in the newest of all countries, they have the credit of being a more ancient nation than any, and reckon, in their genealogies, a prodigious number of years, counting months, that is, as years. That the Romans, at first, comprehended the whole year within ten, and not twelve months, plainly appears by the name of the last, December, meaning the tenth month; and that March was the first is likewise evident, for the fifth month after it was called Quintilis, and the sixth Sextilis, and so the rest; whereas, if January and February had, in this account, preceded March, Quintilis would have been fifth in name and seventh in reckoning. It was also natural that March, dedicated to Mars, should be Romulus' first and April, named from Venus, or Aphrodite, his second month; in it they sacrifice to Venus, and the women bathe on the calends, or first day of it, with myrtle garlands on their heads. But others, because of its being *p* and not *ph*, will not allow of the derivation of this word from Aphrodite, but say it is called April from *aperio*, Latin for to open, because that this month is high spring, and opens and discloses the buds and flowers. The next is called May, from Maia, the mother of Mercury, to whom it is sacred; then June follows, so called from Juno; some, however, derive them from the two ages, old and young, *majores*, being their name for older, and *juniores* for younger men. To the other months they gave denominations according to their order; so the fifth was called Quintilis, Sextilis the sixth, and the rest, September, October, November, and December. Afterwards Quintilis received the name of Julius, from Cæsar, who defeated Pompey; as also Sextilis that of Augustus, from the second Cæsar, who had that title. Domitian, also, in imitation, gave the two other following months his own names, of Germanicus and Domitianus; but, on his being slain, they recovered their ancient denominations of September and October. The two last are the only ones that have kept their names throughout without any alteration. Of the months which were added or transposed in their order by Numa, February comes from *februa;* and is as much a Purification month; in it they make offerings to the dead, and celebrate the Lupercalia, which, in most points, resembles a purification. January was also called from Janus, and precedence given to it by Numa before March, which was dedicated to the god Mars; because, as I conceive, he wished to take every opportunity of intimating that the arts and studies of peace are to be preferred before those of war. For this Janus, whether in remote antiquity he were a demigod or a king, was certainly a great lover of civil and social unity, and one who reclaimed men from brutal and savage living; for which reason they figure him with two faces, to represent the two states and conditions out of the one of which he brought mankind, to lead them into the other. His temple at

Rome has two gates, which they call the gates of war, because they stand open in the time of war, and shut in the times of peace; of which latter there was very seldom an example, for, as the Roman empire was enlarged and extended, it was so encompassed with barbarous nations and enemies to be resisted, that it was seldom or never at peace. Only in the time of Augustus Cæsar, after he had overcome Antony, this temple was shut; as likewise once before, when Marcus Atilius and Titus Manlius were consuls; but then it was not long before, wars breaking out, the gates were again opened. But, during the reign of Numa, those gates were never seen open a single day, but continued constantly shut for a space of forty-three years together; such an entire and universal cessation of war existed. For not only had the people of Rome itself been softened and charmed into a peaceful temper by the just and mild rule of a pacific prince, but even the neighbouring cities, as if some salubrious and gentle air had blown from Rome upon them, began to experience a change of feeling, and partook in the general longing for the sweets of peace and order, and for life employed in the quiet tillage of soil, bringing up of children, and worship of the gods. Festival days and sports, and the secure and peaceful interchange of friendly visits and hospitalities prevailed all through the whole of Italy. The love of virtue and justice flowed from Numa's wisdom as from a fountain, and the serenity of his spirit diffused itself, like a calm, on all sides; so that the hyperboles of poets were flat and tame to express what then existed; as that—

Over the iron shield the spiders hang their threads,

or that—

Rust eats the pointed spear and double-edged sword.
No more is heard the trumpet's brazen roar,
Sweet sleep is banished from our eyes no more.

For during the whole reign of Numa, there was neither war, nor sedition, nor innovation in the state, nor any envy or ill-will to his person, nor plot or conspiracy from views of ambition. Either fear of the gods that were thought to watch over him, or reverence for his virtue, or divine felicity of fortune that in his days preserved human innocence, made his reign, by whatever means, a living example and verification of that saying which Plato, long afterwards, ventured to pronounce, that the sole and only hope of respite or remedy for human evils was in some happy conjunction of events which should unite in a single person the power of a king and the wisdom of a philosopher, so as to elevate virtue to control and mastery over vice. The wise man is blessed in himself, and blessed also are the auditors who can hear and receive those words which flow from his mouth; and perhaps, too, there is no need of compulsion or menaces to affect the multitude, for the mere sight itself of a shining and conspicuous example of virtue in the life of their prince will bring them spontaneously to virtue, and to a conformity with that blameless and blessed life of goodwill and mutual concord, supported by temperance and justice, which is the highest benefit that human means can confer; and he is the truest ruler who can best introduce it into the hearts and practice of his subjects. It is the praise of Numa that no one seems ever to have discerned this so clearly as he.

As to his children and wives, there is a diversity of reports by several authors; some will have it that he never had any other wife than Tatia; nor more children than one daughter called Pompilia; others will have it that he left also four sons, namely, Pompo, Pinus, Calpus, and Mamercus, everyone of whom had issue, and from them descended the noble and illustrious families of Pomponii, Pinarii, Calpurnii, and Mamerci, which for this reason took also the surname of Rex, or King. But there is a third set of writers who say that these pedigrees are but a piece of flattery used by writers who, to gain favour with these great families, made them fictitious genealogies from the lineage of Numa; and that Pompilia was not the daughter of Tatia, but Lucretia, another wife whom he married after he came to his kingdom; however, all of them agree in opinion that she was married to the son of that Marcius who persuaded him to accept the government, and accompanied him to Rome, where, as a mark of honour, he was chosen into the senate, and after the death of Numa, standing in competition with Tullus Hostilius for the kingdom, and being disappointed of the election, in discontent killed himself; his son Marcius, however, who had married Pompilia, continuing at Rome, was the father of Ancus Marcius, who succeeded Tullus Hostilius in the kingdom, and was but five years of age when Numa died.

Numa lived something above eighty years, and then, as Piso writes, was not taken out of the world by a sudden or acute disease, but died of old age and by a gradual and gentle decline. At his funeral all the glories of his life were consummated, when all the neighbouring states in alliance and amity with Rome met to honour and grace the rites of his interment with garlands and public presents; the senators carried the bier on which his corpse was laid, and the priests followed and accompanied the solemn procession; while a general crowd, in which women and children took part, followed with such cries and weeping as if they had bewailed the death and loss of some most dear relation taken away in the flower of age, and not an old and worn-out king. It is said that his body, by his particular command, was not burnt, but that they made, in conformity with his order, two stone coffins, and buried both under the hill Janiculum, in one of which his body was laid, and the other his sacred books, which, as the Greek legislators their tables, he had written out for himself, but had so long inculcated the contents of them, whilst he lived, into the minds and hearts of the priests, that their understandings became fully possessed with the whole spirit and purpose of them; and he therefore bade that they should be buried with his body, as though such holy precepts could not without irreverence be left to circulate in mere lifeless writings. For this very reason, they say, the Pythagoreans bade that their precepts should not be committed to paper, but rather preserved in the living memories of those who were worthy to receive them; and when some of their out-of-the-way and abstruse geometrical processes had been divulged to an unworthy person, they said the gods threatened to punish this wickedness and profanity by a signal and wide-spreading calamity. With these several instances concurring to show a similarity in the lives of Numa and Pythagoras, we may easily pardon those who seek to establish the fact of a real acquaintance between them.

Valerius Antias writes that the books which were buried in the aforesaid chest or coffin of stone were twelve volumes of holy writ and twelve others of Greek philosophy, and that about four hundred years afterwards, when P. Cornelius and M. Bæbius were consuls, in a time of heavy rains, a violent torrent washed away the earth, and dislodged the chests of stone; and, their covers falling off, one of them was found wholly empty, without the least relic of any human body; in the other were the books before mentioned, which the prætor Petilius having read and perused, made oath in the senate, that, in his opinion, it was not fit for their contents to be made public to the people; whereupon the volumes were all carried to the Comitium, and there burnt.

It is the fortune of all good men that their virtue rises in glory after their deaths, and that the envy which evil men conceive against them never outlives them long; some have the happiness even to see it die before them; but in Numa's case, also, the fortunes of the succeeding kings served as foils to set off the brightness of his reputation. For after him there were five kings, the last of whom ended his old age in banishment, being deposed from his crown; of the other four, three were assassinated and murdered by treason; the other, who was Tullus Hostilius, that immediately succeeded Numa, derided his virtues, and especially his devotion to religious worship, as a cowardly and mean-spirited occupation, and diverted the minds of the people to war; but was checked in these youthful insolences, and was himself driven by an acute and tormenting disease into superstitions wholly different from Numa's piety, and left others also to participate in these terrors when he died by the stroke of a thunderbolt.

THE COMPARISON OF NUMA
WITH LYCURGUS

HAVING THUS FINISHED THE LIVES OF LYCURGUS AND NUMA, WE SHALL NOW, though the work be difficult, put together their points of difference as they lie here before our view. Their points of likeness are obvious; their moderation, their religion, their capacity of government and discipline, their both deriving their laws and constitutions from the gods. Yet in their common glories there are circumstances of diversity; for first Numa accepted and Lycurgus resigned a kingdom; Numa received without desiring it, Lycurgus had it and gave it up; the one from a private person and a stranger was raised by others to be their king; the other from the condition of a prince voluntarily descended to the state of privacy. It was glorious to acquire a throne by justice, yet more glorious to prefer justice before a throne; the same virtue which made the one appear worthy of regal power exalted the other to the disregard of it. Lastly, as the musicians tune their harps, so the one let down the high-flown spirits of the people at Rome to a lower key, as the other screwed them up at Sparta to a higher note, when they were sunken low by dissoluteness and riot. The harder task was that of Lycurgus; for it was not so much his business to persuade his citizens to put off their armour or ungird their swords, as to cast away their gold or silver, and abandon costly furniture and rich tables; nor was it necessary to preach to them, that, laying aside their arms, they should observe the festivals, and sacrifice to the gods, but rather, that, giving up feasting and drinking, they should employ their time in laborious and martial exercises; so that while the one effected all by persuasions and his people's love for him, the other, with danger and hazard of his person, scarcely in the end succeeded. Numa's muse was a gentle and loving inspiration, fitting him well to turn and soothe his people into peace and justice out of their violent and fiery tempers; whereas, if we must admit the treatment of the Helots to be a part of Lycurgus' legislation, a most cruel and iniquitous proceeding, we must own that Numa was by a great deal the more humane and Greek-like legislator, granting even to actual slaves a licence to sit at meat with their masters at the feast of Saturn, that they also might have some taste and relish of the sweets of liberty. For this custom, too, is ascribed to Numa, whose wish was, they conceive, to give a place in the enjoyment of the yearly fruits of the soil to those who had helped to produce them. Others will have it to be in remembrance of the age of Saturn, when there was no distinction between master and slave, but all lived as brothers and as equals in a condition of equality.

In general, it seems that both aimed at the same design and intent, which was to bring their people to moderation and frugality; but of other virtues, the one set his affection most on fortitude, and the other on justice; unless we will attribute their different ways to the different habits and temperaments which they had to work upon by their enactments; for Numa did not out of cowardice or fear affect peace, but because he would not be guilty of injustice; nor did Lycurgus promote a spirit of war in his people that they might do injustice to others, but that they might protect themselves by it.

In bringing the habits they formed in their people to a just and happy mean, mitigating them where they exceeded, and strengthening them where they were deficient, both were compelled to make great innovations. The frame of government which Numa formed was democratic and popular to the last extreme, goldsmiths and flute players and shoemakers constituting his promiscuous, many-coloured commonalty. Lycurgus was rigid and aristocratical, banishing all the base and mechanic arts to the company of servants and strangers, and allowing the true citizens no implements but the spear and shield, the trade of war only, and the service of Mars, and no other knowledge or study, but that of obedience to their commanding officers, and victory over their enemies. Every sort of money-making was forbid them as freemen; and to make them thoroughly so and keep them so through their whole lives, every conceivable concern with money was handed over, with the cooking and the waiting at table, to slaves and helots. But Numa made none of these distinctions; he only suppressed military rapacity, allowing free scope to every other means of obtaining wealth; nor did he endeavour to do away with inequality in this respect, but permitted riches to be amassed to any extent, and paid no attention to the gradual and continual augmentation and influx of poverty; which it was his business at the outset, whilst there was no great disparity in the estates of men, and whilst people still lived much in one manner, to obviate, as Lycurgus did, and take measures of precaution against the mischiefs of avarice, mischiefs not of small importance, but the real seed and first beginning of all the great and extensive evils of after-times. The re-division of estates, Lycurgus is not, it seems to me, to be blamed for making, nor Numa for omitting; this equality was the basis and foundation of the one commonwealth; but at Rome, where the lands had been lately divided, there was nothing to urge any re-division or any disturbance of the first arrangement, which was probably still in existence.

With respect to wives and children, and that community which both, with a sound policy, appointed, to prevent all jealousy, their methods, however, were different. For when a Roman thought himself to have a sufficient number of children, in case his neighbour who had none should come and request his wife of him, he had a lawful power to give her up to him who desired her, either for a certain time, or for good. The Lacedæmonian husband, on the other hand, might allow the use of his wife to any other that desired to have children by her, and yet still keep her in his house, the original marriage obligation still subsisting as at first. Nay, many husbands, as we have said, would invite men whom they thought likely to procure them fine and good-looking children into their houses. What is the difference, then, between the two customs? Shall we say that the Lacedæmonian system is one of an extreme and entire unconcern about their wives, and would cause most people endless disquiet and annoyance with pangs and jealousies? The Roman course wears an air of a more delicate acquiescence, draws the veil of a new contract over the change, and concedes the general insupportableness of mere community? Numa's directions, too, for the care of young women, are better adapted to the female sex and to propriety; Lycurgus' are altogether unreserved and unfeminine, and have given a great handle to the poets, who call them (Ibycus, for example) *Phœnomerides*, bare-thighed; and give them the character (as does Euripides) of being wild after husbands—

> These with the young men from the house go out,
> With thighs that show, and robes that fly about.

For in fact the skirts of the frock worn by unmarried girls were not sewn together at the lower part, but used to fly back and show the whole thigh bare as they walked. The thing is most distinctly given by Sophocles—

> —She, also, the young maid,
> Whose frock, no robe yet o'er it laid,
> Folding back, leaves her bare thigh free,
> Hermione.

And so their women, it is said, were bold and masculine, overbearing to their husbands in the first place, absolute mistresses in their houses, giving their opinions about public matters freely, and speaking openly even on the most important subjects. But the matrons, under the government of Numa, still indeed received from their husbands all that high respect and honour which had been paid them under Romulus as a sort of atonement for the violence done to them; nevertheless, great modesty was enjoined upon them; all busy intermeddling forbidden, sobriety insisted on, and silence made habitual. Wine they were not to touch at all, nor to speak, except in their husband's company, even on the most ordinary subjects. So that once when a woman had the confidence to plead her own cause in a court of judicature, the senate, it is said, sent to inquire of the oracle what the prodigy did portend; and, indeed, their general good behaviour and submissiveness is justly proved by the record of those that were otherwise; for as the Greek historians record in their annals the names of those who first unsheathed the sword of civil war, or murdered their brothers, or were parricides, or killed their mothers, so the Roman writers report it as the first example, that Spurius Carvilius divorced his wife, being a case that never before happened, in the space of two hundred and thirty years from the foundation of the city; and that one Thalæa, the wife of Pinarius, had a quarrel (the first instance of the kind) with her mother-in-law, Gegania, in the reign of Tarquinius Superbus; so successful was the legislator in securing order and good conduct in the marriage relation. Their respective regulations for marrying the young women are in accordance with those for their education. Lycurgus made them brides when they were of full age and inclination for it. Intercourse, where nature was thus consulted, would produce, he thought, love and tenderness, instead of the dislike and fear attending an unnatural compulsion; and their bodies, also, would be better able to bear the trials of breeding and of bearing children, in his judgment the one end of marriage.

The Romans, on the other hand, gave their daughters in marriage as early as twelve years old, or even under; thus they thought their bodies alike and minds would be delivered to the future husband pure and undefiled.

The way of Lycurgus seems the more natural with a view to the birth of children; the other, looking to a life to be spent together, is more moral. However, the rules which Lycurgus drew up for superintendence of children, their collection into companies, their discipline and association, as also his exact regulations for their meals, exercises, and sports, argue Numa no more than an ordinary lawgiver. Numa left the whole matter simply to be decided by the parent's wishes or necessities; he might, if he pleased, make his son a husbandman or carpenter, coppersmith or musician; as if it were of no importance for them to be directed and trained up from the beginning to one and the same common end, or as though it would do for them to be like passengers on shipboard, brought thither each for his own ends and by his own choice, uniting to act for the common good only in time of danger upon occasion of their private fears, in general looking simply to their own interest.

We may forbear, indeed, to blame common legislators, who may be deficient in power or knowledge. But when a wise man like Numa had received the sovereignty over a new and docile people, was there anything that would better deserve his attention than the education of children, and the training up of the young, not to contrariety and discordance of character, but to the unity of the common model of virtue, to which from their cradle they should have been formed and moulded? One benefit among many that Lycurgus obtained by his course was the permanence which it secured to his laws. The obligation of oaths to preserve them would have availed but little, if he had not, by discipline and education, infused them into the children's characters, and imbued their whole early life with a love of his government. The result was that the main points and fundamentals of his legislation continued for above five hundred years, like some deep and thoroughly ingrained tincture, retaining their hold upon the nation. But Numa's whole design and aim, the continuance of peace and goodwill, on his death vanished with him; no sooner did he expire his last breath than the gates of Janus' temple flew wide open, and, as if war had, indeed, been kept and caged up within those walls, it rushed forth to fill all Italy with blood and slaughter; and thus that best and justest fabric of things was of no long continuance, because it wanted that cement which should have kept all together, education. What, then, some may say, has not Rome been advanced and bettered by her wars? A question that will need a long answer, if it is to be one to satisfy men who take the *better* to consist in riches, luxury, and dominion rather than in security, gentleness, and that independence which is accompanied by justice.

However, it makes much for Lycurgus, that, after the Romans had deserted the doctrine and discipline of Numa, their empire grew and their power increased so much; whereas so soon as the Lacedæmonians fell from the institutions of Lycurgus, they sank from the highest to the lowest state, and, after forfeiting their supremacy over the rest of Greece, were themselves in danger of absolute extirpation. Thus much, meantime, was peculiarly signal and almost divine in the circumstances of Numa, that he was an alien, and yet courted to come and accept a kingdom, the frame of which though he entirely altered, yet he performed it by mere persuasion, and ruled a city that as yet had scarce become one city, without recurring to arms or any violence (such as Lycurgus used, supporting himself by the aid of the nobler citizens against the commonalty), but, by mere force of wisdom and justice, established union and harmony amongst all.

SOLON

Didymus, the grammarian, in his answer to Asclepiades concerning Solon's Tables of Law, mentions a passage of one Philocles, who states that Solon's father's name was Euphorion, contrary to the opinion of all others who have written concerning him; for they generally agree that he was the son of Execestides, a man of moderate wealth and power in the city, but of a most noble stock, being descended from Codrus; his mother, as Heraclides Ponticus affirms, was cousin to Pisistratus' mother, and the two at first were great friends, partly because they were akin, and partly because of Pisistratus' noble qualities and beauty. And they say Solon loved him; and that is the reason, I suppose, that when afterwards they differed about the government, their enmity never produced any hot and violent passion, they remembered their old kindnesses, and retained—

Still in its embers living the strong fire

of their love and dear affection. For that Solon was not proof against beauty, nor of courage to stand up to passion and meet it—

Hand to hand as in the ring,

we may conjecture by his poems, and one of his laws, in which there are practices forbidden to slaves, which he would appear, therefore, to recommend to freemen. Pisistratus, it is stated, was similarly attached to one Charmus; he it was who dedicated the figure of Love in the Academy, where the runners in the sacred torch race light their torches. Solon, as Hermippus writes, when his father had ruined his estate in doing benefits and kindnesses to other men, though he had friends enough that were willing to contribute to his relief, yet was ashamed to be beholden to others, since he was descended from a family who were accustomed to do kindnesses rather than receive them; and therefore applied himself to merchandise in his youth; though others assure us that he travelled rather to get learning and experience than to make money. It is certain that he was a lover of knowledge, for when he was old he would say, that he—

> Each day grew older, and learnt something new;

and yet no admirer of riches, esteeming as equally wealthy the man—

> Who hath both gold and silver in his hand,
> Horses and mules, and acres of wheat-land,
> And him whose all is decent food to eat,
> Clothes to his back and shoes upon his feet,
> And a young wife and child, since so 'twill be,
> And no more years than will with that agree;

and in another place—

> Wealth I would have, but wealth by wrong procure
> I would not; justice, e'en if slow, is sure.

And it is perfectly possible for a good man and a statesman, without being solicitous for superfluities, to show some concern for competent necessaries. In his time, as Hesiod says—"Work was a shame to none," nor was distinction made with respect to trade, but merchandise was a noble calling, which brought home the good things which the barbarous nations enjoyed, was the occasion of friendship with their kings, and a great source of experience. Some merchants have built great cities, as Protis, the founder of Massilia, to whom the Gauls, near the Rhone, were much attached. Some report also, that Thales and Hippocrates the mathematician traded; and that Plato defrayed the charges of his travels by selling oil in Egypt. Solon's softness and profuseness, his popular rather than philosophical tone about pleasure in his poems, have been ascribed to his trading life; for, having suffered a thousand dangers, it was natural they should be recompensed with some gratifications and enjoyments; but that he accounted himself rather poor than rich is evident from the lines—

> Some wicked men are rich, some good are poor,
> We will not change our virtue for their store:
> Virtue's a thing that none can take away;
> But money changes owners all the day.

At first he used his poetry only in trifles, not for any serious purpose, but simply to pass away his idle hours; but afterwards he introduced moral sentences and state matters, which he did, not to record them merely as an historian, but to justify his own actions, and sometimes to correct, chastise, and stir up the Athenians to noble performances. Some report that he designed to put his laws into heroic verse, and that they began thus:

> We humbly beg a blessing on our laws
> From mighty Jove, and honour, and applause.

In philosophy, as most of the wise men then, he chiefly esteemed the political part of morals; in physics, he was very plain and antiquated, as appears by this:

> It is the clouds that make the snow and hail,
> And thunder comes from lightning without fail;
> The sea is stormy when the winds have blown,
> But it deals fairly when 'tis left alone.

And, indeed, it is probable that at that time Thales alone had raised philosophy above mere practice into speculation; and the rest of the wise men were so called from prudence in political concerns. It is said, that they had an interview at Delphi, and another at Corinth, by the procurement of Periander, who made a meeting for them, and a supper. But their reputation was chiefly raised by sending the tripod to them all, by their modest refusal, and complaisant yielding to one another. For, as the story goes, some of the Coans fishing with a net, some strangers, Milesians, bought the draught at a venture; the net brought up a golden tripod, which, they say, Helen, at her return from Troy, upon the remembrance of an old prophecy, threw in there. Now, the strangers at first contesting with the fishers about the tripod, and the cities espousing the quarrel so far as to engage themselves in a war, Apollo decided the controversy by commanding to present it to the wisest man; and first it was sent to Miletus to Thales, the Coans freely presenting him with that for which they fought against the whole body of the Milesians; but Thales declaring Bias the wiser person, it was sent to him; from him to another; and so, going round them all, it came to Thales a second time; and, at last, being carried from Miletus to Thebes, was there dedicated to Apollo Ismenius. Theophrastus writes that it was first presented to Bias at Priene; and next to Thales at Miletus, and so through all it returned to Bias, and was afterwards sent to Delphi. This is the general report, only some, instead of a tripod, say this present was a cup sent by Crœsus; others, a piece of plate that one Bathycles had left. It is stated, that Anacharsis and Solon, and Solon and Thales, were familiarly acquainted and some have delivered parts of their discourse; for, they say, Anacharsis, coming to Athens, knocked at Solon's door, and told him, that he, being a stranger, was come to be his guest, and contract a friendship with him; and Solon replying, "It is better to make friends at home," Anacharsis replied, "Then you that are at home make friendship with me." Solon, somewhat surprised at the readiness of the repartee, received him kindly, and kept him sometime with him, being already engaged in public business and the compilation of his laws; which, when Anacharsis understood, he laughed at him for imagining the dishonesty and covetousness of his countrymen could be restrained by written laws, which were like spiders' webs, and would catch, it is true, the weak and poor, but easily be broken by the mighty and rich. To this Solon rejoined that men keep their promises when neither side can get anything by the breaking of them; and he would so fit his laws to the citizens, that all should understand it was more eligible to be just than to break the laws. But the event rather agreed with the conjecture of Anacharsis than Solon's hope. Anacharsis, being once at the Assembly, expressed his wonder at the fact that in Greece wise men spoke and fools decided.

Solon went, they say, to Thales, at Miletus, and wondered that Thales took no care to get him a wife and children. To this, Thales made no answer for the present; but a few days after procured a stranger to pretend that he had left Athens ten days ago; and Solon inquiring what news there, the man, according to his instructions, replied, "None but a young man's funeral, which the whole city attended; for he was the son, they said, of an honourable man, the most virtuous of the citizens, who was not then at home, but had been travelling a long time." Solon replied, "What a miserable man is he! But what was his name?" "I have heard it," says the man, "but have now forgotten it, only there was a great talk of his wisdom and his justice." Thus Solon was drawn on by every answer, and his fears heightened, till at last, being extremely concerned, he mentioned his own name, and asked the stranger if that young man was called Solon's son; and the stranger assenting, he began to beat his head, and to do and say all that is usual with men in transports of grief. But Thales took his hand, and, with a smile, said, "These things, Solon, keep me from marriage and rearing children, which are too great for even your constancy to support; however, be not concerned at the report, for it is a fiction." This Hermippus relates, from Patæcus, who boasted that he had Æsop's soul.

However, it is irrational and poor-spirited not to seek conveniences for fear of losing them, for upon the same account we should not allow ourselves to like wealth, glory, or wisdom, since we may fear to be deprived of all these; nay, even virtue itself, than which there is no greater nor more desirable possession, is often suspended by sickness or drugs. Now Thales, though unmarried, could not be free from solicitude unless he likewise felt no care for his friends, his kinsman, or his country; yet we are told he adopted Cybisthus, his sister's son. For the soul, having a principle of kindness in itself, and being born to love, as well as perceive, think, or remember, inclines and fixes upon some stranger, when a man has none of his own to embrace. And alien or illegitimate objects insinuate themselves into his affections, as into some estate that lacks lawful heirs; and with affection come anxiety and care; insomuch that you may see men that use the strongest language against the marriage-bed and the fruit of it, when some servant's or concubine's child is sick or dies, almost killed with grief, and abjectly lamenting. Some have given way to shameful and desperate sorrow at the loss of a dog or horse; others have borne the death of virtuous children without any extravagant or unbecoming grief, have passed the rest of their lives like men, and according to the principles of reason. It is not affection, it is weakness that brings men, unarmed against fortune by reason, into these endless pains and terrors; and they indeed have not even the present enjoyment of what they dote upon, the possibility of the future loss causing them continual pangs, tremors, and distresses. We must not provide against the loss of wealth by poverty, or of friends by refusing all acquaintance, or of children by having none, but by morality and reason. But of this too much.

Now, when the Athenians were tired with a tedious and difficult war that they conducted against the Megarians for the island Salamis, and made a law that it should be death for any man, by writing or speaking, to assert that the city ought to endeavour to recover it, Solon, vexed at the disgrace, and perceiving thousands of the youth wished for somebody to begin, but did not dare to stir first for fear of the law, counterfeited a distraction, and by his own family it was spread about the city that he was mad. He then secretly composed some elegiac verses, and getting them by heart, that it might seem extempore, ran out into the market place with a cap upon his head, and, the people gathering about him, got upon the herald's stand, and sang that elegy which begins thus:

> I am a herald come from Salamis the fair,
> My news from thence my verses shall declare.

The poem is called Salamis; it contains an hundred verses very elegantly written; when it had been sung, his friends commended it, and especially Pisistratus exhorted the citizens to obey his directions; insomuch that they recalled the law, and renewed the war under Solon's conduct. The popular tale is, that with Pisistratus he sailed to Colias, and, finding the women, according to the custom of the country there, sacrificing to Ceres, he sent a trusty friend to Salamis, who should pretend himself a renegade, and advise them, if they desired to seize the chief Athenian women, to come with him at once to Colias; the Megarians presently sent off men in the vessel with him; and Solon, seeing it put off from the island, commanded the women to be gone, and some beardless youths, dressed in their clothes, their shoes and caps, and privately armed with daggers, to dance and play near the shore till the enemies had landed and the vessel was in their power. Things being thus ordered, the Megarians were lured with the appearance, and, coming to the shore, jumped out, eager who should first seize a prize, so that not one of them escaped; and the Athenians set sail for the island and took it.

Others say that it was not taken this way, but that he first received this oracle from Delphi:

> Those heroes that in fair Asopia rest,
> All buried with their faces to the west,
> Go and appease with offerings of the best;

and that Solon, sailing by night to the island, sacrificed to the heroes Periphemus and Cychreus, and then taking five hundred Athenian volunteers (a law having passed that those that took the island should be highest in the government), with a number of fisher-boats and one thirty-oared ship, anchored in a bay of Salamis that looks towards Nisæa; and the Megarians that were then in the island, hearing only an uncertain report, hurried to their arms, and sent a ship to reconnoitre the enemies. This ship Solon took, and, securing the Megarians, manned it with Athenians, and gave them orders to sail to the island with as much privacy as possible; meantime he, with the other soldiers, marched against the Megarians by land, and whilst they were fighting, those from the ship took the city. And this narrative is confirmed by the following solemnity, that was afterwards observed: An Athenian ship used to sail silently at first to the island, then, with noise and a great shout, one leapt out armed, and with a loud cry ran to the promontory Sciradium to meet those that approached upon the land. And just by there stands a temple which Solon dedicated to Mars.

For he beat the Megarians, and as many as were not killed in the battle he sent away upon conditions.

The Megarians, however, still contending, and both sides having received considerable losses, they chose the Spartans for arbitrators. Now, many affirm that Homer's authority did Solon a considerable kindness, and that, introducing a line into the Catalogue of Ships, when the matter was to be determined, he read the passage as follows:

> Twelve ships from Salamis stout Ajax brought,
> And ranked his men where the Athenians fought.

The Athenians, however, call this but an idle story, and report that Solon made it appear to the judges, that Philæus and Eurysaces, the sons of Ajax, being made citizens of Athens, gave them the island, and that one of them dwelt at Brauron in Attica, the other at Melite; and they have a township of Philaidæ, to which Pisistratus belonged, deriving its name from this Philæus. Solon took a farther argument against the Megarians from the dead bodies, which, he said, were not buried after their fashion, but according to the Athenian; for the Megarians turn the corpse to the east, the Athenians to the west. But Hereas the Megarian denies this, and affirms that they likewise turn the body to the west, and also that the Athenians have a separate tomb for everybody, but the Megarians put two or three into one. However, some of Apollo's oracles, where he calls Salamis Ionian, made much for Solon. This matter was determined by five Spartans, Critolaidas, Amompharetus, Hypsechidas, Anaxilas, and Cleomenes.

For this, Solon grew famed and powerful; but his advice in favour of defending the oracle at Delphi, to give aid, and not to suffer the Cirrhæans to profane it, but to maintain the honour of the god, got him most repute among the Greeks; for upon his persuasion the Amphictyons undertook the war, as amongst others, Aristotle affirms, in his enumeration of the victors at the Pythian games, where he makes Solon the author of this counsel. Solon, however, was not general in that expedition, as Hermippus states, out of Evanthes the Samian; for Æschines the orator says no such thing, and, in the Delphian register, Alcmæon, not Solon, is named as commander of the Athenians.

Now the Cylonian pollution had a long while disturbed the common-wealth, ever since the time when Megacles the archon persuaded the conspirators with Cylon that took sanctuary in Minerva's temple to come down and stand to a fair trial. And they, tying a thread to the image, and holding one end of it, went down to the tribunal; but when they came to the temple of the Furies, the thread broke of its own accord, upon which, as if the goddess had refused them protection, they were seized by Megacles and the other magistrates; as many as were without the temples were stoned, these that fled for sanctuary were butchered at the altar, and only those escaped who made supplication to the wives of the magistrates. But they from that time were considered under pollution, and regarded with hatred. The remainder of the faction of Cylon grew strong again, and had continual quarrels with the family of Megacles; and now the quarrel being at its height, and the people divided, Solon, being in reputation, interposed with the chiefest of the Athenians, and by entreaty and admonition persuaded the polluted to submit to a trial and the decision of three hundred noble citizens. And Myron of Phlya being their accuser, they were found guilty, and as many as were then alive were banished, and the bodies of the dead were dug up, and scattered beyond the confines of the country. In the midst of these distractions, the Megarians falling upon them, they lost Nisæa and Salamis again; besides, the city was disturbed with superstitious fears and strange appearances, and the priests declared that the sacrifices intimated some villainies and pollutions that were to be expiated. Upon this, they sent for Epimenides the Phæstian from Crete, who is counted the seventh wise man by those that will not admit Periander into the number. He seems to have been thought a favourite of heaven, possessed of knowledge in all the supernatural and ritual parts of religion; and, therefore, the men of his age called him a new Curies, and son of a nymph named Balte. When he came to Athens, and grew acquainted with Solon, he served him in many instances, and prepared the way for his legislation. He made them moderate in their forms of worship, and abated their mourning by ordering some sacrifices presently after the funeral, and taking off those severe and barbarous ceremonies which the women usually practised; but the greatest benefit was his purifying and sanctifying the city, by certain propitiatory and expiatory lustrations, and foundations of sacred buildings, by that means making them more submissive to justice, and more inclined to harmony. It is reported that, looking upon Munychia, and considering a long while, he said to those that stood by, "How blind is man in future things! For did the Athenians foresee what mischief this would do their city, they would even eat it with their own teeth to be rid of it." A similar anticipation is ascribed to Thales; they say he commanded his friends to bury him in an obscure and contemned quarter of the territory of Miletus, saying that it should someday be the marketplace of the Milesians. Epimenides, being much honoured, and receiving from the city rich offers of large gifts and privileges, requested but one branch of the sacred olive, and, on that being granted, returned.

The Athenians, now the Cylonian sedition was over and the polluted gone into banishment, fell into their old quarrels about the government, there being as many different parties as there were diversities in the country. The Hill quarter favoured democracy, the Plain, oligarchy, and those that lived by the Seaside stood for a mixed sort of government, and so hindered either of the other parties from prevailing. And the disparity of fortune between the rich and the poor, at that time, also reached its height; so that the city seemed to be in a truly dangerous condition, and no other means for freeing it from disturbances and settling it to be possible but a despotic power. All the people were indebted to the rich; and either they tilled their land for their creditors, paying them a sixth part of the increase, and were, therefore, called Hectemorii and Thetes, or else they engaged their body for the debt, and might be seized, and either sent into slavery at home, or sold to strangers; some (for no law forbade it) were forced to sell their children, or fly their country to avoid the cruelty of their creditors; but the most part and the bravest of them began to combine together and encourage one another to stand to it, to choose a leader, to liberate the condemned debtors, divide the land, and change the government.

Then the wisest of the Athenians, perceiving Solon was of all men the only one not implicated in the troubles, that he had not joined in the exactions of the rich, and was not involved in the necessities of the poor, pressed him to succour the commonwealth and compose the differences. Though Phanias the Lesbian affirms, that Solon, to save his country, put a trick upon both parties, and privately promised the poor a division of the lands, and the rich security for their debts. Solon, however, himself says, that it was reluctantly at first that he engaged in state affairs, being afraid of the pride of one party and the greediness of the other; he was chosen archon, however, after Philombrotus, and empowered to be an arbitrator and lawgiver; the rich consenting because he was wealthy, the poor because he was honest. There was a saying of his current before the election, that, when things are *even* there never can be war, and this pleased both parties, the wealthy and the poor; the one conceiving him to mean, when all have their fair proportion; the others, when all are absolutely equal. Thus, there being great hopes on both sides, the chief men pressed Solon to take the government into his own hands, and, when he was once settled, manage the business freely and according to his pleasure; and many of the commons, perceiving it would be a difficult change to be effected by law and reason, were willing to have one wise and just man set over the affairs; and some say that Solon had this oracle from Apollo—

> Take the mid-seat, and be the vessel's guide;
> Many in Athens are upon your side.

But chiefly his familiar friends chid him for disaffecting monarchy only because of the name, as if the virtue of the ruler could not make it a lawful form; Eubœa had made this experiment when it chose Tynnondas, and Mitylene, which had made Pittacus its prince; yet this could not shake Solon's resolution; but, as they say, he replied to his friends, that it was true a tyranny was a very fair spot, but it had no way down from it; and in a copy of verses to Phocus he writes—

> that I spared my land,
> And withheld from usurpation and from violence my hand,
> And forbore to fix a stain and a disgrace on my good name,
> I regret not; I believe that it will be my chiefest fame.

From which it is manifest that he was a man of great reputation before he gave his laws. The several mocks that were put upon him for refusing the power, he records in these words:

> Solon surely was a dreamer, and a man of simple mind;
> When the gods would give him fortune, he of his own will declined;
> When the net was full of fishes, over-heavy thinking it,
> He declined to haul it up, through want of heart and want of wit.
> Had but I that chance of riches and of kingship, for one day,
> I would give my skin for flaying, and my house to die away.

Thus he makes the many and the low people speak of him. Yet, though he refused the government, he was not too mild in the affair; he did not show himself mean and submissive to the powerful, nor make his laws to pleasure those that chose him. For where it was well before, he applied no remedy, nor altered anything, for fear lest—

> Overthrowing altogether and disordering the state,

he should be too weak to new-model and recompose it to a tolerable condition; but what he thought he could effect by persuasion upon the pliable, and by force upon the stubborn, this he did, as he himself says—

> With force and justice working both in one.

And, therefore, when he was afterwards asked if he had left the Athenians the best laws that could be given, he replied, "The best they could receive." The way which, the moderns say, the Athenians have of softening the badness of a thing, by ingeniously giving it some pretty and innocent appellation, calling harlots, for example, mistresses, tributes customs, a garrison a guard, and the jail the chamber, seem originally to have been Solon's contrivance, who called cancelling debts Seisacthea, a relief, or disencumbrance. For the first thing which he settled was, that what debts remained should be forgiven, and no man, for the future, should engage the body of his debtor for security. Though some, as Androtion, affirm that the debts were not cancelled, but the interest only lessened, which sufficiently pleased the people; so that they named this benefit the Seisacthea, together with the enlarging of their measures, and raising the value of their money; for he made a pound, which before passed for seventy-three drachmas, go for a hundred; so that, though the number of pieces in the payment was equal, the value was less; which proved a considerable benefit to those that were to discharge great debts, and no loss to the creditors. But most agree that it was the taking off the debts that was called Seisacthea, which is confirmed by some places in his poem, where he takes honour to himself, that—

> The mortgage-stones that covered her, by me
> Removed—the land that was a slave is free;

that some who had been seized for their debts he had brought back from other countries, where—

> —so far their lot to roam,
> They had forgot the language of their home;

and some he had set at liberty—

> Who here in shameful servitude were held.

While he was designing this, a most vexatious thing happened; for when he had resolved to take off the debts, and was considering the proper form and fit beginning for it, he told some of his friends, Conon, Clinias, and Hipponicus, in whom he had a great deal of confidence, that he would not meddle with the lands, but only free the people from their debts; upon which they, using their advantage, made haste and borrowed some considerable sums of money, and purchased some large farms; and when the law was enacted, they kept the possessions, and would not return the money; which brought Solon into great suspicion and dislike, as if he himself had not been abused, but was concerned in the contrivance. But he presently stopped this suspicion, by releasing his debtors of five talents (for he had lent so much), according to the law; others, as Polyzelus the Rhodian, say fifteen; his friends, however, were ever afterward called Chreocopidæ, repudiators.

In this he pleased neither party, for the rich were angry for their money, and the poor that the land was not divided, and, as Lycurgus ordered in his commonwealth, all men reduced to equality. He, it is true, being the eleventh from Hercules, and having reigned many years in Lacedæmon, had got a great reputation and friends and power, which he could use in modelling his state; and applying force more than persuasion, insomuch that he lost his eye in the scuffle, was able to employ the most effectual means for the safety and harmony of a state, by not permitting any to be poor or rich in his commonwealth. Solon could not rise to that in his polity, being but a citizen of the middle classes; yet he acted fully up to the height of his power, having nothing but the goodwill and good opinion of his citizens to rely on; and that he offended the most part, who looked for another result, he declares in the words—

> Formerly they boasted of me vainly; with averted eyes
> Now they look askance upon me; friends no more, but enemies.

And yet had any other man, he says, received the same power—

> He would not have forborne, nor let alone,
> But made the fattest of the milk his own.

Soon, however, becoming sensible of the good that was done, they laid by their grudges, made a public sacrifice, calling it Seisacthea, and chose Solon to new-model and make laws for the commonwealth, giving him the entire power over everything, their magistracies, their assemblies, courts, and councils; that he should appoint the number, times of meeting, and what estate they must have that could be capable of these, and dissolve or continue any of the present constitutions, according to his pleasure.

First, then, he repealed all Draco's laws, except those concerning homicide, because they were too severe, and the punishment too great; for death was appointed for almost all offences, insomuch that those that were convicted of idleness were to die, and those that stole a cabbage or an apple to suffer even as villains that committed sacrilege or murder. So that Demades, in after time, was thought to have said very happily, that Draco's laws were written not with ink but blood; and he himself, being once asked why he made death the punishment of most offences, replied, "Small ones deserve that, and I have no higher for the greater crimes."

Next, Solon, being willing to continue the magistracies in the hands of the rich men, and yet receive the people into the other part of the government, took an account of the citizens' estates, and those that were worth five hundred measures of fruit, dry and liquid, he placed in the first rank, calling them Pentacosiomedimni; those that could keep an horse, or were worth three hundred measures, were named Hippada Teluntes, and made the second class; the Zeugitæ, that had two hundred measures, were in the third; and all the others were called Thetes, who were not admitted to any office, but could come to the assembly, and act as jurors; which at first seemed nothing, but afterwards was found an enormous privilege, as almost every matter of dispute came before them in this latter capacity. Even in the cases which he assigned to the archon's cognisance, he allowed an appeal to the courts. Besides, it is said that he was obscure and ambiguous in the wording of his laws, on purpose to increase the honour of his courts; for since their differences could not be adjusted by the letter, they would have to bring all their causes to the judges, who thus were in a manner masters of the laws. Of this equalisation he himself makes mention in this manner:

> Such power I gave the people as might do,
> Abridged not what they had, now lavished new,
> Those that were great in wealth and high in place
> My counsel likewise kept from all disgrace.
> Before them both I held my shield of might,
> And let not either touch the other's right.

And for the greater security of the weak commons, he gave general liberty of indicting for an act of injury; if anyone was beaten, maimed, or suffered any violence, any man that would and was able might prosecute the wrongdoer; intending by this to accustom the citizens, like members of the same body, to resent and be sensible of one another's injuries. And there is a saying of his agreeable to his law, for, being asked what city was best modelled, "That," said he, "where those that are not injured try and punish the unjust as much as those that are."

When he had constituted the Areopagus of those who had been yearly archons, of which he himself was a member therefore, observing that the people, now free from their debts, were unsettled and imperious, he formed another council of four hundred, a hundred out of each of the four tribes, which was to inspect all matters before they were propounded to the people, and to take care that nothing but what had been first examined should be brought before the general assembly. The upper council, or Areopagus, he made inspectors and keepers of the laws, conceiving that the commonwealth, held by these two councils, like anchors, would be less liable to be tossed by tumults, and the people be more quiet. Such is the general statement, that Solon instituted the Areopagus; which seems to be confirmed, because Draco makes no mention of the Areopagites, but in all causes of blood refers to the Ephetæ; yet Solon's thirteenth table contains the eighth law set down in these very words: "Whoever before Solon's archonship were disfranchised, let them be restored, except those that, being condemned by the Areopagus, Ephetæ, or in the Prytaneum by the kings, for homicide, murder, or designs against the government, were in banishment when this law was made"; and these words seem to show that the Areopagus existed before Solon's laws, for who could be condemned by that council before his time, if he was the first that instituted the court? Unless, which is probable, there is some ellipsis, or want of precision in the language, and it should run thus: "Those that are convicted of such offences as belong to the cognisance of the Areopagites, Ephetæ, or the Prytanes, when this law was made," shall remain still in disgrace, whilst others are restored; of this the reader must judge.

Amongst his other laws, one is very peculiar and surprising, which disfranchises all who stand neuter in a sedition; for it seems he would not have anyone remain insensible and regardless of the public good, and securing his private affairs, glory that he has no feeling of the distempers of his country; but at once join with the good party and those that have the right upon their side, assist and venture with them, rather than keep out of harm's way and watch who would get the better. It seems an absurd and foolish law which permits an heiress, if her lawful husband fail her, to take his nearest kinsman; yet some say this law was well contrived against those who, conscious of their own unfitness, yet, for the sake of the portion, would match with heiresses, and make use of law to put a violence upon nature; for now, since she can quit him for whom she pleases, they would either abstain from such marriages, or continue them with disgrace, and suffer for their covetousness and designed affront; it is well done, moreover, to confine her to her husband's nearest kinsman, that the children may be of the same family. Agreeable to this is the law that the bride and bridegroom shall be shut into a chamber, and eat a quince together; and that the husband of an heiress shall consort with her thrice a month; for though there be no children, yet it is an honour and due affection which an husband ought to pay to a virtuous, chaste wife; it takes off all petty differences, and will not permit their little quarrels to proceed to a rupture.

In all other marriages he forbade dowries to be given; the wife was to have three suits of clothes, a little inconsiderable household stuff, and that was all; for he would not have marriages contracted for gain or an estate, but for pure love, kind affection, and birth of children. When the mother of Dionysius desired him to marry her to one of his citizens, "Indeed," said he, "by my tyranny I have broken my country's laws, but cannot put a violence upon those of nature by an unseasonable marriage." Such disorder is never to be suffered in a commonwealth, nor such unseasonable and unloving and unperforming marriages, which attain no due end or fruit; any provident governor or lawgiver might say to an old man that takes a young wife what is said to Philoctetes in the tragedy—

Truly, in a fit state thou to marry!

and if he find a young man, with a rich and elderly wife, growing fat in his place, like the partridges, remove him to a young woman of proper age. And of this enough.

Another commendable law of Solon's is that which forbids men to speak evil of the dead; for it is pious to think the deceased sacred, and just, not to meddle with those that are gone, and politic, to prevent the perpetuity of discord. He likewise forbade them to speak evil of the living in the temples, the courts of justice, the public offices, or at the games, or else to pay three drachmas to the person, and two to the public. For never to be able to control passion shows a weak nature and ill-breeding; and always to moderate it is very hard, and to some impossible. And laws must look to possibilities, if the maker designs to punish few in order to their amendment, and not many to no purpose.

He is likewise much commended for his law concerning wills; for before him none could be made, but all the wealth and estate of the deceased belonged to his family; but he by permitting them, if they had no children, to bestow it on whom they pleased, showed that he esteemed friendship a stronger tie than kindred, and affection than necessity; and

made every man's estate truly his own. Yet he allowed not all sorts of lega-
cies, but those only which were not extorted by the frenzy of a disease,
charms, imprisonment, force, or the persuasions of a wife; with good reason thinking that being seduced into wrong was as bad as being forced,
and that between deceit and necessity, flattery and compulsion, there was
little difference, since both may equally suspend the exercise of reason.

He regulated the walks, feasts, and mourning of the women, and took
away everything that was either unbecoming or immodest; when they
walked abroad, no more than three articles of dress were allowed them; an
obol's worth of meat and drink; and no basket above a cubit high; and at
night they were not to go about unless in a chariot with a torch before them.
Mourners tearing themselves to raise pity, and set wailings, and at one man's
funeral to lament for another, he forbade. To offer an ox at the grave was
not permitted, nor to bury above three pieces of dress with the body, or visit
the tombs of any besides their own family, unless at the very funeral; most of
which are likewise forbidden by our laws, but this is further added in ours,
that those that are convicted of extravagance in their mournings are to be
punished as soft and effeminate by the censors of women.

Observing the city to be filled with persons that flocked from all parts
into Attica for security of living, and that most of the country was barren
and unfruitful, and that traders at sea import nothing to those that could
give them nothing in exchange, he turned his citizens to trade, and made
a law that no son be obliged to relieve a father who had not bred him up
to any calling. It is true, Lycurgus, having a city free from all strangers, and
land, according to Euripides—

Large for large hosts, for twice their number much,

and, above all, an abundance of labourers about Sparta, who should not be
left idle, but be kept down with continual toil and work, did well to take off
his citizens from laborious and mechanical occupations, and keep them to
their arms, and teach them only the art of war. But Solon, fitting his laws
to the state of things, and not making things to suit his laws, and finding
the ground scarce rich enough to maintain the husbandmen, and altogether incapable of feeding an unoccupied and leisured multitude,
brought trades into credit, and ordered the Areopagites to examine how
every man got his living, and chastise the idle. But that law was yet more
rigid which, as Heraclides Ponticus delivers, declared the sons of unmarried mothers not obliged to relieve their fathers; for he that avoids the honourable form of union shows that he does not take a woman for children,

but for pleasure, and thus gets his just reward, and has taken away from himself every title to upbraid his children, to whom he has made their very birth a scandal and reproach.

Solon's laws in general about women are his strangest; for he permitted anyone to kill an adulterer that found him in the act; but if anyone forced a free woman, a hundred drachmas was the fine; if he enticed her, twenty; except those that sell themselves openly, that is, harlots, who go openly to those that hire them. He made it unlawful to sell a daughter or a sister, unless, being yet unmarried, she was found wanton. Now it is irrational to punish the same crime sometimes very severely and without remorse, and sometimes very lightly, and as it were in sport, with a trivial fine; unless there being little money then in Athens, scarcity made those mulcts the more grievous punishment. In the valuation for sacrifices, a sheep and a bushel were both estimated at a drachma; the victor in the Isthmian games was to have for reward an hundred drachmas; the conqueror in the Olympian, five hundred; he that brought a wolf, five drachmas; for a whelp, one; the former sum, as Demetrius the Phalerian asserts, was the value of an ox, the latter, of a sheep. The prices which Solon, in his sixteenth table, sets on choice victims, were naturally far greater; yet they, too, are very low in comparison of the present. The Athenians were, from the beginning, great enemies to wolves, their fields being better for pasture than corn. Some affirm their tribes did not take their names from the sons of Ion, but from the different sorts of occupation that they followed; the soldiers were called Hoplitæ, the craftsmen Ergades, and, of the remaining two, the farmers Gedeontes, and the shepherds and graziers Ægicores.

Since the country has but few rivers, lakes, or large springs, and many used wells which they had dug, there was a law made, that, where there was a public well within a *hippicon*, that is, four furlongs, all should draw at that; but when it was farther off, they should try and procure a well of their own; and if they had dug ten fathoms deep and could find no water, they had liberty to fetch a pitcherful of four gallons and a half in a day from their neighbours'; for he thought it prudent to make provision against want, but not to supply laziness. He showed skill in his orders about planting, for anyone that would plant another tree was not to set it within five feet of his neighbour's field; but if a fig or an olive not within nine; for their roots spread farther, nor can they be planted near all sorts of trees without damage, for they draw away the nourishment, and in some cases are noxious by their effluvia. He that would dig a pit or a ditch was to dig it at the distance of its own depth from his neighbour's ground; and he that would raise stocks of bees was not to place them within three hundred feet of those which another had already raised.

He permitted only oil to be exported, and those that exported any other fruit, the archon was solemnly to curse, or else pay an hundred drachmas himself; and this law was written in his first table, and, therefore, let none think it incredible, as some affirm, that the exportation of figs was once unlawful, and the informer against the delinquents called a sycophant. He made a law, also, concerning hurts and injuries from beasts, in which he commands the master of any dog that bit a man to deliver him up with a log about his neck, four and a half feet long; a happy device for men's security. The law concerning naturalising strangers is of doubtful character; he permitted only those to be made free of Athens who were in perpetual exile from their own country, or came with their whole family to trade there; this he did, not to discourage strangers, but rather to invite them to a permanent participation in the privileges of the government; and, besides, he thought those would prove the more faithful citizens who had been forced from their own country, or voluntarily forsook it. The law of public entertainment (*parasitein* is his name for it) is also peculiarly Solon's; for if any man came often, or if he that was invited refused, they were punished, for he concluded that one was greedy, the other a contemner of the state.

All his laws he established for an hundred years, and wrote them on wooden tables or rollers, named axones, which might be turned round in oblong cases; some of their relics were in my time still to be seen in the Prytaneum, or common hall at Athens. These, as Aristotle states, were called cyrbes, and there is a passage of Cratinus the comedian—

> By Solon, and by Draco, if you please,
> Whose Cyrbes make the fires that parch our peas.

But some say those are properly cyrbes, which contain laws concerning sacrifices and the rites of religion, and all the others axones. The council all jointly swore to confirm the laws, and everyone of the Thesmothetæ vowed for himself at the stone in the market place, that if he broke any of the statutes, he would dedicate a golden statue, as big as himself, at Delphi.

Observing the irregularity of the months, and that the moon does not always rise and set with the sun, but often in the same day overtakes and gets before him, he ordered the day should be named the Old and New, attributing that part of it which was before the conjunction to the old moon, and the rest to the new, he being the first, it seems, that understood that verse of Homer—

> The end and the beginning of the month,

and the following day he called the new moon. After the twentieth he did not count by addition, but, like the moon itself in its wane, by subtraction; thus up to the thirtieth.

Now when these laws were enacted, and some came to Solon everyday, to commend or dispraise them, and to advise, if possible, to leave out or put in something, and many criticised and desired him to explain, and tell the meaning of such and such a passage, he, knowing that to do it was useless, and not to do it would get him ill-will, and desirous to bring himself out of all straits, and to escape all displeasure and exceptions, it being a hard thing, as he himself says—

> In great affairs to satisfy all sides,

as an excuse for travelling, bought a trading vessel, and, having leave for ten years' absence, departed, hoping that by that time his laws would have become familiar.

His first voyage was for Egypt, and he lived, as he himself says—

> Near Nilus' mouth, by fair Canopus' shore,

and spent sometime in study with Psenophis of Heliopolis, and Sonchis the Saite, the most learned of all the priests; from whom, as Plato says, getting knowledge of the Atlantic story, he put it into a poem, and proposed to bring it to the knowledge of the Greeks. From thence he sailed to Cyprus, where he was made much of by Philocyprus, one of the kings there, who had a small city built by Demophon, Theseus' son, near the river Clarius, in a strong situation, but incommodious and uneasy of access. Solon persuaded him, since there lay a fair plain below, to remove, and build there a pleasanter and more spacious city. And he stayed himself, and assisted in gathering inhabitants, and in fitting it both for defence and convenience of living; insomuch that many flocked to Philocyprus, and the other kings imitated the design; and, therefore, to honour Solon, he called the city Soli, which was formerly named Æpea. And Solon himself, in his Elegies, addressing Philocyprus, mentions this foundation in these words:

Long may you live, and fill the Solian throne.
Succeeded still by children of your own;
And from your happy island while I sail,
Let Cyprus send for me a favouring gale;
May she advance, and bless your new command,
Prosper your town, and send me safe to land.

That Solon should discourse with Crœsus, some think not agreeable with chronology; but I cannot reject so famous and well-attested a narrative, and, what is more, so agreeable to Solon's temper, and so worthy his wisdom and greatness of mind, because, forsooth, it does not agree with some chronological canons, which thousands have endeavoured to regulate, and yet, to this day, could never bring their differing opinions to any agreement. They say, therefore, that Solon, coming to Crœsus at his request, was in the same condition as an inland man when first he goes to see the sea; for as he fancies every river he meets with to be the ocean, so Solon, as he passed through the court, and saw a great many nobles richly dressed, and proudly attended with a multitude of guards and footboys, thought everyone had been the king, till he was brought to Crœsus, who was decked with every possible rarity and curiosity, in ornaments of jewels, purple, and gold, that could make a grand and gorgeous spectacle of him. Now when Solon came before him, and seemed not at all surprised, nor gave Crœsus those compliments he expected, but showed himself to all discerning eyes to be a man that despised the gaudiness and petty ostentation of it, he commanded them to open all his treasure houses, and carry him to see his sumptuous furniture and luxuries, though he did not wish it; Solon could judge of him well enough by the first sight of him; and, when he returned from viewing all, Crœsus asked him if ever he had known a happier man than he. And when Solon answered that he had known one Tellus, a fellow-citizen of his own, and told him that this Tellus had been an honest man, had had good children, a competent estate, and died bravely in battle for his country, Crœsus took him for an ill-bred fellow and a fool, for not measuring happiness by the abundance of gold and silver, and preferring the life and death of a private and mean man before so much power and empire. He asked him, however, again, if, besides Tellus, he knew any other man more happy. And Solon replying, Yes, Cleobis and Biton, who were loving brothers, and extremely dutiful sons to their mother, and, when the oxen delayed her, harnessed themselves to the wagon, and drew her to Juno's temple, her neighbours all calling her happy, and she herself rejoicing; then, after sacrificing and feasting, they went to rest, and never rose again, but died in the midst of their honour a painless and tranquil death. "What," said Crœsus, angrily, "and dost not thou reckon us amongst the happy men at all?" Solon, unwilling either to flatter or exasperate him more, replied, "The gods, O king, have given the Greeks all other gifts in moderate degree; and so our wisdom, too, is a cheerful and a homely, not a noble and kingly wisdom; and this, observing the numerous misfortunes that attend all conditions, forbids us to grow insolent upon our present enjoyments, or to admire any man's happiness that may yet, in course of time, suffer change. For the uncertain future has yet to come, with every possible variety of fortune; and him only to whom the divinity has continued happiness unto the end we call happy; to salute as happy one that is still in the midst of life and hazard, we think as little safe and conclusive as to crown and proclaim as victorious the wrestler that is yet in the ring." After this, he was dismissed, having given Crœsus some pain, but no instruction.

Æsop, who wrote the fables, being then at Sardis upon Crœsus' invitation, and very much esteemed, was concerned that Solon was so ill received, and gave him this advice: "Solon, let your converse with kings be either short or seasonable." "Nay, rather," replied Solon, "either short or reasonable." So at this time Crœsus despised Solon; but when he was overcome by Cyrus, had lost his city, was taken alive, condemned to be burnt, and laid bound upon the pile before all the Persians and Cyrus himself, he cried out as loud as possibly he could three times, "O Solon! "and Cyrus being surprised, and sending some to inquire what man or god this Solon was, who alone he invoked in this extremity, Crœsus told him the whole story, saying, "He was one of the wise men of Greece, whom I sent for, not to be instructed, or to learn anything that I wanted, but that he should see and be a witness of my happiness; the loss of which was, it seems, to be a greater evil than the enjoyment was a good; for when I had them they were goods only in opinion but now the loss of them has brought upon me intolerable and real evils. And he, conjecturing from what then was, this that now is, bade look to the end of my life, and not rely and grow proud upon uncertainties." When this was told Cyrus, who was a wiser man than Crœsus, and saw in the present example Solon's maxim confirmed, he not only freed Crœsus from punishment, but honoured him as long as he lived; and Solon had the glory, by the same saying, to save one king and instruct another.

When Solon was gone, the citizens began to quarrel; Lycurgus headed the Plain; Megacles, the son of Alcmæon, those to the Seaside; and

Pisistratus the Hill-party, in which were the poorest people, the Thetes, and greatest enemies to the rich; insomuch that, though the city still used the new laws, yet all looked for and desired a change of government, hoping severally that the change would be better for them, and put them above the contrary faction. Affairs standing thus, Solon returned, and was reverenced by all, and honoured; but his old age would not permit him to be as active, and to speak in public, as formerly; yet, by privately conferring with the heads of the factions, he endeavoured to compose the differences, Pisistratus appearing the most tractable; for he was extremely smooth and engaging in his language, a great friend to the poor, and moderate in his resentments; and what nature had not given him, he had the skill to imitate; so that he was trusted more than the others, being accounted a prudent and orderly man, one that loved equality, and would be an enemy to any that moved against the present settlement. Thus he deceived the majority of people; but Solon quickly discovered his character, and found out his design before anyone else; yet did not hate him upon this, but endeavoured to humble him, and bring him off from his ambition, and often told him and others, that if anyone could banish the passion for preeminence from his mind, and cure him of his desire of absolute power, none would make a more virtuous man or a more excellent citizen. Thespis, at this time, beginning to act tragedies, and the thing, because it was new, taking very much with the multitude, though it was not yet made a matter of competition, Solon, being by nature fond of hearing and learning something new, and now, in his old age, living idly, and enjoying himself, indeed, with music and with wine, went to see Thespis himself, as the ancient custom was, act: and after the play was done, he addressed him, and asked him if he was not ashamed to tell so many lies before such a number of people; and Thespis replying that it was no harm to say or do so in play, Solon vehemently struck his staff against the ground: "Ah," said he, "if we honour and commend such play as this, we shall find it someday in our business."

Now when Pisistratus, having wounded himself, was brought into the market place in a chariot, and stirred up the people, as if he had been thus treated by his opponents because of his political conduct, and a great many were enraged and cried out, Solon, coming dose to him, said, "This, O son of Hippocrates, is a bad copy of Homer's Ulysses; you do, to trick your countrymen, what he did to deceive his enemies." After this, the people were eager to protect Pisistratus, and met in an assembly, where one Ariston making a motion that they should allow Pisistratus fifty clubmen for a guard to his person, Solon opposed it, and said much to the same purport as what he has left us in his poems—

> You dote upon his words and taking phrase;

and again—

> True, you are singly each a crafty soul,
> But all together make one empty fool.

But observing the poor men bent to gratify Pisistratus, and tumultuous, and the rich fearful and getting out of harm's way, he departed, saying he was wiser than some and stouter than others; wiser than those that did not understand the design, stouter than those that, though they understood it, were afraid to oppose the tyranny. Now, the people, having passed the law, were not nice with Pisistratus about the number of his clubmen, but took no notice of it, though he enlisted and kept as many as he would, until he seized the Acropolis. When that was done, and the city in an uproar, Megacles, with all his family, at once fled; but Solon, though he was now very old, and had none to back him, yet came into the market place and made a speech to the citizens, partly blaming their inadvertency and meanness of spirit, and in part urging and exhorting them not thus tamely to lose their liberty; and likewise then spoke that memorable saying, that, before, it was an easier task to stop the rising tyranny, but now the great and more glorious action to destroy it, when it was begun already, and had gathered strength. But all being afraid to side with him, he returned home, and, taking his arms, he brought them out and laid them in the porch before his door, with these words: "I have done my part to maintain my country and my laws," and then he busied himself no more. His friends advising him to fly, he refused, but wrote poems, and thus reproached the Athenians in them:

> If now you suffer, do not blame the Powers,
> For they are good, and all the fault was ours,
> All the strongholds you put into his hands,
> And now his slaves must do what he commands.

And many telling him that the tyrant would take his life for this, and asking what he trusted to, that he ventured to speak so boldly, he replied, "To my old age." But Pisistratus, having got the command, so extremely courted Solon, so honoured him, obliged him, and sent to see him, that Solon gave him his advice, and approved many of his actions; for he retained most of Solon's laws, observed them himself, and compelled his friends to obey. And he himself, though already absolute ruler, being accused of murder before the Areopagus, came quietly to clear himself; but his accuser did not appear. And he added other laws, one of which is that the maimed in the wars should be maintained at the public charge; this Heraclides Ponticus records, and that Pisistratus followed Solon's example in this, who had decreed it in the case of one Thersippus, that was maimed; and Theophrastus asserts that it was Pisistratus, not Solon, that made that law against laziness, which was the reason that the country was more productive, and the city tranquiller.

Now Solon, having begun the great work in verse, the history or fable of the Atlantic Island, which he had learned from the wise men in Sais, and thought convenient for the Athenians to know, abandoned it; not, as Plato says, by reason of want of time, but because of his age, and being discouraged at the greatness of the task; for that he had leisure enough, such verses testify, as—

> Each day grow older, and learn something new;

and again—

> But now the Powers, of Beauty, Song, and Wine,
> Which are most men's delights, are also mine.

Plato, willing to improve the story of the Atlantic Island, as if it were a fair estate that wanted an heir and came with some title to him, formed, indeed, stately entrances, noble enclosures, large courts, such as never yet introduced any story, fable, or poetic fiction; but, beginning it late, ended his life before his work; and the reader's regret for the unfinished part is the greater, as the satisfaction he takes in that which is complete is extraordinary. For as the city of Athens left only the temple of Jupiter Olympius unfinished, so Plato, amongst all his excellent works, left this only piece about the Atlantic Island imperfect. Solon lived after Pisistratus seized the government, as Heraclides Ponticus asserts, a long time; but Phanias the Eresian says not two full years; for Pisistratus began his tyranny when Comias was archon, and Phanias says Solon died under Hegestratus, who succeeded Comias. The story that his ashes were scattered about the island Salamis is too strange to be easily believed, or be thought anything but a mere fable; and yet it is given, amongst other good authors, by Aristotle, the philosopher.

POPLICOLA
[*PUBLICOLA*]

SUCH WAS SOLON. TO HIM WE COMPARE POPLICOLA, WHO RECEIVED THIS later title from the Roman people for his merit, as a noble accession to his former name, Publius Valerius. He descended from Valerius, a man amongst the early citizens, reputed the principal reconciler of the differences betwixt the Romans and Sabines, and one that was most instrumental in persuading their kings to assent to peace and union. Thus descended, Publius Valerius, as it is said, whilst Rome remained under its kingly government, obtained as great a name from his eloquence as from his riches, charitably employing the one in liberal aid to the poor, the other with integrity and freedom in the service of justice; thereby giving assurance, that, should the government fall into a republic, he would become a chief man in the community. The illegal and wicked accession of Tarquinius Superbus to the crown, with his making it, instead of kingly rule, the instrument of insolence and tyranny, having inspired the people with a hatred to his reign, upon the death of Lucretia (she killing herself after violence had been done to her), they took an occasion of revolt; and Lucius Brutus, engaging in the change, came to Valerius before all others, and, with his zealous assistance, deposed the kings. And whilst the people inclined towards the electing one leader instead of their king, Valerius acquiesced, that to rule was rather Brutus' due, as the author of the democracy. But when the name of monarchy was odious to the people, and a divided power appeared more grateful in the prospect, and two were chosen to hold it, Valerius, entertaining hopes that he might be elected consul with Brutus, was disappointed; for, instead of Valerius, notwithstanding the endeavours of Brutus, Tarquinius Collatinus was chosen, the husband of Lucretia, a man noways his superior in merit. But the nobles dreading the return of their kings, who still used all endeavours abroad and solicitations at home, were resolved upon a chieftain of an intense hatred to them, and noways likely to yield.

Now Valerius was troubled that his desire to serve his country should be doubted, because he had sustained no private injury from the insolence of the tyrants. He withdrew from the senate and practice of the bar, quitting all public concerns; which gave an occasion of discourse, and fear, too, lest his anger should reconcile him to the king's side, and he should prove the ruin of the state, tottering as yet under the uncertainties of a change. But Brutus being doubtful of some others, and determined to give the test to the senate upon the altars, upon the day appointed Valerius came with cheerfulness into the forum, and was the first man that took the oath, in no way to submit or yield to Tarquin's propositions, but rigorously to maintain liberty; which gave great satisfaction to the senate and assurance to the consuls, his action soon after showing the sincerity of his oath. For ambassadors came from Tarquin, with popular and specious proposals, whereby they thought to seduce the people, as though the king had cast off all insolence, and made moderation the only measure of his desires. To this embassy the consuls thought fit to give public audience, but Valerius opposed it, and would not permit that the poorer people, who entertained more fear of war than of tyranny, should have any occasion offered them, or any temptations to new designs. Afterwards other ambassadors arrived, who declared their king would recede from his crown, and lay down his arms, only capitulating for a restitution to himself, his friends, and allies, of their moneys and estates to support them in their banishment. Now, several inclining to the request, and Collatinus in particular favouring it, Brutus, a man of vehement and unbending nature, rushed into the forum, there proclaiming his fellow-consul to be a traitor, in granting subsidies to tyranny, and supplies for a war to those to whom it was monstrous to allow so much as subsistence in exile. This caused an assembly of the citizens, amongst whom the first that spake was Caius Minucius, a private man, who advised Brutus, and urged the Romans to keep the property, and employ it against the tyrants, rather than to remit it to the tyrants, to be used against themselves. The Romans, however, decided that whilst they had enjoyed the liberty they had fought for, they should not sacrifice peace for the sake of money, but send out the tyrants' property after them. This question, however, of his property was the least part of Tarquin's design; the demand sounded the feelings of the people, and was preparatory to a conspiracy which the ambassadors endeavoured to excite, delaying their return, under pretence of selling some of the goods and reserving others to be sent away, till, in fine, they corrupted two of the most eminent families in Rome, the Aquillian, which had three, and the Vitellian, which had two senators. These all were, by the mother's side, nephews to Collatinus; besides which Brutus had a special alliance to the Vitellii from his marriage with their sister, by whom he had several children; two of whom, of their own age, their near relations and daily companions, the Vitellii seduced to join in the plot, to ally themselves to the great house and royal hopes of the Tarquins, and gain emancipation from the violence and imbecility united of their father, whose austerity to offenders they termed violence, while the imbecility which he had long feigned, to protect himself from the tyrants, still, it appears, was, in name at least, ascribed to him. When upon these inducements the youths came to confer with the Aquillii, and thought it convenient to bind themselves in a solemn and dreadful oath, by tasting the blood of a murdered man, and touching his entrails. For which design they met at the house of the Aquillii. The building chosen for the transaction was, as was natural, dark and unfrequented, and a slave named Vindicius had, as it chanced, concealed himself there, not out of design or any intelligence of the affair, but, accidentally being within, seeing with how much haste and concern they came in, he was afraid to be discovered, and placed himself behind a chest, where he was able to observe their actions and overhear their debates. Their resolutions were to kill the consuls, and they wrote letters to Tarquin to this effect, and gave them to the ambassadors, who were lodging upon the spot with the Aquillii, and were present at the consultation.

Upon their departure, Vindicius secretly quitted the house, but was at a loss what to do in the matter, for to arraign the sons before the father Brutus, or the nephews before the uncle Collatinus, seemed equally (as indeed it was) shocking; yet he knew no private Roman to whom he could intrust secrets of such importance. Unable, however, to keep silence, and burdened with his knowledge, he went and addressed himself to Valerius, whose known freedom and kindness of temper were an inducement; as he was a person to whom the needy had easy access, and who never shut his gates against the petitions or indigences of humble people. But when Vindicius came and made a complete discovery to him, his brother Marcus and his own wife being present, Valerius was struck with amazement, and by no means would dismiss the discoverer, but confined him to the room, and placed his wife as a guard to the door, sending his brother in the interim to beset the king's palace, and seize, if possible, the writings there, and secure the domestics, whilst he, with his constant attendance of clients and friends, and a great retinue of attendants, repaired to the house of the Aquillii, who were, as it chanced, absent from home; and so, forcing an entrance through the gates, they lit upon the letters then lying in the lodgings of the ambassadors. Meantime the Aquillii returned in all haste, and, coming to blows about the gate, endeavoured a recovery of the letters. The other party made a resistance, and throwing their gowns around their opponents' necks, at last, after much struggling on both sides, made their way with them their prisoners through the streets into the forum. The like engagement happened about the king's palace, where Marcus seized some other letters which it was designed should be conveyed away in the goods, and, laying hands on such of the king's people as he could find, dragged them also into the forum. When the consuls had quieted the tumult, Vindicius was brought out by the orders of Valerius, and the accusation stated, and the letters were opened, to which the traitors could make no plea. Most of the people standing mute and sorrowful, some only, out of kindness to Brutus, mentioning banishment, the tears of Collatinus, attended with Valerius' silence, gave some hopes of mercy. But Brutus, calling his two sons by their names, "Canst not thou," said he, "O Titus, or thou, Tiberius, make any defence against the indictment?" The question being thrice proposed, and no reply made, he turned himself to the lictors and cried, "What remains is your duty." They immediately seized the youths, and, stripping them of their clothes, bound their hands behind them and scourged their bodies with their rods; too tragical a scene for others to look at; Brutus, however, is said not to have turned aside his face, nor allowed the least glance of pity to soften and smooth his aspect of rigour and austerity, but sternly watched his children suffer, even till the lictors, extending them on the ground, cut off their heads with an axe; then departed, committing the rest to the judgment of his colleague. An action truly open alike to the highest commendation and the strongest censure; for either the greatness of his virtue raised him above the impressions of sorrow, or the extravagance of his misery took away all sense of it; but neither seemed common, or the result of humanity, but either divine or brutish. Yet it is more reasonable that our judgment should yield to his reputation, than that his merit should suffer detraction by the weakness of our judgment; in the Romans' opinion, Brutus did a greater work in the establishment of the government than Romulus in the foundation of the city.

Upon Brutus' departure out of the forum, consternation, horror, and silence for sometime possessed all that reflected on what was done; the easiness and tardiness, however, of Collatinus gave confidence to the Aquillii to request sometime to answer their charge, and that Vindicius, their servant, should be remitted into their hands, and no longer harboured amongst their accusers. The consul seemed inclined to their proposal, and was proceeding to dissolve the assembly; but Valerius would not suffer Vindicius, who was surrounded by his people, to be surrendered, nor the meeting to withdraw without punishing the traitors; and at length laid violent hands upon the Aquillii, and, calling Brutus to his assistance, exclaimed against the unreasonable course of Collatinus, to impose upon his colleague the necessity of taking away the lives of his own sons, and yet have thoughts of gratifying some women with the lives of traitors and public enemies. Collatinus, displeased at this, and commanding Vindicius to be taken away, the lictors made their way through the crowd and seized their man, and struck all who endeavoured a rescue. Valerius' friends headed the resistance, and the people cried out for Brutus, who, returning, on silence being made, told them he had been competent to pass sentence by himself upon his own sons, but left the rest to the suffrages of the free citizens: "Let every man speak that wishes, and persuade whom he can." But there was no need of oratory, for, it being referred to the vote, they were returned condemned by all the suffrages, and were accordingly beheaded.

Collatinus' relationship to the kings had, indeed, already rendered him suspicious, and his second name, too, had made him obnoxious to the people, who were loth to hear the very sound of Tarquin; but after this had happened, perceiving himself an offence to everyone, he relinquished his charge and departed from the city. At the new elections in his room, Valerius obtained, with high honour, the consulship, as a just reward of his zeal; of which he thought Vindicius deserved a share, whom he made, first of all freedmen, a citizen of Rome, and gave him the privilege of voting in what tribe soever he was pleased to be enrolled; other freedmen received the right of suffrage a long time after from Appius, who thus courted popularity; and from this Vindicius, a perfect manumission is called to this day *vindicta*. This done, the goods of the kings were exposed to plunder, and the palace to ruin.

The pleasantest part of the field of Mars, which Tarquin had owned, was devoted to the service of that god; but, it happening to be harvest season, and the sheaves yet being on the ground, they thought it not proper to commit them to the flail, or unsanctify them with any use; and, therefore, carrying them to the riverside, and trees withal that were cut down, they cast all into the water, dedicating the soil, free from all occupation, to the deity. Now, these thrown in, one upon another, and closing together, the stream did not bear them far, but where the first were carried down and came to a bottom, the remainder, finding no farther conveyance, were stopped and interwoven one with another; the stream working the mass into a firmness, and washing down fresh mud. This, settling there, became an accession of matter, as well as cement, to the rubbish, insomuch that the violence of the waters could not remove it, but forced and compressed it all together. Thus its bulk and solidity gained it new subsidies, which gave it extension enough to stop on its way most of what the stream brought down. This is now a sacred island, lying by the city, adorned with the temples of the gods, and walks, and is called in the Latin tongue *inter duos pontes*. Though some say this did not happen at the dedication of Tarquin's field, but in aftertimes, when Tarquinia, a vestal priestess, gave an adjacent field to the public, and obtained great honours in consequence, as, amongst the rest, that of all women her testimony alone should be received; she had also the liberty to marry, but refused it; thus some tell the story.

Tarquin, despairing of a return to his kingdom by the conspiracy, found a kind reception amongst the Tuscans, who, with a great army, proceeded to restore him. The consuls headed the Romans against them, and made their rendezvous in certain holy places, the one called the Arsian grove, the other the Æsuvian meadow. When they came into action, Aruns, the son of Tarquin, and Brutus, the Roman consul, not accidentally encountering each other, but out of hatred and rage, the one to avenge tyranny and enmity to his country, the other his banishment, set spurs to their horses, and, engaging with more fury than forethought, disregarding their own security, fell together in the combat. This dreadful onset hardly was followed by a more favourable end; both armies, doing and receiving equal damage, were separated by a storm. Valerius was much concerned, not knowing what the result of the day was, and seeing his men as well dismayed at the sight of their own dead, as rejoiced at the loss of the enemy; so apparently equal in the number was the slaughter on either side. Each party, however, felt surer of defeat from the actual sight of their own dead, than they could feel of victory from conjecture about those of their adversaries. The night being come (and such as one may presume must follow such a battle), and the armies laid to rest, they say that the grove shook, and uttered a voice, saying that the Tuscans had lost one man more than the Romans; clearly a divine announcement; and the

Romans at once received it with shouts and expressions of joy; whilst the Tuscans, through fear and amazement, deserted their tents, and were for the most part dispersed. The Romans, falling upon the remainder, amounting to nearly five thousand, took them prisoners, and plundered the camp; when they numbered the dead, they found on the Tuscans' side eleven thousand and three hundred, exceeding their own loss but by one man. This fight happened upon the last of February, and Valerius triumphed in honour of it, being the first consul that drove in with a four-horse chariot; which sight both appeared magnificent, and was received with an admiration free from envy or offence (as some suggest) on the part of the spectators; it would not otherwise have been continued with so much eagerness and emulation through all the after ages. The people applauded likewise the honours he did to his colleague, in adding to his obsequies a funeral oration: which was so much liked by the Romans, and found so good a reception, that it became customary for the best men to celebrate the funerals of great citizens with speeches in their commendation; and their antiquity in Rome is affirmed to be greater than in Greece, unless, with the orator Anaximenes, we make Solon the first author.

Yet some part of Valerius' behaviour did give offence and disgust to the people, because Brutus, whom they esteemed the father of their liberty, had not presumed to rule without a colleague, but united one and then another to him in his commission; while Valerius, they said, centring all authority in himself, seemed not in any sense a successor to Brutus in the consulship, but to Tarquin in the tyranny; he might make verbal harangues to Brutus' memory, yet, when he was attended with all the rods and axes, proceeding down from a house than which the king's house that he had demolished had not been statelier, those actions showed him an imitator of Tarquin. For, indeed, his dwelling-house on the Velia was somewhat imposing in appearance, hanging over the forum, and overlooking all transactions there; the access to it was hard, and to see him far off coming down, a stately and royal spectacle. But Valerius showed how well it were for men in power and great offices to have ears that give admittance to truth before flattery; for upon his friends telling him that he displeased the people, he contended not, neither resented it, but while it was still night, sending for a number of work-people, pulled down his house and levelled it with the ground; so that in the morning the people, seeing and flocking together, expressed their wonder and their respect for his magnanimity, and their sorrow, as though it had been a human being, for the large and beautiful house which was thus lost to them by an unfounded jealousy, while its owner, their consul, without a roof of his own, had to beg a lodging with his friends. For his friends received him, till a place the people gave him was furnished with a house, though less stately than his own, where now stands the temple, as it is called, of Vica Pota.

He resolved to render the government, as well as himself, instead of terrible, familiar and pleasant to the people, and parted the axes from the rods, and always, upon his entrance into the assembly, lowered these also to the people, to show, in the strongest way, the republican foundation of the government; and this the consuls observe to this day. But the humility of the man was but a means, not, as they thought, of lessening himself, but merely to abate their envy by this moderation; for whatever he detracted from his authority he added to his real power, the people still submitting with satisfaction, which they expressed by calling him Poplicola, or people-lover, which name had the preeminence of the rest, and, therefore, in the sequel of his narrative we shall use no other.

He gave free leave to any to sue for the consulship; but before the admittance of a colleague, mistrusting the chances, lest emulation or ignorance should cross his designs, by his sole authority enacted his best and most important measures. First, he supplied the vacancies of the senators, whom either Tarquin long before had put to death, or the war lately cut off; those that he enrolled, they write, amounted to a hundred and sixty-four; afterwards he made several laws which added much to the people's liberty, in particular one granting offenders the liberty of appealing to the people from the judgment of the consuls; a second, that made it death to usurp any magistracy without the people's consent; a third, for the relief of poor citizens, which, taking off their taxes, encouraged their labours; another, against disobedience to the consuls, which was no less popular than the rest, and rather to the benefit of the commonalty than to the advantage of the nobles, for it imposed upon disobedience the penalty of ten oxen and two sheep; the price of a sheep being ten obols, of an ox, an hundred. For the use of money was then infrequent amongst the Romans, but their wealth in cattle great; even now pieces of property are called *peculia* from *pecus*, cattle; and they had stamped upon their most ancient money an ox, a sheep, or a hog; and surnamed their sons Suillii, Bubulci, Caprarii, and Porcii, from *capræ*, goats, and *porci*, hogs.

Amidst this mildness and moderation, for one excessive fault he instituted one excessive punishment; for he made it lawful without trial to take away any man's life that aspired to a tyranny, and acquitted the slayer, if he produced evidence of the crime; for though it was not probable for a man, whose designs were so great, to escape all notice; yet because it was possible he might, although observed, by force anticipate judgment, which the usurpation itself would then preclue, he gave a licence to any to anticipate the usurper. He was honoured likewise for the law touching the treasury; for because it was necessary for the citizens to contribute out of their estates to the maintenance of wars, and he was unwilling himself to be concerned in the care of it, or to permit his friends, or indeed to let the public money pass into any private house, he allotted the temple of Saturn for the treasury, in which to this day they deposit the tribute-money, and granted the people the liberty of choosing two young men as quæstors, or treasurers. The first were Publius Veturius and Marcus Minucius; and a large sum was collected, for they assessed one hundred and thirty thousand, excusing orphans and widows from the payment. After these dispositions, he admitted Lucretius, the father of Lucretia, as his colleague, and gave him the precedence in the government, by resigning the fasces to him, as due to his years, which privilege of seniority continued to our time. But within a few days Lucretius died, and in a new election Marcus Horatius succeeded in that honour, and continued consul for the remainder of the year.

Now, whilst Tarquin was making preparations in Tuscany for a second war against the Romans, it is said a great portent occurred. When Tarquin was king, and had all but completed the buildings of the Capitol, designing, whether from oracular advice or his own pleasure, to erect an earthen chariot upon the top, he intrusted the workmanship to Tuscans of the city Veii, but soon after lost his kingdom. The work thus modelled, the Tuscans set in a furnace, but the clay showed not those passive qualities which usually attend its nature, to subside and be condensed upon the evaporation of the moisture, but rose and swelled out to that bulk, that, when solid and firm, notwithstanding the removal of the roof and opening the walls of the furnace, it could not be taken out without much difficulty. The soothsayers looked upon this as a divine prognostic of success and power to those that should possess it; and the Tuscans resolved not to deliver it to the Roman, who demanded it, but answered that it rather belonged to Tarquin than to those who had sent him into exile. A few days after, they had a horse-race there, with the usual shows and solemnities, and as the charioteer with his garland on his head was quietly driving the victorious chariot out of the ring, the horses, upon no apparent occasion, taking fright, either by divine instigation or by accident, hurried away their driver at full speed to Rome; neither did his holding them in prevail, nor his voice, but he was forced along with violence till, coming to the Capitol, he was thrown out by the gate called Ratumena. This occurrence raised wonder and fear in the Veientines, who now permitted the delivery of the chariot.

The building of the temple of the Capitoline Jupiter had been vowed by Tarquin, the son of Demaratus, when warring with the Sabines; Tarqinius Superbus, his son or grandson, built but could not dedicate it, because he lost his kingdom before it was quite finished. And now that it was completed with all its ornaments, Poplicola was ambitious to dedicate it; but the nobility envied him that honour, as, indeed, also, in some degree, those his prudence in making laws and conduct in wars entitled him to. Grudging him, at any rate, the addition of this, they urged Horatius to sue for the dedication, and, whilst Poplicola was engaged in some military expedition, voted it to Horatius, and conducted him to the Capitol, as though, were Poplicola present, they could not have carried it. Yet, some write, Poplicola was by lot destined against his will to the expedition, the other to the dedication; and what happened in the performance seems to intimate some ground for this conjecture; for, upon the Ides of September, which happens about the full moon of the month Metagitnion, the people having assembled at the Capitol and silence being enjoined, Horatius, after the performance of other ceremonies, holding the doors, according to custom, was proceeding to pronounce the words of dedication, when Marcus, the brother of Poplicola, who had got a place on purpose beforehand near the door, observing his opportunity, cried, "O consul, thy son lies dead in the camp"; which made a great impression upon all others who heard it, yet in nowise discomposed Horatius, who returned merely the reply, "Cast the dead out whither you please; I am not a mourner"; and so completed the dedication. The news was not true, but Marcus thought the lie might avert him from his performance; but it argues him a man of wonderful self-possession, whether he at once saw through the cheat, or, believing it as true, showed no discomposure.

The same fortune attended the dedication of the second temple; the first, as has been said, was built by Tarquin, and dedicated by Horatius; it was burnt down in the civil wars. The second, Sylla built, and, dying before the dedication, left that honour to Catulus; and when this was demolished in the Vitellian sedition, Vespasian, with the same success that attended him in other things, began a third and lived to see it finished, but did not live to see it again destroyed, as it presently was; but was as fortunate in dying before its destruction, as Sylla was the reverse in dying before the dedication of his. For immediately after Vespasian's death it was consumed by fire. The fourth, which now exists, was both built and dedicated by Domitian. It is said Tarquin expended forty thousand pounds of silver in the very foundations; but the whole wealth of the richest private man in Rome would not discharge the cost of the gilding of this temple in our days, it amounting to above twelve thousand talents; the pillars were cut out of Pentelican marble, of a length most happily proportioned to their thickness; these we saw at Athens; but when they were cut anew at Rome and polished, they did not gain so much in embellishment as they lost in symmetry, being rendered too taper and slender. Should anyone who wonders at the costliness of the Capitol visit anyone gallery in Domitian's palace, or hall, or bath, or the apartments of his concubines, Epicharmus' remark upon the prodigal, that—

> 'Tis not beneficence, but truth to say,
> A mere disease of giving things away,

would be in his mouth in application to Domitian. It is neither piety, he would say, nor magnificence, but, indeed, a mere disease of building, and a desire, like Midas, of converting everything into gold or stone. And thus much for this matter.

Tarquin, after the great battle wherein he lost his son in combat with Brutus, fled to Clusium, and sought aid from Lars Porsenna, then one of those most powerful princes of Italy, and a man of worth and generosity; who assured him of assistance, immediately sending his commands to Rome that they should receive Tarquin as their king, and, upon the Romans' refusal, proclaimed war, and, having signified the time and place where he intended his attack, approached with a great army. Poplicola was, in his absence, chosen consul a second time, and Titus Lucretius his colleague, and, returning to Rome, to show a spirit yet loftier than Porsenna's, built the city Sigliura when Porsenna was already in the neighbourhood; and walling it at great expense, there placed a colony of seven hundred men, as being little concerned at the war. Nevertheless, Porsenna, making a sharp assault, obliged the defendants to retire to Rome, who had almost in their entrance admitted the enemy into the city with them; only Poplicola by sallying out at the gate prevented them, and, joining battle by Tiber side, opposed the enemy, that pressed on with their multitude, but at last, sinking under desperate wounds, was carried out of the fight. The same fortune fell upon Lucretius, so that the Romans, being dismayed, retreated into the city for their security, and Rome was in great hazard of being taken, the enemy forcing their way on to the wooden bridge, where Horatius Cocles, seconded by two of the first men in Rome, Herminius and Lartius, made head against them. Horatius obtained this name from the loss of one of his eyes in the war, or, as others write, from the depressure of his nose, which, leaving nothing in the middle to separate them, made both eyes appear but as one; and hence, intending, to say Cyclops, by a mispronunciation they called him Cocles. This Cocles kept the bridge, and held back the enemy, till his own party broke it down behind, and then with his armour dropped into the river, and swam to the hither side, with a wound in his hip from a Tuscan spear. Poplicola, admiring his courage, proposed at once that the Romans should everyone make him a present of a day's provisions, and afterwards give him as much land as he could plough round in one day, and besides erected a brazen statute to his honour in the temple of Vulcan, as a requital for the lameness caused by his wound.

But Porsenna laying close siege to the city, and a famine raging amongst the Romans, also a new army of the Tuscans making incursions into the country, Poplicola, a third time chosen consul, designed to make, without sallying out, his defence against Porsenna, but, privately stealing forth against the new army of the Tuscans, put them to flight and slew five thousand. The story of Mucius is variously given; we, like others, must follow the commonly received statement. He was a man endowed with every virtue, but most eminent in war; and, resolving to kill Porsenna, attired himself in the Tuscan habit, and using the Tuscan language, came to the camp, and approaching the seat where the king sat amongst his nobles, but not certainly knowing the king, and fearful to inquire, drew out his sword, and stabbed one who he thought had most the appearance of king. Mucius was taken in the act, and whilst he was under examination, a pan of fire was brought to the king, who intended to sacrifice; Mucius thrust his right hand into the flame, and whilst it burnt stood looking at Porsenna with a steadfast and undaunted countenance; Porsenna at last in admiration dismissed him, and returned his sword, reaching it from his seat; Mucius received it in his left hand, which occasioned the name of Scævola, left-handed, and said, "I have overcome the terrors of Porsenna, yet am vanquished by his generosity, and gratitude obliges me to disclose what no punishment could extort"; and assured him then, that three hundred Romans, all of the same resolution, lurked about his camp, only waiting for an opportunity; he, by lot appointed to the enterprise, was not sorry that he had miscarried in it, because so brave and good a man deserved rather to be a friend to the Romans than an enemy. To this

Porsenna gave credit, and thereupon expressed an inclination to a truce, not, I presume, so much out of fear of the three hundred Romans, as in admiration of the Roman courage. All other writers call this man Mucius Scævola, yet Athendrous, son of Sandon, in a book addressed to Octavia, Cæsar's sister, avers he was also called Postumus.

Poplicola, not so much esteeming Porsenna's enmity dangerous to Rome as his friendship and alliance serviceable, was induced to refer the controversy with Tarquin to his arbitration, and several times undertook to prove Tarquin the worst of men, and justly deprived of his kingdom. But Tarquin proudly replied he would admit no judge, much less Porsenna, that had fallen away from his engagements; and Porsenna, resenting this answer, and mistrusting the equity of his cause, moved also by the solicitations of his son Aruns, who was earnest for the Roman interest, made a peace on these conditions, that they should resign the land they had taken from the Tuscans, and restore all prisoners and receive back their deserters. To confirm the peace, the Romans gave as hostages ten sons of patrician parents, and as many daughters, amongst whom was Valeria, the daughter of Poplicola.

Upon these assurances, Porsenna ceased from all acts of hostility, and the young girls went down to the river to bathe, at that part where the winding of the bank formed a bay and made the waters stiller and quieter; and, seeing no guard, nor anyone coming or going over, they were encouraged to swim over, notwithstanding the depth and violence of the stream. Some affirm that one of them, by name Clœlia, passing over on horseback, persuaded the rest to swim after; but, upon their safe arrival, presenting themselves to Poplicola, he neither praised nor approved their return, but was concerned lest he should appear less faithful than Porsenna, and this boldness in the maidens should argue treachery in the Romans; so that, apprehending them, he sent them back to Porsenna. But Tarquin's men, having intelligence of this, laid a strong ambuscade on the other side for those that conducted them; and while these were skirmishing together, Valeria, the daughter of Poplicola, rushed through the enemy, and fled, and with the assistance of three of her attendants made good her escape, whilst the rest were dangerously hedged in by the soldiers; but Aruns, Porsenna's son, upon tidings of it, hastened to their rescue, and, putting the enemy to flight, delivered the Romans. When Porsenna saw the maidens returned, demanding who was the author and adviser of the act, and understanding Clœlia to be the person, he looked on her with a cheerful and benignant countenance, and, commanding one of his horses to be brought, sumptuously adorned, made her a present of it. This is produced as evidence by those who affirm that only Clœlia passed the river on horseback; those who deny it call it only the honour the Tuscan did to her courage; a figure, however, on horseback, stands in the Via Sacra, as you go to the Palatium, which some say is the statue of Clœlia, others of Valeria. Porsenna, thus reconciled to the Romans, gave them a fresh instance of his generosity, and commanded his soldiers to quit the camp merely with their arms, leaving their tents, full of corn and other stores, as a gift to the Romans. Hence, even down to our time, when there is a public sale of goods, they cry Porsenna's first, by way of perpetual commemoration of his kindness. There stood also, by the senate-house, a brazen statue of him, of plain and antique workmanship.

Afterwards, the Sabines, making incursions upon the Romans, Marcus Valerius, brother to Poplicola, was made consul, and with him Postumius Tubertus. Marcus, through the management of affairs by the conduct and direct assistance of Poplicola, obtained two great victories, in the latter of which he slew thirteen thousand Sabines without the loss of one Roman, and was honoured, as an accession to his triumph, with an house built in the Palatium at the public charge; and whereas the doors of other houses opened inward into the house, they made this to open outward into the street, to intimate their perpetual public recognition of his merit by thus continually making way for him. The same fashion in their doors the Greeks, they say, had of old universally, which appears from their comedies, where those that are going out make a noise at the door within, to give notice to those that pass by or stand near the door, that the opening the door into the street might occasion no surprisal.

The year after, Poplicola was made consul the fourth time, when a confederacy of the Sabines and Latins threatened a war; a superstitious fear also overran the city on the occasion of general miscarriages of their women, no single birth coming to its due time. Poplicola, upon consultation of the Sibylline books, sacrificing to Pluto, and renewing certain games commanded by Apollo, restored the city to more cheerful assurance in the gods, and then prepared against the menaces of men. There were appearances of great preparation, and of a formidable confederacy. Amongst the Sabines there was one Appius Clausus, a man of a great wealth and strength of body, but most eminent for his high character and for his eloquence; yet, as is usually the fate of great men, he could not escape the envy of others, which was much occasioned by his dissuading the war and seeming to promote the Roman interest, with a view, it is thought, to obtaining absolute power in his own country for himself. Knowing how welcome these reports would be to the multitude, and how offensive to the army and the abettors of the war, he was afraid to stand a trial, but, having a considerable body of friends and allies to assist him, raised a tumult amongst the Sabines, which delayed the war. Neither was Poplicola wanting, not only to understand the grounds of the sedition, but to promote and increase it, and he despatched emissaries with instructions to Clausus, that Poplicola was assured of his goodness and justice, and thought it indeed unworthy in any man, however injured, to seek revenge upon his fellow-citizens; yet if he pleased, for his own security, to leave his enemies and come to Rome, he should be received, both in public and private, with the honour his merit deserved, and their own glory required. Appius, seriously weighing the matter, came to the conclusion that it was the best resource which necessity left him, and advising with his friends, and they inviting others in the same manner, he came to Rome, bringing five thousand families, with their wives and children; people of the quietest and steadiest temper of all the Sabines. Poplicola, informed of their approach, received them with all the kind offices of a friend, and admitted them at once to the franchise, allotting to everyone two acres of land by the river Anio, but to Clausus twenty-five acres, and gave him a place in the senate; a commencement of political power which he used so wisely, that he rose to the highest reputation, was very influential, and left the Claudian house behind him, inferior to none in Rome.

The departure of these men rendered things quiet amongst the Sabines; yet the chief of the community would not suffer them to settle into peace but resented that Clausus now, by turning deserter, should disappoint that revenge upon the Romans, which, while at home, he had unsuccessfully opposed. Coming with a great army, they sat down before Fidenæ, and placed an ambuscade of two thousand men near Rome, in wooded and hollow spots, with a design that some few horsemen, as soon as it was day, should go out and ravage the country, commanding them upon their approach to the town so to retreat as to draw the enemy into the ambush. Poplicola, however, soon advertised of these designs by deserters, disposed his forces to their respective charges. Postumius Balbus, his son-in-law, going out with three thousand men in the evening, was ordered to take the hills, under which the ambush lay, there to observe their motions; his colleague, Lucretius, attended with a body of the lightest and boldest men, was appointed to meet the Sabine horse; whilst he, with the rest of the army, encompassed the enemy. And a thick mist rising accidentally,

Postumius, early in the morning, with shouts from the hills, assailed the ambuscade, Lucretius charged the light-horse, and Poplicola besieged the camp; so that on all sides defeat and ruin came upon the Sabines, and without any resistance the Romans killed them in their flight, their very hopes leading them to their death, for each division, presuming that the other was safe, gave up all thought of fighting or keeping their ground; and these quitting the camp to retire to the ambuscade, and the ambuscade flying to the camp, fugitives thus met fugitives, and found those from whom they expected succour as much in need of succour from themselves. The nearness, however, of the city Fidenæ was the preservation of the Sabines, especially those that fled from the camp; those that could not gain the city either perished in the field, or were taken prisoners. This victory, the Romans, though usually ascribing such success to some god, attributed to the conduct of one captain; and it was observed to be heard amongst the soldiers, that Poplicola had delivered their enemies lame and blind, and only not in chains, to be despatched by their swords. From the spoil and prisoners great wealth accrued to the people.

Poplicola, having completed his triumph, and bequeathed the city to the care of the succeeding consuls, died; thus closing a life which, so far as human life may be, had been full of all that is good and honourable. The people, as though they had not duly rewarded his deserts when alive, but still were in his debt, decreed him a public interment, everyone contributing his *quadrans* towards the charge; the women, besides, by private consent, mourned a whole year, a signal mark of honour to his memory. He was buried, by the people's desire, within the city, in the part called Velia, where his posterity had likewise privilege of burial; now, however, none of the family are interred there, but the body is carried thither and set down, and someone places a burning torch under it and immediately takes it away, as an attestation of the deceased's privilege, and his receding from his honour; after which the body is removed.

THE COMPARISON OF POPLICOLA WITH SOLON

THERE IS SOMETHING SINGULAR IN THE PRESENT PARALLEL WHICH HAS not occurred in any other of the lives; that the one should be the imitator of the other, and the other his best evidence. Upon the survey of Solon's sentence to Crœsus in favour of Tellus' happiness, it seems more applicable to Poplicola; for Tellus, whose virtuous life and dying well had gained him the name of the happiest man, yet was never celebrated in Solon's poems for a good man, nor have his children or any magistracy of his deserved a memorial; but Poplicola's life was the most eminent amongst the Romans, as well for the greatness of his virtue as his power, and also since his death many amongst the distinguished families, even in our days, the Poplicolæ, Messalæ, and Valerii, after a lapse of six hundred years, acknowledge him as the fountain of their honour. Besides, Tellus, though keeping his post and fighting like a valiant soldier, was yet slain by his enemies; but Poplicola, the better fortune, slew his, and saw his country victorious under his command. And his honours and triumphs brought him, which was Solon's ambition, to a happy end; the ejaculation which, in his verses against Mimnermus about the continuance of man's life, he himself made—

> Mourned let me die; and may I, when life ends,
> Occasion sighs and sorrows to my friends,

is evidence to Poplicola's happiness; his death did not only draw tears from his friends and acquaintance, but was the object of universal regret and sorrow through the whole city, the women deplored his loss as that of a son, brother, or common father. "Wealth I would have," said Solon, "but wealth by wrong procure would not," because punishment would follow. But Poplicola's riches were not only justly his, but he spent them nobly in doing good to the distressed. So that if Solon was reputed the wisest man, we must allow Poplicola to be the happiest; for what Solon wished for as the greatest and most perfect good, this Poplicola had, and used and enjoyed to his death.

And as Solon may thus be said to have contributed to Poplicola's glory, so did also Poplicola to his, by his choice of him as his model in the formation of republican institutions; in reducing, for example, the excessive powers and assumption of the consulship. Several of his laws, indeed, he actually transferred to Rome, as his empowering the people to elect their officers, and allowing offenders the liberty of appealing to the people, as Solon did to the jurors. He did not, indeed, create a new senate, as Solon did, but augmented the old to almost double its number. The appointment of treasurers again, the quæstors, has a like origin; with the intent that the chief magistrate should not, if of good character, be withdrawn from greater matters; or, if bad, have the greater temptation to injustice, by holding both the government and treasury in his hands. The aversion to tyranny was stronger in Poplicola; anyone who attempted usurpation could, by Solon's law, only be punished upon conviction; but Poplicola made it death before a trial. And though Solon justly gloried, that, when arbitrary power was absolutely offered to him by circumstances, and when his countrymen would have willingly seen him accept it, he yet declined it; still Poplicola merited no less, who, receiving a despotic command, converted it to a popular office, and did not employ the whole legal power which he held. We must allow, indeed, that Solon was before Poplicola in observing that—

> A people always minds its rulers best
> When it is neither humoured nor oppressed.

The remission of debts was peculiar to Solon; it was his great means for confirming the citizens' liberty; for a mere law to give all men equal rights is but useless, if the poor must sacrifice those rights to their debts, and, in the very seats and sanctuaries of equality, the courts of justice, the offices of state, and the public discussions, be more than anywhere at the beck and bidding of the rich. A yet more extraordinary success was, that, although usually civil violence is caused by any remission of debts, upon this one occasion this dangerous but powerful remedy actually put an end to the civil violence already existing, Solon's own private worth and reputation overbalancing all the ordinary ill-repute and discredit of the change. The beginning of his government was more glorious, for he was entirely original, and followed no man's example, and, without the aid of any ally, achieved his most important measures by his own conduct; yet the close of Poplicola's life was more happy and desirable, for Solon saw the dissolution of his own commonwealth, Poplicola maintained the state in good order to the civil wars. Solon, leaving his laws, as soon as he had made them, engraven in wood, but destitute of a defender, departed from Athens; whilst Poplicola, remaining both in and out of office, laboured to establish the government. Solon, though he actually knew of Pisistratus' ambition, yet was not able to suppress it, but had to yield to usurpation in its infancy; whereas Poplicola utterly subverted and dissolved a potent monarchy, strongly settled by long continuance; uniting thus to virtues equal to those, and purposes identical with those of Solon, the good fortune and the power that alone could make them effective.

In military exploits, Daimachus of Platæa will not even allow Solon the conduct of the war against the Megarians, as was before intimated; but Poplicola was victorious in the most important conflicts, both as a private soldier and commander. In domestic politics, also, Solon, in play, as it were, and by counterfeiting madness induced the enterprise against Salamis; whereas Poplicola, in the very beginning, exposed himself to the greatest risk, took arms against Tarquin, detected the conspiracy, and, being principally concerned both in preventing the escape of and afterwards punishing the traitors, not only expelled the tyrants from the city, but extirpated their very hopes. And as, in cases calling for contest and resistance and manful opposition, he behaved with courage and resolution, so, in instances where peaceable language, persuasion, and concession were requisite, he was yet more to be commended; and succeeded in gaining happily to reconciliation and friendship, Porsenna, a terrible and invincible enemy. Some may, perhaps, object that Solon recovered Salamis, which they had lost, for the Athenians; whereas Poplicola receded from part of what the Romans were at that time possessed of; but judgment is to be made of actions according to the times in which they were performed. The conduct of a wise politican is ever suited to the present posture of affairs; often by foregoing a part he saves the whole, and by yielding in a small matter secures a greater; and so Poplicola, by restoring what the Romans had lately usurped, saved their undoubted patrimony, and procured, moreover, the stores of the enemy for those who were only too thankful to secure their city. Permitting the decision of the controversy to his adversary, he not only got the victory, but likewise what he himself would willingly have given to purchase the victory, Porsenna putting an end to the war, and leaving them all the provision of his camp, from the sense of the virtue and gallant disposition of the Romans which their consul had impressed upon him.

an end to the war, and learning them all the provision of his camp from the
sense of the virtue and gallant disposition of the Romans which their cour-
sel had impressed upon him

THEMISTOCLES

THE BIRTH OF THEMISTOCLES WAS SOMEWHAT TOO OBSCURE TO DO HIM
honour. His father, Neocles, was not of the distinguished people of
Athens, but of the township Phrearrhi, and of the tribe Leontis; and by his
mother's side, as it is reported, he was base-born—

> I am not of the noble Grecian race,
> I'm poor Abrotonon, and born in Thrace;
> Let the Greek women scorn me, if they please,
> I was the mother of Themistocles.

Yet Phanias writes that the mother of Themistocles was not of Thrace
but of Caria, and that her name was not Abrotonon, but Euterpe, and
Neanthes adds farther that she was of Halicarnassus in Caria. And, as illegitimate children, including those that were of half-blood or had but one
parent an Athenian, had to attend at the Cynosarges (a wrestling-place
outside the gates, dedicated to Hercules, who was also of half-blood
amongst the gods, having had a mortal woman for his mother), Themistocles
persuaded several of the young men of high birth to accompany him to
anoint and exercise themselves together at Cynosarges; an ingenious
device for destroying the distinction between the noble and the base-born,
and between those of the whole and those of the half-blood of Athens.
However, it is certain that he was related to the house of Lycomedæ; for
Simonides records that he rebuilt the chapel of Phlya, belonging to that
family, and beautified it with pictures and other ornaments, after it had
been burnt by the Persians.

It is confessed by all that from his youth he was of a vehement and
impetuous nature, of a quick apprehension, and a strong and aspiring

bent for action and great affairs. The holidays and intervals in his studies he did not spend in play or idleness, as other children, but would be always inventing or arranging some oration or declamation to himself, the subject of which was generally the excusing or accusing his companions, so that his master would often say to him, "You, my boy, will be nothing small, but great one way or other, for good or else for bad." He received reluctantly and carelessly instructions given him to improve his manners and behaviour, or to teach him any pleasing or graceful accomplishment, but whatever was said to improve him in sagacity, or in management of affairs, he would give attention to, beyond one of his years, from confidence in his natural capacities for such things. And thus afterwards, when in company where people engaged themselves in what are commonly thought the liberal and elegant amusements, he was obliged to defend himself against the observations of those who considered themselves highly accomplished, by the somewhat arrogant retort, that he certainly could not make use of any stringed instrument, could only, were a small and obscure city put into his hands, make it great and glorious. Notwithstanding this, Stesimbrotus says that Themistocles was a hearer of Anaxagoras, and that he studied natural philosophy under Melissus, contrary to chronology; Melissus commanded the Samians in the siege by Pericles, who was much Themistocles' junior; and with Pericles, also, Anaxagoras was intimate. They, therefore, might rather be credited who report, that Themistocles was an admirer of Mnesiphilus the Phrearrhian, who was neither rhetorician nor natural philosopher, but a professor of that which was then called wisdom, consisting in a sort of political shrewdness and practical sagacity, which had begun and continued, almost like a sect of philosophy, from Solon: but those who came afterwards, and mixed it with pleadings and legal artifices, and transformed the practical part of it into a mere art of speaking and an exercise of words, were generally called sophists. Themistocles resorted to Mnesiphilus when he had already embarked in politics.

In the first essays of his youth he was not regular nor happily balanced; he allowed himself to follow mere natural character, which, without the control of reason and instruction, is apt to hurry, upon either side, into sudden and violent courses, and very often to break away and determine upon the worst; as he afterwards owned himself, saying, that the wildest colts make the best horses, if they only get properly trained and broken in. But those who upon this fasten stories of their own invention, as of his being disowned by his father, and that his mother died for grief of her son's ill-fame, certainly calumniate him; and there are others who relate, on the contrary, how that to deter him from public business, and to let him see how the vulgar behave themselves towards their leaders when they have at last no farther use of them, his father showed him the old galleys as they lay forsaken and cast about upon the sea-shore.

Yet it is evident that his mind was early imbued with the keenest interest in public affairs, and the most passionate ambition for distinction. Eager from the first to obtain the highest place, he unhesitatingly accepted the hatred of the most powerful and influential leaders in the city, but more especially of Aristides, the son of Lysimachus, who always opposed him. And yet all this great enmity between them arose, it appears, from a very boyish occasion, both being attached to the beautiful Stesilaus of Ceos, as Ariston the philosopher tells us; ever after which they took opposite sides, and were rivals in politics. Not but that the incompatibility of their lives and manners may seem to have increased the difference, for Aristides was of a mild nature, and of a nobler sort of character, and, in public matters, acting always with a view, not to glory or popularity, but to the best interest of the state consistently with safety and honesty, he was often forced to oppose Themistocles, and interfere against the increase of his influence, seeing him stirring up the people to all kinds of enterprises, and introducing various innovations. For it is said that Themistocles was so transported with the thoughts of glory and so inflamed with the passion for great actions, that, though he was still young when the battle of Marathon was fought against the Persians, upon the skilful conduct of the general, Miltiades, being everywhere talked about, he was observed to be thoughtful and reserved, alone by himself; he passed the nights without sleep, and avoided all his usual places of recreation, and to those who wondered at the change, and inquired the reason of it, he gave the answer, that "the trophy of Miltiades would not let him sleep." And when others were of opinion that the battle of Marathon would be an end to the war, Themistocles thought that it was but the beginning for far greater conflicts, and for these, to the benefit of all Greece, he kept himself in continual readiness, and his city also in proper training, foreseeing from far before what would happen.

And, first of all, the Athenians being accustomed to divide amongst themselves the revenue proceeding from the silver mines at Laurium, he was the only man that durst propose to the people that this distribution should cease, and that with the money ships should be built to make war against the Æginetans, who were the most flourishing people in all

Greece, and by the number of their ships held the sovereignty of the sea; and Themistocles thus was more easily able to persuade them, avoiding all mention of danger from Darius or the Persians, who were at a great distance, and their coming very uncertain, and at that time not much to be feared; but by a seasonable employment of the emulation and anger felt by the Athenians against the Æginetans, he induced them to preparation. So that with this money an hundred ships were built, with which they afterwards fought against Xerxes. And henceforward, little by little, turning and drawing the city down towards the sea, in the belief that, whereas by land they were not a fit match for their next neighbours, with their ships they might be able to repel the Persians and command Greece, thus, as Plato says, from steady soldiers he turned them into mariners and seamen tossed about the sea, and gave occasion for the reproach against him, that he took away from the Athenians the spear and the shield, and bound them to the bench and the oar. These measures he carried in the assembly, against the opposition, as Stesimbrotus relates, of Miltiades; and whether or no he hereby injured the purity and true balance of government may be a question for philosophers, but that the deliverance of Greece came at that time from the sea, and that these galleys restored Athens again after it was destroyed, were others wanting, Xerxes himself would be sufficient evidence, who, though his land-forces were still entire, after his defeat at sea, fled away, and thought himself no longer able to encounter the Greeks; and, as it seems to me, left Mardonius behind him, not out of any hopes he could have to bring them into subjection, but to hinder them from pursuing him.

Themistocles is said to have been eager in the acquisition of riches, according to some, that he might be the more liberal; for loving to sacrifice often, and to be splendid in his entertainment of strangers, he required a plentiful revenue; yet he is accused by others of having been parsimonious and sordid to that degree that he would sell provisions which were sent to him as a present. He desired Diphilides, who was a breeder of horses, to give him a colt, and when he refused it, threatened that in a short time he would turn his house into a wooden horse, intimating that he would stir up dispute and litigation between him and some of his relations.

He went beyond all men in the passion for distinction. When he was still young and unknown in the world, he entreated Episcles of Hermione, who had a good hand at the lute and was much sought after by the Athenians, to come and practise at home with him, being ambitious of having people inquire after his house and frequent his company. When he came to the Olympic games, and was so splendid in his equipage and entertainments, in his rich tents and furniture, that he strove to outdo Cimon, he displeased the Greeks, who thought that such magnificence might be allowed in one who was a young man and of a great family, but was a great piece of insolence in one as yet undistinguished, and without title or means for making any such display. In a dramatic contest, the play he paid for won the price, which was then a matter that excited much emulation; he put up a tablet in record of it, with the inscription: "Themistocles of Phrearrhi was at the charge of it; Phrynichus made it; Adimantus was archon." He was well liked by the common people, would salute every particular citizen by his own name, and always show himself a just judge in questions of business between private men; he said to Simonides, the poet of Ceos, who desired something of him, when he was commander of the army, that was not reasonable, "Simonides, you would be no good poet if you wrote false measure, nor should I be a good magistrate if for favour I made false law." And at another time, laughing at Simonides, he said, that he was a man of little judgment to speak against the Corinthians, who were inhabitants of a great city, and to have his own picture drawn so often, having so ill-looking a face.

Gradually growing to be great, and winning the favour of the people, he at last gained the day with his faction over that of Aristides, and procured his banishment by ostracism. When the king of Persia was now advancing against Greece, and the Athenians were in consultation who should be general, and many withdrew themselves of their own accord, being terrified with the greatness of the danger, there was one Epicydes, a popular speaker, son to Euphemides, a man of an elegant tongue, but of a faint heart, and a slave to riches, who was desirous of the command, and was looked upon to be in a fair way to carry it by the number of votes; but Themistocles, fearing that, if the command should fall into such hands, all would be lost, bought off Epicydes and his pretensions, it is said, for a sum of money.

When the king of Persia sent messengers into Greece, with an interpreter, to demand earth and water, as an acknowledgment of subjection, Themistocles, by the consent of the people, seized upon the interpreter, and put him to death, for presuming to publish the barbarian orders and decrees in the Greek language; this is one of the actions he is commended for, as also for what he did to Arthmius of Zelea, who brought gold from the king of Persia to corrupt the Greeks, and was, by an order from Themistocles, degraded and disfranchised, he and his children and his posterity; but that which most of all redounded to his credit was, that he put an end to all the civil wars of Greece, composed their differences, and persuaded them to lay aside all enmity during the war with the Persians; and in this great work, Chileus the Arcadian was, it is said, of great assistance to him.

Having taken upon himself the command of the Athenian forces, he immediately endeavoured to persuade the citizens to leave the city, and to embark upon their galleys, and meet with the Persians at a great distance from Greece; but many being against this, he led a large force, together with the Lacedæmonians, into Tempe, that in this pass they might maintain the safety of Thessaly, which had not as yet declared for the king; but when they returned without performing anything, and it was known that not only the Thessalians, but all as far as Bœotia, was going over to Xerxes, then the Athenians more willingly hearkened to the advice of Themistocles to fight by sea, and sent him with a fleet to guard the straits of Artemisium.

When the contingents met here, the Greeks would have the Lacedæmonians to command, and Eurybiades to be their admiral; but the Athenians, who surpassed all the rest together in number of vessels, would not submit to come after any other, till Themistocles, perceiving the danger of the contest, yielded his own command to Eurybiades, and got the Athenians to submit, extenuating the loss by persuading them, that if in this war they behaved themselves like men, he would answer for it after that, that the Greeks, of their own will, would submit to their command. And by this moderation of his, it is evident that he was the chief means of the deliverance of Greece, and gained the Athenians the glory of alike surpassing their enemies in valour, and their confederates in wisdom.

As soon as the Persian armada arrived at Aphetæ, Eurybiades was astonished to see such a vast number of vessels before him, and being informed that two hundred more were sailing around behind the island of Sciathus, he immediately determined to retire farther into Greece, and to sail back into some part of Peloponnesus, where their land army and their fleet might join, for he looked upon the Persian forces to be altogether unassailable by sea. But the Eubœans, fearing that the Greeks would forsake them, and leave them to the mercy of the enemy, sent Pelagon to confer privately with Themistocles, taking with him a good sum of money, which, as Herodotus reports, he accepted and gave to Eurybiades. In this affair none of his own countrymen opposed him so much as Architeles, captain of the sacred galley, who, having no money to supply his seamen, was eager to go home; but Themistocles so incensed the Athenians against them, that they set upon him and left him not so much as his supper, at which Architeles was much surprised, and took it very ill; but Themistocles immediately sent him in a chest a service of provisions, and at the bottom of it a talent of silver, desiring him to sup tonight, and tomorrow provide for his seamen; if not, he would report it among the Athenians that he had received money from the enemy. So Phanias the Lesbian tells the story.

Though the fights between the Greeks and Persians in the straits of Eubœa were not so important as to make any final decision of the war, yet the experience which the Greeks obtained in them was of great advantage; for thus, by actual trial and in real danger, they found out that neither number of ships, nor riches and ornaments, nor boasting shouts, nor barbarous songs of victory, were any way terrible to men that knew how to fight, and were resolved to come hand to hand with their enemies; these things they were to despise, and to come up close and grapple with their foes. This Pindar appears to have seen, and says justly enough of the fight at Artemisium, that—

> There the sons of Athens set
> The stone that freedom stands on yet.

For the first step towards victory undoubtedly is to gain courage. Artemisium is in Eubœa, beyond the city of Histiæa, a sea-beach open to the north; most nearly opposite to it stands Olizon, in the country which formally was under Philoctetes; there is a small temple there, dedicated to Diana, surnamed of the Dawn, and trees about it, around which again stand pillars of white marble; and if you rub them with your hand, they send forth both the smell and colour of saffron. On one of these pillars these verses are engraved:

> With numerous tribes from Asia's region brought
> The sons of Athens on these waters fought;
> Erecting, after they had quelled the Mede,
> To Artemis this record of the deed.

There is a place still to be seen upon this shore, where, in the middle of a great heap of sand, they take out from the bottom a dark powder like ashes, or something that has passed the fire; and here, it is supposed, the shipwrecks and bodies of the dead were burnt.

But when news came from Thermopylæ to Artemisium informing them that king Leonidas was slain, and that Xerxes had made himself master of all the passages by land, they returned back to the interior of Greece, the Athenians having the command of the rear, the place of honour and danger, and much elated by what had been done.

As Themistocles sailed along the coasts, he took notice of the harbours and fit places for the enemy's ships to come to land at, and engraved large letters in such stones as he found there by chance, as also in others which he set up on purpose near to the landing-places, or where they were to water; in which inscriptions he called upon the Ionians to forsake the Medes, if it were possible, and to come over to the Greeks, who were their proper founders and fathers, and were now hazarding all for their liberties; but, if this could not be done, at any rate to impede and disturb the Persians in all engagements. He hoped that these writings would prevail with the Ionians to revolt, or raise some trouble by making their fidelity doubtful to the Persians.

Now, though Xerxes had already passed through Doris and invaded the country of Phocis, and was burning and destroying the cities of the Phocians, yet the Greeks sent them no relief; and, though the Athenians earnestly desired them to meet the Persians in Bœotia, before they could come into Attica, as they themselves had come forward by sea at Artemisium, they gave no ear to their requests, being wholly intent upon Peloponnesus, and resolved to gather all their forces together within the Isthmus, and to build a wall from sea to sea in that narrow neck of land; so that the Athenians were enraged to see themselves betrayed, and at the same time afflicted and dejected at their own destitution. For to fight alone against such a numerous army was to no purpose, and the only expedient now left them was to leave their city and cling to their ships; which the people were very unwilling to submit to, imagining that it would signify little now to gain a victory, and not understanding how there could be deliverance any longer after they had once forsaken the temples of their gods and exposed the tombs and monuments of their ancestors to the fury of their enemies.

Themistocles, being at a loss, and not able to draw the people over to his opinion by any human reason, set his machines to work, as in a theatre, and employed prodigies and oracles. The serpent of Minerva, kept in the inner part of her temple, disappeared; the priest gave it out to the people that the offerings which were set for it were found untouched, and declared, by the suggestion of Themistocles, that the goddess had left the city, and taken her flight before them towards the sea. And he often urged them with the oracle which bade them trust to walls of wood, showing them that walls of wood could signify nothing else but ships; and that the island of Salamis was termed in it, not miserable or unhappy, but had the epithet of divine, for that it should one day be associated with a great good fortune of the Greeks. At length his opinion prevailed, and he obtained a decree that the city should be committed to the protection of Minerva, "Queen of Athens"; that they who were of age to bear arms should embark, and that each should see to sending away his children, women, and slaves where he could. This decree being confirmed, most of the Athenians removed their parents, wives, and children to Trœzen, where they were received with eager goodwill by the Trœzenians, who passed a vote that they should be maintained at the public charge, by a daily payment of two obols to everyone, and leave be given to the children to gather fruit where they pleased, and schoolmasters paid to instruct them. This vote was proposed by Nicagoras.

There was no public treasure at that time in Athens; but the council of Areopagus, as Aristotle says, distributed to everyone that served eight drachmas, which was a great help to the manning of the fleet; but Clidemus ascribes this also to the art of Themistocles. When the Athenians were on their way down to the haven of Piræus, the shield with the head of Medusa was missing; and he, under the pretext of searching for it, ransacked all places, and found among their goods considerable sums of money concealed, which he applied to the public use; and with this the soldiers and seamen were well provided for their voyage.

When the whole city of Athens were going on board, it afforded a spectacle worthy alike of pity and admiration, to see them thus send away their fathers and children before them, and, unmoved with their cries and tears, passed over into the island. But that which stirred compassion most of all was, that many old men, by reason of their great age, were left behind; and even the tame domestic animals could not be seen without some pity, running about the town and howling, as desirous to be carried along with their masters that had kept them; among which it is reported that Xanthippus, the father of Pericles, had a dog that would not endure to stay behind, but leaped into the sea, and swam along by the galley's side till he came to the island of Salamis, where he fainted away and died, and that spot in the island, which is still called the Dog's Grave, is said to be his.

Among the great actions of Themistocles at this crisis, the recall of Aristides was not the least, for, before the war, he had been ostracised by the party which Themistocles headed, and was in banishment; but now, perceiving that the people regretted his absence, and were fearful that he might go over to the Persians to revenge himself, and thereby ruin the affairs of Greece, Themistocles proposed a decree that those who were banished for a time might return again, to give assistance by word and deed to the cause of Greece with the rest of their fellow-citizens.

Eurybiades, by reason of the greatness of Sparta, was admiral of the Greek fleet, but yet was fainthearted in time of danger, and willing to weigh anchor and set sail for the isthmus of Corinth, near which the land army lay encamped; which Themistocles resisted; and this was the occasion of the well-known words, when Eurybiades, to check his impatience, told him that at the Olympic games they that start up before the rest are lashed; "And they," replied Themistocles, "that are left behind are not crowned." Again, Eurybiades lifting up his staff as if he were going to strike, Themistocles said, "Strike if you will, but hear"; Eurybiades, wondering much at his moderation, desired him to speak, and Themistocles now brought him to a better understanding. And when one who stood by him told him that it did not become those who had neither city nor house to lose, to persuade others to relinquish their habitations and forsake their countries, Themistocles gave this reply: "We have indeed left our houses and our walls, base fellow, not thinking it fit to become slaves for the sake of things that have no life nor soul; and yet our city is the greatest of all Greece, consisting of two hundred galleys, which are here to defend you, if you please; but if you run away and betray us, as you did once before, the Greeks shall soon hear news of the Athenians possessing as fair a country, and as large and free a city, as that they have lost." These expressions of Themistocles made Eurybiades suspect that if he retreated the Athenians would fall off from him. When one of Eretria began to oppose him, he said, "Have you anything to say of war, that are like an ink-fish? You have a sword, but no heart." Some say that while Themistocles was thus speaking upon the deck, an owl was seen flying to the right hand of the fleet, which came and sate upon the top of the mast; and this happy omen so far disposed the Greeks to follow his advice, that they presently prepared to fight. Yet, when the enemy's fleet was arrived at the haven of Phalerum, upon the coast of Attica, and with the number of their ships concealed all the shore, and when they saw the king himself in person come down with his land army to the seaside, with all his forces united, then the good counsel of Themistocles was soon forgotten, and the Peloponnesians cast their eyes again towards the isthmus, and took it very ill if anyone spoke against their returning home; and, resolving to depart that night, the pilots had orders what course to steer.

Themistocles, in great distress that the Greeks should retire, and lose the advantage of the narrow seas and strait passage, and slip home every-one to his own city, considered with himself, and contrived that stratagem that was carried out by Sicinnus. This Sicinnus was a Persian captive, but a great lover of Themistocles, and the attendant of his children. Upon this occasion, he sent him privately to Xerxes, commanding him to tell the king that Themistocles, the admiral of the Athenians, having espoused his interest, wished to be the first to inform him that the Greeks were ready to make their escape, and that he counselled him to hinder their flight, to set upon them while they were in this confusion and at a distance from their land army, and hereby destroy all their forces by sea. Xerxes was very joyful at this message, and received it as from one who wished him all that was good, and immediately issued instructions to the commanders of his ships, that they should instantly set out with two hundred galleys to encompass all the islands, and enclose all the straits and passages, that none of the Greeks might escape, and that they should afterwards follow with the rest of their fleet at leisure. This being done, Aristides, the son of Lysimachus, was the first man that perceived it, and went to the tent of Themistocles, not out of any friendship, for he had been formerly ban-ished by his means, as has been related, but to inform him how they were encompassed by their enemies. Themistocles, knowing the generosity of Aristides, and much struck by his visit at that time, imparted to him all that he had transacted by Sicinnus, and entreated him that, as he would be more readily believed among the Greeks, he would make use of his credit to help to induce them to stay and fight their enemies in the narrow seas. Aristides applauded Themistocles, and went to the other commanders and captains of the galleys, and encouraged them to engage; yet they did not perfectly assent to him, till a galley of Tenos, which deserted from the Persians, of which Panætius was commander, came in, while they were still doubting, and confirmed the news that all the straits and passages were beset; and then their rage and fury, as well as their necessity, provoked them all to fight.

As soon as it was day, Xerxes placed himself high up, to view his fleet, and how it was set in order. Phanodemus says, he sat upon a promontory above the temple of Hercules, where the coast of Attica is separated from the island by a narrow channel; but Acestodorus writes, that it was in the confines of Megara, upon those hills which are called the Horns, where he sat in a chair of gold, with many secretaries about him to write down all that was done in the fight.

When Themistocles was about to sacrifice, close to the admiral's galley, there were three prisoners brought to him, fine looking men, and richly dressed in ornamented clothing and gold, said to be the children of Artayctes and Sandauce, sister to Xerxes. As soon as the prophet Euphrantides saw them, and observed that at the same time the fire blazed out from the offerings with a more than ordinary flame, and a man sneezed on the right, which was an intimation of a fortunate event, he took Themistocles by the hand, and bade him consecrate the three young men for sacrifices and offer them up with prayers for victory to Bacchus the Devourer; so should the Greeks not only save themselves, but also obtain victory. Themistocles was much disturbed at this strange and terrible prophecy, but the common people, who in any difficult crisis and great exigency ever look for relief rather to strange and extravagant than to reasonable means, calling upon Bacchus with one voice, led the captives to the altar, and compelled the execution of the sacrifice as the prophet had commanded. This is reported by Phanias the Lesbian, a philosopher well read in history.

The number of the enemy's ships the poet Æschylus gives in his tragedy called the Persians, as on his certain knowledge, in the following words:

> Xerxes, I know, did into battle lead
> One thousand ships; of more than usual speed
> Seven and two hundred. So it is agreed.

The Athenians had an hundred and eighty; in every ship eighteen men fought upon the deck, four of whom were archers and the rest men at arms.

As Themistocles had fixed upon the most advantageous place, so, with no less sagacity, he chose the best time of fighting; for he would not run the prows of his galleys against the Persians, nor begin the fight till the time of day was come, when there regularly blows in a fresh breeze from the open sea, and brings in with it a strong swell into the channel; which was no inconvenience to the Greek ships, which were low-built, and little above the water, but did much to hurt the Persians, which had high sterns and lofty decks, and were heavy and cumbrous in their movements, as it presented them broadside to the quick charges of the Greeks, who kept their eyes upon the motions of Themistocles, as their best example, and more particularly because, opposed to his ship, Ariamenes, admiral to Xerxes, a brave man and by far the best and worthiest of the king's brothers, was seen throwing darts and shooting arrows from his huge galley, as from the walls of a castle. Aminias the Decelean and Sosicles the Pedian, who sailed in the same vessel, upon the ships meeting stem to stem, and transfixing each the other with their brazen prows, so that they were fastened together, when Ariamenes attempted to board theirs, ran at him with their pikes, and thrust him into the sea; his body, as it floated amongst other shipwrecks, was known to Artemisia, and carried to Xerxes.

It is reported that, in the middle of the fight, a great flame rose into the air above the city of Eleusis, and that sounds and voices were heard through all the Thriasian plain, as far as the sea, sounding like a number of men accompanying and escorting the mystic Iacchus, and that a mist seemed to form and rise from the place from whence the sounds came, and, passing forward, fell upon the galleys. Others believed that they saw apparitions, in the shape of armed men, reaching out their hands from the island of Ægina before the Grecian galleys; and supposed they were the Æacidæ, whom they had invoked to their aid before the battle. The first man that took a ship was Lycomedes the Athenian, captain of the galley, who cut down its ensign, and dedicated it to Apollo the Laurel-crowned. And as the Persians fought in a narrow arm of the sea, and could bring but part of their fleet to fight, and fell foul of one another, the Greeks thus equalled them in strength, and fought with them till the evening forced them back, and obtained, as says Simonides, that noble and famous victory, than which neither amongst the Greeks nor barbarians was ever known more glorious exploit on the seas; by the joint valour, indeed, and zeal of all who fought, but by the wisdom and sagacity of Themistocles.

After this sea-fight, Xerxes, enraged at his ill-fortune, attempted, by casting great heaps of earth and stones into the sea, to stop up the channel and make a dam, upon which he might lead his land-forces over into the island of Salamis.

Themistocles, being desirous to try the opinion of Aristides, told him that he proposed to set sail for the Hellespont, to break the bridge of ships, so as to shut up, he said, Asia a prisoner within Europe; but Aristides, disliking the design, said: "We have hitherto fought with an enemy who has regarded little else but his pleasure and luxury; but if we shut him up within Greece, and drive him to necessity, he that is master of such great forces will no longer sit quietly with an umbrella of gold over his head, looking upon the fight for his pleasure; but in such a strait will attempt all things; he will be resolute, and appear himself in person upon all occasions, he will soon correct his errors, and supply what he has formerly omitted through remissness, and will be better advised in all things. Therefore, it is noways our interest, Themistocles," he said, "to take away the bridge that is already made, but rather to build another, if it were possible, that he might make his retreat with the more expedition." To which Themistocles answered: "If this be requisite, we must immediately use all diligence, art, and industry, to rid ourselves of him as soon as may be"; and to this purpose he found out among the captives one of the King of Persia's eunuchs, named Arnaces, whom he sent to the king, to inform him that the Greeks, being now victorious by sea, had decreed to sail to the Hellespont, where the boats were fastened together, and destroy the bridge; but that Themistocles, being concerned for the king, revealed this to him, that he might hasten towards the Asiatic seas, and pass over into his own dominions; and in the meantime would cause delays and hinder the confederates from pursuing him. Xerxes no sooner heard this, but, being very much terrified, he proceeded to retreat out of Greece with all speed. The prudence of Themistocles and Aristides in this was afterwards more fully understood at the battle of Platæa, where Mardonius, with a very small fraction of the forces of Xerxes, put the Greeks in danger of losing all.

Herodotus writes, that of all the cities of Greece, Ægina was held to have performed the best service in the war; while all single men yielded to Themistocles, though, out of envy, unwillingly; and when they returned to the entrance of Peloponnesus, where the several commanders delivered their suffrages at the altar, to determine who was most worthy, everyone gave the first vote for himself and the second for Themistocles. The Lacedæmonians carried him with them to Sparta, where, giving the rewards of valour to Eurybiades, and of wisdom and conduct to Themistocles, they crowned him with olive, presented him with the best chariot in the city, and sent three hundred young men to accompany him to the confines of their country. And at the next Olympic games, when Themistocles entered the course, the spectators took no farther notice of those who were contesting the prizes, but spent the whole day in looking upon him, showing him to the strangers, admiring him, and applauding him by clapping their hands, and other expressions of joy, so that he himself, much gratified, confessed to his friends that he then reaped the fruit of all his labours for the Greeks.

He was, indeed, by nature, a great lover of honour, as is evident from the anecdotes recorded of him. When chosen admiral by the Athenians, he would not quite conclude any single matter of business, either public or private, but deferred all till the day they were to set sail, that, by despatching a great quantity of business all at once, and having to meet a great variety of people, he might make an appearance of greatness and power. Viewing the dead bodies cast up by the sea, he perceived bracelets and necklaces of gold about them, yet passed on, only showing them to a friend that followed him, saying, "Take you these things, for you are not Themistocles." He said to Antiphates, a handsome young man, who had formerly avoided, but now in his glory courted him, "Time, young man, has taught us both a lesson." He said that the Athenians did not honour him or admire him, but made, as it were, a sort of plane-tree of him; sheltered themselves under him in bad weather, and as soon as it was fine, plucked his leaves and cut his branches. When the Seriphian told him that he had not obtained this honour by himself, but by the greatness of the city, he replied, "You speak truth; I should never have been famous if I had been of Seriphus; nor you, had you been of Athens." When another of the generals, who thought he had performed considerable service for the Athenians, boastingly compared his actions with those of Themistocles, he told him that once upon a time the Day after the Festival found fault with the Festival: "On you there is nothing but hurry and trouble and preparation, but, when I come, everybody sits down quietly and enjoys himself"; which the Festival admitted was true, but "if I had not come first, you would not have come at all." "Even so," he said, "if Themistocles had not come before, where had you been now?" Laughing at his own son, who got his mother, and, by his mother's means, his father also, to indulge him, he told him that he had the most power of anyone in Greece: "For the Athenians command the rest of Greece, I command the Athenians, your mother commands me, and you command your mother." Loving to be singular in all things, when he had land to sell, he ordered the crier to give notice that there were good neighbours near it. Of two who made love to his daughter, he preferred the man of worth to the one who was rich, saying he desired a man without riches, rather than riches without a man. Such was the character of his sayings.

After these things, he began to rebuild and fortify the city of Athens, bribing, as Theopompus reports, the Lacedæmonian ephors not to be against it, but, as most relate it, overreaching and deceiving them. For, under the pretext of an embassy, he went to Sparta, whereupon the Lacedæmonians charging him with rebuilding the walls, and Poliarchus coming on purpose from Ægina to denounce it, he denied the fact, bidding them to send people to Athens to see whether it were so or no; by which delay he got time for the building of the wall, and also placed these ambassadors in the hands of his countrymen as hostages for him; and so, when the Lacedæmonians knew the truth, they did him no hurt, but, suppressing all display of their anger for the present, sent him away.

Next he proceeded to establish the harbour of Piræus, observing the great natural advantages of the locality, and desirous to unite the whole city with the sea, and to reverse, in a manner, the policy of ancient Athenian kings, who, endeavouring to withdraw their subjects from the sea, and to accustom them to live, not by sailing about, but by planting and tilling the earth, spread the story of the dispute between Minerva and Neptune for the sovereignty of Athens, in which Minerva, by producing to the judges an olive tree, was declared to have won; whereas Themistocles did not only knead up, as Aristophanes says, the port and the city into one, but made the city absolutely the dependent and the adjunct of the port, and the land of the sea, which increased the power and confidence of the people against the nobility; the authority coming into the hands of sailors and boatswains and pilots. Thus it was one of the orders of the thirty tyrants, that the hustings in the assembly, which had faced towards the sea, should be turned round towards the land; implying their opinion that the empire by sea had been the origin of the democracy, and that the farming population were not so much opposed to oligarchy.

Themistocles, however, formed yet higher designs with a view to naval supremacy. For, after the departure of Xerxes, when the Grecian fleet was arrived at Pagasæ, where they wintered, Themistocles, in a public oration to the people of Athens, told them that he had a design to perform something that would tend greatly to their interests and safety, but was of such a nature that it could not be made generally public. The Athenians ordered him to impart it to Aristides only; and, if he approved of it, to put it in practice. And when Themistocles had discovered to him that his design was to burn the Grecian fleet in the haven of Pagasæ, Aristides coming out to the people, gave this report of the stratagem contrived by Themistocles, that no proposal could be more politic, or more dishonourable; on which the Athenians commanded Themistocles to think no farther of it.

When the Lacedæmonians proposed, at the general council of the Amphictyonians, that the representatives of those cities which were not in the league, nor had fought against the Persians, should be excluded, Themistocles, fearing that the Thessalians, with those of Thebes, Argos, and others, being thrown out of the council, the Lacedæmonians would become wholly masters of the votes, and do what they pleased, supported the deputies of the cities, and prevailed with the members then sitting to alter their opinion on this point, showing them that there were but one-and-thirty cities which had partaken in the war, and that most of these, also, were very small; how intolerable would it be, if the rest of Greece should be excluded, and the general council should come to be ruled by two or three great cities. By this, chiefly, he incurred the displeasure of the Lacedæmonians, whose honours and favours were now shown to Cimon, with a view to making him the opponent of the state policy of Themistocles.

He was also burdensome to the confederates, sailing about the islands and collecting money from them. Herodotus says, that, requiring money of those of the island of Andros, he told them that he had brought with him two goddesses, Persuasion and Force; and they answered him that they had also two great goddesses, which prohibited them from giving him any money, Poverty and Impossibility. Timocreon, the Rhodian poet, reprehends him somewhat bitterly for being wrought upon by money to let some who were banished return, while abandoning himself, who was his guest and friend. The verses are these:

> Pausanias you may praise, and Xanthippus, he be for,
> For Leutychidas, a third; Aristides, I proclaim,
> From the sacred Athens came.
> The one true man of all; for Themistocles Latona doth abhor,
> The liar, traitor, cheat, who to gain his filthy pay,
> Timocreon, his friend, neglected to restore
> To his native Rhodian shore;
> Three silver talents took and departed (curses with him) on his way,
> Restoring people here, expelling there, and killing here,
> Filling evermore his purse: and at the Isthmus gave a treat,
> To be laughed at, of cold meat,
> Which they ate, and prayed the gods someone else might give the
>   feast another year.

But after the sentence and banishment of Themistocles, Timocreon reviles him yet more immoderately and wildly in a poem that begins thus:

> Unto all the Greeks repair,
> O Muse, and tell these verses there,
> As is fitting and is fair.

* * *

The story is, that it was put to the question whether Timocreon should be banished for siding with the Persians, and Themistocles gave his vote against him. So when Themistocles was accused of intriguing with the Medes, Timocreon made these lines upon him:

> So now Timocreon, indeed, is not the sole friend of the Mede,
> There are some knaves besides; nor is it only mine that fails,
> But other foxes have lost tails.

When the citizens of Athens began to listen willingly to those who traduced and reproached him, he was forced, with somewhat obnoxious frequency, to put them in mind of the great services he had performed, and ask those who were offended with him whether they were weary with receiving benefits often from the same person, so rendering himself more odious. And he yet more provoked the people by building a temple to Diana with the epithet of Aristobule, or Diana of Best Counsel; intimating thereby, that he had given the best counsel, not only to the Athenians, but to all Greece. He built this temple near his own house, in the district called Melite, where now the public officers carry out the bodies of such as are executed, and throw the halters and clothes of those that are strangled or otherwise put to death. There is to this day a small figure of Themistocles in the temple of Diana of Best Counsel, which represents him to be a person not only of a noble mind, but also of a most heroic aspect. At length the Athenians banished him, making use of the ostracism to humble his eminence and authority, as they ordinarily did with all whom they thought too powerful, or, by their greatness, disproportionable to the equality thought requisite in a popular government. For the ostracism was instituted, not so much to punish the offender, as to mitigate and pacify the violence of the envious, who delighted to humble eminent men, and who, by fixing this disgrace upon them, might vent some part of their rancour.

Themistocles being banished from Athens, while he stayed at Argos the detection of Pausanias happened, which gave such advantage to his enemies, that Leobotes of Agraule, son of Alcmæon, indicted him of treason, the Spartans supporting him in the accusation.

When Pausanias went about this treasonable design, he concealed it at first from Themistocles, though he were his intimate friend; but when he saw him expelled out of the commonwealth, and how impatiently he took his banishment, he ventured to communicate it to him, and desired his assistance, showing him the king of Persia's letters, and exasperating him against the Greeks, as a villainous, ungrateful people. However, Themistocles immediately rejected the proposals of Pausanias, and wholly refused to be a party in the enterprise, though he never revealed his communications, nor disclosed the conspiracy to any man, either hoping that Pausanias would desist from his intentions, or expecting that so inconsiderate an attempt after such chimerical objects would be discovered by other means.

After that Pausanias was put to death, letters and writings being found concerning this matter, which rendered Themistocles suspected, the Lacedæmonians were clamorous against him, and his enemies among the Athenians accused him; when, being absent from Athens, he made his defence by letters, especially against the points that had been previously alleged against him. In answer to the malicious detractions of his enemies, he merely wrote to the citizens, urging that he who was always ambitious to govern, and not of a character or a disposition to serve, would never sell himself and his country into slavery to a barbarous and hostile nation.

Notwithstanding this, the people, being persuaded by his accusers, sent officers to take him and bring him away to be tried before a council of the Greeks, but, having timely notice of it, he passed over into the island of Corcyra, where the state was under obligations to him; for, being chosen as arbitrator in a difference between them and the Corinthians, he decided the controversy by ordering the Corinthians to pay down twenty talents, and declaring the town and island of Leucas a joint colony from both cities. From thence he fled into Epirus, and, the Athenians and Lacedæmonians still pursuing him, he threw himself upon chances of safety that seemed all but desperate. For he fled for refuge to Admetus, king of the Molossians, who had formerly made some request to the Athenians, when Themistocles was in the height of his authority, and had been disdainfully used and insulted by him, and had let it appear plain enough, that, could he lay hold of him, he would take his revenge. Yet in this misfortune, Themistocles, fearing the recent hatred of his neighbours and fellow-citizens more than the old displeasure of the king, put himself at his mercy and became an humble suppliant to Admetus, after a peculiar manner different from the custom of other countries. For taking the king's son, who was then a child, in his arms, he laid himself down at his hearth, this being the most sacred and only manner of supplication among the Molossians, which was not to be refused. And some say that his wife, Phthia, intimated to Themistocles this way of petitioning, and placed her young son with him before the hearth; others, that king Admetus, that he might be under a religious obligation not to deliver him up to his pursuers, prepared and enacted with him a sort of stage play to this effect. At this time Epicrates of Acharnæ privately conveyed his wife and children out of Athens, and sent them hither, for which afterwards Cimon condemned him and put him to death; as Stesimbrotus reports, and yet somehow, either forgetting this himself, or making Themistocles to be little mindful of it, says presently that he sailed into Sicily, and desired in marriage the daughter of Hiero, tyrant of Syracuse, promising to bring the Greeks under his power; and, on Hiero refusing him, departed thence into Asia; but this is not probable.

For Theophrastus writes, in his work on Monarchy, that when Hiero sent race horses to the Olympian games, and erected a pavilion sumptuously furnished, Themistocles made an oration to the Greeks, inciting them to pull down the tyrant's tent, and not to suffer his horses to run. Thucydides says, that, passing overland to the Ægæan Sea, he took ship at Pydna in the bay Therme, not being known to anyone in the ship, till, being terrified to see the vessel driven by the winds near to Naxos, which was then besieged by the Athenians, he made himself known to the master and pilot, and partly entreating them, partly threatening that if they went on shore he would accuse them, and make the Athenians to believe that they did not take him in out of ignorance, but that he had corrupted them with money from the beginning, he compelled them to bear off and stand out to sea, and sail forward towards the coast of Asia.

A great part of his estate was privately conveyed away by his friends, and sent after him by sea into Asia; besides which, there was discovered and confiscated to the value of fourscore talents, as Theophrastus writes; Theopompus says an hundred; though Themistocles was never worth three talents before he was concerned in public affairs.

When he arrived at Cyme, and understood that all along the coast there were many laid wait for him, and particularly Ergoteles and Pythodorus (for the game was worth the hunting for such as were thankful to make money by any means, the king of Persia having offered by public proclamation two hundred talents to him that should take him), he fled to Ægæ, a small city of the Æolians, where no one knew him but only his host Nicogenes, who was the richest man in Æolia, and well known to the great men of Inner Asia. While Themistocles lay hid for some days in his house, one night, after a sacrifice and supper ensuing, Olbius, the attendant upon Nicogenes' children, fell into a sort of frenzy and fit of inspiration, and cried out in verse—

Night shall speak, and night instruct thee,
By the voice of night conduct thee.

After this, Themistocles, going to bed, dreamed that he saw a snake coil itself up upon his belly, and so creep to his neck; then, as soon as it touched his face, it turned into an eagle, which spread its wings over him, and took him up and flew away with him a great distance; then there appeared a herald's golden wand, and upon this at last it set him down securely, after infinite terror and disturbance.

His departure was effected by Nicogenes by the following artifice: The barbarous nations, and amongst them the Persians especially, are extremely jealous, severe, and suspicious about their women, not only their wives, but also their bought slaves and concubines, whom they keep so strictly that no one ever sees them abroad; they spend their lives shut up within doors, and, when they take a journey, are carried in close tents, curtained in on all sides, and set upon a wagon. Such a travelling carriage being prepared for Themistocles, they hid him in it, and carried him on his journey, and told those whom they met or spoke with upon the road that they were conveying a young Greek woman out of Ionia to a nobleman at court.

Thucydides and Charon of Lampsacus say that Xerxes was dead, and that Themistocles had an interview with his son; but Ephorus, Dinon, Clitarchus, Heraclides, and many others, write that he came to Xerxes. The chronological tables better agree with the account of Thucydides, and yet neither can their statements be said to be quite set at rest.

When Themistocles was come to the critical point, he applied himself first to Artabanus, commander of a thousand men, telling him that he was a Greek, and desired to speak with the king about important affairs concerning which the king was extremely solicitous. Artabanus answered him: "O stranger, the laws of men are different, and one thing is honourable to one man, and to others another; but it is honourable for all to honour and observe their own laws. It is the habit of the Greeks, we are told, to honour, above all things, liberty and equality; but amongst our many excellent laws, we account this the most excellent, to honour the king, and to worship him, as the image of the great preserver of the universe; if, then, you shall consent to our laws, and fall down before the king and worship him, you may both see him and speak to him; but if your mind be otherwise, you must make use of others to intercede for you, for it is not the national custom here for the king to give audience to anyone that doth not fall down before him." Themistocles, hearing this, replied: "Artabanus, I, that come hither to increase the power and glory of the king, will not only submit myself to his laws, since so it hath pleased the god who exalteth the Persian empire to this greatness, but will also cause many more to be worshippers and adorers of the king. Let not this, therefore, be an impediment why I should not communicate to the king what I have to impart." Artabanus asking him, "Who must we tell him that you are? For your words signify you to be no ordinary person," Themistocles answered, "No man, O Artabanus, must be informed of this before the king himself." Thus Phanias relates; to which Eratosthenes, in his treatise on Riches, adds, that it was by the means of a woman of Eretria, who was kept by Artabanus, that he obtained this audience and interview with him.

When he was introduced to the king, and had paid his reverence to him, he stood silent, till the king commanding the interpreter to ask him who he was, he replied, "O king, I am Themistocles the Athenian, driven into banishment by the Greeks. The evils that I have done to the Persians are numerous; but my benefits to them yet greater, in withholding the Greeks from pursuit, so soon as the deliverance of my own country allowed me to show kindness also to you. I come with a mind suited to my present calamities; prepared alike for favours and for anger; to welcome your gracious reconciliation, and to deprecate your wrath. Take my own countrymen for witnesses of the services I have done for Persia, and make use of this occasion to show the world your virtue, rather than to satisfy your indignation. If you save me, you will save your suppliant; if otherwise, will destroy an enemy of the Greeks." He talked also of divine admonitions, such as the vision which he saw at Nicogenes' house, and the direction given him by the oracle of Dodona, where Jupiter commanded him to go to him that had a name like his, by which he understood that he was sent from Jupiter to him, seeing that they both were great, and had the name of kings.

The king heard him attentively, and, though he admired his temper and courage, gave him no answer at that time; but, when he was with his intimate friends, rejoiced in his great good fortune, and esteemed himself very happy in this, and prayed to his god Arimanius, that all his enemies might be ever of the same mind with the Greeks, to abuse and expel the bravest men amongst them. Then he sacrificed to the gods, and presently fell to drinking, and was so well pleased, that in the night, in the middle of his sleep, he cried out for joy three times, "I have Themistocles the Athenian."

In the morning, calling together the chief of his court, he had Themistocles brought before him, who expected no good of it, when he saw, for example, the guards fiercely set against him as soon as they learnt his name, and giving him ill language. As he came forward towards the king, who was seated, the rest keeping silence, passing by Roxanes, a commander of a thousand men, he heard him, with a slight groan, say, without stirring out of his place, "You subtle Greek serpent, the king's good genius hath brought thee thither." Yet, when he came into the presence, and again fell down, the king saluted him, and spake to him kindly, telling him he was now indebted to him two hundred talents; for it was just and reasonable that he should receive the reward which was proposed to whosoever should bring Themistocles; and promising much more, and encouraging him, he commanded him to speak freely what he would concerning the affairs' of Greece. Themistocles replied, that a man's discourse was like to a rich Persian carpet, the beautiful figures and patterns of which can only be shown by spreading and extending it out; when it is contracted and folded up, they are obscure and lost; and, therefore, he desired time. The king being pleased with the comparison, and bidding him take what time he would, he desired a year; in which time, having learnt the Persian language sufficiently, he spoke with the king by himself without the help of an interpreter, it being supposed that he discoursed only about the affairs of Greece; but there happening, at the same time, great alterations at court, and removals of the king's favourites, he drew upon himself the envy of the great people, who imagined that he had taken the boldness to speak concerning them. For the favours shown to other strangers were nothing in comparison with the honours conferred on him; the king invited him to partake of his own pastimes and recreations both at home and abroad, carrying him with him a-hunting, and made him his intimate so far that he permitted him to see the queen-mother, and converse frequently with her. By the king's command, he also was made acquainted with the Magian learning.

When Demaratus the Lacedæmonian, being ordered by the king to ask whatsoever he pleased, that it should immediately be granted him, desired that he might make his public entrance, and be carried in state through the city of Sardis, with the tiara set in the royal manner upon his head, Mithropaustes, cousin to the king, touched him on the head, and told him that he had no brains for the royal tiara to cover, and if Jupiter should give him his lightning and thunder, he would not any the more be

Jupiter for that; the king also repulsed him with anger, resolving never to be reconciled to him, but to be inexorable to all supplications on his behalf. Yet Themistocles pacified him, and prevailed with him to forgive him. And it is reported that the succeeding kings, in whose reigns there was a greater communication between the Greeks and Persians, when they invited any considerable Greek into their service, to encourage him, would write, and promise him that he should be as great with them as Themistocles had been. They relate, also, how Themistocles, when he was in great prosperity, and courted by many, seeing himself splendidly served at his table, turned to his children and said, "Children, we had been undone if we had not been undone." Most writers say that he had three cities given him, Magnesia, Myus, and Lampsacus, to maintain him in bread, meat, and wine. Neanthes of Cyzicus, and Phanias, add two more, the city of Palæscepsis, to provide him with clothes, and Percote, with bedding and furniture for his house.

As he was going down towards the sea-coast to take measures against Greece, a Persian whose name was Epixyes, governor of the upper Phrygia, laid wait to kill him, having for that purpose provided a long time before a number of Pisidians, who were to set upon him when he should stop to rest at a city that is called Lion's-head. But Themistocles, sleeping in the middle of the day, saw the Mother of the gods appear to him in a dream and say unto him, "Themistocles, keep back from the Lion's-head, for fear you fall into the lion's jaws; for this advice I expect that your daughter Mnesiptolema should be my servant." Themistocles was much astonished, and when he had made his vows to the goddess, left the broad road, and, making a circuit, went another way, changing his intended station to avoid that place, and at night took up his rest in the fields. But one of the sumpter-horses, which carried the furniture for his tent, having fallen that day into the river, his servants spread out the tapestry, which was wet, and hung it up to dry; in the meantime the Pisidians made towards them with their swords drawn, and, not discerning exactly by the moon what it was that was stretched out, thought it to be the tent of Themistocles, and that they should find him resting himself within it; but when they came near, and lifted up the hangings, those who watched there fell upon them and took them. Themistocles, having escaped this great danger, in admiration of the goodness of the goddess that appeared to him, built, in memory of it, a temple in the city of Magnesia, which is dedicated to Dindymene, Mother of the gods, in which he consecrated and devoted his daughter Mnesiptolema to her service.

When he came to Sardis, he visited the temples of the gods, and observing, at his leisure, their buildings, ornaments, and the number of their offerings, he saw in the temple of the Mother of the gods the statue of a virgin in brass, two cubits high, called the water-bringer. Themistocles had caused this to be made and set up when he was surveyor of the waters at Athens, out of the fines of those whom he detected in drawing off and diverting the public water by pipes for their private use; and whether he had some regret to see this image in captivity, or was desirous to let the Athenians see in what great credit and authority he was with the king, he entered into a treaty with the governor to persuade him to send this statue back to Athens, which so enraged the Persian officer, that he told him he would write the king word of it. Themistocles, being affrighted hereat, got access to his wives and concubines, by presents of money to whom he appeased the fury of the governor; and afterwards behaved with more reserve and circumspection, fearing the envy of the Persians, and did not, as Theopompus writes, continue to travel about Asia, but lived quietly in his own house in Magnesia, where for a long time he passed his days in great security, being courted by all, and enjoying rich presents, and honoured equally with the greatest persons in the Persian empire; the king, at that time, not minding his concerns with Greece, being taken up with the affairs of inner Asia.

But when Egypt revolted, being assisted by the Athenians, and the Greek galleys roved about as far as Cyprus and Cilicia, and Cimon had made himself master of the seas, the king turned his thoughts thither, and, bending his mind chiefly to resist the Greeks, and to check the growth of their power against him, began to raise forces, and send out commanders, and to despatch messengers to Themistocles at Magnesia, to put him in mind of his promise, and to summon him to act against the Greeks. Yet this did not increase his hatred nor exasperate him against the Athenians, neither was he in any way elevated with the thoughts of the honour and powerful command he was to have in this war; but judging, perhaps, that the object would not be attained, the Greeks having at that time, beside other great commanders, Cimon, in particular, who was gaining wonderful military successes; but chiefly being ashamed to sully the glory of his former great actions, and of his many victories and trophies, he determined to put a conclusion to his life, agreeable to its previous course. He sacrificed to the gods, and invited his friends; and, having entertained them and shaken hands with them, drank bull's blood, as is the usual story; as others state, a poison producing instant death; and ended his days in the city of Magnesia, having lived sixty-five years, most of which he had spent in politics and in wars, in government and command. The king being informed of the cause and manner of his death, admired him more than ever, and continued to show kindness to his friends and relations.

Themistocles left three sons by Archippe, daughter to Lysander of Alopece—Archeptolis, Poleuctus, and Cleophantus. Plato, the philosopher, mentions the last as a most excellent horseman, but otherwise insignificant person; of two sons yet older than these, Neocles and Diocles, Neocles died when he was young by the bite of a horse, and Diocles was adopted by his grandfather, Lysander. He had many daughters, of whom Mnesiptolema, whom he had by a second marriage, was wife to Archeptolis, her brother by another mother; Italia was married to Panthoides, of the island of Chios; Sybaris to Nicomedes the Athenian. After the death of Themistocles, his nephew, Phrasicles, went to Magnesia, and married, with her brothers' consent, another daughter, Nicomache, and took charge of her sister Asia, the youngest of all the children.

The Magnesians possess a splendid sepulchre of Themistocles, placed in the middle of their market place. It is not worth while taking notice of what Andocides states in his address to his Friends concerning his remains, how the Athenian robbed his tomb, and threw his ashes into the air; for he feigns this, to exasperate the oligarchical faction against the people; and there is no man living but knows that Phylarchus simply invents in his history, where he all but uses an actual stage machine, and brings in Neocles and Demopolis as the sons of Themistocles, to incite or move compassion, as if he were writing a tragedy. Diodorus the cosmographer says, in his work on Tombs, but by conjecture rather than of certain knowledge, that near to the haven of Piræus where the land runs out like an elbow from the promontory of Alcimus, when you have doubled the cape and passed inward where the sea is always calm, there is a large piece of masonry, and upon this the Tomb of Themistocles, in the shape of an altar; and Plato the comedian confirms this, he believes, in these verses:

> Thy tomb is fairly placed upon the strand,
> Where merchants still shall greet it with the land;
> Still in and out 'twill see them come and go,
> And watch the galleys as they race below.

Various honours also and privileges were granted to the kindred of Themistocles at Magnesia, which were observed down to our times, and were enjoyed by another Themistocles of Athens, with whom I had an ultimate acquaintance and friendship in the house of Ammonius the philosopher.

CAMILLUS

AMONG THE MANY REMARKABLE THINGS THAT ARE RELATED OF FURIUS Camillus it seems singular and strange above all, that he, who continually was in the highest commands, and obtained the greatest successes, was five times chosen dictator, triumphed four times, and was styled a second founder of Rome, yet never was so much as once consul. The reason of which was the state and temper of the commonwealth at that time; for the people, being at dissension with the senate, refused to return consuls, but in their stead elected other magistrates, called military tribunes, who acted, indeed, with full consular power, but were thought to exercise a less obnoxious amount of authority, because it was divided among a larger number; for to have the management of affairs intrusted to the hands of six persons rather than two was some satisfaction to the opponents of oligarchy. This was the condition of the times when Camillus was in the height of his actions and glory, and, although the government in the meantime had often proceeded to consular elections, yet he could never persuade himself to be consul against the inclination of the people. In all his other administrations, which were many and various, he so behaved himself, that, when alone in authority, he exercised his power as in common, but the honour of all actions redounded entirely to himself, even when in joint commission with others; the reason of the former was his moderation in command; of the latter, his great judgment and wisdom, which gave him without controversy the first place.

The house of the Furii was not, at that time, of any considerable distinction; he, by his own acts, first raised himself to honour, serving under Postumius Tubertis, dictator, in the great battle against the Æquians and Volscians. For riding out from the rest of the army, and in the charge receiving a wound in his thigh, he for all that did not quit the fight, but, letting the dart drag in the wound, and engaging with the bravest of the enemy, put them to flight; for which action, among other rewards bestowed on him, he was created censor, an office in those days of great repute and authority. During his censorship one very good act of his is recorded, that, whereas the wars had made many widows, he obliged such as had no wives, some by fair persuasion, others by threatening to set fines on their heads, to take them in marriage; another necessary one, in causing orphans to be rated, who before were exempted from taxes, the frequent wars requiring more than ordinary expenses to maintain them. What, however, pressed them most was the siege of Veii. Some call this people Veientani. This was the head city of Tuscany, not inferior to Rome, either in number of arms or multitude of soldiers, insomuch that, presuming on her wealth and luxury, and priding herself upon her refinement and sumptuousness, she engaged in many honourable contests with the Romans for glory and empire. But now they abandoned their former ambitious hopes, having been weakened by great defeats, so that, having fortified themselves with high and strong walls, and furnished the city with all sorts of weapons offensive and defensive, as likewise with corn and all manner of provisions, they cheerfully endured a siege, which, though tedious to them, was no less troublesome and distressing to the besiegers. For the Romans, having never been accustomed to stay away from home except in summer, and for no great length of time, and constantly to winter at home, were then first compelled by the tribunes to build forts in the enemy's country, and raising strong works about their camp, to join winter and summer together. And now, the seventh year of the war drawing to an end, the commanders began to be suspected as too slow and remiss in driving on the siege, insomuch that they were discharged and others chosen for the war, among whom was Camillus, then second time tribune. But at present he had no hand in the siege, the duties that fell by lot to him being to make war upon the Faliscans and Capenates, who, taking advantage of the Romans being occupied on all hands, had carried ravages into their country, and, through all the Tuscan war, given them much annoyance, but were now reduced by Camillus, and with great loss shut up within their walls.

And now, in the very heat of the war, a strange phenomenon in the Alban lake, which, in the absence of any known cause and explanation by natural reasons, seemed as great a prodigy as the most incredible that are reported, occasioned great alarm. It was the beginning of autumn, and the summer now ending had, to all observation, been neither rainy nor much troubled with southern winds; and many of the lakes, brooks, and springs of all sorts with which Italy abounds, some were wholly dried up, others drew very little water with them; all the rivers, as is usual in summer, ran in a very low and hollow channel. But the Alban lake, that is fed by no other waters but its own, and is on all sides encircled with fruitful mountains, without any cause, unless it were divine, began visibly to rise and swell, increasing to the feet of the mountains, and by degrees reaching the level of the very tops of them, and all this without any waves or agitation. At first it was the wonder of shepherds and herdsmen; but when the earth, which, like a great dam, held up the lake from falling into the lower grounds, through the quantity and weight of water was broken down, and in a violent stream it ran through the ploughed fields and plantations to discharge itself in the sea, it not only struck terror into the Romans, but was thought by all the inhabitants of Italy to portend some extraordinary event. But the greatest talk of it was in the camp that besieged Veii, so that in the town itself, also, the occurrence became known.

As in long sieges it commonly happens that parties on both sides meet often and converse with one another, so it chanced that a Roman had gained much confidence and familiarity with one of the besieged, a man versed in ancient prophecies, and of repute for more than ordinary skill in divination. The Roman, observing him to be overjoyed at the story of the lake, and to mock at the siege, told him that this was not the only prodigy that of late had happened to the Romans; others more wonderful yet than this had befallen them, which he was willing to communicate to him, that he might the better provide for his private interests in these public distempers. The man greedily embraced the proposal, expecting to hear some wonderful secrets; but when, by little and little, he had led him on in conversation and insensibly drawn him a good way from the gates of the city, he snatched him up by the middle, being stronger than he, and, by the assistance of others that came running from the camp, seized and delivered him to the commanders. The man, reduced to this necessity, and sensible now that destiny was not to be avoided, discovered to them the secret oracles of Veii; that it was not possible the city should be taken, until the Alban lake, which now broke forth and had found out new passages, was drawn back from that course, and so diverted that it could not mingle with the sea. The senate, having heard and satisfied themselves about the matter, decreed to send to Delphi, to ask counsel of the god. The messengers were persons of the highest repute, Licinius Cossus,

Valerius Potitus, and Fabius Ambustus; who, having made their voyage by sea and consulted the god, returned with other answers, particularly that there had been a neglect of some of their national rites relating to the Latin feasts; but the Alban water the oracle commanded, if it were possible, they should keep from the sea, and shut it up in its ancient bounds; but if that was not to be done, then they should carry it off by ditches and trenches into the lower grounds, and so dry it up; which message being delivered, the priests performed what related to the sacrifices, and the people went to work and turned the water.

And now the senate, in the tenth year of the war, taking away all other commands, created Camillus dictator, who chose Cornelius Scipio for his general of horse. And in the first place he made vows unto the gods, that, if they would grant a happy conclusion of the war, he would celebrate to their honour the great games, and dedicate a temple to the goddess whom the Romans call Matuta, the Mother, though, from the ceremonies which are used, one would think she was Leucothea. For they take a servant-maid into the secret part of the temple, and there cuff her, and drive her out again, and they embrace their brothers' children in place of their own; and, in general, the ceremonies of the sacrifice remind one of the nursing of Bacchus by Ino, and the calamities occasioned by her husband's concubine. Camillus, having made these vows, marched into the country of the Faliscans, and in a great battle overthrew them and the Capenates, their confederates; afterwards he turned to the siege of Veii, and, finding that to take it by assault would prove a difficult and hazardous attempt, proceeded to cut mines underground, the earth about the city being easy to break up, and allowing such depth for the works as would prevent their being discovered by the enemy. This design going on in a hopeful way, he openly gave assaults to the enemy, to keep them to the walls, whilst they that worked underground in the mines were, without being perceived, arrived within the citadel, close to the temple of Juno, which was the greatest and most honoured in all the city. It is said that the prince of the Tuscans was at that very time at sacrifice, and that the priest, after he had looked into the entrails of the beast, cried out with a loud voice that the gods would give victory to those that should complete those offerings; and that the Romans who were in the mines, hearing the words, immediately pulled down the floor, and, ascending with noise and clashing weapons, frightened away the enemy, and, snatching up the entrails, carried them to Camillus. But this may look like a fable. The city, however, being taken by storm, and the soldiers busied in pillaging and gathering an infinite quantity of riches and spoils, Camillus, from the high tower, viewing what was done, at first wept for pity; and when they that were by congratulated his success, he lifted up his hands to heaven, and broke out into this prayer: "O most mighty Jupiter, and ye gods that are judges of good and evil actions, ye know that not without just cause, but constrained by necessity, we have been forced to revenge ourselves on the city of our unrighteous and wicked enemies. But if, in the vicissitude of things, there may be any calamity due, to counterbalance this great felicity, I beg that it may be diverted from the city and army of the Romans, and fall, with as little hurt as may be, upon my own head." Having said these words, and just turning about (as the custom of the Romans is to turn to the right after adoration or prayer), he stumbled and fell, to the astonishment of all that were present. But, recovering himself presently from the fall, he told them that he had received what he had prayed for, a small mischance, in compensation for the greatest good fortune.

Having sacked the city, he resolved, according as he had vowed, to carry Juno's image to Rome; and, the workmen being ready for that purpose, he sacrificed to the goddess, and made his supplications that she would be pleased to accept of their devotion toward her, and graciously vouchsafe to accept of a place among the gods that presided at Rome; and the statue, they say, answered in a low voice that she was ready and willing to go. Livy writes, that, in praying, Camillus touched the goddess, and invited her, and that some of the standers-by cried out that she was willing and would come. They who stand up for the miracle and endeavour to maintain it have one great advocate on their side in the wonderful fortune of the city, which, from a small and contemptible beginning, could never have attained to that greatness and power without many signal manifestations of the divine presence and cooperation. Other wonders of the like nature, drops of sweat seen to stand on statues, groans heard from them, the figures seen to turn round and to close their eyes, are recorded by many ancient historians; and we ourselves could relate divers wonderful things, which we have been told by men of our own time, that are not lightly to be rejected; but to give too easy credit to such things, or wholly to disbelieve them, is equally dangerous, so incapable is human infirmity of keeping any bounds, or exercising command over itself, running off sometimes to superstition and dotage, at other times to the contempt and neglect of all that is supernatural. But moderation is best, and to avoid all extremes.

Camillus, however, whether puffed up with the greatness of his achievement in conquering a city that was the rival of Rome, and had held out a ten years' siege, or exalted with the felicitations of those that were about him, assumed to himself more than became a civil and legal magistrate; among other things, in the pride and haughtiness of his triumph, driving through Rome in a chariot drawn with four white horses, which no general either before or since ever did; for the Romans consider such a mode of conveyance to be sacred, and specially set apart to the king, and father of the gods. This alienated the hearts of his fellow-citizens, who were not accustomed to such pomp and display.

The second pique they had against him was his opposing the law by which the city was to be divided; for the tribunes of the people brought forward a motion that the people and senate should be divided into two parts, one of which should remain at home, the other, as the lot should decide, remove to the new-taken city. By which means they should not only have much more room, but, by the advantage of two great and magnificent cities, be better able to maintain their territories and their fortunes in general. The people, therefore, who were numerous and indigent, greedily embraced it, and crowded continually to the forum, with tumultuous demands to have it put to the vote. But the senate and the noblest citizens judging the proceedings of the tribunes to tend rather to a destruction than a division of Rome, greatly averse to it, went to Camillus for assistance, who, fearing the result if it came to a direct contest, contrived to occupy the people with other business, and so staved it off. He thus became unpopular. But the greatest and most apparent cause of their dislike against him arose from the tenths of the spoil; the multitude having here if not a just, yet a plausible case against him. For it seems, as he went to the siege of Veii, he had vowed to Apollo that if he took the city he would dedicate to him the tenth of the spoil. The city being taken and sacked, whether he was loth to trouble the soldiers at that time, or that through the multitude of business he had forgotten his vow, he suffered them to enjoy that part of the spoils also. Sometime afterwards, when his authority was laid down, he brought the matter before the senate, and the priests, at the same time, reported, out of the sacrifices, that there were intimations of divine anger, requiring propitiations and offerings. The senate decreed the obligations to be in force.

But seeing it was difficult for everyone to produce the very same things they had taken, to be divided anew, they ordained that everyone upon oath should bring into the public the tenth part of his gains. This occasioned many annoyances and hardships to the soldiers, who were poor men, and had endured much in the war, and now were forced, out of what they had gained and spent, to bring in so great a proportion. Camillus, being assaulted by their clamour and tumults, for want of a better excuse, betook himself to the poorest of defences, confessing he had forgotten his vow; they in turn complained that he had vowed the tenth of the enemy's goods, and now levied it out of the tenth of the citizens'. Nevertheless, everyone having brought in his due proportion, it was decreed that out of it a bowl of massy gold should be made, and sent to Delphi. And when there was great scarcity of gold in the city, and the magistrates were considering where to get it, the Roman ladies, meeting together and consulting among themselves, out of the golden ornaments they wore contributed as much as went to the making of the offering, which in weight came to eight talents of gold. The senate, to give them the honour they had deserved, ordained that funeral orations should be used at the obsequies of women as well as men, it having never before been a custom that any women after death should receive any public eulogy. Choosing out, therefore, three of the noblest citizens as a deputation, they sent them in a vessel of war, well manned and sumptuously adorned. Storm and calm at sea may both, they say, alike be dangerous; as they at this time experienced, being brought almost to the very brink of destruction, and, beyond all expectation, escaping. For near the isles of Æolus the wind slacking, galleys of the Lipareans came upon them, taking them for pirates; and, when they held up their hands as suppliants, forbore indeed from violence, but took their ship in tow, and carried her into the harbour, where they exposed to sale their goods and persons as lawful prize, they being pirates; and scarcely, at last, by the virtue and interest of one man, Timasitheus by name, who was in office as general, and used his utmost persuasion, they were, with much ado, dismissed. He, however, himself sent out some of his own vessels with them, to accompany them in their voyage and assist them at the dedication; for which he received honours at Rome, as he had deserved.

And now the tribunes of the people again resuming their motion for the division of the city, the war against the Faliscans luckily broke out, giving liberty to the chief citizens to choose what magistrates they pleased, and to appoint Camillus military tribune, with five colleagues; affairs then requiring a commander of authority and reputation, as well as experience. And when the people had ratified the election, he marched with his forces into the territories of the Faliscans, and laid siege to Falerii, a well-fortified city, and plentifully stored with all necessaries of war. And although he perceived it would be no small work to take it, and no little time would be required for it, yet he was willing to exercise the citizens and keep them abroad, that they might have no leisure, idling at home, to follow the tribunes in factions and seditions; a very common remedy, indeed, with the Romans, who thus carried off, like good physicians, the ill humours of their commonwealth. The Falerians, trusting in the strength of their city, which was well fortified on all sides, made so little account of the siege, that all, with the exception of those that guarded the walls, as in times of peace, walked about the streets in their common dress; the boys went to school, and were led by their master to play and exercise about the town walls; for the Falerians, like the Greeks, used to have a single teacher for many pupils, wishing their children to live and be brought up from the beginning in each other's company.

This schoolmaster, designing to betray the Falerians by their children, led them out everyday under the town wall, at first but a little way, and, when they had exercised, brought them home again. Afterwards by degrees he drew them farther and farther, till by practice he had made them bold and fearless, as if no danger was about them; and at last, having got them all together, he brought them to the outposts of the Romans, and delivered them up, demanding to be led to Camillus. Where being come, and standing in the middle, he said that he was the master and teacher of these children, but preferring his favour before all other obligations, he was come to deliver up his charge to him, and, in that, the whole city. When Camillus had heard him out, he was astounded at the treachery of the act, and, turning to the standers-by, observed that "war, indeed, is of necessity attended with much injustice and violence! Certain laws, however, all good men observe even in war itself, nor is victory so great an object as to induce us to incur for its sake obligations for base and impious acts. A great general should rely on his own virtue, and not on other men's vices." Which said, he commanded the officers to tear off the man's clothes, and bind his hands behind him, and give the boys rods and scourges, to punish the traitor and drive him back to the city. By this time the Falerians had discovered the treachery of the schoolmaster, and the city, as was likely, was fall of lamentations and cries for their calamity, men and women of worth running in distraction about the walls and gates; when, behold, the boys came whipping their master on naked and bound, calling Camillus their preserver and god and father. Insomuch that it struck not only into the parents, but the rest of the citizens that saw what was done, such admiration and love of Camillus' justice, that, immediately meeting in assembly, they sent ambassadors to him, to resign whatever they had to his disposal.

Camillus sent them to Rome, where, being brought into the senate, they spoke to this purpose: that the Romans, preferring justice before victory, had taught them rather to embrace submission than liberty; they did not so much confess themselves to be inferior in strength, as they must acknowledge them to be superior in virtue. The senate remitted the whole matter to Camillus, to judge and order as he thought fit; who, taking a sum of money of the Falerians, and, making a peace with the whole nation of the Faliscans, returned home.

But the soldiers, who had expected to have the pillage of the city, when they came to Rome empty-handed, railed against Camillus among their fellow-citizens, as a hater of the people, and one that grudged all advantage to the poor. Afterwards, when the tribunes of the people again brought their motion for dividing the city to the vote, Camillus appeared openly against it, shrinking from no unpopularity, and inveighing boldly against the promoters of it, and so urging and constraining the multitude that contrary to their inclinations they rejected the proposal but yet hated Camillus. Insomuch that though a great misfortune befell him in his family (one of his two sons dying of a disease), commiseration for this could not in the least make them abate their malice. And indeed he took this loss with immoderate sorrow, being a man naturally of a mild and tender disposition, and when the accusation was preferred against him, kept his house, and mourned amongst the women of his family.

His accuser was Lucius Apuleius; the charge, appropriation of the Tuscan spoils; certain brass gates, part of those spoils, were said to be in his possession. The people were exasperated against him, and it was plain they would take hold of any occasion to condemn him. Gathering, therefore, together his friends and fellow-soldiers, and such as had borne command with him, a considerable number in all, he besought them that they would not suffer him to be unjustly overborne by shameful accusations, and left the mock and scorn of his enemies. His friends, having advised and consulted among themselves, made answer, that, as to the sentence, they did not see how they could help him, but that they would contribute to whatsoever fine should be set upon him. Not able to endure so great an indignity, he resolved, in his anger, to leave the city, and go into exile; and so, having taken leave of his wife and his son, he went silently to the gate of the city, and there stopping and turning round, stretched out his hands to the Capitol, and prayed to the gods, that if, without any fault of his own, but merely through the malice and violence of the people, he was driven out into banishment, the Romans might quickly repent of it; and that all mankind might witness their need for the assistance, and desire for the return of Camillus.

Thus, like Achilles, having left his imprecations on the citizens, he went into banishment; so that, neither appearing nor making defence, he was condemned in the sum of fifteen thousand *ases,* which, reduced to silver, make one thousand five hundred drachmas; for the *as* was the money of the time, ten of such copper pieces making the *denarius,* or piece of ten. And there is not a Roman but believes that immediately upon the prayers of Camillus, a sudden judgment followed, and that he received a revenge for the injustice done unto him; which though we cannot think was pleasant, but rather grievous and bitter to him, yet was very remarkable, and noised over the whole world; such a punishment visited the city of Rome, an era of such loss and danger and disgrace so quickly succeeded; whether it thus fell out by fortune, or it be the office of some god not to see injured virtue go unavenged.

The first token that seemed to threaten some mischief to ensue was the death of the censor Julius; for the Romans have a religious reverence for the office of a censor, and esteem it sacred. The second was that, just before Camillus went into exile, Marcus Cædicius, a person of no great distinction, nor of the rank of senator, but esteemed a good and respectable man, reported to the military tribunes a thing worthy their consideration; that, going along the night before in the street called the New Way, and being called by somebody in a loud voice, he turned about, but could see no one, but heard a voice greater than human, which said these words, "Go, Marcus Cædicius, and early in the morning tell the military tribunes that they are shortly to expect the Gauls." But the tribunes made a mock and sport with the story, and a little after came Camillus' banishment.

The Gauls are of the Celtic race, and are reported to have been compelled by their numbers to leave their country, which was insufficient to sustain them all, and to have gone in search of other homes. And being, many thousands of them, young men and able to bear arms, and carrying with them a still greater number of women and young children, some of them, passing the Riphæan mountains, fell upon the Northern Ocean, and possessed themselves of the farthest parts of Europe; others, seating themselves between the Pyrenean mountains and the Alps, lived there a considerable time, near to the Senones and Celtorii; but, afterwards tasting wine which was then first brought them out of Italy, they were all so much taken with the liquor, and transported with the hitherto unknown delight, that, snatching up their arms and taking their families along with them, they marched directly to the Alps, to find out the country which yielded such fruit, pronouncing all others barren and useless. He that first brought wine among them and was the chief instigator of their coming into Italy is said to have been one Aruns, a Tuscan, a man of noble extraction, and not of bad natural character, but involved in the following misfortune. He was guardian to an orphan, one of the richest of the country, and much admired for his beauty, whose name was Lucumo. From his childhood he had been bred up with Aruns in his family, and when now grown up did not leave his house, professing to wish for the enjoyment of his society. And thus for a great while he secretly enjoyed Aruns' wife, corrupting her, and himself corrupted by her. But when they were both so far gone in their passion that they could neither refrain their lust nor conceal it, the young man seized the woman and openly sought to carry her away. The husband, going to law, and finding himself overpowered by the interest and money of his opponent, left his country and, hearing of the state of the Gauls, went to them, and was the conductor of their expedition into Italy.

At their first coming they at once possessed themselves of all that country which anciently the Tuscans inhabited, reaching from the Alps to both the seas, as the names themselves testify; for the North or Adriatic Sea is named from the Tuscan city Adria, and that to the south the Tuscan Sea simply. The whole country is rich in fruit trees, has excellent pasture, and is well watered with rivers. It had eighteen large and beautiful cities, well provided with all the means for industry and wealth, and all the enjoyments and pleasures of life. The Gauls cast out the Tuscans, and seated themselves in them. But this was long before.

The Gauls at this time were besieging Clusium, a Tuscan city. The Clusinians sent to the Romans for succour, desiring them to interpose with the barbarians by letters and ambassadors. There were sent three of the family of the Fabii, persons of high rank and distinction in the city. The Gauls received them courteously, from respect to the name of Rome, and, giving over the assault which was then making upon the walls, came to conference with them; when the ambassadors asking what injury they had received of the Clusinians that they thus invaded their city, Brennus, King of the Gauls, laughed and made answer: "The Clusinians do us injury, in that, being able only to till a small parcel of ground, they must needs possess a great territory, and will not yield any part to us who are strangers, many in number, and poor. In the same nature, O Romans, formerly the Albans, Fidenates, and Ardeates, and now lately the Veientines and Capenates, and many of the Faliscans and Volscians, did you injury; upon whom ye make war if they do not yield you part of what they possess, make slaves of them, waste and spoil their country, and ruin their cities; neither in so doing are cruel or unjust, but follow that most ancient of all laws, which gives the possessions of the feeble to the strong; which begins with God and ends in the beasts; since all these, by nature, seek the stronger to have advantage over the weaker. Cease, therefore, to pity the Clusinians whom we besiege, lest ye teach the Gauls to be kind and compassionate to those that are oppressed by you." By this answer the Romans, perceiving that Brennus was not to be treated with, went into Clusium, and encouraged and stirred up the inhabitants to make a sally with them upon the barbarians, which they did either to try their strength or to show their own. The sally being made, and the fight growing hot about the walls, one of the Fabii, Quintus Ambustus, being well mounted, and setting spurs to his horse, made full against a Gaul, a man of huge bulk and stature, whom he saw riding out at a distance from the rest. At the first he was not recognised, through the quickness of the conflict and the glittering of his armour, that precluded any view of him; but when he had overthrown the Gaul, and was going to gather the spoils, Brennus knew him; and, invoking the gods to be witness, that, contrary to the known and common law of nations, which is holily observed by all mankind, he who had come as an ambassador had now engaged in hostility against him, he drew off his men, and bidding Clusium farewell, led his army directly to Rome. But not wishing that it should look as if they took advantage of that injury, and were ready to embrace any occasion of quarrel, he sent a herald to demand the man in punishment, and in the meantime marched leisurely on.

The senate being met at Rome, among many others that spoke against the Fabii, the priests called fecials were the most decided, who, on the religious ground, urged the senate that they should lay the whole guilt and penalty of the fact upon him that committed it, and so exonerate the rest. These fecials Numa Pompilius, the mildest and justest of kings, constituted guardians of peace, and the judges and determiners of all causes by which war may justifiably be made. The senate referring the whole matter to the people, and the priests there, as well as in the senate, pleading against Fabius, the multitude, however, so little regarded their authority, that in scorn and contempt of it they chose Fabius and the rest of his brothers military tribunes. The Gauls, on hearing this, in great rage threw aside every delay, and hastened on with all the speed they could make. The places through which they marched, terrified with their numbers and the splendour of their preparations for war, and in alarm at their violence and fierceness, began to give up their territories as already lost, with little doubt but their cities would quickly follow; contrary, however, to expectation, they did no injury as they passed, nor took anything from the fields; and, as they went by any city, cried out that they were going to Rome; that the Romans only were their enemies, and that they took all others for their friends.

Whilst the barbarians were thus hastening with all speed, the military tribunes brought the Romans into the field to be ready to engage them, being not inferior to the Gauls in number (for they were no less than forty thousand foot), but most of them raw soldiers, and such as had never handled a weapon before. Besides, they had wholly neglected all religious usages, had not obtained favourable sacrifices, nor made inquiries of the prophets, natural in danger and before battle. No less did the multitude of commanders distract and confound their proceedings; frequently before, upon less occasions, they had chosen a single leader, with the title of dictator, being sensible of what great importance it is in critical times to have the soldiers united under one general with the entire and absolute control placed in his hands. Add to all, the remembrance of Camillus' treatment, which made it now seem a dangerous thing for officers to command without humouring their soldiers. In this condition they left the city, and encamped by the river Allia, about ten miles from Rome; and not far from the place where it falls into the Tiber; and here the Gauls came upon them, and, after a disgraceful resistance, devoid of order and discipline, they were miserably defeated. The left wing was immediately driven into the river, and there destroyed; the right had less damage by declining the shock, and from the low grounds getting to the tops of the hills, from whence most of them afterwards dropped into the city; the rest, as many as escaped, the enemy being weary of the slaughter, stole by night to Veii, giving up Rome and all that was in it for lost.

This battle was fought about the summer solstice, the moon being at full, the very same day in which the sad disaster of the Fabii had happened, when three hundred of that name were at one time cut off by the Tuscans. But from this second loss and defeat the day got the name of Alliensis from the river Allia, and still retains it. The question of unlucky days, whether we should consider any to be so, and whether Heraclitus did well in upbraiding Hesiod for distinguishing them into fortunate and unfortunate, as ignorant that the nature of everyday is the same, I have examined in another place; but upon occasion of the present subject, I think it will not be amiss to annex a few examples relating to this matter. On the fifth of their month Hippodromius, which corresponds to the Athenian Hecatombæon, the Bœotians gained two signal victories, the one at Leuctra, the other at Ceressus, about three hundred years before, when they overcame Lattamyas and the Thessalians, both which asserted the liberty of Greece. Again, on the sixth of Boëdromion, the Persians were worsted by the Greeks at Marathon; on the third, at Platæa, as also at Mycale; on the twenty-fifth, at Arbela. The Athenians, about the full moon in Boëdromion, gained their sea-victory at Naxos under the conduct of Chabrias; on the twentieth, at Salamis, as we have shown in our treatise on Days. Thargelion was a very unfortunate month to the barbarians, for in it Alexander overcame Darius' generals on the Granicus; and the Carthaginians, on the twenty-fourth, were beaten by Timoleon in Sicily, on which same day and month Troy seems to have been taken, as Ephorus, Callisthenes, Damastes, and Phylarchus state. On the other hand, the month Metagitnion, which in Bœotia is called Panemus, was not very lucky to the Greeks; for on its seventh day they were defeated by Antipater, at the battle in Cranon, and utterly ruined; and before, at Chæronea, were defeated by Philip; and on the very same day, same month, and same year, those that went with Archidamus into Italy were there cut off by the barbarians. The Carthaginians also observe the twenty-first of the same month, as bringing with it the largest number and the severest of their losses. I am not ignorant that, about the Feast of Mysteries, Thebes was destroyed the second time by Alexander; and after that, upon the very twentieth of Boëdromion, on which day they lead forth the mystic Iacchus, the Athenians received a garrison of the Macedonians. On the selfsame day the Romans lost their army under Cæpio by the Cimbrians, and in a subsequent year, under the conduct of Lucullus, overcame the Armenians and Tigranes. King Attalus and Pompey died both on their birthdays. One could reckon up several that have had variety of fortune on the same day. This day, meantime, is one of the unfortunate ones to the Romans, and for its sake two others in every month; fear and superstition, as the custom of it is, more and more prevailing. But I have discussed this more accurately in my Roman Questions.

And now, after the battle, had the Gauls immediately pursued those that fled, there had been no remedy but Rome must have wholly been ruined, and those who remained in it utterly destroyed; such was the terror that those who escaped the battle brought with them into the city, and with such distraction and confusion were themselves in turn infected. But the Gauls, not imagining their victory to be so considerable, and overtaken with the present joy, fell to feasting and dividing the spoil, by which means they gave leisure to those who were for leaving the city to make their escape, and to those that remained to anticipate and prepare for their coming. For they who resolved to stay at Rome, abandoning the rest of the city, betook themselves to the Capitol, which they fortified with the help of missiles and new works. One of their principal cares was of their holy things, most of which they conveyed into the Capitol. But the consecrated fire the vestal virgins took, and fled with it, as likewise their other sacred things. Some write that they have nothing in their charge but the ever-living fire which Numa had ordained to be worshipped as the principle of all things; for fire is the most active thing in nature, and all production is either motion, or attended with motion; all the other parts of matter, so long as they are without warmth, lie sluggish and dead, and require the accession of a sort of soul or vitality in the principle of heat; and upon that accession, in whatever way, immediately receive a capacity either of acting or being acted upon. And thus Numa, a man curious in such things, and whose wisdom made it thought that he conversed with the Muses, consecrated fire, and ordained it to be kept ever burning, as an image of that eternal power which orders and actuates all things. Others say that this fire was kept burning in front of the holy things, as in Greece, for purification, and that there were other things hid in the most secret part of the temple, which were kept from the view of all, except those virgins whom they call vestals. The most common opinion was, that the image of Pallas, brought into Italy by Æneas, was laid up there; others say that the Samothracian images lay there, telling a story how that Dardanus carried them to Troy, and when he had built the city, celebrated those rites, and dedicated those images there; that after Troy was taken, Æneas stole them away, and kept them till his coming into Italy. But they who profess to know more of the matter affirm that there are two barrels, not of any great size, one of which stands open and has nothing in it, the other full and sealed up; but that neither of them may be seen but by the most holy virgins. Others think that they who say this are misled by the fact that the virgins put most of their holy things into two barrels at this time of the Gaulish invasion, and hid them underground in the temple of Quirinus; and that from hence that place to this day bears the name of Barrels.

However it be, taking the most precious and important things they had, they fled away with them, shaping their course along the riverside, where Lucius Albinius, a simple citizen of Rome, who among others was making his escape, overtook them, having his wife, children, and goods in a cart;

and, seeing the virgins, dragging along in their arms the holy things of the gods, in a helpless and weary condition, he caused his wife and children to get down, and, taking out his goods, put the virgins in the cart, that they might make their escape to some of the Greek cities. This devout act of Albinius, and the respect he showed thus signally to the gods at a time of such extremity, deserved not to be passed over in silence. But the priests that belonged to other gods, and the most elderly of the senators, men who had been consuls and had enjoyed triumphs, could not endure to leave the city; but, putting on their sacred and splendid robes, Fabius the high priest performing the office, they made their prayers to the gods, and, devoting themselves, as it were, for their country, sate themselves down in their ivory chairs in the forum, and in that posture expected the event.

On the third day after the battle, Brennus appeared with his army at the city, and, finding the gates wide open and no guards upon the walls, first began to suspect it was some design or stratagem, never dreaming that the Romans were in so desperate a condition. But when he found it to be so indeed, he entered at the Colline gate, and took Rome, in the three hundred and sixtieth year, or a little more, after it was built; if, indeed, it can be supposed probable that an exact chronological statement has been preserved of events which were themselves the cause of chronological difficulties about things of later date; of the calamity itself, however, and of the fact of the capture, some faint rumours seem to have passed at the time into Greece. Heraclides Ponticus, who lived not long after these times, in his book upon the Soul, relates that a certain report came from the west, that an army, proceeding from the Hyperboreans, had taken a Greek city called Rome, seated somewhere upon the great sea. But I do not wonder that so fabulous and high-flown an author as Heraclides should embellish the truth of the story with expressions about Hyperboreans and the great sea. Aristotle the philosopher appears to have heard a correct statement of the taking of the city by the Gauls, but he calls its deliverer Lucius; whereas Camillus' surname was not Lucius, but Marcus. But this is a matter of conjecture.

Brennus, having taken possession of Rome, set a strong guard about the Capitol, and, going himself down into the forum, was there struck with amazement at the sight of so many men sitting in that order and silence, observing that they neither rose at his coming, nor so much as changed colour or countenance, but remained without fear or concern leaning upon their staves, and sitting quietly, looking at each other. The Gauls, for a great while, stood wondering at the strangeness of the sight, not daring to approach or touch them, taking them for an assembly of superior beings. But when one, bolder than the rest, drew near to Marcus Papirius, and, putting forth his hand, gently touched his chin and stroked his long beard, Papirius with his staff struck him a severe blow on the head; upon which the barbarian drew his sword and slew him. This was the introduction to the slaughter; for the rest, following his example, set upon them all and killed them, and despatched all others that came in their way; and so went on to the sacking and pillaging the houses, which they continued for many days ensuing. Afterwards, they burnt them down to the ground and demolished them, being incensed at those who kept the Capitol, because they would not yield to summons; but, on the contrary, when assailed, had repelled them, with some loss, from their defences. This provoked them to ruin the whole city, and to put to the sword all that came to their hands, young and old, men, women, and children.

And now, the siege of the Capitol having lasted a good while, the Gauls began to be in want of provision; and dividing their forces, part of them stayed with their king at the siege, the rest went to forage the country, ravaging the towns and villages where they came, but not all together in a body, but in different squadrons and parties; and to such a confidence had success raised them, that they carelessly rambled about without the least fear or apprehension of danger. But the greatest and best ordered body of their forces went to the city of Ardea, where Camillus then sojourned, having, ever since his leaving Rome, sequestered himself from all business, and taken to a private life; but now he began to rouse up himself, and consider not how to avoid or escape the enemy, but to find out an opportunity to be revenged upon them. And perceiving that the Ardeatians wanted not men, but rather enterprise, through the inexperience and timidity of their officers, he began to speak with the young men, first to the effect that they ought not to ascribe the misfortune of the Romans to the courage of their enemy, nor attribute the losses they sustained by rash counsel to the conduct of men who had no title to victory; the event had been only an evidence of the power of fortune: that it was a brave thing even with danger to repel a foreign and barbarous invader whose end in conquering was, like fire, to lay waste and destroy, but if they would be courageous and resolute he was ready to put an opportunity into their hands to gain a victory, without hazard at all. When he found the young men embraced the thing, he went to the magistrates and council of the city, and, having persuaded them also, he mustered all that could bear arms, and drew them up within the walls, that they might not be perceived by the enemy, who was near; who, having scoured the country, and returned heavy-laden with booty, lay encamped in the plains in a careless and negligent posture, so that, with the night ensuing upon debauch and drunkenness, silence prevailed through all the camp. When Camillus learned this from his scouts, he drew out the Ardeatians, and in the dead of the night, passing in silence over the ground that lay between, came up to their works, and, commanding his trumpets to sound and his men to shout and halloo, he struck terror into them from all quarters; while drunkenness impeded and sleep retarded their movements. A few, whom fear had sobered, getting into some order, for a while resisted; and so died with their weapons in their hands. But the greatest part of them, buried in wine and sleep, were surprised without their arms, and despatched; and as many of them as by the advantage of the night got out of the camp were the next day found scattered abroad and wandering in the fields, and were picked up by the horse that pursued them.

The fame of this action soon fled through the neighbouring cities, and stirred up the young men from various quarters to come and join themselves with him. But none were so much concerned as those Romans who escaped in the battle of Allia, and were now at Veii, thus lamenting with themselves, "O heavens, what a commander has Providence bereaved Rome of, to honour Ardea with his actions! And that city, which brought forth and nursed so great a man, is lost and gone, and we, destitute of a leader and shut up within strange walls, sit idle, and see Italy ruined before our eyes. Come, let us send to the Ardeatians to have back our general, or else, with weapons in our hands, let us go thither to him; for he is no longer a banished man, nor we citizens, having no country but what is in the possession of the enemy." To this they all agreed, and sent to Camillus to desire him to take the command; but he answered, that he would not until they that were in the Capitol should legally appoint him; for he esteemed them, so long as they were in being, to be his country; that if they should command him he would readily obey; but against their consent he would intermeddle with nothing. When this answer was returned, they admired the modesty and temper of Camillus; but they could not tell how to find a messenger to carry the intelligence to the Capitol, or rather, indeed, it seemed altogether impossible for anyone to get to the citadel whilst the enemy was in full possession of the city. But among the young men there was one Pontius Cominius, of ordinary birth, but ambitious of honour, who proffered himself to run the hazard, and took no letters with him to those in the Capitol, lest, if he were intercepted, the enemy might learn the intentions of Camillus; but, putting on a poor dress and carrying corks under it, he boldly travelled the greatest part of the way by day, and came to the city when it was dark; the bridge he could not pass, as it was guarded by the barbarians; so that taking his clothes, which were neither many nor heavy, and binding them about his head, he laid his body upon the corks, and swimming with them, got over to the city. And avoiding those quarters where he perceived the enemy was awake, which he guessed at by the lights and noise, he went to the Carmental gate, where there was greatest silence, and where the hill of the Capitol is steepest and rises with craggy and broken rock. By this way he got up, though with much difficulty, by the hollow of the cliff, and presented himself to the guards, saluting them, and telling them his name; he was taken in, and carried to the commanders. And a senate being immediately called, he related to them in order the victory of Camillus, which they had not heard of before, and the proceedings of the soldiers, urging them to confirm Camillus in the command, as on him alone all their fellow-countrymen outside the city would rely. Having heard and consulted of the matter, the senate declared Camillus dictator, and sent back Pontius the same way that he came, who, with the same success as before, got through the enemy without being discovered, and delivered to the Romans outside the decision of the senate, who joyfully received it. Camillus, on his arrival, found twenty thousand of them ready in arms; with which forces, and those confederates he brought along with him, he prepared to set upon the enemy.

But at Rome some of the barbarians, passing by chance near the place at which Pontius by night had got into the Capitol, spied in several places marks of feet and hands, where he had laid hold and clambered, and places where the plants that grew to the rock had been rubbed off, and the earth had slipped, and went accordingly and reported it to the king, who, coming in person, and viewing it, for the present said nothing, but in the evening, picking out such of the Gauls as were nimblest of body, and by living in the mountains were accustomed to climb, he said to them, "The enemy themselves have shown us a way how to come at them, which we knew not of before, and have taught us that it is not so difficult and impossible but that men may overcome it. It would be a great shame, having begun well, to fail in the end, and to give up a place as impregnable, when the enemy himself lets us see the way by which it may be taken; for where it was easy for one man to get up, it will not be hard for many, one after another; nay, when many shall undertake it, they will be aid and strength to each other. Rewards and honours shall be bestowed on every man as he shall acquit himself."

When the king had thus spoken, the Gauls cheerfully undertook to perform it, and in the dead of night a good party of them together, with great silence, began to climb the rock, clinging to the precipitous and difficult ascent, which yet upon trial offered a way to them, and proved less difficult than they had expected. So that the foremost of them having gained the top of all, and put themselves into order, they all but surprised the outworks, and mastered the watch, who were fast asleep; for neither man nor dog perceived their coming. But there were sacred geese kept near the temple of Juno, which at other times were plentifully fed, but now, by reason that corn and other provisions were grown scarce for all, were but in a poor condition. The creature is by nature of quick sense, and apprehensive of the least noise, so that these, being moreover watchful through hunger, and restless, immediately discovered the coming of the Gauls, and, running up and down with their noise and cackling, they raised the whole camp, while the barbarians on the other side, perceiving themselves discovered, no longer endeavoured to conceal their attempt, but with shouting and violence advanced to the assault. The Romans, everyone in haste snatching up the next weapon that came to hand, did what they could on the sudden occasion. Manlius, a man of consular dignity, of strong body and great spirit, was the first that made head against them, and, engaging with two of the enemy at once, with his sword cut off the right arm of one just as he was lifting up his blade to strike, and, running his target full in the face of the other, tumbled him headlong down the steep rock; then mounting the rampart, and there standing with others that came running to his assistance, drove down the rest of them, who, indeed, to begin, had not been many, and did nothing worthy of so bold an attempt. The Romans, having thus escaped this danger, early in the morning took the captain of the watch and flung him down the rock upon the heads of their enemies, and to Manlius for his victory voted a reward, intended more for honour than advantage, bringing him, each man of them as much as he received for his daily allowance, which was half a pound of bread and one eighth of a pint of wine.

Henceforward, the affairs of the Gauls were daily in a worse and worse condition; they wanted provisions, being withheld from foraging through fear of Camillus, and sickness also was amongst them, occasioned by the number of carcases that lay in heaps unburied. Being lodged among the ruins, the ashes, which were very deep, blown about by the winds and combining with the sultry heats, breathed up, so to say, a dry and searching air, the inhalation of which was destructive to their health. But the chief cause was the change from their natural climate, coining as they did out of shady and hilly countries, abounding in means of shelter from the heat, to lodge in low, and, in the autumn season, very unhealthy ground; added to which was the length and tediousness of the siege, as they had now sate seven months before the Capitol. There was, therefore, a great destruction among them, and the number of the dead grew so great that the living gave up burying them. Neither, indeed, were things on that account any better with the besieged, for famine increased upon them, and despondency with not hearing anything of Camillus, it being impossible to send anyone to him, the city was so guarded by the barbarians. Things being in this sad condition on both sides, a motion of treaty was made at first by some of the outposts, as they happened to speak with one another; which being embraced by the leading men, Sulpicius, tribune of the Romans, came to a parley with Brennus, in which it was agreed, that the Romans laying down a thousand weight of gold, the Gauls upon the receipt of it should immediately quit the city and territories. The agreement being confirmed by oath on both sides, and the gold brought forth, the Gauls used false dealing in the weight, secretly at first, but afterwards openly pulled back and disturbed the balance; at which the Romans indignantly complaining, Brennus, in a scoffing and insulting manner, pulled off his sword and belt, and threw them both into the scales; and when Sulpicius asked what that meant, "What should it mean," says he, "but woe to the conquered?" which afterwards became a proverbial saying. As for the Romans, some were so incensed that they were for taking their gold back again and returning to endure the siege. Others were for passing by and dissembling a petty injury, and not to account that the indignity of the thing lay in paying more than was due, since the paying anything at all was itself a dishonour only submitted to as a necessity of the times.

Whilst this difference remained still unsettled, both amongst themselves and with the Gauls, Camillus was at the gates with his army; and having learned what was going on, commanded the main body of his forces to follow slowly after him in good order, and himself with the choicest of his men hastening on, went at once to the Romans; where, all giving way to him, and receiving him as their sole magistrate, with profound silence and order, he took the gold out of the scales, and delivered it to his officers and commanded the Gauls to take their weights and scales and depart; saying that it was customary with the Romans to deliver their country with iron, not with gold. And when Brennus began to rage, and say that he was unjustly dealt with in such a breach of contract, Camillus answered that it was never legally made, and the agreement of no force or obligation; for that himself being declared dictator, and there being no other magistrate by law, the engagement had been made with men who had no power to enter into it; but now they might say anything they had to urge, for he was come with full power by law to grant pardon to such as should ask it, or inflict punishment on the guilty, if they did not repent. At this, Brennus broke into violent anger, and an immediate quarrel ensued; both sides drew their swords and attacked, but in confusion, as could not be otherwise amongst houses, and in narrow lanes and places where it was impossible to form in any order. But Brennus, presently recollecting himself, called off his men, and, with the loss of a few only, brought them to their camp; and rising in the night with all his forces, left the city, and advancing about eight miles, encamped upon the way to Gabii. As soon as day appeared, Camillus came up with him, splendidly armed himself, and his soldiers full of courage and confidence; and there engaging with him in a sharp conflict, which lasted a long while, overthrew his army with great slaughter, and took their camp. Of those that fled, some were presently cut off by the pursuers; others, and these were the greatest number, dispersed hither and thither, and were despatched by the people that came sallying out from the neighbouring towns and villages.

Thus Rome was strangely taken, and more strangely recovered, having been seven whole months in the possession of the barbarians, who entered her a little after the Ides of July, and were driven out about the Ides of February following. Camillus triumphed, as he deserved, having saved his country that was lost, and brought the city, so to say, back again to itself. For those that had fled abroad, together with their wives and children, accompanied him as he rode in; and those who had been shut up in the Capitol, and were reduced almost to the point of perishing with hunger, went out to meet him, embracing each other as they met, and weeping for joy, and, through the excess of the present pleasure, scarce believing in its truth. And when the priests and ministers of the gods appeared bearing the sacred things, which in their flight they had either hid on the spot, or conveyed away with them, and now openly showed in safety, the citizens who saw the blessed sight felt as if with these the gods themselves were again returned unto Rome. After Camillus had sacrificed to the gods, and purified the city according to the directions of those properly instructed, he restored the existing temples, and erected a new one to Rumour, or Voice, informing himself of the spot in which that voice from heaven came by night to Marcus Casdicius, foretelling the coming of the barbarian army.

It was a matter of difficulty, and a hard task, amidst so much rubbish, to discover and re-determine the consecrated places; but by the zeal of Camillus, and the incessant labour of the priests, it was at last accomplished. But when it came also to rebuilding the city, which was wholly demolished, despondency seized the multitude, and a backwardness to engage in a work for which they had no materials; at a time, too, when they rather needed relief and repose from their past labours, than any new demands upon their exhausted strength and impaired fortunes. Thus insensibly they turned their thoughts again towards Veii, a city ready-built and well-provided, and gave an opening to the arts of flatterers eager to gratify their desires, and lent their ears to seditious language flung out against Camillus; as that, out of ambition and self-glory, he withheld them from a city fit to receive them, forcing them to live in the midst of ruins, and to re-erect a pile of burnt rubbish, that he might be esteemed not the chief magistrate only and general of Rome, but, to the exclusion of Romulus, its founder also. The senate, therefore, fearing a sedition, would not suffer Camillus, though desirous, to lay down his authority within the year, though no dictator had ever held it above six months.

They themselves, meantime, used their best endeavours, by kind persuasions and familiar addresses, to encourage and appease the people, showing them the shrines and tombs of their ancestors, calling to their remembrance the sacred spots and holy places which Romulus and Numa or any other of their kings had consecrated and left to their keeping; and among the strongest religious arguments, urged the head, newly separated from the body, which was found in laying the foundation of the Capitol, marking it as a place destined by fate to be the head of all Italy; and the holy fire which had just been rekindled again, since the end of the war, by the vestal virgins; "What a disgrace it would be to them to lose and extinguish this, leaving the city it belonged to, to be either inhabited by strangers and newcomers, or left a wild pasture for cattle to graze on?" Such reasons as these, urged with complaint and expostulation, sometimes in private upon individuals, and sometimes in their public assemblies, were met, on the other hand, by laments and protestations of distress and helplessness; entreaties that, reunited as they just were, after a sort of shipwreck, naked and destitute, they would not constrain them to patch up the pieces of a ruined and shattered city, when they had another at hand ready-built and prepared.

Camillus thought good to refer it to general deliberation, and himself spoke largely and earnestly in behalf of his country, as also many others. At last, calling to Lucius Lucretius, whose place it was to speak first, he commanded him to give his sentence, and the rest as they followed, in order. Silence being made, and Lucretius just about to begin, by chance a centurion passing by outside with his company of the day-guard called out with a loud voice to the ensign-bearer to halt and fix his standard, for this was the best place to stay in. This voice, coming in that moment of time, and at that crisis of uncertainty and anxiety for the future, was taken as a direction what was to be done; so that Lucretius, assuming an attitude of devotion, gave sentence in concurrence with the gods, as he said, as likewise did all that followed. Even among the common people it created a wonderful change of feeling; everyone now cheered and encouraged his neighbour, and set himself to the work, proceeding in it, however, not by any regular lines or divisions, but everyone pitching upon that plot of ground which came next to hand, or best pleased his fancy; by which haste and hurry in building, they constructed their city in narrow and ill-designed lanes, and with houses huddled together one upon another; for it is said that within the compass of the year the whole city was built up anew, both in its public walls and private buildings. The persons, however, appointed by Camillus to resume and mark out, in this general confusion, all consecrated places, coming, in their way round the Palatium, to the chapel of Mars, found the chapel itself indeed destroyed and burnt to the ground, like everything else, by the barbarians; but whilst they were clearing the place, and carrying away the rubbish, lit upon Romulus' augural staff, buried under a great heap of ashes. This sort of staff is crooked at one end, and is called *lituus;* they make use of it in quartering out the regions of the heavens when engaged in divination from the flight of birds; Romulus, who was himself a great diviner, made use of it. But when he disappeared from the earth, the priests took his staff and kept it, as other holy things, from the touch of man; and when they now found that, whereas all other things were consumed, this staff had altogether escaped the flames, they began to conceive happier hopes of Rome, and to augur from this token its future everlasting safety.

And now they had scarcely got a breathing time from their trouble, when a new war came upon them; and the Æquians, Volscians, and Latins all at once invaded their territories, and the Tuscans besieged Sutrium, their confederate city. The military tribunes who commanded the army, and were encamped about the hill Mæcius, being closely besieged by the

Latins and the camp in danger to be lost, sent to Rome, where Camillus was a third time chosen dictator. Of this war two different accounts are given; I shall begin with the more fabulous. They say that the Latins (whether out of pretence, or real design to revive the ancient relationship of the two nations) sent to desire of the Romans some free-born maidens in marriage; that when the Romans were at a loss how to determine (for on one hand they dreaded a war, having scarcely yet settled and recovered themselves, and on the other side suspected that this asking of wives was, in plain terms, nothing else but a demand for hostages, though covered over with the specious name of intermarriage and alliance), a certain handmaid, by name Tutula, or, as some call her, Philotis, persuaded the magistrates to send with her some of the most youthful and best-looking maid-servants, in the bridal dress of noble virgins, and leave the rest to her care and management; that the magistrates, consenting, chose out as many as she thought necessary for her purpose, and adorning them with gold and rich clothes, delivered them to the Latins, who were encamped not far from the city; that at night the rest stole away the enemy's swords, but Tutula or Philotis, getting to the top of a wild fig tree, and spreading out a thick woollen cloth behind her, held out a torch towards Rome, which was the signal concerted between her and the commanders, without the knowledge, however, of any other of the citizens, which was the reason that their issuing out from the city was tumultuous, the officers pushing their men on, and they calling upon one another's names, and scarce able to bring themselves into order; that setting upon the enemy's works, who either were asleep or expected no such matter, they took the camp and destroyed most of them; and that this was done on the Nones of July, which was then called Quintilis, and that the feast that is observed on that day is a commemoration of what was then done. For in it, first, they run out of the city in great crowds, and call out aloud several familiar and common names, Caius, Marcus, Lucius, and the like in representation of the way in which they called to one another when they went out in such haste. In the next place, the maid-servants, gaily dressed, run about, playing and jesting upon all they meet, and amongst themselves, also, use a kind of skirmishing, to show they helped in the conflict against the Latins; and while eating and drinking, they sit shaded over with boughs of wild fig tree, and the day they call Nonæ; Caprotinæ, as some think from that wild fig tree on which the maid-servant held up her torch, the Roman name for a wild fig tree being *caprificus*. Others refer most of what is said or done at this feast to the fate of Romulus, for, on this day, he vanished outside the gates in a sudden darkness and storm (some think it an eclipse of the sun), and from this the day was called Nonæ Caprotinæ, the Latin for a goat being *capra,* and the place where he disappeared having the name of Goat's Marsh, as is stated in his life.

But the general stream of writers prefer the other account of this war, which they thus relate. Camillus, being the third time chosen dictator, and learning that the army under the tribunes was besieged by the Latins and Volscians, was constrained to arm, not only those under, but also those over, the age of service; and taking a large circuit round the mountain Mæcius, undiscovered by the enemy, lodged his army on their rear, and then by many fires gave notice of his arrival. The besieged, encouraged by this, prepared to sally forth and join battle; but the Latins and Volscians, fearing this exposure to an enemy on both sides, drew themselves within their works, and fortified their camp with a strong palisade of trees on every side, resolving to wait for more supplies from home, and expecting, also, the assistance of the Tuscans, their confederates. Camillus, detecting their object, and fearing to be reduced to the same position to which he had brought them, namely, to be besieged himself, resolved to lose no time: and finding their rampart was all of timber, and observing that a strong wind constantly at sun-rising blew off from the mountains, after having prepared a quantity of combustibles, about break of day he drew forth his forces, commanding a part with their missiles to assault the enemy with noise and shouting on the other quarter, whilst he, with those that were to fling in the fire, went to that side of the enemy's camp to which the wind usually blew, and there waited his opportunity. When the skirmish was begun, and the sun risen, and a strong wind set in from the mountains, he gave the signal of onset; and heaving in an infinite quantity of fiery matter, filled all their rampart with it, so that the flame being fed by the close timber and wooden palisades, went on and spread into all quarters. The Latins, having nothing ready to keep it off or extinguish it, when the camp was now almost full of fire, were driven back within a very small compass, and at last forced by necessity to come into their enemy's hands, who stood before the works ready armed and prepared to receive them; of these very few escaped, while those that stayed in the camp were all a prey to the fire, until the Romans, to gain the pillage, extinguished it.

These things performed, Camillus, leaving his son Lucius in the camp to guard the prisoners and secure the booty, passed into the enemy's country, where, having taken the city of the Æquians and reduced the Volscians to obedience, he then immediately led his army to Sutrium, not having heard what had befallen the Sutrians, but making haste to assist them, as if they were still in danger and besieged by the Tuscans. They, however, had already surrendered their city to their enemies, and destitute of all things, with nothing left but their clothes, met Camillus on the way, leading their wives and children, and bewailing their misfortune. Camillus himself was struck with compassion, and perceiving the soldiers weeping, and commiserating their case, while the Sutrians hung about and clung to them, resolved not to defer revenge, but that very day to lead his army to Sutrium; conjecturing that the enemy, having just taken a rich and plentiful city, without an enemy left within it, nor any from without to be expected, would be found abandoned to enjoyment and unguarded. Neither did his opinion fail him; he not only passed through their country without discovery, but came up to their very gates and possessed himself of the walls, not a man being left to guard them, but their whole army scattered about in the houses, drinking and making merry. Nay, when at last they did perceive that the enemy had seized the city, they were so overloaded with meat and wine, that few were able so much as to endeavour to escape, but either waited shamefully for their death within doors, or surrendered themselves to the conqueror. Thus the city of the Sutrians was twice taken in one day; and they who were in possession lost it, and they who had lost regained it, alike by the means of Camillus. For all which actions he received a triumph, which brought him no less honour and reputation than the two former ones; for those citizens who before most regarded him with an evil eye, and ascribed his successes to a certain luck rather than real merit, were compelled by these last acts of his to allow the whole honour to his great abilities and energy.

Of all the adversaries and enviers of his glory, Marcus Manlius was the most distinguished, he who first drove back the Gauls when they made their night attack upon the Capitol, and who for that reason had been named Capitolinus. This man, affecting the first place in the commonwealth, and not able by noble ways to outdo Camillus' reputation, took that ordinary course towards usurpation of absolute power, namely, to gain the multitude, those of them especially that were in debt; defending some by pleading their causes against their creditors, rescuing others by force, and not suffering the law to proceed against them; insomuch that in a short time he got great numbers of indigent people about him, whose tumults and uproars in the forum struck terror into the principal citizens. After that Quintius Capitolinus, who was made dictator to suppress these disorders, had committed Manlius to prison, the people immediately changed their apparel, a thing never done but in great and public calamities, and the senate, fearing some tumult, ordered him to be released. He, however, when set at liberty, changed not his course, but was rather the more insolent in his proceedings, filling the whole city with faction and sedition. They chose, therefore, Camillus again military tribune; and a day being appointed for Manlius to answer to his charge, the prospect from the place where his trial was held proved a great impediment to his accusers, for the very spot where Manlius by night fought with the Gauls overlooked the forum from the Capitol, so that, stretching forth his hands that way, and weeping, he called to their remembrance his past actions, raising compassion in all that beheld him. Insomuch that the judges were at a loss what to do, and several times adjourned the trial, unwilling to acquit him of the crime, which was sufficiently proved, and yet unable to execute the law while his noble action remained, as it were, before their eyes. Camillus, considering this, transferred the court outside the gate to the Peteline Grove, from whence there is no prospect of the Capitol. Here his accuser went on with his charge, and his judges were capable of remembering and duly resenting his guilty deeds. He was convicted, carried to the Capitol, and flung headlong from the rock; so that one and the same spot was thus the witness of his greatest glory, and monument of his most unfortunate end. The Romans, besides, razed his house, and built there a temple to the goddess they call Moneta, ordaining for the future that none of the patrician order should ever dwell on the Capitoline.

And now Camillus, being called to his sixth tribuneship, desired to be excused, as being aged, and perhaps not unfearful of the malice of fortune, and those reverses which seem to ensue upon great prosperity. But the most apparent pretence was the weakness of his body, for he happened at that time to be sick; the people, however, would admit of no excuses, but, crying that they wanted not his strength for horse or for foot service, but only his counsel and conduct, constrained him to undertake the command, and with one of his fellow-tribunes to lead the army immediately against the enemy. These were the Prænestines and Volscians, who, with large forces, were laying waste the territory of the Roman confederates. Having marched out with his army, he sat down and encamped near the enemy, meaning himself to protract the war, or if there should come any necessity or occasion of fighting, in the meantime to regain his strength. But Lucius Furius, his colleague, carried away with the desire of glory, was not to be held in, but, impatient to give battle, inflamed the inferior officers of the army with the same eagerness; so that Camillus, fearing he might seem out of envy to be wishing to rob the young men of the glory of a noble exploit, consented, though unwillingly, that he should draw out the forces, whilst himself, by reason of weakness, stayed behind with a few in the camp. Lucius, engaging rashly, was discomfited, when Camillus, perceiving the Romans to give ground and fly, could not contain himself, but, leaping from his bed, with those he had about him ran to meet them at the gates of the camp, making his way through the flyers to oppose the pursuers; so that those who had got within the camp turned back at once and followed him, and those that came flying from without made head again and gathered about him, exhorting one another not to forsake their general. Thus the enemy, for that time, was stopped in his pursuit. The next day Camillus, drawing out his forces and joining battle with them, overthrew them by main force, and, following close upon them, entered pell-mell with them into their camp, and took it, slaying the greatest part of them. Afterwards, having heard that the city Satricum was taken by the Tuscans, and the inhabitants, all Romans, put to the sword, he sent home to Rome the main body of his forces and heaviest-armed, and taking with him the lightest and most vigorous soldiers, set suddenly upon the Tuscans, who were in the possession of the city, and mastered them, slaying some and expelling the rest; and so, returning to Rome with great spoils, gave signal evidence of their superior wisdom, who, not mistrusting the weakness and age of a commander endued with courage and conduct, had rather chosen him who was sickly and desirous to be excused, than younger men who were forward and ambitious to command.

When, therefore, the revolt of the Tusculans was reported, they gave Camillus the charge of reducing them, choosing one of his five colleagues to go with him. And when everyone was eager for the place, contrary to the expectation of all, he passed by the rest and chose Lucius Furius, the very same man who lately, against the judgment of Camillus, had rashly hazarded and nearly lost a battle; willing, as it should seem, to dissemble that miscarriage, and free him from the shame of it. The Tusculans, hearing of Camillus' coming against them, made a cunning attempt at revoking their act of revolt; their fields, as in times of highest peace, were full of ploughmen and shepherds; their gates stood wide open, and their children were being taught in the schools; of the people, such as were tradesmen, he found in their workshops, busied about their several employments, and the better sort of citizens walking in the public places in their ordinary dress; the magistrates hurried about to provide quarters for the Romans, as if they stood in fear of no danger and were conscious of no fault. Which arts, though they could not dispossess Camillus of the conviction he had of their treason, yet induced some compassion for their repentance; he commanded them to go to the senate and deprecate their anger, and joined himself as an intercessor in their behalf, so that their city was acquitted of all guilt and admitted to Roman citizenship. These were the most memorable actions of his sixth tribuneship.

After these things, Licinius Stolo raised a great sedition in the city, and brought the people to dissension with the senate, contending, that of two consuls one should be chosen out of the commons, and not both out of the patricians. Tribunes of the people were chosen, but the election of consuls was interrupted and prevented by the people. And as this absence of any supreme magistrate was leading to yet further confusion, Camillus was the fourth time created dictator by the senate, sorely against the people's will, and not altogether in accordance with his own; he had little desire for a conflict with men whose past services entitled them to tell him that he had achieved far greater actions in war along with them than in politics with the patricians, who, indeed, had only put him forward now out of envy; that, if successful, he might crush the people, or failing, be crushed himself. However, to provide as good a remedy as he could for the present, knowing the day on which the tribunes of the people intended to prefer the law, he appointed it by proclamation for a general muster, and called the people from the forum into the Campus, threatening to set heavy fines upon such as should not obey. On the other side, the tribunes of the people met his threats by solemnly protesting they would fine him in fifty thousand drachmas of silver, if he persisted in obstructing the people from giving their suffrages for the law. Whether it were, then, that he feared another banishment or condemnation, which would ill become his age and past great actions, or found himself unable to stem the current of the multitude, which ran strong and violent, he betook himself, for the present, to his house, and afterwards, for some days together professing sickness, finally laid down his dictatorship. The senate created another dictator; who, choosing Stolo, leader of the sedition, to be his general of horse, suffered that law to be enacted and ratified, which was most grievous to the patricians, namely, that no person whatsoever should possess above five hundred acres of land. Stolo was much distinguished by the victory he had gained; but, not long after, was found himself to possess more than he had allowed to others, and suffered the penalties of his own law.

And now the contention about election of consuls coming on (which was the main point and original cause of the dissension, and had throughout furnished most matter of division between the senate and the people), certain intelligence arrived, that the Gauls again, proceeding from the Adriatic Sea, were marching in vast numbers upon Rome. On the very heels of the report followed manifest acts also of hostility; the country through which they marched was all wasted, and such as by flight could not make their escape to Rome were dispersing and scattering among the mountains. The terror of this war quieted the sedition; nobles and commons, senate and people together unanimously chose Camillus the fifth time dictator; who, though very aged, not wanting much of fourscore years, yet, considering the danger and necessity of his country, did not, as before, pretend sickness, or depreciate his own capacity, but at once undertook the charge and enrolled soldiers. And, knowing that the great force of the barbarians lay chiefly in their swords, with which they laid about them in a rude and inartificial manner, hacking and hewing the head and shoulders, he caused headpieces entire of iron to be made for most of his men, smoothing and polishing the outside, that the enemy's swords lighting upon them, might either slide off or be broken; and fitted also their shields with a little rim of brass, the wood itself not being sufficient to bear off the blows. Besides, he taught his soldiers to use their long javelins in close encounter, and, by bringing them under their enemy's swords, to receive their strokes upon them

When the Gauls drew near, about the river Anio, dragging a heavy camp after them, and loaded with infinite spoil, Camillus drew forth his forces and planted himself upon a hill of easy ascent, and which had many dips in it, with the object that the greatest of his army might lie concealed, and those who appeared might be thought to have betaken themselves, through fear, to those upper grounds. And the more to increase this opinion in them, he suffered them, without any disturbance, to spoil and pillage even to his very trenches, keeping himself quiet within his works, which were well fortified; till, at last, perceiving that part of the enemy were scattered about the country foraging, and that those that were in the camp did nothing day and night but drink and revel, in the nighttime he drew up his lightest-armed men, and sent them out before to impede the enemy while forming into order, and to harass them when they should first issue out of their camp; and early in the morning brought down his main body, and set them in battle array in the lower grounds, a numerous and courageous army, not, as the barbarians had supposed, an inconsiderable and fearful division. The first thing that shook the courage of the Gauls was, that their enemies had, contrary to their expectation, the honour of being aggressors. In the next place, the light-armed men, falling upon them before they could get into their usual order or range themselves in their proper squadrons, so disturbed and pressed upon them, that they were obliged to fight at random, without any order at all. But at last, when Camillus brought on his heavy-armed legions, the barbarians, with their swords drawn, went vigorously to engage them; the Romans, however, opposing their javelins and receiving the force of their blows on those parts of their defences which were well guarded with steel, turned the edge of their weapons, being made of soft and ill-tempered metal, so that their swords bent and doubled up in their hands; and their shields were pierced through and through, and grew heavy with the javelins that struck upon them. And thus forced to quit their own weapons, they endeavoured to take advantage of those of their enemies, laid hold of the javelins with their hands, and tried to pluck them away. But the Romans, perceiving them now naked and defenceless, betook themselves to their swords, which they so well used that in a little time great slaughter was made in the foremost ranks, while the rest fled over all parts of the level country; the hills and upper grounds Camillus had secured beforehand, and their camp they knew it would not be difficult for the enemy to take, as, through confidence of victory, they had left it unguarded. This fight, it is stated, was thirteen years after the sacking of Rome; and from henceforward the Romans took courage, and surmounted the apprehensions they had hitherto entertained of the barbarians, whose previous defeat they had attributed rather to pestilence and a concurrence of mischances than to their own superior valour. And, indeed, this fear had been formerly so great that they made a law, that priests should be excused from service in war, unless in an invasion from the Gaul.

This was the last military action that ever Camillus performed; for the voluntary surrender of the city of the Velitrani was but a mere accessory to it. But the greatest of all civil contests, and the hardest to be managed, was still to be fought out against the people; who, returning home full of victory and success, insisted, contrary to established law, to have one of the consuls chosen out of their own body. The senate strongly opposed it, and would not suffer Camillus to lay down his dictatorship, thinking that, under the shelter of his great name and authority, they should be better able to contend for the power of his aristocracy. But when Camillus was sitting upon the tribunal, despatching public affairs, an officer, sent by the tribunes of the people, commanded him to rise and follow him, laying his hand upon him, as ready to seize and carry him away; upon which, such a noise and tumult as was never heard before filled the whole forum; some that were about Camillus thrusting the officer from the bench, and the multitude below calling out to him to bring Camillus down. Being at a loss what to do in these difficulties, he yet laid not down his authority, but, taking the senators along with him, he went to the senate-house; but before he entered, besought the gods that they would bring these troubles to a happy conclusion, solemnly vowing, when the tumult was ended, to build a temple to Concord. A great conflict of opposite opinions arose in the senate; but, at last, the most moderate and most acceptable to the people prevailed, and consent was given, that of two consuls, one should be chosen from the commonalty. When the dictator proclaimed this determination of the senate to the people, at the moment pleased and reconciled with the senate, as indeed could not otherwise be, they accompanied Camillus home, with all expressions and acclamations of joy; and the next day, assembling together, they voted a temple of Concord to be built, according to Camillus' vow, facing the assembly and the forum; and to the feasts, called the Latin holidays, they added one day more, making four in all; and ordained that, on the present occasion, the whole people of Rome should sacrifice with garlands on their heads.

In the election of consuls held by Camillus, Marcus Æmilius was chosen of the patricians, and Lucius Sextius the first of the commonalty; and this was the last of all Camillus' actions. In the year following, a pestilential sickness infected Rome, which, besides an infinite number of the common people, swept away most of the magistrates, among whom was Camillus; whose death cannot be called immature, if we consider his great age, or greater actions, yet was he more lamented than all the rest put together that then died of that distemper.

PERICLES

CÆSAR ONCE, SEEING SOME WEALTHY STRANGERS AT ROME, CARRYING UP and down with them in their arms and bosoms young puppy-dogs and monkeys, embracing and making much of them, took occasion not unnaturally to ask whether the women in their country were not used to bear children; by that prince-like reprimand gravely reflecting upon persons who spend and lavish upon brute beasts that affection and kindness which nature has implanted in us to be bestowed on those of our own kind. With like reason may we blame those who misuse that love of inquiry and observation which nature has implanted in our souls, by expending it on objects unworthy of the attention either of their eyes or their ears, while they disregard such as are excellent in themselves, and would do them good.

The mere outward sense, being passive in responding to the impression of the objects that come in its way and strike upon it, perhaps cannot help entertaining and taking notice of everything that addresses it, be it what it will, useful or unuseful; but, in the exercise of his mental perception every man, if he chooses, has a natural power to turn himself upon all occasions, and to change and shift with the greatest ease to what he shall himself judge desirable. So that it becomes a man's duty to pursue and make after the best and choicest of everything, that he may not only employ his contemplation, but may also be improved by it. For as that colour is more suitable to the eye whose freshness and pleasantness stimulates and strengthens the sight, so a man ought to apply his intellectual perception to such objects as, with the sense of delight, are apt to call it forth, and allure it to its own proper good and advantage.

Such objects we find in the acts of virtue, which also produce in the minds of mere readers about them an emulation and eagerness that may lead them on to imitation. In other things there does not immediately follow upon the admiration and liking of the thing done any strong desire of doing the like. Nay, many times, on the very contrary, when we are pleased with the work, we slight and set little by the workman or artist himself, as, for instance, in perfumes and purple dyes, we are taken with the things themselves well enough, but do not think dyers and perfumers otherwise than low and sordid people. It was not said amiss by Antisthenes, when people told him that one Ismenias was an excellent piper. "It may be so," said he, "but he is but a wretched human being, otherwise he would not have been an excellent piper." And King Philip, to the same purpose, told his son Alexander, who once at a merry-meeting played a piece of music charmingly and skilfully, "Are you not ashamed, son, to play so well?" For it is enough for a king or prince to find leisure sometimes to hear others sing, and he does the muses quite honour enough when he pleases to be but present, while others engage in such exercises and trials of skill.

He who busies himself in mean occupations produces, in the very pains he takes about things of little or no use, an evidence against himself of his negligence and indisposition to what is really good. Nor did any generous and ingenuous young man, at the sight of the statue of Jupiter at Pisa, ever desire to be a Phidias, or on seeing that of Juno at Argos, long to be a Polycletus, or feel induced by his pleasure in their poems to wish to be an Anacreon or Philetas or Archilochus. For it does not necessarily follow, that, if a piece of work please for its gracefulness, therefore he that wrought it deserves our admiration. Whence it is that neither do such things really profit or advantage the beholders, upon the sight of which no zeal arises for the imitation of them, nor any impulse or inclination, which may prompt any desire or endeavour of doing the like. But virtue, by the bare statement of its actions, can so affect men's minds as to create at once both admiration of the things done and desire to imitate the doers of them. The goods of fortune we would possess and would enjoy; those of virtue we long to practise and exercise: we are content to receive the former from others, the latter we wish others to experience from us. Moral good is a practical stimulus; it is no sooner seen, than it inspires an impulse to practice, and influences the mind and character not by a mere imitation which we look at, but by the statement of the fact creates a moral purpose which we form.

And so we have thought fit to spend our time and pains in writing of the lives of famous persons; and have composed this tenth book upon that subject, containing the life of Pericles, and that of Fabius Maximus, who carried on the war against Hannibal, men alike, as in their other virtues and good parts, so especially in their mind and upright temper and demeanour, and in that capacity to bear the cross-grained humours of their fellow-citizens and colleagues in office, which made them both most useful and serviceable to the interests of their countries. Whether we take a right aim at our intended purpose, it is left to the reader to judge by what he shall here find.

Pericles was of the tribe Acamantis, and the township Cholargus, of the noblest birth both on his father's and mother's side. Xanthippus, his father, who defeated the King of Persia's generals in the battle of Mycale, took to wife Agariste, the grandchild of Clisthenes, who drove out the sons of Pisistratus, and nobly put an end to their tyrannical usurpation, and, moreover, made a body of laws, and settled a model of government admirably tempered and suited for the harmony and safety of the people.

His mother, being near her time, fancied in a dream that she was brought to bed of a lion, and a few days after was delivered of Pericles, in other respects perfectly formed, only his head was somewhat longish and out of proportion. For which reason almost all the images and statues that were made of him have the head covered with a helmet, the workmen apparently being willing not to expose him. The poets of Athens called him *Schinocephalos*, or squill-head, from *schinos*, a squill, or sea-onion. One of the comic poets, Cratinus, in the Chirons, tells us that—

> Old Chronos once took queen Sedition to wife:
> Which two brought to life
> That tryant far-famed,
> Whom the gods the supreme skull-compeller have named:

and, in the Nemesis, addresses him—

> Come, Jove, thou head of Gods.

And a second, Teleclides, says, that now, in embarrassment with political difficulties, he sits in the city—

> Fainting underneath the load
> Of his own head: and now abroad
> From his huge gallery of a pate
> Sends forth trouble to the state.

And a third, Eupolis, in the comedy called the Demi, in a series of questions about each of the demagogues, whom he makes in the play to come up from hell, upon Pericles being named last, exclaims—

And here by way of summary, now we've done,
Behold, in brief, the heads of all in one.

The master that taught him music, most authors are agreed, was Damon (whose name, they say, ought to be pronounced with the first syllable short). Though Aristotle tells us that he was thoroughly practised in all accomplishments of this kind by Pythoclides. Damon, it is not unlikely, being a sophist, out of policy sheltered himself under the profession of music to conceal from people in general his skill in other things, and under this pretence attended Pericles, the young athlete of politics, so to say, as his training-master in these exercises. Damon's lyre, however, did not prove altogether a successful blind; he was banished the country by ostracism for ten years, as a dangerous intermeddler and a favourer of arbitrary power, and, by this means, gave the stage occasion to play upon him. As, for instance, Plato, the comic poet, introduces a character who questions him—

Tell me, if you please,
Since you're the Chiron who taught Pericles.

Pericles, also, was a hearer of Zeno, the Eleatic, who treated of natural philosophy in the same manner as Parmenides did, but had also perfected himself in an art of his own for refuting and silencing opponents in argument; as Timon of Phlius describes it—

Also the two-edged tongue of mighty Zeno, who,
Say what one would, could argue it untrue.

But he that saw most of Pericles, and furnished him most especially with a weight and grandeur of sense, superior to all arts of popularity, and in general gave him his elevation and sublimity of purpose and of character, was Anaxagoras of Clazomenæ; whom the men of those times called by the name of Nous, that is, mind, or intelligence, whether in admiration of the great and extraordinary gift he had displayed for the science of nature, or because that he was the first of the philosophers who did not refer the first ordering of the world to fortune or chance, nor to necessity or compulsion, but to a pure, unadulterated intelligence, which in all other existing mixed and compound things acts as a principle of discrimination, and of combination of like with like.

For this man, Pericles entertained an extraordinary esteem and admiration, and filling himself with this lofty and, as they call it, up-in-the-air sort of thought, derived hence not merely, as was natural, elevation of purpose and dignity of language, raised far above the base and dishonest buffooneries of mob eloquence, but, besides this, a composure of countenance, and a serenity and calmness in all his movements, which no occurrence whilst he was speaking could disturb, a sustained and even tone of voice, and various other advantages of a similar kind, which produced the greatest effect on his hearers. Once, after being reviled and ill-spoken of all day long in his own hearing by some vile and abandoned fellow in the open market place, where he was engaged in the despatch of some urgent affair, he continued his business in perfect silence, and in the evening returned home composedly, the man still dogging him at the heels, and pelting him all the way with abuse and foul language; and stepping into his house, it being by this time dark, be ordered one of his servants to take a light, and to go along with the man and see him safe home. Ion, it is true, the dramatic poet, says that Pericles' manner in company was somewhat over-assuming and pompous; and that into his high-bearing there entered a good deal of slightingness and scorn of others; he reserves his commendation for Cimon's ease and pliancy and natural grace in society. Ion, however, who must needs make virtue, like a show of tragedies, include some comic scenes, we shall not altogether rely upon; Zeno used to bid those who called Pericles' gravity the affectation of a charlatan, to go and affect the like themselves; inasmuch as this mere counterfeiting might in time insensibly instil into them a real love and knowledge of those noble qualities.

Nor were these the only advantages which Pericles derived from Anaxagoras' acquaintance; he seems also to have become, by his instructions, superior to that superstition with which an ignorant wonder at appearances, for example, in the heavens, possesses the minds of people unacquainted with their causes, eager for the supernatural, and excitable through an inexperience which the knowledge of natural causes removes, replacing wild and timid superstition by the good hope and assurance of an intelligent piety.

There is a story, that once Pericles had brought to him from a country farm of his a ram's head with one horn, and that Lampon, the diviner, upon seeing the horn grow strong and solid out of the midst of the forehead, gave it as his judgment, that, there being at that time two potent factions, parties, or interests in the city, the one of Thucydides and the other of Pericles, the government would come about to that one of them in whose ground or estate this token or indication of fate had shown itself. But that Anaxagoras, cleaving the skull in sunder, showed to the bystanders that the brain had not filled up its natural place, but being oblong, like an egg, had collected from all parts of the vessel which contained it in a point to that place from whence the root of the horn took its rise. And that, for that time, Anaxagoras was much admired for his explanation by those that were present; and Lampon no less a little while after, when Thucydides was overpowered, and the whole affairs of the state and government came into the hands of Pericles.

And yet, in my opinion, it is no absurdity to say that they were both in the right, both natural philosopher and diviner, one justly detecting the cause of this event, by which it was produced, the other the end for which it was designed. For it was the business of the one to find out and give an account of what it was made, and in what manner and by what means it grew as it did; and of the other to foretell to what end and purpose it was so made, and what it might mean or portend. Those who say that to find out the cause of a prodigy is in effect to destroy its supposed signification as such, do not take notice, that, at the same time, together with divine prodigies, they also do away with signs and signals of human art and concert, as, for instance, the clashings of quoits, fire-beacons, and the shadows of sundials, everyone of which has its cause, and by that cause and contrivance is a sign of something else. But these are subjects, perhaps, that would better befit another place.

Pericles, while yet but a young man, stood in considerable apprehension of the people, as he was thought in face and figure to be very like the tyrant Pisistratus, and those of great age remarked upon the sweetness of his voice, and his volubility and rapidity in speaking, and were struck with amazement at the resemblance. Reflecting, too, that he had a considerable estate, and was descended of a noble family, and had friends of great influence, he was fearful all this might bring him to be banished as a dangerous person, and for this reason meddled not at all with state affairs, but in military service showed himself of a brave and intrepid nature. But when Aristides was now dead, and Themistocles driven out, and Cimon was for the most part kept abroad by the expeditions he made in parts out of Greece, Pericles, seeing things in this posture, now advanced and took his side, not with the rich and few, but with the many and poor, contrary to his natural bent, which was far from democratical; but, most likely fearing he might fall under suspicion of aiming at arbitrary power, and seeing Cimon on the side of the aristocracy, and much beloved by the better and more distinguished people, he joined the party of the people, with a view at once both to secure himself and procure means against Cimon.

He immediately entered, also, on quite a new course of life and management of his time. For he was never seen to walk in any street but that which led to the market place and council-hall, and he avoided invitations of friends to supper, and all friendly visiting and intercourse whatever; in all the time he had to do with the public, which was not a little, he was never known to have gone to any of his friends to a supper, except that once when his near kinsman Euryptolemus married, he remained present till the ceremony of the drink-offering, and then immediately rose from table and went his way. For these friendly meetings are very quick to defeat any assumed superiority, and in intimate familiarity an exterior of gravity is hard to maintain. Real excellence, indeed, is most recognised when most openly looked into; and in really good men, nothing which meets the eyes of external observers so truly deserves their admiration, as their daily common life does that of their nearer friends. Pericles, however, to avoid any feeling of commonness, or any satiety on the part of the people, presented himself at intervals only, not speaking to every business, nor at all times coming into the assembly, but, as Critolaus says, reserving himself, like the Salaminian galley, for great occasions, while matters of lesser importance were despatched by friends or other speakers under his direction. And of this number we are told Ephialtes made one, who broke the power of the council of Areopagus, giving the people, according to Plato's expression, so copious and so strong a draught of liberty, that growing wild and unruly, like an unmanageable horse, it, as the comic poets say—

—got beyond all keeping in,
Champing at Eubœa, and among the islands leaping in.

The style of speaking most consonant to his form of life and the dignity of his views he found, so to say, in the tones of that instrument with which Anaxagoras had furnished him; of his teaching he continually availed himself, and deepened the colours of rhetoric with the dye of natural science. For having, in addition to his great natural genius, attained, by the study of nature, to use the words of the divine Plato, this height of intelligence, and this universal consummating power, and drawing hence whatever might be of advantage to him in the art of speaking, he showed himself far superior to all others. Upon which account, they say, he had his nickname given him, though some are of opinion he was named the Olympian from the public buildings with which he adorned the city; and others again, from his great power in public affairs, whether of war or peace. Nor is it unlikely that the confluence of many attributes may have conferred it on him. However, the comedies represented at the time, which, both in good earnest and in merriment, let fly many hard words at him, plainly show that he got that appellation especially from his speaking; they speak of his "thundering and lightning" when he harangued the people, and of his wielding a dreadful thunderbolt in his tongue.

A saying also of Thucydides, the son of Melesias, stands on record, spoken by him by way of pleasantry upon Pericles' dexterity. Thucydides was one of the noble and distinguished citizens, and had been his greatest opponent; and, when Archidamus, the King of the Lacedæmonians, asked him whether he or Pericles were the better wrestler, he made this answer: "When I," said he, "have thrown him and given him a fair fall, by persisting that he had no fall, he gets the better of me, and makes the bystanders, in spite of their own eyes, believe him." The truth, however, is, that Pericles himself was very careful what and how he was to speak, insomuch that, whenever he went up to the hustings, he prayed the gods that no one word might unawares slip from him unsuitable to the matter and the occasion.

He has left nothing in writing behind him, except some decrees; and there are but very few of his sayings recorded; one, for example, is, that he said Ægina must, like a gathering in a man's eye, be removed from Piræus; and another, that he said he saw already war moving on its way towards them out of Peloponnesus. Again, when on a time Sophocles, who was his fellow-commissioner in the generalship, was going on board with him, and praised the beauty of a youth they met with in the way to the ship, "Sophocles," said he, "a general ought not only to have clean hands but also clean eyes." And Stesimbrotus tells us that, in his encomium on those who fell in battle at Samos, he said they were become immortal, as the gods were. "For," said he, "we do not see them themselves, but only by the honours we pay them, and by the benefits they do us, attribute to them immortality; and the like attributes belong also to those that die in the service of their country."

Since Thucydides describes the rule of Pericles as an aristocratical government, that went by the name of a democracy, but was, indeed, the supremacy of a single great man, while many others say, on the contrary, that by him the common people were first encouraged and led on to such evils as appropriations of subject territory, allowances for attending theatres, payments for performing public duties, and by these bad habits were, under the influence of his public measures, changed from a sober, thrifty people, that maintained themselves by their own labours, to lovers of expense, intemperance, and licence, let us examine the cause of this change by the actual matters of fact.

At the first, as has been said, when he set himself against Cimon's great authority, he did caress the people. Finding himself come short of his competitor in wealth and money, by which advantages the other was enabled to take care of the poor, inviting everyday someone or other of the citizens that was in want to supper, and bestowing clothes on the aged people, and breaking down the hedges and enclosures of his grounds, that all that would might freely gather what fruit they pleased, Pericles, thus outdone in popular arts, by the advice of one Damonides of Œa, as Aristotle states, turned to the distribution of the public moneys; and in a short time having bought the people over, what with moneys allowed for shows and for service on juries, and what with other forms of pay and largess, he made use of them against the council of Areopagus of which he himself was no member, as having never been appointed by lot either chief archon, or lawgiver, or king, or captain. For from of old these offices were conferred on persons by lot, and they who had acquitted themselves duly in the discharge of them were advanced to the court of Areopagus. And so Pericles, having secured his power in interest with the populace, directed the exertions of his party against this council with such success, that most of these causes and matters which had been used to be tried there were, by the agency of Ephialtes, removed from its cognisance; Cimon, also, was banished by ostracism as a favourer of the Lacedæmonians and a hater of the people, though in wealth and noble birth he was among the first, and had won several most glorious victories over the barbarians, and had filled the city with money and spoils of war; as is recorded in the history of his life. So vast an authority had Pericles obtained among the people.

The ostracism was limited by law to ten years; but the Lacedæmonians, in the meantime, entering with a great army into the territory of Tanagra, and the Athenians going out against them, Cimon, coming from his banishment before his time was out, put himself in arms and array with those of his fellow-citizens that were of his own tribe, and desired by his deeds to wipe off the suspicion of his favouring the Lacedæmonians, by venturing his own person along with his countrymen. But Pericles' friends, gathering in a body, forced him to retire as a banished man. For which cause also Pericles seems to have exerted himself more in that than in any battle, and to have been conspicuous above all for his exposure of himself to danger. All Cimon's friends, also, to a man, fell together side by side, whom Pericles had accused with him of taking part with the Lacedæmonians. Defeated in this battle on their own frontiers, and expecting a new and perilous attack with return of spring, the Athenians now felt regret and sorrow for the loss of Cimon, and repentance for their expulsion of him. Pericles, being sensible of their feelings, did not hesitate or delay to gratify it, and himself made the motion for recalling him home. He, upon his return, concluded a peace betwixt the two cities; for the Lacedæmonians entertained as kindly feelings towards him as they did the reverse towards Pericles and the other popular leaders.

Yet some there are who say that Pericles did not propose the order for Cimon's return till some private articles of agreement had been made between them, and this by means of Elpinice, Cimon's sister; that Cimon, namely, should go out to sea with a fleet of two hundred ships, and be commander-in-chief abroad, with a design to reduce the King of Persia's territories, and that Pericles should have the power at home.

This Elpinice, it was thought, had before this time procured some favour for her brother Cimon at Pericles' hands, and induced him to be more remiss and gentle in urging the charge when Cimon was tried for his life; for Pericles was one of the committee appointed by the commons to plead against him. And when Elpinice came and besought him in her brother's behalf, he answered, with a smile, "O Elpinice, you are too old a woman to undertake such business as this." But, when he appeared to impeach him, he stood up but once to speak, merely to acquit himself of his commission, and went out of court, having done Cimon the least prejudice of any of his accusers.

How, then, can one believe Idomeneus, who charges Pericles as if he had by treachery procured the murder of Ephialtes, the popular statesman, one who was his friend, and of his own party in all his political course, out of jealousy, forsooth, and envy of his great reputation? This historian, it seems, having raked up these stories, I know not whence, has befouled with them a man who, perchance, was not altogether free from fault or blame, but yet had a noble spirit, and a soul that was bent on honour; and where such qualities are, there can no such cruel and brutal passion find harbour or gain admittance. As to Ephialtes, the truth of the story, as Aristotle has told it, is this: that having made himself formidable to the oligarchical party, by being an uncompromising asserter of the people's rights in calling to account and prosecuting those who any way wronged them, his enemies, lying in wait for him, by the means of Aristodicus the Tanagræan, privately despatched him.

Cimon, while he was admiral, ended his days in the Isle of Cyprus. And the aristocratical party, seeing that Pericles was already before this grown to be the greatest and foremost man of all the city, but nevertheless wishing there should be somebody set up against him, to blunt and turn the edge of his power, that it might not altogether prove a monarchy, put forward Thucydides of Alopece, a discreet person, and a near kinsman of Cimon's, to conduct the opposition against him; who, indeed, though less skilled in warlike affairs than Cimon was, yet was better versed in speaking and political business and keeping close guard in the city, and, engaging with Pericles on the hustings, in a short time brought the government to an equality of parties. For he would not suffer those who were called the honest and good (persons of worth and distinction) to be scattered up and down and mix themselves and be lost among the populace, as formerly, diminishing and obscuring their superiority amongst the masses; but taking them apart by themselves and uniting them in one body, by their combined weight he was able, as it were upon the balance, to make a counterpoise to the other party.

For, indeed, there was from the beginning a sort of concealed split, or seam, as it might be in a piece of iron, marking the different popular and aristocratical tendencies; but the open rivalry and contention of these two opponents made the gash deep, and severed the city into the two parties of the people and the few. And so Pericles, at that time, more than at any other, let loose the reins to the people, and made his policy subservient to their pleasure, contriving continually to have some great public show or solemnity, some banquet, or some procession or other in the town to please them, coaxing his countrymen like children with such delights and pleasures as were not, however, unedifying. Besides that every year he sent out threescore galleys, on board of which there were numbers of the citizens, who were in pay eight months, learning at the same time and practising the art of seamanship.

He sent, moreover, a thousand of them into the Chersonese as planters, to share the land among them by lot, and five hundred more into the isle of Naxos, and half that number to Andros, a thousand into Thrace to dwell among the Bisaltæ, and others into Italy, when the city Sybaris, which now was called Thurii, was to be re-peopled. And this he did to ease and discharge the city of an idle, and, by reason of their idleness, a busy meddling crowd of people; and at the same time to meet the necessities and restore the fortunes of the poor townsmen, and to intimidate, also, and check their allies from attempting any change, by posting such garrisons, as it were, in the midst of them.

That which gave most pleasure and ornament to the city of Athens, and the greatest admiration and even astonishment to all strangers, and that which now is Greece's only evidence that the power she boasts of and her ancient wealth are no romance or idle story, was his construction of the public and sacred buildings. Yet this was that of all his actions in the government which his enemies most looked askance upon and cavilled at in the popular assemblies, crying out how that the commonwealth of Athens had lost its reputation and was ill-spoken of abroad for removing the common treasure of the Greeks from the isle of Delos into their own custody; and how that their fairest excuse for so doing, namely, that they took it away for fear the barbarians should seize it, and on purpose to secure it in a safe place, this Pericles had made unavailable, and how that "Greece cannot but resent it as an insufferable affront, and consider herself to be tyrannised over openly, when she sees the treasure, which was contributed by her upon a necessity for the war, wantonly lavished out by us upon our city, to gild her all over, and to adorn and set her forth, as it were some vain woman, hung round with precious stones and figures and temples, which cost a world of money."

Pericles, on the other hand, informed the people, that they were in no way obliged to give any account of those moneys to their allies, so long as they maintained their defence, and kept off the barbarians from attacking them; while in the meantime they did not so much as supply one horse or man or ship, but only found money for the service; "which money," said he, "is not theirs that give it, but theirs that receive it, if so be they perform the conditions upon which they receive it." And that it was good reason, that, now the city was sufficiently provided and stored with all things necessary for the war, they should convert the overplus of its wealth to such undertakings as would hereafter, when completed, give them eternal honour, and, for the present, while in process, freely supply all the inhabitants with plenty. With their variety of workmanship and of occasions for service, which summon all arts and trades and require all hands to be employed about them, they do actually put the whole city, in a manner, into state-pay; while at the same time she is both beautiful and maintained by herself. For as those who are of age and strength for war are provided for and maintained in the armaments abroad by their pay out of the public stock, so, it being his desire and design that the undisciplined mechanic multitude that stayed at home should not go without their share of public salaries, and yet should not have them given them for sitting still and doing nothing, to that end he thought fit to bring in among them, with the approbation of the people, these vast projects of buildings and designs of work, that would be of some continuance before they were finished, and would give employment to numerous arts, so that the part of the people that stayed at home might, no less than those that were at sea or in garrisons or on expeditions, have a fair and just occasion of receiving the benefit and having their share of the public moneys.

The materials were stone, brass, ivory, gold, ebony, cypresswood; and the arts or trades that wrought and fashioned them were smiths and carpenters, moulders, founders and braziers, stone-cutters, dyers, goldsmiths, ivory-workers, painters, embroiderers, turners; those again that conveyed them to the town for use, merchants and mariners and ship-masters by sea, and by land cartwrights, cattle-breeders, wagoners, rope-makers, flax-workers, shoemakers and leather-dressers, road-makers, miners. And every trade in the same nature, as a captain in an army has his particular company of soldiers under him, had its own hired company of journeymen and labourers belonging to it banded together as in array, to be as it were the instrument and body for the performance of the service. Thus, to say all in a word, the occasions and services of these public works distributed plenty through every age and condition.

As then grew the works up, no less stately in size than exquisite in form, the workmen striving to outvie the material and the design with the beauty of their workmanship, yet the most wonderful thing of all was the rapidity of their execution.

Undertakings, anyone of which singly might have required, they thought, for their completion, several successions and ages of men, were everyone of them accomplished in the height and prime of one man's political service. Although they say, too, that Zeuxis once, having heard Agatharchus the painter boast of despatching his work with speed and ease, replied, "I take a long time." For ease and speed in doing a thing do not give the work lasting solidity or exactness of beauty; the expenditure of time allowed to a man's pains beforehand for the production of a thing is repaid by way of interest with a vital force for the preservation when once produced. For which reason Pericles' works are especially admired, as having been made quickly, to last long. For every particular piece of his work was immediately, even at that time, for its beauty and elegance, antique; and yet in its vigour and freshness looks to this day as if it were just executed. There is a sort of bloom of newness upon those works of his, preserving them from the touch of time, as if they had some perennial spirit and undying vitality mingled in the composition of them.

Phidias had the oversight of all the works, and was surveyor-general, though upon the various portions other great masters and workmen were employed. For Callicrates and Ictinus built the Parthenon; the chapel at Eleusis, where the mysteries were celebrated, was begun by Corœbus, who erected the pillars that stand upon the floor or pavement, and joined them to the architraves; and after his death Metagenes of Xypete added the frieze and the upper line of columns; Xenocles of Cholargus roofed or arched the lantern on top of the temple of Castor and Pollux; and the long wall, which Socrates says he himself heard Pericles propose to the people, was undertaken by Callicrates. This work Cratinus ridicules, as long in finishing—

'Tis long since Pericles, if words would do it,
Talked up the wall; yet adds not one mite to it.

The Odeum, or music-room, which in its interior was full of seats and ranges of pillars, and outside had its roof made to slope and descend from one single point at the top, was constructed, we are told, in imitation of the King of Persia's Pavilion; this likewise by Pericles' order; which Cratinus again, in his comedy called the Thracian Women, made an occasion of raillery—

So, we see here,
Jupiter Long-pate Pericles appear,
Since ostracism time, he's laid aside his head,
And wears the new Odeum in its stead.

Pericles, also eager for distinction, then first obtained the decree for a contest in musical skill to be held yearly at the Panathenæa, and he himself, being chosen judge, arranged the order and method in which the competitors should sing and play on the flute and on the harp. And both at that time, and at other times also, they sat in this music-room to see and hear all such trials of skill.

The propylæa, or entrances to the Acropolis, were finished in five years' time, Mnesicles being the principal architect. A strange accident happened in the course of building, which showed that the goddess was not averse to the work, but was aiding and cooperating to bring it to perfection. One of the artificers, the quickest and the handiest workman among them all, with a slip of his foot fell down from a great height, and lay in a miserable condition, the physicians having no hope of his recovery. When Pericles was in distress about this, Minerva appeared to him at night in a dream, and ordered a course of treatment, which he applied, and in a short time and with great ease cured the man. And upon this occasion it was that he set up a brass statue of Minerva, surnamed Health, in the citadel near the altar, which they say was there before. But it was Phidias who wrought the goddess' image in gold, and he has his name inscribed on the pedestal as the workman of it; and indeed the whole work in a manner was under his charge, and he had, as we have said already, the oversight over all the artists and workmen, through Pericles' friendship for him; and this, indeed, made him much envied, and his patron shamefully slandered with stories, as if Phidias were in the habit of receiving, for Pericles' use, freeborn women that came to see the works. The comic writers of the town, when they had got hold of this story, made much of it, and bespattered him with all the ribaldry they could invent, charging him falsely with the wife of Menippus, one who was his friend and served as lieutenant under him in the wars; and with the birds kept by Pyrilampes, an acquaintance of Pericles, who, they pretended, used to give presents of peacocks to Pericles' female friends. And how can one wonder at any number of strange assertions from men whose whole lives were devoted to mockery, and who were ready at anytime to sacrifice the reputation of their superiors to vulgar envy and spite, as to some evil genius, when even Stesimbrotus the Thracian has dared to lay to the charge of Pericles a monstrous and fabulous piece of criminality with his son's wife? So very difficult a matter is it to trace and find out the truth of anything by history, when, on the one hand, those who afterwards write it find long periods of time intercepting their view, and, on the other hand, the contemporary records of any actions and lives, partly through envy and ill-will, partly through favour and flattery, pervert and distort truth.

When the orators, who sided with Thucydides and his party, were at one time crying out, as their custom was, against Pericles, as one who squandered away the public money, and made havoc of the state revenues, he rose in the open assembly and put the question to the people, whether they thought that he had laid out much; and they saying, "Too much, a great deal," "Then," said he, "since it is so, let the cost not go to your account, but to mine; and let the inscription upon the buildings stand in my name." When they heard him say thus, whether it were out of a surprise to see the greatness of his spirit or out of emulation of the glory of the works, they cried aloud, bidding him to spend on, and lay out what he thought fit from the public purse, and to spare no cost, till all were finished.

At length, coming to a final contest with Thucydides which of the two should ostracise the other out of the country, and having gone through this peril, he threw his antagonist out, and broke up the confederacy that had been organised against him. So that now all schism and division being at an end, and the city brought to evenness and unity, he got all Athens and all affairs that pertained to the Athenians into his own hands, their tributes, their armies, and their galleys, the islands, the sea, and their wide-extended power, partly over other Greeks and partly over barbarians, and all that empire, which they possessed, founded and fortified upon subject nations and royal friendships and alliances.

After this he was no longer the same man he had been before, nor as tame and gentle and familiar as formerly with the populace, so as readily to yield to their pleasures and to comply with the desires of the multitude, as a steersman shifts with the winds. Quitting that loose, remiss, and, in some cases, licentious court of the popular will, he turned those soft and flowery modulations to the austerity of aristocratical and regal rule; and employing this uprightly and undeviatingly for the country's best interests, he was able generally to lead the people along, with their own wills and consents, by persuading and showing them what was to be done; and sometimes, too, urging and pressing them forward extremely against their will, he made them, whether they would or no, yield submission to what was for their advantage. In which, to say the truth, he did but like a skilful physician, who, in a complicated and chronic disease, as he sees occasion, at one while allows his patient the moderate use of such things as please him, at another while gives him keen pains and drug to work the cure. For there arising and growing up, as was natural, all manner of distempered feelings among a people which had so vast a command and dominion, he alone, as a great master, knowing how to handle and deal fitly with each one of them, and, in an especial manner, making that use of hopes and fears, as his two chief rudders, with the one to check the career of their confidence at anytime, with the other to raise them up and cheer them when under any discouragement, plainly showed by this, that rhetoric, or the art of speaking, is, in Plato's language, the government of the souls of men, and that her chief business is to address the affections and passions, which are as it were the strings and keys to the soul, and require a skilful and careful touch to be played on as they should be. The source of this predominance was not barely his power of language, but, as Thucydides assures us, the reputation of his life, and the confidence felt in his character; his manifest freedom from every kind of corruption, and superiority to all considerations of money. Notwithstanding he had made the city of Athens, which was great of itself, as great and rich as can be imagined, and though he were himself in power and interest more than equal to many kings and absolute rulers, who some of them also bequeathed by will their power to their children, he, for his part, did not make the patrimony his father left him greater than it was by one drachma.

Thucydides, indeed, gives a plain statement of the greatness of his power; and the comic poets, in their spiteful manner, more than hint at it, styling his companions and friends the new Pisistratidæ, and calling on him to abjure any intention of usurpation, as one whose eminence was too great to be any longer proportionable to and compatible with a democracy or popular government. And Teleclides says the Athenians had surrendered up to him—

The tribute of the cities, and with them, the cities too, to do with them as
　　he pleases, and undo;
To build up, if he likes, stone walls around a town; and again, if so he likes,
　　to pull them down;
Their treaties and alliances, power, empire, peace, and war, their wealth
　　and their success forever more.

Nor was all this the luck of some happy occasion; nor was it the mere bloom and grace of a policy that flourished for a season; but having for forty years together maintained the first place among statesmen such as Ephialtes and Leocrates and Myronides and Cimon and Tolmides and Thucydides were, after the defeat and banishment of Thucydides, for no less than fifteen years longer, in the exercise of one continuous unintermitted command in the office, to which he was annually re-elected, of General, he preserved his integrity unspotted; though otherwise he was not altogether idle or careless in looking after his pecuniary advantage; his paternal estate, which of right belonged to him, he so ordered that it might neither through negligence be wasted or lessened, nor yet, being so fall of business as he was, cost him any great trouble or time with taking care of it; and put it into such a way of management as he thought to be the most easy for himself, and the most exact. All his yearly products and profits he sold together in a lump, and supplied his household needs afterwards by buying everything that he or his family wanted out of the market. Upon which account, his children, when they grew to age, were not well pleased with his management, and the women that lived with him were treated with little cost, and complained of his way of housekeeping, where everything was ordered and set down from day to day, and reduced to the greatest exactness; since there was not there, as is usual in a great family and a plentiful estate, anything to spare, or over and above; but all that went out or came in, all disbursements and all receipts, proceeded as it were by number and measure. His manager in all this was a single servant, Evangelus by name, a man either naturally gifted or instructed by Pericles so as to excel everyone in this art of domestic economy.

All this, in truth, was very little in harmony with Anaxagoras' wisdom; if, indeed, it be true that he, by a kind of divine impulse and greatness of spirit, voluntarily quitted his house, and left his land to lie fallow and to be grazed by sheep like a common. But the life of a contemplative philosopher and that of an active statesman are, I presume, not the same thing; for the one merely employs, upon great and good objects of thought, an intelligence that requires no aid of instruments nor supply of any external materials; whereas the other, who tempers and applies his virtue to human uses, may have occasion for affluence, not as a matter of necessity, but as a noble thing; which was Pericles' case, who relieved numerous poor citizens.

However, there is a story that Anaxagoras himself, while Pericles was taken up with public affairs, lay neglected, and that, now being grown old, he wrapped himself up with a resolution to die for want of food; which being by chance brought to Pericles' ear, he was horror-struck, and instantly ran thither, and used all the arguments and entreaties he could to him, lamenting not so much Anaxagoras' condition as his own, should he lose such a counsellor as he had found him to be; and that, upon this, Anaxagoras unfolded his robe, and showing himself, made answer: "Pericles," said he, "even those who have occasion for a lamp supply it with oil."

The Lacedæmonians beginning to show themselves troubled at the growth of the Athenian power, Pericles, on the other hand, to elevate the people's spirit yet more, and to raise them to the thought of great actions, proposed a decree, to summon all the Greeks in what part soever, whether of Europe or Asia, every city, little as well as great, to send their deputies to Athens to a general assembly, or convention, there to consult and advise concerning the Greek temples which the barbarians had burnt down, and the sacrifices which were due from them upon vows they had made to their gods for the safety of Greece when they fought against the barbarians; and also concerning the navigation of the sea, that they might henceforward pass to and fro and trade securely and be at peace among themselves.

Upon this errand there were twenty men, of such as were above fifty years of age, sent by commission; five to summon the Ionians and Dorians in Asia, and the islanders as far as Lesbos and Rhodes; five to visit all the places in the Hellespont and Thrace, up to Byzantium; and other five besides these to go to Bœotia and Phocis and Peloponnesus, and from hence to pass through the Locrians over to the neighbouring continent as far as Acarnania and Ambracia; and the rest to take their course through Eubœa to the Œtæns and the Malian Gulf, and to the Achæans of Phthiotis and the Thessalians; all of them to treat with the people as they passed, and persuade them to come and take their part in the debates for settling the peace and jointly regulating the affairs of Greece.

Nothing was effected, nor did the cities meet by their deputies, as was desired; the Lacedæmonians, as it is said, crossing the design underhand, and the attempt being disappointed and baffled first in Peloponnesus. I thought fit, however, to introduce the mention of it, to show the spirit of the man and the greatness of his thoughts.

In his military conduct, he gained a great reputation for wariness; he would not by his goodwill engage in any fight which had much uncertainty or hazard; he did not envy the glory of generals whose rash adventures fortune favoured with brilliant success, however they were admired by others; nor did he think them worthy his imitation, but always used to say to his citizens that, so far as lay in his power, they should continue immortal, and live forever. Seeing Tolmides, the son of Tolmæus, upon the confidence of his former successes, and flushed with the honour his military actions had procured him, making preparations to attack the Bœotians in their own country when there was no likely opportunity, and that he had prevailed with the bravest and most enterprising of the youth to enlist themselves as volunteers in the service, who besides his other force made up a thousand, he endeavoured to withhold him and to advise him from it in the public assembly, telling him in a memorable saying of his, which still goes about, that, if he would not take Pericles' advice, yet he would not do amiss to wait and be ruled by time, the wisest counsellor of all. This saying, at that time, was but slightly commended; but within a few days after, when news was brought that Tolmides himself had been defeated and slain in battle near Coronea, and that many brave citizens had fallen with him, it gained him great repute as well as goodwill among the people, for wisdom and for love of his countrymen.

But of all his expeditions, that to the Chersonese gave most satisfaction and pleasure, having proved the safety of the Greeks who inhabited there.

For not only by carrying along with him a thousand fresh citizens of Athens he gave new strength and vigour to the cities, but also by belting the neck of land, which joins the peninsula to the continent, with bulwarks and forts from sea to sea, he put a stop to the inroads of the Thracians, who lay all about the Chersonese, and closed the door against a continual and grievous war, with which that country had been long harassed, lying exposed to the encroachments and influx of barbarous neighbours, and groaning under the evils of a predatory population both upon and within its borders.

Nor was he less admired and talked of abroad for his sailing around the Peloponnesus, having set out from Pegæ, or The Fountains, the port of Megara, with a hundred galleys. For he not only laid waste the sea-coast, as Tolmides had done before, but also, advancing far up into the mainland with the soldiers he had on board, by the terror of his appearance drove many within their walls; and at Nemea, with main force, routed and raised a trophy over the Sicyonians, who stood their ground and joined battle with him. And having taken on board a supply of soldiers into the galleys out of Achaia, then in league with Athens, he crossed with the fleet to the opposite continent, and, sailing along by the mouth of the river Achelous, overran Acarnania and shut up the Œniadæ within their city walls, and having ravaged and wasted their country, weighed anchor for home with the double advantage of having shown himself formidable to his enemies, and at the same time safe and energetic to his fellow citizens; for there was not so much as any chance miscarriage that happened, the whole voyage through, to those who were under his charge.

Entering also the Euxine Sea with a large and finely equipped fleet, he obtained for the Greek cities any new arrangements they wanted, and entered into friendly relations with them; and to the barbarous nations, and kings and chiefs round about them, displayed the greatness of the power of the Athenians, their perfect ability and confidence to sail wherever they had a mind, and to bring the whole sea under their control. He left the Sinopians thirteen ships of war, with soldiers under the command of Lamachus, to assist them against Timesileus the tyrant; and when he and his accomplices had been thrown out, obtained a decree that six hundred of the Athenians that were willing should sail to Sinope and plant themselves there with the Sinopians, sharing among them the houses and land which the tyrant and his party had previously held.

But in other things he did not comply with the giddy impulses of the citizens, nor quit his own resolutions to follow their fancies, when, carried away with the thought of their strength and great success, they were eager to interfere again in Egypt, and to disturb the King of Persia's maritime dominions. Nay, there were a good many who were, even then, possessed with that unblest and inauspicious passion for Sicily, which afterward the orators of Alcibiades' party blew up into a flame. There were some also who dreamt of Tuscany and Carthage, and not without plausible reason in their present large dominion and prosperous course of their affairs.

But Pericles curbed this passion for foreign conquest, and unsparingly pruned and cut down their ever busy fancies for a multitude of undertakings; and directed their power for the most part to securing and consolidating what they had already got, supposing it would be quite enough for them to do, if they could keep the Lacedæmonians in check; to whom he entertained all along a sense of opposition; which, as upon many other occasions, so he particularly showed by what he did in the time of the holy war. The Lacedæmonians, having gone with an army to Delphi, restored Apollo's temple, which the Phocians had got into their possession, to the Delphians; immediately after their departure, Pericles, with another army, came and restored the Phocians. And the Lacedæmonians, having engraven the record of their privilege of consulting the oracle before others, which the Delphians gave them, upon the forehead of the brazen wolf which stands there, he, also, having received from the Phocians the like privilege for the Athenians, had it cut upon the same wolf of brass on his right side.

That he did well and wisely in thus restraining the exertions of the Athenians within the compass of Greece, the events themselves that happened afterward bore sufficient witness. For, in the first place, the Eubœans revolted, against whom he passed over with forces; and then, immediately after, news came that the Megarians were turned their enemies; and a hostile army was upon the borders of Attica, under the conduct of Plistoanax, King of the Lacedæmonians. Wherefore Pericles came with his army back again in all haste out of Eubœa, to meet the war which threatened at home; and did not venture to engage a numerous and brave army eager for battle; but perceiving that Plistoanax was a very young man, and governed himself mostly by the counsel and advice of Cleandrides, whom the ephors had sent with him, by reason of his youth, to be a kind of guardian and assistant to him, he privately made trial of this man's integrity, and, in a short time, having corrupted him with money, prevailed with him to withdraw the Peloponnesians out of Attica. When the army had retired and dispersed into their several states, the Lacedæmonians in anger fined their king in so large a sum of money, that, unable to pay it, he quitted Lacedæmon; while Cleandrides fled, and had sentence of death passed upon him in his absence. This was the father of Gylippus, who overpowered the Athenians in Sicily. And it seems that this covetousness was an hereditary disease transmitted from father to son; for Gylippus also afterwards was caught in foul practices, and expelled from Sparta for it. But this we have told at large in the account of Lysander.

When Pericles, in giving up his accounts of this expedition, stated a disbursement of ten talents, as laid out upon fit occasion, the people, without any question, nor troubling themselves to investigate the mystery, freely allowed of it. And some historians, in which number is Theophrastus the philosopher, have given it as a truth that Pericles every year used to send privately the sum of ten talents to Sparta, with which he complimented those in office, to keep off the war; not to purchase peace neither, but time, that he might prepare at leisure, and be the better able to carry on war hereafter.

Immediately after this, turning his forces against the revolters, and passing over into the island of Eubœa with fifty sail of ships and five thousand men in arms, he reduced their cities, and drove out the citizens of the Chalcidians, called Hippobotæ, horse-feeders, the chief persons for wealth and reputation among them; and removing all the Histiæans out of the country, brought in a plantation of Athenians in their room; making them his one example of severity, because they had captured an Attic ship and killed all on board.

After this, having made a truce between the Athenians and Lacedæmonians for thirty years, he ordered, by public decree, the expedition against the isle of Samos, on the ground, that, when they were bid to leave off their war with the Milesians they had not complied. And as these measures against the Samians are thought to have been taken to please Aspasia, this may be a fit point for inquiry about the woman, what art or charming, faculty she had that enabled her to captivate, as she did, the greatest statesmen, and to give the philosophers occasion to speak so much about her, and that, too, not to her disparagement. That she was a Milesian by birth, the daughter of Axiochus, is a thing acknowledged. And they say it was in emulation of Thargelia, a courtesan of the old Ionian times, that she made her addresses to men of great power. Thargelia was a great beauty, extremely charming, and at the same time sagacious; she had numerous suitors among the Greeks, and brought all who had to do with her over to the Persian interest, and by their means, being men of the greatest power and station, sowed the seeds of the Median faction up and down in several cities. Aspasia, some say, was courted and caressed by Pericles upon account of her knowledge and skill in politics. Socrates himself would sometimes go to visit her, and some of his acquaintance with him; and those who frequented her company would carry their wives with them to listen to her. Her occupation was anything but creditable, her house being a home for young courtesans. Æschines tells us, also, that Lysicles, a sheep-dealer, a man of low birth and character, by keeping Aspasia company after Pericles' death, came to be a chief man in Athens. And in Plato's Menexenus, though we do not take the introduction as quite serious, still thus much seems to be historical, that she had the repute of being resorted to by many of the Athenians for instruction in the art of speaking. Pericles' inclination for her seems, however, to have rather proceeded from the passion of love. He had a wife that was near of kin to him, who had been married first to Hipponicus, by whom she had Callias, surnamed the Rich; and also she brought Pericles, while she lived with him, two sons, Xanthippus and Paralus. Afterwards, when they did not well agree, nor like to live together, he parted with her, with her own consent, to another man, and himself took Aspasia, and loved her with wonderful affection; everyday, both as he went out and as he came in from the market place, he saluted and kissed her.

In the comedies she goes by the nicknames of the new Omphale and Deianira, and again is styled Juno. Cratinus, in downright terms, calls her a harlot.

> To find him a Juno the goddess of lust
> Bore that harlot past shame,
> Aspasia by name.

It should seem also that he had a son by her; Eupolis, in his Demi, introduced Pericles asking after his safety, and Myronides replying—

> My son? He lives: a man he had been long,
> But that the harlot-mother did him wrong.

Aspasia, they say, became so celebrated and renowned, that Cyrus, also who made war against Artaxerxes for the Persian monarchy, gave her whom he loved the best of all his concubines the name of Aspasia, who before that was called Milto. She was a Phocæan by birth, the daughter of one Hermotimus, and, when Cyrus fell in battle, was carried to the king, and had great influence at court. These things coming into my memory as I am writing this story, it would be unnatural for me to omit them.

Pericles, however, was particularly charged with having proposed to the assembly the war against the Samians, from favour to the Milesians, upon the entreaty of Aspasia. For the two states were at war for the possession of Priene; and the Samians, getting the better, refused to lay down their arms and to have the controversy betwixt them decided by arbitration before the Athenians. Pericles, therefore, fitting out a fleet, went and broke up the oligarchical government at Samos, and taking fifty of the principal men of the town as hostages, and as many of their children, sent them to the isle of Lemnos, there to be kept, though he had offers, as some relate, of a talent apiece for himself from each one of the hostages, and of many other presents from those who were anxious not to have a democracy. Moreover, Pisuthnes the Persian, one of the king's lieutenants, bearing some goodwill to the Samians, sent him ten thousand pieces of gold to excuse the city. Pericles, however, would receive none of all this; but after he had taken that course with the Samians which he thought fit, and set up a democracy among them, sailed back to Athens.

But they, however, immediately revolted, Pisuthnes having privily got away their hostages for them, and provided them with means for the war. Whereupon Pericles came out with a fleet a second time against them, and found them not idle nor slinking away, but manfully resolved to try for the dominion of the sea. The issue was, that after a sharp sea-fight about the island called Tragia, Pericles obtained a decisive victory, having with forty-four ships routed seventy of the enemy's, twenty of which were carrying soldiers.

Together with his victory and pursuit, having made himself master of the port, he laid siege to the Samians, and blocked them up, who yet, one way or another, still ventured to make sallies, and fight under the city walls. But after that another greater fleet from Athens was arrived, and that the Samians were now shut up with a close leaguer on every side, Pericles, taking with him sixty galleys, sailed out into the main sea, with the intention, as most authors give the account, to meet a squadron of Phœnician ships that were coming for the Samians' relief, and to fight them at as great distance as could be from the island; but, as Stesimbrotus says, with a design of putting over to Cyprus, which does not seem to be probable. But, whichever of the two was his intention, it seems to have been a miscalculation. For on his departure, Melissus, the son of Ithagenes, a philosopher, being at that time the general in Samos, despising either the small number of the ships that were left or the inexperience of the commanders, prevailed with the citizens to attack the Athenians. And the Samians having won the battle, and taken several of the men prisoners, and disabled several of the ships, were masters of the sea, and brought into port all necessaries they wanted for the war, which they had not before. Aristotle says, too, that Pericles had been once before this worsted by this Melissus in a sea-fight.

The Samians, that they might requite an affront which had before been put upon them, branded the Athenians, whom they took prisoners, in their foreheads, with the figure of an owl. For so the Athenians had marked them before with a Samæna, which is a sort of ship, low and flat in the prow, so as to look snub-nosed, but wide and large and well-spread in the hold, by which it both carries a large cargo and sails well. And it was so called, because the first of that kind was seen at Samos, having been built by order of Polycrates the tyrant. These brands upon the Samians' foreheads, they say, are the allusion in the passage of Aristophanes, where he says—

For, oh, the Samians are a lettered people.

Pericles, as soon as news was brought him of the disaster that had befallen his army, made all the haste he could to come in to their relief, and having defeated Melissus, who bore up against him, and put the enemy to flight, he immediately proceeded to hem them in with a wall, resolving to master them and take the town, rather with some cost and time than with the wounds and hazards of his citizens. But as it was a hard matter to keep back the Athenians, who were vexed at the delay, and were eagerly bent to fight, he divided the whole multitude into eight parts, and arranged by lot that that part which had the white bean should have leave to feast and take their ease while the other seven were fighting. And this is the reason, they say, that people, when at anytime they have been merry, and enjoyed themselves, called it white day, in allusion to this white bean.

Ephorus the historian tells us besides, that Pericles made use of engines of battery in this siege, being much taken with the curiousness of the invention, with the aid and presence of Artemon himself, the engineer, who, being lame, used to be carried about in a litter, where the works required his attendance, and for that reason was called Periphoretus. But Heraclides Ponticus disproves this out of Anacreon's poems, where mention is made of this Artemon Periphoretus several ages before the Samian war, or any of these occurrences. And he says that Artemon, being a man who loved his ease, and had a great apprehension of danger, for the most part kept close within doors, having two of his servants to hold a brazen shield over his head, that nothing might fall upon him from above; and if he were at anytime forced upon necessity to go abroad, that he was carried about in a little hanging bed, close to the very ground, and that for this reason he was called Periphoretus.

In the ninth month, the Samians surrendering themselves and delivering up the town, Pericles pulled down their walls, and seized their shipping, and set a fine of a large sum of money upon them, part of which they paid down at once, and they agreed to bring in the rest by a certain time, and gave hostages for security. Duris the Samian makes a tragical drama out of these events, charging the Athenians and Pericles with a great deal of cruelty, which neither Thucydides, nor Ephorus, nor Aristotle have given any relation of, and probably with little regard to truth; how, for example, he brought the captains and soldiers of the galleys into the market place at Miletus, and there having bound them fast to boards for ten days, then, when they were already all but half dead, gave order to have them killed by beating out their brains with clubs, and their dead bodies to be flung out into the open streets and fields, unburied. Duris, however, who, even where he has no private feeling concerned, is not wont to keep his narratives within the limits of truth, is the more likely upon this occasion to have exaggerated the calamities which befell his country, to create odium against the Athenians. Pericles, however, after the reduction of Samos, returning back to Athens, took care that those who died in the war should be honourably buried, and made a funeral harangue, as the custom is, in their commendation at their graves, for which he gained great admiration. As he came down from the stage on which he spoke, the rest of the women came and complimented him, taking him by the hand, and crowning him with garlands and ribbons, like a victorious athlete in the games; but Elpinice, coming near to him, said, "These are brave deeds, Pericles, that you have done, and such as deserve our chaplets; who have lost us many a worthy citizen, not in a war with Phœnicians or Medes, like my brother Cimon, but for the overthrow of an allied and kindred city." As Elpinice spoke these words, he, smiling quietly, as it is said, returned her answer with this verse:

> Old women should not seek to be perfumed.

Ion says of him, that upon this exploit of his, conquering the Samians, he indulged very high and proud thoughts of himself: whereas Agamemnon was ten years taking a barbarous city, he had in nine months' time vanquished and taken the greatest and most powerful of the Ionians. And indeed it was not without reason that he assumed this glory to himself, for, in real truth, there was much uncertainty and great hazard in this great war, if so be, as Thucydides tells us, the Samian, state were within a very little of wresting the whole power and dominion of the sea out of the Athenians' hands.

After this was over, the Peloponnesian war beginning to break out in full tide, he advised the people to send help to the Corcyræans, who were attacked by the Corinthians, and to secure to themselves an island possessed of great naval resources, since the Peloponnesians were already all but in actual hostilities against them. The people readily consenting to the motion, and voting an aid and succour for them, he despatched Lacedæmonius, Cimon's son, having only ten ships with him, as it were out of a design to affront him; for there was a great kindness and friendship betwixt Cimon's family and the Lacedæmonians; so, in order that Lacedæmonius might lie the more open to a charge, or suspicion at least, of favouring the Lacedæmonians and playing false, if he performed no considerable exploit in this service, he allowed him a small number of ships, and sent him out against his will; and indeed he made it somewhat his business to hinder Cimon's sons from rising in the state, professing that by their very names they were not to be looked upon as native and true Athenians, but foreigners and strangers, one being called Lacedæmonius, another Thessalus, and the third Eleus; and they were all three of them, it was thought, born of an Arcadian woman. Being, however, ill spoken of on account of these ten galleys, as having afforded but a small supply to the people that were in need, and yet given a great advantage to those who might complain of the act of intervention, Pericles sent out a larger force afterwards to Corcyra, which arrived after the fight was over. And when now the Corinthians, angry and indignant with the Athenians, accused them publicly at Lacedæmon, the Megarians joined with them, complaining that they were, contrary to common right and the articles of peace sworn to among the Greeks, kept out and driven away from every market and from all ports under the control of the Athenians. The Æginetans, also, professing to be ill-used and treated with violence, made supplications in private to the Lacedæmonians for redress, though not daring openly to call the Athenians in question. In the meantime, also, the city Potidæa, under the dominion of the Athenians, but a colony formerly of the Corinthians, had revolted, and was beset with a formal siege, and was a further occasion of precipitating the war.

Yet notwithstanding all this, there being embassies sent to Athens, and Archidamus, the King of the Lacedæmonians, endeavouring to bring the greater part of the complaints and matters in dispute to a fair determination, and to pacify and allay the hearts of the allies, it is very likely that the war would not upon any other grounds of quarrel have fallen upon the Athenians, could they have been prevailed with to repeal the ordinance against the Megarians, and to be reconciled to them. Upon which account, since Pericles was the man who mainly opposed it, and stirred up the people's passions to persist in their contention with the Megarians, he was regarded as the sole cause of the war.

They say, moreover, that ambassadors went, by order, from Lacedæmon to Athens about this very business, and that when Pericles was urging a certain law which made it illegal to take down or withdraw the tablet of the decree, one of the ambassadors, Polyalces by name, said, "Well, do not take it down then, but *turn* it; there is no law, I suppose, which forbids that"; which, though prettily said, did not move Pericles from his resolution. There may have been, in all likelihood, something of a secret grudge and private animosity which he had against the Megarians. Yet, upon a public and open charge against them, that they had appropriated part of the sacred land on the frontier, he proposed a decree that a herald should be sent to them, and the same also to the Lacedæmonians, with an accusation of the Megarians; an order which certainly shows equitable and friendly proceeding enough. And after that the herald who was sent, by name Anthemocritus, died, and it was believed that the Megarians had contrived his death, then Charinus proposed a decree against them, that there should be an irreconcilable and implacable enmity thenceforward betwixt the two commonwealths; and that if anyone of the Megarians should but set his foot in Attica, he should be put to death; and that the commanders, when they take the usual oath, should, over and above that, swear that they will twice every year make an inroad into the Megarian country; and that Anthemocritus should be buried near the Thracian Gates, which are now called the Dipylon, or Double Gate.

On the other hand, the Megarians, utterly denying and disowning the murder of Anthemocritus, throw the whole matter upon Aspasia and Pericles, availing themselves of the famous verses in the Acharnians—

> To Megara some of our madcaps ran,
> And stole Simætha thence, their courtesan.
> Which exploit the Megarians to outdo,
> Came to Aspasia's house, and took off two.

The true occasion of the quarrel is not so easy to find out. But of inducing the refusal to annul the decree, all alike charge Pericles. Some say he met the request with a positive refusal, out of high spirit and a view of the state's best interest, accounting that the demand made in those embassies was designed for a trial of their compliance, and that a concession would be taken for a confession of weakness as if they durst not do otherwise; while other some there are who say that it was rather out of arrogance and a wilful spirit of contention, to show his own strength, that he took occasion to slight the Lacedæmonians. The worst motive of all, which is confirmed by most witnesses, is to the following effect: Phidias the Moulder had, as has before been said, undertaken to make the statue of Minerva. Now he, being admitted to friendship with Pericles, and a great favourite of his, had many enemies upon this account, who envied and maligned him; who also, to make trial in a case of his, what kind of judges the commons would prove, should there be occasion to bring Pericles himself before them, having tampered with Menon, one who had been a workman with Phidias, stationed him in the market place, with a petition desiring public security upon his discovery and impeachment of Phidias. The people admitting the man to tell his story, and the prosecution proceeding in the assembly, there was nothing of theft or cheat proved against him; for Phidias, from the very first beginning, by the advice of Pericles, had so wrought and wrapt the gold that was used in the work about the statue, that they might take it all off, and make out the just weight of it, which Pericles at that time bade the accuser do. But the reputation of his works was what brought envy upon Phidias, especially that where he represents the fight of the Amazons upon the goddess' shield, he had introduced a likeness of himself as a bald old man holding up a great stone with both hands, and had put in a very fine representation of Pericles fighting with an Amazon. And the position of the hand which holds out the spear in front of the face, was ingeniously contrived to conceal in some degree the likeness, which meantime showed itself on either side.

Phidias then was carried away to prison, and there died of a disease; but, as some say, of poison, administered by the enemies of Pericles, to raise a slander, or a suspicion at least, as though he had procured it. The informer Menon, upon Glycon's proposal, the people made free from payment of taxes and customs, and ordered the generals to take care that nobody should do him any hurt. About the same time, Aspasia was indicted of impiety, upon the complaint of Hermippus the comedian, who also laid further to her charge that she received into her house freeborn women for the uses of Pericles. And Diopithes proposed a decree, that public accusations should be laid against persons who neglected religion, or taught new doctrines about things above, directing suspicion, by means of Anaxagoras, against Pericles himself. The people receiving and admitting these accusations and complaints, at length, by this means, they came to enact a decree, at the motion of Dracontides, that Pericles should bring in the accounts of the moneys he had expended, and lodge them with the Prytanes; and that the judges, carrying their suffrage from the altar in the Acropolis, should examine and determine the business in the city. This last clause Hagnon took out of the decree, and moved that the causes should be tried before fifteen hundred jurors, whether they should be styled prosecutions for robbery, or bribery, or any kind of malversation. Aspasia, Pericles begged off, shedding, as Æschines says, many tears at the trial, and personally entreating the jurors. But fearing how it might go with Anaxagoras, he sent him out of the city. And finding that in Phidias' case he had miscarried with the people, being afraid of impeachment, he kindled the war, which hitherto had lingered and smothered, and blew it up into a flame; hoping, by that means, to disperse and scatter these complaints and charges, and to allay their jealousy; the city usually throwing herself upon him alone, and trusting to his sole conduct, upon the urgency of great affairs and public dangers, by reason of his authority and the sway he bore.

These are given out to have been the reasons which induced Pericles not to suffer the people of Athens to yield to the proposals of the Lacedæmonians; but their truth is uncertain.

The Lacedæmonians, for their part, feeling sure that if they could once remove him, they might be at what terms they pleased with the Athenians, sent them word that they should expel the "Pollution" with which Pericles on the mother's side was tainted, as Thucydides tells us. But the issue proved quite contrary to what those who sent the message expected; instead of bringing Pericles under suspicion and reproach, they raised him into yet greater credit and esteem with the citizens, as a man whom their enemies most hated and feared. In the same way, also, before Archidamus, who was at the head of the Peloponnesians, made his invasion into Attica, he told the Athenians beforehand, that if Archidamus, while he laid waste the rest of the country, should forbear and spare his estate, either on the ground of friendship or right of hospitality that was betwixt them, or on purpose to give his enemies an occasion of traducing him; that then he did freely bestow upon the state all his land and the buildings upon it for the public use. The Lacedæmonians, therefore, and their allies, with a great army, invaded the Athenian territories, under the conduct of King Archidamus, and laying waste the country, marched on as far as Acharnæ, and there pitched their camp, presuming that the Athenians would never endure that, but would come out and fight them for their country's and their honour's sake. But Pericles looked upon it as dangerous to engage in battle, to the risk of the city itself, against sixty thousand men-at-arms of Peloponnesians and Bœotians; for so many they were in number that made the inroad at first; and he endeavoured to appease those who were desirous to fight, and were grieved and discontented to see how things went, and gave them good words, saying, that "trees, when they are lopped and cut, grow up again in a short time, but men, being once lost, cannot easily be recovered." He did not convene the people into an assembly, for fear lest they should force him to act against his judgment; but, like a skilful steersman or pilot of a ship, who, when a sudden squall comes on, out at sea, makes all his arrangements, sees that all is tight and fast, and then follows the dictates of his skill, and minds the business of the ship, taking no notice of the tears and entreaties of the sea-sick and fearful passengers, so he, having shut up the city gates, and placed guards at all posts for security, followed his own reason and judgment, little regarding those that cried out against him and were angry at his management, although there were a great many of his friends that urged him with requests, and many of his enemies threatened and accused him for doing as he did, and many made songs and lampoons upon him, which were sung about the town to his disgrace, reproaching him with the cowardly exercise of his office of general, and the tame abandonment of everything to the enemy's hands.

Cleon, also, already was among his assailants, making use of the feeling against him as a step to the leadership of the people, as appears in the anapæstic verses of Hermippus—

> Satyr-king, instead of swords,
> Will you always handle words?
> Very brave indeed we find them,
> But a Teles lurks behind them.
>
> Yet to gnash your teeth you're seen
> When the little dagger keen,
> Whetted everyday anew,
> Of sharp Cleon touches you.

Pericles, however, was not at all moved by any attacks, but took all patiently, and submitted in silence to the disgrace they threw upon him and the ill-will they bore him; and, sending out a fleet of a hundred galleys to Peloponnesus, he did not go along with it in person, but stayed behind, that he might watch at home and keep the city under his own control, till the Peloponnesians broke up their camp and were gone. Yet to soothe the common people, jaded and distressed with the war, he relieved them with distributions of public moneys, and ordained new divisions of subject land. For having turned out all the people of Ægina, he parted the island among the Athenians according to lot. Some comfort, also, and ease in their miseries, they might receive from what their enemies endured. For the fleet, sailing round the Peloponnese, ravaged a great deal of the country, and pillaged and plundered the towns and smaller cities; and by land he himself entered with an army the Megarian country, and made havoc of it all. Whence it is clear that the Peloponnesians, though they did the Athenians much mischief by land, yet suffering as much themselves from them by sea, would not have protracted the war to such a length, but would quickly have given it over, as Pericles at first foretold they would, had not some divine power crossed human purposes.

In the first place, the pestilential disease, or plague, seized upon the city, and ate up all the flower and prime of their youth and strength. Upon occasion of which, the people, distempered and afflicted in their souls, as well as in their bodies, were utterly enraged like madmen against Pericles, and, like patients grown delirious, sought to lay violent hands on their physician, or, as it were, their father. They had been possessed, by his enemies, with the belief that the occasion of the plague was the crowding of the country people together into the town, forced as they were now, in the heat of the summer-weather, to dwell many of them together even as they could, in small tenements and stifling hovels, and to be tied to a lazy course of life within doors, whereas before they lived in a pure, open, and free air. The cause and author of all this, said they, is he who on account of the war has poured a multitude of people in upon us within the walls, and uses all these men that he has here upon no employ or service, but keeps them pent up like cattle, to be overrun with infection from one another, affording them neither shift of quarters nor any refreshment.

With the design to remedy these evils, and do the enemy some inconvenience, Pericles got a hundred and fifty galleys ready, and having embarked many tried soldiers, both foot and horse, was about to sail out, giving great hope to his citizens, and no less alarm to his enemies, upon the sight of so great a force. And now the vessels having their complement of men, and Pericles being gone aboard his own galley, it happened that the

sun was eclipsed, and it grew dark on a sudden, to the affright of all, for this
was looked upon as extremely ominous. Pericles, therefore, perceiving the
steersman seized with fear and at a loss what to do, took his cloak and held
it up before the man's face, and screening him with it so that he could not
see, asked him whether he imagined there was any great hurt, or the sign
of any great hurt in this, and he answering No, "Why," said he, "and what
does that differ from this, only that what has caused that darkness there, is
something greater than a cloak?" This is a story which philosophers tell
their scholars. Pericles, however, after putting out to sea, seems not to have
done any other exploit befitting such preparations, and when he had laid
siege to the holy city Epidaurus, which gave him some hope of surrender,
miscarried in his design by reason of the sickness. For it not only seized
upon the Athenians, but upon all others, too, that held any sort of communication with the army. Finding after this the Athenians ill-affected and
highly displeased with him, he tried and endeavoured what he could to
appease and re-encourage them. But he could not pacify or allay their
anger, nor persuade or prevail with them any way, till they freely passed
their votes upon him, resumed their power, took away his command from
him, and fined him in a sum of money; which by their account that say
least, was fifteen talents, while they who reckon most, name fifty. The name
prefixed to the accusation was Cleon, as Idomeneus tells us; Simmias,
according to Theophrastus; and Heraclides Ponticus gives it as Lacratidas.

After this, public troubles were soon to leave him unmolested; the people, so to say, discharged their passion in their stroke, and lost their stings
in the wound. But his domestic concerns were in an unhappy condition,
many of his friends and acquaintance having died in the plague time, and
those of his family having long since been in disorder and in a kind of
mutiny against him. For the eldest of his lawfully begotten sons, Xanthippus
by name, being naturally prodigal, and marrying a young and expensive
wife, the daughter of Tisander, son of Epilycus, was highly offended at his
father's economy in making him but a scanty allowance, by little and little
at a time. He sent, therefore, to a friend one day and borrowed some
money of him in his father Pericles' name, pretending it was by his order.
The man coming afterward to demand the debt, Pericles was so far from
yielding to pay it, that he entered an action against him. Upon which the
young man, Xanthippus, thought himself so ill-used and disobliged that
he openly reviled his father; telling first, by way of ridicule, stories about
his conversations at home, and the discourses he had with the sophists
and scholars that came to his house. As, for instance, how one who was a

practiser of the five games of skill, having with a dart or javelin unawares against his will struck and killed Epitimus the Pharsalian, his father spent a whole day with Protagoras in a serious dispute, whether the javelin, or the man that threw it, or the masters of the games who appointed these sports, were, according to the strictest and best reason, to be accounted the cause of this mischance. Besides this, Stesimbrotus tells us that it was Xanthippus who spread abroad among the people the infamous story concerning his own wife; and in general that this difference of the young man's with his father, and the breach betwixt them, continued never to be healed or made up till his death. For Xanthippus died in the plague time of the sickness. At which time Pericles also lost his sister, and the greatest part of his relations and friends, and those who had been most useful and serviceable to him in managing the affairs of state. However, he did not shrink or give in upon these occasions, nor betray or lower his high spirit and the greatness of his mind under all his misfortunes; he was not even so much as seen to weep or to mourn, or even attend the burial of any of his friends or relations, till at last he lost his only remaining legitimate son. Subdued by this blow, and yet striving still, as far as he could, to maintain his principle, and to preserve and keep up the greatness of his soul, when he came, however, to perform the ceremony of putting a garland of flowers upon the head of the corpse, he was vanquished by his passion at the sight, so that he burst into exclamations, and shed copious tears, having never done any such thing in his life before.

The city having made trial of other generals for the conduct of war, and orators for business of state, when they found there was no one who was of weight enough for such a charge, or of authority sufficient to be trusted with so great a command, regretted the loss of him, and invited him again to address and advise them, and to reassume the office of general. He, however, lay at home in dejection and mourning; but was persuaded by Alcibiades and others of his friends to come abroad and show himself to the people; who having, upon his appearance, made their acknowledgments, and apologised for their untowardly treatment of him, he undertook the public affairs once more; and, being chosen general, requested that the statute concerning base-born children, which he himself had formerly caused to be made, might be suspended; that so the name and race of his family might not, for absolute want of a lawful heir to succeed, be wholly lost and extinguished. The case of the statute was thus: Pericles, when long ago at the height of his power in the state, having then, as has been said, children lawfully begotten, proposed a law that those only should be reputed true citizens of Athens who were born of such parents as were both Athenians. After this, the King of Egypt having sent to the people, by way of present, forty thousand bushels of wheat, which were to be shared out among the citizens, a great many actions and suits about legitimacy occurred, by virtue of that edict; cases which, till that time, had not been known nor taken notice of; and several persons suffered by false accusations. There were little less than five thousand who were convicted and sold for slaves; those who, enduring the test, remained in the government and passed muster for true Athenians were found upon the poll to be fourteen thousand and forty persons in number.

It looked strange, that a law, which had been carried so far against so many people, should be cancelled again by the same man that made it; yet the present calamity and distress which Pericles laboured under in his family broke through all objections, and prevailed with the Athenians to pity him, as one whose losses and misfortunes had sufficiently punished his former arrogance and haughtiness. His sufferings deserved, they thought, their pity, and even indignation, and his request was such as became a man to ask and men to grant; they gave him permission to enrol his son in the register of his fraternity, giving him his own name. This son afterward, after having defeated the Peloponnesians at Arginusæ, was, with his fellow-generals, put to death by the people.

About the time when his son was enrolled, it should seem the plague seized Pericles, not with sharp and violent fits, as it did others that had it, but with a dull and lingering distemper, attended with various changes and alterations, leisurely, by little and little, wasting the strength of his body, and undermining the noble faculties of his soul. So that Theophrastus, in his Morals, when discussing whether men's characters change with their circumstances, and their moral habits, disturbed by the ailings of their bodies, start aside from the rules of virtue, has left it upon record, that Pericles, when he was sick, showed one of his friends that came to visit him an amulet or charm that the women had hung about his neck; as much as to say, that he was very sick indeed when he would admit of such a foolery as that was.

When he was now near his end, the best of the citizens and those of his friends who were left alive, sitting about him, were speaking of the greatness of his merit, and his power, and reckoning up his famous actions and the number of his victories; for there were no less than nine trophies, which, as their chief commander and conqueror of their enemies, he had set up for the honour of the city. They talked thus together among themselves, as though he were unable to understand or mind what they said, but had now lost his consciousness. He had listened, however, all the while, and attended to all, and, speaking out among them, said that he wondered they should commend and take notice of things which were as much owing to fortune as to anything else, and had happened to many other commanders, and, at the same time, should not speak or make mention of that which was the most excellent and greatest thing of all. "For," said he, "no Athenian, through my means, ever wore mourning."

He was indeed a character deserving our high admiration not only for his equitable and mild temper, which all along in the many affairs of his life, and the great animosities which he incurred, he constantly maintained; but also for the high spirit and feeling which made him regard it the noblest of all his honours that, in the exercise of such immense power, he never had gratified his envy or his passion, nor ever had treated any enemy as irreconcilably opposed to him. And to me it appears that this one thing gives that otherwise childish and arrogant title a fitting and becoming significance; so dispassionate a temper, a life so pure and unblemished, in the height of power and place, might well be called Olympian, in accordance with our conceptions of the divine beings, to whom, as the natural authors of all good and of nothing evil, we ascribe the rule and government of the world. Not as the poets represent, who, while confounding us with their ignorant fancies, are themselves confuted by their own poems and fictions, and call the place, indeed, where they say the gods make their abode, a secure and quiet seat, free from all hazards and commotions, untroubled with winds or with clouds, and equally through all time illumined with a soft serenity and a pure light as though such were a home most agreeable for a blessed and immortal nature; and yet, in the meanwhile, affirm that the gods themselves are full of trouble and enmity and anger and other passions, which no way become or belong to even men that have any understanding. But this will, perhaps, seem a subject fitter for some other consideration, and that ought to be treated of in some other place.

The course of public affairs after his death produced a quick and speedy sense of the loss of Pericles. Those who, while he lived, resented his great authority, as that which eclipsed themselves, presently after his quitting the stage, making trial of other orators and demagogues, readily acknowledged that there never had been in nature such a disposition as his was, more moderate and reasonable in the height of that state he took upon him, or more grave and impressive in the mildness which he used.

And that invidious arbitrary power, to which formerly they gave the name of monarchy and tyranny, did then appear to have been the chief bulwark of public safety; so great a corruption and such a flood of mischief and vice followed which he, by keeping weak and low, had withheld from notice, and had prevented from attaining incurable height through a licentious impunity.

FABIUS

Having related the memorable actions of Pericles, our history now proceeds to the life of Fabius. A son of Hercules and a nymph, of some woman of that country, who brought him forth on the banks of Tiber, was, it is said, the first Fabius, the founder of the numerous and distinguished family of the name. Others will have it that they were first called Fodii, because the first of the race delighted in digging pitfalls for wild beasts *fodere,* being still the Latin for to dig, and *fossa* for a ditch, and that in process of time, by the change of the two letters, they grew to be called Fabii. But be these things true or false, certain it is that this family for a long time yielded a great number of eminent persons. Our Fabius, who was fourth in descent from that Fabius Rullus who first brought the honourable surname of Maximus into his family, was also, by way of personal nickname, called Verrucosus, from a wart on his upper lip; and in his childhood they in like manner named him Ovicula, or The Lamb, on account of his extreme mildness of temper. His slowness in speaking, his long labour and pains in learning, his deliberation in entering into the sports of other children, his easy submission to everybody, as if he had no will of his own, made those who judge superficially of him, the greater number, esteem him insensible and stupid; and few only saw that this tardiness proceeded from stability, and discerned the greatness of his mind, and the lionlikeness of his temper. But as soon as he came into employments, his virtues exerted and showed themselves; his reputed want of energy then was recognised by people in general as a freedom of passion; his slowness in words and actions, the effect of a true prudence; his want of rapidity and his sluggishness, as constancy and firmness.

Living in a great commonwealth, surrounded by many enemies, he saw the wisdom of inuring his body (nature's own weapon) to warlike exercises, and disciplining his tongue for public oratory in a style conformable to his life and character. His eloquence, indeed, had not much of popular ornament, nor empty artifice, but there was in it great weight of sense; it was strong and sententious, much after the way of Thucydides. We have yet extant his funeral oration upon the death of his son, who died consul, which he recited before the people.

He was five times consul, and in his first consulship had the honour of a triumph for the victory he gained over the Ligurians, whom he defeated in a set battle, and drove them to take shelter in the Alps, from whence they never after made any inroad or depredation upon their neighbours. After this, Hannibal came into Italy, who, at his first entrance, having gained a great battle near the river Trebia, traversed all Tuscany with his victorious army, and, desolating the country round about, filled Rome itself with astonishment and terror. Besides the more common signs of thunder and lightning then happening, the report of several unheard-of and utterly strange portents much increased the popular consternation. For it was said that some targets sweated blood; that at Antium, when they reaped their corn, many of the ears were filled with blood; that it had rained red-hot stones; that the Falerians had seen the heavens open and several scrolls falling down, in one of which was plainly written, "Mars himself stirs his arms." But these prodigies had no effect upon the impetuous and fiery temper of the consul Flaminius, whose natural promptness had been much heightened by his late unexpected victory over the Gauls, when he fought them contrary to the order of the senate and the advice of his colleague. Fabius, on the other side, thought it not seasonable to engage with the enemy; not that he much regarded the prodigies, which he thought too strange to be easily understood, though many were alarmed by them; but in regard that the Carthaginians were but few, and in want of money and supplies, he deemed it best not to meet in the field a general whose army had been tried in many encounters, and whose object was a battle, but to send aid to their allies, control the movements of the various subject cities, and let the force and vigour of Hannibal waste away and expire, like a flame, for want of the aliment.

These weighty reasons did not prevail with Flaminius, who protested he would never suffer the advance of the enemy to the city, nor be reduced, like Camillus in former time, to fight for Rome within the walls of Rome. Accordingly he ordered the tribunes to draw out the army into the field; and though he himself, leaping on horseback to go out, was no sooner mounted but the beast, without any apparent cause, fell into so violent a fit of trembling and bounding that he cast his rider headlong on the ground; he was no ways deterred, but proceeded as he had begun, and marched forward up to Hannibal, who was posted near the Lake Thrasymene in Tuscany. At the moment of this engagement, there happened so great an earthquake, that it destroyed several towns, altered the course of rivers, and carried off parts of high cliffs, yet such was the eagerness of the combatants, that they were entirely insensible of it.

In this battle Flaminius fell, after many proofs of his strength and courage, and round about him all the bravest of the army; in the whole, fifteen thousand were killed, and as many made prisoners. Hannibal, desirous to bestow funeral honours upon the body of Flaminius, made diligent search after it, but could not find it among the dead, nor was it ever known what became of it. Upon the former engagement near Trebia, neither the general who wrote, nor the express who told the news, used straightforward and direct terms, nor related it otherwise than as a drawn battle, with equal loss on either side; but on this occasion as soon as Pomponius the prætor had the intelligence, he caused the people to assemble, and, without disguising or dissembling the matter, told them plainly, "We are beaten, O Romans, in a great battle; the consul Flaminius is killed; think, therefore, what is to be done for your safety." Letting loose his news like a gate of wind upon an open sea, he threw the city into utter confusion: in such consternation, their thoughts found no support or stay. The danger at hand at last awakened their judgments into a resolution to choose a dictator, who by the sovereign authority of his office, and by his personal wisdom and courage, might be able to manage the public affairs. Their choice unanimously fell upon Fabius, whose character seemed equal to the greatness of the office; whose age was so far advanced as to give him experience, without taking from him the vigour of action; his body could execute what his soul designed; and his temper was a happy compound of confidence and cautiousness.

Fabius, being thus installed in the office of dictator, in the first place gave the command of the horse to Lucius Minucius; and next asked leave of the senate for himself, that in time of battle he might serve on horseback, which by an ancient law amongst the Romans was forbid to their generals; whether it were, that, placing their greatest strength in their foot, they would have their commanders-in-chief posted amongst them, or else to let them know, that, how great and absolute soever their authority were, the people and senate were still their masters, of whom they must ask leave. Fabius, however, to make the authority of his charge more observable, and to render the people more submissive and obedient to him, caused himself to be accompanied with the full body of four-and-twenty lictors; and, when the surviving consul came to visit him, sent him word to dismiss his lictors with their fasces, the ensigns of authority, and appear before him as a private person.

The first solemn action of his dictatorship was very fitly a religious one: an admonition to the people, that their late overthrow had not befallen them through want of courage in their soldiers, but through the neglect of divine ceremonies in the general. He therefore exhorted them not to fear the enemy, but by extraordinary honour to propitiate the gods. This he did not to fill their minds with superstition, but by religious feeling to raise their courage, and lessen their fear of the enemy by inspiring the belief that Heaven was on their side. With this view, the secret prophecies called the Sibylline Books were consulted; sundry predictions found in them were said to refer to the fortunes and events of the time; but none except the consulter was informed. Presenting himself to the people, the dictator made a vow before them to offer in sacrifice the whole product of the next season, all Italy over, of the cows, goats, swine, sheep, both in the mountains and the plains; and to celebrate musical festivities with an expenditure of the precise sum of 333 sestertia and 333 denarii, with one-third of a denarius over. The sum total of which is, in our money, 83,583 drachmas and 2 obols. What the mystery might be in that exact number is not easy to determine, unless it were in honour of the perfection of the number three, as being the first of odd numbers, the first that contains in itself multiplication, with all other properties whatsoever belonging to numbers in general.

In this manner Fabius, having given the people better heart for the future, by making them believe that the gods took their side, for his own part placed his whole confidence in himself, believing that the gods bestowed victory and good fortune by the instrumentality of valour and of prudence; and thus prepared he set forth to oppose Hannibal, not with intention to fight him, but with the purpose of wearing out and wasting the vigour of his arms by lapse of time, of meeting his want of resources by superior means, by large numbers the smallness of his forces. With this design, he always encamped on the highest grounds, where the enemy's horse could have no access to him. Still he kept pace with them; when they marched he followed them; when they encamped he did the same, but at such a distance as not to be compelled to an engagement, and always keeping upon the hills, free from the insults of their horse; by which means he gave them no rest, but kept them in a continual alarm.

But this his dilatory way gave occasion in his own camp for suspicion of want of courage; and this opinion prevailed yet more in Hannibal's army. Hannibal was himself the only man who was not deceived, who discerned his skill and detected his tactics, and saw, unless he could by art or force bring him to battle, that the Carthaginians, unable to use the arms in which they were superior, and suffering the continual drain of lives and treasure in which they were inferior, would in the end come to nothing. He resolved, therefore, with all the arts and subtleties of war to break his measures, and to bring Fabius to an engagement, like a cunning wrestler, watching every opportunity to get good hold and close with his adversary. He at one time attacked, and sought to distract his attention, tried to draw him off in various directions, and endeavoured in all ways to tempt him from his safe policy. All this artifice, though it had no effect upon the firm judgment and conviction of the dictator, yet upon the common soldier, and even upon the general of the horse himself, it had too great an operation: Minucius, unseasonably eager for action, bold and confident, humoured the soldiery, and himself contributed to fill them with wild eagerness and empty hopes, which they vented in reproaches upon Fabius, calling him Hannibal's pedagogue, since he did nothing else but follow him up and down and wait upon him. At the same time, they cried up Minucius for the only captain worthy to command the Romans; whose vanity and presumption rose so high in consequence, that he insolently jested at Fabius' encampment upon the mountains, saying that he seated them there as on a theatre, to behold the flames and desolation of their country. And he would sometimes ask the friends of the general, whether it were not his meaning, by thus leading them from mountain to mountain, to carry them at last (having no hopes on earth) up into heaven, or to hide them in the clouds from Hannibal's army? When his friends reported these things to the dictator, persuading him that, to avoid the general obloquy, he should engage the enemy, his answer was, "I should be more fainthearted than they make me, if, through fear of idle reproaches, I should abandon my own convictions. It is no inglorious thing to have fear for the safety of our country, but to be turned from one's course by men's opinions, by blame, and by misrepresentation, shows a man unfit to hold an office such as this, which, by such conduct, he makes the slaves of those whose errors it is his business to control."

An oversight of Hannibal occurred soon after. Desirous to refresh his horse in some good pasture-grounds, and to draw off his army, he ordered his guides to conduct him to the district of Casinum. They, mistaking his bad pronunciation, led him and his army to the town of Casilinum, on the frontier of Campania which the river Lothronus, called by the Romans Vulturnus, divides in two parts. The country around is enclosed by mountains, with a valley opening towards the sea, in which the river overflowing forms a quantity of marsh land with deep banks of sand, and discharges itself into the sea on a very unsafe and rough shore. While Hannibal was proceeding hither, Fabius, by his knowledge of the roads, succeeded in making his way around before him, and despatched four thousand choice men to seize the exit from it and stop him up, and lodged the rest of his army upon the neighbouring hills, in the most advantageous places; at the same time detaching a party of his lightest armed men to fall upon Hannibal's rear; which they did with such success, that they cut off eight hundred of them, and put the whole army in disorder. Hannibal, finding the error and the danger he was fallen into, immediately crucified the guides; but considered the enemy to be so advantageously posted, that there was no hope of breaking through them; while his soldiers began to be despondent and terrified, and to think themselves surrounded with embarrassments too difficult to be surmounted.

Thus reduced, Hannibal had recourse to stratagem; he caused two thousand head of oxen which he had in his camp to have torches or dry fagots well fastened to their horns, and lighting them in the beginning of the night, ordered the beasts to be driven on towards the heights commanding the passages out of the valley and the enemy's posts; when this was done, he made his army in the dark leisurely march after them. The oxen at first kept a slow orderly pace, and with their lighted heads resembled an army marching by night, astonishing the shepherds and herdsmen of the hills about. But when the fire burnt down the horns of the beasts to the quick, they no longer observed their sober pace, but unruly and wild with their pain, ran dispersed about, tossing their heads and scattering the fire round about them upon each other and setting light as they passed to the trees. This was a surprising spectacle to the Romans on guard upon the heights. Seeing flames which appeared to come from men advancing with torches, they were possessed with the alarm that the enemy was approaching in various quarters, and that they were being surrounded; and, quitting their post, abandoned the pass, and precipitately retired to their camp on the hills. They were no sooner gone, but the light-armed of Hannibal's men, according to his order, immediately seized the heights, and soon after the whole army, with all the baggage, came up and safely marched through the passes.

Fabius, before the night was over, quickly found out the trick; for some of the beasts fell into his hands; but for fear of an ambush in the dark, he kept his men all night to their arms in the camp. As soon as it was day, he attacked the enemy in the rear, where, after a good deal of skirmishing in the uneven ground, the disorder might have become general, but that Hannibal detached from his van a body of Spaniards, who, of themselves active and nimble, were accustomed to the climbing of mountains. These briskly attacked the Roman troops, who were in heavy armour, killed a good many, and left Fabius no longer in condition to follow the enemy. This action brought the extreme of obloquy and contempt upon the dictator; they said it was now manifest that he was not only inferior to his adversary, as they had always thought, in courage, but even in that conduct, foresight, and generalship, by which he had proposed to bring the war to an end.

And Hannibal, to enhance their anger against him, marched with his army close to the lands and possessions of Fabius, and, giving orders to his soldiers to burn and destroy all the country about, forbade them to do the least damage in the estates of the Roman general, and placed guards for their security. This, when reported at Rome, had the effect with the people which Hannibal desired. Their tribunes raised a thousand stories against him, chiefly at the instigation of Metilius, who, not so much out of hatred to him as out of friendship to Minucius, whose kinsman he was, thought by depressing Fabius to raise his friend. The senate on their part were also offended with him for the bargain he had made with Hannibal about the exchange of prisoners, the conditions of which were that, after exchange made of man for man, if any on either side remained, they should be redeemed at the price of two hundred and fifty drachmas a head. Upon the whole account, there remained two hundred and forty Romans unexchanged, and the senate now not only refused to allow money for the ransoms, but also reproached Fabius for making a contract, contrary to the honour and interest of the commonwealth, for redeeming men whose cowardice had put them in the hands of the enemy. Fabius heard and endured all this with invincible patience; and, having no money by him, and on the other side being resolved to keep his word with Hannibal and not to abandon the captives, he despatched his son to Rome to sell land, and to bring with him the price, sufficient to discharge the ransoms; which was punctually performed by his son and delivery accordingly made to him of the prisoners, amongst whom many, when they were released, made proposals to repay the money; which Fabius in all cases declined.

About this time, he was called to Rome by the priests, to assist, according to the duty of his office, at certain sacrifices, and was thus forced to leave the command of the army with Minucius; but before he parted, not only charged him as his commander-in-chief, but besought and entreated him not to come, in his absence, to a battle with Hannibal. His commands, entreaties, and advice were lost upon Minucius, or his back was no sooner turned but the new general immediately sought occasions to attack the enemy. And notice being brought him that Hannibal had sent out a great part of his army to forage, he fell upon a detachment of the remainder, doing great execution, and driving them to their very camp, with no little terror to the rest, who apprehended their breaking in upon them; and when Hannibal had recalled his scattered forces to the camp, he, nevertheless, without any loss, made his retreat, a success which aggravated his boldness and presumption, and filled the soldiers with rash confidence. The news spread to Rome, where Fabius, on being told it, said that what he most feared was Minucius' success; but the people, highly elated, hurried to the forum to listen to an address from Metilius the tribune, in which he infinitely extolled the valour of Minucius, and fell bitterly upon Fabius, accusing him for want not merely of courage, but even of loyalty; and not only him, but also many other eminent and considerable persons; saying that it was they that had brought the Carthaginians into Italy, with the design to destroy the liberty of the people; for which end they had at once put the supreme authority into the hands of a single person, who by his slowness and delays might give Hannibal leisure to establish himself in Italy, and the people of Carthage time and opportunity to supply him with fresh succours to complete his conquest.

Fabius came forward with no intention to answer the tribune, but only said, that they should expedite the sacrifices, that so he might speedily return to the army to punish Minucius, who had presumed to fight contrary to his orders; words which immediately possessed the people with the belief that Minucius stood in danger of his life. For it was in the power of the dictator to imprison and to put to death, and they feared that Fabius, of a mild temper in general, would be as hard to be appeased when once irritated, as he was slow to be provoked. Nobody dared to raise his voice in opposition; Metilius alone, whose office of tribune gave him security to say what he pleased (for in the time of a dictatorship that magistrateal one preserves his authority), boldly applied himself to the people in the behalf of Minucius; that they should not suffer him to be made a sacrifice to the enmity of Fabius, nor permit him to be destroyed, like the son of Manlius Torquatus, who was beheaded by his father for a victory fought and triumphantly won against order; he exhorted them to take away from Fabius that absolute power of a dictator, and to put it into more worthy hands, better able and more inclined to use it for the public good. These impressions very much prevailed upon the people, though not so far as wholly to dispossess Fabius of the dictatorship. But they decreed that Minucius should have an equal authority with the dictator in the conduct of the war; which was a thing then without precedent, though a little later it was again practised after the disaster at Cannæ; when the dictator, Marcus Junius, being with the army, they chose at Rome Fabius Buteo dictator, that he might create new senators, to supply the numerous places of those who were killed. But as soon as, once acting in public, he had filled those vacant places with a sufficient number, he immediately dismissed his lictors, and withdrew from all his attendance, and mingling like a common person with the rest of the people, quietly went about his own affairs in the forum.

The enemies of Fabius thought they had sufficiently humiliated and subdued him by raising Minucius to be his equal in authority; but they mistook the temper of the man, who looked upon their folly as not his loss, but like Diogenes, who, being told that some persons derided him, made answer, "But I am not derided," meaning that only those were really insulted on whom such insults made an impression, so Fabius, with great tranquillity and unconcern, submitted to what happened, and contributed a proof to the argument of the philosophers that a just and good man is not capable of being dishonoured. His only vexation arose from his fear lest this ill counsel, by supplying opportunities to the diseased military ambition of his subordinate, should damage the public cause. Lest the rashness of Minucius should now at once run headlong into some disaster, he returned back with all privacy and speed to the army; where he found Minucius so elevated with his new dignity, that, a joint-authority not contenting him, he required by turns to have the command of the army every other day. This Fabius rejected, but was contented that the army should be divided; thinking each general singly would better command his part, than partially command the whole. The first and fourth legions he took for his own division, the second and third he delivered to Minucius; so also of the auxiliary forces each had an equal share.

Minucius, thus exalted, could not contain himself from boasting of his success in humiliating the high and powerful office of the dictatorship. Fabius quietly reminded him that it was, in all wisdom, Hannibal, and not Fabius, whom he had to combat; but if he must needs contend with his colleague, it had best be in diligence and care for the preservation of Rome; that it might not be said, a man so favoured by the people served them worse than he who had been ill-treated and disgraced by them.

The young general, despising these admonitions as the false humility of age, immediately removed with the body of his army, and encamped by himself. Hannibal, who was not ignorant of all these passages, lay watching his advantage from them. It happened that between his army and that of Minucius there was a certain eminence, which seemed a very advantageous and not difficult post to encamp upon; the level field around it appeared, from a distance, to be all smooth and even, though it had many inconsiderable ditches and dips in it, not discernible to the eye. Hannibal, had he pleased, could easily have possessed himself of this ground; but he had reserved it for a bait, or train, in proper season, to draw the Romans to an engagement. Now that Minucius and Fabius were divided, he thought the opportunity fair for his purpose; and, therefore, having in the nighttime lodged a convenient number of his men in these ditches and hollow places, early in the morning he sent forth a small detachment, who, in the sight of Minucius, proceeded to possess themselves of the rising ground. According to his expectation, Minucius swallowed the bait, and first sent out his light troops, and after them some horse, to dislodge the enemy; and, at last, when he saw Hannibal in person advancing to the assistance of his men, marched down with his whole army drawn up. He engaged with the troops on the eminence, and sustained their missiles; the combat for sometime was equal; but as soon as Hannibal perceived that the whole army was now sufficiently advanced within the toils he had set for them, so that their backs were open to his men whom he had posted in the hollows, he gave the signal; upon which they rushed forth from various quarters, and with loud cries furiously attacked Minucius in the rear. The surprise and the slaughter was great, and struck universal alarm and disorder through the whole army. Minucius himself lost all his confidence; he looked from officer to officer, and found all alike unprepared to face the danger, and yielding to a flight, which, however, could not end in safety. The Numidian horsemen were already in full victory riding about the plain, cutting down the fugitives.

Fabius was not ignorant of this danger of his countrymen; he foresaw what would happen from the rashness of Minucius, and the cunning of Hannibal; and, therefore, kept his men to their arms, in readiness to wait the event; nor would he trust to the reports of others, but he himself, in front of his camp, viewed all that passed. When, therefore, he saw the army of Minucius encompassed by the enemy, and that by their countenance and shifting their ground they appeared more disposed to flight than to resistance, with a great sigh, striking his hand upon his thigh, he said to those about him, "O Hercules! How much sooner than I expected, though later than he seemed to desire, hath Minucius destroyed himself!" He then commanded the ensigns to be led forward, and the army to follow, telling them, "We must make haste to rescue Minucius, who is a valiant man, and a lover of his country; and if he hath been too forward to engage the enemy, at another time we will tell him of it." Thus, at the head of his men, Fabius marched up to the enemy, and first cleared the plain of the Numidians; and next fell upon those who were charging the Romans in the rear, cutting down all that made opposition, and obliging the rest to save themselves by a hasty retreat, lest they should be environed as the Romans had been. Hannibal, seeing so sudden a change of affairs, and Fabius, beyond the force of his age, opening his way through the ranks up the hillside, that he might join Minucius, warily forbore, sounded a retreat, and drew off his men into their camp; while the Romans on their part were no less contented to retire in safety. It is reported that upon this occasion Hannibal said jestingly to his friends: "Did not I tell you, that this cloud which always hovered upon the mountains would, at sometime or other, come down with a storm upon us?"

Fabius, after his men had picked up the spoils of the field, retired to his own camp, without saying any harsh or reproachful thing to his colleague; who, also, in his part, gathering his army together, spoke and said to them: "To conduct great matters and never commit a fault is above the force of human nature; but to learn and improve by the faults we have committed is that which becomes a good and sensible man. Some reasons I may have to accuse fortune, but I have many more to thank her; for in a few hours she hath cured a long mistake, and taught me that I am not the man who should command others, but have need of another to command me; and that we are not to contend for victory over those to whom it is our advantage to yield. Therefore in everything else henceforth the dictator must be your commander; only in showing gratitude towards him I will still be your leader, and always be the first to obey his orders." Having said this, he commanded the Roman eagles to move forward, and all his men to follow him to the camp of Fabius. The soldiers, then, as he entered, stood amazed at the novelty of the sight, and were anxious and doubtful what the meaning might be. When he came near the dictator's tent, Fabius went forth to meet him, on which he at once laid his standards at his feet, calling him with a loud voice his father; while the soldiers with him saluted the soldiers here as their patrons, the term employed by freedmen to those who gave them their liberty. After silence was obtained, Minucius said, "You have this day, O dictator, obtained two victories; one by your valour and conduct over Hannibal, and another by your wisdom and goodness over your colleague; by one victory you preserved, and by the other instructed us; and when we were already suffering one shameful defeat from Hannibal, by another welcome one from you we were restored to honour and safety. I can address you by no nobler name than that of a kind father, though a father's beneficence falls short of that I have received from you. From a father I individually received the gift of life; to you I owe its preservation not for myself only, but for all these who are under me." After this, he threw himself into the arms of the dictator; and in the same manner the soldiers of each army embraced one another with gladness and tears of joy.

Not long after, Fabius laid down the dictatorship, and consuls were again created. Those who immediately succeeded observed the same method in managing the war, and avoided all occasions of fighting Hannibal in a pitched battle; they only succoured their allies, and preserved the towns from falling off to the enemy. But afterwards, when Terentius Varro, a man of obscure birth, but very popular and bold, had obtained the consulship, he soon made it appear that by his rashness and ignorance he would stake the whole commonwealth on the hazard. For it was his custom to declaim in all assemblies, that, as long as Rome employed generals like Fabius, there never would be an end of the war; vaunting that whenever he should get sight of the enemy, he would that same day free Italy from the strangers. With these promises he so prevailed, that he raised a greater army than had ever yet been sent out of Rome. There were enlisted eighty-eight thousand fighting men; but what gave confidence to the populace, only terrified the wise and experienced, and none more than Fabius; since if so great a body, and the flower of the Roman youth, should be cut off, they could not see any new resource for the safety of Rome. They addressed themselves, therefore, to the other consul, Æmilius Paulus, a man of great experience in war, but unpopular, and fearful also of the people, who once before upon some impeachment had condemned him; so that he needed encouragement to withstand his colleague's temerity. Fabius told him, if he would profitably serve his country, he must no less oppose Varro's ignorant eagerness than Hannibal's conscious readiness, since both alike conspired to decide the fate of Rome by a battle. "It is more reasonable," he said to him, "that you should believe me than Varro, in matters relating to Hannibal, when I tell you that if for this year you abstain from fighting with him, either his army will perish of itself, or else he will be glad to depart of his own will. This evidently appears, inasmuch as, notwithstanding his victories, none of the countries or towns of Italy come in to him, and his army is not now the third part of what it was at first." To this Paulus is said to have replied, "Did I only consider myself, I should rather choose to he exposed to the weapons of Hannibal than once more to the suffrages of my fellow-citizens, who are urgent for what you disapprove; yet since the cause of Rome is at stake, I will rather seek in my conduct to please and obey Fabius than all the world besides."

These good measures were defeated by the importunity of Varro; whom, when they were both come to the army, nothing would content but a separate command, that each consul should have his day; and when his turn came, he posted his army close to Hannibal, at a village called Cannæ, by the river Aufidus. It was no sooner day, but he set up the scarlet coat flying over his tent, which was the signal of battle. This boldness of the consul, and the numerousness of his army, double theirs, startled the Carthaginians; but Hannibal commanded them to their arms, and with a small train rode out to take a full prospect of the enemy as they were now forming in their ranks, from a rising ground not far distant. One of his followers, called Gisco, a Carthaginian of equal rank with himself, told him that the numbers of the enemy were astonishing; to which Hannibal replied with a serious countenance, "There is one thing, Gisco, yet more astonishing, which you take no notice of," and when Gisco inquired what, answered, that "in all those great numbers before us, there is not one man called Gisco." This unexpected jest of their general made all the company laugh, and as they came down from the hill they told it to those whom they met, which caused a general laughter amongst them all, from which they were hardly able to recover themselves. The army, seeing Hannibal's attendants come back from viewing the enemy in such a laughing condition, concluded that it must be profound contempt of the enemy, that made their general at this moment indulge in such hilarity.

According to his usual manner, Hannibal employed stratagems to advantage himself. In the first place, he so drew up his men that the wind was at their backs, which at that time blew with a perfect storm of violence, and, sweeping over the great plains of sand, carried before it a cloud of dust over the Carthaginian army into the faces of the Romans, which much disturbed them in the fight. In the next place, all his best men he put into his wings; and in the body which was somewhat more advanced than the wings, placed the worst and the weakest of his army. He commanded those in the wings, that, when the enemy had made a thorough charge upon that middle advance body, which he knew would recoil, as not being able to withstand their shock, and when the Romans in their pursuit should be far enough engaged within the two wings, they should, both on the right and the left, charge them in the flank, and endeavour to encompass them. This appears to have been the chief cause of the Roman loss. Pressing upon Hannibal's front, which gave ground, they reduced the form of his army into a perfect half-moon, and gave ample opportunity to the captains of the chosen troops to charge them right and left on their flanks, and to cut off and destroy all who did not fall back before the Carthaginian wings united in their rear. To this general calamity, it is also said, that a strange mistake among the cavalry much contributed. For the horse of Æmilius receiving a hurt and throwing his master, those about him immediately alighted to aid the consul; and the Roman troops, seeing their commanders thus quitting their horses, took it for a sign that they should all dismount and charge the enemy on foot. At the sight of this, Hannibal was heard to say, "This pleases me better than if they had been delivered to me bound hand and foot." For the particulars of this engagement, we refer our reader to those authors who have written at large upon the subject.

The consul Varro, with a thin company, fled to Venusia; Æmilius Paulus, unable any longer to oppose the flight of his men, or the pursuit of the enemy, his body all covered with wounds, and his soul no less wounded with grief, sat himself down upon a stone, expecting the kindness of a despatching blow. His face was so disfigured, and all his person so stained with blood, that his very friends and domestics passing by knew him not. At last Cornelius Lentulus, a young man of patrician race, perceiving who he was, alighted from his horse, and, tendering it to him, desired him to get up and save a life so necessary to the safety of the commonwealth, which, at this time, would dearly want so great a captain. But nothing could prevail upon him to accept of the offer; he obliged young

Lentulus, with tears in his eyes, to remount his horse; then standing up, he gave him his hand, and commanded him to tell Fabius Maximus that Æmilius Paulus had followed his directions to his very last, and had not in the least deviated from those measures which were agreed between them; but that it was his hard fate to be overpowered by Varro in the first place, and secondly by Hannibal. Having despatched Lentulus with this commission, he marked where the slaughter was greatest, and there threw himself upon the swords of the enemy. In this battle it is reported that fifty thousand Romans were slain, four thousand prisoners taken in the field, and ten thousand in the camp of both consuls.

The friends of Hannibal earnestly persuaded him to follow up his victory, and pursue the flying Romans into the very gates of Rome, assuring him that in five days' time he might sup in the Capitol; nor is it easy to imagine what consideration hindered him from it. It would seem rather that some supernatural or divine intervention caused the hesitation and timidity which he now displayed, and which made Barcas, a Carthaginian, tell him with indignation, "You know, Hannibal, how to gain a victory, but not how to use it." Yet it produced a marvellous revolution in his affairs; he, who hitherto had not one town, market, or seaport in his possession, who had nothing for the subsistence of his men but what he pillaged from day to day, who had no place of retreat or basis of operation, but was roving, as it were, with a huge troop of banditti, now became master of the best provinces and towns of Italy, and of Capua itself, next to Rome the most flourishing and opulent city, all which came over to him, and submitted to his authority.

It is the saying of Euripides, that "a man is in ill-case when he must try a friend," and so neither, it would seem, is a state in a good one, when it needs an able general. And so it was with the Romans; the counsels and actions of Fabius, which, before the battle, they had branded as cowardice and fear, now, in the other extreme, they accounted to have been more than human wisdom; as though nothing but a divine power of intellect could have seen so far, and foretold contrary to the judgment of all others, a result which, even now it had arrived, was hardly credible. In him, therefore, they placed their whole remaining hopes; his wisdom was the sacred altar and temple to which they fled for refuge, and his counsels, more than anything, preserved them from dispersing and deserting their city, as in the time when the Gauls took possession of Rome. He, whom they esteemed fearful and pusillanimous when they were, as they thought, in a prosperous condition, was now the only man, in this general and unbounded dejection and confusion, who showed no fear, but walked the streets with an assured and serene countenance, addressed his fellow-citizens, checked the women's lamentations, and the public gatherings of those who wanted thus to vent their sorrows. He caused the senate to meet, he heartened up the magistrates, and was himself as the soul and life of every office.

He placed guards at the gates of the city to stop the frightened multitude from flying; he regulated and confined their mournings for their slain friends, both as to time and place; ordering that each family should perform such observances within private walls, and that they should continue only the space of one month, and then the whole city should be purified. The feast of Ceres happening to fall within this time, it was decreed that the solemnity should be intermitted, lest the fewness, and the sorrowful countenance of those who should celebrate it, might too much expose to the people the greatness of their loss; besides that, the worship most acceptable to the gods is that which comes from cheerful hearts. But those rites which were proper for appeasing their anger, and procuring auspicious signs and presages, were by the direction of the augurs carefully performed. Fabius Pictor, a near kinsman to Maximus, was sent to consult the oracle of Delphi; and about the same time, two vestals having been detected to have been violated, the one killed herself, and the other, according to custom, was buried alive.

Above all, let us admire the high spirit and equanimity of this Roman commonwealth; that when the consul Varro came beaten and flying home, full of shame and humiliation, after he had so disgracefully and calamitously managed their affairs, yet the whole senate and people went forth to meet him at the gates of the city, and received him with honour and respect. And, silence being commanded, the magistrates and chief of the senate, Fabius amongst them, commended him before the people, because he did not despair of the safety of the commonwealth, after so great a loss, but was come to take the government into his hands, to execute the laws, and aid his fellow-citizens in their prospect of future deliverance

When word was brought to Rome that Hannibal, after the fight, had marched with his army into other parts of Italy, the hearts of the Romans began to revive, and they proceeded to send out generals and armies. The most distinguished commands were held by Fabius Maximus and Claudius Marcellus, both generals of great fame, though upon opposite grounds. For Marcellus, as we have set forth in his life, was a man of action and high spirit, ready and bold with his own hand, and, as Homer describes his warriors, fierce, and delighting in fights. Boldness, enterprise, and daring to match those of Hannibal, constituted his tactics, and marked his engagements. But Fabius adhered to his former principles, still persuaded that, by following close and not fighting him, Hannibal and his army would at last be tried out and consumed, like a wrestler in too high condition, whose very excess of strength makes him the more likely suddenly to give way and lose it. Posidonius tells us that the Romans called Marcellus their sword, and Fabius their buckler; and that the vigour of the one, mixed with the steadiness of the other, made a happy compound that proved the salvation of Rome. So that Hannibal found by experience that encountering the one, he met with a rapid, impetuous river, which drove him back, and still made some breach upon him; and by the other, though silently and quietly passing by him, he was insensibly washed away and consumed; and, at last, was brought to this, that he dreaded Marcellus when he was in motion, and Fabius when he sat still. During the whole course of this war, he had still to do with one or both of these generals; for each of them was five times consul, and, as prætors or proconsuls or consuls, they had always a part in the government of the army, till, at last, Marcellus fell into the trap which Hannibal had laid for him, and was killed in his fifth consulship. But all his craft and subtlety were unsuccessful upon Fabius, who only once was in some danger of being caught, when counterfeit letters came to him from the principal inhabitants of Metapontum, with promises to deliver up their town if he would come before it with his army, and intimations that they should expect him. This train had almost drawn him in; he resolved to march to them with part of his army, and was diverted only by consulting the omens of the birds, which he found to be inauspicious; and not long after it was discovered that the letters had been forged by Hannibal, who, for his reception, had laid an ambush to entertain him. This, perhaps, we must rather attribute to the favour of the gods than to the prudence of Fabius.

In preserving the towns and allies from revolt by fair and gentle treatment, and in not using rigour, or showing a suspicion upon every light suggestion, his conduct was remarkable. It is told of him, that being informed of a certain Marsian, eminent for courage and good birth, who had been speaking underhand with some of the soldiers about deserting, Fabius was so far from using severity against him, that he called for him, and told him he was sensible of the neglect that had been shown to his merit and good service, which, he said, was a great fault in the commanders who reward more by favour than by desert; "but henceforth, whenever you are aggrieved," said Fabius, "I shall consider it your fault, if you apply yourself to anyone but to me"; and when he had so spoken, he bestowed an excellent horse, and other presents upon him; and, from that time forwards, there was not a faithfuller and more trusty man in the whole army. With good reason he judged, that, if those who have the government of horses and dogs endeavour by gentle usage to cure their angry and untractable tempers, rather than by cruelty and beating, much more should those who have the command of men try to bring them to order and discipline by the mildest and fairest means, and not treat them worse than gardeners do those wild plants, which, with care and attention, lose gradually the savageness of their nature, and bear excellent fruit.

At another time, some of his officers informed him that one of their men was very often absent from his place, and out at nights; he asked them what kind of man he was; they all answered, that the whole army had not a better man, that he was a native of Lucania, and proceeded to speak of several actions which they had seen him perform. Fabius made strict inquiry, and discovered at last that these frequent excursions which he ventured upon were to visit a young girl, with whom he was in love. Upon which he gave private order to some of his men to find out the woman and secretly convey her into his own tent; and then sent for the Lucanian, and, calling him aside, told him, that he very well knew how often he had been out away from the camp at night, which was a capital transgression against military discipline and the Roman laws, but he knew also how brave he was, and the good services he had done; therefore, in consideration of them, he was willing to forgive him his fault; but to keep him in good order, he was resolved to place one over him to be his keeper, who should be accountable for his good behaviour. Having said this, he produced the woman, and told the soldier, terrified and amazed at the adventure, "This is the person who must answer for you; and by your future behaviour we shall see whether your night rambles were on account of love, or for any other worse design."

Another passage there was, something of the same kind, which gained him possession of Tarentum. There was a young Tarentine in the army that had a sister in Tarentum, then in possession of the enemy, who entirely loved her brother, and wholly depended upon him. He, being informed that a certain Bruttian, whom Hannibal had made a commander of the garrison, was deeply in love with his sister, conceived hopes that he might possibly turn it to the advantage of the Romans. And having first communicated his design to Fabius, he left the army as a deserter in show, and went over to Tarentum. The first days passed, and the Bruttian abstained from visiting the sister; for neither of them knew that the brother had notice of the amour between them. The young Tarentine, however, took an occasion to tell his sister how he had heard that a man of station and authority had made his addresses to her, and desired her, therefore, to tell him who it was; "for," said he, "if he be a man that has bravery and reputation, it matters not what countryman he is, since at this time the sword mingles all nations, and makes them equal; compulsion makes all things honourable; and in a time when right is weak, we may be thankful if might assumes a form of gentleness." Upon this the woman sends for her friend, and makes the brother and him acquainted; and whereas she henceforth showed more countenance to her lover than formerly, in the same degrees that her kindness increased, his friendship, also, with the brother advanced. So that at last our Tarentine thought this Bruttian officer well enough prepared to receive the offers he had to make him, and that it would be easy for a mercenary man, who was in love, to accept, upon the terms proposed, the large rewards promised by Fabius. In conclusion, the bargain was struck, and the promise made of delivering the town. This is the common tradition, though some relate the story otherwise, and say, that this woman, by whom the Bruttian was inveigled to betray the town, was not a native of Tarentum, but a Bruttian born, and was kept by Fabius as his concubine; and being a countrywoman and an acquaintance of the Bruttian governor, he privately sent her to him to corrupt him.

Whilst these matters were thus in process, to draw off Hannibal from scenting the design, Fabius sends orders to the garrison in Rhegium, that they should waste and spoil the Bruttian country, and should also lay siege to Caulonia, and storm the place with all their might. These were a body of eight thousand men, the worst of the Roman army, who had most of them been runaways, and had been brought home by Marcellus from Sicily, in dishonour, so that the loss of them would not be any great grief to the Romans. Fabius, therefore, threw out these men as a bait for Hannibal, to divert him from Tarentum; who instantly caught at it, and led his forces to Caulonia; in the meantime, Fabius sat down before Tarentum. On the sixth day of the siege, the young Tarentine slips by night out of the town, and, having carefully observed the place where the Bruttian commander, according to agreement, was to admit the Romans, gave an account of the whole matter to Fabius; who thought it not safe to rely wholly upon the plot, but, while proceeding with secrecy to the post, gave order for a general assault to be made on the other side of the town, both by land and sea. This being accordingly executed, while the Tarentines hurried to defend the town on the side attacked, Fabius received the signal from the Bruttian, scaled the walls, and entered the town unopposed.

Here, we must confess, ambition seems to have overcome him. To make it appear to the world that he had taken Tarentum by force and his own prowess, and not by treachery, he commanded his men to kill the Bruttians before all others; yet he did not succeed in establishing the impression he desired, but merely gained the character of perfidy and cruelty. Many of the Tarentines were also killed, and thirty thousand of them were sold for slaves; the army had the plunder of the town, and there was brought into the treasury three thousand talents. Whilst they were carrying off everything else as plunder, the officer who took the inventory asked what should be done with their gods, meaning the pictures and statues; Fabius answered, "Let us leave their angry gods to the Tarentines." Nevertheless, he removed the colossal statue of Hercules, and had it set up in the Capitol, with one of himself on horseback, in brass, near it; proceedings very different from those of Marcellus on a like occasion, and which, indeed, very much set off in the eyes of the world his clemency and humanity, as appears in the account of his life.

Hannibal, it is said, was within five miles of Tarentum, when he was informed that the town was taken. He said openly, "Rome then has also got a Hannibal; as we won Tarentum, so have we lost it." And, in private with some of his confidants, he told them, for the first time, that he always thought it difficult, but now he held it impossible, with the forces he then had, to master Italy.

Upon this success, Fabius had a triumph decreed him at Rome, much more splendid than his first; they looked upon him now as a champion who had learned to cope with his antagonist, and could now easily foil his arts and prove his best skill ineffectual. And, indeed, the army of Hannibal was at this time partly worn away with continual action, and partly weakened and become dissolute with overabundance and luxury. Marcus Livius, who was governor of Tarentum when it was betrayed to Hannibal, and then retired into the citadel, which he kept till the town was retaken, was annoyed at these honours and distinctions, and, on one occasion, openly declared in the senate, that by his resistance, more than by any action of Fabius, Tarentum had been recovered; on which Fabius laughingly replied: "You say very true, for if Marcus Livius had not lost Tarentum, Fabius Maximus had never recovered it." The people, amongst other marks of gratitude, gave his son the consulship of the next year; shortly after whose entrance upon his office, there being some business on foot about provision for the war, his father, either by reason of age and infirmity, or perhaps out of design to try his son, came up to him on horseback. While he was still at a distance, the young consul observed it, and bade one of his lictors command his father to alight, and tell him if he had any business with the consul, he should come on foot. The standers-by seemed offended at the imperiousness of the son towards a father so venerable for his age and his authority, and turned their eyes in silence towards Fabius. He, however, instantly alighted from his horse, and with open arms came up, almost running, and embraced his son, saying, "Yes, my son, you do well, and understand well what authority you have received, and over whom you are to use it. This was the way by which we and our forefathers advanced the dignity of Rome, preferring ever her honour and service to our own fathers and children."

And, in fact, it is told that the great-grandfather of our Fabius, who was undoubtedly the greatest man of Rome in his time, both in reputation and authority, who had been five times consul, and had been honoured with several triumphs for victories obtained by him, took pleasure in serving as lieutenant under his own son, when he went as consul to his command. And when afterwards his son had a triumph bestowed upon him for his good service, the old man followed, on horseback, his triumphant chariot, as one of his attendants; and made it his glory, that while he really was, and was acknowledged to be, the greatest man in Rome, and held a father's full power over his son, he yet submitted himself to the laws and the magistrate.

But the praises of our Fabius are not bounded here. He afterwards lost his son, and was remarkable for bearing the loss with the moderation becoming a pious father and a wise man, and as it was the custom amongst the Romans, upon the death of any illustrious person, to have a funeral oration recited by some of the nearest relations, he took upon himself that office, and delivered a speech in the forum, which he committed afterwards to writing.

After Cornelius Scipio, who was sent into Spain, had driven the Carthaginians, defeated by him in many battles, out of the country, and had gained over to Rome many towns and nations with large resources, he was received at his coming home with unexampled joy and acclamation of the people; who, to show their gratitude, elected him consul for the year ensuing. Knowing what high expectation they had of him, he thought the

occupation of contesting Italy with Hannibal a mere old man's employment, and proposed no less a task to himself than to make Carthage the
seat of the war, fill Africa with arms and devastation, and so oblige
Hannibal, instead of invading the countries of others, to draw back and
defend his own. And to this end he proceeded to exert all the influence
he had with the people. Fabius, on the other side, opposed the undertaking with all his might, alarming the city, and telling them that nothing but
the temerity of a hot young man could inspire them with such dangerous
counsels, and sparing no means, by word or deed, to prevent it. He prevailed with the senate to espouse his sentiments; but the common people
thought that he envied the fame of Scipio, and that he was afraid lest this
young conqueror should achieve some great and noble exploit, and have
the glory, perhaps, of driving Hannibal out of Italy, or even of ending the
war, which had for so many years continued and been protracted under
his management.

To say the truth, when Fabius first opposed this project of Scipio, he
probably did it out of caution and prudence, in consideration only of the
public safety, and of the danger which the commonwealth might incur;
but when he found Scipio everyday increasing in the esteem of the people, rivalry and ambition led him further, and made him violent and personal in his opposition. For he even applied to Crassus, the colleague of
Scipio, and urged him not to yield the command to Scipio, but that, if his
inclinations were for it, he should himself in person lead the army to
Carthage. He also hindered the giving money to Scipio for the war; so that
he was forced to raise it upon his own credit and interest from the cities
of Etruria, which were extremely attached to him. On the other side,
Crassus would not stir against him, nor remove out of Italy, being, in his
own nature, averse to all contention, and also having, by his office of high
priest, religious duties to retain him. Fabius, therefore, tried other ways to
oppose the design; he impeded the levies, and he declaimed, both in the
senate and to the people, that Scipio was not only himself flying from
Hannibal, but was also endeavouring to drain Italy of all its forces, and to
spirit away the youth of the country to a foreign war, leaving behind them
their parents, wives, and children, and the city itself, a defenceless prey to
the conquering and undefeated enemy at their doors. With this he so far
alarmed the people, that at last they would only allow Scipio for the war
the legions which were in Sicily, and three hundred, whom he particularly
trusted, of those men who had served with him in Spain. In these transactions, Fabius seems to have followed the dictates of his own wary temper.

But, after that Scipio was gone over into Africa, when news almost immediately came to Rome of wonderful exploits and victories, of which the fame was confirmed by the spoils he sent home; of a Numidian king taken prisoner; of a vast slaughter of their men; of two camps of the enemy burnt and destroyed, and in them a great quantity of arms and horses; and when, hereupon, the Carthaginians were compelled to send envoys to Hannibal to call him home, and leave his idle hopes in Italy, to defend Carthage; when, for such eminent and transcending services the whole people of Rome cried up and extolled the actions of Scipio, even then, Fabius contended that a successor should be sent in his place, alleging for it only the old reason of the mutability of fortune, as if she would be weary of long favouring the same person. With this language many did begin to feel offended; it seemed to be morosity and ill-will, the pusillanimity of old age, or a fear, that had now become exaggerated, of the skill of Hannibal. Nay, when Hannibal had put his army on shipboard, and taken his leave of Italy, Fabius still could not forbear to oppose and disturb the universal joy of Rome, expressing his fears and apprehensions, telling them that the commonwealth was never in more danger than now, and that Hannibal was a more formidable enemy under the walls of Carthage than ever he had been in Italy; that it would be fatal to Rome whenever Scipio should encounter his victorious army, still warm with the blood of so many Roman generals, dictators, and consuls slain. And the people were, in some degree, startled with these declamations, and were brought to believe that the further off Hannibal was, the nearer was their danger. Scipio, however, shortly afterwards fought Hannibal, and utterly defeated him, humbled the pride of Carthage beneath his feet, gave his countrymen joy and exultation beyond all their hopes, and—

Long shaken on the seas restored the state.

Fabius Maximus, however, did not live to see the prosperous end of this war, and the final overthrow of Hannibal, nor to rejoice in the reestablished happiness and security of the commonwealth; for about the time that Hannibal left Italy, he fell sick and died. At Thebes, Epaminondas died so poor that he was buried at the public charge; one small iron coin was all, it is said, that was found in his house. Fabius did not need this, but the people, as a mark of their affection, defrayed the expenses of his funeral by a private contribution from each citizen of the smallest piece of coin; thus owning him their common father, and making his end no less honourable than his life.

THE COMPARISON OF FABIUS
WITH PERICLES

WE HAVE HERE HAD TWO LIVES RICH IN EXAMPLES, BOTH OF CIVIL AND military excellence. Let us first compare the two men in their warlike capacity. Pericles presided in his commonwealth when it was in its most flourishing and opulent condition, great and growing in power; so that it may be thought it was rather the common success and fortune that kept him from any fall or disaster. But the task of Fabius, who undertook the government in the worst and most difficult times, was not to preserve and maintain the well-established felicity of a prosperous state, but to raise and uphold a sinking and ruinous commonwealth. Besides, the victories of Cimon, the trophies of Myronides and Leocrates, with the many famous exploits of Tolmides, were employed by Pericles rather to fill the city with festive entertainments and solemnities than to enlarge and secure its empire. Whereas, Fabius, when he took upon him the government, had the frightful object before his eyes of Roman armies destroyed, of their generals and consuls slain, of lakes and plains and forests strewed with the dead bodies, and rivers stained with the blood of his fellow-citizens; and yet, with his mature and solid counsels, with the firmness of his resolution, he, as it were, put his shoulder to the falling commonwealth, and kept it up from foundering through the failings and weaknesses of others. Perhaps it may be more easy to govern a city broken and tamed with calamities and adversity, and compelled by danger and necessity to listen to wisdom, than to set a bridle on wantonness and temerity, and rule a people pampered and restive with long prosperity as were the Athenians when Pericles held the reins of government. But then again, not to be daunted nor discomposed with the vast heap of calamities under which the people of Rome at that time groaned and succumbed, argues a courage in Fabius and a strength of purpose more than ordinary.

We may set Tarentum retaken against Samos won by Pericles, and the conquest of Eubœa we may well balance with the towns of Campania; though Capua itself was reduced by the consuls Fulvius and Appius. I do not find that Fabius won any set battle but that against the Ligurians, for which he had his triumph; whereas Pericles erected nine trophies for as many victories obtained by land and by sea. But no action of Pericles can be compared to that memorable rescue of Minucius, when Fabius redeemed both him and his army from utter destruction; a noble act combining the highest valour, wisdom, and humanity. On the other side, it does not appear that Pericles was ever so overreached as Fabius was by Hannibal with his flaming oxen. His enemy there had, without his agency, put himself accidentally into his power, yet Fabius let him slip in the night, and, when day came, was worsted by him, was anticipated in the moment of success, and mastered by his prisoner. If it is the part of a good general, not only to provide for the present, but also to have a clear foresight of things to come, in this point Pericles is the superior; for he admonished the Athenians, and told them beforehand the ruin the war would bring upon them, by their grasping more than they were able to manage. But Fabius was not so good a prophet, when he denounced to the Romans that the undertaking of Scipio would be the destruction of the commonwealth. So that Pericles was a good prophet of bad success, and Fabius was a bad prophet of success that was good. And, indeed, to lose an advantage through diffidence is no less blamable in a general than to fall into danger for want of foresight; for both these faults, though of a contrary nature, spring from the same root, want of judgment and experience.

As for their civil policy, it is imputed to Pericles that he occasioned the war, since no terms of peace, offered by the Lacedæmonians, would content him. It is true, I presume, that Fabius, also, was not for yielding any point to the Carthaginians, but was ready to hazard all, rather than lessen the empire of Rome. The mildness of Fabius towards his colleague Minucius does, by way of comparison, rebuke and condemn the exertions of Pericles to banish Cimon and Thucydides, noble, aristocratic men, who by his means suffered ostracism. The authority of Pericles in Athens was much greater than that of Fabius in Rome. Hence it was more easy for him to prevent miscarriages arising from the mistakes and insufficiency of other officers; only Tolmides broke loose from him, and, contrary to his persuasions, unadvisedly fought with the Bœotians, and was slain. The greatness of his influence made all others submit and conform themselves to his judgment. Whereas Fabius, sure and unerring himself, for want of that general power, had not the means to obviate the miscarriages of others; but it had been happy for the Romans if his authority had been greater, for so, we may presume, their disasters had been fewer.

As to liberality and public spirit, Pericles was eminent in never taking any gifts, and Fabius, for giving his own money to ransom his soldiers, though the sum did not exceed six talents. Than Pericles, meantime, no man had ever greater opportunities to enrich himself, having had presents offered him from so many kings and princes and allies, yet no man was ever more free from corruption. And for the beauty and magnificence of temples and public edifices with which he adorned his country, it must be confessed, that all the ornaments and structures of Rome, to the time of the Cæsars, had nothing to compare, either in greatness of design or of expense, with the lustre of those which Pericles only erected at Athens.

ALCIBIADES

ALCIBIADES, AS IT IS SUPPOSED, WAS ANCIENTLY DESCENDED FROM Eurysaces, the son of Ajax, by his father's side; and by his mother's side from Alcmæon. Dinomache, his mother, was the daughter of Megacles. His father, Clinias, having fitted out a galley at his own expense, gained great honour in the sea-fight at Artemisium, and was afterwards slain in the battle of Coronea, fighting against the Bœotians. Pericles and Ariphron, the sons of Xanthippus, nearly related to him, became the guardians of Alcibiades. It has been said not untruly that the friendship which Socrates felt for him has much contributed to his fame; and certain it is, that, though we have no account from any writer concerning the mother of Nicias or Demosthenes, of Lamachus or Phormion, of Thrasybulus or Theramenes, notwithstanding these were all illustrious men of the same period, yet we know even the nurse of Alcibiades, that her country was Lacedæmon, and her name Amycla; and that Zopyrus was his teacher and attendant; the one being recorded by Antisthenes, and the other by Plato.

It is not, perhaps, material to say anything of the beauty of Alcibiades, only that it bloomed with him in all the ages of his life, in his infancy, in his youth, and in his manhood; and, in the peculiar character becoming to each of these periods, gave him, in everyone of them, a grace and a charm. What Euripides says, that—

Of all fair things the autumn, too, is fair,

is by no means universally true. But it happened so with Alcibiades, amongst few others, by reason of his happy constitution and natural vigour of body. It is said that his lisping, when he spoke, became him well, and gave a grace and persuasiveness to his rapid speech. Aristophanes takes notice of it in the verses in which he jests at Theorus; "How like a *colax* he is," says Alcibiades, meaning a *corax;* on which it is remarked,

> How very happily he lisped the truth.

Archippus also alludes to it in a passage where he ridicules the son of Alcibiades:

> That people may believe him like his father,
> He walks like one dissolved in luxury,
> Lets his robe trail behind him on the ground,
> Carelessly leans his head, and in his talk
> Affects to lisp.

His conduct displayed many great inconsistencies and variations, not unnaturally, in accordance with the many and wonderful vicissitudes of his fortunes; but among the many strong passions of his real character, the one most prevailing of all was his ambition and desire of superiority, which appears in several anecdotes told of his sayings whilst he was a child. Once being hard pressed in wrestling, and fearing to be thrown, he got the hand of his antagonist to his mouth, and bit it with all his force; and when the other loosed his hold presently, and said, "You bite, Alcibiades, like a woman." "No," replied he, "like a lion." Another time as he played at dice in the street, being then but a child, a loaded cart came that way, when it was his turn to throw; at first he called to the driver to stop, because he was to throw in the way over which the cart was to pass; but the man giving him no attention and driving on, when the rest of the boys divided and gave way, Alcibiades threw himself on his face before the cart and, stretching himself out, bade the carter pass on now if he would; which so startled the man, that he put back his horses, while all that saw it were terrified, and, crying out, ran to assist Alcibiades. When he began to study, he obeyed all his other masters fairly well, but refused to learn upon the flute, as a sordid thing, and not becoming a free citizen; saying that to play on the lute or the harp does not in any way disfigure a man's body or face, but one is hardly to be known by the most intimate friends when playing on the flute. Besides, one who plays on the harp may speak or sing at the same time; but the use of the flute stops the mouth, intercepts the voice, and prevents all articulation. "Therefore," said he, "let the Theban youths pipe, who do not know how to speak, but we Athenians, as our ancestors have told us, have Minerva for our patroness, and Apollo for our protector, one of whom threw away the flute, and the other stripped the flute player of his skin."

Thus, between raillery and good earnest, Alcibiades kept not only himself but others from learning, as it presently became the talk of the young boys, how Alcibiades despised playing on the flute, and ridiculed those who studied it. In consequence of which, it ceased to be reckoned amongst the liberal accomplishments, and became generally neglected.

It is stated in the invective which Antiphon wrote against Alcibiades, that once, when he was a boy, he ran away to the house of Democrates, one of those who made a favourite of him, and that Ariphon had determined to cause proclamation to be made for him, had not Pericles diverted him from it, by saying, that if he were dead, the proclaiming of him could only cause it to be discovered one day sooner, and if he were safe, it would be a reproach to him as long as he lived. Antiphon also says, that he killed one of his own servants with the blow of a staff in Sibyrtius' wrestling ground. But it is unreasonable to give credit to all that is objected by an enemy, who makes open profession of his design to defame him.

It was manifest that the many well-born persons who were continually seeking his company, and making their court to him, were attracted and captivated by his brilliant and extraordinary beauty only. But the affection which Socrates entertained for him is a great evidence of the natural noble qualities and good disposition of the boy, which Socrates, indeed, detected both in and under his personal beauty; and, hearing that his wealth and station, and the great number both of strangers and Athenians who flattered and caressed him, might at last corrupt him, resolved, if possible, to interpose, and preserve so hopeful a plant from perishing in the flower, before its fruit came to perfection. For never did fortune surround and enclose a man with so many of those things which we vulgarly call goods, or so protect him from every weapon of philosophy, and fence him from every access of free and searching words, as she did Alcibiades; who, from the beginning, was exposed to the flatteries of those who sought merely his gratification, such as might well unnerve him, and indispose him to listen to any real adviser or instructor. Yet such was the happiness of his genius, that he discerned Socrates from the rest, and admitted him, whilst he drove away the wealthy and the noble who made court to him. And, in a little time, they grew intimate, and Alcibiades, listening now to language entirely free from every thought of unmanly fondness and silly displays of affection, finding himself with one who sought to lay open to him the deficiencies of his mind, and repress his vain and foolish arrogance—

Dropped like the craven cock his conquered wing.

He esteemed these endeavours of Socrates as most truly a means which the gods made use of for the care and preservation of youth, and began to think meanly of himself and to admire him; to be pleased with his kindness, and to stand in awe of his virtue; and, unawares to himself, there became formed in his mind that reflex image and reciprocation of Love, or Anteros, that Plato talks of. It was a matter of general wonder, when people saw him joining Socrates in his meals and his exercises, living with him in the same tent, whilst he was reserved and rough to all others who made their addresses to him, and acted, indeed, with great insolence to some of them. As in particular to Anytus, the son of Anthemion, one who was very fond of him, and invited him to an entertainment which he had prepared for some strangers. Alcibiades refused the invitation; but, having drunk to excess at his own house with some of his companions, went thither with them to play some frolic; and, standing at the door of the room where the guests were enjoying themselves, and seeing the tables covered with gold and silver cups, he commanded his servants to take away the one-half of them, and carry them to his own house; and then, disdaining so much as to enter into the room himself, as soon as he had done this, went away. The company was indignant, and exclaimed at his rude and insulting conduct; Anytus, however, said, on the contrary, he had shown great consideration and tenderness in taking only a part when he might have taken all.

He behaved in the same manner to all others who courted him except only one stranger, who, as the story is told, having but a small estate, sold it all for about a hundred staters, which he presented to Alcibiades, and besought him to accept. Alcibiades, smiling and well pleased at the thing, invited him to supper, and, after a very kind entertainment, gave him his gold again, requiring him, moreover, not to fail to be present the next day, when the public revenue was offered to farm, and to outbid all others. The man would have excused himself, because the contract was so large, and would cost many talents; but Alcibiades, who had at that time a private pique against the existing farmers of the revenue, threatened to have him beaten if he refused. The next morning, the stranger, coming to the market place, offered a talent more than the existing rate; upon which the farmers, enraged and consulting together, called upon him to name his sureties, concluding that he could find none. The poor man, being startled at the proposal, began to retire; but Alcibiades, standing at a distance, cried out to the magistrates, "Set my name down, he is a friend of mine; I will be security for him." When the other bidders heard this, they perceived that all their contrivance was defeated; for their way was, with the profits of the second year to pay the rent for the year preceding; so that, not seeing any other way to extricate themselves out of the difficulty, they began to entreat the stranger, and offered him a sum of money. Alcibiades would not suffer him to accept of less than a talent; but when that was paid down, he commanded him to relinquish the bargain, having by this device relieved his necessity.

Though Socrates had many and powerful rivals, yet the natural good qualities of Alcibiades gave his affection the mastery. His words overcame him so much, as to draw tears from his eyes, and to disturb his very soul. Yet sometimes he would abandon himself to flatterers, when they proposed to him varieties of pleasure, and would desert Socrates; who, then, would pursue him, as if he had been a fugitive slave. He despised everyone else, and had no reverence or awe for anyone but him. Cleanthes the philosopher, speaking of one to whom he was attached, says his only hold on him was by his ears, while his rivals had all the others offered them; and there is no question that Alcibiades was very easily caught by pleasure; and the expression used by Thucydides about the excesses of his habitual course of living gives occasion to believe so. But those who endeavoured to corrupt Alcibiades took advantage chiefly of his vanity and ambition, and thrust him on unseasonably to undertake great enterprises, persuading him, that as soon as he began to concern himself in public affairs, he would not only obscure the rest of the generals and statesmen, but outdo the authority and the reputation which Pericles himself had gained in Greece. But in the same manner as iron which is softened by the fire grows hard with the cold and all its parts are closed again, so, as often as Socrates observed Alcibiades to be misled by luxury or pride, he reduced and corrected him by his addresses, and made him humble and modest, by showing him in how many things he was deficient, and how very far from perfection in virtue.

When he was past his childhood, he went once to a grammar-school, and asked the master for one of Homer's books; and he making answer that he had nothing of Homer's, Alcibiades gave him a blow with his fist, and went away. Another schoolmaster telling him that he had Homer corrected by himself; "How?" said Alcibiades, "and do you employ your time in teaching children to read? You, who are able to amend Homer, may well undertake to instruct men." Being once desirous to speak with Pericles, he went to his house and was told there that he was not at leisure, but busied in considering how to give up his accounts to the Athenians; Alcibiades, as he went away, said, it "were better for him to consider how he might avoid giving up his accounts at all."

Whilst he was very young, he was a soldier in the expedition against Potidæa, where Socrates lodged in the same tent with him, and stood next to him in battle. Once there happened a sharp skirmish, in which they both behaved with signal bravery; but Alcibiades receiving a wound, Socrates threw himself before him to defend him, and beyond any question saved him and his arms from the enemy, and so in all justice might have challenged the prize of valour. But the generals appearing eager to adjudge the honour to Alcibiades, because of his rank, Socrates, who desired to increase his thirst after glory of a noble kind, was the first to give evidence for him, and pressed them to crown him, and to decree to him the complete suit of armour. Afterwards, in the battle of Delium, when the Athenians were routed, and Socrates with a few others was retreating on foot, Alcibiades, who was on horseback, observing it, would not pass on, but stayed to shelter him from the danger, and brought him safe off, though the enemy pressed hard upon them, and cut off many. But this happened sometime after.

He gave a box on the ear to Hipponicus, the father of Callias, whose birth and wealth made him a person of great influence and repute. And this he did unprovoked by any passion or quarrel between them, but only because, in a frolic, he had agreed with his companions to do it. People were justly offended at this insolence when it became known through the city; but early the next morning, Alcibiades went to his house and knocked at the door, and being admitted to him, took off his outer garment, and presenting his naked body, desired him to scourge and chastise him as he pleased. Upon this Hipponicus forgot all his resentment, and not only pardoned him, but soon after gave him his daughter Hipparete in marriage. Some say that it was not Hipponicus, but his son Callias, who gave Hipparete to Alcibiades, together with a portion of ten talents, and that after, when she had a child, Alcibiades forced him to give ten talents more, upon pretence that such was the agreement if she brought him any children. Afterwards, Callias, for fear of coming to his death by his means, declared, in a full assembly of the people, that, if he should happen to die without children, the state should inherit his house and all his goods. Hipparete was a virtuous and dutiful wife, but, at last, growing impatient of the outrages done to her by her husband's continual entertaining of courtesans, as well strangers as Athenians, she departed from him and retired to her brother's house. Alcibiades seemed not at all concerned at this, and lived on still in the same luxury; but the law requiring that she should deliver to the archon in person, and not by proxy, the instrument by which she claimed a divorce, when, in obedience to the law, she presented herself before him to perform this, Alcibiades came in, caught her up, and carried her home through the market place, no one daring to oppose him nor to take her from him. She continued with him till her death, which happened not long after, when Alcibiades had gone to Ephesus. Nor is this violence to be thought so very enormous or unmanly. For the law, in making her who desires to be divorced appear in public, seems to design to give her husband an opportunity of treating with her, and endeavouring to retain her.

Alcibiades had a dog which cost him seventy minas, and was a very large one, and very handsome. His tail, which was his principal ornament, he caused to be cut off, and his acquaintances exclaiming at him for it, and telling him that all Athens was sorry for the dog, and cried out upon him for this action, he laughed, and said, "Just what I wanted has happened then. I wished the Athenians to talk about this, that they might not say something worse of me."

It is said that the first time he came into the assembly was upon occasion of a largess of money which he made to the people. This was not done by design, but as he passed along he heard a shout, and inquiring the cause, and having learned that there was a donative making to the people, he went in amongst them and gave money also. The multitude thereupon applauding him, and shouting, he was so transported at it, that he forgot a quail which he had under his robe, and the bird, being frightened with the noise, flew off; upon which the people made louder acclamations than before, and many of them started up to pursue the bird; and one Antiochus, a pilot, caught it and restored it to him, for which he was ever after a favourite with Alcibiades.

He had great advantages for entering public life; his noble birth, his riches, the personal courage he had shown in divers battles, and the multitude of his friends and dependents, threw open, so to say, folding doors for his admittance. But he did not consent to let his power with the people rest on anything, rather than on his own gift of eloquence. That he was a master in the art of speaking, the comic poets bear him witness; and the most eloquent of public speakers, in his oration against Midias, allows that Alcibiades, among other perfections, was a most accomplished orator. If, however, we give credit to Theophrastus, who of all philosophers was the most curious inquirer, and the greatest lover of history, we are to understand that Alcibiades had the highest capacity for inventing, for discerning what was the right thing to be said for any purpose, and on any occasion; but aiming not only at saying what was required, but also at saying it well, in respect, that is, of words and phrases, when these did not readily occur, he would often pause in the middle of his discourse for want of the apt word, and would be silent and stop till he could recollect himself, and had considered what to say.

His expenses in horses kept for the public games, and in the number of his chariots, were matter of great observation; never did anyone but he, either private person or king, send seven chariots to the Olympic games. And to have carried away at once the first, the second, and the fourth prize, as Thucydides says, or the third, as Euripides relates it, outdoes far away every distinction that ever was known or thought of in that kind. Euripides celebrates his success in this manner:

> —But my song to you,
> Son of Clinias, is due.
> Victory is noble; how much more
> To do as never Greek before;
> To obtain in the great chariot race
> The first, the second, and third place;
> With easy step advanced to fame
> To bid the herald three times claim
> The olive for one victor's name.

The emulation displayed by the deputations of various states in the presents which they made to him, rendered this success yet more illustrious. The Ephesians erected a tent for him, adorned magnificently; the city of Chios furnished him with provender for his horses and with great numbers of beasts for sacrifice; and the Lesbians sent him wine and other provisions for the many great entertainments which he made. Yet in the midst of all this he escaped not without censure, occasioned either by the ill-nature of his enemies or by his own misconduct. For it is said, that one Diomedes, an Athenian, a worthy man and a friend to Alcibiades, passionately desiring to obtain the victory at the Olympic games, and having heard much of a chariot which belonged to the state at Argos, where he knew that Alcibiades had great power and many friends, prevailed with him to undertake to buy the chariot. Alcibiades did indeed buy it, but then claimed it for his own, leaving Diomedes to rage at him, and to call upon the gods and men to bear witness to the injustice. It would seem there was a suit at law commenced

upon this occasion, and there is yet extant an oration concerning the chariot, written by Isocrates in defence of the son of Alcibiades. But the plaintiff in this action is named Tisias, and not Diomedes.

As soon as he began to intermeddle in the government, which was
when he was very young, he quickly lessened the credit of all who aspired
to the confidence of the people except Phæax, the son of Erasistratus, and
Nicias, the son of Niceratus, who alone could contest it with him. Nicias
was arrived at a mature age, and was esteemed their first general. Phæax was
but a rising statesman like Alcibiades; he was descended from noble ancestors, but was his inferior, as in many other things, so, principally, in eloquence. He possessed rather the art of persuading in private conversation
than of debate before the people, and was, as Eupolis said of him—

The best of talkers, and of speakers worst.

There is extant an oration written by Phæax against Alcibiades, in which,
amongst other things, it is said, that Alcibiades made daily use at his table
of many gold and silver vessels, which belonged to the commonwealth, as
if they had been his own.

There was a certain Hyperbolus, of the township of Perithœdæ, whom
Thucydides also speaks of as a man of bad character, a general butt for
the mockery of all the comic writers of the time, but quite unconcerned
at the worst things they could say, and, being careless of glory, also insensible of shame; a temper which some people call boldness and courage,
whereas it is indeed impudence and recklessness. He was liked by
nobody, yet the people made frequent use of him, when they had a mind
to disgrace or calumniate any persons in authority. At this time, the people, by his persuasions, were ready to proceed to pronounce the sentence
of ten years' banishment, called ostracism. This they made use of to
humiliate and drive out of the city such citizens as outdid the rest in
credit and power, indulging not so much perhaps their apprehensions as
their jealousies in this way. And when, at this time, there was no doubt but
that the ostracism would fall upon one of those three, Alcibiades contrived to form a coalition of parties, and, communicating his project to
Nicias, turned the sentence upon Hyperbolus himself. Others say, that it
was not with Nicias, but Phæax, that he consulted, and by help of his
party procured the banishment of Hyperbolus, when he suspected nothing less. For, before that time, no mean or obscure person had ever fallen
under the punishment, so that Plato, the comic poet, speaking of
Hyperbolus, might well say—

> The man deserved the fate; deny't who can?
> Yes, but the fate did not deserve the man;
> Not for the like of him and his slave-brands
> Did Athens put the sherd into our hands.

But we have given elsewhere a fuller statement of what is known to us of the matter.

Alcibiades was not less disturbed at the distinctions which Nicias gained amongst the enemies of Athens than at the honours which the Athenians themselves paid to him. For though Alcibiades was the proper appointed person to receive all Lacedæmonians when they came to Athens, and had taken particular care of those that were made prisoners at Pylos, yet, after they had obtained the peace and restitution of the captives, by the procurement chiefly of Nicias, they paid him very special attentions. And it was commonly said in Greece, that the war was begun by Pericles, and that Nicias made an end of it, and the peace was generally called the peace of Nicias. Alcibiades was extremely annoyed at this, and being full of envy, set himself to break the league. First, therefore, observing that the Argives, as well out of fear as hatred to the Lacedæmonians, sought for protection against them, he gave them a secret assurance of alliance with Athens. And communicating, as well in person as by letters, with the chief advisers of the people there, he encouraged them not to fear the Lacedæmonians, nor make concessions to them, but to wait a little, and keep their eyes on the Athenians, who, already, were all but sorry they had made peace, and would soon give it up. And afterwards, when the Lacedæmonians had made a league with the Bœotians, and had not delivered up Panactum entire, as they ought to have done by the treaty, but only after first destroying it, which gave great offence to the people of Athens, Alcibiades laid hold of that opportunity to exasperate them more highly. He exclaimed fiercely against Nicias, and accused him of many things, which seemed probable enough: as that, when he was general, he made no attempt himself to capture their enemies that were shut up in the isle of Sphacteria, but, when they were afterwards made prisoners by others, he procured their release and sent them back to the Lacedæmonians, only to get favour with them; that he would not make use of his credit with them to prevent their entering into this confederacy with the Bœotians and Corinthians, and yet, on the other side, that he sought to stand in the way of those Greeks who were inclined to make an alliance and friendship with Athens, if the Lacedæmonians did not like it.

It happened, at the very time when Nicias was by these arts brought into disgrace with the people, that ambassadors arrived from Lacedæmon, who, at their first coming, said what seemed very satisfactory, declaring that they had full powers to arrange all matters in dispute upon fair and equal terms. The council received their propositions, and the people were to assemble on the morrow to give them audience. Alcibiades grew very apprehensive of this, and contrived to gain a secret conference with the ambassadors. When they were met, he said: "What is it you intend, you men of Sparta? Can you be ignorant that the council always act with moderation and respect towards ambassadors, but that the people are full of ambition and great designs? So that, if you let them know what full powers your commission gives you, they will urge and press you to unreasonable conditions. Quit, therefore, this indiscreet simplicity, if you expect to obtain equal terms from the Athenians, and would not have things extorted from you contrary to your inclinations, and begin to treat with the people upon some reasonable articles, not avowing yourselves plenipotentiaries; and I will be ready to assist you, out of goodwill to the Lacedæmonians." When he had said thus, he gave them his oath for the performance of what he promised, and by this way drew them from Nicias to rely entirely upon himself, and left them full of admiration of the discernment and sagacity they had seen in him. The next day, when the people were assembled and the ambassadors introduced, Alcibiades, with great apparent courtesy, demanded of them, With what powers they were come? They made answer that they were not come as plenipotentiaries.

Instantly upon that, Alcibiades, with a loud voice, as though he had received and not done the wrong, began to call them dishonest prevaricators, and to urge that such men could not possibly come with a purpose to say or do anything that was sincere. The council was incensed, the people were in a rage, and Nicias, who knew nothing of the deceit and the imposture, was in the greatest confusion, equally surprised and ashamed at such a change in the men. So thus the Lacedæmonian ambassadors were utterly rejected, and Alcibiades was declared general, who presently united the Argives, the Eleans, and the people of Mantinea, into a confederacy with the Athenians.

No man commended the method by which Alcibiades effected all this, yet it was a great political feat thus to divide and shake almost all Peloponnesus, and to combine so many men in arms against the Lacedæmonians in one day before Mantinea; and, moreover, to remove the war and the danger so far from the frontier of the Athenians, that even success would profit the enemy but little, should they be conquerors, whereas, if they were defeated, Sparta itself was hardly safe.

After this battle at Mantinea, the select thousand of the army of the Argives attempted to overthrow the government of the people in Argos, and make themselves masters of the city; and the Lacedæmonians came to their aid and abolished the democracy. But the people took arms again, and gained the advantage, and Alcibiades came in to their aid and completed the victory, and persuaded them to build long walls, and by that means to join their city to the sea, and so to bring it wholly within reach of the Athenian power. To this purpose he procured them builders and masons from Athens, and displayed the greatest zeal for their service, and gained no less honour and power to himself than to the commonwealth of Athens. He also persuaded the people of Patræ to join their city to the sea, by building long walls; and when someone told them, by way of warning, that the Athenians would swallow them up at last, Alcibiades made answer, "Possibly it may be so, but it will be by little and little, and beginning at the feet, whereas the Lacedæmonians will begin at the head and devour you all at once." Nor did he neglect either to advise the Athenians to look to their interests by land, and often put the young men in mind of the oath which they had made at Agraulos, to the effect that they would account wheat and barley, and vines and olives, to be the limits of Attica; by which they were taught to claim a title to all land that was cultivated and productive.

But with all these words and deeds, and with all this sagacity and eloquence, he intermingled exorbitant luxury and wantonness, in his eating and drinking and dissolute living; wore long purple robes like a woman, which dragged after him as he went through the market place; caused the planks of his galley to be cut away, that so he might lie the softer, his bed not being placed on the boards, but hanging upon girths. His shield, again, which was richly gilded, had not the usual ensigns of the Athenians, but a Cupid, holding a thunderbolt in his hand, was painted upon it. The sight of all this made the people of good repute in the city feel disgust and abhorrence, and apprehension also, at his free living, and his contempt of law, as things monstrous in themselves, and indicating designs of usurpation. Aristophanes has well expressed the people's feelings toward him—

They love, and hate, and cannot do without him.

And still more strongly, under a figurative expression,

> Best rear no lion in your state, 'tis true;
> But treat him like a lion if you do.

The truth is, his liberalities, his public shows, and other munificence to the people, which were such as nothing could exceed, the glory of his ancestors, the force of his eloquence, the grace of his person, his strength of body, joined with his great courage and knowledge in military affairs, prevailed upon the Athenians to endure patiently his excesses, to indulge many things to him, and, according to their habit, to give the softest names to his faults, attributing them to youth and good nature. As, for example, he kept Agatharcus, the painter, a prisoner till he had painted his whole house, but then dismissed him with a reward. He publicly struck Taureas, who exhibited certain shows in opposition to him and contended with him for the prize. He selected for himself one of the captive Melian women, and had a son by her, whom he took care to educate. This the Athenians styled great humanity, and yet he was the principal cause of the slaughter of all the inhabitants of the isle of Melos who were of age to bear arms, having spoken in favour of that decree. When Aristophon, the painter, had drawn Nemea sitting and holding Alcibiades in her arms, the multitudes seemed pleased with the piece, and thronged to see it, but older people disliked and disrelished it, and looked on these things as enormities, and movements towards tyranny. So that it was not said amiss by Archestratus, that Greece could not support a second Alcibiades. Once, when Alcibiades succeeded well in an oration which he made, and the whole assembly attended upon him to do him honour, Timon the misanthrope did not pass slightly by him, nor avoid him, as did others, but purposely met him, and taking him by the hand, said, "Go on boldly, my son, and increase in credit with the people, for thou wilt one day bring them calamities enough." Some that were present laughed at the saying, and some reviled Timon; but there were others upon whom it made a deep impression; so various was the judgment which was made of him and so irregular his own character.

The Athenians, even in the lifetime of Pericles, had already cast a longing eye upon Sicily; but did not attempt anything till after his death. Then, under pretence of aiding their confederates, they sent succours upon all occasions to those who were oppressed by the Syracusans, preparing the way for sending over a greater force. But Alcibiades was the person who inflamed this desire of theirs to the height, and prevailed with them no longer to proceed secretly, and by little and little, in their design, but to sail out with a great fleet, and undertake at once to make themselves masters of the island. He possessed the people with great hopes, and he himself entertained yet greater; and the conquest of Sicily, which was the utmost bound of their ambition, was but the mere outset of his expectation. Nicias endeavoured to divert the people from the expedition, by representing to them that the taking of Syracuse would be a work of great difficulty; but Alcibiades dreamed of nothing less than the conquest of Carthage and Libya, and by the accession of these conceiving himself at once made master of Italy and Peloponnesus, seemed to look upon Sicily as little more than a magazine for the war. The young men were soon elevated with these hopes, and listened gladly to those of riper years, who talked wonders of the countries they were going to; so that you might see great numbers sitting in the wrestling grounds and public places, drawing on the ground the figure of the island and the situation of Libya and Carthage. Socrates the philosopher and Meton the astrologer are said, however, never to have hoped for any good to the commonwealth from this war; the one, it is to be supposed, presaging what would ensue, by the intervention of his attendant Genius; and the other, either upon rational consideration of the project or by use of the art of divination, conceived fears for its issue, and, feigning madness, caught up a burning torch, and seemed as if he would have set his own house on fire. Others report, that he did not take upon him to act the madman, but secretly in the night set his house on fire, and the next morning besought the people, that for his comfort, after such a calamity, they would spare his son from the expedition. By which artifice he deceived his fellow-citizens, and obtained of them what he desired.

Together with Alcibiades, Nicias, much against his will, was appointed general; and he endeavoured to avoid the command, not the less on account of his colleague. But the Athenians thought the war would proceed more prosperously, if they did not send Alcibiades free from all restraint, but tempered his heat with the caution of Nicias. This they chose the rather to do, because Lamachus, the third general, though he was of mature years, yet in several battles had appeared no less hot and rash than Alcibiades himself. When they began to deliberate of the number of forces, and of the manner of making the necessary provisions, Nicias made another attempt to oppose the design, and to prevent the war; but Alcibiades contradicted him, and carried his point with the people. And one Demostratus, an orator, proposing to give the generals absolute power over the preparations and the whole management of the war, it was presently decreed so. When all things were fitted for the voyage, many unlucky omens appeared. At that very time the feast of Adonis happened in which the women were used to expose, in all parts of the city, images resembling dead men carried out to their burial, and to represent funeral solemnities by lamentations and mournful songs. The mutilation, however, of the images of Mercury, most of which, in one night, had their faces all disfigured, terrified many persons who were wont to despise most things of that nature. It was given out that it was done by the Corinthians, for the sake of the Syracusans, who were their colony, in hopes that the Athenians, by such prodigies, might be induced to delay or abandon the war. But the report gained no credit with the people, nor yet the opinion of those who would not believe that there was anything ominous in the matter, but that it was only an extravagant action, committed, in that sort of sport which runs into licence, by wild young men coming from a debauch. Alike enraged and terrified at the thing, looking upon it to proceed from a conspiracy of persons who designed some commotions in the state, the council, as well as the assembly of the people, which were held frequently in a few days' space, examined diligently everything that might administer ground for suspicion. During this examination, Androcles, one of the demagogues, produced certain slaves and strangers before them who accused Alcibiades and some of his friends of defacing other images in the same manner, and of having profanely acted the sacred mysteries at a drunken meeting, where one Theodoras represented the herald, Polytion the torchbearer, and Alcibiades the chief priest, while the rest of the party appeared as candidates for initiation, and received the title of Initiates. These were the matters contained in the articles of information which Thessalus, the son of Cimon, exhibited against Alcibiades, for his impious mockery of the goddesses Ceres and Proserpine. The people were highly exasperated and incensed against Alcibiades upon this accusation, which being aggravated by Androcles, the most malicious of all his enemies, at first disturbed his friends exceedingly. But when they perceived that all the seamen designed for Sicily were for him, and the soldiers also, and when the Argive and Mantinean auxiliaries, a thousand men at arms, openly declared that they had undertaken this distant maritime expedition for the sake of Alcibiades, and that, if he was ill-used, they would all go home, they recovered their courage, and became eager to make use of the present opportunity for justifying him. At this his enemies were again discouraged, fearing lest the people should be more gentle to him in their sentence, because of the occasion they had for his service. Therefore, to obviate this, they contrived that some other orators, who did not appear to be enemies to Alcibiades, but really hated him no less than those who avowed it, should stand up in the assembly and say that it was a very absurd thing that one who was created general of such an army with absolute power, after his troops were assembled, and the confederates were come, should lose the opportunity, whilst the people were choosing his judges by lot, and appointing times for the hearing of the cause. And, therefore, let him set sail at once, good fortune attend him; and when the war should be at an end, he might then in person make his defence according to the laws.

Alcibiades perceived the malice of this postponement, and, appearing in the assembly, represented that it was monstrous for him to be sent with the command of so large an army, when he lay under such accusations and calumnies; that he deserved to die, if he could not clear himself of the crimes objected to him; but when he had so done, and had proved his innocence, he should then cheerfully apply himself to the war, as standing no longer in fear of false accusers. But he could not prevail with the people, who commanded him to sail immediately. So he departed, together with the other generals, having with them near 140 galleys, 5,100 men at arms, and about 1,300 archers, slingers, and light-armed men, and all the other provisions corresponding.

Arriving on the coast of Italy, he landed at Rhegium, and there stated his views of the manner in which they ought to conduct the war. He was opposed by Nicias; but Lamachus being of his opinion, they sailed for Sicily forthwith, and took Catana. This was all that was done while he was there, for he was soon after recalled by the Athenians to abide his trial. At first, as we before said, there were only some slight suspicions advanced against Alcibiades, and accusations by certain slaves and strangers. But afterwards, in his absence, his enemies attacked him more violently, and confounded together the breaking the images with the profanation of the mysteries, as though both had been committed in pursuance of the same conspiracy for changing the government. The people proceeded to imprison all that were accused, without distinction, and without hearing them, and repented now, considering the importance of the charge, that they had not immediately brought Alcibiades to his trial and given judgment against him. Any of his friends or acquaintance who fell into the people's hands, whilst they were in this fury, did not fail to meet with very severe usage. Thucydides has omitted to name the informers, but others mention

Dioclides and Teucer. Amongst whom is Phrynichus, the comic poet, in whom we find the following:

> O dearest Hermes! Only do take care,
> And mind you do not miss your footing there;
> Should you get hurt, occasion may arise
> For a new Dioclides to tell lies.

To which he makes Mercury return this answer:

> will so, for I feel no inclination
> To reward Teucer for more information.

The truth is, his accusers alleged nothing that was certain or solid against him. One of them, being asked how he knew the men who defaced the images, replying, that he saw them by the light of the moon, made a palpable misstatement, for it was just new moon when the fact was committed. This made all men of understanding cry out upon the thing; but the people were as eager as ever to receive further accusations, nor was their first heat at all abated, but they instantly seized and imprisoned everyone that was accused. Amongst those who were detained in prison for their trials was Andocides the orator, whose descent the historian Hellanicus deduces from Ulysses. He was always supposed to hate popular government, and to support oligarchy. The chief ground of his being suspected of defacing the images was because the great Mercury, which stood near his house, and was an ancient monument of the tribe Ægeïs, was almost the only statue of all the remarkable ones which remained entire. For this cause, it is now called the Mercury of Andocides, all men giving it that name, though the inscription is evidence to the contrary. It happened that Andocides, amongst the rest who were prisoners upon the same account, contracted particular acquaintance and intimacy with one Timæus, a person inferior to him in repute, but of remarkable dexterity and boldness. He persuaded Andocides to accuse him and some few others of this crime, urging to him that, upon his confession, he would be, by the decree of the people, secure of his pardon, whereas the event of judgment is uncertain to all men, but to great persons, such as he was, most formidable. So that it was better for him, if he regarded himself, to save his life by falsity, than to suffer an infamous death, as really guilty of the crime. And if he had regard to the public good, it was commendable to sacrifice a few suspected men, by that means to rescue many excellent persons from the fury of the people. Andocides was prevailed upon, and accused himself and some others, and, by the terms of the decree, obtained his pardon, while all the persons named by him, except some few who had saved themselves by flight, suffered death. To gain the greater credit to his information, he accused his own servants amongst others. But notwithstanding this, the people's anger was not wholly appeased; and being now no longer diverted by the mutilators, they were at leisure to pour out their whole rage upon Alcibiades. And, in conclusion, they sent the galley named Salaminian to recall him. But they expressly commanded those that were sent to use no violence, nor seize upon his person, but address themselves to him in the mildest terms, requiring him to follow them to Athens in order to abide his trial, and clear himself before the people. For they feared mutiny and sedition in the army in an enemy's country, which indeed it would have been easy for Alcibiades to effect, if he had wished it. For the soldiers were dispirited upon his departure, expecting for the future tedious delays, and that the war would be drawn out into a lazy length by Nicias, when Alcibiades, who was the spur to action, was taken away. For though Lamachus was a soldier, and a man of courage, poverty deprived him of authority and respect in the army. Alcibiades, just upon his departure, prevented Messena from falling into the hands of the Athenians. There were some in that city who were upon the point of delivering it up, but he, knowing the persons, gave information to some friends of the Syracusans, and so defeated the whole contrivance. When he arrived at Thurii, he went on shore, and, concealing himself there, escaped those who searched after him. But to one who knew him, and asked him if he durst not trust his own native country, he made answer, "In everything else, yes; but in a matter that touches my life, I would not even my own mother, lest she might by mistake throw in the black ball instead of the white." When, afterwards, he was told that the assembly had pronounced judgment of death against him, all he said was, "I will make them feel that I am alive."

The information against him was conceived in this form:

"Thessalus, the son of Cimon, of the township of Lacia, lays information that Alcibiades, the son of Clinias of the township of the Scambonidæ, has committed a crime against the goddesses Ceres and Proserpine, by representing in derision the holy mysteries, and showing them to his companions in his own house. Where, being habited in such robes as are used by the chief priest when he shows the holy things, he named himself the chief priest, Polytion the torchbearer, and Theodoras, of the township of

Phegæa, the herald; and saluted the rest of his company as Initiates and Novices, all which was done contrary to the laws and institutions of the Eumolpidæ, and the heralds and priests of the temple at Eleusis."

He was condemned as contumacious upon his not appearing, his property confiscated, and it was decreed that all the priests and priestesses should solemnly curse him. But one of them, Theano, the daughter of Menon, of the township of Agraule, is said to have opposed that part of the decree, saying that her holy office obliged her to make prayers, but not execrations.

Alcibiades, lying under these heavy decrees and sentences, when first he fled from Thurii, passed over into Peloponnesus and remained sometime at Argos. But being there in fear of his enemies, and seeing himself utterly hopeless of return to his native country, he sent to Sparta, desiring safe conduct, and assuring them that he would make them amends by his future services for all the mischief he had done them while he was their enemy. The Spartans giving him the security he desired, he went eagerly, was well received, and, at his very first coming, succeeded in inducing them, without any further caution or delay, to send aid to the Syracusans; and so roused and excited them, that they forthwith despatched Gylippus into Sicily to crush the forces which the Athenians had in Sicily. A second point was to renew the war upon the Athenians at home. But the third thing, and the most important of all, was to make them fortify Decelea, which above everything reduced and wasted the resources of the Athenians.

The renown which he earned by these public services was equalled by the admiration he attracted to his private life; he captivated and won over everybody by his conformity to Spartan habits. People who saw him wearing his hair close cut, bathing in cold water, eating coarse meal, and dining on black broth, doubted, or rather could not believe, that he ever had a cook in his house, or had ever seen a perfumer, or had worn a mantle of Milesian purple. For he had, as it was observed, this peculiar talent and artifice for gaining men's affections, that he could at once comply with and really embrace and enter into their habits and ways of life, and change faster than the chameleon. One colour, indeed, they say the chameleon cannot assume: it cannot itself appear white; but Alcibiades, whether with good men or with bad, could adapt himself to his company, and equally wear the appearance of virtue or vice. At Sparta, he was devoted to athletic exercises, was frugal and reserved; in Ionia, luxurious, gay, and indolent; in Thrace, always drinking; in Thessaly, ever on horseback; and when he lived with Tisaphernes the Persian satrap, he exceeded the Persians themselves in magnificence and pomp. Not that his natural disposition changed so easily, nor that his real character was so variable, but, whether he was sensible that by pursuing his own inclinations he might give offence to those with whom he had occasion to converse, he transformed himself into any shape, and adopted any fashion, that he observed to be most agreeable to them. So that to have seen him at Lacedæmon, a man, judging by the outward appearance, would have said, "'Tis not Achilles' son, but he himself; the very man" that Lycurgus designed to form; while his real feeling and acts would have rather provoked the exclamation, "'Tis the same woman still." For while king Agis was absent, and abroad with the army, he corrupted his wife Timæa, and had a child born by her. Nor did she even deny it, but when she was brought to bed of a son, called him in public Leotychides, but, amongst her confidants and attendants, would whisper that his name was Alcibiades, to such a degree was she transported by her passion for him. He, on the other side, would say, in his vain way, he had not done this thing out of mere wantonness of insult, nor to gratify a passion, but that his race might one day be kings over the Lacedæmonians.

There were many who told Agis that this was so, but time itself gave the greatest confirmation to the story. For Agis, alarmed by an earthquake, had quitted his wife, and for ten months after was never with her; Leotychides, therefore, being born after these ten months, he would not acknowledge him for his son; which was the reason that afterwards he was not admitted to the succession.

After the defeat which the Athenians received in Sicily, ambassadors were despatched to Sparta at once from Chios and Lesbos and Cyzicus, to signify their purpose of revolting from the Athenians. The Bœotians interposed in favour of the Lesbians, and Pharnabazus of the Cyzicenes, but the Lacedæmonians, at the persuasion of Alcibiades, chose to assist Chios before all others. He himself, also, went instantly to sea, procured the immediate revolt of almost all Ionia, and, cooperating with the Lacedæmonian generals, did great mischief to the Athenians. But Agis was his enemy, hating him for having dishonoured his wife, and also impatient of his glory, as almost every enterprise and every success was ascribed to Alcibiades. Others, also, of the most powerful and ambitious amongst the Spartans were possessed with jealousy of him, and at last prevailed with the magistrates in the city to send orders into Ionia that he should be killed. Alcibiades, however, had secret intelligence of this, and in apprehension of the result, while he communicated all affairs to the Lacedæmonians, yet took care not to put himself into their power. At last he retired to

Tisaphernes, the King of Persia's satrap, for his security, and immediately became the first and most influential person about him. For this barbarian, not being himself sincere, but a lover of guile and wickedness, admired his address and wonderful subtlety. And, indeed, the charm of daily intercourse with him was more than any character could resist or any disposition escape. Even those who feared and envied him could not but take delight, and have a sort of kindness for him, when they saw him and were in his company. So that Tisaphernes, otherwise a cruel character, and, above all other Persians, a hater of the Greeks, was yet so won by the flatteries of Alcibiades, that he set himself even to exceed him in responding to them. The most beautiful of his parks, containing salubrious streams and meadows, where he had built pavilions, and places of retirement royally and exquisitely adorned, received by his direction the name of Alcibiades, and was always so called and so spoken of.

Thus Alcibiades, quitting the interests of the Spartans, whom he could no longer trust, because he stood in fear of Agis, endeavoured to do them ill offices, and render them odious to Tisaphernes, who by his means was hindered from assisting them vigorously, and from finally ruining the Athenians. For his advice was to furnish them but sparingly with money, and so wear them out, and consume them insensibly; when they had wasted their strength upon one another, they would both become ready to submit to the king. Tisaphernes readily pursued his counsel, and so openly expressed the liking and admiration which he had for him, that Alcibiades was looked up to by the Greeks of both parties, and the Athenians, now in their misfortunes, repented them of their severe sentence against him. And he, on the other side, began to be troubled for them, and to fear lest, if that commonwealth were utterly destroyed, he should fall into the hands of the Lacedæmonians, his enemies.

At that time the whole strength of the Athenians was in Samos. Their fleet maintained itself here, and issued from these headquarters to reduce such as had revolted, and protect the rest of their territories; in one way or other still contriving to be a match for their enemies at sea. What they stood in fear of was Tisaphernes and the Phœnician fleet of one hundred and fifty galleys, which was said to be already under sail; if those came, there remained then no hopes for the commonwealth of Athens. Understanding this, Alcibiades sent secretly to the chief men of the Athenians, who were then at Samos, giving them hopes that he would make Tisaphernes their friend; he was willing, he implied, to do some favour, not to the people, not in reliance upon them, but to the better citizens, if only, like brave men, they would make the attempt to put down the insolence of the people, and, by taking upon them the government, would endeavour to save the city from ruin. All of them gave a ready ear to the proposal made by Alcibiades, except only Phrynichus, of the township of Dirades, one of the generals, who suspected, as the truth was, that Alcibiades concerned not himself whether the government were in the people or the better citizens, but only sought by any means to make way for his return into his native country, and to that end inveighed against the people, thereby to gain the others, and to insinuate himself into their good opinion. But when Phrynichus found his counsel to be rejected and that he was himself become a declared enemy of Alcibiades, he gave secret intelligence to Astyochus, the enemy's admiral, cautioning him to beware of Alcibiades and to seize him as a double dealer, unaware that one traitor was making discoveries to another. For Astyochus, who was eager to gain the favour of Tisaphernes, observing the credit Alcibiades had with him, revealed to Alcibiades all that Phrynichus had said against him. Alcibiades at once despatched messengers to Samos, to accuse Phrynichus of the treachery. Upon this, all the commanders were enraged with Phrynichus, and set themselves against him; he, seeing no other way to extricate himself from the present danger, attempted to remedy one evil by a greater. He sent to Astyochus to reproach him for betraying him, and to make an offer to him at the same time to deliver into his hands both the army and the navy of the Athenians. This occasioned no damage to the Athenians, because Astyochus repeated his treachery and revealed also this proposal to Alcibiades. But this again was foreseen by Phrynichus, who, expecting a second accusation from Alcibiades to anticipate him, advertised the Athenians beforehand that the enemy was ready to sail in order to surprise them, and therefore advised them to fortify their camp, and be in a readiness to go aboard their ships. While the Athenians were intent upon doing these things, they received other letters from Alcibiades, admonishing them to beware of Phrynichus, as one who designed to betray their fleet to the enemy, to which they then gave no credit at all, conceiving that Alcibiades, who knew perfectly the counsels and preparations of the enemy, was merely making use of that knowledge, in order to impose upon them in this false accusation of Phrynichus. Yet, afterwards, when Phrynichus was stabbed with a dagger in the market place by Hermon, one of the guards, the Athenians, entering into an examination of the cause, solemnly condemned Phrynichus of treason, and decreed crowns to Hermon and his associates. And now the friends of Alcibiades, carrying all before them at

Samos, despatched Pisander to Athens, to attempt a change of government, and to encourage the aristocratical citizens to take upon themselves the government, and overthrow the democracy, representing to them, that upon these terms, Alcibiades would procure them the friendship and alliance of Tisaphernes.

This was the colour and pretence made use of by those who desired to change the government of Athens to an oligarchy. But as soon as they prevailed, and had got the administration of affairs into their hands, under the name of the Five Thousand (whereas, indeed, they were but four hundred), they slighted Alcibiades altogether, and prosecuted the war with less vigour; partly because they durst not yet trust the citizens, who secretly detested this change, and partly because they thought the Lacedæmonians, who always befriended the government of the few, would be inclined to give them favourable terms.

The people in the city were terrified into submission, many of those who had dared openly to oppose the four hundred having been put to death. But those who were at Samos, indignant when they heard this news, were eager to set sail instantly for the Piræus; sending for Alcibiades, they declared him general, requiring him to lead them on to put down the tyrants. He, however, in that juncture, did not, as it might have been thought a man would, on being suddenly exalted by the favour of a multitude, think himself under an obligation to gratify and submit to all the wishes of those who, from a fugitive and an exile, had created him general of so great an army, and given him the command of such a fleet. But, as became a great captain, he opposed himself to the precipitate resolutions which their rage led them to, and, by restraining them from the great error they were about to commit, unequivocally saved the commonwealth. For if they then sailed to Athens, all Ionia and the islands and the Hellespont would have fallen into the enemies' hands without opposition, while the Athenians, involved in civil war, would have been fighting with one another within the circuit of their own walls. It was Alcibiades, alone, or, at least, principally, who prevented all this mischief; for he not only used persuasion to the whole army, and showed them the danger, but applied himself to them, one by one, entreating some, and constraining others. He was much assisted, however, by Thrasybulus of Stiria, who having the loudest voice, as we are told, of all the Athenians, went along with him, and cried out to those who were ready to be gone. A second great service which Alcibiades did for them was, his undertaking that the Phœnician fleet, which the Lacedæmonians expected to be sent to them by the King of Persia, should either come in aid of the Athenians or otherwise should not come at all. He sailed off with all expedition in order to perform this, and the ships, which had already been seen as near as Aspendus, were not brought any further by Tisaphernes, who thus deceived the Lacedæmonians; and it was by both sides believed that they had been diverted by the procurement of Alcibiades. The Lacedæmonians, in particular, accused him, that he had advised the Barbarian to stand still, and suffer the Greeks to waste and destroy one another, as it was evident that the accession of so great a force to either party would enable them to take away the entire dominion of the sea from the other side.

Soon after this, the four hundred usurpers were driven out, the friends of Alcibiades vigorously assisting those who were for the popular government. And now the people in the city not only desired, but commanded Alcibiades to return home from his exile. He, however, desired not to owe his return to the mere grace and commiseration of the people, and resolved to come back, not with empty hands, but with glory, and after some service done. To this end, he sailed from Samos with a few ships, and cruised on the sea of Cnidos, and about the isle of Cos, but receiving intelligence there that Mindarus, the Spartan admiral, had sailed with his whole army into the Hellespont, and that the Athenians had followed him, he hurried back to succour the Athenian commanders, and, by good fortune, arrived with eighteen galleys at a critical time. For both the fleets having engaged near Abydos, the fight between them had lasted till night, the one side having the advantage on one quarter, and the other on another. Upon his first appearance, both sides formed a false impression; the enemy was encouraged and the Athenians terrified. But Alcibiades suddenly raised the Athenian ensign in the admiral ship, and fell upon those galleys of the Peloponnesians which had the advantage and were in pursuit. He soon put these to flight, and followed them so close that he forced them on shore, and broke the ships in pieces, the sailors abandoning them and swimming away in spite of all the efforts of Pharnabazus, who had come down to their assistance by land and did what he could to protect them from the shore. In fine, the Athenians, having taken thirty of the enemy's ships, and recovered all their own, erected a trophy. After the gaining of so glorious a victory, his vanity made him eager to show himself to Tisaphernes, and, having furnished himself with gifts and presents, and an equipage suitable to his dignity, he set out to visit him. But the thing did not succeed as he had imagined, for Tisaphernes had been long suspected by the Lacedæmonians, and was afraid to fall into disgrace with his king upon that account, and therefore thought that Alcibiades arrived very opportunely, and immediately caused him to be seized, and sent away prisoner to Sardis; fancying, by this act of injustice, to clear himself from all former imputations.

But about thirty days after, Alcibiades escaped from his keeping, and having got a horse, fled to Clazomenæ, where he procured Tisaphernes additional disgrace by professing he was a party to his escape. From there he sailed to the Athenian camp, and, being informed there that Mindarus and Pharnabazus were together at Cyzicus, he made a speech to the soldiers, telling them that sea-fighting, land-fighting, and, by the gods, fighting against fortified cities too, must be all one for them, as unless they conquered everywhere, there was no money for them. As soon as ever he got them on shipboard, he hastened to Proconnesus, and gave command to seize all the small vessels they met, and guard them safely in the interior of the fleet, that the enemy might have no notice of his coming; and a great storm of rain, accompanied with thunder and darkness, which happened at the same time, contributed much to the concealment of his enterprise. Indeed, it was not only undiscovered by the enemy, but the Athenians themselves were ignorant of it, for he commanded them suddenly on board, and set sail when they had abandoned all intention of it. As the darkness presently passed away, the Peloponnesian fleet was seen riding out at sea in front of the harbour of Cyzicus. Fearing, if they discovered the number of his ships, they might endeavour to save themselves by land, he commanded the rest of the captains to slacken, and follow him slowly, whilst he, advancing with forty ships, showed himself to the enemy, and provoked them to fight. The enemy, being deceived as to their numbers, despised them, and, supposing they were to contend with those only, made themselves ready and began the fight. But as soon as they were engaged, they perceived the other part of the fleet coming down upon them, at which they were so terrified that they fled immediately. Upon that, Alcibiades, breaking through the midst of them with twenty of his best ships, hastened to the shore, disembarked, and pursued those who abandoned their ships and fled to land, and made a great slaughter of them. Mindarus and Pharnabazus, coming to their succour, were utterly defeated. Mindarus was slain upon the place, fighting valiantly; Pharnabazus saved himself by flight. The Athenians slew great numbers of their enemies, won much spoil, and took all their ships. They also made themselves masters of Cyzicus, which was deserted by Pharnabazus, and destroyed its Peloponnesian garrison, and thereby not only secured to themselves the Hellespont, but by force drove the Lacedæmonians from out of the rest of the sea. They intercepted some letters written to the ephors, which gave an account of this fatal overthrow, after their short laconic manner. "Our hopes are at an end. Mindarus is slain. The men starve. We know not what to do."

The soldiers who followed Alcibiades in this last fight were so exalted with their success, and felt that degree of pride, that, looking on themselves as invincible, they disdained to mix with the other soldiers, who had been often overcome. For it happened not long before, Thrasyllus had received a defeat near Ephesus, and, upon that occasion, the Ephesians erected their brazen trophy to the disgrace of the Athenians. The soldiers of Alcibiades reproached those who were under the command of Thrasyllus with this misfortune, at the same time magnifying themselves and their own commander, and it went so far that they would not exercise with them, nor lodge in the same quarters. But soon after, Pharnabazus, with a great force of horse and foot, falling upon the soldiers of Thrasyllus, as they were laying waste the territory of Abydos, Alcibiades came to their aid, routed Pharnabazus, and together with Thrasyllus pursued him till it was night; and in this action the troops united, and returned together to the camp, rejoicing and congratulating one another. The next day he erected a trophy, and then proceeded to lay waste with fire and sword the whole province which was under Pharnabazus, where none ventured to resist; and he took divers priests and priestesses, but released them without ransom. He prepared next to attack the Chalcedonians, who had revolted from the Athenians, and had received a Lacedæmonian governor and garrison. But having intelligence that they had removed their corn and cattle out of the fields, and were conveying it all to the Bithynians, who were their friends, he drew down his army to the frontier of the Bithynians, and then sent a herald to charge them with this proceeding. The Bithynians, terrified at his approach, delivered up to him the booty, and entered into alliance with him.

Afterwards he proceeded to the siege of Chalcedon, and enclosed it with a wall from sea to sea. Pharnabazus advanced with his forces to raise the siege, and Hippocrates, the governor of the town, at the same time, gathering together all the strength he had, made a sally upon the Athenians. Alcibiades divided his army so as to engage both at once, and not only forced Pharnabazus to a dishonourable flight, but defeated Hippocrates, and killed him and a number of the soldiers with him. After this he sailed into the Hellespont, in order to raise supplies of money, and took the city of Selymbria, in which action, through his precipitation, he exposed himself to great danger. For some within the town had undertaken to betray it into his hands, and, by agreement, were to give him a signal by a lighted torch about midnight. But one of the conspirators beginning to repent himself of the design, the rest, for fear of being discovered, were driven to give the signal before the appointed hour. Alcibiades, as soon as he saw the torch lifted up in the air, though his army was not in readiness to march, ran instantly towards the walls, taking with him about thirty men only, and commanding the rest of the army to follow him with all possible speed. When he came hither, he found the gate opened for him and entered with his thirty men, and about twenty more light-armed men, who were come up to them. They were no sooner in the city, but he perceived the Selymbrians all armed, coming down upon him; so that there was no hope of escaping if he stayed to receive them; and, on the other hand, having been always successful till that day, wherever he commanded, he could not endure to be defeated and fly. So, requiring silence by sound of a trumpet, he commanded one of his men to make proclamation that the Selymbrians should not take arms against the Athenians. This cooled such of the inhabitants as were fiercest for the fight, for they supposed that all their enemies were within the walls, and it raised the hopes of others who were disposed to an accommodation. Whilst they were parleying, and propositions making on one side and the other, Alcibiades' whole army came up to the town. And now, conjecturing rightly that the Selymbrians were well inclined to peace, and fearing lest the city might be sacked by the Thracians, who came in great numbers to his army to serve as volunteers, out of kindness for him, he commanded them all to retreat without the walls. And upon the submission of the Selymbrians, he saved them from being pillaged, only taking of them a sum of money, and, after placing an Athenian garrison in the town, departed.

During this action, the Athenian captains who besieged Chalcedon concluded a treaty with Pharnabazus upon these articles: That he should give them a sum of money; that the Chalcedonians should return to the subjection of Athens, and that the Athenians should make no inroad into the province whereof Pharnabazus was governor; and Pharnabazus was also to provide safe conducts for the Athenian ambassadors to the King of Persia. Afterwards, when Alcibiades returned thither, Pharnabazus required that he also should be sworn to the treaty; but he refused it, unless Pharnabazus would swear at the same time. When the treaty was sworn to on both sides, Alcibiades went against the Byzantines, who had revolted from the Athenians, and drew a line of circumvallation about the city. But Anaxilaus and Lycurgus, together with some others, having undertaken to betray the city to him upon his engagement to preserve the lives and property of the inhabitants, he caused a report to be spread abroad, as if by reason of some unexpected movement in Ionia, he should be obliged to raise the siege. And, accordingly, that day he made a show to depart with his whole fleet; but returned the same night, and went ashore with all his men at arms, and, silently and undiscovered, marched up to the walls. At the same time, his ships rowed into the harbour with all possible violence, coming on with much fury, and with great shouts and outcries. The Byzantines, thus surprised and astonished, while they all hurried to the defence of their port and shipping, gave opportunity to those who favoured the Athenians securely to receive Alcibiades into the city. Yet the enterprise was not accomplished without fighting, for the Peloponnesians, Bœotians, and Megarians, not only repulsed those who came out of the ships, and forced them on board again, but, hearing that the Athenians were entered on the other side, drew up in order, and went to meet them. Alcibiades, however, gained the victory after some sharp fighting, in which he himself had the command of the right wing, and Theramenes of the left, and took about three hundred, who survived of the enemy, prisoners of war. After the battle, not one of the Byzantines was slain, or driven out of the city, according to the terms upon which the city was put into his hands, that they should receive no prejudice in life or property. And thus Anaxilaus, being afterwards accused at Lacedæmon for this treason, neither disowned nor professed to be ashamed of the action; for he urged that he was not a Lacedæmonian, but a Byzantine, and saw not Sparta, but Byzantium, in extreme danger; the city so blockaded that it was not possible to bring in any new provisions, and the Peloponnesians and Bœotians, who were in garrison, devouring the old stores, whilst the Byzantines, with their wives and children, were starving, that he had not, therefore, betrayed his country to enemies, but had delivered it from the calamities of war, and had but followed the example of the most worthy Lacedæmonians, who esteemed nothing to be honourable and just, but what was profitable for their country. The Lacedæmonians, upon hearing his defence, respected it, and discharged all that were accused.

And now Alcibiades began to desire to see his native country again, or rather to show his fellow-citizens a person who had gained so many victories for them. He set sail for Athens, the ships that accompanied him being adorned with great numbers of shields and other spoils, and towing after them many galleys taken from the enemy, and the ensigns and ornaments of many others which he had sunk and destroyed; all of them together amounting to two hundred. Little credit, perhaps, can be given to what Duris the Samian, who professed to be descended from Alcibiades, adds, that Chrysogonus, who had gained a victory at the Pythian games, played upon his flute for the galleys, whilst the oars kept time with the music; and that Callippides, the tragedian, attired in his buskins, his purple robes, and other ornaments used in the theatre, gave the word to the rowers, and that the admiral galley entered into the port with a purple sail. Neither Theopompus, nor Ephorus, nor Xenophon, mention them. Nor, indeed, is it credible, that one who returned from so long an exile, and such variety of misfortunes, should come home to his countrymen in the style of revellers breaking up from a drinking-party. On the contrary, he ventured the harbour full of fear, nor would he venture to go on shore, till, standing on the deck, he saw Euryptolemus, his cousin, and others of his friends and acquaintance, who were ready to receive him, and invited him to land. As soon as he was landed, the multitude who came out to meet him scarcely seemed so much as to see any of the other captains, but came in throngs about Alcibiades, and saluted him with loud acclamations, and still followed him; those who could press near him crowned him with garlands, and they who could not come up so close yet stayed to behold him afar off, and the old men pointed him out, and showed him to the young ones. Nevertheless, this public joy was mixed with some tears, and the present happiness was alloyed by the remembrance of the miseries they had endured. They made reflections, that they could not have so unfortunately miscarried in Sicily, or been defeated in any of their other expectations, if they had left the management of their affairs formerly, and the command of their forces, to Alcibiades, since, upon his undertaking the administration, when they were in a manner driven from the sea, and could scarce defend the suburbs of their city by land, and, at the same time, were miserably distracted with intestine factions, he had raised them up from this low and deplorable condition, and had not only restored them to their ancient dominion of the sea, but had also made them everywhere victorious over their enemies on land.

There had been a decree for recalling him from his banishment already passed by the people, at the instance of Critias, the son of Callæschrus, as appears by his elegies, in which he puts Alcibiades in mind of this service:

From my proposal did that edict come,
Which from your tedious exile brought you home.
The public vote at first was moved by me,
And my voice put the seal to the decree.

The people being summoned to an assembly, Alcibiades came in amongst them, and first bewailed and lamented his own sufferings, and, in gentle terms complaining of the usage he had received, imputed all to his hard fortune, and some ill-genius that attended him: then he spoke at large of their prospects, and exhorted them to courage and good hope. The people crowned him with crowns of gold, and created him general, both at land and sea, with absolute power. They also made a decree that his estate should be restored to him, and that the Eumolpidæ and the holy herald should absolve him from the curses which they had solemnly pronounced against him by sentence of the people. Which when all the rest obeyed, Theodoras, the high priest, excused himself, "For," said he, "if he is innocent, I never cursed him."

But notwithstanding the affairs of Alcibiades went so prosperously, and so much to his glory, yet many were still somewhat disturbed, and looked upon the time of his arrival to be ominous. For on the day that he came into the port, the feast of the goddess Minerva, which they call the Plynteria, was kept. It is the twenty-first day of Thargelion, when the Praxiergidæ solemnise their secret rites, taking all the ornaments from off her image, and keeping the part of the temple where it stands close covered. Hence the Athenians esteem this day most inauspicious, and never undertake anything of importance upon it; and, therefore, they imagined that the goddess did not receive Alcibiades graciously and propitiously, thus hiding her face and rejecting him. Yet, notwithstanding, everything succeeded according to his wish. When the one hundred galleys, that were to return with him, were fitted out and ready to sail, an honourable zeal detained him till the celebration of the mysteries was over. Forever since Decelea had been occupied, as the enemy commanded the roads leading from Athens to Eleusis, the procession, being conducted by sea, had not been performed with any proper solemnity; they were forced to omit the sacrifices and dances and other holy ceremonies, which had usually been performed in the way, when they led forth Iacchus. Alcibiades, therefore, judged it would be a glorious action, which would do honour to the gods and gain him esteem with men, if he restored the ancient splendour to these rites, escorting the procession again by land, and protecting it with his army in the face of the enemy. For either, if Agis stood still and did not oppose, it would very much diminish and obscure his reputation, or, in the other alternative, Alcibiades would engage in a holy war, in the cause of the gods, and in defence of the most sacred and solemn ceremonies; and this in the sight of his country, where he should have all his fellow-citizens witness of his valour. As soon as he had resolved upon this design, and had communicated it to the Eumolpidæ and heralds, he placed sentinels on the tops of the hills, and at the break of day sent forth his scouts. And then taking with him the priests and Initiates and the Initiators, and encompassing them with his soldiers, he conducted them with great order and profound silence; an august and venerable procession, wherein all who did not envy him said he performed at once the office of a high priest and of a general. The enemy did not dare to attempt anything against them, and thus he brought them back in safety to the city. Upon which, as he was exalted in his own thought, so the opinion which the people had of his conduct was raised that degree, that they looked upon their armies as irresistible and invincible while he commanded them; and he so won, indeed, upon the lower and meaner sort of people, that they passionately desired to have him "tyrant" over them, and some of them did not scruple to tell him so, and to advise him to put himself out of the reach of envy, by abolishing the laws and ordinances of the people, and suppressing the idle talkers that were ruining the state, that so he might act and take upon him the management of affairs, without standing in fear of being called to an account.

How far his own inclinations led him to usurp sovereign power is uncertain, but the most considerable persons in the city were so much afraid of it, that they hastened him on shipboard as speedily as they could, appointing the colleagues whom he chose, and allowing him all other things as he desired. Thereupon he set sail with a fleet of one hundred ships, and, arriving at Andros, he there fought with and defeated as well the inhabitants as the Lacedæmonians who assisted them. He did not, however, take the city; which gave the first occasion to his enemies for all their accusations against him. Certainly, if ever man was ruined by his own glory, it was Alcibiades. For his continual success had produced such an idea of his courage and conduct, that if he failed in anything he undertook, it was imputed to his neglect, and no one would believe it was through want of power. For they thought nothing was too hard for him, if he went about it in good earnest. They fancied, everyday, that they should hear news of the reduction of Chios, and of the rest of Ionia, and grew impatient that things were not effected as fast and as rapidly as they could wish for them. They never considered how extremely money was wanting, and that, having to carry on war with an enemy who had supplies of all things from a great king, he was often forced to quit his armament in order to procure money and provisions for the subsistence of his soldiers. This it was which gave occasion for the last accusation which was made against him. For Lysander, being sent from Lacedæmon with a commission to be admiral of their fleet, and being furnished by Cyrus with a great sum of money, gave every sailor four obols a day, whereas before they had but three. Alcibiades could hardly allow his men three obols, and therefore was constrained to go into Caria to furnish himself with money. He left the care of the fleet, in his absence, to Antiochus, an experienced seaman, but rash and inconsiderate, who had express orders from Alcibiades not to engage, though the enemy provoked him. But he slighted and disregarded these directions to that degree, that, having made ready his own galley and another, he stood for Ephesus, where the enemy lay, and, as he sailed before the heads of their galleys, used every provocation possible, both in words and deeds. Lysander at first manned out a few ships, and pursued him. But all the Athenian ships coming in to his assistance, Lysander, also, brought up his whole fleet, which gained an entire victory. He slew Antiochus himself, took many men and ships, and erected a trophy.

As soon as Alcibiades heard this news, he returned to Samos, and loosing from hence with his whole fleet, came and offered battle to Lysander. But Lysander, content with the victory he had gained, would not stir. Amongst others in the army who hated Alcibiades, Thrasybulus, the son of Thrason, was his particular enemy, and went purposely to Athens to accuse him, and to exasperate his enemies in the city against him. Addressing the people, he represented that Alcibiades had ruined their affairs and lost their ships by mere self-conceited neglect of his duties, committing the government of the army, in his absence, to men who gained his favour by drinking and scurrilous talking, whilst he wandered up and down at pleasure to raise money, giving himself up to every sort of luxury and excess amongst the courtesans of Abydos and Ionia at a time when the enemy's navy were on the watch close at hand. It was also objected to him, that he had fortified a castle near Bisanthe in Thrace, for a safe retreat for himself, as one that either could not, or would not, live in his own country. The Athenians gave credit to these informations, and showed the resentment and displeasure which they had conceived against him by choosing other generals.

As soon as Alcibiades heard of this, he immediately forsook the army, afraid of what might follow; and, collecting a body of mercenary soldiers, made war upon his own account against those Thracians who called themselves free, and acknowledged no king. By this means he amassed to himself a considerable treasure, and, at the same time, secured the bordering Greeks from the incursions of the barbarians.

Tydeus, Menander, and Adimantus, the new-made generals, were at that time posted at Ægospotami, with all the ships which the Athenians had left. From whence they were used to go out to sea every morning, and offer battle to Lysander, who lay near Lampsacus; and when they had done so, returning back again, lay, all the rest of the day, carelessly and without order, in contempt of the enemy. Alcibiades, who was not far off, did not think so slightly of their danger, nor neglect to let them know it, but, mounting his horse, came to the generals, and represented to them that they had chosen a very inconvenient station, where there was no safe harbour, and where they were distant from any town; so that they were constrained to send for their necessary provisions as far as Sestos. He also pointed out to them their carelessness in suffering the soldiers, when they went ashore, to disperse and wander up and down at their pleasure, while the enemy's fleet, under the command of one general, and strictly obedient to discipline, lay so very near them. He advised them to remove the fleet to Sestos. But the admirals not only disregarded what he said, but Tydeus, with insulting expressions, commanded him to be gone, saying, that now not he, but others, had the command of the forces. Alcibiades, suspecting something of treachery in them, departed, and told his friends, who accompanied him out of the camp, that if the generals had not used him with such insupportable contempt, he would within a few days have forced the Lacedæmonians, however unwilling, either to have fought the Athenians at sea or to have deserted their ships. Some looked upon this as a piece of ostentation only; others said, the thing was probable, for that he might have brought down by land great numbers of the Thracian cavalry and archers, to assault and disorder them in their camp. The event, however, soon made it evident how rightly he had judged of the errors which the Athenians committed. For Lysander fell upon them on a sudden, when they least suspected it, with such fury that Conon alone, with eight galleys, escaped him; all the rest, which were about two hundred, he took and carried away, together with three thousand prisoners, whom he put to death. And within a short time after, he took Athens itself, burnt all the ships which he found there, and demolished their long walls.

After this, Alcibiades, standing in dread of the Lacedæmonians, who were now masters both at sea and land, retired into Bithynia. He sent thither great treasure before him, took much with him, but left much more in the castle where he had before resided. But he lost a great part of his wealth in Bithynia, being robbed by some Thracians who lived in those parts, and thereupon determined to go to the court of Artaxerxes, not doubting but that the king, if he would make trial of his abilities, would find him not inferior to Themistocles, besides that he was recommended by a more honourable cause. For he went not, as Themistocles did, to offer his service against his fellow-citizens, but against their enemies, and to implore the king's aid for the defence of his country. He concluded that Pharnabazus would most readily procure him a safe conduct, and therefore went into Phrygia to him, and continued to dwell there sometime, paying him great respect, and being honourably treated by him. The Athenians, in the meantime, were miserably afflicted at their loss of empire; but when they were deprived of liberty also, and Lysander set up thirty despotic rulers in the city, in their ruin now they began to turn to those thoughts which, while safety was yet possible, they would not entertain; they acknowledged and bewailed their former errors and follies, and judged this second ill-usage of Alcibiades to be all the most inexcusable. For he was rejected without any fault committed by himself, and only because they were incensed against his subordinate for having shamefully lost a few ships, they much more shamefully deprived the commonwealth of its most valiant and accomplished general. Yet in this sad state of affairs they had still some faint hopes left them, nor would they utterly despair of the Athenian commonwealth while Alcibiades was safe. For they persuaded themselves that if before, when he was an exile, he could not content himself to live idly and at ease, much less now, if he could find any favourable opportunity, would he endure the insolence of the Lacedæmonians, and the outrages of the Thirty. Nor was it an absurd thing in the people to entertain such imaginations, when the Thirty themselves were so very solicitous to be informed and to get intelligence of all his actions and designs. In fine, Critias represented to Lysander that the Lacedæmonians could never securely enjoy the dominion of Greece till the Athenian democracy was absolutely destroyed; and, though now the people of Athens seemed quietly and patiently to submit to so small a number of governors, yet so long as Alcibiades lived, the knowledge of this fact would never suffer them to acquiesce in their present circumstances.

Yet Lysander would not be prevailed upon by these representations, till at last he received secret orders from the magistrates of Lacedæmon, expressly requiring him to get Alcibiades despatched: whether it was that they feared his energy and boldness in enterprising what was hazardous, or that it was done to gratify King Agis. Upon receipt of this order, Lysander sent away a messenger to Pharnabazus, desiring him to put it in execution. Pharnabazus committed the affair to Magæus, his brother, and to his uncle Susamithres. Alcibiades resided at that time in a small village in Phrygia, together with Timandra, a mistress of his. As he slept, he had this dream: he thought himself attired in his mistress' habit, and that she, holding him in her arms, dressed his head and painted his face as if he had been a woman; others say, he dreamed that he saw Magæus cut off his head and burn his body; at any rate, it was but a little while before his death that he had these visions. Those who were sent to assassinate him had not courage enough to enter the house, but surrounded it first, and set it on fire. Alcibiades, as soon as he perceived it, getting together great quantities of clothes and furniture, threw them upon the fire to choke it, and, having wrapped his cloak about his left arm, and holding his naked sword in his right, he cast himself into the middle of the fire, and escaped securely through it before his clothes were burnt. The barbarians, as soon as they saw him, retreated and none of them durst stay to wait for him, or to engage with him, but, standing at a distance, they slew him with their darts and arrows. When he was dead the barbarians departed, and Timandra took up his dead body, and, covering and wrapping it up in her own robes, she buried it as decently and as honourably as her circumstances would allow. It is said, that the famous Lais, who was called the Corinthian, though she was a native of Hyccara, a small town in Sicily, from whence she was brought a captive, was the daughter of this Timandra. There are some who agree with this account of Alcibiades' death in all points, except that they impute the cause of it neither to Pharnabazus, nor Lysander, nor the Lacedæmonians; but they say he was keeping with him a young lady of a noble house, whom he had debauched, and that her brothers, not being able to endure the indignity, set fire by night to the house where he was living, and, as he endeavoured to save himself from the flames, slew him with their darts, in the manner just related.

CORIOLANUS

The patrician house of the Marcii in Rome produced many men of distinction, and among the rest, Ancus Marcius, grandson to Numa by his daughter, and king after Tullus Hostilius; of the same family were also Publius and Quintus Marcius, which two conveyed into the city the best and most abundant supply of water they have at Rome. As likewise Censorinus, who, having been twice chosen censor by the people, afterwards himself induced them to make a law that nobody should bear that office twice. But Caius Marcius, of whom I now write, being left an orphan, and brought up under the widowhood of his mother, has shown us by experience, that, although the early loss of a father may be attended with other disadvantages, yet it can hinder none from being either virtuous or eminent in the world, and that it is no obstacle to true goodness and excellence; however bad men may be pleased to lay the blame of their corruptions upon that misfortune and the neglect of them in their minority. Nor is he less an evidence to the truth of their opinion who conceive that a generous and worthy nature without proper discipline, like a rich soil without culture, is apt with its better fruits to produce also much that is bad and faulty. While the force and vigour of his soul, and a persevering constancy in all he undertook, led him successfully into many noble achievements, yet, on the other side, also, by indulging the vehemence of his passion, and through an obstinate reluctance to yield or accommodate his humours and sentiments to those of a people about him, he rendered himself incapable of acting and associating with others. Those who saw with admiration how proof his nature was against all the softnesses of pleasure, the hardships of service, and the allurements of gain, while allowing to that universal firmness of his the respective names of temperance, fortitude, and justice, yet in the life of the citizen and the statesman, could not choose but be disgusted at the severity and rugged-ness of his deportment, and with his overbearing, haughty, and imperious temper. Education and study, and the favours of the muses, confer no greater benefit on those that seek them than these humanising and civilis-ing lessons, which teach our natural qualities to submit to the limitations prescribed by reason, and to avoid the wildness of extremes.

Those were times at Rome in which that kind of worth was most esteemed which displayed itself in military achievements; one evidence of which we find in the Latin word for virtue, which is properly equivalent to manly courage. As if valour and all virtue had been the same thing, they used as the common term the name of the particular excellence. But Marcius, having a more passionate inclination than any of that age for feats of war, began at once, from his very childhood, to handle arms; and feel-ing that adventitious implements and artificial arms would effect little, and be of small use to such as have not their native and natural weapons well fixed and prepared for service, he so exercised and inured his body to all sorts of activity and encounter, that besides the lightness of a racer, he had a weight in close seizures and wrestlings with an enemy, from which it was hard for any to disengage himself; so that his competitors at home in dis-plays of bravery, loth to own themselves inferior in that respect, were wont to ascribe their deficiencies to his strength of body, which they say no resist-ance and no fatigue could exhaust.

The first time he went out to the wars, being yet a stripling, was when Tarquinius Superbus, who had been King of Rome and was afterwards expelled, after many unsuccessful attempts, now entered upon his last effort, and proceeded to hazard all as it were upon a single throw. A great number of the Latins and other people of Italy joined their forces, and were marching with him toward the city, to procure his restoration; not, however, so much out of a desire to serve and oblige Tarquin, as to gratify their own fear and envy at the increase of the Roman greatness; which they were anxious to check and reduce. The armies met and engaged in a decisive battle, in the vicissitudes of which Marcius, while fighting bravely in the dictator's presence, saw a Roman soldier struck down at a little dis-tance, and immediately stepped in and stood before him, and slew his assailant. The general, after having gained the victory, crowned him for this act, one of the first, with a garland of oaken branches; it being the Roman custom thus to adorn those who had saved the life of a citizen; whether that the law intended some special honour to the oak, in mem-ory of the Arcadians, a people the oracle had made famous by the name of acorn-eaters; or whether the reason of it was because they might easily, and in all places where they fought, have plenty of oak for that purpose; or, finally, whether the oaken wreath, being sacred to Jupiter, the guardian of the city, might, therefore, be thought a proper ornament for one who preserved a citizen. And the oak, in truth, is the tree which bears the most and the prettiest fruit of any that grow wild, and is the strongest of all that are under cultivation; its acorns were the principal diet of the first mortals, and the honey found in it gave them drink. I may say, too, it furnished fowl and other creatures as dainties, in producing mistletoe for bird-lime to ensnare them. In this battle, meantime, it is stated that Castor and Pollux appeared, and immediately after the battle were seen at Rome just by the fountain where their temple now stands, with their horses foaming with sweat, and told the news of the victory to the people in the forum. The fifteenth of July, being the day of this conquest, became consequently a solemn holiday sacred to the Twin Brothers.

It may be observed, in general, that when young men arrive early at fame and repute, if they are of a nature but slightly touched with emulation, this early attainment is apt to extinguish their thirst and satiate their appetite; whereas the first distinctions of more solid and weighty characters do but stimulate and quicken them and take them away like a wind in the pursuit of honour; they look upon these marks and testimonies to their virtue not as a recompense received for what they have already done, but as a pledge given by themselves of what they will perform hereafter, ashamed now to forsake or underlive the credit they have won, or, rather, not to exceed and obscure all that is gone before by the lustre of their following actions. Marcius, having a spirit of this noble make, was ambitious always to surpass himself, and did nothing, how extraordinary soever, but he thought he was bound to outdo it at the next occasion; and ever desiring to give continual fresh instances of his prowess, he added one exploit to another, and heaped up trophies upon trophies, so as to make it matter of contest also among his commanders, the latter still vying with the earlier which should pay him the greatest honour and speak highest in his commendation. Of all the numerous wars and conflicts in those days there was not one from which he returned without laurels and rewards. And, whereas others made glory the end of their daring, the end of his glory was his mother's gladness; the delight she took to hear him praised and to see him crowned, and her weeping for joy in his embraces rendered him in his own thoughts the most honoured and most happy person in the world. Epaminondas is similarly said to have acknowledged his feeling, that it was the greatest felicity of his whole life that his father and mother survived to hear of his successful generalship and his victory of Leuctra. And he had the advantage, indeed, to have both his parents partake with him, and enjoy the pleasure of his good fortune. But Marcius, believing himself bound to pay his mother Volumnia all that gratitude and duty which would have belonged to his father, had he also been alive, could never satiate himself in his tenderness and respect to her. He took a wife, also, at her request and wish, and continued, even after he had children, to live still with his mother, without parting families.

The repute of his integrity and courage had, by this time, gained him a considerable influence and authority in Rome, when the senate, favouring the wealthier citizens, began to be at variance with the common people, who made sad complaints of the rigorous and inhuman usage they received from the money-lenders. For as many as were behind with them, and had any sort of property, they stripped of all they had, by the way of pledges and sales; and such as through former exactions were reduced already to extreme indigence, and had nothing more to be deprived of, these they led away in person and put their bodies under constraint, notwithstanding the scars and wounds that they could show in attestation of their public services in numerous campaigns; the last of which had been against the Sabines, which they undertook upon a promise made by their rich creditors that they would treat them with more gentleness for the future, Marcus Valerius, the consul, having, by order from the senate, engaged also for the performance of it. But when, after they had fought courageously and beaten the enemy, there was, nevertheless, no moderation or forbearance used, and the senate also professed to remember nothing of that agreement, and sat without testifying the least concern to see them dragged away like slaves and their goods seized upon as formerly, there began now to be open disorders and dangerous meetings in the city; and the enemy, also, aware of the popular confusion, invaded and laid waste the country. And when the consuls now gave notice, that all who were of an age to bear arms should make their personal appearance, but found no one regard the summons, the members of the government, then coming to consult what course should be taken, were themselves again divided in opinion; some thought it most advisable to comply a little in favour of the poor, by relaxing their overstrained rights, and mitigating the extreme rigour of the law, while others withstood this proposal; Marcius in particular, with more vehemence than the rest, alleging that the business of money on either side was not the main thing in question, urged that this disorderly proceeding was but the first insolent step towards open revolt against the laws, which it would become the wisdom of the government to check at the earliest moment.

There had been frequent assemblies of the whole senate, within a small compass of time, about this difficulty, but without any certain issue; the poor commonalty, therefore, perceiving there was likely to be no redress of their grievances, on a sudden collected in a body, and, encouraging each other in their resolution, forsook the city, with one accord, and seizing the hill which is now called the Holy Mount, sat down by the river Anio, without committing any sort of violence or seditious outrage, but merely exclaiming, as they went along, that they had this long time past been, in fact, expelled and excluded from the city by the cruelty of the rich; that Italy would everywhere afford them the benefit of air and water and a place of burial, which was all they could expect in the city, unless it were, perhaps, the privilege of being wounded and killed in time of war for the defence of their creditors. The senate, apprehending the consequences, sent the most moderate and popular men of their own order to treat with them.

Menenius Agrippa, their chief spokesman, after much entreaty to the people, and much plainspeaking on behalf of the senate, concluded, at length, with the celebrated fable. "It once happened," he said, "that all the other members of a man mutinied against the stomach, which they accused as the only idle, uncontributing part in the whole body, while the rest were put to hardships and the expense of much labour to supply and minister to its appetites. The stomach, however, merely ridiculed the silliness of the members, who appeared not to be aware that the stomach certainly does receive the general nourishment, but only to return it again, and redistribute it amongst the rest. Such is the case," he said, "ye citizens, between you and the senate. The counsels and plans that are there duly digested, convey and secure to all of you your proper benefit and support."

A reconciliation ensued, the senate acceding to the request of the people for the annual election of five protectors for those in need of succour, the same that are now called the tribunes of the people; and the first two they pitched upon were Junius Brutus and Sicinnius Vellutus, their leaders in the secession.

The city being thus united, the commons stood presently to their arms, and followed their commanders to the war with great alacrity. As for Marcius, though he was not a little vexed himself to see the populace prevail so far, and gain ground of the senators, and might observe many other patricians have the same dislike of the late concessions, he yet besought them not to yield at least to the common people in the zeal and forwardness they now showed for their country's service, but to prove that they were superior to them, not so much in power and riches, as in merit and worth.

The Romans were now at war with the Volscian nation, whose principal city was Corioli, when, therefore, Cominius the consul had invested this important place, the rest of the Volscians, fearing it would be taken, mustered up whatever force they could from all parts, to relieve it, designing to give the Romans battle before the city, and so attack them on both sides. Cominius, to avoid this inconvenience, divided his army, marching himself with one body to encounter the Volscians on their approach from without and leaving Titus Lartius, one of the bravest Romans of his time, to command the other and continue the siege. Those within Corioli, despising now the smallness of their number, made a sally upon them, and prevailed at first, and pursued the Romans into their trenches. Here it was that Marcius, flying out with a slender company, and cutting those in pieces that first engaged him, obliged the other assailants to slacken their speed; and then, with loud cries, called upon the Romans to renew the battle. For he had, what Cato thought a great point in a soldier, not only strength of hand and stroke, but also a voice and look that of themselves were a terror to an enemy. Divers of his own party now rallying and making up to him, the enemies soon retreated; but Marcius, not content to see them draw off and retire, pressed hard upon the rear, and drove them, as they fled away in haste, to the very gates of their city; where, perceiving the Romans to fall back from their pursuit, beaten off by the multitude of darts poured in upon them from the walls, and that none of his followers had the hardiness to think of falling in pell-mell among the fugitives and so entering a city full of enemies in arms, he, nevertheless, stood and urged them to the attempt, crying out, that fortune had now set open Corioli, not so much to shelter the vanquished, as to receive the conquerors. Seconded by a few that were willing to venture with him, he bore along through the crowd, made good his passage, and thrust himself into the gate through the midst of them, nobody at first daring to resist him. But when the citizens on looking about saw that a very small number had entered, they now took courage, and came up and attacked them. A combat ensued of the most extraordinary description, in which Marcius, by strength of hand, and swiftness of foot, and daring of soul, overpowering everyone that he assailed, succeeded in driving the enemy to seek refuge, for the most part, in the interior of the town, while those remaining submitted, and threw down their arms; thus affording Lartius abundant opportunity to bring in the rest of the Romans with ease and safety.

Corioli being thus surprised and taken, the greater part of the soldiers employed themselves in spoiling and pillaging it, while Marcius indignantly reproached them, and exclaimed that it was a dishonourable and unworthy thing, when the consul and their fellow-citizens had now perhaps encountered the other Volscians, and were hazarding their lives in battle, basely to misspend the time in running up and down for booty, and, under a pretence of enriching themselves, keep out of danger. Few paid him any attention, but, putting himself at the head of these, he took the road by which the consul's army had marched before him, encouraging his companions, and beseeching them, as they went along, not to give up, and praying often to the gods, too, that he might be so happy as to arrive before the fight was over, and come seasonably up to assist Cominius, and partake in the peril of the action.

It was customary with the Romans of that age, when they were moving into battle array, and were on the point of taking up their bucklers, and girding their coats about them, to make at the same time an unwritten will, or verbal testament, and to name who should be their heirs, in the hearing of three or four witnesses. In this precise posture Marcius found them at his arrival, the enemy being advanced within view.

They were not a little disturbed by his first appearance, seeing him covered with blood and sweat, and attended with a small train; but when he hastily made up to the consul with gladness in his looks, giving him his hand, and recounting to him how the city had been taken, and when they saw Cominius also embrace and salute him, everyone took fresh heart; those that were near enough hearing, and those that were at a distance guessing, what had happened; and all cried out to be led to battle. First, however, Marcius desired to know of him how the Volscians had arrayed their army and where they had placed their best men and on his answering that he took the troops of the Antiates in the centre to be their prime warriors that would yield to none in bravery, "Let me demand and obtain of you," said Marcius, "that we may be posted against them." The consul granted the request, with much admiration for his gallantry. And when the conflict began by the soldiers darting at each other, and Marcius sallied out before the rest, the Volscians opposed to him were not able to make head against him; wherever he fell in, he broke their ranks, and made a lane through them; but the parties turning again, and enclosing him on each side with their weapons, the consul, who observed the danger he was in, despatched some of the choicest men he had for his rescue. The conflict then growing warm and sharp about Marcius and many falling dead in a little space, the Romans bore so hard upon their enemies, and pressed them with such violence, that they forced them at length to abandon their ground, and to quit the field. And going now to prosecute the victory, they besought Marcius, tired out with his toils, and faint and heavy through the loss of blood, that he would retire to the camp. He replied, however, that weariness was not for conquerors, and joined with them in the pursuit. The rest of the Volscian army was in like manner defeated, great numbers killed, and no less taken captive.

The day after, when Marcius, with the rest of the army, presented themselves at the consul's tent, Cominius rose, and having rendered all due acknowledgment to the gods for the success of that enterprise, turned next to Marcius, and first of all delivered the strongest encomium upon his rare exploits, which he had partly been an eyewitness of himself, in the late battle, and had partly learned from the testimony of Lartius. And then he required him to choose a tenth part of all the treasure and horses and captives that had fallen into their hands, before any division should be made to others; besides which, he made him the special present of a horse with trappings and ornaments, in honour of his actions. The whole army applauded; Marcius, however, stepped forth, and declaring his thankful acceptance of the horse, and his gratification at the praises of his general, said, that all other things, which he could only regard rather as mercenary advantages than any significations of honour, he must waive, and should be content with the ordinary proportion of such rewards. "I have only," said he, "one special grace to beg, and this I hope you will not deny me. There was a certain hospitable friend of mine among the Volscians, a man of probity and virtue, who is become a prisoner, and from former wealth and freedom is now reduced to servitude. Among his many misfortunes let my intercession redeem him from the one of being sold as a common slave." Such a refusal and such a request on the part of Marcius were followed with yet louder acclamations; and he had many more admirers of this generous superiority to avarice, than of the bravery he had shown in battle. The very persons who conceived some envy and despite to see him so specially honoured, could not but acknowledge, that one who so nobly could refuse reward, was beyond others worthy to receive it; and were more charmed with that virtue which made him despise advantage, than with any of those former actions that have gained him his title to it. It is the higher accomplishment to use money well than to use arms; but not to need it is more noble than to use it.

When the noise of approbation and applause ceased, Cominius, resuming, said: "It is idle, fellow-soldiers, to force and obtrude those other gifts of ours on one who is unwilling to accept them; let us, therefore, give him one of such a kind that he cannot well reject it; let us pass a vote, I mean, that he shall hereafter be called Coriolanus, unless you think that his performance at Corioli has itself anticipated any such resolution." Hence, therefore, he had this third name of Coriolanus, making it all the plainer that Caius was a personal proper name, and the second, or surname, Marcius, one common to his house and family; the third being a subsequent addition which used to be imposed either from some particular act or fortune, bodily characteristic, or good quality of the bearer. Just as the Greeks, too, gave additional names in old time, in some cases from some achievement, Soter, for example, and Callinicus; or personal appearance, as Physcon and Grypus; good qualities, Euergetes and Philadelphus; good fortune, Eudæmon, the title of the second Battus. Several monarchs have also had names given them in mockery, as Antigonus was called Doson, and Ptolemy, Lathyrus. This sort of title was yet more common among the Romans. One of the Metelli was surnamed Diadematus, because he walked about for a long time with a bandage on his head to conceal a scar; and another, of the same family, got the name of Celer, from the rapidity he displayed in giving a funeral entertainment of gladiators within a few days after his father's death, his speed and energy in doing which was thought extraordinary. There are some, too, who even at this day take names from certain casual incidents at their nativity: a child that is born when his father is away from home is called Proculus; or Postumus, if after his decease; and when twins come into the world, and one dies at the birth, the survivor has the name of Vopiscus. From bodily peculiarities they derive not only their Syllas and Nigers, but their Cæci and Claudii; wisely endeavouring to accustom their people not to reckon either the loss of sight, or any other bodily misfortune, as a matter of disgrace to them, but to answer to such names without shame, as if they were really their own. But this discussion better befits another place.

The war against the Volscians was no sooner at an end, than the popular orators revived domestic troubles, and raised another sedition, without any new cause or complaint or just grievance to proceed upon, but merely turning the very mischiefs that unavoidably ensued from their former contests into a pretext against the patricians. The greatest part of their arable land had been left unsown and without tillage, and the time of war allowing them no means or leisure to import provision from other countries, there was an extreme scarcity. The movers of the people then observing that there was no corn to be bought, and that if there had been they had no money to buy it, began to calumniate the wealthy with false stories and whisper it about, as if they, out of their malice, had purposely contrived the famine. Meanwhile, there came an embassy from the Velitrani, proposing to deliver up their city to the Romans, and desiring they would send some new inhabitants to people it, as a late pestilential disease had swept away so many of the natives, that there was hardly a tenth part remaining of their whole community. This necessity of the Velitrani was considered by all more prudent people as most opportune in the present state of affairs; since the dearth made it needful to ease the city of its superfluous members, and they were in hope also, at the same time, to dissipate the gathering sedition by ridding themselves of the more violent and heated partisans, and discharging, so to say, the elements of disease and disorder in the state. The consuls, therefore, singled out such citizens to supply the desolation at Velitræ, and gave notice to others, that they should be ready to march against the Volscians, with the politic design of preventing intestine broils by employment abroad, and in the hope that when rich as well as poor, plebeians and patricians, should be mingled again in the same army and the same camp, and engage in one common service for the public, it would mutually dispose them to reconciliation and friendship.

But Sicinnius and Brutus, the popular orators, interposed, crying out that the consuls disguised the most cruel and barbarous action in the world under that mild and plausible name of a colony, and were simply precipitating so many poor citizens into a mere pit of destruction, bidding them settle down in a country where the air was charged with disease, and the ground covered with dead bodies, and expose themselves to the evil influence of a strange and angered deity. And then, as if it would not satisfy their hatred to destroy some by hunger, and offer others to the mercy of a plague, they must proceed to involve them also in a needless war of their own making, that no calamity might be wanting to complete the punishment of the citizens for refusing to submit to that of slavery to the rich.

By such addresses, the people were so possessed, that none of them would appear upon the consular summons to be enlisted for the war; and they showed entire aversion to the proposal for a new plantation; so that the senate was at a loss what to say or do. But Marcius, who began now to bear himself higher and to feel confidence in his past actions, conscious, too, of the admiration of the best and greatest men of Rome, openly took the lead in opposing the favourers of the people. The colony was despatched to Velitræ, those that were chosen by lot being compelled to depart upon high penalties; and when they obstinately persisted in refusing to enrol themselves for the Volscian service, he mustered up his own clients, and as many others as could be wrought upon by persuasion, and with these made inroad into the territories of the Antiates, where, finding a considerable quantity of corn, and collecting much booty, both of cattle and prisoners, he reserved nothing for himself in private, but returned safe to Rome, while those that ventured out with him were seen laden with pillage, and driving their prey before them. This sight filled those that had stayed at home with regret for their perverseness, with envy at their fortunate fellow-citizens, and with feelings of dislike to Marcius, and hostility to his growing reputation and power, which might probably be used against the popular interest.

Not long after he stood for the consulship: when, however, the people began to relent and incline to favour him, being sensible what a shame it would be to repulse and affront a man of his birth and merit, after he had done them so many signal services. It was usual for those who stood for offices among them to solicit and address themselves personally to the citizens, presenting themselves in the forum with the toga on alone, and no tunic under it; either to promote their supplications by the humility of their dress, or that such as had received wounds might more readily display those marks of their fortitude. Certainly, it was not out of suspicion of bribery and corruption that they required all such petitioners for their favour to appear ungirt and open, without any close garment; as it was much later, and many ages after this, that buying and selling crept in at their elections, and money became an ingredient in the public suffrages; proceeding thence to attempt their tribunals, and even attack their camps, till, by hiring the valiant, and enslaving iron to silver, it grew master of the state, and turned their commonwealth into a monarchy. For it was well and truly said that the first destroyer of the liberties of a people is he who first gave them bounties and largesses. At Rome the mischief seems to have stolen secretly in, and by little and little, not being at once discerned and taken notice of. It is not certainly known who the man was that did there first either bribe the citizens, or corrupt the courts; whereas, in Athens, Anytus, the son of Anthemion, is said to have been the first that gave money to the judges, when on his trial, toward the latter end of the Peloponnesian war, for letting the fort of Pylos fall into the hands of the enemy; in a period while the pure and golden race of men were still in possession of the Roman forum.

Marcius, therefore, as the fashion of candidates was, showing the scars and gashes that were still visible on his body, from the many conflicts in which he had signalised himself during a service of seventeen years together, they were, so to say, put out of countenance at this display of merit, and told one another that they ought in common modesty to create him consul. But when the day of election was now come, and Marcius appeared in the forum, with a pompous train of senators attending him, and the patricians all manifested greater concern, and seemed to be exerting greater efforts, than they had ever done before on the like occasion, the commons then fell off again from the kindness they had conceived for him, and in the place of their late benevolence, began to feel something of indignation and envy; passions assisted by the fear they entertained, that if a man of such aristocratic temper and so influential among the patricians should be invested with the power which that office would give him, he might employ it to deprive the people of all that liberty which was yet left them. In conclusion, they rejected Marcius. Two other names were announced, to the great mortification of the senators, who felt as if the indignity reflected rather upon themselves than on Marcius. He, for his part, could not bear the affront with any patience. He had always indulged his temper, and had regarded the proud and contentious element of human nature as a sort of nobleness and magnanimity; reason and discipline had not imbued him with that solidity and equanimity which enters so largely into the virtues of the statesman. He had never learned how essential it is for anyone who undertakes public business, and desires to deal with mankind, to avoid above all things that self-will, which, as Plato says, belongs to the family of solitude; and to pursue, above all things, that capacity so generally ridiculed, of submission to ill-treatment. Marcius, straightforward and direct, and possessed with the idea that to vanquish and overbear all opposition is the true part of bravery, and never imagining that it was the weakness and womanishness of his nature that broke out, so to say, in these ulcerations of anger, retired, full of fury and bitterness against the people. The young patricians, too, all that were proudest and most conscious of their noble birth, had always been devoted to his interest, and, adhering to him now, with a fidelity that did him no good, aggravated his resentment with the expression of their indignation and condolence. He had been their captain, and their willing instructor in the arts of war, when out upon expeditions, and their model in that true emulation and love of excellence which makes men extol, without envy or jealousy, each other's brave achievements.

In the midst of these distempers, a large quantity of corn reached Rome, a great part bought up in Italy, but an equal amount sent as a present from Syracuse, from Gelo, then reigning there. Many began now to hope well of their affairs, supposing the city, by this means, would be delivered at once, both of its want and discord. A council, therefore, being presently held, the people came flocking about the senate-house, eagerly awaiting the issue of that deliberation, expecting that the market prices would now be less cruel, and that what had come as gift would be distributed as such. There were some within who so advised the senate; but Marcius, standing up, sharply inveighed against those who spoke in favour of the multitude, calling them flatterers of the rabble, traitors to the nobility, and alleging, that, by such gratifications, they did but cherish those ill seeds of boldness and petulance that had been sown among the people, to their own prejudice, which they should have done well to observe and stifle at their first appearance, and not have suffered the plebeians to grow so strong, by granting them magistrates of such authority as the tribunes. They were, indeed, even now formidable to the state since everything they desired was granted them; no constraint was put on their will; they refused obedience to the consuls and, overthrowing all law and magistracy, gave the title of magistrate to their private factious leaders. "When things are come to such a pass for us to sit here and decree largesses and bounties for them, like those Greeks where the populace is supreme and absolute, what would it be else," said he, "but to take their disobedience into pay and maintain it for the common ruin of us all? They certainly cannot look upon these liberalities as a reward of public service, which they know they have so often deserted; nor yet of those secessions, by which they openly renounce their country; much less of the calumnies and slanders they have been always so ready to entertain against the senate; but will rather conclude that a bounty, which seems to have no other visible cause or reason, must needs be the effect of our fear and flattery; and will, therefore, set no limit to their disobedience, nor ever cease from disturbances and sedition. Concession is mere madness; if we have any wisdom and resolution at all, we shall, on the contrary, never rest till we have recovered from them that tribunician power they have extorted from us; as being a plain subversion of the consulship, and a perpetual ground of separation in our city that is no longer one, as heretofore, but has in this received such a wound and rupture as is never likely to close and unite again, or suffer us to be of one mind, and to give over inflaming our distempers, and being a torment to each other."

Marcius, with much more to this purpose, succeeded, to an extraordinary degree, in inspiring the younger men with the same furious sentiments, and had almost all the wealthy on his side, who cried him up as the only person their city had, superior alike to force and flattery; some of the older men, however, opposed him, suspecting the consequences. As, indeed, there came no good of it; for the tribunes, who were present, perceiving how the proposal of Marcius took, ran out into the crowd with exclamations, calling on the plebeians to stand together, and come in to their assistance. The assembly met, and soon became tumultuous. The sum of what Marcius had spoken, having been reported to the people, excited them to such fury, that they were ready to break in upon the senate. The tribunes prevented this, by laying all the blame on Coriolanus, whom, therefore, they cited by their messengers to come before them and defend himself. And when he contemptuously repulsed the officers who brought him the summons, they came themselves, with the Ædiles, or overseers of the market, proposing to carry him away by force, and, accordingly, began to lay hold on his person. The patricians, however, coming to his rescue, not only thrust off the tribunes, but also beat the Ædiles, that were their seconds in the quarrel; night approaching, put an end to the contest. But, as soon as it was day, the consuls, observing the people to be highly exasperated, and that they ran from all quarters and gathered in the forum, were afraid for the whole city, so that, convening the senate afresh, they desired them to advise how they might best compose and pacify the incensed multitude by equitable language and indulgent decrees; since, if they wisely considered the state of things, they would find that it was no time to stand upon terms of honour and a mere point of glory; such a critical conjuncture called for gentle methods, and for temperate and humane counsels. The majority, therefore, of the senators giving way, the consuls proceeded to pacify the people in the best manner they were able, answering gently to such imputations and charges as had been cast upon the senate, and using much tenderness and moderation in the admonitions and reproofs they gave them. On the point of the price of provisions, they said there should be no difference at all between them. When a great part of the commonalty was grown cool, and it appeared from their orderly and peaceful behaviour that they had been very much appeased by what they had heard, the tribunes, standing up, declared, in the name of the people, that since the senate was pleased to act soberly and do them reason, they, likewise, should be ready to yield in all that was fair and equitable on their side; they must insist, however, that Marcius should give in his answer to the several charges as follows: first, could he deny that he instigated the senate to overthrow the government and annul the privileges of the people? And, in the next place, when called to account for it, did he not disobey the summons? And, lastly, by the blows and other public affronts to the Ædiles, had he not done all he could to commence a civil war?

These articles were brought in against him, with a design either to humble Marcius, and show his submission, if, contrary to his nature, he should now court and sue the people; or, if he should follow his natural disposition, which they rather expected from their judgment of his character, then that he might thus make the breach final between himself and the people.

He came, therefore, as it were, to make his apology, and clear himself; in which belief the people kept silence, and gave him a quiet hearing. But when, instead of the submissive and deprecatory language expected from him, he began to use not only an offensive kind of freedom, seeming rather to accuse than apologise, but, as well by the tone of his voice as the air of his countenance, displayed a security that was not far from disdain and contempt of them, the whole multitude then became angry, and gave evident signs of impatience and disgust; and Sicinnius, the most violent of the tribunes, after a little private conference with his colleagues, proceeded solemnly to pronounce before them all, that Marcius was condemned to die by the tribunes of the people, and bid the Ædiles take him to the Tarpeian rock, and without delay throw him headlong from the precipice. When they, however, in compliance with the order, came to seize upon his body, many, even of the plebeian party, felt it to be a horrible and extravagant act; the patricians, meantime, wholly beside themselves with distress and horror, hurried up with cries to the rescue; and while some made actual use of their hands to hinder the arrest, and surrounding Marcius, got him in among them, others, as in so great a tumult no good could be done by words, stretched out theirs, beseeching the multitude that they would not proceed to such furious extremities; and at length, the friends and acquaintance of the tribunes, wisely perceiving how impossible it would be to carry off Marcius to punishment without much bloodshed and slaughter of the nobility, persuaded them to forbear everything unusual and odious; not to despatch him by any sudden violence, or without regular process, but refer the cause to the general suffrage of the people. Sicinnius then, after a little pause, turning to the patricians, demanded what their meaning was, thus forcibly to rescue Marcius out of the people's hands, as they were going to punish him; when it was replied by them, on the other side, and the question put, "Rather, how came it into your minds, and what is it you design, thus to drag one of the worthiest men of Rome, without trial, to a barbarous and illegal execution?" "Very well," said Sicinnius, "you shall have no ground in this respect for quarrel or complaint against the people. The people grant your request, and your partisan shall be tried. We appoint you, Marcius," directing his speech to him, "the third market-day ensuing, to appear and defend yourself, and to try if you can satisfy the Roman citizens of your innocence, who will then judge your case by vote." The patricians were content with such a truce and respite for that time, and gladly returned home, having for the present brought off Marcius in safety.

During the interval before the appointed time (for the Romans hold their sessions every ninth day, which from that cause are called *mundinæ* in Latin), a war fell out with the Antiates, likely to be of some continuance, which gave them hope they might one way or other elude the judgment. The people, they presumed, would become tractable, and their indignation lessen and languish by degrees in so long a space, if occupation and war did not wholly put it out of their mind. But when, contrary to expectation, they made a speedy agreement with the people of Antium, and the army came back to Rome, the patricians were again in great perplexity, and had frequent meetings to consider how things might be arranged, without either abandoning Marcius, or yet giving occasion to the popular orators to create new disorders. Appius Claudius, whom they counted among the senators most averse to the popular interest, made a solemn declaration, and told them beforehand, that the senate would utterly destroy itself and betray the government, if they should once suffer the people to assume the authority of pronouncing sentence upon any of the patricians; but the oldest senators and most favourable to the people maintained, on the other side, that the people would not be so harsh and severe upon them, as some were pleased to imagine, but rather become more gentle and humane upon the concession of that power, since it was not contempt of the senate, but the impression of being contemned by it, which made them pretend to such a prerogative. Let that be once allowed them as a mark of respect and kind feeling, and the mere possession of this power of voting would at once dispossess them of their animosity.

When, therefore, Marcius saw that the senate was in pain and suspense upon his account, divided, as it were, betwixt their kindness for him and their apprehensions from the people, he desired to know of the tribunes what the crimes were they intended to charge him with, and what the heads of the indictment they would oblige him to plead to before the people; and being told by them that he was to be impeached for attempting usurpation, and that they would prove him guilty of designing to establish arbitrary government, stepping forth upon this, "Let me go then," he said, "to clear myself from that imputation before an assembly of them; I freely offer myself to any sort of trial, nor do I refuse any kind of punishment whatsoever; only," he continued, "let what you now mention be really made my accusation, and do not you play false with the senate." On their consenting to these terms, he came to his trial. But when the people met together, the tribunes, contrary to all former practice, extorted first, that votes should be taken, not by centuries, but tribes; a change, by which the indigent and factious rabble, that had no respect for honesty and justice, would be sure to carry it against those who were rich and well known, and accustomed to serve the state in war. In the next place, whereas they had engaged to prosecute Marcius upon no other head but that of tyranny, which could never be made out against him, they relinquished this plea, and urged instead, his language in the senate against an abasement of the price of corn, and for the overthrow of the tribunician power; adding further, as a new impeachment, the distribution that was made by him of the spoil and booty he had taken from the Antiates, when he overran their country, which he had divided among those that had followed him, whereas it ought rather to have been brought into the public treasury; which last accusation did, they say, more discompose Marcius than all the rest, as he had not anticipated he should ever be questioned on that subject, and, therefore, was less provided with any satisfactory answer to it on the sudden. And when, by way of excuse, he began to magnify the merits of those who had been partakers with him in the action, those that had stayed at home, being more numerous than the other, interrupted him with outcries. In conclusion, when they came to vote, a majority of three tribes condemned him; the penalty being perpetual banishment. The sentence of his condemnation being pronounced, the people went away with greater triumph and exultation than they had ever shown for any victory over enemies; while the senate was in grief and deep dejection, repenting now and vexed to the soul that they had not done and suffered all things rather than give way to the insolence of the people, and permit them to assume and abuse so great an authority. There was no need then to look at men's dresses, or other marks of distinction, to know one from another: anyone who was glad was, beyond all doubt, a plebeian, anyone who looked sorrowful, a patrician.

Marcius alone, himself, was neither stunned nor humiliated. In mien, carriage, and countenance he bore the appearance of entire composure, and, while all his friends were full of distress, seemed the only man that was not touched with his misfortune. Not that either reflection taught him, or gentleness of temper made it natural for him, to submit: he was wholly possessed, on the contrary, with a profound and deep-seated fury, which passes with many for no pain at all. And pain, it is true, transmuted, so to say, by its own fiery heat into anger, loses every appearance of depression and feebleness; the angry man makes a show of energy, as the man in a high fever does of natural heat, while, in fact, all this action of the soul is but mere diseased palpitation, distension, and inflammation. That such was his distempered state appeared presently plainly enough in his actions. On his return home, after saluting his mother and his wife, who were all in tears and full of loud lamentations, and exhorting them to moderate the sense they had of his calamity, he proceeded at once to the city gates, whither all the nobility came to attend him; and so not so much as taking anything with him, or making any request to the company, he departed from them, having only three or four clients with him. He continued solitary for a few days in a place in the country, distracted with a variety of counsels, such as rage and indignation suggested to him; and proposing to himself no honourable or useful end, but only how he might best satisfy his revenge on the Romans, he resolved at length to raise up a heavy war against them from their nearest neighbours. He determined, first to make trial of the Volscians, whom he knew to be still vigorous and flourishing, both in men and treasure, and he imagined their force and power was not so much abated as their spite and anger increased by the late overthrows they had received from the Romans.

There was a man of Antium, called Tullus Aufidius, who, for his wealth and bravery and the splendour of his family, had the respect and privilege of a king among the Volscians, but whom Marcius knew to have a particular hostility to himself, above all other Romans. Frequent menaces and challenges had passed in battle between them, and those exchanges of defiance to which their hot and eager emulation is apt to prompt young soldiers had added private animosity to their national feelings of opposition. Yet for all this, considering Tullus to have a certain generosity of temper, and knowing that no Volscian, so much as he, desired an occasion to requite upon the Romans the evils they had done, he did what much confirms the saying, that—

> Hard and unequal is with wrath the strife,
> Which makes us buy its pleasure with our life.

Putting on such a dress as would make him appear to any whom he might meet most unlike what he really was, like Ulysses—

> The town he entered of his mortal foes.

His arrival at Antium was about evening, and, though several met him in the streets, yet he passed along without being known to any and went directly to the house of Tullus, and, entering undiscovered, went up to the fire-hearth, and seated himself there without speaking a word, covering up his head. Those of the family could not but wonder, and yet they were afraid either to raise or question him, for there was a certain air of majesty both in his posture and silence, but they recounted to Tullus, being then at supper, the strangeness of this accident. He immediately rose from table and came in, and asked who he was and for what business he came thither; and then Marcius, unmuffling himself, and pausing awhile, "If," said he, "you cannot call me to mind, Tullus, or do not believe your eyes concerning me, I must of necessity be my own accuser. I am Caius Marcius, the author of so much mischief to the Volscians; of which, were I seeking to deny it, the surname of Coriolanus I now bear would be a sufficient evidence against me. The one recompense I have received for all the hardships and perils I have gone through was the title that proclaims my enmity to your nation, and this is the only thing which is still left me. Of all other advantages, I have been stripped and deprived by the envy and outrage of the Roman people, and the cowardice and treachery of the magistrates and those of my own order. I am driven out as an exile, and become an humble suppliant at your hearth, not so much for safety and protection (should I have come hither, had I been afraid to die?) as to seek vengeance against those that expelled me; which, methinks, I have already obtained, by putting myself into your hands. If, therefore, you have really a mind to attack your enemies, come then, make use of that affliction you see me in to assist the enterprise, and convert my personal infelicity into a common blessing to the Volscians; as, indeed, I am likely to be more serviceable in fighting for than against you, with the advantage which I now possess, of knowing all the secrets of the enemy that I am attacking. But if you decline to make any further attempts I am neither desirous to live myself, nor will it be well in you to preserve a person who has been your rival and adversary of old, and now, when he offers you his service, appears unprofitable and useless to you."

Tullus, on hearing this, was extremely rejoiced, and giving him his right hand, exclaimed, "Rise, Marcius, and be of good courage; it is a great happiness you bring to Antium, in the present use you make of yourself; expect everything that is good from the Volscians." He then proceeded to feast and entertain him with every display of kindness, and for several days after they were in close deliberation together on the prospects of a war.

While this design was forming, there were great troubles and commotions at Rome, from the animosity of the senators against the people, heightened just now by the late condemnation of Marcius. Besides that their soothsayers and priests, and even private persons, reported signs and prodigies not to be neglected; one of which is stated to have occurred as follows: Titus Latinus, a man of ordinary condition, but of a quiet and virtuous character, free from all superstitious fancies, and yet more from vanity and exaggeration, had an apparition in his sleep, as if Jupiter came and bade him tell the senate, that it was with a bad and unacceptable dancer that they had headed his procession. Having beheld the vision, he said, he did not much attend to it at the first appearance; but after he had seen and slighted it a second and third time, he had lost a hopeful son, and was himself struck with a palsy. He was brought into the senate on a litter to tell this, and the story goes that he had no sooner delivered his message there, but he at once felt his strength return and got up on his legs, and went home alone without need of any support. The senators, in wonder and surprise, made a diligent search into the matter. That which his dream alluded to was this: some citizen had, for some heinous offence, given up a servant of his to the rest of his fellows with charge to whip him first through the market, and then to kill him; and while they were executing this command, and scourging the wretch, who screwed and turned himself into all manner of shapes and unseemly motions, through the pain he was in, the solemn procession in honour of Jupiter chanced to follow at their heels. Several of the attendants on which were, indeed, scandalised at the sight, yet no one of them interfered, or acted further in the matter than merely to utter some common reproaches and execrations on a master who inflicted so cruel a punishment. For the Romans treated their slaves with great humanity in these times, when, working and labouring themselves, and living together among them, they naturally were more gentle and familiar with them. It was one of the severest punishments for a slave who had committed a fault to have to take the piece of wood which supports the pole of a wagon, and carry it about through the neighbourhood; a slave who had once undergone the shame of this, and been thus seen by the household and the neighbours, had no longer any trust or credit among them, and had the name of *furcifer; furca* being the Latin word for a prop, or support.

When, therefore, Latinus had related his dream, and the senators were considering who this disagreeable and ungainly dancer could be, some of the company, having been struck with the strangeness of the punishment, called to mind and mentioned the miserable slave who was lashed through the streets and afterwards put to death. The priests, when consulted, confirmed the conjecture; the master was punished; and orders given for a new celebration of the procession and the spectacles in honour of the god. Numa, in other respects also a wise arranger of religious offices, would seem to have been especially judicious in his direction, with a view to the attentiveness of the people, that, when the magistrates or priests performed any divine worship, a herald should go before, and proclaim with a loud voice, *Hoc age*, Do this you are about, and so warn them to mind whatever sacred action they were engaged in, and not suffer any business or worldly avocation to disturb and interrupt it; most of the things which men do of this kind being in manner forced from them, and effected by constraint. It is usual with the Romans to recommence their sacrifices and processions and spectacles, not only upon such a cause as this, but for any slighter reason. If but one of the horses which drew the chariot, called Tensæ, upon which the images of their gods were placed, happened to fail and falter, or if the driver took hold of the reins with his left hand, they would decree that the whole operation should commence anew; and, in latter ages, one and the same sacrifice was performed thirty times over, because of the occurrence of some defect or mistake or accident in the service. Such was the Roman reverence and caution in religious matters.

Marcius and Tullus were now secretly discoursing of their project with the chief men of Antium, advising them to invade the Romans while they were at variance among themselves. And when shame appeared to hinder them from embracing the motion, as they had sworn to a truce and cessation of arms for the space of two years, the Romans themselves soon furnished them with a pretence, by making proclamation, out of some jealousy or slanderous report, in the midst of the spectacles, that all the Volscians who had come to see them should depart the city before sunset. Some affirm that this was a contrivance of Marcius, who sent a man privately to the consuls, falsely to accuse the Volscians of intending to fall upon the Romans during the games, and to set the city on fire. This public affront roused and inflamed their hostility to the Romans; and Tullus, perceiving it, made his advantage of it, aggravating the fact, and working on their indignation, till he persuaded them, at last, to despatch ambassadors to Rome, requiring the Romans to restore that part of their country and those towns which they had taken from the Volscians in the late war. When the Romans heard the message, they indignantly replied that the Volscians were the first that took up arms, but the Romans would be the last to lay them down. This answer being brought back, Tullus called a general assembly of the Volscians; and the vote passing for a war, he then proposed that they should call in Marcius, laying aside the remembrance of former grudges, and assuring themselves that the services they should now receive from him as a friend and associate would abundantly outweigh any harm or damage he had done them when he was their enemy. Marcius was accordingly summoned, and having made his entrance, and spoken to the people, won their good opinion of his capacity, his skill, counsel, and boldness, not less by his present words than by his past actions. They joined him in commission with Tullus, to have full power as the general of their forces in all that related to the war. And he, fearing lest the time that would be requisite to bring all the Volscians together in full preparation might be so long as to lose him the opportunity of action, left order with the chief persons and magistrates of the city to provide other things, while he himself, prevailing upon the most forward to assemble and march out with him as volunteers without staying to be enrolled, made a sudden inroad into the Roman confines, when nobody expected him, and possessed himself of so much booty, that the Volscians found they had more than they could either carry away or use in the camp. The abundance of provision which he gained, and the waste and havoc of the country which he made, were, however, of themselves and in his account, the smallest results of that invasion; the great mischief he intended, and his special object in all, was to increase at Rome the suspicions entertained of the patricians, and to make them upon worse terms with the people. With this view, while spoiling all the fields and destroying the property of other men, he took special care to preserve their farms and lands untouched, and would not allow his soldiers to ravage there, or seize upon anything which belonged to them. From hence their invectives and quarrels against one another broke out afresh, and rose to a greater height than ever; the senators reproaching those of the commonalty with their late injustice to Marcius; while the plebeians, on their side, did not hesitate to accuse

them of having, out of spite and revenge, solicited him to this enterprise, and thus, when others were involved in the miseries of a war by
their means, they sat like unconcerned spectators, as being furnished
with a guardian and protector abroad of their wealth and fortunes, in
the very person of the public enemy. After this incursion and exploit,
which was of great advantage to the Volscians, as they learned by it to
grow more hardy and to contemn their enemy, Marcius drew them off,
and returned in safety.

But when the whole strength of the Volscians was brought together in
the field, with great expedition and alacrity, it appeared so considerable a
body, that they agreed to leave part in garrison, for the security of their
towns, and with the other part to march against the Romans. Marcius now
desired Tullus to choose which of the two charges would be most agreeable to him. Tullus answered that since he knew Marcius to be equally
valiant with himself, and far more fortunate, he would have him take the
command of those that were going out to the war, while he made it his
care to defend their cities at home, and provide all conveniences for the
army abroad. Marcius, thus reinforced, and much stronger than before,
moved first towards the city called Circæum, a Roman colony. He received
its surrender and did the inhabitants no injury; passing thence, he
entered and laid waste the country of the Latins, where he expected the
Romans would meet him, as the Latins were their confederates and allies,
and had often sent to demand succours from them. The people, however,
on their part, showing little inclination for the service, and the consuls
themselves being unwilling to run the hazard of a battle, when the time of
their office was almost ready to expire, they dismissed the Latin ambassadors without any effect; so that Marcius, finding no army to oppose him,
marched up to their cities, and having taken by force Toleria, Lavici, Peda,
and Bola, all of which offered resistance, not only plundered their houses,
but made a prey likewise of their persons. Meantime he showed particular
regard for all such as came over to his party, and, for fear they might sustain any damage against his will, encamped at the greatest distance he
could, and wholly abstained from the lands of their property.

After, however, that he had made himself master of Bola, a town not
above ten miles from Rome, where he found great treasure, and put
almost all the adults to the sword; and when on this, the other Volscians
that were ordered to stay behind and protect their cities, hearing of his
achievements and success, had not patience to remain any longer at
home, but came hastening in their arms to Marcius, saying that he alone

was their general and the sole commander they would own; with all this, his name and renown spread throughout all Italy, and universal wonder prevailed at the sudden and mighty revolution in the fortunes of two nations which the loss and the accession of a single man had effected.

All at Rome was in great disorder; they were utterly averse from fighting, and spent their whole time in cabals and disputes and reproaches against each other; until news was brought that the enemy had laid close siege to Lavinium, where were the images and sacred things of their tutelar gods, and from whence they derived the origin of their nation, that being the first city which Æneas built in Italy. These tidings produced a change as universal as it was extraordinary in the thoughts and inclinations of the people, but occasioned a yet stranger revulsion of feelings among the patricians. The people now were for repealing the sentence against Marcius, and calling him back into the city; whereas the senate, being assembled to preconsider the decree, opposed and finally rejected the proposal, either out of the mere humour of contradicting and withstanding the people in whatever they should desire, or because they were unwilling, perhaps, that he should owe his restoration to their kindness; or having now conceived a displeasure against Marcius himself, who was bringing distress upon all alike, though he had not been ill-treated by all, and was become a declared enemy to his whole country, though he knew well enough that the principal and all the better men condoled with him and suffered in his injuries.

This resolution of theirs being made public, the people could proceed no further, having no authority to pass anything by suffrage, and enact it for a law, without a previous decree from the senate. When Marcius heard of this, he was more exasperated than ever, and, quitting the siege of Lavinium, marched furiously towards Rome, and encamped at a place called the Cluilian ditches, about five miles from the city. The nearness of his approach did, indeed, create much terror and disturbance, yet it also ended their dissensions for the present; as nobody now, whether consul or senator, durst any longer contradict the people in their design of recalling Marcius; but, seeing their women running affrighted up and down the streets, and the old men at prayer in every temple with tears and supplications, and that, in short, there was a general absence among them both of courage and wisdom to provide for their own safety, they came at last to be all of one mind, that the people had been in the right to propose as they did a reconciliation with Marcius, and that the senate was guilty of a fatal error to begin a quarrel with him when it was a time to forget offences, and they should have studied rather to appease him. It was, therefore, unanimously agreed by all parties, that ambassadors should be despatched, offering him return to his country, and desiring he would free them from the terrors and distresses of the war. The persons sent by the senate with this message were chosen out of his kindred and acquaintance, who naturally expected a very kind reception at their first interview, upon the score of that relation and their old familiarity and friendship with him; in which, however, they were much mistaken. Being led through the enemy's camp, they found him sitting in state amidst the chief men of the Volscians, looking insupportably proud and arrogant. He bade them declare the cause of their coming, which they did in the most gentle and tender terms, and with a behaviour suitable to their language. When they had made an end of speaking, he returned them a sharp answer, full of bitterness and angry resentment, as to what concerned himself and the ill-usage he had received from them; but as general of the Volscians, he demanded restitution of the cities and the lands which had been seized upon during the late war, and that the same rights and franchises should be granted them at Rome, which had been before accorded to the Latins; since there could be no assurance that a peace would be firm and lasting without fair and just conditions on both sides. He allowed them thirty days to consider and resolve.

The ambassadors being departed, he withdrew his forces out of the Roman territory. This, those of the Volscians who had long envied his reputation, and could not endure to see the influence he had with the people, laid hold of, as the first matter of complaint against him. Among them was also Tullus himself, not for any wrong done him personally by Marcius, but through the weakness incident to human nature, he could not help feeling mortified to find his own glory thus totally obscured, and himself overlooked and neglected now by the Volscians, who had so great an opinion of their new leader, that he alone was all to them, while other captains, they thought, should be content with that share of power which he might think fit to accord. From hence the first seeds of complaint and accusation were scattered about in secret, and the malcontents met and heightened each other's indignation, saying, that to retreat as he did was in effect to betray and deliver up though not their cities and their arms, yet what was as bad, the critical times and opportunities for action, on which depend the preservation or the loss of everything else; since in less than thirty days' space, for which he had given a respite for the war, there might happen the greatest changes in the world. Yet Marcius spent not any part of the time idly, but attacked the confederates of the enemy, ravaged their land, and took from them seven great and populous cities in that interval. The Romans, in the meanwhile, durst not venture out to their relief; but were utterly fearful, and showed no more disposition or capacity for action than if their bodies had been struck with a palsy, and became destitute of sense and motion. But when the thirty days were expired, and Marcius appeared again with his whole army, they sent another embassy, to beseech him that he would moderate his displeasure and would withdraw the Volscian army, and then make any proposals he thought best for both parties; the Romans would make no concessions to menaces, but if it were his opinion that the Volscians ought to have any favour shown them, upon laying down their arms they might obtain all they could in reason desire.

The reply of Marcius was, that he should make no answer to this as general of the Volscians, but, in the quality still of a Roman citizen, he would advise and exhort them, as the case stood, not to carry it so high, but think rather of just compliance, and return to him, before three days were at an end, with a ratification of his previous demands; otherwise, they must understand that they could not have any further freedom of passing through his camp upon idle errands.

When the ambassadors were come back, and had acquainted the senate with the answer, seeing the whole state now threatened as it were by a tempest, and the waves ready to overwhelm them, they were forced, as we say in extreme perils, to let down the sacred anchor. A decree was made, that the whole order of their priests, those who initiated in the mysteries or had the custody of them, and those who, according to the ancient practice of the country, divined from birds, should all and everyone of them go in full procession to Marcius with their pontifical array, and the dress and habit which they respectively used in their several functions, and should urge him, as before, to withdraw his forces, and then treat with his countrymen in favour of the Volscians. He consented so far, indeed, as to give the deputation an admittance into his camp, but granted nothing at all, nor so much as expressed himself more mildly; but without capitulating or receding, bade them once for all choose whether they would yield or fight, since the old terms were the only terms of peace. When this solemn application proved ineffectual, the priests, too, returning unsuccessful, they determined to sit still within the city and keep watch about their walls, intending only to repulse the enemy, should he offer to attack them, and placing their hopes chiefly in time and in extraordinary accidents of fortune; as to themselves, they felt incapable of doing anything for their own deliverance; mere confusion and terror and ill-boding reports possessed the whole city; till at last a thing happened not unlike what we so often find represented, without, however, being accepted as true by people in general, in Homer. On some great and unusual occasion we find him say—

> But him the blue-eyed goddess did inspire;

and elsewhere—

> But some immortal turned my mind away,
> To think what others of the deed would say;

and again—

> Were't his own thought or were't a god's command?

People are apt, in such passages, to censure and disregard the poet, as if, by the introduction of mere impossibilities and idle fictions, he were denying the action of a man's own deliberate thought and free choice; which is not, in the least, the case in Homer's representation, where the ordinary, probable, and habitual conclusions that common reason leads to are continually ascribed to our own direct agency. He certainly says frequently enough—

> But I consulted with my own great soul;

or, as in another passage—

> He spoke. Achilles, with quick pain possessed,
> Resolved two purposes in his strong breast;

and in a third—

> —Yet never to her wishes won
> The just mind of the brave Bellerophon.

But where the act is something out of the way and extraordinary, and seems in a manner to demand some impulse of divine possession and sudden inspiration to account for it, here he does introduce divine agency, not to destroy, but to prompt the human will; not to create in us another agency, but offering images to stimulate our own; images that in no sort or kind make our action involuntary, but give occasion rather to spontaneous action, aided and sustained by feelings of confidence and hope. For either we must totally dismiss and exclude divine influences from every kind of causality and origination in what we do, or else what other way can we conceive in which divine aid and cooperation can act? Certainly we cannot suppose that the divine beings actually and literally turn our bodies and direct our hands and our feet this way or that, to do what is right: it is obvious that they must actuate the practical and elective element of our nature, by certain initial occasions, by images presented to the imagination, and thoughts suggested to the mind, such either as to excite it to, or avert and withhold it from, any particular course.

In the perplexity which I have described, the Roman women went, some to other temples, but the greater part, and the ladies of highest rank, to the altar of Jupiter Capitolinus. Among these suppliants was Valeria, sister to the great Poplicola, who did the Romans eminent service both in peace and war. Poplicola himself was now deceased, as is told in the history of his life; but Valeria lived still, and enjoyed great respect and honour at Rome, her life and conduct no way disparaging her birth. She, suddenly seized with the sort of instinct or emotion of mind which I have described, and happily lighting, not without divine guidance, on the right expedient, both rose herself, and bade the others rise, and went directly with them to the house of Volumnia, the mother of Marcius. And coming in and finding her sitting with her daughter-in-law, and with her little grandchildren on her lap, Valeria, then surrounded by her female companions, spoke in the name of them all:

"We that now make our appearance, O Volumnia, and you, Vergilia, are come as mere women to women, not by direction of the senate, or an order from the consuls, or the appointment of any other magistrate; but the divine being himself, as I conceive, moved to compassion by our prayers, prompted us to visit you in a body, and request a thing on which our own and the common safety depends, and which, if you consent to it, will raise your glory above that of the daughters of the Sabines, who won over their fathers and their husbands from mortal enmity to peace and friendship. Arise and come with us to Marcius; join in our supplication, and bear for your country this true and just testimony on her behalf; that, notwithstanding the many mischiefs that have been done her, yet she has never outraged you, nor so much as thought of treating you ill, in all her resentment, but does now restore you safe into his hands, though there be small likelihood she should obtain from him any equitable terms."

The words of Valeria were seconded by the acclamations of the other women, to which Volumnia made answer:

"I and Vergilia, my countrywomen, have an equal share with you all in the common miseries, and we have the additional sorrow, which is wholly ours, that we have lost the merit and good fame of Marcius, and see his person confined, rather than protected, by the arms of the enemy. Yet I account this the greatest of all misfortunes, if indeed the affairs of Rome be sunk to so feeble a state as to have their last dependence upon us. For it is hardly imaginable he should have any consideration left for us, when he has no regard for the country which he was wont to prefer before his mother and wife and children. Make use, however, of our service; and lead us, if you please, to him; we are able, if nothing more, at least to spend our last breath in making suit to him for our country."

Having spoken thus, she took Vergilia by the hand, and the young children, and so accompanied them to the Volscian camp. So lamentable a sight much affected the enemies themselves, who viewed them in respectful silence. Marcius was then sitting in his place, with his chief officers about him, and, seeing the party of women advance toward them, wondered what should be the matter; but perceiving at length that his mother was at the head of them, he would fain have hardened himself in his former inexorable temper, but, overcome by his feelings, and confounded at what he saw, he did not endure they should approach him sitting in state, but came down hastily to meet them, saluting his mother first, and embracing her a long time, and then his wife and children, sparing neither tears nor caresses, but suffering himself to be borne away and carried headlong, as it were, by the impetuous violence of his passion.

When he had satisfied himself, and observed that his mother Volumnia was desirous to say something, the Volscian council being first called in, he heard her to the following effect: "Our dress and our very persons, my son, might tell you, though we should say nothing ourselves, in how forlorn a condition we have lived at home since your banishment and absence from us; and now consider with yourself, whether we may not pass for the most unfortunate of all women, to have that sight, which should be the sweetest that we could see, converted, through I know not what fatality, to one of all others the most formidable and dreadful— Volumnia to behold her son, and Vergilia her husband, in arms against the walls of Rome. Even prayer itself, whence others gain comfort and relief in all manner of misfortunes, is that which most adds to our confusion and distress; since our best wishes are inconsistent with themselves, nor can we at the same time petition the gods for Rome's victory and your preservation, but what the worst of our enemies would imprecate as a curse, is the very object of our vows. Your wife and children are under the sad necessity, that they must either be deprived of you or of their native soil. As for myself, I am resolved not to wait till war shall determine this alternative for me; but if I cannot prevail with you to prefer amity and concord to quarrel and hostility, and to be the benefactor to both parties rather than the destroyer of one of them, be assured of this from me, and reckon steadfastly upon it, that you shall not be able to reach your country, unless you trample first upon the corpse of her that brought you into life. For it will be ill in me to wait and loiter in the world till the day wherein I shall see a child of mine, either led in triumph by his own countrymen, or triumphing over them. Did I require you to save your country by ruining the Volscians, then, I confess, my son, the case would be hard for you to solve. It is base to bring destitution on our fellow-citizens; it is unjust to betray those who have placed their confidence in us. But, as it is, we do but desire a deliverance equally expedient for them and us; only more glorious and honourable on the Volscian side, who, as superior in arms, will be thought freely to bestow the two greatest of blessings, peace and friendship, even when they themselves receive the same. If we obtain these, the common thanks will be chiefly due to you as the principal cause; but if they be not granted, you alone must expect to bear the blame from both nations. The chance of all war is uncertain, yet thus much is certain in the present, that you, by conquering Rome, will only get the reputation of having undone your country; but if the Volscians happen to be defeated under your conduct, then the world will say, that, to satisfy a revengeful humour, you brought misery on your friends and patrons."

Marcius listened to his mother while she spoke without answering her a word; and Volumnia, seeing him stand mute also for a long time after she had ceased, resumed: "O my son," said she, "what is the meaning of this silence? Is it a duty to postpone everything to a sense of injuries, and wrong to gratify a mother in a request like this? Is it the characteristic of a great man to remember wrongs that have been done him, and not the part of a great and good man to remember benefits such as those that children receive from parents, and to requite them with honour and respect? You, methinks, who are so relentless in the punishment of the ungrateful, should not be more careless than others to be grateful yourself. You have punished your country already; you have not yet paid your debt to me. Nature and religion, surely unattended by any constraint, should have won your consent to petitions so worthy and so just as these; but if it must be so, I will even use my last resource." Having said this, she threw herself down at his feet, as did also his wife and children; upon which Marcius, crying out, "O mother! What is it you have done to me!" raised her up from the ground, and pressing her right hand with more than ordinary vehemence, "You have gained a victory," said he, "fortunate enough for the Romans, but destructive to your son; whom you, though none else, have defeated." After which, and a little private conference with his mother and his wife, he sent them back again to Rome, as they desired.

The next morning, he broke up his camp, and led the Volscians homeward, variously affected with what he had done; some of them complaining of him and condemning his act, others, who were inclined to a peaceful conclusion, unfavourable to neither. A third party, while much disliking his proceedings, yet could not look upon Marcius as a treacherous person, but thought it pardonable in him to be thus shaken and driven to surrender at last, under such compulsion. None, however, opposed his commands; they all obediently followed him, though rather from admiration of his virtue, than any regard they now had to his authority. The Roman people, meantime, more effectually manifested how much fear and danger they had been in while the war lasted, by their deportment after they were freed from it. Those that guarded the walls had no sooner given notice that the Volscians were dislodged and drawn off, but they set open all their temples in a moment, and began to crown themselves with garlands and prepare for sacrifice, as they were wont to do upon tidings brought of any signal victory. But the joy and transport of the whole city was chiefly remarkable in the honours and marks of affection paid to the women, as well by the senate as the people in general; everyone declaring that they were, beyond all question, the instruments of the public safety. And the senate having passed a decree that whatsoever they would ask in the way of any favour or honour should be allowed and done for them by the magistrates, they demanded simply that a temple might be erected to Female Fortune, the expense of which they offered to defray out of their own contributions, if the city would be at the cost of sacrifices, and other matters pertaining to the due honour of the gods, out of the common treasury. The senate, much commending their public spirit, caused the temple to be built and a statue set up in it at the public charge; they, however, made up a sum among themselves for a second image of Fortune, which the Romans say uttered, as it was putting up, words to this effect, "Blessed of the gods, O women, is your gift."

These words, they profess, were repeated a second time, expecting our belief of what seems pretty nearly an impossibility. It may be possible enough that statues may seem to sweat, and to run with tears, and to stand with certain dewy drops of a sanguine colour; for timber and stones are frequently known to contract a kind of scurf and rottenness, productive of moisture; and various tints may form on the surfaces, both from within and from the action of the air outside; and by these signs it is not absurd to imagine that the deity may forewarn us. It may happen, also, that images and statues may sometimes make a noise not unlike that of a moan or groan, through a rupture or violent internal separation of the parts; but that an articulate voice, and such express words, and language so clear and exact and elaborate, should proceed from inanimate things is, in my judgment, a thing utterly out of possibility. For it was never known that either the soul of man, or the deity himself, uttered vocal sounds and language, alone, without an organised body and members fitted for speech. But where history seems in a manner to force our assent by the concurrence of numerous and credible witnesses, we are to conclude that an impression distinct from sensation affects the imaginative part of our nature, and then carries away the judgment, so as to believe it to be a sensation; just as in sleep we fancy we see and hear, without really doing either. Persons, however, whose strong feelings of reverence to the deity, and tenderness for religion, will not allow them to deny or invalidate anything of this kind, have certainly a strong argument for their faith, in the wonderful and transcendent character of the divine power; which admits no manner of comparison with ours, either in its nature or its action, the modes or the strength of its operations. It is no contradiction to reason that it should do things that we cannot do, and effect what for us is impracticable: differing from us in all respects, in its acts yet more than in other points we may well believe it to be unlike us and remote from us. Knowledge of divine things for the most part, as Heraclitus says, is lost to us by incredulity.

When Marcius came back to Antium, Tullus, who thoroughly hated and greatly feared him, proceeded at once to contrive how he might immediately despatch him, as, if he escaped now, he was never likely to give him such another advantage. Having therefore got together and suborned several partisans against him, he required Marcius to resign his charge and give the Volscians an account of his administration. He, apprehending the danger of a private condition, while Tullus held the office of general and exercised the greatest power among his fellow-citizens, made answer, that he was ready to lay down his commission, whenever those from whose common authority he had received it should think fit to recall it, and that in the meantime he was ready to give the Antiates satisfaction, as to all particulars of his conduct, if they were desirous of it.

An assembly was called, and popular speakers, as had been concerted, came forward to exasperate and incense the multitude; but when Marcius stood up to answer, the more unruly and tumultuous part of the people became quiet on a sudden, and out of reverence allowed him to speak without the least disturbance; while all the better people, and such as were satisfied with a peace, made it evident by their whole behaviour, that they would give him a favourable hearing, and judge and pronounce according to equity.

Tullus, therefore, began to dread the issue of the defence he was going to make for himself; for he was an admirable speaker, and the former services he had done the Volscians had procured and still preserved for him greater kindness than could be outweighed by any blame for his late conduct. Indeed, the very accusation itself was a proof and testimony of the greatness of his merits, since people could never have complained or thought themselves wronged, because Rome was not brought into their power, but that by his means they had come so near to taking it. For these reasons, the conspirators judged it prudent not to make any further delays, nor to test the general feeling; but the boldest of their faction crying out that they ought not to listen to a traitor, nor allow him still to retain office and play the tyrant among them, fell upon Marcius in a body, and slew him there, none of those that were present offering to defend him. But it quickly appeared that the action was in nowise approved by the majority of the Volscians, who hurried out of their several cities to show respect to his corpse; to which they gave honourable interment, adorning his sepulchre with arms and trophies, as the monument of a noble hero and a famous general. When the Romans heard tidings of his death, they gave no other signification either of honour or of anger towards him, but simply granted the request of the women, that they might put themselves into mourning and bewail him for ten months, as the usage was upon the loss of a father or a son or a brother; that being the period fixed for the longest lamentation by the laws of Numa Pompilius, as is more amply told in the account of him.

Marcius was no sooner deceased, but the Volscians felt the need of his assistance. They quarrelled first with the Æquians, their confederates and their friends, about the appointment of the general of their joint forces, and carried their dispute to the length of bloodshed and slaughter; and were then defeated by the Romans in a pitched battle, where not only

Tullus lost his life, but the principal flower of their whole army was cut in pieces; so that they were forced to submit and accept of peace upon very dishonourable terms, becoming subjects of Rome, and pledging themselves to submission.

THE COMPARISON OF ALCIBIADES
WITH CORIOLANUS

HAVING DESCRIBED ALL THEIR ACTIONS THAT SEEM TO DESERVE commemoration, their military ones, we may say, incline the balance very decidedly upon neither side. They both, in pretty equal measure, displayed on numerous occasions the daring and courage of the soldier, and the skill and foresight of the general; unless, indeed, the fact that Alcibiades was victorious and successful in many contests both by sea and land, ought to gain him the title of a more complete commander. That so long as they remained and held command in their respective countries they eminently sustained, and when they were driven into exile yet more eminently damaged, the fortunes of those countries, is common to both. All the sober citizens felt disgust at the petulance, the low flattery, and base seductions which Alcibiades, in his public life, allowed himself to employ with the view of winning the people's favour; and the ungraciousness, pride, and oligarchical haughtiness which Marcius, on the other hand, displayed in his, were the abhorrence of the Roman populace. Neither of these courses can be called commendable; but a man who ingratiates himself by indulgence and flattery is hardly so censurable as one who, to avoid the appearance of flattering, insults. To seek power by servility to the people is a disgrace, but to maintain it by terror, violence, and oppression is not a disgrace only, but an injustice.

Marcius, according to our common conceptions of his character, was undoubtedly simple and straightforward; Alcibiades, unscrupulous as a public man, and false. He is more especially blamed for the dishonourable and treacherous way in which, as Thucydides relates, he imposed upon the Lacedæmonian ambassadors, and disturbed the continuance of the peace. Yet this policy, which engaged the city again in war, nevertheless placed it in a powerful and formidable position, by the accession, which Alcibiades obtained for it, of the alliance of Argos and Mantinea. And Coriolanus also, Dionysius relates, used unfair means to excite war between the Romans and the Volscians, in the false report which he spread about the visitors at the Games; and the motive of this action seems to make it the worse of the two; since it was not done, like the other, out of ordinary political jealousy, strife, and competition. Simply to gratify anger from which, as Ion says, no one ever yet got any return, he threw whole districts of Italy into confusion, and sacrificed to his passion against his country numerous innocent cities. It is true, indeed, that Alcibiades also, by his resentment, was the occasion of great disasters to his country, but he relented as soon as he found their feelings to be changed; and after he was driven out a second time, so far from taking pleasure in the errors and inadvertencies of their commanders, or being indifferent to the danger they were thus incurring, he did the very thing that Aristides is so highly commended for doing to Themistocles; he came to the generals who were his enemies, and pointed out to them what they ought to do. Coriolanus, on the other hand, first of all attacked the whole body of his countrymen, though only one portion of them had done him any wrong, while the other, the better and nobler portion, had actually suffered, as well as sympathised, with him. And, secondly, by the obduracy with which he resisted numerous embassies and supplications, addressed in propitiation of his single anger and offence, he showed that it had been to destroy and overthrow, not to recover and regain his country, that he had excited bitter and implacable hostilities against it. There is, indeed, one distinction that may be drawn. Alcibiades, it may be said, was not safe among the Spartans, and had the inducements at once of fear and of hatred to lead him again to Athens; whereas Marcius could not honourably have left the Volscians, when they were behaving so well to him: he, in the command of their forces and the enjoyment of their entire confidence, was in a very different position from Alcibiades, whom the Lacedæmonians did not so much wish to adopt into their service, as to use and then abandon. Driven about from house to house in the city, and from general to general in the camp, the latter had no resort but to place himself in the hands of Tisaphernes; unless, indeed, we are to suppose that his object in courting favour with him was to avert the entire destruction of his native city, whither he wished himself to return.

As regards money, Alcibiades, we are told, was often guilty of procuring it by accepting bribes, and spent it ill in luxury and dissipation. Coriolanus declined to receive it, even when pressed upon him by his commanders as an honour; and one great reason for the odium he incurred with the populace in the discussions about their debts was, that he trampled upon the poor, not for money's sake, but out of pride and insolence.

Antipater, in a letter written upon the death of Aristotle the philosopher, observes, "Amongst his other gifts he had that of persuasiveness"; and the absence of this in the character of Marcius made all his great actions and noble qualities unacceptable to those whom they benefited: pride, and self-will, the consort, as Plato calls it, of solitude, made him insufferable. With the skill which Alcibiades, on the contrary, possessed to treat everyone in the way most agreeable to him, we cannot wonder that all his successes were attended with the most exuberant favour and honour; his very errors, at times, being accompanied by something of grace and felicity. And so in spite of great and frequent hurt that he had done the city, he was repeatedly appointed to office and command; while Coriolanus stood in vain for a place which his great services had made his due. The one, in spite of the harm he occasioned, could not make himself hated, nor the other, with all the admiration he attracted, succeeded in being beloved by his countrymen.

Coriolanus, moreover, it should be said, did not as a general obtain any successes for his country, but only for his enemies against his country. Alcibiades was often of service to Athens, both as a soldier and as a commander. So long as he was personally present, he had the perfect mastery of his political adversaries; calumny only succeeded in his absence. Coriolanus was condemned in person at Rome; and in like manner killed by the Volscians, not indeed with any right or justice, yet not without some pretext occasioned by his own acts; since, after rejecting all conditions of peace in public, in private he yielded to the solicitations of the women and, without establishing peace, threw up the favourable chances of war. He ought, before retiring, to have obtained the consent of those who had placed their trust in him; if indeed he considered their claims on him to be the strongest. Or, if we say that he did not care about the Volscians, but merely had prosecuted the war, which he now abandoned, for the satisfaction of his own resentment, then the noble thing would have been, not to spare his country for his mother's sake, but his mother in and with his country; since both his mother and his wife were part and parcel of that endangered country. After harshly repelling public supplications, the entreaties of ambassadors, and the prayers of priests, to concede all as a private favour to his mother was less an honour to her than a dishonour to the city which thus escaped, in spite, it would seem, of its own demerits through the intercession of a single woman. Such a grace could, indeed, seem merely invidious, ungracious, and unreasonable in the eyes of both parties; he retreated without listening to the persuasions of his opponents or asking the consent of his friends. The origin of all lay in his unsociable, supercilious, and self-willed disposition, which, in all cases, is offensive to most people; and when combined with a passion for distinction passes into absolute savageness and mercilessness. Men decline to ask favours of the people, professing not to need any honours from them; and then are indignant if they do not obtain them. Metellus, Aristides, and Epaminondas certainly did not beg favours of the multitude; but that was because they, in real truth, did not value the gifts which a popular body can either confer or refuse; and when they were more than once driven into exile, rejected at elections, and condemned in courts of justice, they showed no resentment at the ill-humour of their fellow-citizens, but were willing and contented to return and be reconciled when the feeling altered and they were wished for. He who least likes courting favour, ought also least to think of resenting neglect; to feel wounded at being refused a distinction can only arise from an overweening appetite to have it.

Alcibiades never professed to deny that it was pleasant to him to be honoured, and distasteful to him to be overlooked; and, accordingly, he always tried to place himself upon good terms with all that he met; Coriolanus' pride forbade him to pay attentions to those who could have promoted his advancement, and yet his love of distinction made him feel hurt and angry when he was disregarded. Such are the faulty parts of his character, which in all other respects was a noble one. For his temperance, continence, and probity he claims to be compared with the best and purest of the Greeks; not in any sort or kind with Alcibiades, the least scrupulous and most entirely careless of human beings in all these points.

TIMOLEON

I<small>T WAS FOR THE SAKE OF OTHERS THAT</small> I <small>FIRST COMMENCED WRITING</small>
biographies; but I find myself proceeding and attaching myself to it for my
own; the virtues of these great men serving me as a sort of looking-glass,
in which I may see how to adjust and adorn my own life. Indeed, it can be
compared to nothing but daily living and associating together; we receive,
as it were, in our inquiry, and entertain each successive guest, view—

Their stature and their qualities,

and select from their actions all that is noblest and worthiest to know.

Ah, and what greater pleasure can one have?

or what more effective means to one's moral improvement? Democritus
tells us we ought to pray that of the phantasms appearing in the circum-
ambient air, such may present themselves to us as are propitious, and that
we may rather meet with those that are agreeable to our natures and are
good than the evil and unfortunate; which is simply introducing into philosophy a doctrine untrue in itself, and leading to endless superstitions.
My method, on the contrary, is, by the study of history, and by the familiarity acquired in writing, to habituate my memory to receive and retain
images of the best and worthiest characters. I thus am enabled to free
myself from any ignoble, base, or vicious impressions, contracted from
the contagion of ill company that I may be unavoidably engaged in; by the
remedy of turning my thoughts in a happy and calm temper to view these
noble examples. Of this kind are those of Timoleon the Corinthian and
Paulus Æmilius, to write whose lives is my present business; men equally
famous, not only for their virtues, but success; insomuch that they have left

it doubtful whether they owe their greatest achievements to good fortune, or their own prudence and conduct.

The affairs of the Syracusans, before Timoleon was sent into Sicily, were in this posture; after Dion had driven out Dionysius the tyrant, he was slain by treachery, and those that had assisted him in delivering Syracuse were divided among themselves; and thus the city by a continual change of governors, and a train of mischiefs that succeeded each other, became almost abandoned; while of the rest of Sicily, part was now utterly depopulated and desolate through long continuance of war, and most of the cities that had been left standing were in the hands of barbarians and soldiers out of employment, that were ready to embrace every turn of government. Such being the state of things, Dionysius takes the opportunity, and in the tenth year of his banishment, by the help of some mercenary troops he had got together, forces out Nysæus, then master of Syracuse, recovers all afresh, and is again settled in his dominion; and as at first he had been strangely deprived of the greatest and most absolute power that ever was by a very small party, so now, in a yet stranger manner, when in exile and of mean condition, he became the sovereign of those who had ejected him. All therefore that remained in Syracuse had to serve under a tyrant, who at the best was of an ungentle nature, and exasperated now to a degree of savageness by the late misfortunes and calamities he had suffered. The better and more distinguished citizens, having timely retired thence to Hicetes, ruler of the Leontines, put themselves under his protection, and chose him for their general in the war; not that he was much preferable to any open and avowed tyrant, but they had no other sanctuary at present, and it gave them some ground of confidence that he was of a Syracusan family, and had forces able to encounter those of Dionysius.

In the meantime the Carthaginians appeared before Sicily with a great navy, watching when and where they might make a descent upon the island; and terror at this fleet made the Sicilians incline to send an embassy into Greece to demand succours from the Corinthians, whom they confided in rather than others, not only upon the account of their near kindred, and the great benefits they had often received by trusting them, but because Corinth had ever shown herself attached to freedom and averse from tyranny and had engaged in many noble wars, not for empire or aggrandisement, but for the sole liberty of the Greeks. But Hicetes, who made it the business of his command not so much to deliver the Syracusans from other tyrants, as to enslave them to himself, had already entered into some secret conferences with those of Carthage, while in public he commended the design of his Syracusan clients, and despatched ambassadors from himself, together with theirs, into Peloponnesus; not that he really desired any relief to come from there, but in case the Corinthians, as was likely enough, on account of the troubles of Greece and occupation at home, should refuse their assistance, hoping then he should be able with less difficulty to dispose and incline things for the Carthaginian interest, and so make use of these foreign pretenders, as instruments and auxiliaries for himself, either against the Syracusans or Dionysius, as occasion served. This was discovered a while after.

The ambassadors being arrived, and their request known, the Corinthians, who had always a great concern for all their colonies and plantations, but especially for Syracuse, since by good fortune there was nothing to molest them in their own country, where they were enjoying peace and leisure at that time, readily and with one accord passed a vote for their assistance. And when they were deliberating about the choice of a captain for the expedition, and the magistrates were urging the claims of various aspirants for reputation, one of the crowd stood up and named Timoleon, son of Timodemus, who had long absented himself from public business, and had neither any thoughts of, nor the least pretensions to, an employment of that nature. Some god or other, it might rather seem, had put it in the man's heart to mention him; such favour and goodwill on the part of Fortune seemed at once to be shown in his election, and to accompany all his following actions, as though it were on purpose to commend his worth, and add grace and ornament to his personal virtues. As regards his parentage, both Timodemus his father, and his mother Demariste, were of high rank in the city; and as for himself, he was noted for his love of his country, and his gentleness of temper, except in his extreme hatred to tyrants and wicked men. His natural abilities for war were so happily tempered, that while a rare prudence might be seen in all the enterprises of his younger years, an equal courage showed itself in the last exploits of his declining age. He had an elder brother, whose name was Timophanes, who was every way unlike him, being indiscreet and rash, and infected by the suggestions of some friends and foreign soldiers, whom he kept always about him, with a passion for absolute power. He seemed to have a certain force and vehemence in all military service, and even to delight in dangers, and thus he took much with the people, and was advanced to the highest charges, as a vigorous and effective warrior; in the obtaining of which offices and promotions, Timoleon much assisted him, helping to conceal or at least to extenuate his errors, embellishing by his

praise whatever was commendable in him, and setting off his good qualities to the best advantage.

It happened once in the battle fought by the Corinthians against the
forces of Argos and Cleonæ, that Timoleon served among the infantry,
when Timophanes, commanding their cavalry, was brought into extreme
danger; as his horse being wounded fell forward and threw him headlong
amidst the enemies, while part of his companions dispersed at once in a
panic, and the small number that remained, bearing up against a great
multitude, had much ado to maintain any resistance. As soon, therefore,
as Timoleon was aware of the accident, he ran hastily in to his brother's
rescue, and covering the fallen Timophanes with his buckler, after having
received abundance of darts, and several strokes by the sword upon his
body and his armour, he at length with much difficulty obliged the enemies to retire, and brought off his brother alive and safe. But when the
Corinthians, for fear of losing their city a second time, as they had once
before, by admitting their allies, made a decree to maintain four hundred
mercenaries for its security, and gave Timophanes the command over
them, he, abandoning all regard to honour and equity, at once proceeded
to put into execution his plans for making himself absolute, and bringing
the place under his own power; and having cut off many principal citizens,
uncondemned and without trial, who were most likely to hinder his
designs, he declared himself tyrant of Corinth; a procedure that infinitely
afflicted Timoleon, to whom the wickedness of such a brother appeared
to be his own reproach and calamity. He undertook to persuade him by
reasoning, that desisting from that wild and unhappy ambition, he would
bethink himself how he should make the Corinthians some amends, and
find out an expedient to remedy and correct the evils he had done them.
When his single admonition was rejected and contemned by him, he
makes a second attempt, taking with him Æschylus his kinsman, brother
to the wife of Timophanes, and a certain diviner, that was his friend, whom
Theopompus in his history calls Satyrus, but Ephorus and Timæus mention in theirs by the name of Orthagoras. After a few days, then, he returns
to his brother with this company, all three of them surrounding and
earnestly importuning him upon the same subject, that now at length he
would listen to reason, and be of another mind. But when Timophanes
began first to laugh at the men's simplicity, and presently broke out into
rage and indignation against them, Timoleon stepped aside from him and
stood weeping with his face covered, while the other two, drawing out
their swords, despatched him in a moment.

On the rumour of this act being soon scattered about, the better and more generous of the Corinthians highly applauded Timoleon for the hatred of wrong and the greatness of soul that had made him, though of a gentle disposition and full of love and kindness for his family, think the obligations to his country stronger than the ties of consanguinity, and prefer that which is good and just before gain and interest and his own particular advantage. For the same brother, who with so much bravery had been saved by him when he fought valiantly in the cause of Corinth, he had now as nobly sacrificed for enslaving her afterwards by a base usurpation. But then, on the other side, those that knew not how to live in a democracy, and had been used to make their humble court to the men of power, though they openly professed to rejoice at the death of the tyrant, nevertheless, secretly reviling Timoleon, as one that had committed an impious and abominable act, drove him into melancholy and dejection. And when he came to understand how heavily his mother took it, and that she likewise uttered the saddest complaints and most terrible imprecations against him, he went to satisfy and comfort her as to what had happened; and finding that she would not endure so much as to look upon him, but caused her doors to be shut, that he might have no admission into her presence, with grief at this he grew so disordered in his mind and so disconsolate, that he determined to put an end to his perplexity with his life, by abstaining from all manner of sustenance. But through the care and diligence of his friends, who were very instant with him, and added force to their entreaties, he came to resolve and promise at last, that he would endure living, provided it might be in solitude, and remote from company; so that, quitting all civil transactions and commerce with the world for a long while after his first retirement, he never came into Corinth, but wandered up and down the fields, full of anxious and tormenting thoughts, and spent his time in desert places, at the farthest distance from society and human intercourse. So true it is that the minds of men are easily shaken and carried off from their own sentiments through the casual commendation or reproof of others, unless the judgments that we make, and the purposes we conceive, be confirmed by reason and philosophy, and thus obtain strength and steadiness. An action must not only be just and laudable in its own nature, but it must proceed likewise from motives and a lasting principle, that so we may fully and constantly approve the thing, and be perfectly satisfied in what we do; for otherwise, after having put our resolution into practice, we shall out of pure weakness come to be troubled at the performance, when the grace and godliness, which rendered it before so amiable and pleasing to us, begin to decay and wear out of our fancy; like greedy people, who, seizing on the more delicious morsels of any dish with a keen appetite, are presently disgusted when they grow full, and find themselves oppressed and uneasy now by what they before so greedily desired. For a succeeding dislike spoils the best of actions, and repentance makes that which was never so well done become base and faulty; whereas the choice that is founded upon knowledge and wise reasoning does not change by disappointment, or suffer us to repent, though it happen perchance to be less prosperous in the issue. And thus, Phocion, of Athens, having always vigorously opposed the measures of Leosthenes, when success appeared to attend them, and he saw his countrymen rejoicing and offering sacrifice in honour of their victory, "I should have been as glad," said he to them, "that I myself had been the author of what Leosthenes has achieved for you, as I am that I gave you my own counsel against it." A more vehement reply is recorded to have been made by Aristides the Locrian, one of Plato's companions, to Dionysius the elder, who demanded one of his daughters in marriage: "I had rather," said he to him, "see the virgin in her grave than in the palace of a tyrant." And when Dionysius, enraged at the affront, made his sons be put to death a while after, and then again insultingly asked, whether he were still in the same mind as to the disposal of his daughters, his answer was, "I cannot but grieve at the cruelty of your deeds, but am not sorry for the freedom of my own words." Such expressions as these may belong perhaps to a more sublime and accomplished virtue.

The grief, however, of Timoleon at what had been done, whether it arose from commiseration of his brother's fate or the reverence he bore his mother, so shattered and broke his spirits, that for the space of almost twenty years he had not offered to concern himself in any honourable or public action. When, therefore, he was pitched upon for a general, and, joyfully accepted as such by the suffrages of the people, Teleclides, who was at that time the most powerful and distinguished man in Corinth, began to exhort him that he would act now like a man of worth and gallantry: "For," said he, "if you do bravely in this service we shall believe that you delivered us from a tyrant; but if otherwise that you killed your brother." While he was yet preparing to set sail, and enlisting soldiers to embark with him, there came letters to the Corinthians from Hicetes, plainly disclosing his revolt and treachery. For his ambassadors had no sooner gone for Corinth, but he openly joined the Carthaginians, negotiating that they might assist him to throw out Dionysius, and become master of Syracuse in his room. And fearing he might be disappointed of his aim if troops and a commander should come from Corinth before this were effected, he sent a letter of advice thither, in all haste, to prevent their setting out, telling them they need not be at any cost and trouble upon his account, or run the hazard of a Sicilian voyage, especially since the Carthaginians, alliance with whom against Dionysius the slowness of their motions had compelled him to embrace, would dispute their passage, and lay in wait to attack them with a numerous fleet. This letter being publicly read, if any had been cold and indifferent before as to the expedition in hand, the indignation they now conceived against Hicetes so exasperated and inflamed them all that they willingly contributed to supply Timoleon, and endeavoured with one accord to hasten his departure.

When the vessels were equipped, and his soldiers every way provided for, the female priest of Proserpina had a dream or vision wherein she and her mother Ceres appeared to them in a travelling garb, and were heard to say that they were going to sail with Timoleon into Sicily; whereupon the Corinthians, having built a sacred galley, devoted it to them, and called it the galley of the goddesses. Timoleon went in person to Delphi, where he sacrificed to Apollo, and, descending into the place of prophecy, was surprised with the following marvellous occurrence. A riband, with crowns and figures of victory embroidered upon it, slipped off from among the gifts that were there consecrated and hung up in the temple, and fell directly down upon his head; so that Apollo seemed already to crown him with success, and send him thence to conquer and triumph. He put to sea only with seven ships of Corinth, two of Corcyra, and a tenth which was furnished by the Leucadians; and when he was now entered into the deep by night, and carried with a prosperous gale, the heaven seemed all on a sudden to break open, and a bright spreading flame to issue forth from it and hover over the ship he was in; and, having formed itself into a torch, not unlike those that are used in the mysteries, it began to steer the same course, and run along in their company, guiding them by its light to that quarter of Italy where they designed to go ashore. The soothsayers affirmed that this apparition agreed with the dream of the holy woman, since the goddesses were now visibly joining in the expedition, and sending this light from heaven before them: Sicily being thought sacred to Proserpina, as poets feign that the rape was committed there, and that the island was given her in dowry when she married Pluto.

These early demonstrations of divine favour greatly encouraged his whole army; so that making all the speed they were able, by a voyage across the open sea, they were soon passing along the coast of Italy. But the tidings that came from Sicily much perplexed Timoleon, and disheartened his soldiers. For Hicetes, having already beaten Dionysius out of the field, and reduced most of the quarters of Syracuse itself, now hemmed him in and besieged him in the citadel and what is called the Island, whither he was fled for his last refuge; while the Carthaginians, by agreement, were to make it their business to hinder Timoleon from landing in any port of Sicily; so that he and his party being driven back, they might with ease and at their own leisure divide the island among themselves. In pursuance of which design the Carthaginians sent away twenty of their galleys to Rhegium, having aboard them certain ambassadors from Hicetes to Timoleon, who carried instructions suitable to these proceedings, specious amusements, and plausible stories, to colour and conceal dishonest purposes. They had order to propose and demand that Timoleon himself, if he liked the offer, should come and advise with Hicetes and partake of all his conquests, but that he might send back his ships and forces to Corinth, since the war was in a manner finished, and the Carthaginians had blocked up the passage, determined to oppose them if they should try to force their way towards the shore. When, therefore, the Corinthians met with these envoys at Rhegium, and received their message, and saw the Phœnician vessels riding at anchor in the bay, they became keenly sensible of the abuse that was put upon them, and felt a general indignation against Hicetes, and great apprehensions for the Siceliots, whom they now plainly perceived to be as it were a prize and recompense to Hicetes on one side for his perfidy, and to the Carthaginians on the other for the sovereign power they secured to him. For it seemed utterly impossible to force and overbear the Carthaginian ships that lay before them and were double their number, as also to vanquish the victorious troops which Hicetes had with him in Syracuse, to take the lead of which very troops they had undertaken their voyage.

The case being thus, Timoleon, after some conference with the envoys of Hicetes and the Carthaginian captains, told them he should readily submit to their proposals (to what purpose would it be to refuse compliance?): he was desirous only, before his return to Corinth, that what had passed between them in private might be solemnly declared before the people of Rhegium, a Greek city, and a common friend to the parties; this, he said, would very much conduce to his own security and discharge: and they likewise would more strictly observe articles of agreement, on behalf of the Syracusans, which they had obliged themselves to in the presence of so many witnesses. The design of all which was only to divert their attention, while he got an opportunity of slipping away from their fleet; a contrivance that all the principal Rhegians were privy and assisting to, who had a great desire that the affairs of Sicily should fall into Corinthian hands, and dreaded the consequences of having barbarian neighbours. An assembly was therefore called, and the gates shut, that the citizens might have no liberty to turn to other business; and a succession of speakers came forward, addressing the people at great length, to the same effect, without bringing the subject to any conclusion, making way each for another and purposely spinning out the time, till the Corinthian galleys should get clear of the haven; the Carthaginian commanders being detained there without any suspicion, as also Timoleon still remained present, and gave signs as if he were just preparing to make an oration. But upon secret notice that the rest of the galleys were already gone off, and that his alone remained waiting for him, by the help and concealment of those Rhegians that were about the hustings and favoured his departure, he made shift to slip away through the crowd, and running down to the port, set sail with all speed; and having reached his other vessels, they came all safe to Tauromenium in Sicily, whither they had been formerly invited, and where they were now kindly received by Andromachus, then ruler of the city. This man was father of Timæus the historian, and incomparably the best of all those that bore sway in Sicily at that time, governing his citizens according to law and justice and openly professing an aversion and enmity to all tyrants; upon which account he gave Timoleon leave to muster up his troops there, and to make that city the seat of war, persuading the inhabitants to join their arms with the Corinthian forces, and assist them in the design of delivering Sicily.

But the Carthaginians who were left in Rhegium perceiving, when the assembly was dissolved, that Timoleon had given them the go-by, were not a little vexed to see themselves outwitted, much to the amusement of the Rhegians, who could not but smile to find Phœnicians complain of being cheated. However, they despatched a messenger aboard one of their galleys to Tauromenium, who, after much blustering in the insolent barbaric way, and many menaces to Andromachus if he did not forthwith send the Corinthians off, stretched out his hand with the inside upward, and then turning it down again, threatened he would handle their city even so, and turn it topsy-turvy in as little time, and with as much ease. Andromachus, laughing at the man's confidence, made no other reply, but, imitating his gesture, bid him hasten his own departure, unless he had a mind to see that kind of dexterity practised first upon the galley which brought him hither.

Hicetes, informed that Timoleon had made good his passage, was in great fear of what might follow, and sent to desire the Carthaginians that a large number of galleys might be ordered to attend and secure the coast. And now it was that the Syracusans began wholly to despair of safety, seeing the Carthaginians possessed of their haven, Hicetes master of the town, and Dionysius supreme in the citadel; while Timoleon had as yet but a slender hold of Sicily, as it were by the fringe or border of it, in the small city of the Tauromenians, with a feeble hope and a poor company; having but a thousand soldiers at the most, and no more provisions, either of corn or money, than were just necessary for the maintenance and the pay of that inconsiderable number. Nor did the other towns of Sicily confide in him, overpowered as they were with violence and outrage, and embittered against all that should offer to lead armies by the treacherous conduct chiefly of Callipus, an Athenian, and Pharax, a Lacedæmonian captain, both of whom, after giving out that the design of their coming was to introduce liberty and to depose tyrants, so tyrannised themselves, that the reign of former oppressors seemed to be a golden age in comparison, and the Sicilians began to consider those more happy who had expired in servitude, than any that had lived to see such a dismal freedom.

Looking, therefore, for no better usage from the Corinthian general, but imagining that it was only the same old course of things once more, specious pretences and false professions to allure them by fair hopes and kind promises into the obedience of a new master, they all, with one accord, unless it were the people of Adranum, suspected the exhortations, and rejected the overtures that were made them in his name. These were inhabitants of a small city, consecrated to Adranus, a certain god that was in high veneration throughout Sicily, and, as it happened, they were then at variance among themselves, insomuch that one party called in Hicetes and the Carthaginians to assist them, while the other sent proposals to Timoleon. It so fell out that these auxiliaries, striving which should be soonest, both arrived at Adranum about the same time; Hicetes bringing with him at least five thousand men, while all the force Timoleon could make did not exceed twelve hundred. With these he marched out of Tauromenium, which was about three hundred and forty furlongs distant from that city. The first day he moved but slowly, and took up his quarters betimes after a short journey; but the day following he quickened his pace, and, having passed through much difficult ground, towards evening received advice that Hicetes was just approaching Adranum, and pitching his camp before it; upon which intelligence, his captains and other officers caused the vanguard to halt, that the army being refreshed, and having reposed a while, might engage the enemy with better heart. But Timoleon, coming up in haste, desired them not to stop for that reason, but rather use all possible diligence to surprise the enemy, whom probably they would now find in disorder, as having lately ended their march and being taken up at present in erecting tents and preparing supper; which he had no sooner said, but laying hold of his buckler and putting himself in the front, he led them on as it were to certain victory. The braveness of such a leader made them all follow him with like courage and assurance. They were now within less than thirty furlongs of Adranum, which they quickly traversed, and immediately fell in upon the enemy, who were seized with confusion, and began to retire at their first approaches; one consequence of which was that, amidst so little opposition, and so early and general a flight, there were not many more than three hundred slain, and about twice the number made prisoners. Their camp and baggage, however, was all taken. The fortune of this onset soon induced the Adranitans to unlock their gates, and to embrace the interest of Timoleon, to whom they recounted, with a mixture of affright and admiration, how, at the very minute of the encounter, the doors of their temple flew open of their own accord, that the javelin also, which their god held in his hand, was observed to tremble at the point, and that drops of sweat had been seen running down his face; prodigies that not only presaged the victory then obtained, but were an omen, it seemed, of all his future exploits, to which this first happy action gave the occasion.

For now the neighbouring cities and potentates sent deputies, one upon another, to seek his friendship and make offer of their service. Among the rest Mamercus, the tyrant of Catana, an experienced warrior and a wealthy prince, made proposals of alliance with him, and what was of greater importance still, Dionysius himself, being now grown desperate, and well-nigh forced to surrender, despising Hicetes who had been thus shamefully baffled, and admiring the valour of Timoleon, found means to advertise him and his Corinthians that he should be content to deliver up himself and the citadel into their hands. Timoleon, gladly embracing this unlooked-for advantage, sends away Euclides and Telemachus, two Corinthian captains, with four hundred men, for the seizure and custody of the castle, with directions to enter not all at once, or in open view, that being impracticable so long as the enemy kept guard, but by stealth, and in small companies. And so they took possession of the fortress and the palace of Dionysius, with all the stores and ammunition he had prepared and laid up to maintain the war. They found a good number of horses, every variety of engines, a multitude of darts, and weapons to arm seventy thousand men (a magazine that had been formed from ancient time), besides two thousand soldiers that were then with him, whom he gave up with the rest for Timoleon's service. Dionysius himself, putting his treasure aboard, and taking a few friends, sailed away unobserved by Hicetes, and being brought to the camp of Timoleon, there first appeared in the humble dress of a private person, and was shortly after sent to Corinth with a single ship and a small sum of money. Born and educated in the most splendid court and the most absolute monarchy that ever was, which he held and kept up for the space of ten years succeeding his father's death, he had, after Dion's expedition, spent twelve other years in a continual agitation of wars and contests, and great variety of fortune, during which time all the mischiefs he had committed in his former reign were more than repaid by the ills he himself then suffered, since he lived to see the deaths of his sons in the prime and vigour of their age, and the rape of his daughters in the flower of their virginity, and the wicked abuse of his sister and his wife, who, after being first exposed to all the lawless insults of the soldiery, was then murdered with her children, and cast into the sea; the particulars of which are more exactly given in the life of Dion.

Upon the news of his landing at Corinth, there was hardly a man in Greece who had not the curiosity to come and view the late formidable tyrant, and say some words to him; part, rejoicing at his disasters, were led thither out of mere spite and hatred, that they might have the pleasure of trampling, as it were, on the ruins of his broken fortune; but others, letting their attention and their sympathy turn rather to the changes and revolutions of his life, could not but see in them a proof of the strength and potency with which divine and unseen causes operate amidst the weakness of human and visible things. For neither art nor nature did in that age produce anything comparable to this work and wonder of fortune which showed the very same man, that was not long before supreme monarch of Sicily, loitering about perhaps in the fish market, or sitting in a perfumer's shop drinking the diluted wine of taverns, or squabbling in the street with common women, or pretending to instruct the singing women of the theatre, and seriously disputing with them about the measure and harmony of pieces of music that were performed there. Such behaviour on his part was variously criticised. He was thought by many to act thus out of pure compliance with his own natural indolent and vicious inclinations; while finer judges were of the opinion, that in all this he was playing a politic part, with a design to be contemned among them, and that the Corinthians might not feel any apprehension or suspicion of his being uneasy under his reverse of fortune, or solicitous to retrieve it; to avoid which danger, he purposely and against his true nature affected an appearance of folly and want of spirit in his private life and amusements.

However it be, there are sayings and repartees of his left still upon record, which seem to show that he not ignobly accommodated himself to his present circumstances; as may appear in part from the ingenuousness of the avowal he made on coming to Leucadia, which, as well as Syracuse, was a Corinthian colony, where he told the inhabitants that he found himself not unlike boys who had been in fault, who can talk cheerfully with their brothers, but are ashamed to see their father; so likewise he, he said, could gladly reside with them in that island, whereas he felt a certain awe upon his mind which made him averse to the sight of Corinth, that was a common mother to them both. The thing is further evident from the reply he once made to a stranger in Corinth, who deriding him in a rude and scornful manner about the conferences he used to have with philosophers, whose company had been one of his pleasures while yet a monarch, and demanding, in fine, what he was the better now for all those wise and learned discourses of Plato, "Do you think," said he, "I have made no profit of his philosophy when you see me bear my change of fortune as I do?" And when Aristoxenus the musician, and several others, desired to know how Plato offended him, and what had been the ground of his displeasure with him, he made answer that, of the many evils attaching to the condition of sovereignty, the one greatest infelicity was that none of those who were accounted friends would venture to speak freely, or tell the plain truth; and that by means of such he had been deprived of Plato's kindness. At another time, when one of those pleasant companions that are desirous to pass for wits, in mockery to Dionysius, as if he were still the tyrant, shook out the folds of his cloak, as he was entering into a room where he was, to show there were no concealed weapons about him, Dionysius, by way of retort, observed, that he would prefer he would do so on leaving the room, as a security that he was carrying nothing off with him. And when Philip of Macedon, at a drinking party, began to speak in banter about the verses and tragedies which his father, Dionysius the elder, had left behind him, and pretended to wonder how he could get anytime from his other business to compose such elaborate and ingenious pieces, he replied, very much to the purpose, "It was at those leisurable hours, which such as you and I, and those we call happy men, bestow upon our cups." Plato had not the opportunity to see Dionysius at Corinth, being already dead before he came thither; but Diogenes of Sinope, at their first meeting in the street there, saluted him with the ambiguous expression, "O Dionysius, how little you deserve your present life!" Upon which Dionysius stopped and replied, "I thank you, Diogenes, for your condolence." "Condole with you!" replied Diogenes; "do you not suppose that, on the contrary, I am indignant that such a slave as you, who, if you had your due, should have been let alone to grow old and die in the state of tyranny, as your father did before you, should now enjoy the ease of private persons, and be here to sport and frolic in our society?" So that when I compare those sad stories of Philistus, touching the daughters of Leptines, where he makes pitiful moan on their behalf, as fallen from all the blessings and advantages of powerful greatness to the miseries of an humble life, they seem to me like the lamentations of a woman who has lost her box of ointment, her purple dresses, and her golden trinkets. Such anecdotes will not, I conceive, be thought either foreign to my purpose of writing Lives, or unprofitable in themselves, by such readers as are not in too much haste, or busied and taken up with other concerns.

But if the misfortune of Dionysius appears strange and extraordinary, we shall have no less reason to wonder at the good fortune of Timoleon, who, within fifty days after his landing in Sicily, both recovered the citadel of Syracuse and sent Dionysius an exile into Peloponnesus. This lucky beginning so animated the Corinthians, that they ordered him a supply of two thousand foot and two hundred horse, who, reaching Thurii, intended to cross over thence into Sicily; but finding the whole sea beset with Carthaginian ships, which made their passage impracticable, they were constrained to stop there, and watch their opportunity: which time, however, was employed in a noble action. For the Thurians, going out to war against their Bruttian enemies, left their city in charge with these Corinthian strangers, who defended it as carefully as if it had been their own country, and faithfully resigned it up again.

Hicetes, in the interim, continued still to besiege the castle of Syracuse, and hindered all provisions from coming in by sea to relieve the Corinthians that were in it. He had engaged also, and despatched towards Adranum, two unknown foreigners to assassinate Timoleon, who at no time kept any standing guard about his person, and was then altogether secure, diverting himself, without any apprehension, among the citizens of the place, it being a festival in honour of their gods. The two men that were sent, having casually heard that Timoleon was about to sacrifice, came directly into the temple with poniards under their cloaks, and pressing in among the crowd, by little and little got up close to the altar; but, as they were just looking for a sign from each other to begin the attempt, a third person struck one of them over the head with a sword, upon whose sudden fall, neither he that gave the blow, nor the partisan of him that received it, kept their stations any longer; but the one, making way with his bloody sword, put no stop to his flight, till he gained the top of a certain lofty precipice, while the other, laying hold of the altar, besought Timoleon to spare his life, and he would reveal to him the whole conspiracy. His pardon being granted, he confessed that both himself and his dead companion were sent thither purposely to slay him. While this discovery was made, he that killed the other conspirator had been fetched down from his sanctuary of the rock, loudly and often protesting, as he came along, that there was no injustice in the fact, as he had only taken righteous vengeance for his father's blood, whom this man had murdered before in the city of Leontini; the truth of which was attested by several there present, who could not choose but wonder too at the strange dexterity of fortune's operations, the facility with which she makes one event the spring and motion to something wholly different, uniting every scattered accident and loose particular and remote action, and interweaving them together to serve her purpose; so that things that in themselves seem to have no connection or interdependence whatsoever, become in her hands, so to say, the end and the beginning of each other. The Corinthians, satisfied as to the innocence of this seasonable feat, honoured and rewarded the author with a present of ten pounds in their money, since he had, as it were, lent the use of his just resentment to the tutelar genius that seemed to be protecting Timoleon, and had not pre-expended this anger, so long ago conceived, but had reserved and deferred, under fortune's guidance, for his preservation, the revenge of a private quarrel.

But this fortunate escape had effects and consequences beyond the present, as it inspired the highest hopes and future expectations of Timoleon, making people reverence and protect him as a sacred person sent by heaven to revenge and redeem Sicily. Hicetes, having missed his aim in this enterprise, and perceiving, also, that many went off and sided with Timoleon, began to chide himself for his foolish modesty, that, when so considerable a force of the Carthaginians lay ready to be commanded by him, he had employed them hitherto by degrees and in small numbers, introducing their reinforcements by stealth and clandestinely, as if he had been ashamed of the action. Therefore, now laying aside his former nicety, he calls in Mago, their admiral, with his whole navy, who presently set sail, and seized upon the port with a formidable fleet of at least a hundred and fifty vessels, landing there sixty thousand foot, which were all lodged within the city of Syracuse; so that, in all men's opinion, the time anciently talked of and long expected, wherein Sicily should be subjugated by barbarians, was now come to its fatal period. For in all their preceding wars and many desperate conflicts with Sicily, the Carthaginians had never been able, before this, to take Syracuse; whereas Hicetes now receiving them and putting them into their hands, you might see it become now as it were a camp of barbarians. By this means, the Corinthian soldiers that kept the castle found themselves brought into great danger and hardship; as, besides that their provision grew scarce, and they began to be in want, because the havens were strictly guarded and blocked up, the enemy exercised them still with skirmishes and combats about their walls, and they were not only obliged to be continually in arms, but to divide and prepare themselves for assaults and encounters of every kind, and to repel every variety of the means of offence employed by a besieging army.

Timoleon made shift to relieve them in these straits, sending corn from Catana by small fishing boats and little skiffs, which commonly gained a passage through the Carthaginian galleys in times of storm, stealing up when the blockading ships were driven apart and dispersed by the stress of weather; which Mago and Hicetes observing, they agreed to fall upon Catana, from whence these supplies were brought in to the besieged, and accordingly put off from Syracuse, taking with them the best soldiers in their whole army. Upon this Neon the Corinthian, who was captain of those that kept the citadel, taking notice that the enemies who stayed there behind were very negligent and careless in keeping guard, made a sudden sally upon them as they lay scattered, and, killing some and putting others to flight, he took and possessed himself of that quarter which they call Acradina, and was thought to be the strongest and most impregnable part of Syracuse, a city made up and compacted, as it were, of several towns put together. Having thus stored himself with corn and money, he did not abandon the place, nor retire again into the castle, but fortifying the precincts of Acradina, and joining it by works to the citadel, he undertook the defence of both. Mago and Hicetes were now come near to Catana, when a horseman, despatched from Syracuse, brought them tidings that Acradina was taken; upon which they returned, in all haste, with great disorder and confusion, having neither been able to reduce the city they went against, nor to preserve that they were masters of.

These successes, indeed, were such as might leave foresight and courage a pretence still of disputing it with fortune, which contributed most to the result. But the next following event can scarcely be ascribed to anything but pure felicity. The Corinthian soldiers who stayed at Thurii, partly for fear of the Carthaginian galleys which lay in wait for them under the command of Hanno, and partly because of tempestuous weather which had lasted for many days, and rendered the sea dangerous, took a resolution to march by land over the Bruttian territories, and what with persuasion and force together, made good their passage through those barbarians to the city of Rhegium, the sea being still rough and raging as before. But Hanno, not expecting the Corinthians would venture out, and supposing it would be useless to wait there any longer, bethought himself, as he imagined, of a most ingenious and clever stratagem apt to delude and ensnare the enemy; in pursuance of which he commanded the seamen to crown themselves with garlands, and adorning his galleys with bucklers both of the Greek and Carthaginian make, he sailed away for Syracuse in this triumphant equipage, and using all his oars as he passed under the castle with much shouting and laughter, cried out, on purpose to dishearten the besieged, that he was come from vanquishing and taking the Corinthian succours, which he fell upon at sea as they were passing over into Sicily. While he was thus trifling and playing his tricks before Syracuse, the Corinthians, now come as far as Rhegium, observing the coast clear, and that the wind was laid, as it were by miracle, to afford them in all appearance a quiet and smooth passage, went immediately aboard on such little barks and fishing boats as were then at hand, and got over to Sicily with such complete safety and in such an extraordinary calm, that they drew their horses by the reins, swimming along by them as the vessels went across.

When they were all landed, Timoleon came to receive them, and by their means at once obtained possession of Messena, from whence he marched in good order to Syracuse, trusting more to his late prosperous achievements than his present strength, as the whole army he had then with him did not exceed the number of four thousand: Mago, however, was troubled and fearful at the first notice of his coming, and grew more apprehensive and jealous still upon the following occasion. The marshes about Syracuse, that receive a great deal of fresh water, as well from springs as from lakes and rivers discharging themselves into the sea, breed abundance of eels, which may be always taken there in great quantities by any that will fish for them. The mercenary soldiers that served on both sides were wont to follow the sport together at their vacant hours, and upon any cessation of arms; who being all Greeks, and having no cause of private enmity to each other, as they would venture bravely in fight, so in times of truce used to meet and converse amicably together. And at this present time, while engaged about this common business of fishing, they fell into talk together; and some expressing their admiration of the neighbouring sea, and others telling how much they were taken with the convenience and commodiousness of the buildings and public works, one of the Corinthian party took occasion to demand of the others: "And is it possible that you who are Grecians born should be so forward to reduce a city of this greatness, and enjoying so many rare advantages, into the state of barbarism; and lend your assistance to plant Carthaginians, that are the worst and bloodiest of men, so much the nearer to us? Whereas you should rather wish there were many more Sicilies to lie between them and Greece. Have you so little sense as to believe, that they come hither with an army, from the Pillars of Hercules and the Atlantic Sea, to hazard themselves for the establishment of Hicetes? Who, if he had had the consideration which becomes a general, would never have thrown out his ancestors and founders to bring in the enemies of his country in the room of them, when he might have enjoyed all suitable honour and command, with consent of Timoleon and the rest of Corinth." The Greeks that were in pay with Hicetes, noising these discourses about their camp, gave Mago some ground to suspect, as indeed he had long sought for a pretence to be gone, that there was treachery contrived against him; so that, although Hicetes entreated him to tarry, and made it appear how much stronger they were than the enemy, yet, conceiving they came far more short of Timoleon in respect of courage and fortune than they surpassed him in number, he presently went aboard and set sail for Africa, letting Sicily escape out of his hands with dishonour to himself, and for such uncertain causes, that no human reason could give an account of his departure.

The day after he went away, Timoleon came up before the city in array for a battle. But when he and his company heard of this sudden flight, and saw the docks all empty, they could not forbear laughing at the cowardice of Mago, and in mockery caused proclamation to be made through the city that a reward would be given to anyone who could bring them tidings whither the Carthaginian fleet had conveyed itself from them. However, Hicetes resolving to fight it out alone, and not quitting his hold of the city, but sticking close to the quarters he was in possession of, places that were well fortified and not easy to be attacked, Timoleon divided his forces into three parts, and fell himself upon the side where the river Anapas ran, which was most strong and difficult of access; and he commanded those that were led by Isias, a Corinthian captain, to make their assault from the post of Acradina, while Dinarchus and Demaretus, that brought him the last supply from Corinth, were, with a third division, to attempt the quarter called Epipolæ. A considerable impression being made from every side at once, the soldiers of Hicetes were beaten off and put to flight; and this—that the city came to be taken by storm, and fall suddenly into their hands, upon the defeat and rout of the enemy—we must in all justice ascribe to the valour of the assailants and the wise conduct of their general; but that not so much as a man of the Corinthians was either slain or wounded in the action, this the good fortune of Timoleon seems to challenge for her own work, as though, in a sort of rivalry with his own personal exertions, she made it her aim to exceed and obscure his actions by her favours, that those who heard him commended for his noble deeds might rather admire the happiness than the merit of them. For the fame of what was done not only passed through all Sicily, and filled Italy with wonder, but even Greece itself, after a few days, came to ring with the greatness of his exploit; insomuch that those of Corinth, who had as yet no certainty that their auxiliaries were landed on the island, had tidings brought them at the same time that they were safe and were conquerors. In so prosperous a course did affairs run, and such was the speed and celerity of execution with which fortune, as with a new ornament, set off the native lustres of the performance.

Timoleon, being master of the citadel, avoided the error which Dion had been guilty of. He spared not the place for the beauty and sumptuousness of its fabric, and, keeping clear of those suspicions which occasioned first the unpopularity and afterwards the fall of Dion, made a public crier give notice that all the Syracusans who were willing to have a hand in the work should bring pick-axes and mattocks, and other instruments, and help him to demolish the fortifications of the tyrants. When they all came up with one accord, looking upon that order and that day as the surest foundation of their liberty, they not only pulled down the castle, but overturned the palaces and monuments adjoining, and whatever else might preserve any memory of former tyrants. Having soon levelled and cleared the place, he there presently erected courts for administration of justice, ratifying the citizens by this means, and building popular government on the fall and ruin of tyranny. But since he had recovered a city destitute of inhabitants, some of them dead in civil wars and insurrections, and others being fled to escape tyrants, so that through solitude and want of people the great market place of Syracuse was overgrown with such quantity of rank herbage that it became a pasture for their horses, the grooms lying along in the grass as they fed by them; while also other towns, very few excepted, were become full of stags and wild boars, so that those who had nothing else to do went frequently a-hunting, and found game in the suburbs and about the walls; and not one of those who possessed themselves of castles, or made garrisons in the country, could be persuaded to quit their present abode, or would accept an invitation to return back into the city, so much did they all dread and abhor the very name of assemblies and forms of government and public speaking, that had produced the greater part of those usurpers who had successively assumed a dominion over them—Timoleon, therefore, with the Syracusans that remained, considering this vast desolation, and how little hope there was to have it otherwise supplied, thought good to write to the Corinthians, requesting that they would send a colony out of Greece to re-people Syracuse. For else the land about it would lie unimproved; and besides this, they expected to be involved in a greater war from Africa, having news brought them that Mago had killed himself, and that the Carthaginians, out of rage for his ill-conduct in the late expedition, had caused his body to be nailed upon a cross, and that they were raising a mighty force, with design to make their descent upon Sicily the next summer.

These letters from Timoleon being delivered at Corinth, and the ambassadors of Syracuse beseeching them at the same time that they would take upon them the care of their poor city, and once again become the founders of it, the Corinthians were not tempted by any feeling of cupidity to lay hold of the advantage. Nor did they seize and appropriate the city to themselves, but going about first to the games that are kept as sacred in Greece, and to the most numerously attended religious assemblages, they made publication by heralds, that the Corinthians, having destroyed the usurpation at Syracuse and driven out the tyrant, did thereby invite the Syracusan exiles, and any other Siceliots, to return and inhabit the city, with full enjoyment of freedom under their own laws, the land being divided among them in just and equal proportions. And after this, sending messengers into Asia and the several islands where they understood that most of the scattered fugitives were then residing, they bade them all repair to Corinth, engaging that the Corinthians would afford them vessels and commanders, and a safe convoy, at their own charges, to Syracuse. Such generous proposals, being thus spread about, gained them the just and honourable recompense of general praise and benediction, for delivering the country from oppressors, and saving it from barbarians, and restoring it at length to the rightful owners of the place. These, when they were assembled at Corinth, and found how insufficient their company was, besought the Corinthians that they might have a supplement of other persons, as well out of their city as the rest of Greece, to go with them as joint colonists; and so raising themselves to the number of ten thousand, they sailed together to Syracuse. By this time great multitudes, also, from Italy and Sicily had flocked in to Timoleon, so that, as Athanis reports, their entire body amounted now to sixty thousand men. Among these he divided the whole territory, and sold the houses for a thousand talents; by which method he both left it in the power of the old Syracusans to redeem their own, and made it a means also for raising a stock for the community, which had been so much impoverished of late and was so unable to defray other expenses, and especially those of a war, that they exposed their very statues to sale, a regular process being observed, and sentence of auction passed upon each of them by majority of votes, as if they had been so many criminals taking their trial; in the course of which it is said that while condemnation was pronounced upon all other statues, that of the ancient usurper Gelo was exempted, out of admiration and honour and for the sake of the victory he gained over the Carthaginian forces at the river Himera.

Syracuse being thus happily revived, and replenished again by the general concourse of inhabitants from all parts, Timoleon was desirous now to rescue other cities from the like bondage, and wholly and once for all to extirpate arbitrary government out of Sicily. And for this purpose marching in to the territories of those that used it, he compelled Hicetes first to renounce the Carthaginian interest, and, demolishing the fortresses which were held by him, to live henceforth among the Leontinians as a private person. Leptines, also, the tyrant of Apollonia and divers other little towns, after some resistance made, seeing the danger he was in of being taken by force, surrendered himself; upon which Timoleon spared his life, and sent him away to Corinth, counting it a glorious thing that the mother city should expose to the view of other Greeks these Sicilian tyrants, living now in an exiled and a low condition. After this he returned to Syracuse, that he might have leisure to attend to the establishment of the new constitution, and assist Cephalus and Dionysius, who were sent from Corinth to make laws, in determining the most important points of it. In the meanwhile, desirous that his hired soldiers should not want action, but might rather enrich themselves by some plunder from the enemy, he despatched Dinarchus and Demaretus with a portion of them into the part of the island belonging to the Carthaginians, where they obliged several cities to revolt from the barbarians, and not only lived in great abundance themselves, but raised money from their spoil to carry on the war.

Meantime, the Carthaginians landed at the promontory of Lilybæum, bringing with them an army of seventy thousand men on board two hundred galleys, besides a thousand other vessels laden with engines of battery, chariots, corn, and other military stores, as if they did not intend to manage the war by piecemeal and in parts as heretofore, but to drive the Greeks altogether and at once out of all Sicily. And indeed it was a force sufficient to overpower the Siceliots, even though they had been at perfect union among themselves, and had never been enfeebled by intestine quarrels. Hearing that part of their subject territory was suffering devastation, they forthwith made toward the Corinthians with great fury, having Asdrubal and Hamilcar for their generals; the report of whose numbers and strength coming suddenly to Syracuse, the citizens were so terrified, that hardly three thousand, among so many myriads of them, had the courage to take up arms and join Timoleon. The foreigners, serving for pay, were not above four thousand in all, and about a thousand of these grew fainthearted by the way, and forsook Timoleon in his march towards the enemy, looking on him as frantic and distracted, destitute of the sense which might have been expected from his time of life, thus to venture out against an army of seventy thousand men, with no more than five thousand foot and a thousand horse; and, when he should have kept those forces to defend the city, choosing rather to remove them eight days' journey from Syracuse, so that if they were beaten from the field, they would have no retreat, nor any burial if they fell upon it. Timoleon, however, reckoned it some kind of advantage, that these had thus discovered themselves before the battle, and encouraging the rest, led them with all speed to the river Crimesus, where it was told him the Carthaginians were drawn together.

As he was marching up an ascent, from the top of which they expected to have a view of the army and of the strength of the enemy, there met him by chance a train of mules loaded with parsley; which his soldiers conceived to be an ominous occurrence or ill-boding token, because this is the herb with which we not unfrequently adorn the sepulchres of the dead; and there is a proverb derived from the custom, used of one who is dangerously sick, that he has need of nothing but parsley. So to ease their minds, and free them from any superstitious thoughts or forebodings of evil, Timoleon halted, and concluded an address suitable to the occasion, by saying, that a garland of triumph was here luckily brought them, and had fallen into their hands of its own accord, as an anticipation of victory: the same with which the Corinthians crown the victors in the Isthmian games, accounting chaplets of parsley the sacred wreath proper to their country; parsley being at that time still the emblem of victory at the Isthmian, as it is now at the Nemean sports; and it is not so very long ago that the pine first began to be used in its place.

Timoleon, therefore, having thus bespoke his soldiers, took part of the parsley, and with it made himself a chaplet first, his captains and their companies all following the example of their leader. The soothsayers then, observing also two eagles on the wing towards them, one of which bore a snake struck through with her talons, and the other, as she flew, uttered a loud cry indicating boldness and assurance, at once showed them to the soldiers, who with one consent fell to supplicate the gods, and call them in to their assistance. It was now about the beginning of summer, and conclusion of the month called Thargelion, not far from the solstice; and the river sending up a thick mist, all the adjacent plain was at first darkened with the fog, so that for a while they could discern nothing from the enemy's camp; only a confused buzz and undistinguished mixture of voices came up to the hill from the distant motions and clamours of so vast a multitude. When the Corinthians had mounted, and stood on the top, and had laid down their bucklers to take breath and repose themselves, the sun coming round and drawing up the vapours from below, the gross foggy air that was now gathered and condensed above formed in a cloud upon the mountains; and, all the under places being clear and open, the river Crimesus appeared to them again, and they could descry the enemies passing over it, first with their formidable four-horse chariots of war, and then ten thousand footmen bearing white shields, whom they guessed to be all Carthaginians, from the splendour of their arms, and the slowness and order of their march. And when now the troops of various other nations, flowing in behind them, began to throng for passage in a tumultuous and unruly manner, Timoleon, perceiving that the river gave them opportunity to single off whatever number of their enemies they had a mind to engage at once, and bidding his soldiers observe how their forces were divided into two separate bodies by the intervention of the stream, some being already over, and others still to ford it, gave Demaretus command to fall in upon the Carthaginians with his horse, and disturb their ranks before they should be drawn up into form of battle; and coming down into the plain himself forming his right and left wing of other Sicilians, intermingling only a few strangers in each, he placed the natives of Syracuse in the middle, with the stoutest mercenaries he had about his own person; and waiting a little to observe the action of his horse, when they saw they were not only hindered from grappling with the Carthaginians by the armed chariots that ran to and fro before the army, but forced continually to wheel about to escape having their ranks broken, and so to repeat their charges anew, he took his buckler in his hand, and crying out to the foot that they should follow him with courage and confidence, he seemed to speak with a more than human accent, and a voice stronger than ordinary; whether it were that he naturally raised it so high in the vehemence and ardour with his mind to assault the enemy, or else, as many then thought, some god or other spoke with him. When his soldiers quickly gave an echo to it, and besought him to lead them on without any further delay, he made a sign to the horse, that they should draw off from the front where the chariots were, and pass sidewards to attack their enemies in the flank; then, making his vanguard firm by joining man to man and buckler to buckler, he caused the trumpet to sound, and so bore in upon the Carthaginians.

They, for their part, stoutly received and sustained his first onset; and having their bodies armed with breast-plates of iron, and helmets of brass on their heads, besides great bucklers to cover and secure them, they could easily repel the charge of the Greek spears. But when the business came to a decision by the sword, where mastery depends no less upon art than strength, all on a sudden from the mountain-tops violent peals of thunder and vivid flashes of lightning broke out; following upon which the darkness, that had been hovering about the higher grounds and the crests of the hills, descending to the place of battle and bringing a tempest of rain and of wind and hail along with it, was driven upon the Greeks behind, and fell only at their backs, but discharged itself in the very faces of the barbarians, the rain beating on them, and the lightning dazzling them without cessation; annoyances that in many ways distressed at any rate the inexperienced, who had not been used to such hardships, and, in particular, the claps of thunder, and the noise of the rain and hail beating on their arms, kept them from hearing the commands of their officers. Besides which, the very mud also was a great hindrance to the Carthaginians, who were not lightly equipped, but, as I said before, loaded with heavy armour; and then their shirts underneath getting drenched, the foldings about the bosom filled with water, grew unwieldy and cumbersome to them as they fought, and made it easy for the Greeks to throw them down, and, when they were once down, impossible for them, under that weight, to disengage themselves and rise again with weapons in their hands. The river Crimesus, too, swollen partly by the rain, and partly by the stoppage of its course with the numbers that were passing through, overflowed its banks; and the level ground by the side of it, being so situated as to have a number of small ravines and hollows of the hillside descending upon it, was now filled with rivulets and currents that had no certain channel, in which the Carthaginians stumbled and rolled about, and found themselves in great difficulty. So that, in fine, the storm bearing still upon them, and the Greeks having cut in pieces four hundred men of their first ranks, the whole body of their army began to fly. Great numbers were overtaken in the plain, and put to the sword there; and many of them, as they were making their way back through the river, falling foul upon others that were yet coming over, were borne away and overwhelmed by the waters; but the major part, attempting to get up the hill so as to make their escape, were intercepted and destroyed by the light-armed troops. It is said that, of ten thousand who lay dead after the fight, three thousand, at least, were Carthaginian citizens; a heavy loss and great grief to their countrymen; those that fell being men inferior to none among them as to birth, wealth, or reputation. Nor do their records mention that so many native Carthaginians were ever cut off before in any-one battle; as they usually employed Africans, Spaniards, and Numidians in their wars, so that if they chanced to be defeated, it was still at the cost and damage of other nations.

The Greeks easily discovered of what condition and account the slain were by the richness of their spoils; for when they came to collect the booty, there was little reckoning made either of brass or iron, so abundant were better metals, and so common were silver and gold. Passing over the river, they became masters of their camp and carriages. As for captives, a great many of them were stolen away and sold privately by the soldiers, but about five thousand were brought in and delivered up for the benefit of the public; two hundred of their chariots of war were also taken. The tent of Timoleon then presented a most glorious and magnificent appearance, being heaped up and hung round with every variety of spoils and military ornaments, among which there were a thousand breastplates of rare workmanship and beauty, and bucklers to the number of ten thousand. The victors being but few to strip so many that were vanquished, and having such valuable booty to occupy them, it was the third day after the fight before they could erect and finish the trophy of their conquest. Timoleon sent tidings of his victory to Corinth, with the best and goodliest arms he had taken as a proof of it; that he thus might render his country an object of emulation to the whole world, when, of all the cities of Greece, men should there alone behold the chief temples adorned, not with Grecian spoils, nor offerings obtained by the bloodshed and plunder of their own countrymen and kindred, and attended, therefore, with sad and unhappy remembrances, but with such as had been stripped from barbarians and enemies to their nation, with the noblest titles inscribed upon them, titles telling of the justice as well as fortitude of the conquerors; namely, that the people of Corinth, and Timoleon their general, having redeemed the Greeks of Sicily from Carthaginian bondage, made oblation of these to the gods, in grateful acknowledgment of their favour.

Having done this, he left his hired soldiers in the enemy's country to drive and carry away all they could throughout the subject-territory of Carthage, and so marched with the rest of his army to Syracuse, where he issued an edict for banishing the thousand mercenaries who had basely deserted him before the battle, and obliged them to quit the city before sunset. They, sailing into Italy, lost their lives there by the hands of the Bruttians, in spite of a public assurance of safety previously given them; thus receiving, from the divine power, a just reward of their own treachery. Mamercus, however, the tyrant of Catana, and Hicetes, after all, either envying Timoleon the glory of his exploits, or fearing him as one that would keep no agreement, or having any peace with tyrants, made a league with the Carthaginians, and pressed them much to send a new army and commander into Sicily, unless they would be content to hazard all and to be wholly ejected out of that island. And in consequence of this, Gisco was despatched with a navy of seventy sail. He took numerous Greek mercenaries also into pay, that being the first time they had ever been enlisted for the Carthaginian service; but then it seems the Carthaginians began to admire them, as the most irresistible soldiers of all mankind. Uniting their forces in the territory of Messena, they cut off four hundred of Timoleon's paid soldiers, and within the dependencies of Carthage, at a place called Hieræ, destroyed, by an ambuscade, the whole body of mercenaries that served under Euthymus the Leucadian; which accidents, however, made the good fortune of Timoleon accounted all the more remarkable, as these were the men that, with Philomelus of Phocis and Onomarchus, had forcibly broken into the temple of Apollo at Delphi, and were partakers with them in the sacrilege; so that being hated and shunned by all, as persons under a curse, they were constrained to wander about in Peloponnesus; when, for want of others, Timoleon was glad to take them into service in his expedition for Sicily, where they were successful in whatever enterprise they attempted under his conduct. But now, when all the important dangers were past, on his sending them out for the relief and defence of his party in several places, they perished and were destroyed at a distance from him, not all together, but in small parties; and the vengeance which was destined for them, so accommodating itself to the good fortune which guarded Timoleon as not to allow any harm or prejudice for good men to arise from the punishment of the wicked, the benevolence and kindness which the gods had for Timoleon was thus as distinctly recognised in his disasters as in his successes.

What most annoyed the Syracusans was their being insulted and mocked by the tyrants; as, for example, by Mamercus, who valued himself much upon his gift for writing poems and tragedies, and took occasion, when coming to present the gods with the bucklers of the hired soldiers whom he had killed, to make a boast of his victory in an insulting elegiac inscription:

> These shields with purple, gold, and ivory wrought,
> Were won by us that but with poor ones fought.

After this, while Timoleon marched to Calauria, Hicetes made an inroad into the borders of Syracuse, where he met with considerable booty, and having done much mischief and havoc, returned back to Calauria itself, in contempt of Timoleon and the slender force he had then with him. He, suffering Hicetes to pass forward, pursued him with his horsemen and light infantry, which Hicetes perceiving, crossed the river Damyrias, and then stood in a posture to receive him; the difficulty of the passage, and the height and steepness of the bank on each side, giving advantage enough to make him confident. A strange contention and dispute, meantime, among the officers of Timoleon a little retarded the conflict; no one of them was willing to let another pass over before him to engage the enemy; each man claiming it as a right to venture first and begin the onset; so that their fording was likely to be tumultuous and without order, a mere general struggle which should be the foremost. Timoleon, therefore, desiring to decide the quarrel by lot, took a ring from each of the pretenders, which he cast into his own cloak, and, after he had shaken all together, the first he drew out had, by good fortune, the figure of a trophy engraved as a seal upon it; at the sight of which the young captains all shouted for joy, and, without waiting any longer to see how chance would determine it for the rest, took every man his way through the river with all the speed they could make, and fell to blows with the enemies, who were not able to bear up against the violence of their attack, but fled in haste and left their arms behind them all alike, and a thousand dead upon the place.

Not long after, Timoleon, marching up to the city of the Leontines, took Hicetes alive, and his son Eupolemus, and Euthymus, the commander of his horse, who were bound and brought to him by their own soldiers. Hicetes and the stripling his son were then executed as tyrants and traitors; and Euthymus, though a brave man, and one of singular courage, could obtain no mercy, because he was charged with contemptuous language in disparagement of the Corinthians when they first sent their forces into Sicily; it is said that he told the Leontini in a speech that the news did not sound terrible, nor was any great danger to be feared because of—

Corinthian women coming out of doors.

So true it is that men are usually more stung and galled by reproachful words than hostile actions: and they bear an affront with less patience than an injury; to do harm and mischief by deeds is counted pardonable from the enemies, as nothing less can be expected in a state of war; whereas virulent and contumelious words appear to be the expression of needless hatred, and to proceed from an excess of rancour.

When Timoleon came back to Syracuse, the citizens brought the wives and daughters of Hicetes and his son to a public trial, and condemned and put them to death. This seems to be the least pleasing action of Timoleon's life; since if he had interposed, the unhappy women would have been spared. He would appear to have disregarded the thing, and to have given them up to the citizens, who were eager to take vengeance for the wrongs done to Dion, who expelled Dionysius; since it was this very Hicetes who took Arete the wife and Aristomache the sister of Dion with a son that had not yet passed his childhood, and threw them all together into the sea alive, as related in the life of Dion.

After this, he moved towards Catana against Mamercus, who gave him battle near the river Abolus, and was overthrown and put to flight, losing above two thousand men, a considerable part of whom were the Phœnician troops sent by Gisco to his assistance. After this defeat the Carthaginians sued for peace; which was granted on the conditions that they should confine themselves to the country within the river Lycus, that those of the inhabitants who wished to remove to the Syracusan territories should be allowed to depart with their whole families and fortunes, and, lastly, that Carthage should renounce all engagements to the tyrants. Mamercus, now forsaken and despairing of success, took ship for Italy with the design of bringing in the Lucanians against Timoleon and the people of Syracuse: but the men in his galleys turning back and landing again and delivering up Catana to Timoleon, thus obliged him to fly for his own safety to Messena, where Hippo was tyrant. Timoleon, however, coming up against them, and besieging the city both by sea and land, Hippo, fearful of the event, endeavoured to slip away in a vessel; which the people of Messena surprised as it was putting off, and seizing on his person, and bringing all their children from school into the theatre, to witness the glorious spectacle of a tyrant punished, they first publicly scourged and then put him to death. Mamercus made surrender of himself to Timoleon, with the proviso that he should be tried at Syracuse and Timoleon should take no part in his accusation. Thither he was brought accordingly, and presenting himself to plead before the people, he essayed to pronounce an oration he had long before composed in his own defence; but finding himself interrupted by noise and clamours, and observing from their aspect and demeanour that the assembly was inexorable, he threw off his upper garment, and running across the theatre as hard as he could, dashed his head against one of the stones under the seats with intention to have killed himself; but he had not the fortune to perish as he designed, but was taken up alive, and suffered the death of a robber.

Thus did Timoleon cut the nerves of tyranny and put a period to the wars; and, whereas, at his first entering upon Sicily, the island was as it were become wild again, and was hateful to the very natives on account of the evils and miseries they suffered there, he so civilised and restored it, and rendered it so desirable to all men, that even strangers now came by sea to inhabit those towns and places which their own citizens had formerly forsaken and left desolate. Agrigentum and Gela, two famous cities that had been ruined and laid waste by the Carthaginians after the Attic war, were then peopled again, the one by Megellus and Pheristus from Elea, the other by Gorgus, from the island of Ceos, partly with new settlers, partly with the old inhabitants whom they collected again from various parts; to all of whom Timoleon not only afforded a secure and peaceful abode after so obstinate a war, but was further so zealous in assisting and providing for them that he was honoured among them as their founder.

Similar feelings also possessed to such a degree all the rest of the Sicilians that there was no proposal for peace, nor reformation of laws, nor assignation of land, nor reconstruction of government, which they could think well of, unless he lent his aid as a chief architect, to finish and adorn the work, and superadd some touches from his own hand, which might render it pleasing both to God and man.

Although Greece had in his time produced several persons of extraordinary worth, and much renowned for their achievements, such as Timotheus and Agesilaus and Pelopidas and (Timoleon's chief model) Epaminondas, yet the lustre of their best actions was obscured by a degree of violence and labour, insomuch that some of them were matter of blame and of repentance; whereas there is not anyone act of Timoleon's, setting aside the necessity he was placed under in reference to his brother, to which, as Timæus observes, we may not fitly apply that exclamation of Sophocles—

> O gods! What Venus, or what grace divine,
> Did here with human workmanship combine?

For as the poetry of Antimachus, and the painting of Dionysius, the artists of Colophon, though full of force and vigour, yet appeared to be strained and elaborate in comparison with the pictures of Nicomachus and the verses of Homer, which, besides their general strength and beauty, have the peculiar charm of seeming to have been executed with perfect ease and readiness; so the expeditions and acts of Epaminondas or Agesilaus, that were full of toil and effort, when compared with the easy and natural as well as noble and glorious achievements of Timoleon, compel our fair and unbiased judgment to pronounce the latter not indeed the effect of fortune, but the success of fortunate merit. Though he himself indeed ascribed that success to the sole favour of fortune; and both in the letters which he wrote to his friends at Corinth, and in the speeches he made to the people of Syracuse, he would say, that he was thankful unto God, who, designing to save Sicily, was pleased to honour him with the name and title of the deliverance he vouchsafed it. And having built a chapel in his house, he there sacrificed to Good Hap, as a deity that had favoured him, and devoted the house itself to the Sacred Genius; it being a house which the Syracusans had selected for him, as a special reward and monument of his brave exploits, granting him together with it the most agreeable and beautiful piece of land in the whole country, where he kept his residence for the most part, and enjoyed a private life with his wife and children, who came to him from Corinth. For he returned thither no more, unwilling to be concerned in the broils and tumults of Greece, or to expose himself to public envy (the fatal mischief which great commanders continually run into, from the insatiable appetite for honours and authority); but wisely chose to spend the remainder of his days in Sicily, and there partake of the blessings he himself had procured, the greatest of which was to behold so many cities flourish, and so many thousands of people live happy through his means.

As, however, not only, as Simonides says, "on every lark must grow a crest," but also in every democracy there must spring up a false accuser, so was it at Syracuse: two of their popular spokesmen, Laphystius and Demænetus by name, fell to slander Timoleon. The former of whom requiring him to put in sureties that he would answer to an indictment that would be brought against him, Timoleon would not suffer the citizens, who were incensed at this demand, to oppose it or hinder the proceeding, since he of his own accord had been, he said, at all that trouble, and run so many dangerous risks for this very end and purpose, that everyone who wished to try matters by law should freely have recourse to it. And when Demænetus, in a full audience of the people, laid several things to his charge which had been done while he was general, he made no reply to him, but only said he was much indebted to the gods for granting the request he had so often made them, namely, that he might live to see the Syracusans enjoy that liberty of speech which they now seemed to be masters of.

Timoleon, therefore, having by confession of all done the greatest and the noblest things of any Greek of his age, and alone distinguished himself in those actions to which their orators and philosophers, in their harangues and panegyrics at their solemn national assemblies, used to exhort and incite the Greeks, and being withdrawn beforehand by happy fortune, unspotted and without blood, from the calamities of civil war, in which ancient Greece was soon after involved; having also given full proof, as of his sage conduct and manly courage to the barbarians and tyrants, so of his justice and gentleness to the Greeks, and his friends in general; having raised, too, the greater part of those trophies he won in battle without any tears shed or any mourning worn by the citizens either of Syracuse or Corinth, and within less than eight years' space delivered Sicily from its inveterate grievances and intestine distempers, and given it up free to the native inhabitants, began, as he was now growing old, to find his eyes fail, and awhile after became perfectly blind. Not that he had done anything himself which might occasion this defect, or was deprived of his sight by any outrage of fortune; it seems rather to have been some inbred and hereditary weakness that was founded in natural causes, which by length of time came to discover itself. For it is said, that several of his kindred and family were subject to the like gradual decay, and lost all use of their eyes, as he did, in their declining years. Athanis the historian tells us that even during the war against Hippo and Mamercus, while he was in his camp at Mylæ, there appeared a white speck within his eye, from whence all could foresee the deprivation that was coming on him; this, however, did not hinder him then from continuing the siege, and prosecuting the war, till he got both the tyrants into his power; but upon his coming back to Syracuse, he presently resigned the authority of sole commander, and besought the citizens to excuse him from any further service, since things were already brought to so fair an issue. Nor is it so much to be wondered that he himself should bear the misfortune without any marks of trouble; but the respect and gratitude which the Syracusans showed him when he was entirely blind may justly deserve our admiration. They used to go themselves to visit him in troops and brought all the strangers that travelled through their country to his house and manor, that they also might have the pleasure to see their noble benefactor; making it the great matter of their joy and exultation, that when, after so many brave and happy exploits, he might have returned with triumph into Greece, he should disregard all the glorious preparations that were there made to receive him, and choose rather to stay here and end his days among them. Of the various things decreed and done in honour of Timoleon, I consider one most signal testimony to have been the vote which they passed, that, whenever they should be at war with any foreign nation, they should make use of none but a Corinthian general. The method, also, of their proceeding in council was a noble demonstration of the same deference for his person. For, determining matters of less consequence themselves, they always called him to advise in the more difficult cases, and such as were of greater moment. He was, on these occasions, carried through the market place in a litter, and brought in, sitting, into the theatre, where the people with one voice saluted him by his name; and then, after returning the courtesy, and pausing for a time, till the noise of their gratulations and blessings began to cease, he heard the business in debate, and delivered his opinion. This being confirmed by a general suffrage, his servants went back with the litter through the midst of the assembly, the people waiting on him out with acclamations and applauses, and then returning to consider other public matters, which they could despatch in his absence. Being thus cherished in his old age, with all the respect and tenderness due to a common father, he was seized with a very slight indisposition, which, however, was sufficient, with the aid of time, to put a period to his life. There was an allotment then of certain days given, within the space of which the Syracusans were to provide whatever should be necessary for his burial, and all the neighbouring country people and strangers were to make their appearance in a body; so that the funeral pomp was set out with great splendour and magnificence in all other respects, and the bier, decked with ornaments and trophies, was borne by a select body of young men over that ground where the palace and castle of Dionysius stood before they were demolished by Timoleon. There attended on the solemnity several thousands of men and women, all crowned with flowers, and arrayed in fresh and clean attire, which made it look like the procession of a public festival; while the language of all, and their tears mingling with their praise and benediction of the dead Timoleon, manifestly showed that it was not any superficial honour, or commanded homage, which they paid him, but the testimony of a just sorrow for his death, and the expression of true affection. The bier at length being placed upon the pile of wood that was kindled to consume his corpse, Demetrius, one of their loudest criers, proceeded to read a proclamation to the following purpose: "The people of Syracuse have made a special decree to inter Timoleon, the son of Timodemus, the Corinthian, at the common expense of two hundred minas, and to honour his memory forever, by the establishment of annual prizes to be competed for in music, and horse-races, and all sorts of bodily exercise; and this, because he suppressed the tyrants, overthrew the barbarians, replenished the principal cities, that were desolate, with new inhabitants, and then restored the Sicilian Greeks to the privilege of living by their own laws." Besides this, they made a tomb for him in the market place, which they afterwards built round with colonnades, and attached to it places of exercise for the young men, and gave it the name of the Timoleonteum. And keeping to that form and order of civil policy and observing those laws and constitutions which he left them, they lived themselves a long time in great prosperity.

ÆMILIUS PAULUS

ALMOST ALL HISTORIANS AGREE THAT THE ÆMILII WERE ONE OF THE ancient and patrician houses in Rome; and those authors who affirm that King Numa was pupil to Pythagoras tell us that the first who gave name to his posterity was Mamercus, the son of Pythagoras, who, for his grace and address in speaking, was called Æmilius. Most of this race that have risen through their merit to reputation also enjoyed good fortune: and even the misfortune to Lucius Paulus at the battle of Cannæ gave testimony to his wisdom and valour. For not being able to persuade his colleague not to hazard the battle, he, though against his judgment, joined with him in the contest, but was no companion in his flight: on the contrary, when he that was so resolute to engage deserted him in the midst of danger he kept the field and died fighting. This Æmilius had a daughter named Æmilia, who was married to Scipio the Great, and a son Paulus, who is the subject of my present history.

In his early manhood, which fell at a time when Rome was flourishing with illustrious characters, he was distinguished for not attaching himself to the studies usual with the young men of mark of that age, nor treading the same paths to fame. For he did not practise oratory with a view to pleading causes, nor would he stoop to salute, embrace, and entertain the vulgar, which were the usual insinuating arts by which many grew popular. Not that he was incapable of either, but he chose to purchase a much more lasting glory by his valour, justice, and integrity, and in these virtues he soon oustripped all his equals.

The first honourable office he aspired to was that of ædile, which he carried against twelve competitors of such merit that all of them in process of time were consuls. Being afterwards chosen into the number of priests

called augurs, appointed amongst the Romans to observe and register divinations made by the flight of birds or prodigies in the air, he so carefully
studied the ancient customs of his country, and so thoroughly understood
the religion of his ancestors, that this office, which was before only
esteemed a title of honour and merely upon that account sought after, by
this means rose to the rank of one of the highest arts, and gave a confirmation to the correctness of the definition, which some philosophers have
given of religion, that it is the science of worshipping the gods. When he
performed any part of his duty, he did it with great skill and utmost care,
making it, when he was engaged in it, his only business, not omitting anyone ceremony, or adding the least circumstance, but always insisting, with
his companions of the same order, even on points that might seem inconsiderable, and urging upon them, that though they might think the Deity
was easily pacified, and ready to forgive faults of inadvertency, yet any
such laxity was a very dangerous thing for a commonwealth to allow;
because no man ever began the disturbance of his country's peace by a
notorious breach of its laws; and those who are careless in trifles give a
precedent for remissness in important duties. Nor was he less severe in
requiring and observing the ancient Roman discipline in military affairs;
not endeavouring, when he had the command, to ingratiate himself with
his soldiers by popular flattery, though this custom prevailed at that time
amongst many, who, by favour and gentleness to those that were under
them in their first employment, sought to be promoted to a second; but,
by instructing them in the laws of military discipline with the same care
and exactness a priest would use in teaching ceremonies and dreadful
mysteries, and by severity to such as transgressed and contemned those
laws, he maintained his country in its former greatness, esteeming victory
over enemies itself but as an accessory to the proper training and disciplining of the citizens.

Whilst the Romans were engaged in war with Antiochus the Great,
against whom their most experienced commanders were employed, there
arose another war in the west, and they were all up in arms in Spain.
Thither they sent Æmilius, in the quality of prætor, not with six axes,
which number other prætors were accustomed to have carried before
them, but with twelve; so that in his prætorship he was honoured with the
dignity of a consul. He twice overcame the barbarians in battle, thirty
thousand of whom were slain: successes chiefly to be ascribed to the wisdom and conduct of the commander, who by his great skill in choosing
the advantage of the ground, and making the onset at the passage of a

river, gave his soldiers an easy victory. Having made himself master of two hundred and fifty cities, whose inhabitants voluntarily yielded, and bound themselves by oath to fidelity, he left the province in peace, and returned to Rome, not enriching himself a drachma by the war. And, indeed, in general, he was but remiss in making money; though he always lived freely and generously on what he had, which was so far from being excessive, that after his death there was barely enough left to answer his wife's dowry.

His first wife was Papiria, the daughter of Maso, who had formerly been consul. With her he lived a considerable time in wedlock, and then divorced her, though she had made him the father of noble children; being mother of the renowned Scipio and Fabius Maximus. The reason of this separation has not come to our knowledge; but there seems to be a truth conveyed in the account of another Roman's being divorced from his wife, which may be applicable here. This person being highly blamed by his friends, who demanded, Was she not chaste? Was she not fair? Was she not fruitful? Holding out his shoe, asked them, Whether it was not new? And well made? Yet, added he, none of you can tell where it pinches me. Certain it is, that great and open faults have often led to no separation; while mere petty repeated annoyances, arising from unpleasantness or incongruity of character, have been the occasion of such estrangement as to make it impossible for man and wife to live together with any content.

Æmilius, having thus put away Papiria, married a second wife, by whom he had two sons, whom he brought up in his own house, transferring the two former into the greatest and the most noble families of Rome. The elder was adopted into the house of Fabius Maximus, who was five times consul; the younger by the son of Scipio Africanus, his cousin-german, and was by him named Scipio.

Of the daughters of Æmilius, one was married to the son of Cato, the other to Ælius Tubero, a most worthy man, and the one Roman who best succeeded in combining liberal habits with poverty. For there were sixteen near relations, all of them of the family of the Ælii, possessed of but one farm, which sufficed them all, whilst one small house, or rather cottage, contained them, their numerous offspring, and their wives; amongst whom was the daughter of our Æmilius, who, although her father had been twice consul, and had twice triumphed, was not ashamed of her husband's poverty, but proud of his virtue that kept him poor. Far otherwise it is with the brothers and relations of this age, who, unless whole tracts of land, or at least walls and rivers, part their inheritances, and keep them at a distance, never cease from mutual quarrels. History suggests a variety of good counsel of this sort, by the way, to those who desire to learn and improve.

To proceed: Æmilius, being chosen consul, waged war with the Ligurians, or Ligustines, a people near the Alps. They were a bold and warlike nation, and their neighbourhood to the Romans had begun to give them skill in the arts of war. They occupy the further parts of Italy ending under the Alps, and those parts of the Alps themselves which are washed by the Tuscan sea and face toward Africa, mingled there with Gauls and Iberians of the coast. Besides, at that time they had turned their thoughts to the seas, and sailing as far as the Pillars of Hercules in light vessels fitted for that purpose, robbed and destroyed all that trafficked in those parts. They, with an army of forty thousand, waited the coming of Æmilius, who brought with him not above eight thousand, so that the enemy was five to one when they engaged; yet he vanquished and put them to flight, forcing them to retire into their walled towns, and in this condition offered them fair conditions of accommodation; it being the policy of the Romans not utterly to destroy the Ligurians, because they were a sort of guard and bulwark against the frequent attempts of the Gauls to overrun Italy. Trusting wholly therefore to Æmilius, they delivered up their towns and shipping into his hands. He, at the utmost, razed only the fortifications and delivered their towns to them again, but took away all their shipping with him, leaving them no vessels bigger than those of three oars, and set at liberty great numbers of prisoners they had taken both by sea and land, strangers as well as Romans. These were the acts most worthy of remark in his first consulship.

Afterwards he frequently intimated his desire of being a second time consul, and was once candidate; but meeting with a repulse and being passed by, he gave up all thought of it, and devoted himself to his duties as augur, and to the education of his children, whom he not only brought up, as he himself had been, in the Roman and ancient discipline, but also with unusual zeal in that of Greece. To this purpose he not only procured masters to teach them grammar, logic, and rhetoric, but had for them also preceptors in modelling and drawing, managers of horses and dogs, and instructors in field sports, all from Greece. And, if he was not hindered by public affairs, he himself would be with them at their studies, and see them perform their exercises, being the most affectionate father in Rome.

This was the time, in public matters, when the Romans were engaged in war with Perseus, King of the Macedonians, and great complaints were made of their commanders, who, either through their want of skill or courage, were conducting matters so shamefully, that they did less hurt to the enemy than they received from him. They that not long before had forced Antiochus the Great to quit the rest of Asia, to retire beyond Mount Taurus, and confine himself to Syria, glad to buy his peace with fifteen thousand talents; they that not long since had vanquished King Philip in Thessaly, and freed the Greeks from the Macedonian yoke; nay, had overcome Hannibal himself, who far surpassed all kings in daring and power— thought it scorn that Perseus should think himself an enemy fit to match the Romans, and to be able to wage war with them so long on equal terms, with the remainder only of his father's routed forces; not being aware that Philip after his defeat had greatly improved both the strength and discipline of the Macedonian army. To make which appear, I shall briefly recount the story from the beginning.

Antigonus, the most powerful amongst the captains and successors of Alexander, having obtained for himself and his posterity the title of king, had a son named Demetrius, father to Antigonus, called Gonatas, and he had a son Demetrius, who, reigning some short time, died and left a young son called Philip. The chief men of Macedon, fearing great confusion might arise in his minority, called in Antigonus, cousin-german to the late king, and married him to the widow, the mother of Philip. At first they only styled him regent and general, but when they found by experience that he governed the kingdom with moderation and to general advantage, gave him the title of king. This was he that was surnamed Doson, as if he was a great promiser and a bad performer. To him succeeded Philip, who in his youth gave great hopes of equalling the best of kings, and that he one day would restore Macedon to its former state and dignity, and prove himself the one man able to check the power of the Romans, now rising and extending over the whole world. But, being vanquished in a pitched battle by Titus Flaminius near Scotussa, his resolution failed, and he yielded himself and all that he had to the mercy of the Romans, well contented that he could escape with paying a small tribute. Yet afterwards, recollecting himself, he bore it with great impatience, and thought he lived rather like a slave that was pleased with ease, than a man of sense and courage, whilst he held his kingdom at the pleasure of his conquerors; which made him turn his whole mind to war, and prepare himself with as much cunning and privacy as possible. To this end, he left his cities on the high roads and sea-coast ungarrisoned, and almost desolate, that they might seem inconsiderable; in the meantime, collecting large forces up the country, and furnishing his inland posts, strongholds, and towns, with arms, money, and men fit for service, he thus provided himself for war, and yet kept his preparations close. He had in his armoury arms for thirty thousand men; in granaries, in places of strength, eight millions of bushels of corn, and as much ready money as would defray the charge of maintaining ten thousand mercenary soldiers for ten years in defence of the country. But before he could put these things into motion, and carry his designs into effect, he died for griefs and anguish of mind, being sensible he had put his innocent son Demetrius to death, upon the calumnies of one that was far more guilty. Perseus, his son that survived, inherited his hatred to the Romans as well as his kingdom, but was incompetent to carry out his designs, through want of courage and the viciousness of a character in which, among faults and diseases of various sorts, covetousness bore the chief place. There is a statement also of his not being true-born; that the wife of King Philip took him from his mother, Gnathænion (a woman of Argos, that earned her living as a seamstress), as soon as he was born, and passed him upon her husband as her own. And this might be the chief cause of his contriving the death of Demetrius; as he might well fear that, so long as there was a lawful successor in the family, there was no security that his spurious birth might not be revealed.

Notwithstanding all this, and though his spirit was so mean and temper so sordid, yet trusting to the strength of his resources, he engaged in a war with the Romans, and for a long time maintained it; repulsing and even vanquishing some generals of consular dignity, and some great armies and fleets. He routed Publius Licinius, who was the first that invaded Macedonia, in a cavalry battle, slew twenty-five hundred practiced soldiers, and took six hundred prisoners; and surprising their fleet as they rode at anchor before Orens, he took twenty ships of burden with all their lading, sunk the rest that were freighted with corn, and, besides this, made himself master of four galleys with five banks of oars. He fought a second battle with Hostilius, a consular officer, as he was making his way into the country at Elimiæ, and forced him to retreat; and, when he afterwards by stealth designed an invasion through Thessaly, challenged him to fight, which the other feared to accept. Nay more, to show his contempt to the Romans, and that he wanted employment, as a war by the by, he made an expedition against the Dardanians, in which he slew ten thousand of those barbarian people, and brought a great spoil away. He privately, moreover, solicited the Gauls (also called Basternæ), a warlike nation, and famous for horsemen, dwelling near the Danube; and incited the Illyrians, by the means of Genthius their king, to join with him in the war. It was also reported that the barbarians, allured by promise of rewards, were to make an irruption into Italy, through the lower Gaul by the shore of the Adriatic Sea.

The Romans, being advertised of these things, thought it necessary no longer to choose their commanders by favour or solicitation, but of their own motion to select a general of wisdom and capacity for the management of great affairs. And such was Paulus Æmilius, advanced in years, being nearly threescore, yet vigorous in his own person, and rich in valiant sons and sons-in-law, besides a great number of influential relations and friends, all of whom joined in urging him to yield to the desires of the people, who called him to the consulship. He at first manifested some shyness of the people and withdrew himself from their importunity, professing reluctance to hold office; but, when they daily came to his doors, urging him to come forth to the place of election, and pressing him with noise and clamour, he acceded to their request. When he appeared amongst the candidates, it did not look as if it were to sue for the consulship, but to bring victory and success, that he came down into the Campus; they all received him there with such hopes and such gladness, unanimously choosing him a second time consul; nor would they suffer the lots to be cast, as was usual, to determine which province should fall to his share, but immediately decreed him the command of the Macedonian war. It is told, that when he had been proclaimed general against Perseus, and was honourably accompanied home by great numbers of people, he found his daughter Tertia, a very little girl, weeping, and taking her to him asked her why she was crying. She, catching him about the neck and kissing him, said, "O father, do you not know that Perseus is dead?" meaning a little dog of that name that was brought up in the house with her; to which Æmilius replied, "Good fortune, my daughter; I embrace the omen." This Cicero, the orator, relates in his book on divination.

It was the custom for such as were chosen consuls, from a stage designed for such purposes, to address the people, and return them thanks for their favour. Æmilius, therefore, having gathered an assembly, spoke and said that he sued for the first consulship, because he himself stood in need of such honour; but for the second, because they wanted a general; upon which account he thought there was no thanks due: if they judged they could manage the war by any other to more advantage, he would willingly yield up his charge; but, if they confided in him, they were not to make themselves his colleagues in his office, or raise reports, and criticise his actions, but, without talking, supply him with means and assistance necessary to the carrying on of the war; for if they proposed to command their own commander they would render this expedition more ridiculous than the former. By this speech he inspired great reverence for him amongst the citizens and great expectations of future success; all were well pleased that they had passed by such as sought to be preferred by flattery, and fixed upon a commander endued with wisdom and courage to tell them the truth. So entirely did the people of Rome, that they might rule, and become masters of the world, yield obedience and service to reason and superior virtue.

That Æmilius, setting forward to the war, by a prosperous voyage and successful journey, arrived with speed and safety at his camp I attribute to good fortune; but, when I see how the war under his command was brought to a happy issue, partly by his own daring boldness, partly by his good counsel, partly by the ready administration of his friends, partly by his presence of mind and skill to embrace the most proper advice in the extremity of danger, I cannot ascribe any of his remarkable and famous actions (as I can those of other commanders) to his so much celebrated good fortune; unless you will say that the covetousness of Perseus was the good fortune of Æmilius. The truth is, Perseus' fear of spending his money was the destruction and utter ruin of all those splendid and great preparations with which the Macedonians were in high hopes to carry on the war with success. For there came at his request ten thousand horsemen of the Basternæ, and as many foot, who were to keep pace with them, and supply their places in case of failure; all of them professed soldiers, men skilled neither in tilling of land, nor in navigation of ships, nor able to get their living by grazing, but whose only business and single art and trade it was to fight and conquer all that resisted them. When these came into the district of Mædica, and encamped and mixed with the king's soldiers, being men of great stature, admirable at their exercises, great boasters, and loud in their threats against their enemies, they gave new courage to the Macedonians, who were ready to think the Romans would not be able to confront them, but would be struck with terror at their looks and motions, they were so strange and so formidable to behold. When Perseus had thus encouraged his men, and elevated them with these great hopes, as soon as a thousand gold pieces were demanded for each captain, he was so amazed and beside himself at the vastness of the amount, that out of mere stinginess he drew back and let himself lose their assistance, as if he had been some steward, not the enemy of the Romans, and would have to give an exact account of the expenses of the war to those with whom he waged it. Nay, when he had his foes as tutors, to instruct him what he had to do, who, besides their other preparations, had a hundred thousand men drawn together and in readiness for their service; yet he that was to engage against so considerable a force, and in a war that was maintaining such numbers as this, nevertheless doled out his money, and put seals on his bags, and was as fearful of touching it, as if it had belonged to some-one else. And all this was done by one, not descended from Lydians or Phœnicians, but who could pretend to some share of the virtues of Alexander and Philip, whom he was allied to by birth; men who con-quered the world by judging that empire was to be purchased by money, not money by empire. Certainly it became a proverb, that not Philip, but his gold, took the cities of Greece. And Alexander, when he undertook his expedition against the Indians, and found his Macedonians encumbered and appear to march heavily with their Persian spoils, first set fire to his own carriages, and thence persuaded the rest to imitate his example, that thus freed they might proceed to the war without hindrance. Whereas Perseus, abounding in wealth, would not preserve himself, his children, and his kingdom, at the expense of a small part of his treasure; but chose rather to be carried away with numbers of his subjects with the name of the wealthy captive, and show the Romans what great riches he had hus-banded and preserved for them. For he not only played false with the Gauls, and sent them away, but also, after alluring Genthius, King of the Illyrians, by the hopes of three hundred talents, to assist him in the war, he caused the money to be counted out in the presence of his messengers, and to be sealed up. Upon which Genthius, thinking himself possessed of what he desired, committed a wicked and shameful act: he seized and imprisoned the ambassadors sent to him from the Romans. Whence Perseus, concluding that there was no need of money to make Genthius an enemy to the Romans, but that he had given a lasting earnest of his enmity, and by his flagrant injustice sufficiently involved himself in the war, defrauded the unfortunate king of his three hundred talents, and without any concern beheld him, his wife, and children, in a short time after, carried out of their kingdom, as from their nest, by Lucius Anicius, who was sent against him with an army.

Æmilius, coming against such an adversary, made light indeed of him, but admired his preparation and power. For he had four thousand horse, and not much fewer than forty thousand full-armed foot of the phalanx; and planting himself along the seaside, at the foot of Mount Olympus, in ground with no access on any side, and on all sides fortified with fences and bulwarks of wood, remained in great security, thinking by delay and expense to weary out Æmilius. But he, in the meantime, busy in thought, weighed all counsels and all means of attack, and perceiving his soldiers, from their former want of discipline, to be impatient of delay, and ready on all occasions to teach their general his duty, rebuked them, and bade them not meddle with what was not their concern, but only take care that they and their arms were in readiness, and to use their swords like Romans when their commander should think fit to employ them. Further, he ordered that the sentinels by night should watch without javelins, that thus they might be more careful and surer to resist sleep, having no arms to defend themselves against any attacks of an enemy.

What most annoyed the army was the want of water; for only a little, and that foul, flowed out, or rather came by drops from a spring adjoining the sea; but Æmilius, considering that he was at the foot of the high and woody mountain Olympus, and conjecturing by the flourishing growth of the trees that there were springs that had their course underground, dug a great many holes and wells along the foot of the mountain, which were presently filled with pure water escaping from its confinement into the vacuum they afforded. Although there are some, indeed, who deny that there are reservoirs of water lying ready provided out of sight, in the places from whence springs flow, and that when they appear, they merely issue and run out; on the contrary, they say, they are then formed and come into existence for the first time, by the liquefaction of the surrounding matter; and that this change is caused by density and cold, when the moist vapour, by being closely pressed together, becomes fluid. As women's breasts are not like vessels full of milk always prepared and ready to flow from them; but their nourishment being changed in their breasts, is there made milk, and from thence is pressed out. In like manner, places of the earth that are cold and full of springs, do not contain any hidden waters or receptacles which are capable, as from a source always ready and furnished, of supplying all the brooks and deep rivers; but by compressing and condensing the vapours and air they turn them into that substance. And thus places that are dug open flow by that pressure, and afford the more water (as the breasts of women do milk by their being sucked), the vapour thus moistening and becoming fluid; whereas ground that remains idle and undug is not capable of producing any water, whilst it wants the motion which is the cause of liquefaction. But those that assert this opinion give occasion to the doubtful to argue, that on the same ground there should be no blood in living creatures, but that it must be formed by the wound, some sort of spirit or flesh being changed into a liquid and flowing matter. Moreover, they are refuted by the fact that men who dig mines, either in sieges or for metals, meet with rivers, which are not collected by little and little (as must necessarily be, if they had their being at the very instant the earth was opened), but break out at once with violence; and upon the cutting through a rock, there often gush out great quantities of water, which then as suddenly cease. But of this enough.

Æmilius lay still for some days, and it is said that there were never two great armies so nigh that enjoyed so much quiet. When he had tried and considered all things, he was informed that there was yet one passage left unguarded, through Perrhæbia by the temple of Apollo and the Rock. Gathering, therefore, more hope from the place being left defenceless than fear from the roughness and difficulty of the passage, he proposed it for consultation. Amongst those that were present at the council, Scipio, surnamed Nasica, son-in-law to Scipio Africanus, who afterwards was so powerful in the senate-house, was the first that offered himself to command those that should be sent to encompass the enemy. Next to him, Fabius Maximus, eldest son of Æmilius, although yet very young, offered himself with great zeal. Æmilius, rejoicing, gave them, not so many as Polybius states, but, as Nasica himself tells us in a brief letter which he wrote to one of the kings with an account of the expedition, three thousand Italians that were not Romans, and his left wing consisting of five thousand. Taking with him, besides these, one hundred and twenty horsemen, and two hundred Thracians and Cretans intermixed that Harpalus had sent, he began his journey towards the sea, and encamped near the temple of Hercules, as if he designed to embark, and so to sail round and environ the enemy. But when the soldiers had supped and it was dark, he made the captains acquainted with his real intentions, and marching all night in the opposite directions away from the sea, till he came under the temple of Apollo, there rested his army. At this place Mount Olympus rises in height more than ten furlongs, as appears by the epigram made by the man that measured it:

> The summit of Olympus, at the site
> Where stands Apollo's temple, has a height
> Of full ten furlongs by the line, and more,
> Ten furlongs, and one hundred feet, less four.
> Eumelus' son, Xenagoras, reached the place.
> Adieu, O king, and do thy pilgrim grace.

It is allowed, say the geometricians, that no mountain in height or sea in depth exceeds ten furlongs, and yet it seems probable that Xenagoras did not take his admeasurement carelessly, but according to the rules of art, and with instruments for the purpose. Here it was that Nasica passed the night.

A Cretan deserted, who fled to the enemy during the march, discovered to Perseus the design which the Romans had to encompass him: for he, seeing that Æmilius lay still, had not suspected any such attempt. He was startled at the news, yet did not put his army in motion, but sent ten thousand mercenary soldiers, and two thousand Macedonians, under command of Milo, with order to hasten and possess themselves of the passes. Polybius relates that the Romans found these men asleep when they attacked them; but Nasica says there was a sharp and severe conflict on the top of the mountain, that he himself encountered a mercenary Thracian, pierced him through with his javelin, and slew him; and that the enemy being forced to retreat, Milo stripped to his coat and fled shamefully without his armour, while he followed without danger, and conveyed the whole army down into the country.

After this event, Perseus, now grown fearful, and fallen from his hopes, removed his camp in all haste; he was under the necessity either to stop before Pydna, and there run the hazard of a battle, or disperse his army into cities, and there expect the event of the war, which, having once made its way into his country, could not be driven out without great slaughter and bloodshed. But Perseus, being told by his friends that he was much superior in number, and that men fighting in the defence of their wives and children must needs feel all the more courage, especially when all was done in the sight of their king, who himself was engaged in equal danger, was thus again encouraged; and, pitching his camp, prepared himself to fight, viewed the country, and gave out the commands, as if he designed to set upon the Romans as soon as they approached. The place was a field fit for the action of a phalanx, which requires smooth standing and even ground, and also had divers little hills, one joining another, fit for the motions whether in retreat or advance of light troops and skirmishers. Through the middle ran the rivers Æson and Leucus, which though not very deep, it being the latter end of summer, yet were likely enough to give the Romans some trouble.

As soon as Æmilius had rejoined Nasica, he advanced in battle array against the enemy; but when he found how they were drawn up, and the number of their forces, he regarded them with admiration and surprise, and halted, considering within himself. The young commanders, eager to fight, riding along by his side, pressed him not to delay, and most of all

Nasica, flushed with his late success on Olympus. To whom Æmilius answered with a smile: "So would I do were I of your age; but many victories have taught me the ways in which men are defeated, and forbid me to engage soldiers weary with a long march against an army drawn up and prepared for battle."

Then he gave command that the front of his army, and such as were in sight of the enemy, should form as if ready to engage, and those in the rear should cast up the trenches and fortify the camp; so that the hindmost in succession wheeling off by degrees and withdrawing, their whole order was insensibly broken up, and the army encamped without noise or trouble.

When it was night, and, supper being over, all were turning to sleep and rest, on a sudden the moon, which was then at full and high in the heavens, grew dark, and by degrees losing her light, passed through various colours, and at length was totally eclipsed. The Romans, according to their custom, clattering brass pans and lifting up fire-brands and torches into the air, invoked the return of her light; the Macedonians behaved far otherwise: terror and amazement seized their whole army, and a rumour crept by degrees into their camp that this eclipse portended even that of their king. Æmilius was no novice in these things, nor was ignorant of the nature of the seeming irregularities of eclipses—that in a certain revolution of time, the moon in her course enters the shadow of the earth and is there obscured, till, passing the region of darkness, she is again enlightened by the sun. Yet being a devout man, a religious observer of sacrifices and the art of divination, as soon as he perceived the moon beginning to regain her former lustre, he offered up to her eleven heifers. At the break of day he sacrificed as many as twenty in succession to Hercules, without any token that his offering was accepted; but at the one-and-twentieth, the signs promised victory to defenders. He then vowed a hecatomb and solemn sports to Hercules, and commanded his captains to make ready for battle, staying only till the sun should decline and come round to the west, lest, being in their faces in the morning, it should dazzle the eyes of his soldiers. Thus he whiled away the time in his tent, which was open towards the plain where his enemies were encamped.

When it grew towards evening, some tell us, Æmilius himself used a stratagem to induce the enemy to begin the fight; that he turned loose a horse without a bridle, and sent some of the Romans to catch him, upon whose following the beast the battle began. Others relate that the Thracians, under the command of one Alexander, set upon the Roman beasts of burden that were bringing forage to the camp; that to oppose these, a party of seven hundred Ligurians were immediately detached; and that, relief coming still from both armies, the main bodies at last engaged Æmilius, like a wise pilot, foreseeing by the present waves and motion of the armies the greatness of the following storm, came out of his tent, went through the legions, and encouraged his soldiers. Nasica, in the meantime, who had ridden out to the skirmishers, saw the whole force of the enemy on the point of engaging. First marched the Thracians, who, he himself tells us, inspired him with most terror; they were of great stature, with bright and glittering shields and black frocks under them, their legs armed with greaves, and they brandished, as they moved, straight and heavily ironed spears over their right shoulders. Next the Thracians marched the mercenary soldiers, armed after different fashions; with these Pæonians were mingled. These were succeeded by a third division, of picked men, native Macedonians, the choicest for courage and strength, in the prime of life, gleaming with gilt armour and scarlet coats. As these were taking their places they were followed from the camp by the troops in phalanx called the Brazen Shields, so that the whole plain seemed alive with the flashing of steel and the glistening of brass; and the hills also with their shouts, as they cheered each other on. In this order they marched, and with such boldness and speed, that those that were first slain died at but two furlongs distance from the Roman camp.

The battle being begun, Æmilius came in and found that the foremost of the Macedonians had already fixed the ends of their spears into the shields of his Romans, so that it was impossible to come near them with their swords. When he saw this, and observed that the rest of the Macedonians took the targets that hung on their left shoulders, and brought them round before them, and all at once stooped their pikes against their enemies' shields, and considered the great strength of this wall of shields, and the formidable appearance of a front thus bristling with arms, he was seized with amazement and alarm; nothing he had ever seen before had been equal to it; and in aftertimes he frequently used to speak both of the sight and of his own sensations. These, however, he dissembled, and rode through his army without either breastplate or helmet, with a serene and cheerful countenance.

On the contrary, as Polybius relates, no sooner was the battle begun, but the Macedonian king basely withdrew to the city Pydna, under a pretence of sacrificing to Hercules; a god that is not wont to regard the faint offerings of cowards, or to fulfil unsanctioned vows. For truly it can hardly be a thing that heaven would sanction, that he that never shoots should carry away the prize; he triumph that slinks from the battle; he that takes no pains meet with success, or the wicked man prosper. But to Æmilius' petitions the god listened; he prayed for victory with his sword in his hand, and fought while entreating divine assistance.

A certain Posidonius, who has at some length written a history of Perseus, and professes to have lived at the time, and to have been himself engaged in these events, denies that Perseus left the field either through fear or pretence of sacrificing, but that, the very day before the fight, he received a kick from a horse on his thigh; that though very much disabled, and dissuaded by all his friends, he commanded one of his riding-horses to be brought, and entered the field unarmed; that amongst an infinite number of darts that flew about on all sides, one of iron lighted on him, and though not with the point, yet by a glance struck him with such force on his left side that it tore his clothes and so bruised his flesh that the mark remained a long time after. This is what Posidonius says in defence of Perseus.

The Romans not being able to make a breach in the phalanx, one Salius, a commander of the Pelignians, snatched the ensign of his company and threw it amongst the enemies; on seeing which, the Pelignians (as amongst the Italians it is always thought the greatest breach of honour to abandon a standard) rushed with great violence towards the place, where the conflict grew very fierce and the slaughter terrible on both sides. For these endeavoured to cut the spears asunder with their swords, or to beat them back with their shields, or put them by with their hands; and, on the other side, the Macedonians held their long sarissas in both hands, and pierced those that came in their way quite through their armour, no shield or corslet being able to resist the force of that weapon. The Pelignians and Marrucinians were thrown headlong to the ground, having without consideration, with mere animal fury, rushed upon a certain death. Their first ranks being slain, those that were behind were forced to give back; it cannot be said they fled, but they retreated towards Mount Olocrus. When Æmilius saw this, Posidonius relates, he rent his clothes, some of his men being ready to fly, and the rest not willing to engage with a phalanx into which they could not hope to make any entrance—a sort of palisade, as it were, impregnable and unapproachable, with its close array of long spears everywhere meeting the assailant. Nevertheless, the unequalness of the ground would not permit a widely extended front to be so exactly drawn up as to have their shields everywhere joined; and Æmilius perceived that there were a great many interstices and breaches in the Macedonian phalanx, as it usually happens in all great armies, according to the different efforts of the combatants, who in one part press forward with eagerness, and in another are forced to fall back. Taking, therefore, this occasion, with all speed he broke up his men into their cohorts, and gave them order to fall into the intervals and openings of the enemy's body, and not to make one general attack upon them all, but to engage, as they were divided, in several partial battles. These commands Æmilius gave to his captains, and they to their soldiers; and no sooner had they entered the spaces and separated their enemies, but they charged them, some on their sides where they were naked and exposed, and others, making a circuit, behind; and thus destroyed the force of the phalanx, which consists in common action and close union. And now, come to fight man to man, or in small parties, the Macedonians smote in vain upon firm and long shields with their little swords, whilst their slight bucklers were not able to sustain the weight and force of the Roman swords, which pierced through all their armour to their bodies; they turned, in fine, and fled.

The conflict was obstinate. And here Marcus, the son of Cato, and son-in-law of Æmilius, whilst he showed all possible courage, let fall his sword. Being a young man carefully brought up and disciplined, and, son of so renowned a father, bound to give proof of more than ordinary virtue, he thought his life but a burden, should he live and permit his enemies to enjoy this spoil. He hurried hither and thither, and wherever he espied a friend or companion, declared his misfortune, and begged their assistance; a considerable number of brave men being thus collected, with one accord they made their way through their fellows after their leader, and fell upon the enemy; whom after a sharp conflict, many wounds, and much slaughter, they repulsed, possessed the place that was now deserted and free, and set themselves to search for the sword, which at last they found covered with a great heap of arms and dead bodies. Overjoyed with this success, they raised the song of triumph, and, with more eagerness than ever, charged the foes that yet remained firm and unbroken. In the end, three thousand of the chosen men, who kept their ground and fought valiantly to the last, were all cut in pieces, while the slaughter of such as fled was also very great. The plain and the lower part of the hills were filled with dead bodies, and the water of the river Leucus, which the Romans did not pass till the next day after the battle, was then mingled with blood. For it is said there fell more than twenty-five thousand of the enemy; of the Romans, as Posidonius relates, a hundred; as Nasica, only fourscore. This battle, though so great, was very quickly decided, it being three in the afternoon when they first engaged, and not four when the enemy was vanquished; the rest of the day was spent in pursuit of the fugitives, whom they followed about thirteen or fourteen miles, so that it was far in the night when they returned.

All the others were met by their servants with torches, and brought back with joy and great triumph to their tents, which were set out with lights, and decked with wreaths of ivy and laurel. But the general himself was in great grief. Of the two sons that served under him in the war, the youngest was missing, whom he held most dear, and whose courage and good qualities he perceived much to excel those of his brothers. Bold and eager for distinction, and still a mere child in age, he concluded that he had perished, whilst for want of experience he had engaged himself too far amongst his enemies. His sorrow and fears became known to the army; the soldiers, quitting their suppers, ran about with lights, some to Æmilius' tent, some out of the trenches, to seek him amongst such as were slain in the first onset. There was nothing but grief in the camp, and the plain was filled with the cries of men calling out for Scipio; for, from his very youth, he was an object of admiration; endowed above any of his equals with the good qualities requisite either for command or counsel. At length, when it was late, and they almost despaired, he returned from the pursuit with only two or three of his companions all covered with the fresh blood of his enemies, having been, like some dog of noble breed, carried away by the pleasure, greater than he could control, of his first victory. This was that Scipio that afterwards destroyed Carthage and Numantia, and was, without dispute, the first of the Romans in merit, and had the greatest authority amongst them. Thus Fortune, deferring her displeasure and jealousy of such great success to some other time, let Æmilius at present enjoy this victory, without any detraction or diminution.

As for Perseus, from Pydna he fled to Pella with his cavalry, which was as yet almost entire. But when the foot came up with them, and, upbraiding them as cowards and traitors, tried to pull them off their horses, and fell to blows, Perseus, fearing the tumult, forsook the common road, and, lest he should be known, pulled off his purple, and carried it before him, and took his crown in his hand and, that he might the better converse with his friends, alighted from his horse and led him. Of those that were about him, one stopped, pretending to tie his shoe that was loose, another to water his horse, a third to drink himself; and thus lagging behind, by degrees left him, they having not so much reason to fear their enemies as his cruelty; for he, disordered by his misfortune, sought to clear himself by laying the cause of the overthrow upon everybody else. He arrived at Pella in the night, where Euctus and Eudæus, two of his treasurers, came to him, and, what with their reflecting on his former faults, and their free and ill-timed admonitions and counsels, so exasperated him, that he killed them both, stabbing them with his own dagger. After this, nobody stuck to him but Evander the Cretan, Archedemus the Ætolian, and Neon the Bœotian. Of the common soldiers there followed him only those from Crete, not out of any goodwill, but because they were as constant to his riches as the bees to their hive. For he carried a great treasure with him, out of which he had suffered them to take cups, bowls, and other vessels of silver and gold, to the value of fifty talents. But when he was come to Amphipolis, and afterwards to Galepsus, and his fears were a little abated, he relapsed into his old and constitutional disease of covetousness, and lamented to his friends that he had, through inadvertency, allowed some gold plate which had belonged to Alexander the Great to go into the hands of the Cretans, and besought those that had it, with tears in his eyes, to exchange with him again for money. Those that understood him thoroughly knew very well that he only played the Cretan with the Cretans, but those that believed him, and restored what they had, were cheated; as he not only did not pay the money, but by craft got thirty talents more of his friends into his hands (which in a short time after fell to the enemy), and with them sailed to Samothrace, and there fled to the temple of Castor and Pollux for refuge.

The Macedonians were always accounted great lovers of their kings, but now, as if their chief prop was broken, they all gave way together, and submitted to Æmilius, and in two days made him master of their whole country. This seems to confirm the opinion which ascribes whatever he did to good fortune. The omen, also, that happened at Amphipolis has a supernatural character. When he was sacrificing there, and the holy rites were just begun, on a sudden, lightning fell upon the altar, set the wood on fire, and completed the immolation of the sacrifice. The most signal manifestation, however, of preternatural agency appears in the story of the rumour of his success. For on the fourth day after Perseus was vanquished at Pydna, whilst the people at Rome were seeing the horse-races, a report suddenly rose at the entrance of the theatre that Æmilius had defeated Perseus in a great battle, and was reducing all Macedonia under his power; and from thence it spread amongst the people, and created general joy, with shoutings and acclamations for that whole day through the city. But when no certain author was found of the news, and everyone alike had taken it at random, it was abandoned for the present and thought no more of, until, a few days after, certain intelligence came, and then the first was looked upon as no less than a miracle, having, under an appearance of fiction, contained what was real and true. It is reported also, that the news of the battle fought in Italy, near the river Sagra, was conveyed into Peloponnesus the same day, and of that at Mycale against the Medes, to Platæa. When the Romans had defeated the Tarquins, who were combined with the Latins, a little after there were seen at Rome two tall and comely men, who professed to bring the news from the camp. They were conjectured to be Castor and Pollux. The first man that spoke to them in the forum, near the fountain where they were cooling their horses, which were all of a foam, expressed surprise at the report of the victory, when, it is said, they smiled, and gently touched his beard with their hands, the hair of which from being black was, on the spot, changed to yellow. This gave credit to what they said, and fixed the name of Ahenobarbus, or Brazen-beard, on the man. And a thing which happened in our own time will make all these credible. For when Antonius rebelled against Domitian, and Rome was in consternation, expecting great wars from the quarter of Germany, all on a sudden, and nobody knows upon what account, the people spontaneously gave out a rumour of victory, and the news ran current through the city, that Antonius himself was slain, his whole army destroyed, and not so much as a part of it escaped; nay, this belief was so strong and positive, that many of the magistrates offered up sacrifice. But when, at length, the author was sought for, and none was to be found, it vanished by degrees, everyone shifting it off from himself to another, and, at last, was lost in the numberless crowd, as in a vast ocean, and, having no solid ground to support its credit, was in a short time not so much as named in the city. Nevertheless, when Domitian marched out with his forces to the war, he met with messengers and letters that gave him a relation of the victory; and the rumour, it was found, had come the very day it was gained, though the distance between the places was more than twenty-five hundred miles. The truth of this no man of our time is ignorant of.

But to proceed. Cnæus Octavius, who was joined in command with Æmilius, came to an anchor with his fleet under Samothrace, where, out of respect to the gods, he permitted Perseus to enjoy the benefit of refuge, but took care that he should not escape by sea. Notwithstanding, Perseus secretly persuaded Oroandes of Crete, master of a small vessel, to convey him and his treasure away. He, however, playing the true Cretan, took in the treasure, and bade him come, in the night, with his children and most necessary attendants, to the port by the temple of Ceres; but, as soon as it was evening, set sail without him. It had been sad enough for Perseus to be forced to let down himself, his wife, and children through a narrow window by a wall—people altogether unaccustomed to hardship and flying; but that which drew a far sadder sigh from his heart was, when he was told by a man, as he wandered on the shore, that he had seen Oroandes under sail in the main sea; it being now about daybreak. So, there being no hopes left of escaping, he fled back again to the wall, which he and his wife recovered, though they were seen by the Romans, before they could reach them. His children he himself had delivered into the hands of Ion, one that had been his favourite, but now proved his betrayer, and was the chief cause that forced him (beasts themselves will do so when their young ones are taken) to come and yield himself up to those that had them in their power. His greatest confidence was in Nasica, and it was for him he called, but he not being there, he bewailed his misfortune, and, seeing there was no possible remedy, surrendered himself to Octavius. And here, in particular, he made it manifest that he was possessed with a vice more sordid than covetousness itself, namely, the fondness of life; by which he deprived himself even of pity, the only thing that fortune never takes away from the most wretched. He desired to be brought to Æmilius, who arose from his seat, and, accompanied with his friends, went to receive him, with tears in his eyes, as a great man fallen by the anger of the gods and his own ill-fortune; when Perseus—the most shameful of sights— threw himself at his feet, embraced his knees, and uttered unmanly cries and petitions, such as Æmilius was not able to bear, nor would vouchsafe to hear: but looking on him with a sad and angry countenance he said, "Why, unhappy man, do you thus take pains to exonerate fortune of your heaviest charge against her, by conduct that will make it seem that you are not unjustly in calamity, and that it is not your present condition, but your former happiness, that was more than your deserts? And why depreciate also my victory, and make my conquests insignificant, by proving yourself a coward, and a foe beneath a Roman? Distressed valour challenges great respect, even from enemies; but cowardice, though never so successful, from the Romans has always met with scorn." Yet for all this he took him up, gave him his hand, and delivered him into the custody of Tubero. Meantime, he himself carried his sons, his sons-in-law, and others of chief rank, especially of the younger sort, back with him into his tent, where for a long time he sat down without speaking one word, insomuch that they all wondered at him. At last, he began to discourse of fortune and human affairs. "Is it meet," said he, "for him that knows he is but man, in his greatest prosperity to pride himself, and be exalted at the conquest of a city, nation, or kingdom, and not rather well to weigh this change of fortune, in which all warriors may see an example of their common frailty, and learn a lesson that there is nothing durable or constant? For what time can men select to think themselves secure, when that of victory itself forces us more than any to dread our own fortune? And a very little consideration on the law of things, and how all are hurried round, and each man's station changed, will introduce sadness in the midst of the greatest joy. Or can you, when you see before your eyes the succession of Alexander himself, who arrived at the height of power and ruled the greatest empire, in the short space of an hour trodden underfoot—when you behold a king, that was but even now surrounded with so numerous an army, receiving nourishment to support his life from the hands of his conquerors— can you, I say, believe there is any certainty in what we now possess, whilst there is such a thing as chance? No, young men, cast off that vain pride and empty boast of victory; sit down with humility, looking always for what is yet to come, and the possible future reverses which the divine displeasure may eventually make the end of our present happiness." It is said that Æmilius, having spoken much more to the same purpose, dismissed the young men properly humbled, and with their vainglory and insolence thoroughly chastened and curbed by his address.

When this was done, he put his army into garrisons, to refresh themselves, and went himself to visit Greece, and to spend a short time in relaxations equally honourable and humane. For as he passed, he eased the people's grievances, reformed their governments, and bestowed gifts upon them; to some corn, to others oil out of the king's storehouses, in which, they report, there were such vast quantities laid up, that receivers and petitioners were lacking before they could be exhausted. In Delphi he found a great square pillar of white marble, designed for the pedestal of King Perseus' golden statue, on which he commanded his own to be placed, alleging that it was but just that the conquered should give place to the conquerors. In Olympia he is said to have uttered the saying everybody has heard, that Phidias had carved Homer's Jupiter. When the ten commissioners arrived from Rome, he delivered up again to the Macedonians their cities and country, granting them to live at liberty, and according to their own laws, only paying the Romans the tribute of a hundred talents, double which sum they had been wont to pay to their kings. Then he celebrated all manner of shows and games, and sacrifices to the gods, and made great entertainments and feasts; the charge of all which he liberally defrayed out of the king's treasury; and showed that he understood the ordering and placing of his guests, and how every man should be received, answerably to their rank and quality, with such nice exactness, that the Greeks were full of wonder, finding the care of these matters of pleasure did not escape him, and that though involved in such important business, he could observe correctness in these trifles. Nor was it least gratifying to him, that, amidst all the magnificent and splendid preparations, he himself was always the most grateful sight, and greatest pleasure to those he entertained. And he told those that seemed to wonder at his diligence, that there was the same spirit shown in marshalling a banquet as an army; in rendering the one formidable to the enemy, the other acceptable to the guests. Nor did men less praise his liberality, and the greatness of his soul, than his other virtues; for he would not so much as see those great quantities of silver and gold, which were heaped together out of the king's palaces, but delivered them to the quæstors, to be put into the public treasury. He only permitted his own sons, who were great lovers of learning, to take the king's books; and when he distributed rewards due to extraordinary valour, he gave his son-in-law, Ælius Tubero, a bowl that weighed five pounds. This is that Tubero we have already mentioned, who was one of sixteen relations that lived together, and were all maintained out of one little farm; and it is said that this was the first plate that ever entered the house of the Ælii, brought thither as an honour and reward of virtue; before this time, neither they nor their wives ever made use either of silver or gold.

Having thus settled everything well, taking his leave of the Greeks, and exhorting the Macedonians, that, mindful of the liberty they had received from the Romans, they should endeavour to maintain it by their obedience to the laws, and concord amongst themselves, he departed for Epirus, having orders from the senate to give the soldiers that followed him in the war against Perseus the pillage of the cities of that country. That he might set upon them all at once by surprise and unawares, he summoned ten of the principal men out of each, whom he commanded, on such an appointed day, to bring all the gold and silver they had either in their private houses or temples; and, with everyone of these, as if it were for this very purpose, and under a pretence of searching for and receiving the gold, he sent a centurion and a guard of soldiers; who, the set day being come, rose all at once, and at the very self-same time fell upon them, and proceeded to ransack the cities; so that in one hour a hundred and fifty thousand persons were made slaves, and threescore and ten cities sacked. Yet what was given to each soldier, out of so vast a destruction and utter ruin, amounted to no more than eleven drachmas; so that men could only shudder at the issue of a war, where the wealth of a whole nation thus divided turned to so little advantage and profit to each particular man.

When Æmilius had done this—an action perfectly contrary to his gentle and mild nature—he went down to Oricus, where he embarked his army for Italy. He sailed up the river Tiber in the king's galley, that had sixteen banks of oars, and was richly adorned with captured arms and with cloths of purple and scarlet; so that, the vessel rowing slowly against the stream, the Romans that crowded on the shore to meet him had a foretaste of his following triumph. But the soldiers, who had cast a covetous eye on the treasures of Perseus, when they did not obtain as much as they thought they deserved, were secretly enraged and angry with Æmilius for this, but openly complained that he had been a severe and tyrannical commander over them; nor were they ready to show their desire of his triumph. When Servius Galba, who was Æmilius' enemy, though he commanded as tribune under him, understood this, he had the boldness plainly to affirm that a triumph was not to be allowed him; and sowed various calumnies amongst the soldiers, which yet further increased their ill-will. Nay more, he desired the tribunes of the people, because the four hours that were remaining of the day could not suffice for the accusation, to let him put it off till another. But when the tribunes commanded him to speak then, if he had anything to say, he began a long oration, filled with all manner of reproaches, in which he spent the remaining part of the time, and the tribunes, when it was dark, dismissed the assembly. The soldiers growing more vehement on this, thronged all to Galba, and entering into a conspiracy, early in the morning beset the capitol, where the tribunes had appointed the following assembly to be held.

As soon as it was day it was put to the vote, and the first tribe was proceeding to refuse the triumph; and the news spread amongst the people and to the senate. The people were indeed much grieved that Æmilius should meet with such ignominy; but this was only in words, which had no effect. The chief of the senate exclaimed against it as a base action, and excited one another to repress the boldness and insolence of the soldiers, which would ere long become altogether ungovernable and violent, were they now permitted to deprive Æmilius of his triumph. Forcing a passage through the crowd, they came up in great numbers, and desired the tribunes to defer polling till they had spoken what they had to say to the people. All things thus suspended, and silence being made, Marcus Servilius stood up, a man of consular dignity, and who had killed twenty-three of his enemies that had challenged him in single combat. "It is now more than ever," said he, "dear to my mind how great a commander our Æmilius Paulus is, when I see he was able to perform such famous and great exploits with an army so full of sedition and baseness; nor can I sufficiently wonder, that a people that seemed to glory in the triumphs over Illyrians and Ligurians, should now through envy refuse to see the Macedonian king led alive, and all the glory of Philip and Alexander, in captivity to the Roman power. For is it not a strange thing for you, who upon a slight rumour of victory that came by chance into the city, did offer sacrifices and put up your requests unto the gods that you might see the report verified, now, when the general is returned with an undoubted conquest, to defraud the gods of honour, and yourselves of joy, as if you feared to behold the greatness of his warlike deed, or were resolved to spare your enemy? And of the two, much better were it to put a stop to the triumph, out of pity to him, than out of envy to your general; yet to such a height of power is malice arrived amongst you, that a man without one scar to show on his skin, that is smooth and sleek with ease and home-keeping habits, will undertake to define the office and duties of a general before us, who with our own wounds have been taught how to judge of the valour or the cowardice of commanders." And, at the same time, putting aside his garment, he showed an infinite number of scars upon his breast, and, turning about, he exposed some parts of his person which it is usual to conceal; and, addressing Galba, said: "You deride me for these, in which I glory before my fellow-citizens, for it is in their service, in which I have ridden night and day, that I received them; but go collect the votes, whilst I follow after, and note the base and ungrateful, and such as choose rather to be flattered and courted than commanded by their general." It is said this speech so stopped the soldiers' mouths, and altered their minds, that all the tribes decreed a triumph for Æmilius; which was performed after this manner.

The people erected scaffolds in the forum, in the circuses, as they call their buildings for horse-races, and in all other parts of the city where they could best behold the show. The spectators were clad in white garments; all the temples were open, and full of garlands and perfumes; the ways were cleared and kept open by numerous officers, who drove back all who crowded into or ran across the main avenue. This triumph lasted three days. On the first, which was scarcely long enough for the sight, were to be seen the statues, pictures, and colossal images which were taken from the enemy, drawn upon two hundred and fifty chariots. On the second was carried in a great many wagons the finest and richest armour of the Macedonians, both of brass and steel, all newly polished and glittering; the pieces of which were piled up and arranged purposely with the greatest art, so as to seem to be tumbled in heaps carelessly and by chance: helmets were thrown upon shields, coats of mail upon greaves; Cretan targets, and Thracian bucklers and quivers of arrows, lay huddled amongst horses' bits, and through these there appeared the points of naked swords, intermixed with long Macedonian sarissas. All these arms were fastened together with just so much looseness that they struck against one another as they were drawn along, and made a harsh and alarming noise, so that, even as spoils of a conquered enemy, they could not be beheld without dread. After these wagons loaded with armour there followed three thousand men who carried the silver that was coined, in seven hundred and fifty vessels, each of which weighed three talents, and was carried by four men. Others brought silver bowls and goblets and cups, all disposed in such order as to make the best show, and all curious as well for their size as the solidity of their embossed work.

On the third day, early in the morning, first came the trumpeters, who did not sound as they were wont in a procession or solemn entry, but such a charge as the Romans use when they encourage the soldiers to fight. Next followed young men wearing frocks with ornamented borders, who led to the sacrifice a hundred and twenty stalled oxen, with their horns gilded, and their heads adorned with ribbons and garlands; and with these were boys that carried basins for libation, of silver and gold. After this was brought the gold coin, which was divided into vessels that weighed three talents, like those that contained the silver; they were in number seventy-seven. These were followed by those that brought the consecrated bowl which Æmilius had caused to be made, that weighed ten talents, and was set with precious stones. Then were exposed to view the cups of Antigonus and Seleucus, and those of the Thericlean make, and all the gold plate that was used at Perseus' table. Next to these came Perseus' chariot, in which his armour was placed, and on that his diadem. And, after a little intermission, the king's children were led captives, and with them a train of their attendants, masters, and teachers, all shedding tears, and stretching out hands to the spectators, and making the children themselves also beg and entreat their compassion. There were two sons and a daughter, whose tender age made them but little sensible of the greatness of their misery, which very insensibility of their condition rendered it the more deplorable; insomuch that Perseus himself was scarcely regarded as he went along, whilst pity fixed the eyes of the Romans upon the infants; and many of them could not forbear tears, and all beheld the sight with a mixture of sorrow and pleasure, until the children were passed.

After his children and their attendants came Perseus himself, clad all in black, and wearing the boots of his country, and looking like one altogether stunned and deprived of reason, through the greatness of his misfortunes. Next followed a great company of his friends and familiars, whose countenances were disfigured with grief, and who let the spectators see, by their tears and their continual looking upon Perseus, that it was his fortune they so much lamented, and that they were regardless of their own. Perseus sent to Æmilius to entreat that he might not be led in pomp, but be left out of the triumph; who, deriding, as was but just, his cowardice and fondness of life, sent him this answer, that as for that, it had been before, and was now, in his own power; giving him to understand that the disgrace could be avoided by death; which the fainthearted man not having the spirit for, and made effeminate by I know not what hopes, allowed himself to appear as a part of his own spoils. After these were carried four hundred crowns, all made of gold, sent from the cities by their respective deputations to Æmilius, in honour of his victory. Then he himself came, seated on a chariot magnificently adorned (a man well worthy to be looked at, even without these ensigns of power), dressed in a robe of purple, interwoven with gold, and holding a laurel branch in his right hand. All the army, in like manner, with boughs of laurel in their hands, divided into their bands and companies, followed the chariot of their commander; some singing verses, according to the usual custom, mingled with raillery; others, songs of triumph and the praise of Æmilius' deeds; who, indeed, was admired and accounted happy by all men, and unenvied by everyone that was good; except so far as it seems the province of some god to lessen that happiness which is too great and inordinate, and so to mingle the affairs of human life that no one should be entirely free and exempt from calamities; but, as we read in Homer, that those should think themselves truly blessed whom fortune has given an equal share of good and evil.

Æmilius had four sons, of whom Scipio and Fabius, as is already related, were adopted into other families; the other two, whom he had by a second wife, and who were yet but young, he brought up in his own house. One of these died at fourteen years of age, five days before his father's triumph, the other at twelve, three days after; so that there was no Roman without a deep sense of his suffering, and who did not shudder at the cruelty of fortune, that had not scrupled to bring so much sorrow into a house replenished with happiness, rejoicing, and sacrifices, and to inter-mingle tears and laments with songs of victory and triumph.

Æmilius, however, reasoning justly that courage and resolution was not merely to resist armour and spears, but all the shocks of ill-fortune, so met and so adapted himself to these mingled and contrasting circumstances, as to outbalance the evil with the good, and his private concerns with those of the public; and thus did not allow anything either to take away from the grandeur, or sully the dignity of his victory. For as soon as he had buried the first of his sons (as we have already said), he triumphed; and the sec-ond dying almost as soon as his triumph was over, he gathered together an assembly of the people, and made an oration to them, not like a man that stood in need of comfort from others, but one that undertook to support his fellow-citizens in their grief for the sufferings he himself underwent.

"I," he said, "who never yet feared anything that was human, have, amongst such as were divine, always had a dread of Fortune as faithless and inconstant; and, for the very reason that in this war she had been as a favourable gale in all my affairs, I still expected some change and reflux of things. In one day I passed the Ionian sea, and reached Corcyra from Brundisium; thence in five more I sacrificed at Delphi, and in other five days came to my forces in Macedonia, where, after I had finished the usual sacrifices for the purifying of the army, I entered on my duties, and, in space of fifteen days, put an honourable period to the war. Still retaining a jealousy of Fortune, even from the smooth current of my affairs, and see-ing myself secure and free from the danger of any enemy, I chiefly dreaded the change of the goddess at sea, whilst conveying home my victorious army, vast spoils, and a captive king. Nay, indeed, after I was returned to you safe, and saw the city full of joy, congratulating, and sacrifices, yet still I dis-trusted, well knowing that Fortune never conferred any great benefits that were unmixed and unattended with probabilities of reverse. Nor could my mind, that was still as it were in labour, and always foreseeing something to befall this city, free itself from this fear, until this great misfortune befell me in my own family, and till, in the midst of those days set apart for triumph, I carried two of the best sons, my only destined successors, one after another to their funerals. Now, therefore, I am myself safe from danger, at least as to what was my greatest care; and I trust and am verily persuaded that for the time to come Fortune will prove constant and harmless unto you; since she has sufficiently wreaked her jealousy at our great success on me and mine, and has made the conqueror as marked an example of human instability as the captive whom he led in triumph, with this only difference, that Perseus, though conquered, does yet enjoy his children, while the conqueror, Æmilius, is deprived of his." This was the generous and magnanimous oration Æmilius is said to have spoken to the people, from a heart truly sincere and free from all artifice.

Although he very much pitied the condition of Perseus, and studied to befriend him in what he was able, yet he could procure no other favour than his removal from the common prison, the *Carcer*, into a more cleanly and humane place of security, where, whilst he was guarded, it is said, he starved himself to death. Others state his death to be of the strangest and most unusual character: that the soldiers who were his guard, having conceived a spite and hatred against him for some reason, and finding no other way to grieve and afflict him, kept him from sleep, took pains to disturb him when he was disposed to rest, and found out contrivances to keep him continually awake, by which means at length he was utterly worn out, and expired. Two of his children, also, died soon after him; the third, who was named Alexander, they say proved an exquisite artist in turning and graving small figures, and learned so perfectly to speak and write the Roman language, that he became clerk to the magistrates, and behaved himself in his office with great skill and conduct.

They ascribed to Æmilius' conquest of Macedonia this most acceptable benefit to the people, that he brought so vast a quantity of money into the public treasury, that they never paid any taxes, until Hirtius and Pansa were consuls, which was in the first war between Antony and Cæsar. This also was peculiar and remarkable in Æmilius, that though he was extremely beloved and honoured by the people, yet he always sided with the nobles; nor would he either say or do anything to ingratiate himself with the multitude, but constantly adhered to the nobility, in all political matters, which in aftertimes was cast in Scipio Africanus' teeth by Appius; these two being in their time the most considerable men in the city, and standing in competition for the office of censor. The one had on his side the nobles and the senate, to which party the Appii were always attached; the other, although his own interest was great, yet made use of the favour and love of the people. When, therefore, Appius saw Scipio come to the market place, surrounded with men of mean rank, and such as were but newly made free, yet were very fit to manage a debate, to gather together the rabble, and to carry whatsoever they designed by importunity and noise, crying out with a loud voice: "Groan now," said he, "O Æmilius Paulus, if you have knowledge in your grave of what is done above, that your son aspires to be censor, by the help of Æmilius, the common crier, and Licinius Philonicus." Scipio always had the goodwill of the people, because he was constantly heaping favours on them; but Æmilius, although he still took part with the nobles, yet was as much the people's favourite as those who most sought popularity and used every art to obtain it. This they made manifest, when, amongst other dignities, they thought him worthy of the office of censor, a trust accounted most sacred and of great authority, as well in other things, as in the strict examination into men's lives. For the censors had power to expel a senator, and enrol whom they judged most fit in his room, and to disgrace such young men as lived licentiously, by taking away their horses. Besides this, they were to value and assess each man's estate, and register the number of the people. There were numbered by Æmilius 347,452 men. He declared Marcus Æmilius Lepidus first senator, who had already four times held that honour, and he removed from their office three of the senators of the least note. The same moderation he and his fellow-censor, Marcius Philippus, used at the muster of the knights.

Whilst he was thus busy about many and weighty affairs he fell sick of a disease, which at first seemed hazardous; and although after a while it proved without danger, yet was troublesome and difficult to be cured: so that by the advice of his physicians he sailed to Velia, in south Italy, and there dwelt a long time near the sea, where he enjoyed all possible quietness. The Romans, in the meanwhile, longed for his return, and oftentimes by their expressions in the theatres gave public testimony of their great desire and impatience to see him. When, therefore, the time drew nigh that a solemn sacrifice was of necessity to be offered, and he found, as he thought, his body strong enough, he came back again to Rome, and there performed the holy rites with the rest of the priests, the people in the meantime crowding about him and congratulating his return. The next day he sacrificed again to the gods for his recovery; and, having finished the sacrifice, returned to his house and sat down to dinner, when, all on a sudden and when no change was expected, he fell into a fit of delirium and, being quite deprived of his senses, the third day after ended a life in which he had wanted no manner of thing which is thought to conduct to happiness. Nay, his very funeral pomp had something in it remarkable and to be admired, and his virtue was graced with the most solemn and happy rites at his burial; consisting, not in gold and ivory, or in the usual sumptuousness and splendour of such preparations, but in the goodwill, honour, and love, not only of his fellow-citizens, but of his enemies themselves. For as many Spaniards, Ligurians, and Macedonians as happened to be present at the solemnity, that were young and of vigorous bodies, took up the bier and carried it; whilst the more aged followed, called Æmilius the benefactor and preserver of their countries. For not only at the time of his conquest had he acted to all with kindness and clemency, but, through the whole course of his life, he continued to do them good and look after their concerns, as if they had been his familiars and relations. They report that the whole of his estate scarce amounted to three hundred and seventy thousand drachmas; to which he left his two sons co-heirs; but Scipio, who was the youngest, being adopted into the more wealthy family of Africanus, gave it all to his brother. Such are said to have been the life and manners of Æmilius.

THE COMPARISON OF TIMOLEON
WITH ÆMILIUS PAULUS

SUCH BEING THE STORY OF THESE TWO GREAT MEN'S LIVES, WITHOUT DOUBT in the comparison very little difference will be found between them. They made war with two powerful enemies: the one against the Macedonians, and the other with the Carthaginians; and the success was in both cases glorious. One conquered Macedon from the seventh succeeding heir of Antigonus; the other freed Sicily from usurping tyrants, and restored the island to its former liberty. Unless, indeed, it be made a point of Æmilius' side, that he engaged with Perseus when his forces were entire, and composed of men that had often successfully fought with the Romans; whereas Timoleon found Dionysius in a despairing condition, his affairs being reduced to the last extremity; or, on the contrary, it be urged in favour of Timoleon, that he vanquished several tyrants, and a powerful Carthaginian army, with which an inconsiderable number of men gathered together from all parts, not with such an army as Æmilius had, of well-disciplined soldiers, experienced in war, and accustomed to obey; but with such as through the hopes of gain restored to them, unskilled in fighting and ungovernable. And when actions are equally glorious, and the means to compass them unequal, the greatest esteem is certainly due to that general who conquers with the small power.

Both have the reputation of having behaved themselves with an uncorrupted integrity in all the affairs they managed; but Æmilius had the advantage of being, from his infancy, by the laws and customs of his country brought up to the proper management of public affairs, which Timoleon brought himself to by his own efforts. And this is plain; for at that time all the Romans were uniformly orderly and obedient, respectful to the laws and to their fellow-citizens: whereas it is remarkable that not one of the Greek generals commanding in Sicily could keep himself uncorrupted, except Dion, and of him many entertained a jealousy that he would establish a monarchy there, after the Lacedæmonian manner. Timæus writes, that the Syracusans sent even Gylippus home dishonourably, and with a reputation lost by the unsatiable covetousness he displayed when he commanded the army. And numerous historians tell us of the wicked and perfidious acts committed by Pharax the Spartan and Callippus the Athenian, with the view of making themselves kings of Sicily. Yet what were these men, and what strength had they, to entertain such a thought? The first of them was a follower of Dionysius, when he was expelled from Syracuse, and the other a hired captain of foot under Dion, and came into Sicily with him. But Timoleon, at the request and prayers of the Syracusans, was sent to be their general, and had no need to seek for power, but had a perfect title, founded on their own offers, to hold it; and yet no sooner had he freed Sicily from her oppressors, but he willingly surrendered it.

It is truly worthy our admiration in Æmilius, that though he conquered so great and so rich a realm as that of Macedon, yet he would not touch, nor see any of the money, nor did he advantage himself one farthing by it, though he was very generous of his own to others. I would not intend any reflection on Timoleon for accepting of a house and handsome estate in the country, which the Syracusans presented him with; there is no dishonour in accepting; but yet there is greater glory in a refusal, and the supremest virtue is shown in not wanting what it might fairly take. And as that body is, without doubt, the most strong and healthful which can the easiest support extreme cold and excessive heat in the change of seasons, and that the most firm and collected mind which is not puffed up with prosperity nor dejected with adversity; so the virtue of Æmilius was eminently seen in his countenance and behaviour, continuing as noble and lofty upon the loss of two dear sons, as when he achieved his greatest victories and triumphs. But Timoleon, after he had justly punished his brother, a truly heroic action, let his reason yield to a causeless sorrow, and humiliated with grief and remorse, forbore for twenty years to appear in any public place, or meddle with any affairs of the commonwealth. It is truly very commendable to abhor and shun the doing any base action; but to stand in fear of every kind of censure or disrepute may argue a gentle and open-hearted, but not an heroic temper.

PELOPIDAS

CATO MAJOR, HEARING SOME COMMEND ONE THAT WAS RASH, AND inconsiderately daring in a battle, said, "There is a difference between a man's prizing valour at a great rate, and valuing life at little"; a very just remark. Antigonus, we know, at least, had a soldier, a venturous fellow, but of wretched health and constitution; the reason of whose ill-look he took the trouble to inquire into; and, on understanding from him that it was a disease, commanded his physicians to employ their utmost skill, and if possible recover him; which brave hero, when once cured, never afterwards sought danger or showed himself venturous in battle; and, when Antigonus wondered and upbraided him with his change, made no secret of the reason, and said, "Sir, you are the cause of my cowardice, by freeing me from those miseries which made me care little for life." With the same feeling, the Sybarite seems to have said of the Spartans, that it was no commendable thing in them to be so ready to die in the wars, since by that they were freed from such hard labour and miserable living. In truth, the Sybarites, a soft and dissolute people, might well imagine they hated life, because in their eager pursuit of virtue and glory they were not afraid to die; but, in fact, the Lacedæmonians found their virtue secured them happiness alike in living or in dying; as we see in the epitaph that says—

> They died, but not as lavish of their blood,
> Or thinking death itself was simply good;
> Their wishes neither were to live nor die,
> But to do both alike commendably.

An endeavour to avoid death is not blamable, if we do not basely desire to live; nor a willingness to die good and virtuous, if it proceeds from a contempt of life. And therefore Homer always takes care to bring his bravest and most daring heroes well armed into battle; and the Greek lawgivers punished those that threw away their shields, but not him that lost his sword or spear; intimating that self-defence is more a man's business than offence. This is especially true of a governor of a city, or a general; for it, as Iphicrates divides it out, the light-armed are the hands; the horse the feet; the infantry the breast; and the general the head; and, when he puts himself upon danger, not only ventures his own person, but all those whose safety depends on his; and so on the contrary. Callicratidas, therefore, though otherwise a great man, was wrong in his answer to the augur who advised him, the sacrifice being unlucky, to be careful of his life; "Sparta," said he, "will not miss one man." It is true, Callicratidas, when simply serving in any engagement either at sea or land, was but a single person, but as a general, he united in his life the lives of all, and could hardly be called one when his death involved the ruin of so many. The saying of old Antigonus was better, who, when he was to fight at Andros, and one told him, "The enemy's ships are more than ours"; replied, "For how many then wilt thou reckon me?" intimating that a brave and experienced commander is to be highly valued, one of the first duties of whose office indeed it is to save him on whose safety depends that of others. And therefore I applaud Timotheus, who, when Chares showed the wounds he had received, and his shield pierced by a dart, told him, "Yet how ashamed I was, at the siege of Samos, when a dart fell near me, for exposing myself, more like a boy than like a general in command of a large army." Indeed, where the general's hazarding himself will go far to decide the result, there he must fight and venture his person, and not mind their maxims, who would have a general die, if not *of,* at least *in* old age; but when the advantage will be but small if he gets the better, and the loss considerable if he falls, who then would desire, at the risk of the commander's life, a piece of success which a common soldier might obtain? This I thought fit to premise before the lives of Pelopidas and Marcellus, who were both great men, but who both fell by their own rashness. For, being gallant men, and having gained their respective countries great glory and reputation by their conduct in war against terrible enemies, the one, as history relates, overthrowing Hannibal, who was till then invincible; the other, in a set battle beating the Lacedæmonians, then supreme both at sea and land; they ventured at last too far and were heedlessly prodigal of their lives, when there was the greatest need of men and commanders such as they. And this agreement in their characters and their deaths is the reason why I compare their lives.

Pelopidas, the son of Hippoclus, was descended, as likewise Epaminondas was, from an honourable family in Thebes; and, being brought up to opulence, and having a fair estate left him whilst he was young, he made it his business to relieve the good and deserving amongst the poor, that he might show himself lord and not slave of his estate. For amongst men, as Aristotle observes, some are too narrow-minded to use their wealth, and some are loose and abuse it; and these live perpetual slaves to their pleasures, as the others to their gain. Others permitted themselves to be obliged by Pelopidas, and thankfully made use of his liberality and kindness; but amongst all his friends he could never persuade Epaminondas to be a sharer in his wealth. He, however, stepped down into his poverty, and took pleasure in the same poor attire, spare diet, unwearied endurance of hardships, and unshrinking boldness in war; like Capaneus in Euripides, who had—

Abundant wealth and in that wealth no pride,

he was ashamed anyone should think that he spent more upon his person than the meanest Theban. Epaminondas made his familiar and hereditary poverty more light and easy by his philosophy and single life; but Pelopidas married a woman of good family, and had children; yet still thinking little of his private interests, and devoting all his time to the public, he ruined his estate: and, when his friends admonished and told him how necessary that money which he neglected was: "Yes," he replied, "necessary to Nicodemus," pointing to a blind cripple.

Both seemed equally fitted by nature for all sorts of excellence; but bodily exercises chiefly delighted Pelopidas, learning Epaminondas; and the one spent his spare hours in hunting and the Palæstra, the other in hearing lectures or philosophising. And, amongst a thousand points for praise in both, the judicious esteem nothing equal to that constant benevolence and friendship, which they inviolably preserved in all their expeditions, public actions, and administration of the commonwealth. For if anyone looks on the administrations of Aristides and Themistocles, of Cimon and Pericles, of Nicias and Alcibiades, what confusion, what envy, what mutual jealousy appears? And if he then casts his eye on the kindness and reverence that Pelopidas showed Epaminondas, he must needs confess that these are more truly and more justly styled colleagues in government and command than the others, who strove rather to overcome one another than their enemies. The true cause of this was their virtue; whence it came that they did not make their actions aim at wealth and glory, an endeavour sure to lead to bitter and contentious jealousy; but both from the beginning being inflamed with a divine desire of seeing their country glorious by their exertions, they used to that end one another's excellences as their own. Many, indeed, think this strict and entire affection is to be dated from the battle at Mantinea, where they both fought, being part of the succours that were sent from Thebes to the Lacedæmonians, their then friends and allies. For, being placed together amongst the infantry, and engaging the Arcadians, when the Lacedæmonian wing, in which they fought, gave ground, and many fled, they closed their shields together and resisted the assailants. Pelopidas, having received seven wounds in the forepart of his body, fell upon an heap of slain friends and enemies; but Epaminondas, though he thought him past recovery, advanced to defend his arms and body, and singly fought a multitude, resolving rather to die than forsake his helpless Pelopidas. And now, he being much distressed, being wounded in the breast by a spear, and in the arm by a sword, Agesipolis, the King of the Spartans, came to his succour from the other wing, and beyond hope delivered both.

After this the Lacedæmonians pretended to be friends to Thebes, but in truth looked with jealous suspicions on the designs and power of the city, and chiefly hated the party of Ismenias and Androclides, in which Pelopidas also was an associate, as tending to liberty and the advancement of the commonalty. Therefore Archias, Leontidas, and Philip, all rich men, and of oligarchical principles, and immoderately ambitious, urged Phœbidas the Spartan, as he was on his way past the city with a considerable force, to surprise the Cadmea, and, banishing the contrary faction, to establish an oligarchy, and by that means subject the city to the supremacy of the Spartans. He, accepting the proposal, at the festival of Ceres unexpectedly fell on the Thebans, and made himself master of the citadel. Ismenias was taken, carried to Sparta, and in a short time murdered; but Pelopidas, Pherenicus, Androclides, and many more that fled were publicly proclaimed outlaws. Epaminondas stayed at home, being not much looked after, as one whom philosophy had made inactive and poverty incapable.

The Lacedæmonians cashiered Phœbidas, and fined him one hundred thousand drachmas, yet still kept a garrison in the Cadmea; which made all Greece wonder at their inconsistency, since they punished the doer, but approved the deed. And though the Thebans, having lost their polity, and being enslaved by Archias and Leontidas, had no hopes to get free from this tyranny, which they saw guarded by the whole military power of the Spartans, and had no means to break the yoke, unless these could be deposed from their command of sea and land; yet Leontidas and his associates, understanding the exiles lived at Athens in favour with the people, and with honour from all the good and virtuous, formed secret designs against their lives, and, suborning some unknown fellows, despatched Androclides, but were not successful on the rest. Letters, besides, were sent from Sparta to the Athenians, warning them neither to receive nor countenance the exiles, but expel them as declared common enemies of the confederacy. But the Athenians, from their natural hereditary inclination to be kind, and also to make a grateful return to the Thebans, who had very much assisted them in restoring their democracy, and had publicly enacted, that if any Athenian would march armed through Bœotia against the tyrants, that no Bœotian should either see or hear it, did the Thebans no harm.

Pelopidas, though one of the youngest, was active in privately exciting each single exile; and often told them at their meetings that it was both dishonourable and impious to neglect their enslaved and engarrisoned country, and, lazily contented with their own lives and safety, depend on the decree of the Athenians, and through fear fawn on every smooth-tongued orator that was able to work upon the people: no, they must venture for this great prize, taking Thrasybulus' bold courage for example, and as he advanced from Thebes and broke the power of the Athenian tyrants, so they should march from Athens and free Thebes. When by this method he had persuaded them, they privately despatched some persons to those friends they had left at Thebes, and acquainted them with their designs. Their plans being approved, Charon, a man of the greatest distinction, offered his house for their reception; Phillidas contrived to get himself made secretary to Archias and Philip, who then held the office of polemarch or chief captain; and Epaminondas had already inflamed the youth. For, in their exercises, he had encouraged them to challenge and wrestle with the Spartans, and again, when he saw them puffed up with victory and success, sharply told them, that it was the greatest shame to be such cowards as to serve those whom in strength they so much excelled.

The day of action being fixed, it was agreed upon by the exiles that Pherenicus with the rest should stay at the Thriasian plain while some few of the younger men tried the first danger, by endeavouring to get into the city; and, if they were surprised by their enemies, the others should take care to provide for their children and parents. Pelopidas first offered to undertake the business; then Melon, Damoclides, and Theopompus, men of noble families, who, in other things loving and faithful to one another, were rivals constant only in glory and courageous exploits. They were twelve in all, and having taken leave of those that stayed behind, and sent a messenger to Charon, they went forward, clad in short coats, and carrying hounds and hunting-poles with them, that they might be taken for hunters beating over the fields, and prevent all suspicion in those that met them on the way. When the messenger came to Charon, and told him they were approaching, he did not change his resolution at the sight of danger, but, being a man of his word, offered them his house. But one Hipposthenidas, a man of no ill principles, a lover of his country, and a friend to the exiles, but not of as much resolution as the shortness of time and the character of the action required, being as it were dizzied at the greatness of the approaching enterprise; and beginning now for the first time to comprehend that, relying on that weak assistance which could be expected from the exiles, they were undertaking no less a task than to shake the government, and overthrow the whole power of Sparta; went privately to his house and sent a friend to Melon and Pelopidas, desiring them to forbear for the present, to return to Athens and expect a better opportunity. The messenger's name was Chlidon, who, going home in haste and bringing out his horse, asked for the bridle; but, his wife, not knowing where it was, and, when it could not be found, telling him she had lent it to a friend, first they began to chide, then to curse one another, and his wife wished the journey might prove ill to him and those that sent him; insomuch that Chlidon's passion made him waste a great part of the day in this quarrelling, and then, looking on this chance as an omen, he laid aside all thoughts of his journey, and went away to some other business. So nearly had these great and glorious designs, even in their very birth, lost their opportunity.

But Pelopidas and his companions, dressing themselves like countrymen, divided, and, whilst it was yet day, entered at different quarters of the city. It was, besides, a windy day, and now it just began to snow, which contributed much to their concealment, because most people were gone indoors to avoid the weather. Those, however, that were concerned in the design received them as they came, and conducted them to Charon's house, where the exiles and others made up forty-eight in number. The tyrant's affairs stood thus: the secretary, Phillidas, as I have already observed, was an accomplice in and privy to all the contrivance of the exiles, and he a while before had invited Archias, with others, to an entertainment on that day, to drink freely, and meet some women of the town, on purpose that when they were drunk, and given up to their pleasures, he might deliver them over to the conspirators. But before Archias was thoroughly heated notice was given him that the exiles were privately in the town; a true report indeed, but obscure, and not well confirmed: nevertheless, though Phillidas endeavoured to divert the discourse, Archias sent one of his guards to Charon, and commanded him to attend immediately. It was evening, and Pelopidas and his friends with him in the house were putting themselves into a fit posture for action, having their breastplates on already, and their swords girt: but at the sudden knocking at the door, one stepping forth to inquire the matter, and learning from the officer that Charon was sent for by the polemarch, returned in great confusion and acquainted those within; and immediately conjectured that the whole plot was discovered, and they should be cut in pieces, before so much as achieving any action to do credit to their bravery: yet all agreed that Charon should obey and attend the polemarch to prevent suspicion. Charon was, indeed, a man of courage and resolution in all dangers, yet in this case he was extremely concerned, lest any should suspect that he was the traitor and the death of so many brave citizens be laid on him. And, therefore, when he was ready to depart, he brought his son out of the women's apartment, a little boy as yet, but one of the best looking and strongest of all those of his age, and delivered him to Pelopidas with these words: "If you find me a traitor, treat the boy as an enemy without any mercy." The concern which Charon showed drew tears from many; but all protested vehemently against his supposing anyone of them so mean-spirited and base, at the appearance of approaching danger, as to suspect or blame him; and therefore desired him not to involve his son, but to set him out of harm's way: that so he, perhaps escaping the tyrant's power, might live to revenge the city and his friends. Charon, however, refused to remove him, and asked, "What life, what safety could be more honourable, than to die bravely with his father and such generous companions?" Thus, imploring the protection of the gods, and saluting and encouraging them all, he departed, considering with himself, and composing his voice and countenance, that he might look as little like as possible to what in fact he really was.

When he was come to the door, Archias with Phillidas came out to him, and said, "I have heard, Charon, that there are some men just come, and lurking in the town, and that some of the citizens are resorting to them." Charon was at first disturbed, but asking, "Who are they? And who conceals them?" and finding Archias did not thoroughly understand the matter, he concluded that none of those privy to the design had given this information, and replied, "Do not disturb yourselves for an empty rumour: I will look into it, however, for no report in such a case is to be neglected." Phillidas, who stood by, commended him, and leading back Archias, got him deep in drink, still prolonging the entertainment with the hopes of the women's company at last. But when Charon returned, and found the men prepared, not as if they hoped for safety and success, but to die bravely and with the slaughter of their enemies, he told Pelopidas and his friends the truth, but pretended to others in the house that Archias talked to him about something else, inventing a story for the occasion. This storm was just blowing over, when fortune brought another; for a messenger came with a letter from one Archias, the Hierophant at Athens, to his namesake Archias, who was his friend and guest. This did not merely contain a vague conjectural suspicion, but, as it appeared afterwards, disclosed every particular of the design. The messenger being brought in to Archias, who was now pretty well drunk, and delivering the letter, said to him, "The writer of this desired it might be read at once; it is on urgent business." Archias, with a smile, replied, "Urgent business tomorrow," and so receiving the letter, he put it under his pillow, and returned to what he had been speaking of with Phillidas, and these words of his are a proverb to this day amongst the Greeks.

Now when the opportunity seemed convenient for action, they set out in two companies; Pelopidas and Damoclides with their party went against Leontidas and Hypates, that lived near together; Charon and Melon against Archias and Philip, having put on women's apparel over their breastplates, and thick garlands of fir and pine to shade their faces; and so, as soon as they came to the door, the guests clapped and gave an huzza, supposing them to be the women they expected. But when the conspirators had looked about the room, and carefully marked all that were at the entertainment, they drew their swords, and making at Archias and Philip amongst the tables, disclosed who they were. Phillidas persuaded some few of his guests to sit still, and those that got up and endeavoured to assist the polemarch, being drunk, were easily despatched. But Pelopidas and his party met with a harder task; as they attempted Leontidas, a sober and formidable man, and when they came to his house found his door shut, he being already gone to bed. They knocked a long time before anyone would answer, but at last, a servant that heard them, coming out and unbarring the door, as soon as the gate gave way, they rushed in, and, overturning the man, made all haste to Leontidas' chamber. But Leontidas, guessing at the matter by the noise and running, leaped from his bed and drew his dagger, but forgot to put out the lights, and by that means make them fall foul of one another in the dark. As it was, being easily seen by reason of the light, he received them at his chamber door and stabbed Cephisodorus, the first man that entered: on his falling, the next that he engaged was Pelopidas; and the passage being narrow and Cephisodorus' body lying in the way, there was a fierce and dangerous conflict. At last Pelopidas prevailed, and having killed Leontidas, he and his companions went in pursuit of Hypates, and after the same manner broke into his house. He perceived the design, and fled to his neighbours; but they closely followed, and caught and killed him.

This done they joined Melon, and sent to hasten the exiles they had left in Attica: and called upon the citizens to maintain their liberty, and taking down the spoils from the porches, and breaking open all the armourers' shops that were near, equipped those that came to their assistance. Epaminondas and Gorgidas came in already armed, with a gallant train of young men and the best of the old. Now the city was in a great excitement and confusion, a great noise and hurry, lights set up in every house, men running here and there; however, the people did not as yet gather into a body, but, amazed at the proceedings, and not clearly understanding the matter, waited for the day. And, therefore, the Spartan officers were thought to have been in fault for not falling on at once, since their garrison consisted of about fifteen hundred men, and many of the citizens ran to them; but, alarmed with the noise, the fires, and the confused running of the people, they kept quietly within the Cadmea. As soon as day appeared, the exiles from Attica came in armed, and there was a general assembly of the people. Epaminondas and Gorgidas brought forth Pelopidas and his party, encompassed by the priests, who held out garlands, and exhorted the people to fight for their country and their gods. The assembly, at their appearance, rose up in a body and with shouts and acclamations received the men as their deliverers and benefactors.

Then Pelopidas, being chosen chief captain of Bœotia, together with Melon and Charon, proceeded at once to blockade the citadel, and stormed it on all sides, being extremely desirous to expel the Lacedæmonians, and free the Cadmea, before an army could come from Sparta to their relief. And he just so narrowly succeeded, that they, having surrendered on terms and departed, on their way home met Cleombrotus at Megara marching towards Thebes with a considerable force. The Spartans condemned and executed Herippidas and Arcissus, two of their governors, at Thebes, and Lysanoridas the third, being severely fined, fled to

Peloponnesus. This action so closely resembling that of Thrasybulus, in the courage of the actors, the danger, the encounters, and equally crowned with success, was called the sister of it by the Greeks. For we can scarcely find any other examples where so small and weak a party of men by bold courage overcame such numerous and powerful enemies, or brought greater blessings to their country by so doing. But the subsequent change of affairs made this action the more famous; for the war which forever ruined the pretensions of Sparta to command, and put an end to the supremacy she then exercised alike by sea and by land, proceeded from that night, in which Pelopidas not surprising any fort, or castle, or citadel, but coming, the twelfth man, to a private house, loosed and broke, if we may speak truth in metaphor, the chains of the Spartan sway, which before seemed of adamant and indissoluble.

But now the Lacedæmonians invading Bœotia with a great army, the Athenians, affrighted at the danger, declared themselves no allies to Thebes, and prosecuting those that stood for the Bœotian interest, executed some, and banished and fined others: and the cause of Thebes, destitute of allies, seemed in a desperate condition. But Pelopidas and Gorgidas, holding the office of captains of Bœotia, designing to breed a quarrel between the Lacedæmonians and Athenians, made this contrivance. One Sphodrias, a Spartan, a man famous indeed for courage in battle, but of no sound judgment, full of ungrounded hopes and foolish ambition, was left with an army at Thespiæ, to receive and succour the Theban renegades. To him Pelopidas and his colleagues privately sent a merchant, one of their friends, with money, and, what proved more efficient, advice—that it more became a man of his worth to set upon some great enterprise, and that he should, making a sudden incursion on the unprotected Athenians, surprise the Piræus; since nothing could be so grateful to Sparta as to take Athens; and the Thebans, of course, would not stir to the assistance of men whom they now hated and looked upon as traitors. Sphodrias, being at last wrought upon, marched into Attica by night with his army, and advanced as far as Eleusis; but there his soldiers' hearts failing, after exposing his project and involving the Spartans in a dangerous war, he retreated to Thespiæ. After this the Athenians zealously sent supplies to Thebes, and putting to sea, sailed to many places, and offered support and protection to all those of the Greeks who were willing to revolt.

The Thebans, meantime, singly, having many skirmishes with the Spartans in Bœotia, and fighting some battles, not great indeed, but important as training and instructing them, thus had their minds raised, and their bodies inured to labour, and gained both experience and courage by these frequent encounters, insomuch that we have it related that Antalcidas, the Spartan, said to Agesilaus, returning wounded from Bœotia, "Indeed, the Thebans have paid you handsomely for instructing them in the art of war, against their wills." In real truth, however, Agesilaus was not their master in this, but those that prudently and opportunely, as men do young dogs, set them on their enemies, and brought them safely off after they had tasted the sweets of victory and resolution. Of all those leaders, Pelopidas deserves the most honour: as after they had once chosen him general, he was every year in command as long as he lived; either captain of the sacred band, or, what was most frequent, chief captain of Bœotia. About Platæa and Thespiæ the Spartans were routed and put to flight, and Phœbidas, that surprised the Cadmea, slain; and at Tanagra a considerable force was worsted, and the leader Panthoides killed. But these encounters, though they raised the victors' spirits, did not thoroughly dishearten the unsuccessful; for there was no set battle, or regular fighting, but mere incursions on advantage, in which, according to occasion, they charged, retired again, or pursued. But the battle at Tegyræ, which seemed a prelude to Leuctra, won Pelopidas great reputation; for none of the other commanders could claim any hand in the design, nor the enemies any show of victory. The city of the Orchomenians siding with the Spartans, and having received two companies for its guard, he kept a constant eye upon it, and watched his opportunity. Hearing that the garrison had moved into Locris, and hoping to find Orchomenus defenceless, he marched with his sacred band and some few horsemen. But when he approached the city, and found that a reinforcement of the garrison was on its march from Sparta, he made a circuit round the foot of the mountains, and retreated with his little army through Tegyræ, that being the only way he could pass. For the river Melas, almost as soon as it rises, spreads itself into marshes and navigable pools, and makes all the plain between impassable. A little below the marshes stands the temple and oracle of Apollo Tegyræus, forsaken not long before that time, having flourished till the Median wars, Echecrates then being priest. Here they profess that the god was born; the neighbouring mountain is called Delos, and there the river Melas comes again into a channel; beyond the temples rise two springs, admirable for the sweetness, abundance, and coolness of the streams; one they called Phœnix, the other Elæa, even to the present time, as if Lucina had not been delivered between two trees, but fountains. A place hard by, called Ptoum, is shown, where they say she was affrighted by the appearance of a boar; and the stories of the Python and Tityus are in like manner appropriated by these localities. I omit many of the points that are used as arguments. For our tradition does not rank this god amongst those that were born, and then made immortal, as Hercules and Bacchus, whom their virtue raised above a mortal and passible condition; but Apollo is one of the eternal unbegotten deities, if we may collect any certainty concerning these things, from the statements of the oldest and wisest in such subjects.

As the Thebans were retreating from Orchomenus towards Tegyræ, the Spartans, at the same time marching from Locris, met them. As soon as they came in view, advancing through the straits, one told Pelopidas, "We are fallen into our enemy's hands"; he replied, "And why not they into ours?" and immediately commanded his horse to come up from the rear and charge, while he himself drew his infantry, being three hundred in number, into a close body, hoping by that means, at whatsoever point he made the attack, to break his way through his more numerous enemies. The Spartans had two companies (the company consisting, as Ephorus states, of five hundred; Callisthenes says seven hundred; others, as Polybius, nine hundred); and their leaders, Gorgoleon and Theopompus, confident of success, advanced upon the Thebans. The charge being made with much fury, chiefly where the commanders were posted, the Spartan captains that engaged Pelopidas were first killed; and those immediately around them suffering severely, the whole army was thus disheartened, and opened a lane for the Thebans as if they desired to pass through and escape. But when Pelopidas entered, and turning against those that stood their ground, still went on with a bloody slaughter, an open flight ensued amongst the Spartans. The pursuit was carried but a little way, because they feared the neighbouring Orchomenians and the reinforcements from Lacedæmon; they had succeeded, however, in fighting a way through their enemies, and overpowering their whole force; and, therefore, erecting a trophy, and spoiling the slain, they returned home extremely encouraged with their achievements. For in all the great wars there had ever been against Greeks or barbarians, the Spartans were never before beaten by a smaller company than their own; nor, indeed, in a set battle, when their number was equal. Hence their courage was thought irresistible, and their high repute before the battle made a conquest already of enemies, who thought themselves no match for the men of Sparta even on equal terms. But this battle first taught the other Greeks, that not only Eurotas, or the country between Babyce and Cnacion, breeds men of courage and resolution, but that where the youth are ashamed of baseness, and ready to venture in a good cause, where they fly disgrace more than danger, there, wherever it be, are found the bravest and most formidable opponents.

Gorgidas, according to some, first formed the Sacred Band of three hundred chosen men, to whom, as being a guard for the citadel, the State allowed provision, and all things necessary for exercise: and hence they were called the city band, as citadels of old were usually called cities. Others say that it was composed of young men attached to each other by personal affection, and a pleasant saying of Pammenes is current, that Homer's Nestor was not well skilled in ordering an army, when he advised the Greeks to rank tribe and tribe, and family and family together, that—

So tribe might tribe, and kinsmen kinsmen aid.

but that he should have joined lovers and their beloved. For men of the same tribe or family little value one another when dangers press; but a band cemented by friendship grounded upon love is never to be broken, and invincible; since the lovers, ashamed to be base in sight of their beloved, and the beloved before their lovers, willingly rush into danger for the relief of one another. Nor can that be wondered at since they have more regard for their absent lovers than for others present; as in the instance of the man who, when his enemy was going to kill him, earnestly requested him to run him through the breast, that his lover might not blush to see him wounded in the back. It is a tradition likewise that Iolaüs, who assisted Hercules in his labours and fought at his side, was beloved of him; and Aristotle observes that, even in his time, lovers plighted their faith at Iolaüs' tomb. It is likely, therefore, that this band was called sacred on this account; as Plato calls a lover a divine friend. It is stated that it was never beaten till the battle at Chæronea: and when Philip, after the fight, took a view of the slain, and came to the place where the three hundred that fought his phalanx lay dead together, he wondered, and understanding that it was the band of lovers, he shed tears and said, "Perish any man who suspects that these men either did or suffered anything that was base."

It was not the disaster of Laius, as the poets imagine, that first gave rise to this form of attachment amongst the Thebans, but their lawgivers, designing to soften whilst they were young their natural fierceness, brought, for example, the pipe into great esteem, both in serious and sportive occasions, and gave great encouragement to these friendships in the Palæstra, to temper the manners and characters of the youth. With a view to this they did well, again, to make Harmony, the daughter of Mars and Venus, their tutelar deity; since, where force and courage is joined with gracefulness and winning behaviour, a harmony ensues that combines all the elements of society in perfect consonance and order. Gorgidas distributed this Sacred Band all through the front ranks of the infantry, and thus made their gallantry less conspicuous; not being united in one body, but mingled with so many others of inferior resolution, they had no fair opportunity of showing what they could do. But Pelopidas, having sufficiently tried their bravery at Tegyræ, where they had fought alone and around his own person, never afterward divided them, but, keeping them entire, and as one man, gave them the first duty in the greatest battles. For as horses ran brisker in a chariot than singly, not that their joint force divides the air with greater ease, but because being matched one against the other emulation kindles and inflames their courage; thus he thought brave men, provoking one another to noble actions, would prove most serviceable, and most resolute, where all were united together.

Now when the Lacedæmonians had made peace with the other Greeks, and united all their strength against the Thebans only, and their king, Cleombrotus, had passed the frontier with ten thousand foot and one thousand horse, and not only subjection, as heretofore, but total dispersion and annihilation threatened, and Bœotia was in a greater fear than ever—Pelopidas, leaving his house, when his wife followed him on his way, and with tears begged him to be careful of his life, made answer, "Private men, my wife, should be advised to look to themselves, generals to save others." And when he came to the camp, and found the chief captains disagreeing, he, first, joined the side of Epaminondas, who advised to fight the enemy; though Pelopidas himself was not then in office as chief captain of Bœotia, but in command of the Sacred Band, and trusted as it was fit a man should be, who had given his country such proofs of his zeal for its freedom. And so when a battle was agreed on, and they encamped in front of the Spartans at Leuctra, Pelopidas saw a vision, which much discomposed him. In that plain lie the bodies of the daughters of one Scedasus, called from the place Leuctridæ, having been buried there after having been ravished by some Spartan strangers. When this base and lawless deed was done, and their father could get no satisfaction at Lacedæmon, with bitter imprecations on the Spartans, he killed himself at his daughters' tombs: and from that time the prophecies and oracles still warned them to have a great care of the divine vengeance at Leuctra. Many, however, did not understand the meaning, being uncertain about the place, because there was a little maritime town of Laconia called Leuctron, and near Megalopolis in Arcadia a place of the same name; and the villainy was committed long before this battle.

Now Pelopidas, being asleep in the camp, thought he saw the maidens weeping about their tombs, and cursing the Spartans, and Scedasus commanding, if they desired the victory, to sacrifice a virgin with chestnut hair to his daughters. Pelopidas looked on this as an harsh and impious injunction, but rose and told it to the prophets and commanders of the army, some of whom contended that it was fit to obey, and adduced as examples from the ancients, Menœceus, son of Creon; Macaria, daughter of Hercules; and from later times, Pherecydes the philosopher, slain by the Lacedæmonians, and his skin, as the oracles advised, still kept by their kings. Leonidas, again, warned by the oracle, did as it were sacrifice himself for the good of Greece; Themistocles offered human victims to Bacchus Omestes, before the engagement at Salamis; and success showed their actions to be good. On the contrary, Agesilaus, going from the same place, and against the same enemies that Agamemnon did, and being commanded in a dream at Aulis to sacrifice his daughter, was so weak as to disobey; the consequence of which was, that his expedition was unsuccessful and inglorious. But some on the other side urged that such a barbarous and impious obligation could not be pleasing to any Superior Beings; that typhons and giants did not preside over the world, but the general father of gods and men; that it was absurd to imagine any divinities or powers delighted in slaughter and sacrifices of men; or, if there were such, they were to be neglected as weak and unable to assist; such unreasonable and cruel desires could only proceed from, and live in, weak and depraved minds.

The commanders thus disputing, and Pelopidas being in a great perplexity, a mare colt, breaking from the herd, ran through the camp, and when she came to the place where they were stood still; and whilst some admired her bright chestnut colour, others her mettle, or the strength and fury of her neighing, Theocritus, the augur, took thought, and cried out to Pelopidas, "O good friend! Look, the sacrifice is come; expect no other virgin, but use that which the gods have sent thee." With that they took the colt, and, leading her to the maidens' sepulchres, with the usual solemnity and prayers, offered her with joy, and spread through the whole army the account of Pelopidas' dream, and how they had given the required sacrifice.

In the battle, Epaminondas, bending his phalanx to the left, that, as much as possible, he might divide the right wing, composed of Spartans, from the other Greeks, and distress Cleombrotus by a fierce charge in column on that wing, the enemies perceived the design, and began to change their order, to open and extend their right wing, and, as they far exceeded him in number, to encompass Epaminondas. But Pelopidas with the three hundred came rapidly up, before Cleombrotus could extend his line, and close up his divisions, and so fell upon the Spartans while in disorder; though the Lacedæmonians, the expertest and most practised soldiers of all mankind, used to train and accustom themselves to nothing so much as to keep themselves from confusion upon any change of position, and to follow any leader, or right-hand man, and form in order, and fight on what part soever dangers press. In this battle, however, Epaminondas with his phalanx, neglecting the other Greeks, and charging them alone, and Pelopidas coming up with such incredible speed and fury, so broke their courage and baffled their art that there began such a flight and slaughter amongst the Spartans as was never before known. And so Pelopidas, though in no high office, but only captain of a small band, got as much reputation by the victory as Epaminondas, who was general and chief captain of Bœotia.

Into Peloponnesus, however, they both advanced together as colleagues in supreme command, and gained the greater part of the nations there from the Spartan confederacy; Elis, Argos, all Arcadia, and much of Laconia itself. It was the dead of winter, and but few of the last days of the month remained, and, in the beginning of the next, new officers were to succeed, and whoever failed to deliver up his charge forfeited his head. Therefore, the other chief captains fearing the law, and to avoid the sharpness of the winter, advised a retreat. But Pelopidas joined with Epaminondas, and, encouraging his countrymen, led them against Sparta, and, passing the Eurotas, took many of the towns, and wasted the country as far as the sea. This army consisted of seventy thousand Greeks, of which number the Thebans could not make the twelfth part; but the reputation of the men made all their allies contented to follow them as leaders, though no articles to that effect had been made. For, indeed, it seems the first and paramount law, that he that wants a defender is naturally a subject to him that is able to defend: as mariners, though in a calm or in the port they grow insolent, and brave the pilot, yet when a storm comes, and danger is at hand, they all attend, and put their hopes in him. So the Argives, Eleans, and Arcadians, in their congresses, would contend with the Thebans for superiority in command, yet in a battle, or any hazardous undertaking, of their own will followed their Theban captains. In this expedition they united all Arcadia into one body, and expelling the Spartans that inhabited Messenia, they called back the old Messenians, and established them in Ithome in one body—and, returning through Cenchreæ, they dispersed the Athenians, who designed to set upon them in the straits, and hinder their march.

For these exploits, all the other Greeks loved their courage and admired their success; but among their own citizens, envy, still increasing with their glory, prepared them no pleasing nor agreeable reception. Both were tried for their lives, because they did not deliver up their command in the first month, Bucatius, as the law required, but kept it four months longer, in which time they did these memorable actions in Messenia, Arcadia, and Laconia. Pelopidas was first tried, and therefore in greatest danger, but both were acquitted. Epaminondas bore the accusation and trial very patiently, esteeming it a great and essential part of courage and generosity not to resent injuries in political life. But Pelopidas, being a man of a fiercer temper, and stirred on by his friends to revenge the affront, took the following occasion. Meneclidas, the orator, was one of those that had met with Melon and Pelopidas at Charon's house; but not receiving equal honour, and being powerful in his speech, but loose in his manners, and ill-natured, he abused his natural endowments, even after this trial, to accuse and calumniate his betters. He excluded Epaminondas from the chief captaincy, and for a long time kept the upper hand of him, but he was not powerful enough to bring Pelopidas out of the people's favour, and therefore endeavoured to raise a quarrel between him and Charon. And since it is some comfort to the envious to make those men, whom themselves cannot excel, appear worse than others, he studiously enlarged upon Charon's actions in his speeches to the people, and made panegyrics on his expeditions and victories; and, of the victory which the horsemen won at Platæa, before the battle at Leuctra, under Charon's command, he endeavoured to make the following sacred memorial. Androcydes, the Cyzicenian, had undertaken to paint a previous battle for the city, and was at work in Thebes; and when the revolt began, and the war came on, the Thebans kept the picture that was then almost finished. This picture Meneclidas persuaded them to dedicate, inscribed with Charon's name, designing by that means to obscure the glory of Epaminondas and Pelopidas. This was a ludicrous piece of pretension, to set a single victory, where only one Gerandas, an obscure Spartan, and forty more were slain, above such numerous and important battles. This motion Pelopidas opposed as contrary to law, alleging that it was not the custom of the Thebans to honour any single man, but to attribute the victory to their country; yet in all the contest he extremely commended Charon, and confined himself to showing Meneclidas to be a troublesome and envious fellow, asking the Thebans, if they had done nothing that was excellent . . . insomuch that Meneclidas was severely fined; and he, being unable to pay, endeavoured afterwards to disturb the government. These things give us some light into Pelopidas' life.

Now when Alexander, the tyrant of Pheræ, made open war against some of the Thessalians, and had designs against all, the cities sent an embassy to Thebes, to desire succours and a general; and Pelopidas, knowing that Epaminondas was detained by the Peloponnesian affairs, offered himself to lead the Thessalians, being unwilling to let his courage and skill lie idle, and thinking it unfit that Epaminondas should be withdrawn from his present duties. When he came into Thessaly with his army, he presently took Larissa, and endeavoured to reclaim Alexander, who submitted, and bring him, from being a tyrant, to govern gently, and according to law: but finding him untractable and brutish, and hearing great complaints of his lust and cruelty, Pelopidas began to be severe, and used him roughly, insomuch that the tyrant stole away privately with his guard. But Pelopidas, leaving the Thessalians fearless of the tyrant, and friends amongst themselves, marched into Macedonia, where Ptolemy was then at war with Alexander, the King of Macedon; both parties having sent for him to hear and determine their differences, and assist the one that appeared injured. When he came, he reconciled them, calling back the exiles; and receiving for hostages Philip the king's brother, and thirty children of the nobles, he brought them to Thebes; showing the other Greeks how wide a reputation the Thebans had gained for honesty and courage. This was that Philip who afterwards endeavoured to enslave the Greeks; then he was a boy, lived with Pammenes in Thebes; and hence some conjecture that he took Epaminondas' actions for the rule of his own; and perhaps, indeed, he did take example from his activity and skill in war, which, however, was but a small portion of his virtues; of his temperance, justice, generosity, and mildness, in which he was truly great, Philip enjoyed no share either by nature or imitation.

After this, upon a second complaint of the Thessalians against Alexander of Pheræ, as a disturber of the cities, Pelopidas was joined with Ismenias, in an embassy to him; but led no forces from Thebes, not expecting any war, and therefore was necessitated to make use of the Thessalians upon the emergency. At the same time, also, Macedon was in confusion again, as Ptolemy had murdered the king, and seized the government: but the king's friends sent for Pelopidas, and he being willing to interpose in the matter, but having no soldiers of his own, enlisted some mercenaries in the country, and with them marched against Ptolemy. When they faced one another Ptolemy corrupted these mercenaries with a sum of money, and persuaded them to revolt to him; but yet fearing the very name and reputation of Pelopidas, he came to him as his superior, submitted, begged his pardon, and protested that he kept the government only for the brothers of the dead king, and would prove a friend to the friends, and an enemy to the enemies of Thebes; and, to confirm this, he gave his son, Philoxenus, and fifty of his companions, for hostages. These Pelopidas sent to Thebes; but he himself, being vexed at the treachery of the mercenaries, and understanding that most of their goods, their wives, and children lay at Pharsalus, so that if he could take them the injury would be sufficiently revenged, got together some of the Thessalians, and marched to Pharsalus. When he just entered the city, Alexander, the tyrant, appeared before it with an army; but Pelopidas and his friends, thinking that he came to clear himself from those crimes that were laid to his charge, went to him; and though they knew very well that he was profligate and cruel, yet they imagined that the authority of Thebes, and their own dignity and reputation, would secure them from violence. But the tyrant, seeing them come unarmed and alone, seized them, and made himself master of Pharsalus. Upon this his subjects were much intimidated, thinking that after so great and so bold an iniquity he would spare none, but behave himself toward all, and in all matters, as one despairing of his life.

The Thebans, when they heard of this, were very much enraged, and despatched an army, Epaminondas being then in disgrace, under the command of other leaders. When the tyrant brought Pelopidas to Pheræ, at first he permitted those that desired it to speak with him, imagining that this disaster would break his spirit, and make him appear contemptible. But when Pelopidas advised the complaining Pheræans to be comforted, as if the tyrant was now certain in a short time to smart for his injuries, and sent to tell him, "that it was absurd daily to torment and murder his wretched innocent subjects, and yet spare him, who, he well knew, if ever he got his liberty, would be bitterly revenged"; the tyrant, wondering at his boldness and freedom of speech, replied, "And why is Pelopidas in haste to die?" He, hearing of it, rejoined, "That you may be the sooner ruined, being then more hated by the gods than now." From that time he forbade any to converse with him; but Thebe, the daughter of Jason and wife to Alexander, hearing from the keepers of the bravery and noble behaviour of Pelopidas, had a great desire to see and speak with him. Now when she came into the prison, and, as a woman, could not at once discern his greatness in his calamity, only judging by the meanness of his attire and general appearance, that he was used basely and not befitting a man of his reputation, she wept. Pelopidas, at first not knowing who she was, stood amazed; but when he understood, saluted her by her father's name—Jason and he having been friends and familiars—and she saying, "I pity your wife, sir," he replied, "And I you, that though not in chains, can endure Alexander." This touched the woman, who already hated Alexander for his cruelty and injustice, for his general debaucheries, and for his abuse of her youngest brother. She, therefore, often went to Pelopidas, and, speaking freely of the indignities she suffered, grew more enraged and more exasperated against Alexander.

The Theban generals that were sent into Thessaly did nothing, but, being either unskilful or unfortunate, made a dishonourable retreat, for which the city fined each of them ten thousand drachmas, and sent Epaminondas with their forces. The Thessalians, inspirited by the fame of this general, at once began to stir, and the tyrant's affairs were at the verge of destruction; so great was the fear that possessed his captains and his friends, and so eager the desire of his subjects to revolt, in hope of his speedy punishment. But Epaminondas, more solicitous for the safety of Pelopidas than his own glory, and fearing that if things came to extremity Alexander would grow desperate, and, like a wild beast, turn and worry him, did not prosecute the war to the utmost; but, hovering still over him with his army, he so handled the tyrant as not to leave him any confidence, and yet not to drive him to despair and fury. He was aware of his savageness, and the little value he had for right and justice, insomuch that sometimes he buried men alive, and sometimes dressed them in bears' and boars' skins, and then baited them with dog, or shot at them for his divertisement. At Melibœa and Scotussa, two cities, his allies, he called all the inhabitants to an assembly, and then surrounded them and cut them to pieces with his guards. He consecrated the spear with which he killed his uncle Polyphron, and, crowning it with garlands, sacrificed to it as a god, and called it Tychon. And once seeing a tragedian act Euripides' Troades, he left the theatre; but sending for the actor, bade him not to be concerned at his departure, but act as he had been used to do, as it was not in contempt of him that he departed, but because he was ashamed that his citizens should see him, who never pitied any man that he murdered, weep at the sufferings of Hecuba and Andromache. This tyrant, however, alarmed at the very name, report, and appearance of an expedition under the conduct of Epaminondas, presently—

Dropped like a craven cock his conquered wing.

and sent an embassy to entreat and offer satisfaction. Epaminondas refused to admit such a man as an ally to the Thebans, but granted him a truce of thirty days, and Pelopidas and Ismenias being delivered up, returned home.

Now the Thebans, understanding that the Spartans and Athenians had sent an embassy to the Persians for assistance, themselves, likewise, sent Pelopidas; an excellent design to increase his glory, no man having ever before passed through the dominions of the king with greater fame and reputation. For the glory that he won against the Spartans did not creep slowly or obscurely; but, after the fame of the first battle at Leuctra was gone abroad, the report of new victories continually following, exceedingly increased, and spread his celebrity far and near. Whatever satraps or generals or commanders he met, he was the object of their wonder and discourse. "This is the man," they said, "who hath beaten the Lacedæmonians from sea and land, and confined that Sparta within Taygetus and Eurotas, which, but a little before, under the conduct of Agesilaus, was entering upon a war with the great king about Susa and Ecbatana." This pleased Artaxerxes, and he was the more inclined to show Pelopidas attention and honour, being desirous to seem reverenced, and attended by the greatest. But when he saw him and heard his discourse, more solid than the Athenians, and not so haughty as the Spartans, his regard was heightened, and, truly acting like a king, he openly showed the respect that he felt for him; and this the other ambassadors perceived. Of all other Greeks he had been thought to have done Antalcidas, the Spartan, the greatest honour, by sending him that garland dipped in an unguent, which he himself had worn at an entertainment. Indeed, he did not deal so delicately with Pelopidas, but, according to the custom, gave him the most splendid and considerable presents, and granted him his desires—that the Grecians should be free, Messenia inhabited, and the Thebans accounted the king's hereditary friends. With these answers, but not accepting one of the presents, except what was a pledge of kindness and goodwill, he returned. This behaviour of Pelopidas ruined the other ambassadors; the Athenians condemned and executed their Timagoras, and, indeed, if they did it for receiving so many presents from the king, their sentence was just and good; as he not only took gold and silver, but a rich bed, and slaves to make it, as if the Greeks were unskilful in that art; besides eighty cows and herdsmen, professing he needed cows'milk for some distemper; and, lastly, he was carried in a litter to the seaside, with a present of four talents for his attendants. But the Athenians, perhaps, were not so much irritated at his greediness for the presents. For Epicrates the baggage-carrier not only confessed to the people that he had received gifts from the king, but made a motion, that instead of nine archons, they should yearly choose nine poor citizens to be sent ambassadors to the king, and enriched by his presents, and the people only laughed at the joke. But they were vexed that the Thebans obtained their desires, never considering that Pelopidas' fame was more powerful than all their rhetorical discourse, with a man who still inclined to the victorious in arms. This embassy, having obtained the restitution of Messenia, and the freedom of the other Greeks, got Pelopidas a great deal of goodwill at his return.

At this time, Alexander the Pheræan, falling back to his old nature, and having seized many of the Thessalian cities, and put garrisons upon the Achæans of Phthiotis, and the Magnesians, the cities, hearing that Pelopidas was returned, sent an embassy to Thebes requesting succours, and him for their leader. The Thebans willingly granted their desire; and now when all things were prepared, and the general beginning to march, the sun was eclipsed, and darkness spread over the city at noonday. Now when Pelopidas saw them startled at the prodigy, he did not think it fit to force on men who were afraid and out of heart, nor to hazard seven thousand of his citizens; and therefore with only three hundred horse volunteers, set forward himself to Thessaly, much against the will of the augurs and his fellow-citizens in general, who all imagined this marked portent to have reference to this great man. But he was heated against Alexander for the injuries he had received, and hoped likewise, from the discourse which formerly he had with Thebe, that his family by this time was divided and in disorder. But the glory of the expedition chiefly excited him; for he was extremely desirous at this time, when the Lacedæmonians were sending out military officers to assist Dionysius the Sicilian tyrant, and the Athenians took Alexander's pay, and honoured him with a brazen statue as a benefactor, that the Thebans should be seen, alone, of all the Greeks, undertaking the cause of those who were oppressed by tyrants, and destroying the violent and illegal forms of government in Greece.

When Pelopidas was come to Pharsalus, he formed an army, and presently marched against Alexander; and Alexander understanding that Pelopidas had few Thebans with him, and that his own infantry was double the number of the Thessalians, faced him at Thetidium. Someone told Pelopidas, "The tyrant meets us with a great army"; "So much the better," he replied, "for then we shall overcome the more." Between the two armies lay some steep high hills about Cynoscephalæ, which both parties endeavoured to take by their foot. Pelopidas commanded his horse, which were good and many, to charge that of the enemies; they routed and pursued them through the plain. But Alexander meantime took the hills, and charging the Thessalian foot that came up later, and strove to climb the steep and craggy ascent, killed the foremost, and the others, much distressed, could do the enemies no harm. Pelopidas, observing this, sounded a retreat to his horse, and gave orders that they should charge the enemies that kept their ground; and he himself, taking his shield, quickly joined those that fought about the hills, and advancing to the front, filled his men with such courage and alacrity, that the enemies imagined they came with other spirits and other bodies to the onset. They stood two or three charges, but finding these come on stoutly, and the horse, also, returning from the pursuit, gave ground, and retreated in order. Pelopidas now perceiving, from the rising ground, that the enemy's army was, though not yet routed, full of disorder and confusion, stood and looked about for Alexander; and when he saw him in the right wing, encouraging and ordering his mercenaries, he could not moderate his anger, but inflamed at the sight, and blindly following his passion, regardless alike of his own life and his command, advanced far before his soldiers, crying out and challenging the tyrant who did not dare to receive him, but retreating, hid himself amongst his guard. The foremost of the mercenaries that came hand to hand were driven back by Pelopidas, and some killed; but many at a distance shot through his armour and wounded him, till the Thessalians, in anxiety for the result, ran down the hill to his relief, but found him already slain. The horse came up also, and routed the phalanx, and following the pursuit a great way filled the whole country with the slain, which were above three thousand.

No one can wonder that the Thebans then present should show great grief at the death of Pelopidas, calling him their father, deliverer, and instructor in all that was good and commendable. But the Thessalians and the allies, outdoing in their public edicts all the just honours that could be paid to human courage, gave, in their display of feeling, yet stronger demonstrations of the kindness they had for him. It is stated that none of the soldiers, when they heard of his death, would put off their armour, unbridle their horses, or dress their wounds, but still hot and with their arms on, ran to the corpse, and, as if he had been yet alive and could see what they did, heaped up spoils about his body. They cut off their horses' manes and their own hair, many kindled no fire in their tents, took no supper, and silence and sadness was spread over all the army; as if they had not gained the greatest and most glorious victory, but were overcome by the tyrant and enslaved. As soon as it was known in the cities, the magistrates, youths, children, and priests came out to meet the body, and brought trophies, crowns, and suits of golden armour; and, when he was to be interred, the elders of the Thessalians came and begged the Thebans that they might give the funeral; and one of them said, "Friends, we ask a favour of you, that will prove both an honour and comfort to us in this our great misfortune. The Thessalians shall never again wait on the living Pelopidas, shall never give honours of which he can be sensible, but if we may have his body, adorn his funeral, and inter him, we shall hope to show that we esteem his death a greater loss to the Thessalians than to the Thebans. You have lost only a good general, we both a general and our liberty. For how shall we dare to desire from you another captain, since we cannot restore Pelopidas?"

The Thebans granted their request, and there was never a more splendid funeral in the opinion of those who do not think the glory of such solemnities consists only in gold, ivory, and purple; as Philistus did, who extravagantly celebrates the funeral of Dionysius, in which his tyranny concluded like the pompous exit of some great tragedy. Alexander the Great, at the death of Hephæstion, not only cut off the manes of his horses and his mules, but took down the battlements from the city walls, that even the towns might seem mourners, and instead of their former beauteous appearance, look bald at his funeral. But such honours, being commanded and forced from the mourners, attended with feelings of jealousy towards those who received them, and of hatred towards those who exacted them, were no testimonies of love and respect, but of the barbaric pride, luxury, and insolence of those who lavished their wealth in these vain and undesirable displays. But that a man of common rank, dying in a strange country, neither his wife, children, nor kinsmen present, none either asking or compelling it, should be attended, buried, and crowned by so many cities that strove to exceed one another in the demonstrations of their love, seems to be the sum and completion of happy fortune. For the death of happy men is not, as Æsop observes, most grievous, but most blessed, since it secures their felicity, and puts it out of fortune's power. And that Spartan advised well, who, embracing Diagoras, that had himself been crowned in the Olympic Games, and saw his sons and grandchildren victors, said, "Die, Diagoras, for thou canst not be a god." And yet who would compare all the victories in the Pythian and Olympian Games put together with one of those enterprises of Pelopidas, of which he success-fully performed so many? Having spent his life in brave and glorious actions, he died at last in the chief command, for the thirteenth time, of the Bœotians, fighting bravely and in the act of slaying a tyrant, in defence of the liberty of the Thessalians.

His death, as it brought grief, so likewise it produced advantage to the allies; for the Thebans, as soon as they heard of his fall, delayed not their revenge, but presently sent seven thousand foot and seven hundred horse, under the command of Malcitas and Diogiton. And they, finding Alexander weak and without forces, compelled him to restore the cities he had taken, to withdraw his garrisons from the Magnesians and Achæans of Phthiotis, and swear to assist the Thebans against whatsoever enemies they should require. This contented the Thebans, but punishment overtook the tyrant for his wickedness, and the death of Pelopidas was revenged by Heaven in the following manner. Pelopidas, as I have already mentioned, had taught his wife Thebe not to fear the outward splendour and show of the tyrant's defences, since she was admitted within them. She, of herself, too, dreaded his inconstancy, and hated his cruelty; and therefore, con-spiring with her three brothers, Tisiphonus, Pytholaus, and Lycophron, made the following attempt upon him. All other apartments were full of the tyrant's night guards, but their bed-chamber was an upper room, and before the door lay a chained dog to guard it, which would fly at all but the tyrant and his wife and one servant that fed him. When Thebe, there-fore, designed to kill her husband, she hid her brothers all day in a room hard by, and she, going in alone, according to her usual custom, to Alexander, who was asleep already, in a little time came out again, and commanded the servant to lead away the dog, for Alexander wished to rest quietly. She covered the stairs with wool, that the young men might make no noise as they came up; and then, bringing up her brothers with their weapons, and leaving them at the chamber door, she went in, and brought away the tyrant's sword that hung over his head, and showed it them for confirmation that he was fast asleep. The young men appearing fearful, and unwilling to do the murder, she chid them, and angrily vowed she would wake Alexander and discover the conspiracy; and so, with a lamp in her hand, she conducted them in, they being both ashamed and afraid, and brought them to the bed; when one of them caught him by the feet, the other pulled him backwards by the hair, and the third ran him through. The death was more speedy, perhaps, than was fit; but, in that he was the first tyrant that was killed by the contrivance of his wife, and as his corpse was abused, thrown out, and trodden under foot by the Pheræans, he seems to have suffered what his villainies deserved.

MARCELLUS

THEY SAY THAT MARCUS CLAUDIUS, WHO WAS FIVE TIMES CONSUL OF THE Romans, was the son of Marcus; and that he was the first of his family called Marcellus; that is, *martial,* as Posidonius affirms. He was, indeed, by long experience, skilful in the art of war, of a strong body, valiant of hand, and by natural inclinations addicted to war. This high temper and heat he showed conspicuously in battle; in other respects he was modest and obliging, and so far studious of Greek learning and discipline, as to honour and admire those that excelled in it, though he did not himself attain a proficiency in them equal to his desire, by reason of his employments. For if ever there were any men whom, as Homer says, Heaven

> From their first youth unto their utmost age
> Appointed the laborious wars to wage,

certainly they were the chief Romans of that time; who in their youth had war with the Carthaginians in Sicily, in their middle age with the Gauls in the defence of Italy itself; and at last, when now grown old, struggled again with Hannibal and the Carthaginians, and wanted in their latest years what is granted to most men, exemption from military toils; their rank and their great qualities still making them be called upon to undertake the command.

Marcellus, ignorant or unskilful of no kind of fighting, in single combat surpassed himself; he never declined a challenge, and never accepted without killing his challenger. In Sicily, he protected and saved his brother Otacilius when surrounded in battle, and slew the enemies that pressed upon him; for which act he was by the generals, while he was yet but young, presented with crowns and other honourable rewards; and, his good qualities more and more displaying themselves, he was created Curule Ædile by the people and by the high priests Augur; which is that priesthood to which chiefly the law assigns the observation of auguries. In his ædileship, a certain mischance brought him to the necessity of bringing an impeachment into the senate. He had a son named Marcus, of great beauty, in the flower of his age, and no less admired for the goodness of his character. This youth, Capitolinus, a bold and ill-mannered man, Marcellus' colleague, sought to abuse. The boy at first himself repelled him; but when the other again persecuted him, told his father. Marcellus, highly indignant, accused the man in the senate: where he, having appealed to the tribunes of the people, endeavoured by various shifts and exceptions to elude the impeachment; and, when the tribunes refused their protection, by flat denial rejected the charge. As there was no witness of the fact, the senate thought fit to call the youth himself before them: on witnessing whose blushes and tears, and shame mixed with the highest indignation, seeking no further evidence of the crime, they condemned Capitolinus, and set a fine upon him; of the money of which Marcellus caused silver vessels for libation to be made, which he dedicated to the gods.

After the end of the first Punic war, which lasted one-and-twenty years, the seed of Gallic tumults sprang up, and began again to trouble Rome. The Insubrians, a people inhabiting the subalpine region of Italy, strong in their own forces, raised from among the other Gauls aids of mercenary soldiers, called Gæsatæ. And it was a sort of miracle, and special good fortune for Rome, that the Gallic war was not coincident with the Punic, but that the Gauls had with fidelity stood quiet as spectators, while the Punic war continued, as though they had been under engagement to await and attack the victors, and now only were at liberty to come forward. Still the position itself, and the ancient renown of the Gauls, struck no little fear into the minds of the Romans, who were about to undertake a war so near home and upon their own borders; and regarded the Gauls, because they had once taken their city, with more apprehension than any people, as is apparent from the enactment which from that time forth provided, that the high priests should enjoy an exemption from all military duty, except only in Gallic insurrections.

The great preparations, also, made by the Romans for war (for it is not reported that the people of Rome ever had at one time so many legions in arms, either before or since), and their extraordinary sacrifices, were plain arguments of their fear. For though they were most averse to barbarous and cruel rites, and entertained more than any nation the same pious and reverent sentiments of the gods with the Greeks; yet, when this war was coming upon them, they then, from some prophecies in the Sibyls' books, put alive underground a pair of Greeks, one male, the other female; and likewise two Gauls, one of each sex, in the market called the beast market: continuing even to this day to offer to these Greeks and Gauls certain ceremonial observances in the month of November.

In the beginning of this war, in which the Romans sometimes obtained remarkable victories, sometimes were shamefully beaten, nothing was done toward the determination of the contest until Flaminius and Furius, being consuls, led large forces against the Insubrians. At the time of their departure, the river that runs through the country of Picenum was seen flowing with blood; there was a report that three moons had once been seen at Ariminum; and, in the consular assembly, the augurs declared that the consuls had been unduly and inauspiciously created. The senate, therefore, immediately sent letters to the camp, recalling the consuls to Rome with all possible speed, and commanding them to forbear from acting against the enemies, and to abdicate the consulship on the first opportunity. These letters being brought to Flaminius, he deferred to open them till, having defeated and put to flight the enemy's forces, he wasted and ravaged their borders. The people, therefore, did not go forth to meet him when he returned with huge spoils; nay, because he had not instantly obeyed the command in the letters, by which he was recalled, but slighted and contemned them, they were very near denying him the honour of a triumph. Nor was the triumph sooner passed than they deposed him, with his colleague, from the magistracy, and reduced them to the state of private citizens. So much were all things at Rome made to depend upon religion; they would not allow any contempt of the omens and the ancient rites, even though attended with the highest success: thinking it to be of more importance to the public safety that the magistrates should reverence the gods, than that they should overcome their enemies. Thus Tiberius Sempronius, whom for his probity and virtue the citizens highly esteemed, created Scipio Nasica and Caius Marcius consuls to succeed him; and when they were gone into their provinces, lit upon books concerning the religious observances, where he found something he had not known before; which was this. When the consul took his auspices, he sat without the city in a house, or tent, hired for that occasion; but, if it happened that he, for any urgent cause, returned into the city, without having yet seen any certain signs, he was obliged to leave that first building, or tent, and to seek another to repeat the survey from. Tiberius, it appears, in ignorance of this, had twice used the same building before announcing the new consuls. Now, understanding his error, he referred the matter to the senate: nor did the senate neglect this minute fault, but soon wrote expressly of it to Scipio Nasica and Caius Marcius; who, leaving their provinces and without delay returning to Rome, laid down their magistracy. This happened at a later period. About the same time, too, the priesthood was taken away from two men of very great honour, Cornelius Cethegus and Quintus Sulpicius: from the former, because he had not rightly held out the entrails of a beast slain for sacrifice; from the latter, because, while he was immolating, the tufted cap which the Flamens wear had fallen from his head. Minucius, the dictator, who had already named Caius Flaminius master of the horse, they deposed from his command, because the squeak of a mouse was heard, and put others into their places. And yet, notwithstanding, by observing so anxiously these little niceties they did not run into any superstition, because they never varied from nor exceeded the observances of their ancestors.

So soon as Flaminius with his colleague had resigned the consulate, Marcellus was declared consul by the presiding officers called Interrexes; and, entering into the magistracy, chose Cnæus Cornelius his colleague. There was a report that, the Gauls proposing a pacification, and the senate also inclining to peace, Marcellus inflamed the people to war; but a peace appears to have been agreed upon, which the Gæsatæ broke; who, passing the Alps, stirred up the Insubrians (they being thirty thousand in number, and the Insubrians more numerous by far); and proud of their strength, marched directly to Acerræ, a city seated on the north of the river Po. From thence Britomartus, king of the Gæsatæ, taking with him ten thousand soldiers, harassed the country round about. News of which being brought to Marcellus, leaving his colleague at Acerræ with the foot and all the heavy arms and a third part of the horse, and carrying with him the rest of the horse and six hundred light-armed foot, marching night and day without remission, he stayed not till he came up to these ten thousand near a Gaulish village called Clastidium, which not long before had been reduced under the Roman jurisdiction. Nor had he time to refresh his soldiers or to give them rest. For the barbarians, that were then present, immediately observed his approach, and contemned him, because he had very few foot with him. The Gauls were singularly skilful in horsemanship, and thought to excel in it; and as at present they also exceeded Marcellus in number, they made no account of him. They, therefore, with their king at their head, instantly charged upon him, as if they would trample him under their horses' feet, threatening all kinds of cruelties. Marcellus, because his men were few, that they might not be encompassed and charged on all sides by the enemy, extended his wings of horse, and, riding about, drew out his wings of foot in length, till he came near to the enemy. Just as he was in the act of turning round to face the enemy, it so happened that his horse, startled with their fierce look and their cries, gave back, and carried him forcibly aside. Fearing lest this accident, if converted into an omen, might discourage his soldiers, he quickly brought his horse round to confront the enemy, and made a gesture of adoration to the sun, as if he had wheeled about not by chance, but for a purpose of devotion. For it was customary to the Romans, when they offered worship to the gods, to turn round; and in this moment of meeting the enemy, he is said to have vowed the best of the arms to Jupiter Feretrius.

The king of the Gauls beholding Marcellus, and from the badges of his authority conjecturing him to be the general, advanced some way before his embattled army, and with a loud voice challenged him, and, brandishing his lance, fiercely ran in full career at him; exceeding the rest of the Gauls in stature, and with his armour, that was adorned with gold and silver and various colours, shining like lightning. These arms seeming to Marcellus, while he viewed the enemy's army drawn up in battalia, to be the best and fairest, and thinking them to be those he had vowed to Jupiter, he instantly ran upon the king, and pierced through his breastplate with his lance; then pressing upon him with the weight of his horse, threw him to the ground, and with two or three strokes more slew him. Immediately he leapt from his horse, laid his hand upon the dead king's arm and, looking up towards Heaven, thus spoke: "O Jupiter Feretrius, arbiter of the exploits of captains, and of the acts of commanders in war and battles, be thou witness that I, a general, have slain a general: I, a consul, have slain a king with my own hand, third of all the Romans; and that to thee I consecrate these first and most excellent of the spoils. Grant to us to despatch the relics of the war with the same course of fortune." Then the Roman horse joining battle not only with the enemy's horse, but also with the foot who attacked them, obtained a singular and unheard-of victory. For never before or since have so few horse defeated such numerous forces of horse and foot together. The enemies being to a great number slain, and the spoils collected, he returned to his colleague, who was conducting the war, with ill-success, against the enemies near the greatest and most populous of the Gallic cities, Milan. This was their capital, and, therefore, fighting valiantly in defence of it, they were not so much besieged by Cornelius, as they besieged him. But Marcellus having returned, and the Gæsatæ retiring as soon as they were certified of the death of the king and the defeat of his army, Milan was taken. The rest of their towns, and all they had, the Gauls delivered up of their own accord to the Romans, and had peace upon equitable conditions granted to them.

Marcellus alone, by a decree of the senate, triumphed. The triumph was in magnificence, opulence, spoils, and the gigantic bodies of the captives most remarkable. But the most grateful and most rare spectacle of all was the general himself, carrying the arms of the barbarian king to the god to whom he had vowed them. He had taken a tall and straight stock of an oak, and had lopped and formed it to a trophy. Upon this he fastened and hung about the arms of the king, arranging all the pieces in their suitable places. The procession advancing solemnly, he, carrying this trophy, ascended the chariot; and thus, himself the fairest and most glorious triumphant image, was conveyed into the city. The army adorned with shining armour followed in order, and with verses composed for the occasion, and with songs of victory celebrated the praises of Jupiter and of their general. Then entering the temple of Jupiter Feretrius, he dedicated his gift; the third, and to our memory the last, that ever did so. The first was Romulus, after having slain Acron, king of the Cæninenses: the second, Cornelius Cossus, who slew Tolumnius the Etruscan: after them Marcellus, having killed Britomartus, king of the Gauls; after Marcellus, no man. The god to whom these spoils were consecrated is called Jupiter *Feretrius,* from the trophy carried on the *feretrum,* one of the Greek words which at that time still existed in great numbers in Latin: or, as others say, it is the surname of the Thundering Jupiter derived from *ferire,* to strike. Others there are who would have the name to be deduced from the *strokes* that are given in fight; since even now in battles, when they press upon their enemies, they constantly call out to each other, *strike,* in Latin *feri.* Spoils in general they call Spolia, and these in particular Opima; though, indeed, they say that Numa Pompilius, in his commentaries, makes mention of first, second, and third Spolia Opima; and that he prescribes that the first taken be consecrated to Jupiter Feretrius, the second to Mars, the third to Quirinus; as also that the reward of the first be three hundred *asses;* of the second, two hundred; of the third, one hundred. The general account, however, prevails, that those spoils only are Opima which the general first takes in set battle, and takes from the enemy's chief captain whom he has slain with his own hand. But of this enough. The victory and the ending of the war was so welcome to the people of Rome, that they sent to Apollo of Delphi, in testimony of their gratitude, a present of a golden cup of an hundred pound weight, and gave a great part of the spoil to their associate cities, and took care that many presents should be sent also to Hiero, King of the Syracusans, their friend and ally.

When Hannibal invaded Italy, Marcellus was despatched with a fleet to Sicily. And when the army had been defeated at Cannæ, and many thousands of them perished, and a few had saved themselves by flying to Canusium, and all feared lest Hannibal, who had destroyed the strength of the Roman army, should advance at once with his victorious troops to Rome, Marcellus first sent for the protection of the city fifteen hundred soldiers from the fleet. Then, by decree of the senate, going to Canusium, having heard that many of the soldiers had come together in that place, he led them out of the fortifications to prevent the enemy from ravaging the country. The chief Roman commanders had most of them fallen in battles; and the citizens complained that the extreme caution of Fabius Maximus, whose integrity and wisdom gave him the highest authority, verged upon timidity and inaction. They confided in him to keep them out of danger, but could not expect that he would enable them to retaliate. Fixing, therefore, their thoughts upon Marcellus, and hoping to combine his boldness, confidence, and promptitude with Fabius' caution and prudence, and to temper the one by the other, they sent, sometimes both with consular command, sometimes one as consul, the other as proconsul, against the enemy. Posidonius writes, that Fabius was called the buckler, Marcellus the sword of Rome. Certainly, Hannibal himself confessed that he feared Fabius as a schoolmaster, Marcellus as an adversary: the former, lest he should be hindered from doing mischief; the latter, lest he should receive harm himself.

And first, when among Hannibal's soldiers, proud of their victory, carelessness and boldness had grown to a great height, Marcellus, attacking all their stragglers and plundering parties, cut them off, and by little and little diminished their forces. Then carrying aid to the Neopolitans and Nolans, he confirmed the minds of the former, who, indeed, were of their own accord faithful enough to the Romans; but in Nola he found a state of discord, the senate not being able to rule and keep in the common people, who were generally favourers of Hannibal. There was in the town one Bantius, a man renowned for his high birth and courage. This man, after he had fought most fiercely at Cannæ, and had killed many of the enemies, at last was found lying in a heap of dead bodies, covered with darts, and was brought to Hannibal, who so honoured him, that he not only dismissed him without ransom, but also contracted friendship with him, and made him his guest. In gratitude for this great favour, he became one of the strongest partisans of Hannibal, and urged the people to revolt. Marcellus could not be induced to put to death a man of such eminence, and who had endured such dangers in fighting on the Roman side; but, knowing himself able, by the general kindliness of his disposition, and in particular by the attractiveness of his address, to gain over a character whose passion was for honour, one day when Bantius saluted him, he asked him who he was; not that he knew him not before, but seeking an occasion of further conference. When Bantius had told who he was, Marcellus, seeming surprised with joy and wonder, replied: "Are you that Bantius whom the Romans commend above the rest that fought at Cannæ, and praise as the one man that not only did not forsake the consul Paulus Æmilius, but received in his own body many darts thrown at him?" Bantius owning himself to be that very man, and showing his scars: "Why, then," said Marcellus, "did not you, having such proofs to show of your affection to us, come to me at my first arrival here? Do you think that we are unwilling to requite with favour those who have well deserved, and who are honoured even by our enemies?" He followed up his courtesies by a present of a war-horse and five hundred drachmas in money. From that time Bantius became the most faithful assistant and ally of Marcellus, and a most keen discoverer of those that attempted innovation and sedition.

These were many, and had entered into a conspiracy to plunder the baggage of the Romans, when they should make an irruption against the enemy. Marcellus, therefore, having marshalled his army within the city, placed the baggage near to the gates, and, by an edict, forbade the Nolans to go to the walls. Thus, outside the city, no arms could be seen; by which prudent device he allured Hannibal to move with his army in some disorder to the city, thinking that things were in a tumult there. Then Marcellus, the nearest gate being, as he had commanded, thrown open, issuing forth with the flower of his horse in front, charged the enemy. By and by the foot, sallying out of another gate, with a loud shout joined in the battle. And while Hannibal opposes part of his forces to these, the third gate also is opened, out of which the rest break forth, and on all quarters fall upon the enemies, who were dismayed at this unexpected encounter, and did but feebly resist those with whom they had been first engaged, because of their attack by these others who sallied out later. Here Hannibal's soldiers, with much bloodshed and many wounds, were beaten back to their camp, and for the first time turned their backs to the Romans. There fell in this action, as it is related, more than five thousand of them; of the Romans, not above five hundred. Livy does not affirm that either the victory or the slaughter of the enemy was so great; but certain it is that the adventure brought great glory to Marcellus, and to the Romans, after their calamities, a great revival of confidence, as they began now to entertain a hope that the enemy with whom they contended was not invincible, but liable like themselves to defeats.

Therefore, the other consul being deceased, the people recalled Marcellus, that they might put him into his place; and, in spite of the magistrates, succeeded in postponing the election till his arrival, when he was by all the suffrages created consul. But because it happened to thunder, the augurs accounting that he was not legitimately created, and yet not daring, for fear of the people, to declare their sentence openly, Marcellus voluntarily resigned the consulate, retaining however his command. Being created proconsul, and returning to the camp at Nola, he proceeded to harass those that followed the party of the Carthaginians; on whose coming with speed to succour them, Marcellus declined a challenge to a set battle, but when Hannibal had sent out a party to plunder, and now expected no fight, he broke out upon him with his army. He had distributed to the foot long lances, such as are commonly used in naval fights; and instructed them to throw them with great force at convenient distances against the enemies, who were inexperienced in that way of darting, and used to fight with short darts hand to hand. This seems to have been the cause of the total rout and open flight of all the Carthaginians who were then engaged; there fell of them five thousand; four elephants were killed, and two taken; but what was of the greatest moment, on the third day after, more than three hundred horse, Spaniards and Numidians mixed, deserted to him, a disaster that had never to that day happened to Hannibal, who had kept together in harmony an army of barbarians, collected out of many various and discordant nations. Marcellus and his successors in all this war made good use of the faithful service of these horsemen.

He now was a third time created consul, and sailed over into Sicily. For the success of Hannibal had excited the Carthaginians to lay claim to that whole island; chiefly because, after the murder of the tyrant Hieronymus, all things had been in tumult and confusion at Syracuse. For which reason the Romans also had sent before to that city a force under the conduct of Appius, as prætor. While Marcellus was receiving that army, a number of Roman soldiers cast themselves at his feet, upon occasion of the following calamity. Of those that survived the battle at Cannæ, some had escaped by flight, and some were taken alive by the enemy; so great a multitude, that it was thought there were not remaining Romans enough to defend the wall of the city. And yet the magnanimity and constancy of the city was such, that it would not redeem the captives from Hannibal, though it might have done so for a small ransom; a decree of the senate forbade it, and chose rather to leave them to be killed by the enemy, or sold out of Italy; and commanded that all who had saved themselves by flight should be transported into Sicily, and not permitted to return into Italy, until the war with Hannibal should be ended. These, therefore, when Marcellus was arrived in Sicily, addressed themselves to him in great numbers; and casting themselves at his feet, with much lamentation and tears humbly besought him to admit them to honourable service; and promised to make it appear by their future fidelity and exertions that that defeat had been received rather by misfortune than by cowardice. Marcellus, pitying them, petitioned the senate by letters, that he might have leave at all times to recruit his legions out of them. After much debate about the thing, the senate decreed they were of opinion that the commonwealth did not require the service of cowardly soldiers; if Marcellus perhaps thought otherwise, he might make use of them, provided no one of them be honoured on any occasion with a crown or military gift, as a reward of his virtue or courage. This decree stung Marcellus; and on his return to Rome, after the Sicilian war was ended, he upbraided the senate that they had denied to him, who had so highly deserved of the republic, liberty to relieve so great a number of citizens in great calamity.

At this time Marcellus, first incensed by injuries done him by Hippocrates, commander of the Syracusans (who, to give proof of his good affection to the Carthaginians, and to acquire the tyranny to himself, had killed a number of Romans at Leontini), besieged and took by force the city of Leontini; yet violated none of the townsmen; only deserters, as many as he took, he subjected to the punishment of the rods and axe. But Hippocrates, sending a report to Syracuse, that Marcellus had put all the adult population to the sword, and then coming upon the Syracusans, who had risen in tumult upon that false report, made himself master of the city. Upon this Marcellus moved with his whole army to Syracuse, and encamping near the wall, sent ambassadors into the city to relate to the Syracusans the truth of what had been done in Leontini. When these could not prevail by treaty, the whole power being now in the hands of Hippocrates, he proceeded to attack the city both by land and by sea. The land forces were conducted by Appius: Marcellus, with sixty galleys, each with five rows of oars, furnished with all sorts of arms and missiles, and a huge bridge of planks laid upon eight ships chained together, upon which was carried the engine to cast stones and darts, assaulted the walls, relying on the abundance and magnificence of his preparations, and on his own previous glory; all which, however, were, it would seem, but trifles for Archimedes and his machines.

These machines he had designed and contrived, not as matters of any importance, but as mere amusements in geometry; in compliance with King Hiero's desire and request, some little time before, that he should reduce to practice some part of his admirable speculation in science, and by accommodating the theoretic truth to sensation and ordinary use, bring it more within the appreciation of the people in general. Eudoxus and Archytas had been the first originators of this far-famed and highly prized art of mechanics, which they employed as an elegant illustration of geometrical truths, and as means of sustaining experimentally, to the satisfaction of the senses, conclusions too intricate for proof by words and diagrams. As, for example, to solve the problem, so often required in constructing geometrical figures, given the two extremes, to find the two mean lines of a proportion, both these mathematicians had recourse to the aid of instruments, adapting to their purpose certain curves and sections of lines. But what with Plato's indignation at it, and his invectives against it as the mere corruption and annihilation of the one good of geometry which was thus shamefully turning its back upon the unembodied objects of pure intelligence to recur to sensation, and to ask help (not to be obtained without base supervisions and depravation) from matter; so it was that mechanics came to be separated from geometry, and, repudiated and neglected by philosophers, took its place as a military art. Archimedes, however, in writing to King Hiero, whose friend and near relation he was, had stated that given the force, any given weight might be moved, and even boasted, we are told, relying on the strength of demonstration, that if there were another earth, by going into it he could remove this. Hiero being struck with amazement at this, and entreating him to make good this problem by actual experiment, and show some great weight moved by a small engine, he fixed accordingly upon a ship of burden out of the king's arsenal, which could not be drawn out of the dock without great labour and many men; and, loading her with many passengers and a full freight, sitting himself the while far off, with no great endeavour, but only holding the head of the pulley in his hand and drawing the cords by degrees, he drew the ship in a straight line, as smoothly and evenly as if she had been in the sea. The king, astonished at this, and convinced of the power of the art, prevailed upon Archimedes to make him engines accommodated to all the purposes, offensive and defensive, of a siege. These the king himself never made use of, because he spent almost all his life in a profound quiet and the highest affluence. But the apparatus was, in most opportune time, ready at hand for the Syracusans, and with it also the engineer himself.

When, therefore, the Romans assaulted the walls in two places at once, fear and consternation stupefied the Syracusans, believing that nothing was able to resist that violence and those forces. But when Archimedes began to ply his engines, he at once shot against the land forces all sorts of missile weapons, and immense masses of stone that came down with incredible noise and violence; against which no man could stand; for they knocked down those upon whom they fell in heaps, breaking all their ranks and files. In the meantime huge poles thrust out from the walls over the ships sunk some by the great weights which they let down from on high upon them; others they lifted up into the air by an iron hand or beak like a crane's beak and, when they had drawn them up by the prow, and set them on end upon the poop, they plunged them to the bottom of the sea; or else the ships, drawn by engines within, and whirled about, were dashed against steep rocks that stood jutting out under the walls, with great destruction of the soldiers that were aboard them. A ship was frequently lifted up to a great height in the air (a dreadful thing to behold), and was rolled to and fro, and kept swinging, until the mariners were all thrown out, when at length it was dashed against the rocks, or let fall. At the engine that Marcellus brought upon the bridge of ships, which was called *Sambuca*, from some resemblance it had to an instrument of music, while it was as yet approaching the wall, there was discharged a piece of rock of ten talents weight, then a second and a third, which, striking upon it with immense force and a noise like thunder, broke all its foundation to pieces, shook out all its fastenings, and completely dislodged it from the bridge. So Marcellus, doubtful what counsel to pursue, drew off his ships to a safer distance, and sounded a retreat to his forces on land. They then took a resolution of coming up under the walls, if it were possible, in the night; thinking that as Archimedes used ropes stretched at length in playing his engines, the soldiers would now be under the shot, and the darts would, for want of sufficient distance to throw them, fly over their heads without effect. But he, it appeared, had long before framed for such occasions engines accommodated to any distance, and shorter weapons; and had made numerous small openings in the walls, through which, with engines of a shorter range, unexpected blows were inflicted on the assailants. Thus, when they who thought to deceive the defenders came close up to the walls, instantly a shower of darts and other missile weapons was again cast upon them. And when stones came tumbling down perpendicularly upon their heads, and, as it were, the whole wall shot out arrows at them, they retired. And now, again, as they were going off, arrows and darts of a longer range inflicted a great slaughter among them, and their ships were driven one against another; while they themselves were not able to retaliate in any way. For Archimedes had provided and fixed most of his engines immediately under the wall; whence the Romans, seeing that indefinite mischief overwhelmed them from no visible means, began to think they were fighting with the gods.

Yet Marcellus escaped unhurt, and deriding his own artificers and engineers, "What," said he, "must we give up fighting with this geometrical Briareus, who plays pitch-and-toss with our ships, and, with the multitude of darts which he showers at a single moment upon us, really outdoes the hundred-handed giants of mythology?" And doubtless, the rest of the Syracusans were but the body of Archimedes' designs, one soul moving and governing all; for, laying aside all other arms, with this alone they infested the Romans and protected themselves. In fine, when such terror had seized upon the Romans, that, if they did but see a little rope or a piece of wood from the wall, instantly crying out, that there it was again, Archimedes was about to let fly some engine at them, they turned their backs and fled, Marcellus desisted from conflicts and assaults, putting all his hope in a long siege. Yet Archimedes possessed so high a spirit, so profound a soul, and such treasures of scientific knowledge, that though these inventions had now obtained him the renown of more than human sagacity, he yet would not deign to leave behind him any commentary or writing on such subjects; but, repudiating as sordid and ignoble the whole trade of engineering, and every sort of art that lends itself to mere use and profit, he placed his whole affection and ambition in those purer speculations where there can be no reference to the vulgar needs of life; studies, the superiority of which to all others is unquestioned, and in which the only doubt can be whether the beauty and grandeur of the subjects examined, of the precision and cogency of the methods and means of proof, most deserve our admiration. It is not possible to find in all geometry more difficult and intricate questions, or more simple and lucid explanations. Some ascribe this to his natural genius; while others think that incredible effort and toil produced these, to all appearances, easy and unlaboured results. No amount of investigation of yours would succeed in attaining the proof, and yet, once seen, you immediately believe you would have discovered it; by so smooth and so rapid a path he leads you to the conclusion required. And thus it ceases to be incredible that (as is commonly told of him) the charm of his familiar and domestic Siren made him forget his food and neglect his person, to that degree that when he was occasionally carried by absolute violence to bathe or have his body anointed, he used to trace geometrical figures in the ashes of the fire, and diagrams in the oil on his body, being in a state of entire preoccupation, and, in the truest sense, divine possession with his love and delight in science. His discoveries were numerous and admirable; but he is said to have requested his friends and relations that, when he was dead, they would place over his tomb a sphere containing a cylinder, inscribing it with the ratio which the containing solid bears to the contained.

Such was Archimedes, who now showed himself, and so far as lay in him the city also, invincible. While the siege continued, Marcellus took Megara, one of the earliest founded of the Greek cities in Sicily, and capturing also the camp of Hippocrates at Acilæ, killed above eight thousand men, having attacked them whilst they were engaged in forming their fortifications. He overran a great part of Sicily; gained over many towns from the Carthaginians, and overcame all that dared to encounter him. As the siege went on, one Damippus, a Lacedæmonian, putting to sea in a ship from Syracuse, was taken. When the Syracusans much desired to redeem this man, and there were many meetings and treaties about the matter betwixt them and Marcellus, he had opportunity to notice a tower into which a body of men might be secretly introduced, as the wall near to it was not difficult to surmount, and it was itself carelessly guarded. Coming often thither, and entertaining conferences about the release of Damippus, he had pretty well calculated the height of the tower, and got ladders prepared. The Syracusans celebrated a feast to Diana; this juncture of time, when they were given up entirely to wine and sport, Marcellus laid hold of, and before the citizens perceived it, not only possessed himself of the tower, but, before the break of day, filled the wall around with soldiers, and made his way into the Hexapylum. The Syracusans now beginning to stir, and to be alarmed at the tumult, he ordered the trumpets everywhere to sound, and thus frightened them all into flight, as if all parts of the city were already won, though the most fortified, and the fairest, and most ample quarter was still ungained. It is called Acradina, and was divided by a wall from the outer city, one part of which they call Neapolis, the other Tycha. Possessing himself of these, Marcellus, about break of day, entered through the Hexapylum, all his officers congratulating him. But looking down from the higher places upon the beautiful and spacious city below, he is said to have wept much, commiserating the calamity that hung over it, when his thoughts represented to him how dismal and foul the face of the city would be in a few hours, when plundered and sacked by the soldiers. For among the officers of his army there was not one man that durst deny the plunder of the city to the soldiers' demands; nay, many were instant that it should be set on fire and laid level to the ground: but this Marcellus would not listen to. Yet he granted, but with great unwillingness and reluctance, that the money and slaves should be made prey; giving orders, at the same time, that none should violate any free person, nor kill, misuse, or make a slave of any of the Syracusans. Though he had used this moderation, he still esteemed the condition of that city to be pitiable, and, even amidst the congratulations and joy, showed his strong feelings of sympathy and commiseration at seeing all the riches accumulated during a long felicity now dissipated in an hour. For it is related that no less prey and plunder was taken here than afterward in Carthage. For not long after they obtained also the plunder of the other parts of the city, which were taken by treachery; leaving nothing untouched but the king's money, which was brought into the public treasury. But nothing afflicted Marcellus so much as the death of Archimedes, who was then, as fate would have it, intent upon working out some problem by a diagram, and having fixed his mind alike and his eyes upon the subject of his speculation, he never noticed the incursion of the Romans, nor that the city was taken. In this transport of study and contemplation, a soldier, unexpectedly coming up to him, commanded him to follow to Marcellus; which he declining to do before he had worked out his problem to a demonstration, the soldier, enraged, drew his sword and ran him through. Others write that a Roman soldier, running upon him with a drawn sword, offered to kill him; and that Archimedes, looking back, earnestly besought him to hold his hand a little while, that he might not leave what he was then at work upon inconclusive and imperfect; but the soldier, nothing moved by his entreaty, instantly killed him. Others again relate that, as Archimedes was carrying to Marcellus mathematical instruments, dials, spheres, and angles, by which the magnitude of the sun might be measured to the sight, some soldiers seeing him, and thinking that he carried gold in a vessel, slew him. Certain it is that his death was very afflicting to

Marcellus; and that Marcellus ever after regarded him that killed him as a murderer; and that he sought for his kindred and honoured them with signal favours.

Indeed, foreign nations had held the Romans to be excellent soldiers and formidable in battle; but they had hitherto given no memorable example of gentleness, or humanity, or civil virtue; and Marcellus seems first to have shown to the Greeks that his countrymen were most illustrious for their justice. For such was his moderation to all with whom he had anything to do, and such his benignity also to many cities and private men, that, if anything hard or severe was decreed concerning the people of Enna, Megara, or Syracuse, the blame was thought to belong rather to those upon whom the storm fell, than to those who brought it upon them. One example of many I will commemorate. In Sicily there is a town called Engyum, not indeed great, but very ancient and ennobled by the presence of the goddesses, called the Mothers. The temple, they say, was built by the Cretans; and they show some spears and brazen helmets, inscribed with the names of Meriones, and (with the same spelling as in Latin) of Ulysses, who consecrated them to the goddesses. This city highly favouring the party of the Carthaginians, Nicias, the most eminent of the citizens, counselled them to go over to the Romans; to that end acting freely and openly in harangues to their assemblies, arguing the imprudence and madness of the opposite course. They, fearing his power and authority, resolved to deliver him in bonds to the Carthaginians. Nicias, detecting the design, and seeing that his person was secretly kept in watch, proceeded to speak irreligiously to the vulgar of the Mothers, and showed many signs of disrespect, as if he denied and contemned the received opinion of the presence of those goddesses; his enemies the while rejoicing that he, of his own accord, sought the destruction hanging over his head. When they were just now about to lay hands upon him, an assembly was held, and here Nicias, making a speech to the people concerning some affair then under deliberation, in the midst of his address, cast himself upon the ground; and soon after, while amazement (as usually happens on such surprising occasions) held the assembly immovable, raising and turning his head round, he began in a trembling and deep tone, but by degrees raised and sharpened his voice. When he saw the whole theatre struck with horror and silence, throwing off his mantle and rending his tunic he leaps up half naked, and runs towards the door, crying out aloud that he was driven by the wrath of the Mothers. When no man durst, out of religious fear, lay hands upon him or stop him, but all gave way before him, he ran out of the gate, not omitting any shriek or gesture of men possessed and mad. His wife, conscious of his counter-feiting, and privy to his design, taking her children with her, first cast herself as a suppliant before the temple of the goddesses; then, pretending to seek her wandering husband, no man hindering her, went out of the town in safety; and by this means they all escaped to Marcellus at Syracuse. After many other such affronts offered him by the men of Engyum, Marcellus, having taken them all prisoners and cast them into bonds, was preparing to inflict upon them the last punishment; when Nicias, with tears in his eyes, addressed himself to him. In fine, casting himself at Marcellus' feet, and deprecating for his citizens, he begged most earnestly their lives, chiefly those of his enemies. Marcellus, relenting, set them all at liberty, and rewarded Nicias with ample lands and rich presents. This history is recorded by Posidonius the philosopher.

Marcellus, at length recalled by the people of Rome to the immediate war at home, to illustrate his triumph, and adorn the city, carried away with him a great number of the most beautiful ornaments of Syracuse. For, before that, Rome neither had, nor had seen, any of those fine and exquisite rarities; nor was any pleasure taken in graceful and elegant pieces of workmanship. Stuffed with barbarous arms and spoils stained with blood, and everywhere crowned with triumphal memorials and trophies, she was no pleasant or delightful spectacle for the eyes of peaceful or refined spectators; but, as Epaminondas named the fields of Bœotia the stage of Mars; and Xenophon called Ephesus the workhouse of war; so, in my judgment, may you call Rome, at that time (to use the words of Pindar), "the precinct of the peaceless Mars." Whence Marcellus was more popular with the people in general, because he had adorned the city with beautiful objects that had all the charms of Grecian grace and symmetry; but Fabius Maximus, who neither touched nor brought away anything of this kind from Tarentum, when he had taken it, was more approved of by the elder men. He carried off the money and valuables, but forbade the statues to be moved; adding, as it is commonly related, "Let us leave to the Tarentines these offended gods." They blamed Marcellus, first for placing the city in an invidious position, as it seemed now to celebrate victories and lead processions of triumph, not only over men, but also over the gods as captives; then, that he had diverted to idleness, and vain talk about curious arts and artificers, the common people, which, bred up in wars and agriculture, had never tasted of luxury and sloth, and, as Euripides said of Hercules, had been—

Rude, unrefined, only for great things good,

so that now they misspent much of their time in examining and criticising trifles. And yet, notwithstanding this reprimand, Marcellus made it his glory to the Greeks themselves, that he had taught his ignorant countrymen to esteem and admire the elegant and wonderful productions of Greece.

But when the envious opposed his being brought triumphant into the city, because there were some relics of the war in Sicily, and a third triumph would be looked upon with jealousy, he gave way. He triumphed upon the Alban mount, and thence entered the city in *ovation*, as it is called in Latin, in Greek *eua;* but in this ovation he was neither carried in a chariot, nor crowned with laurel, nor ushered by trumpets sounding; but went afoot with shoes on, many flutes or pipes sounding in concert, while he passed along, wearing a garland of myrtle, in a peaceable aspect, exciting rather love and respect than fear. Whence I am, by conjecture, led to think that, originally, the difference observed betwixt ovation and triumph did not depend upon the greatness of the achievements, but the manner of performing them. For they who, having fought a set battle, and slain the enemy, returned victors, led that martial, terrible triumph, and, as the ordinary custom then was in frustrating the army, adorned the arms and the soldiers with a great deal of laurel. But they who without force, by colloquy, persuasion, and reasoning, had done the business, to these captains custom gave the honour of the unmilitary and festive ovation. For the pipe is the badge of peace, and myrtle the plant of Venus, who more than the rest of the gods and goddesses abhors force and war. It is called ovation, not as most think, from the Greek *euasmus,* because they act it with shouting and cries of *Eua:* for so do they also the proper triumphs. The Greeks have wrested the word to their own language, thinking that this honour, also, must have some connection with Bacchus, who in Greek has the titles of Euius and Thriambus. But the thing is otherwise. For it was the custom for commanders, in their triumph, to immolate an ox, but in their ovation, a sheep: hence they named it *Ovation,* from the Latin *ovis.* It is worth observing, how exactly opposite the sacrifices appointed by the Spartan legislator are to those of the Romans. For at Lacedæmon, a captain, who had performed the work he had undertook by cunning, or courteous treaty, on laying down his command, immolated an ox; he that did the business by battle, offered a cock; the Lacedæmonians, though most warlike, thinking exploit performed by reason and wisdom to be more excellent and more congruous to man, than one effected by mere force and courage. Which of the two is to be preferred I leave to the determination of others.

Marcellus being the fourth time consul, his enemies suborned the Syracusans to come to Rome to accuse him, and to complain that they had suffered indignities and wrongs, contrary to the conditions granted them. It happened that Marcellus was in the capitol offering sacrifice when the Syracusans petitioned the senate, yet sitting, that they might have leave to accuse him and present their grievances. Marcellus' colleague, eager to protect him in his absence, put them out of the court. But Marcellus himself came as soon as he heard of it. And first, in his curule chair as consul, he referred to the senate the cognisance of other matters: but when these were transacted, rising from his seat, he passed as a private man into the place where the accused were wont to make their defence, and gave free liberty to the Syracusans to impeach him. But they, struck with consternation by his majesty and confidence, stood astonished; and the power of his presence now, in his robe of state, appeared far more terrible and severe than it had done when he was arrayed in armour. Yet, reanimated at length by Marcellus' rivals, they began their impeachment, and made an oration in which pleas of justice mingled with lamentation and complaint; the sum of which was, that being allies and friends of the people of Rome, they had, notwithstanding, suffered things which other commanders had abstained from inflicting upon enemies. To this Marcellus answered that they had committed many acts of hostility against the people of Rome, and had suffered nothing but what enemies conquered and captured in war cannot possibly be protected from suffering: that it was their own fault they had been made captives, because they refused to give ear to his frequent attempts to persuade them by gentle means: neither were they forced into war by the power of tyrants, but had rather chosen the tyrants themselves for the express object that they might make war. The orations ended, and the Syracusans, according to the custom, having retired, Marcellus left his colleague to ask the sentences, and, withdrawing with the Syracusans, stayed expecting at the doors of the senate-house; not in the least discomposed in spirit, either with alarm at the accusation, or by anger against the Syracusans; but with perfect calmness and serenity attending the issue of the cause. The sentences at length being all asked, and a decree of the senate made in vindication of Marcellus, the Syracusans, with tears flowing from their eyes, cast themselves at his knees, beseeching him to forgive themselves there present, and to be moved by the misery of the rest of their city, which would ever be mindful of, and grateful for, his benefits. Thus Marcellus, softened by their tears and distress, was not only reconciled to the deputies, but ever afterwards continued to find opportunity of doing kindness to the Syracusans. The liberty which he had restored to them, and their rights, laws, and goods that were left, the senate confirmed. Upon which account the Syracusans, besides other signal honours, made a law, that if Marcellus should at anytime come into Sicily, or any of his posterity, the Syracusans should wear garlands and offer public sacrifice to the gods.

After this he moved against Hannibal. And whereas the other consuls and commanders, since the defeat received at Cannæ, had all made use of the same policy against Hannibal, namely, to decline coming to a battle with him; and none had had the courage to encounter him in the field and put themselves to the decision by the sword; Marcellus entered upon the opposite course, thinking that Italy would be destroyed by the very delay by which they looked to wear out Hannibal; and that Fabius, who, adhering to his cautious policy, waited to see the war extinguished, while Rome itself meantime wasted away (like timid physicians, who, dreading to administer remedies, stay waiting, and believe that what is the decay of the patient's strength is the decline of the disease), was not taking a right course to heal the sickness of his country. And first, the great cities of the Samnites, which had revolted, came into his power; in which he found a large quantity of corn and money, and three thousand of Hannibal's soldiers, that were left for the defence. After this, the proconsul Cnæus Fulvius with eleven tribunes of the soldiers being slain in Apulia, and the greatest part of the army also at the same time cut off, he despatched letters to Rome, and bade the people be of good courage, for that he was now upon the march against Hannibal, to turn his triumph into sadness. On these letters being read, Livy writes that the people were not only not encouraged, but more discouraged than before. For danger, they thought, was but the greater in proportion as Marcellus was of more value than Fulvius. He, as he had written, advancing into the territories of the Lucanians, came up to him at Numistro, and, the enemy keeping himself upon the hills, pitched his camp in a level plain, and the next day drew forth his army in order for fight. Nor did Hannibal refuse the challenge. They fought long and obstinately on both sides, victory yet seeming undecided, when, after three hours' conflict, night hardly parted them. The next day, as soon as the sun was risen, Marcellus again brought forth his troops, and ranged them among the dead bodies of the slain, challenging Hannibal to solve the question by another trial. When he dislodged and drew off, Marcellus, gathering up the spoils of the enemies, and burying the bodies of his slain soldiers, closely followed him. And though

Hannibal often used stratagems, and laid ambushes to entrap Marcellus, yet he never could circumvent him. By skirmishes, meantime, in all of which he was superior, Marcellus gained himself such high repute, that, when the time of the Comitia at Rome was near at hand, the senate thought fit rather to recall the other consul from Sicily than to withdraw Marcellus from his conflict with Hannibal; and on his arrival they bid him name Quintus Fulvius dictator. For the dictator is created neither by the people nor by the senate, but the consul of the prætor, before the popular assembly, pronounces him to be dictator whom he himself chooses. Hence he is called dictator, *dicere* meaning to name. Others say that he is named dictator because his word is a *law,* and he orders what he pleases, without submitting it to the vote. For the Romans call the orders of magistrates *Edicts.*

And now because Marcellus' colleague, who was recalled from Sicily, had a mind to name another man dictator, and would not be forced to change his opinion, he sailed away by night back to Sicily. So the common people made an order that Quintus Fulvius should be chosen dictator: and the senate, by an express, commanded Marcellus to nominate him. He obeying proclaimed him dictator according to the order of the people; but the office of proconsul was continued to himself for a year. And having arranged with Fabius Maximus that, while he besieged Tarentum, he would, by following Hannibal and drawing him up and down, detain him from coming to the relief of the Tarentines, he overtook him at Canusium: and as Hannibal often shifted his camp, and still declined the combat, he everywhere sought to engage him. At last, pressing upon him while encamping, by light skirmishes he provoked him to a battle; but night again divided them in the very heat of the conflict. The next day Marcellus again showed himself in arms, and brought up his forces in array. Hannibal, in extreme grief, called his Carthaginians together to an harangue: and vehemently prayed them to fight today worthily of all their former success; "For you see," said he, "how, after such great victories, we have not liberty to respire, nor to repose ourselves, though victors; unless we drive this man back." Then the two armies, joining battle, fought fiercely; when the event of an untimely movement showed Marcellus to have been guilty of an error. The right wing being hard pressed upon, he commanded one of the legions to be brought up to the front. This change disturbing the array and posture of the legions gave the victory to the enemies; and there fell two thousand seven hundred Romans. Marcellus, after he had retreated into his camp, called his soldiers together. "I see," said he, "many Roman arms and bodies, but I see not so much as one Roman." To their entreaties for his pardon, he returned a refusal while they remained beaten, but promised to give it so soon as they should overcome; and he resolved to bring them into the field again the next day, that the fame of their victory might arrive at Rome before that of their flight. Dismissing the assembly, he commanded barley instead of wheat to be given to those companies that had turned their backs. These rebukes were so bitter to the soldiers, that though a great number of them were grievously wounded, yet they relate there was not one to whom the general's oration was not more painful and smarting than his wounds.

The day breaking, a scarlet toga, the sign of instant battle, was displayed. The companies marked with ignominy begged they might be posted in the foremost place, and obtained their request. Then the tribunes bring forth the rest of the forces, and draw them up. On news of which, "O strange!" said Hannibal, "what will you do with this man, who can bear neither good nor bad fortune? He is the only man who neither suffers us to rest when he is victor, nor rests himself when he is overcome. We shall have, it seems, perpetually to fight with him; as in good success his confidence, and in ill success his shame, still urges him to some further enterprise." Then the armies engaged. When the fight was doubtful, Hannibal commanded the elephants to be brought into the first battalion, and to be driven upon the van of the Romans. When the beasts, trampling upon many, soon caused disorder, Flavius, a tribune of soldiers, snatching an ensign, meets them, and wounding the first elephant with the spike at the bottom of the ensign staff, puts him to flight. The beast turned around upon the next, and drove back both him and the rest that followed. Marcellus, seeing this, pours in his horse with great force upon the elephants, and upon the enemy disordered by their flight. The horse, making a fierce impression, pursued the Carthaginians home to their camp, while the elephants, wounded and running upon their own party, caused a considerable slaughter. It is said more than eight thousand were slain; of the Roman army three thousand, and almost all wounded. This gave Hannibal opportunity to retire in the silence of the night, and to remove to greater distance from Marcellus; who was kept from pursuing by the number of his wounded men, and removed, by gentle marches, into Campania, and spent the summer at Sinuessa, engaged in restoring them.

But as Hannibal, having disentangled himself from Marcellus, ranged with his army round about the country, and wasted Italy free from all fear, at Rome Marcellus was evil spoken of. His detractors induced Publicius

Bibulus, tribune of the people, an eloquent and violent man, to undertake his accusation. He, by assiduous harangues, prevailed upon the people to withdraw from Marcellus the command of the army; "Seeing that Marcellus," said he, "after brief exercise in the war, has withdrawn as it might be from the wrestling ground to the warm baths to refresh himself." Marcellus, on hearing this, appointed lieutenants over his camp and hasted to Rome to refute the charges against him: and there found ready drawn up an impeachment consisting of these calumnies. At the day prefixed, in the Flaminian circus, into which place the people had assembled themselves, Bibulus rose and accused him. Marcellus himself answered, briefly and simply, but the first and most approved men of the city spoke largely and in high terms, very freely advising the people not to show themselves worse judges than the enemy, condemning Marcellus of timidity, from whom alone of all their captains the enemy fled, and as perpetually endeavoured to avoid fighting with him as to fight with others. When they made an end of speaking, the accuser's hope to obtain judgment so far deceived him, that Marcellus was not only absolved, but the fifth time created consul.

No sooner had he entered upon this consulate, but he suppressed a great commotion in Etruria, that had proceeded near to revolt, and visited and quieted the cities. Then, when the dedication of the temple, which he had vowed out of his Sicilian spoils to Honour and Virtue, was objected to by the priests, because they denied that one temple could be lawfully dedicated to two gods, he began to adjoin another to it, resenting the priests' opposition, and almost converting the thing into an omen. And, truly, many other prodigies also affrighted him; some temples had been struck with lightning, and in Jupiter's temple mice had gnawed the gold; it was reported, also, that an ox had spoken, and that a boy had been born with a head like an elephant's. All which prodigies had indeed been attended to, but due reconciliation had not been obtained from the gods. The aruspices therefore detained him at Rome, glowing and burning with desire to return to the war. For no man was ever inflamed with so great desire of anything as was he to fight a battle with Hannibal. It was the subject of his dreams in the night, the topic of all his consultations with his friends and familiars, nor did he present to the gods any other wish, but that he might meet Hannibal in the field. And I think that he would most gladly have set upon him, with both armies environed within a single camp. Had he not been even loaded with honours, and had he not given proofs in many ways of his maturity of judgment and of prudence equal to that of any commander, you might have said that he was agitated by a youthful ambition, above what became a man of that age, for he had passed the sixtieth year of his life when he began his fifth consulship.

The sacrifices having been offered, and all that belonged to the propitiation of the gods performed, according to the prescription of the diviners, he at last with his colleague went forth to carry on the war. He tried all possible means to provoke Hannibal, who at that time had a standing camp betwixt Bantia and Venusia. Hannibal declined an engagement, but having obtained intelligence that some troops were on their way to the town of Locri Epizephyrii, placing an ambush under the little hill of Petelia, he slew two thousand five hundred soldiers. This incensed Marcellus to revenge; and he therefore moved nearer Hannibal. Betwixt the two camps was a little hill, a tolerably secure post covered with wood; it had steep descents on either side and there were springs of water seen trickling down. This place was so fit and advantageous that the Romans wondered that Hannibal, who had come thither before them, had not seized upon it, but had left it to the enemies. But to him the place had seemed commodious indeed for a camp, but yet more commodious for an ambuscade; and to that use he chose to put it. So in the wood and the hollows he hid a number of archers and spearmen, confident that the commodiousness of the place would allure the Romans. Nor was he deceived in his expectation. For presently in the Roman camp they talked and disputed, as if they had all been captains, how the place ought to be seized, and what great advantage they should thereby gain upon the enemies, chiefly if they transferred their camp thither, at any rate, if they strengthened the place with a fort. Marcellus resolved to go, with a few horse, to view it. Having called a diviner he proceeded to sacrifice. In the first victim the aruspex showed him the liver without a head; in the second the head appeared of unusual size, and all the other indications highly promising. When these seemed sufficient to free them from the dread of the former, the diviners declared that they were all the more terrified by the latter; because entrails too fair and promising, when they appear after others that are maimed and monstrous, render the change doubtful and suspicious. But—

Nor fire nor brazen wall can keep out fate;

as Pindar observes. Marcellus, therefore, taking with him his colleague Crispinus, and his son, a tribune of soldiers, with two hundred and twenty horse at most (among whom there was not one Roman, but all were

Etruscans, except forty Fregellans, of whose courage and fidelity he had on all occasions received full proof), goes to view the place. The hill was covered with woods all over; on the top of it sat a scout concealed from the sight of the enemy, but having the Roman camp exposed to his view. Upon signs received from him, the men that were placed in ambush stirred not till Marcellus came near; and then all starting up in an instant, and encompassing him from all sides, attacked him with darts, struck about and wounded the backs of those that fled, and pressed upon those who resisted. These were the forty Fregellans. For though the Etruscans fled in the very beginning of the fight, the Fregellans formed themselves into a ring, bravely defending the consuls, till Crispinus, struck with two darts, turned his horse to fly away; and Marcellus' side was run through with a lance with a broad head. Then the Fregellans, also, the few that remained alive, leaving the fallen consul, and rescuing young Marcellus, who also was wounded, got into the camp by flight. There were slain not much above forty; five lictors and eighteen horsemen came alive into the enemy's hands. Crispinus also died of his wounds a few days after. Such a disaster as the loss of both consuls in a single engagement was one that had never before befallen the Romans.

Hannibal, little valuing the other events, as soon as he was told of Marcellus' death, immediately hasted to the hill. Viewing the body, and continuing for sometime to observe its strength and shape, he allowed not a word to fall from him expressive of the least pride or arrogancy, nor did he show in his countenance any sign of gladness, as another perhaps would have done, when his fierce and troublesome enemy had been taken away; but amazed by so sudden and unexpected an end, taking off nothing but his ring, gave order to have the body properly clad and adorned and honourably burned. The relics put into a silver urn, with a crown of gold to cover it, he sent back to his son. But some of the Numidians, setting upon these that were carrying the urn, took it from them by force, and cast away the bones; which being told to Hannibal, "It is impossible, it seems then," he said, "to do anything against the will of God!" He punished the Numidians; but took no further care of sending or re-collecting the bones; conceiving that Marcellus so fell, and so lay unburied, by a certain fate. So Cornelius Nepos and Vaerius Maximus have left upon record: but Livy and Augustus Cæsar affirm that the urn was brought to his son, and honoured with a magnificent funeral. Besides the monuments raised for him at Rome, there was dedicated to his memory at Catana, in Sicily, an ample wrestling place called after him; statues and pictures, out of those he took from Syracuse, were set up in Samothrace, in the temple of the gods, named Cabiri, and in that of Minerva at Lindus, where also there was a statue of him, says Posidonius, with the following inscription:

> This was, O stranger, once Rome's star divine,
> Claudius Marcellus of an ancient line;
> To fight her wars seven times her consul made,
> Low in the dust her enemies he laid.

The writer of the inscription has added to Marcellus' five consulates his two proconsulates. His progeny continued in high honour even down to Marcellus, son of Octavia, sister of Augustus, whom she bore to her husband Caius Marcellus; and who died a bridegroom, in the year of his ædileship, having not long before married Cæsar's daughter. His mother, Octavia, dedicated the library to his honour and memory, and Cæsar the theatre which bears his name.

THE COMPARISON OF PELOPIDAS
WITH MARCELLUS

THESE ARE THE MEMORABLE THINGS I HAVE FOUND IN HISTORIANS concerning Marcellus and Pelopidas. Betwixt which two great men, though in natural character and manners they nearly resemble each other, because both were valiant and diligent, daring and high-spirited, there was yet some diversity in the one point, that Marcellus in many cities which he reduced under his power committed great slaughter; but Epaminondas and Pelopidas never after any victory put men to death, or reduced citizens to slavery. And we are told, too, that the Thebans would not, had these been present, have taken the measures they did against the Orchomenians. Marcellus' exploits against the Gauls are admirable and ample; when, accompanied by a few horse, he defeated and put to flight a vast number of horse and foot together (an action you cannot easily in historians find to have been done by any other captain), and took their king prisoner. To which honour Pelopidas aspired, but did not attain; he was killed by the tyrant in the attempt. But to these you may perhaps oppose those two most glorious battles at Leuctra and Tegryæ; and we have no statement of any achievement of Marcellus, by stealth or ambuscade, such as were those of Pelopidas, when he returned from exile, and killed the tyrants at Thebes; which, indeed, may claim to be called the first in rank of all achievements ever performed by secrecy and cunning. Hannibal was, indeed, a most formidable enemy for the Romans; but so for that matter were the Lacedæmonians for the Thebans. And that these were, in the fights of Leuctra and Tegyræ, beaten and put to flight by Pelopidas is confessed, whereas Polybius writes that Hannibal was never so much as once vanquished by Marcellus, but remained invincible in all encounters till Scipio came. I myself, indeed, have followed rather Livy,

Cæsar, Cornelius Nepos and, among the Greeks, king Juba, in stating that the troops of Hannibal were in some encounters routed and put to flight by Marcellus; but certainly these defeats conducted little to the sum of the war. It would seem as if they had been merely feints of some sort on the part of the Carthaginians. What was indeed truly and really admirable was, that the Romans, after the defeat of so many armies, the slaughter of so many captains, and, in fine, the confusion of almost the whole Roman empire, still showed a courage equal to their losses, and were as willing as their enemies to engage in new battles. And Marcellus was the one man who overcame the great and inveterate fear and dread, and revived, raised, and confirmed the spirits of the soldiers to that degree of emulation and bravery that would not let them easily yield the victory, but made them contend for it to the last. For the same men, whom continual defeats had accustomed to think themselves happy, if they could but save themselves by running from Hannibal, were by him taught to esteem it base and ignominious to return safe but unsuccessful; to be ashamed to confess that they had yielded one step in the terrors of the fight; and to grieve to extremity if they were not victorious.

In short, as Pelopidas was never overcome in any battle, where himself was present and commanded in chief, and as Marcellus gained more victories than any of his contemporaries, truly he that could not be easily overcome, considering his many successes, may fairly be compared with him who was undefeated. Marcellus took Syracuse; whereas Pelopidas was frustrated of his hope of capturing Sparta. But in my judgment it was more difficult to advance his standard even to the walls of Sparta, and to be the first of mortals that ever passed the river Eurotas in arms, than it was to reduce Sicily; unless, indeed, we say that that adventure is with more of right to be attributed to Epaminondas, as was also the Leuctrian battle; whereas Marcellus' renown, and the glory of his brave actions, came entire and undiminished to him alone. For he alone took Syracuse; and without his colleague's help defeated the Gauls, and, when all others declined, alone, without one companion, ventured to engage with Hannibal; and changing the aspect of the war first showed the example of daring to attack him.

I cannot commend the death of either of these great men; the suddenness and strangeness of their ends gives me a feeling rather of pain and distress. Hannibal has my admiration who, in so many severe conflicts, more than can be reckoned in one day, never received so much as one wound. I honour Chrysantes also (in Xenophon's Cyropædia), who, having raised his sword in the act of striking his enemy, so soon as a retreat was sounded, left him, and retired sedately and modestly. Yet the anger which provoked Pelopidas to pursue revenge in the heat of fight may excuse him.

> The first thing for a captain is to gain
> Safe victory; the next to be with honour slain,

as Euripides says. For then he cannot be said to *suffer* death; it is rather to be called an action. The very object, too, of Pelopidas' victory, which consisted in the slaughter of the tyrant, presenting itself to his eyes, did not wholly carry him away unadvisedly: he could not easily expect again to have another equally glorious occasion for the exercise of his courage in a noble and honourable cause. But Marcellus, when it made little to his advantage, and when no such violent ardour as present danger naturally calls out transported him to passion, throwing himself into danger, fell into an unexplored ambush; he, namely, who had borne five consulates, led three triumphs, won the spoils and glories of kings and victories, to act the part of a mere scout, or sentinel, and to expose all his achievements to be trod under foot by the mercenary Spaniards and Numidians, who sold themselves and their lives to the Carthaginians; so that even they themselves felt unworthy, and almost grudged themselves the unhoped-for success of having cut off, among a few Fregellan scouts, the most valiant, the most potent, and most renowned of the Romans. Let no man think that we have thus spoken out of a design to accuse these noble men; it is merely an expression of frank indignation in their own behalf, at seeing them thus wasting all their other virtues upon that of bravery and throwing away their lives, as if the loss would be only felt by themselves, and not by their country, allies, and friends.

After Pelopidas' death, his friends, for whom he died, made a funeral for him; the enemies, by whom he had been killed, made one for Marcellus. A noble and happy lot indeed the former; yet there is something higher and greater in the admiration rendered by enemies to the virtue that had been their own obstacle, than in the grateful acknowledgments of friends. Since, in the one case, it is virtue alone that challenges itself the honour; while, in the other, it may be rather men's personal profit and advantage that is the real origin of what they do.

ARISTIDES

ARISTIDES, THE SON OF LYSIMACHUS, WAS OF THE TRIBE ANTIOCHIS, AND township of Alopece. As to wealth, statements differ; some say he passed his life in extreme poverty, and left behind him two daughters whose indigence long kept them unmarried; but Demetrius, the Phalerian, in opposition to this general report, professes in his Socrates to know a farm at Phalerum going by Aristides' name, where he was interred; and, as marks of his opulence, adduces first, the office of archon eponymus, which he obtained by the lot of the bean; which was confined to the highest assessed families, called the Pentacosiomedimni; second, the ostracism, which was not usually inflicted on the poorer citizens, but on those of great houses, whose station exposed them to envy; third and last, that he left certain tripods in the temple of Bacchus, offerings for his victory in conducting the representation of dramatic performances, which were even in our age still to be seen, retaining this inscription upon them, "The tribe Antiochis obtained the victory: Aristides defrayed the charges: Archestratus' play was acted." But this argument, though in appearance the strongest, is of the least moment of any. For Epaminondas, who all the world knows was educated, and lived his whole life in much poverty, and also Plato, the philosopher, exhibited magnificent shows, the one an entertainment of fluteplayers, the other of dithyrambic singers; Dion, the Syracusan, supplying the expenses of the latter, and Pelopidas those of Epaminondas. For good men do not allow themselves in any inveterate and irreconcilable hostility to receiving presents from their friends, but while looking upon those that are accepted to be hoarded up and with avaricious intentions as sordid and mean, they do not refuse such as, apart from all profit, gratify the pure love of honour and magnificence. Panætius, again, shows that

Demetrius was deceived concerning the tripod by an identity of name. For, from the Persian war to the end of the Peloponnesian, there are upon record only two of the name of Aristides who defrayed the expense of representing plays and gained the prize, neither of which was the same with the son of Lysimachus; but the father of the one was Xenophilus, and the other lived at a much later time, as the way of writing, which is that in use since the time of Euclides, and the addition of the name of Archestratus prove, a name which, in the time of the Persian war, no writer mentions, but which several, during the Peloponnesian war, record as that of a dramatic poet. The argument of Panætius requires to be more closely considered. But as for the ostracism, everyone was liable to it, whom his reputation, birth, or eloquence raised above the common level; insomuch that even Damon, preceptor to Pericles, was thus banished, because he seemed a man of more than ordinary sense. And, moreover, Idomeneus says that Aristides was not made archon by the lot of the bean, but the free election of the people. And if he held the office after the battle of Platæa, as Demetrius himself has written, it is very probable that his great reputation and success in the war made him be preferred for his virtue to an office which others received in consideration of their wealth. But Demetrius manifestly is eager not only to exempt Aristides, but Socrates likewise, from poverty, as from a great evil; telling us that the latter had not only a house of his own, but also seventy minæ put out at interest with Crito.

Aristides being the friend and supporter of that Clisthenes, who settled the government after the expulsion of the tyrants, and emulating and admiring Lycurgus, the Lacedæmonian, above all politicians, adhered to the aristocratical principles of government; and had Themistocles, son to Neocles, his adversary on the side of the populace. Some say that, being boys and bred up together from their infancy, they were always at variance with each other in all their words and actions, as well serious as playful, and that in this their early contention they soon made proof of their natural inclinations; the one being ready, adventurous, and subtle, engaging readily and eagerly in everything; the other of a staid and settled temper, intent on the exercise of justice, not admitting any degree of falsity, indecorum, or trickery, no, not so much as at his play. Ariston of Chios says the first origin of the enmity which rose to so great a height was a love affair; they were rivals for the affection of the beautiful Stesilaus of Ceos, and were passionate beyond all moderation, and did not lay aside their animosity when the beauty that had excited it passed away; but, as if it had only exercised them in it, immediately carried their heats and differences into public business.

Themistocles, therefore, joining an association of partisans, fortified himself with considerable strength; insomuch that when someone told him that were he impartial he would make a good magistrate; "I wish," replied he, "I may never sit on that tribunal where my friends shall not plead a greater privilege than strangers." But Aristides walked, so to say, alone on his own path in politics, being unwilling, in the first place, to go along with his associates in ill-doing, or to cause them vexation by not gratifying their wishes; and, secondly, observing that many were encouraged by the support they had in their friends to act injuriously, he was cautious; being of opinion that the integrity of his words and actions was the only right security for a good citizen.

However, Themistocles making many dangerous alterations, and withstanding and interrupting him in the whole series of his actions, Aristides also was necessitated to set himself against all Themistocles did, partly in self-defence, and partly to impede his power from still increasing by the favour of the multitude; esteeming it better to let slip some public conveniences, rather than that he by prevailing should become powerful in all things. In fine, when he once had opposed Themistocles in some measures that were expedient, and had got the better of him, he could not refrain from saying, when he left the assembly, that unless they sent Themistocles and himself to the barathrum, there could be no safety for Athens. Another time, when urging some proposal upon the people, though there were much opposition and stirring against it, he yet was gaining the day; but just as the president of the assembly was about to put it to the vote, perceiving by what had been said in debate the inexpediency of his advice, he let it fall. Also he often brought in his bills by other persons, lest Themistocles, through party spirit against him, should be any hindrance to the good of the public.

In all the vicissitudes of public affairs, the constancy he showed was admirable, not being elated with honours, and demeaning himself tranquilly and sedately in adversity; holding the opinion that he ought to offer himself to the service of his country without mercenary views and irrespectively of any reward, not only of riches, but even of glory itself. Hence it came, probably, that at the recital of these verses of Æschylus in the theatre, relating to Amphiaraus—

> For not at seeming just, but being so
> He aims; and from his depth of soil below
> Harvests of wise and prudent counsels grow,

the eyes of all the spectators turned on Aristides, as if this virtue, in an especial manner, belonged to him.

He was a most determined champion for justice, not only against feelings of friendship and favour, but wrath and malice. Thus it is reported of him that when prosecuting the law against one who was his enemy, on the judges after accusation refusing to hear the criminal, and proceeding immediately to pass sentence upon him, he rose in haste from his seat and joined in petition with him for a hearing, and that he might enjoy the privilege of the law. Another time, when judging between two private persons, on the one declaring his adversary had very much injured Aristides; "Tell me rather, good friend," he said, "what wrong he has done you; for it is your cause, not my own, which I now sit judge of." Being chosen to the charge of the public revenue, he made it appear, that not only those of his time, but the preceding officers, had alienated much treasure, and especially Themistocles—

> Well known he was an able man to be,
> But with his fingers apt to be too free.

Therefore, Themistocles associating several persons against Aristides, and impeaching him when he gave in his accounts, caused him to be condemned of robbing the public; so Idomeneus states; but the best and chiefest men of the city much resenting it, he was not only exempted from the fine imposed upon him, but likewise again called to the same employment. Pretending now to repent him of his former practice, and carrying himself with more remissness, he became acceptable to such as pillaged the treasury by not detecting or calling them to an exact account. So that those who had their fill of the public money began highly to applaud Aristides, and sued to the people making interest to have him once more chosen treasurer. But when they were upon the point of election, he reproved the Athenians. "When I discharged my office well and faithfully," said he, "I was insulted and abused; but now that I have allowed the public thieves in a variety of malpractices, I am considered an admirable patriot. I am more ashamed, therefore, of this present honour than of the former sentence; and I commiserate your condition, with whom it is more praiseworthy to oblige ill men than to conserve the revenue of the public." Saying thus, and proceeding to expose the thefts that had been committed, he stopped the mouths of those who cried him up and vouched for him, but gained real and true commendations from the best men.

When Datis, being sent by Darius under pretence of punishing the Athenians for their burning of Sardis, but in reality to reduce the Greeks under his dominion, landed at Marathon and laid waste the country, among the ten commanders appointed by the Athenians for the war, Miltiades was of the greatest name; but the second place, both for reputation and power, was possessed by Aristides; and when his opinion to join battle was added to that of Miltiades, it did much to incline the balance. Every leader by his day having the command in chief, when it came to Aristides' turn he delivered it into the hands of Miltiades, showing his fellow-officers that it is not dishonourable to obey and follow wise and able men, but, on the contrary, noble and prudent. So appeasing their rivalry, and bringing them to acquiesce in one and the best advice, he confirmed Miltiades in the strength of an undivided and unmolested authority. For now everyone, yielding his day of command, looked for orders only to him. During the fight the main body of the Athenians being the hardest put to it, the barbarians, for a long time, making opposition there against the tribes Leontis and Antiochis, Themistocles and Aristides being ranged together fought valiantly; the one being of the tribe Leontis, the other of the Antiochis. But after they had beaten the barbarians back to their ships, and perceived that they sailed not for the isles, but were driven in by the force of sea and wind towards the country of Attica, fearing lest they should take the city, unprovided of defence, they hurried away thither with nine tribes, and reached it the same day. Aristides, being left with his tribe at Marathon to guard the plunder and prisoners, did not disappoint the opinion they had of him. Amidst the profusion of gold and silver, all sorts of apparel, and other property, more than can be mentioned, that were in the tents and the vessels which they had taken, he neither felt the desire to meddle with anything himself, nor suffered others to do it; unless it might be some who took away anything unknown to him; as Callias, the torchbearer, did. One of the barbarians, it seems, prostrated himself before this man, supposing him to be a king by his hair and fillet; and, when he had so done, taking him by the hand, showed him a great quantity of gold hid in a ditch. But Callias, most cruel and impious of men, took away the treasure, but slew the man, lest he should tell of him. Hence, they say, the comic poets gave his family the name of *Laccopluti*, or enriched by the ditch, alluding to the place where Callias found the gold. Aristides, immediately after this, was archon; although Demetrius, the Phalerian, says he held the office a little before he died after the battle of Platæa. But in the records of the successors of Xanthippides, in whose year Mardonius was overthrown at Platæa, amongst very many there mentioned, there is not so much as one of the same name as Aristides; while immediately after Phænippus, during whose term of office they obtained the victory of Marathon, Aristides is registered.

Of all his virtues, the common people were most affected with his justice, because of its continual and common use; and thus, although of mean fortune and ordinary birth, he possessed himself of the most kingly and divine appellation of Just: which kings, however, and tyrants have never sought after; but have taken delight to be surnamed besiegers of cities, thunderers, conquerors, or eagles again, and hawks; affecting, it seems, the reputation which proceeds from power and violence, rather than that of virtue. Although the divinity, to whom they desire to compare and assimilate themselves, excels, it is supposed, in three things, immortality, power, and virtue; of which three the noblest and divinest is virtue. For the elements and vacuum have an everlasting existence; earthquakes, thunders, storms, and torrents have great power; but in justice and equity nothing participates except by means of reason and the knowledge of that which is divine. And thus, taking the three varieties of feeling commonly entertained towards the deity, the sense of his happiness, fear, and honour of him, people would seem to think him blest and happy for his exemption from death and corruption, to fear and dread him for his power and dominion, but to love, honour, and adore him for his justice. Yet though thus disposed, they covet that immortality which our nature is not capable of, and that power the greatest part of which is at the disposal of fortune; but give virtue, the only divine good really in our reach, the last place, most unwisely; since justice makes the life of such as are in prosperity, power, and authority the life of a god, and injustice turns it to that of a beast.

Aristides, therefore, had at first the fortune to be beloved for this surname, but at length envied. Especially when Themistocles spread a rumour amongst the people that, by determining and judging all matters privately, he had destroyed the courts of judicature, and was secretly making way for a monarchy in his own person, without the assistance of guards. Moreover the spirit of the people, now grown high, and confident with their late victory, naturally entertained feelings of dislike to all of more than common fame and reputation. Coming together, therefore, from all parts into the city, they banished Aristides by the ostracism, giving their jealousy of his reputation the name of fear of tyranny. For ostracism was not the punishment of any criminal act, but was speciously said to be the mere depression and humiliation of excessive greatness and power; and was in fact a gentle relief and mitigation of envious feeling, which was thus allowed to vent itself in inflicting no intolerable injury, only a ten years' banishment. But after it came to be exercised upon base and villainous fellows, they desisted from it; Hyperbolus being the last whom they banished by the ostracism.

The cause of Hyperbolus' banishment is said to have been this. Alcibiades and Nicias, men that bore the greatest sway in the city, were of different factions. As the people, therefore, were about to vote the ostracism, and obviously to decree it against one of them, consulting together and uniting their parties they contrived the banishment of Hyperbolus. Upon which the people, being offended, as if some contempt or affront was put upon the thing, left off and quite abolished it. It was performed, to be short, in this manner. Everyone taking an *ostracon*, a sherd, that is, or piece of earthenware, wrote upon it the citizen's name he would have banished, and carried it to a certain part of the market place surrounded with wooden rails. First, the magistrates numbered all the sherds in gross (for if there were less than six thousand, the ostracism was imperfect); then, laying every name by itself, they pronounced him whose name was written by the larger number banished for ten years, with the enjoyment of his estate. As therefore, they were writing the names on the sherds, it is reported that an illiterate clownish fellow, giving Aristides his sherd, supposing him a common citizen, begged him to write *Aristides* upon it; and he being surprised and asking if Aristides had ever done him any injury, "None at all," said he, "neither know I the man; but I am tired of hearing him everywhere called the Just." Aristides, hearing this, is said to have made no reply, but returned the sherd with his own name inscribed. At his departure from the city, lifting up his hands to heaven, he made a prayer (the reverse, it would seem, of that of Achilles), that the Athenians might never have any occasion which should constrain them to remember Aristides.

Nevertheless, three years after, when Xerxes marched through Thessaly and Bœotia into the country of Attica, repealing the law, they decreed the return of the banished: chiefly fearing Aristides, lest, joining himself to the enemy, he should corrupt and bring over many of his fellow-citizens to the party of the barbarians; much mistaking the man, who, already before the decree, was exerting himself to excite and encourage the

Greeks to the defence of their liberty. And afterwards, when Themistocles was general with absolute power, he assisted him in all ways both in action and counsel; rendering, in consideration of the common security, the greatest enemy he had the most glorious of men. For when Eurybiades was deliberating to desert the isle of Salamis, and the galleys of the barbarians putting out by night to sea surrounded and beset the narrow passage and islands, and nobody was aware how they were environed, Aristides, with great hazard, sailed from Ægina through the enemy's fleet; and coming by night to Themistocles' tent and calling him out by himself; "if we have any discretion," said he, "Themistocles, laying aside at this time our vain and childish contention, let us enter upon a safe and honourable dispute, vying with each other for the preservation of Greece; you in the ruling and commanding, I in the subservient and advising part; even indeed, as I now understand you to be alone adhering to the best advice, in counselling without any delay to engage in the straits. And in this, though our own party oppose, the enemy seems to assist you. For the sea behind, and all around us, is covered with their fleet; so that we are under a necessity of approving ourselves men of courage, and fighting whether we will or no; for there is no room left us for flight." To which Themistocles answered, "I would not willingly, Aristides, be overcome by you on this occasion; and shall endeavour, in emulation of this good beginning, to outdo it in my actions." Also relating to him the stratagem he had framed against the barbarians, he entreated him to persuade Eurybiades and show him how it was impossible they should save themselves without an engagement; as he was the more likely to be believed. Whence, in the council of war, Cleocritus, the Corinthian, telling Themistocles that Aristides did not like his advice as he was present and said nothing, Aristides answered, that he should not have held his peace if Themistocles had not been giving the best advice; and that he was now silent not out of any goodwill to the person, but in approbation of his counsel.

Thus the Greek captains were employed. But Aristides perceiving Psyttalea, a small island that lies within the straits over against Salamis, to be filled by a body of the enemy, put aboard his small boats the most forward and courageous of his countrymen, and went ashore upon it; and, joining battle with the barbarians, slew them all, except such more remarkable persons as were taken alive. Amongst these were three children of Sandauce, the king's sister, whom he immediately sent away to Themistocles, and it is stated that, in accordance with a certain oracle, they were by the command of Euphrantides, the seer, sacrificed to

Bacchus, called Omestes, or the devourer. But Aristides, placing armed men all around the island, lay in wait for such as were cast upon it, to the intent that none of his friends should perish, nor any of his enemies escape. For the closest engagement of the ships, and the main fury of the whole battle, seems to have been about this place; for which reason a trophy was erected in Psyttalea.

After the fight, Themistocles, to sound Aristides, told him they had performed a good piece of service, but there was a better yet to be done, the keeping Asia in Europe, by sailing forthwith to the Hellespont and cutting in sunder the bridge. But Aristides, with an exclamation, bid him think no more of it, but deliberate and find out means for removing the Mede, as quickly as possible, out of Greece; lest being enclosed, through want of means to escape, necessity should compel him to force his way with so great an army. So Themistocles once more despatched Arnaces, the eunuch, his prisoner, giving him in command privately to advertise the king that he had diverted the Greeks from their intention of setting sail for the bridges, out of the desire he felt to preserve him.

Xerxes, being much terrified with this, immediately hasted to the Hellespont. But Mardonius was left with the most serviceable part of the army, about three hundred thousand men, and was a formidable enemy, confident in his infantry and writing messages of defiance to the Greeks: "You have overcome by sea men accustomed to fight on land, and unskilled at the oar; but there lies now the open country of Thessaly; and the plains of Bœotia offer a broad and worthy field for brave men, either horse or foot, to contend in." But he sent privately to the Athenians, both by letter and word of mouth from the king, promising to rebuild their city, to give them a vast sum of money, and constitute them lords of all Greece, on condition they were not engaged in the war. The Lacedæmonians, receiving news of this, and fearing, despatched an embassy to the Athenians, entreating that they would send their wives and children to Sparta, and receive support from them for their superannuated. For, being despoiled both of their city and country, the people were suffering extreme distress. Having given audience to the ambassadors, they returned an answer, upon the motion of Aristides, worthy of the highest admiration; declaring, that they forgave their enemies if they thought all things purchasable by wealth, than which they knew nothing of greater value; but that they felt offended at the Lacedæmonians for looking only to their present poverty and exigence, without any remembrance of their valour and magnanimity, offering them their victuals to fight in the cause of Greece.

Aristides, making this proposal and bringing back the ambassadors into the assembly, charged them to tell the Lacedæmonians, that all the treasure on the earth or under it was of less value with the people of Athens than the liberty of Greece. And, showing the sun to those who came from Mardonius, "As long as that retains the same course, so long," said he, "shall the citizens of Athens wage war with the Persians for the country which has been wasted, and the temples that have been profaned and burnt by them." Moreover, he proposed a decree that the priests should anathematise him who sent any herald to the Medes, or deserted the alliance of Greece.

When Mardonius made a second incursion into the country of Attica, the people passed over again into the isle of Salamis. Aristides, being sent to Lacedæmon, reproved them for their delay and neglect in abandoning Athens once more to the barbarians; and demanded their assistance for that part of Greece which was not yet lost. The Ephori, hearing this, made show of sporting all day, and of carelessly keeping holy day (for they were then celebrating the Hyacinthian festival), but in the night, selecting five thousand Spartans, each of whom was attended by seven Helots, they sent them forth unknown to those from Athens. And when Aristides again reprehended them, they told him in derision that he either doted or dreamed, for the army was already at Oresteum, in their march towards the *strangers,* as they called the Persians. Aristides answered that they jested unseasonably, deluding their friends instead of their enemies. Thus says Idomeneus. But in the decree of Aristides, not himself, but Cimon, Xanthippus, and Myronides are appointed ambassadors.

Being chosen general for the war, he repaired to Platæa with eight thousand Athenians, where Pausanias, generalissimo of all Greece, joined him with the Spartans; and the forces of the other Greeks came into them. The whole encampment of the barbarians extended all along the bank of the river Asopus, their numbers being so great there was no enclosing them all, but their baggage and most valuable things were surrounded with a square bulwark, each side of which was the length of ten furlongs.

Tisamenus, the Elean, had prophesied to Pausanias and all the Greeks, and foretold them victory if they made no attempt upon the enemy, but stood on their defence. But Aristides sending to Delphi, the god answered that the Athenians should overcome their enemies in case they made supplication to Jupiter and Juno of Cithæron, Pan, and the nymphs Sphragitides, and sacrificed to the heroes Androcrates, Leucon, Pisander, Damocrates, Hypsion, Actæon, and Polyidus; and if they fought within their own territories in the plain of Ceres Eleusinia and Proserpine. Aristides was perplexed upon the tidings of this oracle; since the heroes to whom it commanded him to sacrifice had been chieftains of the Platæans, and the cave of the nymphs Sphragitides was on the top of Mount Cithæron, on the side facing the setting sun of summer time; in which place, as the story goes, there was formerly an oracle, and many that lived in the district were inspired with it, whom they called *Nympholepti,* possessed with the nymphs. But the plain of Ceres Eleusinia, and the offer of victory to the Athenians, if they fought in their own territories, recalled them again, and transferred the war into the country of Attica. In this juncture, Arimnestus, who commanded the Platæans, dreamed that Jupiter, the Saviour, asked him what the Greeks had resolved upon; and that he answered, "Tomorrow, my Lord, we march our army to Eleusis, and there give the barbarians battle according to the directions of the oracle of Apollo." And that the god replied they were utterly mistaken, for that the places spoken of by the oracle were within the bounds of Platæa, and if they sought there they should find them. This manifest vision having appeared to Arimnestus, when he awoke he sent for the most aged and experienced of his countrymen, with whom, communicating and examining the matter, he found that near Hysiæ, at the foot of Mount Cithæron, there was a very ancient temple called the temple of Ceres Eleusinia and Proserpine. He therefore forthwith took Aristides to the place, which was very convenient for drawing up an army of foot, because the slopes at the bottom of the mountain Cithæron rendered the plain, where it comes up to the temple, unfit for the movements of cavalry. Also, in the same place, there was the fane of Androcrates, environed with a thick shady grove. And that the oracle might be accomplished in all particulars for the hope of victory, Arimnestus proposed, and the Platæans decreed, that the frontiers of their country towards Attica should be removed, and the land given to the Athenians, that they might fight in defence of Greece in their own proper territory. This zeal and liberality of the Platæans became so famous that Alexander, many years after, when he had obtained the dominion of all Asia, upon erecting the walls of Platæa, caused proclamation to be made, by the herald at the Olympic games, that the king did the Platæans this favour in consideration of their nobleness and magnanimity, because, in the war with the Medes, they freely gave up their land and zealously fought with the Greeks.

The Tegeatans, contesting the post of honour with the Athenians, demanded that, according to custom, the Lacedæmonians being ranged on the right wing of the battle, they might have the left, alleging several matters in commendation of their ancestors. The Athenians being indignant at the claim, Aristides came forward: "To contend with the Tegeatans," said he, "for noble descent and valour, the present time permits not; but this we say to you, O you Spartans, and you the rest of the Greeks, that place neither takes away nor contributes courage; we shall endeavour by crediting and maintaining the post you assign us to reflect no dishonour on our former performances. For we are come, not to differ with our friends, but to fight our enemies; not to extol our ancestors, but ourselves to behave as valiant men. This battle will manifest how much each city, captain, and private soldier is worth to Greece." The council of war, upon this address, decided for the Athenians, and gave them the other wing of the battle.

All Greece being in suspense, and especially the affairs of the Athenians unsettled, certain persons of great families and possessions having been impoverished by the war, and seeing all their authority and reputation in the city vanished with their wealth, and others in possession of their honours and places, convened privately at a house in Platæa, and conspired for the dissolution of the democratic government; and, if the plot should not succeed, to ruin the cause and betray all to the barbarians. These matters being in agitation in the camp, and many persons already corrupted, Aristides, perceiving the design, and dreading the present juncture of time, determined neither to let the business pass unanimadverted upon, nor yet altogether to expose it; not knowing how many the accusation might reach, and willing to set bounds to his justice with a view to the public convenience. Therefore, of many that were concerned he apprehended eight only, two of whom, who were first proceeded against and most guilty, Æschines of Lampra and Agesias of Acharnæ, made their escape out of the camp. The rest he dismissed; giving opportunity to such as thought themselves concealed to take courage and repent; intimating that they had in the war a great tribunal, where they might clear their guilt by manifesting their sincere and good intentions towards their country.

After this, Mardonius made trial of the Grecian courage, by sending his whole number of horse, in which he thought himself much the stronger, against them, while they were all pitched at the foot of Mount Cithæron, in strong and rocky places, except the Megarians. They, being three thousand in number, were encamped on the plain, where they were damaged by the horse charging and making inroads upon them on all hands. They sent, therefore, in haste to Pausanias, demanding relief, as not being able alone to sustain the great numbers of the barbarians. Pausanias, hearing this, and perceiving the tents of the Megarians already hid by the multitude of darts and arrows, and themselves driven together into a narrow space, was at a loss himself how to aid them with his battalion of heavy-armed Lacedæmonians. He proposed it, therefore, as a point of emulation in valour and love of distinction, to the commanders and captains who were around him, if any would voluntarily take upon them the defence and succour of the Megarians. The rest being backward, Aristides undertook the enterprise for the Athenians, and sent Olympiodorus, the most valiant of his inferior officers, with three hundred chosen men and some archers under his command. These being soon in readiness, and running upon the enemy, as soon as Masistius, who commanded the barbarians' horse, a man of wonderful courage and of extraordinary bulk and comeliness of person, perceived it, turning his steed he made towards them. And they sustaining the shock and joining battle with him, there was a sharp conflict, as though by this encounter they were to try the success of the whole war. But after Masistius' horse received a wound and flung him, and he falling could hardly raise himself through the weight of his armour, the Athenians, pressing upon him with blows, could not easily get at his person, armed as he was, his breast, his head, and his limbs all over, with gold and brass and iron; but one of them at last, running him in at the visor of his helmet, slew him; and the rest of the Persians, leaving the body, fled. The greatness of the Greek success was known, not by the multitude of the slain (for an inconsiderable number were killed), but by the sorrow the barbarians expressed. For they shaved themselves, their horses, and mules for the death of Masistius, and filled the plain with howling and lamentation; having lost a person, who, next to Mardonius himself, was by many degrees the chief among them, both for valour and authority.

After this skirmish of the horse, they kept from fighting a long time; for the soothsayers, by the sacrifices, foretold the victory both to Greeks and Persians, if they stood upon the defensive part only, but if they became aggressors, the contrary. At length Mardonius, when he had but a few days' provision, and the Greek forces increased continually by some or other that came in to them, impatient of delay, determined to lie still no longer, but passing Asopus by daybreak, to fall unexpectedly upon the Greeks; and signified the same over night to the captains of his host. But about midnight, a certain horseman stole into the Greek camp, and coming to the watch, desired them to call Aristides, the Athenian, to him. He coming speedily, "I am," said the stranger, "Alexander, king of the Macedonians, and am arrived here through the greatest danger in the world for the good-will I bear you, lest a sudden onset should dismay you, so as to behave in the fight worse than usual. For tomorrow Mardonius will give you battle, urged, not by any hope of success or courage, but by want of victuals; since, indeed, the prophets prohibit him the battle, the sacrifices and oracles being unfavourable; and the army is in despondency and consternation; but necessity forces him to try his fortune, or sit still and endure the last extremity of want." Alexander, thus saying, entreated Aristides to take notice and remember him, but not to tell any other. But he told him, it was not convenient to conceal the matter from Pausanias (because he was general); as for any other, he would keep it secret from them till the battle was fought; but if the Greeks obtained the victory, that then no one should be ignorant of Alexander's goodwill and kindness towards them. After this, the king of the Macedonians rode back again, and Aristides went to Pausanias' tent and told him; and they sent for the rest of the captains and gave orders that the army should be in battle array.

Here, according to Herodotus, Pausanias spoke to Aristides, desiring him to transfer the Athenians to the right wing of the army opposite to the Persians (as they would do better service against them, having been experienced in their way of combat, and emboldened with former victories), and to give him the left, where the Medizing Greeks were to make their assault. The rest of the Athenian captains regarded this as an arrogant and interfering act on the part of Pausanias; because, while permitting the rest of the army to keep their stations, he removed them only from place to place, like so many Helots, opposing them to the greatest strength of the enemy. But Aristides said they were altogether in the wrong. If so short a time ago they contested the left wing with the Tegeatans, and gloried in being preferred before them, now, when the Lacedæmonians give them place in the right, and yield them in a manner the leading of the army, how is it they are discontented with the honour that is done them, and do not look upon it as an advantage to have to fight, not against their countrymen and kindred, but barbarians, and such as were by nature their enemies? After this, the Athenians very readily changed places with the Lacedæmonians, and there went words amongst them as they were encouraging each other that the enemy approached with no better arms or stouter hearts than those who fought the battle of Marathon; but had the same bows and arrows, and the same embroidered coats and gold, and the same delicate bodies and effeminate minds within; "While we have the same weapons and bodies, and our courage augmented by our victories; and fight not like others in defence of our country only, but for the trophies of Salamis and Marathon; that they may not be looked upon as due to Miltiades or fortune, but to the people of Athens." Thus, therefore, were they making haste to change the order of their battle. But the Thebans, understanding it by some deserters, forthwith acquainted Mardonius; and he, either for fear of the Athenians, or a desire to engage the Lacedæmonians, marched over his Persians to the other wing, and commanded the Greeks of his party to be posted opposite to the Athenians. But this change was observed on the other side, and Pausanias, wheeling about again, ranged himself on the right, and Mardonius, also, as at first, took the left wing over against the Lacedæmonians. So the day passed without action.

After this the Greeks determined in council to remove their camp some distance, to possess themselves of a place convenient for watering; because the springs near them were polluted and destroyed by the barbarian cavalry. But night being come, and the captains setting out towards the place designed for their camping, the soldiers were not very ready to follow, and keep in a body, but, as soon as they had quitted their first entrenchments, made towards the city of Platæa; and there was much tumult and disorder as they dispersed to various quarters and proceeded to pitch their tents. The Lacedæmonians, against their will, had the fortune to be left by the rest. For Amompharetus, a brave and daring man, who had long been burning with desire of the fight, and resented their many lingerings and delays, calling the removal of the camp a mere running away and flight, protested he would not desert his post, but would there remain with his company and sustain the charge of Mardonius. And when Pausanias came to him and told him he did do these things by the common vote and determination of the Greeks, Amompharetus taking up a great stone and flinging it at Pausanias' feet, and "By this token," said he, "do I give my suffrage for the battle, nor have I any concern with the cowardly consultations and decrees of other men," Pausanias, not knowing what to do in the present juncture, sent to the Athenians, who were drawing off, to stay to accompany him; and so he himself set off with the rest of the army for Platæ, hoping thus to make Amompharetus move.

Meantime, day came upon them; and Mardonius (for he was not ignorant of their deserting their camp), having his army in array, fell upon the Lacedæmonians with great shouting and noise of barbarous people, as if they were not about to join battle, but crush the Greeks in their flight. Which within a very little came to pass. For Pausanias, perceiving what was done, made a halt, and commanded everyone to put themselves in order for the battle; but either through his anger with Amompharetus, or the disturbance he was in by reason of the sudden approach of the enemy, he forgot to give the signal to the Greeks in general. Whence it was that they did not come in immediately or in a body to their assistance, but by small companies and straggling, when the fight was already begun. Pausanias, offering sacrifice, could not procure favourable omens, and so commanded the Lacedæmonians, setting down their shields at their feet, to abide quietly and attend his directions, making no resistance to any of their enemies. And he sacrificing again a second time, the horse charged, and some of the Lacedæmonians were wounded. At this time, also, Callicrates, who, we are told, was the most comely man in the army, being shot with an arrow and upon the point of expiring, said that he lamented not his death (for he came from home to lay down his life in the defence of Greece), but that he died without action. The case was indeed hard, and the forbearance of the men wonderful; for they let the enemy charge without repelling them; and, expecting their proper opportunity from the gods and their general, suffered themselves to be wounded and slain in their ranks. And some say, that while Pausanias was at sacrifice and prayers, some space out of the battle array, certain Lydians, falling suddenly upon him, plundered and scattered the sacrifice: and that Pausanias and his company, having no arms, beat them with staves and whips; and that, in imitation of this attack, the whipping the boys about the altar, and after it the Lydian procession, are to this day practised in Sparta.

Pausanias, therefore, being troubled at these things, while the priests went on offering one sacrifice after another, turns himself towards the temple with tears in his eyes, and lifting up his hands to heaven besought Juno of Cithæron, and the other tutelar gods of the Platæans, if it were not in the fates for the Greeks to obtain the victory, that they might not perish without performing some remarkable thing, and by their actions demonstrating to their enemies that they waged war with men of courage and soldiers. While Pausanias was thus in the act of supplication, the sacrifices appeared propitious, and the soothsayers foretold victory. The word being given, the Lacedæmonian battalion of foot seemed, on the sudden, like someone fierce animal, setting up his bristles, and betaking himself to the combat; and the barbarians perceived that they encountered with men who would fight it to the death. Therefore, holding their wicker-shields before them, they shot their arrows amongst the Lacedæmonians. But they, keeping together in the order of a phalanx, and falling upon the enemies, forced their shields out of their hands, and, striking with their pikes at the breasts and faces of the Persians, overthrew many of them, who, however, fell not either unrevenged or without courage. For taking hold of the spears with their bare hands, they broke many of them, and betook themselves not without effect to the sword; and making use of their falchions and scimitars, and wresting the Lacedæmonians' shields from them, and grappling with them, it was a long time that they made resistance.

Meanwhile, for sometime, the Athenians stood still, waiting for the Lacedæmonians to come up. But when they heard much noise as of men engaged in fight, and a messenger, they say, came from Pausanias, to advertise them of what was going on, they soon hasted to their assistance. And as they passed through the plain to the place where the noise was, the Greeks, who took part with the enemy, came upon them. Aristides, as soon as he saw them, going a considerable space before the rest, cried out to them, conjuring them by the guardian gods of Greece to forbear the fight, and be no impediment or stop to those who were going to succour the defenders of Greece. But when he perceived they gave no attention to him, and had prepared themselves for the battle, then turning from the present relief of the Lacedæmonians, he engaged them, being five thousand in number. But the greatest part soon gave way and retreated, as the barbarians also were put to flight. The sharpest conflict is said to have been against the Thebans, the chiefest and most powerful persons among them at that time siding zealously with the Medes, and leading the multitude not according to their own inclination, but as being subjects of an oligarchy.

The battle being thus divided, the Lacedæmonians first beat off the Persians; and a Spartan, named Arimnestus, slew Mardonius by a blow on the head with a stone, as the oracle in the temple of Amphiaraus had foretold to him. For Mardonius sent a Lydian thither, and another person, a Carian, to the cave of Trophonius. This latter the priest of the oracle answered in his own language. But the Lydian sleeping in the temple of Amphiaraus, it seemed to him that a minister of the divinity stood before him and commanded him to be gone; and on his refusing to do it, flung a great stone at his head, so that he thought himself slain with the blow. Such is the story. They drove the fliers within their walls of wood; and, a little time after, the Athenians put the Thebans to flight, killing three hundred of the chiefest and of greatest note among them in the actual fight itself. For when they began to fly, news came that the army of the barbarians was besieged within their palisade; and so giving the Greeks opportunity to save themselves, they marched to assist at the fortifications; and coming in to the Lacedæmonians, who were altogether unhandy and unexperienced in storming, they took the camp with great slaughter of the enemy. For of three hundred thousand, forty thousand only are said to have escaped with Artabazus; while on the Greeks' side there perished in all thirteen hundred and sixty; of which fifty-two were Athenians, all of the tribe Æantis, that fought, says Clidemus, with the greatest courage of any; and for this reason the men of this tribe used to offer sacrifice for the victory, as enjoined by the oracle, to the nymphs Sphragitides at the expense of the public; ninety-one were Lacedæmonians, and sixteen Tegeatans. It is strange, therefore, upon what grounds Herodotus can say, that they only, and none other, encountered the enemy, for the number of the slain and their monuments testify that the victory was obtained by all in general; and if the rest had been standing still, while the inhabitants of three cities only had been engaged in the fight, they would not have set on the altar the inscription—

> The Greeks, when, by their courage and their might,
> They had repelled the Persian in the fight,
> The common altar of freed Greece to be,
> Reared this to Jupiter who guards the free.

They fought this battle on the fourth day of the month Boëdromion, according to the Athenians, but according to the Bœotians, on the twenty-seventh of Panemus—on which day there is still a convention of the Greeks at Platæa, and the Platæans still offer sacrifice for the victory to Jupiter of freedom. As for the difference of days, it is not to be wondered at, since even at the present time, when there is a far more accurate knowledge of astronomy, some begin the month at one time, and some at another.

After this, the Athenians not yielding the honour of the day to the Lacedæmonians, nor consenting they should erect a trophy, things were not far from being ruined by dissension among the armed Greeks; had not Aristides, by much soothing and counselling the commanders, especially Leocrates and Myronides, pacified and persuaded them to leave the thing to the decision of the Greeks. And on their proceeding to discuss the matter, Theogiton, the Megarian, declared the honour of the victory was to be given some other city, if they would prevent a civil war; after him Cleocritus of Corinth rising up, made people think he would ask the palm for the Corinthians (for next to Sparta and Athens, Corinth was in greatest estimation); but he delivered his opinion, to the general admiration, in favour of the Platæans; and counselled to take away all contention by giving them the reward and glory of the victory, whose being honoured could be distasteful to neither party. This being said, first Aristides gave consent in the name of the Athenians, and Pausanias, then, for the Lacedæmonians. So, being reconciled, they set apart eighty talents for the Platæans, with which they built the temple and dedicated the image to Minerva, and adorned the temple with pictures, which even to this very day retain their lustre. But the Lacedæmonians and Athenians each erected a trophy apart by themselves. On their consulting the oracle about offering sacrifice, Apollo answered that they should dedicate an altar to Jupiter of freedom, but should not sacrifice till they had extinguished the fires throughout the country, as having been defiled by the barbarians, and had kindled unpolluted fire at the common altar at Delphi. The magistrates of Greece, therefore, went forthwith and compelled such as had fire to put it out; and Euchidas, a Platæan, promising to fetch fire, with all possible speed, from the altar of the god, went to Delphi, and having sprinkled and purified his body crowned himself with laurel; and taking the fire from the altar ran back to Platæa, and got back there before sunset, performing in one day a journey of a thousand furlongs; and saluting his fellow-citizens and delivering them the fire, he immediately fell down, and in a short time after expired. But the Platæans, taking him up, interred him in the temple of Diana Euclia, setting this inscription over him: "Euchidas ran to Delphi and back again in one day." Most people believe that Euclia is Diana, and call her by that name. But some say she was the daughter of Hercules, by Myrto, the daughter of Menœtius, and sister of Patroclus, and dying a virgin, was worshipped by the Bœotians and Locrians. Her altar and image are set up in all their market places, and those of both sexes that are about marrying sacrifice to her before the nuptials.

A general assembly of all the Greeks being called, Aristides proposed a decree that the deputies and religious representatives of the Greek states should assemble annually at Platæa, and every fifth year celebrate the Eleutheria or games of freedom. And that there should be a levy upon all Greece for the war against the barbarians of ten thousand spearmen, one thousand horse, and a hundred sail of ships; but the Platæans to be exempt, and sacred to the service of the gods, offering sacrifice for the welfare of Greece. These things being ratified, the Platæans undertook the performance of annual sacrifice to such as were slain and buried in that place; which they still perform in the following manner. On the sixteenth day of Mæmacterion (which with the Bœotians is Alalcomenus) they make their procession, which, beginning by break of day, is led by a trumpeter sounding for onset; then follow certain chariots loaded with myrrh and garlands; and then a black bull; then come the young men of free birth carrying libations of wine and milk in large two-handed vessels, and jars of oil and precious ointments, none of servile condition being permitted to have any hand in this ministration, because the men died in defence of freedom; after all comes the chief magistrate of Platæa (for whom it is unlawful at other times either to touch iron or wear any other coloured garment but white), at that time apparelled in a purple robe; and, taking a water pot out of the city record-office, he proceeds, bearing a sword in his hand, through the middle of the town to the sepulchres. Then drawing water out of a spring, he washes and anoints the monuments, and sacrificing the bull upon a pile of wood, and making supplication to Jupiter and Mercury of the earth, invites those valiant men who perished in the defence of Greece to the banquet and the libations of blood. After this, mixing a bowl of wine, and pouring out for himself, he says, "I drink to those who lost their lives for the liberty of Greece." These solemnities the Platæans observe to this day.

Aristides perceived that the Athenians, after their return into the city, were eager for a democracy; and deeming the people to deserve consideration on account of their valiant behaviour, as also that it was a matter of difficulty, they being well armed, powerful, and full of spirit with their victories, to oppose them by force, he brought forward a decree that everyone might share in the government and the archons be chosen out of the whole body of the Athenians. And on Themistocles telling the people in assembly that he had some advice for them, which could not be given in public, but was most important for the advantage and security of the city, they appointed Aristides alone to hear and consider it with him. And on his acquainting Aristides that his intent was to set fire to the arsenal of the Greeks, for by that means should the Athenians become supreme masters of all Greece, Aristides, returning to the assembly, told them that nothing was more advantageous than what Themistocles designed, and nothing more unjust. The Athenians, hearing this, gave Themistocles order to desist; such was the love of justice felt by the people, and such the credit and confidence they reposed in Aristides.

Being sent in joint commission with Cimon to the war, he took notice that Pausanias and the other Spartan captains made themselves offensive by imperiousness and harshness to the confederates; and by being himself gentle and considerate with them, and by the courtesy and disinterested temper which Cimon, after his example, manifested in the expeditions, he stole away the chief command from the Lacedæmonians, neither by weapons, ships, or horses, but by equity and wise policy. For the Athenians being endeared to the Greeks by the justice of Aristides and by Cimon's moderation, the tyranny and selfishness of Pausanias rendered them yet more desirable. He on all occasions treated the commanders of the confederates haughtily and roughly; and the common soldiers he punished with stripes, or standing under the iron anchor for a whole day together; neither was it permitted for any to provide straw for themselves to lie on, or forage for their horses, or to come near the springs to water before the Spartans were furnished, but servants with whips drove away such as approached. And when Aristides once was about to complain and expostulate with Pausanias, he told him with an angry look that he was not at leisure, and gave no attention to him. The consequence was that the sea captains and generals of the Greeks, in particular, the Chians, Samians, and Lesbians, came to Aristides and requested him to be their general, and to receive the confederates into his command, who had long desired to relinquish the Spartans and come over to the Athenians. But he answered that he saw both equity and necessity in what they said, but their fidelity required the test of some action, the commission of which would make it impossible for the multitude to change their minds again. Upon which Uliades, the Samian, and Antagoras of Chios, conspiring together, ran in near Byzantium on Pausanias' galley, getting her between them as she was sailing before the rest. But when Pausanias, beholding them, arose up and furiously threatened soon to make them know that they had been endangering not his galley, but their own countries, they bid him go his way, and thank Fortune that fought for him at Platæa; for hitherto, in reverence to that, the Greeks had forborne from inflicting on him the punishment he deserved. In fine, they all went off and joined the Athenians. And here the magnanimity of the Lacedæmonians was wonderful. For when they perceived that their generals were becoming corrupted by the greatness of their authority, they voluntarily laid down the chief command, and left off sending anymore of them to the wars, choosing rather to have citizens of moderation and consistent in the observance of their customs, than to possess the dominion of all Greece.

Even during the command of the Lacedæmonians, the Greeks paid a certain contribution towards the maintenance of the war; and being desirous to be rated city by city in their due proportion, they desired Aristides of the Athenians, and gave him command, surveying the country and revenue, to assess everyone according to their ability and what they were worth. But he, being so largely empowered, Greece as it were submitting all her affairs to his sole management, went out poor and returned poorer; laying the tax not only without corruption and injustice, but to the satisfaction and convenience of all. For as the ancients celebrated the age of Saturn, so did the confederates of Athens Aristides' taxation, terming it the happy time of Greece; and that more especially, as the sum was in a short time doubled, and afterwards trebled. For the assessment which Aristides made was four hundred and sixty talents. But to this Pericles added very near one third part more; for Thucydides says that in the beginning of the Peloponnesian war the Athenians had coming in from their confederates six hundred talents. But after Pericles' death, the demagogues, increasing by little and little, raised it to the sum of thirteen hundred talents; not so much through the war's being so expensive and changeable either by its length or ill success, as by their alluring the people to spend upon largesses and playhouse allowances, and in erecting statues and temples. Aristides, therefore, having acquired a wonderful and great reputation by this levy of the tribute, Themistocles is said to have derided him, as if this had been not the commendation of a man, but a money-bag; a retaliation, though not in the same kind, for some free words which Aristides had used. For he, when Themistocles once was saying that he thought the highest virtue of a general was to understand and foreknow the measures the enemy would take, replied, "This, indeed, Themistocles, is simply necessary, but the excellent thing in a general is to keep his hands from taking money."

Aristides, moreover, made all the people of Greece swear to keep the league, and himself took the path in the name of the Athenians, flinging wedges of red-hot iron into the sea, after curses against such as should make breach of their vow. But afterwards, it would seem, when things were in such a state as constrained them to govern with a stronger hand, he bade the Athenians to throw the perjury upon him, and manage affairs as convenience required. And, in general, Theophrastus tells us, that Aristides was, in his own private affairs, and those of his fellow-citizens, rigorously just, but that in public matters he acted often in accordance with his country's policy, which demanded, sometimes, not a little injustice. It is reported of him that he said in a debate, upon the motion of the Samians for removing the treasure from Delos to Athens, contrary to the league, that the thing indeed was not just but was expedient.

In fine, having established the dominion of his city over so many people, he himself remained indigent; and always delighted as much in the glory of being poor, as in that of his trophies; as is evident from the following story. Callias, the torchbearer, was related to him; and was prosecuted by his enemies in a capital cause, in which, after they had slightly argued the matters on which they indicted him, they proceeded, besides the point, to address the judges: "You know," said they, "Aristides, the son of Lysimachus, who is the admiration of all Greece. In what a condition do you think his family is in at his house, when you see him appear in public in such a threadbare cloak? Is it not probable that one who, out of doors, goes thus exposed to the cold, must want food and other necessaries at home? Callias, the wealthiest of the Athenians, does nothing to relieve either him or his wife and children in their poverty, though he is his own cousin, and has made use of him in many cases, and often reaped advantage by his interest with you." But Callias, perceiving the judges were moved more particularly by this, and were exasperated against him, called in Aristides, requiring him to testify that when he frequently offered him divers presents, and entreated him to accept them, he had refused, answering that it became him better to be proud of his poverty than Callias of his wealth; since there are many to be seen that make a good or bad use of riches, but it is difficult, comparatively, to meet with one who supports poverty in a noble spirit; those only should be ashamed of it who incurred it against their wills. On Aristides deposing these facts in favour of Callias, there was none who heard them that went not away desirous rather to be poor like Aristides than rich as Callias. Thus Æschines, the scholar of Socrates, writes. But Plato declares that, of all the great renowned men in the city of Athens, he was the only one worthy of consideration; for Themistocles, Cimon, and Pericles filled the city with porticoes, treasure, and many other vain things, but Aristides guided his public life by the rule of justice. He showed his moderation very plainly in his conduct towards Themistocles himself. For though Themistocles had been his adversary in all his undertakings, and was the cause of his banishment, yet when he afforded a similar opportunity of revenge, being accused to the city, Aristides bore him no malice; but while Alcmæon, Cimon, and many others were prosecuting and impeaching him, Aristides alone neither did nor said any ill against him, and no more triumphed over his enemy in his adversity than he had envied him his prosperity.

Some say Aristides died in Pontus, during a voyage upon the affairs of the public. Others that he died of old age at Athens being in great honour and veneration amongst his fellow-citizens. But Craterus, the Macedonian, relates his death as follows. After the banishment of Themistocles, he says, the people growing insolent, there sprung up a number of false and frivolous accusers, impeaching the best and most influential men and exposing them to the envy of the multitude, whom their good fortune and power had filled with self-conceit. Amongst these, Aristides was condemned of bribery upon the accusation of Diophantus of Amphitrope, for taking money from the Ionians when he was collector of the tribute; and being unable to pay the fine, which was fifty mimæ, sailed to Ionia, and died there. But of this Craterus brings no written proof, neither the sentence of his condemnation, nor the decree of the people; though in general it is tolerably usual with him to set down such things and to cite his authors. Almost all others who have spoken of the misdeeds of the people towards their generals collect them all together, and tell us of the banishment of Themistocles, Miltiades' bonds, Pericles' fine, and the death of Paches in the judgment-hall, who, upon receiving sentence, killed himself on the hustings, with many things of the like nature. They add the banishment of Aristides; but of this his condemnation they make no mention.

Moreover, his monument is to be seen at Phalerum, which they say was built him by the city, he not having left enough even to defray funeral charges. And it is stated that his two daughters were publicly married out of the prytaneum, or State-house, by the city, which decreed each of them three thousand drachmas for her portion; and that upon his son Lysimachus the people bestowed a hundred minas of money, and as many acres of planted land, and ordered him besides, upon the motion of Alcibiades, four drachmas a day. Furthermore, Lysimachus leaving a daughter, named Polycrite, as Callisthenes says, the people voted her, also, the same allowance for food with those that obtained the victory in the Olympic Games. But Demetrius the Phalerian, Hieronymus the Rhodian, Aristoxenus the musician, and Aristotle (if the Treatise of Nobility is to be reckoned among the genuine pieces of Aristotle) say that Myrto, Aristides' granddaughter, lived with Socrates the philosopher, who indeed had another wife, but took her into his house, being a widow, by reason of her indigence and want of the necessaries of life. But Panætius sufficiently confutes this in his book concerning Socrates. Demetrius the Phalerian, in his Socrates, says he knew one Lysimachus, son to the daughter of Aristides, extremely poor, who used to sit near what is called the Iaccheum, and sustained himself by a table for interpreting dreams; and that, upon his proposal and representations, a decree was passed by the people to give the mother and aunt of this man half a drachma a day. The same Demetrius, when he was legislating himself, decreed each of these women a drachma *per diem*. And it is not to be wondered at, that the people of Athens should take such care of people living in the city, since hearing the granddaughter of Aristogiton was in a low condition in the isle of Lemnos, and so poor nobody would marry her, they brought her back to Athens, and marrying her to a man of good birth, gave a farm at Potamus as her marriage-portion; and of similar humanity and bounty the city of Athens, even in our age, has given numerous proofs, and is justly admired and respected in consequence.

MARCUS CATO

MARCUS CATO, WE ARE TOLD, WAS BORN AT TUSCULUM, THOUGH (TILL HE betook himself to civil and military affairs) he lived and was bred up in the country of the Sabines, where his father's estate lay. His ancestors seeming almost entirely unknown, he himself praises his father Marcus, as a worthy man and a brave soldier, and Cato, his great-grandfather, too, as one who had often obtained military prizes, and who, having lost five horses under him, received, on the account of his valour, the worth of them out of the public exchequer. Now it being the custom among the Romans to call those who, having no repute by birth, made themselves eminent by their own exertions, new men or upstarts, they called even Cato himself so, and so he confessed himself to be as to any public distinction or employment, but yet asserted that in the exploits and virtues of his ancestors he was very ancient. His third name originally was not Cato, but Priscus, though afterwards he had the surname of Cato, by reason of his abilities; for the Romans call a skilful or experienced man *Catus*. He was of a ruddy complexion and grey-eyed; as the writer, who, with no goodwill, made the following epigram upon him lets us see:

> Porcius, who snarls at all in every place,
> With his grey eyes, and with his fiery face,
> Even after death will scarce admitted be
> Into the infernal realms by Hecate.

He gained, in early life, a good habit of body by working with his own hands, and living temperately, and serving in war; and seemed to have an equal proportion both of health and strength. And he exerted and practised his eloquence through all the neighbourhood and little villages;

thinking it as requisite as a second body, and an all but necessary organ to one who looks forward to something above a mere humble and inactive life. He would never refuse to be counsel for those who needed him, and was, indeed, early reckoned a good lawyer, and, ere long, a capable orator.

Hence his solidity and depth of character showed itself gradually more and more to those with whom he was concerned, and claimed, as it were, employment in great affairs and places of public command. Nor did he merely abstain from taking fees for his counsel and pleading, but did not even seem to put any high price on the honour which proceeded from such kind of combats, seeming much more desirous to signalise himself in the camp and in real fights; and while yet but a youth, had his breast covered with scars he had received from the enemy: being (as he himself says) but seventeen years old when he made his first campaign; in the time when Hannibal, in the height of his success, was burning and pillaging all Italy. In engagements he would strike boldly, without flinching, stand firm to his ground, fix a bold countenance upon his enemies, and with a harsh threatening voice accost them, justly thinking himself and telling others that such a rugged kind of behaviour sometimes terrifies the enemy more than the sword itself. In his marches he bore his own arms on foot, whilst one servant only followed, to carry the provision for his table, with whom he is said never to have been angry or hasty whilst he made ready his dinner or supper, but would, for the most part, when he was free from military duty, assist and help him himself to dress it. When he was with the army, he used to drink only water; unless, perhaps, when extremely thirsty, he might mingle it with a little vinegar, or if he found his strength fail him, take a little wine.

The little country house of Manius Curius, who had been thrice carried in triumph, happened to be near his farm; so that often going thither, and contemplating the small compass of the place, and plainness of the dwelling, he formed an idea of the mind of the person, who being one of the greatest of the Romans, and having subdued the most warlike nations, nay, had driven Pyrrhus out of Italy, now, after three triumphs, was contented to dig in so small a piece of ground, and live in such a cottage. Here it was that the ambassadors of the Samnites, finding him boiling turnips in the chimney corner, offered him a present of gold; but he sent them away with this saying; that he, who was content with such a supper, had no need of gold; and that he thought it more honourable to conquer those who possessed the gold, than to possess the gold itself. Cato, after reflecting upon these things, used to return and, reviewing his own farm, his servants, and housekeeping, increase his labour and retrench all superfluous expenses.

When Fabius Maximus took Tarentum, Cato, being then but a youth, was a soldier under him; and being lodged with one Nearchus, a Pythagorean, desired to understand some of his doctrine, and hearing from him the language, which Plato also uses—that pleasure is evil's chief bait; the body the principal calamity of the soul; and that those thoughts which most separate and take it off from the affections of the body most enfranchise and purify it; he fell in love the more with frugality and temperance. With this exception, he is said not to have studied Greek until when he was pretty old; and in rhetoric to have then profited a little by Thucydides, but more by Demosthenes; his writings, however, are considerably embellished with Greek sayings and stories; nay, many of these, translated word for word, are placed with his own opophthegms and sentences.

There was a man of the highest rank, and very influential among the Romans, called Valerius Flaccus, who was singularly skilful in discerning excellence yet in the bud, and also much disposed to nourish and advance it. He, it seems, had lands bordering upon Cato's; nor could he but admire when he understood from his servants the manner of his living, how he laboured with his own hands, went on foot betimes in the morning to the courts to assist those who wanted his counsel: how, returning home again, when it was winter, he would throw a loose frock over his shoulders, and in the summer time would work without anything on among his domestics, sit down with them, eat of the same bread, and drink of the same wine. When they spoke, also, of other good qualities, his fair dealing and moderation, mentioning also some of his wise sayings, he ordered that he should be invited to supper; and thus becoming personally assured of his fine temper and his superior character, which, like a plant, seemed only to require culture and a better situation, he urged and persuaded him to apply himself to state affairs at Rome. Thither, therefore, he went, and by his pleading soon gained many friends and admirers; but, Valerius chiefly assisting his promotion, he first of all got appointed tribune in the army, and afterwards was made quæstor, or treasurer. And now becoming eminent and noted, he passed, with Valerius himself, through the greatest commands, being first his colleague as consul, and then censor. But among all the ancient senators, he most attached himself to Fabius Maximus; not so much for the honour of his person, and the greatness of his power, as that he might have before him his habit and manner of life, as the best examples to follow; and so he did not hesitate to oppose Scipio the Great, who, being then but a young man, seemed to set himself against the power of Fabius, and to be envied by him. For being sent together with him as treasurer, when he saw him, according to his natural custom, make great expenses, and distribute among the soldiers without sparing, he freely told him that the expense in itself was not the greatest thing to be considered, but that he was corrupting the frugality of the soldiers, by giving them the means to abandon themselves to unnecessary pleasures and luxuries. Scipio answered, that he had no need for so accurate a treasurer (bearing on as he was, so to say, full sail to the war), and that he owed the people an account of his actions, and not of the money he spent. Hereupon Cato returned from Sicily and, together with Fabius, made loud complaints in the open senate of Scipio's lavishing unspeakable sums, and childishly loitering away his time in wrestling matches and comedies, as if he were not to make war, but holiday; and thus succeeded in getting some of the tribunes of the people sent to call him back to Rome, in case the accusations should prove true. But Scipio demonstrating, as it were, to them, by his preparations, the coming victory, and, being found merely to be living pleasantly with his friends, when there was nothing else to do, but in no respect because of that easiness and liberality at all the more negligent in things of consequence and moment, without impediment, set sail toward the war.

Cato grew more and more powerful by his eloquence, so that he was commonly called the Roman Demosthenes; but his manner of life was yet more famous and talked of. For oratorical skill was, as an accomplishment, commonly studied and sought after by all young men; but he was very rare who would cultivate the old habits of bodily labour, or prefer a light supper, and a breakfast which never saw the fire, or be in love with poor clothes and a homely lodging, or could set his ambition rather on doing without luxuries than on possessing them. For now the state, unable to keep its purity by reason of its greatness, and having so many affairs, and people from all parts under its government, was fain to admit many mixed customers and new examples of living. With reason, therefore, everybody admired Cato, when they saw others sink under labours and grow effeminate by pleasures; and yet beheld him unconquered by either, and that not only when he was young and desirous of honour, but also when old and grey-headed, after a consulship and triumph; like some famous victor in the games, persevering in his exercise and maintaining his character to the very last. He himself says that he never wore a suit of clothes which cost more than a hundred drachmas; and that, when he was general and consul, he drank the same wine which his workmen did; and that the meat or fish which was bought in the meat-market for his dinner did not cost above thirty *asses*. All which was for the sake of the commonwealth, that so his body might be the hardier for the war. Having a piece of embroidered Babylonian tapestry left him, he sold it; because none of his farmhouses were so much as plastered. Nor did he ever buy a slave for above fifteen hundred drachmas; as he did not seek for effeminate and handsome ones, but able sturdy workmen, horse-keepers and cow-herds: and these he thought ought to be sold again, when they grew old, and no useless servants fed in the house. In short, he reckoned nothing a good bargain which was superfluous; but whatever it was, though sold for a farthing, he would think it a great price, if you had no need of it; and was for the purchase of lands for sowing and feeding, rather than grounds for sweeping and watering.

Some imputed these things to petty avarice, but others approved of him, as if he had only the more strictly denied himself for the rectifying and amending of others. Yet certainly, in my judgment, it marks an over-rigid temper for a man to take the work out of his servants as out of brute beasts, turning them off and selling them in their old age, and thinking there ought to be no further commerce between man and man than whilst there arises some profit by it. We see that kindness or humanity has a larger field than bare justice to exercise itself in; law and justice we cannot, in the nature of things, employ on others than men; but we may extend our goodness and charity even to irrational creatures and such acts flow from a gentle nature, as water from an abundant spring. It is doubtless the part of a kind-natured man to keep even worn-out horses and dogs, and not only take care of them when they are foals and whelps, but also when they are grown old. The Athenians, when they built their Hecatompedon, turned those mules loose to feed freely which they had observed to have done the hardest labour. One of these (they say) came once of itself to offer its service, and ran along with, nay, and went before, the teams which drew the wagons up to the acropolis, as if it would incite and encourage them to draw more stoutly; upon which there passed a vote that the creature should be kept at the public charge even till it died. The graves of Cimon's horses, which thrice won the Olympian races, are yet to be seen close by his own monument. Old Xanthippus, too (amongst many others who buried the dogs they had bred up), entombed his which swam after his galley to Salamis, when the people fled from Athens, on the top of a cliff, which they call the Dog's Tomb to this day. Nor are we to use living creatures like old shoes or dishes and throw them away when they are worn out or broken with service; but if it were for nothing else, but by way of study and practice in humanity, a man ought always to prehabituate himself in these things to be of a kind and sweet disposition. As to myself, I would not so much as sell my draught ox on the account of his age, much less for a small piece of money sell a poor old man, and so chase him, as it were, from his own country, by turning him not only out of the place where he has lived a long while, but also out of the manner of living he has been accustomed to, and that more especially when he would be as useless to the buyer as to the seller. Yet Cato for all this glories that he left that very horse in Spain which he used in the wars when he was consul, only because he would not put the public to the charge of his freight. Whether these acts are to be ascribed to the greatness or pettiness of his spirit, let everyone argue as they please.

For his general temperance, however, and self-control he really deserves the highest admiration. For when he commanded the army, he never took for himself, and those that belonged to him, above three bushels of wheat for a month, and somewhat less than a bushel and a half a day of barley for his baggage-cattle. And when he entered upon the government of Sardinia, where his predecessors had been used to require tents, bedding and clothes upon the public account, and to charge the state heavily with the cost of provisions and entertainments for a great train of servants and friends, the difference he showed in his economy was something incredible. There was nothing of any sort for which he put the public to expense; he would walk without a carriage to visit the cities, with one only of the common town officers, who carried his dress, and a cup to offer libation with. Yet though he seemed thus easy and sparing to all who were under his power, he, on the other hand, showed most inflexible severity and strictness in what related to public justice, and was rigorous and precise in what concerned the ordinances of the commonwealth; so that the Roman government never seemed more terrible, nor yet more mild than under his administration.

His very manner of speaking seemed to have such a kind of idea with it; for it was courteous, and yet forcible; pleasant, yet overwhelming; facetious, yet austere; sententious, and yet vehement; like Socrates, in the description of Plato, who seemed outwardly to those about him to be but a simple, talkative, blunt fellow; whilst at the bottom he was full of such gravity and matter, as would even move tears and touch the very hearts of his auditors. And, therefore, I know not what has persuaded some to say that Cato's style was chiefly like that of Lysias. However, let us leave those to judge of these things who profess most to distinguish between the several kinds of oratorical style in Latin; whilst we write down some of his memorable sayings; being of the opinion that a man's character appears much more by his words than, as some think it does, by his looks.

Being once desirous to dissuade the common people of Rome from their unseasonable and impetuous clamour for largesses and distributions of corn, he began thus to harangue them: "It is a difficult task, O citizens, to make speeches to the belly, which has no ears." Reproving, also, their sumptuous habits, he said it was hard to preserve a city where a fish sold for more than an ox. He had a saying, also, that the Roman people were like sheep; for they, when single, do not obey, but when all together in a flock, they follow their leaders: "So you," said he, "when you have got together in a body, let yourselves be guided by those whom singly you would never think of being advised by." Discoursing of the power of women: "Men," said he, "usually command women; but we command all men, and the women command us." But this, indeed, is borrowed from the sayings of Themistocles, who, when his son was making many demands of him by means of the mother, said, "O woman, the Athenians govern the Greeks; I govern the Athenians, but you govern me, and your son governs you; so let him use his power sparingly, since, simple as he is, he can do more than all the Greeks together." Another saying of Cato's was, that the Roman people did not only fix the value of such and such purple dyes, but also of such and such habits of life: "For," said he, "as dyers most of all dye such colours as they see to be most agreeable, so the young men learn, and zealously affect, what is most popular with you." He also exhorted them that, if they were grown great by their virtue and temperance, they should not change for the worse; but if intemperance and vice had made them great, they should change for the better; for by that means they were grown indeed quite great enough. He would say, likewise, of men who wanted to be continually in office, that apparently they did not know their road; since they could not do without beadles to guide them on it. He also reproved the citizens for choosing still the same men as their magistrates: "For you will seem," said he, "either not to esteem government worth much, or to think few worthy to hold it." Speaking, too, of a certain enemy of his, who lived a very base and discreditable life: "It is considered," he said, "rather as a curse than a blessing on him, that this fellow's mother prays that she may leave him behind her." Pointing at one who had sold the land which his father had left him, and which lay near the seaside, he pretended to express his wonder at his being stronger even than the sea itself; for what it washed away with a great deal of labour, he with a great deal of ease drank away. When the senate, with a great deal of splendour, received King Eumenes on his visit to Rome, and the chief citizens strove who should be most about him, Cato appeared to regard him with suspicion and apprehension; and when one that stood by, too, took occasion to say that he was a very good prince and a great lover of the Romans: "It may be so," said Cato; "but by nature this same animal of a king is a kind of man-eater"; nor, indeed, were there ever kings who deserved to be compared with Epaminondas, Pericles, Themistocles, Manius Curius, or Hamilcar, surnamed Barcas. He used to say, too, that his enemies envied him because he had to get up everyday before light and neglect his own business to follow that of the public. He would also tell you that he had rather be deprived of the reward for doing well than not to suffer the punishment for doing ill; and that he could pardon all offenders but himself.

The Romans having sent three ambassadors to Bithynia, of whom one was gouty, another had his skull trepanned, and the other seemed little better than a fool, Cato, laughing, gave out that the Romans had sent an embassy which had neither feet, head, nor heart. His interest being entreated by Scipio, on account of Polybius, for the Achæan exiles, and there happening to be a great discussion in the senate about it, some being for, and some against their return, Cato, standing up, thus delivered himself: "Here do we sit all day long, as if we had nothing to do but beat our brains whether these old Greeks should be carried to their graves by the bearers here or by those in Achæa." The senate voting their return, it seems that a few days after Polybius' friends further wished that it should be further moved in the senate that the said banished persons should receive again the honours which they first had in Achæa; and to this purpose they sounded Cato for his opinion; but he, smiling, answered, that Polybius, Ulysses like, having escaped out of the Cyclops' den, wanted, it would seem, to go back again because he had left his cap and belt behind him. He used to assert, also, that wise men profited more by fools, than fools by wise men; for that wise men avoided the faults of fools, but that fools would not imitate the good examples of wise men. He would profess, too, that he was more taken with young men that blushed than with those who looked pale; and that he never desired to have a soldier that moved his hands too much in marching, and his feet too much in fighting; or snored louder than he shouted. Ridiculing a fat, overgrown man: "What use," said he, "can the state turn a man's body to, when all between the throat and groin is taken up by the belly?" When one who was much given to pleasures desired his acquaintance, begging his pardon, he said he could not live with a man whose palate was of a quicker sense than his heart. He would likewise say that the soul of a lover lived in the body of another: and that in his whole life he most repented of three things; one was, that he had trusted a secret to a woman; another that he went by water when he might have gone by land; the third, that he had remained one whole day without doing any business of moment. Applying himself to an old man who was committing some vice: "Friend," said he, "old age has of itself blemishes enough; do not you add to it the deformity of vice." Speaking to a tribune, who was reputed a poisoner, and was very violent for the bringing in of a bill, in order to make a certain law: "Young man," cried he, "I know not which would be better, to drink, what you mix, or confirm what you would put up for a law." Being reviled by a fellow who lived a profligate and wicked life: "A contest," replied he, "is unequal between you and me: for you can hear ill words easily, and can as easily give them: but it is unpleasant to me to give such, and unusual to hear them." Such was his manner of expressing himself in his memorable sayings.

Being chosen consul, with his friend and familiar Valerius Flaccus, the government of that part of Spain which the Romans called the Hither Spain fell to his lot. Here, as he was engaged in reducing some of the tribes by force, and bringing over others by good words, a large army of barbarians fell upon him, so that there was danger of being disgracefully forced out again. He therefore called upon his neighbours, the Celtiberians, for help; and on their demanding two hundred talents for their assistance, everybody else thought it intolerable that even the Romans should promise barbarians a reward for their aid; but Cato said there was no discredit or harm in it; for, if they overcame, they would pay them out of the enemy's purse, and not out of their own; but if they were overcome, there would be nobody left either to demand the reward or to pay it. However, he won that battle completely, and, after that, all his other affairs succeeded splendidly. Polybius says that, by his command, the walls of all the cities on this side the river Bætis were in one day's time demolished, and yet there were a great many of them full of brave and warlike men. Cato himself says that he took more cities than he stayed days in Spain. Neither is this a mere rhodomontade, if it be true that the number was four hundred. And though the soldiers themselves had got much in the fights, yet he distributed a pound of silver to every man of them, saying, it was better that many of the Romans should return home with silver, rather than a few with gold. For himself, he affirms, that of all the things that were taken, nothing came to him beyond what he ate and drank. "Neither do I find fault," continued he, "with those that seek to profit by these spoils, but I had rather compete in valour with the best, than in wealth with the richest, or with the most covetous in love of money." Nor did he merely keep himself clear from taking anything, but even all those who more immediately belonged to him. He had five servants with him in the army; one of whom called Paccus, bought three boys out of those who were taken captive; which Cato coming to understand, the man, rather than venture into his presence, hanged himself. Cato sold the boys, and carried the price he got for them into the public exchequer.

Scipio the Great, being his enemy, and desiring, whilst he was carrying all things so successfully, to obstruct him, and take the affairs of Spain into his own hands, succeeded in getting himself appointed his successor in the government, and, making all possible haste, put a term to Cato's authority. But he, taking with him a convoy of five cohorts of foot and five hundred horse to attend him home, overthrew by the way the Lacetanians, and taking from them six hundred deserters, caused them all to be beheaded; upon which Scipio seemed to be in indignation, but Cato, in mock disparagement of himself, said, "Rome would become great indeed if the most honourable and great men would not yield up the first place of valour to those who were more obscure, and when they who were of the commonalty (as he himself was) would contend in valour with those who were most eminent in birth and honour." The senate having voted to change nothing of what had been established by Cato, the government passed away under Scipio to no manner of purpose, in idleness and doing nothing; and so diminished his credit much more than Cato's. Nor did Cato, who now received a triumph, remit after this and slacken the reins of virtue, as many do, who strive not so much for virtue's sake, as for vainglory, and having attained the highest honours, as the consulship and triumphs, pass the rest of their life in pleasure and idleness, and quit all public affairs. But he, like those who are just entered upon public life for the first time, and thirst after gaining honour and glory in some new office, strained himself, as if he were but just setting out; and offering still publicly his service to his friends and citizens, would give up neither his pleadings nor his soldiery.

He accompanied and assisted Tiberius Sempronius, as his lieutenant, when he went into Thrace and to the Danube; and, in the quality of tribune, went with Manius Acilius into Greece, against Antiochus the Great, who, after Hannibal, more than anyone struck terror into the Romans. For having reduced once more under a single command almost the whole of Asia, all, namely, that Seleucus Nicator had possessed, and having brought into obedience many warlike nations of the barbarians, he longed to fall upon the Romans, as if they only were now worthy to fight with him. So across he came with his forces, pretending, as a specious cause of the war, that it was to free the Greeks, who had indeed no need of it, they having been but newly delivered from the power of king Philip and the Macedonians, and made independent, with the free use of their own laws, by the goodness of the Romans themselves: so that all Greece was in commotion and excitement, having been corrupted by the hopes of royal aid which the popular leaders in their cities put them into. Manius, therefore, sent ambassadors to the different cities; and Titus Flaminius (as is written in the account of him) suppressed and quieted most of the attempts of the innovators, without any trouble. Cato brought over the Corinthians, those of Patræ and Ægium, and spent a good deal of time at Athens. There is also an oration of his said to be extant which he spoke in Greek to the people; in which he expressed his admiration of the virtue of the ancient Athenians, and signified that he came with a great deal of pleasure to be a spectator of the beauty and greatness of their city. But this is a fiction; for he spoke to the Athenians by an interpreter, though he was able to have spoken himself; but he wished to observe the usage of his own country, and laughed at those who admired nothing but what was in Greek. Jesting upon Postumius Albinus, who had written an historical work in Greek, and requested that allowances might be made for his attempt, he said that allowance indeed might be made if he had done it under the express compulsion of an Amphictyonic decree. The Athenians, he says, admired the quickness and vehemence of his speech; for an interpreter would be very long in repeating what he expressed with a great deal of brevity; but on the whole he professed to believe that the words of the Greeks came only from their lips, whilst those of the Romans came from their hearts.

Now Antiochus, having occupied with his army the narrow passages about Thermopylæ, and added palisades and walls to the natural fortifications of the place, sat down there, thinking he had done enough to divert the war; and the Romans, indeed, seemed wholly to despair of forcing the passage; but Cato, calling to mind the compass and circuit which the Persians had formerly made to come at this place, went forth in the night, taking along with him part of the army. Whilst they were climbing up, the guide, who was a prisoner, missed the way, and wandering up and down by impracticable and precipitous paths, filled the soldiers with fear and despondency. Cato, perceiving the danger, commanded all the rest to halt, and stay where they were, whilst he himself, taking along with him one Lucius Manlius, a most expert man at climbing mountains, went forward with a great deal of labour and danger, in the dark night, and without the least moonshine, among the wild olive trees and steep craggy rocks, there being nothing but precipices and darkness before their eyes, till they struck into a little pass which they thought might lead down into the enemy's camp. There they put up marks upon some conspicuous peaks which surmount the hill called Callidromon, and, returning again, they led the army along with them to the said marks, till they got into their little path again, and there once made a halt; but when they began to go further, the path deserted them at a precipice, where they were in another strait and fear; nor did they perceive that they were all this while near the enemy. And now the day began to give some light, when they seemed to hear a noise, and presently after to see the Greek trenches and the guard at the foot of the rock. Here, therefore, Cato halted his forces, and commanded the troops from Firmum only, without the rest, to stick by him, as he had always found them faithful and ready. And when they came up and formed around him in close order, he thus spoke to them: "I desire," he said, "to take one of the enemy alive, that so I may understand what men these are who guard the passage; their number; and with what discipline, order, and preparation they expect us; but this feat," continued he, "must be an act of a great deal of quickness and boldness, such as that of lions, when they dart upon some timorous animal." Cato had no sooner thus expressed himself, but the Firmans forthwith rushed down the mountain, just as they were, upon the guard, and, falling unexpectedly upon them, affrighted and dispersed them all. One armed man they took, and brought to Cato, who quickly learned from him that the rest of the forces lay in the narrow passage about the king; that those who kept the tops of the rocks were six hundred choice Ætolians. Cato, therefore, despising the smallness of their number and carelessness, forthwith drawing his sword, fell upon them with a great noise of trumpets and shouting. The enemy, perceiving them thus tumbling, as it were, upon them from the precipices, flew to the main body, and put all things into disorder there.

In the meantime, whilst Manius was forcing the works below, and pouring the thickest of his forces into the narrow passages, Antiochus was hit in the mouth with a stone, so that his teeth being beaten out by it, he felt such excessive pain, that he was fain to turn away with his horse; nor did any part of his army stand the shock of the Romans. Yet, though there seemed no reasonable hope of flight, where all paths were so difficult, and where there were deep marshes and steep rocks, which looked as if they were ready to receive those who should stumble, the fugitives, neverthe-less, crowding and pressing together in the narrow passages, destroyed even one another in their terror of the swords and blows of the enemy. Cato (as it plainly appears) was never oversparing of his own praises, and seldom shunned boasting of any exploit; which quality, indeed, he seems to have thought the natural accompaniment of great actions; and with these particular exploits he was highly puffed up; he says that those who saw him that day pursuing and slaying the enemies were ready to assert that Cato owed not so much to the public as the public did to Cato; nay, he adds, that Manius the consul, coming hot from the fight, embraced him for a great while, when both were all in a sweat; and then cried out with joy that neither he himself, no, nor all the people together, could make him a recompense equal to his actions. After the fight he was sent to Rome that he himself might be the messenger of it: and so, with a favourable wind, he sailed to Brundusium, and in one day got from thence to Tarentum; and having travelled four days more, upon the fifth, count-ing from the time of his landing, he arrived at Rome, and so brought the first news of the victory himself; and filled the whole city with joy and sac-rifices, and the people with the belief that they were able to conquer every sea and every land.

These are pretty nearly all the eminent actions of Cato relating to mil-itary affairs: in civil policy, he was of opinion that one chief duty consisted in accusing and indicting criminals. He himself prosecuted many, and he would also assist others who prosecuted them, nay, would even procure such, as he did the Petilii against Scipio; but not being able to destroy him, by reason of the nobleness of his family, and the real greatness of his mind, which enabled him to trample all calumnies under foot, Cato at last would meddle no more with him; yet joining with the accusers against Scipio's brother Lucius, he succeeded in obtaining a sentence against him, which condemned him to the payment of a large sum of money to the state; and being insolvent, and in danger of being thrown into jail, he was, by the interposition of the tribunes of the people, with much ado dis-missed. It is also said of Cato, that when he met a certain youth, who had effected the disgrace of one of his father's enemies, walking in the market place, he shook him by the hand, telling him, that this was what we ought to sacrifice to our dead parents—not lambs and goats, but the tears and condemnations of their adversaries. But neither did he himself escape with impunity in his management of affairs; for if he gave his enemies but the least hold, he was still in danger, and exposed to be brought to justice. He is reported to have escaped at least fifty indictments; and one above the rest, which was the last, when he was eighty-six years old, about which time he uttered the well-known saying, that it was hard for him who had lived with one generation of men, to plead now before another. Neither did he make this the least of his lawsuits; for, four years after, when he was fourscore and ten, he accused Servilius Galba: so that his life and actions extended, we may say, as Nestor's did, over three ordinary ages of man. For, having had many contests, as we have related, with Scipio the Great, about affairs of state, he continued them down to Scipio the younger, who was the adopted grandson of the former, and the son of that Paulus who overthrew Perseus and the Macedonians.

Ten years after his consulship, Cato stood for the office of censor, which was indeed the summit of all honour, and in a manner the highest step in civil affairs; for besides all other power, it had also that of an inquisition into everyone's life and manners. For the Romans thought that no marriage, or rearing of children, nay, no feast or drinking-bout, ought to be permitted according to everyone's appetite or fancy, without being examined and inquired into; being indeed of opinion that a man's character was much sooner perceived in things of this sort than in what is done publicly and in open day. They chose, therefore, two persons, one out of the patricians, the other out of the commons, who were to watch, correct, and punish, if anyone ran too much into voluptuousness, or transgressed the usual manner of life of his country; and these they called Censors. They had power to take away a horse, or expel out of the senate anyone who lived intemperately and out of order. It was also their business to take an estimate of what everyone was worth, and to put down in registers everybody's birth and quality; besides many other prerogatives. And therefore the chief nobility opposed his pretensions to it. Jealousy prompted the patricians, who thought that it would be a stain to everybody's nobility, if men of no original honour should rise to the highest dignity and power; while others, conscious of their own evil practices and of the violation of the laws and customs of their country, were afraid of the austerity of the man; which, in an office of such great power, was likely to prove most uncompromising and severe. And so, consulting among themselves, they brought forward seven candidates in opposition to him, who sedulously set themselves to court the people's favour by fair promises, as though what they wished for was indulgent and easy government. Cato, on the contrary, promising no such mildness, but plainly threatening evil livers, from the very hustings openly declared himself, and exclaiming that the city needed a great and thorough purgation, called upon the people, if they were wise, not to choose the gentlest, but the roughest of physicians; such a one, he said, he was, and Valerius Flaccus, one of the patricians, another; together with him, he doubted not but he should do something worth the while, and that by cutting to pieces and burning like a hydra all luxury and voluptuousness. He added, too, that he saw all the rest endeavouring after the office with ill intent, because they were afraid of those who would exercise it justly, as they ought. And so truly great and so worthy of great men to be its leaders was, it would seem, the Roman people, that they did not fear the severity and grim countenance of Cato, but rejecting those smooth promisers who were ready to do all things to ingratiate themselves, they took him, together with Flaccus; obeying his recommendations not as though he were a candidate, but as if he had had the actual power of commanding and governing already.

Cato named, as chief of the senate, his friend and colleague Lucius Valerius Flaccus, and expelled, among many others, Lucius Quintius, who had been consul seven years before, and (which was greater honour to him than the consulship) brother to that Titus Flaminius who overthrew King Philip. The reason he had for his expulsion was this. Lucius, it seems took along with him in all his commands a youth whom he had kept as his companion from the flower of his age, and to whom he gave as much power and respect as to the chiefest of his friends and relations.

Now it happened that Lucius being consular governor of one of the provinces, the youth setting himself down by him, as he used to do, among other flatteries with which he played upon him, when he was in his cups, told him he loved him so dearly that, "though there was a show of gladiators to be seen at Rome, and I," he said, "had never beheld one in my life; and though I, as it were, longed to see a man killed, yet I made all possible haste to come to you." Upon this Lucius, returning his fondness, replied, "Do not be melancholy on that account; I can remedy that." Ordering therefore, forthwith, one of those condemned to die to be brought to the feast, together with the headsman and axe, he asked the youth if he wished to see him executed. The boy answering that he did, Lucius commanded the executioner to cut off his neck; and this several historians mention; and Cicero, indeed, in his dialogue *de Senectute*, introduces Cato relating it himself. But

Livy says that he that was killed was a Gaulish deserter, and that Lucius did not execute him by the stroke of the executioner, but with his own hand; and that it is so stated in Cato's speech.

Lucius being thus expelled out of the senate by Cato, his brother took it very ill, and appealing to the people, desired that Cato should declare his reasons; and when he began to relate this transaction of the feast, Lucius endeavoured to deny it; but Cato challenging him to a formal investigation, he fell off and refused it, so that he was then acknowledged to suffer deservedly. Afterwards, however, when there was some show at the theatre, he passed by the seats where those who had been consuls used to be placed, and taking his seat a great way off, excited the compassion of the common people, who presently with a great noise made him go forward, and as much as they could tried to set right and salve over what had happened. Manilius, also, who, according to the public expectation, would have been next consul, he threw out of the senate, because, in the presence of his daughter, and in open day, he had kissed his wife. He said that, as for himself, his wife never came into his arms except when there was great thunder; so that it was for jest with him, that it was a pleasure for him, when Jupiter thundered.

His treatment of Lucius, likewise the brother of Scipio, and one who had been honoured with a triumph, occasioned some odium against Cato; for he took his horse from him, and was thought to do it with a design of putting an affront on Scipio Africanus, now dead. But he gave most general annoyance by retrenching people's luxury; for though (most of the youth being thereby already corrupted) it seemed almost impossible to take it away with an open hand and directly, yet going, as it were, obliquely around, he caused all dress, carriages, women's ornaments, household furniture, whose price exceeded one thousand five hundred drachmas, to be rated at ten times as much as they were worth; intending by thus making the assessments greater, to increase the taxes paid upon them. He also ordained that upon every thousand *asses* of property of this kind, three should be paid, so that people, burdened with these extra charges, and seeing others of as good estates, but more frugal and sparing, paying less into the public exchequer, might be tried out of their prodigality. And thus, on the one side, not only those were disgusted at Cato who bore the taxes for the sake of their luxury, but those, too, who on the other side laid by their luxury for fear of the taxes. For people in general reckon that an order not to display their riches is equivalent to the taking away of their riches, because riches are seen much more in superfluous than in necessary things. Indeed this was what excited the wonder of Ariston the philosopher; that we account those who possess superfluous things more happy than those who abound with what is necessary and useful. But when one of his friends asked Scopas, the rich Thessalian, to give him some article of no great utility, saying that it was not a thing that he had any great need or use for himself, "In truth," replied he, "it is just these useless and unnecessary things that make my wealth and happiness." Thus the desire of riches does not proceed from a natural passion within us, but arises rather from vulgar out-of-doors opinion of other people.

Cato, notwithstanding, being little solicitous as to those who exclaimed against him, increased his austerity. He caused the pipes, through which some persons brought the public water into their houses and gardens, to be cut, and threw down all buildings which jutted out into the common streets. He beat down also the price in contracts for public works to the low-est, and raised it in contracts for farming the taxes to the highest sum; by which proceedings he drew a great deal of hatred upon himself. Those who were of Titus Flaminius' party cancelled in the senate all the bargains and contracts made by him for the repairing and carrying on of the sacred and public buildings as unadvantageous to the commonwealth. They incited also the boldest of the tribunes of the people to accuse him and to fine him two talents. They likewise much opposed him in building the court or basilica, which he caused to be erected at the common charge, just by the senate-house, in the market place, and called by his own name, the Porcian. However, the people, it seems, liked his censorship wondrously well; for, setting up a statue for him in the temple of the goddess of Health, they put an inscription under it, not recording his commands in war or his triumph, but to the effect that this was Cato the Censor, who, by his good discipline and wise and temperate ordinances, reclaimed the Roman commonwealth when it was declining and sinking down into vice. Before this honour was done to himself, he used to laugh at those who loved such kind of things, saying, that they did not see that they were tak-ing pride in the workmanship of brass-founders and painters; whereas the citizens bore about his best likeness in their breasts. And when any seemed to wonder that he should have never a statue, while many ordinary per-sons had one, "I would," said he, "much rather be asked, why I have not one, than why I have one." In short, he would not have any honest citizen endure to be praised, except it might prove advantageous to the common-wealth. Yet still he had passed the highest commendation on himself; for he tells us that those who did anything wrong, and were found fault with, used to say it was not worthwhile to blame them, for they were not Catos. He also adds, that they who awkwardly mimicked some of his actions were called left-handed Catos; and that the senate in perilous times would cast their eyes on him, as upon a pilot in a ship, and that often when he was not present they put off affairs of greatest consequence. These things are indeed also testified of him by others; for he had a great authority in the city, alike for his life, his eloquence, and his age.

He was also a good father, an excellent husband to his wife, and an extraordinary economist; and as he did not manage his affairs of this kind carelessly, and as things of little moment, I think I ought to record a little further whatever was commendable in him in these points. He married a wife more noble than rich; being of opinion that the rich and the high-born are equally haughty and proud; but that those of noble blood would be more ashamed of base things, and consequently more obedient to their husbands in all that was fit and right. A man who beat his wife or child laid violent hands, he said, on what was most sacred; and a good husband he reckoned worthy of more praise than a great senator; and he admired the ancient Socrates for nothing so much as for having lived a temperate and contented life with a wife who was a scold, and children who were half-witted.

As soon as he had a son born, though he had never such urgent business upon his hands, unless it were some public matter, he would be by when his wife washed it and dressed it in its swaddling clothes. For she herself suckled it, nay, she often too gave her breast to her servants' children, to produce, by suckling the same milk, a kind of natural love in them to her son. When he began to come to years of discretion, Cato himself would teach him to read, although he had a servant, a very good grammarian, called Chilo, who taught many others; but he thought not fit, as he himself said, to have his son reprimanded by a slave, or pulled, it may be, by the ears when found tardy in his lesson: nor would he have him owe to a servant the obligation of so great a thing as his learning; he himself, therefore (as we were saying), taught him his grammar, law, and his gymnastic exercises. Nor did he only show him, too, how to throw a dart, to fight in armour, and to ride, but to box also and to endure both heat and cold, and to swim over the most rapid and rough rivers. He says, likewise, that he wrote histories, in large characters, with his own hand, that so his son, without stirring out of the house, might learn to know about his countrymen and forefathers; nor did he less abstain from speaking anything obscene before his son, than if it had been in the presence of the sacred virgins, called vestals. Nor would he ever go into the bath with him; which seems indeed to have been the common custom of the Romans. Sons-in-law used to avoid bathing with fathers-in-law, disliking to see one another naked; but having, in time, learned of the Greeks to strip before men, they have since taught the Greeks to do it even with the women themselves.

Thus, like an excellent work, Cato formed and fashioned his son to virtue; nor had he any occasion to find fault with his readiness and docility; but as he proved to be of too weak a constitution for hardships, he did not insist on requiring of him any very austere way of living. However, though delicate in health, he proved a stout man in the field, and behaved himself valiantly when Paulus Æmilius fought against Perseus; where when his sword was struck from him by a blow, or rather slipped out of his hand by reason of its moistness, he so keenly resented it, that he turned to some of his friends about him, and taking them along with him again fell upon the enemy; and having by a long fight and much force cleared the place, at length found it among great heaps of arms, and the dead bodies of friends as well as enemies piled one upon another. Upon which Paulus, his general, much commended the youth; and there is a letter of Cato's to his son, which highly praised his honourable eagerness for the recovery of his sword. Afterwards he married Tertia, Æmilius Paulus' daughter, and sister to Scipio; nor was he admitted into this family less for his own worth than his father's. So that Cato's care in his son's education came to a very fitting result.

He purchased a great many slaves out of the captives taken in war, but chiefly brought up the young ones, who were capable to be, as it were, bro-ken and taught like whelps and colts. None of these ever entered another man's house, except sent either by Cato himself or his wife. If anyone of them were asked what Cato did, they answered merely that they did not know. When a servant was at home, he was obliged either to do some work or sleep, for indeed Cato loved those most who used to lie down often to sleep, accounting them more docile than those who were wakeful, and more fit for anything when they were refreshed with a little slumber. Being also of opinion that the great cause of the laziness and misbehaviour of slaves was their running after their pleasures, he fixed a certain price for them to pay for permission amongst themselves, but would suffer no con-nections out of the house. At first, when he was but a poor soldier, he would not be difficult in anything which related to his eating, but looked upon it as a pitiful thing to quarrel with a servant for the belly's sake; but afterwards, when he grew richer, and made any feasts for his friends and colleagues in office, as soon as supper was over he used to go with a leather thong and scourge those who had waited or dressed the meat care-lessly. He always contrived, too, that his servants should have some differ-ence one among another, always suspecting and fearing a good understanding between them. Those who had committed anything worthy of death, he punished if they were found guilty by the verdict of their fellow-servants. But being after all much given to the desire of gain, he looked upon agriculture rather as a pleasure than profit; resolving, therefore, to lay out his money in safe and solid things, he purchased ponds, hot baths, grounds full of fuller's earth, remunerative lands, pastures, and woods; from all which he drew large returns, nor could Jupiter himself, he used to say, do him much damage. He was also given to the form of usury, which is considered most odious, in traffic by sea; and that thus—he desired that those whom he put out his money to should have many partners; when the number of them and their ships came to be fifty, he himself took one share through Quintio his freedman, who therefore was to sail with the adventurers, and take a part in all their proceedings, so that thus there was no danger of losing his whole stock, but only a little part, and that with a prospect of great profit. He likewise lent money to those of his slaves who wished to borrow, with which they bought also other young ones, whom, when they had taught and bred up at his charges, they would sell again at the year's end; but some of them Cato would keep for himself, giving just as much for them as another had offered. To incline his son to be of his kind or temper, he used to tell him that it was not like a man, but rather like a widow woman, to lessen an estate. But the strongest indication of Cato's avaricious humour was when he took the boldness to affirm that he was a most wonderful, nay, a godlike man, who left more behind him than he had received.

He was now grown old, when Carneades the Academic, and Diogenes the Stoic, came as deputies from Athens to Rome, praying for release from a penalty of five hundred talents laid on the Athenians, in a suit, to which they did not appear, in which the Oropians were plaintiffs and Sicyonians judges. All the most studious youth immediately waited on these philoso-phers, and frequently, with admiration, heard them speak. But the grace-fulness of Carneades' oratory, whose ability was really greatest, and his reputation equal to it, gathered large and favourable audiences, and ere long filled, like a wind, all the city with the sound of it. So that it soon began to be told that a Greek, famous even to admiration, winning and carrying all before him, had impressed so strange a love upon the young men, that quitting all their pleasures and pastimes, they ran mad, as it were, after philosophy; which indeed much pleased the Romans in general; nor could they but with much pleasure see the youth receive so welcomely the Greek literature, and frequent the company of learned men. But Cato, on the other side, seeing the passion for words flowing into the city, from the beginning took it ill, fearing lest the youth should be diverted that way, and so should prefer the glory of speaking well before that of arms and doing well. And when the fame of the philosophers increased in the city, and Caius Acilius, a person of distinction, at his own request, became their interpreter to the senate at their first audience, Cato resolved, under some specious pretence, to have all philosophers cleared out of the city; and, coming into the senate, blamed the magistrates for letting these deputies stay so long a time without being despatched, though they were persons that could easily persuade the people to what they pleased; that therefore in all haste something should be determined about their petition, that so they might go home again to their own schools, and declaim to the Greek children, and leave the Roman youth to be obedient, as hitherto, to their own laws and governors.

Yet he did this not out of any anger, as some think, to Carneades; but because he wholly despised philosophy, and out of a kind of pride scoffed at the Greek studies and literature; as, for example, he would say, that Socrates was a prating, seditious fellow, who did his best to tyrannise over his country, to undermine the ancient customs, and to entice and withdraw the citizens to opinions contrary to the laws. Ridiculing the school of Isocrates, he would add, that his scholars grew old men before they had done learning with him, as if they were to use their art and plead causes in the court of Minos in the next world. And to frighten his son from anything that was Greek, in a more vehement tone than became one of his age, he pronounced, as it were, with the voice of an oracle, that the Romans would certainly be destroyed when they began once to be infected with Greek literature; though time indeed has shown the vanity of this his prophecy; as, in truth, the city of Rome has risen to its highest fortune while entertaining Grecian learning. Nor had he an aversion only against the Greek philosophers, but the physicians also; for having, it seems, heard how Hippocrates, when the king of Persia sent for him, with offers of a fee of several talents, said, that he would never assist barbarians who were enemies to the Greeks; he affirmed, that this was now become a common oath taken by all physicians, and enjoined his son to have a care and avoid them; for that he himself had written a little book of prescriptions for curing those who were sick in his family; he never enjoined fasting to anyone, but ordered them either vegetables, or the meat of a duck, pigeon, or leveret; such kind of diet being of light digestion and fit for sick folks, only it made those who ate it dream a little too much; and by the use of this kind of physic, he said, he not only made himself and those about him well, but kept them so.

However, for this his presumption he seemed not to have escaped unpunished; for he lost both his wife and his son; though he himself, being of a strong, robust constitution, held out longer; so that he would often, even in his old days, address himself to women, and when he was past a lover's age, married a young woman, upon the following pretence: Having lost his own wife, he married his son to the daughter of Paulus Æmilius, who was sister to Scipio; so that being now a widower himself, he had a young girl who came privately to visit him, but the house being very small, and a daughter-in-law also in it, this practice was quickly discovered; for the young woman seeming once to pass through it a little too boldly, the youth, his son, though he said nothing, seemed to look somewhat indignantly upon her. The old man perceiving and understanding that what he did was disliked, without finding any fault or saying a word, went away, as his custom was, with his usual companions to the market: and among the rest, he called aloud to one Salonius, who had been a clerk under him, and asked him whether he had married his daughter? He answered no, nor would he, till he had consulted him. Said Cato, "Then I have found out a fit son-in-law for you, if he should not displease by reason of his age; for in all other points there is no fault to be found in him; but he is indeed, as I said, extremely old." However, Salonius desired him to undertake the business, and to give the young girl to whom he pleased, she being a humble servant of his, who stood in need of his care and patronage. Upon this Cato, without anymore ado, told him he desired to have the damsel himself. These words, as may well be imagined, at first astonished the man, conceiving that Cato was as far off from marrying, as he from a likelihood of being allied to the family of one who had been consul and had triumphed; but perceiving him in earnest, he consented willingly; and going onwards to the forum, they quickly completed the bargain.

Whilst the marriage was in hand, Cato's son, taking some of his friends along with him, went and asked his father if it were for any offence he brought in a stepmother upon him? But Cato cried out, "Far from it, my son, I have no fault to find with you or anything of yours; only I desire to have many children, and to leave the commonwealth more such citizens as you are." Pisistratus, the tyrant of Athens, made, they say, this answer to his sons, when they were grown men, when he married his second wife, Timonassa of Argos, by whom he had, it is said, Iophon and Thessalus. Cato had a son by this second wife, to whom, from his mother, he gave the surname of Salonius. In the meantime, his eldest died in his prætorship; of whom Cato often makes mention in his books, as having been a good man. He is said, however, to have borne the loss moderately and like a philosopher, and was nothing the more remiss in attending to affairs of state; so that he did not, as Lucius Lucullus and Metellus Pius did, grow languid in his old age, as though public business were a duty once to be discharged, and then quitted; nor did he, like Scipio Africanus, because envy had struck at his glory, turn from the public, and change and pass away the rest of his life without doing anything; but as one persuaded Dionysius, that the most honourable tomb he could have would be to die in the exercise of his dominion; so Cato thought that old age to be the most honourable which was busied in public affairs; though he would, now and then, when he had leisure, recreate himself with husbandry and writing.

And, indeed, he composed various books and histories; and in his youth he addicted himself to agriculture for profit's sake; for he used to say he had but two ways of getting—agriculture and parsimony; and now, in his old age, the first of these gave him both occupation and a subject of study. He wrote one book on country matters, in which he treated particularly even of making cakes and preserving fruit; it being his ambition to be curious and singular in all things. His suppers, at his country house, used also to be plentiful; he daily invited his friends and neighbours about him, and passed the time merrily with them; so that his company was not only agreeable to those of the same age, but even to younger men; for he had had experience in many things, and had been concerned in much, both by word and deed, that was worth the hearing. He looked upon a good table as the best place for making friends; where the commendations of brave and good citizens were usually introduced, and little said of base and unworthy ones; as Cato would not give leave in his company to have anything, either good or ill, said about them.

Some will have the overthrow of Carthage to have been one of his last acts of state; when, indeed, Scipio the younger did by his valour give it the last blow, but the war, chiefly by the counsel and advice of Cato, was undertaken on the following occasion. Cato was sent to the Carthaginians and Masinissa, King of Numidia, who were at war with one another, to know the cause of their difference. He, it seems, had been a friend of the Romans from the beginning; and they, too, since they were conquered by

Scipio, were of the Roman confederacy, having been shorn of their power by loss of territory and a heavy tax. Finding Carthage, not (as the Romans thought) low and in an ill condition, but well manned, full of riches and all sorts of arms and ammunition, and perceiving the Carthaginians carry it high, he conceived that it was not a time for the Romans to adjust affairs between them and Masinissa; but rather that they themselves would fall into danger, unless they should find means to check this rapid new growth of Rome's ancient irreconcilable enemy. Therefore, returning quickly to Rome, he acquainted the senate that the former defeats and blows given to the Carthaginians had not so much diminished their strength, as it had abated their imprudence and folly; that they were not become weaker, but more experienced in war, and did only skirmish with the Numidians to exercise themselves the better to cope with the Romans: that the peace and league they had made was but a kind of suspension of war which awaited a fairer opportunity to break out again.

Moreover, they say that, shaking his gown, he took occasion to let drop some African figs before the senate. And on their admiring the size and beauty of them, he presently added, that the place that bore them was but three days' sail from Rome. Nay, he never after this gave his opinion, but at the end he would be sure to come out with this sentence, "ALSO, CARTHAGE, METHINKS, OUGHT UTTERLY TO BE DESTROYED." But Publius Scipio Nasica would always declare his opinion to the contrary, in these words, "It seems requisite to me that Carthage should still stand." For seeing his countrymen to be grown wanton and insolent, and the people made, by their prosperity, obstinate and disobedient to the senate, and drawing the whole city, whither they would, after them, he would have had the fear of Carthage to serve as a bit to hold the contumacy of the multitude; and he looked upon the Carthaginians as too weak to overcome the Romans, and too great to be despised by them. On the other side, it seemed a perilous thing to Cato that a city which had been always great, and was now grown sober and wise, by reason of its former calamities, should still lie, as it were, in wait for the follies and dangerous excesses of the over-powerful Roman people; so that he thought it the wisest course to have all outward dangers removed, when they had so many inward ones among themselves.

Thus Cato, they say, stirred up the third and last war against the Carthaginians: but no sooner was the said war begun, than he died, prophesying of the person that should put an end to it who was then only a young man; but, being tribune in the army, he in several fights gave proof of his courage and conduct. The news of which being brought to Cato's ears at Rome, he thus expressed himself:

> The only wise man of them all is he,
> The others e'en as shadows flit and flee.

This prophecy Scipio soon confirmed by his actions.

Cato left no posterity, except one son by his second wife, who was named, as we said, Cato Salonius; and a grandson by his eldest son, who died. Cato Salonius died when he was prætor, but his son Marcus was afterwards consul, and he was grandfather of Cato the philosopher, who for virtue and renown was one of the most eminent personages of his time.

THE COMPARISON OF ARISTIDES
WITH MARCUS CATO

HAVING MENTIONED THE MOST MEMORABLE ACTIONS OF THESE GREAT men, if we now compare the whole life of the one with that of the other, it will not be easy to discern the difference between them, lost as it is amongst such a number of circumstances in which they resemble each other. If, however, we examine them in detail, as we might some piece of poetry, or some picture, we shall find this common to them both, that they advanced themselves to great honour and dignity in the commonwealth by no other means than their own virtue and industry. But it seems when Aristides appeared, Athens was not at its height of grandeur and plenty, the chief magistrates and officers of his time being men only of moderate and equal fortunes among themselves. The estimate of the greatest estates then was five hundred medimns; that of the second, or knights, three hundred; of the third and last, called Zeugitæ, two hundred. But Cato, out of a petty village from a country life, leaped into the commonwealth, as it were into a vast ocean; at a time when there were no such governors as the Curii, Fabricii, and Hostilii. Poor labouring men were not then advanced from the plough and spade to be governors and magistrates; but greatness of family, riches, profuse gifts, distributions, and personal application were what the city looked to; keeping a high hand, and, in a manner, insulting over those that courted preferment. It was not as great a matter to have Themistocles for an adversary, a person of mean extraction and small fortune (for he was not worth, it is said, more than four or five talents when he first applied himself to public affairs), as to contest with a Scipio Africanus, a Servius Galba, and a Quintius Flamininus, having no other aid but a tongue free to assert right.

Besides, Aristides at Marathon, and again at Platæa, was but one commander out of ten; whereas Cato was chosen consul with a single colleague, having many competitors, and with a single colleague, also, was preferred before seven most noble and eminent pretenders to be censor. But Aristides was never principal in any action; for Miltiades carried the day at Marathon, at Salamis, Themistocles, and at Platæa, Herodotus tells us, Pausanias got the glory of that noble victory: and men like Sophanes, and Aminias, Callimachus, and Cynægyrus, behaved themselves so well in all those engagements as to contest it with Aristides even for the second place. But Cato not only in his consulship was esteemed the chief in courage and conduct in the Spanish war, but even whilst he was only serving as tribune at Thermopylæ, under another's command, he gained the glory of the victory, for having, as it were, opened a wide gate for the Romans to rush in upon Antiochus, and for having brought the war on his back, whilst he only minded what was before his face. For that victory, which was beyond dispute all Cato's own work, cleared Asia out of Greece, and by that means made way afterwards for Scipio into Asia. Both of them, indeed, were always victorious in war; but at home Aristides stumbled, being banished and oppressed by the faction of Themistocles; yet Cato, notwithstanding he had almost all the chief and most powerful of Rome for his adversaries, and wrestled with them even to his old age, kept still his footing. Engaging also in many public suits, sometimes plaintiff, sometimes defendant, he cast the most, and came off clear with all; thanks to his eloquence, that bulwark and powerful instrument to which more truly, than to chance or his fortune, he owed it, that he sustained himself unhurt to the last. Antipater justly gives it as a high commendation to Aristotle, the philosopher, writing of him after his death, that among his other virtues, he was endowed with a faculty of persuading people which way he pleased.

Questionless, there is no perfecter endowment in man than political virtue, and of this Economics is commonly esteemed not the least part; for a city, which is a collection of private households, grows into a stable commonwealth by the private means of prosperous citizens that compose it. Lycurgus by prohibiting gold and silver in Sparta, and making iron, spoiled by the fire, the only currency, did not by these measures discharge them from minding their household affairs, but cutting off luxury, the corruption and tumour of riches, he provided there should be an abundant supply of all necessary and useful things for all persons, as much as any other law-maker ever did; being more apprehensive of a poor, needy, and indigent member of a community, than of the rich and haughty. And in this management of domestic concerns, Cato was as great as in the government of public affairs; for he increased his estate, and became a master to others in economy and husbandry; upon which subjects he collected in his writings many useful observations. On the contrary Aristides, by his poverty, made justice odious, as if it were the pest and impoverisher of a family, and beneficial to all, rather than to those that were endowed with it. Yet Hesiod urges us alike to just dealing and care of our households, and inveighs against idleness as the origin of injustice; and Homer admirably says:

> Work was not dear, nor household cares to me,
> Whose increase rears the thriving family;
> But well-rigged ships were always my delight,
> And wars, and darts, and arrows of the fight:

as if the same characters carelessly neglected their own estates, and lived by injustice and rapine from others. For it is not as the physicians say of oil, that, outwardly applied, it is very wholesome, but taken inwardly detrimental, that thus a just man provides carefully for others, and is heedless of himself and his own affairs; but in this Aristides' political virtues seem to be defective; since, according to most authors, he took no care to leave his daughters a portion, or himself enough to defray his funeral charges: whereas Cato's family produced senators and generals to the fourth generation; his grandchildren, and their children, came to the highest preferments. But Aristides, who was the principal man of Greece, through extreme poverty reduced some of his to get their living by jugglers' tricks, others, for want, to hold out their hands for public alms; leaving none means to perform any noble action, or worthy his dignity.

Yet why should this needs follow? Since poverty is dishonourable not in itself, but when it is a proof of laziness, intemperance, luxury, and carelessness; whereas in a person that is temperate, industrious, just, and valiant, and who uses all his virtues for the public good, it shows a great and lofty mind. For he has no time for great matters who concerns himself with petty ones; nor can he relieve many needs of others, who himself has many needs of his own. What most of all enables a man to serve the public is not wealth, but content and independence; which, requiring no superfluity at home, distracts not the mind from the common good. God alone is entirely exempt from all want: of human virtues, that which needs least is the most absolute and most divine. For as a body bred to a good habit requires nothing exquisite either in clothes or food, so a sound man and a sound household keep themselves up with a small matter. Riches ought to be proportioned to the use we have of them; for he that scrapes together a great deal, making use of but little, is not independent; for if he wants them not, it is folly in him to make provision for things which he does not desire; or if he does desire them, and restrains his enjoyment out of sordidness, he is miserable. I would fain know of Cato himself, if we seek riches that we may enjoy them, why is he proud of having a great deal, and being contented with little? But if it be noble, as it is, to feed on coarse bread, and drink the same wine with our hinds, and not to covet purple, and plastered houses, neither Aristides, nor Epaminondas, nor Manius Curius, nor Caius Fabricius wanted necessaries, who took no pains to get those things whose use they approved not. For it was not worth the while of a man who esteemed turnips a most delicate food, and who boiled them himself, whilst his wife made bread, to brag so often of a halfpenny, and write a book to show how a man may soonest grow rich; the very good of being contented with little is because it cuts off at once the desire and the anxiety for superfluities. Hence Aristides, it is told, said, on the trial of Callias, that it was for them to blush at poverty who were poor against their wills; they who like him were willingly so might glory in it. For it is ridiculous to think Aristides' neediness imputable to his sloth, who might fairly enough by the spoil of one barbarian, or seizing one tent, have become wealthy. But enough of this.

Cato's expeditions added no great matter to the Roman empire, which already was so great, as that in a manner it could receive no addition; but those of Aristides are the noblest, most splendid, and distinguished actions the Grecians ever did, the battles at Marathon, Salamis, and Platæa. Nor indeed is Antiochus, nor the destruction of the walls of the Spanish towns, to be compared with Xerxes, and the destruction by sea and land of so many myriads of enemies; in all of which noble exploits Aristides yielded to none, though he left the glory and the laurels, like the wealth and money, to those who needed and thirsted more greedily after them: because he was superior to those also. I do not blame Cato for perpetually boasting and preferring himself before all others, though in one of his orations he says that it is equally absurd to praise and dispraise one's self: yet he who does not so much as desire others' praises, seems to me more perfectly virtuous, than he who is always extolling himself. A mind free from ambition is a main help to political gentleness; ambition, on the contrary, is hard-hearted, and the greatest fomenter of envy; from which Aristides was wholly exempt; Cato very subject to it. Aristides assisted Themistocles in matters of highest importance, and, as his subordinate officer, in a manner raised Athens: Cato, by opposing Scipio, almost broke and defeated his expedition against the Carthaginians, in which he overthrew Hannibal, who till then was even invincible; and, at last, by continually raising suspicions and calumnies against him, he chased him from the city, and inflicted a disgraceful sentence on his brother for robbing the state.

Finally, that temperance which Cato always highly cried up, Aristides preserved truly pure and untainted. But Cato's marriage, unbecoming his dignity and age, is a considerable disparagement, in this respect, to his character. For it was not decent for him at that age to bring home to his son and his wife a young woman, the daughter of a common paid clerk in the public service: but whether it were for his own gratification or out of anger at his son, both the fact and the pretence were unworthy. For the reason he pretended to his son was false: for if he desired to get more as worthy children, he ought to have married a well-born wife; not to have contented himself, so long as it was unnoticed, with a woman to whom he was not married; and, when it was discovered, he ought not to have chosen such a father-in-law as was easiest to be got, instead of one whose affinity might be honourable to him.

PHILOPŒMEN

CLEANDER WAS A MAN OF HIGH BIRTH AND GREAT POWER IN THE CITY OF
Mantinea, but by the chances of the time happened to be driven from
thence. There being an intimate friendship betwixt him and Craugis, the
father of Philopœmen, who was a person of great distinction, he settled at
Megalopolis, where, while his friend lived, he had all he could desire.
When Craugis died, he repaid the father's hospitable kindness in the care
of the orphan son; by which means Philopœmen was educated by him, as
Homer says Achilles was by Phoenix, and from his infancy moulded to
lofty and noble inclinations. But Ecdemus and Demophanes had the principal tuition of him, after he was past the years of childhood. They were
both Megalopolitans; they had been scholars in the academic philosophy,
and friends to Arcesilaus, and had, more than any of their contemporaries, brought philosophy to bear upon action and state affairs. They had
freed their country from tyranny by the death of Aristodemus, whom they
caused to be killed; they had assisted Aratus in driving out the tyrant
Nicocles from Sicyon; and, at the request of the Cyreneans, whose city was
in a state of extreme disorder and confusion, went thither by sea, and succeeded in establishing good government and happily settling their commonwealth. And among their best actions they themselves counted the
education of Philopœmen, thinking they had done a general good to
Greece by giving him the nurture of philosophy. And indeed all Greece
(which looked upon him as a kind of latter birth brought forth, after so
many noble leaders, in her decrepit age) loved him wonderfully; and, as
his glory grew, increased his power. And one of the Romans, to praise him,
calls him the last of the Greeks; as if after him Greece had produced no
great man, nor who deserved the name of Greek.

His person was not, as some fancy, deformed; for his likeness is yet to be seen at Delphi. The mistake of the hostess of Megara was occasioned, it would seem, merely by his easiness of temper and his plain manners. This hostess having word brought her that the general of the Achæans was coming to her house in the absence of her husband, was all in a hurry about providing his supper. Philopœmen, in an ordinary cloak, arriving in this point of time, she took him for one of his own train who had been sent on before, and bid him lend her his hand in her household work. He forthwith threw off his cloak, and fell to cutting up the firewood. The husband returning, and seeing him at it, "What," says he, "may this mean, O Philopœmen?" "I am," replied he in his Doric dialect, "paying the penalty of my ugly looks." Titus Flamininus, jesting with him upon his figure, told him one day he had well-shaped hands and feet, but no belly: and he was indeed slender in the waist. But this raillery was meant to the poverty of his fortune; for he had good horse and foot, but often wanted money to entertain and play them. These are common anecdotes told of Philopœmen.

The love of honour and distinction was, in his character, not unalloyed with feelings of personal rivalry and resentment. He made Epaminondas his great example, and came not far behind him in activity, sagacity, and incorruptible integrity; but his hot contentious temper continually carried him out of the bounds of that gentleness, composure, and humanity which had marked Epaminondas, and this made him thought a pattern rather of military than of civil virtue. He was strongly inclined to the life of a soldier even from his childhood, and he studied and practised all that belonged to it, taking great delight in managing of horses and handling of weapons. Because he was naturally fitted to excel in wrestling, some of his friends and tutors recommended his attention to athletic exercises. But he would first be satisfied whether it would not interfere with his becoming a good soldier. They told him, as was the truth, that the one life was directly opposite to the other; the requisite state of body, the ways of living, and the exercises all different: the professed athlete sleeping much and feeding plentifully, punctually regular in his set times of exercise and rest, and apt to spoil all by every little excess or breach of his usual method; whereas the soldier ought to train himself in every variety of change and irregularity, and, above all, to bring himself to endure hunger and loss of sleep without difficulty. Philopœmen, hearing this, not only laid by all thoughts of wrestling and contemned it then, but when he came to be general, discouraged it by all marks of reproach and dishonour he could imagine, as a thing which made men, otherwise excellently fit for war, to be utterly useless and unable to fight on necessary occasions.

When he left off his masters and teachers, and began to bear arms in the incursions which his citizens used to make upon the Lacedæmonians for pillage and plunder, he would always march out the first and return the last. When there was nothing to do, he sought to harden his body, and make it strong and active by hunting, or labouring in his ground. He had a good estate about twenty furlongs from the town, and thither he would go everyday after dinner and supper; and when night came, throw himself upon the first mattress in his way, and there sleep as one of the labourers. At break of day he would rise with the rest, and work either in the vineyard or at the plough; from thence return again to the town, and employ his time with his friends or the magistrates in public business. What he got in the wars he laid out on horses, or arms, or in ransoming captives; but endeavoured to improve his own property the justest way, by tillage; and this not slightly, by way of diversion, but thinking it his strict duty so to manage his own fortune as to be out of the temptation of wronging others.

He spent much time on eloquence and philosophy, but selected his authors, and cared only for those by whom he might profit in virtue. In Homer's fictions his attention was given to whatever he thought apt to raise the courage. Of all other books he was most devoted to the commentaries of Evangelus on military tactics, and took delight, at leisure hours, in the histories of Alexander; thinking that such reading, unless undertaken for mere amusement and idle conversation, was to the purpose for action. Even in speculations on military subjects it was his habit to neglect maps and diagrams, and to put the theorems to practical proof on the ground itself. He would be exercising his thoughts and considering as he travelled, and arguing with those about him of the difficulties of steep or broken ground, what might happen at rivers, ditches, or mountain-passes, in marching in close or in open, in this or in that particular form of battle. The truth is, he indeed took an immoderate pleasure in military operations and in warfare, to which he devoted himself, as the special means for exercising all sorts of virtue, and utterly contemned those who were not soldiers, as drones and useless in the commonwealth.

When he was thirty years of age, Cleomenes, King of the Lacedæmonians, surprised Megalopolis by night, forced the guards, broke in, and seized the market place. Philopœmen came out upon the alarm, and fought with desperate courage, but could not beat the enemy out again; yet he succeeded in effecting the escape of the citizens, who got away while he made head against the pursuers, and amused Cleomenes, till, after losing his horse and receiving several wounds, with much ado he came off himself, being the last man in the retreat. The Megalopolitans escaped to Messene, whither Cleomenes sent to offer them their town and goods again. Philopœmen perceiving them to be only too glad at the news, and eager to return, checked them with a speech, in which he made them sensible, that what Cleomenes called restoring the city was, rather, possessing himself of the citizens; and through their means securing also the city for the future. The mere solitude would, of itself, ere long force him away, since there was no staying to guard empty houses and naked walls. These reasons withheld the Megalopolitans, but gave Cleomenes a pretext to pillage and destroy a great part of the city, and carry away a great booty.

Awhile after, King Antigonus coming down to succour the Achæans, they marched with their united forces against Cleomenes; who, having seized the avenues, lay advantageously posted on the hills of Sellasia. Antigonus drew up close by him, with a resolution to force him in his strength. Philopœmen, with his citizens, was that day placed among the horse, next to the Illyrian foot, a numerous body of bold fighters who completed the line of battle, forming, together with the Achæans, the reserve. Their orders were to keep their ground, and not engage till from the other wing, where the king fought in person, they should see a red coat lifted up on the point of a spear. The Achæans obeyed their order and stood fast, but the Illyrians were led on by their commanders to the attack. Euclides, the brother of Cleomenes, seeing the foot thus severed from the horse, detached the best of his light-armed men, commanding them to wheel about, and charge the unprotected Illyrians in the rear. This charge putting things in confusion, Philopœmen, considering those light-armed men would be easily repelled, went first to the king's officers to make them sensible what the occasion required. But they not minding what he said, but slighting him as a hare-brained fellow (as indeed he was not yet of any repute sufficient to give credit to a proposal of such importance), he charged with his own citizens, at the first encounter disordered, and soon after put the troops to flight with great slaughter. Then, to encourage the king's army further, to bring them all upon the enemy while he was in confusion, he quitted his horse, and fighting with extreme difficulty in his heavy horseman's dress, in rough uneven ground, full of water-courses and hollows, had both his thighs struck through with a thonged javelin. It was thrown with great force, so that the head came out on the other side, and made a severe, though not a mortal, wound. There he stood awhile, as if he had been shackled, unable to move. The fastening which joined the thong to the javelin made it difficult to get it drawn out, nor would any about him venture to do it. But the fight being now at the hottest, and likely to be quickly decided, he was transported with the desire of partaking in it, and struggled and strained so violently, setting one leg forward, the other back, that at last he broke the shaft in two; and thus, got the pieces pulled out. Being in this manner set at liberty, he caught up his sword, and running through the midst of those who were fighting in the first ranks, animated his men, and set them afire with emulation. Antigonus after the victory asked the Macedonians, to try them, how it happened the horse had charged without orders before the signal? They answering, that they were against their wills forced to it by a young man of Megalopolis, who had fallen in before his time: "This young man," replied Antigonus, smiling, "did like an experienced commander."

This, as was natural, brought Philopœmen into great reputation. Antigonus was earnest to have him in his service, and offered him very advantageous conditions, both as to command and pay. But Philopœmen, who knew that his nature brooked not to be under another, would not accept them; yet not enduring to live idle, and hearing of wars in Crete for practice' sake he passed over thither. He spent sometime among those very warlike, and, at the same time, sober and temperate men, improving much by experience in all sorts of service; and then returned with so much fame that the Achæans presently chose him commander of the horse. These horsemen at that time had neither experience nor bravery, it being the custom to take any common horses, the first and cheapest they could procure, when they were to march; and on almost all occasions they did not go themselves, but hired others in their places, and stayed at home. Their former commanders winked at this, because, it being an honour among the Achæans to serve on horseback, these men had great power in the commonwealth, and were able to gratify or molest whom they pleased. Philopœmen, finding them in this condition, yielded not to any such considerations, nor would pay it over as formerly; but went himself from town to town, where, speaking with the young men, one by one, he endeavoured to excite a spirit of ambition and love of honour among them, using punishment also, where it was necessary. And then by public exercises, reviews, and contests in the presence of numerous spectators, in a little time he made them wonderfully strong and bold, and, which is reckoned of greatest consequence in military service, light and agile. With use and industry they grew so perfect, to such a command of their horses, such a ready exactness in wheeling round in their troops, that in any change of posture the whole body seemed to move with all the facility and promptitude, and, as it were, with the single will of one man. In the great battle which they fought with the Ætolians and Eleans by the river Larissus, he set them an example himself. Damophantus, general of the Elean horse, singled out Philopœmen, and rode with full speed at him. Philopœmen awaited his charge, and, before receiving the stroke, with a violent blow of his spear threw him dead to the ground: upon whose fall the enemy fled immediately. And now Philopœmen was in everybody's mouth, as a man who in actual fighting with his own hand yielded not to the youngest, nor in good conduct to the oldest, and there came not into the field any better soldier or commander.

Aratus, indeed, was the first who raised the Achæans, inconsiderable till then, into reputation and power, by uniting their divided cities into one commonwealth, and establishing amongst them a humane and truly Grecian form of government; and hence it happened, as in running waters, where, when a few little particles of matter once stop, others stick to them, and one part strengthening another, the whole becomes firm and solid; so in a general weakness, when every city relying only on itself, all Greece was giving way to an easy dissolution, the Achæans, first forming themselves into a body, and then drawing in their neighbours round about, some by protection, delivering them from their tyrants, others by peaceful consent and by naturalisation, designed at last to bring all Peloponnesus into one community. Yet while Aratus lived, they depended much on the Macedonians, courting first Ptolemy, then Antigonus and Philip, who all took part continually in whatever concerned the affairs of Greece. But when Philopœmen came to a command, the Achæans, feeling themselves a match for the most powerful of their enemies, declined foreign support. The truth is, Aratus, as we have written in his life, was not of so warlike a temper, but did most by policy and gentleness, and friendships with foreign princes; but Philopœmen being a man both of execution and command, a great soldier, and fortunate in his first attempts, wonderfully heightened both the power and courage of the Achæans, accustomed to victory under his conduct.

But first he altered what he found amiss in their arms and form of battle. Hitherto they had used light, thin bucklers, too narrow to cover the body, and javelins much shorter than pikes. By which means they were skilful in skirmishing at a distance, but in a close fight had much the disadvantage.

Then in drawing their forces up for battle, they were never accustomed to form in regular divisions; and their line being unprotected either by the thick array of projecting spears or by their shields, as in the Macedonian phalanx, where the soldiers close and their shields touch, they were easily opened and broken. Philopœmen reformed all this, persuading them to change the narrow target and short javelin into a large shield and long pike; to arm their heads, bodies, thighs, and legs; and instead of loose skirmishing, fight firmly and foot to foot. After he had brought them all to wear full armour, and by that means into the confidence of thinking themselves now invincible, he turned what before had been idle profusion and luxury into an honourable expense. For being long used to vie with each other in their dress, and furniture of their houses, and service of their tables, and to glory in outdoing one another, the disease by custom was grown incurable, and there was no possibility of removing it altogether. But he diverted the passion, and brought them, instead of these superfluities, to love useful and more manly display, and reducing their other expenses, to take delight in appearing magnificent in their equipage of war. Nothing then was to be seen in the shops but plate breaking up, or melting down, gilding of breastplate, and studding bucklers and bits with silver; nothing in the places of exercise, but horses managing, and young men exercising their arms; nothing in the hands of the women, but helmets and crests of feathers to be dyed, and military cloaks and riding-frocks to be embroidered; the very sight of all which, quickening and raising their spirits, made them contemn dangers, and feel ready to venture on any honourable dangers. Other kinds of sumptuosity give us pleasure but make us effeminate; the tickling of the sense slackening the vigour of the mind; but magnificence of this kind strengthens and heightens the courage; as Homer makes Achilles at the sight of his new arms exulting with joy, and on fire to use them. When Philopœmen had obtained of them to arm, and set themselves out in this manner, he proceeded to train them, mustering and exercising them perpetually; in which they obeyed him with great zeal and eagerness. For they were wonderfully pleased with their new form of battle, which being so knit and cemented together, seemed almost incapable of being broken. And then their arms, which for their riches and beauty they wore with pleasure, becoming light and easy to them with constant use, they longed for nothing more than to try them with an enemy, and fight in earnest.

The Achæans at that time were at war with Machanidas, the tyrant of Lacedæmon, who, having a strong army, watched all opportunities of becoming entire master of Peloponnesus. When intelligence came that he was fallen upon the Mantineans, Philopœmen forthwith took the field, and marched towards him. They met near Mantinea, and drew up in sight of the city. Both, besides the whole strength of their several cities, had a good number of mercenaries in pay. When they came to fall on, Machanidas, with his hired soldiers, beat the spearmen and the Tarentines whom Philopœmen had placed in the front. But when he should have charged immediately into the main battle, which stood close and firm, he hotly followed the chase; and instead of attacking the Achæans, passed on beyond them, while they remained drawn up in their place. With so untoward a beginning the rest of the confederates gave themselves up for lost; but Philopœmen, professing to make it a matter of small consequence, and observing the enemy's oversight, who had thus left an opening in their main body, and exposed their own phalanx, made no sort of motion to oppose them, but let them pursue the chase freely, till they had placed themselves at a great distance from him. Then seeing the Lacedæmonians before him deserted by their horse, with their flanks quite bare, he charged suddenly, and surprised them without a commander, and not so much as expecting an encounter, as, when they saw Machanidas driving the beaten enemy before him, they thought the victory already gained. He overthrew them with great slaughter (they report above four thousand killed in the place), and then faced about against Machanidas, who was returning with his mercenaries from the pursuit. There happened to be a broad deep ditch between them, alongside of which both rode their horses for a while, the one trying to get over and fly, the other to hinder him. It looked less like the contest between two generals than like the last defence of some wild beast brought to bay by the keen huntsman Philopœmen, and forced to fight for his life. The tyrant's horse was mettled and strong; and feeling the bloody spurs in his sides, ventured to take the ditch. He had already so far reached the other side, as to have planted his fore-feet upon it, and was struggling to raise himself with these, when Simmias and Polyænus, who used to fight by the side of Philopœmen, came up on horseback to his assistance. But Philopœmen, before either of them, himself met Machanidas; and perceiving that the horse with his head high reared covered his master's body, turned his own a little, and holding his javelin by the middle, drove it against the tyrant with all his force, and tumbled him dead into the ditch. Such is the precise posture in which he stands at Delphi in the brazen statue which the Achæans set up of him, in admiration of his valour in this single combat, and conduct during the whole day.

We are told that at the Nemean games, a little after this victory, Philopœmen being then general the second time, and at leisure on the occasion of the solemnity, first showed the Greeks his army drawn up in full array as if they were to fight, and executed with it all the manœuvres of a battle with wonderful order, strength, and celerity. After which he went into the theatre, while the musicians were singing for the prize, followed by the young soldiers in their military cloaks and their scarlet frocks under their armour, all in the very height of bodily vigour, and much alike in age, showing a high respect to their general; yet breathing at the same time a noble confidence in themselves, raised by success in many glorious encounters. Just at their coming in, it so happened that the musician Pylades, with a voice well suited to the lofty style of poet, was in the act of commencing the Persians of Timotheus—

Under his conduct Greece was glorious and was free.

The whole theatre at once turned to look at Philopœmen, and clapped with delight; their hopes venturing once more to return to their country's former reputation; and their feelings almost rising to the height of their ancient spirit.

It was with the Achæans as with young horses, which go quietly with their usual riders, but grow unruly and restive under strangers. The soldiers, when any service was in hand, and Philopœmen not at their head, grew dejected and looked about for him; but if he once appeared, came presently to themselves, and recovered their confidence and courage, being sensible that this was the only one of their commanders whom the enemy could not endure to face; but, as appeared in several occasions, were frighted with his very name. Thus we find that Philip, King of Macedon, thinking to terrify the Achæans into subjection again, if he could rid his hands of Philopœmen, employed some persons privately to assassinate him. But the treachery coming to light, he became infamous, and lost his character through Greece. The Bœotians besieging Megara, and ready to carry the town by storm, upon a groundless rumour that Philopœmen was at hand with succour, ran away, and left their scaling ladders at the wall behind them. Nabis (who was tyrant of Lacedæmon after Machanidas) had surprised Messene at a time when Philopœmen was out of command. He tried to persuade Lysippus, then general of the Achæans, to succour Messene: but not prevailing with him, because, he said, the enemy being now within it, the place was irrecoverably lost, he resolved to go himself, without order or commission, followed merely by his own immediate fellow-citizens, who went with him as their general by commission from nature, which had made him fittest to command. Nabis, hearing of his coming, thought it not convenient to stay; but stealing out of the furthest gate with his men, marched away with all the speed he could, thinking himself a happy man if he could get off with safety. And he did escape; but Messene was rescued.

All hitherto makes for the praise and honour of Philopœmen. But when at the request of the Gortynians he went away into Crete to command for them, at a time when his own country was distressed by Nabis, he exposed himself to the charge of either cowardice, or unseasonable ambition of honour amongst foreigners. For the Megalopolitans were then so pressed, that, the enemy being master of the field and encamping almost at their gates, they were forced to keep themselves within their walls, and sow their very streets. And in the meantime, across the seas, waging war and commanding in chief in a foreign nation, furnished his ill-wishers with matter enough for their reproaches. Some said he took the offer of the Gortynians, because the Achæans chose other generals, and left him but a private man. For he could not endure to sit still, but looking upon war and command in it as his great business, always coveted to be employed. And this agrees with what he once aptly said of King Ptolemy. Somebody was praising him for keeping his army and himself in an admirable state of discipline and exercise: "And what praise," replied Philopœmen, "for a king of his years, to be always preparing, and never performing?" However, the Megalopolitans, thinking themselves betrayed, took it so ill that they were about to banish him. But the Achæans put an end to that design by sending their general, Aristæus, to Megalopolis, who, though he were at difference with Philopœmen about affairs of the commonwealth, yet would not suffer him to be banished. Philopœmen finding himself upon this account out of favour with his citizens, induced divers of the little neighbouring places to renounce obedience to them, suggesting to them to urge that from the beginning they were not subject to their taxes or laws, or any way under their command. In these pretences he openly took their part, and fomented seditious movements amongst the Achæans in general against Megalopolis. But these things happened a while after.

While he stayed in Crete, in the service of the Gortynians, he made war not like a Peloponnesian and Arcanian, fairly in the open field, but fought with them at their own weapon, and turning their stratagems and tricks against themselves, showed them they played craft against skill, and were but children to an experienced soldier. Having acted here with great bravery, and great reputation to himself, he returned into Peloponnesus, where he found Philip beaten by Titus Quintius, and Nabis at war both with the Romans and Achæans. He was at once chosen general against Nabis, but venturing to fight by sea, met, like Epaminondas, with a result very contrary to the general expectation and his own former reputation. Epaminondas, however, according to some statements, was backward by design, unwilling to give his countrymen an appetite for the advantages of the sea, lest from good soldiers they should by little and little turn, as Plato says, to ill mariners. And therefore he returned from Asia and the Islands without doing anything, on purpose. Whereas Philopœmen, thinking his skill in land-service would equally avail at sea, learned how great a part of valour experience is, and how much it imparts in the management of things to be accustomed to them. For he was not only put to the worst in the fight for want of skill, but having rigged up an old ship, which had been a famous vessel forty years before, and shipped his citizens in her, she foundering, he was in danger of losing them all. But finding the enemy, as if he had been driving out of the sea, had, in contempt of him besieged Gythium, he presently set sail again, and taking them unexpectedly, dispersed and careless after their victory, landed in the night, burnt their camp, and killed a great number.

A few days after, as he was marching through a rough country, Nabis came suddenly upon him. The Achæans were dismayed, and in such difficult ground where the enemy had secured the advantage, despaired to get off with safety. Philopœmen made a little halt, and, viewing the ground, soon made it appear that the one important thing in war is skill in drawing up an army. For by advancing only a few paces, and, without any confusion or trouble, altering his order according to the nature of the place, he immediately relieved himself from every difficulty, and then charging, put the enemy to flight. But when he saw they fled, not towards the city, but dispersed every man a different way all over the field, which for wood and hills, brooks and hollows, was not passable by horse, he sounded a retreat, and encamped by broad daylight. Then foreseeing the enemy would endeavour to steal scatteringly into the city in the dark, he posted strong parties of the Achæans all along the watercourses and sloping ground near the walls. Many of Nabis' men fell into their hands. For returning not in a body, but as the chance of flight had disposed of everyone, they were caught like birds ere they could enter into the town.

These actions obtained him distinguished marks of affection and honour in all the theatres of Greece, but not without the secret ill-will of Titus Flamininus, who was naturally eager for glory, and thought it but reasonable a consul of Rome should be otherwise esteemed by the Achæans than a common Arcadian; especially as there was no comparison between what he and what Philopœmen had done for them, he having by one proclamation restored all Greece, as much as had been subject to Philip and the Macedonians, to liberty. After this, Titus made peace with Nabis, and Nabis was circumvented and slain by the Ætolians. Things being then in confusion at Sparta, Philopœmen laid hold of the occasion, and coming upon them with an army, prevailed with some by persuasion, with others by fear, till he brought the whole city over to the Achæans. As it was no small matter for Sparta to become a member of Achæa, this action gained him infinite praise from the Achæans, for having strengthened their confederacy by the addition of so great and powerful a city, and not a little goodwill from the nobility of Sparta itself, who hoped they had now procured an ally who would defend their freedom. Accordingly, having raised a sum of one hundred and twenty silver talents by the sale of the house and goods of Nabis, they decreed him the money, and sent a deputation in the name of the city to present it. But here the honesty of Philopœmen showed itself clearly to be a real, uncounterfeited virtue. For, first of all, there was not a man among them who would undertake to make him this offer of a present, but everyone excusing himself, and shifting it off upon his fellow, they laid the office at last on Timolaus, with whom he had lodged at Sparta. Then Timolaus came to Megalopolis, and was entertained by Philopœmen; but struck into admiration with the dignity of his life and manners, and the simplicity of his habits, judging him to be utterly inaccessible to any such considerations, he said nothing, but pretending other business, returned without a word mentioned of the present. He was sent again, and did just as formerly. But the third time with much ado, and faltering in his words, he acquainted Philopœmen with the goodwill of the city of Sparta to him. Philopœmen listened obligingly and gladly; and then went himself to Sparta, where he advised them, not to bribe good men and their friends, of whose virtue they might be sure without charge to themselves; but to buy off and silence ill citizens, who disquieted the city with their seditious speeches in the public assemblies; for it was better to bar liberty of speech in enemies than friends. Thus it appeared how much Philopœmen was above bribery.

Diophanes being afterwards general of the Achæans, and hearing the Lacedæmonians were bent on new commotions, resolved to chastise them; they, on the other side, being set upon war, were embroiling all Peloponnesus. Philopœmen on this occasion did all he could to keep Diophanes quiet and to make him sensible that as the times went, while

Antiochus and the Romans were disputing their pretensions with vast armies in the heart of Greece, it concerned a man in his position to keep a watchful eye over them, and dissembling, and putting up with any less important grievances, to preserve all quiet at home. Diophanes would not be ruled, but joined with Titus, and both together falling into Daconia, marched directly to Sparta. Philopœmen, upon this, took, in his indignation, a step which certainly was not lawful, nor in the strictest sense just, but boldly and loftily conceived. Entering into the town himself, he, a private man as he was, refused admission to both the consul of Rome and the general of the Achæans, quieted the disorders in the city, and reunited it on the same terms as before to the Achæan confederacy.

Yet afterwards, when he was general himself, upon some new misdemeanour of the Lacedæmonians, he brought back those who had been banished, put, as Polybius writes, eighty, according to Aristocrates three hundred and fifty, Spartans to death, razed the walls, took away a good part of their territory and transferred it to the Megalopolitans, forced out of the country and carried into Achæa all who had been made citizens of Sparta by tyrants, except three thousand who would not submit to banishment. These he sold for slaves, and with the money, as if to exult over them, built a colonnade at Megalopolis. Lastly, unworthily trampling upon the Lacedæmonians in their calamities, and gratifying his hostility by a most oppressive and arbitrary action, he abolished the laws of Lycurgus, and forced them to educate their children and live after the manner of the Achæans; as though, while they kept to the discipline of Lycurgus, there was no humbling their haughty spirits. In their present distress and adversity they allowed Philopœmen thus to cut the sinews of their commonwealth asunder, and behave themselves humbly and submissively. But afterwards, in no long time, obtaining the support of the Romans, they abandoned their new Achæan citizenship; and as much as in so miserable and ruined a condition they could, re-established their ancient discipline.

When the war betwixt Antiochus and the Romans broke out in Greece, Philopœmen was a private man. He repined grievously when he saw Antiochus lay idle at Chalcis, spending his time in unreasonable courtship and weddings, while his men lay dispersed in several towns, without order, or commanders, and minding nothing but their pleasures. He complained much that he was not himself in office, and said he envied the Romans their victory; and that if he had had the fortune to be then in command, he would have surprised and killed the whole army in the taverns.

When Antiochus was overcome, the Romans pressed harder upon Greece, and encompassed the Achæans with their power; the popular leaders in the several cities yielded before them; and their power speedily, under the divine guidance, advanced to the consummation due to it in the revolutions of fortune. Philopœmen, in this conjecture, carried himself like a good pilot in a high sea, sometimes shifting sail, and sometimes yielding, but still steering steady; and omitting no opportunity nor effort to keep all who were considerable, whether for eloquence or riches, fast to the defence of their common liberty.

Aristænus, a Megalopolitan of great credit among the Achæans, but always a favourer of the Romans, saying one day in the senate that the Romans should not be opposed, or displeased in any way, Philopœmen heard him with an impatient silence; but at last, not able to hold longer, said angrily to him, "And why be in such haste, wretched man, to behold the end of Greece?" Manius, the Roman consul, after the defeat of Antiochus, requested the Achæans to restore the banished Lacedæmonians to their country, which motion was seconded and supported by all the interest of Titus. But Philopœmen crossed it, not from ill-will to the men, but that they might be beholden to him and the Achæans, not to Titus and the Romans. For when he came to be general himself, he restored them. So impatient was his spirit of any subjection and so prone his nature to contest everything with men in power.

Being now three score and ten, and the eighth time general, he was in hope to pass in quiet, not only the year of his magistracy, but his remaining life. For as our diseases decline, as it is supposed with our declining bodily strength, so the quarrelling humour of the Greeks abated much with their failing political greatness. But fortune or some divine retributive power threw him down in the close of his life, like a successful runner who stumbles at the goal. It is reported, that being in company where one was praised for a great commander, he replied, there was no great account to be made of a man who had suffered himself to be taken alive by his enemies.

A few days after, news came that Dinocrates the Messenian, a particular enemy to Philopœmen, and for his wickedness and villainies generally hated, had induced Messene to revolt from the Achæans, and was about to seize upon a little place called Colonis. Philopœmen lay then sick of a fever at Argos. Upon the news he hasted away, and reached Megalopolis, which was distant above four hundred furlongs, in a day. From thence he immediately led out the horse, the noblest of the city, young men in the vigour of their age, and eager to proffer their service, both from attachment to

Philopœmen and zeal for the cause. As they marched towards Messene, they met with Dinocrates, near the hill of Evander, charged and routed him. But five hundred fresh men, who, being left for a guard to the country, came in late, happening to appear, the flying enemy rallied again about the hills. Philopœmen, fearing to be enclosed, and solicitous for his men, retreated over ground extremely disadvantageous, bringing up the rear himself. As he often faced, and made charges upon the enemy, he drew them upon himself; though they merely made movements at a distance, and shouted about him, nobody daring to approach him. In his care to save every single man, he left his main body so often, that at last he found himself alone among the thickest of his enemies. Yet even then none durst come up to him, but being pelted at a distance, and driven to stony steep places, he had great difficulty, with much spurring, to guide his horse aright. His age was no hindrance to him, for with perpetual exercise it was both strong and active; but being weakened with sickness, and tired with his long journey, his horse stumbling, he fell encumbered with his arms, and faint, upon a hard and rugged piece of ground. His head received such a shock with the fall that he lay awhile speechless, so that the enemy, thinking him dead, began to turn and strip him. But when they saw him lift up his head and open his eyes, they threw themselves all together upon him, bound his hands behind him, and carried him off, every kind of insult and contumely being lavished on him who truly had never so much as dreamed of being led in triumph by Dinocrates.

The Messenians, wonderfully elated with the news, thronged in swarms to the city gates. But when they saw Philopœmen in a posture so unsuitable to the glory of his great actions and famous victories, most of them, struck with grief and cursing the deceitful vanity of human fortune, even shed tears of compassion at the spectacle. Such tears by little and little turned to kind words, and it was almost in everybody's mouth that they ought to remember what he had done for them, and how he had preserved the common liberty, by driving away Nabis. Some few, to make their court to Dinocrates, were for torturing and then putting him to death as a dangerous and irreconcilable enemy; all the more formidable to Dinocrates, who had taken him a prisoner, should he after this misfortune regain his liberty. They put him at last into a dungeon underground, which they called the treasury, a place into which there came no air nor light from abroad; and which, having no doors, was closed with a great stone. This they rolled into the entrance and fixed, and placing a guard about it, left him. In the meantime Philopœmen's soldiers, recovering themselves after their flight, and fearing he was dead when he appeared nowhere, made a stand, calling him with loud cries, and reproaching one another with their unworthy and shameful escape; having betrayed their general, who, to preserve their lives, had lost his own. Then returning after much inquiry and search, hearing at last that he was taken they sent away messengers round about with the news. The Achæans resented the misfortune deeply, and decreed to send and demand him; and in the meantime drew their army together for his rescue.

While these things passed in Achæa, Dinocrates, fearing that any delay would save Philopœmen, and resolving to be beforehand with the Achæans, as soon as night had dispersed the multitude, sent in the executioner with poison, with orders not to stir from him till he had taken it. Philopœmen had then laid down, wrapt up in his cloak, not sleeping, but oppressed with grief and trouble; but seeing light, and a man with poison by him, struggled to sit up; and, taking the cup, asked the man if he heard anything of the horsemen, particularly Lycortas? The fellow answering, that most part had got off safe, he nodded, and looking cheerfully upon him, "It is well," he said, "that we have not been every way unfortunate"; and without a word more, drank it off, and laid him down again. His weakness offering but little resistance to the poison, it despatched him presently.

The news of his death filled all Achæa with grief and lamentation. The youth, with some of the chief of the several cities, met at Megalopolis with a resolution to take revenge without delay. They chose Lycortas general, and falling upon the Messenians, put all to fire and sword, till they all with one consent made their submission. Dinocrates, with as many as had voted for Philopœmen's death, anticipated their vengeance and killed themselves. Those who would have had him tortured, Lycortas put in chains and reserved for severer punishment. They burnt his body, and put the ashes into an urn, and then marched homeward, not as in an ordinary march, but with a kind of solemn pomp, half triumph, half funeral, crowns of victory on their heads, and tears in their eyes, and their captive enemies in fetters by them. Polybius, the general's son, carried the urn, so covered with garlands and ribbons as scarcely to be visible; and the noblest of the Achæans accompanied him. The soldiers followed rally armed and mounted, with looks neither altogether sad as in mourning, nor lofty as in victory. The people from all towns and villages in their way flocked out to meet him, as at his return from conquest, and, saluting the urn, fell in with the company and followed on to Megalopolis; where, when the old men, the women and children were mingled with the rest, the whole city was filled with sighs, complaints and cries, the loss of Philopœmen seeming to them the loss of their own greatness, and of their rank among the Achæans. Thus he was honourably buried according to his worth, and the prisoners were stoned about his tomb.

Many statues were set up, and many honours decreed to him by the several cities. One of the Romans in the time of Greece's affliction, after the destruction of Corinth, publicly accusing Philopœmen, as if he had been still alive, of having been the enemy of Rome, proposed that these memorials should be all removed. A discussion ensued, speeches were made, and Polybius answered the sycophant at large. And neither Mummius nor the lieutenants would suffer the honourable monuments of so great a man to be defaced, though he had often crossed both Titus and Manius. They justly distinguished, and as became honest men, betwixt usefulness and virtue—what is good in itself, and what is profitable to particular parties—judging thanks and reward due to him who does a benefit from him who receives it, and honour never to be denied by the good to the good. And so much concerning Philopœmen.

FLAMININUS[1]

WHAT TITUS QUINTIUS FLAMININUS, WHOM WE SELECT AS A PARALLEL TO Philopœmen, was in personal appearance, those who are curious may see by the brazen statue of him, which stands in Rome near that of the great Apollo, brought from Carthage, opposite to the Circus Maximus, with a Greek inscription upon it. The temper of his mind is said to have been of the warmest both in anger and in kindness, not indeed equally so in both respects; as in punishing he was ever moderate, never inflexible; but whatever courtesy or good turn he set about, he went through with it, and was as perpetually kind and obliging to those on whom he had poured his favours, as if they, not he, had been the benefactors; exerting himself for the security and preservation of what he seemed to consider his noblest possessions, those to whom he had done good. But being ever thirsty after honour, and passionate for glory, if anything of a greater and more extraordinary nature were to be done, he was eager to be the doer of it himself; and took more pleasure in those that needed, than in those that were capable of conferring favours; looking on the former as objects for his virtue, and on the latter as competitors in glory.

Rome had then many sharp contests going on, and her youth betaking themselves early to the wars, learned betimes the art of commanding; and Flamininus, having passed through the rudiments of soldiery, received his first charge in the war against Hannibal, as tribune under Marcellus, then consul. Marcellus, indeed, falling into an ambuscade, was cut off. But Titus, receiving the appointment of governor, as well of Tarentum, then retaken, as of the country about it, grew no less famous for his administration of justice, than for his military skill. This obtained him the office of leader and founder of two colonies which were sent into the cities of

Narnia and Cossa; which filled him with loftier hopes, and made him aspire to step over those previous honours which it was usual first to pass through, the offices of tribune of the people, prætor and ædile, and to level his aim immediately at the consulship. Having these colonies, and all their interest ready at his service, he offered himself as candidate; but the tribunes of the people, Fulvius and Manius,[2] and their party, strongly opposed him; alleging how unbecoming a thing it was that a man of such raw years, one who was yet, as it were, untrained, uninitiated in the first sacred rites and mysteries of government, should, in contempt of the laws, intrude and force himself into the sovereignty.

However, the senate remitted it to the people's choice and suffrage; who elected him (though not then arrived at his thirtieth year) consul with Sextus Ælius. The war against Philip and the Macedonians fell to Titus by lot, and some kind fortune, propitious at that time to the Romans, seems to have so determined it; as neither the people nor the state of things which were now to be dealt with were such as to require a general who would always be upon the point of force and mere blows, but rather were accessible to persuasion and gentle usage. It is true that the kingdom of Macedon furnished supplies enough to Philip for actual battle with the Romans; but to maintain a long and lingering war he must call in aid from Greece; must thence procure his supplies; there find his means of retreat; Greece, in a word, would be his resource for all the requisites of his army. Unless, therefore, the Greeks could be withdrawn from siding with Philip, this war with him must not expect its decision from a single battle. Now Greece (which had not hitherto held much correspondence with the Romans, but first began an intercourse on this occasion) would not so soon have embraced a foreign authority, instead of the commanders she had been inured to, had not the general of these strangers been of a kind, gentle nature, one who worked rather by fair means than force; of a persuasive address in all applications to others, and no less courteous and open to all addresses of others to him; and above all bent and determined on justice. But the story of his actions will best illustrate these particulars.

Titus observed that both Sulpicius and Publius, who had been his predecessors in that command, had not taken the field against the Macedonians till late in the year; and then, too, had not set their hands properly to the war, but had kept skirmishing and scouting here and there for passes and provisions, and never came to close fighting with Philip. He resolved not to trifle away a year, as they had done, at home in ostentation of the honour, and in domestic administration, and only then to join the army, with the pitiful hope of protracting the term of office through a second year, acting as consul in the first, and as general in the latter. He was, moreover, infinitely desirous to employ his authority with effect upon the war, which made him slight those home honours and prerogatives. Requesting, therefore, of the senate, that his brother Lucius might act with him as admiral of the navy, and taking with him to be the edge, as it were, of the expedition three thousand still young and vigorous soldiers, of those who, under Scipio, had defeated Asdrubal in Spain, and Hannibal in Africa, he got safe into Epirus; and found Publius encamped with his army, over against Philip, who had long made good the pass over the river Apsus, and the straits there; Publius not having been able, for the natural strength of the place, to effect anything against him. Titus therefore took upon himself the conduct of the army, and, having dismissed Publius, examined the ground. The place is in strength not inferior to Tempe, though it lacks the trees and green woods, and the pleasant meadows and walks that adorn Tempe. The Apsus, making its way between vast and lofty mountains which all but meet above a single deep ravine in the midst, is not unlike the river Peneus in the rapidity of its current and in its general appearance. It covers the foot of those hills, and leaves only a craggy, narrow path cut out beside the stream, not easily passable at anytime for an army, but not at all when guarded by an enemy.

There were some, therefore, who would have had Titus make a circuit through Dassaretis, and take an easy and safe road by the district of Lyncus. But he, fearing that if he should engage himself too far from the sea in barren and untilled countries, and Philip should decline fighting, he might, through want of provisions, be constrained to march back again to the seaside without effecting anything, as his predecessor had done before him, embraced the resolution of forcing his way over the mountains. But Philip, having possessed himself of them with his army, showered down his darts and arrows from all parts upon the Romans. Sharp encounters took place, and many fell wounded and slain on both sides, and there seemed but little likelihood of thus ending the war; when some of the men, who fed their cattle thereabouts, came to Titus with a discovery, that there was a roundabout way which the enemy neglected to guard: through which they undertook to conduct his army, and to bring it, within three days at furthest, to the top of the hills. To gain the surer credit with him, they said that Charops, son of Machatas, a leading man in Epirus, who was friendly to the Romans, and aided them (though, for fear of Philip, secretly), was privy to the design. Titus gave their information belief, and sent a captain with four thousand foot and three hundred horse; these herdsmen being their guides, but kept in bonds. In the daytime they lay still under the covert of the hollow and woody places, but in the night they marched by moonlight, the moon being then at the full. Titus, having detached this party, lay quiet with his main body, merely keeping up the attention of the enemy by some slight skirmishing. But when the day arrived that those who stole round were expected upon the top of the hill, he drew up his forces early in the morning, as well the light-armed as the heavy, and, dividing them into three parts, himself led the van, marching his men up the narrow passage along the bank, darted at by the Macedonians and engaging, in this difficult ground, hand to hand with his assailants; whilst the other two divisions on either side of him threw themselves with great alacrity among the rocks. Whilst they were struggling forward, the sun rose, and a thin smoke, like a mist, hanging on the hills, was seen rising at a distance, unperceived by the enemy, being behind them, as they stood on the heights; and the Romans, also, as yet under suspense, in the toil and difficulty they were in, could only doubtfully construe the sight according to their desires. But as it grew thicker and thicker, blackening the air, and mounting to a greater height, they no longer doubted but it was the fire-signal of their companions; and, raising a triumphant shout, forcing their way onwards, they drove the enemy back into the roughest ground; while the other party echoed back their acclamations from the top of the mountain.

The Macedonians fled with all the speed they could make; there fell, indeed, not more than two thousand of them; for the difficulties of the place rescued them from pursuit. But the Romans pillaged their camp, seized upon their money and slaves, and, becoming absolute masters of the pass, traversed all Epirus; but with such order and discipline, with such temperance and moderation, that, though they were far from the sea, at a great distance from their vessels, and stinted of their monthly allowance of corn, and though they had much difficulty in buying, they nevertheless abstained altogether from plundering the country, which had provisions enough of all sorts in it. For intelligence being received that Philip, making a flight, rather than a march, through Thessaly, forced the inhabitants from the towns to take shelter in the mountains, burnt down the towns themselves, and gave up as spoil to his soldiers all the property which it had been found impossible to remove, abandoning, as it would seem, the whole country to the Romans, Titus was, therefore, very desirous, and entreated his soldiers that they would pass through it as if it were their own, or as if a place trusted into their hands; and, indeed, they quickly perceived, by the event, what benefit they derived from this moderate and orderly conduct. For they no sooner set foot in Thessaly, but the cities opened their gates, and the Greeks, within Thermopylæ, were all eagerness and excitement to ally themselves with them. The Achæans abandoned their alliance with Philip, and voted to join with the Romans in actual arms against him; and the Opuntians, though the Ætolians, who were zealous allies of the Romans, were willing and desirous to undertake the protection of the city, would not listen to proposals from them; but sending for Titus, intrusted and committed themselves to his charge.

It is told of Pyrrhus, that when first, from an adjacent hill or watchtower which gave him a prospect of the Roman army, he descried them drawn up in order, he observed, that he saw nothing barbarian-like in this barbarian line of battle. And all who came near Titus could not choose but say as much of him, at their first view. For they who had been told by the Macedonians of an invader, at the head of a barbarian army, carrying everywhere slavery and destruction on his sword's point; when, in lieu of such an one, they met a man, in the flower of his age, of a gentle and humane aspect, a Greek in his voice and language, and a lover of honour, were wonderfully pleased and attracted; and when they left him, they filled the cities, wherever they went, with favourable feelings for him, and with the belief that in him they might find the protector and assertor of their liberties. And when afterwards, on Philip's professing a desire for peace, Titus made a tender to him of peace and friendship, upon the condition that the Greeks be left to their own laws, and that he should withdraw his garrisons, which he refused to comply with, now after these proposals the universal belief even of the favourers and partisans of Philip was, that the Romans came not to fight against the Greeks, but for the Greeks against the Macedonians.

Accordingly, all the rest of Greece came to peaceable terms with him. But as he marched into Bœotia, without committing the least act of hostility, the nobility and chief men of Thebes came out of their city to meet him, devoted under the influence of Brachylles to the Macedonian alliance, but desirous at the same time to show honour and deference to Titus; as they were, they conceived, in amity with both parties. Titus received them in the most obliging and courteous manner, but kept going gently on, questioning and inquiring of them, and sometimes entertaining them with narratives of his own, till his soldiers might a little recover from the weariness of their journey. Thus passing on, he and the Thebans came together into their city, not much to their satisfaction; but yet they could not well deny him entrance, as a good number of his men attended him in. Titus, however, now he was within, as if he had not had the city at his mercy, came forward and addressed them, urging them to join the Roman interest. King Attalus followed to the same effect. And he, indeed, trying to play the advocate, beyond what it seems his age could bear, was seized, in the midst of his speech, with a sudden flux or dizziness, and swooned away; and, not long after, was conveyed by ship into Asia, and died there. The Bœotians joined the Roman alliance.

But now, when Philip sent an embassy to Rome, Titus despatched away agents on his part, too, to solicit the senate, if they should continue the war, to continue him in his command, or if they determined an end to that, that he might have the honour of concluding the peace. Having a great passion for distinction, his fear was, that if another general were commissioned to carry on the war, the honour even of what was passed would be lost to him; and his friends transacted matters so well on his behalf, that Philip was unsuccessful in his proposals, and the management of the war was confirmed in his hands. He no sooner received the senate's determination, but, big with hopes, he marched directly into Thessaly, to engage Philip; his army consisting of twenty-six thousand men, out of which the Ætolians furnished six thousand foot and four hundred horse. The forces of Philip were much about the same number. In this eagerness to encounter, they advanced against each other, till both were near Scotussa, where they resolved to hazard a battle. Nor had the approach of these two formidable armies the effect that might have been supposed, to strike into the generals a mutual terror of each other; it rather inspired them with ardour and ambition; on the Romans' part, to be the conquerors of Macedon, a name which Alexander had made famous amongst them for strength and valour; whilst the Macedonians, on the other hand, esteeming of the Romans as an enemy very different from the Persians, hoped, if victory stood on their side, to make the name of Philip more glorious than that of Alexander. Titus, therefore, called upon his soldiers to play the part of valiant men, because they were now to act their parts upon the most illustrious theatre of the world, Greece, and to contend with the bravest antagonists. And Philip, on the other side, commenced a harangue to his men, as usual before an engagement, and to be the better heard (whether it were merely a mischance, or the result of unseasonable haste, not observing what he did), mounted an eminence outside their camp, which proved to be a burying-place; and much disturbed by the despondency that seized his army at the unluckiness of the omen, all that day kept in his camp, and declined fighting.

But on the morrow, as day came on, after a soft and rainy night, the clouds changing into a mist filled all the plain with thick darkness; and a dense foggy air descending, by the time it was full day, from the adjacent mountains into the ground betwixt the two camps, concealed them from each other's view. The parties sent out on either side, some for ambuscade, some for discovery, falling in upon one another quickly after they were thus detached, began the fight at what are called the Cynos Cephalæ, a number of sharp tops of hills that stand close to one another, and have the name from some resemblance in their shape. Now many vicissitudes and changes happening, as may well be expected, in such an uneven field of battle, sometimes hot pursuit, and sometimes as rapid a flight, the generals on both sides kept sending in succours from the main bodies, as they saw their men pressed or giving ground, till at length the heavens clearing up, let them see what was going on, upon which the whole armies engaged. Philip, who was in the right wing, from the advantage of the higher ground which he had, threw on the Romans the whole weight of his phalanx, with a force which they were unable to sustain; the dense array of spears, and the pressure of the compact mass overpowering them. But the king's left wing being broken up by the hilliness of the place, Titus observing it, and cherishing little or no hopes on that side where his own gave ground, makes in all haste to the other, and there charges in upon the Macedonians; who, in consequence of the inequality and roughness of the ground, could not keep their phalanx entire, nor line their ranks to any great depth (which is the great point of their strength), but were forced to fight man for man under heavy and unwieldy armour. For the Macedonian phalanx is like some single powerful animal, irresistible so long as it is embodied into one, and keeps its order, shield touching shield, all as in a piece; but if it be once broken, not only is the joint force lost, but the individual soldiers also who composed it lose each one his own single strength, because of the nature of their armour; and because each of them is strong, rather, as he makes a part of the whole, than in himself. When these were routed, some gave chase to the flyers, others charged the flanks of those Macedonians who were still fighting, so that the conquering wing, also, was quickly disordered, took to flight, and threw down its arms. There were then slain no less than eight thousand, and about five thousand were taken prisoners; and the Ætolians were blamed as having been the main occasion that Philip himself got safe off.

For whilst the Romans were in pursuit, they fell to ravaging and plundering the camp, and did it so completely, that when the others returned, they found no booty in it.

This bred at first hard words, quarrels, and misunderstandings betwixt them. But, afterwards, they galled Titus more by ascribing the victory to themselves, and prepossessing the Greeks with reports to that effect; insomuch that poets, and people in general in the songs that were sung or written in honour of the action, still ranked the Ætolians foremost. One of the pieces most current was the following epigram:

> Naked and tombless see, O passerby,
> The thirty thousand men of Thessaly,
> Slain by the Ætolians and the Latin band,
> That came with Titus from Italia's land;
> Alas for mighty Macedon! That day,
> Swift as a roe, King Philip fled away.

This was composed by Alcæus in mockery of Philip, exaggerating the number of the slain. However, being everywhere repeated, and by almost everybody, Titus was more nettled at it than Philip. The latter merely retorted upon Alcæus with some elegiac verses of his own:

> Naked and leafless see, O passerby,
> The cross that shall Alcæus crucify.

But such little matters extremely fretted Titus, who was ambitious of a reputation among the Greeks; and he therefore acted in all after-occurrences by himself, paying but very slight regard to the Ætolians. This offended them in their turn; and when Titus listened to terms of accommodation, and admitted an embassy upon the proffers of the Macedonian king, the Ætolians made it their business to publish through all the cities of Greece, that this was the conclusion of all; that he was selling Philip a peace at a time when it was in his hand to destroy the very roots of the war, and to overthrow the power which had first inflicted servitude upon Greece. But whilst with these and the like rumours the Ætolians laboured to shake the Roman confederates, Philip, making overtures of submission of himself and his kingdom to the discretion of Titus and the Romans, put an end to those jealousies, as Titus, by accepting them, did to the war. For he reinstated Philip in his kingdom of Macedon, but made it a condition that he should quit Greece, and that he should pay one thousand talents; he took from him also all his shipping, save ten vessels; and sent away Demetrius, one of his sons, hostage to Rome; improving his opportunity to the best advantage, and taking wise precautions for the future. For Hannibal the African, a professed enemy to the Roman name, an exile from his own country, and not long since arrived at King Antiochus' court, was already stimulating that prince, not to be wanting to the good fortune that had been hitherto so propitious to his affairs; the magnitude of his successes having gained him the surname of the Great. He had begun to level his aim at universal monarchy, but above all he was eager to measure himself with the Romans. Had not, therefore, Titus upon a principle of prudence and foresight, lent an ear to peace, and had Antiochus found the Romans still at war in Greece with Philip, and had these two, the most powerful and warlike princes of that age, confederated for their common interests against the Roman state, Rome might once more have run no less a risk, and been reduced to no less extremities, than she had experienced under Hannibal. But now, Titus opportunely introducing this peace between the wars, despatching the present danger before the new one had arrived, at once disappointed Antiochus of his first hopes and Philip of his last.

When the ten commissioners, delegated to Titus from the senate, advised him to restore the rest of Greece to their liberty, but that Corinth, Chalcis, and Demetrias should be kept garrisoned for security against Antiochus; the Ætolians on this, breaking out into loud accusations, agitated all the cities, calling upon Titus to strike off the shackles of Greece (so Philip used to term those three cities), and asking the Greeks whether it were not matter of much consolation to them that, though their chains weighed heavier, yet they were now smoother and better polished than formerly, and whether Titus were not deservedly admired by them as their benefactor, who had unshackled the feet of Greece, and tied her up by the neck; Titus, vexed and angry at this, made it his request to the senate, and at last prevailed in it, that the garrisons in these cities should be dismissed, that so the Greeks might be no longer debtors to him for a partial, but for an entire favour. It was now the time of the celebration of the Isthmian games; and the seats around the racecourse were crowded with an unusual multitude of spectators; Greece, after long wars, having regained not only peace, but hopes of liberty, and being able once more to keep holiday in safety. A trumpet sounded to command silence; and the crier, stepping forth amidst the spectators, made proclamation, that the Roman senate and Titus Quintius, the proconsular general, having vanquished King Philip and the Macedonians, restored the Corinthians, Locrians, Phocians,

Eubœans, Achæans of Phthiotis, Magnetians, Thessalians, and Perrhæbians to their own lands, laws, and liberties; remitting all impositions upon them, and withdrawing all garrisons from their cities. At first, many heard not at all, and others not distinctly, what was said; but there was a confused and uncertain stir among the assembled people, some wondering, some asking, some calling out to have it proclaimed again. When, therefore, fresh silence was made, the crier raising his voice, succeeded in making himself generally heard; and recited the decree again. A shout of joy followed it, so loud that it was heard as far as the sea. The whole assembly rose and stood up; there was no further thought of the entertainment; all were only eager to leap up and salute and address their thanks to the deliverer and champion of Greece. What we often hear alleged, in proof of the force of human voices, was actually verified upon this occasion. Crows that were accidentally flying over the course fell down dead into it. The disruption of the air must be the cause of it; for the voices being numerous, and the acclamation violent, the air breaks with it and can no longer give support to the birds, but lets them tumble, like one that should attempt to walk upon a vacuum; unless we should rather imagine them to fall and die, shot with the noise as a dart. It is possible, too, that there may be a circular agitation of the air, which, like marine whirlpools, may have a violent direction of this sort given to it from the excess of its fluctuation.

But for Titus; the sports being now quite at an end, so beset was he on every side, and by such multitudes, that had he not, foreseeing the probable throng and concourse of the people, timely withdrawn, he would scarce, it is thought, have ever got clear of them. When they had tired themselves with acclamations all about his pavilion, and night was now come, wherever friends or fellow-citizens met, they joyfully saluted and embraced each other, and went home to feast and carouse together. And there, no doubt, redoubling their joy, they began to recollect and talk of the state of Greece, what wars she had incurred in defence of her liberty, and yet was never perhaps mistress of a more settled or grateful one than this which other men's labours had won for her; almost without one drop of blood, or one citizen's loss to be mourned for, she had this day had put into her hands the most glorious of rewards, and best worth the contending for. Courage and wisdom are, indeed, rarities amongst men, but of all that is good, a just man it would seem is the most scarce. Such as Agesilaus, Lysander, Nicias, and Alcibiades, knew how to play the general's part, how to manage a war, how to bring off their men victorious by land and sea; but how to employ that success to generous and honest purposes they had not known. For should a man except the achievement at Marathon, the sea-fight at Salamis, the engagements at Platæa and Thermopylæ, Cimon's exploits at Eurymedon, and on the coasts of Cyprus, Greece fought all her battles against, and to enslave, herself; she erected all her trophies to her own shame and misery, and was brought to ruin and desolation almost wholly by the guilt and ambition of her great men. A foreign people, appearing just to retain some embers, as it were, some faint remainders of a common character derived to them from their ancient sires, a nation from whom it was a mere wonder that Greece should reap any benefit by word or thought, these are they who have retrieved Greece from her severest dangers and distresses, have rescued her out of the hands of insulting lords and tyrants, and reinstated her in her former liberties.

Thus they entertained their tongues and thoughts: whilst Titus by his actions made good what had been proclaimed. For he immediately despatched away Lentulus to Asia, to set the Bargylians free, Titillius to Thrace, to see the garrisons of Philip removed out of the towns and islands there, while Publius Villius set sail, in order to treat with Antiochus about the freedom of the Greeks under him. Titus himself passed on to Chalcis, and sailing thence to Magnesia, dismantled the garrisons there, and surrendered the government into the people's hands. Shortly after, he was appointed at Argos to preside in the Nemean games, and did his part in the management of that solemnity singularly well; and made a second publication there by the crier of liberty to the Greeks; and, visiting all the cities, he exhorted them to the practice of obedience to law, of constant justice, and unity, and friendship one towards another. He suppressed their factions, brought home their political exiles; and, in short, his conquest over the Macedonians did not seem to give him a more lively pleasure, than to find himself prevalent in reconciling Greeks with Greeks; so that their liberty seemed now the least part of the kindness he conferred upon them.

The story goes, that when Lycurgus the orator had rescued Xenocrates the philosopher from the collectors who were hurrying him away to prison for non-payment of the alien tax, and had them punished for the licence they had been guilty of, Xenocrates afterwards meeting the children of Lycurgus, "My sons," said he, "I am nobly repaying your father for his kindness; he has the praises of the whole people in return for it." But the returns which attended Titus Quintius and the Romans, for their beneficence to the Greeks, terminated not in empty praises only; for these proceedings gained them, deservedly, credit and confidence, and thereby power, among all nations, for many not only admitted the Roman commanders, but even sent and entreated to be under their protection; neither was this done by popular governments alone, or by single cities; but kings oppressed by kings cast themselves into these protecting hands. Insomuch that in a very short time (though perchance not without divine influence in it) all the world did homage to them. Titus himself thought more highly of his liberation of Greece than of any other of his actions, as appears by the inscription with which he dedicated some silver targets, together with his own shield, to Apollo at Delphi:

> Ye Spartan Tyndarids, twin sons of Jove,
> Who in swift horsemanship have placed your love,
> Titus, of great Æneas' race, leaves this
> In honour of the liberty of Greece.

He offered also to Apollo a golden crown, with this inscription:

> This golden crown upon thy locks divine,
> O blest Latonia's son, was set to shine
> By the great captain of the Ænean name.
> O Phœbus, grant the noble Titus fame!

The same event has twice occurred to the Greeks in the city of Corinth. Titus, then, and Nero again in our days, both at Corinth, and both alike at the celebration of the Isthmian games, permitted the Greeks to enjoy their own laws and liberty. The former (as has been said) proclaimed it by the crier; but Nero did it in the public meeting-place from the tribunal, in a speech which he himself made to the people. This, however, was long after.

Titus now engaged in a most gallant and just war upon Nabis, that most profligate and lawless tyrant of the Lacedæmonians, but in the end disappointed the expectations of the Greeks. For when he had an opportunity of taking him, he purposely let it slip, and struck up a peace with him, leaving Sparta to bewail an unworthy slavery; whether it were that he feared, if the war should be protracted, Rome would send a new general who might rob him of the glory of it; or that emulation and envy of Philopœmen (who had signalised himself among the Greeks upon all other occasions, but in that war especially had done wonders both for matter of courage and counsel, and whom the Achæans magnified in their theatres, and put into the same balance of glory with Titus), touched him to the quick; and that he scorned that an ordinary Arcadian, who had commanded in a few encounters upon the confines of his native district, should be spoken of in terms of equality with a Roman consul, waging war as the protector of Greece in general. But, besides, Titus was not without an apology too for what he did, namely, that he put an end to the war only when he foresaw that the tyrant's destruction must have been attended with the ruin of the other Spartans.

The Achæans, by various decrees, did much to show Titus honour: none of these returns, however, seemed to come up to the height of the actions that merited them, unless it were one present they made him, which affected and pleased him beyond all the rest; which was this. The Romans, who in the war with Hannibal had the misfortune to be taken captives, were sold about here and there, and dispersed into slavery; twelve hundred in number were at that time in Greece. The reverse of their fortune always rendered them objects of compassion; but more particularly, as well might be, when they now met, some with their sons, some with their brothers, others with their acquaintance; slaves with their free, and captives with their victorious countrymen. Titus, though deeply concerned on their behalf, yet took none of them from their masters by constraint. But the Achæans, redeeming them at five pounds a man, brought them all together into one place, and made a present of them to him, as he was just going on shipboard, so that he now sailed away with the fullest satisfaction; his generous actions having procured him as generous returns, worthy a brave man and a lover of his country. This seemed the most glorious part of all his succeeding triumph; for these redeemed Romans (as it is the custom for slaves, upon their manumission, to shave their heads and wear felt hats) followed in that habit in the procession. To add to the glory of this show, there were the Grecian helmets, the Macedonian targets and long spears, borne with the rest of the spoils in public view, besides vast sums of money; Tuditanus says, 3,713 pounds weight of massy gold, 43,270 of silver, 14,514 pieces of coined gold, called Philippics, which was all over and above the thousand talents which Philip owed, and which the Romans were afterwards prevailed upon, chiefly by the mediation of Titus, to remit to Philip, declaring him their ally and confederate, and sending him home his hostage son.

Shortly after, Antiochus entered Greece with a numerous fleet and a powerful army, soliciting the cities there to sedition and revolt; abetted in all and seconded by the Ætolians, who for this long time had borne a grudge and secret enmity to the Romans, and now suggested to him, by the way of a cause and pretext of war, that he came to bring the Greeks liberty. When, indeed, they never wanted it less, as they were free already, but, in lack of really honourable grounds, he was instructed to employ these lofty professions. The Romans, in the interim, in the great apprehension of revolutions and revolt in Greece, and of his great reputation for military strength, despatched the consul Manius Acilius to take the charge of the war, and Titus, as his lieutenant, out of regard to the Greeks: some of whom he no sooner saw, but he confirmed them in the Roman interests; others, who began to falter, like a timely physician, by the use of the strong remedy of their own affection for himself, he was able to arrest in the first stage of the disease, before they had committed themselves to any great error. Some few there were whom the Ætolians were beforehand with, and had so wholly perverted that he could do no good with them; yet these, however angry and exasperated before, he saved and protected when the engagement was over. For Antiochus, receiving a defeat at Thermopylæ, not only fled the field, but hoisted sail instantly for Asia. Manius, the consul, himself invaded and besieged a part of the Ætolians, while King Philip had permission to reduce the rest. Thus while, for instance, the Dolopes and Magnesians on the one hand, the Athamanes and Aperantians on the other, were ransacked by the Macedonians, and while Manius laid Heraclea waste, and besieged Naupactus, then in the Ætolians' hands, Titus, still with a compassionate care for Greece, sailed across from Peloponnesus to the consul: and began first of all to chide him, that the victory should be owing alone to his arms, and yet he should suffer Philip to bear away the prize and profit of the war, and set wreaking his anger upon a single town, whilst the Macedonians overran several nations and kingdoms. But as he happened to stand then in view of the besieged, they no sooner spied him out, but they call to him from their wall, they stretch forth their hands, they supplicate and entreat him. At the time, he said not a word more, but turning about with tears in his eyes, went his way. Some little while after he discussed the matter so effectually with Manius, that he won him over from his passion, and prevailed with him to give a truce and time to the Ætolians to send deputies to Rome to petition the senate for terms of moderation.

But the hardest task, and that which put Titus to the greatest difficulty, was to entreat with Manius for the Chalcidians, who had incensed him on account of a marriage which Antiochus had made in their city, even whilst the war was on foot; a match noways suitable in point of age, he an elderly man being enamoured with a mere girl; and as little proper for the time, in the midst of a war. She was the daughter of one Cleoptolemus, and is said to have been wonderfully beautiful. The Chalcidians, in consequence, embraced the king's interests with zeal and alacrity, and let him make their city the basis of his operations during the war. Thither, therefore, he made with all speed, when he was routed and fled; and reaching Chalcis, without making any stay, taking this young lady, and his money and friends with him, away he sails to Asia. And now Manius' indignation carrying him in all haste against the Chalcidians, Titus hurried after him, endeavouring to pacify and to entreat him; and at length succeeded both with him and the chief men among the Romans.

The Chalcidians, thus owing their lives to Titus, dedicated to him all the best and most magnificent of their sacred buildings, inscriptions upon which may be seen to run thus to this day: THE PEOPLE DEDICATE THIS GYM-NASIUM TO TITUS AND TO HERCULES; so again: THE PEOPLE CONSECRATE THE DELPHINIUM TO TITUS AND TO HERCULES; and what is yet more, even in our time, a priest of Titus was formerly elected and declared; and after sacrifice and libation, they sing a set song, much of which for the length of it we omit, but shall transcribe the closing verses—

> The Roman Faith, whose aid of yore
> Our vows were offered to implore,
> We worship now and evermore.
> To Rome, to Titus, and to Jove,
> O maidens, in the dances move.
> Dances and Io-Pæans too
> Unto the Roman Faith are due,
> O Saviour Titus, and to you.

Other parts of Greece also heaped honours upon him suitable to his merits, and what made all those honours true and real, was the surprising goodwill and affection which his moderation and equity of character had won for him. For if he were at anytime at variance with anybody in matters of business, or out of emulation and rivalry (as with Philopœmen, and again with Diophanes, when in office as general of the Achæns), his resentment never went far, nor did it ever break out into acts; but when it had vented itself in some citizen-like freedom of speech, there was an end of it. In fine, nobody charged malice or bitterness upon his nature, though many imputed hastiness and levity to it; in general, he was the most attractive and agreeable of companions, and could speak, too, both with grace and forcibly. For instance, to divert the Achæans from the conquest of the isle of Zacynthus,

"If," said he, "they put their head too far out of Peloponnesus, they may hazard themselves as much as a tortoise out of its shell." Again, when he and Philip first met to treat of a cessation and peace, the latter complaining that Titus came with a mighty train, while he himself came alone and unattended, "Yes," replied Titus, "you have left yourself alone by killing your friends." At another time, Dinocrates, the Messenian, having drunk too much at a merrymeeting in Rome, danced there in woman's clothes, and the next day addressed himself to Titus for assistance in his design to get Messene out of the hands of the Achæans. "This," replied Titus, "will be matter for consideration; my only surprise is that a man with such purposes on his hands should be able to dance and sing at drinking parties." When, again, the ambassadors of Antiochus were recounting to those of Achæa the various multitudes composing their royal master's forces, and ran over a long catalogue of hard names, "I supped once," said Titus, "with a friend, and could not forbear expostulating with him at the number of dishes he had provided, and said I wondered where he had furnished himself with such a variety; 'Sir,' replied he, 'to confess the truth, it is all hog's flesh differently cooked.' And so, men of Achæa, when you are told of Antiochus' lancers, and pikemen, and foot-guards, I advise you not to be surprised; since in fact they are all Syrians, differently armed."

After his achievements in Greece, and when the war with Antiochus was at an end, Titus was created censor; the most eminent office, and, in a manner, the highest preferment, in the commonwealth. The son of Marcellus, who had been five times consul, was his colleague. These, by virtue of their office, cashiered four senators of no great distinction, and admitted to the roll of citizens all freeborn residents. But this was more by constraint than their own choice; for Terentius Culeo, then tribune of the people, to spite the nobility, spurred on the populace to order it to be done. At this time, the two greatest and most eminent persons in the city, Africanus Scipio and Marcus Cato, were at variance. Titus named Scipio first member of the senate; and involved himself in a quarrel with Cato, on the following unhappy occasion. Titus had a brother, Lucius Flamininus, very unlike him in all points of character, and, in particular, low and dissolute in his pleasures, and flagrantly regardless of all decency. He kept as a companion a boy whom he used to carry about with him, not only when he had troops under his charge, but even when the care of a province was committed to him. One day at a drinking-bout, when the youngster was wantoning with Lucius, "I love you, sir, so dearly," said he, "that preferring your satisfaction to my own, I came away without seeing the gladiators, though I have never seen a man killed in my life." Lucius, delighted with what the boy said, answered, "Let not that trouble you; I can satisfy that longing," and with that orders a condemned man to be fetched out of the prison, and the executioner to be sent for, and commands him to strike off the man's head, before they rose from table. Valerius Antias only so far varies the story as to make it a woman for whom he did it. But Livy says that in Cato's own speech the statement is that a Gaulish deserter coming with his wife and children to the door, Lucius took him into the banqueting-room, and killed him with his own hand, to gratify his paramour. Cato, it is probable, might say this by way of aggravation of the crime; but that the slain was no such fugitive, but a prisoner, and one condemned to die, not to mention other authorities, Cicero tells us in his treatise on Old Age, where he brings in Cato, himself, giving that account of the matter.

However, this is certain; Cato, during his censorship, made a severe scrutiny into the senators' lives in order to the purging and reforming the house, and expelled Lucius, though he had been once consul before, and though the punishment seemed to reflect dishonour on his brother also. Both of them presented themselves to the assembly of the people in a suppliant manner, not without tears in their eyes, requesting that Cato might show the reason and cause of his fixing such a stain upon so honourable a family. The citizens thought it a modest and moderate request. Cato, however, without any retraction or reserve, at once came forward, and standing up with his colleague interrogated Titus as to whether he knew the story of the supper. Titus answered in the negative, Cato related it, and challenged Lucius to a formal denial of it. Lucius made no reply, whereupon the people adjudged the disgrace just and suitable, and waited upon Cato home from the tribunal in great state. But Titus still so deeply resented his brother's degradation, that he allied himself with those who had long borne a grudge against Cato; and winning over a major part of the senate, he revoked and made void all the contracts, leases, and bargains made by Cato, relating to public revenues, and also got numerous actions and accusations brought against him; carrying on against a lawful magistrate and excellent citizens, for the sake of one who was indeed his relation, but was unworthy to be so, and had but gotten his deserts, a course of bitter and violent attacks, which it would be hard to say were either right or patriotic. Afterwards, however, at a public spectacle in the theatre, at which the senators appeared as usual, sitting, as became their rank, in the first seats, when Lucius was spied at the lower end, seated in a mean, dishonourable place, it made a great impression upon the people, nor could they endure the sight, but kept calling out to him to move, until he did move, and went in among those of consular dignity, who received him into their seats.

This natural ambition of Titus was well enough looked upon by the world whilst the wars we have given a relation of afforded competent fuel to feed it; as, for instance, when after the expiration of his consulship, he had a command as military tribune, which nobody pressed upon him. But being now out of all employ in the government, and advanced in years, he showed his defects more plainly; allowing himself, in this inactive remainder of life, to be carried away with the passion for reputation, as uncontrollably as any youth. Some such transport, it is thought, betrayed him into a proceeding against Hannibal, which lost him the regard of many. For Hannibal, having fled his country, first took sanctuary with Antiochus; but he, having been glad to obtain a peace, after the battle in Phrygia, Hannibal was put to shift for himself, by a second flight, and, after wandering through many countries, fixed at length in Bithynia, proffering his service to King Prusias. Everyone at Rome knew where he was, but looked upon him, now in his weakness and old age, with no sort of apprehension, as one whom fortune had quite cast off. Titus, however, coming thither as ambassador, though he was sent from the senate to Prusias upon another errand, yet seeing Hannibal resident there, it stirred up resentment in him to find that he was yet alive. And though Prusias used much intercession and entreaties in favour of him, as his suppliant and familiar friend, Titus was not to be entreated. There was an ancient oracle, it seems, which prophesied thus of Hannibal's end:

Libyssan earth shall Hannibal inclose.

He interpreted this to be meant of the African Libya, and that he should be buried in Carthage; as if he might yet expect to return and end his life there. But there is a sandy place in Bithynia, bordering on the sea, and near it a little village called Libyssa. It was Hannibal's chance to be staying here, and, having ever from the beginning had a distrust of the easiness and cowardice of Prusias, and a fear of the Romans, he had, long before, ordered seven underground passages to be dug from his house, leading from his lodging and running a considerable distance in various opposite directions, all undiscernible from without. As soon, therefore, as he heard what Titus had ordered, he attempted to make his escape through these mines; but finding them beset with the king's guards, he resolved upon making away with himself. Some say that, wrapping his upper garment about his neck, he commanded his servant to set his knee against his back, and not to cease twisting and pulling it till he had completely strangled him. Others say he drank bull's blood, after the example of Themistocles and Midas. Livy writes that he had poison in readiness, which he mixed for the purpose, and that, taking the cup in his hand, "Let us ease," said he, "the Romans of their continual dread and care, who think it long and tedious to await the death of a hated old man. Yet Titus will not bear away a glorious victory, nor one worthy of those ancestors who sent to caution Pyrrhus, an enemy, and a conqueror too, against the poison prepared for him by traitors."

Thus various are the reports of Hannibal's death; but when the news of it came to the senator's ears, some felt indignation against Titus for it, blaming as well his officiousness as his cruelty; who when there was nothing to urge it, out of mere appetite for distinction to have it said that he had caused Hannibal's death, sent him to his grave when he was now like a bird that in its old age has lost its feathers, and incapable of flying, is let alone to live tamely without molestation.

They began also now to regard with increased admiration the clemency and magnanimity of Scipio Africanus, and called to mind how he, when he had vanquished in Africa the till then invincible and terrible Hannibal, neither banished him his country, nor exacted of his countrymen that they should give him up. At a parley just before they joined battle, Scipio gave him his hand, and in the peace made after it, he put no hard article upon him, nor insulted over his fallen fortune. It is told, too, that they had another meeting afterwards, at Ephesus, and that when Hannibal, as they were walking together, took the upper hand, Africanus let it pass, and walked on without the least notice of it; and that then they began to talk of generals, and Hannibal affirmed that Alexander was the greatest commander the world had seen, next to him Pyrrhus, and the third was himself; Africanus, with a smile, asked, "What would you have said, if I had not defeated you?" "I would not then, Scipio," he replied, "have made myself the third, but the first commander." Such conduct was much admired in Scipio, and that of Titus, who had as it were insulted the dead whom another had slain, was no less generally found fault with. Not but that there were some who applauded the action, looking upon a living Hannibal as a fire, which only wanted blowing to become a flame. For when he was in the prime and flower of his age, it was not his body nor his hand that had been so formidable, but his consummate skill and experience, together with his innate malice and rancour against the

Roman name, things which do not impair with age. For the temper and bent of the soul remains constant, while fortune continually varies; and some new hope might easily rouse to a fresh attempt those whose hatred made them enemies to the last. And what really happened afterwards does to a certain extent tend yet further to the exculpation of Titus. Aristonicus, of the family of a common musician, upon the reputation of being the son of Eumenes, filled all Asia with tumults and rebellion. Then again, Mithridates, after his defeats by Sylla and Fimbria, and vast slaughter as well among his prime officers as common soldiers, made head again, and proved a most dangerous enemy, against Lucullus, both by sea and land. Hannibal was never reduced to so contemptible a state as Caius Marius; he had the friendship of a king, and the free exercise of his faculties, employment and charge in the navy, and over the horse and foot, of Prusias; whereas those who but now were laughing to hear of Marius wandering about Africa, destitute and begging, in no long time after were seen entreating his mercy in Rome, with his rods at their backs, and his axes at their necks. So true it is, that looking to the possible future, we can call nothing that we see either great or small; as nothing puts an end to the mutability and vicissitude of things but what puts an end to their very being. Some authors accordingly tell us that Titus did not do this of his own head, but that he was joined in commission with Lucius Scipio, and that the whole object of the embassy was to effect Hannibal's death. And now, as we find no further mention in history of anything done by Titus, either in war or in the administration of the government, but simply that he died in peace, it is time to look upon him as he stands in comparison with Philopœmen.

THE COMPARISON OF PHILOPŒMEN
WITH FLAMININUS

FIRST THEN, AS FOR THE GREATNESS OF THE BENEFITS WHICH TITUS
conferred on Greece, neither Philopœmen, nor many braver men than
he, can make good the parallel. They were Greeks fighting against Greeks,
but Titus, a stranger to Greece, fought for her. And at the very time when
Philopœmen went over into Crete, destitute of means to succour his
besieged countrymen, Titus, by a defeat given to Philip in the heart of
Greece, set them and their cities free. Again, if we examine the battles they
fought, Philopœmen, whilst he was the Achæans' general, slew more
Greeks than Titus, in aiding the Greeks, slew Macedonians. As to their failings, ambition was Titus' weak side, and obstinacy Philopœmen's; in the
former, anger was easily kindled; in the latter, it was as hardly quenched.
Titus reserved to Philip the royal dignity; he pardoned the Ætolians, and
stood their friend; but Philopœmen, exasperated against his country,
deprived it of its supremacy over the adjacent villages. Titus was ever constant to those he had once befriended; the other, upon any offence, as
prone to cancel kindnesses. He who had once been a benefactor to the
Lacedæmonians, afterwards laid their walls level with the ground, wasted
their country, and in the end changed and destroyed the whole frame
of their government. He seems, in truth, to have prodigalled away his own
life through passion and perverseness; for he fell upon the Messenians,
not with that conduct and caution that characterised the movements of
Titus, but with unnecessary and unreasonable haste.

The many battles he fought, and the many trophies he won, may make
us ascribe to Philopœmen the more thorough knowledge of war. Titus
decided the matter betwixt Philip and himself in two engagements; but
Philopœmen came off victorious in ten thousand encounters, to all which

fortune had scarcely any pretence, so much were they owing to his skill. Besides, Titus got his renown, assisted by the power of a flourishing Rome; the other flourished under a declined Greece, so that his successes may be accounted his own; in Titus' glory Rome claims a share. The one had brave men under him, the other made his brave, by being over them. And though Philopœmen was unfortunate, certainly, in always being opposed to his countrymen, yet this misfortune is at the same time a proof of his merit. Where the circumstances are the same, superior success can only be ascribed to superior merit. And he had, indeed, to do with the two most warlike nations of all Greece, the Cretans on the one hand, and the Lacedæmonians on the other, and he mastered the craftiest of them by art and the bravest of them by valour. It may also be said that Titus, having his men armed and disciplined to his hand, had in a manner his victories made for him; whereas Philopœmen was forced to introduce a discipline and tactics of his own, and to new-mould and model his soldiers; so that what is of greatest import towards insuring a victory was in his case his own creation, while the other had it ready provided for his benefit. Philopœmen effected many gallant things with his own hand, but Titus none; so much so that one Archedemus, an Ætolian, made it a jest against him that while he, the Ætolian, was running with his drawn sword, where he saw the Macedonians drawn up closest and fighting hardest, Titus was standing still, and with hands stretched out to heaven, praying to the gods for aid.

It is true Titus acquitted himself admirably, both as a governor and as an ambassador; but Philopœmen was no less serviceable and useful to the Achæans in the capacity of a private man than in that of a commander. He was a private citizen when he restored the Messenians to their liberty, and delivered their city from Nabis; he was also a private citizen when he rescued the Lacedæmonians, and shut the gates of Sparta against the general Diophanes and Titus. He had a nature so truly formed for command that he could govern even the laws themselves for the public good; he did not need to wait for the formality of being elected into command by the governed, but employed their service, if occasion required, at his own discretion; judging that he who understood their real interests was more truly their supreme magistrate, than he whom they had elected to the office. The equity, clemency, and humanity of Titus towards the Greeks display a great and generous nature; but the actions of Philopœmen, full of courage, and forward to assert his country's liberty against the Romans, have something yet greater and nobler in them. For it is not as hard a task to gratify the indigent and distressed, as to bear up against and to dare to incur the anger of the powerful. To conclude, since it does not appear to be easy, by any review or discussion, to establish the true difference of their merits and decide to which a preference is due, will it be an unfair award in the case, if we let the Greek bear away the crown for military conduct and warlike skill, and the Roman for justice and clemency?

PYRRHUS

OF THE THESPROTIANS AND MOLOSSIANS AFTER THE GREAT INUNDATION, the first king, according to some historians, was Phæthon, one of those who came into Epirus with Pelasgus. Others tell us that Deucalion and Pyrrha, having set up the worship of Jupiter at Dodona, settled there among the Molossians. In after time, Neoptolemus, Achilles' son, planting a colony, possessed these parts himself, and left a succession of kings, who, after him, was named Pyrrhidæ, as he in his youth was called Pyrrhus, and of his legitimate children, one born of Lanassa, daughter of Cleodæus, Hyllus' son, had also that name. From him Achilles came to have divine honours in Epirus, under the name of Aspetus, in the language of the country. After these first kings, those of the following intervening times becoming barbarous, and insignificant both in their power and their lives, Tharrhypas is said to have been the first who, by introducing Greek manners and learning, and humane laws into his cities, left any fame of himself. Alcetas was the son of Tharrhypas, Arybas of Alcetas, and of Arybas and Troas his queen, Æacides; he married Phthia, the daughter of Menon, the Thessalian, a man of note at the time of the Lamiac war, and of highest command in the confederate army next to Leosthenes. To Æacides were born of Phthia, Deidamia and Troas, daughters, and Pyrrhus, a son.

The Molossians, afterwards falling into factions and expelling Æacides, brought in the sons of Neoptolemus, and such friends of Æacides as they could take were all cut off; Pyrrhus, yet an infant, and searched for by the enemy, had been stolen away and carried off by Androclides and Angelus; who, however, being obliged to take with them a few servants, and women to nurse the child, were much impeded and retarded in their flight, and when they were now overtaken, they delivered the infant to Androcleon, Hippias, and Neander, faithful and able young fellows, giving them in charge to make for Megara, a town of Macedon, with all their might, while they themselves, partly by entreaty, and partly by force, stopped the course of the pursuers till late in the evening. At last, having hardly forced them back, they joined those who had the care of Pyrrhus: but the sun being already set, at the point of attaining their object they suddenly found themselves cut off from it. For on reaching the river that runs by the city they found it looking formidable and rough, and endeavouring to pass over, they discovered it was not fordable; late rains having heightened the water and made the current violent. The darkness of the night added to the horror of all, so that they durst not venture of themselves to carry over the child and the women that attended it; but, perceiving some of the country people on the other side, they desired them to assist their passage, and showed them Pyrrhus, calling out aloud, and importuning them. They, however, could not hear for the noise and roaring of the water. Thus time was spent while those called out, and the others did not understand what was said, till one recollecting himself, stripped off a piece of bark from an oak, and wrote on it with the tongue of a buckle, stating the necessities and the fortunes of the child, and then rolling it about a stone, which was made use of to give force to the motion, threw it over to the other side, or, as some say, fastened it to the end of a javelin, and darted it over. When the men on the other shore read what was on the bark, and saw how time pressed, without delay they cut down some trees, and lashing them together, came over to them. And it so fell out, that he who first got ashore, and took Pyrrhus in his arms, was named Achilles, the rest being helped over by others as they came to hand.

Thus being safe, and out of the reach of pursuit, they addressed themselves to Glaucias, then King of the Illyrians, and finding him sitting at home with his wife, they laid down the child before them. The king began to weigh the matter, fearing Cassander, who was a mortal enemy of Æacides, and, being in deep consideration, said nothing for a long time; while Pyrrhus, crawling about on the ground, gradually got near and laid hold with his hand upon the king's robe, and so helping himself upon his feet against the knees of Glaucias first moved laughter, and then pity, as a little, humble, crying petitioner. Some say he did not throw himself before Glaucias, but catching hold of an altar of the gods, and spreading his hands about it, raised himself up by that; and that Glaucias took the act as an omen. At present, therefore, he gave Pyrrhus into the charge of his wife, commanding he should be brought up with his own children; and a little later, the enemies sending to demand him, and Cassander himself offering two hundred talents, he would not deliver him up; but when he was twelve years old, bringing him with an army into Epirus, made him king. Pyrrhus in the air of his face had something more of the terrors than of the augustness of kingly power; he had not a regular set of upper teeth, but in the place of them one continued bone, with small lines marked on it, resembling the divisions of a row of teeth. It was a general belief he could cure the spleen by sacrificing a white cock and gently pressing with his right foot on the spleen of the persons as they lay down on their backs, nor was anyone so poor or inconsiderable as not to be welcome, if he desired it, to the benefit of his touch. He accepted the cock for the sacrifice as a reward, and was always much pleased with the present. The large toe of that foot was said to have a divine virtue; for after his death, the rest of the body being consumed, this was found unhurt, and untouched by the fire. But of these things hereafter.

Being now about seventeen years old, and the government in appearance well settled, he took a journey out of the kingdom to attend the marriage of one of Glaucias' sons, with whom he was brought up; upon which opportunity the Molossians again rebelling, turned out all of his party, plundered his property, and gave themselves up to Neoptolemus. Pyrrhus having thus lost the kingdom, and being in want of all things, applied to Demetrius, the son of Antigonus, the husband of his sister Deidamia, who, while she was but a child, had been in name the wife of Alexander, son of Roxana, but their affairs afterwards proving unfortunate, when she came to age, Demetrius married her. At the great battle of Ipsus, where so many kings were engaged, Pyrrhus, taking part with Demetrius, though yet but a youth, routed those that encountered him, and highly signalised himself among all the soldiery; and afterwards, when Demetrius' fortunes were low, he did not forsake him then, but secured for him the cities of Greece with which he was intrusted; and upon articles of agreement being made between Demetrius and Ptolemy, he went over as an hostage for him into Egypt, where both in hunting and other exercises he gave Ptolemy an ample proof of his courage and strength. Here observing Berenice in greatest power, and of all Ptolemy's wives highest in esteem for virtue and understanding, he made his court principally to her. He had a particular art of gaining over the great to his own interest, as on the other hand he readily overlooked such as were below him; and being also well-behaved and temperate in his life, among all the young princes then at court he was thought most fit to have Antigone for his wife, one of the daughters of Berenice by Philip, before she married Ptolemy.

After this match, advancing in honour, and Antigone being a very good wife to him, having procured a sum of money, and raised an army, he so ordered matters as to be sent into his kingdom of Epirus, and arrived there to the great satisfaction of many, from their hate to Neoptolemus, who was governing in a violent and arbitrary way. But fearing lest Neoptolemus should enter into alliance with some neighbouring princes, he came to terms and friendship with him, agreeing that they should share the government between them. There were people, however, who, as time went on, secretly exasperated them, and fomented jealousies between them. The cause chiefly moving Pyrrhus is said to have had this beginning. It was customary for the kings to offer sacrifice to Mars at Passaro, a place in the Molossian country, and that done to enter into a solemn covenant with the Epirots; they to govern according to law, these to preserve the government as by law established. This was performed in the presence of both kings, who were there with their immediate friends, giving and receiving many presents; here Gelo, one of the friends of Neoptolemus, taking Pyrrhus by the hand, presented him with two pair of draught oxen. Myrtilus, his cup-bearer, being then by, begged these of Pyrrhus, who not giving them to him, but to another, Myrtilus extremely resented it, which Gelo took notice of, and, inviting him to a banquet (amidst drinking and other excesses, as some relate, Myrtilus being then in the flower of his youth), he entered into discourse, persuading him to adhere to Neoptolemus, and destroy Pyrrhus by poison. Myrtilus received the design, appearing to approve and consent to it, but privately discovered it to Pyrrhus, by whose command he recommended Alexicrates, his chief cup-bearer, to Gelo, as a fit instrument for their design, Pyrrhus being very desirous to have proof of the plot by several evidences. So Gelo, being deceived, Neoptolemus, who was no less deceived, imagining the design went prosperously on, could not forbear, but in his joy spoke of it among his friends, and once at an entertainment at his sister Cadmea's talked openly of it, thinking none heard but themselves. Nor was anyone there but Phænarete the wife of Samon, who had the care of Neoptolemus' flocks and herds. She, turning her face towards the wall upon a couch, seemed fast asleep, and having heard all that passed, unsuspected, next day came to Antigone, Pyrrhus' wife, and told her what she had heard Neoptolemus say to his sister. On understanding which Pyrrhus for the present said little, but on a sacrifice day, making an invitation for

Neoptolemus, killed him; being satisfied before that the great men of the Epirots were his friends, and that they were eager for him to rid himself of Neoptolemus, and not to content himself with a mere petty share of the government, but to follow his own natural vocation to great designs, and now when a just ground of suspicion appeared, to anticipate Neoptolemus by taking him off first.

In memory of Berenice and Ptolemy he named his son by Antigone, Ptolemy, and having built a city in the peninsula of Epirus, called it Berenicis. From this time he began to revolve many and vast projects in his thoughts; but his first special hope and design lay near home, and he found means to engage himself in the Macedonian affairs under the following pretext. Of Cassander's sons, Antipater, the eldest, killed Thessalonica, his mother, and expelled his brother Alexander, who sent to Demetrius entreating his assistance, and also called in Pyrrhus; but Demetrius being retarded by multitude of business, Pyrrhus, coming first, demanded in reward of his service the districts called Tymphæa and Parauæa in Macedon itself, and of their new conquests, Ambracia, Acarnania, and Amphilochia. The young prince giving way, he took possession of these countries, and secured them with good garrisons, and proceeded to reduce for Alexander himself other parts of the kingdom which he gained from Antipater. Lysimachus, designing to send aid to Antipater, was involved in much other business, but knowing Pyrrhus would not disoblige Ptolemy, or deny him anything, sent pretended letters to him as from Ptolemy, desiring him to give up his expedition, upon the payment of three hundred talents to him by Antipater. Pyrrhus, opening the letter, quickly discovered the fraud of Lysimachus; for it had not the accustomed style of salutation, "The father to the son, health," but "King Ptolemy to Pyrrhus, the king, health"; and reproaching Lysimachus, he notwithstanding made a peace, and they all met to confirm it by a solemn oath upon sacrifice. A goat, a bull, and a ram being brought out, the ram on a sudden fell dead. The others laughed, but Theodotus the prophet forbade Pyrrhus to swear, declaring that Heaven by that portended the death of one of the three kings, upon which he refused to ratify the peace.

The affairs of Alexander being now in some kind of settlement, Demetrius arrived, contrary, as soon appeared, to the desire and indeed not without the alarm of Alexander. After they had been a few days together, their mutual jealousy led them to conspire against each other; and Demetrius, taking advantage of the first occasion, was beforehand with the young king, and slew him, and proclaimed himself King of

Macedon. There had been formerly no very good understanding between him and Pyrrhus; for besides the inroads he made into Thessaly, the innate disease of princes, ambition of greater empire, had rendered them formidable and suspected neighbours to each other, especially since Deidamia's death; and both having seized Macedon, they came into conflict for the same object, and the difference between them had the stronger motives. Demetrius having first attacked the Ætolians and subdued them, left Pantauchus there with a considerable army, and marched direct against Pyrrhus, and Pyrrhus, as he thought, against him; but by mistake of the ways they passed by one another, and Demetrius falling into Epirus wasted the country, and Pyrrhus, meeting with Pantauchus, prepared for an engagement. The soldiers fell to, and there was a sharp and terrible conflict, especially where the generals were. Pantauchus, in courage, dexterity, and strength of body, being confessedly the best of all Demetrius' captains, and having both resolution and high spirit, challenged Pyrrhus to fight hand to hand; on the other side Pyrrhus, professing not to yield to any king in valour and glory, and esteeming the fame of Achilles more truly to belong to him for his courage than for his blood, advanced against Pantauchus through the front of the army. First they used their lances, then came to a close fight, and managed their swords both with art and force; Pyrrhus receiving one wound, but returning two for it, one in the thigh and the other near the neck, repulsed and overthrew Pantauchus, but did not kill him outright, as he was rescued by his friends. But the Epirots exulting in the victory of their king, and admiring his courage, forced through and cut in pieces the phalanx of the Macedonians, and pursuing those that fled, killed many, and took five thousand prisoners.

This fight did not so much exasperate the Macedonians with anger for their loss, or with hatred to Pyrrhus, as it caused esteem and admiration of his valour, and great discourse of him among those that saw what he did, and were engaged against him in the action. They thought his countenance, his swiftness, and his motions expressed those of the great Alexander, and that they beheld here an image and resemblance of his rapidity and strength in fight; other kings merely by their purple and their guards, by the formal bending of their necks and lofty tone of their speech, Pyrrhus only by arms and in action, represented Alexander. Of his knowledge of military tactics and the art of a general, and his great ability that way, we have the best information from the commentaries he left behind him. Antigonus, also, we are told, being asked who was the greatest soldier, said, "Pyrrhus, if he lives to be old," referring only to those of his own time; but Hannibal of all great commanders esteemed Pyrrhus for skill and conduct the first, Scipio the second, and himself the third, as is related in the life of Scipio. In a word, he seemed ever to make this all his thought and philosophy, as the most kingly part of learning: other curiosities he held in no account. He is reported, when asked at a feast whether he thought Python or Caphisias the best musician to have said, Polysperchon was the best soldier, as though it became a king to examine and understand only such things. Towards his familiars he was mild and not easily incensed; zealous and even vehement in returning kindnesses. Thus when Aeropus was dead, he could not bear it with moderation, saying, he indeed had suffered what was common to human nature, but condemning and blaming himself, that by puttings off and delays he had not returned his kindness in time. For our debts may be satisfied to the creditor's heirs, but not to have made the acknowledgment of received favours, while they to whom it is due can be sensible of it, afflicts a good and worthy nature. Some thinking it fit that Pyrrhus should banish a certain ill-tongued fellow in Ambracia, who had spoken very indecently of him, "Let him rather," said he, "speak against us here to a few, than rambling about to a great many." And others who in their wine had made reflections upon him, being afterward questioned for it, and asked by him whether they had said such words, on one of the young fellows answering, "Yes, all that, king: and should have said more if we had had more wine"; he laughed and discharged them. After Antigone's death, he married several wives to enlarge his interest and power. He had the daughter of Autoleon, King of the Pæonians, Bircenna, Bardyllis the Illyrian's daughter, Lanassa, daughter of Agathocles the Syracusan, who brought with her in dower the city of Corcyra, which had been taken by Agathocles. By Antigone he had Ptolemy, Alexander by Lanassa, and Helenus, his youngest son, by Bircenna: he brought them up all in arms, hot and eager youths, and by him sharpened and whetted to war from their very infancy. It is said, when one of them, while yet a child, asked him to which he would leave the kingdom, he replied, to him that had the sharpest sword, which indeed was much like that tragical curse of Œdipus to his sons:

> Not by the lot decide,
> But within the sword the heritage divide.

So unsocial and wild-beast-like is the nature of ambition and cupidity.

After this battle Pyrrhus, returning gloriously home, enjoyed his fame and reputation, and being called "Eagle" by the Epirots, "By you," said he,

"I am an eagle; for how should I not be such, while I have your arms as wings to sustain me?" A little after, having intelligence that Demetrius was dangerously sick, he entered on a sudden into Macedonia, intending only an incursion, and to harass the country; but was very near seizing upon all, and taking the kingdom without a blow. He marched as far as Edessa unresisted, great numbers deserting and coming in to him. This danger excited Demetrius beyond his strength, and his friends and commanders in a short time got a considerable army together, and with all their forces briskly attacked Pyrrhus, who, coming only to pillage, would not stand a fight, but retreating, lost part of his army, as he went off, by the close pursuit of the Macedonians. Demetrius, however, although he had easily and quickly forced Pyrrhus out of the country, yet did not slight him, but having resolved upon great designs, and to recover his father's kingdom with an army of one hundred thousand men, and a fleet of five hundred ships, would neither embroil himself with Pyrrhus, nor leave the Macedonians so active and troublesome a neighbour; and since he had no leisure to continue the war with him, he was willing to treat and conclude a peace, and to turn his forces upon the other kings. Articles being agreed upon, the designs of Demetrius quickly discovered themselves by the greatness of his preparation. And the other kings, being alarmed, sent to Pyrrhus ambassadors and letters, expressing their wonder that he should choose to let his own opportunity pass by, and wait till Demetrius could use his; and whereas he was now able to chase him out of Macedon involved in designs and disturbed, he should expect till Demetrius at leisure, and grown great, should bring the war home to his own door, and make him fight for his temples and sepulchres in Molossia; especially having so lately, by his means, lost Corcyra and his wife together. For Lanassa had taken offence at Pyrrhus for too great an inclination to those wives of his that were barbarians, and so withdrew to Corcyra, and desiring to marry some king, invited Demetrius, knowing of all the kings he was most ready to entertain offers of marriage; so he sailed thither, married Lanassa, and placed a garrison in the city. The kings having written thus to Pyrrhus, themselves likewise contrived to find Demetrius work, while he was delaying and making his preparations. Ptolemy, setting out with a great fleet, drew off many of the Greek cities. Lysimachus out of Thrace wasted the upper Macedon; and Pyrrhus, also taking arms at the same time, marched to Berœa, expecting, as it fell out, that Demetrius, collecting his forces against Lysimachus, would leave the lower country undefended. That very night he seemed in his sleep to be called by Alexander the Great, and approaching saw him sick abed, but was received with very kind words, and much respect, and promised zealous assistance. He making bold to reply, "How, sir, can you, being sick, assist me?" "With my name," said he, and mounting Nisæan horse, seemed to lead the way. At the sight of this vision he was much assured, and with swift marches overrunning all the interjacent places, takes Berœa, and making his headquarters there, reduced the rest of the country by his commanders. When Demetrius received intelligence of this, and perceived likewise the Macedonians ready to mutiny in the army, he was afraid to advance further, lest, coming near Lysimachus, a Macedonian king, and of great fame, they should revolt to him. So returning, he marched directly against Pyrrhus, as a stranger, and hated by the Macedonians. But while he lay encamped there near him, many who came out of Berœa infinitely praised Pyrrhus as invincible in arms, a glorious warrior, who treated those he had taken kindly and humanely. Several of these Pyrrhus himself sent privately, pretending to be Macedonians, and saying, now was the time to be delivered from the severe government of Demetrius by coming over to Pyrrhus, a gracious prince and a lover of soldiers. By this artifice a great part of the army was in a state of excitement, and the soldiers began to look every way about inquiring for Pyrrhus. It happened he was without his helmet, till understanding they did not know him, he put it on again, and so was quickly recognised by his lofty crest and the goat's horns he wore upon it. Then the Macedonians, running to him, desired to be told his password, and some put oaken boughs upon their heads, because they saw them worn by the soldiers about him. Some persons even took the confidence to say to Demetrius himself, that he would be well advised to withdraw and lay down the government. And he, indeed, seeing the mutinous movements of the army to be only too consistent with what they said, privately got away, disguised in a broad hat and a common soldier's coat. So Pyrrhus became master of the army without fighting, and was declared King of the Macedonians.

But Lysimachus now arriving, and claiming the defeat of Demetrius as the joint exploit of them both, and that therefore the kingdom should be shared between them, Pyrrhus, not as yet quite assured of the Macedonians, and in doubt of their faith, consented to the proposition of Lysimachus, and divided the country and cities between them accordingly. This was for the present useful, and prevented a war; but shortly after they found the partition not so much a peaceful settlement as an occasion of further complaint and difference. For men whose ambition neither seas, nor mountains, nor unpeopled deserts can limit, nor the bounds dividing

Europe from Asia confine their vast desires, it would be hard to expect to forbear from injuring one another when they touch and are close together. These are ever naturally at war, envying and seeking advantages of one another, and merely make use of those two words, peace and war, like current coin, to serve their occasions, not as justice but as expediency suggests, and are really better men when they openly enter on a war, than when they give to the mere forbearance from doing wrong, for want of opportunity, the sacred names of justice and friendship. Pyrrhus was an instance of this; for setting himself against the rise of Demetrius again, and endeavouring to hinder the recovery of his power, as it were from a kind of sickness, he assisted the Greeks, and came to Athens, where, having ascended the Acropolis, he offered sacrifice to the goddess, and the same day came down again, and told the Athenians he was much gratified by the goodwill and the confidence they had shown to him; but if they were wise he advised them never to let any king come thither again, or open their city gates to him. He concluded also a peace with Demetrius, but shortly after he was gone into Asia, at the persuasion of Lysimachus, he tampered with the Thessalians to revolt, and besieged his cities in Greece; finding he could better preserve the attachment of the Macedonians in war than in peace, and being of his own inclination not much given to rest. At last, after Demetrius had been overthrown in Syria, Lysimachus, who had secured his affairs, and had nothing to do, immediately turned his whole forces upon Pyrrhus, who was in quarters at Edessa, and falling upon and seizing his convoy of provisions, brought first a great scarcity into the army; then partly by letters, partly by spreading rumours abroad, he corrupted the principal officers of the Macedonians, reproaching them that they had made one their master who was both a stranger and descended from those who had ever been servants to the Macedonians, and that they had thrust the old friends and familiars of Alexander out of the country. The Macedonian soldiers being much prevailed upon, Pyrrhus withdrew himself with his Epirots and auxiliary forces, relinquishing Macedon, just after the same manner he took it. So little reason have kings to condemn popular governments for changing sides as suits their interests, as in this they do but imitate them who are the great instructors of unfaithfulness and treachery; holding him the wisest that makes the least account of being an honest man.

Pyrrhus having thus retired into Epirus, and left Macedon, fortune gave him a fair occasion of enjoying himself in quiet, and peaceably governing his own subjects; but he who thought it a nauseous course of life not to be doing mischief to others, or receiving some from them, like Achilles, could not endure repose—

—But sad and languished far,
Desiring battle and the shout of war,

and gratified his inclination by the following pretext for new troubles. The Romans were at war with the Tarentines, who, not being able to go on with the war, nor yet, through the foolhardiness and the viciousness of their popular speakers, to come to terms and give it up, proposed now to make Pyrrhus their general, and engage him in it, as of all the neighbouring kings the most at leisure, and the most skilful as a commander. The more grave and discreet citizens opposing these counsels, were partly overborne by the noise and violence of the multitude; while others, seeing this, absented themselves from the assemblies; only one Meton, a very sober man, on the day this public decree was to be ratified, when the people were now seating themselves, came dancing into the assembly like one quite drunk, with a withered garland and a small lamp in his hand, and a woman playing on a flute before him. And as in great multitudes met at such popular assemblies no decorum can be well observed, some clapped him, others laughed, none forbade him, but called to the woman to play, and to him to sing to the company, and when they thought he was going to do so, "'Tis right of you, O men of Tarentum," he said, "not to hinder any from making themselves merry that have a mind to it, while it is yet in their power; and if you are wise, you will take out your pleasure of your freedom while you can, for you must change your course of life, and follow other diet when Pyrrhus comes to town." These words made a great impression upon many of the Tarentines, and a confused murmur went about that he had spoken much to the purpose; but some who feared they should be sacrificed if a peace were made with the Romans, reviled the whole assembly for so tamely suffering themselves to be abused by a drunken sot, and crowding together upon Meton, thrust him out. So the public order was passed and ambassadors sent into Epirus, not only in their own names, but in those of all the Italian Greeks, carrying presents to Pyrrhus, and letting him know they wanted a general of reputation and experience; and that they could furnish him with large forces of Lucanians, Messapians, Samnites, and Tarentines, amounting to twenty thousand horse, and three hundred and fifty thousand foot. This did not only quicken Pyrrhus, but raised an eager desire for the expedition in the Epirots.

There was one Cineas, a Thessalian, considered to be a man of very good sense, a disciple of the great orator Demosthenes, who, of all that were famous at that time for speaking well, most seemed, as in a picture, to revive in the minds of the audience the memory of his force and vigour of eloquence; and being always about Pyrrhus, and sent about in his service to several cities, verified the saying of Euripides, that—

—the force of words
Can do whate'er is done by conquering swords.

And Pyrrhus was used to say, that Cineas had taken more towns with his words than he with his arms, and always did him the honour to employ him in his most important occasions. This person, seeing Pyrrhus eagerly preparing for Italy, led him one day when he was at leisure into the following reasonings: "The Romans, sir, are reported to be great warriors and conquerors of many warlike nations; if God permit us to overcome them, how should we use our victory?" "You ask," said Pyrrhus, "a thing evident of itself. The Romans once conquered, there is neither Greek nor barbarian city that will resist us, but we shall presently be masters of all Italy, the extent and resources and strength of which anyone should rather profess to be ignorant of than yourself." Cineas after a little pause, "And having subdued Italy, what shall we do next?" Pyrrhus not yet discovering his intention, "Sicily," he replied, "next holds out her arms to receive us, a wealthy and populous island, and easy to be gained; for since Agathocles left it, only faction and anarchy, and the licentious violence of the demagogues prevail." "You speak," said Cineas, "what is perfectly probable, but will the possession of Sicily put an end to the war?" "God grant us," answered Pyrrhus, "victory and success in that, and we will use these as forerunners of greater things; who could forbear from Libya and Carthage then within reach, which Agathocles, even when forced to fly from Syracuse, and passing the sea only with a few ships, had all but surprised? These conquests once perfected, will any assert that of the enemies who now pretend to despise us, anyone will dare to make further resistance?" "None," replied Cineas, "for then it is manifest we may with such mighty forces regain Macedon, and make an absolute conquest of Greece; and when all these are in our power what shall we do then?" Said Pyrrhus, smiling, "We will live at our ease, my dear friend, and drink all day, and divert ourselves with pleasant conversation." When Cineas had led Pyrrhus with his argument to this point: "And what hinders us now, sir, if we have a mind to be merry, and entertain one another, since we have at hand without trouble all those necessary things, to which through much blood and great labour, and infinite hazards and mischief done to ourselves and to others, we design at last to arrive?" Such reasonings rather troubled Pyrrhus with the thought of the happiness he was quitting, than any way altered his purpose, being unable to abandon the hopes of what he so much desired.

And first, he sent away Cineas to the Tarentines with three thousand men; presently after, many vessels for transport of horse, and galleys, and flat-bottomed boats of all sorts arriving from Tarentum, he shipped upon them twenty elephants, three thousand horse, twenty thousand foot, two thousand archers, and five hundred slingers. All being thus in readiness, he set sail, and being half-way over, was driven by the wind, blowing, contrary to the season of the year, violently from the north, and carried from his course, but by the great skill and resolution of his pilots and seamen, he made the land with infinite labour, and beyond expectation. The rest of the fleet could not get up, and some of the dispersed ships, losing the coast of Italy, were driven into the Libyan and Sicilian Sea; others, not able to double the cape of Japygium, were overtaken by the night; and, with a boisterous and heavy sea, throwing them upon a dangerous and rocky shore, they were all very much disabled except the royal galley. She, while the sea bore upon her sides, resisted with her bulk and strength, and avoided the force of it, till the wind coming about, blew directly in their teeth from the shore, and the vessel keeping up with her head against it, was in danger of going to pieces; yet on the other hand, to suffer themselves to be driven off to sea again, which was thus raging and tempestuous, with the wind shifting about every way, seemed to them the most dreadful of all their present evils. Pyrrhus, rising up, threw himself overboard. His friends and guards strove eagerly who should be most ready to help him, but night and the sea, with its noise and violent surge, made it extremely difficult to do this; so that hardly, when with the morning the wind began to subside, he got ashore, breathless and weakened in body, but with high courage and strength of mind resisting his hard fortune. The Messapians, upon whose shore they were thrown by the tempest, came up eagerly to help them in the best manner they could; and some of the straggling vessels that had escaped the storm arrived; in which were a very few horse, and not quite two thousand foot, and two elephants.

With these Pyrrhus marched straight to Tarentum, where Cineas, being informed of his arrival, led out the troops to meet him. Entering the town, he did nothing unpleasing to the Tarentines, nor put any force upon them, till the ships were all in harbour, and the greatest part of the army got together; but then perceiving that the people, unless some strong compulsion was used to them, were not capable either of saving others or being saved themselves, and were rather intending, while he engaged for them in the field, to remain at home bathing and feasting themselves, he first shut up the places of public exercise, and the walks, where, in their idle way, they fought their country's battles and conducted her campaigns in their talk; he prohibited likewise all festivals, revels, and drinking-parties as unseasonable, and summoning them to arms, showed himself rigorous and inflexible in carrying out the conscription for service in the war. So that many, not understanding what it was to be commanded, left the town, calling it mere slavery not to do as they pleased. He now received intelligence that Lævinus, the Roman consul, was upon his march with a great army, and plundering Lucania as he went. The confederate forces were not come up to him, yet he thought it impossible to suffer so near an approach of an enemy, and drew out with his army, but first sent an herald to the Romans to know if before the war they would decide the differences between them and the Italian Greeks by his arbitrament and mediation. But Lævinus returning answer that the Romans neither accepted him as arbitrator nor feared him as an enemy, Pyrrhus advanced, and encamped in the plain between the cities of Pandosia and Heraclea, and having notice the Romans were near, and lay on the other side of the river Siris, he rode up to take a view of them, and seeing their order, the appointment of the watches, their method and the general form of their encampment, he was amazed, and addressing one of his friends next to him: "This order," said he, "Megacles, of the barbarians, is not at all barbarian in character; we shall see presently what they can do"; and growing a little more thoughtful of the event, resolved to expect the arriving of the confederate troops. And to hinder the Romans, if in the meantime they should endeavour to pass the river, he planted men all along the bank to oppose them. But they, hastening to anticipate the coming up of the same forces which he had determined to wait for, attempted the passage with their infantry, where it was fordable, and with the horse in several places, so that the Greeks, fearing to be surrounded, were obliged to retreat, and Pyrrhus, perceiving this, and being much surprised, bade his foot officers draw their men up in line of battle, and continue in arms, while he himself with three thousand horse advanced, hoping to attack the Romans as they were coming over, scattered and disordered. But when he saw a vast number of shields appearing above the water, and the horse following them in good order, gathering his men in a closer body, himself at the head of them, he began the charge, conspicuous by his rich and beautiful armour, and letting it be seen that his reputation had not outgone what he was able effectually to perform. While exposing his hands and body in the fight, and bravely repelling all that engaged him, he still guided the battle with a steady and undisturbed reason, and such presence of mind, as if he had been out of the action and watching it from a distance, passing still from point to point, and assisting those whom he thought most pressed by the enemy. Here Leonnatus the Macedonian, observing one of the Italians very intent upon Pyrrhus, riding up towards him, and changing places as he did, and moving as he moved: "Do you see, sir," said he, "that barbarian on the black horse with white feet? He seems to be one that designs some great and dangerous thing, for he looks constantly at you, and fixes his whole attention, full of vehement purpose, on you alone, taking no notice of others. Be on your guard, sir, against him." "Leonnatus," said Pyrrhus, "it is impossible for any man to avoid his fate; but neither he nor any other Italian shall have much satisfaction in engaging with me." While they were in this discourse, the Italian, lowering his spear and quickening his horse, rode furiously at Pyrrhus, and run his horse through with his lance; at the same instant Leonnatus ran his through. Both horses falling, Pyrrhus' friends surrounded him and brought him off safe, and killed the Italian, bravely defending himself. He was by birth a Frentanian, captain of a troop, and named Oplacus.

This made Pyrrhus use greater caution, and now seeing his horse give ground, he brought up the infantry against the enemy, and changing his scarf and his arms with Megacles, one of his friends, and obscuring himself, as it were, in his, charged upon the Romans, who received and engaged him, and a great while the success of the battle remained undetermined; and it is said there were seven turns of fortune both of pursuing and being pursued. And the change of his arms was very opportune for the safety of his person, but had like to have overthrown his cause and lost him the victory; for several falling upon Megacles, the first that gave him his mortal wound was one Dexous, who, snatching away his helmet and his robe, rode at once to Lævinus, holding them up, and saying aloud he had killed Pyrrhus. These spoils being carried about and shown among the ranks, the Romans were transported with joy, and shouted aloud; while equal discouragement and terror prevailed among the Greeks, until Pyrrhus, understanding what had happened, rode about the army with his face bare, stretching out his hand to his soldiers, and telling them aloud it was he. At last, the elephants more particularly began to distress the Romans, whose horses, before they came near, not enduring them, went back with their riders; and upon this, he commanded the Thessalian cavalry to charge them in their disorder, and routed them with great loss. Dionysius affirms near fifteen thousand of the Romans fell; Hieronymus, no more than seven thousand. On Pyrrhus' side, the same Dionysius makes thirteen thousand slain, the other under four thousand; but they were the flower of his men, and amongst them his particular friends as well as officers whom he most trusted and made use of. However, he possessed himself of the Romans' camp which they deserted, and gained over several confederate cities, and wasted the country round about, and advanced so far that he was within about thirty-seven miles of Rome itself. After the fight many of the Lucanians and Samnites came in and joined him, whom he chid for their delay, but yet he was evidently well pleased and raised in his thoughts, that he had defeated so great an army of the Romans with the assistance of the Tarentines alone.

The Romans did not remove Lævinus from the consulship; though it is told that Caius Fabricius said, that the Epirots had not beaten the Romans, but only Pyrrhus, Lævinus; insinuating that their loss was not through want of valour but of conduct; but filled up their legions, and enlisted fresh men with all speed, talking high and boldly of war, which struck Pyrrhus with amazement. He thought it advisable by sending first to make an experiment whether they had any inclination to treat, thinking that to take the city and make an absolute conquest was no work for such an army as his was at that time, but to settle a friendship, and bring them to terms, would be highly honourable after his victory. Cineas was despatched away, and applied himself to several of the great ones, with presents for themselves and their ladies from the king; but not a person would receive any, and answered, as well men as women, that if an agreement were publicly concluded, they also should be ready, for their parts, to express their regard to the king. And Cineas, discoursing with the senate in the most persuasive and obliging manner in the world, yet was not heard with kindness or inclination, although Pyrrhus offered also to return all the prisoners he had taken in the fight without ransom, and promised his assistance for the entire conquest of all Italy, asking only their friendship for himself, and security for the Tarentines, and nothing further. Nevertheless, most were well inclined to a peace, having already received one great defeat, and fearing another from an additional force of the native Italians, now joining with Pyrrhus. At this point Appius

Claudius, a man of great distinction, but who, because of his great age and loss of sight, had declined the fatigue of public business, after these propositions had been made by the king, hearing a report that the senate was ready to vote the conditions of peace, could not forbear, but commanding his servants to take him up, was carried in his chair through the forum to the senate-house. When he was set down at the door, his sons and sons-in-law took him up in their arms, and, walking close round about him, brought him into the senate. Out of reverence for so worthy a man, the whole assembly was respectfully silent.

And a little after raising up himself: "I bore," said he, "until this time, the misfortune of my eyes with some impatience, but now while I hear of these dishonourable motions and resolves of yours, destructive to the glory of Rome, it is my affliction, that being already blind, I am not deaf too. Where is now that discourse of yours that became famous in all the world, that if he, the great Alexander, had come into Italy, and dared to attack us when we were young men, and our fathers, who were then in their prime, he had not now been celebrated as invincible, but either flying hence, or falling here, had left Rome more glorious? You demonstrate now that all that was but foolish arrogance and vanity, by fearing Molossians and Chaonians, ever the Macedonian's prey, and by trembling at Pyrrhus who was himself but an humble servant to one of Alexander's lifeguard, and comes here, not so much to assist the Greeks that inhabit among us, as to escape from his enemies at home, a wanderer about Italy, and yet dares to promise you the conquest of it all by that army which has not been able to preserve for him a little part of Macedon. Do not persuade yourselves that making him your friend is the way to send him back, it is the way rather to bring over other invaders from thence, contemning you as easy to be reduced, if Pyrrhus goes off without punishment for his outrages on you, but, on the contrary, with the reward of having enabled the Tarentines and Samnites to laugh at the Romans." When Appius had done, eagerness for the war seized on every man, and Cineas was dismissed with this answer, that when Pyrrhus had withdrawn his forces out of Italy, then, if he pleased, they would treat with him about friendship and alliance, but while he stayed there in arms, they were resolved to prosecute the war against him with all their force, though he should have defeated a thousand Lævinuses. It is said that Cineas, while he was managing this affair, made it his business carefully to inspect the manners of the Romans, and to understand their methods of government, and having conversed with their noblest citizens, he afterwards told Pyrrhus, among other things, that the senate seemed to him an assembly of kings, and as for the people, he feared lest it might prove that they were fighting with a Lernæan hydra, for the consul had already raised twice as large an army as the former, and there were many times over the same number of Romans able to bear arms.

Then Caius Fabricius came in embassy from the Romans to treat about the prisoners that were taken, one whom Cineas had reported to be a man of highest consideration among them as an honest man and a good soldier, but extremely poor. Pyrrhus received him with much kindness, and privately would have persuaded him to accept of his gold, not for any evil purpose, but calling it a mark of respect and hospitable kindness. Upon Fabricius' refusal, he pressed him no further, but the next day, having a mind to discompose him, as he had never seen an elephant before, he commanded one of the largest, completely armed, to be placed behind the hangings, as they were talking together. Which being done, upon a sign given, the hanging was drawn aside, and the elephant, raising his trunk over the head of Fabricius, made an horrid and ugly noise. He, gently turning about and smiling, said to Pyrrhus, "Neither your money yesterday, nor this beast today, makes any impression upon me." At supper, amongst all sorts of things that were discoursed of, but more particularly Greece and the philosophers there, Cineas, by accident, had occasion to speak of Epicurus, and explained the opinions his followers hold about the gods and the commonwealth, and the objects of life, placing the chief happiness of man in pleasure, and declining public affairs as an injury and disturbance of a happy life, removing the gods afar off both from kindness or anger, or any concern for us at all, to a life wholly without business and flowing in pleasures. Before he had done speaking, "O Hercules!" Fabricius cried out to Pyrrhus, "may Pyrrhus and the Samnites entertain themselves with this sort of opinions as long as they are in war with us." Pyrrhus, admiring the wisdom and gravity of the man, was the more transported with desire of making friendship instead of war with the city, and entreated him, personally, after the peace should be concluded, to accept of living with him as the chief of his ministers and generals. Fabricius answered quietly, "Sir, this will not be for your advantage, for they who now honour and admire you, when they have had experience of me, will rather choose to be governed by me than by you." Such was Fabricius. And Pyrrhus received his answer without any resentment or tyrannic passion; nay, among his friends he highly commended the great mind of Fabricius, and intrusted the prisoners to him alone, on condition that if the senate should not vote a peace, after they had conversed with their friends and celebrated the festival of Saturn, they should be remanded. And, accordingly, they were sent back after the holidays; it being decreed pain of death for any that stayed behind.

After this, Fabricius taking the consulate, a person came with a letter to the camp written by the king's principal physician, offering to take off Pyrrhus by poison, and so end the war without further hazard to the Romans, if he might have a reward proportionable to his service. Fabricius, hating the villainy of the man, and disposing the other consul to the same opinion, sent despatches immediately to Pyrrhus to caution him against the treason. His letter was to this effect: "Caius Fabricius and Quinrus Æmilius, consuls of the Romans, to Pyrrhus the king, health. You seem to have made an ill-judgment both of your friends and enemies; you will understand by reading this letter sent to us, that you are at war with honest men, and trust villains and knaves. Nor do we disclose this to you out of any favour to you, but lest your ruin might bring a reproach upon us, as if we had ended the war, by treachery, as not able to do it by force." When Pyrrhus had read the letter and made inquiry into the treason, he punished the physician, and as an acknowledgment to the Romans sent to Rome the prisoners without ransom, and again employed Cineas to negotiate a peace for him. But they, regarding it as at once too great a kindness from an enemy, and too great a reward for not doing an ill thing to accept their prisoners so, released in return an equal number of the Tarentines and Samnites, but would admit of no debate of alliance or peace until he had removed his arms and forces out of Italy, and sailed back to Epirus with the same ships that brought him over. Afterwards, his affairs demanding a second fight, when he had refreshed his men, he decamped, and met the Romans about the city Asculum, where, however, he was much incommoded by a woody country unfit for his horse, and a swift river, so that the elephants, for want of sure treading, could not get up with the infantry. After many wounded and many killed, night put an end to the engagement. Next day, designing to make the fight on even ground, and have the elephants among the thickest of the enemy, he caused a detachment to possess themselves of those incommodious grounds, and, mixing slingers and archers among the elephants, with full strength and courage, he advanced in a close and well-ordered body. The Romans, not having those advantages of retreating and falling on as they pleased, which they had before, were obliged to fight man to man upon plain ground, and, being anxious to drive back the infantry before the elephants could get up, they fought fiercely with their swords among the Macedonian spears, not sparing themselves, thinking only to wound and kill, without regard to what they suffered. After a long and obstinate fight, the first giving ground is reported to have been where Pyrrhus himself engaged with extraordinary courage; but they were most carried away by the overwhelming force of the elephants, not being able to make use of their valour, but overthrown as it were by the irruption of a sea or an earthquake, before which it seemed better to give way than to die without doing anything, and not gain the least advantage by suffering the utmost extremity, the retreat to their camp not being far. Hieronymus says there fell six thousand of the Romans, and of Pyrrhus' men, the king's own commentaries reported three thousand five hundred and fifty lost in this action. Dionysius, however, neither gives any account of two engagements at Asculum, nor allows the Romans to have been certainly beaten, stating that once only after they had fought till sunset, both armies were unwillingly separated by the night, Pyrrhus being wounded by a javelin in the arm, and his baggage plundered by the Samnites, that in all there died of Pyrrhus' men and the Romans above fifteen thousand. The armies separated; and, it is said, Pyrrhus replied to one that gave him joy of his victory that one other such would utterly undo him. For he had lost a great part of the forces he brought with him, and almost all his particular friends and principal commanders; there were no others there to make recruits, and he found the confederates in Italy backward. On the other hand, as from a fountain continually flowing out of the city, the Roman camp was quickly and plentifully filled up with fresh men, not at all abating in courage for the loss they sustained, but even from their very anger gaining new force and resolution to go on with the war.

Among these difficulties he fell again into new hopes and projects distracting his purposes. For at the same time some persons arrived from Sicily, offering into his hands the cities of Agrigentum, Syracuse, and Leontini, and begging his assistance to drive out the Carthaginians and rid the island of tyrants; and others brought him news out of Greece that Ptolemy, called Ceranus, was slain in a fight, and his army cut in pieces by the Gauls, and that now, above all others, was his time to offer himself to the Macedonians, in great need of a king. Complaining much of fortune for bringing him so many occasions of great things all together at a time, and thinking that to have both offered to him was to lose one of them, he was doubtful, balancing in his thoughts. But the affairs of Sicily seeming to hold out the greater prospects, Africa lying so near, he turned himself to them, and presently despatched away Cineas, as he used to do, to make terms beforehand with the cities. Then he placed a garrison in Tarentum, much to the Tarentines' discontent, who required him either to perform what he came for, and continue with them in a war against the Romans, or leave the city as he found it. He returned no pleasing answer, but commanded them to be quiet and attend his time, and so sailed away. Being arrived in Sicily, what he had designed in his hopes was confirmed effectually, and the cities frankly surrendered to him; and wherever his arms and force were necessary, nothing at first made any considerable resistance. For advancing with thirty thousand foot, and twenty-five hundred horse, and two hundred ships, he totally routed the Phœnicians, and overran their whole province, and Eryx being the strongest town they held, and having a great garrison in it, he resolved to take it by storm. The army being in readiness to give the assault, he put on his arms, and coming to the head of his men made a vow of plays and sacrifices in honour to Hercules, if he signalised himself in that day's action before the Greeks that dwelt in Sicily, as became his great descent and his fortunes. The sign being given by sound of trumpet, he first scattered the barbarians with his shot, and then brought his ladders to the wall, and was the first that mounted upon it himself, and, the enemy appearing in great numbers, he beat them back; some he threw down from the walls on each side, others he laid dead in a heap round about him with his sword, nor did he receive the least wound, but by his very aspect inspired terror in the enemy; and gave a clear demonstration that Homer was in the right, and pronounced according to the truth of fact, that fortitude alone, of all the virtues, is wont to display itself in divine transports and frenzies. The city being taken, he offered to Hercules most magnificently, and exhibited all varieties of shows and plays.

A sort of barbarous people about Messena, called Mamertines, gave much trouble to the Greeks, and put several of them under contribution. These being numerous and valiant (from whence they had their name, equivalent in the Latin tongue to *warlike*,[3]) he first intercepted the collectors of the contribution money, and cut them off, then beat them in open fight, and destroyed many of their places of strength. The Carthaginians being now inclined to composition, and offering him a round sum of money, and to furnish him with shipping, if a peace were concluded, he told them plainly, aspiring still to greater things, there was but one way for a friendship and right understanding between them, if they, wholly abandoning Sicily, would consent to make the African sea the limit between them and the Greeks. And being elevated with his good fortune, and the strength of his forces, and pursuing those hopes in prospect of which he first sailed thither, his immediate aim was at Africa; and as he had abundance of shipping, but very ill equipped, he collected seamen, not by fair and gentle dealing with the cities, but by force in a haughty and insolent way, and menacing them with punishments. And as at first he had not acted thus, but had been unusually indulgent and kind, ready to believe, and uneasy to none; now of a popular leader becoming a tyrant by these severe proceedings, he got the name of an ungrateful and a faithless man. However, they gave way to these things as necessary, although they took them very ill from him; and especially when he began to show suspicion of Thœnon and Sosistratus, men of the first position in Syracuse, who invited him over into Sicily, and when he was come, put the cities into his power, and were most instrumental in all he had done there since his arrival, whom he now would neither suffer to be about his person, nor leave at home; and when Sosistratus out of fear withdrew himself, and then he charged Thœnon, as in a conspiracy with the other, and put him to death, with this all his prospects changed, not by little and little, nor in a single place only, but a mortal hatred being raised in the cities against him, some fell off to the Carthaginians, others called in the Mamertines. And seeing revolts in all places, and desires of alteration, and a potent faction against him, at the same time he received letters from the Samnites and Tarentines, who were beaten quite out of the field, and scarce able to secure their towns against the war, earnestly begging his help. This served as a colour to make his relinquishing Sicily no flight, nor a despair of good success; but in truth not being able to manage Sicily, which was as a ship labouring in a storm, and willing to be out of her, he suddenly threw himself over into Italy. It is reported that at his going off he looked back upon the island, and said to those about him, "How brave a field of war do we leave, my friends, for the Romans and Carthaginians to fight in," which, as he then conjectured, fell out indeed not long after.

When he was sailing off, the barbarians having conspired together, he was forced to a fight with the Carthaginians in the very road, and lost many of his ships; with the rest he fled into Italy. There, about one thousand Mamertines, who had crossed the sea a little before, though afraid to engage him in open field, setting upon him where the passages were difficult, put the whole army in confusion. Two elephants fell, and a great part of his rear was cut off. He, therefore, coming up in person, repulsed the enemy, but ran into great danger among men long trained and bold in war. His being wounded in the head with a sword, and retiring a little out of the fight, much increased their confidence, and one of them advancing a good way before the rest, large of body and in bright armour, with an haughty voice challenged him to come forth if he were alive. Pyrrhus, in great anger, broke away violently from his guards, and, in his fury, besmeared with blood, terrible to look upon, made his way through his own men, and struck the barbarian on the head with his sword such a blow, as with the strength of his arm, and the excellent temper of the weapon, passed downward so far that his body being cut asunder fell in two pieces. This stopped the course of the barbarians, amazed and confounded at Pyrrhus, as one more than man; so that continuing his march all the rest of the way undisturbed, he arrived at Tarentum with twenty thousand foot and three thousand horse, where, reinforcing himself with the choicest troops of the Tarentines, he advanced immediately against the Romans, who then lay encamped in the territories of the Samnites, whose affairs were extremely shattered, and their counsels broken, having been in many fights beaten by the Romans. There was also a discontent amongst them at Pyrrhus for his expedition into Sicily, so that not many came in to join him.

He divided his army into two parts, and despatched the first into Lucania to oppose one of the consuls there, so that he should not come in to assist the other; the rest he led against Manius Curius, who had posted himself very advantageously near Beneventum, and expected the other consul's forces, and partly because the priests had dissuaded him by unfavourable omens, was resolved to remain inactive. Pyrrhus, hastening to attack these before the other could arrive, with his best men, and the most serviceable elephants, marched in the night toward their camp. But being forced to go round about, and through a very woody country, their lights failed them, and the soldiers lost their way. A council of war being called, while they were in debate, the night was spent, and, at the break of day, his approach, as he came down the hills, was discovered by the enemy, and put the whole camp into disorder and tumult. But the sacrifices being auspicious, and the time absolutely obliging them to fight, Manius drew his troops out of the trenches, and attacked the vanguard, and, having routed them all, put the whole army into consternation, so that many were cut off and some of the elephants taken. This success drew on Manius into the level plain, and here, in open battle, he defeated part of the enemy; but, in other quarters, finding himself overpowered by the elephants and forced back to his trenches, he commanded out those who were left to guard them, a numerous body, standing thick at the ramparts, all in arms and fresh. These coming down from their strong position, and charging the elephants, forced them to retire; and they in the flight turning back upon their own men, caused great disorder and confusion, and gave into the hands of the Romans the victory and the future supremacy. Having obtained from these efforts, and these contests, the feeling as well as the fame of invincible strength, they at once reduced Italy under their power, and not long after Sicily too.

Thus fell Pyrrhus from his Italian and Sicilian hopes, after he had consumed six years in these wars, and though unsuccessful in his affairs, yet preserved his courage unconquerable among all these misfortunes, and was held, for military experience, and personal valour and enterprise, much the bravest of all the princes of his time, only what he got by great actions he lost again by vain hopes, and by new desires of what he had not, kept nothing of what he had. So that Antigonus used to compare him to a player with dice, who had excellent throws, but knew not how to use them. He returned into Epirus with eight thousand foot and five hundred horse, and for want of money to pay them, was fain to look out for a new war to maintain the army. Some of the Gauls joining him, he invaded Macedonia, where Antigonus, son of Demetrius, governed, designing merely to plunder and waste the country. But after he had made himself master of several towns, and two thousand men came over to him, he began to hope for something greater, and adventured upon Antigonus himself, and meeting him at a narrow passage, put the whole army in disorder. The Gauls, who brought up Antigonus' rear, were very numerous and stood firm, but after a sharp encounter, the greatest part of them were cut off, and they who had the charge of the elephants being surrounded every way, delivered up both themselves and the beasts, Pyrrhus, taking this advantage, and advising more with his good fortune than his reason, boldly set upon the main body of the Macedonian foot, already surprised with fear, and troubled at the former loss. They declined any action or engagement with him; and he, holding out his hand and calling aloud both to the superior and under officers by name, brought over the foot from Antigonus, who, flying away secretly, was only able to retain some of the seaport towns. Pyrrhus, among all these kindnesses of fortune, thinking what he had effected against the Gauls the most advantageous for his glory, hung up their richest and goodliest spoils in the temple of Minerva Itonis, with this inscription:

> Pyrrhus, descendant of Molossian kings,
> These shields to thee, Itonian goddess, brings,
> Won from the valiant Gaul when in the fight
> Antigonus and all his host took flight;
> 'Tis not today or yesterday alone
> That for brave deeds the Æacidæ are known.

After this victory in the field, he proceeded to secure the cities, and having possessed himself of Ægæ, beside other hardships put upon the people there, he left in the town a garrison of Gauls, some of those in his own army, who being insatiably desirous of wealth, instantly dug up the tombs of the kings that lay buried there, and took away the riches, and insolently scattered about their bones. Pyrrhus, in appearance, made no great matter of it, either deferring it on account of the pressure of other business, or wholly passing it by, out of fear of punishing those barbarians; but this made him very ill spoken of among the Macedonians, and his affairs being yet unsettled and brought to no firm consistence, he began to entertain new hopes and projects, and in raillery called Antigonus a shameless man, for still wearing his purple and not changing it for an ordinary dress; but upon Cleonymus, the Spartan, arriving and inviting him to Lacedæmon, he frankly embraced the overture. Cleonymus was of royal descent, but seeming too arbitrary and absolute, had no great respect nor credit at home; and Areus was king there. This was the occasion of an old and public grudge between him and the citizens; but, beside that, Cleonymus, in his old age, had married a young lady of great beauty and royal blood, Chilonis, daughter of Leotychides, who, falling desperately in love with Acrotatus, Areus' son, a youth in the flower of manhood, rendered this match both uneasy and dishonourable to Cleonymus, as there was none of the Spartans who did not very well know how much his wife slighted him; so these domestic troubles added to his public discontent. He brought Pyrrhus to Sparta with an army of twenty-five thousand foot, two thousand horse, and twenty-four elephants. So great a preparation made it evident to the whole world that he came, not so much to gain Sparta for Cleonymus, as to take all Peloponnesus for himself, although he expressly denied this to the Lacedæmonian ambassadors that came to him at Megalopolis, affirming he came to deliver the cities from the slavery of Antigonus, and declaring he would send his younger sons to Sparta, if he might, to be brought up in Spartan habits, that so they might be better bred than all other kings. With these pretensions amusing those who came to meet him in his march, as soon as ever he entered Laconia he began to plunder and waste the country, and on the ambassadors complaining that he began the war upon them before it was proclaimed: "We know," said he, "very well that neither do you Spartans, when you design anything, talk of it beforehand." One Mandroclidas, then present, told him, in the broad Spartan dialect: "If you are a god, you will do us no harm, we are wronging no man; but if you are a man, there may be another stronger than you."

He now marched away directly for Lacedæmon, and being advised by Cleonymus to give the assault as soon as he arrived, fearing, as it is said, lest the soldiers, entering by night, should plunder the city, he answered, they might do it as well next morning, because there were but few soldiers in town, and those unprovided against his sudden approach, as Areus was not there in person, but gone to aid the Gortynians in Crete. And it was this alone that saved the town, because he despised it as not tenable, and so imagining no defence would be made, he sat down before it that night. Cleonymus' friends, and the Helots, his domestic servants, had made great preparation at his house, as expecting Pyrrhus there at supper. In the night the Lacedæmonians held a consultation to ship over all the women into Crete, but they unanimously refused, and Archidamia came into the senate with a sword in her hand, in the name of them all, asking if the men expected the women to survive the ruins of Sparta. It was next resolved to draw a trench in a line directly over against the enemy's camp, and, here and there in it, to sink wagons in the ground, as deep as the naves of the wheel, that, so being firmly fixed, they might obstruct the passage of the elephants. When they had just begun the work, both maids and women came to them, the married women with their robes tied like girdles round their underfrocks, and the unmarried girls in their single frocks only, to assist the elder men at the work. As for the youth that were next day to engage, they left them to their rest, and undertaking their proportion, they themselves finished a third part of the trench, which was in breadth six cubits, four in depth, and eight hundred feet long, as Phylarchus says; Hieronymus makes it somewhat less. The enemy beginning to move by break of day, they brought their arms to the young men, and giving them also in charge the trench, exhorted them to defend and keep it bravely, as it would be happy for them to conquer in the view of their whole country, and glorious to die in the arms of their mothers and wives, falling as became Spartans. As for Chilonis, she retired with a halter about her neck, resolving to die so rather than fall into the hands of Cleonymus, if the city were taken.

Pyrrhus himself, in person, advanced with his foot to force through the shields of the Spartans ranged against him, and to get over the trench, which was scarce passable, because the looseness of the fresh earth afforded no firm footing for the soldiers. Ptolemy, his son, with two thousand Gauls, and some choice men of the Chaonians, went around the trench, and endeavoured to get over where the wagons were. But they, being so deep in the ground, and placed close together, not only made his passage, but also the defence of the Lacedæmonians, very troublesome. Yet now the Gauls had got the wheels out of the ground, and were drawing off the wagons toward the river, when young Acrotatus, seeing the danger, passing through the town with three hundred men, surrounded Ptolemy undiscerned, taking the advantage of some slopes of the ground, until he fell upon his rear, and forced him to wheel about. And thrusting one another into the ditch, and falling among the wagons, at last with much loss, not without difficulty, they withdrew. The elderly men and all the women saw this brave action of Acrotatus, and when he returned back into the town to his first post, all covered with blood and fierce and elate with victory, he seemed to the Spartan women to have become taller and more beautiful than before, and they envied Chilonis so worthy a lover. And some of the old men followed him, crying aloud, "Go on, Acrotatus, be happy with Chilonis, and beget brave sons for Sparta." Where Pyrrhus himself fought was the hottest of the action and many of the Spartans did gallantly, but in particular one Phyllius signalised himself, made the best resistance, and killed most assailants; and when he found himself ready to sink with the many wounds he had received, retiring a little out of his place behind another, he fell down among his fellow-soldiers, that the enemy might not carry off his body. The fight ended with the day, and Pyrrhus, in his sleep, dreamed that he drew thunderbolts upon Lacedæmon, and set it all on fire, and rejoiced at the sight; and waking, in this transport of joy, he commanded his officers to get all things ready for a second assault, and relating his dream among his friends, supposing it to mean that he should take the town by storm, the rest assented to it with admiration, but Lysimachus was not pleased with the dream, and told him he feared lest as places struck with lightning are held sacred, and not to be trodden upon, so the gods might by this let him know the city should not be taken. Pyrrhus replied, that all these things were but idle talk, full of uncertainty, and only fit to amuse the vulgar; their thought, with their swords in their hands, should always be—

The one good omen is King Pyrrhus' cause,

and so got up, and drew out his army to the walls by break of day. The Lacedæmonians, in resolution and courage, made a defence even beyond their power; the women were all by, helping them to arms, and bringing bread and drink to those that desired it, and taking care of the wounded. The Macedonians attempted to fill up the trench, bringing huge quantities of materials and throwing them upon the arms and dead bodies, that lay there and were covered over. While the Lacedæmonians opposed this with all their force, Pyrrhus, in person, appeared on their side of the trench and wagons, pressing on horseback toward the city, at which the men who had that post calling out, and the women shrieking and running about, while Pyrrhus violently pushed on, and beat down all that disputed his way, his horse received a shot in the belly from a Cretan arrow, and, in his convulsions as he died, threw off Pyrrhus on slippery and steep ground. And all about him being in confusion at this, the Spartans came boldly up, and making good use of their missiles, forced them off again. After this Pyrrhus, in other quarters also, put an end to the combat, imagining the Lacedæmonians would be inclined to yield, as almost all of them were wounded, and very great numbers killed outright; but the good fortune of the city, either satisfied with the experiment upon the bravery of the citizens, or willing to prove how much even in the last extremities such interposition may effect, brought, when the Lacedæmonians had now but very slender hopes left, Aminias, the Phocian, one of Antigonus' commanders, from Corinth to their assistance, with a force of mercenaries; and they were no sooner received into the town, but Areus, their king, arrived there himself, too, from Crete, with two thousand men more. The women upon this went all home to their houses, finding it no longer necessary for them to meddle with the business of the war; and they also were sent back, who, though not of military age, were by necessity forced to take arms, while the rest prepared to fight Pyrrhus.

He, upon the coming of these additional forces, was indeed possessed with a more eager desire and ambition than before to make himself master of the town; but his designs not succeeding, and receiving fresh losses everyday, he gave over the siege, and fell to plundering the country, determining to winter thereabout. But fate is unavoidable, and a great feud happening at Argos between Aristeas and Aristippus, two principal citizens, after Aristippus had resolved to make use of the friendship of Antigonus, Aristeas to anticipate him invited Pyrrhus thither. And he always revolving hopes upon hopes, and treating all his successes as occasions of more, and his reverses as defects to be amended by new enterprises, allowed neither losses nor victories to limit him in his receiving or giving trouble, and so presently went for Argos. Areus, by frequent ambushes, and seizing positions where the ways were most unpracticable, harassed the Gauls and Molossians that brought up the rear. It had been told Pyrrhus by one of the priests that found the liver of the sacrificed beast imperfect that some of his near relations would be lost; in this tumult and disorder of his rear, forgetting the prediction, he commanded out his son Ptolemy with some of his guards to their assistance, while he himself led on the main body rapidly out of the pass. And the fight being very warm where Ptolemy was (for the most select men of the Lacedæmonians, commanded by Evalcus, were there engaged), one Oryssus of Aptera in Crete, a stout man and swift of foot, running on one side of the young prince, as he was fighting bravely, gave him a mortal wound and slew him. On his fall those about him turned their backs, and the Lacedæmonian horse, pursuing and cutting off many, got into the open plain, and found themselves engaged with the enemy before they were aware, without their infantry; Pyrrhus, who had received the ill news of his son, and was in great affliction, drew out his Molossian horse against them, and charging at the head of his men, satiated himself with the blood and slaughter of the Lacedæmonians, as indeed he always showed himself a terrible and invincible hero in actual fight, but now he exceeded all he had ever done before in courage and force. On his riding his horse up to Evalcus, he by declining a little to one side, had almost cut off Pyrrhus' hand in which he held the reins, but lighting on the reins, only cut them; at the same instant Pyrrhus, running him through with his spear, fell from his horse, and there on foot as he was proceeded to slaughter all those choice men that fought about the body of Evalcus; a severe additional loss to Sparta, incurred after the war itself was now at an end, by the mere animosity of the commanders. Pyrrhus having thus offered, as it were, a sacrifice to the ghost of his son, and fought a glorious battle in honour of his obsequies, and having vented much of his pain in action against the enemy, marched away to Argos. And having intelligence that Antigonus was already in possession of the high grounds, he encamped about Nauplia, and the next day despatched a herald to Antigonus calling him a villain, and challenging him to descend into the plain field and fight with him for the kingdom. He answered, that his conduct should be measured by times as well as by arms, and that if Pyrrhus had no leisure to live, there were ways enough open to death. To both the kings, also, came ambassadors from Argos, desiring each party to retreat, and to allow the city to remain in friendship with both, without falling into the hands of either. Antigonus was persuaded, and sent his son as a hostage to the Argives; but Pyrrhus, although he consented to retire, yet, as he sent no hostage, was suspected. A remarkable portent happened at this time to Pyrrhus; the heads of the sacrificed oxen, lying apart from the bodies, were seen to thrust out their tongues and lick up their own gore. And in the city of Argos, the priestess of Apollo Lycius rushed out of the temple, crying she saw the city full of carcasses and slaughter, and an eagle coming out to fight, and presently vanishing again.

In the dead of the night, Pyrrhus, approaching the walls, and finding the gate called Diamperes set open for them by Aristeas, was undiscovered long enough to allow all his Gauls to enter and take possession of the marketplace. But the gate being too low to let in the elephants, they were obliged to take down the towers which they carried on their backs, and put them on again in the dark and in disorder, so that time being lost, the city took the alarm, and the people ran, some to Aspis the chief citadel, and other places of defence, and sent away to Antigonus to assist them. He, advancing within a short distance, made an halt, but sent in some of his principal commanders, and his son with a considerable force. Areus came thither, too, with one thousand Cretans, and some of the most active men among the Spartans, and all falling on at once upon the Gauls, put them in great disorder. Pyrrhus, entering in with noise and shouting near the Cylarabis, when the Gauls returned the cry, noticed that it did not express courage and assurance, but was the voice of men distressed, and that had their hands full. He, therefore, pushed forward in haste the van of his horse that marched but slowly and dangerously, by reason of the drains and sinks of which the city is full. In this night engagement there was infinite uncertainty as to what was being done, or what orders were given; there was much mistaking and struggling in the narrow streets; all generalship was useless in that darkness and noise and pressure; so both sides continued without doing anything, expecting daylight. At the first dawn, Pyrrhus, seeing the great citadel Aspis full of enemies, was disturbed, and remarking, among a variety of figures dedicated in the market place, a wolf and a bull of brass, as it were ready to attack one another, he was struck with alarm, recollecting an oracle that formerly predicted fate had determined his death when he should see a wolf fighting with a bull. The Argives say these figures were set up in record of a thing that long ago had happened there. For Danaus, at his first landing in the country, near the Pyramia in Thyreatis, as he was on his way towards Argos, espied a wolf fighting with a bull, and conceiving the wolf to represent him (for this stranger fell upon a native as he designed to do), stayed to see the issue of the fight, and the wolf prevailing, he offered vows to Apollo Lycius, and thus made his attempt upon the town, and succeeded; Gelanor, who was then king, being displaced by a faction. And this was the cause of dedicating those figures.

Pyrrhus, quite out of heart at this sight, and seeing none of his designs succeed, thought best to retreat, but fearing the narrow passage at the gate, sent to his son Helenus, who was left without the town with a great part of his forces, commanding him to break down part of the wall, and assist the retreat if the enemy pressed hard upon them. But what with haste and confusion, the person that was sent delivered nothing clearly; so that quite mistaking, the young prince with the best of his men and the remaining elephants marched straight through the gates into the town to assist his father. Pyrrhus was now making good his retreat, and while the marketplace afforded them ground enough both to retreat and fight, frequently repulsed the enemy that bore upon him. But when he was forced out of that broad place into the narrow street leading to the gate, and fell in with those who came the other way to his assistance, some did not hear him call out to them to give back, and those who did, however eager to obey him, were pushed forward by others behind, who poured in at the gate. Besides, the largest of his elephants falling down on his side in the very gate, and lying roaring on the ground, was in the way of those that would have got out. Another of the elephants already in the town, called Nicon, striving to take up his rider, who, after many wounds received, was fallen off his back, bore forward upon those that were retreating, and, thrusting upon friends as well as enemies, tumbled them all confusedly upon one another, till having found the body, and taken it up with his trunk, he carried it on his tusks, and, returning in a fury, trod down all before him. Being thus pressed and crowded together, not a man could do anything for himself, but being wedged, as it were, together into one mass, the whole multitude rolled and swayed this way and that altogether, and did very little execution either upon the enemy in their rear, or on any of them who were intercepted in the mass, but very much harm to one another. For he who had either drawn his sword or directed his lance could neither restore it again, nor put his sword up; with these weapons they wounded their own men, as they happened to come in the way, and they were dying by mere contact with each other.

Pyrrhus, seeing this storm and confusion of things, took off the crown he wore upon his helmet, by which he was distinguished, and gave it to one nearest his person, and trusting to the goodness of his horse, rode in among the thickest of the enemy, and being wounded with a lance through his breastplate, but not dangerously, nor indeed very much, he turned about upon the man who struck him, who was an Argive, not of any illustrious birth, but the son of a poor old woman; she was looking upon the fight among other women from the top of a house, and perceiving her son engaged with Pyrrhus, and affrighted at the danger he was in, took up a tile with both hands and threw it at Pyrrhus. This falling on his head below the helmet, and bruising the vertebræ of the lower part of the neck, stunned and blinded him; his hands let go the reins, and sinking down from his horse he fell just by the tomb of Licymnius. The common soldiers knew not who it was; but one Zopyrus, who served under Antigonus, and two or three others running thither, and knowing it was Pyrrhus, dragged him to a doorway hard by, just as he was recovering a little from the blow. But when Zopyrus drew out an Illyrian sword, ready to cut off his head, Pyrrhus gave him so fierce a look that, confounded with terror, and sometimes his hands trembling and then again endeavouring to do it, full of fear and confusion, he could not strike him right, but cutting over his mouth and chin, it was a long time before he got off the head. By this time what had happened was known to a great many, and Alcyoneus hastening to the place, desired to look upon the head, and see whether he knew it, and taking it in his hand rode away to his father, and threw it at his feet, while he was sitting with some of his particular favourites. Antigonus, looking upon it, and knowing it, thrust his son from him, and struck him with his staff, calling him wicked and barbarous, and covering his eyes with his robe shed tears, thinking of his own father and grandfather, instances in his own family of the changefulness of fortune, and caused the head and body of Pyrrhus to be burned with all due solemnity. After this, Alcyoneus, discovering Helenus under a mean disguise in a threadbare coat, used him very respectfully, and brought him to his father. When Antigonus saw him, "This, my son," said he, "is better; and yet even now you have not done wholly well in allowing these clothes to remain, to the disgrace of those who it seems now are the victors." And treating Helenus with great kindness, and as became a prince, he restored him to his kingdom of Epirus, and gave the same obliging reception to all Pyrrhus' principal commanders, his camp and whole army having fallen into his hands.

CAIUS MARIUS

WE ARE ALTOGETHER IGNORANT OF ANY THIRD NAME OF CAIUS MARIUS; AS also of Quintus Sertorius, that possessed himself of Spain; or of Lucius Mummius that destroyed Corinth, though this last was surnamed Achaicus from his conquests, as Scipio was called Africanus, and Metellus, Macedonicus. Hence Posidonius draws his chief argument to confute those that hold the third to be the Roman proper name, as Camillus, Marcellus, Cato; as in this case, those that had but two names would have no proper name at all. He did not, however, observe that by his own reasoning he must rob the women absolutely of their names; for none of them have the first, which Posidonius imagines the proper name with the Romans. Of the other two, one was common to the whole family, Pompeii, Manlii, Cornelii (as with us Greeks, the Heraclidæ, and Pelopidæ), the other titular, and personal, taken either from their natures, or actions, or bodily characteristics, as Macrinus, Torquatus, Sylla; such as are Mnemon, Grypus, or Callinicus among the Greeks. On the subject of names, however, the irregularity of custom, would we insist upon it, might furnish us with discourse enough.

There is a likeness of Marius in stone at Ravenna, in Gaul, which I myself saw, quite corresponding with that roughness of character that is ascribed to him. Being naturally valiant and warlike, and more acquainted also with the discipline of the camp than of the city, he could not moderate his passion when in authority. He is said never to have either studied Greek, or to have use of that language in any matter of consequence; thinking it ridiculous to bestow time in that learning, the teachers of which were little better than slaves. So after his second triumph, when at the dedication of a temple he presented some shows after the Greek fashion, coming into the theatre, he only sat down and immediately departed. And, accordingly, as Plato used to say to Xenocrates the philosopher, who was thought to show more than ordinary harshness of disposition, "I pray you, good Xenocrates, sacrifice to the Graces"; so if any could have persuaded Marius to pay his devotions to the Greek Muses and Graces, he had never brought his incomparable actions, both in war and peace, to so unworthy a conclusion, or wrecked himself, so to say, upon an old age of cruelty and vindictiveness, through passion, ill-timed ambition, and insatiable cupidity. But this will further appear by and by from the facts.

He was born of parents altogether obscure and indigent, who supported themselves by their daily labour; his father of the same name with himself, his mother called Fulcinia. He had spent a considerable part of his life before he saw and tasted the pleasures of the city; having passed previously in Cirrhæaton, a village of the territory of Arpinum, a life, compared with city delicacies, rude and unrefined, yet temperate, and conformable to the ancient Roman severity. He first served as a soldier in the war against the Celtiberians, when Scipio Africanus besieged Numantia; where he signalised himself to his general by courage far above his comrades, and particularly by his cheerfully complying with Scipio's reformation of his army, being almost ruined by pleasures and luxury. It is stated, too, that he encountered and vanquished an enemy in single combat, in his general's sight. In consequence of all this he had several honours conferred upon him; and once when at an entertainment a question arose about commanders, and one of the company (whether really desirous to know, or only in complaisance) asked Scipio where the Romans, after him, should obtain such another general, Scipio, gently clapping Marius on the shoulder as he sat next him, replied, "Here, perhaps." So promising was his early youth of his future greatness, and so discerning was Scipio to detect the distant future in the present first beginnings. It was this speech of Scipio, we are told, which, like a divine admonition, chiefly emboldened Marius to aspire to a political career. He sought, and by the assistance of Cæcilius Metellus, of whose family he as well as his father were dependents, obtained the office of tribune of the people. In which place, when he brought forward a bill for the regulation of voting, which seemed likely to lessen the authority of the great men in the courts of justice, the consul Cotta opposed him, and persuaded the senate to declare against the law, and called Marius to account for it. He, however, when this decree was prepared, coming into the senate, did not behave like a young man newly and undeservedly advanced to authority, but, assuming all the courage that his future actions would have warranted, threatened Cotta, unless he recalled the decree, to throw him into prison. And on his turning to Metellus, and asking his vote, and Metellus, rising up to concur with the consul, Marius, calling for the officer outside, commanded him to take Metellus into custody. He appealed to the other tribunes, but not one of them assisted him; so that the senate, immediately complying, withdrew the decree. Marius came forth with glory to the people and confirmed his law, and was henceforth esteemed a man of undaunted courage and assurance, as well as a vigorous opposer of the senate in favour of the commons. But he immediately lost their opinion of him by a contrary action; for when a law for the distribution of corn was proposed, he vigorously and successfully resisted it, making himself equally honoured by both parties, in gratifying neither, contrary to the public interest.

After his tribuneship, he was candidate for the office of chief ædile; there being two orders of them, one the curules, from the stool with crooked feet on which they sat when they performed their duty; the other and inferior, called ædiles of the people. As soon as they have chosen the former, they give their voices again for the latter. Marius, finding he was likely to be put by for the greater, immediately changed and stood for the less; but because he seemed too forward and hot, he was disappointed of that also. And yet though he was in one day twice frustrated of his desired preferment (which never happened to any before), yet he was not at all discouraged, but a little while after sought for the prætorship and was nearly suffering a repulse, and then, too, though he was returned last of all, was nevertheless accused of bribery.

Cassius Sabaco's servant, who was observed within the rails among those who voted, chiefly occasioned the suspicion, as Sabaco was an intimate friend of Marius; but on being called to appear before the judges, he alleged, that being thirsty by reason of the heat, he called for cold water, and that his servant brought him a cup, and as soon as he had drunk, departed; he was, however, excluded from the senate by the succeeding censors, and not undeservedly either, as was thought, whether it might be for his false evidence, or his want of temperance. Caius Herennius was also cited to appear as evidence, but pleaded that it was not customary for a *patron* (the Roman word for *protector*) to witness against his clients, and that the law excused them from that harsh duty; and both Marius and his parents had always been clients to the family of Herennii. And when the judges would have accepted of this plea, Marius himself opposed it, and told Herennius, that when he was first created magistrate he ceased to be his client; which was not altogether true. For it is not every office that frees clients and their posterity from the observance due to their patrons, but only those to which the law has assigned a curule chair. Notwithstanding, though at the beginning of the suit it went somewhat hard with Marius, and he found the judges no way favourable to him, yet at last, their voices being equal, contrary to all expectation, he was acquitted.

In his prætorship he did not get much honour, yet after it he obtained the further Spain; which province he is said to have cleared of robbers, with which it was much infested, the old barbarous habits still prevailing, and the Spaniards, in those days, still regarding robbery as a piece of valour. In the city he had neither riches nor eloquence to trust to, with which the leading men of the time obtained power with the people, but his vehement disposition, his indefatigable labours, and his plain way of living, of themselves gained him esteem and influence; so that he made an honourable match with Julia, of the distinguished family of the Cæsars, to whom that Cæsar was nephew who was afterwards so great among the Romans, and, in some degree, from his relationship, made Marius his example, as in his life we have observed.

Marius is praised for both temperance and endurance, of which latter he gave a decided instance in an operation of surgery. For having, as it seems, both his legs full of great tumours, and disliking the deformity, he determined to put himself into the hands of an operator; when, without being tied, he stretched out one of his legs, and silently, without changing countenance, endured most excessive torments in the cutting, never either flinching or complaining; but when the surgeon went to the other, he declined to have it done, saying, "I see the cure is not worth the pain."

The consul Cæcilius Metellus, being declared general in the war against Jugurtha in Africa, took with him Marius for lieutenant; where, eager himself to do great deeds and services that would get him distinction, he did not, like others, consult Metellus' glory and the serving his interest, and attributing his honour of lieutenancy not to Metellus, but to fortune, which had presented him with a proper opportunity and theatre of great actions, he exerted his utmost courage. That war, too, affording several difficulties, he neither declined the greatest, nor disdained undertaking the least of them, but surpassing his equals in counsel and conduct, and matching the very common soldiers in labour and abstemiousness, he gained great popularity with them; as indeed any voluntary partaking with people in their labour is felt as an easing of that labour, as it seems to take away the constraint and necessity of it. It is the most obliging sight in the world to the Roman soldier to see a commander eat the same bread as himself, or lie upon an ordinary bed, or assist the work in the drawing a trench and raising a bulwark. For they do not so much admire those that confer honours and riches upon them, as those that partake of the same labour and danger with themselves; but love them better that will vouchsafe to join in their work, than those that encourage their idleness.

Marius thus employed, and thus winning the affections of the soldiers, before long filled both Africa and Rome with his fame, and some, too, wrote home from the army that the war with Africa would never be brought to a conclusion unless they chose Caius Marius consul. All which was evidently unpleasing to Metellus; but what more especially grieved him was the calamity of Turpillius. This Turpillius had, from his ancestors, been a friend of Metellus, and kept up a constant hospitality with him, and was now serving in the war in command of the smiths and carpenters of the army. Having the charge of a garrison in Vaga, a considerable city, and trusting too much to the inhabitants, because he treated them civilly and kindly, he unawares fell into the enemy's hands. They received Jugurtha into the city; yet nevertheless, at their request, Turpillius was dismissed safe and without receiving any injury; whereupon he was accused of betraying it to the enemy. Marius, being one of the council of war, was not only violent against him himself, but also incensed most of the others, so that Metellus was forced, much against his will, to put him to death. Not long after the accusation proved false, and when others were comforting Metellus, who took heavily the loss of his friend, Marius, rather insulting and arrogating it to himself, boasted in all companies that he had involved Metellus in the guilt of putting his friend to death.

Henceforward they were at open variance; and it is reported that Metellus once, when Marius was present, said insultingly, "You, sir, design to leave us to go home and stand for the consulship, and will not be content to wait and be consul with this boy of mine?" Metellus' son being a mere boy at the time. Yet for all this Marius being very importunate to be gone, after several delays, he was dismissed about twelve days before the election of consuls; and performed that long journey from the camp to the seaport of Utica in two days and a night, and there doing sacrifice before he went on shipboard, it is said the augur told him that heaven promised him some incredible good fortune, and such as was beyond all expectation. Marius, not a little elated with his good omen, began his voyage, and in four days, with a favourable wind, passed the sea; he was welcomed with great joy by the people, and being brought into the assembly by one of the tribunes, sued for the consulship, inveighing in all ways against Metellus, and promising either to slay Jugurtha or take him alive.

He was elected triumphantly, and at once proceeded to levy soldiers contrary both to law and custom, enlisting slaves and poor people; whereas former commanders never accepted of such, but bestowed arms, like other favours, as a matter of distinction, on persons who had the proper qualification, a man's property being thus a sort of security for his good behaviour. These were not the only occasions of ill-will against Marius; some haughty speeches, uttered with great arrogance and contempt, gave great offence to the nobility; as, for example, his saying that he had carried off the consulship as a spoil from the effeminacy of the wealthy and high-born citizens, and telling the people that he gloried in wounds he had himself received for them, as much as others did in the monuments of dead men, and images of their ancestors. Often speaking of the commanders that had been unfortunate in Africa, naming Bestia, for example, and Albinus, men of very good families, but unfit for war, and who had miscarried through want of experience, he asked the people about him if they did not think that the ancestors of these nobles had much rather have left a descendant like him, since they themselves grew famous not by nobility, but by their valour and great actions? This he did not say merely out of vanity and arrogance, or that he were willing, without any advantage, to offend the nobility; but the people always delighting in affronts and scurrilous contumelies against the senate, making boldness of speech their measure of greatness of spirit, continually encouraged him in it, and strengthened his inclination not to spare persons of repute, so he might gratify the multitude.

As soon as he arrived again in Africa, Metellus, no longer able to control his feelings of jealousy, and his indignation that now when he had really finished the war, and nothing was left but to secure the person of Jugurtha, Marius, grown great merely through his ingratitude to him, should come to bereave him both of his victory and triumph, could not bear to have any interview with him; but retired himself, whilst Rutilius, his lieutenant, surrendered up the army to Marius, whose conduct, however, in the end of the war, met with some sort of retribution, as Sylla deprived him of the glory of the action as he had done Metellus. I shall state the circumstances briefly here as they are given at large in the life of Sylla. Bocchus was king of the more distant barbarians, and was father-in-law to Jugurtha, yet sent him little or no assistance in his war, professing fears of his unfaithfulness, and really jealous of his growing power; but after Jugurtha fled, and in his distress came to him as his last hope, he received him as a suppliant, rather because ashamed to do otherwise than out of real kindness; and when he had him in his power, he openly entreated Marius on his behalf, and interceded for him with bold words, giving out that he would by no means deliver him. Yet privately designing to betray him, he sent for Lucius Sylla, quæstor to Marius, and who had on a previous occasion befriended Bocchus in the war. When Sylla, relying on his word, came to him, the African began to doubt and repent of his purpose, and for several days was unresolved with himself, whether he should deliver Jugurtha or retain Sylla; at length he fixed upon his former treachery, and put Jugurtha alive into Sylla's possession. Thus was the first occasion given of that fierce and implacable hostility which so nearly ruined the whole Roman empire. For many that envied Marius attributed the success wholly to Sylla, and Sylla himself got a seal made, on which was engraved Bocchus betraying Jugurtha to him, and constantly used it, irritating the hot and jealous temper of Marius, who was naturally greedy of distinction, and quick to resent any claim to share in his glory, and whose enemies took care to promote the quarrel, ascribing the beginning and chief business of the war to Metellus and its conclusion to Sylla; that so the people might give over admiring and esteeming Marius as the worthiest person.

But these envyings and calumnies were soon dispersed and cleared away from Marius by the danger that threatened Italy from the west; when the city, in great need of a good commander, sought about whom she might set at the helm to meet the tempest of so great a war, no one would have anything to say to any members of noble or potent families who offered themselves for the consulship, and Marius, though then absent, was elected.

Jugurtha's apprehension was only just known, when the news of the invasion of the Teutones and Cimbri began. The accounts at first exceeded all credit, as to the number and strength of the approaching army, but in the end report proved much inferior to truth, as they were three hundred thousand effective fighting men, besides a far greater number of women and children. They professed to be seeking new countries to sustain these great multitudes, and cities where they might settle and inhabit, in the same way as they had heard the Celti before them had driven out the Tyrrhenians, and possessed themselves of the best part of Italy. Having had no commerce with the southern nations, and travelling over a wide extent of country, no man knew what people they were, or whence they came, that thus like a cloud burst over Gaul and Italy; yet by their grey eyes and the largeness of their stature they were conjectured to be some of the German races dwelling by the northern sea; besides that, the Germans call plunderers Cimbri.

There are some that say that the country of the Celti, in its vast size and extent, reaches from the furthest sea and the arctic regions to the lake Mæotis eastward, and to that part of Scythia which is near Pontus, and that there the nations mingle together; that they did not swarm out of their country all at once, or on a sudden, but advancing by force of arms, in the summer season, every year, in the course of time they crossed the whole continent. And thus, though each party had several appellations, yet the whole army was called by the common name of Celto-Scythians. Others say that the Cimmerii, anciently known to the Greeks, were only a small part of the nation, who were driven out upon some quarrel among the Scythians, and passed all along from the lake Mæotis to Asia, under the conduct of one Lygdamis; and that the greater and more warlike part of them still inhabit the remotest regions lying upon the outer ocean. These, they say, live in a dark and woody country hardly penetrable by the sunbeams, the trees are so close and thick, extending into the interior as far as the Hercynian forest; and their position on the earth is under that part of heaven where the pole is so elevated that, by the declination of the parallels, the zenith of the inhabitants seems to be but little distant from it; and that their days and nights being almost of an equal length, they divide their year into one of each. This was Homer's occasion for the story of Ulysses calling up the dead, and from this region the people, anciently called Cimmerii, and afterwards, by an easy change, Cimbri, came into Italy. All this, however, is rather conjecture than an authentic history.

Their numbers, most writers agree, were not less, but rather greater than was reported. They were of invincible strength and fierceness in their wars, and hurried into battle with the violence of a devouring flame; none could withstand them: all they assaulted became their prey. Several of the greatest Roman commanders with their whole armies, that advanced for the defence of Transalpine Gaul, were ingloriously overthrown, and, indeed, by their faint resistance, chiefly gave them the impulse of marching towards Rome. Having vanquished all they had met, and found abundance of plunder, they resolved to settle themselves nowhere till they should have razed the city and wasted all Italy. The Romans, being from all parts alarmed with this news, sent for Marius to undertake the war, and nominated him the second time consul, though the law did not permit anyone that was absent, or that had not waited a certain time after his first consulship, to be again created. But the people rejected all opposers, for they considered this was not the first time that the law gave place to the common interest; nor the present occasion less urgent than that when, contrary to law, they made Scipio consul, not in fear for the destruction of their own city, but desiring the ruin of that of the Carthaginians.

Thus it was decided; and Marius, bringing over his legions out of Africa on the very first day of January, which the Romans count the beginning of the year, received the consulship, and then, also, entered in triumph, showing Jugurtha a prisoner to the people, a sight they had despaired of ever beholding, nor could any, so long as he lived, hope to reduce the enemy in Africa; so fertile in expedients was he to adapt himself to every turn of fortune, and so bold as well as subtle. When, however, he was led in triumph, it is said that he fell distracted, and when he was afterwards thrown into prison, where some tore off his clothes by force, and others, whilst they struggled for his golden earring, with it pulled off the tip of his ear, and when he was, after this, cast naked into the dungeon, in his amazement and confusion, with a ghastly laugh, he cried out, "O Hercules! How cold your bath is!" Here for six days struggling with hunger, and to the very last minute desirous of life, he was overtaken by the just reward of his villainies. In this triumph was brought, as is stated, of gold three thousand and seven pounds weight, of silver bullion five thousand seven hundred and seventy-five, of money in gold and silver coin two hundred and eighty-seven thousand drachmas. After the solemnity, Marius called together the senate in the capitol, and entered, whether through inadvertency or unbecoming exultation with his good fortune, in his triumphal habit; but presently observing the senate offended at it, went out, and returned in his ordinary purple-bordered robe.

On the expedition he carefully disciplined and trained his army whilst they were on their way, giving them practice in long marches, and running of every sort, and compelling every man to carry his own baggage and prepare his own victuals; insomuch that thenceforward laborious soldiers, who did their work silently without grumbling, had the name of "Marius' mules." Some, however, think the proverb had a different occasion; that when Scipio besieged Numantia, and was careful to inspect not only their horses and arms, but their mules and carriages too, and see how well equipped and in what readiness each one's was, Marius brought forth his horse which he had fed extremely well, and a mule in better case, stronger and gentler than those of others; that the general was very well pleased, and often afterwards mentioned Marius' beasts; and that hence the soldiers, when speaking jestingly in the praise of a drudging laborious fellow, called him Marius' mule.

But to proceed; very great fortune seemed to attend Marius, for by the enemy in a manner changing their course, and falling first upon Spain, he had time to exercise his soldiers, and confirm their courage, and, which was most important, to show them what he himself was. For that fierce manner of his in command, and inexorableness in punishing, when his men became used not to do amiss or disobey, was felt to be wholesome and advantageous, as well as just, and his violent spirit, stern voice, and harsh aspect, which in a little while grew familiar to them, they esteemed terrible not to themselves, but only to their enemies. But his uprightness in judging more especially pleased the soldiers, one remarkable instance of which is as follows. One Caius Lusius, his own nephew, had a command under him in the army, a man not in other respects of bad character, but shamefully licentious with young men. He had one young man under his command called Trebonius, with whom notwithstanding many solicitations he could never prevail. At length one night be sent a messenger for him and Trebonius came, as it was not lawful for him to refuse when he was sent for, and being brought into his tent, when Lusius began to use violence with him, he drew his sword and ran him through. This was done whilst Marius was absent. When he returned, he appointed Trebonius a time for his trial, where, whilst many accused him, and not anyone appeared in his defence, he himself boldly related the whole matter, and brought witness of his previous conduct to Lusius, who had frequently offered him considerable presents. Marius, admiring his conduct and much pleased, commanded the garland, the usual Roman reward of valour, to be brought, and himself crowned Trebonius with it, as having performed an excellent action, at a time that very much wanted such good examples.

This being told at Rome, proved no small help to Marius towards his third consulship; to which also conduced the expectation of the barbarians at the summer season, the people being unwilling to trust their fortunes with any other general but him. However, their arrival was not so early as was imagined, and the time of Marius' consulship was again expired. The election coming on, and his colleague being dead, he left the command of the army to Manius Aquilius, and hastened to Rome, where, several eminent persons being candidates for the consulship,

Lucius Saturninus, who more than any of the other tribunes swayed the populace, and of whom Marius himself was very observant, exerted his eloquence with the people, advising them to choose Marius consul. He playing the modest part, and professing to decline the office, Saturninus called him traitor to his country if, in such apparent danger, he would avoid command. And though it was not difficult to discover that he was merely helping Marius in putting this pretence upon the people, yet, considering that the present juncture much required his skill, and his good fortunes too, they voted him the fourth time consul, and made Catulus Lutatius his colleague, a man very much esteemed by the nobility and not unagreeable to the commons.

Marius, having notice of the enemy's approach, with all expedition passed the Alps, and pitching his camp by the river Rhone, took care first for plentiful supplies of victuals: lest at anytime he should be forced to fight at a disadvantage for want of necessaries. The carriage of provision for the army from the sea, which was formerly long and expensive, he made speedy and easy. For the mouth of the Rhone, by the influx of the sea, being barred and almost filled up with sand and mud mixed with clay, the passage there became narrow, difficult, and dangerous for the ships that brought their provisions. Hither, therefore, bringing his army, then at leisure, he drew a great trench; and by turning the course of a great part of the river, brought it to a convenient point on the shore where the water was deep enough to receive ships of considerable burden, and where there was a calm and easy opening to the sea. And this still retains the name it took from him.

The enemy dividing themselves into two parts, the Cimbri arranged to go against Catulus higher up through the country of the Norici, and to force that passage; the Teutones and Ambrones to march against Marius by the seaside through Liguria. The Cimbri were a considerable time in doing their part. But the Teutones and Ambrones with all expedition passing over the interjacent country, soon came in sight, in numbers beyond belief, of a terrible aspect, and uttering strange cries and shouts. Taking up a great part of the plain with their camp, they challenged Marius to battle; he seemed to take no notice of them, but kept his soldiers within their fortification, and sharply reprehended those that were too forward and eager to show their courage, and who, out of passion, would needs be fighting, calling them traitors to their country, and telling them they were not now to think of the glory of triumphs and trophies, but rather how they might repel such an impetuous tempest of war and save Italy.

Thus he discoursed privately with his officers and equals, but placed the soldiers by turns upon the bulwarks to survey the enemy, and so made them familiar with their shape and voice, which were indeed altogether extravagant and barbarous, and he caused them to observe their arms, and the way of using them, so that in a little time what at first appeared terrible to their apprehensions, by often viewing became familiar. For he very rationally supposed that the strangeness of things often makes them seem formidable when they are not so; and that by our better acquaintance, even things which are really terrible lose much of their frightfulness. This daily converse not only diminished some of the soldiers' fears, but their indignation warmed and inflamed their courage when they heard the threats and insupportable insolence of their enemies; who not only plundered and depopulated all the country round, but would even contemptuously and confidently attack the ramparts.

Complaints of the soldiers now began to come to Marius' ears. "What effeminacy does Marius see in us, that he should thus like women lock us up from encountering our enemies? Come on, let us show ourselves men, and ask him if he expects others to fight for Italy; and means merely to employ us in servile offices, when he would dig trenches, cleanse places of mud and dirt, and turn the course of the rivers? It was to do such works as these, it seems, that he gave us all our long training; he will return home, and boast of these great performances of his consulships to the people. Does the defeat of Carbo and Cæpio, who were vanquished by the enemy, affright him? Surely they were much inferior to Marius both in glory and valour, and commanded a much weaker army: at the worst, it is better to be in action, though we suffer for it like them, than to sit idle spectators of the destruction of our allies and companions." Marius, not a little pleased to hear this, gently appeased them, pretending that he did not distrust their valour, but that he took his measures as to the time and place of victory from some certain oracles.

And, in fact, he used solemnly to carry about in a litter a Syrian woman, called Martha, a supposed prophetess, and to do sacrifice by her directions. She had formerly been driven away by the senate, to whom she addressed herself, offering to inform them about these affairs, and to foretell future events; and after this betook herself to the women, and gave them proofs of her skill, especially Marius' wife, at whose feet she sat when she was viewing a contest of gladiators, and correctly foretold which of them should overcome. She was for this and the like predictings sent by her to Marius and the army, where she was very much looked up to, and, for the most part, carried about in a litter. When she went to sacrifice, she wore a purple robe lined and buckled up, and had in her hand a little spear trimmed with ribbons and garlands. This theatrical show made many question whether Alarms really gave any credit to her himself, or only played the counterfeit, when he showed her publicly, to impose upon the soldiers.

What, however, Alexander the Myndian relates about the vultures does really deserve admiration; that always before Marius' victories there appeared two of them, and accompanied the army, which were known by their brazen collars (the soldiers having caught them and put these about their necks and so let them go, from which time they in a manner knew and saluted the soldiers), and whenever these appeared in their marches, they used to rejoice at it, and thought themselves sure of some success. Of the many other prodigies that then were taken notice of, the greater part were but of the ordinary stamp; it was, however, reported that at Ameria and Tuder, two cities in Italy, there were seen at nights in the sky flaming darts and shields, now waved about, and then again clashing against one another, all in accordance with the postures and motions soldiers use in fighting; that at length one party retreating, and the other pursuing, they all disappeared westward. Much about the same time came Bataces, one of Cybele's priests, from Pessinus, and reported how the goddess had declared to him out of her oracle that the Romans should obtain the victory. The senate giving credit to him, and voting the goddess a temple to be built in hopes of the victory, Aulus Pompeius, a tribune, prevented Bataces, when he would have gone and told the people this same story, calling him impostor, and ignominiously pulling him off the hustings; which action in the end was the main thing that gained credit for the man's story, for Aulus had scarce dissolved the assembly, and returned home, when a violent fever seized him, and it was matter of universal remark, and in everybody's mouth, that he died within a week after.

Now the Teutones, whilst Marius lay quiet, ventured to attack his camp; from whence, however, being encountered with showers of darts, and losing several of their men, they determined to march forward, hoping to reach the other side of the Alps without opposition, and, packing up their baggage, passed securely by the Roman camp, where the greatness of their number was especially made evident by the long time they took in their march, for they were said to be six days continually going on in passing Marius' fortifications; they marched pretty near, and revilingly asked the Romans if they would send any commands by them to their wives, for they would shortly be with them. As soon as they were passed and had gone on a little distance ahead, Marius began to move, and follow them at his leisure, always encamping at some small distance from them; choosing also strong positions, and carefully fortifying them, that he might quarter with safety. Thus they marched till they came to the place called Sextilius' Waters, from whence it was but a short way before being amidst the Alps, and here Marius put himself in readiness for the encounter.

He chose a place for his camp of considerable strength, but where there was a scarcity of water; designing, it is said, by this means, also, to put an edge on his soldiers' courage; and when several were not a little distressed, and complained of thirst, pointing to a river that ran near the enemy's camp; "There," said he, "you may have drink, if you will buy it with your blood." "Why, then," replied they, "do you not lead us to them, before our blood is dried up in us?" He answered, in a softer tone, "Let us first fortify our camp," and the soldiers, though not without repining, proceeded to obey. Now a great company of their boys and camp followers, having neither drink for themselves nor for their horses, went down to that river; some taking axes and hatchets, and some, too, swords and darts with their pitchers, resolving to have water though they fought for it. These were first encountered by a small party of the enemies; for most of them had just finished bathing, and were eating and drinking, and several were still bathing, the country thereabouts abounding in hot springs; so that the Romans partly fell upon them whilst they were enjoying themselves and occupied with the novel sights and pleasantness of the place. Upon hearing the shouts, great numbers still joining in the fight, it was not a little difficult for Marius to contain his soldiers, who were afraid of losing the camp servants; and the more warlike part of the enemies, who had overthrown Manlius and Cæpio (they were called Ambrones, and were in number, one with another, above thirty thousand), taking the alarm, leaped up and hurried to arms.

These, though they had just been gorging themselves with food, and were excited and disordered with drink, nevertheless did not advance with an unruly step, or in mere senseless fury, nor were their shouts mere inarticulate cries; but clashing their arms in concert and keeping time as they leapt and bounded onward, they continually repeated their own name, "Ambrones!" either to encourage one another, or to strike the greater terror into their enemies. Of all the Italians in Marius' army, the Ligurians were the first that charged; and when they caught the word of the enemy's confused shout, they, too, returned the same, as it was an ancient name also in their country, the Ligurians always using it when speaking of their descent. This acclamation, bandied from one army to the other before they joined, served to rouse and heighten their fury, while the men on either side strove, with all possible vehemence, the one to overshout the other.

The river disordered the Ambrones; before they could draw up all their army on the other side of it, the Ligurians presently fell upon the van, and began to charge them hand to hand. The Romans, too, coming to their assistance, and from the higher ground pouring upon the enemy, forcibly repelled them, and the most of them (one thrusting another into the river) were there slain, and filled it with their blood and dead bodies. Those that got safe over, not daring to make head, were slain by the Romans, as they fled to their camp and wagons; where the women meeting them with swords and hatchets, and making a hideous outcry, set upon those that fled as well as those that pursued, the one as traitors, the other as enemies, and mixing themselves with the combatants, with their bare arms pulling away the Romans' shields, and laying hold on their swords, endured the wounds and slashing of their bodies to the very last with undaunted resolution. Thus the battle seems to have happened at that river rather by accident than by the design of the general.

After the Romans were retired from the great slaughter of the Ambrones, night came on; but the army was not indulged, as was the usual custom, with songs of victory, drinking in their tents, and mutual entertainments and (what is most welcome to soldiers after successful fighting) quiet sleep, but they passed that night, above all others, in fears and alarm. For their camp was without either rampart or palisade, and there remained thousands upon thousands of their enemies yet unconquered; to whom were joined as many of the Ambrones as escaped. There were heard from these all through the night wild bewailings, nothing like the sighs and groans of men, but a sort of wild-beast-like howling and cursing joined with threats and lamentations rising from the vast multitude, and echoed among the neighbouring hills and hollow banks of the river. The whole plain was filled with hideous noise, insomuch that the Romans were not a little afraid, and Marius himself was apprehensive of a confused tumultuous night engagement. But the enemy did not stir either this night or the next day, but were employed in disposing and drawing themselves up to the greatest advantage.

Of this occasion Marius made good use; for there were beyond the enemies some wooded ascents and deep valleys thickly set with trees, whither he sent Claudius Marcellus, secretly, with three thousand regular soldiers, giving him orders to post them in ambush there, and show themselves at the rear of the enemies when the fight was begun. The others, refreshed with victuals and sleep, as soon as it was day he drew up before the camp, and commanded the horse to sally out into the plain, at the sight of which the Teutones could not contain themselves till the Romans should come down and fight them on equal terms, but hastily arming themselves, charged in their fury up the hillside. Marius, sending officers to all parts, commanded his men to stand still and keep their ground; when they came within reach, to throw their javelins, then use their swords, and joining their shields, force them back; pointing out to them that the steepness of the ground would render the enemy's blows inefficient, nor could their shields be kept close together, the inequality of the ground hindering the stability of their footing.

This counsel he gave them, and was the first that followed it; for he was inferior to none in the use of his body, and far excelled all in resolution. The Romans accordingly stood for their approach, and, checking them in their advance upwards, forced them little by little to give way and yield down the hill, and here, on the level ground, no sooner had the Ambrones begun to restore their van into a posture of resistance, but they found their rear disordered. For Marcellus had not let slip the opportunity; but as soon as the shout was raised among the Romans on the hills, he, setting his men in motion, fell in upon the enemy behind, at full speed, and with loud cries, and routed those nearest him, and they, breaking the ranks of those that were before them, filled the whole army with confusion. They made no long resistance after they were thus broke in upon, but having lost all order, fled.

The Romans, pursuing them, slew and took prisoners above one hundred thousand, and possessing themselves of their spoil, tents, and carriages, voted all that was not purloined to Marius' share, which, though so magnificent a present, yet was generally thought less than his conduct deserved in so great a danger. Other authors give a different account, both about the division of the plunder and the number of the slain. They say, however, that the inhabitants of Massilia made fences round their vineyards with the bones, and that the ground, enriched by the moisture of the putrefied bodies (soaked with the rain of the following winter), yielded at the season a prodigious crop, and fully justified Archilochus, who said, that the fallows thus are fattened. It is an observation, also, that extraordinary rains pretty generally fall after great battles; whether it be that some divine power thus washes and cleanses the polluted earth with showers from above, or that moist and heavy evaporations, steaming forth from the blood and corruption, thicken the air, which naturally is subject to alteration from the smallest causes.

After the battle, Marius chose out from amongst the barbarians' spoils and arms those that were whole and handsome, and that would make the greatest show in his triumph; the rest he heaped upon a large pile, and offered a very splendid sacrifice. Whilst the army stood round about with their alms and garlands, himself attired (as the fashion is on such occasions) in the purple-bordered robe, and taking a lighted torch, and with both hands lifting it up towards heaven, he was then going to put it to the pile, when some friends were espied with all haste coming towards him on horseback. Upon which everyone remained in silence and expectation. They, upon their coming up, leapt off and saluted Marius, bringing him the news of his fifth consulship, and delivered him letters to that effect. This gave the addition of no small joy to the solemnity; and while the soldiers clashed their arms and shouted, the officers again crowned Marius with a laurel wreath, and he thus set fire to the pile, and finished his sacrifice.

But whatever it be which interferes to prevent the enjoyment of prosperity ever being pure and sincere, and still diversifies human affairs with the mixture of good and bad, whether fortune or divine displeasure or the necessity of the nature of things, within a few days Marius received an account of his colleague, Catulus, which, as a cloud in serenity and calm, terrified Rome with the apprehension of another imminent storm. Catulus, who marched against the Cimbri, despairing of being able to defend the passes of the Alps, lest, being compelled to divide his forces into several parties, he should weaken himself, descended again into Italy, and posted his army behind the river Adige; where he occupied the passages with strong fortifications on both sides the river, and made a bridge, that so he might cross to the assistance of his men on the other side, if so be the enemy, having forced their way through the mountain passes, should storm the fortresses. The barbarians, however, came on with such insolence and contempt of their enemies, that to show their strength and courage, rather than out of any necessity, they went naked in the showers of snow, and through the ice and deep snow climbed up to the tops of the hills, and from thence, placing their broad shields under their bodies, let themselves slide from the precipices along their vast slippery descents.

When they had pitched their camp at a little distance from the river, and surveyed the passage, they began to pile it up, giant-like, tearing down the neighbouring hills; and brought trees pulled up by the roots, and heaps of earth to the river, damming up its course; and with great heavy materials which they rolled down the stream and dashed against the bridge, they forced away the beams which supported it; in consequence of which the greatest part of the Roman soldiers, much affrighted, left the camp and fled. Here Catulus showed himself a generous and noble general, in preferring the glory of his people before his own; for when he could not prevail with his soldiers to stand to their colours, but saw how they all deserted them, he commanded his own standard to be taken up, and running to the foremost of those that fled, he led them forward, choosing rather that the disgrace should fall upon himself than upon his country, and that they should not seem to fly, but, following their captain, to make a retreat. The barbarians assaulted and took the fortress on the other side the Adige; where much admiring the few Romans there left, who had shown extreme courage, and had fought worthily of their country, they dismissed them upon terms, swearing them upon their brazen bull, which was afterwards taken in the battle, and carried, they say, to Catulus' house, as the chief trophy of victory.

Thus falling in upon the country destitute of defence, they wasted it on all sides. Marius was presently sent for to the city; where, when he arrived, everyone supposing he would triumph, the senate, too, unanimously voting it, he himself did not think it convenient: whether that he were not willing to deprive his soldiers and officers of their share of the glory, or that, to encourage the people in this juncture, he would leave the honour due to his past victory on trust, as it were, in the hands of the city and its future fortune; deferring it now to receive it afterwards with the greater splendour. Having left such orders as the occasion required, he hastened to Catulus, whose drooping spirits he much raised, and sent for his own army from Gaul; and as soon as it came, passing the river Po, he endeavoured to keep the barbarians out of that part of Italy which lies south of it.

They professed they were in expectation of the Teutones, and saying they wondered they were so long in coming deferred the battle; either that they were really ignorant of their defeat or were willing to seem so. For they certainly much maltreated those that brought them such news, and, sending to Marius, required some part of the country for themselves and their brethren, and cities fit for them to inhabit. When Marius inquired of the ambassadors who their brethren were, upon their saying the Teutones, all that were present began to laugh; and Marius scoffingly answered them, "Do not trouble yourself for your brethren, for we have already provided lands for them, which they shall possess forever." The ambassadors, understanding the mockery, broke into insults, and threatened that the Cimbri would make him pay for this and the Teutones, too, when they came. "They are not far off," replied Marius, "and it will be unkindly done of you to go away before greeting your brethren." Saying so, he commanded the kings of the Teutones to be brought out, as they were, in chains; for they were taken by the Sequani among the Alps, before they could make their escape. This was no sooner made known to the Cimbri, but they with all expedition came against Marius, who then lay still and guarded his camp.

It is said that, against this battle Marius first altered the construction of the Roman javelins. For before at the place where the wood was joined to the iron it was made fast with two iron pins; but now Marius let one of them alone as it was, and pulling out the other, put a weak wooden peg in its place, thus contriving that when it was driven into the enemy's shield, it should not stand right out, but the wooden peg breaking, the iron should bend, and so the javelin should hold fast by its crooked point and drag. Bœorix, King of the Cimbri, came with a small party of horse to the Roman camp, and challenged Marius to appoint the time and place where they might meet and fight for the country. Marius answered that the Romans never consulted their enemies when to fight, however, he would gratify the Cimbri so far; and so they fixed upon the third day after and for the place, the plain near Vercellæ, which was convenient enough for the Roman horse, and afforded room for the enemy to display their numbers.

They observed the time appointed, and drew out their forces against each other. Catulus commanded twenty thousand three hundred, and Marius thirty-two thousand, who were placed in the two wings, leaving Catulus the centre. Sylla, who was present at the fight, gives this account; saying, also, that Marius drew up his army in this order, because he expected that the armies would meet on the wings since it generally happens that in such extensive fronts the centre falls back, and thus he would have the whole victory to himself and his soldiers, and Catulus would not be even engaged. They tell us, also, that Catulus himself alleged this in vindication of his honour, accusing, in various ways, the enviousness of Marius. The infantry of the Cimbri marched quietly out of their fortifications, having their flanks equal to their front; every side of the army taking up thirty furlongs. Their horse, that were in number fifteen thousand, made a very splendid appearance. They wore helmets, made to resemble the head and jaws of wild beasts, and other strange shapes, and heightening these with plumes of feathers, they made themselves appear taller than they were. They had breastplates of iron and white glittering shields; and for their offensive arms everyone had two darts, and when they came hand to hand, they used large and heavy swords.

The cavalry did not fall directly upon the front of the Romans, but, turning to the right, they endeavoured to draw them on in that direction by little and little, so as to get them between themselves and their infantry, who were placed in the left wing. The Roman commanders soon perceived the design, but could not contain the soldiers; for one happening to shout out that the enemy fled, they all rushed to pursue them, while the whole barbarian foot came on, moving like a great ocean. Here Marius, having washed his hands, and lifting them up towards heaven, vowed an hecatomb to the gods; and Catulus, too, in the same posture, solemnly promised to consecrate a temple to the "Fortune of that day." They say, too, that Marius, having the victim shown to him as he was sacrificing, cried out with a loud voice, "The victory is mine."

However, in the engagement, according to the accounts of Sylla and his friends, Marius met with what might be called a mark of divine displeasure. For a great dust being raised, which (as it might very probably happen) almost covered both the armies, he, leading on his forces to the pursuit, missed the enemy, and having passed by their array, moved for a good space, up and down the field; meanwhile the enemy, by chance, engaged with Catulus, and the heat of the battle was chiefly with him and his men, among whom Sylla says he was; adding, that the Romans had great advantage of the heat and sun that shone in the faces of the Cimbri. For they, well able to endure cold, and having been bred up (as we observed before) in cold and shady countries, were overcome with the excessive heat; they sweated extremely, and were much out of breath, being forced to hold their shields before their faces; for the battle was fought not long after the summer solstice, or, as the Romans reckon, upon the third day before the new moon of the month now called August and then Sextilis. The dust, too, gave the Romans no small addition to their courage, inasmuch as it hid the enemy. For afar off they could not discover their number; but everyone advancing to encounter those that were nearest to them, they came to fight hand to hand before the sight of so vast a multitude had struck terror into them. They were so much used to labour, and so well exercised, that in all the heat and toil of the encounter, not one of them was observed either to sweat or to be out of breath; so much so, that Catulus himself, they say, recorded it in commendation of his soldiers.

Here the greatest part and most valiant of the enemies were cut in pieces; for those that fought in the front, that they might not break their ranks, were fast tied to one another, with long chains put through their belts. But as they pursued those that fled to their camp they witnessed a most fearful tragedy; the women, standing in black clothes on their wagons, slew all that fled, some their husbands, some their brethren, others their fathers; and strangling their little children with their own bands, threw them under the wheels and the feet of the cattle, and then killed themselves. They tell of one who hung herself from the end of the pole of a wagon, with her children tied dangling at her heels. The men, for want of trees, tied themselves, some to the horns of the oxen, others by the neck to their legs, that so pricking them on, by the starting and springing of the beasts, they might be torn and trodden to pieces. Yet for all they thus massacred themselves, above sixty thousand were taken prisoners, and those that were slain were said to be twice as many.

The ordinary plunder was taken by Marius' soldiers, but the other spoils, as ensigns, trumpets, and the like, they say, were brought to Catulus' camp; which he used for the best argument that the victory was obtained by himself and his army. Some dissensions arising, as was natural, among the soldiers, the deputies from Parma, being then present, were made judges of the controversy; whom Catulus' men carried about among their slain enemies and manifestly showed them that they were slain by their javelins, which were known by the inscriptions, having Catulus' name cut in the wood. Nevertheless the whole glory of the action was ascribed to Marius, on account of his former victory, and under colour of his present authority; the populace more especially styling him the third founder of their city, as having diverted a danger no less threatening than was that when the Gauls sacked Rome; and everyone, in their feasts and rejoicings at home with their wives and children, made offerings and libations in honour of "*The Gods and Marius*"; and would have had him solely have the honour of both the triumphs. However, he did not do so, but triumphed together with Catulus, being desirous to show his moderation even in such great circumstances of good fortune; besides he was not a little afraid of the soldiers in Catulus' army, lest, if he should wholly bereave their general of the honour, they should endeavour to hinder him of his triumph.

Marius was now in his fifth consulship, and he sued for his sixth in such a manner as never any man before him had done, even for his first; he courted the people's favour and ingratiated himself with the multitude by every sort of complaisance; not only derogating from the state and dignity of his office, but also belying his own character, by attempting to seem popular and obliging, for which nature had never designed him. His passion for distinction did, indeed, they say, make him exceedingly timorous in any political matters, or in confronting public assemblies; and that undaunted presence of mind he always showed in battle against the enemy forsook him when he was to address the people; he was easily upset by the most ordinary commendation or dispraise. It is told of him, that having at one time given the freedom of the city to one thousand men of Camerinum who had behaved valiantly in this war, and this seeming to be illegally done, upon someone or other calling him to an account for it, he answered, that the law spoke too softly to be heard in such a noise of war; yet he himself appeared to be more disconcerted and overcome by the clamour made in the assemblies. The need they had of him in time of war procured him power and dignity; but in civil affairs, when he despaired of getting the first place, he was forced to betake himself to the favour of the people, never caring to be a good man so that he were but a great one.

He thus became very odious to all the nobility; and above all, he feared Metellus, who had been so ungratefully used by him, and whose true virtue made him naturally an enemy to those that sought influence with the people, not by the honourable course, but by subservience and complaisance. Marius, therefore, endeavoured to banish him from the city, and for this purpose he contracted a close alliance with Glaucia and Saturninus, a couple of daring fellows, who had the great mass of the indigent and seditious multitude at their control; and by their assistance he enacted various laws, and bringing the soldiers, also, to attend the assembly, he was enabled to overpower Metellus. And as Rutilius relates (in all other respects a fair and faithful authority, but, indeed, privately an enemy to Marius), he obtained his sixth consulship by distributing vast sums of money among the tribes, and by this bribery kept out Metellus, and had Valerius Flaccus given him as his instrument, rather than his colleague, in the consulship. The people had never before bestowed so many consulships on anyone man, except on Valerius Corvinus only, and he, too, they say, was forty-five years between his first and last; but Marius, from his first, ran through five more, with one current of good fortune.

In the last, especially, he contracted a great deal of hatred, by committing several gross misdemeanours in compliance with the desires of Saturninus; among which was the murder of Nonius whom Saturninus slew because he stood in competition with him for the tribuneship. And when, afterwards, Saturninus, on becoming tribune, brought forward his law for the division of lands, with a clause enacting that the senate publicly swear to confirm whatever the people should vote, and not to oppose them in anything, Marius, in the senate, cunningly feigned to be against this provision, and said that he would not take any such oath, nor would any man, he thought, who was wise; for if there were no ill design in the law, still it would be an affront to the senate to be compelled to give their approbation, and not to do it willingly and upon persuasion. This he said, not that it was agreeable to his own sentiments, but that he might entrap Metellus beyond any possibility of escape. For Marius, in whose ideas virtue and capacity consisted largely in deceit, made very little account of what he had openly professed to the senate; and knowing that Metellus was one of a fixed resolution, and, as Pindar has it, esteemed "truth the first principle of heroic virtue," he hoped to ensnare him into a declaration before the senate, and on his refusing, as he was sure to do, afterwards to take the oath, he expected to bring him into such odium with the people as should never be wiped off. The design succeeded to his wish. As soon as Metellus had declared that he would not swear to it, the senate adjourned. A few days after on Saturninus citing the senators to make their appearance, and take the oath before the people, Marius stepped forth, amidst a profound silence, everyone being intent to hear him, and bidding farewell to those fine speeches he had before made in the senate, said, that his back was not so broad that he should think himself bound, once for all, by any opinion once given on so important a matter; he would willingly swear and submit to the law, if so be it were one, a proviso which he added as a mere cover for his effrontery. The people, in great joy at his taking the oath, loudly clapped and applauded him, while the nobility stood by ashamed and vexed at his inconstancy; but they submitted out of fear of the people, and all in order took the oath, till it came to Metellus' turn. But he, though his friends begged and entreated him to take it, and not to plunge himself irrecoverably into the penalties which Saturninus had provided for those that should refuse it, would not flinch from his resolution, nor swear; but, according to his fixed custom, being ready to suffer anything rather than do a base, unworthy action, he left the forum, telling those that were with him that to do wrong things is base, and to do well where there is no danger, common; the good man's characteristic is to do so where there is danger.

Hereupon Saturninus put it to the vote, that the consuls should place Metellus under their interdict, and forbid him fire, water, and lodging.

There were enough, too, of the basest of people ready to kill him. Nevertheless, when many of the better sort were extremely concerned, and gathered about Metellus, he would not suffer them to raise a sedition upon his account, but with this calm reflection left the city, "Either when the posture of affairs is mended and the people repent, I shall be recalled, or if things remain in their present condition, it will be best to be absent." But what great favour and honour Metellus received in his banishment, and in what manner he spent his time at Rhodes, in philosophy, will be more fitly our subject when we write his life.

Marius, in return for this piece of service, was forced to connive at Saturninus, now proceeding to the very height of insolence and violence, and was, without knowing it, the instrument of mischief beyond endurance, the only course of which was through outrages and massacres to tyranny and the subversion of the government. Standing in some awe of the nobility, and, at the same time, eager to court the commonalty, he was guilty of a most mean and dishonest action. When some of the great men came to him at night to stir him up against Saturninus, at the other door, unknown to them, he let him in; then making the same pretence of some disorder of body to both, he ran from one party to the other, and staying at one time with them and another with him, he instigated and exasperated them one against another. At length when the senate and equestrian order conceited measures together, and openly manifested their resentment, he did bring his soldiers into the forum, and driving the insurgents into the capitol, and then cutting off the conduits, forced them to surrender by want of water. They, in this distress, addressing themselves to him, surrendered, as it is termed, on the *public faith*. He did his utmost to save their lives, but so wholly in vain, that when they came down into the forum they were all basely murdered. Thus he had made himself equally odious both to the nobility and commons, and when the time was come to create censors, though he was the most obvious man, yet he did not petition for it; but fearing the disgrace of being repulsed, permitted others, his inferiors, to be elected, though he pleased himself by giving out that he was not willing to disoblige too many by undertaking a severe inspection into their lives and conduct.

There was now an edict preferred to recall Metellus from banishment; this he vigorously, but in vain, opposed both by word and deed, and was at length obliged to desist. The people unanimously voted for it; and he, not able to endure the sight of Metellus' return, made a voyage to Cappadocia and Galatia; giving out that he had to perform the sacrifices which he had vowed to Cybele; but actuated really by other less apparent reasons. For, in fact, being a man altogether ignorant of civil life and ordinary politics, he received all his advancement from war; and supposing his power and glory would by little and little decrease by his lying quietly out of action, he was eager by every means to excite some new commotions, and hoped that by setting at variance some of the kings, and by exasperating Mithridates, especially, who was then apparently making preparations for war, he himself should be chosen general against him, and so furnish the city with new matter of triumph, and his own house with the plunder of Pontus and the riches of its king. Therefore, though Mithridates entertained him with all imaginable attention and respect, yet he was not at all wrought upon or softened by it; but said, "O king, either endeavour to be stronger than the Romans, or else quietly submit to their commands." With which he left Mithridates as he indeed had often heard the fame of the bold speaking of the Romans, but now for the first time experienced it.

When Marius returned again to Rome, he built a house close by the forum, either, as he himself gave out, that he was not willing his clients should be tried with going far, or that he imagined distance was the reason why more did not come. This, however, was not so; the real reason was, that, being inferior to others in agreeableness of conversation and the arts of political life, like a mere tool and implement of war, he was thrown aside in time of peace. Amongst all those whose brightness eclipsed his glory, he was most incensed against Sylla, who had owed his rise to the hatred which the nobility bore Marius; and had made his disagreement with him the one principle of his political life. When Bocchus, King of Numidia, who was styled the associate of the Romans, dedicated some figures of Victory in the capitol, and with them a representation in gold of himself delivering Jugurtha to Sylla, Marius upon this was almost distracted with rage and ambition, as though Sylla had arrogated this honour to himself, and endeavoured forcibly to pull down these presents; Sylla, on the other side, as vigorously resisted him; but the Social War, then on a sudden threatening the city, put a stop to this sedition when just ready to break out. For the most warlike and best-peopled countries of all Italy formed confederacy together against Rome, and were within a little of subverting the empire; as they were indeed strong, not only in their weapons and the valour of their soldiers, but stood nearly upon equal terms with the Romans as to the skill and daring of their commanders.

As much glory and power as this war, so various in its events and so uncertain as to its success, conferred upon Sylla, so much it took away from

Marius, who was thought tardy, unenterprising, and timid, whether it were that his age was now quenching his former heat and vigour (for he was above sixty-five years old), or that having, as he himself said, some distemper that affected his muscles, and his body being unfit for action, he did service above his strength. Yet, for all this, he came off victor in a considerable battle, wherein he slew six thousand of the enemies, and never once gave them any advantage over him; and when he was surrounded by the works of the enemy, he contained himself, and though insulted over, and challenged, did not yield to the provocation. The story is told that when Publius Silo, a man of the greatest repute and authority among the enemies, said to him, "If you are indeed a great general, Marius, leave your camp and fight a battle," he replied, "If you are one, make me do so." And another time, when the enemy gave them a good opportunity of a battle, and the Romans through fear durst not charge, so that both parties retreated, he called an assembly of his soldiers, and said, "It is no small question whether I should call the enemies or you the greater cowards, for neither did they dare to face your backs, nor you to confront theirs." At length, professing to be worn out with the infirmity of his body, he laid down his command.

Afterwards when the Italians were worsted, there were several candidates suing with the aid of the popular leaders for the chief command in the war with Mithridates. Sulpicius, tribune of the people, a bold and confident man, contrary to everybody's expectation, brought forward Marius, and proposed him as proconsul and general in that war. The people were divided; some were on Marius' side, others voted for Sylla, and jeeringly bade Marius go to the baths at Baiæ, to cure his body, worn out, as himself confessed, with age and catarrhs. Marius had indeed, there, about Misenum, a villa more effeminately and luxuriously furnished than seemed to become one that had seen service in so many and great wars and expeditions. This same house Cornelia bought for seventy-five thousand drachmas, and not long after Lucius Lucullus, for two million five hundred thousand; so rapid and so great was the growth of Roman sumptuosity. Yet, in spite of all this, out of a mere boyish passion for distinction, affecting to shake off his age and weakness, he went down daily to the Campus Martius, and exercising himself with the youth, showed himself still nimble in his armour, and expert in riding; though he was undoubtedly grown bulky in his old age, and inclining to excessive faintness and corpulency.

Some people were pleased with this, and went continually to see him competing and displaying himself in these exercises; but the better sort that saw him pitied the cupidity and ambition that made one who had risen from utter poverty to extreme wealth, and out of nothing into greatness, unwilling to admit any limit to his high fortune, or to be content with being admired, and quietly enjoying what he had already got; why, as if he still were indigent, should he at so great an age leave his glory and his triumphs to go into Cappadocia and the Euxine Sea, to fight Archelaus and Neoptolemus, Mithridates' generals? Marius' pretences for this action of his seemed very ridiculous; for he said he wanted to go and teach his son to be a general.

The condition of the city, which had long been unsound and diseased, became hopeless now that Marius found so opportune an instrument for the public destruction as Sulpicius' insolence. This man professed, in all other respects, to admire and imitate Saturninus; only he found fault with him for backwardness and want of spirit in his designs. He, therefore, to avoid this fault, got six hundred of the equestrian order about him as his guard, whom he named anti-senators; and with these confederates he set upon the consuls, whilst they were at the assembly, and took the son of one of them who fled from the forum and slew him. Sylla, being hotly pursued, took refuge in Marius' house, which none could suspect, by that means escaping those that sought him, who hastily passed by there, and, it is said, was safely conveyed by Marius himself out at the other door, and came to the camp. Yet Sylla, in his memoirs, positively denies that he fled to Marius, saying he Was carried thither to consult upon the matters to which Sulpicius would have forced him, against his will, to consent; that he, surrounding him with drawn swords, hurried him to Marius, and constrained him thus, till he went thence to the forum and removed, as they required him to do, the interdict on business.

Sulpicius, having thus obtained the mastery, decreed the command of the army to Marius, who proceeded to make preparations for his march, and sent two tribunes to receive the charge of the army from Sylla. Sylla hereupon exasperating his soldiers, who were about thirty-five thousand full-armed men, led them towards Rome. First falling upon the tribunes Marius had sent, they slew them; Marius having done as much for several of Sylla's friends in Rome, and now offering their freedom to the slaves on condition of their assistance in the war; of whom, however, they say, there were but three who accepted his proposal. For some small time he made head against Sylla's assault, but was soon overpowered and fled; those that were with him, as soon as he had escaped out of the city, were dispersed, and night coming on, he hastened to a country-house of his, called Solonium. Hence he sent his son to some neighbouring farms of his father-in-law,

Mucius, to provide necessaries; he went himself to Ostia, where his friend Numerius had prepared him a ship, and hence, not staying for his son, he took with him his son-in-law Granius, and weighed anchor.

Young Marius, coming to Mucius' farms, made his preparations; and the day breaking, was almost discovered by the enemy. For there came thither a party of horse that suspected some such matter; but the farm steward, foreseeing their approach, hid Marius in a cart full of beans, then yoking in his team and driving toward the city, met those that were in search of him. Marius, thus conveyed home to his wife, took with him some necessaries, and came at night to the seaside; where, going on board a ship that was bound for Africa, he went away thither. Marius, the father, when he had put to sea, with a strong gale passing along the coast of Italy, was in no small apprehension of one Geminius, a great man at Terracina, and his enemy; and therefore bade the seamen hold off from that place. They were indeed willing to gratify him, but the wind now blowing in from the sea and making the waves swell to a great height, they were afraid the ship would not be able to weather out the storm, and Marius, too, being indisposed and sea-sick, they made for land, and not without some difficulty reached the shore near Circeium.

The storm now increasing and their victuals failing, they left their ship, and wandered up and down without any certain purpose, simply as in great distresses people shun the present as the greatest evil, and rely upon the hopes of uncertainties. For the land and sea were both equally unsafe for them; it was dangerous to meet with people, and it was no less so to meet with none, on account of their want of necessaries. At length, though late, they lighted upon a few poor shepherds, that had not anything to relieve them; but knowing Marius, advised him to depart as soon as might be, for they had seen a little beyond that place a party of horse that were gone in search of him. Finding himself in a great strait, especially because those that attended him were not able to go further, being spent with their long fasting, for the present he turned aside out of the road, and hid himself in a thick wood, where he passed the night in great wretchedness. The next day, pinched with hunger, and willing to make use of the little strength he had, before it were all exhausted, he travelled by the seaside, encouraging his companions not to fall away from him before the fulfilment of his final hopes, for which, in reliance on some old predictions, he professed to be sustaining himself. For when he was yet but very young, and lived in the country, he caught in the skirt of his garment an eagle's nest, as it was falling, in which were seven young ones, which his parents seeing and much admiring, consulted the augurs about it, who told them he should become the greatest man in the world, and that the fates had decreed he should seven times be possessed of the supreme power and authority. Some are of opinion that this really happened to Marius, as we have related it; others say, that those who then and through the rest of his exile heard him tell these stories, and believed him, have merely repeated a story that is altogether fabulous; for an eagle never hatches more than two; and even Musæus was deceived, who, speaking of the eagle, says that—

She lays three eggs, hatches two, and rears one.

However this be, it is certain Marius, in his exile and greatest extremities, would often say that he should attain a seventh consulship.

When Marius and his company were now about twenty furlongs distant from Minturnæ, a city in Italy, they espied a troop of horse making up toward them with all speed, and by chance, also, at the same time, two ships under sail. Accordingly, they ran everyone with what speed and strength they could to the sea, and plunging into it swam to the ships. Those that were with Granius, reaching one of them, passed over to an island opposite, called Ænaria; Marius himself, whose body was heavy and unwieldy, was with great pains and difficulty kept above the water by two servants, and put into the other ship. The soldiers were by this time come to the seaside, and from thence called out to the seamen to put to shore, or else to throw out Marius, and then they might go whither they would. Marius besought them with tears to the contrary, and the masters of the ship, after frequent changes, in a short space of time, of their purpose, inclining first to one, then to the other side, resolved at length to answer the soldiers that they would not give up Marius. As soon as they had ridden off in a rage, the seamen, again changing their resolution, came to land, and casting anchor at the mouth of the river Liris, where it overflows and makes a marsh, they advised him to land, refresh himself on shore, and take some care of his discomposed body, till the wind came fairer; which, said they, will happen at such an hour, when the wind from the sea will calm, and that from the marshes rise. Marius, following their advice, did so, and when the seamen had set him on shore, he laid him down in an adjacent field, suspecting nothing less than what was to befall him. They, as soon as they had got into the ship, weighed anchor and departed, as thinking it neither honourable to deliver Marius into the hands of those that sought him, nor safe to protect him.

He thus, deserted by all, lay a good while silently on the shore; at length collecting himself, he advanced with pain and difficulty, without any path, till, wading through deep bogs and ditches full of water and mud, he came upon the hut of an old man that worked in the fens, and falling at his feet besought him to assist and preserve one who, if he escaped the present danger, would make him returns beyond his expectation. The poor man, whether he had formerly known him, or were then moved with his superior aspect, told him that if he wanted only rest his cottage would be convenient; but if he were flying from anybody's search, he would hide him in a more retired place. Marius desiring him to do so, he carried him into the fens and bade him hide himself in an hollow place by the riverside, where he laid upon him a great many reeds, and other things that were light, and would cover, but not oppress him. But within a very short time he was disturbed with a noise and tumult from the cottage, for Geminius had sent several from Terracina in pursuit of him; some of whom happening to come that way, frightened and threatened the old man for having entertained and hid an enemy of the Romans. Whereupon Marius, arising and stripping himself, plunged into a puddle full of thick muddy water; and even there he could not escape their search, but was pulled out covered with mire, and carried away naked to Minturnæ and delivered to the magistrates. For there had been orders sent through all the towns to make public search for Marius, and if they found him to kill him; however, the magistrates thought convenient to consider a little better of it first, and sent him prisoner to the house of one Fannia.

This woman was supposed not very well affected towards him upon an old account. One Tinnius had formerly married this Fannia; from whom she afterwards, being divorced, demanded her portion, which was considerable, but her husband accused her of adultery; so the controversy was brought before Marius in his sixth consulship. When the case was examined thoroughly, it appeared both that Fannia had been incontinent, and that her husband, knowing her to be so, had married and lived a considerable time with her. So that Marius was severe enough with both, commanding him to restore her portion, and laying a fine of four copper coins upon her by way of disgrace. But Fannia did not then behave like a woman that had been injured, but as soon as she saw Marius, remembered nothing less than old affronts; took care of him according to her ability, and comforted him. He made her his returns and told her he did not despair, for he had met with a lucky omen, which was thus. When he was brought to Fannia's house, as soon as the gate was opened, an ass came running out to drink at a spring hard by, and giving a bold and encouraging look, first stood still before him, then brayed aloud and pranced by him. From which Marius drew his conclusion, and said, that the fates designed his safety, rather by sea than land, because the ass neglected his dry fodder, and turned from it to the water. Having told Fannia this story, he bade the chamber door to be shut and went to rest.

Meanwhile the magistrates and councillors of Minturnæ consulted together, and determined not to delay any longer, but immediately to kill Marius; and when none of their citizens durst undertake the business, a certain soldier, a Gaulish or Cimbrian horseman (the story is told both ways), went in with his sword drawn to him. The room itself was not very light, that part of it especially where he then lay was dark, from whence Marius' eyes, they say, seemed to the fellow to dart out flames at him, and a loud voice to say, out of the dark, "Fellow, darest thou kill Caius Marius?" The barbarian hereupon immediately fled, and leaving his sword in the place, rushed out of doors, crying only this, "I cannot kill Caius Marius." At which they were all at first astonished, and presently began to feel pity, and remorse, and anger at themselves for making so unjust and ungrateful a decree against one who had preserved Italy, and whom it was bad enough not to assist. "Let him go," said they, "where he please to banishment, and find his fate somewhere else; we only entreat pardon of the gods for thrusting Marius distressed and deserted out of our city."

Impelled by thoughts of this kind, they went in a body into the room, and taking him amongst them, conducted him towards the seaside; on his way to which, though everyone was very officious to him, and all made what haste they could, yet a considerable time was likely to be lost. For the grove of Marica (as she is called), which the people hold sacred and make it a point of religion not to let anything that is once carried into it be taken out, lay just in their road to the sea, and if they should go round about, they must needs come very late thither. At length one of the old men cried out and said, there was no place so sacred but they might pass through it for Marius' preservation; and thereupon, first of all, he himself, taking up some of the baggage that was carried for his accommodation to the ship, passed through the grove, all the rest immediately, with the same readiness, accompanying him. And one Belæus (who afterwards had a picture of these things drawn, and put it in a temple at the place of embarkation), having by this time provided him a ship, Marius went on board, and hoisting sail, was by fortune thrown upon the island Ænaria, where meeting with Granius, and his other friends, he sailed with them for Africa. But their water failing them in the way, they were forced to put in near Eryx, in Sicily, where was a Roman quæstor on the watch, who all but captured Marius himself on his landing, and did kill sixteen of his retinue that went to fetch water. Marius, with all expedition loosing thence, crossed the sea to the isle of Meninx, where he first heard the news of his son's escape with Cethegus, and of his going to implore the assistance of Hiempsal, King of Numidia.

With this news, being somewhat comforted, he ventured to pass from that isle towards Carthage. Sextilius, a Roman, was then governor in Africa; one that had never received either any injury or any kindness from Marius; but who from compassion, it was hoped, might lend him some help. But he was scarce got ashore with a small retinue when an officer met him, and said, "Sextilius, the governor, forbids you, Marius, to set foot in Africa; if you do, he says he will put the decree of the senate in execution, and treat you as an enemy to the Romans." When Marius heard this, he wanted words to express his grief and resentment, and for a good while held his peace, looking sternly upon the messenger, who asked him what he should say, or what answer he should return to the governor? Marius answered him with a deep sigh: "Go tell him that you have seen Caius Marius sitting in exile among the ruins of Carthage"; appositely applying the example of the fortune of that city to the change of his own condition.

In the interim, Hiempsal, King of Numidia, dubious of what he should determine to do, treated young Marius and those that were with him very honourably; but when they had a mind to depart, he still had some pretence or other to detain them, and it was manifest he made these delays upon no good design. However, there happened an accident that made well for their preservation. The hard fortune which attended young Marius, who was of a comely aspect, touched one of the king's concubines, and this pity of hers was the beginning and occasion of love for him. At first he declined the woman's solicitations, but when he perceived that there was no other way of escaping, and that her offers were more serious than for the gratification of intemperate passion, he accepted her kindness, and she finding means to convey them away, he escaped with his friends and fled to his father. As soon as they had saluted each other, and were going by the seaside, they saw some scorpions fighting, which Marius took for an ill omen, whereupon they immediately went on board a little fisher-boat, and made towards Cercinas, an island not far distant from the continent. They had scarce put off from shore when they espied some horse, sent after them by the king, with all speed making towards that very place from which they were just retired. And Marius thus escaped a danger, it might be said, as great as any he ever incurred.

At Rome news came that Sylla was engaged with Mithridates' generals in Bœotia; the consuls, from factious opposition, were fallen to downright fighting, wherein Octavius prevailing, drove Cinna out of the city for attempting despotic government, and made Cornelius Merula consul in his stead; while Cinna, raising forces in other parts of Italy, carried the war against them. As soon as Marius heard of this he resolved, with all expedition, to put to sea again, and taking with him from Africa some Mauritanian horse, and a few of the refugees out of Italy, all together not above one thousand, he, with this handful, began his voyage. Arriving at Telamon, in Etruria, and coming ashore, he proclaimed freedom for the slaves; and many of the countrymen, also, and shepherds thereabouts, who were already freemen, at the hearing his name, flocked to him to the seaside. He persuaded the youngest and strongest to join him, and in a small time got together a competent force with which he filled forty ships. Knowing Octavius to be a good man and willing to execute his office with the greatest justice imaginable, and Cinna to be suspected by Sylla, and in actual warfare against the established government, he determined to join himself and his forces with the latter. He therefore sent a message to him, to let him know that he was ready to obey him as consul.

When Cinna had joyfully received his offer, naming him proconsul, and sending him the fasces and other ensigns of authority, he said that grandeur did not become his present fortune; but wearing an ordinary habit, and still letting his hair grow as it had done, from that very day he first went into banishment, and being now above threescore and ten years old, he came slowly on foot, designing to move people's compassion; which did not prevent, however, his natural fierceness of expression from still predominating, and his humiliation still let it appear that he was not so much dejected as exasperated by the change of his condition. Having saluted Cinna and the soldiers, he immediately prepared for action, and soon made a considerable alteration in the posture of affairs. He first cut off the provision ships, and plundering all the merchants, made himself master of the supplies of corn; then bringing his navy to the seaport towns, he took them, and at last, becoming master of Ostia by treachery, he pillaged that town, and slew a multitude of the inhabitants, and, blocking up the river, took from the enemy all hopes of supply by the sea; then marched with his army toward the city, and posted himself upon the hill called Janiculum.

The public interest did not receive so great damage from Octavius' unskilfulness in his management of affairs as from his omitting needful measures through too strict observance of the law. As when several advised him to make the slaves free, he said that he would not give slaves the privilege of the country from which he then, in defence of the laws, was driving away Marius. When Metellus, son to that Metellus who was general in the war in Africa, and afterwards banished through Marius' means, came to Rome, being thought a much better commander than Octavius, the soldiers, deserting the consul, came to him and desired him to take the command of them and preserve the city; that they, when they had got an experienced valiant commander, should fight courageously, and come off conquerors. But when Metellus, offended at it, commanded them angrily to return to the consul, they revolted to the enemy. Metellus, too, seeing the city in desperate condition, left it; but a company of Chaldæans, sacrificers, and interpreters of the Sibyl's books persuaded Octavius that things could turn out happily, and kept him at Rome. He was, indeed, of all the Romans the most upright and just, and maintained the honour of the consulate, without cringing or compliance, as strictly in accordance with ancient laws and usages as though they had been immutable mathematical truths; and yet fell, I know not how, into some weaknesses, giving more observance to fortunetellers and diviners, than to men skilled in civil and military affairs. He therefore, before Marius entered the city, was pulled down from the rostra and murdered by those that were sent before by Marius; and it is reported there was a Chaldæan writing found in his gown when he was slain. And it seemed a thing very unaccountable, that of two famous generals, Marius should be often successful by the observing divinations, and Octavius ruined by the same means.

When affairs were in this posture, the senate assembled, and sent a deputation to Cinna and Marius, desiring them to come into the city peaceably and spare the citizens. Cinna, as consul, received the embassy, sitting in the curule chair, and returned a kind answer to the messengers; Marius stood by him and said nothing, but gave sufficient testimony, by the gloominess of his countenance and the sternness of his looks, that he would in a short time fill the city with blood. As soon as the council arose, they went toward the city, where Cinna entered with his guards, but Marius stayed at the gates, and, dissembling his rage, professed that he was then an exile and banished his country by course of law; that if his presence were necessary, they must, by a new decree, repeal the former act by which he was banished; as though he were, indeed, a religious observer of the laws, and as if he were returning to a city free from fear or oppression. Hereupon the people were assembled, but before three or four tribes had given their votes, throwing up his pretences and his legal scruples about his banishment, he came into the city with a select guard of the slaves who had joined him, whom he called Bardyæi. These proceeded to murder a number of citizens, as he gave command, partly by word of mouth, partly by the signal of his nod. At length Ancharius, a senator, and one that had been prætor, coming to Marius, and not being re-saluted by him, they with their drawn swords slew him before Marius' face; and henceforth this was their token, immediately to kill all those who met Marius and saluting him were taken no notice of, nor answered with the like courtesy; so that his very friends were not without dreadful apprehensions and horror, whensoever they came to speak with him.

When they had now butchered a great number, Cinna grew more remiss and cloyed with murders; but Marius' rage continued still fresh and unsatisfied, and he daily sought for all that were any way suspected by him. Now was every road and every town filled with those that pursued and hunted them that fled and hid themselves; and it was remarkable that there was no more confidence to be placed, as things stood, either in hospitality or friendship; for there were found but a very few that did not betray those that fled to them for shelter. And thus the servants of Cornutus deserve the greater praise and admiration, who, having concealed their master in the house, took the body of one of the slain, cut off the head, put a gold ring on the finger, and showed it to Marius' guards, and buried it with the same solemnity as if it had been their own master. This trick was perceived by nobody, and so Cornutus escaped, and was conveyed by his domestics into Gaul.

Marcus Antonius, the orator, though he, too, found a true friend, had ill-fortune. The man was but poor and a plebeian, and as he was entertaining a man of the greatest rank in Rome, trying to provide for him with the best he could, he sent his servant to get some wine of a neighbouring vintner. The servant carefully tasting it and bidding him draw better, the fellow asked him what was the matter, that he did not buy new and ordinary wine as he used to do, but richer and of a greater price; he without any designs told him, as his old friend and acquaintance, that his master entertained Marcus Antonius, who was concealed with him. The villainous vintner, as soon as the servant was gone, went himself to Marius, then at supper, and being brought into his presence, told him he would deliver Antonius into his hands. As soon as he heard it, it is said he gave a great shout, and clapped his hands for joy, and had very nearly risen up and gone to the place himself; but being detained by his friends, he sent Annius, and some soldiers with him, and commanded him to bring Antonius' head to him with all speed. When they came to the house, Annius stayed at the door, and the soldiers went upstairs into the chamber; where, seeing Antonius, they endeavoured to shuffle off the murder from one another; for so great it seems were the graces and charms of his oratory, that as soon as he began to speak and beg his life, none of them durst touch or so much as look upon him; but hanging down their heads, everyone fell a-weeping. When their stay seemed something tedious, Annius came up himself and found Antonius discoursing, and the soldiers astonished and quite softened by it, and calling them cowards, went himself and cut off his head.

Catulus Lutatius, who was colleague with Marius, and his partner in the triumph over the Cimbri, when Marius replied to those that interceded for him and begged his life, merely with the words, "He must die," shut himself up in a room, and making a great fire, smothered himself. When maimed and headless carcasses were now frequently thrown about and trampled upon the streets, people were not so much moved with compassion at the sight, as struck into a kind of horror and consternation. The outrages of those that were called Bardyæi was the greatest grievance. These murdered the masters of families in their own houses, abused their children, and ravished their wives, and were uncontrollable in their rapine and murders, till those of Cinna's and Sertorius' party, taking counsel together, fell upon them in the camp and killed them every man.

In the interim, as if a change of wind was coming on, there came news from all parts that Sylla, having put an end to the war with Mithridates, and taken possession of the provinces, was returning into Italy with a great army. This gave some small respite and intermission to these unspeakable calamities. Marius and his friends believing war to be close at hand, Marius was chosen consul the seventh time, and appearing on the very calends of January, the beginning of the year, threw one Sextus Lucinus from the Tarpeian precipice; an omen, as it seemed, portending the renewed misfortunes both of their party and of the city. Marius, himself now worn out with labour and sinking under the burden of anxieties, could not sustain his spirits, which shook within him with the apprehension of a new war and fresh encounters and dangers, the formidable character of which he knew by his own experience. He was not now to hazard the war with Octavius or Merula, commanding an inexperienced multitude or seditious rabble; but

Sylla himself was approaching, the same who had formerly banished him, and since that, had driven Mithridates as far as the Euxine Sea.

Perplexed with such thoughts as these, and calling to mind his banishment, and the tedious wanderings and dangers he underwent, both by sea and land, he fell into despondency, nocturnal frights, and unquiet sleep, still fancying that he heard someone telling him, that—

—the lion's lair
Is dangerous, though the lion be not there.

Above all things fearing to lie awake, he gave himself up to drinking deep and besotting himself at night in a way most unsuitable to his age, by all means provoking sleep, as a diversion of his thoughts. At length, on the arrival of a messenger from the sea, he was seized with new alarms, and so what with his fear for the future, and what with the burden and satiety of the present, on some slight predisposing cause, he fell into a pleurisy, as Posidonius the philosopher relates, who says he visited and conversed with him when he was sick, about some business relating to his embassy. Caius Piso, an historian, tells us that Marius, walking after supper with his friends, fell into a conversation with them about his past life, and after reckoning up the several changes of his condition that from the beginning had happened to him, said, that it did not become a prudent man to trust himself any longer with fortune; and, thereupon taking leave of those that were with him, he kept his bed seven days, and then died.

Some say his ambition betrayed itself openly in his sickness, and that he ran into an extravagant frenzy, fancying himself to be general in the war against Mithridates, throwing himself into such postures and motions of his body as he had formerly used when he was in battle, with frequent shouts and loud cries. With so strong and invincible a desire of being employed in that business had he been possessed through his pride and emulation. Though he had now lived seventy years, and was the first man that ever was chosen seven times consul, and had an establishment and riches sufficient for many kings, he yet complained of his ill fortune, that he must now die before he had attained what he desired. Plato, when he saw his death approaching, thanked the guiding providence and fortune of his life, first, that he was born a man and a Grecian, not a barbarian or a brute, and next, that he happened to live in Socrates' age. And so, indeed, they say Antipater of Tarsus, in like manner, at his death, calling to mind the happiness that he had enjoyed, did not so much as omit his prosperous voyage to Athens; thus recognising every favour of his indulgent fortune with the greatest acknowledgments, and carefully saving all to the last in that safest of human treasure-chambers, the memory. Unmindful and thoughtless persons, on the contrary, let all that occurs to them slip away from them as time passes on. Retaining and preserving nothing, they lose the enjoyment of their present prosperity by fancying something better to come; whereas by fortune we may be prevented to this, but that cannot be taken from us. Yet they reject their present success, as though it did not concern them, and do nothing but dream of future uncertainties; not indeed unnaturally; as till men have by reason and education laid a good foundation for external superstructures, in the seeking after and gathering them they can never satisfy the unlimited desires of their mind.

Thus died Marius on the seventeenth day of his seventh consulship, to the great joy and content of Rome, which thereby was in good hopes to be delivered from the calamity of a cruel tyranny; but in a small time they found that they had only changed their old and worn-out master for another, young and vigorous; so much cruelty and savageness did his son Marius show in murdering the noblest and most approved citizens. At first, being esteemed resolute and daring against his enemies, he was named the son of Mars, but afterwards, his actions betraying his contrary disposition, he was called the son of Venus. At last, besieged by Sylla in Præneste, where he endeavoured in many ways, but in vain, to save his life, when on the capture of the city there was no hope of escape, he killed himself with his own hand.

LYSANDER

THE TREASURE-CHAMBER OF THE ACANTHIANS AT DELPHI HAS THIS inscription: "The spoils which Brasidas and the Acanthians took from the Athenians." And, accordingly, many take the marble statue, which stands within the building by the gates, to be Brasidas'; but, indeed, it is Lysander's, representing him with his hair at full length, after the old fashion, and with an ample beard. Neither is it true, as some give out, that because the Argives, after their great defeat, shaved themselves for sorrow, that the Spartans contrarywise triumphing in their achievements, suffered their hair to grow; neither did the Spartans come to be ambitious of wearing long hair, because the Bacchiadæ, who fled from Corinth to Lacedæmon, looked mean and unsightly, having their heads all close cut. But this, also, is indeed one of the ordinances of Lycurgus, who, as it is reported, was used to say, that long hair made good-looking men more beautiful, and ill-looking men more terrible.

Lysander's father is said to have been Aristoclitus, who was not indeed of the royal family but yet of the stock of the Heraclidæ. He was brought up in poverty, and showed himself obedient and conformable, as ever anyone did, to the customs of his country; of a manly spirit, also, and superior to all pleasures, excepting only that which their good actions bring to those who are honoured and successful; and it is accounted no base thing in Sparta for their young men to be overcome with this kind of pleasure. For they are desirous, from the very first, to have their youth susceptible to good and bad repute, to feel pain at disgrace, and exultation at being commended; and anyone who is insensible and unaffected in these respects is thought poor-spirited and of no capacity for virtue. Ambition and the passion for distinction were thus implanted in his character by his

Laconian education, nor, if they continued there, must we blame his natural disposition much for this. But he was submissive to great men, beyond what seems agreeable to the Spartan temper, and could easily bear the haughtiness of those who were in power, when it was any way for his advantage, which some are of opinion is no small part of political discretion. Aristotle, who says all great characters are more or less atrabilious, as Socrates and Plato and Hercules were, writes that Lysander, not indeed early in life, but when he was old, became thus affected. What is singular in his character is that he endured poverty very well, and that he was not at all enslaved or corrupted by wealth, and yet he filled his country with riches and the love of them, and took away from them the glory of not admiring money; importing amongst them an abundance of gold and silver after the Athenian war, though keeping not one drachma for himself. When Dionysius, the tyrant, sent his daughters some costly gowns of Sicilian manufacture, he would not receive them, saying he was afraid they would make them look more unhandsome. But a while after, being sent ambassador from the same city to the same tyrant, when he had sent him a couple of robes, and bade him choose which of them he would, and carry to his daughter: "She," said he, "will be able to choose best for herself," and taking both of them, went his way.

The Peloponnesian war having now been carried on a long time, and it being expected, after the disaster of the Athenians in Sicily, that they would at once lose the mastery of the sea, and ere long be routed everywhere, Alcibiades, returning from banishment, and taking the command, produced a great change, and made the Athenians again a match for their opponents by sea; and the Lacedæmonians, in great alarm at this, and calling up fresh courage and zeal for the conflict, feeling the want of an able commander and of a powerful armament, sent out Lysander to be admiral of the seas. Being at Ephesus, and finding the city well affected towards him, and favourable to the Lacedæmonian party, but in ill condition, and in danger to become barbarised by adopting the manners of the Persians, who were much mingled among them, the country of Lydia bordering upon them, and the king's generals being quartered there for a long time, he pitched his camp there, and commanded the merchant ships all about to put in thither, and proceeded to build ships of war there; and thus restored their ports by the traffic he created, and their market by the employment he gave, and filled their private houses and their workshops with wealth, so that from that time the city began, first of all, by Lysander's means, to have some hopes of growing to that stateliness and grandeur which now it is at.

Understanding that Cyrus, the king's son, was come to Sardis, he went up to talk with him, and to accuse Tisaphernes, who, receiving a command to help the Lacedæmonians, and to drive the Athenians from the sea, was thought, on account of Alcibiades, to have become remiss and unwilling, and by paying the seamen slenderly to be ruining the fleet. Now Cyrus was willing that Tisaphernes might be found in blame, and be ill reported of, as being, indeed, a dishonest man, and privately at feud with himself. By these means, and by their daily intercourse together, Lysander, especially by the submissiveness of his conversation, won the affection of the young prince, and greatly roused him to carry on the war; and when he would depart, Cyrus gave him a banquet, and desired him not to refuse his good-will, but to speak and ask whatever he had a mind to, and that he should not be refused anything whatsoever: "Since you are so very kind," replied Lysander, "I earnestly request you to add one penny to the seamen's pay, that instead of three pence, they may now receive four pence." Cyrus, delighted with his public spirit, gave him ten thousand darics, out of which he added the penny to the seamen's pay, and by the renown of this in a short time emptied the ships of the enemies, as many would come over to that side which gave the most pay, and those who remained, being disheartened and mutinous, daily created trouble to the captains. Yet for all Lysander had so distracted and weakened his enemies, he was afraid to engage by sea, Alcibiades being an energetic commander, and having the superior number of ships, and having been hitherto, in all battles, unconquered both by sea and land.

But afterwards, when Alcibiades sailed from Samos to Phocæa, leaving Antiochus, the pilot, in command of all his forces, this Antiochus, to insult Lysander, sailed with two galleys into the port of the Ephesians, and with mocking and laughter proudly rowed along before the place where the ships lay drawn up. Lysander, in indignation, launched at first a few ships only and pursued him, but as soon as he saw the Athenians come to his help, he added some other ships, and, at last, they fell to a set battle together; and Lysander won the victory, and taking fifteen of their ships, erected a trophy. For this, the people in the city being angry, put Alcibiades out of command, and finding himself despised by the soldiers in Samos, and ill spoken of, he sailed from the army into the Chersonese. And this battle, although not important in itself, was made remarkable by its consequences to Alcibiades.

Lysander, meanwhile, invited to Ephesus such persons in the various cities as he saw to be bolder and haughtier-spirited than the rest, proceeded to lay the foundations of that government by bodies of ten, and those revolutions which afterwards came to pass, stirring up and urging them to unite in clubs and apply themselves to public affairs, since as soon as ever the Athenians should be put down, the popular government, he said, should be suppressed and they should become supreme in their several countries. And he made them believe these things by present deeds, promoting those who were his friends already to great employments, honours, and offices, and, to gratify their covetousness, making himself a partner in injustice and wickedness. So much so, that all flocked to him, and courted and desired him, hoping, if he remained in power, that the highest wishes they could form would all be gratified. And therefore, from the very beginning, they could not look pleasantly upon Callicratidas, when he came to succeed Lysander as admiral; nor, afterwards, when he had given them experience that he was a most noble and just person, were they pleased with the manner of his government, and its straightforward, Dorian, honest character. They did, indeed, admire his virtue, as they might the beauty of some hero's image; but their wishes were for Lysander's zealous and profitable support of the interests of his friends and partisans, and they shed tears, and were much disheartened when he sailed from them. He himself made them yet more disaffected to Callicratidas; for what remained of the money which had been given him to pay the navy, he sent back again to Sardis, bidding them, if they would, apply to Callicratidas himself, and see how he was able to maintain the soldiers. And, at the last, sailing away, he declared to him that he delivered up the fleet in possession and command of the sea. But Callicratidas, to expose the emptiness of these high pretensions, said, "In that case, leave Samos on the left hand, and sailing to Miletus, there deliver up the ships to me; for if we are masters of the sea, we need not fear sailing by our enemies in Samos." To which Lysander answering, that not himself but he commanded the ships, sailed to Peloponnesus, leaving Callicratidas in great perplexity. For neither had he brought any money from home with him, nor could he endure to tax the towns or force them, being in hardship enough. Therefore, the only course that was to be taken was to go and beg at the doors of the king's commanders, as Lysander had done; for which he was most unfit of any man, being of a generous and great spirit, and one who thought it more becoming for the Greeks to suffer any damage from one another, than to flatter and wait at the gates of barbarians, who, indeed, had gold enough, but nothing else that was commendable. But being compelled by necessity, he proceeded to Lydia, and went at once to Cyrus' house, and sent in word that Callicratidas, the admiral, was there to speak with him; one of those who kept the gates replied, "Cyrus, O stranger, is not now at leisure, for he is drinking." To which Callicratidas answered, most innocently, "Very well, I will wait till he has done his draught." This time, therefore, they took him for some clownish fellow, and he withdrew, merely laughed at by the barbarians; but when, afterwards, he came a second time to the gate, and was not admitted, he took it hardly and set off for Ephesus, wishing a great many evils to those who first let themselves be insulted over by these barbarians, and taught them to be insolent because of their riches; and added vows to those who were present, that as soon as ever he came back to Sparta, he would do all he could to reconcile the Greeks, that they might be formidable to barbarians, and that they should cease henceforth to need their aid against one another. But Callicratidas, who entertained purposes worthy a Lacedæmonian, and showed himself worthy to compete with the very best of Greece, for his justice, his greatness of mind and courage, not long after, having been beaten in a sea fight at Arginusæ, died.

And now, affairs going backwards, the associates in the war sent an embassy to Sparta, requiring Lysander to be their admiral, professing themselves ready to undertake the business much more zealously if he was commander; and Cyrus also sent to request the same thing. But because they had a law which would not suffer anyone to be admiral twice, and wished, nevertheless, to gratify their allies, they gave the title of admiral to one Aracus, and sent Lysander nominally as vice-admiral, but, indeed, with full powers. So he came out, long wished for by the greatest part of the chief persons and leaders in the towns, who hoped to grow to greater power still by his means, when the popular governments should be everywhere destroyed.

But to those who loved honest and noble behaviour in their commanders, Lysander, compared with Callicratidas, seemed cunning and subtle, managing most things in the war by deceit, extolling what was just when it was profitable, and when it was not, using that which was convenient, instead of that which was good; and not judging truth to be in nature better than falsehood, but setting a value upon both according to interest. He would laugh at those who thought Hercules' posterity ought not to use deceit in war: "For where the lion's skin will not reach, you must patch it out with the fox's." Such is the conduct recorded of him in the business about Miletus; for when his friends and connections, whom he had promised to assist in suppressing popular government, and expelling their political opponents, had altered their minds, and were reconciled to their enemies, he pretended openly as if he was pleased with it, and was desirous to further the reconciliation, but privately he railed at and abused them, and provoked them to set upon the multitude. And as soon as ever he perceived a new attempt to be commencing, he at once came up and entered into the city, and the first of the conspirators he lit upon, he pretended to rebuke, and spoke roughly, as if he would punish them; but the others, meantime, he bade be courageous, and to fear nothing, now he was with them. And all this acting and dissembling was with the object that the most considerable men of the popular party might not fly away, but might stay in the city and be killed; which so fell out, for all who believed him were put to death.

There is a saying also, recorded by Androclides, which makes him guilty of great indifference to the obligations of an oath. His recommendation, according to this account, was to "cheat boys with dice, and men with oaths," an imitation of Polycrates of Samos, not very honourable to a lawful commander, to take example, namely, from a tyrant; nor in character with Laconian usages, to treat gods as ill as enemies, or, indeed, even more injuriously; since he who overreaches by an oath admits that he fears his enemy, while he despises his God.

Cyrus now sent for Lysander to Sardis, and gave him some money, and promised him some more, youthfully protesting in favour to him, that if his father gave him nothing, he would supply him of his own; and if he himself should be destitute of all, he would cut up, he said, to make money, the very throne upon which he sat to do justice, it being made of gold and silver; and, at last, on going up into Media to his father, he ordered that he should receive the tribute of the towns, and committed his government to him, and so taking his leave, and desiring him not to fight by sea before he returned, for he would come back with a great many ships out of Phœnicia and Cilicia, departed to visit the king.

Lysander's ships were too few for him to venture to fight, and yet too many to allow of his remaining idle; he set out, therefore, and reduced some of the islands, and wasted Ægina and Salamis; and from thence landing in Attica, and saluting Agis, who came from Decelea to meet him, he made a display to the land-forces of the strength of the fleet as though he could sail where he pleased, and were absolute master by sea. But hearing the Athenians pursued him, he fled another way through the island into Asia. And finding the Hellespont without any defence, he attacked Lampsacus with his ships by sea; while Thorax, acting in concert with him with the land army, made an assault on the walls; and so having taken the city by storm, he gave it up to his soldiers to plunder. The fleet of the Athenians, a hundred and eighty ships, had just arrived at Elæus in the Chersonese; and hearing the news, that Lampsacus was destroyed, they presently sailed to Sestos; where, taking in victuals, they advanced to Ægos Potami, over against their enemies, who were still stationed about Lampsacus. Amongst other Athenian captains who were now in command was Philocles, he who persuaded the people to pass a decree to cut off the right thumb of the captives in the war, that they should not be able to hold the spear, though they might the oar.

Then they all rested themselves, hoping they should have battle the next morning. But Lysander had other things in his head; he commanded the mariners and pilots to go on board at dawn, as if there should be a battle as soon as it was day, and to sit there in order, and without any noise, excepting what should be commanded, and in like manner that the land army should remain quietly in their ranks by the sea. But the sun rising, and the Athenians sailing up with their whole fleet in line, and challenging them to battle, though he had had his ships all drawn up and manned before daybreak, nevertheless did not stir. He merely sent some boats to those who lay foremost, and bade them keep still and stay in their order; not to be disturbed, and none of them to sail out and offer battle. So about evening, the Athenians sailing back, he would not let the seamen go out of the ships before two or three, which he had sent to espy, were returned, after seeing the enemies disembark. And thus they did the next day, and the third, and so to the fourth. So that the Athenians grew extremely confident, and disdained their enemies as if they had been afraid and daunted. At this time, Alcibiades, who was in his castle in the Chersonese, came on horseback to the Athenian army, and found fault with their captains, first of all that they had pitched their camp neither well nor safely on an exposed and open beach, a very bad landing for the ships, and secondly, that where they were they had to fetch all they wanted from Sestos, some considerable way off; whereas if they sailed round a little way to the town and harbour of Sestos, they would be at a safer distance from an enemy, who lay watching their movements, at the command of a single general, terror of whom made every order rapidly executed. This advice, however, they would not listen to; and Tydeus answered disdainfully, that not he, but others, were in office now. So Alcibiades, who even suspected there must be treachery, departed.

But on the fifth day, the Athenians having sailed towards them, and gone back again as they were used to do, very proudly and full of contempt, Lysander sending some ships, as usual, to look out, commanded the masters of them that when they saw the Athenians go to land, they should row back again with all their speed, and that when they were about half-way across, they should lift up a brazen shield from the fore-deck, as the sign of battle. And he himself sailing round, encouraged the pilots and masters of the ships, and exhorted them to keep all their men to their places, seamen and soldiers alike, and as soon as ever the sign should be given, to row boldly to their enemies. Accordingly, when the shield had been lifted up from the ships, and the trumpet from the admiral's vessel had sounded for the battle, the ships rowed up, and the foot soldiers strove to get along by the shore to the promontory. The distance there between the two continents is fifteen furlongs, which, by zeal and eagerness of the rowers, was quickly traversed. Conon, one of the Athenian commanders, was the first who saw from the land the fleet advancing, and shouted out to embark, and in the greatest distress bade some and entreated others, and some he forced to man the ships. But all his diligence signified nothing, because the men were scattered about; for as soon as they came out of the ships, expecting no such matter, some went to market, others walked about the country, or went to sleep in their tents, or got their dinners ready, being, through their commanders' want of skill, as far as possible from any thought of what was to happen; and the enemy now coming up with shouts and noise, Conon, with eight ships, sailed out, and making his escape, passed from thence to Cyprus, to Evagoras. The Peloponnesians falling upon the rest, some they took quite empty, and some they destroyed while they were filling; the men, meantime coming unarmed and scattered to help, died at their ships, or, flying by land, were slain, their enemies disembarking and pursuing them. Lysander took three thousand prisoners, with the generals, and the whole fleet, excepting the sacred ship Paralus, and those which fled with Conon. So taking their ships in tow, and having plundered their tents, with pipe and songs of victory, he sailed back to Lampsacus, having accomplished a great work with small pains, and having finished in one hour a war which had been protracted in its continuance, and diversified in its incidents and in its fortunes, to a degree exceeding belief, compared with all before it. After altering its shape and character a thousand times, and after having been the destruction of more commanders than all the previous wars of Greece put together, it was now put an end to by the good counsel and ready conduct of one man.

Some, therefore, looked upon the result as a divine intervention, and there were certain who affirmed that the stars of Castor and Pollux were seen on each side of Lysander's ship, when he first set sail from the haven toward his enemies, shining about the helm; and some say the stone which fell down was a sign of this slaughter. For a stone of a great size did fall, according to the common belief, from heaven, at Ægos Potami, which is shown to this day, and held in great esteem by the Chersonites. And it is said that Anaxagoras foretold that the occurrence of a slip or shake among the bodies fixed in the heavens, dislodging anyone of them, would be followed by the fall of the whole of them. For no one of the stars is now in the same place in which it was at first; for they, being, according to him, like stones and heavy, shine by the refraction of the upper air round about them, and are carried along forcibly by the violence of the circular motion by which they were originally withheld from falling, when cold and heavy bodies were first separated from the general universe. But there is a more probable opinion than this maintained by some, who say that falling stars are no effluxes, nor discharges of ethereal fire, extinguished almost at the instant of its igniting by the lower air; neither are they the sudden combustion and blazing up of a quantity of the lower air let loose in great abundance into the upper region; but the heavenly bodies, by a relaxation of the force of their circular movement, are carried by an irregular course, not in general into the inhabited part of the earth, but for the most part into the wide sea; which is the cause of their not being observed. Daimachus, in his treatise on Religion, supports the view of Anaxagoras. He says, that before this stone fell, for seventy-five days continually, there was seen in the heavens a vast fiery body, as if it had been a flaming cloud, not resting, but carried about with several intricate and broken movements, so that the flaming pieces, which were broken off by this commotion and running about, were carried in all directions, shining as falling stars do. But when it afterwards came down to the ground in this district, and the people of the place recovering from their fear and astonishment came together, there was no fire to be seen, neither any sign of it; there was only a stone lying, big indeed, but which bore no proportion, to speak of, to that fiery compass. It is manifest that Daimachus needs to have indulgent hearers; but if what he says be true, he altogether proves those to be wrong who say that a rock broken off from the top of some mountain, by winds and tempests, and caught and whirled about like a top, as soon as this impetus began to slacken and cease, was precipitated and fell to the ground. Unless, indeed, we choose to say that the phenomenon which was observed for so many days was really fire, and that the change in the atmosphere ensuing on its extinction was attended with violent winds and agitations, which might be the cause of this stone being carried off. The exacter treatment of this subject belongs, however, to a different kind of writing.

Lysander, after the three thousand Athenians whom he had taken prisoners were condemned by the commissioners to die, called Philocles the general, and asked him what punishment he considered himself to deserve, for having advised the citizens, as he had done, against the Greeks; but he, being nothing cast down at his calamity, bade him not to accuse him of matters of which nobody was a judge, but to do to him, now he was a conqueror, as he would have suffered, had he been overcome. Then washing himself, and putting on a fine cloak, he led the citizens the way to the slaughter, as Theophrastus writes in his history. After this Lysander, sailing about to the various cities, bade all the Athenians he met go into Athens, declaring that he would spare none, but kill every man whom he found out of the city, intending thus to cause immediate famine and scarcity there, that they might not make the siege laborious to him, having provisions sufficient to endure it. And suppressing the popular governments and all other constitutions, he left one Lacedæmonian chief officer in every city, with ten rulers to act with him, selected out of the societies which he had previously formed in the different towns. And doing thus as well in the cities of his enemies as of his associates, he sailed leisurely on, establishing, in a manner, for himself supremacy over the whole of Greece. Neither did he make choice of rulers by birth or by wealth, but bestowed the offices on his own friends and partisans, doing everything to please them, and putting absolute power of reward and punishment into their hands. And thus, personally appearing on many occasions of bloodshed and massacre, and aiding his friends to expel their opponents, he did not give the Greeks a favourable specimen of the Lacedæmonian government; and the expression of Theopompus, the comic poet, seemed but poor, when he compared the Lacedæmonians to tavern women, because when the Greeks had first tasted the sweet wine of liberty, they then poured vinegar into the cup; for from the very first it had a rough and bitter taste, all government by the people being suppressed by Lysander, and the boldest and least scrupulous of the oligarchical party selected to rule the cities.

Having spent some little time about these things, and sent some before to Lacedæmon to tell them he was arriving with two hundred ships, he united his forces in Attica with those of the two kings Agis and Pausanias, hoping to take the city without delay. But when the Athenians defended themselves, he with his fleet passed again to Asia, and in like manner destroyed the forms of government in all the other cities, and placed them under the rule of ten chief persons, many in everyone being killed, and many driven into exile; and in Samos he expelled the whole people, and gave their cities to the exiles whom he brought back. And the Athenians still possessing Sestos, he took it from them, and suffered not the Sestians themselves to dwell in it, but gave the city and country to be divided out among the pilots and masters of the ships under him; which was his first act that was disallowed by the Lacedæmonians, who brought the Sestians back again into their country. All Greece, however, rejoiced to see the Æginetans, by Lysander's aid, now again, after a long time, receiving back their cities, and the Melians and Scionæans restored, while the Athenians were driven out, and delivered up the cities.

But when he now understood they were in bad case in the city because of the famine, he sailed to Piræus, and reduced the city, which was compelled to surrender on what conditions he demanded. One hears it said by Lacedæmonians that Lysander wrote to the Ephors thus: "Athens is taken"; and that these magistrates wrote back to Lysander, "Taken is enough." But this saying was invented for its neatness' sake: for the true decree of the magistrates was on this manner: "The government of the Lacedæmonians has made these orders; pull down the Piræus and the long walls; quit all the towns, and keep to your own land; if you do these things, you shall have peace, if you wish it, restoring also your exiles. As concerning the number of the ships, whatsoever there be judged necessary to appoint, that do." This scroll of conditions the Athenians accepted, Theramenes, son of Hagnon, supporting it. At which time, too, they say that when Cleomenes, one of the young orators, asked him how he durst act and speak contrary to Themistocles, delivering up the walls to the Lacedæmonians, which he had built against the will of the Lacedæmonians, he said, "O young man, I do nothing contrary to Themistocles; for he raised these walls for the safety of the citizens, and we pull them down for their safety; and if walls make a city happy, then Sparta must be the most wretched of all, as it has none."

Lysander, as soon as he had taken all the ships except twelve, and the walls of the Athenians, on the sixteenth day of the month Munychion, the same on which they had overcome the barbarians at Salamis, then proceeded to take measures for altering the government. But the Athenians taking that very unwillingly, and resisting, he sent to the people and informed them that he found that the city had broken the terms, for the walls were standing when the days were past within which they should have been pulled down. He should, therefore, consider their case anew, they having broken their first articles. And some state, in fact, the proposal was made in the congress of the allies, that the Athenians should all be sold as slaves; on which occasion, Erianthus, the Theban, gave his vote to pull down the city, and turn the country into sheep-pasture; yet afterwards, when there was a meeting of the captains together, a man of Phocis, singing the first chorus in Euripides' Electra, which begins—

> Electra, Agamemnon's child, I come
> Unto thy desert home,

they were all melted with compassion, and it seemed to be a cruel deed to destroy and pull down a city which had been so famous, and produced such men.

Accordingly Lysander, the Athenians yielding up everything, sent for a number of flute-women out of the city, and collected together all that were in the camp, and pulled down the walls, and burnt the ships to the sound of the flute, the allies being crowned with garlands, and making merry together, as counting that day the beginning of their liberty. He proceeded also at once to alter the government, placing thirty rulers in the city and ten in the Piræus: he put, also, a garrison into the Acropolis, and made Callibius, a Spartan, the governor of it; who afterwards taking up his staff to strike Autolycus, the athlete, about whom Xenophon wrote his "Banquet," on his tripping up his heels and throwing him to the ground, Lysander was not vexed at it, but chid Callibius, telling him he did not know how to govern freemen. The thirty rulers, however, to gain Callibius' favour, a little after killed Autolycus.

Lysander, after this, sails out to Thrace, and what remained of the public money, and the gifts and crowns which he had himself received, numbers of people, as might be expected, being anxious to make presents to a man of such great power, who was, in a manner, the lord of Greece, he sends to Lacedæmon by Gylippus, who had commanded formerly in Sicily. But he, it is reported, unsewed the sacks at the bottom, took a considerable amount of silver out of everyone of them, and sewed them up again, not knowing there was a writing in everyone stating how much there was. And coming into Sparta, what he had thus stolen away he hid under the tiles of his house, and delivered up the sacks to the magistrates, and showed the seals were upon them. But afterwards, on their opening the sacks and counting it, the quantity of the silver differed from what the writing expressed; and the matter causing some perplexity to the magistrates,

Gylippus' servant tells them in a riddle, that under the tiles lay many owls; for, as it seems, the greatest part of the money then current bore the Athenian stamp of the owl. Gylippus having committed so foul and base a deed, after such great and distinguished exploits before, removed himself from Lacedæmon.

But the wisest of the Spartans, very much on account of this occurrence, dreading the influence of money, as being what had corrupted the greatest citizens, exclaimed against Lysander's conduct, and declared to the Ephors that all the silver and gold should be sent away, as mere "alien mischiefs." These consulted about it; and Theopompus says it was Sciraphidas, but Ephorus that it was Phlogidas, who declared they ought not to receive any gold or silver into the city; but to use their own country coin, which was iron, and was first of all dipped in vinegar when it was red-hot, that it might not be worked up anew, but because of the dipping might be hard and unpliable. It was also, of course, very heavy and troublesome to carry, and a great deal of it in quantity and weight was but a little in value. And perhaps all the old money was so, coin consisting of iron, or, in some countries, copper skewers, whence it comes that we still find a great number of small pieces of money retain the name of *obolus,* and the drachma is six of these, because so much may be grasped in one's hand. But Lysander's friends being against it, and endeavouring to keep the money in the city, it was resolved to bring in this sort of money to be used publicly, enacting, at the same time, that if anyone was found in possession of any privately, he should be put to death, as if Lycurgus had feared the coin, and not the covetousness resulting from it, which they did not repress by letting no private man keep any, so much as they encouraged it, by allowing the state to possess it; attaching thereby a sort of dignity to it, over and above its ordinary utility. Neither was it possible, that what they saw so much esteemed publicly they should privately despise as unprofitable; and that everyone should think that thing could be nothing worth for his own personal use, which was so extremely valued and desired for the use of the state. And moral habits, induced by public practices, are far quicker in making their way into men's private lives, than the failings and faults of individuals are in infecting the city at large. For it is probable that the parts will be rather corrupted by the whole if that grows bad; while the vices which flow from a part into the whole find many correctives and remedies from that which remains sound. Terror and the law were now to keep guard over the citizens' houses, to prevent any money entering into them: but their minds could no longer be expected to remain superior to the desire of it when wealth in general was thus set up to be striven after, as a high and noble object. On this point, however, we have given our censure of the Lacedæmonians in one of our other writings.

Lysander erected out of the spoils brazen statues at Delphi of himself, and of everyone of the masters of the ships, as also figures of the golden stars of Castor and Pollux, which vanished before the battle at Leuctra. In the treasury of Brasidas and the Acanthians there was a trireme made of gold and ivory, of two cubits, which Cyrus sent Lysander in honour of his victory. But Alexandrides of Delphi writes, in his history, that there was also a deposit of Lysander's, a talent of silver, and fifty-two minas, besides eleven staters; a statement not consistent with the generally received account of his poverty. And at that time, Lysander, being in fact of greater power than any Greek before, was yet thought to show a pride, and to affect a superiority greater even than his power warranted. He was the first, as Duris says in his history, among the Greeks to whom the cities reared altars as to a god, and sacrificed; to him were songs of triumph first sung, the beginning of one of which still remains recorded:

> Great Greece's general from spacious Sparta we
> Will celebrate with songs of victory.

And the Samians decreed that their solemnities of Juno should be called the Lysandria; and out of the poets he had Chœrilus always with him, to extol his achievements in verse; and to Antilochus, who had made some verses in his commendation, being pleased with them, he gave a hat full of silver; and when Antimachus of Colophon, and one Niceratus of Heraclea, competed with each other in a poem on the deeds of Lysander, he gave the garland to Niceratus; at which Antimachus, in vexation, suppressed his poem; but Plato, being then a young man and admiring Antimachus for his poetry, consoled him for his defeat by telling him that it is the ignorant who are the sufferers by ignorance, as truly as the blind by want of sight. Afterwards, when Aristonus, the musician, who had been a conqueror six times at the Pythian games, told him as a piece of flattery, that if he were successful again, he would proclaim himself in the name of Lysander, "that is," he answered, "as his slave?"

This ambitious temper was indeed only burdensome to the highest personages and to his equals, but through having so many people devoted to serve him, an extreme haughtiness and contemptuousness grew up, together with ambition, in his character. He observed no sort of moderation, such as befitted a private man, either in rewarding or in punishing;

the recompense of his friends and guests was absolute power over cities, and irresponsible authority and the only satisfaction of his wrath was the destruction of his enemy; banishment would not suffice. As for example, at a later period, fearing lest the popular leaders of the Milesians should fly, and desiring also to discover those who lay hid, he swore he would do them no harm, and on their believing him and coming forth, he delivered them up to the oligarchical leaders to be slain, being in all no less than eight hundred. And, indeed, the slaughter in general of those of the popular party in the towns exceeded all computation; as he did not kill only for offences against himself, but granted these favours without sparing, and joined in the execution of them, to gratify the many hatreds and the much cupidity of his friends everywhere round about him. From whence the saying of Eteocles, the Lacedæmonian, came to be famous, that "Greece could not have borne two Lysanders." Theophrastus says, that Archestratus said the same thing concerning Alcibiades. But in his case what had given most offence was a certain licentious and wanton self-will; Lysander's power was feared and hated because of his unmerciful disposition. The Lacedæmonians did not at all concern themselves for any other accusers; but afterwards, when Pharnabazus, having been injured by him, he having pillaged and wasted his country, sent some to Sparta to inform against him, the Ephors taking it very ill, put one of his friends and fellow-captains, Thorax, to death, taking him with some silver privately in his possession; and they sent him a scroll, commanding him to return home. This scroll is made up thus: When the Ephors send an admiral or general on his way, they take two round pieces of wood, both exactly of a length and thickness, and cut even to one another; they keep one themselves, and the other they give to the person they send forth; and these pieces of wood they call Scytales. When, therefore, they have occasion to communicate any secret or important matter, making a scroll of parchment long and narrow like a leathern thong, they roll it about their own staff of wood, leaving no space void between, but covering the surface of the staff with the scroll all over. When they have done this, they write what they please on the scroll, as it is wrapped about the staff; and when they have written, they take off the scroll, and send it to the general without the wood. He, when he has received it, can read nothing of the writing, because the words and letters are not connected, but all broken up; but taking his own staff, he winds the slip of the scroll about it, so that this folding, restoring all the parts into the same order that they were in before, and putting what comes first into connection with what follows, brings the whole consecutive contents to view round the outside. And this scroll is called a *staff*, after the name of the wood, as a thing measured is by the name of the measure.

But Lysander, when the staff came to him to the Hellespont, was troubled, and fearing Pharnabazus' accusations most, made haste to confer with him, hoping to end the difference by a meeting together. When they met, he desired him to write another letter to the magistrates, stating that he had not been wronged, and had no complaint to prefer. But he was ignorant that Pharnabazus, as it is in the proverb, played Cretan against Cretan; for pretending to do all that was desired, openly he wrote such a letter as Lysander wanted, but kept by him another, written privately; and when they came to put on the seals, changed the tablets, which differed not at all to look upon, and gave him the letter which had been written privately. Lysander, accordingly, coming to Lacedæmon, and going, as the custom is, to the magistrates' office, gave Pharnabazus' letter to the Ephors, being persuaded that the greatest accusation against him was now withdrawn; for Pharnabazus was beloved by the Lacedæmonians, having been the most zealous on their side in the war of all the king's captains. But after the magistrates had read the letter they showed it him, and he understanding now that—

> Others beside Ulysses deep can be,
> Not the one wise man of the world is he,

in extreme confusion, left them at the time. But a few days after, meeting the Ephors, he said he must go to the temple of Ammon, and offer the god the sacrifices which he had vowed in war. For some state it as a truth, that when he was besieging the city of Aphytæ in Thrace, Ammon stood by him in his sleep; whereupon raising the siege, supposing the god had commanded it, he bade the Aphytæans sacrifice to Ammon, and resolved to make a journey into Libya to propitiate the god. But most were of opinion that the god was but the pretence, and that in reality he was afraid of the Ephors, and that impatience of the yoke at home, and dislike of living under authority, made him long for some travel and wandering, like a horse just brought in from open feeding and pasture to the stable, and put again to his ordinary work. For that which Ephorus states to have been the cause of this travelling about, I shall relate by and by.

And having hardly and with difficulty obtained leave of the magistrates to depart, he set sail. But the kings, while he was on his voyage, considering that keeping, as he did, the cities in possession by his own friends and partisans, he was in fact their sovereign and the lord of Greece, took measures for restoring the power to the people, and for throwing his friends out. Disturbances commencing again about these things, and, first of all, the Athenians from Phyle setting upon their thirty rulers and over-powering them, Lysander, coming home in haste, persuaded the Lacedæmonians to support the oligarchies and to put down the popular governments, and to the thirty in Athens, first of all, they sent a hundred talents for the war, and Lysander himself, as general, to assist them. But the kings envying him, and fearing lest he should take Athens again, resolved that one of themselves should take the command. Accordingly Pausanias went, and in words, indeed, professed as if he had been for the tyrant against the people, but in reality exerted himself for peace, that Lysander might not by the means of his friends become lord of Athens again. This he brought easily to pass; for, reconciling the Athenians, and quieting the tumults, he defeated the ambitious hope of Lysander, though shortly after, on the Athenians rebelling again, he was censured for having thus taken, as it were, the bit out of the mouth of the people, which, being freed from the oligarchy, would now break out again into affronts and insolence; and Lysander regained the reputation of a person who employed his command not in gratification of others, not for applause, but strictly for the good of Sparta.

His speech, also, was bold and daunting to such as opposed him. The Argives, for example, contended about the bounds of their land, and thought they brought juster pleas than the Lacedæmonians; holding out his sword, "He," said Lysander, "that is master of this, brings the best argu-ment about the bounds of territory." A man of Megara, at some confer-ence, talking freedom with him, "This language, my friend," said he, "should come from a city." To the Bœotians, who were acting a doubtful part, he put the question, whether he should pass through their country with spears upright or levelled. After the revolt of the Corinthians, when, on coming to their walls, he perceived the Lacedæmonians hesitating to make the assault, and a hare was seen to leap through the ditch: "Are you not ashamed," he said, "to fear an enemy, for whose laziness the very hares sleep upon their walls?"

When King Agis died, leaving a brother Agesilaus, and Leontychides, who was supposed his son, Lysander, being attached to Agesilaus, persuaded him to lay claim to the kingdom, as being a true descendant of Hercules; Leontychides lying under the suspicion of being the son of Alcibiades, who lived privately in familiarity with Timæa, the wife of Agis, at the time he was a fugitive in Sparta. Agis, they say, computing the time, satisfied himself that she could not have conceived by him, and had hitherto always neglected and manifestly disowned Leontychides; but now when he was carried sick to Heræa, being ready to die, what by importunities of the young man himself, and of his friends, in the presence of many he declared Leontychides to be his; and desiring those who were present to bear witness to this to the Lacedæmonians, died. They accordingly did so testify in favour of Leontychides. And Agesilaus, being otherwise highly reputed of, and strong in the support of Lysander, was, on the other hand, prejudiced by Diopithes, a man famous for his knowledge of oracles, who adduced this prophecy in reference to Agesilaus' lameness:

> Beware, great Sparta, lest there come of thee,
> Though sound thyself, an halting sovereignty;
> Troubles, both long and unexpected too,
> And storms of deadly warfare shall ensue.

When many, therefore, yielded to the oracle, and inclined to Leontychides, Lysander said that Diopithes did not take the prophecy rightly; for it was not that the god would be offended if any lame person ruled over the Lacedæmonians, but that the kingdom would be a lame one if bastards and false-born should govern with the posterity of Hercules. By this argument, and by his great influence among them, he prevailed, and Agesilaus was made king.

Immediately, therefore, Lysander spurred him on to make an expedition into Asia, putting him in hopes that he might destroy the Persians, and attain the height of greatness. And he wrote to his friends in Asia, bidding them request to have Agesilaus appointed to command them in the war against the barbarians; which they were persuaded to, and sent ambassadors to Lacedæmon to entreat it. And this would seem to be a second favour done Agesilaus by Lysander, not inferior to his first in obtaining him the kingdom. But with ambitious natures, otherwise not ill qualified for command, the feeling of jealousy of those near them in reputation continually stands in the way of the performance of noble actions; they make those their rivals in virtue, whom they ought to use as their helpers to it. Agesilaus took Lysander, among the thirty counsellors that accompanied him, with intentions of using him as his especial friend; but when they were come into Asia, the inhabitants there, to whom he was but little known, addressed themselves to him but little and seldom; whereas Lysander, because of their frequent previous intercourse, was visited and attended by large numbers, by his friends out of observance, and by others out of fear;

and just as in tragedies it not uncommonly is the case with the actors, the person who represents a messenger or servant is much taken notice of, and plays the chief part, while he who wears the crown and sceptre is hardly heard to speak, even so was it about the counsellor, he had all the real honours of the government, and to the king was left the empty name of power. This disproportionate ambition ought very likely to have been in some way softened down, and Lysander should have been reduced to his proper second place, but wholly to cast off and to insult and affront for glory's sake one who was his benefactor and friend was not worthy Agesilaus to allow in himself. For, first of all, he gave him no opportunity for any action, and never set him in any place of command; then, for whomsoever he perceived him exerting his interest, these persons he always sent away with a refusal, and with less attention than any ordinary suitors, thus silently undoing and weakening his influence.

Lysander, miscarrying in everything, and perceiving that his diligence for his friends was but a hindrance to them, forbore to help them, entreating them that they would not address themselves to, nor observe him, but that they would speak to the king, and to those who could be of more service to friends than at present he could; most, on hearing this, forbore to trouble him about their concerns, but continued their observances to him, waiting upon him in the walks and places of exercise; at which Agesilaus was more annoyed than ever, envying him the honour; and, finally, when he gave many of the officers places of command and the governments of cities, he appointed Lysander carver at his table, adding, by way of insult to the Ionians, "Let them go now, and pay their court to my carver." Upon this, Lysander thought fit to come and speak with him; and a brief laconic dialogue passed between them as follows: "Truly, you know very well, O Agesilaus, how to depress your friends"; "Those friends," replied he, "who would be greater than myself; but those who increase my power, it is just should share in it." "Possibly, O Agesilaus," answered Lysander, "in all this there may be more said on your part than done on mine, but I request you, for the sake of observers from without, to place me in any command under you where you may judge I shall be the least offensive, and most useful."

Upon this he was sent ambassador to the Hellespont; and though angry with Agesilaus, yet did not neglect to perform his duty, and having induced Spithridates the Persian, being offended with Pharnabazus, a gallant man, and in command of some forces, to revolt, he brought him to Agesilaus. He was not, however, employed in any other service, but having completed his time returned to Sparta, without honour, angry with Agesilaus, and hating more than ever the whole Spartan government, and resolved to delay no longer, but while there was yet time, to put into execution the plans which he appears sometime before to have concerted for a revolution and change in the constitution. These were as follows. The Heraclidæ who joined with the Dorians, and came into Peloponnesus, became a numerous and glorious race in Sparta, but not every family belonging to it had the right of succession in the kingdom, but the kings were chosen out of two only, called the Eurypontidæ and the Agiadæ; the rest had no privilege in the government by their nobility of birth, and the honours which followed from merit lay open to all who could obtain them. Lysander who was born of one of these families, when he had risen into great renown for his exploits, and had gained great friends and power, was vexed to see the city, which had increased to what it was by him, ruled by others not at all better descended than himself, and formed a design to remove the government from the two families, and to give it in common to all the Heraclidæ; or, as some say, not to the Heraclidæ only, but to all Spartans; that the reward might not belong to the posterity of Hercules, but to those who were like Hercules, judging by that personal merit which raised even him to the honour of the Godhead; and he hoped that when the kingdom was thus to be competed for, no Spartan would be chosen before himself.

Accordingly he first attempted and prepared to persuade the citizens privately, and studied an oration composed for this purpose by Cleon, the Halicarnassian. Afterwards perceiving so unexpected and great an innovation required bolder means of support, he proceeded, as it might be on the stage, to avail himself of machinery, and to try the effects of divine agency upon his countrymen. He collected and arranged for his purpose answers and oracles from Apollo, not expecting to get any benefit from Cleon's rhetoric, unless he should first alarm and overpower the minds of his fellow-citizens by religious and superstitious terrors, before bringing them to the consideration of his arguments. Ephorus relates, after he had endeavoured to corrupt the oracle of Apollo, and had again failed to persuade the priestess of Dodona by means of Pherecles, that he went to Ammon, and discoursed with the guardians of the oracle there, proffering them a great deal of gold, and that they, taking this ill, sent some to Sparta to accuse Lysander; and on his acquittal the Libyans, going away, said, "You will find us, O Spartans, better judges, when you come to dwell with us in Libya," there being a certain ancient oracle that the Lacedæmonians should dwell in Libya. But as the whole intrigue and the course of the contrivance was no ordinary one, nor lightly undertaken, but depended as it went on, like some mathematical proposition, on a variety of important admissions, and proceeded through a series of intricate and difficult steps to its conclusion, we will go into it at length, following the account of one who was at once an historian and a philosopher.

There was a woman in Pontus who professed to be pregnant by Apollo, which many, as was natural, disbelieved, and many also gave credit to, and when she had brought forth a man-child, several, not unimportant persons, took an interest in its rearing and bringing up. The name given the boy was Silenus, for some reason or other. Lysander, taking this for the groundwork, frames and devises the rest himself, making use of not a few, nor these insignificant champions of his story, who brought the report of the child's birth into credit without any suspicion. Another report, also, was procured from Delphi and circulated in Sparta, that there were some very old oracles which were kept by the priests in private writings; and they were not to be meddled with, neither was it lawful to read them, till one in aftertimes should come, descended from Apollo, and, on giving some known token to the keepers, should take the books in which the oracles were. Things being thus ordered beforehand, Silenus, it was intended, should come and ask for the oracles, as being the child of Apollo, and those priests who were privy to the design were to profess to search narrowly into all particulars, and to question him concerning his birth; and, finally, were to be convinced, and, as to Apollo's son, to deliver up to him the writings. Then he, in the presence of many witnesses, should read, amongst other prophecies, that which was the object of the whole contrivance, relating to the office of the kings, that it would be better and more desirable to the Spartans to choose their kings out of the best citizens. And now, Silenus being grown up to a youth, and being ready for the action, Lysander miscarried in his drama through the timidity of one of his actors, or assistants, who just as he came to the point lost heart and drew back. Yet nothing was found out while Lysander lived, but only after his death.

He died before Agesilaus came back from Asia, being involved, or perhaps more truly having himself involved Greece, in the Bœotian war. For it is stated both ways; and the cause of it some make to be himself, others the Thebans, and some both together; the Thebans, on the one hand, being charged with casting away the sacrifices at Aulis, and that being bribed with the king's money brought by Androclides and Amphitheus, they had, with the object of entangling the Lacedæmonians in a Grecian war, set upon the Phocians, and wasted their country; it being said, on the other hand, that Lysander was angry that the Thebans had preferred a claim to the tenth part of the spoils of the war, while the rest of the confederates submitted without complaint; and because they expressed indignation about the money which Lysander sent to Sparta, but more especially, because from them the Athenians had obtained the first opportunity of freeing themselves from the thirty tyrants, whom Lysander had made, and to support whom the Lacedæmonians issued a decree that political refugees from Athens might be arrested in whatever country they were found, and that those who impeded their arrest should be excluded from the confederacy. In reply to this the Thebans issued counter decrees of their own, truly in the spirit and temper of the actions of Hercules and Bacchus, that every house and city in Bœotia should be opened to the Athenians who required it, and that he who did not help a fugitive who was seized should be fined a talent for damages, and if anyone should bear arms through Bœotia to Attica against the tyrants, that none of the Thebans should either see or hear of it. Nor did they pass these humane and truly Greek decrees without at the same time making their acts conformable to their words. For Thrasybulus, and those who with him occupied Phyle, set out upon that enterprise from Thebes, with arms and money, and secrecy and a point to start from, provided for them by the Thebans. Such were the causes of complaint Lysander had against Thebes. And being now grown violent in his temper through the atrabilious tendency which increased upon him in his old age, he urged the Ephors and persuaded them to place a garrison in Thebes, and taking the commander's place, he marched forth with a body of troops. Pausanias, also, the king, was sent shortly after with an army. Now Pausanias, going round by Cithæron, was to invade Bœotia; Lysander, meantime, advanced through Phocis to meet him, with a numerous body of soldiers. He took the city of the Orchomenians, who came over to him of their own accord, and plundered Lebadea. He despatched also letters to Pausanias, ordering him to move from Platæa to meet him at Haliartus, and that himself would be at the walls of Haliartus by break of day. These letters were brought to the Thebans, the carrier of them falling into the hands of some Theban scouts. They, having received aid from Athens, committed their city to the charge of the Athenian troops, and sallying out about the first sleep, succeeded in reaching Haliartus a little before Lysander, and part of them entered into the city. He upon this first of all resolved, posting his army upon a hill, to stay for Pausanias; then as the day advanced, not being able to rest, he bade his men take up their arms, and encouraging the allies, led them in a column along the road to the walls. But those Thebans who had remained outside, taking the city on the left hand, advanced against the rear of their enemies, by the fountain which is called Cissusa; here they tell the story that the nurses washed the infant Bacchus after his birth; the water of it is of a bright wine-colour, clear, and most pleasant to drink; and not far off the Cretan storax grows all about, which the Haliartians adduce in token of Rhadamanthus having dwelt there, and they show his sepulchre, calling it Alea. And the monument also of Alcmena is hard by; for there, as they say, she was buried, having married Rhadamanthus after Amphitryon's death. But the Thebans inside the city, forming in order of battle with the Haliartians, stood still for sometime, but on seeing Lysander with a party of those who were foremost approaching, on a sudden opening the gates and falling on, they killed him with the soothsayer at his side, and a few others: for the greater part immediately fled back to the main force. But the Thebans not slackening, but closely pursuing them, the whole body turned to fly towards the hills. There were one thousand of them slain; there died, also, of the Thebans three hundred, who were killed with their enemies, while chasing them into craggy and difficult places. These had been under suspicion of favouring the Lacedæmonians, and in their eagerness to clear themselves in the eyes of their fellow-citizens, exposed themselves in the pursuit, and so met their death. News of the disaster reached Pausanias as he was on the way from Platæa to Thespiæ, and having set his army in order he came to Haliartus; Thrasybulus, also, came from Thebes, leading the Athenians.

Pausanias proposing to request the bodies of the dead under truce, the elders of the Spartans took it ill, and were angry among themselves, and coming to the king, declared that Lysander should not be taken away upon any conditions; if they fought it out by arms about his body, and conquered, then they might bury him; if they were overcome, it was glorious to die upon the spot with their commander. When the elders had spoken these things, Pausanias saw it would be a difficult business to vanquish the Thebans, who had but just been conquerors; that Lysander's body also lay near the walls, so that it would be hard for them, though they overcame, to take it away without a truce; he therefore sent a herald, obtained a truce, and withdrew his forces, and carrying away the body of Lysander, they buried it in the first friendly soil they reached on crossing the Bœotian frontier, in the country of the Panopæans; where the monument still stands as you go on the road from Delphi to Chæronea. Now the army quartering there, it is said that a person of Phocis, relating the battle to one who was not in it, said, the enemies fell upon them just after Lysander had passed over the Hoplites; surprised at which a Spartan, a friend of Lysander, asked what Hoplites he meant, for he did not know the name. "It was there," answered the Phocian, "that the enemy killed the first of us; the rivulet by the city is called Hoplites." On hearing which the Spartan shed tears and observed how impossible it is for any man to avoid his appointed lot; Lysander, it appears, having received an oracle as follows:

> Sounding Hoplites see thou bear in mind,
> And the earthborn dragon following behind.

Some, however, say that Hoplites does not run by Haliartus, but is a water-course near Coronea, falling into the river Philarus, not far from the town in former times called Hoplias, and now Isomantus.

The man of Haliartus who killed Lysander, by name Neochorus, bore on his shield the device of a dragon; and this, it was supposed, the oracle signified. It is said also that at the time of the Peloponnesian war, the Thebans received an oracle from the sanctuary of Ismenus, referring at once to the battle at Delium, and to this which thirty years after took place at Haliartus. It ran thus:

> Hunting the wolf, observe the utmost bound,
> And the hill Orchalides where foxes most are found.

By the words, "the utmost bound," Delium being intended, where Bœotia touches Attica, and by Orchalides, the hill now called Alopecus, which lies in the parts of Haliartus towards Helicon.

But such a death befalling Lysander, the Spartans took it so grievously at the time, that they put the king to a trial for his life, which he not daring to await, fled to Tegea, and there lived out his life in the sanctuary of Minerva. The poverty also of Lysander being discovered by his death made his merit more manifest, since from so much wealth and power, from all the homage of the cities, and of the Persian kingdom, he had not in the least degree, so far as money goes, sought any private aggrandisement, as Theopompus in his history relates, whom anyone may rather give credit to when he commends than when he finds fault, as it is more agreeable to him to blame than to praise. But subsequently, Ephorus says, some contro-versy arising among the allies at Sparta, which made it necessary to consult the writings which Lysander had kept by him, Agesilaus came to his house, and finding the book in which the oration on the Spartan constitution was written at length, to the effect that the kingdom ought to be taken from the Eurypontidæ and Agiadæ, and to be offered in common, and a choice made out of the best citizens, at first he was eager to make it public, and to show his countrymen the real character of Lysander. But Lacratidas, a wise man, and at that time chief of the Ephors, hindered Agesilaus, and said they ought not to dig up Lysander again, but rather to bury with him a discourse, composed so plausibly and subtly. Other honours, also, were paid him, after his death; and amongst these they imposed a fine upon those who had engaged themselves to marry his daughters, and then when Lysander was found to be poor, after his decease, refused them; because when they thought him rich they had been observant of him, but now his poverty had proved him just and good, they forsook him. For there was, it seems, in Sparta, a punishment for not marrying, for a late, and for a bad marriage; and to the last penalty those were most especially liable who sought alliances with the rich instead of with the good and with their friends. Such is the account we have found given of Lysander.

SYLLA

LUCIUS CORNELIUS SYLLA WAS DESCENDED OF A PATRICIAN OR NOBLE family. Of his ancestors, Rufinus, it is said, had been consul, and incurred a disgrace more signal than his distinction. For being found possessed of more than ten pounds of silver plate, contrary to the law, he was for this reason put out of the senate. His posterity continued ever after in obscurity, nor had Sylla himself any opulent parentage. In his younger days he lived in hired lodgings, at a low rate, which in aftertimes was adduced against him as proof that he had been fortunate above his quality. When he was boasting and magnifying himself for his exploits in Libya, a person of noble station made answer, "And how can you be an honest man, who, since the death of a father who left you nothing, have become so rich?" The time in which he lived was no longer an age of pure and upright manners, but had already declined, and yielded to the appetite for riches and luxury; yet still, in the general opinion, they who deserted the hereditary poverty of their family were as much blamed as those who had run out a fair patrimonial estate. And afterwards, when he had seized the power into his hands, and was putting many to death, a freedman, suspected of having concealed one of the proscribed, and for that reason sentenced to be thrown down the Tarpeian rock, in a reproachful way recounted how they had lived long together under the same roof, himself for the upper rooms paying two thousand sesterces, and Sylla for the lower three thousand; so that the difference between their fortunes then was no more than one thousand sesterces, equivalent in Attic coin to two hundred and fifty drachmas. And thus much of his early fortune.

His general personal appearance may be known by his statues; only his blue eyes, of themselves extremely keen and glaring, were rendered all the more forbidding and terrible by the complexion of his face, in which white was mixed with rough blotches of fiery red. Hence, it is said, he was surnamed Sylla, and in allusion to it one of the scurrilous jesters at Athens made the verse upon him—

> Sylla is a mulberry sprinkled o'er with meal.

Nor is it out of place to make use of marks of character like these, in the case of one who was by nature so addicted to raillery, that in his youthful obscure years he would converse freely with players and professed jesters, and join them in all their low pleasures. And when supreme master of all, he was often wont to muster together the most impudent players and stage-followers of the town, and to drink and bandy jests with them without regard to his age or the dignity of his place, and to the prejudice of important affairs that required his attention. When he was once at table, it was not in Sylla's nature to admit of anything that was serious, and whereas at other times he was a man of business and austere of countenance, he underwent all of a sudden, at his first entrance upon wine and good-fellowship, a total revolution, and was gentle and tractable with common singers and dancers, and ready to oblige anyone that spoke with him. It seems to have been a sort of diseased result of this laxity that he was so prone to amorous pleasures, and yielded without resistance to any temptation of voluptuousness, from which even in his old age he could not refrain. He had a long attachment for Metrobius, a player. In his first amours, it happened that he made court to a common but rich lady, Nicopolis by name, and what by the air of his youth, and what by long intimacy, won so far on her affections, that she rather than he was the lover, and at her death she bequeathed him her whole property. He likewise inherited the estate of a step-mother who loved him as her own son. By these means he had pretty well advanced his fortunes.

He was chosen quæstor to Marius in his first consulship, and set sail with him for Libya, to war upon Jugurtha. Here, in general, he gained approbation; and more especially, by closing in dexterously with an accidental occasion, made a friend of Bocchus, King of Numidia. He hospitably entertained the king's ambassadors on their escape from some Numidian robbers, and after showing them much kindness, sent them on their journey with presents, and an escort to protect them. Bocchus had long hated and dreaded his son-in-law, Jugurtha, who had now been worsted in the field and had fled to him for shelter; and it so happened he was at this time entertaining a design to betray him. He accordingly invited Sylla to come to him, wishing the seizure and surrender of Jugurtha to be effected rather through him, than directly by himself. Sylla, when he had communicated the business to Marius, and received from him a small detachment, voluntarily put himself into this imminent danger; and confiding in a barbarian, who had been unfaithful to his own relations, to apprehend another man's person, made surrender of his own. Bocchus, having both of them now in his power, was necessitated to betray one or other, and after long debate with himself, at last resolved on his first design, and gave up Jugurtha into the hands of Sylla.

For this Marius triumphed, but the glory of the enterprise, which through people's envy of Marius was ascribed to Sylla, secretly grieved him. And the truth is, Sylla himself was by nature vainglorious, and this being the first time that from a low and private condition he had risen to esteem amongst the citizens and tasted of honour, his appetite for distinction carried him to such a pitch of ostentation, that he had a representation of this action engraved on a signet ring, which he carried about with him, and made use of ever after. The impress was Bocchus delivering, and Sylla receiving, Jugurtha. This touched Marius to the quick; however, judging Sylla to be beneath his rivalry, he made use of him as lieutenant, in his second consulship, and in his third as tribune; and many considerable services were effected by his means. When acting as lieutenant he took Copillus, chief of the Tectosages, prisoner, and compelled the Marsians, a great and populous nation, to become friends and confederates of the Romans.

Henceforward, however, Sylla, perceiving that Marius bore a jealous eye over him, and would no longer afford him opportunities of action, but rather opposed his advance, attached himself to Catulus, Marius' colleague, a worthy man, but not energetic enough as a general. And under this commander, who intrusted him with the highest and most important commissions, he rose at once to reputation and to power. He subdued by arms most part of the Alpine barbarians; and when there was a scarcity in the armies, he took that care upon himself and brought in such a store of provisions as not only to furnish the soldiers of Catulus with abundance, but likewise to supply Marius. This, as he writes himself, wounded Marius to the very heart. So slight and childish were the first occasions and motives of that enmity between them, which, passing afterwards through a long course of civil bloodshed and incurable divisions to find its end in tyranny, and the confusion of the whole state, proved Euripides to have been truly wise and thoroughly acquainted with the causes of disorders in the body politic, when he forewarned all men to beware of Ambition, as of all the higher Powers the most destructive and pernicious to her votaries.

Sylla, by this time thinking that the reputation of his arms abroad was sufficient to entitle him to a part in the civil administration, betook himself immediately from the camp to the assembly, and offered himself as a candidate for a prætorship, but failed. The fault of this disappointment he wholly ascribes to the populace, who, knowing his intimacy with King Bocchus, and for that reason expecting, that if he was made ædile before his praetorship, he would then show them magnificent hunting-shows and combats between Libyan wild beasts, chose other prætors, on purpose to force him into the ædileship. The vanity of this pretext is sufficiently disproved by matter-of-fact. For the year following, partly by flatteries to the people, and partly by money, he got himself elected prætor. Accordingly, once while he was in office, on his angrily telling Cæsar that he should make use of his authority against him, Cæsar answered him with a smile, "You do well to call it your own, as you bought it." At the end of his prætorship he was sent over into Cappadocia, under the pretence of reestablishing Ariobarzanes in his kingdom, but in reality to keep in check the restless movements of Mithridates, who was gradually procuring himself as vast a new acquired power and dominion as was that of his ancient inheritance. He carried over with him no great forces of his own, but making use of the cheerful aid of the confederates, succeeded, with considerable slaughter of the Cappadocians, and yet greater of the Armenian succours, in expelling Gordius and establishing Ariobarzanes as king.

During his stay on the banks of the Euphrates, there came to him Orobazus, a Parthian, ambassador from King Arsaces, as yet there having been no correspondence between the two nations. And this also we may lay to the account of Sylla's felicity, that he should be the first Roman to whom the Parthians made address for alliance and friendship. At the time of which reception, the story is, that, having ordered three chairs of state to be set, one for Ariobarzanes, one for Orobazus, and a third for himself, he placed himself in the middle, and so gave audience. For this the King of Parthia afterwards put Orobazus to death. Some people commended Sylla for his lofty carriage towards the barbarians; others again accused him of arrogance and unseasonable display. It is reported that a certain Chaldæan, of Orobazus' retinue, looking Sylla wistfully in the face, and observing carefully the motions of his mind and body, and forming a judgment of his nature, according to the rules of his art, said that it was impossible for him not to become the greatest of men; it was rather a wonder how he could even then abstain from being head of all.

At his return, Censorinus impeached him of extortion, for having exacted a vast sum of money from a well-affected and associate kingdom. However, Censorinus did not appear at the trial, but dropped his accusation. His quarrel, meantime, with Marius began to break out afresh, receiving new material from the ambition of Bocchus, who, to please the people of Rome, and gratify Sylla, set up in the temple of Jupiter Capitolinus images bearing trophies, and a representation in gold of the surrender of Jugurtha to Sylla. When Marius, in great anger, attempted to pull them down, and others aided Sylla, the whole city would have been in tumult and commotion with this dispute, had not the Social War, which had long lain smouldering, blazed forth at last, and for the present put an end to the quarrel.

In the course of this war, which had many great changes of fortune, and which, more than any, afflicted the Romans, and, indeed, endangered the very being of the Commonwealth, Marius was not able to signalise his valour in any action, but left behind him a clear proof, that warlike excellence requires a strong and still vigorous body. Sylla, on the other hand, by his many achievements, gained himself, with his fellow-citizens, the name of a great commander, while his friends thought him the greatest of all commanders, and his enemies called him the most fortunate. Nor did this make the same sort of impression on him as it made on Timotheus the son of Conon, the Athenian; who, when his adversaries ascribed his successes to his good luck, and had a painting made, representing him asleep, and Fortune by his side, casting her nets over the cities, was rough and violent in his indignation at those who did it, as if, by attributing all to Fortune, they had robbed him of his just honours; and said to the people on one occasion at his return from war, "In this, ye men of Athens, Fortune had no part." A piece of boyish petulance, which the deity, we are told, played back upon Timotheus; who from that time was never able to achieve anything that was great, but proving altogether unfortunate in his attempts, and falling into discredit with the people, was at last banished the city. Sylla, on the contrary, not only accepted with pleasure the credit of such divine felicities and favours, but joining himself and extolling and glorifying what was done, gave the honour of all to Fortune, whether it were out of boastfulness, or a real feeling of divine agency. He remarks, in his Memoirs, that of all his well-advised actions, none proved so lucky in the execution as what he had boldly enterprised, not by calculation, but upon the moment. And, in the character which he gives of himself, that he was born for fortune rather than war, he seems to give Fortune a higher place than merit, and, in short, makes himself entirely the creature of a superior power, accounting even his concord with Metellus, his equal in office, and his connection by marriage, a piece of preternatural felicity. For expecting to have met in him a most troublesome, he found him a most accommodating, colleague. Moreover, in the Memoirs which he dedicated to Lucullus, he admonished him to esteem nothing more trustworthy than what the divine powers advise him by night. And when he was leaving the city with an army, to fight in the Social War, he relates that the earth near the Laverna opened, and a quantity of fire came rushing out of it, shooting up with a bright flame into the heavens. The soothsayers upon this foretold that a person of great qualities, and of a rare and singular aspect, should take the government in hand, and quiet the present troubles of the city. Sylla affirms he was the man, for his golden head of hair made him an extraordinary-looking man, nor had he any shame, after the great actions he had done, in testifying to his own great qualities. And thus much of his opinion as to divine agency.

In general he would seem to have been of a very irregular character, full of inconsistencies with himself; much given to rapine, to prodigality yet more; in promoting or disgracing whom he pleased, alike unaccountable; cringing to those he stood in need of, and domineering over others who stood in need of him, so that it was hard to tell whether his nature had more in it of pride or of servility. As to his unequal distribution of punishments, as, for example, that upon slight grounds he would put to the torture, and again would bear patiently with the greatest wrongs; would readily forgive and be reconciled after the most heinous acts of enmity and yet would visit small and inconsiderable offences with death and confiscation of goods; one might judge that in himself he was really of a violent and revengeful nature, which, however, he could qualify, upon reflection, for his interest. In this very Social War, when the soldiers with stones and clubs had killed an officer of prætorian rank, his own lieutenant, Albinus by name, he passed by this flagrant crime without any inquiry, giving it out moreover in a boast, that the soldiers would behave all the better now, to make amends, by some special bravery, for their breach of discipline. He took no notice of the clamours of those that cried for justice, but designing already to supplant Marius, now that he saw the Social War near its end, he made much of his army, in hopes to get himself declared general of the forces against Mithridates.

At his return to Rome he was chosen consul with Quintus Pompeius, in the fiftieth year of his age, and made a most distinguished marriage with Cæcilia, daughter of Metellus, the chief priest. The common people made a variety of verses in ridicule of the marriage, and many of the nobility also were disgusted at it, esteeming him, as Livy writes, unworthy of this connection, whom before they thought worthy of a consulship. This was not his only wife, for first, in his younger days, he was married to Ilia, by whom he had a daughter; after her to Ælia; and thirdly to Clœlia, whom he dismissed as barren, but honourably, and with professions of respect, adding, moreover, presents. But the match between him and Metella, falling out a few days after, occasioned suspicions that he had complained of Clœlia without due cause. To Metella he always showed great deference, so much so that the people, when anxious for the recall of the exiles of Marius' party, upon his refusal, entreated the intercession of Metella. And the Athenians, it is thought, had harder measure, at the capture of their town, because they used insulting language to Metella in their jests from the walls during the siege. But of this hereafter.

At present esteeming the consulship but a small matter in comparison of things to come, he was impatiently carried away in thought to the Mithridatic War. Here he was withstood by Marius; who out of mad affectation of glory and thirst for distinction, those never dying passions, though he were now unwieldy in body, and had given up service, on account of his age, during the late campaigns, still coveted after command in a distant war beyond the seas. And whilst Sylla was departed for the camp, to order the rest of his affairs there, he sate brooding at home, and at last hatched that execrable sedition, which wrought Rome more mischief than all her enemies together had done, as was indeed foreshown by the gods. For a flame broke forth of its own accord, from under the staves of the ensigns, and was with difficulty extinguished. Three ravens brought their young into the open road, and ate them, carrying the relics into the nest again. Mice having gnawed the consecrated gold in one of the temples, the keepers caught one of them, a female, in a trap; and she bringing forth five young ones in the very trap, devoured three of them. But what was greatest of all, in a calm and clear sky there was heard the sound of a trumpet, with such a loud and dismal blast, as struck terror and amazement into the hearts of the people. The Etruscan sages affirmed that this prodigy betokened the mutation of the age, and a general revolution in the world. For according to them there are in all eight ages, differing one from another in the lives and the characters of men, and to each of these God has allotted a certain measure of time, determined by the circuit of the great year. And when one age is run out, at the approach of another, there appears some wonderful sign from earth or heaven, such as makes it manifest at once to those who have made it their business to study such things, that there has succeeded in the world a new race of men, differing in customs and institutes of life, and more or less regarded by the gods than the preceding. Among other great changes that happen, as they say, at the turn of ages, the art of divination, also, at one time rises in esteem, and is more successful in its predictions, clearer and surer tokens being sent from God, and then, again, in another generation declines as low, becoming mere guesswork for the most part, and discerning future events by dim and uncertain intimations. This was the mythology of the wisest of the Tuscan sages, who were thought to possess a knowledge beyond other men. Whilst the senate sat in consultation with the soothsayers, concerning these prodigies, in the temple of Bellona, a sparrow came flying in, before them all, with a grasshopper in its mouth, and letting fall one part of it, flew away with the remainder. The diviners foreboded commotions and dissensions between the great landed proprietors and the common city populace; the latter, like the grasshopper, being loud and talkative; while the sparrow might represent the "dwellers in the field."

Marius had taken into alliance Sulpicius, the tribune, a man second to none in any villainies, so that it was less the question what others he surpassed, but rather in what respects he most surpassed himself in wickedness. He was cruel, bold, rapacious, and in all these points utterly shameless and unscrupulous; not hesitating to offer Roman citizenship by public sale to freed slaves and aliens, and to count out the price on public money-tables in the forum. He maintained three thousand swordsmen, and had always about him a company of young men of the equestrian class ready for all occasions, whom he styled his Anti-senate. Having had a law enacted, that no senator should contract a debt of above two thousand drachmas, he himself, after death, was found indebted three millions. This was the man whom Marius let in upon the Commonwealth, and who, confounding all things by force and the sword, made several ordinances of dangerous consequence, and amongst the rest one giving Marius the conduct of the Mithridatic war. Upon this the consuls proclaimed a public cessation of business, but as they were holding an assembly near the temple of Castor and Pollux, he let loose the rabble upon them, and amongst many others slew the consul Pompeius' young son in the forum,

Pompeius himself hardly escaping in the crowd. Sylla, being closely pursued into the house of Marius, was forced to come forth and dissolve the cessation; and for his doing this, Sulpicius, having deposed Pompeius, allowed Sylla to continue his consulship, only transferring the Mithridatic expedition to Marius.

There were immediately despatched to Nola tribunes to receive the army, and bring it to Marius; but Sylla, having got first to the camp, and the soldiers, upon hearing the news, having stoned the tribunes, Marius, in requital, proceeded to put the friends of Sylla in the city to the sword, and rifled their goods. Every kind of removal and flight went on, some hastening from the camp to the city, others from the city to the camp. The senate, no more in its own power, but wholly governed by the dictates of Marius and Sulpicius, alarmed at the report of Sylla's advancing with his troops towards the city, sent forth two of the prætors, Brutus and Servilius, to forbid his nearer approach. The soldiers would have slain these prætors in a fury, for their bold language to Sylla; contenting themselves, however, with breaking their rods, and tearing off their purple-edged robes, after much contumelious usage they sent them back, to the sad dejection of the citizens, who beheld their magistrates despoiled of their badges of office, and announcing to them that things were now manifestly come to a rupture past all cure. Marius put himself in readiness, and Sylla with his colleague moved from Nola, at the head of six complete legions, all of them willing to march up directly against the city, though he himself as yet was doubtful in thought, and apprehensive of the danger. As he was sacrificing, Postumius the soothsayer, having inspected the entrails, stretching forth both hands to Sylla, required to be bound and kept in custody till the battle was over, as willing, if they had not speedy and complete success, to suffer the utmost punishment. It is said, also, that there appeared to Sylla himself, in a dream, a certain goddess, whom the Romans learnt to worship from the Cappadocians, whether it be the Moon, or Pallas, or Bellona. This same goddess, to his thinking, stood by him, and put into his hand thunder and lightning, then naming his enemies one by one, bade him strike them, who, all of them, fell on the discharge and disappeared. Encouraged by this vision, and relating it to his colleague, next day he led on towards Rome. About Picinæ being met by a deputation, beseeching him not to attack at once, in the heat of a march, for that the senate had decreed to do him all the right imaginable, he consented to halt on the spot, and sent his officers to measure out the ground, as is usual, for a camp; so that the deputation, believing it, returned. They were no sooner gone, but he sent a party on under the command of Lucius Basillus and Caius Mummius, to secure the city gate, and the walls on the side of the Esquiline hill, and then close at their heels followed himself with all speed. Basillus made his way successfully into the city, but the unarmed multitude, pelting him with stones and tiles from off the houses, stopped his further progress, and beat him back to the wall. Sylla by this time was come up, and seeing what was going on, called aloud to his men to set fire to the houses, and taking a flaming torch, he himself led the way, and commanded the archers to make use of their fire-darts, letting fly at the tops of houses; all which he did, not upon any plan, but simply in his fury, yielding the conduct of that day's work to passion, and as if all he saw were enemies, without respect or pity either to friends, relations, or acquaintance, made his entry by fire, which knows no distinction betwixt friend or foe.

In this conflict, Marius, being driven into the temple of Mother-Earth, thence invited the slaves by proclamation of freedom, but the enemy coming on he was overpowered and fled the city.

Sylla having called a senate, had sentence of death passed on Marius and some few others, amongst whom was Sulpicius, tribune of the people. Sulpicius was killed, being betrayed by his servant, whom Sylla first made free, and then threw him headlong down the Tarpeian rock. As for Marius, he set a price on his life, by proclamation, neither gratefully nor politically, if we consider into whose house, not long before, he put himself at mercy, and safely dismissed. Had Marius at that time not let Sylla go, but suffered him to be slain by the hands of Sulpicius, he might have been lord of all: nevertheless he spared his life, and a few days after, when in a similar position himself, received a different measure.

By these proceedings Sylla excited the secret distaste of the senate; but the displeasure and free indignation of the commonalty showed itself plainly by their actions. For they ignominiously rejected Nonius, his nephew, and Servius, who stood for offices of state by his interest, and elected others as magistrates, by honouring whom they thought they should most annoy him. He made semblance of extreme satisfaction at all this, as if the people by his means had again enjoyed the liberty of doing what seemed best to them. And to pacify the public hostility, he created Lucius Cinna consul, one of the adverse party, having first bound him under oaths and imprecations to be favourable to his interest. For Cinna, ascending the capitol with a stone in his hand, swore solemnly, and prayed with direful curses, that he himself, if he were not true to his friendship with Sylla, might be cast out of the city, as that stone out of his hand; and thereupon cast the stone to the ground, in the presence of many people Nevertheless Cinna had no sooner entered on his charge, but he took measures to disturb the present settlement, having prepared an impeachment against Sylla, got Virginius, one of the tribunes of the people, to be his accuser; but Sylla, leaving him and the court of judicature to themselves, set forth against Mithridates.

About the time that Sylla was making ready to put off with his force from Italy, besides many other omens which befell Mithridates, then staying at Pergamus, there goes a story that a figure of Victory, with a crown in her hand, which the Pergamenians by machinery from above let down on him, when it had almost reached his head, fell to pieces, and the crown tumbling down into the midst of the theatre, there broke against the ground, occasioning a general alarm among the populace, and considerably disquieting Mithridates himself, although his affairs at that time were succeeding beyond expectation. For having wrested Asia from the Romans, and Bithynia and Cappadocia from their kings, he made Pergamus his royal seat, distributing among his friends riches, principalities, and kingdoms. Of his sons, one residing in Pontus and Bosporus held his ancient realm as far as the deserts beyond the lake Mæotis, without molestation; while Ariarathes, another, was reducing Thrace and Macedon, with a great army, to obedience. His generals, with forces under them, were establishing his supremacy in other quarters. Archelaus, in particular, with his fleet, held absolute mastery of the sea, and was bringing into subjection the Cyclades, and all the other islands as far as Malea, and had taken Eubœa itself. Making Athens his headquarters, from thence as far as Thessaly he was withdrawing the states of Greece from the Roman allegiance, without the least ill-success, except at Chæronea. For here Bruttius Sura, lieutenant to Sentius, governor of Macedon, a man of singular valour and prudence, met him, and, though he came like a torrent pouring over Bœotia, made stout resistance, and thrice giving him battle near Chæronea, repulsed and forced him back to the sea. But being commanded by Lucius Lucullus to give place to his successor, Sylla, and resign the war to whom it was decreed, he presently left Bœotia, and retired back to Sentius, although his success had outgone all hopes, and Greece was well disposed to a new revolution, upon account of his gallant behaviour. These were the glorious actions of Bruttius.

Sylla, on his arrival, received by their deputations the compliments of all the cities of Greece, except Athens, against which, as it was compelled by the tyrant Aristion to hold for the king, he advanced with all his forces, and investing the Piræus, laid formal siege to it, employing every variety of engines, and trying every manner of assault; whereas, had he forborn but a little while, he might without hazard have taken the Upper City by famine, it being already reduced to the last extremity, through want of necessaries. But eager to return to Rome, and fearing innovation there, at great risk, with continual fighting and vast expense, he pushed on the war. Besides other equipage, the very work about the engines of battery was supplied with no less than ten thousand yoke of mules, employed daily in that service. And when timber grew scarce, for many of the works failed, some crushed to pieces by their own weight, others taking fire by the continual play of the enemy, he had recourse to the sacred groves, and cut down the trees of the Academy, the shadiest of all the suburbs, and the Lyceum. And a vast sum of money being wanted to carry on the war, he broke into the sanctuaries of Greece, that of Epidaurus and that of Olympia, sending for the most beautiful and precious offerings deposited there. He wrote, likewise, to the Amphictyons at Delphi, that it were better to remit the wealth of the god to him, for that he would keep it more securely, or in case he made use of it, restore as much. He sent Caphis, the Phocian, one of his friends, with this message, commanding him to receive each item by weight. Caphis came to Delphi, but was loth to touch the holy things, and with many tears, in the presence of the Amphictyons, bewailed the necessity. And on some of them declaring they heard the sound of a harp from the inner shrine, he, whether he himself believed it, or was willing to try the effect of religious fear upon Sylla, sent back an express. To which Sylla replied in a scoffing way, that it was surprising to him that Caphis did not know that music was a sign of joy, not anger; he should, therefore, go on boldly, and accept what a gracious and bountiful god offered.

Other things were sent away without much notice on the part of the Greeks in general, but in the case of the silver tun, that only relic of the regal donations, which its weight and bulk made it impossible for any carriage to receive, the Amphictyons were forced to cut it into pieces, and called to mind in so doing, how Titus Flamininus, and Manius Acilius, and again Paulus Æmilius, one of whom drove Antiochus out of Greece, and the others subdued the Macedonian kings, had not only abstained from violating the Greek temples, but had even given them new gifts and honours, and increased the general veneration for them. They, indeed, the lawful commanders of temperate and obedient soldiers, and themselves great in

soul, and simple in expenses, lived within the bounds of the ordinary established charges, accounting it a greater disgrace to seek popularity with their
men, than to feel fear of their enemy. Whereas the commanders of these
times, attaining to superiority by force, not worth, and having need of arms
one against another, rather than against the public enemy, were constrained
to temporise in authority, and in order to pay for the gratifications with
which they purchased the labour of their soldiers, were driven, before they
knew it, to sell the commonwealth itself, and, to gain the mastery over men
better than themselves, were content to become slaves to the vilest of
wretches. These practices drove Alarms into exile, and again brought him
in against Sylla. These made Cinna the assassin of Octavius, and Fimbria of
Flaccus. To which courses Sylla contributed not the least; for to corrupt and
win over those who were under the command of others, he would be munif-
icent and profuse towards those who were under his own; and so, while
tempting the soldiers of other generals to treachery, and his own to dissolute living, he was naturally in want of a large treasury, and especially during that siege.

Sylla had a vehement and an implacable desire to conquer Athens,
whether out of emulation, fighting as it were against the shadow of the
once famous city, or out of anger, at the foul words and scurrilous jests
with which the tyrant Aristion, showing himself daily, with unseemly ges-
ticulations, upon the walls, had provoked him and Metella.

The tyrant Aristion had his very being compounded of wantonness
and cruelly, having gathered into himself all the worst of Mithridates' diseased and vicious qualities, like some fatal malady which the city, after its
deliverance from innumerable wars, many tyrannies and seditions, was in
its last days destined to endure. At the time when a medimnus of wheat
was sold in the city for one thousand drachmas and men were forced to
live on the feverfew growing round the citadel, and to boil down shoes
and oil-bags for their food, he, carousing and feasting in the open face of
day, then dancing in armour, and making jokes at the enemy, suffered the
holy lamp of the goddess to expire for want of oil, and to the chief priestess, who demanded of him the twelfth part of a medimnus of wheat, he
sent the like quantity of pepper. The senators and priests who came as suppliants to beg of him to take compassion on the city, and treat for peace
with Sylla, he drove away and dispersed with a flight of arrows. At last, with
much ado, he sent forth two or three of his revelling companions to parley, to whom Sylla, perceiving that they made no serious overtures towards

an accommodation, but went on haranguing in praise of Theseus, Eumolpus, and the Median trophies, replied, "My good friends, you may put up your speeches and be gone. I was sent by the Romans to Athens, not to take lessons, but to reduce rebels to obedience."

In the meantime news came to Sylla that some old men, talking in the Ceramicus, had been overheard to blame the tyrant for not securing the passages and approaches near the Heptachalcum, the one point where the enemy might easily get over. Sylla neglected not the report, but going in the night, and discovering the place to be assailable, set instantly to work. Sylla himself makes mention in his Memoirs that Marcus Teius, the first man who scaled the wall, meeting with an adversary, and striking him on the headpiece a home-stroke, broke his own sword, but, notwithstanding, did not give ground, but stood and held him fast. The city was certainly taken from that quarter, according to the tradition of the oldest of the Athenians.

When they had thrown down the wall, and made all level betwixt the Piraic and Sacred Gate, about midnight Sylla entered the breach, with all the terrors of trumpets and cornets sounding, with the triumphant shout and cry of an army let loose to spoil and slaughter, and scouring through the streets with swords drawn. There was no numbering the slain; the amount is to this day conjectured only from the space of ground overflowed with blood. For without mentioning the execution done in other quarters of the city, the blood that was shed about the market place spread over the whole Ceramicus within the Double-gate, and, according to most writers, passed through the gate and overflowed the suburb. Nor did the multitudes which fell thus exceed the number of those who, out of pity and love for their country which they believed Was now finally to perish, slew themselves; the best of them, through despair of their country's surviving, dreading themselves to survive, expecting neither humanity nor moderation in Sylla. At length, partly at the instance of Midias and Calliphon, two exiled men, beseeching and casting themselves at his feet, partly by the intercession of those senators who followed the camp, having had his fill of revenge, and making some honourable mention of the ancient Athenians, "I forgive," said he, "the many for the sake of the few, the living for the dead." He took Athens, according to his own Memoirs, on the calends of March, coinciding pretty nearly with the new moon of Anthesterion, on which day it is the Athenian usage to perform various acts in commemoration of the ruins and devastations occasioned by the deluge, that being supposed to be the time of its occurrence.

At the taking of the town, the tyrant fled into the citadel, and was there besieged by Curio, who had that charge given him. He held out a considerable time, but at last yielded himself up for want of water, and divine power immediately intimated its agency in the matter. For on the same day and hour that Curio conducted him down, the clouds gathered in a clear sky, and there came down a great quantity of rain and filled the citadel with water.

Not long after, Sylla won the Piræus, and burnt most of it; amongst the rest, Philo's arsenal, a work very greatly admired.

In the meantime Taxiles, Mithridates' general, coming down from Thrace and Macedon, with an army of one hundred thousand foot, ten thousand horse, and ninety chariots, armed with scythes at the wheels, would have joined Archelaus, who lay with a navy on the coast near Munychia, reluctant to quit the sea, and yet unwilling to engage the Romans in battle, but desiring to protract the war and cut off the enemy's supplies. Which Sylla perceiving much better than himself, passed with his forces into Bœotia, quitting a barren district which was inadequate to maintain an army even in time of peace. He was thought by some to have taken false measures in thus leaving Attica, a rugged country, and ill suited for cavalry to move in, and entering the plain and open fields of Bœotia, knowing as he did the barbarian strength to consist most in horses and chariots. But as was said before, to avoid famine and scarcity, he was forced to run the risk of a battle. Moreover he was in anxiety for Hortensius, a bold and active officer, whom on his way to Sylla with forces from Thessaly, the barbarians awaited in the straits. For these reasons Sylla drew off into Bœotia. Hortensius, meantime, was conducted by Caphis, our countryman, another way unknown to the barbarians, by Parnassus, just under Tithora, which was then not so large a town as it is now, but a mere fort, surrounded by steep precipices whither the Phocians also, in old times, when flying from the invasion of Xerxes, carried themselves and their goods and were saved. Hortensius, encamping here, kept off the enemy by day, and at night descending by difficult passages to Patronis, joined the forces of Sylla who came to meet him. Thus united they posted themselves on a fertile hill in the middle of the plain of Elatea, shaded with trees and watered at the foot. It is called Philobœotus, and its situation and natural advantages are spoken of with great admiration by Sylla.

As they lay thus encamped, they seemed to the enemy a contemptible number, for there were not above fifteen hundred horse, and less than fifteen thousand foot. Therefore the rest of the commanders, over-persuading

Archelaus and drawing up the army, covered the plain with horses, chariots, bucklers, targets. The clamour and cries of so many nations forming for battle rent the air, nor was the pomp and ostentation of their costly array altogether idle and unserviceable for terror; for the brightness of their armour, embellished magnificently with gold and silver, and the rich colours of their Median and Scythian coats, intermixed with brass and shining steel, presented a flaming and terrible sight as they swayed about and moved in their ranks, so much so that the Romans shrunk within their trenches, and Sylla, unable by any arguments to remove their fear, and unwilling to force them to fight against their wills, was fain to sit down in quiet, ill-brooking to become the subject of barbarian insolence and laughter. This, however, above all advantaged him, for the enemy, from contemning of him, fell into disorder amongst themselves, being already less thoroughly under command, on account of the number of their leaders. Some few of them remained within the encampment, but others, the major part, lured out with hopes of prey and rapine, strayed about the country many days' journey from the camp, and are related to have destroyed the city of Panope, to have plundered Lebadea, and robbed the oracle without any orders from their commanders.

Sylla, all this while, chafing and fretting to see the cities all around destroyed, suffered not the soldiery to remain idle, but leading them out, compelled them to divert the Cephisus from its ancient channel by casting up ditches, and giving respite to none, showed himself rigorous in punishing the remiss, that growing weary of labour, they might be induced by hardship to embrace danger. Which fell out accordingly, for on the third day, being hard at work as Sylla passed by, they begged and clamoured to be led against the enemy. Sylla replied, that this demand of war proceeded rather from a backwardness to labour than any forwardness to fight, but if they were in good earnest martially inclined, he bade them take their arms and get up thither, pointing to the ancient citadel of the Parapotamians, of which at present, the city being laid waste, there remained only the rocky hill itself, steep and craggy on all sides, and severed from Mount Hedylium by the breadth of the river Assus, which, running between, and at the bottom of the same hill falling into the Cephisus with an impetuous confluence, makes this eminence a strong position for soldiers to occupy. Observing that the enemy's division, called the Brazen Shields, were making their way up thither, Sylla was willing to take first possession, and by the vigorous efforts of the soldiers, succeeded. Archelaus, driven from hence, bent his forces upon Chæronea. The Chæroneans who bore arms in the Roman camp beseeching Sylla not to abandon the city, he despatched Gabinius, a tribune, with one legion, and sent out also the Chæroneans, who endeavoured, but were not able to get in before Gabinius; so active was he, and more zealous to bring relief than those who had entreated it. Juba writes that Ericius was the man sent, not Gabinius. Thus narrowly did our native city escape.

From Lebadea and the cave of Trophonius there came favourable rumours and prophecies of victory to the Romans, of which the inhabitants of those places gave a fuller account, but as Sylla himself affirms in the tenth book of his Memoirs, Quintus Titius, a man of some repute among the Romans who were engaged in mercantile business in Greece, came to him after the battle won at Chæronea, and declared that Trophonius had foretold another fight and victory on the place, within a short time. After him a soldier, by name Salvenius, brought an account from the god of the future issue of affairs in Italy. As to the vision, they both agreed in this, that they had seen one who in stature and in majesty was similar to Jupiter Olympius.

Sylla, when he had passed over the Assus, marching under the Mount Hedylium, encamped close to Archelaus, who had intrenched himself strongly between the mountains Acontium and Hedylium, close to what are called the Assia. The place of his intrenchment is to this day named from him, Archelaus. Sylla, after one day's respite, having left Murena behind him with one legion and two cohorts to amuse the enemy with continual alarms, himself went and sacrificed on the banks of Cephisus, and the holy rites ended, held on towards Chæronea to receive the forces there and view Mount Thurium, where a party of the enemy had posted themselves. This is a craggy height running up in a conical form to a point called by us Orthopagus; at the foot of it is the river Morius and the temple of Apollo Thurius. The god had his surname from Thuro, mother of Chæron, whom ancient record makes founder of Chæronea. Others assert that the cow, which Apollo gave to Cadmus for a guide, appeared there, and that the place took its name from the beast, Thor being the Phœnician word for cow.

At Sylla's approach to Chæronea, the tribune who had been appointed to guard the city led out his men in arms, and met him with a garland of laurel in his hand; which Sylla accepting, and at the same time saluting the soldiers and animating them to the encounter, two men of Chæronea, Homoloichus and Anaxidamus, presented themselves before him, and offered, with a small party, to dislodge those who were posted on Thurium.

For there lay a path out of sight of the barbarians, from what is called Petrochus along by the Museum, leading right down from above upon Thurium. By this way it was easy to fall upon them and either stone them from above or force them down into the plain. Sylla, assured of their faith and courage by Gabinius, bade them proceed with the enterprise, and meantime drew up the army, and disposing the cavalry on both wings, himself took command of the right; the left being committed to the direction of Murena. In the rear of all, Galba and Hortensius, his lieutenants, planted themselves on the upper grounds with the cohorts of reserve, to watch the motions of the enemy, who, with numbers of horse and swift-footed, light-armed infantry, were noticed to have so formed their wing as to allow it readily to change about and alter its position, and thus gave reason for suspecting that they intended to carry it far out and so to inclose the Romans.

In the meanwhile, the Chæroneans, who had Ericius for commander by appointment of Sylla, covertly making their way around Thurium, and then discovering themselves, occasioned a great confusion and rout among the barbarians, and slaughter, for the most part, by their own hands. For they kept not their place, but making down the steep descent, ran themselves on their own spears, and violently sent each other over the cliffs, the enemy from above pressing on and wounding them where they exposed their bodies; insomuch that there fell three thousand about Thurium. Some of those who escaped, being met by Murena as he stood in array, were cut off and destroyed. Others breaking through to their friends and falling pell-mell into the ranks, filled most part of the army with fear and tumult, and caused a hesitation and delay among the generals, which was no small disadvantage. For immediately upon the discomposure, Sylla coming full speed to the charge, and quickly crossing the interval between the armies, lost them the service of their armed chariots, which require a considerable space of ground to gather strength and impetuosity in their career, a short course being weak and ineffectual, like that of missiles without a full swing. Thus it fared with the barbarians at present, whose first chariots came feebly on and made but a faint impression; the Romans, repulsing them with shouts and laughter, called out, as they do at the races in the circus, for more to come. By this time the mass of both armies met; the barbarians on one side fixed their long pikes, and with their shields locked close together, strove so far as in them lay to preserve their line of battle entire. The Romans, on the other side, having discharged their javelins, rushed on with their drawn swords, and struggled to put by the pikes to get at them the sooner, in the fury that possessed them at seeing in the front of the enemy fifteen thousand slaves, whom the royal commanders had set free by proclamation, and ranged amongst the men of arms. And a Roman centurion is reported to have said at this sight, that he never knew servants allowed to play the masters, unless at the Saturnalia. These men, by their deep and solid array, as well as by their daring courage, yielded but slowly to the legions, till at last by slinging engines, and darts, which the Romans poured in upon them behind, they were forced to give way and scatter.

As Archelaus was extending the right wing to encompass the enemy, Hortensius with his cohorts came down in force, with intention to charge him in the flank. But Archelaus wheeling about suddenly with two thousand horse, Hortensius, out-numbered and hard pressed, fell back towards the higher grounds, and found himself gradually getting separated from the main body and likely to be surrounded by the enemy. When Sylla heard this, he came rapidly up to his succour from the right wing, which as yet had not engaged. But Archelaus, guessing the matter by the dust of his troops, turned to the right wing, from whence Sylla came, in hopes to surprise it without a commander. At the same instant, likewise, Taxiles, with his Brazen Shields, assailed Murena, so that a cry coming from both places, and the hills repeating it around, Sylla stood in suspense which way to move. Deciding to resume his own station, he sent in aid to Murena four cohorts under Hortensius, and commanding the fifth to follow him, returned hastily to the right wing, which of itself held its ground on equal terms against Archelaus; and, at his appearance, with one bold effort forced them back, and, obtaining the mastery, followed them, flying in disorder to the river and Mount Acontium. Sylla, however, did not forget the danger Murena was in; but hasting thither and finding him victorious also, then joined in the pursuit. Many barbarians were slain in the field, many more were cut in pieces as they were making into the camp. Of all the vast multitude, ten thousand only got safe into Chalcis. Sylla writes that there were but fourteen of his soldiers missing, and that two of these returned towards evening; he, therefore, inscribed on the trophies the names of Mars, Victory, and Venus, as having won the day no less by good fortune than by management and force of arms. This trophy of the battle in the plain stands on the place where Archelaus first gave way, near the stream of the Molus; another is erected high on the top of Thurium, where the barbarians were environed, with an inscription in Greek, recording that the glory of the day belonged to Homoloichus and Anaxidamus. Sylla celebrated his victory at Thebes with spectacles, for which he erected a stage, near Œdipus' well. The judges of the performances were Greeks chosen out of other cities; his hostility to the Thebans being implacable, half of whose territory he took away and consecrated to Apollo and Jupiter, ordering that out of the revenue compensation should be made to the gods for the riches himself had taken from them.

After this, hearing that Flaccus, a man of the contrary faction, had been chosen consul, and was crossing the Ionian Sea with an army, professedly to act against Mithridates, but in reality against himself, he hastened towards Thessaly, designing to meet him, but in his march, when near Melitea, received advices from all parts that the countries behind him were overrun and ravaged by no less a royal army than the former. For Dorylaus, arriving at Chalcis with a large fleet, on board of which he brought over with him eighty thousand of the best appointed and best disciplined soldiers of Mithridates' army, at once invaded Bœotia, and occupied the country in hopes to bring Sylla to a battle, making no account of the dissuasions of Archelaus, but giving it out as to the last fight, that without treachery so many thousand men could never have perished. Sylla, however, facing about expeditiously, made it clear to him that Archelaus was a wise man, and had good skill in the Roman valour; insomuch that he himself, after some small skirmishes with Sylla near Tilphossium, was the first of those who thought it not advisable to put things to the decision of the sword, but rather to wear out the war by expense of time and treasure. The ground, however, near Orchomenus, where they then lay encamped, gave some encouragement to Archelaus, being a battlefield admirably suited for any army superior in cavalry. Of all the plains in Bœotia that are renowned for their beauty and extent, this alone, which commences from the city of Orchomenus, spreads out unbroken and clear of trees to the edge of the fens in which the Melas, rising close under Orchomenus, loses itself, the only Greek river which is a deep and navigable water from the very head, increasing also about the summer solstice like the Nile, and producing plants similar to those that grow there, only small and without fruit. It does not run far before the main stream disappears among the blind and woody marsh-grounds; a small branch, however, joins the Cephisus, about the place where the lake is thought to produce the best flute-reeds.

Now that both armies were posted near each other, Archelaus lay still, but Sylla employed himself in cutting ditches from either side; that if possible, by driving the enemies from the firm and open champaign, he might force them into the fens. They, on the other hand, not enduring

this, as soon as their leaders allowed them the word of command, issued
out furiously in large bodies; when not only the men at work were dispersed, but most part of those who stood in arms to protect the work fled
in disorder. Upon this, Sylla leaped from his horse, and snatching hold of
an ensign, rushed through the midst of the rout upon the enemy, crying
out aloud, "To me, O Romans, it will be glorious to fall here. As for you,
when they ask you where you betrayed your general, remember and say, at
Orchomenus." His men rallying again at these words, and two cohorts
coming to his succour from the right wing, he led them to the charge and
turned the day. Then retiring some short distance and refreshing his men,
he proceeded again with his works to block up the enemy's camp. They
again sallied out in better order than before. Here Diogenes, stepson to
Archelaus, fighting on the right wing with much gallantry, made an honourable end. And the archers, being hard pressed by the Romans, and
wanting space for a retreat, took their arrows by handfuls, and striking
with these as with swords, beat them back. In the end, however, they were
all driven into the intrenchment and had a sorrowful night of it with their
slain and wounded. The next day again, Sylla, leading forth his men up to
their quarters, went on finishing the lines of intrenchment, and when they
issued out again with larger numbers to give him battle, fell on them and
put them to the rout, and in the consternation ensuing, none daring to
abide, he took the camp by storm. The marshes were filled with blood,
and the lake with dead bodies, insomuch that to this day many bows, helmets, fragments of iron, breastplates, and swords of barbarian make continue to be found buried deep in mud, two hundred years after the fight.
Thus much of the actions of Chæronea and Orchomenus.

At Rome, Cinna and Carbo were now using injustice and violence
towards persons of the greatest eminence, and many of them to avoid this
tyranny repaired, as to a safe harbour, to Sylla's camp, where, in a short
space, he had about him the aspect of a senate. Metella, likewise, having
with difficulty conveyed herself and children away by stealth, brought him
word that his houses, both in town and country, had been burnt by his
enemies, and entreated his help at home. Whilst he was in doubt what to
do, being impatient to hear of his country being thus outraged, and yet
not knowing how to leave so great a work as the Mithridatic war unfinished, there comes to him Archelaus, a merchant of Delos, with hopes of
an accommodation, and private instructions from Archelaus, the king's
general. Sylla liked the business so well as to desire a speedy conference
with Archelaus in person, and a meeting took place on the seacoast near

Delium, where the temple of Apollo stands. When Archelaus opened the conversation, and began to urge Sylla to abandon his pretensions to Asia and Pontus, and to set sail for the war in Rome, receiving money and ship-ping, and such forces as he should think fitting from the king, Sylla inter-posing, bade Archelaus take no further care for Mithridates, but assume the crown to himself, and become a confederate of Rome, delivering up the navy. Archelaus professing his abhorrence of such treason, Sylla proceeded: "So you, Archelaus, a Cappadocian, and slave, or if it so please you friend, to a barbarian king, would not, upon such vast considerations, be guilty of what is dishonourable, and yet dare to talk to me, Roman gen-eral and Sylla, of treason? As if you were not the selfsame Archelaus who ran away at Chæronea, with few remaining out of one hundred and twenty thousand men; who lay for two days in the fens of Orchomenus, and left Bœotia impassable for heaps of dead carcasses." Archelaus, changing his tone at this, humbly besought him to lay aside the thoughts of war, and make peace with Mithridates. Sylla consenting to this request, articles of agreement were concluded on. That Mithridates should quit Asia and Paphlagonia, restore Bithynia to Nicomedes, Cappadocia to Ariobarzanes, and pay the Romans two thousand talents, and give him seventy ships of war with all their furniture. On the other hand, that Sylla should confirm to him his other dominions, and declare him a Roman confederate. On these terms he proceeded by the way of Thessaly and Macedon towards the Hellespont, having Archelaus with him, and treating him with great attention. For Archelaus being taken dangerously ill at Larissa, he stopped the march of the army, and took care of him, as if he had been one of his own captains, or his colleague in command. This gave suspicion of foul play in the battle of Chæronea; as it was also observed that Sylla had released all the friends of Mithridates taken prisoners in war, except only Aristion the tyrant, who was at enmity with Archelaus, and was put to death by poison; and, above all, ten thousand acres of land in Eubœa had been given to the Cappadocian, and he had received from Sylla the style of friend and ally of the Romans. On all which points Sylla defends him-self in his Memoirs.

The ambassadors of Mithridates arriving and declaring that they accepted of the conditions, only Paphlagonia they could not part with; and as for the ships, professing not to know of any such capitulation, Sylla in a rage exclaimed, "What say you? Does Mithridates then withhold Paphlagonia? And as to the ships, deny that article? I thought to have seen him prostrate at my feet to thank me for leaving him so much as that right hand of his, which has cut off so many Romans. He will shortly, at my coming over into Asia, speak another language; in the meantime, let him at his ease in Pergamus sit managing a war which he never saw." The ambassadors in terror stood silent by, but Archelaus endeavoured with humble supplications to assuage his wrath, laying hold on his right hand and weeping. In conclusion he obtained permission to go himself in person to Mithridates; for that he would either mediate a peace to the satisfaction of Sylla, or if not, slay himself. Sylla having thus despatched him away, made an inroad into Mædica, and after wide depopulations returned back again into Macedon, where he received Archelaus about Philippi, bringing word that all was well, and that Mithridates earnestly requested an interview. The chief cause of this meeting was Fimbria; for he, having assassinated Flaccus, the consul of the contrary faction, and worsted the Mithridatic commanders, was advancing against Mithridates himself, who, fearing this, chose rather to seek the friendship of Sylla.

And so met at Dardanus in the Troad, on one side Mithridates, attended with two hundred ships, and land-forces consisting of twenty thousand men at arms, six thousand horse, and a large train of scythed chariots; on the other, Sylla with only four cohorts and two hundred horse. As Mithridates drew near and put out his hand, Sylla demanded whether he was willing or no to end the war on the terms Archelaus had agreed to, but seeing the king made no answer, "How is this?" he continued, "ought not the petitioner to speak first, and the conqueror to listen in silence?" And when Mithridates, entering upon his plea, began to shift off the war, partly on the gods, and partly to blame the Romans themselves, he took him up, saying that he had heard, indeed, long since from others, and now he knew it himself for truth, that Mithridates was a powerful speaker, who in defence of the most foul and unjust proceedings, had not wanted for specious pretences. Then charging him with and inveighing bitterly against the outrages he had committed, he asked again whether he was willing or no to ratify the treaty of Archelaus? Mithridates answering in the affirmative, Sylla came forward, embraced and kissed him. Not long after he introduced Ariobarzanes and Nicomedes, the two kings, and made them friends. Mithridates, when he had handed over to Sylla seventy ships and five hundred archers, set sail for Pontus.

Sylla, perceiving the soldiers to be dissatisfied with the peace (as it seemed indeed a monstrous thing that they should see the king who was their bitterest enemy, and who had caused one hundred and fifty thousand Romans to be massacred in one day in Asia, now sailing off with the

riches and spoils of Asia, which he had pillaged, and put under contribution for the space of four years), in his defence to them alleged, that he
could not have made head against Fimbria and Mithridates, had they both
withstood him in conjunction. Thence he set out and went in search of
Fimbria, who lay with the army about Thyatira, and pitching his camp not
far off, proceeded to fortify it with a trench. The soldiers of Fimbria came
out in their single coats, and saluting his men, lent ready assistance to the
work; which change Fimbria beholding, and apprehending Sylla as irreconcilable, laid violent hands on himself in the camp.

Sylla imposed on Asia in general a tax of twenty thousand talents, and
despoiled individually each family by the licentious behaviour and long
residence of the soldiery in private quarters. For he ordained that every
host should allow his guest four tetradrachms each day, and moreover
entertain him, and as many friends as he should invite, with a supper; that
a centurion should receive fifty drachmas a day, together with one suit of
clothes to wear within doors, and another when he went abroad.

Having set out from Ephesus with the whole navy, he came the third
day to anchor in the Piræus. Here he was initiated in the mysteries, and
seized for his use the library of Apellicon the Teian, in which were most of
the works of Theophrastus and Aristotle, then not in general circulation.
When the whole was afterwards conveyed to Rome, there, it is said, the
greater part of the collection passed through the hands of Tyrannion
the grammarian, and that Andronicus the Rhodian, having through his
means the command of numerous copies, made the treatises public, and
drew up the catalogues that are now current. The elder Peripatetics
appear themselves, indeed, to have been accomplished and learned men,
but of the writings of Aristotle and Theophrastus they had no large or
exact knowledge, because Theophrastus bequeathing his books to the
heir of Neleus of Scepsis, they came into careless and illiterate hands.

During Sylla's stay about Athens, his feet were attacked by a heavy
benumbing pain, which Strabo calls the first inarticulate sounds of the
gout. Taking, therefore, a voyage to Ædepsus, he made use of the hot
waters there, allowing himself at the same time to forget all anxieties, and
passing away his time with actors. As he was walking along the seashore,
certain fishermen brought him some magnificent fish. Being much
delighted with the gift, and understanding, on inquiry, that they were men
of Halææ, "What," said he, "are there any men of Halææ surviving?" For
after his victory at Orchomenus, in the heat of a pursuit, he had destroyed
three cities of Bœotia, Anthedon, Larymna, and Halææ. The men not

knowing what to say for fear, Sylla, with a smile, bade them cheer up and return in peace, as they had brought with them no insignificant intercessors. The Halæans say that this first gave them courage to re-unite and return to their city.

Sylla, having marched through Thessaly and Macedon to the sea coast, prepared, with twelve hundred vessels, to cross over from Dyrrhachium to Brundisium. Not far from hence is Apollonia, and near it the Nymphæum, a spot of ground where, from among green trees and meadows, there are found at various points springs of fire continually streaming out. Here, they say, a satyr, such as statuaries and painters represent, was caught asleep, and brought before Sylla, where he was asked by several interpreters who he was, and, after much trouble, at last uttered nothing intelligible, but a harsh noise, something between the neighing of a horse and crying of a goat. Sylla, in dismay, and deprecating such an omen, bade it be removed.

At the point of transportation, Sylla being in alarm, lest at their first setting foot upon Italy the soldiers should disband and disperse one by one among the cities, they of their own accord first took an oath to stand firm by him, and not of their goodwill to injure Italy; then seeing him in distress for money, they made, so they say, a free-will offering, and contributed each man according to his ability. However, Sylla would not accept of their offering, but praising their goodwill, and arousing up their courage, went over (as he himself writes) against fifteen hostile generals in command of four hundred and fifty cohorts; but not without the most unmistakable divine intimations of his approaching happy successes. For when he was sacrificing at his first landing near Tarentum, the victim's liver showed the figure of a crown of laurel with two fillets hanging from it. And a little while before his arrival in Campania, near the mountain Hephæus, two stately goats were seen in the daytime, fighting together, and performing all the motions of men in battle. It proved to be an apparition, and rising up gradually from the ground, dispersed in the air, like fancied representations in the clouds, and so vanished out of sight. Not long after, in the selfsame place, when Marius the younger and Norbanus the consul attacked him with two great armies, without prescribing the order of battle, or arranging his men according to their divisions, by the sway only of one common alacrity and transport of courage, he overthrew the enemy, and shut up Norbanus into the city of Capua, with the loss of seven thousand of his men. And this was the reason, he says, that the soldiers did not leave him and disperse into the different towns, but held fast to him, and despised the enemy, though infinitely more in number.

At Silvium (as he himself relates it), there met him a servant of Pontius, in a state of divine possession, saying that he brought him the power of the sword and victory from Bellona, the goddess of war, and if he did not make haste, that the capitol would be burnt, which fell out on the same day the man foretold it, namely, on the sixth day of the month Quintilis, which we now call July.

At Fidentia, also, Marcus Lucullus, one of Sylla's commanders, reposed such confidence in the forwardness of the soldiers, as to dare to face fifty cohorts of the enemy with only sixteen of his own: but because many of them were unarmed delayed the onset. As he stood thus waiting, and considering with himself, a gentle gale of wind, bearing along with it from the neighbouring meadows a quantity of flowers, scattered them down upon the army, on whose shields and helmets they settled, and arranged themselves spontaneously so as to give the soldiers, in the eyes of the enemy, the appearance of being crowned with chaplets. Upon this, being yet further animated, they joined battle, and victoriously slaying eight thousand men, took the camp. This Lucullus was brother to that Lucullus who in aftertimes conquered Mithridates and Tigranes.

Sylla, seeing himself still surrounded by so many armies, and such mighty hostile powers, had recourse to art, inviting Scipio, the other consul, to a treaty of peace. The motion was willingly embraced, and several meetings and consultations ensued, in all which Sylla, still interposing matter of delay and new pretences, in the meanwhile debauched Scipio's men by means of his own, who were as well practised as the general himself in all the artifices of inveigling. For entering into the enemy's quarters and joining in conversation, they gained some by present money, some by promises, others by fair words and persuasions; so that in the end, when Sylla with twenty cohorts drew near, on his men saluting Scipio's soldiers, they returned the greeting and came over, leaving Scipio behind them in his tent, where he was found all alone and dismissed. And having used his twenty cohorts as decoys to ensnare the forty of the enemy, he led them all back into the camp. On this occasion, Carbo was heard to say that he had both a fox and a lion in the breast of Sylla to deal with, and was most troubled with the fox.

Sometime after, at Signia, Marius the younger, with eighty-five cohorts, offered battle to Sylla, who was extremely desirous to have it decided on that very day; for the night before he had seen a vision in his sleep, of Marius the elder, who had been sometime dead, advising his son to beware of the following day, as of fatal consequence to him. For this reason, Sylla, longing to come to a battle, sent off for Dolabella, who lay encamped at some distance. But because the enemy had beset and blocked up the passes, his soldiers got tired with skirmishing and marching at once. To these difficulties was added, moreover, tempestuous rainy weather, which distressed them most of all. The principal officers therefore came to Sylla, and besought him to defer the battle that day, showing him how the soldiers lay stretched on the ground, where they had thrown themselves down in their weariness, resting their heads upon their shields to gain some repose. When, with much reluctance, he had yielded, and given orders for pitching the camp, they had no sooner begun to cast up the rampart and draw the ditch, but Marius came riding up furiously at the head of his troops, in hopes to scatter them in that disorder and confusion. Here the gods fulfilled Sylla's dream. For the soldiers, stirred up with anger, left off their work, and sticking their javelins into the bank, with drawn swords and a courageous shout, came to blows with the enemy, who made but small resistance, and lost great numbers in the flight. Marius fled to Præneste, but finding the gates shut, tied himself round by a rope that was thrown down to him, and was taken up on the walls. Some there are (as Fenestella for one) who affirm that Marius knew nothing of the fight, but, overwatched and spent with hard duty, had reposed himself, when the signal was given, beneath some shade, and was hardly to be awakened at the flight of his men. Sylla, according to his own account, lost only twenty-three men in this fight, having killed of the enemy twenty thousand, and taken alive eight thousand.

The like success attended his lieutenants, Pompey, Crassus, Metellus, Servilius, who with little or no loss cut off vast numbers of the enemy, insomuch that Carbo, the prime supporter of the cause, fled by night from his charge of the army, and sailed over into Libya.

In the last struggle, however, the Samnite Telesinus, like some champion, whose lot it is to enter last of all into the lists and take up the wearied conqueror, came nigh to have foiled and overthrown Sylla before the gates of Rome. For Telesinus with his second, Lamponius the Lucanian, having collected a large force, had been hastening towards Præneste, to relieve Alarms from the siege; but perceiving Sylla ahead of him, and Pompey behind, both hurrying up against him, straitened thus before and behind, as a valiant and experienced soldier, he arose by night, and marching directly with his whole army, was within a little of making his way unexpectedly into Rome itself. He lay that night before the city, at ten furlongs' distance from the Colline gate, elated and full of hope at having thus outgeneralled so many eminent commanders. At break of day, being charged by the noble youth of the city, among many others he overthrew Appius Claudius, renowned for high birth and character. The city, as is easy to imagine, was all in an uproar, the women shrieking and running about, as if it had already been entered forcibly by assault, till at last Balbus, sent forward by Sylla, was seen riding up with seven hundred horse at full speed. Halting only long enough to wipe the sweat from the horses, and then hastily bridling again, he at once attacked the enemy. Presently Sylla himself appeared, and commanding those who were foremost to take immediate refreshment, proceeded to form in order for battle. Dolabella and Torquatus were extremely earnest with him to desist awhile, and not with spent forces to hazard the last hope, having before them in the field, not Carbo or Marius, but two warlike nations bearing immortal hatred to Rome, the Samnites and Lucanians, to grapple with. But he put them by, and commanded the trumpets to sound a charge, when it was now about four o'clock in the afternoon. In the conflict which followed, as sharp a one as ever was, the right wing where Crassus was posted had clearly the advantage; the left suffered and was in distress, when Sylla came to its succour, mounted on a white courser, full of mettle and exceedingly swift, which two of the enemy knowing him by, had their lances ready to throw at him; he himself observed nothing, but his attendant behind him giving the horse a touch, he was, unknown to himself, just so far carried forward that the points, falling beside the horse's tail, stuck in the ground. There is a story that he had a small golden image of Apollo from Delphi, which he was always wont in battle to carry about him in his bosom, and that he then kissed it with these words, "O Apollo Pythius, who in so many battles hast raised to honour and greatness the Fortunate Cornelius Sylla, wilt thou now cast him down, bringing him before the gate of his country, to perish shamefully with his fellow-citizens?" Thus, they say, addressing himself to the god, he entreated some of his men, threatened some, and seized others with his hand, till at length the left wing being wholly shattered, he was forced in the general rout, to betake himself to the camp, having lost many of his friends and acquaintance. Many, likewise, of the city spectators, who had come out, were killed or trodden under foot. So that it was generally believed in the city that all was lost, and the siege of Præneste was all but raised; many fugitives from the battle making their way thither, and urging Lucretius Ofella, who was appointed to keep on the siege, to rise in all haste, for that Sylla had perished, and Rome fallen into the hands of the enemy.

About midnight there came into Sylla's camp messengers from Crassus, to fetch provision for him and his soldiers; for having vanquished the enemy, they had pursued him to the walls of Antemna, and had sat down there. Sylla, hearing this, and that most of the enemy was destroyed, came to Antemna by break of day, where three thousand of the besieged having sent forth a herald, he promised to receive them to mercy, on condition they did the enemy mischief in their coming over. Trusting to his word, they fell foul on the rest of their companions, and made a great slaughter one of another. Nevertheless, Sylla gathered together in the circus, as well these as other survivors of the party, to the number of six thousand, and just as he commenced speaking to the senate, in the temple of Bellona, proceeded to cut them down, by men appointed for that service. The cry of so vast a multitude put to the sword, in so narrow a space, was naturally heard some distance, and startled the senators. He, however, continuing his speech with a calm and unconcerned countenance, bade them listen to what he had to say, and not busy themselves with what was doing out of doors; he had given directions for the chastisement of some offenders. This gave the most stupid of the Romans to understand that they had merely exchanged, not escaped, tyranny. And Marius, being of a naturally harsh temper, had not altered, but merely continued what he had been, in authority; whereas Sylla, using his fortune moderately and unambitiously at first, and giving good hopes of a true patriot, firm to the interests both of the nobility and commonalty, being, moreover, of a gay and cheerful temper from his youth, and so easily moved to pity as to shed tears readily, has, perhaps deservedly, cast a blemish upon offices of great authority, as if they deranged men's former habits and character, and gave rise to violence, pride, and inhumanity. Whether this be a real change and revolution in the mind, caused by fortune, or rather a lurking viciousness of nature, discovering itself in authority, it were matter of another sort of disquisition to decide.

Sylla being thus wholly bent upon slaughter; and filling the city with executions without number or limit, many wholly uninterested persons falling a sacrifice to private enmity, through his permission and indulgence to his friends, Caius Metellus, one of the younger men, made bold in the senate to ask him what end there was of these evils, and at what point he might be expected to stop? "We do not ask you," said he, "to pardon any whom you have resolved to destroy, but to free from doubt those whom you are pleased to save." Sylla answering, that he knew not as yet whom to spare, "Why, then," said he, "tell us whom you will punish."

This Sylla said he would do. These last words, some authors say, were spoken not by Metellus, but by Afidius, one of Sylla's fawning companions. Immediately upon this, without communicating with any of the magistrates, Sylla proscribed eighty persons, and notwithstanding the general indignation, after one day's respite, he posted two hundred and twenty more, and on the third again, as many. In an address to the people on this occasion, he told them he had put up as many names as he could think of; those which had escaped his memory, he would publish at a future time. He issued an edict likewise, making death the punishment of humanity, proscribing any who should dare to receive and cherish a proscribed person without exception to brother, son, or parents. And to him who should slay anyone proscribed person, he ordained two talents reward, even were it a slave who had killed his master, or a son his father. And what was thought most unjust of all, he caused the attainder to pass upon their sons, and sons' sons, and made open sale of all their property. Nor did the proscription prevail only at Rome, but throughout all the cities of Italy the effusion of blood was such, that neither sanctuary of the gods, nor hearth of hospitality, nor ancestral home escaped. Men were butchered in the embraces of their wives, children in the arms of their mothers. Those who perished through public animosity or private enmity were nothing in comparison of the numbers of those who suffered for their riches. Even the murderers began to say, that "his fine house killed this man, a garden that, a third, his hot baths." Quintus Aurelius, a quiet, peaceable man, and one who thought all his part in the common calamity consisted in condoling with the misfortunes of others, coming into the forum to read the list, and finding himself among the proscribed, cried out, "Woe is me, my Alban farm has informed against me." He had not gone far before he was despatched by a ruffian, sent on that errand.

In the meantime, Marius, on the point of being taken, killed himself; and Sylla, coming to Præneste, at first proceeded judicially against each particular person, till at last, finding it a work of too much time, he cooped them up together in one place, to the number of twelve thousand men, and gave order for the execution of them all, his own host alone excepted. But he, brave man, telling him he could not accept the obligation of life from the hands of one who had been the ruin of his country, went in among the rest, and submitted willingly to the stroke. What Lucius Catilina did was thought to exceed all other acts. For having, before matters came to an issue, made away with his brother, he besought Sylla to place him in the list of proscription, as though he had been alive, which was done; and Catiline, to return the kind office, assassinated a certain Marcus Marius, one of the adverse party, and brought the head to Sylla, as he was sitting in the forum, and then going to the holy water of Apollo, which was nigh, washed his hands.

There were other things, besides this bloodshed, which gave offence. For Sylla had declared himself dictator, an office which had then been laid aside for the space of one hundred and twenty years. There was, likewise, an act of grace passed on his behalf, granting indemnity for what was passed, and for the future intrusting him with the power of life and death, confiscation, division of lands, erecting and demolishing of cities, taking away of kingdoms, and bestowing them at pleasure. He conducted the sale of confiscated property after such an arbitrary, imperious way, from the tribunal, that his gifts excited greater odium even than his usurpations; women, mimes, and musicians, and the lowest of the freed slaves had presents made them of the territories of nations and the revenues of cities: and women of rank were married against their will to some of them. Wishing to insure the fidelity of Pompey the Great by a nearer tie of blood, he bade him divorce his present wife, and forcing Æmilia, the daughter of Scaurus and Metella, his own wife, to leave her husband, Manius Glabrio, he bestowed her, though then with child, on Pompey, and she died in childbirth at his house.

When Lucretius Ofella, the same who reduced Marius by siege, offered himself for the consulship, he first forbade him; then, seeing he could not restrain him, on his coming down into the forum with a numerous train of followers, he sent one of the centurions who were immediately about him, and slew him, himself sitting on the tribunal in the temple of Castor, and beholding the murder from above. The citizens apprehending the centurion, and dragging him to the tribunal, he bade them cease their clamouring and let the centurion go, for he had commanded it.

His triumph was, in itself, exceedingly splendid, and distinguished by the rarity and magnificence of the royal spoils; but its yet greatest glory was the noble spectacle of the exiles. For in the rear followed the most eminent and most potent of the citizens, crowned with garlands, and calling Sylla saviour and father, by whose means they were restored to their own country, and again enjoyed their wives and children. When the solemnity was over, and the time come to render an account of his actions, addressing the public assembly, he was as profuse in enumerating the lucky chances of war as any of his own military merits. And, finally, from this felicity he requested to receive the surname of Felix. In writing and transacting business with the Greeks, he styled himself Epaphroditus, and on his trophies which are still extant with us the name is given Lucius Cornelius Sylla Epaphroditus. Moreover, when his wife had brought him forth twins, he named the male Faustus and the female Fausta, the Roman words for what is auspicious and of happy omen. The confidence which he reposed in his good genius, rather than in any abilities of his own, emboldened him, though deeply involved in bloodshed, and though he had been the author of such great changes and revolutions of state, to lay down his authority, and place the right of consular elections once more in the hands of the people. And when they were held, he not only declined to seek that office, but in the forum exposed his person publicly to the people, walking up and down as a private man. And contrary to his will, a certain bold man and his enemy, Marcus Lepidus, was expected to become consul, not so much by his own interest, as by the power and solicitation of Pompey, whom the people were willing to oblige. When the business was over, seeing Pompey going home overjoyed with the success, he called him to him and said, "What a polite act, young man, to pass by Catulus, the best of men, and choose Lepidus, the worst! It will be well for you to be vigilant, now that you have strengthened your opponent against yourself." Sylla spoke this, it may seem, by a prophetic instinct, for, not long after, Lepidus grew insolent and broke into open hostility to Pompey and his friends.

Sylla, consecrating the tenth of his whole substance to Hercules, entertained the people with sumptuous feastings. The provision was so much above what was necessary, that they were forced daily to throw great quantities of meat into the river, and they drank wine forty years old and upwards. In the midst of the banqueting, which lasted many days, Metella died of a disease. And because that the priest forbade him to visit the sick, or suffer his house to be polluted with mourning, he drew up an act of divorce and caused her to be removed into another house whilst alive. Thus far, out of religious apprehension, he observed the strict rule to the very letter, but in the funeral expenses he transgressed the law he himself had made, limiting the amount, and spared no cost. He transgressed, likewise, his own sumptuary laws respecting expenditure in banquets, thinking to allay his grief by luxurious drinking parties and revellings with common buffoons.

Some few months after, at a show of gladiators, when men and women sat promiscuously in the theatre, no distinct places being as yet appointed, there sat down by Sylla a beautiful woman of high birth, by name Valeria, daughter of Messala, and sister to Hortensius the orator. Now it happened that she had been lately divorced from her husband. Passing along behind Sylla, she leaned on him with her hand, and plucking a bit of wool from his garment, so proceeded to her seat. And on Sylla looking up and wondering what it meant, "What harm, mighty sir," said she, "if I also was desirous to partake a little in your felicity?" It appeared at once that Sylla was not displeased, but even tickled in his fancy, for he sent out to inquire her name, her birth, and past life. From this time there passed between them many side glances, each continually turning round to look at the other, and frequently interchanging smiles. In the end, overtures were made, and a marriage concluded on. All which was innocent, perhaps, on the lady's side, but, though she had been never so modest and virtuous, it was scarcely a temperate and worthy occasion of marriage on the part of Sylla, to take fire, as a boy might, at a face and a bold look, incentives not seldom to the most disorderly and shameless passions.

Notwithstanding this marriage, he kept company with actresses, musicians, and dancers, drinking with them on couches night and day. His chief favourites were Roscius the comedian, Sorex the arch mime, and Metrobius the player, for whom, though past his prime, he still professed a passionate fondness. By these courses he encouraged a disease which had begun from unimportant cause; and for a long time he failed to observe that his bowels were ulcerated, till at length the corrupted flesh broke out into lice. Many were employed day and night in destroying them, but the work so multiplied under their hands, that not only his clothes, baths, basins, but his very meat was polluted with that flux and contagion, they came swarming out in such numbers. He went frequently by day into the bath to scour and cleanse his body, but all in vain; the evil generated too rapidly and too abundantly for any ablutions to overcome it. There died of this disease, amongst those of the most ancient times, Acastus, the son of Pelias; of later date, Alcman the poet, Pherecydes the theologian, Callisthenes the Olynthian, in the time of his imprisonment, as also Mucius the lawyer; and if we may mention ignoble, but notorious names, Eunus the fugitive, who stirred up the slaves of Sicily to rebel against their masters, after he was brought captive to Rome, died of this creeping sickness.

Sylla not only foresaw his end, but may be also said to have written of it. For in the two-and-twentieth book of his Memoirs, which he finished two days before his death, he writes that the Chaldeans foretold him, that after he had led a life of honour, he should conclude it in fulness of prosperity. He declares, moreover, that in a vision he had seen his son, who had died not long before Metella, stand by in mourning attire, and beseech his father to cast off further care, and come along with him to his mother Metella, there to live at ease and quietness with her. However, he could not refrain from intermeddling in public affairs. For, ten days before his decease, he composed the differences of the people of Dicæarchia, and prescribed laws for their better government. And the very day before his end, it being told him that the magistrate Granius deferred the payment of a public debt, in expectation of his death, he sent for him to his house, and placing his attendants about him, caused him to be strangled; but through the straining of his voice and body, the imposthume breaking, he lost a great quantity of blood. Upon this, his strength failing him, after spending a troublesome night, he died, leaving behind him two young children by Metella. Valeria was afterwards delivered of a daughter, named Posthuma; for so the Romans call those who are born after the father's death.

Many ran tumultuously together, and joined with Lepidus to deprive the corpse of the accustomed solemnities; but Pompey, though offended at Sylla (for he alone of all his friends was not mentioned in his will), having kept off some by his interest and entreaty, others by menaces, conveyed the body to Rome, and gave it a secure and honourable burial. It is said that the Roman ladies contributed such vast heaps of spices, that besides what was carried on two hundred and ten litters, there was sufficient to form a large figure of Sylla himself, and another representing a lictor, out of the costly frankincense and cinnamon. The day being cloudy in the morning, they deferred carrying forth the corpse till about three in the afternoon, expecting it would rain. But a strong wind blowing full upon the funeral pile, and setting it all in a bright flame, the body was consumed so exactly in good time, that the pyre had begun to smoulder, and the fire was upon the point of expiring, when a violent rain came down, which continued till night. So that his good fortune was firm even to the last, and did as it were officiate at his funeral. His monument stands in the Campus Martius, with an epitaph of his own writing; the substance of it being, that he had not been outdone by any of his friends in doing good turns, nor by any of his foes in doing bad.

THE COMPARISON OF LYSANDER WITH SYLLA

HAVING COMPLETED THIS LIFE ALSO, COME WE NOW TO THE COMPARISON. That which was common to them both was that they were founders of their own greatness, with this difference, that Lysander had the consent of his fellow-citizens, in times of sober judgment, for the honours he received; nor did he force anything from them against their goodwill, nor hold any power contrary to the laws.

In civil strife e'en villains rise to fame.

And so then at Rome, when the people were distempered, and the government out of order, one or other was still raised to despotic power; no wonder, then, if Sylla reigned, when the Glauciæ and Saturnini drove out the Metelli, when sons of consuls were slain in the assemblies, when silver and gold purchased men and arms, and fire and sword enacted new laws and put down lawful opposition. Nor do I blame anyone, in such circumstances, for working himself into supreme power, only I would not have it thought a sign of great goodness to be head of a state so wretchedly discomposed. Lysander, being employed in the greatest commands and affairs of state, by a sober and well-governed city, may be said to have had repute as the best and most virtuous man, in the best and most virtuous commonwealth. And thus, often returning the government into the hands of the citizens, he received it again as often, the superiority of his merit still awarding him the first place. Sylla, on the other hand, when he had once made himself general of an army, kept his command for ten years together, creating himself sometimes consul, sometimes proconsul, and sometimes dictator, but always remaining a tyrant.

It is true Lysander, as was said, designed to introduce a new form of government; by milder methods, however, and more agreeable to law than Sylla, not by force of arms, but persuasion, nor by subverting the whole state at once, but simply by amending the succession of the kings; in a way, moreover, which seemed the naturally just one, that the most deserving should rule, especially in a city which itself exercised command in Greece, upon account of virtue, not nobility. For as the hunter considers the whelp itself, not the bitch, and the horse-dealer the foal, not the mare (for what if the foal should prove a mule?), so likewise were that politician extremely out, who, in the choice of a chief magistrate, should inquire, not what the man is, but how descended. The very Spartans themselves have deposed several of their kings for want of kingly virtues, as degenerated and good for nothing. As a vicious nature, though of an ancient stock, is dishonourable, it must be virtue itself, and not birth, that makes virtue honourable. Furthermore, the one committed his acts of injustice for the sake of his friends; the other extended his to his friends themselves. It is confessed on all hands, that Lysander offended most commonly for the sake of his companions, committing several slaughters to uphold their power and dominion; but as for Sylla, he, out of envy, reduced Pompey's command by land and Dolabella's by sea, although he himself had given them those places; and ordered Lucretius Ofella, who sued for the consulship as the reward of many great services, to be slain before his eyes, exciting horror and alarm in the minds of all men, by his cruelty to his dearest friends.

As regards the pursuit of riches and pleasures, we yet further discover in one a princely, in the other a tyrannical, disposition. Lysander did nothing that was intemperate or licentious, in that full command of means and opportunity, but kept clear, as much as ever man did, of that trite saying—

Lions at home, but foxes out of doors;

and ever maintained a sober, truly Spartan, and well-disciplined course of conduct. Whereas Sylla could never moderate his unruly affections, either by poverty when young, or by years when grown old, but would be still prescribing laws to the citizens concerning chastity and sobriety, himself living all that time, as Sallust affirms, in lewdness and adultery. By these ways he so impoverished and drained the city of her treasures, as to be forced to sell privileges and immunities to allied and friendly cities for money, although he daily gave up the wealthiest and the greatest families to public sale and confiscation. There was no end of his favours vainly spent and thrown away on flatterers; for what hope could there be, or what likelihood of forethought or economy, in his more private moments over wine, when, in the open face of the people, upon the auction of a large estate, which he would have passed over to one of his friends at a small price, because another bid higher, and the officer announced the advance, he broke out into a passion, saying: "What a strange and unjust thing is this, O citizens, that I cannot dispose of my own booty as I please!" But Lysander, on the contrary, with the rest of the spoil, sent home for public use even the presents which were made him. Nor do I commend him for it, for he, perhaps, by excessive liberality, did Sparta more harm than ever the other did Rome by rapine; I only use it as an argument of his indifference to riches. They exercised a strange influence on their respective cities. Sylla, a profuse debauchee, endeavoured to restore sober living amongst the citizens; Lysander, temperate himself, filled Sparta with the luxury he disregarded. So that both were blameworthy, the one for raising himself above his own laws, the other for causing his fellow-citizens to fall beneath his own example. He taught Sparta to want the very things which he himself had learned to do without. And thus much of their civil administration.

As for feats of arms, wise conduct in war, innumerable victories, perilous adventures, Sylla was beyond compare. Lysander, indeed, came off twice victorious in two battles by sea; I shall add to that the siege of Athens, a work of greater fame than difficulty. What occurred in Bœotia, and at Haliartus, was the result, perhaps, of ill fortune; yet it certainly looks like ill counsel, not to wait for the king's forces, which had all but arrived from Platæa, but out of ambition and eagerness to fight, to approach the walls at disadvantage, and so to be cut off by a sally of inconsiderable men. He received his death-wound, not as Cleombrotus, at Leuctra, resisting manfully the assault of an enemy in the field; not as Cyrus or Epaminondas, sustaining the declining battle, or making sure the victory; all these died the death of kings and generals; but he, as it had been some common skirmisher or scout, cast away his life ingloriously, giving testimony to the wisdom of the ancient Spartan maxim, to avoid attacks on walled cities, in which the stoutest warrior may chance to fall by the hand, not only of a man utterly his inferior, but by that of a boy or woman, as Achilles, they say, was slain by Paris in the gates. As for Sylla, it were hard to reckon up how many set battles he won, or how many thousand he slew; he took Rome itself twice, as also the Athenian Piræus, not by famine as Lysander did, but by a series of great battles, driving Archelaus into the sea. And what is most important, there was a vast difference between the commanders they had to deal with. For I look upon it as an easy task, or rather sport, to beat Antiochus, Alcibiades' pilot, or to circumvent Philocles, the Athenian demagogue—

Sharp only at the inglorious point of tongue,

whom Mithridates would have scorned to compare with his groom, or Marius with his lictor. But of the potentates, consuls, commanders, and demagogues, to pass by all the rest who opposed themselves to Sylla, who amongst the Romans so formidable as Marius, what king more powerful than Mithridates? Who of the Italians more warlike than Lamponius and Telesinus? Yet of these, one he drove into banishment, one he quelled, and the others he slew.

And what is more important, in my judgment, than anything yet adduced, is that Lysander had the assistance of the state in all his achievements; whereas Sylla, besides that he was a banished person, and overpowered by a faction, at a time when his wife was driven from home, his houses demolished, adherents slain, himself then in Bœotia, stood embattled against countless numbers of the public enemy, and, endangering himself for the sake of his country, raised a trophy of victory; and not even when Mithridates came with proposals of alliance and aid against his enemies would he show any sort of compliance, or even clemency; did not so much as address him, or vouchsafe him his hand, until he had it from the king's own mouth that he was willing to quit Asia, surrender the navy, and restore Bithynia and Cappadocia to the two kings. Than which action Sylla never performed a braver, or with a nobler spirit, when preferring the public good to the private, and like good hounds, where he had once fixed, never letting go his hold, till the enemy yielded then, and not until then, he set himself to revenge his own private quarrels. We may perhaps let ourselves be influenced, moreover, in our comparison of their characters, by considering their treatment of Athens. Sylla, when he had made himself master of the city, which then upheld the dominion and power of Mithridates in opposition to him, restored her to liberty and the free exercise of her own laws; Lysander, on the contrary, when she had fallen from a vast height of dignity and rule, showed her no compassion, but abolishing her democratic government, imposed on her the most cruel and lawless tyrants. We are now qualified to consider whether we should go far from the truth or no in pronouncing that Sylla performed the more glorious deeds, but Lysander committed the fewer faults, as, likewise, by giving to one the preeminence for moderation and self-control, to the other for conduct and valour.

CIMON

PERIPOLTAS THE PROPHET, HAVING BROUGHT THE KING OPHELTAS, AND those under his command, from Thessaly into Bœotia, left there a family, which flourished a long time after; the greater part of them inhabiting Chæronea, the first city out of which they expelled the barbarians. The descendants of this race, being men of bold attempts and warlike habits, exposed themselves to so many dangers in the invasions of the Mede, and in battles against the Gauls, that at last they were almost wholly consumed.

There was left one orphan of this house, called Damon, surnamed Peripoltas, in beauty and greatness of spirit surpassing all of his age, but rude and undisciplined in temper. A Roman captain of a company that wintered in Chæronea became passionately fond of this youth, who was now pretty nearly grown a man. And finding all his approaches, his gifts, his entreaties, alike repulsed, he showed violent inclinations to assault Damon. Our native Chæronea was then in a distressed condition, too small and too poor to meet with anything but neglect. Damon, being sensible of this, and looking upon himself as injured already, resolved to inflict punishment. Accordingly, he and sixteen of his companions conspired against the captain; but that the design might be managed without any danger of being discovered, they all daubed their faces at night with soot. Thus disguised and inflamed with wine, they set upon him by break of day, as he was sacrificing in the market place; and having killed him, and several others that were with him, they fled out of the city, which was extremely alarmed and troubled at the murder. The council assembled immediately, and pronounced sentence of death against Damon and his accomplices. This they did to justify the city to the Romans. But that evening, as the magistrates were at supper together, according to the custom, Damon and his confederates, breaking into the hall, killed them, and then fled again out of the town. About this time, Lucius Lucullus chanced to be passing that way with a body of troops, upon some expedition, and this disaster having but recently happened, he stayed to examine the matter. Upon inquiry, he found the city was in no wise faulty, but rather that they themselves had suffered; therefore he drew out the soldiers, and carried them away with him. Yet Damon continuing to ravage the country all about, the citizens, by messages and decrees, in appearance favourable, enticed him into the city, and upon his return, made him Gymnasiarch; but afterwards as he was anointing himself in the vapour baths, they set upon him and killed him. For a long while after apparitions continuing to be seen, and groans to be heard in that place, so our fathers have told us, they ordered the gates of the baths to be built up; and even to this day those who live in the neighbourhood believe that they sometimes see spectres and hear alarming sounds. The posterity of Damon, of whom some still remain, mostly in Phocis, near the town of Stiris, are called Asbolomeni, that is, in the Æolian idiom, men daubed with soot: because Damon was thus besmeared when he committed this murder.

But there being a quarrel between the people of Chæronea and the Orchomenians, their neighbours, these latter hired an informer, a Roman, to accuse the community of Chæronea as if it had been a single person of the murder of the Romans, of which only Damon and his companions were guilty; accordingly, the process was commenced, and the cause pleaded before the Prætor of Macedon, since the Romans as yet had not sent governors into Greece.

The advocates who defended the inhabitants appealed to the testimony of Lucullus, who, in answer to a letter the prætor wrote to him, returned a true account of the matter-of-fact. By this means the town obtained its acquittal, and escaped a most serious danger. The citizens, thus preserved, erected a statue to Lucullus in the market place, near that of the god Bacchus.

We also have the same impressions of gratitude; and though removed from the events by the distance of several generations, we yet feel the obligation to extend to ourselves: and as we think an image of the character and habits to be a greater honour than one merely representing the face and the person, we will put Lucullus' life amongst our parallels of illustrious men, and without swerving from the truth, will record his actions. The commemoration will be itself a sufficient proof of our grateful feeling, and he himself would not thank us, if in recompense for a service which consisted in speaking the truth, we should abuse his memory with a false and counterfeit narration. For as we would wish that a painter who is to draw a beautiful face, in which there is yet some imperfection, should neither wholly leave out, nor yet too pointedly express what is defective, because this would deform it, and that spoil the resemblance; so since it is hard, or indeed perhaps impossible, to show the life of a man wholly free from blemish, in all that is excellent we must follow truth exactly, and give it fully; any lapses or faults that occur, through human passions or political necessities, we may regard rather as the shortcomings of some particular virtue, than as the natural effects of vice; and may be content without introducing them, curiously and officiously, into our narrative, if it be but out of tenderness to the weakness of nature, which has never succeeded in producing any human character so perfect in virtue as to be pure from all admixture and open to no criticism. On considering with myself to whom I should compare Lucullus I find none so exactly his parallel as Cimon.

They were both valiant in war, and successful against the barbarians; both gentle in political life, and more than any others gave their countrymen a respite from civil troubles at home, while abroad each of them raised trophies and gained famous victories. No Greek before Cimon, nor Roman before Lucullus, ever carried the scene of war so far from their own country; putting out of the question the acts of Bacchus and Hercules, and any exploit of Perseus against the Ethiopians, Medes, and Armenians, or again of Jason, of which any record that deserves credit can be said to have come down to our days. Moreover in this they were alike, that they did not finish the enterprises they undertook. They brought their enemies near their ruin, but never entirely conquered them. There was yet a great conformity in the free goodwill and lavish abundance of their entertainments and general hospitalities, and in the youthful laxity of their habits. Other points of resemblance, which we have failed to notice, may be easily collected from our narrative itself.

Cimon was the son of Miltiades and Hegesipyle, who was by birth a Thracian, and daughter to the King Olorus, as appears from the poems of Melanthius and Archelaus, written in praise of Cimon. By this means the historian Thucydides was his kinsman by the mother's side; for his father's name also, in remembrance of this common ancestor, was Olorus, and he was the owner of the gold mines in Thrace, and met his death, it is said, by violence, in Scapte Hyle, a district of Thrace; and his remains having afterwards been brought into Attica, a monument is shown as his among those of the family of Cimon, near the tomb of Elpinice, Cimon's sister.

But Thucydides was of the township of Halimus, and Miltiades and his family were Laciadæ. Miltiades, being condemned in a fine of fifty talents of the state, and unable to pay it, was cast into prison, and there died. Thus Cimon was left an orphan very young, with his sister Elpinice, who was also young and unmarried. And at first he had but an indifferent reputation, being looked upon as disorderly in his habits, fond of drinking, and resembling his grandfather, also called Cimon, in character, whose simplicity got him the surname of Coalemus. Stesimbrotus of Thasos, who lived near about the same time with Cimon, reports of him that he had little acquaintance either with music, or any of the other liberal studies and accomplishments, then common among the Greeks; that he had nothing whatever of the quickness and the ready speech of his countrymen in Attica; that he had great nobleness and candour in his disposition, and in his character in general resembled rather a native of Peloponnesus than of Athens; as Euripides describes Hercules—

—Rude
And unrefined, for great things well endued:

for this may fairly be added to the character which Stesimbrotus has given of him.

They accused him, in his younger years, of cohabiting with his own sister Elpinice, who, indeed, otherwise had no very clear reputation, but was reported to have been over-intimate with Polygnotus the painter; and hence, when he painted the Trojan women in the porch, then called the Plesianactium, and now the Pœcile, he made Laodice a portrait of her. Polygnotus was not an ordinary mechanic, nor was he paid for his work, but out of a desire to please the Athenians painted the portico for nothing. So it is stated by the historians, and in the following verses by the poet Melanthius:

Wrought by his hand the deeds of heroes grace
At his own charge our temples and our place.

Some affirm that Elpinice lived with her brother, not secretly, but as his married wife, her poverty excluding her from any suitable match. But afterwards, when Callias, one of the richest men of Athens, fell in love with her, and proffered to pay the fine the father was condemned in, if he could obtain the daughter in marriage, with Elpinice's own consent, Cimon betrothed her to Callias. There is no doubt but that Cimon was, in general, of an amorous temper. For Melanthius, in his elegies, rallies him on his attachment for Asteria of Salamis, and again for a certain Mnestra. And there can be no doubt of his unusually passionate affection for his lawful wife Isodice, the daughter of Euryptolemus, the son of Megacles; nor of his regret, even to impatience, at her death, if any conclusion may be drawn from those elegies of condolence, addressed to him upon his loss of her. The philosopher Panætius is of opinion that Archelaus, the writer on physics, was the author of them, and indeed the time seems to favour that conjecture. All the other points of Cimon's character were noble and good. He was as daring as Miltiades, and not inferior to Themistocles in judgment, and was incomparably more just and honest than either of them. Fully their equal in all military virtues, in the ordinary duties of a citizen at home he was immeasurably their superior. And this, too, when he was very young, his years not yet strengthened by any experience. For when Themistocles, upon the Median invasion, advised the Athenians to forsake their city and their country, and to carry all their arms on shipboard and fight the enemy by sea, in the straits of Salamis; when all the people stood amazed at the confidence and rashness of this advice, Cimon was seen, the first of all men, passing with a cheerful countenance through the Ceramicus, on his way with his companions to the citadel, carrying a bridle in his hand to offer to the goddess, intimating that there was no more need of horsemen now, but of mariners. There, after he had paid his devotions to the goddess, and offered up the bridle, he took down one of the bucklers that hung upon the walls of the temple, and went down to the port; by this example giving confidence to many of the citizens. He was also of a fairly handsome person, according to the poet Ion, tall and large, and let his thick and curly hair grow long. After he had acquitted himself gallantly in this battle of Salamis, he obtained great repute among the Athenians, and was regarded with affection, as well as admiration. He had many who followed after him, and bade him aspire to actions not less famous than his father's battle of Marathon. And when he came forward in political life, the people welcomed him gladly, being now weary of Themistocles; in opposition to whom, and because of the frankness and easiness of his temper, which was agreeable to everyone, they advanced Cimon to the highest employments in the government. The man that contributed most to his promotion was Aristides, who early discerned in his character his natural capacity, and purposely raised him, that he might be a counterpoise to the craft and boldness of Themistocles.

After the Medes had been driven out of Greece, Cimon was sent out as an admiral, when the Athenians had not yet attained their dominion by sea, but still followed Pausanias and the Lacedæmonians; and his fellow-citizens under his command were highly distinguished, both for the excellence of their discipline, and for their extraordinary zeal and readiness. And further, perceiving that Pausanias was carrying on secret communications with the barbarians, and writing letters to the King of Persia to betray Greece, and puffed up with authority and success, was treating the allies haughtily, and committing many wanton injustices, Cimon, taking this advantage, by acts of kindness to those who were suffering wrong, and by his general humane bearing, robbed him of the command of the Greeks, before he was aware, not by arms, but by his mere language and character. The greatest part of the allies, no longer able to endure the harshness and pride of Pausanias, revolted from him to Cimon and Aristides, who accepted the duty, and wrote to the Ephors of Sparta, desiring them to recall a man who was causing dishonour to Sparta and trouble to Greece. They tell of Pausanias, that when he was in Byzantium, he solicited a young lady of a noble family in the city, whose name was Cleonice, to debauch her. Her parents, dreading his cruelty, were forced to consent, and so abandoned their daughter to his wishes. The daughter asked the servants outside the chamber to put out all the lights; so that approaching silently and in the dark towards his bed, she stumbled upon the lamp, which she overturned. Pausanias, who was fallen asleep, awakened and, startled with the noise, thought an assassin had taken that dead time of night to murder him, so that hastily snatching up his poniard that lay by him, he struck the girl, who fell with the blow, and died. After this, he never had rest, but was continually haunted by her, and saw an apparition visiting him in his sleep, and addressing him with these angry words:

> Go on thy way, unto the evil end,
> That doth on lust and violence attend.

This was one of the chief occasions of indignation against him among the confederates, who now, joining their resentments and forces with Cimon's, besieged him in Byzantium. He escaped out of their hands, and, continuing, as it is said, to be disturbed by the apparition, fled to the oracle of the dead at Heraclea, raised the ghost of Cleonice, and entreated her to be reconciled. Accordingly she appeared to him, and answered that, as soon as he came to Sparta, he should speedily be freed from all evils; obscurely foretelling, it would seem, his imminent death. This story is related by many authors.

Cimon, strengthened with the accession of the allies, went as general into Thrace. For he was told that some great men among the Persians, of the king's kindred, being in possession of Eion, a city situated upon the river Strymon, infested the neighbouring Greeks. First he defeated these Persians in battle, and shut them up within the walls of their town. Then he fell upon the Thracians of the country beyond the Strymon, because they supplied Eion with victuals, and driving them entirely out of the country, took possession of it as conqueror, by which means he reduced the besieged to such straits, that Butes, who commanded there for the king, in desperation set fire to the town, and burned himself, his goods, and all his relations, in one common flame. By this means, Cimon got the town, but no great booty; as the barbarians had not only consumed themselves in the fire, but the richest of their effects. However, he put the country about into the hands of the Athenians, a most advantageous and desirable situation for a settlement. For this action, the people permitted him to erect the stone Mercuries, upon the first of which was this inscription:

> Of bold and patient spirit, too, were those,
> Who, where the Strymon under Eion flows,
> With famine and the sword, to utmost need,
> Reduced at last the children of the Mede.

Upon the second stood this:

> The Athenians to their leaders this reward
> For great and useful service did accord;
> Others hereafter shall, from their applause,
> Learn to be valiant in their country's cause.

And upon the third the following:

> With Atreus' sons, this city sent of yore
> Divine Menestheus to the Trojan shore;
> Of all the Greeks, so Homer's verses say,
> The ablest man an army to array:
> So old the title of her sons the name
> Of chiefs and champions in the field to claim.

Though the name of Cimon is not mentioned in these inscriptions, yet his contemporaries considered them to be the very highest honours to him; as neither Miltiades nor Themistocles ever received the like. When Miltiades claimed a garland, Sochares of Decelea stood up in the midst of the assembly and opposed it, using words which, though ungracious, were received with applause by the people: "When you have gained a victory by yourself, Miltiades, then you may ask to triumph so too." What then induced them so particularly to honour Cimon? Was it that under other commanders they stood upon the defensive? But by his conduct, they not only attacked their enemies, but invaded them in their own country, and acquired new territory, becoming masters of Eion and Amphipolis, where they planted colonies, as also they did in the isle of Scyros, which Cimon had taken on the following occasion. The Dolopians were the inhabitants of this isle, a people who neglected all husbandry, and had, for many generations, been devoted to piracy; this they practised to that degree, that at last they began to plunder foreigners that brought merchandise into their ports. Some merchants of Thessaly, who had come to shore near to Ctesium, were not only spoiled of their goods, but themselves put into confinement. These men afterwards escaping from their prison, went and obtained sentence against the Scyrians in a court of Amphictyons, and when the Scyrian people declined to make public restitution, and called upon the individuals who had got the plunder to give it up, these persons, in alarm, wrote to Cimon to succour them, with his fleet, and declared themselves ready to deliver the town into his hands. Cimon, by these means, got the town, expelled the Dolopian pirates, and so opened the traffic of the Ægean sea. And, understanding that the ancient Theseus, the son of Ægeus, when he fled from Athens and took refuge in this isle, was here treacherously slain by King Lycomedes, who feared him, Cimon endeavoured to find out where he was buried. For an oracle had commanded the Athenians to bring home his ashes, and pay him all due honours as a hero; but hitherto they had not been able to learn where he was interred, as the people of Scyros dissembled the knowledge of it, and were not willing to allow a search. But now, great inquiry being made, with some difficulty he found out the tomb and carried the relics into his own galley, and with great pomp and show brought them to Athens, four hundred years, or thereabouts, after his expulsion. This act got Cimon great favour with the people, one mark of which was the judgment, afterwards so famous, upon the tragic poets. Sophocles, still a young man, had just brought forward his first plays; opinions were much divided, and the spectators had taken sides with some heat. So, to determine the case, Apsephion, who was at that time archon, would not cast lots who should be judges; but when Cimon and his brother commanders with him came into the theatre, after they had performed the usual rites to the god of the festival, he would not allow them to retire, but came forward and made them swear (being ten in all, one from each tribe) the usual oath; and so being sworn judges, he made them sit down to give sentence. The eagerness for victory grew all the warmer from the ambition to get the suffrages of such honourable judges. And the victory was at last adjudged to Sophocles, which Æschylus is said to have taken so ill, that he left Athens shortly after, and went in anger to Sicily, where he died, and was buried near the city of Gela.

Ion relates that when he was a young man, and recently come from Chios to Athens, he chanced to sup with Cimon at Laomedon's house. After supper, when they had, according to custom, poured out wine to the honour of the gods, Cimon was desired by the company to give them a song, which he did with sufficient success, and received the commendations of the company, who remarked on his superiority to Themistocles, who, on a like occasion, had declared he had never learnt to sing, nor to play, and only knew how to make a city rich and powerful. After talking of things incident to such entertainments, they entered upon the particulars of the several actions for which Cimon had been famous. And when they were mentioning the most signal, he told them they had omitted one, upon which he valued himself most for address and good contrivance. He gave this account of it. When the allies had taken a great number of the barbarians prisoners in Sestos and Byzantium, they gave him the preference to divide the booty; he accordingly put the prisoners in one lot, and the spoils of their rich attire and jewels in the other. This the allies complained of as an unequal division; but he gave them their choice to take which lot they would, for that the Athenians should be content with that which they refused. Herophytus of Samos advised them to take the ornaments for their share, and leave the slaves to the Athenians; and Cimon went away, and was much laughed at for his ridiculous division. For the allies carried away the golden bracelets, and armlets, and collars, and purple robes, and the Athenians had only the naked bodies of the captives, which they could make no advantage of, being unused to labour. But a little while after, the friends and kinsmen of the prisoners coming from Lydia and Phrygia, redeemed everyone of his relations at a high ransom; so that by this means Cimon got so much treasure that he maintained his whole fleet of galleys with the money for four months; and yet there was some left to lay up in the treasury at Athens.

Cimon now grew rich, and what he gained from the barbarians with honour, he spent yet more honourably upon the citizens. For he pulled down all the enclosures of his gardens and grounds, that strangers, and the needy of his fellow-citizens, might gather of his fruits freely. At home he kept a table, plain, but sufficient for a considerable number; to which any poor townsman had free access, and so might support himself without labour, with his whole time left free for public duties. Aristotle states, however, that this reception did not extend to all the Athenians, but only to his own fellow-townsmen, the Laciadæ. Besides this, he always went attended by two or three young companions, very well clad; and if he met with an elderly citizen in a poor habit, one of these would change clothes with the decayed citizen, which was looked upon as very nobly done. He enjoined them, likewise, to carry a considerable quantity of coin about them, which they were to convey silently into the hands of the better class of poor men, as they stood by them in the market place. This, Cratinus the poet speaks of in one of his comedies, the Archilochi—

> For I, Metrobius too, the scrivener poor,
> Of ease and comfort in my age secure
> By Greece's noblest son in life's decline,
> Cimon, the generous-hearted, the divine,
> Well-fed and feasted hoped till death to be,
> Death which, alas! Has taken him ere me.

Gorgias the Leontine gives him this character, that he got riches that he might use them, and used them that he might get honour by them. And Critias, one of the thirty tyrants, makes it, in his elegies, his wish to have—

> The Scopads' wealth, and Cimon's nobleness,
> And King Agesilaus' success.

Lichas, we know, became famous in Greece, only because on the days of the sports, when the young boys run naked, he used to entertain the strangers that came to see these diversions. But Cimon's generosity outdid all the old Athenian hospitality and good-nature. For though it is the city's just boast that their forefathers taught the rest of Greece to sow corn, and how to use springs of water, and to kindle fire, yet Cimon, by keeping open house for his fellow-citizens, and giving travellers liberty to eat the fruits which the, several seasons produced in his land, seemed to restore to the world that community of goods, which mythology says existed in the reign of Saturn. Those who object to him, that he did this to be popular and gain the applause of the vulgar, are confuted by the constant tenor of the rest of his actions, which all tended to uphold the interests of the nobility and the Spartan policy, of which he gave instances, when together with Aristides he opposed Themistocles, who was advancing the authority of the people beyond its just limits, and resisted Ephialtes, who, to please the multitude, was for abolishing the jurisdiction of the court of Areopagus. And when all of this time, except Aristides and Ephialtes, enriched themselves out of the public money, he still kept his hands clean and untainted, and to his last day never acted or spoke for his own private gain or emolument. They tell us that Rhœsaces, a Persian, who had traitorously revolted from the king his master, fled to Athens, and there, being harassed by sycophants, who were still accusing him to the people, he applied himself to Cimon for redress, and, to gain his favour, laid down in his doorway two cups, the one full of gold and the other of silver Darics. Cimon smiled and asked him whether he wished to have Cimon's hired service or his friendship. He replied, his friendship. "If so," said he, "take away these pieces, for, being your friend, when I shall have occasion for them, I will send and ask for them."

The allies of the Athenians began now to be weary of war and military service, willing to have repose, and to look after their husbandry and traffic. For they saw their enemies driven out of the country, and did not fear any new vexations from them. They still paid the tax they were assessed at, but did not send men and galleys, as they had done before. This the other Athenian generals wished to constrain them to, and by judicial proceedings against defaulters, and penalties which they inflicted on them, made the government uneasy, and even odious. But Cimon practised a contrary method; he forced no man to go that was not willing, but of those that desired to be excused from service he took money and vessels unmanned, and let them yield to the temptation of staying at home, to attend to their private business. Thus they lost their military habits and luxury, and their own folly quickly changed them into unwarlike husbandmen and traders; while Cimon, continually embarking large numbers of Athenians on board his galleys, thoroughly disciplined them in his expeditions, and ere long made them the lords of their own paymasters. The allies, whose indolence maintained them, while they thus went sailing about everywhere, and incessantly bearing arms and acquiring skill, began to fear and flatter them, and found themselves after a while allies no longer, but unwittingly become tributaries and slaves.

Nor did any man ever do more than Cimon did to humble the pride of the Persian king. He was not content with getting rid of him out of

Greece; but following close at his heels, before the barbarians could take breath and recover themselves, he was already at work, and what with his devastations, and his forcible reduction of some places, and the revolts and voluntary accession of others, in the end, from Ionia to Pamphylia, all Asia was clear of Persian soldiers. Word being brought him that the royal commanders were lying in wait upon the coast of Pamphylia with a numerous land army and a large fleet, he determined to make the whole sea on his side the Chelidonian islands so formidable to them that they should never dare to show themselves in it; and setting off from Cnidos and the Triopian headland with two hundred galleys, which had been originally built with particular care by Themistocles, for speed and rapid evolutions, and to which he now gave greater width and roomier decks along the sides to move to and fro upon, so as to allow a great number of full-armed soldiers to take part in the engagements and fight from them, he shaped his course first of all against the town of Phaselis, which though inhabited by Greeks, yet would not quit the interests of Persia, but denied his galleys entrance into their port. Upon this he wasted the country, and drew up his army to their very walls; but the soldiers of Chios, who were then serving under him, being ancient friends to the Phaselites, endeavouring to propitiate the general in their behalf, at the same time shot arrows into the town, to which were fastened letters conveying intelligence. At length he concluded peace with them, upon the conditions that they should pay down ten talents, and follow him against the barbarians. Ephorus says the admiral of the Persian fleet was Tithraustes, and the general of the land army Pherendates; but Callisthenes is positive that Ariomandes, the son of Gobryas, had the supreme command of all the forces. He lay waiting with the whole fleet at the mouth of the river Eurymedon, with no design to fight, but expecting a reinforcement of eighty Phœnician ships on their way from Cyprus. Cimon, aware of this, put out to sea, resolved, if they would not fight a battle willingly, to force them to it. The barbarians, seeing this, retired within the mouth of the river to avoid being attacked; but when they saw the Athenians come upon them, notwithstanding their retreat, they met them with six hundred ships, as Phanodemus relates, but, according to Ephorus, only with three hundred and fifty. However, they did nothing worthy such mighty forces, but immediately turned the prows of their galleys toward the shore, where those that came first threw themselves upon the land, and fled to their army drawn up thereabout, while the rest perished with their vessel or were taken. By this, one may guess at their number, for though a great many escaped out of the fight, and a great many others were sunk, yet two hundred galleys were taken by the Athenians.

When their land army drew toward the seaside, Cimon was in suspense whether he should venture to try and force his way on shore; as he should thus expose his Greeks, wearied with slaughter in the first engagement, to the swords of the barbarians, who were all fresh men, and many times their number. But seeing his men resolute, and flushed with victory, he bade them land, though they were not yet cool from their first battle. As soon as they touched ground, they set up a shout and ran upon the enemy, who stood firm and sustained the first shock with great courage, so that the fight was a hard one, and some principal men of the Athenians in rank and courage were slain. At length, though with much ado, they routed the barbarians, and killing some, took others prisoners, and plundered all their tents and pavilions, which were full of rich spoil. Cimon, like a skilled athlete at the games, having in one day carried off two victories wherein he surpassed that of Salamis by sea and that of Platæa by land, was encouraged to try for yet another success. News being brought that the Phœnician succours, in number eighty sail, had come in sight at Hydrum, he set off with all speed to find them, while they as yet had not received any certain account of the larger fleet, and were in doubt what to think; so that, thus surprised, they lost all their vessels and most of their men with them. This success of Cimon so daunted the King of Persia that he presently made that celebrated peace, by which he engaged that his armies should come no nearer the Grecian sea than the length of a horse's course, and that none of his galleys or vessels of war should appear between the Cyanean and Chelidonian isles. Callisthenes, however, says that he did not agree to any such articles, but that, upon the fear this victory gave him, he did in reality thus act, and kept off so far from Greece, that when Pericles with fifty and Ephialtes with thirty galleys cruised beyond the Chelidonian isles, they did not discover one Persian vessel. But in the collection which Craterus made of the public acts of the people, there is a draft of this treaty given. And it is told, also, that at Athens they erected the altar of Peace upon this occasion, and decreed particular honours to Callias, who was employed as ambassador to procure the treaty.

The people of Athens raised so much money from the spoils of this war, which were publicly sold, that besides other expenses, and raising the south wall of the citadel, they laid the foundation of the long walls, not, indeed, finished till at a later time, which were called the Legs. And the place where they built them being soft and marshy ground, they were forced to sink great weights of stone and rubble to secure the foundation and did all this out of the money Cimon supplied them with. It was he, likewise, who first embellished the upper city with those fine and ornamental places of exercise and resort, which they afterwards so much frequented and delighted in. He set the market place with plane-trees; and the Academy, which was before a bare, dry, and dirty spot, he converted into a well-watered grove, with shady alleys to walk in, and open courses for races.

When the Persians who had made themselves masters of the Chersonese, so far from quitting it, called in the people of the interior of Thrace to help them against Cimon, whom they despised for the smallness of his forces, he set upon them with only four galleys, and took thirteen of theirs; and having driven out the Persians, and subdued the Thracians, he made the whole Chersonese the property of Athens. Next he attacked the people of Thasos, who had revolted from the Athenians; and, having defeated them in a fight at sea, where he took thirty-three of their vessels, he took their town by siege, and acquired for the Athenians all the mines of gold on the opposite coast, and the territory dependent on Thasos. This opened him a fair passage into Macedon, so that he might, it was thought, have acquired a good portion of that country; and because he neglected the opportunity, he was suspected of corruption, and of having been bribed off by King Alexander. So, by the combination of his adversaries, he was accused of being false to his country. In his defence he told the judges that he had always shown himself in his public life the friend, not, like other men, of rich Ionians and Thessalians, to be courted, and to receive presents, but of the Lacedæmonians; for as he admired, so he wished to imitate, the plainness of their habits, their temperance, and simplicity of living, which he preferred to any sort of riches: but that he always had been, and still was, proud to enrich his country with the spoils of her enemies. Stesimbrotus, making mention of this trial, states that Elpinice, in behalf of her brother, addressed herself to Pericles, the most vehement of his accusers, to whom Pericles answered, with a smile, "You are old, Elpinice, to meddle with affairs of this nature." However, he proved the mildest of his prosecutors, and rose up but once all the while, almost as a matter of form, to plead against him. Cimon was acquitted.

In his public life after this he continued, whilst at home, to control and restrain the common people, who would have trampled upon the nobility, and drawn all the power and sovereignty to themselves. But when he afterwards was sent out to war, the multitude broke loose, as it were, and overthrew all the ancient laws and customs they had hitherto observed, and, chiefly at the instigation of Ephialtes, withdrew the cognisance of almost all causes from the Areopagus; so that all jurisdiction now being transferred to them, the government was reduced to a perfect democracy, and this by the help of Pericles, who was already powerful, and had pronounced in favour of the common people. Cimon, when he returned, seeing the authority of this great council so upset, was exceedingly troubled, and endeavoured to remedy these disorders by bringing the courts of law to their former state, and restoring the old aristocracy of the time of Clisthenes. This the others declaimed against with all the vehemence possible, and began to revive those stories concerning him and his sister, and cried out against him as the partisan of the Lacedæmonians. To these calumnies the famous verses of Eupolis the poet upon Cimon refer:

> He was as good as others that one sees,
> But he was fond of drinking and of ease;
> And would at nights to Sparta often roam,
> Leaving his sister desolate at home.

But if, though slothful and a drunkard, he could capture so many towns and gain so many victories, certainly if he had been sober and minded his business, there had been no Grecian commander, either before or after him, that could have surpassed him for exploits of war.

He was, indeed, a favourer of the Lacedæmonians, even from his youth, and he gave the names of Lacedæmonius and Eleus to two sons, twins, whom he had, as Stesimbrotus says, by a woman of Clitorium, whence Pericles often upbraided them with their mother's blood. But Diodorus the geographer asserts that both these, and another son of Cimon's, whose name was Thessalus, were born of Isodice, the daughter of Euryptolemus, the son of Megacles.

However, this is certain, that Cimon was countenanced by the Lacedæmonians in opposition to Themistocles, whom they disliked; and while he was yet very young, they endeavoured to raise and increase his credit in Athens. This the Athenians perceived at first with pleasure, and the favour the Lacedæmonians showed him was in various ways advantageous to them and their affairs, as at that time they were just rising to power, and were occupied in winning the allies to their side. So they seemed not at all offended with the honour and kindness shown to Cimon, who then had the chief management of all the affairs of Greece, and was acceptable to the Lacedæmonians, and courteous to the allies. But afterwards the Athenians, grown more powerful, when they saw

Cimon so entirely devoted to the Lacedæmonians, began to be angry, for he would always in his speeches prefer them to the Athenians, and upon every occasion, when he would reprimand them for a fault, or incite them to emulation, he would exclaim, "The Lacedæmonians would not do thus." This raised the discontent, and got him in some degree the hatred of the citizens; but that which ministered chiefly to the accusation against him fell out upon the following occasion.

In the fourth year of the reign of Archidamus, the son of Zeuxidamus, King of Sparta, there happened in the country of Lacedæmon the greatest earthquake that was known in the memory of man; the earth opened into chasms, and the mountain Taygetus was so shaken, that some of the rocky points of it fell down, and except five houses, all the town of Sparta was shattered to pieces. They say that a little before any motion was perceived, as the young men and the boys just grown up were exercising themselves together in the middle of the portico, a hare, of a sudden, started out just by them, which the young men, though all naked and daubed with oil, ran after for sport. No sooner were they gone from the place, than the gymnasium fell down upon the boys who had stayed behind, and killed them all. Their tomb is to this day called Sismatias. Archidamus, by the present danger made apprehensive of what might follow, and seeing the citizens intent upon removing the most valuable of their goods out of their houses, commanded an alarm to be sounded, as if an enemy were coming upon them, in order that they should collect about him in a body, with arms. It was this alone that saved Sparta at that time, for the Helots were got together from the country about, with design to surprise the Spartans, and overpower those whom the earthquake had spared. But finding them armed and well prepared, they retired into the towns and openly made war with them, gaining over a number of the Laconians of the country districts; while at the same time the Messenians, also, made an attack upon the Spartans, who therefore despatched Periclidas to Athens to solicit succours, of whom Aristophanes says in mockery that he came and—

> In a red jacket, at the altars seated,
> With a white face, for men and arms entreated.

This Ephialtes opposed, protesting that they ought not to raise up or assist a city that was a rival to Athens; but that being down, it were best to keep her so, and let the pride and arrogance of Sparta be trodden under. But Cimon, as Critias says, preferring the safety of Lacedæmon to the aggrandisement of his own country, so persuaded the people, that he soon marched out with a large army to their relief. Ion records, also, the most successful expression which he used to move the Athenians. "They ought not to suffer Greece to be lamed, nor their own city to be deprived of her yoke-fellow."

In his return from aiding the Lacedæmonians, he passed with his army through the territory of Corinth; whereupon Lachartus reproached him for bringing his army into the country without first asking leave of the people. For he that knocks at another man's door ought not to enter the house till the master gives him leave. "But you Corinthians, O Lachartus," said Cimon, "did not knock at the gates of the Cleonæans and Megarians, but broke them down, and entered by force, thinking that all places should be open to the stronger." And having thus rallied the Corinthian, he passed on with his army. Sometime after this, the Lacedæmonians sent a second time to desire succours of the Athenians against the Messenians and Helots, who had seized upon Ithome. But when they came, fearing their boldness and gallantry, of all that came to their assistance, they sent them only back, alleging they were designing innovations. The Athenians returned home, enraged at this usage, and vented their anger upon all those who were favourers of the Lacedæmonians, and seizing some slight occasion, they banished Cimon for ten years, which is the time prescribed to those that are banished by the ostracism. In the meantime, the Lacedæmonians, on their return after freeing Delphi from the Phocians, encamped their army at Tanagra, whither the Athenians presently marched with design to fight them.

Cimon, also, came thither armed, and ranged himself among those of his own tribe which was the Œneis, desirous of fighting with the rest against the Spartans; but the council of five hundred being informed of this, and frighted at it, his adversaries crying out he would disorder the army, and bring the Lacedæmonians to Athens, commanded the officers not to receive him. Wherefore Cimon left the army, conjuring Euthippus, the Anaphlystian, and the rest of his companions, who were most suspected as favouring the Lacedæmonians, to behave themselves bravely against their enemies, and by their actions make their innocence evident to their countrymen. These, being in all a hundred, took the arms of Cimon, and followed his advice; and making a body by themselves, fought so desperately with the enemy, that they were all cut off, leaving the Athenians deep regret for the loss of such brave men, and repentance for having so unjustly suspected them. Accordingly, they did not long retain

their severity toward Cimon, partly upon remembrance of his former services, and partly, perhaps, induced by the juncture of the times. For being
defeated at Tanagra in a great battle, and fearing the Peloponnesians
would come upon them at the opening of the spring, they recalled Cimon
by a decree, of which Pericles himself was author. So reasonable were men's
resentments in those times, and so moderate their anger, that it always gave
way to the public good. Even ambition, the least governable of all human
passions, could then yield to the necessities of the state.

Cimon, as soon as he returned, put an end to the war, and reconciled
the two cities. Peace thus established, seeing the Athenians impatient of
being idle, and eager after the honour and aggrandisement of war, lest they
should set upon the Greeks themselves, or with so many ships cruising
about the isles and Peloponnesus they should give occasions to intestine
wars, or complaints of their allies against them, he equipped two hundred
galleys, with design to make an attempt upon Egypt and Cyprus; purposing,
by this means, to accustom the Athenians to fight against the barbarians,
and enrich themselves honestly by spoiling those who were the natural enemies of Greece. But when all things were prepared, and the army ready to
embark, Cimon had this dream. It seemed to him that there was a furious
bitch barking at him, and mixed with the barking a kind of human voice
uttered these words:

> Come on; for thou shalt shortly be,
> A pleasure to my whelps and me.

This dream was hard to interpret, yet Astyphilus of Posidonia, a man
skilled in divinations, and intimate with Cimon, told him that his death
was presaged by this vision, which he thus explained. A dog is enemy to
him he barks at; and one is always most a pleasure to one's enemies when
one is dead; the mixture of human voice with barking signifies the Medes,
for the army of the Medes is mixed up of Greeks and barbarians. After this
dream, as he was sacrificing to Bacchus, and the priest cutting up the victim, a number of ants, taking up the congealed particles of the blood, laid
them about Cimon's great toe. This was not observed for a good while, but
at the very time when Cimon spied it, the priest came and showed him the
liver of the sacrifice imperfect, wanting that part of it called the head. But
he could not then recede from the enterprise, so he set sail. Sixty of his
ships he sent toward Egypt; with the rest he went and fought the King of
Persia's fleet, composed of Phœnician and Cilician galleys, recovered all
the cities thereabout, and threatened Egypt; designing no less than the

entire ruin of the Persian empire. And the rather, for that he was informed Themistocles was in great repute among the barbarians, having promised the king to lead his army, whenever he should make war upon Greece. But Themistocles, it is said, abandoning all hopes of compassing his designs, very much out of the despair of overcoming the valour and good fortune of Cimon, died a voluntary death. Cimon, intent on great designs, which he was now to enter upon, keeping his navy about the isle of Cyprus, sent messengers to consult the oracle of Jupiter Ammon upon some secret matter. For it is not known about what they were sent, and the god would give them no answer, but commanded them to return again, for that Cimon was already with him. Hearing this, they returned to sea, and as soon as they came to the Grecian army, which was then about Egypt, they understood that Cimon was dead; and computing the time of the oracle, they found that his death had been signified, he being then already with the gods.

He died, some say, of sickness, while besieging Citium, in Cyprus; according to others, of a wound he received in a skirmish with the barbarians. When he perceived he should die, he commanded those under his charge to return, and by no means to let the news of his death be known by the way; this they did with such secrecy that they all came home safe, and neither their enemies nor the allies knew what had happened. Thus, as Phanodemus relates, the Grecian army was, as it were, conducted by Cimon thirty days after he was dead. But after his death there was not one commander among the Greeks that did anything considerable against the barbarians, and instead of uniting against their common enemies, the popular leaders and partisans of war animated them against one another to that degree, that none could interpose their good offices to reconcile them. And while, by their mutual discord, they ruined the power of Greece, they gave the Persians time to recover breath, and repair all their losses. It is true, indeed, Agesilaus carried the arms of Greece into Asia, but it was a long time after; there were, indeed, some brief appearances of a war against the king's lieutenants in the maritime provinces, but they all quickly vanished; before he could perform anything of moment, he was recalled by fresh civil dissensions and disturbances at home. So that he was forced to leave the Persian king's officers to impose what tribute they pleased on the Greek cities in Asia, the confederates and allies of the Lacedæmonians. Whereas, in the time of Cimon, not so much as a letter-carrier, or a single horseman, was ever seen to come within four hundred furlongs of the sea.

The monuments, called Cimonian to this day, in Athens, show that his remains were conveyed home, yet the inhabitants of the city Citium pay particular honour to a certain tomb which they call the tomb of Cimon, according to Nausicrates the rhetorician, who states that in a time of famine, when the crops of their land all failed, they sent to the oracle, which commanded them not to forget Cimon, but give him the honours of a superior being. Such was the Greek commander.

LUCULLUS

THE GRANDFATHER OF LUCULLUS HAD BEEN CONSUL; HIS UNCLE BY THE mother's side was Metellus, surnamed Numidicus. As for his parents, his father was convicted of extortion, and his mother Cæcilia's reputation was bad. The first thing that Lucullus did before ever he stood for any office, or meddled with the affairs of state, being then but a youth, was to accuse the accuser of his father, Servilius the augur, having caught him in offence against the state. This thing was much taken notice of among the Romans, who commended it as an act of high merit. Even without the provocation the accusation was esteemed no unbecoming action, for they delighted to see young men as eagerly attacking injustice as good dogs do wild beasts. But when great animosities ensued, insomuch that some were wounded and killed in the fray, Servilius escaped. Lucullus followed his studies and became a competent speaker, in both Greek and Latin, insomuch that Sylla, when composing the commentaries of his own life and actions, dedicated them to him, as one who could have performed the task better himself. His speech was not only elegant and ready for purposes of mere business, like the ordinary oratory which will in the public market place—

Lash as a wounded tunny does the sea,

but on every other occasion shows itself—

Dried up and perished with the want of wit;

but even in his younger days he addicted himself to the study, simply for its own sake, of the liberal arts; and when advanced in years, after a life of conflicts, he gave his mind, as it were, its liberty, to enjoy in full leisure the refreshment of philosophy; and summoning up his contemplative faculties,

administered a timely check, after his difference with Pompey, to his feelings of emulation and ambition. Besides what has been said of his love of
learning already, one instance more was, that in his youth, upon a suggestion of writing the Marsian war in Greek and Latin verse and prose, arising
out of some pleasantry that passed into a serious proposal, he agreed with
Hortensius the lawyer and Sisenna the historian, that he would take his lot;
and it seems that the lot directed him to the Greek tongue, for a Greek history of that war is still extant.

Among the many signs of the great love which he bore to his brother
Marcus, one in particular is commemorated by the Romans. Though he
was elder brother, he would not step into authority without him, but
deferred his own advance until his brother was qualified to bear a share
with him, and so won upon the people as, when absent, to be chosen
Ædile with him.

He gave many and early proofs of his valour and conduct in the
Marsian war, and was admired by Sylla for his constancy and mildness, and
always employed in affairs of importance, especially in the mint; most of
the money for carrying on the Mithridatic war being coined by him in
Peloponnesus, which, by the soldiers' wants, was brought into rapid circulation and long continued current under the name of Lucullean coin.
After this, when Sylla conquered Athens, and was victorious by land but
found the supplies for his army cut off, the enemy being master at sea,
Lucullus was the man whom he sent into Libya and Egypt to procure him
shipping. It was the depth of winter when he ventured with but three small
Greek vessels, and as many Rhodian galleys, not only into the main sea,
but also among multitudes of vessels belonging to the enemies who were
cruising about as absolute masters. Arriving at Crete he gained it, and
finding the Cyrenians harassed by long tyrannies and wars, he composed
their troubles, and settled their government; putting the city in mind of
that saying which Plato once had oracularly uttered of them, who, being
requested to prescribe laws to them, and mould them into some sound
form of government, made answer that it was a hard thing to give laws to
the Cyrenians, abounding, as they did, in wealth and plenty. For nothing
is more intractable than man when in felicity, nor anything more docile,
when he has been reduced and humbled by fortune. This made the
Cyrenians so willingly submit to the laws which Lucullus imposed upon
them. From thence sailing into Egypt, and pressed by pirates, he lost most
of his vessels; but he himself narrowly escaping, made a magnificent entry
into Alexandria. The whole fleet, a compliment due only to royalty, met

him in full array, and the young Ptolemy showed wonderful kindness to him, appointing him lodging and diet in the palace, where no foreign commander before him had been received. Besides, he gave him gratuities and presents, not such as were usually given to men of his condition, but four times as much; of which, however, he took nothing more than served his necessity and accepted of no gift, though what was worth eighty talents was offered him. It is reported he neither went to see Memphis, nor any of the celebrated wonders of Egypt. It was for a man of no business and much curiosity to see such things, not for him who had left his commander in the field lodging under the ramparts of his enemies.

Ptolemy, fearing the issue of that war, deserted the confederacy, but nevertheless sent a convoy with him as far as Cyprus, and at parting, with much ceremony, wishing him a good voyage, gave him a very precious emerald set in gold. Lucullus at first refused it, but when the king showed him his own likeness cut upon it, he thought he could not persist in a denial, for had he parted with such open offence, it might have endangered his passage. Drawing a considerable squadron together, which he summoned as he sailed by out of all the maritime towns except those suspected of piracy, he sailed for Cyprus, and there understanding that the enemy lay in wait under the promontories for him, he laid up his fleet, and sent to the cities to send in provisions for his wintering among them. But when time served, he launched his ships suddenly, and went off, and hoisting all his sails in the night, while he kept them down in the day, thus came safe to Rhodes. Being furnished with ships at Rhodes, he also prevailed upon the inhabitants of Cos and Cnidus to leave the king's side, and join in an expedition against the Samians. Out of Chios he himself drove the king's party, and set the Colophonians at liberty, having seized Epigonus the tyrant, who oppressed them.

About this time Mithridates left Pergamus, and retired to Pitane, where being closely besieged by Fimbria on the land, and not daring to engage with so bold and victorious a commander, he was concerting means for escape by sea, and sent for all his fleets from every quarter to attend him. Which when Fimbria perceived, having no ships of his own, he sent to Lucullus, entreating him to assist him with his, in subduing the most odious and warlike of kings, lest the opportunity of humbling Mithridates, the prize which the Romans had pursued with so much blood and trouble, should now at last be lost, when he was within the net and easily to be taken. And were he caught, no one would be more highly commended than Lucullus, who stopped his passage and seized him in his flight. Being driven from the land by the one, and met in the sea by the other, he would give matter of renown and glory to them both, and the much applauded actions of Sylla at Orchomenus and about Chæronea would no longer be thought of by the Romans. The proposal was no unreasonable thing; it being obvious to all men, that if Lucullus had hearkened to Fimbria, and with his navy, which was then near at hand, had blocked up the haven, the war soon had been brought to an end, and infinite numbers of mischiefs prevented thereby. But he, whether from the sacredness of friendship between himself and Sylla, reckoning all other considerations of public or of private advantage inferior to it, or out of detestation of the wickedness of Fimbria, whom he abhorred for advancing himself by the late death of his friend and the general of the army, or by a divine fortune sparing Mithridates then, that he might have him an adversary for a time to come, for whatever reason, refused to comply, and suffered Mithridates to escape and laugh at the attempts of Fimbria. He himself alone first, near Lectum, in Troas, in a sea-fight, overcame the king's ships; and afterwards, discovering Neoptolemus lying in wait for him near Tenedos, with a greater fleet, he went aboard a Rhodian quinquereme galley, commanded by Damagoras, a man of great experience at sea, and friendly to the Romans, and sailed before the rest. Neoptolemus made up furiously at him, and commanded the master, with all imaginable might, to charge; but Damagoras, fearing the bulk and massy stem of the admiral, thought it dangerous to meet him prow to prow, and, rapidly wheeling round, bid his men backwater, and so received him astern; in which place, though violently borne upon, he received no manner of harm, the blow being defeated by falling on those parts of the ship which lay under water. By which time, the rest of the fleet coming up to him, Lucullus gave order to turn again, and vigorously falling upon the enemy, put them to flight, and pursued Neoptolemus. After this he came to Sylla, in Chersonesus, as he was preparing to pass the strait, and brought timely assistance for the safe transportation of the army.

Peace being presently made, Mithridates sailed off to the Euxine sea, but Sylla taxed the inhabitants of Asia twenty thousand talents, and ordered Lucullus to gather and coin the money. And it was no small comfort to the cities under Sylla's severity, that a man of not only incorrupt and just behaviour, but also of moderation, should be employed in so heavy and odious an office. The Mitylenæans, who absolutely revolted, he was willing should return to their duty, and submit to a moderate penalty for the offence they had given in the case of Marius. But finding them bent upon their own destruction, he came up to them, defeated them at sea, blocked them up in their city and besieged them; then sailing off from them openly in the day to Elæa, he returned privately, and posting an ambush near the city, lay quiet himself. And on the Mitylenæans coming out eagerly and in disorder to plunder the deserted camp, he fell upon them, took many of them, and slew five hundred, who stood upon their defence. He gained six thousand slaves and a very rich booty.

He was no way engaged in the great and general troubles of Italy which Sylla and Marius created, a happy providence at that time detaining him in Asia upon business. He was as much in Sylla's favour, however, as any of his other friends; Sylla, as was said before, dedicated his Memoirs to him as a token of kindness, and at his death, passing by Pompey, made him guardian to his son; which seems, indeed, to have been the rise of the quarrel and jealousy between them two, being both young men, and passionate for honour.

A little after Sylla's death, he was made consul with Marcus Cotta, about the one hundred and seventy-sixth Olympiad. The Mithridatic war being then under debate, Marcus declared that it was not finished, but only respited for a time, and therefore, upon choice of provinces, the lot falling to Lucullus to have Gaul within the Alps, a province where no great action was to be done, he was ill-pleased. But chiefly, the success of Pompey in Spain fretted him, as, with the renown he got there, if the Spanish war were finished in time, he was likely to be chosen general before anyone else against Mithridates. So that when Pompey sent for money, and signified by letter that, unless it were sent him, he would leave the country and Sertorius, and bring his forces home to Italy, Lucullus most zealously supported his request, to prevent any pretence of his returning home during his own consulship; for all things would have been at his disposal, at the head of so great an army. For Cethegus, the most influential popular leader at that time, owing to his always both acting and speaking to please the people, had, as it happened, a hatred to Lucullus, who had not concealed his disgust at his debauched, insolent, and lawless life. Lucullus, therefore, was at open warfare with him. And Lucius Quintius, also, another demagogue, who was taking steps against Sylla's constitution, and endeavouring to put things out of order, by private exhortations and public admonitions he checked in his designs, and repressed his ambition, wisely and safely remedying a great evil at the very outset.

At this time news came that Octavius, the governor of Cilicia, was dead, and many were eager for the place, courting Cethegus, as the man best able to serve them. Lucullus set little value upon Cilicia itself, no otherwise than as he thought, by his acceptance of it, no other man besides himself might be employed in the war against Mithridates, by reason of its nearness to Cappadocia. This made him strain every effort that that province might be allotted to himself, and to none other; which led him at last into an expedient not so honest or commendable, as it was serviceable for compassing his design, submitting to necessity against his own inclination. There was one Præcia, a celebrated wit and beauty, but in other respects nothing better than an ordinary harlot; who, however, to the charms of her person adding the reputation of one that loved and served her friends, by making use of those who visited her to assist their designs and promote their interests, had thus gained great power. She had seduced Cethegus, the first man at that time in reputation and authority of all the city, and enticed him to her love, and so had made all authority follow her. For nothing of moment was done in which Cethegus was not concerned, and nothing by Cethegus without Præcia. This woman Lucullus gained to his side by gifts and flattery (and a great price it was in itself to so stately and magnificent a dame, to be seen engaged in the same cause with Lucullus), and thus he presently found Cethegus his friend, using his utmost interest to procure Cilicia for him; which when once obtained, there was no more need of applying himself either of Præcia or Cethegus; for all unanimously voted him to the Mithridatic war, by no hands likely to be so successfully managed as his. Pompey was still contending with Sertorius, and Metellus by age unfit for service; which two alone were the competitors who could prefer any claim with Lucullus for that command. Cotta, his colleague, after much ado in the senate, was sent away with a fleet to guard the Propontis, and defend Bithynia.

Lucullus carried with him a legion under his own orders, and crossed over into Asia and took the command of the forces there, composed of men who were all thoroughly disabled by dissoluteness and rapine, and the Fimbrians, as they were called, utterly unmanageable by long want of any sort of discipline. For these were they who under Fimbria had slain Flaccus, the consul and general, and afterwards betrayed Fimbria to Sylla; a wilful and lawless set of men, but warlike, expert and hardy in the field. Lucullus in a short time took down the courage of these, and disciplined the others, who then first, in all probability, knew what a true commander and governor was; whereas in former times they had been courted to service, and took up arms at nobody's command, but their own wills.

The enemy's provisions for war stood thus: Mithridates, like the Sophists, boastful and haughty at first, set upon the Romans, with a very inefficient army, such, indeed, as made a good show, but was nothing for use; but being shamefully routed, and taught a lesson for a second engagement, he reduced his forces to a proper, serviceable shape. Dispensing with the mixed multitudes, and the noisy menaces of barbarous tribes of various languages, and with the ornaments of gold and precious stones, a greater temptation to the victors than security to the bearers, he gave his men broad swords like the Romans', and massy shields; chose horses better for service than show, drew up an hundred and twenty thousand foot in the figure of the Roman phalanx, and had sixteen thousand horse, besides chariots armed with scythes, no less than a hundred. Besides which, he set out a fleet not at all cumbered with gilded cabins, luxurious baths, and women's furniture, but stored with weapons and darts, and other necessaries, and thus made a descent upon Bithynia. Not only did these parts willingly receive him again, but almost all Asia regarded him as their salvation from the intolerable miseries which they were suffering from the Roman money-lenders and revenue farmers. These, afterwards, who like harpies stole away their very nourishment, Lucullus drove away, and at this time, by reproving them, did what he could to make them more moderate, and to prevent a general secession, then breaking out in all parts. While Lucullus was detained in rectifying these matters, Cotta, finding affairs ripe for action, prepared for battle with Mithridates; and news coming from all hands that Lucullus had already entered Phrygia, on his march against the enemy, he, thinking he had a triumph all but actually in his hands, lest his colleague should share in the glory of it, hasted to battle without him. But being routed, both by sea and land, he lost sixty ships with their men, and four thousand foot, and himself was forced into and besieged in Chalcedon, there waiting for relief from Lucullus. There were those about Lucullus who would have had him leave Cotta, and go forward, in hope of surprising the defenceless kingdom of Mithridates. And this was the feeling of the soldiers in general, who were indignant that Cotta should by his ill-counsel not only lose his own army, but hinder them also from conquest, which at that time, without the hazard of a battle, they might have obtained. But Lucullus, in a public address, declared to them that he would rather save one citizen from the enemy, than be master of all that they had.

Archelaus, the former commander in Bœotia under Mithridates, who afterwards deserted him and accompanied the Romans, protested to

Lucullus that, upon his bare coming, he would possess himself of all Pontus. But he answered, that it did not become him to be more cowardly than huntsmen, to leave the wild beasts abroad and seek after sport in their deserted dens. Having so said, he made towards Mithridates with thirty thousand foot and two thousand five hundred horse. But on being come in sight of his enemies, he was astonished at their numbers, and thought to forbear fighting, and wear out time. But Marius, whom Sertorius had sent out of Spain to Mithridates with forces under him, stepping out and challenging him, he prepared for battle. In the very instant before joining battle, without any perceptible alteration preceding, on a sudden the sky opened, and a large luminous body fell down in the midst between the armies, in shape like a hogshead, but in colour like melted silver, insomuch that both armies in alarm withdrew. This wonderful prodigy happened in Phrygia, near Otryæ. Lucullus after this began to think with himself that no human power and wealth could suffice to sustain such great numbers as Mithridates had for any long time in the face of an enemy, and commanded one of the captives to be brought before him, and first of all asked him how many companions had been quartered with him and how much provision he had left behind him, and when he had answered him, commanded him to stand aside; then asked a second and a third the same question; after which, comparing the quantity of provision with the men, he found that in three or four days' time his enemies would be brought to want. This all the more determined him to trust to time, and he took measures to store his camp with all sorts of provision, and thus living in plenty, trusted to watch the necessities of his hungry enemy.

This made Mithridates set out against the Cyzicenians, miserably shattered in the fight at Chalcedon, where they lost no less than three thousand citizens and ten ships. And that he might the safer steal away unobserved by Lucullus, immediately after supper, by the help of a dark and wet night, he went off, and by the morning gained the neighbourhood of the city, and sat down with his forces upon the Adrastean mount. Lucullus, on finding him gone, pursued, but was well pleased not to overtake him with his own forces in disorder; and he sat down near what is called the Thracian village, an admirable position for commanding all the roads and the places whence, and through which, the provisions for Mithridates' camp must of necessity come. And judging now of the event, he no longer kept his mind from his soldiers, but when the camp was fortified and their work finished, called them together, and with great assurance told them that in a few days, without the expense of blood, he would give them victory.

Mithridates besieged the Cyzicenians with ten camps by land, and with his ships occupied the strait that was betwixt their city and the mainland and so blocked them up on all sides; they, however, were fully prepared stoutly to receive him, and resolved to endure the utmost extremity, rather than forsake the Romans. That which troubled them most was, that they knew not where Lucullus was, and heard nothing of him, though at that time his army was visible before them. But they were imposed upon by the Mithridatians, who, showing them the Romans encamped on the hills, said, "Do you see those? Those are the auxiliary Armenians and Medes, whom Tigranes has sent to Mithridates." They were thus overwhelmed with thinking of the vast numbers round them, and could not believe any way of relief was left them, even if Lucullus should come up to their assistance. Demonax, a messenger sent in by Archelaus, was the first who told them of Lucullus' arrival; but they disbelieved his report, and thought he came with a story invented merely to encourage them. At which time it happened that a boy, a prisoner who had run away from the enemy, was brought before them; who, being asked where Lucullus was, laughed at their jesting, as he thought, but, finding them in earnest, with his finger pointed to the Roman camp; upon which they took courage. The lake Dascylitis was navigated with vessels of some little size; one, the biggest of them, Lucullus drew ashore, and carrying her across in a wagon to the sea, filled her with soldiers, who, sailing along unseen in the dead of the night, came safe into the city.

The gods themselves, too, in admiration of the constancy of the Cyzicenians, seem to have animated them with manifest signs, more especially now in the festival of Proserpine, where a black heifer being wanting for sacrifice, they supplied it by a figure made of dough, which they set before the altar. But the holy heifer set apart for the goddess, and at that time grazing with the other herds of the Cyzicenians, on the other side of the strait, left the herd and swam over to the city alone, and offered herself for sacrifice. By night, also, the goddess appearing to Aristagoras, the town clerk, "I am come," said she, "and have brought the Libyan piper against the Pontic trumpeter; bid the citizens, therefore, be of good courage." While the Cyzicenians were wondering what the words could mean, a sudden wind sprung up and caused a considerable motion on the sea. The king's battering engines, the wonderful contrivance of Niconides of Thessaly, then under the walls, by their cracking and rattling soon demonstrated what would follow; after which an extraordinarily tempestuous south wind succeeding shattered, in a short space of time, all the rest of the works, and, by a violent concussion, threw down the wooden tower a hundred cubits high. It is said that in Ilium Minerva appeared to many that night in their sleep, with the sweat running down her person, and showed them her robe torn in one place, telling them that she had just arrived from relieving the Cyzicenians; and the inhabitants to this day show a monument, with an inscription, including a public decree, referring to the fact.

Mithridates, through the knavery of his officers, not knowing for sometime the want of provision in his camp, was troubled in mind that the Cyzicenians should hold out against him. But his ambition and anger fell, when he saw his soldiers in the extremity of want, and feeding on men's flesh; as, in truth, Lucullus was not carrying on the war as mere matter of show and stage play, but, according to the proverb, made the seat of war in the belly, and did everything to cut off their supplies of food. Mithridates, therefore, took advantage of the time while Lucullus was storming a fort, and sent away almost all his horse to Bithynia, with the sumpter cattle, and as many of the foot as were unfit for service. On intelligence of which, Lucullus, while it was yet night, came to his camp, and in the morning, though it was stormy weather, took with him ten cohorts of foot, and the horse, and pursued them under falling snow and in cold so severe that many of his soldiers were unable to proceed; and with the rest coming upon the enemy, near the river Rhyndacus, he overthrew them with so great a slaughter that the very women of Apollonia came out to seize on the booty and strip the slain. Great numbers, as we may suppose, were slain; six thousand horses were taken, with an infinite number of beasts of burden, and no less than fifteen thousand men. All which he led along by the enemy's camp. I cannot but wonder on this occasion at Sallust, who says that this was the first time camels were seen by the Romans, as if he thought those who, long before, under Scipio defeated Antiochus, or those who lately had fought against Archelaus near Orchomenus and Chæronea, had not known what a camel was. Mithridates himself, fully determined upon flight, as mere delays and diversions for Lucullus, sent his admiral Aristonicus to the Greek sea; who, however, was betrayed in the very instant of going off, and Lucullus became master of him, and ten thousand pieces of gold which he was carrying with him to corrupt some of the Roman army. After which, Mithridates himself made for the sea, leaving the foot officers to conduct the army, upon whom Lucullus fell, near the river Granicus, where he took a vast number alive, and slew twenty thousand. It is reported that the total number killed, of fighting men and of others who followed the camp, amounted to something not far short of three hundred thousand.

Lucullus first went to Cyzicus, where he was received with all the joy and gratitude suiting the occasion, and then collected a navy, visiting the shores of the Hellespont. And arriving at Troas, he lodged in the temple of Venus, where, in the night, he thought he saw the goddess coming to him, and saying—

Sleep'st thou, great lion, when the fawns are nigh?

Rising up hereupon, he called his friends to him, it being yet night, and told them his vision; at which instant some Ilians came up and acquainted him that thirteen of the king's quinqueremes were seen off the Achæan harbour, sailing for Lemnos. He at once put to sea, took these, and slew their admiral Isidorus. And then he made after another squadron, who were just come into port, and were hauling their vessels ashore, but fought from the decks, and sorely galled Lucullus' men; there being neither room to sail round them, nor to bear upon them for any damage, his ships being afloat, while their stood secure and fixed on the sand. After much ado, at the only landing-place of the island, he disembarked the choicest of his men, who, falling upon the enemy behind, killed some, and forced others to cut their cables, and thus making from the shore, they fell foul upon one another, or came within the reach of Lucullus' fleet. Many were killed in the action. Among the captives was Marius, the commander sent by Sertorius, who had but one eye. And it was Lucullus' strict command to his men before the engagement, that they should kill no man who had but one eye, that he might rather die under disgrace and reproach.

This being over, he hastened his pursuit after Mithridates, whom he hoped to still find in Bithynia, intercepted by Voconius, whom he sent out before to Nicomedia with part of the fleet to stop his flight. But Voconius, loitering in Samothrace to get initiated and celebrate a feast, let slip his opportunity, Mithridates being passed by with all his fleet. He, hastening into Pontus before Lucullus should come up to him, was caught in a storm, which dispersed his fleet and sunk several ships. The wrecks floated on all the neighbouring shore for many days after. The merchant ship, in which he himself was, could not well in that heavy swell be brought ashore by the masters for its bigness, and it being heavy with water and ready to sink, he left it and went aboard a pirate vessel, delivering himself into the hands of pirates, and thus unexpectedly and wonderfully came safe to Heraclea, in Pontus.

Thus the proud language Lucullus had used to the senate ended without any mischance. For they having decreed him three thousand talents to furnish out a navy, he himself was against it, and sent them word that without any such great and costly supplies, by the confederate shipping alone, he did not in the least doubt but to rout Mithridates from the sea. And so he did, by divine assistance, for it is said that the wrath of Diana of Priapus brought the great tempest upon the men of Pontus, because they had robbed her temple and removed her image.

Many were persuading Lucullus to defer the war, but he rejected their counsel, and marched through Bithynia and Galatia into the king's country, in such great scarcity of provision at first, that thirty thousand Galatians followed, every man carrying a bushel of wheat at his back. But subduing all in his progress before him, he at last found himself in such great plenty that an ox was sold in the camp for a single drachma, and a slave for four. The other booty they made no account of, but left it behind or destroyed it; there being no disposing of it, where all had such abundance. But when they had made frequent incursions with their cavalry, and had advanced as far as Themiscyra, and the plains of the Thermodon, merely laying waste the country before them, they began to find fault with Lucullus, asking "why he took so many towns by surrender, and never one by storm, which might enrich them with the plunder? And now, forsooth, leaving Amisus behind, a rich and wealthy city, of easy conquest, if closely besieged, he will carry us into the Tiberenian and Chaldean wilderness, to fight with Mithridates." Lucullus, little thinking this would be of such dangerous consequence as it afterwards proved, took no notice and slighted it; and was rather anxious to excuse himself to those who blamed his tardiness, in losing time about small, pitiful places not worth the while, and allowing Mithridates opportunity to recruit. "That is what I design," said he, "and sit here contriving by my delay, that he may grow great again, and gather a considerable army, which may induce him to stand, and not fly away before us. For do you not see the wide and unknown wilderness behind? Caucasus is not far off, and a multitude of vast mountains, enough to conceal ten thousand kings that wished to avoid a battle. Besides this, a journey but of few days leads from Cabira to Armenia, where Tigranes reigns, king of kings, and holds in his hands a power that has enabled him to keep the Parthians in narrow bounds, to remove Greek cities bodily into Media, to conquer Syria and Palestine, to put to death the kings of the royal line of Seleucus, and carry away their wives and daughters by violence. This same is relation and son-in-law to

Mithridates, and cannot but receive him upon entreaty, and enter into war with us to defend him; so that, while we endeavour to dispose Mithridates, we shall endanger the bringing in of Tigranes against us, who already has sought occasion to fall out with us, but can never find one so justifiable as the succour of a friend and prince in his necessity. Why, therefore, should we put Mithridates upon this resource, who as yet does not see how he may best fight with us, and disdains to stoop to Tigranes; and not rather allow him time to gather a new army and grow confident again, that we may thus fight with Colchians and Tibarenians, whom we have often defeated already, and not with Medes and Armenians."

Upon these motives, Lucullus sat down before Amisus, and slowly carried on the siege. But the winter being well spent, he left Murena in charge of it, and went himself against Mithridates, then rendezvousing at Cabira, and resolving to await the Romans, with forty thousand foot about him, and fourteen thousand horse, on whom he chiefly confided. Passing the river Lycus, he challenged the Romans into the plains, where the cavalry engaged, and the Romans were beaten. Pomponius, a man of some note, was taken wounded; and sore, and in pain as he was, was carried before Mithridates, and asked by the king if he would become his friend if he saved his life. He answered, "Yes, if you become reconciled to the Romans; if not, your enemy." Mithridates wondered at him, and did him no hurt. The enemy being with their cavalry master of the plains, Lucullus was something afraid, and hesitated to enter the mountains, being very large, woody, and almost inaccessible, when by good luck, some Greeks who had fled into a cave were taken, the eldest of whom, Artemidorus by name, promised to bring Lucullus, and seat him in a place of safety for his army, where there was a fort that overlooked Cabira. Lucullus, believing him, lighted his fires, and marched in the night, and safely passing the defile, gained the place, and in the morning was seen above the enemy, pitching his camp in a place advantageous to descend upon them if he desired to fight, and secure from being forced if he preferred to lie still. Neither side was willing to engage at present. But it is related that some of the king's party were hunting a stag, and some Romans wanting to cut them off, came out and met them. Whereupon they skirmished, more still drawing together to each side, and at last the king's party prevailed, on which the Romans, from their camp seeing their companions fly, were enraged, and ran to Lucullus with entreaties to lead them out, demanding that the sign might be given for battle. But he, that they might know of what consequence the presence and appearance of a wise commander is in time of conflict and danger, ordered them to stand still. But he went down himself into the plains, and meeting with the foremost that fled, commanded them to stand and turn back with him. These obeying, the rest also turned and formed again in a body, and thus, with no great difficulty, drove back the enemies, and pursued them to their camp. After his return, Lucullus inflicted the customary punishment upon the fugitives, and made them dig a trench of twelve foot, working in their frocks unfastened, while the rest stood by and looked on.

There was in Mithridates' camp one Olthacus, a chief of the Dandarians, a barbarous people living near the lake Mæotis, a man remarkable for strength and courage in fight, wise in council, and pleasant and ingratiating in conversation. He, out of emulation, and a constant eagerness which possessed him to outdo one of the other chiefs of his country, promised a great piece of service to Mithridates, no less than the death of Lucullus. The king commended his resolution, and, according to agreement, counterfeited anger, and put some disgrace upon him; whereupon he took horse, and fled to Lucullus, who kindly received him, being a man of great name in the army. After some short trial of his sagacity and perseverance, he found way to Lucullus' board and council. The Dandarian, thinking he had a fair opportunity, commanded his servants to lead his horse out of the camp, while he himself, as the soldiers were refreshing and resting themselves, it being then high noon, went to the general's tent, not at all expecting that entrance would be denied to one who was so familiar with him, and came under pretence of extraordinary business with him. He had certainly been admitted had not sleep, which has destroyed many captains, saved Lucullus. For so it was, and Menedemus, one of the bedchamber, was standing at the door, who told Olthacus that it was altogether unseasonable to see the general, since, after long watching and hard labour, he was but just before laid down to repose himself. Olthacus would not go away upon this denial, but still persisted, saying that he must go in to speak of some necessary affairs, whereupon Menedemus grew angry, and replied that nothing was more necessary than the safety of Lucullus, and forced him away with both hands. Upon which, out of fear, he straightway left the camp, took horse, and without effect returned to Mithridates. Thus in action as in physic, it is the critical moment that gives both the fortunate and the fatal effect.

After this, Sornatius being sent out with ten companies for forage, and pursued by Menander, one of Mithridates' captains, stood his ground, and after a sharp engagement, routed and slew a considerable number of the enemy. Adrianus being sent afterward, with some forces, to procure food enough and to spare for the camp, Mithridates did not let the opportunity slip, but despatched Menemachus and Myro, with a great force, both horse and foot, against him, all which except two men, it is stated, were cut off by the Romans. Mithridates concealed the loss, giving it out that it was a small defeat, nothing near so great as reported, and occasioned by the unskilfulness of the leaders. But Adrianus in great pomp passed by his camp, having many wagons full of corn and other booty, filling Mithridates with distress, and the army with confusion and consternation. It was resolved, therefore, to stay no longer. But when the king's servants sent away their own goods quietly, and hindered others from doing so too, the soldiers in great fury thronged and crowded to the gates, seized on the king's servants and killed them, and plundered the baggage. Dorylaus, the general, in this confusion, having nothing else besides his purple cloak, lost his life for that, and Hermæus the priest was trod underfoot in the gate.

Mithridates, having not one of his guards, nor even a groom remaining with him, got out of the camp in the throng, but had none of his horses with him; until Ptolemy, the eunuch, some little time after, seeing him in the press making his way among the others, dismounted and gave his horse to the king. The Romans were already close upon him in their pursuit, nor was it through want of speed that they failed to catch him, but they were as near as possible doing so. But greediness and a petty military avarice hindered them from acquiring that booty which in so many fights and hazards they had sought after, and lost Lucullus the prize of his victory. For the horse which carried the king was within reach, but one of the mules that carried the treasure either by accident stepping in, or by order of the king so appointed to go between him and the pursuers, they seized and pilfered the gold, and falling out among themselves about the prey, let slip the great prize. Neither was their greediness prejudicial to Lucullus in this only, but also they slew Callistratus, the king's confidential attendant, under suspicion of having five hundred pieces of gold in his girdle; whereas Lucullus had specially ordered that he should be conveyed safe into the camp. Notwithstanding all which, he gave them leave to plunder the camp.

After this, in Cabira, and other strongholds which he took, he found great treasures, and private prisons, in which many Greeks and many of the king's relations had been confined, who, having long since counted themselves no other than dead men, by the favour of Lucullus met not with relief so truly as with a new life and second birth. Nyssa, also, sister of Mithridates, enjoyed the like fortunate captivity; while those who seemed to be most out of danger, his wives and sisters at Phernacia, placed in safety as they thought, miserably perished, Mithridates in his flight sending Bacchides the eunuch to them. Among others there were two sisters of the king, Roxana and Statira, unmarried women forty years old, and two Ionian wives, Berenice of Chios and Monime of Biletus. This latter was the most celebrated among the Greeks, because she so long withstood the king in his courtship to her, though he presented her with fifteen thousand pieces of gold, until a covenant of marriage was made, and a crown was sent her, and she was saluted queen. She had been a sorrowful woman before, and often bewailed her beauty, that had procured her a keeper, instead of a husband, and a watch of barbarians, instead of the home and attendance of a wife; and, removed far from Greece, she enjoyed the pleasure which she proposed to herself only in a dream, being in the meantime robbed of that which is real. And when Bacchides came and bade them prepare for death, as everyone thought most easy and painless, she took the diadem from her head, and fastening the string to her neck, suspended herself with it; which soon breaking, "O wretched headband!" said she, "not able to help me even in this small thing!" And throwing it away she spat on it, and offered her throat to Bacchides. Berenice had prepared a potion for herself, but at her mother's entreaty, who stood by, she gave her part of it. Both drank the potion, which prevailed over the weaker body. But Berenice, having drunk too little, was not released by it, but lingering on unable to die, was strangled by Bacchides for haste. It is said that one of the unmarried sisters drank the poison, with bitter execrations and curses; but Statira uttered nothing ungentle or reproachful, but, on the contrary, commended her brother, who in his own danger neglected not theirs, but carefully provided that they might go out of the world without shame or disgrace.

Lucullus, being a good and humane man, was concerned at these tilings. However, going on, he came to Talaura, from whence four days before his arrival Mithridates had fled, and was got to Tigranes in Armenia. He turned off, therefore, and subdued the Chaldeans and Tibarenians, with the lesser Armenia, and having reduced all their forts and cities, he sent Appius to Tigranes to demand Mithridates. He himself went to Amisus, which still held out under the command of Callimachus, who, by his great engineering skill, and his dexterity at all the shifts and subtleties of a siege, had greatly incommoded the Romans. For which afterward he paid dear enough, and was now outmanœuvred by Lucullus, who, unexpectedly coming upon him at the time of the day when the soldiers used to withdraw and rest themselves, gained part of the wall, and forced him to leave the city, in doing which he fired it; either envying the Romans the booty, or to secure his own escape the better. No man looked after those who went off in the ships, but as soon as the fire had seized on most part of the wall, the soldiers prepared themselves for plunder; while Lucullus, pitying the ruin of the city, brought assistance from without, and encouraged his men to extinguish the flames. But all, being intent upon the prey, and giving no heed to him, with loud outcries, beat and dashed their arms together, until he was compelled to let them plunder, that by that means he might at least save the city from fire. But they did quite the contrary, for in searching the houses with lights and torches everywhere, they were themselves the cause of the destruction of most of the buildings, inasmuch that when Lucullus the next day went in, he shed tears, and said to his friends, that he had often before blessed the fortune of Sylla, but never so much admired it as then, because when he was willing he was also able to save Athens, "but my infelicity is such, that while I endeavour to imitate him, I become like Mummius." Nevertheless, he endeavoured to save as much of the city as he could, and at the same time, also, by a happy providence a fall of rain concurred to extinguish the fire. He himself while present repaired the ruins as much as he could, receiving back the inhabitants who had fled, and settling as many other Greeks as were willing to live there, adding a hundred furlongs of ground to the place.

This city was a colony of Athens, built at that time when she flourished and was powerful at sea, upon which account many who fled from Aristion's tyranny settled here, and were admitted as citizens, but had the ill-luck to fly from evils at home into greater abroad. As many of these as survived Lucullus furnished everyone with clothes, and two hundred drachmas, and sent them away into their own country. On this occasion Tyrannion the grammarian was taken. Murena begged him of Lucullus, and took him and made him a freedman; but in this he abused Lucullus' favour, who by no means liked that a man of high repute for learning should be first made a slave and then freed; for freedom thus speciously granted again was a real deprivation of what he had before. But not in this case alone Murena showed himself far inferior in generosity to the general.

Lucullus was now busy in looking after the cities of Asia, and having no war to divert his time, spent it in the administration of law and justice, the want of which had for a long time left the province a prey to unspeakable and incredible miseries; so plundered and enslaved by tax-farmers and usurers that private people were compelled to sell their sons in the flower of their youth, and their daughters in their virginity, and the states publicly to sell their consecrated gifts, pictures, and statues. In the end their lot was to yield themselves up slaves to their creditors, but before this worse troubles befell them, tortures, inflicted with ropes and by horses, standing abroad to be scorched when the sun was hot, and being driven into ice and clay in the cold; insomuch that slavery was no less than a redemption and joy to them. Lucullus in a short time freed the cities from all these evils and oppressions; for, first of all, he ordered there should be no more taken than one percent. Secondly, where the interest exceeded the principal, he struck it off. The third and most considerable order was, that the creditor should receive the fourth part of the debtor's income; but if any lender had added the interest to the principal, it was utterly disallowed. Insomuch, that in the space of four years all debts were paid and lands returned to their right owners. The public debt was contracted when Asia was fined twenty thousand talents by Sylla, but twice as much was paid to the collectors, who by their usury had by this time advanced it to a hundred and twenty thousand talents. And accordingly they inveighed against Lucullus at Rome, as grossly injured by him, and by their money's help (as, indeed, they were very powerful, and had many of the statesmen in their debt), they stirred up several leading senators against him. But Lucullus was not only beloved by the cities which he obliged, but was also wished for by other provinces, who blessed the good-luck of those who had such a governor over them.

Appius Clodius, who was sent to Tigranes (the same Clodius was brother to Lucullus' wife), being led by the king's guides a roundabout way, unnecessarily long and tedious, through the upper country, being informed by his freedman, a Syrian by nation, of the direct road, left that lengthy and fallacious one; and bidding the barbarians, his guides, adieu, in a few days passed over Euphrates, and came to Antioch upon Daphne. There being commanded to wait for Tigranes, who at that time was reducing some towns in Phœnicia, he won over many chiefs to his side, who unwillingly submitted to the King of Armenia, among whom was Zarbienus, King of the Gordyenians; also many of the conquered cities corresponded privately with him, whom he assured of relief from Lucullus, but ordered them to lie still at present. The Armenian government was an oppressive one, and intolerable to the Greeks, especially that of the present king, who, growing insolent and overbearing with his success, imagined all things valuable and esteemed among men not only were his in fact, but had been purposely created for him alone. From a small and inconsiderable beginning, he had gone on to be the conqueror of many nations, had humbled the Parthian power more than any before him, and filled Mesopotamia with Greeks, whom he carried in numbers out of Cilicia and Cappadocia. He transplanted also the Arabs, who lived in tents, from their country and home, and settled them near him, that by their means he might carry on the trade.

He had many kings waiting on him, but four he always carried with him as servants and guards, who, when he rode, ran by his horse's side in ordinary under-frocks, and attended him, when sitting on his throne, and publishing his decrees to the people, with their hands folded together; which posture of all others was that which most expressed slavery, it being that of men who had bidden adieu to liberty, and had prepared their bodies more for chastisement than the service of their masters. Appius, nothing dismayed or surprised at this theatrical display, as soon as audience was granted him, said he came to demand Mithridates for Lucullus' triumph, otherwise to denounce war against Tigranes: insomuch that though Tigranes endeavoured to receive him with a smooth countenance and a forced smile, he could not dissemble his discomposure to those who stood about him at the bold language of the young man; for it was the first time, perhaps, in twenty-five years, the length of his reign, or, more truly, of his tyranny, that any free speech had been uttered to him. However, he made answer to Appius, that he would not desert Mithridates, and would defend himself, if the Romans attacked him. He was angry, also, with Lucullus for calling him only king in his letter, and not king of kings, and, in his answer, would not give him his title of imperator. Great gifts were sent to Appius, which he refused; but on their being sent again and augmented, that he might not seem to refuse in anger, he took one goblet and sent the rest back, and without delay went off to the general.

Tigranes before this neither vouchsafed to see nor speak with Mithridates, though a near kinsman, and forced out of so considerable a kingdom, but proudly and scornfully kept him at a distance, as a sort of prisoner, in a marshy and unhealthy district; but now, with much profession of respect and kindness, he sent for him, and at a private conference between them in the palace, they healed up all private jealousies between them, punishing their favourites, who bore all the blame; among whom Metrodorus of Scepsis was one, an eloquent and learned man, and so close an intimate as commonly to be called the king's father. This man, as it happened, being employed in an embassy by Mithridates to solicit help against the Romans, Tigranes asked him, "What would you, Metrodorus, advise me to in this affair?" In return to which, either out of goodwill to Tigranes, or a want of solicitude for Mithridates, he made answer, that as ambassador he counselled him to it, but as a friend dissuaded him from it. This Tigranes reported and affirmed to Mithridates, thinking that no irreparable harm would come of it to Metrodorus. But upon this he was presently taken off, and Tigranes was sorry for what he had done, though he had not, indeed, been absolutely the cause of his death; yet he had given the fatal turn to the anger of Mithridates, who had privately hated him before, as appeared from his cabinet papers when taken, among which there was an order that Metrodorus should die. Tigranes buried him splendidly, sparing no cost to his dead body, whom he betrayed when alive. In Tigranes' court died, also, Amphicrates the orator (if, for the sake of Athens, we may also mention him), of whom it is told that he left his country and fled to Seleucia, upon the river Tigris, and, being desired to teach logic among them, arrogantly replied, that the dish was too little to hold a dolphin. He, therefore, came to Cleopatra, daughter of Mithridates, and queen to Tigranes, but, being accused of misdemeanours, prohibited all commerce with his countrymen, ended his days by starving himself. He, in like manner, received from Cleopatra an honourable burial, near Sapha, a place so called in that country.

Lucullus, when he had re-established law and a lasting peace in Asia, did not altogether forget pleasure and mirth, but, during his residence at Ephesus, gratified the cities with sports, festival triumphs, wrestling games, and single combats of gladiators. And they, in requital, instituted others, called Lucullean games, in honour to him, thus manifesting their love to him, which was of more value to him than all the honour. But when Appius came to him and told him he must prepare for war with Tigranes, he went again into Pontus, and, gathering together his army, besieged Sinope, or rather the Cilicians of the king's side who held it; who thereupon killed a number of the Sinopians, and set the city on fire, and by night endeavoured to escape. Which when Lucullus perceived, he entered the city, and killed eight thousand of them who were still left behind; but restored to the inhabitants what was their own, and took special care for the welfare of the city. To which he was chiefly prompted by this vision. One seemed to come to him in his sleep, and say, "Go on a little further, Lucullus, for Autolycus is coming to see thee." When he arose he could not imagine what the vision meant. The same day he took the city, and as he was pursuing the Cilicians, who were flying by sea, he saw a statue lying on the shore, which the Cilicians carried so far, but had not time to carry aboard. It was one of the masterpieces of Sthenis. And one told him that it was the statue of Autolycus, the founder of the city. This Autolycus is reported to have been son to Deimachus, and one of those who, under Hercules, went on the expedition out of Thessaly against the Amazons; from whence in his return with Demoleon and Phlogius, he lost his vessel on a point of the Chersonesus, called Pedalium. He himself, with his companions and their weapons, being saved, came to Sinope, and dispossessed the Syrians there. The Syrians held it, descended from Syrus, as is the story, the son of Apollo and Sinope, the daughter of Asopus. Which as soon as Lucullus heard, he remembered the admonition of Sylla, whose advice it is in his Memoirs to treat nothing as so certain and so worthy of reliance as an intimation given in dreams.

When it was now told him that Mithridates and Tigranes were just ready to transport their forces into Lycaonia and Cilicia, with the object of entering Asia before him, he wondered much why the Armenian, supposing him to entertain any real intentions to fight with the Romans, did not assist Mithridates in his flourishing condition, and join forces when he was fit for service, instead of suffering him to be vanquished and broken in pieces, and now at last beginning the war, when its hopes were grown cold, and throwing himself down headlong with them, who were irrevocably fallen already. But when Machares, the son of Mithridates, and governor of Bosporus, sent him a crown, valued at a thousand pieces of gold, and desired to be enrolled as a friend and confederate of the Romans, he fairly reputed that war at an end, and left Sornatius, his deputy, with six thousand soldiers, to take care of Pontus. He himself, with twelve thousand foot and a little less than three thousand horse, went forth to the second war, advancing, it seemed very plain, with too great and ill-advised speed, into the midst of warlike nations and many thousands upon thousands of horse, into an unknown extent of country, everyway inclosed with deep rivers and mountains, never free from snow; which made the soldiers, already far from orderly, follow him with great unwillingness and opposition. For the same reason, also, the popular leaders at home publicly inveighed and declaimed against him, as one that raised up war after war, not so much for the interest of the republic, as that he himself, being still in commission, might not lay down arms, but go on enriching himself by the public dangers. These men, in the end, effected their purpose. But Lucullus, by long journeys, came to the Euphrates, where, finding the waters high and rough from the winter, he was much troubled for fear of delay and difficulty while he should procure boats and make a bridge of them. But in the evening the flood beginning to retire, and decreasing all through the night, the next day they saw the river far down within his banks, so much so that the inhabitants, discovering the little islands in the river, and the water stagnating among them, a thing which had rarely happened before, made obeisance to Lucullus, before whom the very river was humble and submissive, and yielded an easy and swift passage. Making use of the opportunity, he carried over his army, and met with a lucky sign at landing. Holy heifers are pastured on purpose for Diana Persia, whom, of all the gods, the barbarians beyond Euphrates chiefly adore. They use these heifers only for her sacrifices. At other times they wander up and down undisturbed, with the mark of the goddess, a torch, branded on them; and it is no such light or easy thing, when occasion requires, to seize one of them. But one of these, when the army had passed the Euphrates, coming to a rock consecrated to the goddess, stood upon it, and then, laying down her neck, like others that are forced down with a rope, offered herself to Lucullus for sacrifice. Besides which, he offered also a bull to Euphrates, for his safe passage. That day he tarried there, but on the next, and those that followed, he travelled through Sophene, using no manner of violence to the people who came to him and willingly received his army. And when the soldiers were desirous to plunder a castle that seemed to be well stored within, "That is the castle," said he, "that we must storm," showing them Taurus at a distance; "the rest is reserved for those who conquer there." Wherefore hastening his march, and passing the Tigris, he came over into Armenia.

The first messenger that gave notice of Lucullus' coming was so far from pleasing Tigranes that he had his head cut off for his pains; and no man daring to bring further information, without any intelligence at all, Tigranes sat while war was already blazing around him, giving ear only to those who flattered him, by saying that Lucullus would show himself a great commander if he ventured to wait for Tigranes at Ephesus, and did not at once fly out of Asia at the mere sight of the many thousands that were come against him. He is a man of a strong body that can carry off a great quantity of wine, and of a powerful constitution of mind that can sustain felicity. Mithrobarzanes, one of his chief favourites, first dared to tell him the truth, but had no more thanks for his freedom of speech than to be immediately sent out against Lucullus with three thousand horse, and a great number of foot, with peremptory demands to bring him alive and trample down his army. Some of Lucullus' men were then pitching their camp, and the rest were coming up to them, when the scouts gave notice that the enemy was approaching, whereupon he was in fear lest they should fall upon him, while his men were divided and unarranged; which made him stay to pitch the camp himself, and send out Sextilius the legate, with sixteen hundred horse, and about as many heavy and light arms, with orders to advance towards the enemy, and wait until intelligence came to him that the camp was finished. Sextilius designed to have kept this order; but Mithrobarzanes coming furiously upon him, he was forced to fight. In the engagement, Mithrobarzanes himself was slain, fighting, and all his men, except a few who ran away, were destroyed. After this, Tigranes left Tigranocerta, a great city built by himself, and retired to Taurus, and called all his forces about him.

But Lucullus, giving him no time to rendezvous, sent out Murena to harass and cut off those who marched to Tigranes, and Sextilius, also, to disperse a great company of Arabians then on the way to the king. Sextilius fell upon the Arabians in their camp, and destroyed most of them, and also Murena, in his pursuit after Tigranes through a craggy and narrow pass, opportunely fell upon him. Upon which Tigranes, abandoning all his baggage, fled; many of the Armenians were killed and more taken. After this success, Lucullus went to Tigranocerta, and sitting down before the city, besieged it. In it were many Greeks carried away out of Cilicia, and many barbarians in like circumstances with the Greeks, Adiabenians, Assyrians, Gordyenians, and Cappadocians, whose native cities he had destroyed, and forced away the inhabitants to settle here. It was a rich and beautiful city, every common man, and every man of rank, in imitation of the king, studied to enlarge and adorn it. This made Lucullus more vigorously press the siege, in the belief that Tigranes would not patiently endure it, but even against his own judgment would come down in anger to force him away; in which he was not mistaken. Mithridates earnestly dissuaded him from it, sending messengers and letters to him not to engage, but rather with his horse to try and cut off the supplies. Taxiles, also, who came from Mithridates, and who stayed with his army, very much entreated the king to forbear, and to avoid the Roman arms, things it was not safe to meddle with. To this he hearkened at first, but when the Armenians and Gordyenians in a full body, and the whole forces of Medes and Adiabenians, under their respective kings, joined him; when many Arabians came up from the sea beyond Babylon; and from the Caspian sea, the Albanians and the Iberians their neighbours, and not a few of the free people, without kings, living about the Araxes, by entreaty and hire also came together to him; and all the king's feasts and councils rang of nothing but expectations, boastings, and barbaric threatenings, Taxiles went in danger of his life for giving council against fighting, and it was imputed to envy in Mithridates thus to discourage him from so glorious an enterprise. Therefore Tigranes would by no means tarry for him, for fear he should share in the glory, but marched on with all his army, lamenting to his friends, as it is said, that he should fight with Lucullus alone and not with all the Roman generals together. Neither was his boldness to be accounted wholly frantic or unreasonable, when he had so many nations and kings attending him, and so many tens of thousands of well-armed foot and horse about him. He had twenty thousand archers and slingers, fifty-five thousand horse, of which seventeen thousand were in complete armour, as Lucullus wrote to the senate, a hundred and fifty thousand heavy-armed men, drawn up partly into cohorts, partly into phalanxes, besides various divisions of men appointed to make roads and lay bridges, to drain off waters and cut wood, and to perform other necessary services, to the number of thirty-five thousand, who, being quartered behind the army, added to its strength, and made it the more formidable to behold.

As soon as he had passed Taurus, and appeared with his forces, and saw the Romans beleaguering Tigranocerta, the barbarous people within, with shoutings and acclamations, received the sight, and threatening the Romans from the walls, pointed to the Armenians. In a council of war, some advised Lucullus to leave the siege, and march up to Tigranes, others that it would not be safe to leave the siege, and so many enemies behind. He answered that neither side by itself was right, but together both gave sound advice; and accordingly he divided his army, and left Murena with six thousand foot in charge of the siege, and himself went out with twenty-four cohorts, in which were no more than ten thousand men-at-arms, and with all the horse and slingers and archers and about a thousand sitting down by the river in a large plain, he appeared, indeed, very inconsiderable to Tigranes, and a fit subject for the flattering wits about him. Some of whom jeered, others cast lots for the spoil, and everyone of the kings and commanders came and desired to undertake the engagement alone, and that he would be pleased to sit still and behold. Tigranes himself, wishing to be witty and pleasant upon the occasion, made use of the well-known saying, that they were too many for ambassadors, and too few for soldiers. Thus they continued sneering and scoffing. As soon as day came, Lucullus brought out his forces under arms. The barbarian army stood on the eastern side of the river, and there being a bend of the river westward in that part of it, where it was easiest forded, Lucullus, while he led his army on in haste, seemed to Tigranes to be flying; who thereupon called Taxiles, and in derision said, "Do you not see these invincible Romans flying?" But Taxiles replied, "Would, indeed, O king, that some such unlikely piece of fortune might be destined you; but the Romans do not, when going on a march, put on their best clothes, nor use bright shields, and naked headpieces, as now you see them, with the leathern coverings all taken off, but this is a preparation for war of men just ready to engage with their enemies." While Taxiles was thus speaking, as Lucullus wheeled about, the first eagle appeared, and the cohorts, according to their divisions and companies, formed in order to pass over, when with much ado, and like a man that is just recovering from a drunken fit, Tigranes cried out twice or thrice, "What, are they upon us?" In great confusion, therefore, the army got in array, the king keeping the main body to himself, while the left wing giving in charge to the Adiabenian, and the right to the Mede, in front of which latter were posted most of the heavy-armed cavalry. Some officers advised Lucullus, just as he was going to cross the river, to lie still, that day being one of the unfortunate ones which they call black days, for on it the army under Cæpio, engaging with the Cimbrians, was destroyed. But he returned the famous answer, "I will make it a happy day to the Romans." It was the day before the Nones of October.

Having so said, he bade them take courage, passed over the river, and himself first of all led them against the enemy, clad in a coat of mail, with shining steel scales and a fringed mantle; and his sword might already be seen out of the scabbard, as if to signify that they must without delay come to a hand-to-hand combat with an enemy whose skill was in distant fighting, and by the speed of their advance curtail the space that exposed them to the archery. But when he saw the heavy-armed horse, the flower of the army, drawn up under a hill, on the top of which was a broad and open plain about four furlongs distant, and of no very difficult or troublesome access, he commanded his Thracian and Galatian horse to fall upon their flank, and beat down their lances with their swords. The only defence of these horse-men-at-arms are their lances; they have nothing else that they can use to protect themselves or annoy their enemy, on account of the weight and stiffness of their armour, with which they are, as it were, built up. He himself, with two cohorts, made to the mountain, the soldiers briskly following, when they saw him in arms afoot first toiling and climbing up. Being on the top and standing in an open place, with a loud voice he cried out, "We have overcome, we have overcome, fellow-soldiers!" And having so said, he marched against the armed horsemen, commanding his men not to throw their javelins, but coming up hand to hand with the enemy, to hack their shins and thighs, which parts alone were unguarded in these heavy-armed horsemen. But there was no need of this way of fighting, for they stood not to receive the Romans, but with great clamour and worse flight they and their heavy horses threw themselves upon the ranks of the foot, before ever these could so much as begin the fight, insomuch that without a wound or bloodshed, so many thousands were overthrown. The greatest slaughter was made in the flight, or rather in the endeavouring to fly away, which they could not well do by reason of the depth and closeness of their own ranks, which hindered them. Tigranes at first fled with a few, but seeing his son in the same misfortune, he took the diadem from his head, and with tears gave it him, bidding him save himself by some other road if he could. But the young man, not daring to put it on, gave it to one of his trustiest servants to keep for him. This man, as it happened, being taken, was brought to Lucullus, and so, among the captives, the crown of Tigranes was also taken. It is stated that above a hundred thousand foot were lost, and that of the horse but very few escaped at all. Of the Romans, a hundred were wounded and five killed. Antiochus the philosopher, making mention of this fight in his book about the gods, says that the sun never saw the like. Strabo, a second philosopher, in his historical collection, says that the Romans could not but blush and deride themselves for putting on armour against such pitiful slaves. Livy also says that the Romans never fought an enemy with such unequal forces, for the conquerors were not so much as one-twentieth part of the number of the conquered. The most sagacious and experienced Roman commanders made it a chief commendation of Lucullus that he had conquered two great and potent kings by two most opposite ways, haste and delay. For he wore out the flourishing power of Mithridates by delay and time, and crushed that of Tigranes by haste; being one of the rare examples of generals who made use of delay for active achievement and speed for security.

On this account it was that Mithridates had made no haste to come up to fight, imagining Lucullus would, as he had done before, use caution and delay, which made him march at his leisure to join Tigranes. And first, as he began to meet some straggling Armenians in the way, making off in great fear and consternation, he suspected the worst, and when greater numbers of stripped and wounded men met him and assured him of the defeat, he set out to seek for Tigranes. And finding him destitute and humiliated, he by no means requited him with insolence, but alighting from his horse, and condoling with him on their common loss, he gave him his own royal guard to attend him, and animated him for the future. And they together gathered fresh forces about them. In the city Tigranocerta, the Greeks meantime, dividing from the barbarians, sought to deliver it up to Lucullus, and he attacked and took it. He seized on the treasure himself, but gave the city to be plundered by the soldiers, in which were found, amongst other property, eight thousand talents of coined money. Besides this, also, he distributed eight hundred drachmas to each man out of the spoils. When he understood that many players were taken in the city, whom Tigranes had invited from all parts for opening the theatre which he had built, he made use of them for celebrating his triumphal games and spectacles. The Greeks he sent home, allowing them money for their journey, and the barbarians also, as many as had been forced away from their own dwellings. So that by this one city being dissolved, many, by the restitution of their former inhabitants, were restored. By all of which Lucullus was beloved as a benefactor and founder. Other successes, also, attended him, such as he well deserved, desirous as he was far more of praise for acts of justice and clemency, than for feats in war, these being due partly to the soldiers, and very greatly to fortune, while those are the sure proofs of a gentle and liberal soul; and by such aids Lucullus, at that time, even without the help of arms, succeeded in reducing the barbarians. For the kings of the Arabians came to him, tendering what they had, and with them the Sophenians also submitted. And he so dealt with the Gordyenians, that they were willing to leave their own habitations, and to follow him with their wives and children. Which was for this cause. Zarbienus, King of the Gordyenians, as has been told, being impatient under the tyranny of Tigranes, had by Appius secretly made overtures of confederacy with Lucullus, but, being discovered, was executed, and his wife and children with him, before the Romans entered Armenia. Lucullus forgot not this, but coming to the Gordyenians made a solemn interment in honour of Zarbienus, and adorning the funeral pile with royal robes, and gold, and the spoils of Tigranes, he himself in person kindled the fire, and poured in perfumes with the friends and relations of the deceased, calling him his companion and the confederate of the Romans. He ordered, also, a costly monument to be built for him. There was a large treasure of gold and silver found in Zarbienus' palace, and no less than three million measures of corn, so that the soldiers were provided for, and Lucullus had the high commendation of maintaining the war at its own charge, without receiving one drachma from the public treasury.

After this came an embassy from the King of Parthia to him, desiring amity and confederacy; which being readily embraced by Lucullus, another was sent by him in return to the Parthian, the members of which discovered him to be a double-minded man, and to be dealing privately at the same time with Tigranes, offering to take part with him, upon condition Mesopotamia were delivered up to him. Which as soon as Lucullus understood, he resolved to pass by Tigranes and Mithridates as antagonists already overcome, and to try the power of Parthia, by leading his army against them, thinking it would be a glorious result, thus in one current of war, like an athlete in the games, to throw down three kings one after another, and successively to deal as a conqueror with three of the greatest power under heaven. He sent, therefore, into Pontus to Sornatius and his colleagues, bidding them bring the army thence, and join with him in his expedition out of Gordyene. The soldiers there, however, who had been restive and unruly before, now openly displayed their mutinous temper. No manner of entreaty or force availed with them, but they protested and cried out that they would stay no longer even there, but would go away and desert Pontus. The news of which, when reported to Lucullus, did no small harm to the soldiers about him, who were already corrupted with wealth and plenty, and desirous of ease. And on hearing the boldness of the others, they called them men, and declared they themselves ought to follow their example, for the actions which they had done did now well deserve release from service and repose.

Upon these and worse words, Lucullus gave up the thoughts of invading Parthia, and in the height of summer-time went against Tigranes. Passing over Taurus, he was filled with apprehension at the greenness of the fields before him, so long is the season deferred in this region by the coldness of the air. But nevertheless, he went down, and twice or thrice putting to flight the Armenians who dared to come out against him, he plundered and burnt their villages, and seizing on the provision designed for Tigranes, reduced his enemies to the necessity which he had feared for himself. But when, after doing all he could to provoke the enemy to fight, by drawing entrenchments round their camp and by burning the country before them, he could by no means bring them to venture out, after their frequent defeats before, he rose up and marched to Artaxata, the royal city of Tigranes, where his wives and young children were kept, judging that

Tigranes would never suffer that to go without the hazard of a battle. It is related that Hannibal the Carthaginian, after the defeat of Antiochus by the Romans, coming to Artaxas, King of Armenia, pointed out to him many other matters to his advantage, and observing the great natural capacities and the pleasantness of the site, then lying unoccupied and neglected, drew a model of a city for it, and bringing Artaxas thither, showed it to him and encouraged him to build. At which the king being pleased, and desiring him to oversee the work, erected a large and stately city which was called after his own name, and made metropolis of Armenia.

And in fact, when Lucullus proceeded against it, Tigranes no longer suffered it, but came with his army, and on the fourth day sat down by the Romans, the river Arsanias lying between them, which of necessity Lucullus must pass in his march to Artaxata. Lucullus, after sacrifice to the gods, as if victory were already obtained, carried over his army, having twelve cohorts in the first division in front, the rest being disposed in the rear to prevent the enemy's inclosing them. For there were many choice horse drawn up against him; in the front stood the Mardian horse-archers, and Iberians with long spears, in whom, being the most warlike, Tigranes more confided than in any other of his foreign troops. But nothing of moment was done by them, for though they skirmished with the Roman horse at a distance, they were not able to stand when the foot came up to them; but being broken, and flying on both sides, drew the horse in pursuit after them. Though these were routed, yet Lucullus was not without alarm when he saw the cavalry about Tigranes with great bravery and in large numbers coming upon him; he recalled his horse from pursuing, and he himself, first of all, with the best of his men, engaged the Satrapenians who were opposite him, and before ever they came to close fight routed them with the mere terror. Of three kings in battle against him, Mithridates of Pontus fled away the most shamefully, being not so much as able to endure the shout of the Romans. The pursuit reached a long way, and all through the night the Romans slew and took prisoners, and carried off spoils and treasure, till they were weary. Livy says there were more taken and destroyed in the first battle, but in the second, men of greater distinction.

Lucullus, flushed and animated by this victory, determined to march on into the interior and there complete his conquests over the barbarians, but winter weather came on, contrary to expectation, as early as the autumnal equinox, with storms and frequent snows, and, even in the most clear days, hoar frost and ice, which made the waters scarcely drinkable for the horses by their exceeding coldness, and scarcely passable through the ice breaking and cutting the horses' sinews. The country for the most part being quite uncleared, with difficult passes, and much wood, kept them continually wet, the snow falling thickly on them as they marched in the day, and the ground that they lay upon at night being damp and watery. After the battle they followed not Lucullus many days before they began to be refractory, first of all entreating and sending the tribunes to him, but presently they tumultuously gathered together, and made a shouting all night long in their tents, a plain sign of a mutinous army. But Lucullus as earnestly entreated them, desiring them to have patience, till they took the Armenian Carthage, and overturned the work of their great enemy, meaning Hannibal. But when he could not prevail, he led them back, and crossing Taurus by another road, came into the fruitful and sunny country of Mygdonia, where was a great and populous city, by the barbarians called Nisibis, by the Greeks Antioch of Mygdonia. This was defended by Guras, brother of Tigranes, with the dignity of governor, and by the engineering skill and dexterity of Callimachus, the same who so much annoyed the Romans at Amisus. Lucullus, however, brought his army up to it, and laying close siege, in a short time took it by storm. He used Guras, who surrendered himself, kindly, but gave no attention to Callimachus, though he offered to make discovery of hidden treasures, commanding him to be kept in chains, to be punished for firing the city of Amisus, which had disappointed his ambition of showing favour and kindness to the Greeks.

Hitherto, one would imagine fortune had attended and fought with Lucullus, but afterwards, as if the wind had failed of a sudden, he did all things by force, and as it were against the grain; and showed certainly the conduct and patience of a wise captain, but in the results met with no fresh honour or reputation; and indeed, by bad success and vain embarrassments with his soldiers, he came within a little of losing even what he had before. He himself was not the least cause of all this, being far from inclined to seek popularity with the mass of the soldiers, and more ready to think any indulgence shown to them an invasion of his own authority. But what was worst of all, he was naturally unsociable to his great officers in commission with him, despising others and thinking them worthy of nothing in comparison with himself. These faults, we are told, he had with all his many excellences; he was of a large and noble person, an eloquent speaker, and a wise counsellor, both in the forum and the camp. Sallust says the soldiers were ill-affected to him from the beginning of the war, because they were forced to keep the field two winters at Cyzicus and afterwards at Amisus. Their other winters, also, vexed them, for they either spent them in an enemy's country, or else were confined to their tents in the open field among their confederates; for Lucullus not so much as once went into a Greek confederate town with his army. To this ill-affection abroad, the tribunes yet more contributed at home, invidiously accusing Lucullus as one who for empire and riches prolonged the war, holding, it might almost be said, under his sole power Cilicia, Asia, Bithynia, Paphlagonia, Pontus, Armenia, all as far as the river Phasis; and now of late had plundered the royal city of Tigranes, as if he had been commissioned not so much to subdue as to strip kings. This is what we are told was said by Lucius Quintius, one of the prætors, at whose instance, in particular, the people determined to send one who should succeed Lucullus in his province, and voted, also, to relieve many of the soldiers under him from further service.

Besides these evils, that which most of all prejudiced Lucullus was Publius Clodius, an insolent man, very vicious and bold, brother to Lucullus' wife, a woman of bad conduct, with whom Clodius was himself suspected of criminal intercourse. Being then in the army under Lucullus, but not in as great authority as he expected (for he would fain have been the chief of all, but on account of his character was postponed to many), he ingratiated himself secretly with the Fimbrian troops, and stirred them up against Lucullus, using fair speeches to them, who of old had been used to be flattered in such a manner. These were those whom Fimbria before had persuaded to kill the consul Flaccus, and choose him their leader. And so they listened not unwillingly to Clodius, and called him the soldiers' friend, for the concern he professed for them, and the indignation he expressed at the prospect that "there must be no end of wars and toils, but in fighting with all nations, and wandering throughout all the world they must wear out their lives receiving no other reward for their service than to guard the carriages and camels of Lucullus, laden with gold and precious goblets; while as for Pompey's soldiers, they were all citizens, living safe at home with their wives and children, on fertile lands, or in towns, and that, not after driving Mithridates and Tigranes into wild deserts, and overturning the royal cities of Asia, but after having merely reduced exiles in Spain, or fugitive slaves in Italy. Nay, if indeed we must never have an end of fighting, should we not rather reserve the remainder of our bodies and souls for a general who will reckon his chiefest glory to be the wealth of his soldiers."

By such practices the army of Lucullus, being corrupted, neither followed him against Tigranes, nor against Mithridates, when he now at once returned into Pontus out of Armenia, and was recovering his kingdom, but under pretence of the winter, sat idle in Gordyene, every minute expecting either Pompey, or some other general, to succeed Lucullus. But when news came that Mithridates had defeated Fabius, and was marching against Sornatius and Triarius, out of shame they followed Lucullus. Triarius, ambitiously aiming at victory before ever Lucullus came to him, though he was then very near, was defeated in a great battle, in which it is said that above seven thousand Romans fell, among whom were a hundred and fifty centurions and four-and-twenty tribunes, and that the camp itself was taken. Lucullus, coming up a few days after, concealed Triarius from the search of the angry soldiers. But when Mithridates declined battle, and waited for the coming of Tigranes, who was then on his march with great forces, he resolved before they joined their forces to turn once more and engage with Tigranes. But in the way the mutinous Fimbrians deserted their ranks, professing themselves released from service by a decree, and that Lucullus, the provinces being allotted to others, had no longer any right to command them. There was nothing beneath the dignity of Lucullus which he did not now submit to bear, entreating them one by one, from tent to tent, going up and down humbly and in tears and even taking some like a suppliant by the hand. But they turned away from his salutes, and threw down their empty purses, bidding him engage alone with the enemy, as he alone made advantage of it. At length by the entreaty of the other soldiers, the Fimbrians, being prevailed upon, consented to tarry that summer under him, but if during that time no enemy came to fight them, to be free. Lucullus of necessity was forced to comply with this, or else to abandon the country to the barbarians. He kept them, indeed, with him, but without urging his authority upon them; nor did he lead them out to battle, being contented if they should but stay with him, though he then saw Cappadocia wasted by Tigranes; and Mithridates again triumphing, whom not long before he reported to the senate to be wholly subdued; and commissioners were now arrived to settle the affairs of Pontus, as if all had been quietly in his possession. But when they came, they found him not so much as master of himself, but contemned and derided by the common soldiers, who arrived at that height of insolence against their general, that at the end of summer they put on their armour and drew their swords, and defied their enemies then absent and gone off a long while before, and with great outcries and waving their swords in the air they quitted the camp, proclaiming that the time was expired which they promised to stay with Lucullus. The rest were summoned by letter from Pompey to come and join him; he by the favour of the people and by flattery of their leaders having been chosen general of the army against Mithridates and Tigranes, though the senate and the nobility all thought that Lucullus was injured, having those put over his head who succeeded rather to his triumph than to his commission, and that he was not so truly deprived of his command, as of the glory he had deserved in his command, which he was forced to yield to another.

It was yet more of just matter of pity and indignation to those who were present; for Lucullus remained no longer master of rewards or punishments for any actions done in the war; neither would Pompey suffer any man to go to him, or pay any respect to the orders and arrangements he made with advice of his ten commissioners, but expressly issued edicts to the contrary, and could not but be obeyed by reason of his greater power. Friends, however, on both sides, thought it desirable to bring them together, and they met in a village of Galatia, and saluted each other in a friendly manner, with congratulations on each other's successes. Lucullus was the elder, but Pompey the more distinguished by his more numerous commands and his two triumphs. Both had rods dressed with laurel carried before them for their victories, and as Pompey's laurels were withered with passing through hot and droughty countries, Lucullus' lictors courteously gave Pompey's some of the fresh and green ones which they had, which Pompey's friends counted a good omen, as indeed, of a truth, Lucullus' actions furnished the honours of Pompey's command. The interview, however, did not bring them to any amicable agreement; they parted even less friends than they met. Pompey repealed all the acts of Lucullus, drew off his soldiers, and left him no more than sixteen hundred for his triumph, and even those unwilling to go with him. So wanting was Lucullus, either through natural constitution or adverse circumstances, in that one first and most important requisite of a general, which had he but added to his other many and remarkable virtues, his fortitude, vigilance, wisdom, justice, the Roman empire had not had Euphrates for its boundary, but the utmost ends of Asia and the Hyrcanian sea; as other nations were then disabled by the late conquests of Tigranes, and the power of Parthia had not in Lucullus' time shown itself so formidable as Crassus afterwards found it, nor had as yet gained that consistency, being crippled by wars at home and on its frontiers, and unable even to make head against the encroachments of the Armenians. And Lucullus, as it was, seems to me through others' agency to have done Rome greater harm than he did her advantage by his own. For the trophies in Armenia, near the Parthian frontier, and Tigranocerta, and Nisibis, and the great wealth brought from thence to Rome, with the captive crown of Tigranes carried in triumph, all helped to puff up Crassus, as if the barbarians had been nothing else but spoil and booty, and he, falling among the Parthian archers, soon demonstrated that Lucullus' triumphs were not beholden to the inadvertency and effeminacy of his enemies, but to his own courage and conduct. But of this afterwards.

Lucullus, upon his return to Rome, found his brother Marcus accused by Caius Memmius for his acts as quæstor, done by Sylla's orders; and on his acquittal, Memmius changed the scene, and animated the people against Lucullus himself, urging them to deny him a triumph for appropriating the spoils and prolonging the war. In this great struggle, the nobility and chief men went down, and mingling in person among the tribes, with much entreaty and labour, scarce at length prevailed upon them to consent to his triumph. The pomp of which proved not so wonderful or so wearisome with the length of the procession and the number of things carried in it, but consisted chiefly in vast quantities of arms and machines of the king's with which he adorned the Flaminian circus, a spectacle by no means despicable. In his progress there passed by a few horsemen in heavy armour, ten chariots armed with scythes, sixty friends and officers of the king's, and a hundred and ten brazen-beaked ships of war, which were conveyed along with them, a golden image of Mithridates six feet high, a shield set with precious stones, twenty loads of silver vessels, and thirty-two of golden cups, armour, and money, all carried by men. Besides which, eight mules were laden with golden couches, fifty-six with bullion, and a hundred and seven with coined silver, little less than two million seven hundred thousand pieces. There were tablets, also, with inscriptions, stating what moneys he gave Pompey for prosecuting the piratic war, what he delivered into the treasury, and what he gave to every soldier, which was nine hundred and fifty drachmas each. After all which he nobly feasted the city and adjoining villages or *vici*.

Being divorced from Clodia, a dissolute and wicked woman, he married Servilia, sister to Cato. This also proved an unfortunate match, for she only wanted one of all of Clodia's vices, the criminality she was accused of with her brothers. Out of reverence to Cato, he for a while connived at her impurity and immodesty, but at length dismissed her. When the senate expected great things from him, hoping to find in him a check to the usurpations of Pompey, and that with the greatness of his station and credit he would come forward as the champion of the nobility, he retired from business and abandoned public life; either because he saw the state to be in a difficult and diseased condition, or, as others say, because he was as great as he could well be, and inclined to a quiet and easy life, after those many labours and toils which had ended with him so far from fortunately. There are those who highly commend his change of life, saying that he thus avoided the rock on which Marius split. For he, after the great and glorious deeds of his Cimbrian victories, was not contented to retire upon his honours, but out of an insatiable desire of glory and power, even in his old age, headed a political party against young men, and let himself fall into miserable actions, and yet more miserable sufferings. Better in like manner, they say, had it been for Cicero, after Catiline's conspiracy, to have retired and grown old, and for Scipio, after his Numantine and Carthaginian conquests, to have sat down contented. For the administration of public affairs has, like other things, its proper term, and statesmen, as well as wrestlers, will break down when strength and youth fail. But Crassus and Pompey, on the other hand, laughed to see Lucullus abandoning himself to pleasure and expense, as if luxurious living were not a thing that as little became his years as government of affairs at home or of an army abroad.

And, indeed, Lucullus' life, like the Old Comedy, presents us at the commencement with acts of policy and of war, at the end offering nothing but good eating and drinking, feastings, and revellings, and mere play. For I give no higher name to his sumptuous buildings, porticos, and baths, still less to his paintings and sculptures, and all his industry about these curiosities, which he collected with vast expense, lavishly bestowing all the wealth and treasure which he got in the war upon them, insomuch that even now, with all the advance of luxury, the Lucullean gardens are counted the noblest the emperor has. Tubero the stoic, when he saw his buildings at Naples, where he suspended the hills upon vast tunnels, brought in the sea for moats and fish-ponds round his house, and built pleasure-houses in the waters, called him Xerxes in a gown. He had also fine seats in Tusculum, belvederes, and large open balconies for men's apartments, and porticos to walk in, where Pompey coming to see him, blamed him for making a house which would be pleasant in summer, but uninhabitable in winter; whom he answered with a smile, "You think me, then, less provident than cranes and storks, not to change my home with the season." When a prætor, with great expense and pains, was preparing a spectacle for the people, and asked him to lend him some purple robes for the performers in a chorus, he told him he would go home and see, and if he had got any, would let him have them; and the next day asking how many he wanted, and being told that a hundred would suffice, bade him to take twice as many: on which the poet Horace observes, that a house is but a poor one where the valuables unseen and unthought of do not exceed all those that meet the eye.

Lucullus' daily entertainments were ostentatiously extravagant, not only with purple coverlets, and plate adorned with precious stones, and dancings, and interludes, but with the greatest diversity of dishes and the most elaborate cookery, for the vulgar to admire and envy. It was a happy thought of Pompey in his sickness, when his physician prescribed a thrush for his dinner, and his servants told him that in summer-time thrushes were not to be found anywhere but in Lucullus' fattening coops, that he would not suffer them to fetch one thence, but observing to his physician, "So if Lucullus had not been an epicure, Pompey had not lived," ordered something else that could easily be got to be prepared for him. Cato was his friend and connection, but, nevertheless, so hated his life and habits, that when a young man in the senate made a long and tedious speech in praise of frugality and temperance, Cato got up and said, "How long do you mean to go on making money like Crassus, living like Lucullus, and talking like Cato?" There are some, however, who say the words were said, but not by Cato.

It is plain from the anecdotes on record of him that Lucullus was not only pleased with, but even gloried in his way of living. For he is said to have feasted several Greeks upon their coming to Rome day after day, who of a true Grecian principle, being ashamed, and declining the invitations, where so great an expense was everyday incurred for them, he with a smile told them, "Some of this, indeed my Grecian friends, is for your sakes, but more for that of Lucullus." Once when he supped alone, there being only one course, and that but moderately furnished, he called his steward and reproved him, who professing to have supposed that there would be no need of any great entertainment, when nobody was invited, was answered, "What, did not you know, then, that today Lucullus dines with Lucullus?" Which being much spoken of about the city, Cicero and Pompey one day met him loitering in the forum, the former his intimate friend and familiar, and, though there had been some ill-will between Pompey and him about the command in the war, still they used to see each other and converse on easy terms together. Cicero accordingly saluted him, and asked him whether today were a good time for asking a favour of him, and on his answering, "Very much so," and begging to hear what it was, "Then," said Cicero, "we shall like to dine with you today, just on the dinner that is prepared for yourself." Lucullus being surprised, and requesting a day's time, they refused to grant it, neither suffered him to talk with his servants, for fear he should give order for more than was appointed before. But thus much they consented to, that before their faces he might tell his servants, that today he would sup in the Apollo (for so one of his best dining-rooms was called), and by this evasion he outwitted his guests. For every room, as it seems, had its own assessment of expenditure, dinner at such a price, and all else in accordance; so that the servants, on knowing where he would dine, knew also how much was to be expended, and in what style and form dinner was to be served. The expense for the Apollo was fifty thousand drachmas, and thus much being that day laid out, the greatness of the cost did not so much amaze Pompey and Cicero, as the rapidity of the outlay. One might believe Lucullus thought his money really captive and barbarian, so wantonly and contumeliously did he treat it.

His furnishing a library, however, deserves praise and record, for he collected very many choice manuscripts; and the use they were put to was even more magnificent than the purchase, the library being always open, and the walks and reading-rooms about it free to all Greeks, whose delight it was to leave their other occupations and hasten thither as to the habitation of the Muses, there walking about, and diverting one another. He himself often passed his hours there, disputing with the learned in the walks, and giving his advice to statesmen who required it, insomuch that his house was altogether a home, and in a manner a Greek prytaneum for those that visited Rome. He was fond of all sorts of philosophy, and was well read and expert in them all. But he always from the first specially favoured and valued the Academy; not the New one, which at that time under Philo flourished with the precepts of Carneades, but the Old one, then sustained and represented by Antiochus of Ascalon, a learned and eloquent man. Lucullus with great labour made him his friend and champion, and set him up against Philo's auditors, among whom Cicero was one, who wrote an admirable treatise in defence of his sect, in which he puts the argument in favour of *comprehension* in the mouth of Lucullus, and the opposite argument in his own. The book is called Lucullus. For, as has been said, they were great friends, and took the same side in politics. For Lucullus did not wholly retire from the republic, but only from ambition, and from the dangerous and often lawless struggle for political preeminence, which he left to Crassus and Cato, whom the senators, jealous of Pompey's greatness, put forward as their champions, when Lucullus refused to head them. For his friends' sake he came into the forum and into the senate, when occasion offered to humble the ambition and pride of Pompey, whose settlement, after his conquests over the kings, he got cancelled, and, by the assistance of Cato, hindered a division of lands to his soldiers, which he proposed. So Pompey went over to Crassus and Cæsar's alliance, or rather conspiracy, and filling the city with armed men, procured the ratification of his decrees by force, and drove Cato and Lucullus out of the forum. Which being resented by the nobility, Pompey's party produced one Vettius, pretending they apprehended him in a design against Pompey's life. Who in the senate-house accused others, but before the people named Lucullus, as if he had been suborned by him to kill Pompey. Nobody gave heed to what he said, and it soon appeared that they had put him forward to make false charges and accusations. And after a few days the whole intrigue became yet more obvious, when the dead body of Vettius was thrown out of prison, he being reported, indeed, to have died a natural death, but carrying marks of a halter and blows about him, and seeming rather to have been taken off by those who suborned him. These things kept Lucullus at a greater distance from the republic.

But when Cicero was banished the city, and Cato sent to Cyprus, he quitted public affairs altogether. It is said, too, that before his death his intellects failed him by degrees. But Cornelius Nepos denies that either age or sickness impaired his mind, which was rather affected by a potion, given him by Callisthenes, his freedman. The potion was meant by Callisthenes to strengthen his affection for him, and was supposed to have that tendency, but it stood quite otherwise, and so disabled and unsettled his mind, that while he was yet alive, his brother took charge of his affairs. At his death, as though it had been the death of one taken off in the very height of military and civil glory, the people were much concerned, and flocked together, and would have forcibly taken his corpse, as it was carried into the market place by young men of the highest rank, and have buried it in the field of Mars, where they buried Sylla. Which being altogether unexpected, and necessaries not easily to be procured on a sudden, his brother, after much entreaty and solicitation, prevailed upon them to suffer him to be buried on his Tusculan estate as had been appointed. He himself survived him but a short time, coming not far behind in death, as he did in age and renown, in all respects, a most loving brother.

THE COMPARISON OF LUCULLUS
WITH CIMON

ONE MIGHT BLESS THE END OF LUCULLUS, WHICH WAS SO TIMED AS TO LET him die before the great revolution, which fate, by intestine wars, was already effecting against the established government, and to close his life in a free though troubled commonwealth. And in this, above all other things, Cimon and he are alike. For he died also when Greece was as yet undisordered in its highest felicity; though in the field at the head of his army, not recalled, nor out of his mind, nor sullying the glory of his wars, engagements, and conquests, by making feastings and debauches seem the apparent end and aim of them all; as Plato says scornfully of Orpheus, that he makes an eternal debauch hereafter the reward of those who lived well here. Indeed, ease and quiet, and the study of pleasant and speculative learning, to an old man retiring from command and office, is a most suitable and becoming solace; but to misguide virtuous actions to pleasure as their utmost end, and as the conclusion of campaigns and commands, to keep the feast of Venus, did not become the noble Academy, and the follower of Xenocrates, but rather one that inclined to Epicurus. And this is one surprising point of contrast between them; Cimon's youth was ill reputed and intemperate, Lucullus' well disciplined and sober. Undoubtedly we must give the preference to the change for good, for it argues the better nature, where vice declines and virtue grows. Both had great wealth, but employed it in different ways; and there is no comparison between the south wall of the acropolis built by Cimon, and the chambers and galleries, with their seaviews, built at Naples by Lucullus, out of the spoils of the barbarians. Neither can we compare Cimon's popular and liberal table with the sumptuous oriental one of Lucullus, the former receiving a great many guests everyday at small cost, and the latter expensively spread for a few men of pleasure, unless you will say that different times made the alteration. For who can tell but that Cimon, if he had retired in his old age from business and war to quiet and solitude, might have lived a more luxurious and self-indulgent life, as he was fond of wine and company, and accused, as has been said, of laxity with women? The better pleasures gained in successful action and effort leave the baser appetites no time or place, and make active and heroic men forget them. Had but Lucullus ended his days in the field, and in command, envy and detraction itself could never have accused him. So much for their manner of life.

In war, it is plain they were both soldiers of excellent conduct, both at land and sea. But as in the games they honour those champions who on the same day gain the garland, both in wrestling and in the pancratium, with the name of "Victors and more," so Cimon, honouring Greece with a sea and land victory on the same day, may claim a certain preeminence among commanders. Lucullus received command from his country, whereas Cimon brought it to his. He annexed the territories of enemies to her, who ruled over confederates before, but Cimon made his country, which when he began was a mere follower of others, both rule over confederates, and conquer enemies too, forcing the Persians to relinquish the sea, and inducing the Lacedæmonians to surrender their command. If it be the chiefest thing in a general to obtain the obedience of his soldiers by goodwill, Lucullus was despised by his own army, but Cimon highly prized even by others. His soldiers deserted the one, the confederates came over to the other. Lucullus came home without the forces which he led out; Cimon, sent out at first to serve as one confederate among others, returned home with authority even over these also, having successfully effected for his city three most difficult services, establishing peace with the enemy, dominion over confederates, and concord with Lacedæmon. Both aiming to destroy great kingdoms, and subdue all Asia, failed in their enterprise, Cimon by a simple piece of ill-fortune, for he died when general, in the height of success; but Lucullus no man can wholly acquit of being in fault with his soldiers, whether it were he did not know, or would not comply with, the distastes and complaints of his army, which brought him at last into such extreme unpopularity among them. But did not Cimon also suffer like him in this? For the citizens arraigned him, and did not leave off till they had banished him, that, as Plato says, they might not hear him for the space of ten years. For high and noble minds seldom please the vulgar, or are acceptable to them; for the force they use to straighten their distorted actions gives the same pain as surgeons' bandages do in bringing dislocated bones to their natural position. Both of them, perhaps, come off pretty much with an equal acquittal on this count.

Lucullus very much outwent him in war, being the first Roman who carried an army over Taurus, passed the Tigris, took and burned the royal palaces of Asia in the sight of the kings, Tigranocerta, Cabira, Sinope, and Nisibis, seizing and overwhelming the northern parts as far as the Phasis, the east as far as Media, and making the South and Red Sea his own through the kings of the Arabians. He shattered the power of the kings, and narrowly missed their persons, while like wild beasts they fled away into deserts and thick and impassable woods. In demonstration of this superiority, we see that the Persians, as if no great harm had befallen them under Cimon, soon after appeared in arms against the Greeks, and overcame and destroyed their numerous forces in Egypt. But after Lucullus, Tigranes and Mithridates were able to do nothing; the latter, being disabled and broken in the former wars, never dared to show his army to Pompey outside the camp, but fled away to Bosporus, and there died. Tigranes threw himself, naked and unarmed, down before Pompey, and taking his crown from his head laid it at his feet, complimenting Pompey with what was not his own, but, in real truth, the conquest already effected by Lucullus. And when he received the ensigns of majesty again, he was well pleased, evidently because he had forfeited them before. And the commander, as the wrestler, is to be accounted to have done most who leaves an adversary almost conquered for his successor. Cimon moreover, when he took the command, found the power of the king broken, and the spirits of the Persians humbled by their great defeats and incessant routs under Themistocles, Pausanias, and Leontychides, and thus easily overcame the bodies of men whose souls were quelled and defeated beforehand. But Tigranes had never yet in many combats been beaten, and was flushed with success when he engaged with Lucullus. There is no comparison between the numbers which came against Lucullus and those subdued by Cimon. All which things being rightly considered, it is a hard matter to give judgment. For supernatural favour also appears to have attended both of them, directing the one what to do, the other what to avoid, and thus they have, both of them, so to say, the vote of the gods, to declare them noble and divine characters.

NICIAS

CRASSUS, IN MY OPINION, MAY MOST PROPERLY BE SET AGAINST NICIAS, AND the Parthian disaster compared with that in Sicily. But here it will be well for me to entreat the reader, in all courtesy, not to think that I contend with Thucydides in matters so pathetically, vividly, and eloquently, beyond all imitation, and even beyond himself, expressed by him; nor to believe me guilty of the like folly with Timæus, who, hoping in his history to surpass Thucydides in art, and to make Philistus appear a trifler and a novice, pushes on in his descriptions, through all the battles, sea-fights, and public speeches, in recording which they have been most successful, without meriting so much as to be compared, in Pindar's phrase, to—

> One that on his feet
> Would with the Lydian cars compete.

He simply shows himself all along a half-lettered, childish writer; in the words of Diphilus—

> —of wit obese,
> O'erlarded with Sicilian grease.

Often he sinks to the very level of Xenarchus, telling us that he thinks it ominous to the Athenians that their general, who had victory in his name, was unwilling to take command in the expedition; and that the defacing of the Hermæ was a divine intimation that they should suffer much in the war by Hermocrates, the son of Hermon; and, moreover, how it was likely that Hercules should aid the Syracusans for the sake of Proserpine, by whose means he took Cerberus, and should be angry with the Athenians for protecting the Egesteans, descended from Trojan ancestors, whose city he, for an injury of their king Laomedon, had overthrown. However, all these may be merely other instances of the same happy taste that makes him correct the diction of Philistus, and abuse Plato and Aristotle. This sort of contention and rivalry with others in matter of style, to my mind, in any case, seems petty and pedantic, but when its objects are works of inimitable excellence, it is absolutely senseless. Such actions in Nicias' life as Thucydides and Philistus have related, since they cannot be passed by, illustrating as they do most especially his character and temper, under his many and great troubles, that I may not seem altogether negligent, I shall briefly run over. And such things as are not commonly known, and lie scattered here and there in other men's writings, or are found amongst the old monuments and archives, I shall endeavour to bring together; not collecting mere useless pieces of learning, but adducing what may make his disposition and habit of mind understood.

First of all, I would mention what Aristotle has said of Nicias, that there had been three good citizens eminent above the rest for their hereditary affection and love to the people, Nicias the son of Niceratus, Thucydides the son of Melesias, and Theramenes the son of Hagnon, but the last less than the others; for he had his dubious extraction cast in his teeth, as a foreigner from Ceos, and his inconstancy, which made him side sometimes with one party, sometimes with another, in public life, and which obtained him the nickname of the Buskin.

Thucydides came earlier, and, on the behalf of the nobility, was a great opponent of the measures by which Pericles courted the favour of the people.

Nicias was a younger man, yet was in some reputation even whilst Pericles lived; so much so as to have been his colleague in the office of general, and to have held command by himself more than once. But on the death of Pericles, he presently rose to the highest place, chiefly by the favour of the rich and eminent citizens, who set him up for their bulwark against the presumption and insolence of Cleon; nevertheless, he did not forfeit the goodwill of the commonalty, who, likewise, contributed to his advancement. For though Cleon got great influence by his exertions—

—to please
The old men, who trusted him to find them fees,

yet even those, for whose interest and to gain whose favour he acted, nevertheless observing the avarice, the arrogance, and the presumption of the man, many of them supported Nicias. For his was not that sort of gravity which is harsh and offensive, but he tempered it with a certain caution and deference, winning upon the people, by seeming afraid of them. And being naturally diffident and unhopeful in war, his good fortune supplied his want of courage, and kept it from being detected, as in all his commands he was constantly successful. And his timorousness in civil life, and his extreme dread of accusers, was thought very suitable in a citizen of a free state; and from the people's goodwill towards him, got him no small power over them, they being fearful of all that despised them, but willing to promote one who seemed to be afraid of them; the greatest compliment their betters could pay them being not to contemn them.

Pericles, who by solid virtue and the pure force of argument ruled the commonwealth, had stood in need of no disguises nor persuasions with the people. Nicias, inferior in these respects, used his riches, of which he had abundance, to gain popularity. Neither had he the nimble wit of Cleon to win the Athenians to his purposes by amusing them with bold jests; unprovided with such qualities, he courted them with dramatic exhibitions, gymnastic games, and other public shows, more sumptuous and more splendid than had been ever known in his or in former ages. Amongst his religious offerings, there was extant, even in our days, the small figure of Minerva in the citadel, having lost the gold that covered it; and a shrine in the temple of Bacchus, under the tripods, that were presented by those who won the prize in the shows or plays. For at these he had often carried off the prize, and never once failed. We are told that on one of these occasions, a slave of his appeared in the character of Bacchus, of a beautiful person and noble stature, and with as yet no beard upon his chin; and on the Athenians being pleased with the sight, and applauding a long time, Nicias stood up, and said he could not in piety keep as a slave one whose person had been consecrated to represent a god. And forthwith he set the young man free. His performances at Delos are, also, on record, as noble and magnificent works of devotion. For whereas the choruses which the cities sent to sing hymns to the god were wont to arrive in no order, as it might happen, and, being there met by a crowd of people crying out to them to sing, in their hurry to begin, used to disembark confusedly, putting on their garlands, and changing their dresses as they left the ships, he, when he had to convoy the sacred company, disembarked the chorus at Rhenea, together with the sacrifice, and other holy appurtenances. And having brought along with him from Athens a bridge fitted by measurement for the purpose, and magnificently adorned with gilding and colouring, and with garlands and tapestries: this he laid in the night over the channel betwixt Rhenea and Delos, being no great distance. And at break of day he marched forth with all the procession to the god, and led the chorus, sumptuously ornamented, and singing their hymns, along over the bridge. The sacrifices, the games, and the feast being over, he set up a palm-tree of brass for a present to the god, and bought a parcel of land with ten thousand drachmas which he consecrated; with the revenue the inhabitants of Delos were to sacrifice and to feast, and to pray the gods for many good things to Nicias. This he engraved on a pillar, which he left in Delos to be a record of his bequest. This same palm-tree, afterwards broken down by the wind, fell on the great statue which the men of Naxos presented, and struck it to the ground.

It is plain that much of this might be vainglory, and the mere desire of popularity and applause; yet from other qualities and carriages of the man one might believe all this cost and public display to be the effect of devotion. For he was one of those who dreaded the divine powers extremely, and, as Thucydides tells us, was much given to arts of divination. In one of Pasiphon's dialogues, it is stated that he daily sacrificed to the gods, and keeping a diviner at his house, professed to be consulting always about the commonwealth, but for the most part inquired about his own private affairs, more especially concerning his silver mines; for he owned many works at Laurium, of great value, but somewhat hazardous to carry on. He maintained there a multitude of slaves, and his wealth consisted chiefly in silver. Hence he had many hangers-on about him, begging and obtaining. For he gave to those who could do him mischief no less than to those who deserved well. In short, his timidity was a revenue to rogues, and his humanity to honest men. We find testimony in the comic writers, as when Teleclides, speaking of one of the professed informers, says:

> Charicles gave the man a pound, the matter not to name,
> That from inside a money-bag into the world he came;
> And Nicias, also, paid him four; I know the reason well,
> But Nicias is a worthy man, and so I will not tell.

So, also, the informer whom Eupolis introduces in his Maricas, attacking a good, simple, poor man:

> How long ago did you and Nicias meet?
> I did but see him just now in the street.

> The man has seen him and denies it not,
> 'Tis evident that they are in a plot.

> See you, O citizens! 'tis fact,
> Nicias is taken in the act.

> Taken, Fools! Take so good a man
> In aught that's wrong none will or can.

Cleon, in Aristophanes, makes it one of his threats:

> I'll outscream all the speakers, and make Nicias stand aghast.

Phrynichus also implies his want of spirit and his easiness to be intimated in the verses—

> A noble man he was, I well can say,
> Nor walked like Nicias, cowering on his way.

So cautious was he of informers, and so reserved, that he never would dine out with any citizen, nor allowed himself to indulge in talk and conversation with his friends, nor give himself any leisure for such amusements; but when he was general he used to stay at the office till night, and was the first that came to the council-house, and the last that left it. And if no public business engaged him, it was very hard to have access, or to speak with him, he being retired at home and locked up. And when any came to the door, some friend of his gave them good words, and begged them to excuse him, Nicias was very busy; as if affairs of state and public duties still kept him occupied. He who principally acted this part for him, and contributed most to this state and show, was Hiero, a man educated in Nicias' family, and instructed by him in letters and music. He professed to be the son of Dionysius, surnamed Chalcus, whose poems are yet extant, and had led out the colony to Italy and founded Thurii. This Hiero transacted all his secrets for Nicias with the diviners; and gave out to the people what a toilsome and miserable life he led for the sake of the commonwealth. "He," said Hiero, "can never be either at the bath or at his meat but some public business interferes. Careless of his own and zealous for the public good, he scarcely ever goes to bed till after others have had their first sleep. So that his health is impaired and his body out of order, nor is he cheerful or affable with his friends, but loses them as well as his money in the service of the state, while other men gain friends by public speaking, enrich themselves, fare delicately and make government their amusement." And in fact this was Nicias' manner of life, so that he well might apply to himself the words of Agamemnon:

Vain pomp's the ruler of the life we live
And a slave's service to the crowd we give.

He observed that the people, in the case of men of eloquence, or of eminent parts, make use of their talents upon occasion, but were always jealous of their abilities, and held a watchful eye upon them, taking all opportunities to humble their pride and abate their reputation; as was manifest in their condemnation of Pericles, their banishment of Damon, their distrust of Antiphon the Rhamnusian, but especially in the case of Paches who took Lesbos, who, having to give an account of his conduct, in the very court of justice unsheathed his sword and slew himself. Upon such considerations, Nicias declined all difficult and lengthy enterprises; if he took a command, he was for doing what was safe; and if, as thus was likely, he had for the most part success, he did not attribute it to any wisdom, conduct, or courage of his own, but, to avoid envy, he thanked fortune for all, and gave the glory to the divine powers. And the actions themselves bore testimony in his favour; the city met at that time with several considerable reverses, but he had not a hand in any of them. The Athenians were routed in Thrace by the Chalcidians, Calliades and Xenophon commanding in chief. Demosthenes was the general when they were unfortunate in Ætolia. At Delium they lost a thousand citizens under the conduct of Hippocrates; the plague was principally laid to the charge of Pericles, he, to carry on the war, having shut up close together in the town the crowd of people from the country who, by the change of place, and of their usual course of living, bred the pestilence. Nicias stood clear of all this; under his conduct was taken Cythera, an island most commodious against Laconia, and occupied by the Lacedæmonian settlers; many places, likewise, in Thrace, which had revolted, were taken or won over by him; he shutting up the Megarians within their town, seized upon the isle of Minoa; and soon after, advancing from thence to Nisæa, made himself master there, and then making a descent upon the Corinthian territory, fought a successful battle, and slew a great number of the Corinthians with their captain Lycophron. There it happened that two of his men were left by an oversight, when they carried off the dead, which when he understood, he stopped the fleet, and sent a herald to the enemy for leave to carry off the dead; though by law and custom, he that by a truce craved leave to carry off the dead was hereby supposed to give up all claim to the victory. Nor was it lawful for him that did this to erect a trophy, for his is the victory who is master of the field, and he is not master who asks leave;

as wanting power to take. But he chose rather to renounce his victory and his glory than to let two citizens lie unburied. He scoured the coast of Laconia all along, and beat the Lacedæmonians that made head against him. He took Thyrea, occupied by the Æginetans, and carried the prisoners to Athens.

When Demosthenes had fortified Pylos, and the Peloponnesians brought together both their sea and land forces before it, after the fight, about the number of four hundred native Spartans were left ashore in the isle Sphacteria. The Athenians thought it a great prize, as indeed it was, to take these men prisoners. But the siege, in places that wanted water, being very difficult and untoward, and to convey necessaries about by sea in summer tedious and expensive, in winter doubtful, or plainly impossible, they began to be annoyed, and to repent their having rejected the embassy of the Lacedæmonians, that had been sent to propose a treaty of peace, which had been done at the importunity of Cleon, who opposed it chiefly out of a pique to Nicias; for, being his enemy, and observing him to be extremely solicitous to support the offers of the Lacedæmonians, he persuaded the people to refuse them.

Now, therefore, that the siege was protracted, and they heard of the difficulties that pressed their army, they grew enraged against Cleon. But he turned all the blame upon Nicias, charging it on his softness and cowardice, that the besieged were not yet taken. "Were I general," said he, "they should not hold out so long." The Athenians not unnaturally asked the question, "Why, then, as it is, do not you go with a squadron against them?" And Nicias standing up resigned his command at Pylos to him, and bade him take what forces he pleased along with him, and not be bold in words, out of harm's way, but go forth and perform some real service for the commonwealth. Cleon, at the first, tried to draw back, disconcerted at the proposal, which he had never expected; but the Athenians insisting, and Nicias loudly upbraiding him, he thus provoked, and fired with ambition, took upon him the charge, and said further, that within twenty days after he embarked, he would either kill the enemy, upon the place, or bring them alive to Athens. This the Athenians were readier to laugh at than to believe, as on other occasions, also, his bold assertions and extravagances used to make them sport, and were pleasant enough. As, for instance, it is reported that once when the people were assembled, and had waited his coming a long time, at last he appeared with a garland on his head, and prayed them to adjourn to the next day. "For," said he, "I am not at leisure today; I have sacrificed to the gods, and am to entertain some strangers." Whereupon the Athenians, laughing, rose up, and dissolved the assembly. However, at this time he had good fortune, and in conjunction with Demosthenes, conducted the enterprise so well that within the time he had limited, he carried captive to Athens all the Spartans that had not fallen in battle.

This brought great disgrace on Nicias; for this was not to throw away his shield, but something yet more shameful and ignominious, to quit his charge voluntarily out of cowardice, and voting himself, as it were, out of his command of his own accord, to put into his enemy's hand the opportunity of achieving so brave an action. Aristophanes has a jest against him on this occasion in the Birds:

> Indeed, not now the word that must be said
> Is, do like Nicias, or retire to bed.

And, again, in his Husbandmen:

> I wish to stay at home and farm,
>   What then?
> Who should prevent you?
>   You, my countrymen;
> Whom I would pay a thousand drachmas down,
> To let me give up office and leave town.
> Enough; content; the sum two thousand is,
> With those that Nicias paid to give up his.

Besides all this, he did great mischief to the city by suffering the accession of so much reputation and power to Cleon, who now assumed such lofty airs, and allowed himself in such intolerable audacity, as led to many unfortunate results, a sufficient part of which fell to his own share. Amongst other things, he destroyed all the decorum of public speaking; he was the first who ever broke out into exclamations, flung open his dress, smote his thigh, and ran up and down whilst he was speaking, things which soon after introduced, amongst those who managed the affairs of state, such licence and contempt of decency as brought all into confusion.

Already, too, Alcibiades was beginning to show his strength at Athens, a popular leader, not, indeed, as utterly violent as Cleon, but as the land of Egypt, through the richness of its soil, is said—

> —great plenty to produce,
> Both wholesome herbs, and drugs of deadly juice,

so the nature of Alcibiades was strong and luxuriant in both kinds, and made way for many serious innovations. Thus it fell out that after Nicias had got his hands clear of Cleon, he had not opportunity to settle the city perfectly into quietness. For having brought matters to a pretty hopeful condition, he found everything carried away and plunged again into confusion by Alcibiades, through the wildness and vehemence of his ambition, and all embroiled again in war worse than ever. Which fell out thus. The persons who had principally hindered the peace were Cleon and Brasidas. War setting off the virtue of the one and hiding the villainy of the other, gave to the one occasions of achieving brave actions, to the other opportunity of committing equal dishonesties. Now when these two were in one battle both slain near Amphipolis, Nicias was aware that the Spartans had long been desirous of a peace, and that the Athenians had no longer the same confidence in the war. Both being alike tired, and, as it were by consent, letting fall their hands, he, therefore, in this nick of time, employed his efforts to make a friendship betwixt the two cities, and to deliver the other states of Greece from the evils and calamities they laboured under, and so establish his own good name for success as a statesman for all future time. He found the men of substance, the elder men, and the land-owners and farmers pretty generally all inclined to peace. And when, in addition to these, by conversing and reasoning, he had cooled the wishes of a good many others for war, he now encouraged the hopes of the Lacedæmonians, and counselled them to seek peace. They confided in him, as on account of his general character for moderation and equity, so, also, because of the kindness and care he had shown to the prisoners taken at Pylos and kept in confinement, making their misfortune the more easy to them.

The Athenians and the Spartans had before this concluded a truce for a year, and during this, by associating with one another, they had tasted again the sweets of peace and security and unimpeded intercourse with friends and connections, and thus longed for an end of that fighting and bloodshed, and heard with delight the chorus sing such verses as—

> —my lance I'll leave
> Laid by, for spiders to o'erweave,

and remembered with joy the saying, In peace, they who sleep are awaked by the cock-crow, not by the trumpet. So shutting their ears, with loud reproaches, to the forebodings of those who said that the Fates decreed this to be a war of thrice nine years, the whole question having been debated, they made a peace. And most people thought, now, indeed, they had got an end of all their evils. And Nicias was in every man's mouth, as one especially beloved of the gods, who, for his piety and devotion, had been appointed to give a name to the fairest and greatest of all blessings. For in fact they considered the peace Nicias' work, as the war the work of Pericles; because he, on light occasions, seemed to have plunged the Greeks into great calamities, while Nicias had induced them to forget all the evils they had done each other and to be friends again; and so to this day it is called the Peace of Nicias.

The articles being, that the garrisons and towns taken on either side and the prisoners should be restored, and they to restore the first to whom it should fall by lot, Nicias, as Theophrastus tells us, by a sum of money procured that the lot should fall for the Lacedæmonians to deliver the first. Afterwards, when the Corinthians and the Bœotians showed their dislike of what was done, and by their complaints and accusations were well nigh bringing the war back again, Nicias persuaded the Athenians and the Lacedæmonians, besides the peace, to make a treaty of alliance, offensive and defensive, as a tie and confirmation of the peace, which would make them more terrible to those that held out, and the firmer to each other. Whilst these matters were on foot, Alcibiades, who was no lover of tranquillity, and who was offended with the Lacedæmonians because of their applications and attentions to Nicias, while they overlooked and despised himself, from first to last, indeed, had opposed the peace, though all in vain, but now finding that the Lacedæmonians did not altogether continue to please the Athenians, but were thought to have acted unfairly in having made a league with the Bœotians, and had not given up Panactum, as they should have done, with its fortifications unrazed, nor yet Amphipolis, he laid hold on these occasions for his purpose, and availed himself of everyone of them to irritate the people. And, at length, sending for ambassadors from the Argives, he exerted himself to effect a confederacy between the Athenians and them. And now, when Lacedæmonian ambassadors were come with full powers, and at their preliminary audience by the council seemed to come in all points with just proposals, he, fearing that the general assembly, also, would be won to their offers, overreached them with false professions and oaths of assistance, on the condition that they would not avow that they came with full powers; this, he said, being the only way for them to attain their desires. They being overpersuaded and decoyed from Nicias to follow him, he introduced them to the assembly, and asked them presently whether or no they came in all points with full powers, which, when they denied, he, contrary to their expectation, changing his countenance, called the council to witness their words, and now bade the people beware how they trust or transact anything with such manifest liars, who say at one time one thing, and at another the very opposite upon the same subject. These plenipotentiaries were, as well they might be, confounded at this, and Nicias, also being at a loss what to say, and struck with amazement and wonder, the assembly resolved to send immediately for the Argives, to enter into a league with them. An earthquake, which interrupted the assembly, made for Nicias' advantage; and the next day the people being again assembled after much speaking and soliciting, with great ado he brought it about that the treaty with the Argives should be deferred, and he be sent to the Lacedæmonians, in full expectation that so all would go well.

When he arrived at Sparta, they received him there as a good man, and one well inclined towards them; yet he effected nothing, but, baffled by the party that favoured the Bœotians, he returned home, not only dishonoured and hardly spoken of, but likewise in fear of the Athenians, who were vexed and enraged that through his persuasions they had released so many and such considerable persons, their prisoners, for the men who had been brought from Pylos were of the chiefest families of Sparta, and had those who were highest there in place and power for their friends and kindred. Yet did they not in their heat proceed against him, otherwise than that they chose Alcibiades general, and took the Mantineans and Eleans, who had thrown up their alliance with the Lacedæmonians, into the league, together with the Argives, and sent to Pylos freebooters to infest Laconia, whereby the war began to break out afresh.

But the enmity betwixt Nicias and Alcibiades running higher and higher, and the time being at hand for decreeing the ostracism or banishment, for ten years, which the people, putting the name on a sherd, were wont to inflict at certain times on some person suspected or regarded with jealousy for his popularity or wealth, both were now in alarm and apprehension, one of them, in all likelihood, being to undergo this ostracism; as the people abominated the life of Alcibiades, and stood in fear of his boldness and resolution, as is shown particularly in the history of him; while as for Nicias, his riches made him envied, and his habits of living, in particular his unsociable and exclusive ways, not like those of a fellow-citizen, or even a fellow-man, went against him, and having many times opposed their inclinations, forcing them against their feelings to do what was their interest, he had got himself disliked.

To speak plainly, it was a contest of the young men who were eager for war, against the men of years and lovers of peace, they turning the ostracism upon the one, these upon the other. But—

In civil strife e'en villains rise to fame.

And so now it happened that the city, distracted into two factions, allowed free course to the most impudent and profligate persons, among whom was Hyperbolus of the Perithœdæ, one who could not, indeed, be said to be presuming upon any power, but rather by his presumption rose into power, and by the honour he found in the city, became the scandal of it. He, at this time, thought himself far enough from the ostracism, as more properly deserving the slave's gallows, and made account, that one of these men being despatched out of the way he might be able to play a part against the other that should be left, and openly showed his pleasure at the dissension, and his desire to inflame the people against both of them. Nicias and Alcibiades, perceiving his malice, secretly combined together, and setting both their interests jointly at work, succeeded in fixing the ostracism not on either of them, but even on Hyperbolus. This, indeed, at the first made sport, and raised laughter among the people; but afterwards it was felt as an affront, that the thing should be dishonoured by being employed upon so unworthy a subject; punishment, also, having its proper dignity, and ostracism being one that was appropriate rather for Thucydides, Aristides, and such like persons; whereas for Hyperbolus it was a glory, and a fair ground for boasting on his part, when for his villainy he suffered the same with the best men. As Plato, the comic poet, said of him:

The man deserved the fate, deny who can;
Yes, but the fate did not deserve the man;
Not for the like of him and his slave-brands,
Did Athens put the sherd into our hands.

And, in fact, none ever afterwards suffered this sort of punishment, but Hyperbolus was the last, as Hipparchus the Cholargian, who was kin to the tyrant, was the first.

There is no judgment to be made of fortune; nor can any reasoning bring us to a certainty about it. If Nicias had run the risk with Alcibiades, whether of the two should undergo the ostracism, he had either prevailed, and, his rival being expelled the city, he had remained secure; or, being overcome, he had avoided the utmost disasters, and preserved the reputation of a most excellent commander. Meantime I am not ignorant that

Theophrastus says, that when Hyperbolus was banished, Phæax, not Nicias, contested it with Alcibiades; but most authors differ from him.

It was Alcibiades, at any rate, whom when the Ægestean and Leontine ambassadors arrived and urged the Athenians to make an expedition against Sicily, Nicias opposed, and by whose persuasions and ambition he found himself overborne, who, even before the people could be assembled, had preoccupied and corrupted their judgment with hopes and with speeches; insomuch that the young men at their sports, and the old men in their workshops, and sitting together on the benches, would be drawing maps of Sicily, and making charts showing the seas, the harbours, and general character of the coast of the island opposite Africa. For they made not Sicily the end of the war but rather its starting-point and headquarters from whence they might carry it to the Carthaginians, and possess themselves of Africa, and of the seas as far as the pillars of Hercules. The bulk of the people, therefore, pressing this way, Nicias, who opposed them, found but few supporters, nor those of much influence; for the men of substance, fearing lest they should seem to shun the public charges and ship-money, were quiet against their inclination; nevertheless he did not tire nor give it up, but even after the Athenians decreed a war and chose him in the first place general, together with Alcibiades and Lamachus, when they were again assembled, he stood up, dissuaded them, and protested against the decision, and laid the blame on Alcibiades, charging him with going about to involve the city in foreign dangers and difficulties, merely with a view to his own private lucre and ambition. Yet it came to nothing. Nicias, because of his experience, was looked upon as the fitter for the employment, and his wariness with the bravery of Alcibiades, and the easy temper of Lamachus, all compounded together, promised such security, that he did but confirm the resolution. Demostratus, who, of the popular leaders, was the one who chiefly pressed the Athenians to the expedition, stood up and said he would stop the mouth of Nicias from urging anymore excuses, and moved that the generals should have absolute power, both at home and abroad, to order and to act as they thought best; and this vote the people passed.

The priests, however, are said to have very earnestly opposed the enterprise. But Alcibiades had his diviners of another sort, who from some old prophecies announced that "there shall be great fame of the Athenians in Sicily," and messengers came back to him from Jupiter Ammon with oracles importing that "the Athenians shall take all the Syracusans." Those, meanwhile, who knew anything that boded ill, concealed it lest they might seem to fore-speak ill-luck. For even prodigies that were obvious and plain would not deter them; not the defacing of the Hermæ, all maimed in one night except one, called the Hermes of Andocides, erected by the tribe of Ægeus, placed directly before the house then occupied by Andocides; or what was perpetrated on the altar of the twelve gods, upon which a certain man leaped suddenly up, and then turning round mutilated himself with a stone. Likewise at Delphi there stood a golden image of Minerva, set on a palm-tree of brass, erected by the city of Athens from the spoils they won from the Medes; this was pecked at several days together by crows flying upon it, who also plucked off and knocked down the fruit, made of gold, upon the palm-tree. But the Athenians said these were all but inventions of the Delphians, corrupted by the men of Syracuse. A certain oracle bade them bring from Clazomenæ the priestess of Minerva there; they sent for the woman and found her named *Hesychia, Quietness,* this being, it would seem, what the divine powers advised the city at this time, to be quiet. Whether, therefore, the astrologer Meton feared these presages, or that from human reason he doubted its success (for he was appointed to a command in it), feigning himself mad, he set his house on fire. Others say he did not counterfeit madness, but set his house on fire in the night, and the next morning came before the assembly in great distress, and besought the people, in consideration of the sad disaster, to release his son from the service, who was about to go captain of a galley for Sicily. The genius, also, of the philosopher Socrates, on this occasion, too, gave him intimation by the usual tokens, that the expedition would prove the ruin of the commonwealth; this he imparted to his friends and familiars, and by them it was mentioned to a number of people. Not a few were troubled because the days on which the fleet set sail happened to be the time when the women celebrated the death of Adonis; there being everywhere then exposed to view images of dead men, carried about with mourning and lamentation, and women beating their breasts. So that such as laid any stress on these matters were extremely troubled, and feared lest that all this warlike preparation, so splendid and so glorious, should suddenly, in a little time, be blasted in its very prime of magnificence, and come to nothing.

Nicias, in opposing the voting of this expedition, and neither being puffed up with hopes, nor transported with the honour of his high command so as to modify his judgment, showed himself a man of virtue and constancy. But when his endeavours could not diverge the people from the war, nor get leave for himself to be discharged of the command, but the people, as it were, violently him took up and carried him, and against his will put him in the office of general, this was no longer now a time for his excessive caution and his delays, nor was it for him, like a child, to look back from the ship, often repeating and reconsidering over and over again how that his advice had not been over-ruled by fair arguments, thus blunting the courage of his fellow-commanders and spoiling the season of action. Whereas, he ought speedily to have closed with the enemy and brought the matter to an issue, and put fortune immediately to the test in battle. But, on the contrary, when Lamachus counselled to sail directly to Syracuse, and fight the enemy under their city walls, and Alcibiades advised to secure the friendship of the other towns, and then to march against them, Nicias dissented from them both, and insisted that they should cruise quietly around the island and display their armament, and having landed a small supply of men for the Egesteans, return to Athens, weakening at once the resolution and casting down the spirits of the men. And while, a little while after, the Athenians called home Alcibiades in order to his trial, he being, though joined nominally with another in commission, in effect the only general, made now no end of loitering, of cruising, and considering, till their hopes were grown stale, and all the disorder and consternation which the first approach and view of their forces had cast amongst the enemy was worn off and had left them.

Whilst yet Alcibiades was with the fleet, they went before Syracuse with a squadron of sixty galleys, fifty of them lying in array without the harbour, while the other ten rowed in to reconnoitre, and by a herald called upon the citizens of Leontini to return to their own country. These scouts took a galley of the enemy's, in which they found certain tablets, on which was set down a list of all the Syracusans, according to their tribes. These were wont to be laid up at a distance from the city, in the temple of Jupiter Olympius, but were now brought forth for examination to furnish a muster-roll of young men for the war. These being so taken by the Athenians, and carried to the officers, and the multitude of names appearing, the diviners thought it unpropitious, and were in apprehension lest this should be the only destined fulfilment of the prophecy, that "the Athenians shall take all the Syracusans." Yet, indeed, this was said to be accomplished by the Athenians at another time, when Callippus the Athenian, having slain Dion, became master of Syracuse. But when Alcibiades shortly after sailed away from Sicily, the command fell wholly to Nicias. Lamachus was, indeed, a brave and honest man, and ready to fight fearlessly with his own hand in battle, but so poor and ill-off that, whenever he was appointed general, he used always, in accounting for his outlay of public money, to bring some little reckoning or other of money for his very clothes and shoes. On the contrary, Nicias, as on other accounts, so, also, because of his wealth and station, was very much thought of. The story is told that once upon a time the commission of generals being in consultation together in their public office, he bade Sophocles the poet give his opinion first, as the senior of the board. "I," replied Sophocles, "am the older, but you are the senior." And so now, also, Lamachus, who better understood military affairs, being quite his subordinate, he himself, evermore delaying and avoiding risk, and faintly employing his forces, first by his sailing about Sicily at the greatest distance aloof from the enemy, gave them confidence, then by afterwards attacking Hybla, a petty fortress, and drawing off before he could take it, make himself utterly despised. At the last he retreated to Catana without having achieved anything, save that he demolished Hyccara, an humble town of the barbarians, out of which, the story goes, that Lais the courtesan, yet a mere girl, was sold amongst the other prisoners, and carried thence away to Peloponnesus.

But when the summer was spent, after reports began to reach him that the Syracusans were grown so confident that they would come first to attack him, and troopers skirmishing to the very camp twitted his soldiers, asking whether they came to settle with the Catanians, or to put the Leontines in possession of their city, at last, with much ado, Nicias resolved to sail against Syracuse. And wishing to form his camp safely and without molestation, he procured a man to carry from Catana intelligence to the Syracusans that they might seize the camp of the Athenians unprotected, and all their arms, if on such a day they should march with all their forces to Catana; and that, the Athenians living mostly in the town, the friends of the Syracusans had concerted, as soon as they should perceive them coming, to possess themselves of one of the gates, and to fire the arsenal; that many now were in the conspiracy and awaited their arrival. This was the ablest thing Nicias did in the whole of his conduct of the expedition. For having drawn out all the strength of the enemy, and made the city destitute of men, he set out from Catana, entered the harbour, and chose a fit place for his camp, where the enemy could least incommode him with the means in which they were superior to him, while with the means in which he was superior to them he might expect to carry on the war without impediment.

When the Syracusans returned from Catana, and stood in battle array before the city gates, he rapidly led up the Athenians and fell on them and defeated them, but did not kill many, their horse hindering the pursuit.

And his cutting and breaking down the bridges that lay over the river gave Hermocrates, when cheering up the Syracusans, occasion to say that Nicias was ridiculous, whose great aim seemed to be to avoid fighting, as if fighting were not the thing he came for. However, he put the Syracusans into a very great alarm and consternation, so that instead of fifteen generals then in service, they chose three others, to whom the people engaged by oath to allow absolute authority.

There stood near them the temple of Jupiter Olympius, which the Athenians (there being in it many consecrated things of gold and silver) were eager to take, but were purposely withheld from it by Nicias, who let the opportunity slip, and allowed a garrison of the Syracusans to enter it, judging that if the soldiers should make booty of that wealth it would be no advantage to the public, and he should bear the guilt of the impiety. Not improving in the least this success, which was everywhere famous, after a few days' stay, away he goes to Naxos, and there winters, spending largely for the maintenance of so great an army, and not doing anything except some matters of little consequence with some native Sicilians that revolted to him. Insomuch that the Syracusans took heart again, made excursions to Catana, wasted the country, and fired the camp of the Athenians. For which everybody blamed Nicias, who, with his long reflection, his deliberateness, and his caution, had let slip the time for action. None ever found fault with the man when once at work, for in the brunt he showed vigour and activity enough, but was slow and wanted assurance to engage. When, therefore, he brought again the army to Syracuse, such was his conduct, and with such celerity, and at the same time security, he came upon them, that nobody knew of his approach, when already he had come to shore with his galleys at Thapsus, and had landed his men; and before any could help it, he had surprised Epipolæ, had defeated the body of picked men that came to its succour, took three hundred prisoners, and routed the cavalry of the enemy, which had been thought invincible. But what chiefly astonished the Syracusans, and seemed incredible to the Greeks, was in so short a space of time the walling about of Syracuse, a town not less than Athens, and far more difficult, by the unevenness of the ground, and the nearness of the sea and the marshes adjacent, to have such a wall drawn in a circle round it; yet this, all within a very little, finished by a man that had not even his health for such weighty cares, but lay ill of the stone, which may justly bear the blame for what was left undone. I admire the industry of the general, and the bravery of the soldiers for what they succeeded in. Euripides, after their ruin and disaster, writing their funeral elegy, said that—

Eight victories over Syracuse they gained,
While equal yet to both the gods remained.

And in truth one shall not find eight, but many more victories, won by these men against the Syracusans, till the gods, in real truth, or fortune intervened to check the Athenians in this advance to the height of power and greatness.

Nicias, therefore, doing violence to his body, was present in most actions. But once, when his disease was the sharpest upon him, he lay in the camp with some few servants to attend him. And Lamachus having the command fought the Syracusans, who were bringing a cross-wall from the city along to that of the Athenians, to hinder them from carrying it round; and in the victory, the Athenians hurrying in some disorder to the pursuit, Lamachus getting separated from his men, had to resist the Syracusan horse that came upon him. Before the rest advanced Callicrates, a man of good courage and skill in war. Lamachus, upon a challenge, engaged with him in single combat, and receiving the first wound, returned it so home to Callicrates, that they both fell and died together. The Syracusans took away his body and arms, and at full speed advanced to the wall of the Athenians, where Nicias lay without any troops to oppose to them, yet roused by this necessity, and seeing the danger, he bade those about him go and set on fire all the wood and materials that lay provided before the wall for the engines, and the engines themselves; this put a stop to the Syracusans, saved Nicias, saved the walls and all the money of the Athenians. For when the Syracusans saw such a fire blazing up between them and the wall, they retired.

Nicias now remained sole general, and with great prospects; for cities began to come over to alliance with him, and ships laden with corn from every coast came to the camp, everyone favouring when matters went well. And some proposals from among the Syracusans despairing to defend the city, about a capitulation, were already conveyed to him. And in fact Gylippus, who was on his way with a squadron to their aid from Lacedæmon, hearing on his voyage of the wall surrounding them, and of their distress, only continued his enterprise thenceforth, that, giving Sicily up for lost, he might, if even that should be possible, secure the Italians their cities. For a strong report was everywhere spread about that the Athenians carried all before them, and had a general alike for conduct and for fortune invincible.

And Nicias himself, too, now against his nature grown bold in his present strength and success, especially from the intelligence he received underhand of the Syracusans, believing they would almost immediately surrender the town upon terms, paid no manner of regard to Gylippus coming to their assistance, nor kept any watch of his approach, so that neglected altogether and despised, Gylippus went in a long-boat ashore without the knowledge of Nicias, and, having landed in the remotest parts from Syracuse, mustered up a considerable force, the Syracusans not so much as knowing of his arrival nor expecting him; so that an assembly was summoned to consider the terms to be arranged with Nicias, and some were actually on the way, thinking it essential to have all despatched before the town should be quite walled round, for now there remained very little to be done, and the materials for the building lay all ready along the line.

In this very nick of time and danger arrived Gongylus in one galley from Corinth, and everyone, as may be imagined, flocking about him, he told them that Gylippus would be with them speedily, and that other ships were coming to relieve them. And, ere yet they could perfectly believe Gongylus, an express was brought from Gylippus, to bid them go forth to meet him. So now taking good heart, they armed themselves; and Gylippus at once led on his men from their march in battle array against the Athenians, as Nicias also embattled these. And Gylippus, piling his arms in view of the Athenians, sent a herald to tell them he would give them leave to depart from Sicily without molestation. To this Nicias would not vouchsafe any answer, but some of his soldiers laughing, asked if with the sight of one coarse coat and Laconian staff the Syracusan prospects had become so brilliant that they could despise the Athenians, who had released to the Lacedæmonians three hundred, whom they held in chains, bigger men than Gylippus, and longer-haired? Timæus, also, writes that even the Syracusans made no account of Gylippus, at the first sight mocking at his staff and long hair, as afterwards they found reason to blame his covetousness and meanness. The same author, however, adds that on Gylippus' first appearance, as it might have been at the sight of an owl abroad in the air, there was a general flocking together of men to serve in the war. And this is the truer saying of the two; for in the staff and the cloak they saw the badge and authority of Sparta, and crowded to him accordingly. And not only Thucydides affirms that the whole thing was done by him alone, but so, also, does Philistus, who was a Syracusan and an actual witness of what happened.

However, the Athenians had the better in the first encounter, and slew some few of the Syracusans, and amongst them Gongylus of Corinth. But on the next day Gylippus showed what it is to be a man of experience; for with the same arms, the same horses, and on the same spot of ground, only employing them otherwise, he overcame the Athenians; and they fleeing to their camp, he set the Syracusans to work, and with the stone and materials that had been brought together for finishing the wall of the Athenians, he built a cross-wall to intercept theirs and break it off, so that even if they were successful in the field, they would not be able to do anything. And after this the Syracusans taking courage manned their galleys, and with their horse and followers ranging about took a good many prisoners; and Gylippus going himself to the cities, called upon them to join with him, and was listened to and supported vigorously by them. So that Nicias fell back again to his old views, and, seeing the face of affairs change, desponded, and wrote to Athens, bidding them either send another army, or recall this out of Sicily, and that he might, in any case, be wholly relieved of the command, because of his disease.

Before this the Athenians had been intending to send another army to Sicily, but envy of Nicias' early achievements and high fortune had occasioned, up to this time, many delays; but now they were all eager to send off succours. Eurymedon went before, in midwinter, with money, and to announce that Euthydemus and Menander were chosen out of those that served there under Nicias to be joint commanders with him. Demosthenes was to go after in the spring with a great armament. In the meantime Nicias was briskly attacked, both by sea and land; in the beginning he had the disadvantage on the water, but in the end repulsed and sunk many galleys of the enemy. But by land he could not provide succour in time, so Gylippus surprised and captured Plemmyrium, in which the stores for the navy, and a great sum of money being there kept, all fell into his hands, and many were slain, and many taken prisoners. And what was of greatest importance, he now cut off Nicias' supplies, which had been safely and readily conveyed to him under Plemmyrium, while the Athenians still held it, but now that they were beaten out, he could only procure them with great difficulty, and with opposition from the enemy, who lay in wait with their ships under that fort. Moreover, it seemed manifest to the Syracusans that their navy had not been beaten by strength, but by their disorder in the pursuit. Now, therefore, all hands went to work to prepare for a new attempt that should succeed better than the former. Nicias had no wish for a sea-fight, but said it was mere folly for them, when Demosthenes was coming in all haste with so great a fleet and fresh forces to their succour, to engage the enemy with a less number of ships and ill provided. But, on the other hand, Menander and Euthydemus, who were just commencing their new command, prompted by a feeling of rivalry and emulation of both the generals, were eager to gain some great success before Demosthenes came, and to prove themselves superior to Nicias. They urged the honour of the city, which, said they, would be blemished and utterly lost if they should decline a challenge from the Syracusans. Thus they forced Nicias to a sea-fight; and by the stratagem of Ariston, the Corinthian pilot (his trick, described by Thucydides, about the men's dinners), they were worsted, and lost many of their men, causing the greatest dejection to Nicias, who had suffered so much from having the sole command, and now again miscarried through his colleagues.

But now by this time Demosthenes with his splendid fleet came in sight outside the harbour, a terror to the enemy. He brought along, in seventy-three galleys, five thousand men-at-arms; of darters, archers, and slingers, not less than three thousand; with the glittering of their armour, the flags waving from the galleys, the multitude of coxswains and flute players giving time to the rowers, setting off the whole with all possible warlike pomp and ostentation to dismay the enemy. Now one may believe the Syracusans were again in extreme alarm, seeing no end or prospect of release before them, toiling, as it seemed, in vain, and perishing to no purpose. Nicias, however, was not long overjoyed with the reinforcement, for the first time he conferred with Demosthenes, who advised forthwith to attack the Syracusans, and to put all to the speediest hazard, to win Syracuse, or else return home, afraid, and wondering at his promptness and audacity, he besought him to do nothing rashly and desperately, since delay would be the ruin of the enemy, whose money would not hold out, nor their confederates be long kept together; that when once they came to be pinched with want, they would presently come again to him for terms, as formerly. For, indeed, many in Syracuse held secret correspondence with him, and urged him to stay, declaring that even now the people were quite worn out with the war and weary of Gylippus. And if their necessities should the least sharpen upon them they would give up all.

Nicias glancing darkly at these matters, and unwilling to speak out plainly, made his colleagues imagine that it was cowardice which made him talk in this manner. And saying that this was the old story over again, the well-known procrastinations and delays and refinements with which at first he let slip the opportunity in not immediately falling on the enemy, but suffering the armament to become a thing of yesterday, that nobody was alarmed with, they took the side of Demosthenes, and with ado forced Nicias to comply. And so Demosthenes, taking the land-forces, by night made an assault upon Epipolæ; part of the enemy he slew ere they took the alarm, the rest defending themselves he put to flight. Nor was he content with this victory there, but pushed on further, till he met the Bœotians. For these were the first that made head against the Athenians, and charged them with a shout, spear against spear, and killed many on the place. And now at once there ensued a panic and confusion throughout the whole army; the victorious portion got infected with the fears of the flying part, and those who were still disembarking and coming forward, falling foul of the retreaters, came into conflict with their own party, taking the fugitives for pursuers, and treating their friends as if they were the enemy.

Thus huddled together in disorder, distracted with fear and uncertainties, and unable to be sure of seeing anything, the night not being absolutely dark, nor yielding any steady light, the moon then towards setting, shadowed with the many weapons and bodies that moved to and fro, and glimmering so as not to show an object plain, but to make friends through fear suspected for foes, the Athenians fell into utter perplexity and desperation. For, moreover, they had the moon at their backs, and consequently their own shadows fell upon them, and both hid the number and the glittering of their arms; while the reflection of the moon from the shields of the enemy made them show more numerous and better appointed than, indeed, they were. At last, being pressed on every side, when once they had given way, they took to rout, and in their flight were destroyed, some by the enemy, some by the hand of their friends, and some tumbling down the rocks, while those that were dispersed and straggled about were picked off in the morning by the horsemen and put to the sword. The slain were two thousand; and of the rest few came off safe with their arms.

Upon this disaster, which to him was not wholly an unexpected one, Nicias accused the rashness of Demosthenes; but he, making his excuses for the past, now advised to be gone in all haste, for neither were other forces to come, nor could the enemy be beaten with the present. And, indeed, even supposing they were yet too hard for the enemy in any case, they ought to remove and quit a situation which they understood to be always accounted a sickly one, and dangerous for an army, and was more particularly unwholesome now, as they could see themselves because of the time of year. It was the beginning of autumn, and many now lay sick, and all were out of heart.

It grieved Nicias to hear of flight and departing home, not that he did not fear the Syracusans, but he was worse afraid of the Athenians, their impeachments and sentences; he professed that he apprehended no further harm there, or if it must be, he would rather die by the hand of an enemy than by his fellow-citizens. He was not of the opinion which Leo of Byzantium declared to his fellow-citizens: "I had rather," said he, "perish by you, than with you." As to the matter of place and quarter whither to remove their camp, that, he said, might be debated at leisure. And Demosthenes, his former counsel having succeeded so ill, ceased to press him further; others thought Nicias had reasons for expectation, and relied on some assurance from people within the city, and that this made him so strongly oppose their retreat, so they acquiesced. But fresh forces now coming to the Syracusans and the sickness growing worse in his camp, he, also, now approved of their retreat, and commanded the soldiers to make ready to go aboard.

And when all were in readiness, and none of the enemy had observed them, not expecting such a thing, the moon was eclipsed in the night, to the great fright of Nicias and others, who, for want of experience, or out of superstition, felt alarm at such appearances. That the sun might be darkened about the close of the month, this even ordinary people now understood pretty well to be the effect of the moon; but the moon itself to be darkened, how that could come about, and how, on the sudden, a broad full moon should lose her light, and show such various colours, was not easy to be comprehended; they concluded it to be ominous, and a divine intimation of some heavy calamities. For he who the first, and the most plainly of any, and with the greatest assurance committed to writing how the moon is enlightened and overshadowed, was Anaxagoras; and he was as yet but recent, nor was his argument much known, but was rather kept secret, passing only amongst a few, under some kind of caution and confidence. People would not then tolerate natural philosophers, and theorists, as they then called them, about things above; as lessening the divine power, by explaining away its agency into the operation of irrational causes and senseless forces acting by necessity, without anything of Providence or a free agent. Hence it was that Protagoras was banished, and Anaxagoras cast in prison, so that Pericles had much difficulty to procure his liberty; and Socrates, though he had no concern whatever with this sort of learning, yet was put to death for philosophy. It was only afterwards that the reputation of Plato, shining forth by his life, and because he subjected natural necessity to divine and more excellent principles, took away the obloquy and scandal that had attached to such contemplations, and obtained these studies currency among all people. So his friend Dion, when the moon, at the time he was to embark from Zacynthus to go against Dionysius, was eclipsed, was not in the least disturbed, but went on, and arriving at Syracuse, expelled the tyrant. But it so fell out with Nicias, that he had not at this time a skilful diviner with him; his former habitual adviser who used to moderate much of his superstition, Stilbides, had died a little before. For, in fact, this prodigy, as Philochorus observes, was not unlucky for men wishing to fly, but on the contrary very favourable; for things done in fear require to be hidden, and the light is their foe. Nor was it usual to observe signs in the sun or moon more than three days, as Autoclides states in his Commentaries. But Nicias persuaded them to wait another full course of the moon, as if he had not seen it clear again as soon as ever it had passed the region of shadow where the light was obstructed by the earth.

In a manner abandoning all other cares, he betook himself wholly to his sacrifices, till the enemy came upon them with their infantry, besieging the forts and camp, and placing their ships in a circle about the harbour. Nor did the men in the galleys only, but the little boys everywhere got into the fishing boats and rowed up and challenged the Athenians, and insulted over them. Amongst these a youth of noble parentage, Heraclides by name, having ventured out beyond the rest, an Athenian ship pursued and well-nigh took him. His uncle Pollichus, in fear for him, put out with ten galleys which he commanded, and the rest, to relieve Pollichus, in like manner drew forth; the result of it being a very sharp engagement, in which the Syracusans had the victory, and slew Eurymedon, with many others. After this the Athenian soldiers had no patience to stay longer, but raised an outcry against their officers, requiring them to depart by land; for the Syracusans, upon their victory, immediately shut and blocked up the entrance of the harbour; but Nicias would not consent to this, as it was a shameful thing to leave behind so many ships of burden, and galleys little less than two hundred. Putting, therefore, on board the best of the foot, and the most serviceable darters, they filled one hundred and ten galleys; the rest wanted oars. The remainder of his army Nicias posted along by the seaside, abandoning the great camp and the fortifications adjoining the temple of Hercules; so the Syracusans, not having for a long time performed their usual sacrifice to Hercules, went up now, both priests and captains, to sacrifice.

And their galleys being manned, the diviners predicted from their sacrifices victory and glory to the Syracusans, provided they would not be the aggressors, but fight upon the defensive; for so Hercules overcame all, by only defending himself when set upon. In this confidence they set out; and this proved the hottest and fiercest of all their sea-fights, raising no less concern and passion in the beholders than in the actors; as they could oversee the whole action with all the various and unexpected turns of fortune which, in a short space, occurred in it; the Athenians suffering no less from their own preparations, than from the enemy; for they fought against light and nimble ships, that could attack from any quarter, with theirs laden and heavy. And they were thrown at with stones that fly indifferently any way, for which they could only return darts and arrows, the direct aim of which the motion of the water disturbed, preventing their coming true, point foremost to their mark. This the Syracusans had learned from Ariston the Corinthian pilot, who, fighting stoutly, fell himself in this very engagement, when the victory had already declared for the Syracusans.

The Athenians, their loss and slaughter being very great, their flight by sea cut off, their safety by land so difficult, did not attempt to hinder the enemy towing away their ships, under their eyes, nor demanded their dead, as, indeed, their want of burial seemed a less calamity than the leaving behind the sick and wounded which they now had before them. Yet more miserable still than those did they reckon themselves, who were to work on yet, through more such sufferings, after all to reach the same end.

They prepared to dislodge that night. And Gylippus and his friends seeing the Syracusans engaged in their sacrifices and at their cups, for their victories, and it being also a holiday, did not expect either by persuasion or by force to rouse them up and carry them against the Athenians as they decamped. But Hermocrates, of his own head, put a trick upon Nicias, and sent some of his companions to him, who pretended they came from those that were wont to hold secret intelligence with him, and advised him not to stir that night, the Syracusans having laid ambushes and beset the ways. Nicias, caught with this stratagem, remained, to encounter presently in reality what he had feared when there was no occasion. For they, the next morning, marching before, seized the defiles, fortified the passes where the rivers were fordable, cut down the bridges, and ordered their horsemen to range the plains and ground that lay open, so as to leave no part of the country where the Athenians could move without fighting. They stayed both that day and another night, and then went along as if they were leaving their own, not an enemy's country, lamenting and bewailing for want of necessaries, and for their parting from friends and companions that were not able to help themselves; and, nevertheless, judging the present evils lighter than those they expected to come. But among the many miserable spectacles that appeared up and down in the camp, the saddest sight of all was Nicias himself, labouring under his malady, and unworthily reduced to the scantiest supply of all the accommodations necessary for human wants, of which he in his condition required more than ordinary, because of his sickness, yet bearing up under all this illness, and doing and undergoing more than many in perfect health. And it was plainly evident that all this toil was not for himself, or from any regard to his own life, but that purely for the sake of those under his command he would not abandon hope. And, indeed, the rest were given over to weeping and lamentation through fear or sorrow, but he, whenever he yielded to anything of the kind, did so, it was evident, from reflection upon the shame and dishonour of the enterprise, contrasted with the greatness and glory of the success he had anticipated, and not only the sight of his person, but, also, the recollection of the arguments and the dissuasions he used to prevent this expedition enhanced their sense of the undeservedness of his sufferings, nor had they any heart to put their trust in the gods, considering that a man so religious, who had performed to the divine powers so many and so great acts of devotion, should have no more favourable treatment than the wickedest and meanest of the army.

Nicias, however, endeavoured all the while by his voice, his countenance, and his carriage, to show himself undefeated by these misfortunes. And all along the way shot at, and receiving wounds eight days continually from the enemy, he yet preserved the forces with him in a body entire, till that Demosthenes was taken prisoner with the party that he led, whilst they fought and made a resistance, and so got behind and were surrounded near the country house of Polyzelus. Demosthenes thereupon drew his sword, and wounded but did not kill himself, the enemy speedily running in and seizing upon him. So soon as the Syracusans had gone and informed Nicias of this, and he had sent some horsemen, and by them knew the certainly of the defeat of that division, he then vouchsafed to sue to Gylippus for a truce for the Athenians to depart out of Sicily, leaving hostages for payment of money that the Syracusans had expended in the war.

But now they would not hear of these proposals, but threatening and reviling them, angrily and insultingly continued to ply their missiles at them, now destitute of every necessary. Yet Nicias still made good his retreat all that night, and the next day, through all their darts, made his way to the river Asinarus. There, however, the enemy encountering them, drove some into the stream, while others, ready to die for thirst, plunged in headlong, while they drank at the same time, and were cut down by their enemies. And here was the cruellest and the most immoderate slaughter. Till at last Nicias falling down to Gylippus, "Let pity, O Gylippus," said he, "move you in your victory; not for me, who was destined, it seems, to bring the glory I once had to this end, but for the other Athenians; as you well know that the chances of war are common to all, and the Athenians used them moderately and mildly towards you in their prosperity."

At these words, and at the sight of Nicias, Gylippus was somewhat troubled, for he was sensible that the Lacedæmonians had received good offices from Nicias in the late treaty, and he thought it would be a great and glorious thing for him to carry off the chief commanders of the Athenians alive. He therefore raised Nicias with respect, and bade him be of good cheer, and commanded his men to spare the lives of the rest. But the word of command being communicated slowly, the slain were a far greater number than the prisoners. Many, however, were privately conveyed away by particular soldiers. Those taken openly were hurried together in a mass; their arms and spoils hung up on the finest and largest trees along the river. The conquerors, with garlands on their heads, with their own horses splendidly adorned, and cropping short the manes and tails of those of their enemies, entered the city, having, in the most signal conflict ever waged by Greeks against Greeks, and with the greatest strength and the utmost effort of valour and manhood won a most entire victory.

And a general assembly of the people of Syracuse and their confederates sitting, Eurycles, the popular leader, moved, first, that the day on which they took Nicias should from thenceforward be kept holiday by sacrificing and forbearing all manner of work, and from the river be called the Asinarian Feast. This was the twenty-sixth day of the month Carneus, the Athenian Metagitnion. And that the servants of the Athenians with the other confederates be sold for slaves, and they themselves and the Sicilian auxiliaries be kept and employed in the quarries, except the generals, who should be put to death. The Syracusans favoured the proposals, and when Hermocrates said, that to use well a victory was better than to gain a victory, he was met with great clamour and outcry. When Gylippus, also, demanded the Athenian generals to be delivered to him, that he might carry them to the Lacedæmonians, the Syracusans, now insolent with their good-fortune, gave him ill words. Indeed, before this, even in the war, they had been impatient at his rough behaviour and Lacedæmonian haughtiness, and had, as Timæus tells us, discovered sordidness and avarice in his character, vices which may have descended to him from his father Cleandrides, who was convicted of bribery and banished. And the very man himself, of the one thousand talents which Lysander sent to Sparta, embezzled thirty, and hid them under the tiles of his house, and was detected and shamefully fled his country. But this is related more at large in the life of Lysander. Timæus says that Demosthenes and Nicias did not die, as Thucydides and Philistus have written, by the order of the Syracusans, but that upon a message sent them from Hermocrates, whilst yet the assembly were sitting, by the connivance of some of their guards, they were enabled to put an end to themselves. Their bodies, however, were thrown out before the gates and offered for a public spectacle. And I have heard that to this day in a temple at Syracuse is shown a shield, said to have been Nicias', curiously wrought and embroidered with gold and purple intermixed. Most of the Athenians perished in the quarries by diseases and ill diet, being allowed only one pint of barley everyday, and one half pint of water. Many of them, however, were carried off by stealth, or, from the first, were supposed to be servants, and were sold as slaves. These latter were branded on their foreheads with the figure of a horse. There were, however, Athenians who, in addition to slavery, had to endure even this. But their discreet and orderly conduct was an advantage to them; they were either soon set free, or won the respect of their masters with whom they continued to live. Several were saved for the sake of Euripides, whose poetry, it appears, was in request among the Sicilians more than among any of the settlers out of Greece. And when any travellers arrived that could tell them some passage, or give them any specimen of his verses, they were delighted to be able to communicate them to one another. Many of the captives who got safe back to Athens are said, after they reached home, to have gone and made their acknowledgments to Euripides, relating how that some of them had been released from their slavery by teaching what they could remember of his poems, and others, when straggling after the fight, been relieved with meat and drink for repeating some of his lyrics. Nor need this be any wonder, for it is told that a ship of Caunus fleeing into one of their harbours for protection, pursued by pirates, was not received, but forced back, till one asked if they knew any of Euripides' verses, and on their saying they did, they were admitted, and their ship brought into harbour.

It is said that the Athenians would not believe their loss, in a great degree because of the person who first brought them news of it. For a certain stranger, it seems, coming to Piræus, and there sitting in a barber's shop, began to talk of what had happened, as if the Athenians already knew all that had passed; which the barber hearing, before he acquainted anybody else, ran as fast as he could up into the city, addressed himself to the Archons, and presently spread it about in the public Place. On which, there being everywhere, as may be imagined, terror and consternation, the Archons summoned a general assembly, and there brought in the man and questioned him how he came to know. And he, giving no satisfactory account, was taken for a spreader of false intelligence and a disturber of the city, and was, therefore, fastened to the wheel and racked a long time, till other messengers arrived that related the whole disaster particularly. So hardly was Nicias believed to have suffered the calamity which he had often predicted.

CRASSUS

MARCUS CRASSUS, WHOSE FATHER HAD BORNE THE OFFICE OF A CENSOR, and received the honour of a triumph, was educated in a little house together with his two brothers, who both married in their parents' lifetime; they kept but one table amongst them; all which, perhaps, was not the least reason of his own temperance and moderation in diet. One of his brothers dying, he married his widow, by whom he had his children; neither was there in these respects any of the Romans who lived a more orderly life than he did, though later in life he was suspected to have been too familiar with one of the vestal virgins, named Licinia, who was, nevertheless, acquitted, upon an impeachment brought against her by one Plotinus. Licinia stood possessed of a beautiful property in the suburbs, which Crassus desiring to purchase at a low price, for this reason was frequent in his attentions to her, which gave occasion to the scandal, and his avarice, so to say, serving to clear him of the crime, he was acquitted. Nor did he leave the lady till he had got the estate.

People were wont to say that the many virtues of Crassus were darkened by the one vice of avarice, and indeed he seemed to have no other but that; for it being the most predominant, obscured others to which he was inclined. The arguments in proof of his avarice were the vastness of his estate, and the manner of raising it; for whereas at first he was not worth above three hundred talents, yet, though in the course of his political life he dedicated the tenth of all he had to Hercules, and feasted the people, and gave to every citizen corn enough to serve him three months, upon casting up his accounts, before he went upon his Parthian expedition, he found his possessions to amount to seven thousand one hundred talents; most of which, if we may scandal him with a truth, he got by fire and rapine, making his advantages of the public calamities. For when Sylla seized the city, and exposed to sale the goods of those that he had caused to be slain, accounting them booty and spoils, and, indeed, calling them so too, and was desirous of making as many, and as eminent men as he could, partakers in the crime, Crassus never was the man that refused to accept, or give money for them. Moreover, observing how extremely subject the city was to fire and falling down of houses, by reason of their height and their standing so near together, he bought slaves that were builders and architects, and when he had collected these to the number of more than five hundred, he made it his practice to buy houses that were on fire, and those in the neighbourhood, which, in the immediate danger and uncertainty the proprietors were willing to part with for little or nothing, so that the greatest part of Rome, at one time or other, came into his hands. Yet for all he had so many workmen, he never built anything but his own house, and used to say that those that were addicted to building would undo themselves soon enough without the help of other enemies. And though he had many silver mines, and much valuable land, and labourers to work in it, yet all this was nothing in comparison of his slaves, such a number and variety did he possess of excellent readers, amanuenses, silversmiths, stewards and table-waiters, whose instruction he always attended to himself, superintending in person, while they learned, and teaching them himself, accounting it the main duty of a master to look over the servants that are, indeed, the living tools of housekeeping; and in this, indeed, he was in the right, in thinking, that is, as he used to say, that servants ought to look after all other things, and the master after them. For economy, which in things inanimate is but money-making, when exercised over men becomes policy. But it was surely a mistaken judgment, when he said no man was to be accounted rich that could not maintain an army at his own cost and charges, for war, as Archidamus well observed, is not fed at a fixed allowance, so that there is no saying what wealth suffices for it, and certainly it was one very far removed from that of Marius; for when he had distributed fourteen acres of land a man, and understood that some desired more, "God forbid," said he, "that any Roman should think that too little which is enough to keep him alive and well."

Crassus, however, was very eager to be hospitable to strangers; he kept open house, and to his friends he would lend money without interest, but called it in precisely at the time; so that his kindness was often thought worse than the paying the interest would have been. His entertainments were, for the most part, plain and citizenlike, the company general and

popular; good taste and kindness made them pleasanter than sumptuosity would have done. As for learning he chiefly cared for rhetoric, and
what would be serviceable with large numbers; he became one of the best
speakers at Rome, and by his pains and industry outdid the best natural
orators. For there was no trial how mean and contemptible soever that he
came to unprepared; nay, several times he undertook and concluded a
cause when Pompey and Cæsar and Cicero refused to stand up, upon
which account particularly he got the love of the people, who looked
upon him as a diligent and careful man, ready to help and succour his fellow citizens. Besides, the people were pleased with his courteous and
unpretending salutations and greetings, for he never met any citizen however humble and low, but he returned him his salute by name. He was
looked upon as a man well-read in history, and pretty well versed in
Aristotle's philosophy, in which one Alexander instructed him, a man
whose intercourse with Crassus gave a sufficient proof of his good nature
and gentle disposition; for it is hard to say whether he was poorer when he
entered into his service, or while he continued in it; for being his only
friend that used to accompany him when travelling, he used to receive
from him a cloak for the journey, and when he came home had it
demanded from him again; poor, patient sufferer, when even the philosophy he professed did not look upon poverty as a thing indifferent. But of
this hereafter.

When Cinna and Marius got the power in their hands it was soon perceived that they had not come back for any good they intended to their
country, but to effect the ruin and utter destruction of the nobility. And as
many as they could lay their hands on they slew, amongst whom were
Crassus' father and brother; he himself, being very young, for the moment
escaped the danger; but understanding that he was every way beset and
hunted after by the tyrants, taking with him three friends and ten servants,
with all possible speed he fled into Spain, having formerly been there and
secured a great number of friends, while his father was prætor of that
country. But finding all people in a consternation, and trembling at the
cruelty of Marius, as if he was already standing over them in person, he
durst not discover himself to anybody, but hid himself in a large cave
which was by the seashore, and belonged to Vibius Pacianus, to whom he
sent one of his servants to sound him, his provisions, also, beginning to
fail. Vibius was well pleased at his escape, and inquiring the place of his
abode and the number of his companions, he went not to him himself,
but commanded his steward to provide everyday a good meal's meat, and

carry it and leave it near such a rock, and to return without taking any further notice or being inquisitive, promising him his liberty if he did as he commanded and that he would kill him if he intermeddled. The cave is not far from the sea; a small and insignificant looking opening in the cliffs conducts you in; when you are entered, a wonderfully high roof spreads above you, and large chambers open out one beyond another, nor does it lack either water or light, for a very pleasant and wholesome spring runs at the foot of the cliffs, and natural chinks, in the most advantageous place, let in the light all day long, and the thickness of the rock makes the air within pure and clear, all the wet and moisture being carried off into the spring.

While Crassus remained here, the steward brought them what was necessary, but never saw them, nor knew anything of the matter, though they within saw, and expected him at the customary times. Neither was their entertainment such as just to keep them alive, but given them in abundance and for their enjoyment; for Pacianus resolved to treat him with all imaginable kindness, and considering that he was a young man, thought it well to gratify a little his youthful inclinations; for to give just what is needful seems rather to come from necessity than from a hearty friendship. Once taking with him two female servants, he showed them the place and bade them go in boldly, whom when Crassus and his friends saw, they were afraid of being betrayed and demanded what they were, and what they would have. They, according as they were instructed, answered, they came to wait upon their master, who was hid in that cave. And so Crassus perceiving it was a piece of pleasantry and of goodwill on the part of Vibius, took them in and kept them there with him as long as he stayed, and employed them to give information to Vibius of what they wanted, and how they were. Fenestella says he saw one of them, then very old, and often heard her speak of the time and repeat the story with pleasure.

After Crassus had lain concealed there eight months, on hearing that Cinna was dead, he appeared abroad, and a great number of people flocking to him, out of whom he selected a body of two thousand five hundred, he visited many cities, and, as some write, sacked Malaca, which he himself, however, always denied, and contradicted all who said so. Afterwards, getting together some ships, he passed into Africa, and joined with Metellus Pius, an eminent person that had raised a very considerable force; but upon some difference between him and Metellus, he stayed not long there, but went over to Sylla, by whom he was very much esteemed. When Sylla passed over into Italy, he was anxious to put all the young men that were with him in employment; and as he despatched someone way, and some another, Crassus, on its falling to his share to raise men among the Marsians, demanded a guard, being to pass through the enemy's country, upon which Sylla replied sharply, "I give you for guard your father, your brother, your friends and kindred, whose unjust and cruel murder I am now going to revenge"; and Crassus, being nettled, went his way, broke boldly through the enemy, collected a considerable force, and in all Sylla's wars acted with great zeal and courage. And in these times and occasions, they say, began the emulation and rivalry for glory between him and Pompey; for though Pompey was the younger man, and had the disadvantage to be descended of a father that was disesteemed by the citizens, and hated as much as ever man was, yet in these actions he shone out and was proved so great that Sylla always used, when he came in, to stand up and uncover his head, an honour which he seldom showed to older men and his own equals, and always saluted him *Imperator.* This fired and stung. Crassus, though, indeed, he could not with any fairness claim to be preferred; for he both wanted experience, and his two innate vices, sordidness and avarice, tarnished all the lustre of his actions. For when he had taken Tudertia, a town of the Umbrians, he converted, it was said, all the spoils to his own use, for which he was complained of to Sylla. But in the last and greatest battle before Rome itself when Sylla was worsted, some of his battalions giving ground, and others being quite broken, Crassus got the victory on the right wing, which he commanded, and pursued the enemy till night, and then sent to Sylla to acquaint him with his success, and demand provision for his soldiers. In the time, however, of the proscriptions and sequestrations, he lost his repute again, by making great purchases for little or nothing, and asking for grants. Nay, they say he proscribed one of the Bruttians without Sylla's order, only for his own profit, and that, on discovering this, Sylla never after trusted him in any public affairs. As no man was more cunning than Crassus to ensnare others by flattery, so no man lay more open to it, or swallowed it more greedily than himself. And this particularly was observed of him, that though he was the most covetous man in the world, yet he habitually disliked and cried out against others who were so.

It troubled him to see Pompey so successful in all his undertakings; that he had had a triumph before he was capable to sit in the senate, and that the people had surnamed him Magnus, or the great. When somebody was saying Pompey the Great was coming, he smiled, and asked him, "How big is he?" Despairing to equal him by feats of arms, he betook himself to civil life, where by doing kindnesses, pleading, lending money, by speaking and canvassing among the people for those who had objects to obtain from them, he gradually gained as great honour and power as Pompey had from his many famous expeditions. And it was a curious thing in their rivalry, that Pompey's name and interests in the city were greatest when he was absent, for his renown in war, but when present he was often less successful than Crassus, by reason of his superciliousness and haughty way of living, shunning crowds of people, and appearing rarely in the forum, and assisting only some few, and that not readily, that his interests might be the stronger when he came to use it for himself. Whereas Crassus, being a friend always at hand, ready to be had and easy of access, and always with his hands full of other people's business, with his freedom and courtesy, got the better of Pompey's formality. In point of dignity of person, eloquence of language, and attractiveness of countenance, they were pretty equally excellent. But, however, this emulation never transported Crassus so far as to make him bear enmity or any ill-will; for though he was vexed to see Pompey and Cæsar preferred to him, yet he never mingled any hostility or malice with his jealousy; though Cæsar, when he was taken captive by the corsairs in Asia, cried out, "O Crassus, how glad you will be at the news of my captivity!" Afterwards they lived together on friendly terms, for when Cæsar was going prætor into Spain, and his creditors, he being then in want of money, came upon him and seized his equipage, Crassus then stood by him and relieved him, and was his security for eight hundred and thirty talents. And in general, Rome being divided into three great interests, those of Pompey, Cæsar, and Crassus (for as for Cato, his fame was greater than his power, and he was rather admired than followed), the sober and quiet part were for Pompey, the restless and hot-headed followed Cæsar's ambition, but Crassus trimmed between them, making advantages of both, and changed sides continually, being neither a trusty friend nor an implacable enemy, and easily abandoned both his attachments and his animosities, as he found it for his advantage, so that in short spaces of time the same men and the same measures had him both as their supporter and as their opponent. He was much liked, but was feared as much or even more. At any rate, when Sicinius, who was the greatest troubler of the magistrates and ministers of his time, was asked how it was he let Crassus alone, "Oh," said he, "he carries hay on his horns," alluding to the custom of tying hay to the horns of the bull that used to butt, that people might keep out of his way.

The insurrection of the gladiators and the devastation of Italy, commonly called the war of Spartacus, began upon this occasion. One

Lentulus Batiates trained up a great many gladiators in Capua, most of them Gauls and Thracians, who, not for any fault by them committed, but simply through the cruelty of their master, were kept in confinement for this object of fighting one with another. Two hundred of these formed a plan to escape, but being discovered, those of them who became aware of it in time to anticipate their master, being seventy-eight, got out of a cook's shop chopping-knives and spits, and made their way through the city, and lighting by the way on several wagons that were carrying gladiators' arms to another city, they seized upon them and armed themselves. And seizing upon a defensible place, they chose three captains, of whom Spartacus was chief, a Thracian of one of the nomad tribes, and a man not only of high spirit and valiant, but in understanding, also, and in gentleness superior to his condition, and more of a Grecian than the people of his country usually are. When he first came to be sold at Rome, they say a snake coiled itself upon his face as he lay asleep, and his wife, who at this latter time also accompanied him in his flight, his countrywoman, a kind of prophetess, and one of those possessed with the bacchanal frenzy, declared that it was a sign portending great and formidable power to him with no happy event.

First, then, routing those that came out of Capua against them, and thus procuring a quantity of proper soldiers' arms, they gladly threw away their own as barbarous and dishonourable. Afterwards Clodius, the prætor, took the command against them with a body of three thousand men from Rome, and besieged them within a mountain, accessible only by one narrow and difficult passage, which Clodius kept guarded, encompassed on all other sides with steep and slippery precipices. Upon the top, however, grew a great many wild vines, and cutting down as many of their boughs as they had need of, they twisted them into strong ladders long enough to reach from thence to the bottom, by which, without any danger, they got down all but one, who stayed there to throw them down their arms, and after this succeeded in saving himself. The Romans were ignorant of all this, and, therefore, coming upon them in the rear, they assaulted them unawares and took their camp. Several, also, of the shepherds and herdsmen that were there, stout and nimble fellows, revolted over to them, to some of whom they gave complete arms, and made use of others as scouts and light-armed soldiers. Publius Varinus, the prætor, was now sent against them, whose lieutenant, Furius, with two thousand men, they fought and routed. Then Cossinius was sent with considerable forces, to give his assistance and advice, and him Spartacus missed but very little of capturing in person, as he was bathing at Salinæ; for he with great difficulty made his escape, while Spartacus possessed himself of his baggage, and following the chase with a great slaughter, stormed his camp and took it, where Cossinius himself was slain. After many successful skirmishes with the prætor himself, in one of which he took his lictors and his own horse, he began to be great and terrible; but wisely considering that he was not to expect to match the force of the empire, he marched his army towards the Alps, intending, when he had passed them, that every man should go to his own home, some to Thrace, some to Gaul. But they, grown confident in their numbers, and puffed up with their success, would give no obedience to him, but went about and ravaged Italy; so that now the senate was not only moved at the indignity and baseness, both of the enemy and of the insurrection, but, looking upon it as a matter of alarm and of dangerous consequence, sent out both the consuls to it, as to a great and difficult enterprise. The consul Gellius, falling suddenly upon a party of Germans, who through contempt and confidence had straggled from Spartacus, cut them all to pieces. But when Lentulus with a large army besieged Spartacus, he sallied out upon him, and, joining battle, defeated his chief officers, and captured all his baggage. As he made toward the Alps, Cassius, who was prætor of that part of Gaul that lies about the Po, met him with ten thousand men, but being overcome in the battle, he had much ado to escape himself, with the loss of a great many of his men.

When the senate understood this, they were displeased at the consuls, and ordering them to meddle no further, they appointed Crassus general of the war, and a great many of the nobility went volunteers with him, partly out of friendship, and partly to get honour. He stayed himself on the borders of Picenum, expecting Spartacus would come that way, and sent his lieutenant, Mummius, with two legions, to wheel about and observe the enemy's motions, but upon no account to engage or skirmish. But he, upon the first opportunity, joined battle, and was routed, having a great many of his men slain, and a great many only saving their lives with the loss of their arms. Crassus rebuked Mummius severely, and arming the soldiers again, he made them find sureties for their arms, that they would part with them no more, and five hundred that were the beginners of the flight he divided into fifty tens, and one of each was to die by lot, thus reviving the ancient Roman punishment of decimation, where ignominy is added to the penalty of death, with a variety of appalling and terrible circumstances, presented before the eyes of the whole army, assembled as spectators. When he had thus reclaimed his men, he led them against the enemy; but Spartacus retreated through Lucania toward the sea, and in the straits meeting with some Cilician pirate ships, he had thoughts of attempting Sicily, where, by landing two thousand men, he hoped to new kindle the war of the slaves, which was but lately extinguished, and seemed to need but little fuel to set it burning again. But after the pirates had struck a bargain with him, and received his earnest, they deceived him and sailed away. He thereupon retired again from the sea, and established his army in the peninsula of Rhegium; there Crassus came upon him, and considering the nature of the place, which of itself suggested the undertaking, he set to work to build a wall across the isthmus; thus keeping his soldiers at once from idleness and his foes from forage. This great and difficult work he perfected in a space of time short beyond all expectation, making a ditch from one sea to the other, over the neck of land, three hundred furlongs long, fifteen feet broad, and as much in depth, and above it built a wonderfully high and strong wall. All which Spartacus at first slighted and despised, but when provisions began to fail, and on his proposing to pass further, he found he was walled in, and no more was to be had in the peninsula, taking the opportunity of a snowy, stormy night, he filled up part of the ditch with earth and boughs of trees, and so passed the third part of his army over.

Crassus was afraid lest he should march directly to Rome, but was soon eased of that fear when he saw many of his men break out in a mutiny and quit him, and encamped by themselves upon the Lucanian lake. This lake they say changes at intervals of time, and is sometimes sweet, and sometimes so salt that it cannot be drunk. Crassus falling upon these beat them from the lake, but he could not pursue the slaughter, because of Spartacus suddenly coming up and checking the flight. Now he began to repent that he had previously written to the senate to call Lucullus out of Thrace, and Pompey out of Spain; so that he did all he could to finish the war before they came, knowing that the honour of the action would redound to him that came to his assistance. Resolving, therefore, first to set upon those that had mutinied and encamped apart, whom Caius Cannicius and Castus commanded, he sent six thousand men before to secure a little eminence, and to do it as privately as possible, which that they might do they covered their helmets, but being discovered by two women that were sacrificing for the enemy, they had been in great hazard, had not Crassus immediately appeared, and engaged in a battle which proved a most bloody one. Of twelve thousand three hundred whom he killed, two only

were found wounded in their backs, the rest all having died standing in
their ranks and fighting bravely. Spartacus, after this discomfiture, retired
to the mountains of Petelia, but Quintius, one of Crassus' officers, and
Scrofa, the quæstor, pursued and overtook him. But when Spartacus rallied and faced them, they were utterly routed and fled, and had much ado
to carry off their quæstor, who was wounded. This success, however,
ruined Spartacus, because it encouraged the slaves, who now disdained
any longer to avoid fighting, or to obey their officers, but as they were
upon the march, they came to them with their swords in their hands, and
compelled them to lead them back again through Lucania, against the
Romans, the very thing which Crassus was eager for. For news was already
brought that Pompey was at hand; and people began to talk openly that
the honour of this war was reserved to him, who would come and at once
oblige the enemy to fight and put an end to the war. Crassus, therefore,
eager to fight a decisive battle, encamped very near the enemy, and began
to make lines of circumvallation; but the slaves made a sally and attacked
the pioneers. As fresh supplies came in on either side, Spartacus, seeing
there was no avoiding it, set all his army in array and when his horse was
brought him, he drew out his sword and killed him, saying, if he got the
day he should have a great many better horses of the enemies', and if he
lost it he should have no need of this. And so making directly towards
Crassus himself, through the midst of arms and wounds, he missed him,
but slew two centurions that fell upon him together. At last being deserted
by those that were about him, he himself stood his ground, and, surrounded by the enemy, bravely defending himself, was cut in pieces. But
though Crassus had good fortune, and not only did the part of a good general, but gallantly exposed his person, yet Pompey had much of the credit
of the action. For he met with many of the fugitives, and slew them, and
wrote to the senate that Crassus indeed had vanquished the slaves in a
pitched battle, but that he had put an end to the war, Pompey was honoured with a magnificent triumph for his conquest over Sertorius and
Spain, while Crassus could not himself so much as desire a triumph in its
full form, and indeed it was thought to look but meanly in him to accept
of the lesser honour, called the ovation, for a servile war, and perform a
procession on foot. The difference between this and the other, and the
origin of the name, are explained in the life of Marcellus.

And Pompey being immediately invited to the consulship, Crassus,
who had hoped to be joined with him, did not scruple to request his assistance. Pompey most readily seized the opportunity, as he desired by all

means to lay some obligation upon Crassus, and zealously promoted his interest; and at last he declared in one of his speeches to the people that he should be not less beholden to them for his colleague than for the honour of his own appointment. But once entered upon the employment, this amity continued not long; but differing almost in everything, disagreeing, quarrelling, and contending, they spent the time of their consulship without effecting any measure of consequence, except that Crassus made a great sacrifice to Hercules, and feasted the people at ten thousand tables, and measured them out corn for three months. When their command was now ready to expire, and they were, as it happened, addressing the people, a Roman knight, one Onatius Aurelius, an ordinary private person, living in the country, mounted the hustings, and declared a vision he had in his sleep. "Jupiter," said he, "appeared to me, and commanded me to tell you, that you should not suffer your consuls to lay down their charge before they are made friends." When he had spoken, the people cried out that they should be reconciled. Pompey stood still and said nothing, but Crassus, first offering him his hand, said, "I cannot think, my countrymen, that I do anything humiliating or unworthy of myself, if I make the first offers of accommodation and friendship with Pompey, whom you yourselves styled the Great before he was of man's estate, and decreed him a triumph before he was capable of sitting in the senate."

This is what was memorable in Crassus' consulship, but as for his censorship, that was altogether idle and inactive, for he neither made a scrutiny of the senate, nor took a review of the horsemen, nor a census of the people, though he had as mild a man as could be desired for his colleague, Lutatius Catulus. It is said, indeed, that when Crassus intended a violent and unjust measure, which was the reducing Egypt to be tributary to Rome, Catulus strongly opposed it, and falling out about it, they laid down their office by consent. In the great conspiracy of Catiline, which was very near subverting the government, Crassus was not without some suspicion of being concerned, and one man came forward and declared him to be in the plot; but nobody credited him. Yet Cicero, in one of his orations, clearly charges both Crassus and Cæsar with the guilt of it, though that speech was not published till they were both dead. But in his speech upon his consulship, he declares that Crassus came to him by night, and brought a letter concerning Catiline, stating the details of the conspiracy. Crassus hated him ever after, but was hindered by his son from doing him any injury; for Publius was a great lover of learning and eloquence, and a constant follower of Cicero, insomuch that he put himself into mourning when he was accused, and induced the other young men to do the same. And at last he reconciled him to his father.

Cæsar now returning from his command, and designing to get the consulship, and seeing that Crassus and Pompey were again at variance, was unwilling to disoblige one by making application to the other, and despaired of success without the help of one of them; he therefore made it his business to reconcile them, making it appear that by weakening each other's influence they were promoting the interest of the Ciceros, the Catuli, and the Catos, who would really be of no account if they would join their interests and their factions, and act together in public with one policy and one united power. And so reconciling them by his persuasions, out of the three parties he set up one irresistible power, which utterly subverted the government both of senate and people. Not that he made either Pompey or Crassus greater than they were before, but by their means made himself greatest of all; for by the help of the adherents of both, he was at once gloriously declared consul, which office when he administered with credit, they decreed him the command of an army, and allotted him Gaul for his province, and so placed him as it were in the citadel, not doubting but they should divide the rest at their pleasure between themselves, when they had confirmed him in his allotted command. Pompey was actuated in all this by an immoderate desire of ruling, but Crassus, adding to his old disease of covetousness, a new passion after trophies and triumphs, emulous of Cæsar's exploits, not content to be beneath him in these points, though above him in all others, could not be at rest, till it ended in an ignominious overthrow and a public calamity. When Cæsar came out of Gaul to Lucca, a great many went thither from Rome to meet him. Pompey and Crassus had various conferences with him in secret, in which they came to the resolution to proceed to still more decisive steps, and to get the whole management of affairs into their hands, Cæsar to keep his army, and Pompey and Crassus to obtain new ones and new provinces. To effect all which there was but one way, the getting the consulate a second time, which they were to stand for, and Cæsar to assist them by writing to his friends and sending many of his soldiers to vote.

But when they returned to Rome, their design was presently suspected, and a report was soon spread that this interview had been for no good. When Marcellinus and Domitius asked Pompey in the senate if he intended to stand for the consulship, he answered, perhaps he would, perhaps not; and being urged again, replied, he would ask it of the honest citizens, but not of the dishonest. Which answer appearing too haughty and arrogant, Crassus said, more modestly, that he would desire it if it might be for the advantage of the public, otherwise he would decline it. Upon this some others took confidence and came forward as candidates, among them Domitius. But when Pompey and Crassus now openly appeared for it, the rest were afraid and drew back; only Cato encouraged Domitius, who was his friend and relation, to proceed, exciting him to persist, as though he was now defending the public liberty, as these men, he said, did not so much aim at the consulate as at arbitrary government, and it was not a petition for office, but a seizure of provinces and armies. Thus spoke and thought Cato, and almost forcibly compelled Domitius to appear in the forum, where many sided with them. For there was, indeed, much wonder and question among the people, "Why should Pompey and Crassus want another consulship? And why they two together, and not with some third person? We have a great many men not unworthy to be fellow-consuls with either the one or the other." Pompey's party, being apprehensive of this, committed all manner of indecencies and violences, and amongst other things lay in wait for Domitius, as he was coming thither before daybreak with his friends; his torchbearer they killed, and wounded several others, of whom Cato was one. And these being beaten back and driven into a house, Pompey and Crassus were proclaimed consuls. Not long after, they surrounded the house with armed men, thrust Cato out of the forum, killed some that made resistance, and decreed Cæsar his command for five years longer, and provinces for themselves, Syria and both the Spains, which being divided by lots, Syria fell to Crassus, and the Spains to Pompey.

All were well pleased with the change, for the people were desirous that Pompey should go far from the city, and he, being extremely fond of his wife, was very glad to continue there; but Crassus was so transported with his fortune, that it was manifest he thought he had never had such good luck befall him as now, so that he had much to do to contain himself before company and strangers; but amongst his private friends he let fall many vain and childish words, which were unworthy of his age, and contrary to his usual character, for he had been very little given to boasting hitherto. But then being strangely puffed up, and his head heated, he would not limit his fortune with Parthia and Syria; but looking on the actions of Lucullus against Tigranes and the exploits of Pompey against Mithridates as but child's play, he proposed to himself in his hopes to pass as far as Bactria and India, and the utmost ocean. Not that he was called upon by the decree which appointed him to his office to undertake any expedition against the Parthians, but it was well known that he was eager for it, and Cæsar wrote to him out of Gaul commending his resolution, and inciting him to the war. And when Ateius, the tribune of the people, designed to stop his journey, and many others murmured that one man should undertake a war against a people that had done them no injury, and were at amity with them, he desired Pompey to stand by him and accompany him out of the town, as he had a great name amongst the common people. And when several were ready prepared to interfere and raise an outcry, Pompey appeared with a pleasing countenance, and so mollified the people, that they let Crassus pass quietly. Ateius, however, met him, and first by word of mouth warned and conjured him not to proceed, and then commanded his attendant officer to seize him and detain him; but the other tribunes not permitting it, the officer released Crassus. Ateius, therefore, running to the gate, when Crassus was come thither, set down a chafing-dish with lighted fire in it, and burning incense and pouring libations on it, cursed him with dreadful imprecations, calling upon and naming several strange and horrible deities. In the Roman belief there is so much virtue in these sacred and ancient rites, that no man can escape the effects of them, and that the utterer himself seldom prospers; so that they are not often made use of, and but upon a great occasion. And Ateius was blamed at the time for resorting to them, as the city itself, in whose cause he used them, would be the first to feel the ill effects of these curses and supernatural terrors.

Crassus arrived at Brundusium, and though the sea was very rough, he had not patience to wait, but went on board, and lost many of his ships. With the remnant of his army he marched rapidly through Galatia, where meeting with King Deiotarus, who, though he was very old, was about building a new city, Crassus scoffingly told him, "Your majesty begins to build at the twelfth hour." "Neither do you," said he, "O general, undertake your Parthian expedition very early." For Crassus was then sixty years old, and he seemed older than he was. At his first coming, things went as he would have them, for he made a bridge over the Euphrates, without much difficulty, and passed over his army in safety, and occupied many cities of Mesopotamia, which yielded voluntarily. But a hundred of his men were killed in one, in which Apollonius was tyrant; therefore, bringing his forces against it, he took it by storm, plundered the goods, and sold the inhabitants. The Greeks call this city Zenodotia, upon the taking of which he permitted the army to salute him Imperator, but this was very ill thought of, and it looked as if he despaired a nobler achievement, that he made so much of this little success. Putting garrisons of seven thousand foot and one thousand horse in the new conquests, he returned to take up his winter quarters in Syria, where his son was to meet him coming from Cæsar out of Gaul, decorated with rewards for his valour, and bringing with him one thousand select horse. Here Crassus seemed to commit his first error, and except, indeed, the whole expedition, his greatest; for, whereas he ought to have gone forward and seized Babylon and Seleucia, cities that were ever at enmity with the Parthians, he gave the enemy time to provide against him. Besides, he spent his time in Syria more like an usurer than a general, not in taking an account of the arms, and in improving the skill and discipline of his soldiers, but in computing the revenue of the cities, wasting many days in weighing by scale and balance the treasure that was in the temple of Hierapolis, issuing requisitions for levies of soldiers upon particular towns and kingdoms, and then again withdrawing them on payment of sums of money, by which he lost his credit and became despised. Here, too, he met with the first ill-omen from that goddess, whom some call Venus, others Juno, others Nature, or the Cause that produces out of moisture the first principles and seeds of all things, and gives mankind their earliest knowledge of all that is good for them. For as they were going out of the temple young Crassus stumbled and his father fell upon him.

When he drew his army out of winter quarters, ambassadors came to him from Arsaces, with this short speech: If the army was sent by the people of Rome, he denounced mortal war, but if, as he understood was the case, against the consent of his country, Crassus for his own private profit had invaded his territory, then their king would be more merciful, and taking pity upon Crassus' dotage, would send those soldiers back who had been left not so truly to keep guard on him as to be his prisoners. Crassus boastfully told them he would return his answer at Seleucia, upon which Vagises, the eldest of them, laughed and showed the palm of his hand, saying, "Hair will grow here before you will see Seleucia"; so they returned to their king, Hyrodes, telling him it was war. Several of the Romans that were in garrison in Mesopotamia with great hazard made their escape, and brought word that the danger was worth consideration, urging their own eyewitness of the numbers of the enemy, and the manner of their fighting, when they assaulted their towns; and, as men's manner is, made all seem greater than really it was. By flight it was impossible to escape them, and as impossible to overtake them when they fled, and they had a new and strange sort of darts, as swift as sight, for they pierced whatever they met with, before you could see who threw them; their men-at-arms were so provided that their weapons would cut through anything, and their armour give way to nothing. All which when the soldiers heard their hearts failed them; for till now they thought there was no difference between the Parthians and the Armenians or Cappadocians, whom Lucullus grew weary with plundering, and had been persuaded that the main difficulty of the war consisted only in the tediousness of the march and the trouble of chasing men that durst not come to blows, so that the danger of a battle was beyond their expectation; accordingly, some of the officers advised Crassus to proceed no further at present, but reconsider the whole enterprise, amongst whom in particular was Cassius, the quæstor. The soothsayers, also, told him privately the signs found in the sacrifices were continually adverse and unfavourable. But he paid no heed to them, or to anybody who gave any other advice than to proceed. Nor did Artavasdes, King of Armenia, confirm him a little, who came to his aid with six thousand horse; who, however, were said to be only the king's lifeguard and suit, for he promised ten thousand cuirassiers more, and thirty thousand foot, at his own charge. He urged Crassus to invade Parthia by the way of Armenia, for not only would he be able there to supply his army with abundant provision, which he would give him, but his passage would be more secure in the mountains and hills, with which the whole country was covered, making it almost impassable to horse, in which the main strength of the Parthians consisted. Crassus returned him but cold thanks for his readiness to serve him, and for the splendour of his assistance, and told him he was resolved to pass through Mesopotamia, where he had left a great many brave Roman soldiers; whereupon the Armenian went his way. As Crassus was taking the army over the river at Zeugma, he encountered preternaturally violent thunder, and the lightning flashed in the faces of the troops, and during the storm a hurricane broke upon the bridge, and carried part of it away; two thunderbolts fell upon the very place where the army was going to encamp; and one of the general's horses, magnificently caparisoned, dragged away the groom into the river and was drowned. It is said, too, that when they went to take up the first standard, the eagle of itself turned its head backward; and after he had passed over his army, as they were distributing provisions, the first thing they gave was lentils and salt, which with the Romans are the food proper to funerals, and are offered to the dead. And as Crassus was haranguing his soldiers, he let fall a word which was thought very ominous in the army;

for "I am going," he said, "to break down the bridge, that none of you may return"; and whereas he ought, when he had perceived his blunder, to have corrected himself, and explained his meaning, seeing the men alarmed at the expression, he would not do it out of mere stubbornness. And when at the last general sacrifice the priest gave him the entrails, they slipt out of his hand, and when he saw the standers-by concerned at it, he laughed and said, "See what it is to be an old man; but I shall hold my sword fast enough."

So he marched his army along the river with seven legions, little less than four thousand horse, and as many light-armed soldiers, and the scouts returning declared that not one man appeared, but that they saw the footing of a great many horses which seemed to be retiring in flight, whereupon Crassus conceived great hopes, and the Romans began to despise the Parthians, as men that would not come to combat, hand to hand. But Cassius spoke with him again, and advised him to refresh his army in some of the garrison towns, and remain there till they could get some certain intelligence of the enemy, or at least to make toward Seleucia, and keep by the river, that so they might have the convenience of having provision constantly supplied by the boats, which might always accompany the army, and the river would secure them from being environed, and, if they should fight, it might be upon equal terms.

While Crassus was still considering, and as yet undetermined, there came to the camp an Arab chief named Ariamnes, a cunning and wily fellow, who, of all the evil chances which combined to lead them on to destruction, was the chief and the most fatal. Some of Pompey's old soldiers knew him, and remembered him to have received some kindnesses of Pompey, and to have been looked upon as a friend to the Romans, but he was now suborned by the king's generals, and sent to Crassus to entice him if possible from the river and hills into the wide open plain, where he might be surrounded. For the Parthians desired anything rather than to be obliged to meet the Romans face to face. He, therefore, coming to Crassus (and he had a persuasive tongue), highly commended Pompey as his benefactor, and admired the forces that Crassus had with him, but seemed to wonder why he delayed and made preparations, as if he should not use his feet more than any arms, against men that, taking with them their best goods and chattels, had designed long ago to fly for refuge to the Scythians or Hyrcanians. "If you meant to fight, you should have made all possible haste, before the king should recover courage, and collect his forces together; at present you see Surena and Sillaces opposed to you, to draw you off in pursuit of them, while the king himself keeps out of the way." But this was all a lie, for Hyrodes had divided his army in two parts; with one he in person wasted Armenia, revenging himself upon Artavasdes, and sent Surena against the Romans, not out of contempt, as some pretend, for there is no likelihood that he should despise Crassus, one of the chiefest men of Rome, to go and fight with Artavasdes, and invade Armenia; but much more probably he really apprehended the danger, and therefore waited to see the event, intending that Surena should first run the hazard of a battle, and draw the enemy on. Nor was this Surena an ordinary person, but in wealth, family, and reputation, the second man in the kingdom, and in courage and prowess the first, and for bodily stature and beauty no man like him. Whenever he travelled privately, he had one thousand camels to carry his baggage, two hundred chariots for his concubines, one thousand completely armed men for lifeguards, and a great many more light-armed; and he had at least ten thousand horsemen altogether, of his servants and retinue. The honour had long belonged to his family, that at the king's coronation he put the crown upon his head, and when this very king Hyrodes had been exiled, he brought him in; it was he, also, that took the great city of Seleucia, was the first man that scaled the walls, and with his own hand beat off the defenders. And though at this time he was not above thirty years old, he had a great name for wisdom and sagacity, and, indeed, by these qualities chiefly, he overthrew Crassus, who first through his overweening confidence, and afterwards because he was cowed by his calamities, fell a ready victim to his subtlety. When Ariamnes had thus worked upon him, he drew him from the river into vast plains, by a way that at first was pleasant and easy but afterwards very troublesome by reason of the depth of the sand, no tree, nor any water, and no end of this to be seen; so that they were not only spent with thirst, and the difficulty of the passage, but were dismayed with the uncomfortable prospect of not a bough, not a stream, not a hillock, not a green herb, but in fact a sea of sand, which encompassed the army with its waves. They began to suspect some treachery, and at the same time came messengers from Artavasdes, that he was fiercely attacked by Hyrodes, who had invaded his country, so that now it was impossible for him to send any succours, and that he therefore advised Crassus to turn back, and with joint forces to give Hyrodes battle, or at least that he should march and encamp where horses could not easily come, and keep to the mountains. Crassus, out of anger and perverseness, wrote him no answer, but told them, at present he was not at leisure to mind the Armenians, but he would call upon them another time, and revenge himself upon Artavasdes for his treachery. Cassius and his friends began again to complain, but when they perceived that it merely displeased Crassus, they gave over, but privately railed at the barbarian, "What evil genius, O thou worst of men, brought thee to our camp, and with what charms and potions hast thou bewitched Crassus, that he should march his army through a vast and deep desert, through ways which are rather fit for a captain of Arabian robbers, than for the general of a Roman army?" But the barbarian, being a wily fellow, very submissively exhorted them, and encouraged them to sustain it a little further, and ran about the camp, and professing to cheer up the soldiers, asked them, jokingly, "What, do you think you march through Campania, expecting everywhere to find springs, and shady trees, and baths, and inns of entertainment? Consider you now travel through the confines of Arabia and Assyria." Thus he managed them like children, and before the cheat was discovered, he rode away; not but that Crassus was aware of his going, but he had persuaded him that he would go and contrive how to disorder the affairs of the enemy.

It is related that Crassus came abroad that day not in his scarlet robe, which Roman generals usually wear, but in a black one, which, as soon as he perceived, he changed. And the standard-bearers had much ado to take up their eagles, which seemed to be fixed to the place. Crassus laughed at it, and hastened their march, and compelled his infantry to keep pace with his cavalry, till some few of the scouts returned and told them that their fellows were slain and they hardly escaped, that the enemy was at hand in full force, and resolved to give them battle. On this all was in an uproar; Crassus was struck with amazement, and for haste could scarcely put his army in good order. First, as Cassius advised, he opened their ranks and files that they might take up as much space as could be, to prevent their being surrounded, and distributed the horse upon the wings, but afterwards changing his mind, he drew up his army in a square, and made a front every way, each of which consisted of twelve cohorts, to everyone of which he allotted a troop of horse, that no part might be destitute of the assistance that the horse might give, and that they might be ready to assist everywhere, as need should require. Cassius commanded one of the wings, young Crassus the other, and he himself was in the middle. Thus they marched on till they came to a little river named Balissus, a very inconsiderable one in itself, but very grateful to the soldiers, who had suffered so much by drouth and heat all along their march. Most of the commanders were of the opinion that they ought to remain there that night, and to inform themselves as much as possible of the number of the enemies, and their order, and so march against them at break of day; but Crassus was so carried away by the eagerness of his son, and the horsemen that were with him, who desired and urged him to lead them on and engage, that he commanded those that had a mind to it to eat and drink as they stood in their ranks, and before they had all well done, he led them on, not leisurely and with halts to take breath, as if he was going to battle, but kept on his pace as if he had been in haste, till they saw the enemy, contrary to their expectation, neither so many nor so magnificently armed as the Romans expected. For Surena had hid his main force behind the first ranks, and ordered them to hide the glittering of their armour with coats and skins. But when they approached and the general gave the signal, immediately all the field rung with a hideous noise and terrible clamour. For the Parthians do not encourage themselves to war with cornets and trumpets, but with a kind of kettle-drum, which they strike all at once in various quarters. With these they make a dead, hollow noise, like the bellowing of beasts, mixed with sounds resembling thunder, having, it would seem, very correctly observed that of all our senses hearing most confounds and disorders us, and that the feelings excited through it most quickly disturb and most entirely overpower the understanding.

When they had sufficiently terrified the Romans with their noise, they threw off the covering of their armour, and shone like lightning in their breastplates and helmets of polished Margianian steel, and with their horses covered with brass and steel trappings. Surena was the tallest and finest looking man himself, but the delicacy of his looks and effeminacy of his dress did not promise so much manhood as he really was master of; for his face was painted, and his hair parted after the fashion of the Medes, whereas the other Parthians made a more terrible appearance, with their shaggy hair gathered in a mass upon their foreheads after the Scythian mode. Their first design was with their lances to beat down and force back the first ranks of the Romans, but when they perceived the depth of their battle, and that the soldiers firmly kept their ground, they made a retreat, and pretending to break their order and disperse, they encompassed the Roman square before they were aware of it. Crassus commanded his light-armed soldiers to charge, but they had not gone far before they were received with such a shower of arrows that they were glad to retire amongst the heavy-armed, with whom this was the first occasion of disorder and terror, when they perceived the strength and force of their darts, which pierced their arms, and passed through every kind of covering, hard and soft alike. The Parthians now placing themselves at distances began to shoot from all sides, not aiming at any particular mark (for, indeed, the order of the Romans was so close, that they could not miss if they would), but simply sent their arrows with great force out of strong bent bows, the strokes from which came with extreme violence. The position of the Romans was a very bad one from the first; for if they kept their ranks, they were wounded, and if they tried to charge, they hurt the enemy none the more, and themselves suffered none the less. For the Parthians threw their darts as they fled, an art in which none but the Scythians excel them, and it is, indeed, a cunning practice, for while they thus fight to make their escape, they avoid the dishonour of a flight.

However, the Romans had some comfort to think that when they had spent all their arrows, they would either give over or come to blows; but when they presently understood that there were numerous camels loaded with arrows, and that when the first ranks had discharged those they had, they wheeled off and took more, Crassus seeing no end of it, was out of all heart, and sent to his son that he should endeavour to fall in upon them before he was quite surrounded; for the enemy advanced most upon that quarter, and seemed to be trying to ride around and come upon the rear. Therefore the young man, taking with him thirteen hundred horse, one thousand of which he had from Cæsar, five hundred archers, and eight cohorts of the full-armed soldiers that stood next him, led them up with design to charge the Parthians. Whether it was that they found themselves in a piece of marshy ground, as some think, or else designing to entice young Crassus as far as they could from his father, they turned and began to fly; whereupon he crying out that they durst not stand, pursued them, and with him Censorinus and Megabacchus, both famous, the latter for his courage and prowess, the other for being of a senator's family, and an excellent orator, both intimates of Crassus, and of about the same age. The horse thus pushing on, the infantry stayed a little behind, being exalted with hopes and joy, for they supposed they had already conquered, and now were only pursuing; till when they were gone too far, they perceived the deceit, for they that seemed to fly now turned again, and a great many fresh ones came on. Upon this they made a halt, for they doubted not but now the enemy would attack them, because they were so few. But they merely placed their cuirassiers to face the Romans, and with the rest of their horse rode about scouring the field, and thus stirring up the sand, they raised such a dust that the Romans could neither see nor speak to one another, and being driven in upon one another in one close body, they were thus hit and killed, dying, not by a quick and easy death, but with miserable pains and convulsions; for writhing upon the darts in their bodies, they broke them in their wounds, and when they would by force pluck out the barbed points, they caught the nerves and veins, so that they tore and tortured themselves. Many of them died thus, and those that survived were disabled for any service, and when Publius exhorted them to charge the cuirassiers, they showed him their hands nailed to their shields, and their feet stuck to the ground, so that they could neither fly nor fight. He charged in himself boldly, however, with his horse, and came to close quarters with them, but was very unequal, whether as to the offensive or defensive part; for with his weak and little javelins, he struck against targets that were of tough raw hides and iron, whereas, the lightly-clad bodies of his Gaulish horsemen were exposed to the strong spears of the enemy. For upon these he mostly depended, and with them he wrought wonders; for they would catch hold of the great spears, and close upon the enemy, and so pull them off from their horses, where they could scarce stir by reason of the heaviness of their armour, and many of the Gauls quitting their own horses, would creep under those of the enemy, and stick them in the belly; which, growing unruly with the pain, trampled upon their riders and upon the enemies promiscuously. The Gauls were chiefly tormented by the heat and drouth, being not accustomed to either, and most of their horses were slain by being spurred on against the spears, so that they were forced to retire among the foot, bearing off Publius grievously wounded. Observing a sandy hillock not far off, they made to it, and tying their horses to one another, and placing them in the midst, and joining all their shields together before them, they thought they might make some defence against the barbarians. But it fell out quite contrary, for when they were drawn up in a plain, the front in some measure secured those that were behind; but when they were upon the hill, one being of necessity higher up than another, none were in shelter, but all alike stood equally exposed, bewailing their inglorious and useless fate. There were with Publius two Greeks that lived near there at Carrhæ, Hieronymus and Nicomachus; these men urged him to retire with them and fly to Ichnæ, a town not far from thence, and friendly to the Romans. "No," said he, "there is no death so terrible, for the fear of which Publius would leave his friends that die upon his account"; and bidding them to take care of themselves, he embraced them and sent them away, and, because he could not use his arm, for he was run through with a dart, he opened his side to his armour-bearer, and commanded him to run him through. It is said Censorinus fell in the same manner. Megabacchus slew himself, as did also the rest of best note. The Parthians coming upon the rest with their lances, killed them fighting, nor were there above five hundred taken prisoners. Cutting off the head of Publius, they rode off directly towards Crassus.

His condition was thus. When he had commanded his son to fall upon the enemy, and word was brought him that they fled and that there was a distant pursuit, and perceiving also that the enemy did not press upon him so hard as formerly, for they were mostly gone to fall upon Publius, he began to take heart a little; and drawing his army towards some sloping ground, expected when his son would return from the pursuit. Of the messengers whom Publius sent to him (as soon as he saw his danger), the first were intercepted by the enemy, and slain; the last, hardly escaping, came and declared that Publius was lost, unless he had speedy succours. Crassus was terribly distracted, not knowing what counsel to take, and indeed no longer capable of taking any; overpowered now by fear for the whole army, now by desire to help his son. At last he resolved to move with his forces. Just upon this, up came the enemy with their shouts and noises more terrible than before, their drums sounding again in the ears of the Romans, who now feared a fresh engagement. And they who brought Publius' head upon the point of a spear, riding up near enough that it could be known, scoffingly inquired where were his parents, and what family he was of, for it was impossible that so brave and gallant a warrior should be the son of so pitiful a coward as Crassus. This sight above all the rest dismayed the Romans, for it did not incite them to anger as it might have done, but to horror and trembling, though they say Crassus outdid himself in this calamity, for he passed through the ranks and cried out to them, "This, O my countrymen, is my own peculiar loss, but the fortune and the glory of Rome is safe and untainted so long as you are safe. But if anyone be concerned for my loss of the best of sons, let him show it in revenging him upon the enemy. Take away their joy, revenge their cruelty, nor be dismayed at what is past; for whoever tries for great objects must suffer something. Neither did Lucullus overthrow Tigranes without bloodshed, nor Scipio Antiochus; our ancestors lost one thousand ships about Sicily, and how many generals and captains in Italy? No one of which losses hindered them from overthrowing their conquerors; for the State of Rome did not arrive to this height by fortune, but by perseverance and virtue in confronting danger."

While Crassus thus spoke exhorting them, he saw but few that gave much heed to him, and when he ordered them to shout for battle, he could no longer mistake the despondency of his army, which made but a faint and unsteady noise, while the shout of the enemy was clear and bold. And when they came to the business, the Parthian servants and dependents riding about shot their arrows, and the horsemen in the foremost ranks with their spears drove the Romans close together, except those who rushed upon them for fear of being killed by their arrows. Neither did these do much execution, being quickly despatched; for the strong, thick spear made large and mortal wounds, and often run through two men at once. As they were thus fighting, the night coming on parted them, the Parthians boasting that they would indulge Crassus with one night to mourn his son, unless upon better consideration he would rather go to Arsaces than be carried to him. These, therefore, took up their quarters near them, being flushed with their victory. But the Romans had a sad night of it; for neither taking care for the burial of their dead, nor the cure of the wounded, nor the groans of the expiring, everyone bewailed his own fate. For there was no means of escaping, whether they should stay for the light, or venture to retreat into the vast desert in the dark. And now the wounded men gave them new trouble, since to take them with them would retard their flight, and if they should leave them, they might serve as guides to the enemy by their cries. However, they were all desirous to see and hear Crassus, though they were sensible that he was the cause of all their mischief. But he wrapped his cloak around him, and hid himself, where he lay as an example, to ordinary minds, of the caprice of fortune, but to the wise, of inconsiderateness and ambition; who, not content to be superior to so many millions of men, being inferior to two, esteemed himself as the lowest of all. Then came Octavius, his lieutenant, and Cassius, to comfort him, but he being altogether past helping, they themselves called together the centurions and tribunes, and agreeing that the best way was to fly, they ordered the army out, without sound of trumpet, and at first with silence. But before long, when the disabled men found they were left behind, strange confusion and disorder, with an outcry and lamentation, seized the camp, and a trembling and dread presently fell upon them, as if the enemy were at their heels. By which means, now and then turning out of their way, now and then standing to their ranks, sometimes taking up the wounded that followed, sometimes laying them down, they wasted the time, except three hundred horse, whom Egnatius brought safe to Carrhæ about midnight; where calling, in the Roman tongue, to the watch, as soon as they heard him, he bade them tell Coponius, the governor, that Crassus had fought a very great battle with the Parthians; and having said but this, and not so much as telling his name, he rode away at full speed to Zeugma. And by this means he saved himself and his men, but lost his reputation by deserting his general. However, his message to Coponius was for the advantage of Crassus; for he, suspecting by this hasty and confused delivery of the message that all was not well, immediately ordered the garrison to be in arms, and as soon as he understood that Crassus was upon the way towards him, he went out to meet him, and received him with his army into the town.

The Parthians, although they perceived their dislodgment in the night, yet did not pursue them, but as soon as it was day, they came upon those that were left in the camp, and put no less than four thousand to the sword, and with their light horse picked up a great many stragglers. Varguntinus, the lieutenant, while it was yet dark, had broken off from the main body with four cohorts which had strayed out of the way; and the Parthians encompassing these on a small hill, slew every man of them excepting twenty, who with their drawn swords forced their way through the thickest, and they admiring their courage, opened their ranks to the right and left, and let them pass without molestation to Carrhæ.

Soon after a false report was brought to Surena, that Crassus, with his principal officers, had escaped, and that those who were got into Carrhæ were but a confused rout of insignificant people, not worth further pursuit. Supposing, therefore, that he had lost the very crown and glory of his victory, and yet being uncertain whether it were so or not, and anxious to ascertain the fact, that so he should either stay and besiege Carrhæ or follow Crassus, he sent one of his interpreters to the walls, commanding him in Latin to call for Crassus or Cassius, for that the general, Surena, desired a conference. As soon as Crassus heard this, he embraced the proposal, and soon after there came up a band of Arabians, who very well knew the faces of Crassus and Cassius, as having been frequently in the Roman camp before the battle. They having espied Cassius from the wall, told him that Surena desired a peace, and would give them safe convoy, if they would make a treaty with the king his master, and withdraw all their troops out of Mesopotamia; and this he thought most advisable for them both, before things came to the last extremity; Cassius, embracing the proposal, desired that a time and place might be appointed where Crassus and Surena might have an interview. The Arabians, having charged themselves with the message, went back to Surena, who was not a little rejoiced that Crassus was there to be besieged.

Next day, therefore, he came up with his army, insulting over the Romans, and haughtily demanded of them Crassus and Cassius, bound, if they expected any mercy. The Romans, seeing themselves deluded and mocked, were much troubled at it, but advising Crassus to lay aside his distant and empty hopes of aid from the Armenians, resolved to fly for it; and this design ought to have been kept private, till they were upon their way, and not have been told to any of the people of Carrhæ. But Crassus let this also be known to Andromachus, the most faithless of men, nay, he was so infatuated as to choose him for his guide. The Parthians then, to be sure, had punctual intelligence of all that passed; but it being contrary to their usage, and also difficult for them to fight by night, and Crassus having chosen that time to set out, Andromachus, lest he should get the start too far of his pursuers, led him hither and thither, and at last conveyed him into the midst of morasses and places full of ditches, so that the Romans had a troublesome and perplexing journey of it, and some were who, supposing by these windings and turnings of Andromachus that no good was intended, resolved to follow him no further. And at last Cassius himself returned to Carrhæ, and his guides, the Arabians, advising him to tarry there till the moon was got out of Scorpio, he told them that he was most afraid of Sagittarius, and so with five hundred horse went off to Syria. Others there were who, having got honest guides, took their way by the mountains called Sinnaca, and got into places of security by daybreak; these were five thousand under the command of Octavius, a very gallant man. But Crassus fared worse; day overtook him still deceived by Andromachus, and entangled in the fens and the difficult country. There were with him four cohorts of legionary soldiers, a very few horsemen, and five lictors, with whom having with great difficulty got into the way, and not being a mile and a half from Octavius, instead of going to join him, although the enemy were already upon him, he retreated to another hill, neither so defensible nor impassable for the horse, but lying under the hills at Sinnaca, and continued so as to join them in a long ridge through the plain. Octavius could see in what danger the general was, and himself, at first but slenderly followed, hurried to the rescue. Soon after, the rest, upbraiding one another with baseness in forsaking their officers, marched down, and falling upon the Parthians, drove them from the hill, and compassing Crassus about, and fencing him with their shields, declared proudly, that no arrow in Parthia should ever touch their general, so long as there was a man of them left alive to protect him.

Surena, therefore, perceiving his soldiers less inclined to expose themselves, and knowing that if the Romans should prolong the battle till night, they might then gain the mountains and be out of his reach, betook himself to his usual craft. Some of the prisoners were set free, who had, as it was contrived, been in hearing, while some of the barbarians spoke a set purpose in the camp to the effect that the king did not design the war to be pursued to extremity against the Romans, but rather desired, by his general treatment of Crassus, to make a step towards reconciliation. And the barbarians desisted from fighting, and Surena himself, with his chief officers, riding gently to the hill, unbent his bow and held out his hand, inviting Crassus to an agreement, and saying that it was beside the king's intentions, that they had thus had experience of the courage and the strength of his soldiers; that now he desired no other contention but that of kindness and friendship, by making a truce, and permitting them to go away in safety. These words of Surena the rest received joyfully, and were eager to accept the offer; but Crassus, who had sufficient experience of their perfidiousness, and was unable to see any reason for the sudden change, would give no ear to them, and only took time to consider. But the soldiers cried out and advised him to treat, and then went on to upbraid and affront him, saying that it was very unreasonable that he should bring them to fight with such men armed, whom himself, without their arms, durst not look in the face. He tried first to prevail with them by entreaties, and told them that if they would have patience till evening, they might get into the mountains and passes, inaccessible for horse, and be out of danger, and withal he pointed out the way with his hand, entreating them not to abandon their preservation, now close before them. But when they mutinied and clashed their targets in a threatening manner, he was overpowered and forced to go, and only turning about at parting, said, "You, Octavius and Petronius, and the rest of the officers who are present, see the necessity of going which I lie under, and cannot but be sensible of the indignities and violence offered to me. Tell all men when you have escaped, that Crassus perished rather by the subtlety of his enemies, than by the disobedience of his countrymen."

Octavius, however, would not stay there, but with Petronius went down from the hill; as for the lictors, Crassus bade them be gone. The first that met him were two half-blood Greeks, who, leaping from their horses, made a profound reverence to Crassus, and desired him, in Greek, to send some before him, who might see that Surena himself was coming towards them, his retinue disarmed, and not having so much as their wearing swords along with them. But Crassus answered, that if he had the least concern for his life, he would never have intrusted himself in their hands, but sent two brothers of the name of Roscius to inquire on what terms and in what numbers they should meet. These Surena ordered immediately to be seized, and himself with his principal officers came up on horseback, and greeting him, said, "How is this, then? A Roman commander is on foot, whilst I and my train are mounted." But Crassus replied, that there was no error committed on either side, for they both met according to the custom of their own country. Surena told him that from that time there was a league between the king his master and the Romans, but that Crassus must go with him to the river to sign it, "for you Romans," said he, "have not good memories for conditions," and so saying, reached out his hand to him. Crassus, therefore, gave order that one of his horses should be brought; but Surena told him there was no need, "the king, my master, presents you with this"; and immediately a horse with a golden bit was brought up to him, and himself was forcibly put into the saddle by the grooms, who ran by the side and struck the horse to make the more haste. But Octavius running up, got hold of the bridle, and soon after one of the officers, Petronius, and the rest of the company came up, striving to stop the horse, and pulling back those who on both sides of him forced, Crassus forward. Thus from pulling and thrusting one another, they came to a tumult, and soon after to blows. Octavius, drawing his sword, killed a groom of one of the barbarians, and one of them, getting behind Octavius, killed him. Petronius was not armed, but being struck on the breastplate, fell down from his horse, though without hurt. Crassus was killed by a Parthian, called Pomaxathres; others say by a different man, and that Pomaxathres only cut off his head and right hand after he had fallen. But this is conjecture rather than certain knowledge, for those that were by had not leisure to observe particulars, and were either killed fighting about Crassus, or ran off at once to get to their comrades on the hill. But the Parthians coming up to them, and saying that Crassus had the punishment he justly deserved, and that Surena bade the rest come down from the hill without fear, some of them came down and surrendered themselves, others were scattered up and down in the night, a very few of whom got safe home, and others the Arabians, beating through the country, hunted down and put to death. It is generally said, that in all twenty thousand men were slain and ten thousand taken prisoners.

Surena sent the head and hand of Crassus to Hyrodes the king, into Armenia, but himself by his messengers scattering a report that he was bringing Crassus alive to Seleucia, made a ridiculous procession, which by way of scorn, he called a triumph. For one Caius Paccianus, who of all the prisoners was most like Crassus, being put into a woman's dress of the fashion of the barbarians, and instructed to answer to the title of Crassus and Imperator, was brought sitting upon his horse, while before him went a parcel of trumpeters and lictors upon camels. Purses were hung at the end of the bundles of rods, and the heads of the slain fresh bleeding at the end of their axes. After them followed the Seleucian singing women, repeating scurrilous and abusive songs upon the effeminacy and cowardliness of Crassus. This show was seen by everybody; but Surena calling together the senate of Seleucia, laid before them certain wanton books, of the writings of Aristides, his Milesiaca; neither, indeed, was this any forgery, for they had been found among the baggage of Rustius, and were a good subject to supply Surena with insulting remarks upon the Romans, who were not able even in the time of war to forget such writings and practices. But the people of Seleucia had reason to commend the wisdom of Æsop's fable of the wallet, seeing their general Surena carrying a bag full of loose Milesian stories before him, but keeping behind him a whole Parthian Sybaris in his many wagons full of concubines; like the vipers and asps people talk of, all the foremost and more visible parts fierce and terrible with spears and arrows and horsemen, but the rear terminating in loose women and castanets, music of the lute, and midnight revellings. Rustius, indeed, is not to be excused, but the Parthians had forgot, when they mocked at the Milesian stories, that many of the royal line of their Arsacidæ had been born of Milesian and Ionian mistresses.

Whilst these things were doing, Hyrodes had struck up a peace with the King of Armenia, and made a match between his son Pacorus and the King of Armenia's sister. Their feastings and entertainments in consequence were very sumptuous, and various Grecian compositions, suitable to the occasion, were recited before them. For Hyrodes was not ignorant of the Greek language and literature, and Artavasdes was so expert in it, that he wrote tragedies and orations and histories, some of which are still extant. When the head of Crassus was brought to the door, the tables were just taken away, and one Jason, a tragic actor, of the town of Tralles, was singing the scene in the Bacchæ of Euripides concerning Agave. He was receiving much applause, when Sillaces, coming to the room, and having made obeisance to the king, threw down the head of Crassus into the midst of the company. The Parthians receiving it with joy and acclamations, Sillaces, by the king's command, was made to sit down, while Jason handed over the costume of Pentheus to one of the dancers in the chorus, and taking up the head of Crassus, and acting the part of a bacchante in her frenzy, in a rapturous impassioned manner, sang the lyric passages—

> We've hunted down a mighty chase today,
> And from the mountain bring the noble prey,

to the great delight of all the company; but when the verses of the dialogue followed—

> What happy hand the glorious victim slew?
> I claim that honour to my courage due,

Pomaxathres, who happened to be there at the supper, started up and would have got the head into his own hands, "for it is my due," said he, "and no man's else." The king was greatly pleased, and gave presents, according to the custom of the Parthians, to them, and to Jason, the actor, a talent. Such was the burlesque that was played, they tell us, as the afterpiece to the tragedy of Crassus' expedition. But divine justice failed not to punish both Hyrodes for his cruelty and Surena for his perjury; for Surena not long after was put to death by Hyrodes, out of mere envy to his glory; and Hyrodes himself, having lost his son Pacorus, who was beaten in a battle with the Romans, falling into a disease which turned to a dropsy, had aconite given him by his second son, Phraates; but the poison working only upon the disease, and carrying away the dropsical matter with itself, the king began suddenly to recover, so that Phraates at length was forced to take the shortest course, and strangled him.

THE COMPARISON OF CRASSUS
WITH NICIAS

IN THE COMPARISON OF THESE TWO, FIRST, IF WE COMPARE THE ESTATE OF
Nicias with that of Crassus, we must acknowledge Nicias' to have been
more honestly got. In itself, indeed, one cannot much approve of gaining
riches by working mines, the greatest part of which is done by malefactors
and barbarians, some of them, too, bound, and perishing in those close and
unwholesome places. But if we compare this with the sequestrations of
Sylla, and the contracts for houses ruined by fire, we shall then think
Nicias came very honestly by his money. For Crassus publicly and avowedly
made use of these arts, as other men do of husbandry, and putting out
money to interest; while as for other matters which he used to deny, when
taxed with them, as, namely, selling his voice in the senate for gain's sake,
and injuring allies, and courting women, and conniving at criminals, these
are things which Nicias was never so much as falsely accused of; nay, he was
rather laughed at for giving money to those who made a trade of impeachments, merely out of timorousness, a course, indeed, that would by no
means become Pericles and Aristides, but necessary for him who by nature
was wanting in assurance, even as Lycurgus, the orator, frankly acknowledged to the people; for when he was accused for buying off an evidence,
he said that he was very much pleased that, having administered their
affairs for so long a time, he was at last accused, rather for giving than receiving. Again, Nicias, in his expenses, was of a more public spirit than Crassus,
priding himself much on the dedication of gifts in temples, on presiding
at gymnastic games, and furnishing choruses for the plays, and adorning
processions, while the expenses of Crassus, in feasting and afterwards providing food for so many myriads of people, were much greater than
all that Nicias possessed as well as spent put together. So that one might

wonder at anyone's failing to see that vice is a certain inconsistency and incongruity of habit, after such an example of money dishonourably obtained and waste-fully lavished away.

Let so much be said of their estates; as for their management of public affairs, I see not that any dishonesty, injustice, or arbitrary action can be objected to Nicias, who was rather the victim of Alcibiades' tricks, and was always careful and scrupulous in his dealings with the people. But Crassus is very generally blamed for his changeableness in his friendships and enmities, for his unfaithfulness, and his mean and underhand proceedings; since he himself could not deny that to compass the consulship he hired men to lay violent hands upon Domitius and Cato. Then at the assembly held for assigning the provinces, many were wounded and four actually killed, and he himself, which I had omitted in the narrative of his life, struck with his fist one Lucius Analius, a senator, for contradicting him, so that he left the place bleeding. But as Crassus was to be blamed for his violent and arbitrary courses, so is Nicias no less to be blamed for his timorousness and meanness of spirit, which made him submit and give in to the basest people, whereas in this respect Crassus showed himself lofty-spirited and magnanimous, who having to do not with such as Cleon or Hyperbolus, but with the splendid acts of Cæsar and the three triumphs of Pompey, would not stoop, but bravely bore up against their joint interests, and in obtaining the office of censor, surpassed even Pompey himself. For a statesman ought not to regard how invidious the thing is, but how noble, and by his greatness to overpower envy; but if he will be always aiming at security and quiet, and dread Alcibiades upon the hustings, and the Lacedæmonians at Pylos, and Perdiccas in Thrace, there is room and opportunity enough for retirement, and he may sit out of the noise of business, and weave himself, as one of the sophists says, his triumphal garland of inactivity. His desire of peace, indeed, and of finishing the war was a divine and truly Grecian ambition, nor in this respect would Crassus deserve to be compared to him, though he had enlarged the Roman empire to the Caspian Sea or the Indian Ocean.

In a state where there is a sense of virtue, a powerful man ought not to give way to the ill-affected, or expose the government to those that are incapable of it, nor suffer high trusts to be committed to those who want common honesty. Yet Nicias, by his connivance, raised Cleon, a fellow remarkable for nothing but his loud voice and brazen face, to the command of an army. Indeed, I do not commend Crassus, who in the war with Spartacus was more forward to fight than became a discreet general, though he was urged into it by a point of honour, lest Pompey by his coming should rob him of the glory of the action, as Mummius did Metellus at the taking of Corinth, but Nicias' proceedings are inexcusable. For he did not yield up a mere opportunity of getting honour and advantage to his competitor, but believing that the expedition would be very hazardous, was thankful to take care of himself, and left the commonwealth to shift for itself. And whereas Themistocles, lest a mean and incapable fellow should ruin the state by holding command in the Persian war, bought him off, and Cato, in a most dangerous and critical conjuncture, stood for the tribuneship for the sake of his country, Nicias, reserving himself for trifling expeditions against Minoa and Cythera, and the miserable Melians, if there be occasion to come to blows with the Lacedæmonians, slips off his general's cloak and hands over to the unskilfulness and rashness of Cleon, fleet, men, and arms, and the whole command, where the utmost possible skill was called for. Such conduct, I say, is not to be thought so much carelessness of his own fame, as of the interest and preservation of his country. By this means it came to pass he was compelled to the Sicilian war, men generally believing that he was so much honestly convinced of the difficulty of the enterprise, as ready out of mere love of ease and cowardice to lose the city the conquest of Sicily. But yet it is a great sign of his integrity, that though he was always averse from war, and unwilling to command, yet they always continued to appoint him as the best experienced and ablest general they had. On the other hand Crassus, though always ambitious of command, never attained to it, except by mere necessity in the servile war, Pompey and Metellus and the two brothers Lucullus being absent, although at that time he was at his highest pitch of interest and reputation. Even those who thought most of him seem to have thought him, as the comic poet says—

A brave man anywhere but in the field.

There was no help, however, for the Romans, against his passion for command and for distinction. The Athenians sent out Nicias against his will to the war, and Crassus led out the Romans against theirs; Crassus brought misfortune on Rome, as Athens brought it on Nicias.

Still this is rather ground for praising Nicias, than for finding fault with Crassus. His experience and sound judgment as a general saved him from being carried away by the delusive hopes of his fellow-citizens, and made him refuse to entertain any prospect of conquering Sicily. Crassus, on the other hand, mistook, in entering on a Parthian war as an easy matter. He was eager, while Cæsar was subduing the west, Gaul, Germany, and Britain, to advance for his part to the east and the Indian Sea, by the conquest of Asia, to complete the incursion of Pompey and the attempts of Lucullus, men of prudent temper and of unimpeachable worth, who nevertheless entertained the same projects as Crassus, and acted under the same convictions. When Pompey was appointed to the like command, the senate was opposed to it; and after Cæsar had routed three hundred thousand Germans, Cato recommended that he should be surrendered to the defeated enemy, to expiate in his own person the guilt of breach of faith. The people, meantime (their service to Cato!), kept holiday for fifteen days, and were overjoyed. What would have been their feelings, and how many holidays would they have celebrated, if Crassus had sent news from Babylon of victory, and thence marching onward had converted Media and Persia, the Hyrcanians, Susa and Bactra, into Roman provinces?

If wrong we must do, as Euripides says, and cannot be content with peace and present good things, let it not be for such results as destroying Mende or Scandea, or beating up the exiled Æginetans in the coverts to which like hunted birds they had fled, when expelled from their homes, but let it be for some really great remuneration: nor let us part with justice, like a cheap and common thing, for a small and trifling price. Those who praise Alexander's enterprise and blame that of Crassus, judge of the beginning unfairly by the results.

In actual service, Nicias did much that deserves high praise. He frequently defeated the enemy in battle, and was on the very point of capturing Syracuse; nor should he bear the whole blame of the disaster, which may fairly be ascribed in part to his want of health and to the jealousy entertained of him at home. Crassus, on the other hand, committed so many errors as not to leave fortune room to show him favour. It is no surprise to find such imbecility fall a victim to the power of Parthia; the only wonder is to see it prevailing over the wonted good fortune of Rome. One scrupulously observed, the other entirely slighted the arts of divination: and as both equally perished, it is difficult to see what inference we should draw. Yet the fault of over-caution, supported by old and general opinion, better deserves forgiveness than that of self-willed and lawless transgression.

In his death, however, Crassus had the advantage, as he did not surrender himself, nor submit to bondage, nor let himself be taken in by trickery, but was the victim only of the entreaties of his friends and the perfidy of his enemies; whereas Nicias enhanced the shame of his death by yielding himself up in the hope of disgraceful and inglorious escape.

ENDNOTES

◄░►

[1] The manuscripts generally write the name incorrectly—Flaminius. Titus was the name by which he was commonly known to the Greeks.

[2] Manius Curius is meant.

[3] *Mamers* being another and older form for *Mars*. The Mamertines were descended from Campanian or Oscan mercenaries and spoke a kind of Latin.

INDEX

SUGGESTED READING

❧✦❧

BOARDMAN, JOHN, JASPER GRIFFIN, AND OSWYN MURRAY. *The Oxford Illustrated History of the Classical World.* 2 vols.: *Greece and the Hellenistic World* and *The Roman World.* Oxford and New York: Oxford University Press, 2001.

DUFF, TIM. *Plutarch's "Lives": Exploring Virtue and Vice.* Oxford: Clarendon Press, 1999.

GELZER, MATTIAS. *Caesar: Politician and Statesman.* Trans. Peter Needham. 6th ed. Cambridge: Harvard University Press, 1960.

HAASE, WOLFGANG, ED. *Aufstieg und Niedergang der Römischen Welt.* Vol. 2.33.6. Berlin and New York: Walter de Gruyter, 1992.

HAMILTON, J. R. *Plutarch, "Alexander": A Commentary.* Oxford: Clarendon Press, 1969.

HIRZEL, RUDOLF. *Plutarch.* Das Erbe der Alten, vol. 4. Leipzig: Dieterich'sche Verlagsbuchhandlung Theodor Weicher, 1912.

JONES, C. P. *Plutarch and Rome.* Oxford: Clarendon Press, 1971.

KLEINER, DIANA E. E. *Cleopatra and Rome.* Cambridge, MA: The Belknap Press of Harvard University Press, 2005.

LAMBERTON, ROBERT. *Plutarch.* Hermes Books. New Haven and London: Yale University Press, 2001.

LANE FOX, ROBIN. *Alexander the Great.* London: Penguin Books, 2004.

MOMIGLIANO, ARNOLDO. *The Development of Greek Biography.* Cambridge, MA: Harvard University Press, 1993.

RUSSELL, D. A. *Plutarch.* New York: Scribner, 1973.

SHERBO, ARTHUR. "The Dryden-Cambridge Translation of Plutarch's *Lives.*" *Études anglaises* 32.2 (1979) 177–84.

———. "Dryden as a Cambridge Editor." *Studies in Bibliography* 38 (1985) 251–61.

WINN, JAMES ANDERSON. *John Dryden and His World.* New Haven and London: Yale University Press, 1987.

Look for the following titles, available now from
The Barnes & Noble Library of Essential Reading.

Visit your Barnes & Noble bookstore,
or shop online at *www.bn.com/loer*

NONFICTION

Creative Evolution	Henri Bergson	0760765480
Critique of Judgment	Immanuel Kant	0760762023
Critique of Practical Reason	Immanuel Kant	0760760942
Critique of Pure Reason	Immanuel Kant	0760755949
Dark Night of the Soul, The	St. John of the Cross	0760765871
Democracy and Education	John Dewey	0760765863
Democracy in America	Alexis de Tocqueville	0760752303
Descent of Man and Selection in Relation to Sex, The	Charles Darwin	0760763119
Dialogues concerning Natural Religion	David Hume	0760777713
Discourse on Method	René Descartes	0760756023
Discourses on Livy	Niccolò Machiavelli	0760771731
Dolorous Passion of Our Lord Jesus Christ, The	Anne Catherine Emmerich	0760771715
Early History of Rome, The	Titus Livy	0760770239
Ecce Homo	Friedrich Nietzsche	0760777721
Edison: His Life and Inventions	Frank Lewis Dyer	0760765820
Egyptian Book of the Dead, The	E. A. Wallis Budge	0760768382
Elements, The	Euclid	0760763127
Emile	Jean-Jacques Rousseau	0760773513
Eminent Victorians	Lytton Strachey	0760749930
Encheiridion	Epictetus	0760770204
Enquiry concerning Human Understanding, An	David Hume	0760755922
Essay concerning Human Understanding, An	John Locke	0760760497
Essays, The	Francis Bacon	0760770182
Essence of Christianity, The	Ludwig Feuerbach	076075764X
Ethics and On the Improvement of the Understanding	Benedict de Spinoza	0760768374
Extraordinary Popular Delusions and the Madness of Crowds	Charles Mackay	0760755825
Fall of Troy, The	Quintus of Smyrna	0760768366
Fifteen Decisive Battles of the Western World	Edward Shepherd Creasy	0760754950
Florentine History	Niccolò Machiavelli	0760756015
From Manassas to Appomattox	James Longstreet	0760759200
From Ritual to Romance	Jessie L. Weston	0760773548
Great Democracies, The	Winston S. Churchill	0760768609
Guide for the Perplexed, The	Moses Maimonides	0760757577
Hannibal	Theodore Ayrault Dodge	076076896X
Happy Hunting-Grounds, The	Kermit Roosevelt	0760755817
History of Atlantis, The	Lewis Spence	076077045X

History of the Conquest of Mexico, The	William H. Prescott	0760759227
History of the Conquest of Peru, The	William H. Prescott	076076137X
History of the Donner Party, The	Charles F. McGlashan	0760752427
History of the English Church and People, The	Bede	0760765510
History of Wales, A	J. E. Lloyd	0760752419
How the Other Half Lives	Jacob A. Riis	0760755892
How to Sing	Lilli Lehmann	0760752311
How We Think	John Dewey	0760770387
Hunting the Grisly and Other Sketches	Theodore Roosevelt	0760752338
Imitation of Christ, The	Thomas À. Kempis	0760755914
In His Steps	Charles M. Sheldon	0760755779
Influence of Sea Power upon History, The, 1660–1783	Alfred Thayer Mahan	0760754993
Interesting Narrative of the Life of Olaudah Equiano, The	Olaudah Equiano	0760773505
Interior Castle, The	St. Teresa of Avila	0760770247
Introduction to Logic	Immanuel Kant	0760770409
Introduction to Mathematical Philosophy	Bertrand Russell	0760773408
Introduction to Mathematics	Alfred North Whitehead	076076588X
Investigation of the Laws of Thought, An	George Boole	0760765847
Kingdom of God is Within You, The	Leo Tolstoy	0760765529
Lady's Life in the Rockies, A	Isabella Bird	0760763135
Leonardo da Vinci and a Memory of His Childhood	Sigmund Freud	0760749922
Letters and Saying of Epicurus	Epicurus	0760763283
Leviathan, The	Thomas Hobbes	0760755930
Life of Johnson	James Boswell	0760773483
Lives of the Caesars, The	Suetonius	0760757585
Manners, Customs, and History of the Highlanders of Scotland	Walter Scott	0760758697
Meditations	Marcus Aurelius	076075229X
Memoirs	William T. Sherman	0760773688
Metaphysics	Aristotle	0760773637
Montcalm and Wolfe	Francis Parkman	0760768358
Montessori Method, The	Maria Montessori	0760749957
Mosby's Memoirs	John Singleton Mosby	0760773726

THE BARNES & NOBLE
LIBRARY OF ESSENTIAL READING

This newly developed series has been established to provide affordable access to books of literary, academic, and historic value—works of both well-known writers and those who deserve to be rediscovered. Selected and introduced by scholars and specialists with an intimate knowledge of the works, these volumes present complete, original texts in a modern, readable typeface—welcoming a new generation of readers to influential and important books of the past. With more than 100 titles already in print and more than 100 forthcoming, the Library of Essential Reading offers an unrivaled variety of thought, scholarship, and entertainment. Best of all, these handsome and durable paperbacks are priced to be exceptionally affordable. For a full list of titles, visit *www.bn.com/loer*.